LEO BAECK INSTITUTE
YEAR BOOK

1995

Liberation

By courtesy of Yad Vashem

LEO BAECK INSTITUTE

YEAR BOOK
1995

XL

SECKER & WARBURG · LONDON
PUBLISHED FOR THE INSTITUTE
LONDON · JERUSALEM · NEW YORK

FOUNDER EDITOR: ROBERT WELTSCH (1956–1978)
EDITOR EMERITUS: ARNOLD PAUCKER (1970–1992)

Editorial office: Leo Baeck Institute
4 Devonshire Street, London W1N 2BH

THE LEO BAECK INSTITUTE
was founded in 1955 for the study of the history and culture of German-speaking Central European Jewry

The Institute is named in honour of the man who was the last representative figure of German Jewry in Germany during the Nazi period

LEO BAECK INSTITUTE

JERUSALEM: 33 Bustanai Street
LONDON: 4 Devonshire Street, W1
NEW YORK: 129 East 73rd Street

© Leo Baeck Institute 1995
Published by Martin Secker & Warburg Limited
Michelin House, 81 Fulham Road, London SW3 6RB
ISBN 0 436 20257 3
Photoset by Wilmaset Limited, Birkenhead, Wirral
Printed in Great Britain by Clays Ltd, St Ives plc

J. A. S. Grenville
EDITOR

Julius Carlebach
ASSOCIATE EDITOR

Katy Bannister
Ulla B. Weinberg
ASSISTANT EDITORS

ADVISORY BOARD

Great Britain:	Marianne Calmann	London
	David Cesarani	London
	Ian Kershaw	Sheffield
	Jeremy Noakes	Exeter
	Peter Pulzer	Oxford
	Robert S. Wistrich	London
Germany:	Werner T. Angress	Berlin
	Wolfgang Benz	Berlin
	Ursula Büttner	Hamburg
	Arno Herzig	Hamburg
	Stefi Jersch-Wenzel	Berlin
	Monika Richarz	Hamburg
	Reinhard Rürup	Berlin
United States:	Christopher Browning	Tacoma
	Vicki Caron	Brown
	Peter Gay	Yale
	Marion Kaplan	New York
	Hillel J. Kieval	Washington
	Steven Lowenstein	Los Angeles
	Michael A. Meyer	Cincinnati
	Jehuda Reinharz	Brandeis
	Ismar Schorsch	New York
	David Sorkin	Madison
	Fritz Stern	New York
	Guy Stern	Wayne State
	Bernard Wasserstein	Brandeis
Israel:	Steven Aschheim	Jerusalem
	Avraham Barkai	Lehavoth Habashan
	Evyatar Friesel	Jerusalem
	Michael Graetz	Jerusalem
	Hagit Lavski	Jerusalem
	Robert Liberles	Beersheva
	Paul Mendes-Flohr	Jerusalem
	Chaim Schatzker	Haifa
	Shulamit Volkov	Tel-Aviv
	Moshe Zimmermann	Jerusalem

Contents

Preface by John Grenville and Julius Carlebach   IX

I. GERMAN AND AUSTRIAN JEWS IN THE FIGHT AGAINST NATIONAL-SOCIALIST GERMANY

ARNOLD PAUCKER: Resistance of German and Austrian Jews to the Nazi Regime, 1933–1945   3

JOHN P. FOX: German- and Austrian-Jewish Volunteers in Britain's Armed Forces, 1939–1945   21

GUY STERN: The Jewish Exiles in the Service of US Intelligence. The Post-War Years   51

II. JEWISH CONVERSION FROM THE SEVENTEENTH TO THE NINETEENTH CENTURY

ELISHEVA CARLEBACH: Converts and their Narratives in Early Modern Germany. The Case of Friedrich Albrecht Christiani   65

DEBORAH HERTZ: Why Did the Christian Gentleman Assault the *Jüdischer Elegant*? Four Conversion Stories from Berlin, 1816–1825   85

ALAN LEVENSON: The Conversionary Impulse in Fin de Siècle Germany   107

TODD M. ENDELMAN: Leaving the Jewish Fold in Germany. Comments on the Papers of Elisheva Carlebach, Deborah Hertz and Alan Levenson   123

III. GERMAN JEWS IN THE AGE OF EMANCIPATION

SHMUEL FEINER: Mendelssohn and "Mendelssohn's Disciples". A Re-examination   133

DAVID SORKIN: Religious Reforms and Secular Trends in German-Jewish Life. An Agenda for Research   169

DAGMAR HERZOG: The Rise of the Religious Right and the Recasting of the "Jewish Question". Baden in the 1840s   185

IV. RESPONSES TO PERSECUTION IN THE 1930s. TWO NEW PERSPECTIVES

EDITH RAIM: The Persecution of the Heine Family in Germany, 1933–1939   211

ANDREW CHANDLER: Lambeth Palace, the Church of England and the Jews of Germany and Austria in 1938   225

V. JUDAICA

DAVID ELLENSON: A Disputed Precedent. The Prague Organ in Nineteenth-Century Central-European Legal Literature and Polemics .. 251

EDWARD VAN VOOLEN, IRENE FABER & ANNETTE WEBER: Jewish Ceremonial Silver from Germany in the Jewish Historical Museum, Amsterdam 265

VI. HISTORIOGRAPHICAL REVIEW

KURT PÄTZOLD: Persecution and the Holocaust. A Provisional Review of GDR Historiography 291

VII. BIBLIOGRAPHY FOR 1994 313

VIII. LIST OF CONTRIBUTORS 449

IX. INDEX 453

Illustrations

Liberation	Frontispiece
Resistance	between pp. 6–7
Jews in the British Forces	between pp. 38–39
Jews in the American Army	between pp. 54–55
Hep! Hep! Riot	opposite p. 85
Prague Organs	between pp. 262–263
German-Jewish Ceremonial Silver	between pp. 278–279

Preface

When the first volume of the Year Book was published in 1956, its appearance coincided with the death of Leo Baeck that November, in whose honour the Institutes had been named. Among Leo Baeck's last contributions was the foreword of that Year Book. He wrote of the "epochs" that give shape and meaning to events. With the dispersal of the survivors of German Jewry, an epoch of German-Jewish culture and history had come to an end. Once refugees in many lands, German Jews and their descendants were becoming new citizens of other countries – Britons, Americans, Israelis – and identified with nations on every continent. But the generation of founders did not simply turn a page and repudiate their past. They were determined that if, as they thought, Jewish life in Germany had been obliterated by National Socialism, the long history, struggles, and contributions of German Jewry to German and Central-European history should not be obliterated as well.

In Germany in the 1950s, apart from the writings of predominantly German-Jewish scholars, the thread of academic study from teacher to pupil had been severed by the National-Socialist perversions of what they called "research". Now there was no one to teach and few who wished to learn. A crucial period for the Year Book were the decades from the mid-1950s to the early 1970s. German-Jewish scholars in exile then formed the bridge, keeping knowledge alive, and helped the few Germans who then turned their attention to the German-Jewish past, to discover, first and foremost, the roots of the calamity and of the regression into barbarism that had overtaken German society.

When the Year Book was launched, despite its high aspirations, there was no certainty that sufficient scholars could be found to contribute in the future or that the cost of producing the Year Book and finding an adequate market for it would sustain it. There was even some discussion whether Year Book I was an appropriate title as it would have to be followed by at least one more Year Book! It is worth recalling these uncertainties now that the Year Book is in its fortieth year and well established as the pre-eminent publication in its field.

The Year Book was fortunate in its founders. Here only two among the many names will be cited: Siegfried Moses, President of the Leo Baeck Institute, formerly active in German communal affairs, managing director of the Schocken Department Store in Zwickau, President of the *Zionistische Vereinigung für Deutschland* and Vice-Chairman of the *Reichsvertretung der Juden in Deutschland* until his emigration to Palestine in 1937, there to start a new life and distinguished career. The first editor was Robert Weltsch, once the distinguished editor of the *Jüdische Rundschau*, who also made his new life in Palestine and Israel. This generation of German Jews, conscious of a sense of a common past though now dispersed, were also witnesses of their own times; the articles which formed the greater part of the contents of the first volume reflected this. It highlighted in their own words: "The absorbing story of Jewish Life and Spiritual Resistance in Hitler Germany, 1933–1939".

Siegfried Moses set out the aims of the publication with clarity in the preface. The programme, as proposed then, has remained at the core of the Year Book publication. Many articles since then have been published on the "inner development of German Jewry": the struggle for emancipation, the waves of conversion, the changes in the social and economic structure of German Jewry, religious trends and philosophy, Zionism, education, the many achievements of eminent Jews in the professions – in literature, journalism, the arts; also on the road to catastrophe, antisemitism, the National-Socialist state and emigration; and finally on the impact of Jewish emigrants on the countries where they found refuge.

But the last forty years have also witnessed a broadening of outlook and of research topics. The Year Book has always reflected ongoing scholarship. It was natural that at its beginnings the founders in Jerusalem, profoundly steeped in German culture, should have emphasised *German* Jewry. The vision has widened to German- or Yiddish-speaking Jewry, which encompasses much of Central Europe. The relationship and mutual influences of German Jews and Jewish neighbours, especially in the former Russian and Habsburg empires, is a subject of profound importance. German Jews were never an isolated group. Pride in the achievements of "great men" needed to be supplemented by study of the mass of ordinary, not famous Jews, their social integration, family life and contributions. The relationships of Christians with their Jewish neighbours, not only their negative but also their positive aspects, have become subjects of research. The history of Jewish descendants should not be excluded. In short: not only Jews looking outwards, but also non-Jews looking "inwards" have been of crucial importance to succeeding scholars. The Year Book is no longer confined to the years since emancipation. Indeed its concerns reach back to medieval Jewry of German-speaking lands. More controversially, the editors recognise that a new post-war German-Jewish community has emerged. Its links with the German past may still be tenuous, but are they not to be encouraged?

During the last forty years more than seven hundred articles have been published, based on original research, generally of high quality and of lasting value. The Year Book is now indispensable to students of German-speaking Jewry. History knows no finality; neither does the study of the subjects on which the Year Book focuses.

One important feature of the Year Book which began with volume one and has been continued ever since is the unique bibliography of books and articles on German Jewry. It was compiled by the Wiener Library staff anonymously from 1956 to 1963, then for sixteen years by Bertha Cohn on behalf of the Wiener Library and later the LBI. In 1980 Irmgard Foerg and Annette Pringle took over and worked together for ten years; after Irmgard Foerg retired, Barbara Suchy began her collaboration with Annette Pringle. The bibliography has grown enormously since the early years, reflecting both an increase in scholarship and far more comprehensive bibliographical control. A computer has replaced card indexes. But the idea of a division into subsections, though they have been changed somewhat over the years, has remained the same. It has proved both sound and invaluable to researchers. The task of pulling together the individual entries from forty volumes into one accessible computerised source is under way. Bibliography is a painstaking and meticulous task. Without bibliographers, scholars would be groping in the dark. Meanwhile the two excellent Index Volumes for Year Books I–XX, compiled by Eli Rothschild, and by Janet Langmaid for Year Books XXI–XXXIX, published in 1995, provide sophisticated access. Here, too, the Year Book has been an exemplary role model.

Adequate financial resources are a necessary precondition for the continuity of bringing research to publication. The annual bibliography alone involves not only devoted labour, but considerable expense. That we have found understanding and strong support in the financing of the Year Book in the *Bundesministerium des Inneren* now for many years, irrespective of the political parties in the Federal Government, is deserving of special notice and our appreciation. Nor should it be overlooked that the *Länder*, through the *Kultusministerkonferenz*, have also proved to be steadfast friends of the Year Book and have provided financial help through annual grants.

The Year Book has had just two editors from its inception until 1992: for thirty-seven years Robert Weltsch and Arnold Paucker. This in itself is a unique record of continuity unlikely to be equalled. Together with the current editor and associate editor they will be the last with any roots in pre-war Germany. Very few of the contributors today have such a background. In this sense the Year Book has come of age: it is independent of personal memories, but its contributors are just as committed. Most striking has been the generational change of contributors and their geographical spread. American, Israeli and British scholarship of German-speaking Jewry is no longer alone in the forefront; scholarship in Germany, mainly by those who are not Jews, has made rapid strides since those early days when it still relied on refugee scholars. Today there is a fruitful interchange without any one group able to claim an exclusive leadership role. The three Leo Baeck Institutes in Jerusalem, New York and London are all adapting to change and each have their own full programmes. Contributions are received from Latin America and Australia, any day now they may arrive from China and Japan. This international spread causes new problems for the editors of an English language journal: not all contributors entirely master the necessary linguistic skills. To maintain a high degree of accuracy a hard-working editorial team has been built up over the years in the London office to whom much credit for the reliability of the Year Book is due.

There are always new tasks facing the LBI which are reflected in the Year Book. One of the most immediate is to arouse awareness and stimulate interest in the new *Bundesländer* where in GDR times the study of the history and culture of German-speaking Jews was minimised and considered from inflexible ideological perspectives. A good beginning has been made.

In this Year Book, as in some others, the sections do not follow the usual chronological sequence. The fortieth anniversary of the Year Book also coincides with the Liberation of Europe, with the ending of the Nazi Holocaust and the liberation of the survivors in the camps. The editors have therefore placed a section concerned with German- and Austrian-Jewish resistance and war service with the Allies during the Second World War first. It is an important aspect of the émigré history of German-speaking Jews which requires more research. To include this section seemed especially appropriate as many misapprehensions about the supposed lack of active participation of Jews in the fight against National-Socialist Germany still persist.

John Grenville   *Julius Carlebach*

Ernst Gottfried Lowenthal, a founding Board member of the Leo Baeck Institute, died on 7th August 1994 at the age of 89 in Berlin. In his long life he was devoted both to urgent practical tasks facing German Jews from Weimar to the post-war years and to chronicling German Jews and their achievements: an astoundingly humane and productive record which touched many lives. His roots were as deeply embedded in Germany and German culture as in the Jewish community. Apart from the war years of exile in Great Britain from 1939–1946, he made his home in Germany. His life bridged three eras: Weimar, National-Socialist and post-war Germany; from his editorship of the *Zeitschrift für die Geschichte der Juden in Deutschland* and his work for the C.V. to his activities from 1945 onwards: first as Director of the Jewish Relief Unit and then his involvement in the revival of Jewish community life in Germany and in questions of restitution claims. Of lasting value are his four contributions to the Year Book, entitled 'In the shadow of doom: Post-war publications on Jewish communal history in Germany'. But he was among the first to insist that German-Jewish history should not be seen from the perspective of the Holocaust. To future generations he has bequeathed his uniquely valuable archives of German-Jewish biography. As one of the last survivors of German-Jewish culture in Germany his death is deeply mourned by his Jewish friends internationally and by his many German friends.

J.A.S.G.

German and Austrian Jews in the Fight against National-Socialist Germany

Resistance of German and Austrian Jews to the Nazi Regime 1933–1945

BY ARNOLD PAUCKER

When Jewish resistance studies became part of German-Jewish historiography it was younger historians who had to overcome the misgivings of a more conservative Jewish historians' élite. As this clash of opinions has been evaluated elsewhere,[1] it should be enough to say here that it is the complexities of Jewish resistance in Germany that accounted for opposition to the topic as such and that the issues at stake are by no means entirely dead.

These studies were initiated by the Leo Baeck Institute in London[2] and those who continued them were often closely connected with the Institute – even if their work was not always published under its auspices.[3] Other studies were and are now being undertaken by younger scholars, often Germans.[4] The subject is not exhausted, but the time has come to take stock, to formulate some conclusions and to clarify certain issues. A few introductory remarks are essential.

Most studies of German-Jewish resistance have confined themselves to the political anti-Fascist underground activities of Jews in Germany, but it is imperative to extend them to include armed resistance in Occupied Europe. Often the same people are involved.

The particular character of the resistance of German Jews dictates that it cannot be seen in isolation: it is part of the general history of the resistance. It must always be analysed in relation to a) the German resistance, b) the European resistance forces.

Jewish resistance studies are bound to involve a critical approach to German

---

[1]Arnold Paucker, *Jüdischer Widerstand in Deutschland. Tatsachen und Problematik, Beiträge zum Widerstand 1933–1945*, Berlin 1989 (Gedenkstätte Deutscher Widerstand Berlin 37), pp. 4–5 and *passim*; expanded English version *Jewish Resistance in Germany. The Facts and the Problems*, Publications in English of the Gedenkstätte Deutscher Widerstand, Berlin 1991, pp. 4–5 and *passim*. (Henceforth all references are to this latter version quoted as Paucker, *Jewish Resistance, op. cit.*) But see also note 6.
[2]Helmut Eschwege, 'Resistance of German Jews against the Nazi Regime', in *LBI Year Book XV* (1970), pp. 143–180, was the first of these studies.
[3]The most comprehensive work to date which goes way beyond the confines of Jewish political anti-Fascist resistance is Konrad Kwiet/Helmut Eschwege, *Selbstbehauptung und Widerstand. Deutsche Juden im Kampf um Existenz und Menschenwürde, 1933–1945*, Hamburg 1984 (Hamburger Beiträge zur Sozial- und Zeitgeschichte 19). The project was first suggested and promoted by the London Leo Baeck Institute.
[4]A recent venture was a moving exhibition in Berlin (March-June 1993) with a catalogue volume, Wilfried Löhken/Werner Vathke (eds.), *Juden im Widerstand. Drei Gruppen zwischen Überlebenskampf und politischer Aktion. Berlin 1939–1945*, Berlin 1993.

resistance, steering a middle course between that of scepticism and minimising, and exaggerated claims as to its proportions; while taking account of the special problems its major protagonists posed for the Jewish community in Germany.

In the European context such studies cannot ignore the currently fashionable denigration of European partisan warfare as being of little or no use to the Allied war effort; as marked by internecine armed clashes, or as solely Communist dominated.

All this is related to a rampant revisionist historiography with its polemical onslaught which blurs the moral differences between the Allies and the Nazis; a vicious re-writing of history which also exploits the collapse of the Soviet Union.

Furthermore one cannot – in the general Jewish context – overlook the attitude of Jewish historians to European Jewish resistance, which veers from dismissing it altogether as totally absent or utterly futile,[5] to claims of such magnitude that further careful substantiation is essential.

And finally – German-Jewish historiography has neglected the Austrian angle, which also needs assessment, because there are some differences between German-Jewish and Austrian-Jewish resistance.

While it is essential to stress that our findings must be seen against the general background whilst keeping the currently raging controversies in mind, one cannot even hope to encompass the major facets and problems of the resistance of German-speaking Jews in this brief abstract. This paper should be seen, rather, as a supplement – an attempt to summarise to some extent and to provide further information as yet unpublished or less generally known.

The historiography of German resistance and that of Jewish resistance in Germany went through several phases. In Federal Germany there used not to be much stomach for it. The men of July 20th, yes; perhaps the *Weiße Rose* – but the illegal workers' resistance movement hardly figured and the Jews were seen only as passive victims. For the late German Democratic Republic the true resistants were only the Communists, of course, others vanished into oblivion or were ennobled to Communist status in retrospect; Jewish aspects were conveniently disregarded. And the older generation of Jewish historians just ignored the topic. Twenty-five years ago the author was told that if young Jews had fought in the ranks of the illegal working-class parties, this was not part of Jewish history.[6] We

---

[5]Raul Hilberg in his otherwise so meritorious *Perpetrators. Victims. Bystanders. The Jewish Catastrophe 1933–1945*, London 1993, did not find it necessary to revise the negative conclusions he arrived at in 1961 in his *The Destruction of the European Jews*, despite the evidence assembled by other historians which attests to a considerable Jewish resistance. Cf. the excellent critique of the German edition, *Täter, Opfer, Zuschauer. Die Vernichtung der Juden 1933–1945*, Frankfurt a. Main 1992, by Arno Lustiger in *Der Spiegel* (15th February 1993), pp 54–61. Lustiger rightly contends that at times Jews accounted for 15% of those engaged in military resistance operations in France; there were more than 20,000 Jewish partisans in the East alone.

[6]See Arnold Paucker, 'Eröffnungsrede anläßlich der Ausstellung *Juden im Widerstand*, Berlin den 31. März 1993', in Löhken/Vathke (eds.), *Juden im Widerstand, op. cit.*, p. 206. On the "founder fathers" of the London LBI and their attitudes see also *idem*, 'History in Exile. Writing the Story of German Jewry', in *Zwischenwelt 4. Literatur und Kultur des Exils in Großbritannien*, ed. by Siglinde Bolbescher, Konstantin Kaiser, Donal McLaughlin, J.M. Ritchie, Vienna 1995.

should by now have overcome these stumbling blocks, but recent renewed disputes in the *Bundesrepublik* make one wonder.

Now, too, we should call an end to constant altercation as to whether we talk of Jewish resistance or resistance of Jews in Germany. There is no easy answer as to the motives of those who felt that something had to be done beyond Jewish retrenchment, beyond Zionism, beyond emigration, beyond the raising of Jewish consciousness. One cannot convincingly differentiate between Jewish resistance and resistance of Jews. Naturally, when a group of the *Hashomer Hazair* in a Hamburg cellar manufactures leaflets against the Nazi regime, when the *Borochov-Jugend* in Berlin edits a clandestine counter-journal to Streicher's *Der Stürmer* (well attested from a period when the Nazis had been firmly in the saddle for almost three years),[7] we are speaking of Jewish resistance; and the Jewish motivation was undoubtedly strong. When Jews in the Social-Democratic *Neu Beginnen*[8] or those organised in Communist cadres distributed anti-Fascist propaganda, they acted primarily out of solidarity with the German working class and so we term it resistance of Jews. And yet such a division is simplistic. As Nazi rule became more established and ever harsher and finally murderous, the boundaries between motives, concepts or ideologies became increasingly blurred. Antisemitism and the persecution of the Jews had a greater impact on the feelings and the zeal of certain Left-wing functionaries who developed more of a Jewish identification. And in some Jewish groups, whose engagement had been primarily Jewish before, the feeling of anti-Fascist solidarity grew stronger and the overthrow of Fascism became their central goal. How could it have been otherwise? Under relentless pressure matters were bound to be in constant flux. Historians are in the habit of categorising everything. It is time to throw this artificially inflated division between Jewish resistance and resistance of Jews overboard.

While Jewish resistance in Germany was not exactly a mirror image of, or a counterpart to, German resistance, a strong connection exists and ties can be established between Jews and almost all the German resistance movements.

But we do have a problem here linked to the character and political orientation of the Jewish community – an orientation well-known to be left-of-centre, largely left Liberal or moderate Social Democratic, with an obvious further Jewish mass move by voters to the Democratic Socialists (and to a lesser extent to the

---

[7]Israel Getzler, 'Der Antistürmer. Kampfblatt gegen Antisemitismus und Rassenhass', in *Jüdischer Almanach 1994 des Leo Baeck Instituts*, ed. by Jakob Hessing, Frankfurt a. Main 1993, pp. 44–48.

[8]Despite its "Leninist" antecedents *Org/Neu Beginnen* could be termed a democratic Socialist resistance movement and it is significant that, as in Italy's *Giustizia e Libertà*, the founders Walter Löwenheim (Lowe) ("Miles") and others, and so many of the rank and file, were Jews. Cf. a.o. Gerhard Bry, 'Resistance. Recollections from the Nazi Years', in Monika Richarz (ed.), *Jewish Life in Germany. Memoirs from Three Centuries*, transl. by Stella P. Rosenfeld and Sidney Rosenfeld, Bloomington–Indianapolis 1991, Publication of the Leo Baeck Institute New York, pp. 369–378. See also now Jan Foitzik (ed.), *Walter Loewenheim. Geschichte der Org. (Neu Beginnen) 1929–1935*, Berlin 1994 (Schriften der Gedenkstätte Deutscher Widerstand).

Catholic *Zentrum*), when the Liberal centre faltered in Germany after 1930.[9] Jews therefore under the Nazi dictatorship would continue to sympathise with the aims of those – let us call them "democratic" anti-Fascist groupings – who continued to work underground, and one would expect that they would have joined them, had they been so disposed. While quite a few undoubtedly did, it was not a majority resistance option and neither were the "moderates" the main German resistance bodies.

The two dominant resistance forces – those at least potentially effective – were the National Conservatives and the Communists, deriving any strength they had from very disparate sectors of the German population. Here was the problem sensed by various sections of the Jewish community and its leaders, when they concerned themselves with it at all; and it shows itself so much more strongly to today's historian of German Jewry who is much better acquainted with certain aspects of the German resistance and conversant with later developments. It is a truism that a Jewish community can only flourish in a pluralistic democratic society; the post-war aims of the major German resistance forces – the Conservative *Ständestaat* of the German Right and the Proletarian paradise of the Communists – were not theirs: essentially there was no place for them in either.

We have dealt with the Communist problem elsewhere at length[10] and can restrict ourselves to a few observations later on – so it will be useful to pay more attention to the Conservative option here.

The controversy as to the true character of the National Conservative resistance persists. Certainly they were a very mixed bunch, consisting of Conservatives whose anti-Nazi credentials had been impeccable from the beginning; of Conservatives who had welcomed the "National Revolution" in their loathing of the Weimar Republic and their fear of Bolshevism and only gradually realised that they had fallen into the hands of gangsters; of ex-Nazis who wished to mend their ways; of generals and officers who had supported the war until the debacle of Stalingrad[11] – and beyond. There were many other elements – a motley crowd – whose democratic credentials were doubtful. What

---

[9] On Jewish political options in Weimar Germany see Ernest Hamburger and Peter Pulzer, 'Jews as Voters in the Weimar Republic', in *LBI Year Book XXX* (1985), pp. 3–66. See also Peter Pulzer, 'The Electoral Stance of the Jews, 1930–1933', in his *Jews and the German State. The Political History of a Minority, 1848–1933*, Oxford 1992, pp. 291–323. Pulzer's figures are fairly authoritative, though I still estimate the final move to the SPD as more substantial, adding considerably to the previous Jewish SPD base. I last calculated that in 1932 close to 55% must have voted Socialist, and some 5% Communist. See Arnold Paucker, 'Jewish Self-Defence', in *Die Juden im Nationalsozialistischen Deutschland/The Jews in Nazi Germany 1933–1943*, ed. by Arnold Paucker with Sylvia Gilchrist and Barbara Suchy, Tübingen 1986 (Schriftenreihe wissenschaftlicher Abhandlungen des Leo Baeck Instituts 45), p. 59. (But I accept that further detailed research of the very differentiated voting patterns in July and November 1932 may force us to lower figures of the Jewish SPD vote somewhat.)

[10] Paucker, *Jewish Resistance, op. cit.*, pp. 7–8.

[11] Count Claus Schenk von Stauffenberg, the central figure of the July 1944 Putsch, is on record as having supported the Nazi invasion of the Soviet Union until the end of 1942 (with all this implies) and there are many examples of such an attitude.

By courtesy of Sergej Glanze/Ghost

Fifty Years After
Berlin honours the Jewish Resistance Fighters

Above: Berlin exhibition, 1993
Below: Monument for Baum Group, Berlin, Unter den Linden

Gerd Meyer
(1919–1942)

Martin Kochmann
(1912–1943)

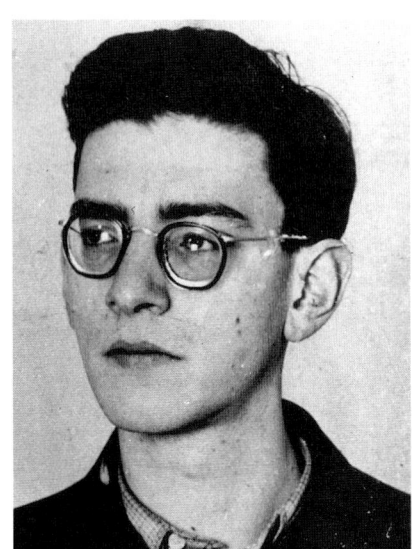

Herbert Budzislawski
(1920–1943)

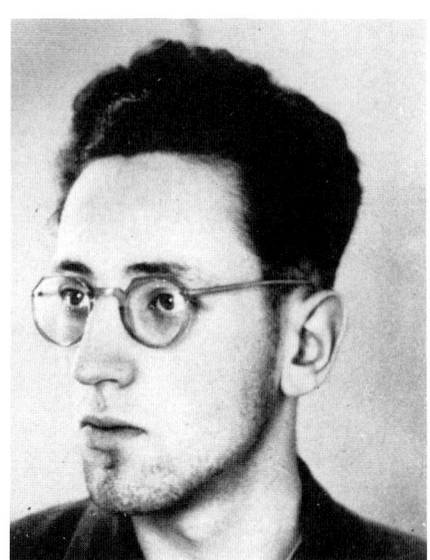

Heinz Rothholz
(1921–1943)

Jewish Resistance in Berlin
Baum Group

*All photos, unless otherwise indicated, by courtesy of R. Biswas, E. Brothers,
H. Cühn, M. Joachim, F. S. Kochman, M. Kreutzer, W. Löhken,
B. Meffert, M. Pikarski, G. Prager, W. Sack, K. Sprittulla and O. Wendt*

Heinz Birnbaum
(1920–1943)

Lotte Rotholz, geb. Jastrow
(1923–1943?)

Alice Hirsch
(1923–1943?)

Heinz Joachim
(1919–1942)

Jewish Resistance in Berlin
Baum Group

Charlotte Holzer, geb. Abraham
(1909–1980)

Richard Holzer
(1911–1975)

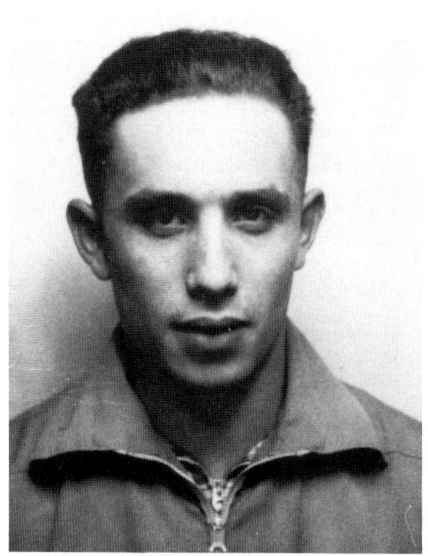

Felix Heymann
(1917–1943)

Suzanne Wesse, geb. Vasseur
(1914–1942)

Jewish Resistance in Berlin
Baum Group

By courtesy of Martin Schönfeld, Berlin

Jewish Resistance in Berlin

Above: Walter Sacks Group
Below: Hanni Meyer, Baum Group; Memorial Plaque in Berlin, Ritterstr. 16

persönlichen Interesses. Eben weil man fühlt, daß dies fast nicht anders sein könne, wird überall ein Mensch, der im reifen Alter seine Religion wechselt, von den meisten verachtet; gleichwohl legen eben diese dadurch an den Tag, daß sie die Religion nicht für Sache vernünftiger Überzeugung, sondern bloß des früh und vor aller Prüfung eingeimpften Glaubens halten.

Diese Schrift ist in Deutschland verfaßt und hergestellt worden. Sie soll zur Klärung der Meinungen über die neue, durch den Sieg des Faschismus in Deutschland geschaffene Lage beitragen. Die Herausgeber wollen und können keinerlei Verantwortung für die in diesem Heft vorgetragenen Auffassungen übernehmen, sie müssen sie den Autoren überlassen. Die Herausgeber glauben aber, der deutschen und der internationalen Arbeiterbewegung einen Dienst zu erweisen, wenn sie es ermöglichen, daß die Diskussion unserer großen Probleme auf breitester Grundlage in vollster Offenheit zustande kommt.

Am 30. Jänner wurde die Koalitionsregierung mit Hitler gebildet. Am 28. Februar leiteten die Nationalsozialisten mit der Brandstiftung im Reichstag ihr Terrorregime gegen die sozialistischen Arbeiterorganisationen in Deutschland ein. Bereits Mitte Juli haben sich alle bürgerlichen Parteien restlos liquidiert,

Vor uns aber steht heute die Aufgabe, unter der terroristischen Herrschaft der deutschen faschistischen Reaktion die Fahne des marxistischen Sozialismus hochzuhalten, unablässig an dem Sturze der Barbarenherrschaft zu arbeiten, um den werktätigen Massen in Deutschland den Weg zum Sozialismus freizumachen. Wir wissen, daß jeder Schritt vorwärts auf diesem Wege auch einen Anstoß für das internationale sozialistische Proletariat bedeutet, die Zeit der Verwirrung zu überwinden und mit neuen Kräften dem sozialistischen Freiheitsziel zuzustreben. In diesem Bewußtsein werden wir kämpfen.

„Die französische abstrakte Eidesformel taugt eben darum gar nichts! das Abstrahieren vom gegebenen Positiven sollte dem eigenen Gedankengang eines jeden, dem Grade seiner Bildung gemäß, überlassen bleiben. Inzwischen hast du recht, den Eid als unleugbares Beispiel praktischer Wirksamkeit der Religion anzuführen. Daß jedoch diese auch außerdem

Neu Beginnen

Anti-Nazi Propaganda smuggled into Germany camouflaged as Schopenhauer's *Über Religion*

Title page, pp. 5 and 62 showing the abrupt changes in the text

Kurt Hirschfeldt
(1898–1971)

Edith Hirschfeldt, geb. Berlow
(b. 1903)

Jewish Resistance
Gemeinschaft für Frieden und Aufbau

Grunewald, June 1943
Gad Beck, David Billard, Jizchak Schwersenz,
Zwi Abrahamson, Poldi Chones

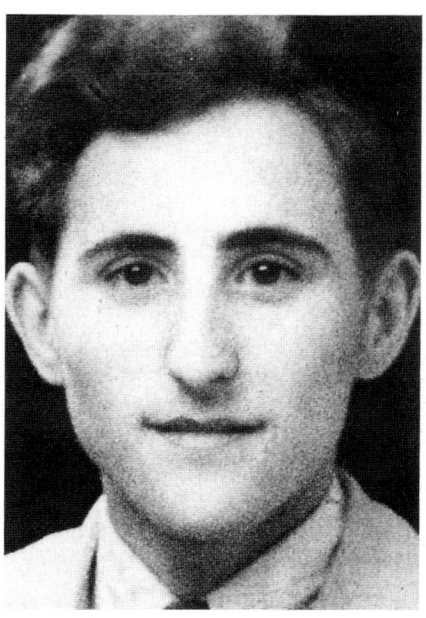

Gad Beck
(b. 1923)

Zionist Underground in Germany
Chug Chaluzi

Vorbereitungslager Rüdnitz, 1939

Above: The house at Rüdnitz (nr. Bernau), a preparation camp for teenagers for the emigration to Palestine
Middle: In the Assembly Room of Rüdnitz a quotation of the eighth line from the *Internationale* in Hebrew; it reads in translation: "Nothing from yesterday, tomorrow everything"
Below: Group photo of the participants; from left to right: last row, 3rd: one of the group leaders (Madrichim), name unknown; same row, 5th: Arthur Hofstädter, second Madrich; middle row, 8th: Erich Lucas, third Madrich

Rights owned by Hans Hirschberg, London. Not to be reproduced without his permission

united them in the end was the realisation that Hitler had led Germany to catastrophe and – let us be fair – many of them were revolted by the mass killings of the Jews in the East. Of the German Right they were still the best; and so many were to die a cruel death.

What do we actually know about the links between the remaining Jewish leadership and the emerging "Conservative" resistance?[12] For lack of documentation and because of the death of Leo Baeck, President of the *Reichsvertretung*, before he could fulfil his promise to write about it, our knowledge is scanty indeed. We have some corroboration of the relations of the *Reichsvertretung/Reichsvereinigung* with a Stuttgart circle of more "Liberal" industrialists and with such Conservative Nationalist politicians as the Lord Mayor of Leipzig, Carl Goerdeler, and the Prussian Finance Minister, Johannes Popitz (both executed after July 1944), but this is certainly not the whole story. Connections with far more Right-wing elements and even with renegade Nazis were involved. What we can piece together is a certain amount of collaboration with something we may politely term "establishment anti-Fascism".

That Jewish leaders were in contact with this sector is a logical outcome of their way of thinking. However liberal in outlook, dictated as it was by the history of the Jewish minority, theirs was a conservative lifestyle and on the whole they did not have much sympathy with working-class aspirations. And some of the prominent Jewish representatives were not really politically minded. But their contacts – especially before war broke out – with Right-wing bureaucrats who remained in the administration were of the utmost importance, as they were able to provide "inside" information and warn of imminent dangers. Some of these had backed the Nazis initially and were soon disabused. Among them were – otherwise reactionary – philosemites and gradually, as the war went wrong, more and more on the Right felt that Hitler had to be overthrown. Relations were gradually established between the Nationalist opposition and the remaining Jewish leaders. The picture painted here is a very generalised one. One has to study the history of the German Conservative-led resistance up to the July 1944 putsch; and one also has to keep in mind that we have no corroboration whatsoever that any Jewish/Conservative links continued after the deportation of Leo Baeck to Terezin in January 1943. But I would put it that these anti-Hitler

---

[12]For some of the following see also Hans Reichmann, 'Excerpts from Leo Baeck's Writings. Foreword: The Fate of a Manuscript', in *LBI Year Book III* (1958), pp. 361–363; *idem*, 'Aufzeichnung über eine Unterredung', in *Worte des Gedenkens für Leo Baeck. Im Auftrag des Councils of Jews from Germany* hrsg. von Eva G. Reichmann, Heidelberg 1959, pp. 237–241, esp. pp. 238–239; Albert H. Friedlander, 'A Muted Protest in War-Time Berlin. Writing on the Legal Position of German Jewry throughout the Centuries. Leo Baeck – Leopold Lucas – Hilde Ottenheimer', in *LBI Year Book XXXVII* (1992), pp. 363–380; Arnold Paucker, 'Preface/Introduction', *ibid*, pp. XIII-XIV. Some lines have been quoted directly here and also later a few lines have been taken from this and earlier Year Book prefaces. It should be emphasised here that we have no evidence of any links between Jewish leaders and the National-Conservative resistance from within the German army. Such connections would have been very unlikely.

Right-wing forces were both the natural and the unnatural allies of a more conservative Jewish leadership.

Some details of this collaboration have come down to us. In view of what we know today, it is more than curious, it is incongruous that it was Baeck's draft of a manifesto to be directed to the German people on the day of the "liberation" – (for which read successful putsch) which in 1942 was apparently chosen in a kind of Conservative essay competition. Baeck was informed that he had "won". No one has ever seen a copy of this aborted "proclamation". It was also at the behest of the Conservative resistance, with a Nazi turncoat as go-between, that Baeck and two close colleagues undertook the compilation of the history of the Jewish *Rechtsstellung* for the benefit of the "freed" German population. This dangerous secret task was in itself an act of courageous defiance of the Nazi regime.

But here is the rub. With some notable exceptions (later from the *Kreisauer Kreis*), the National Conservative conspirators had no intention whatsoever of restoring the full civil rights of the Jews after their "liberation" of Germany. The extermination of the Jews would have been stopped by them at once, but they were not at all keen on having the Jewish emigrants back in a reborn, presumably Conservative, Germany. The best a Jewish remnant could have hoped for was an existence as a second-class citizen, on sufferance. There is not a shred of doubt as to this Conservative "Jewish" programme.[13] The Jewish leadership cannot have been so naive as not to have known that they had put their trust in very doubtful friends, even though the extent of their true intentions must have been hidden from them. And yet the Jewish representatives were quite prepared to co-operate with the most awkward customers and were fully justified in so doing. They were forced to seek any way out – to appeal to and enlist all those forces which seemed to promise some sort of deliverance from persecution and extermination.

Now, briefly, the Communist factor. The position of German Jewry has been outlined before: moderate, middle-class, politically and as to religion mainly liberal, and certainly 95% non- or anti-Communist. Under Nazism this did not change. The Communists were atheists. For years their anti-capitalist underground propaganda had a repellent anti-Jewish tinge – and they were vociferously anti-Zionist as well.[14] It is after 1935 that one can register Communist policy changes; and during the November Pogrom their political (though not

---

[13]This has been so well documented by Christof Dipper, 'Der deutsche Widerstand und die Juden', in the special issue *Juden in Deutschland zwischen Assimilation und Verfolgung* of the journal *Geschichte und Gesellschaft*, ed. by Reinhard Rürup, vol. IX, No. 3 (1983), pp. 349–380, and others in the last twelve years that we can dispense with further evidence here. See also the recent important article by Christof Dipper, 'Der 20. Juli und die "Judenfrage" ', in *Die Zeit*, No. 27 (1st July 1994). It is ironic that men of the older generation in the National Conservative resistance (Goerdeler, Popitz etc.) who were in touch with the Jewish representatives are recorded as making reprehensible statements on the "Jewish Question". Later utterances from the *Kreisauer Kreis* are more acceptable, but somewhat hazy. Altogether extant documentation paints a bleak picture of the attitudes of the Right-wing conspirators.

[14]Paucker, *Jewish Resistance, op. cit.*, p. 8; on Communist propaganda and the "Jewish Question" see in particular David Bankier, 'The German Communist Party and Nazi-Antisemitism, 1933–1938', in *LBI Year Book XXXII* (1987), pp. 325–340.

their practical) support for the Jews was impressive.[15] There was assuredly amongst the Jewish public a certain respect for Communist underground fighters who had been caught, imprisoned, murdered. But in general the barriers were insurmountable. Militant resistance for the Jewish collective was never feasible. Communism as an option just did not exist.

So much for the Jews as a group. But where Jewish youth – against the advice of the official Jewish leadership[16] – engaged in resistance activities, they for the most part joined the Communists, or co-operated with them or accepted their assistance. Unruffled by the vagaries of Komintern policy, undisturbed by the excesses of Communist pronouncements on the "Jewish Question", little concerned as regards the anti-Zionist stance and undeterred by the somewhat controversial division of underground cadres into Gentile and Jewish cells (which should not be described as an application of the Nuremberg Laws, but more fairly presented as a security measure), only the lull in resistance activities during the Hitler-Stalin pact caused dismay within Jewish Communist resistance cells. Of course, one must differentiate between co-operation, fellow travelling (if you like) and the many who had unhesitatingly joined the illegal Communist movement, had a real contempt for the "Jüdische Führer" and showed no concern for the fears of Jewish leadership as to the repercussions anti-Nazi propaganda and later acts of sabotage might have for the remaining Jewish population.[17] It is an incontrovertible fact that the reservations of active Jewish anti-Fascists were few; they opted for the extreme Left and above all for the Communists, because they saw in them the most fanatical, adroit, determined and best organised opponents to the Nazi regime. And at the time they were quite right.[18]

While we have been emphatic about a gradual growth of Jewish conscious-

---

[15]Paucker, *Jewish Resistance*, *op. cit.*, p. 8. But as Jeffrey Herf, 'East German Communists and the Jewish Question. The Case of Paul Merker', in *Journal of Contemporary History*, vol. XXIX, No. 4 (October 1994), pp. 627–661, points out, the exemplary issue of the *Rote Fahne* in support of the Jewish population during the "*Kristallnacht*", whilst a "clear statement of solidarity of German Communists with the Jews, was the only one of its kind from the KPD Politbüro from 1933 to 1945". It would be wrong, however, to extend such strictures to the Communist cadres operating throughout Germany, which often behaved admirably, assisting their Jewish comrades and Jews in general, particularly those on the run.

[16]Paucker, *Jewish Resistance*, *op. cit.*, p. 7.

[17]However, the act of sabotage by the Baum group against the "Soviet Paradise" Exhibition in Berlin's *Lustgarten*, which resulted in Jewish mass executions, was opposed within this resistance organisation itself as too great a risk for Jews and anti-Fascists. Apparently it was condemned by Richard Holzer and Felix Heymann, but they were overruled by Herbert Baum. Charlotte and Richard Holzer in conversation with the author, Berlin 1972; and now Michael Kreutzer, 'Zur Geschichte der Widerstandsgruppen um Herbert Baum', *loc. cit.*, p. 135 (see note 24).

[18]The "Jewish policy" of the KPD has been criticised in some detail in Paucker, *Jewish Resistance*, *op. cit.*, p. 8. Moreover, the ideological contortions and tactical and strategic errors of the Party were blatant. For which now see also Wolfgang Benz/Walter H. Pehle (eds.), *Lexikon des deutschen Widerstandes*, Frankfurt a. Main 1994, *passim*. Nevertheless, in the post-war political climate in the West, Communist resistance was either neglected or unfairly treated. Despite all justified misgivings, the outstanding resistance record of the Communists has to be acknowledged. For the following pages on anti-Fascist activity of Jewish youth and to avoid recapitulation, the reader is also referred to Paucker, *Jewish Resistance*, *op. cit.*, and to Kwiet/Eschwege, *Selbstbehauptung*, *op. cit.*, which remains invaluable.

ness, there is no doubt where the primary allegiance of most of these Jewish anti-Fascists lay. Even the youngest of them identified as a matter of course with the ideological positions of whatever segment of the German underground resistance they belonged to and took part in the political altercations between the various groups (resembling on a much smaller scale and in a completely different way the state of division which persisted in the Jewish community at large). Communist and non-Communist Jewish youth engaged in some justified, but often barren and unprofitable, disputes. We are not speaking here of any betrayals or denunciations; only of political conflict, a disunity which marked the German anti-Fascist forces and in which Jewish comrades fully shared.[19] It did not perhaps hinder resistance all that much, but it did not help it either. However, we know that close ties of personal friendship united some of these Jewish political antagonists.

Yet something more must be said about the motivation and the character of these young Jewish anti-Fascists. I have no hesitation in calling them humanist Socialists and Communists. They were not only fighting German Fascism, they also passionately believed in a world of social justice and freedom and they were confident that their struggle against the Nazi regime would result in such a new society. In that – as we know – they were, of course, sadly mistaken. Another illusion from which they suffered, and which was nourished by the remarkable solidarity with which their Gentile comrades supported them, was the assumption that there was still a solid German working-class force which would eventually rise against Hitler. Another myth. But it would be unjust and unfair to describe even the larger group of Communist Jewish youth by the now fashionable and misleading term "totalitarian anti-Fascists". Undoubtedly there were some budding apparatchiks and potential bullies already amongst them; but what generally distinguished these young Socialists and Communists who chose resistance was their deeply felt conviction that while there could be no true liberty without Socialism, there could be no true Socialism without liberty. Not only do I speak here from personal knowledge of Jewish boys and girls who were executed by the Nazis between 1942 and 1945 and whose memory I honour; the post-war political options and the vicissitudes of some of the survivors in the East after 1945 bear this out as well.

Historians of the resistance have computed that up to 2,500 German Jews were actively engaged in some form of resistance between 1933 and 1945 (and when we add military resistance in Occupied Europe the figure would be larger).[20] All figures are conjecture; some are suspect. How does one work out numbers, percentages and ratio to the German population when documentation is often scanty, when to some extent one has to rely on eyewitness reports and participant observers – and a degree of speculation enters? It is an astounding

---

[19] When, in 1993, interviewing a former member of the Communist Jewish resistance, I pointed to the daring exploits of the *Borochow-Jugend*, he retorted: "But are you aware that they were Trotskyists?" In fact a Communist activist helped them operate. (Getzler, 'Antistürmer', *loc. cit.*, p. 45.)

[20] More cautiously Konrad Kwiet, in 'Problems of Jewish Resistance Historiography', in *LBI Year Book XXIV* (1979), pp. 37–57, claims 2,000. So did this author in Paucker, *Jewish Resistance, op. cit.*, p.11. Further research has shown that this figure actually needs to be upgraded.

figure when compared with the numbers we have for active German resistance fighters. To reach these figures historians have had to take account of trial records, of the number of political prisoners held in German concentration camps (well-documented), and of survivors' reports from former members of Jewish youth movements – such reports can be checked and properly evaluated.

Confronted with such an impressive Jewish presence in the resistance in Germany, one may well argue that Jews, as a disadvantaged minority who had given the Liberal and Socialist movements so many adherents and who now bore the brunt of the Nazi onslaught, had more reasons for resentment and might be expected to join the anti-Fascist resistance in fairly large numbers. However, these activists ran a double risk as Jews and as anti-Nazis:[21] they could be and were exposed, when detected and arrested, to the full rigour of the punishments meted out by a ruthless and vindictive regime.

Who exactly are we talking about here? What contingents and age groups are involved? The largest group was the Jewish component of the clandestine German Left. Outlawed by the regime, Communists, Socialists and others regrouped into an anti-Nazi underground and many Jewish members who had been active in the Weimar Republic, thus a somewhat older age group, joined in – some 1,000 to 1,500 of them. Many of these resistance groups were smashed by the *Gestapo* in the early years of the regime and their members filled the concentration camps; the numbers of Jewish inmates can be established with reasonable accuracy. Many prisoners were released between 1936 and 1939 on condition that they left Germany though there are also cases of daring reinfiltration: a return to resume illegal work in Germany which ranged all the way from skilful to foolhardy and amateurish, with added dangers for the Jewish infiltrators. The second largest group were those who had mostly been too young to become politicised before 1933 and who were enrolled in anti-Nazi activity as members of Jewish youth movements. Their numbers have been assessed at roughly 500 to 600, mostly in cells organised by the Communists and various Socialist movements, which operated throughout Germany within both Zionist[22] and non-Zionist youth organisations, distributing anti-Nazi propaganda material.[23] Of these the groups organised by Herbert Baum between 1933 and 1942, which extended way beyond Berlin – their centre of operation – to other

---

[21]See also Konrad Kwiet, 'Resistance and Opposition. The Example of the German Jews', in David Clay Large (ed.), *Contending with Hitler. Varieties of German Resistance in the Third Reich*, Washington–Cambridge 1991, p. 70.

[22]See for instance Alice and Gerhard Zadek, *Mit dem letzten Zug nach England. Opposition, Exil, Heimkehr*, Berlin 1992, pp. 71ff. and *passim*, which is a good narrative of the activities of young Jews who were members of one of the Baum groups while belonging from 1936 to the Berlin *Hashomer Hazair*. The Zadeks, like so many other members of Herbert Baum groups, left Germany in time, just before the outbreak of the war. Likewise on cells within the *Hashomer Hazair* see Günther Bernd Ginzel, *Jüdischer Alltag in Deutschland 1933–1945*, Düsseldorf 1984, pp. 240–247, esp. note 37.

[23]On the dissemination of anti-Nazi leaflets by Jewish youth see Eric Brothers, 'On the Anti-Fascist Resistance of German Jews', in *LBI Year Book XXXII* (1987), pp. 369–382.

German cities, were by far the most outstanding and numerous.[24] Then there were those Jewish groups which acted independently. Here we deal with a much younger age group; often they were under sixteen when they were first recruited. A further smaller group consisted of somewhat older men and women who were members of the Liberal resistance.[25] There were a few loners,[26] even some National-German orientated former Jewish officers and soldiers who, veterans of the First World War, engaged in furious individual acts of defiance.[27] Finally, there were the links on the higher level, mentioned above.

Now some words about the special function of Jewish women in the resistance.[28] In recent years a fair amount of research has been done on the role of women in the European resistance – which is in consonance with the spread of feminist studies. One need not be a feminist to agree with the view that an assessment of the function, the position of and the specific problems facing Jewish women in the resistance is long overdue. One may argue that women were more adaptable and qualified for undercover work: it has certainly been proven to have been the case in practice. In Germany, with many resistance fighters conscripted into the army, the networks in the *Reich* proper began to rely on women more and more. In the case of Jews things were different, but until the final deportations Jewish women – unlike German women – were used as forced

---

[24]Counting all those recruited by Herbert Baum and his comrades who were active in the pre-war period and managed to emigrate in time, the total number of those affiliated with the Communist-led Baum groups from 1933 to 1942/3 may have reached 150. There were also Jewish boys and girls in other Communist cells. The literature on the Baum groups cannot all be cited here. A most searching new analysis is Michael Kreutzer, 'Die Suche nach einem Ausweg, der es ermöglicht, in Deutschland als Mensch zu leben. Zur Geschichte der Widerstandsgruppen um Herbert Baum', in Löhken/Vathke (eds.), *Juden im Widerstand, op. cit.*, pp. 95–158. Two very important studies of the Baum group and its sabotage of the "Soviet Paradise" Exhibition are: Wolfgang Wippermann, *Die Berliner Gruppe Baum und der jüdische Widerstand, Beiträge zum Widerstand 1933–1945*, Berlin 1982 (Gedenkstätte Deutscher Widerstand Berlin 19); and Wolfgang Scheffler, 'Der Brandanschlag im Berliner Lustgarten im Mai 1942 und seine Folgen. Eine quellenkritische Betrachtung', in *Jahrbuch des Landesarchivs Berlin*, Berlin 1984, pp. 91–118. Furthermore, Kwiet/Eschwege, *Selbstbehauptung, op. cit.*, 'Die Herbert-Baum-Gruppe', p. 114–139, which also lists the literature on the Baum group up to 1984. For the last ten years consult the bibliographies of *LBI Year Books XXX-XL* (1985–1995). See also notes 23 and 64.

[25]The most detailed account of the Liberal option is now Horst R. Sassin, *Liberale im Widerstand. Die Robinsohn-Strassmann-Gruppe 1934–1942*, Hamburg 1993 (Hamburger Beiträge zur Sozial- und Zeitgeschichte 30). See also *idem*, 'Liberals of Jewish Background in the Anti-Nazi Resistance', in *LBI Year Book XXXVII* (1992), pp. 381–396; and *idem, Widerstand, Verfolgung und Emigration Liberaler 1933–1945*, Bonn 1983, a catalogue volume, which accompanied an exhibition of the Friedrich-Naumann-Stiftung. Here the impressive participation of Jews in the Liberal Resistance is well documented. See also Wolfgang Benz, 'Eine liberale Widerstandsgruppe und ihre Ziele. Hans Robinsohns Denkschrift aus dem Jahre 1939', in *Vierteljahrshefte für Zeitgeschichte*, 3 (1981), pp. 437–471. However, the Jewish presence in Germany's liberal resistance groups does not bear comparison with the Left-wing engagement of the great majority of Jews who joined the anti-Nazi resistance.

[26]Kwiet/Eschwege, *Selbstbehauptung, op. cit.*, pp. 243–246.

[27]Cf. Dieter Corbach, *"Ich kann nicht schweigen!" Richard Stern, Köln, Marsilstein 20*, Cologne 1988, p. 13; Erich Leyens, *1933–1938. Under the Nazi Regime*, unpubl. ms., 1990; Kwiet/Eschwege, *Selbstbehauptung, op. cit.*, pp. 240–241.

[28]Simone Erpel, 'Struggle and Survival. Jewish Women in the Anti-Fascist Resistance in Germany', in *LBI Year Book XXXVII* (1992), pp. 397–414. See also (for Europe in general) Ingrid Strobl, 'Vergessene Heldinnen. Jüdische Frauen im Widerstand', in *idem, Das Feld des Vergessens. Jüdischer Widerstand und deutsche "Vergangenheitsbewältigung"*, Berlin–Amsterdam 1994, pp. 45–63.

labour in the factories and there was thus more scope for underground work. That Jewish women were often the core of strength and reliance in groups increasingly harassed and in danger of detection is well established. It was they who sometimes held a group together. Their fortitude under interrogation and torture by the *Gestapo* was astounding.

We have written about a group consisting entirely of Jewish girls, operating in the Berlin area.[29] They all came originally from the *Bund deutsch-jüdischer Jugend*, led by a young woman called Eva Mamlok, who, by all accounts, was possessed of outstanding qualities of leadership and must have been an astute organiser. It is also politically significant that they differed from most Berlin groups in their attitude to Communism. While the Communists lay low during the Hitler-Stalin pact until June 1941, it was precisely this group of girls which undertook anti-war propaganda in Berlin factories from 1939 to 1941. There is only one survivor – all the others were deported and perished in the East.

Most of these young women came originally from once-prosperous Jewish middle-class homes, not exactly the breeding ground for militant and resourceful anti-Fascists. Fighting in the resistance is not the same as opting for the Left in a democracy; it is to risk one's life constantly in a merciless war. One of the most moving stories is that of Helga Beyer of the Breslau *Freie Deutsch-Jüdische Jugend*;[30] recruited into the resistance at the age of thirteen, she acted as a courier smuggling anti-Nazi propaganda across the frontiers. Arrested at the age of seventeen, sent to Ravensbrück concentration camp, she succumbed there in 1942.

In the preceding pages we have described the political Jewish resistance activities within the bounds of Germany itself which necessarily shadowed the pattern of German resistance activities – a non-military resistance even during the war years confined by the special conditions which obtained in the *Reich*. It fully deserves to be called "resistance" as it was punishable by long-term incarceration in prisons and concentration camps, torture and death in times of peace, and by execution once war had broken out.[31] Yet one must not forget that there were other Jewish manifestations of opposition to the Nazi rulers which at least border on resistance. The German Jews were in a special situation which was comparable to that of no other German group. An entire community was put outside the law, or whatever "law" there remained in Germany, and one does not do justice to the Jewish collective if one ignores other forms of defiance practised

---

[29]Paucker, *Jewish Resistance*, op. cit., p. 13; *idem* and Lucien Steinberg, 'Some Notes on Resistance', in *LBI Year Book XVI* (1971), pp. 241–242.

[30]Antje Dertinger, *Weiße Möwe, gelber Stern. Das kurze Leben der Helga Beyer. Ein Bericht*, Berlin–Bonn 1987; Paucker, *Jewish Resistance*, op. cit., pp. 12–13.

[31]The definition of "resistance" accepted by Benz/Pehle (eds.), *Lexikon des deutschen Widerstandes*, op. cit., pp. 9–11, is perhaps over-generous, but the definition applied here to indicate active anti-Nazi underground work is today generally accepted by German historians. Given this restrictive definition, far too little attention is being paid by German historiography to Jewish resistance, judging by the flood of publications issued in connection with the 50th anniversary of the July plot. There is a noticeable dearth of information on Jewish groups in Peter Steinbach/Johannes Tuchel (eds.), *Widerstand gegen den Nationalsozialismus*, Bonn 1994 (Bundeszentrale für politische Bildung, Schriftenreihe 323); and other examples of this neglect could be given. Explanations such as that the structure of the German resistance accounts for this are not convincing.

by them.* As we have shown elsewhere, when rabbis polemicised against the Nazi regime from the pulpit,[32] when Jewish journalists countered antisemitic allegations by articles printed in the controlled and censored Jewish press,[33] this demanded considerable daring and testified to a will to resist.

Of course much of Jewish self-assertion under the Nazi dictatorship cannot qualify as resistance. There are those who claim that suicide in cases of discrimination when faced with deportation could be termed an act of individual resistance. They should be more properly described as anguished protests.[34] But some Jewish reactions to persecution and later to organised annihilation certainly do qualify as forms of resistance.

After the outbreak of hostilities there were thousands of German Jews who went underground to avoid deportation.[35] This was not political anti-Nazi activity, but evasion of deportation; a refusal to comply with the orders of an almighty totalitarian dictatorship which deserves to be classified as resistance in the broadest sense of the term. Some 10,000 German Jews made this attempt; two-thirds of whom were caught sooner or later, but about 3,000 succeeded in this illegal way of life and surfaced in the days of liberation. Admittedly, the precise figures are still a matter of argument. Much tribute is due to the many brave Germans who helped them, but it is quite remarkable how many Jews succeeded in evading the vigilance and constant manhunts of the *Gestapo*. The most spectacular story is that of an entire Zionist Jewish youth group which managed to go into hiding.[36] All this does not fit in with the common picture of a legality-bound, fearful and passive German Jewry.

What about the armed resistance of German and Austrian Jews? We need not waste time discussing this particular option for the official Jewish communities –

---

*See the last page of illustrations in this essay.

[32] Some examples in Paucker, *Jewish Resistance, op. cit.*, pp. 5–6. It needed considerable nerve. Rabbi Joachim Prinz excelled in this. Cf. Joachim Prinz, 'A Rabbi under the Hitler Regime', in Herbert Strauss/Kurt R. Grossmann (eds.), *Gegenwart im Rückblick. Festgabe für die Jüdische Gemeinde zu Berlin 25 Jahre nach dem Neubeginn 1970*, Heidelberg 1970, pp. 231–238. Perhaps the most telling event was Prinz's flourishing of *Der Stürmer* from the pulpit, asking his congregation: "Is this what we really look like?" All this in the presence of *Gestapo* agents who could have arrested him at once, *ibid.*, pp. 233–234. See also Max Nussbaum, 'Ministry under Stress. A Rabbi's Recollections of Nazi Berlin 1939–1940', *ibid.*, pp. 239–247.

[33] Paucker, *Jewish Resistance, op. cit.*, pp. 6 and 17, note 17. The role of Jewish newspapers in this respect has been treated repeatedly in essays and introductions of the *LBI Year Book*. Arno Herzberg, 'The Jewish Press under the Nazi Regime. Its Mission, Suppression and Defiance – A Memoir', in *LBI Year Book XXXVI* (1991), pp. 367–388, must suffice here as one example.

[34] Konrad Kwiet, 'The Ultimate Refuge – Suicide in the Jewish Community under the Nazis', in *LBI Year Book XXIX* (1984), pp. 135–167; Kwiet/Eschwege, *Selbstbehauptung, op. cit.*, 'Der Selbstmord', pp. 194–215.

[35] Avraham Seligmann, 'An Illegal Way of Life in Nazi Germany', in *LBI Year Book XXXVII* (1992), pp. 327–361.

[36] See a.o. Jizchak Schwersenz and Edith Wolff, 'Jüdische Jugend im Untergrund. Eine zionistische Gruppe in Deutschland während des zweiten Weltkrieges. Mit einer historischen Einführung von Shaul Esh', in *Bulletin des Leo Baeck Instituts*, vol. XII, No. 45 (1969), pp. 5–100; Jizchak Schwersenz, *Die versteckte Gruppe*, Berlin 1988; Ferdinand Kroh, *David kämpft. Vom jüdischen Widerstand gegen Hitler*, Reinbek bei Hamburg 1988; Christine Zahn,' "Nicht mitgehen, sondern weggehen!" Chug Chaluzi – eine jüdische Jugendgruppe im Untergrund', in Löhken/Vathke (eds.), *Juden im Widerstand, op. cit.*, pp. 159–205.

it never existed.[37] There is a, perhaps apocryphal, story about militant opposition of Jewish youth to the SS during the *"Kristallnacht"* in defence of a synagogue in Baden.[38] For Austria – allowing the term *"Großdeutschland"* just for once – there was in the last phase of the war some sporadic "military" resistance of Jews. But as for the *Altreich* itself, as there was no armed German resistance, there could be no Jewish one either. Military resistance was only possible outside the frontiers of Germany. It was in Spain in 1936 that armed Jewish resistance began. In the same way as there were German workers who went to Spain because they felt that only there could they wage an armed struggle against Hitler, so there were German Jews: either political refugees already abroad, or young Jews who went from Germany to the assistance of the Spanish Republic, to fight in the International Brigades. And it is to the credit of World Jewry that it supported where it could the legitimate Spanish government, as there was a general recognition that the defence of Spanish freedom and the defeat of Spanish Fascism – with its vicious antisemitic propaganda – was in the Jewish interest (and who knows how the war would have shaped, if France had had at its back a democratic Spain in 1939/1940?). In recent years the Jewish part in the International Brigades has been evaluated by many competent historians. The Jewish contingents, with 400–500 German Jews amongst them, were, in terms of percentage, by far the strongest group.[39] To dismiss the Brigades as just a Communist-run enterprise – as some still do – is facile and ill-informed, a relic of the Cold War. To paraphrase Chaim Herzog, the President of the State of Israel, the story of the Jewish volunteers in Spain is a glorious page in the annals of the Jewish people.

We have to pay attention to the events in Spain if only for the reason that from 1939, and then from 1941, battle-experienced Brigadists were everywhere a central element in the European resistance. Often they were the very kernel of the formations; they were organisers, both Jews and Gentiles alike, and naturally Jewish refugees on the run joined them as well. They could be found across the whole spectrum of the resistance. In France there were some German Jews who commanded sectors of the *Maquis*[40] and active resistance of Jewish women's groups from Germany has also been recorded.[41] The participation of German Jews in the Garibaldi and Matteotti Brigades and in *Giustizia e Libertà* in

---

[37]Paucker, *Jewish Resistance, op. cit.*, p. 3.

[38]Julius Keller, *German Jews Fought Back*, New York–Washington etc., 1975, pp. 89–109. The author introduces his book as "fiction based on historic facts".

[39]The authority is: Arno Lustiger, *Schalom Libertad! Juden im Spanischen Bürgerkrieg*, Frankfurt a. Main 1989, chap. 'Deutschland und Österreich', pp. 223–259; *idem, "Shalom Libertad!" Les Juifs dans la guerre civile espagnole*, chap. 'Allemagne-Autriche', pp. 175–215; *idem*, 'German and Austrian Jews in the International Brigade', in *LBI Year Book XXXV* (1990), pp. 297–320. Also cf. Kwiet/Eschwege, *Selbstbehauptung, op. cit.*, pp. 101–110.

[40]See f.i. Lustiger, 'German and Austrian Jews', *loc. cit.*, p. 314.

[41]See f.i. Juliane Lepsius, 'Widerstand in Südfrankreich. Charlotte Löwenthal', 1992, Deposition in LBI New York Archives.

Northern Italy has now been fully substantiated.[42] Some of them died in battle or were executed by the Germans after capture.

After the collapse of the Italian armies in the Balkans their commanders refused to hand over to the Nazis the numerous Jews who had long been under their protection and interned in humane conditions. It was the constant procrastination of the Italian military authorities which saved these Jews from deportation and aided their subsequent liberation; whereupon many men joined Tito's partisans, briefly as a Jewish brigade, which was then absorbed into a larger partisan unit.[43] Amongst them were quite a number of German Jews. There had been other Jewish escapees from Germany who had joined the Yugoslav partisans even earlier – as there were Jews from Austria in the brigades operating from Slovenia.[44] Amongst those deported to the East there is some evidence of German Jews who did reach partisan formations, where the terrain allowed. Even as far away as Shanghai there were Jewish clandestine activities under Japanese occupation in which Jews from Central Europe shared.[45]

In Eastern Europe the fatalism of the doomed ghetto fighters could only be expressed as: "We can do nothing, but we must do something", but in the West, especially in the years 1943–1945, German Jews fighting in the *Maquis* were still fighting for their lives, though with the knowledge that they were on the winning side, with liberation to hope for.

Jewish historiography has completely neglected Austrian-Jewish resistance and has now to rely largely on the exemplary work of the Austrian Resistance Documentation Centre in Vienna whose research is usually not available in English.[46] As this final section is more in the nature of an appendix, a cursory glance at the Austrian scene, the reader must be referred to the original sources in German. Although the Austrian studies do not single out Jews as such – apart from some notable exceptions – and prefer to treat the "Austrian struggle for

---

[42]Klaus Voigt in his standard work *Zuflucht auf Widerruf. Exil in Italien 1933–1945*, vol. II, Stuttgart 1993, chap. 7, section, 'Im Versteck, auf der Flucht und im Widerstand', pp. 377–401, esp. pp. 399–401, names about thirty refugees in Italy who joined the resistance, particularly *Giustizia e Libertà*. To these must be added a few Communists who came from France or Yugoslavia and were active in the formation of the Garibaldi Brigades. After the liberation in Milan I myself met two German Jews, former members of the International Brigades, who had been with the *Garibaldini*.

[43]Voigt, *Zuflucht auf Widerruf, op. cit.*, p. 239 and *passim*; Jonathan Steinberg, *All or Nothing. The Axis and the Holocaust 1941–1943*, London–New York 1990, pp. 131–133, 170; Lucien Steinberg, 'Le bataillon juif de l'île de Rab', in *Le Monde Juif*, vol. XXV, No. 54 (1969), p. 43–47.

[44]The number of Jews who fought in Tito's partisan armies has been variously estimated as up to 20,000. This figure seems hardly plausible in view of the so much smaller figure of Yugoslav Jewish survivors, but undoubtedly there were thousands of Jews amongst the partisans and the great majority were, of course, Serbian and Croat Jews who had escaped the massacres (Tito's friend and adviser, Mosha Pijade, was Jewish). However, the number of non-Yugoslav Jewish partisans who fought with Tito grew steadily. See also below, p. 19.

[45]James R. Ross, *Escape to Shanghai. A Jewish Community in China*, New York–Toronto etc. 1994, p. 215 and *passim*, gives some details of clandestine activities in Shanghai, such as refugees being recruited for a presumably Allied underground network. Communist Jewish arrivals from Germany also reorganised for political work in the city. Cf. Günter and Genia Nobel, 'Life is Luck – 45 Years after Exile in Shanghai', in *Jewish Culture Club. Visitor's Letter*, Berlin (Autumn 1993), p. 3.

[46]The following concise section is based largely on the material put at my disposal by the *Dokumentationsarchiv des österreichischen Widerstandes* (DÖW) and its publications. The author is indebted to them for their generous assistance.

liberation" as a unified whole, the lives and activities of Austrian-Jewish resistance fighters are given considerable space, and this is fully justified.

When it comes to the Austrian-Jewish community, the gradualism of increasing persecution and consequent adaptation, which is such a significant factor in Germany, was completely absent in Austria. Instead of stage-by-stage degradation and expropriation, there was one fell swoop which left the community in total disarray – and this is also reflected in purely "Jewish" resistance activities. In Germany the outlawing of the Jewish youth movements took years, and it takes time for the penetration of youth groups and the formation of resistance cells. In Austria this had no chance and, consequently, while we do know of a few individuals, for instance from the dissolved *Hashomer Hazair*, who joined the general Austrian resistance,[47] one has to register an absence of organised Jewish resistance groups; such as the Baum groups, the Mamlok group, the *Borochov-Jugend* and others active in Germany. On the other hand though – while the difference between the two countries holds good – there was considerable Jewish participation in various forms of Austrian resistance and again, considering the size of the fast-shrinking Jewish population, here, too, on a quite remarkable scale. As in Germany, the community also resorted to other means of defiance and self-assertion.

One must stress that from 1934 to 1938 Austria had experienced a period of semi-Fascist or authoritarian twilight and that numerous Jews were involved in the clandestine activities of the outlawed Socialist and Communist parties. This was in consonance with the political sympathies of many Jewish intellectuals and young workers, who suffered persecution for their beliefs under the new non-democratic regime.[48] Until wholesale emigration and deportation, these continued their work after the *Anschluß*. Then there had been Spain – and, as with Germany, Jewish participation in the Austrian contingent was formidable. The lives of these Brigadists (there were some 120 of them) have now been meticulously recorded.[49] We know about the conspicuous role they played later in the Belgian and French resistance[50] – from the very beginning – and it must be

---

[47] It is significant that Angelika Jensen, *Die Geschichte der jüdischen Jugendbewegung "Haschomer Hazair" in Österreich von den Anfängen bis 1940*, Vienna 1995, has nothing to say about individual members in the resistance. This is no different from "official" histories of the German *Hashomer Hazair*, which do not tackle the subject either.

[48] Jonny Moser, 'Die Juden Österreichs und der Widerstand gegen das NS-Regime', in *DÖW Jahrbuch 1993*, p. 103.

[49] *Ibid.*, p. 103, gives the figure as 80. However, Hans Landauer in his compilation *Die österreichischen jüdischen Spanienkämpfer*, DÖW, E 19.715, lists about 120 Austrian Jews who fought in the International Brigades or the Republican Army and documents their subsequent fates. See also idem, 'Österreichische Juden als Spanienkämpfer', in *Das Jüdische Echo* (1991), pp. 110–114; idem, 'Weg und Blutzoll der österreichischen Spanienkämpfer in den Jahren 1936–1939', in *DÖW Jahrbuch 1987*, pp. 90–97; 'Weg und Blutzoll der österreichischen Spanienkämpfer in den Jahren 1939–1945', in *DÖW Jahrbuch 1988*, pp. 148–162. Leopold Spira, 'Spanische Erinnerungen. Als Interbrigadist gegen Franco', in *Das Jüdische Echo* (1991), pp. 107–110.

[50] See also DÖW/Ulrich Weinzierl (eds.), *Österreicher im Exil. Belgien 1938–1945. Eine Dokumentation*, Vienna 1987, esp. pp. 110–131; Tilly Spiegel, *Österreicher in der belgischen und französischen Résistance*, Vienna 1969; Moser, 'Die Juden Österreichs', loc. cit., pp. 109ff. See a.o. DÖW/Ulrich Weinzierl (eds.), *Österreicher im Exil. Frankreich 1938–1945*, Vienna 1984, esp. pp. 177–239; F.R. Reiter (ed.), *Unser Kampf. In Frankreich für Österreich. Interviews mit Widerstandskämpfern*, Vienna–Cologne 1984.

emphasised that the Austrian Communists, Jews and Gentiles alike, steered clear of the despicable policy of the French Communist Party during the twelve months from the collapse of France to the invasion of the Soviet Union.[51]

A *Travail-Anti-Allemand* group, active in both Belgium and France, was formed by political refugees from Austria very soon after the occupation. It was attached to the resistance in both countries and in France became affiliated to the *Front National pour la Libération*. Here Jews played a formidable part.[52] Anti-war propaganda was directed to Austrian soldiers in the *Wehrmacht*; Jewish women and their non-Jewish comrades – political refugees from Austria – were engaged in trying to talk them into deserting.[53] From 1943 the Austrian and Austrian-Jewish refugees were involved in military action as part of the general resistance forces.[54] Their share in the liberation of France is well attested.[55]

In Austria itself some Jews were active after 1938 in the monarchist-legitimist *Österreichische Kampffront*, which was quickly liquidated by the *Gestapo*.[56] We know some of their names from the trial records. But, in view of the political orientation of Austrian Jewry, one would not expect many Jews amongst the traditionalist Austrian resistance groups.

The most curious manifestation of partly Jewish anti-Fascist activity in Austria itself is the story of the *Sonderabteilung "NN"*, the *Mischlingsliga* in Vienna and the *Antifaschistische Partei Österreichs*, founded first in 1938 and reformed in

---

[51]In this conjunction it must be stressed that the Austrian Communists were not alone in this. Together with the other Spanish exiles who found refuge in France after Franco's victory, the Spanish Communists adopted a similar stance and fought the German invaders from the outset. Moreover, it is only fair to state that the official line of the French Communist Party from 1939 to 1941 was by no means accepted by all party members. It was opposed in the higher party echelons and amongst the rank and file; let alone by "Jewish" comrades. It was altogether an unnatural situation, and many witnesses can testify to the audible sigh of relief which went through Communist cadres throughout Europe, Great Britain and the Middle East on 22nd June 1941. For them everything had suddenly come "right" again.

[52]Moser, 'Die Juden Österreichs', *loc. cit.*, pp. 109–112.

[53]See Tilly Spiegel, *Frauen und Mädchen im österreichischen Widerstand*, Vienna 1967, p. 39, on women who later returned to Austria for illegal work. See also Strobl, *Das Feld des Vergessens, op. cit.*, pp. 46ff.

[54]Moser, 'Die Juden Österreichs', *loc. cit.*, pp. 109–112; DÖW/Weinzierl (eds.), *Frankreich, op. cit.*, pp. 177–239; Spiegel, *Österreicher in der belgischen und französischen Résistance, op. cit.*

[55]See also Albert Sternfeld, *Betrifft: Österreich. Von Österreich betroffen*, Vienna 1990, *passim*, who links resistance activities with service in the Allied Armies before the collapse of France in 1940 and after the Liberation in 1944. His cautious estimate of 15,000–16,000 volunteers from Austria, largely Jews, tallies with the figures for German Jews, usually estimated as 20,000 in all in the Allied Forces; cf. Paucker, 'Eröffnungsrede', *loc. cit.*, p. 208. On the part played by German Jews in the British war effort see now: Gerhard Hirschfeld, 'Deutsche Emigranten in Großbritannien und ihr Widerstand gegen den Nationalsozialismus', in Klaus-Jürgen Müller/David N. Dilks (eds.), Großbritannien und der deutsche Widerstand 1933–1944, Paderborn–Munich etc. 1994, pp. 107–121. Consult also the essays on military resistance by Arno Lustiger and Yoav Gelber, in *LBI Year Book XXXV* (1990); and by John P. Fox and Guy Stern in *LBI Year Book XXXVII* (1992).*

*See further the essays by John P. Fox, 'German-and Austrian-Jewish Volunteers in Britain's Armed Forces 1939–1945'; and Guy Stern, 'The Jewish Exiles in the Service of US Intelligence. The Post-War Years' in this volume of the Year Book – (Ed.).

[56]DÖW, A. Nr. 15643.

1943 after the Allies had promised to restore independence to Austria.[57] It consisted of half-Jews, but also of Jews and of Austrian-Gentile marriage partners (it is telling that the partners of mixed marriages, as in Germany, had their specific role in the resistance). The *Mischlingsliga*, although it also indulged in a great deal of Austrian patriotic rhetoric, leant nevertheless to the Left and, while ostensibly politically neutral, Communist influence dominated. (Playing the nationalistic card was, of course, in accordance with Communist war-time policy.) The *Mischlingsliga* became – for obvious reasons, most Jews having been deported – the only "Jewish" resistance in Vienna. It co-operated with the Czech underground and with Tito's partisans, for whom it organised supplies, medicines in particular. Apart from propaganda it engaged in industrial sabotage, jointly with Yugoslav and French prisoners of war who worked in Austrian factories. The *Mischlingsliga* had a *Führer*,[58] who issued military orders in authoritarian language, and during the battle for Vienna his "troops", who had trained "for the day", did finally see some military actions. With some 100–200 activists it reached battalion strength, and was entrusted with police functions by the Russians after the Liberation.[59]

The reinfiltration into Austria by Jewish anti-Fascists camouflaged as French voluntary workers is another heroic and tragic chapter of the Austrian resistance. Already in 1940, after the occupation of France, the return "home" of Austrian Communists, where it was not considered "risky", to bolster underground work against the Nazi regime, was ordered by the *Kommunistische Partei Österreichs* (KPÖ) and as a consequence many were betrayed and executed. At that time Jewish Party members most certainly did not fall into the category of possible returnees. However, in 1943 quite a few – with faked papers – joined Gentile comrades and often suffered a similar fate.[60] (Such infiltration, as we have seen, was by no means uncommon in Germany as well, but it took place before 1939. After the outbreak of the war, Jewish anti-Fascists were, as a rule, most unlikely to resume illegal activities there.) Within months of the liberation of France quite a few Austrian Jews who had been fighting with the *Maquis* managed somehow to cross into Yugoslavia to join the Austrian battalions of Tito's partisan armies. And the very last days of the war saw Austrian Jews fighting on Austrian soil, in the Free Austrian *Kampfgruppe Steiermark* which linked up with the Soviet

---

[57]DÖW, A. Nr. 987, 988, 989, 7162, Die Sonderabteilung ... Festschrift etc. (18.3.1943); Gedächtnisprotokoll der Befragung von Herrn Otto Horn (17.2.1971); leaflets, proclamations etc. Otto Franz Max Horn was one of the leaders. This is a fascinating story which deserves a separate study.
[58]Otto Ernst Andreasch (Monti). He was arrested in February 1944 and died in November during an Allied air raid. DÖW, A. Nr. 987–989, p. 4.
[59]DÖW, A. Nr. 7162, p. 9.
[60]Moser, 'Die Juden Österreichs', *loc. cit.*, pp. 110, 112; Spiegel, *Frauen und Mädchen, op. cit.*, p. 39.

Forces[61] and Jewish survivors in Vienna storming SS barracks there together with units of the Red Army.[62]

Jewish historians especially have castigated the Jewish leadership, East and West, for their inertia, impotence and even complicity. They certainly have a point. Jewish representatives, elected or non-elected, were often constitutionally unable to deal with Fascist repression and mass murder. They could not cope; their options were minimal. We who did not have to face their dilemma should not judge them too harshly.

But there is another side to the depressing picture of passivity in the face of annihilation. As we have shown here for German and Austrian Jews – and the same goes of course for European Jewry in general[63] – a great many ordinary Jewish people, above all the young, resisted wherever and whenever they could.[64] They had their share – however small – in the liberation of Europe from Nazi tyranny.

---

[61] Moser, 'Die Juden Österreichs', *loc. cit.*, pp. 112–113. The most detailed study of the *Kampfgruppe Steiermark* (founded at the end of 1943 in the Soviet Union), Christian Fleck, *Koralmpartisanen. Über abweichende Karrieren politisch motivierter Widerstandskämpfer*, Vienna–Cologne 1986, does not discuss individual Jews. One of them, Leo Engelmann, was taken and sentenced to be shot a few weeks before the end of the war. Radomir Luza, 'The Resistance in Austria, 1938–1945', in *Politics and Society in Germany, Austria and Switzerland*, vol. I, issue 2 (Winter 1988), p. 22 (based on his book with the same title, Minneapolis 1984), has a picture of the "Austrian Freedom Batallion" with Friedl Fürnberg and Franz Hunner (really Honner!), Jewish members of the Central Committee of the KPÖ, in the front row.

[62] DÖW, A. Nr. 7162, p. 9.

[63] Arno Lustiger, *Zum Kampf auf Leben und Tod! Das Buch vom Widerstand der Juden 1933–1945*, Cologne 1994.

[64] In view of the brevity of this paper, I have again to point to the many individual studies of particular Jewish groups. Only the most trenchant have been given here. One cannot conclude this paper without mentioning the *Rote Kapelle* to which quite a number of Jews belonged; and the *Gemeinschaft für Frieden und Aufbau*, a resistance group of Jews and Gentiles distributing anti-war propaganda between 1943 and 1945 and liquidated by the *Gestapo* in the last months of the war. See Barbara Schieb-Samizadek 'Die Gemeinschaft für Frieden und Aufbau', in Löhken/Vathke (eds.), *Juden im Widerstand, op. cit.*, pp. 37–81 (and cf. the publications cited there by Lucien Steinberg and others). See also Paucker/Steinberg, 'Some Notes', *loc. cit.* When it comes to the Herbert Baum groups the proliferation of literature has spanned thirty-five years; from Bernhard Mark, 'Die Gruppe von Herbert Baum. Eine jüdische Widerstandsgruppe in den Jahren 1937–1942', in *Blätter für Geschichte*, 14 (1961), pp. 34ff. (in Yiddish), and Margot Pikarski, 'Über die führende Rolle der Parteiorganisation der KPD in der antifaschistischen Widerstandsgruppe Herbert Baum, Berlin 1939–1942', in *Beiträge zur Geschichte der deutschen Arbeiterbewegung*, No. 5, Berlin 1966; to Eric Brothers/Michael Kreutzer, 'Die Widerstandsgruppe um Herbert Baum', in a forthcoming catalogue of an international exhibition in Frankfurt a. Main on Jewish resistance in Europe. See also notes 23 and 24.

German-and Austrian-Jewish Volunteers in Britain's Armed Forces 1939–1945 *

BY JOHN P. FOX

In a brief discussion of the role played by German Jews in the resistance against Nazi Germany – was it "Jewish resistance" or the "resistance of Jews"? – it was noted that at least 20,000 German Jews (men and women)[1] served in Allied military forces during the Second World War, with honour and often paying the ultimate price. Six thousand of those came from Berlin.[2] Given the individual – and often idiosyncratic – characteristics of those concerned and the wide range of their civilian and wartime experiences, it is hardly surprising that the several thousand Jewish refugees from Germany and Austria who served in Britain's armed forces at the time should epitomise many of the dichotomies in wider analyses of Jewish resistance and opposition to the Nazi Third *Reich*. Neither was there any iron-cast homogeneity about the motives and means whereby they volunteered for service in a foreign army against their original homelands.

Within the wider context of European Jewish resistance to Nazism, the

---

*A shortened version of this article was read on 8th January 1994 to the American Historical Association Conference in San Francisco, as part of a special symposium on Jewish resistance during the Second World War organised by the Leo Baeck Institute. I am extremely grateful to the Leo Baeck Institute for having invited me to give that presentation, and for having supported my attendance at the AHA conference. I should also like to acknowledge my special thanks to Dr. Arnold Paucker. It was at his suggestion that I first investigated aspects of German- and Austrian-Jewish refugee involvement with the British war effort during the Second World War, resulting in two publications. The first, 'German and Austrian Jews in Britain's Armed Forces and British and German Citizenship Policies 1939–1945', was published in *LBI Year Book XXXVII* (1992), pp. 415–459. This present contribution is the second. It is thanks also to Dr. Paucker that I was able to establish contact with two former members of Twelve Force, Paul Yogi Mayer and Stephen Dale, and through them other members of that special group. Both my San Francisco conference paper and the present contribution could not have been written without the help vouchsafed me through the replies received from former members of Twelve Force to a questionnaire I sent them. Several of them also made other invaluable and unique information available to me. To them, I extend my grateful thanks.

[1]Norman Bentwich, *I Understand the Risks. The Story of the Refugees from Nazi oppression who fought in the British Forces in the World War*, London 1950, devotes chap. 11 of his book to the subject of 'Alien Women Soldiers'. Although Bentwich mentions many names of individual German and Austrian refugees in his wide-ranging study, only in a few cases is he specific as to their Jewish origins.

[2]See Arnold Paucker, 'Nachwort. Rede anläßlich der Eröffnung der Ausstellung "Juden im Widerstand", Berlin den 31. März 1993', in Wilfried Löhken and Werner Vathke (eds.), *Juden im Widerstand. Drei Gruppen zwischen Überlebenskampf und politischer Aktion, Berlin 1939–1945*, Berlin 1993, pp. 206–208.

personal and collective (but incomplete) story of this heterogeneous group of people illustrates yet other aspects of the history of Jewish refugees from Nazi Germany and Austria; of the Jewish refugee experience in the United Kingdom; of their experience within Britain's armed forces; and of some individual military events of the Second World War. Yet their status as aliens within Britain's armed forces – "enemy aliens" during wartime, as the majority had been unable to gain naturalisation by then – served yet again to underline the ambivalence of their position within a foreign country in conflict with their countries of origin: a conflict in which they clearly opposed the latter. Not wanted within Nazified German and Austrian societies because they were Jews, these people had had no choice but to enter other countries, those, that is, that would accept them, as those nebulously perceived pariahs of the twentieth century: refugees.[3] Apart from a small minority able to enter Palestine, most had to find a safe haven in other, predominantly Gentile, societies whose general attitudes towards foreigners, let alone Jews, had always been ambivalent at best, and downright hostile at worst. The title of a recent Austrian book aptly sums up the dilemmas confronting these Jewish refugees, and the total paradox of their situation in a world where bureaucracy and ethnicity seemed to count for everything: *Die Heimat wurde ihnen fremd, die Fremde nicht zur Heimat*.[4]

As one of the major "safe havens" for Jews fleeing Nazi persecution, the United Kingdom was not all that different from many others. Ambivalence towards the new arrivals, partly because of their Jewishness, but above all because they were foreigners, was often the dominant feature shown by many of its citizens and the bureaucracy which ruled them. Yet if English society was not exactly a milieu flowing with the milk of human kindness for foreigners and alien Jews,[5] why was it that several thousand of these Jewish refugees served that society as members of the British Armed Forces during the Second World War? Alternatively, was this seen less in terms of serving Britain than as a means of bringing about the end of Nazism in Germany? How precisely did such military service come about, especially since after September 1939 alien Jewish refugees from Germany and Austria were officially classified as "enemy aliens"? What did they expect to gain in a personal sense? What did they expect to achieve politically, if anything, with regard to Nazi Germany? What was the nature of their wartime service? Could military service within the United Kingdom be construed as specifically Jewish "resistance" or opposition to Nazism? Or were such notions modified as it merged, of necessity, with the United Kingdom/Allied forms of opposition and

---

[3]See for example, Anna C. Bramwell (ed.), *Refugees in the Age of Total War*, London 1988; Michael R. Marrus, *The Unwanted. European Refugees in the Twentieth Century*, London–New York 1985.
[4]The editor of the book *Die Heimat wurde ihnen fremd, die Fremde nicht zur Heimat. Erinnerungen österreichischer Juden aus dem Exil*, Vienna 1993, is Dr. Adi Wimmer of Klagenfurt University. I am grateful to Mr. A.W. Freud for this reference.
[5]Cf. Marion Berghahn, *German-Jewish Refugees in England. The Ambiguities of Assimilation*, London 1984; Colin Holmes, *Anti-Semitism in British Society 1876–1939*, London 1979; idem, *John Bull's Island. Immigration and British Society, 1871–1971*, London 1988; Tony Kushner, *The Persistence of Prejudice. Antisemitism in British Society During the Second World War*, Manchester 1989.

armed resistance to the Third *Reich*?[6] How many of these refugees intended, from the beginning, to return to a non-Nazi Germany? Alternatively, how many decided – and when – never to return to their homelands because of the apparent tolerance granted there for so long to Nazism and because of the Holocaust?

Given their physical location in the United Kingdom, and that the Allied invasions of Italy and Normandy only commenced in 1943 and 1944, the Jewish refugees discussed here were obviously in a different situation from Jews and other civilians ensnared in Nazi-dominated Europe. Within Europe "resistance" of any kind, by whomsoever, against Nazism was more easily defined and understood, physically and morally, since the enemy was there, to be confronted and dealt with on a daily basis. Yet for any anti-Nazi resistance to be labelled "Jewish" requires it to be more or less uniquely Jewish in nature. Thus, it could be argued that those in the Nazi-created ghettos for Jews in Eastern Europe, who daily and indeed hourly fought a battle for personal, communal and spiritual survival, pursued a truly Jewish form of resistance – as did those who participated in purely Jewish armed insurrections against the Nazi Moloch.[7] Where, however, Jews shared in resistance and opposition against Nazism, it becomes more difficult to label those actions as purely "Jewish" in nature. From this perspective, the alien Jewish refugees who served in British and Allied armed forces during the Second World War had more in common with the Jews who fought in the predominantly non-Jewish partisan bands in the forests of eastern Poland and western Russia – where Jews were often in as much danger from their so-called comrades as from the Nazis[8] – than they did with the Jews of the Polish and Baltic ghettos under Nazism.

Nevertheless, when serving in Britain's armed forces, there were some important differences between the Jewish refugees discussed here and their "Tommy" comrades. The majority of Britons who served during the Second

---

[6]There is, of course, a vast bibliography on the complex subject of German and European resistance to the Nazi Third *Reich*, and only a few of the most significant titles can be referred to here. See for example, M.R.D. Foot, *Resistance. An Analysis of European Resistance to Nazism, 1940–1945*, London 1976; Peter Grasmann, *Sozialdemokraten gegen Hitler 1933–1945*, Munich 1976; Peter Hoffmann, *The History of the German Resistance 1933–1945*, London 1977; Lothar Kettenacker (ed.), *Das "Andere Deutschland" im Zweiten Weltkrieg. Emigration und Widerstand in internationaler Perspektive*, Stuttgart 1977; Henri Michel, *The Shadow War. Resistance in Europe 1939–1945*, London 1972; Werner Rings, *Life with the Enemy. Collaboration and Resistance in Hitler's Europe 1939–1945*, London 1982; Werner Röder, *Die deutschen sozialistischen Exilgruppen in Großbritannien 1940–1945. Ein Beitrag zur Geschichte des Widerstandes gegen den Nationalsozialismus*, 2nd edn., Bonn 1973; Ger van Roon, *German Resistance to Hitler. Count von Moltke and the Kreisau Circle*, London 1971; Hans Rothfels, *Die deutsche Opposition gegen Hitler. Eine Würdigung*, Frankfurt a. Main 1958; Jürgen Schmädeke and Peter Steinbach (eds.), *Der Widerstand gegen den Nationalsozialismus. Die deutsche Gesellschaft und der Widerstand gegen Hitler*, Munich 1985; Walter Schmitthenner and Hans Buchheim (eds.), *Der deutsche Widerstand gegen Hitler. Vier historisch-kritische Studien von Hermann Graml, Hans Mommsen, Hans Joachim Reichhardt und Ernst Wolf*, Cologne–Berlin 1966. Unless books on resistance to Nazism deal specifically with Jewish resistance, the topic is usually ignored in most studies.

[7]See Reuben Ainsztein, *Jewish Resistance in Nazi-Occupied Eastern Europe. With A Historical Survey of the Jew as Fighter and Soldier in the Diaspora*, London 1974; Yisrael Gutman, *The Jews of Warsaw, 1939–1943. Ghetto, Underground, Revolt*, Brighton 1982; Konrad Kwiet and Helmut Eschwege, *Selbstbehauptung und Widerstand. Deutsche Juden im Kampf um Existenz und Menschenwürde 1933–1945*, Hamburg 1984; Yuri Suhl (ed.), *They Fought Back. The Story of Jewish Resistance in Nazi Europe*, London 1968.

[8]See especially the key study by Shmuel Krakowski, *The War of the Doomed. Jewish Armed Resistance in Poland, 1942–1944*, New York–London 1984.

World War did so because they were conscripted. They had no legal or other choice in the matter. That situation likewise determined whatever emotions were felt about serving King and Country in a second war this century against the German *Reich*. Consequently, most simply got on with the job of military service and "duty", and followed orders in the time-honoured fashion.

Given their alien status – apart from the few granted naturalisation by 1939/1940 – Jewish refugees in the United Kingdom could only take up some form of positive action against Nazi Germany by volunteering for service in Britain's armed forces. Yet that only became possible as and when the British government decided its policies in this respect. Nevertheless, when permitted to volunteer and serve, most refugees acknowledged the influence of certain motives which did not, and could not, apply to their British comrades. While most made the important distinction between fighting against Nazism but for their (idealised) Germany,[9] none could forget their own bitter experiences of Nazi Germany's anti-Jewish policies. One refugee's own youthful anti-Nazi activities in 1934 resulted in some typical treatment after he was arrested, to be succeeded four years later by arrest and internment in Sachsenhausen concentration camp as part of the wide-sweeping arrests following the *"Reichskristallnacht"* on 9th/10th November 1938.[10] Moreover, many refugees left behind families and friends who continued to suffer persecution under the Nazis. There were natural feelings, therefore, of wanting to "get even" with the Nazis, while for some such thoughts turned to revenge when news emerged from 1942 onwards of Germany's policies of mass murder in Europe. Understandably, the British private could feel nothing of this. To this extent at least, it could be argued that there were elements of a special "Jewish" contribution to Britain's armed forces during the Second World War. There are other aspects to this special Jewish contribution which also need to be considered. Despite rather obvious manifestations of antisemitism and the strong xenophobia in British society, it is still surprising how many Jewish refugees actually volunteered for military service after September 1939 – although the term "volunteer" needs to be carefully defined within the present context. For most, however, the outbreak of war between the United Kingdom and Germany on 3rd September 1939 dashed the hopes of gaining that which it was felt would resolve most of their difficulties within British society: British citizenship. One condition for that was at least five years' residence in the United Kingdom. Although after 3rd September 1939 the British government agreed to process applications submitted by that date, it refused to accept any others for the duration of the war. The larger number of Jewish refugees, who fled Germany and Austria in 1938 and 1939 because of the

---

[9]Imperial War Museum, Department of Sound Records. Interview with Clive Teddern. 003839/06. R06. Transcript, p. 56; anonymous contribution from a member of Twelve Force (on which, see further below).

[10]See the account, and the consequences which followed, of such youthful Jewish anti-Nazi actions as the printing and distribution of leaflets and the posting of anti-Nazi stickers on walls, lamp-posts etc. in Stephen Dale, *Spanglet. Or By Any Other Name*, privately printed 1993, pp. 31ff.; available in the Wiener Library, London. The description of that author's experiences in 1938 are to be found on pp. 46–50.

"*Reichskristallnacht*" and its consequences,[11] were thus forced to experience the Second World War in the United Kingdom as "enemy aliens". This opprobrium applied whether they remained civilians or became part of the British military anti-Nazi effort.

Although many Jewish refugees felt relief on Neville Chamberlain's declaration of war upon Germany because it appeared to rule out another Munich or other compromise with Hitler,[12] those whose applications for British citizenship immediately foundered now found themselves classified as "enemy" aliens. Moreover, as of 28th September 1939, all aliens from the age of sixteen had to be examined by Aliens Tribunals (of which there were 120) for classification as either an "A" category alien, one to be interned; a "B" category, one to be exempt from internment, but subject to restrictions concerning residence and travel, etc.; and the "C" category, those exempt from both internment and restrictions. While civil libertarians might have seen these tribunals as a retrograde step,[13] they actually helped some Jewish refugees. The issue of a "C" category immediately signified a measure of "approval" for that individual by that final arbiter of the citizen's life, the British civil service. As such, it acted as a kind of internal passport for the alien refugee. This even included entry into Britain's armed forces since, at an inter-ministerial meeting on 12th September 1939 in Whitehall, the War Office agreed to accept aliens into the Army, provided that if they were Germans, Austrians, or Czechs they had been positively vetted and passed by the Aliens Tribunals.[14] Two months later, in November 1939, it was officially announced that aliens aged between nineteen and fifty would be permitted to enlist in certain branches of the armed forces.[15] Although this granted them exemption from registration under Article 22 of the all-embracing Aliens Order, it did nothing to change their (non-British) nationality particulars; a policy maintained rigorously by the British government throughout the war.[16] It was also announced that aliens approved by the Military Intelligence Branch of the War Office would be allowed to join a new army formation of the Auxiliary Military Pioneer Corps (AMPC), known from 1940 simply as the Pioneer Corps.[17]

The AMPC, formed on 17th October 1939 under Army Order 200 of 1939, was essentially an unarmed military labour unit whose members, often known as

---

[11]See the concise, but exemplary, analysis by Hermann Graml, *Antisemitism in the Third Reich*, Oxford 1992. Extensive lists of titles on the subject of the "*Reichskristallnacht*" are to be found in the bibliographies of *LBI Year Book XXXV* (1990), pp. 535–543; and *LBI Year Book XXXVI* (1991), pp. 532–537.

[12]Imperial War Museum, Department of Sound Records. Interview with Professor Hans Grüneberg. 004478/03. RO2. Transcript, p. 14.

[13]On the question of civil liberties in wartime Britain, see Neil Stammers, *Civil Liberties in Britain During the Second World War. A Political Study*, London 1983.

[14]Public Record Office, Kew, Home Office Documents (= HO). HO 213/262. GEN. 29/15/127. Unsigned Record of Meeting in Home Office, 12th September 1939.

[15]Miriam Kochan, *Britain's Internees in the Second World War*, London 1983, p. 17.

[16]See John P. Fox, *loc. cit.*, pp. 415–459.

[17]Bentwich, *Risks*, *op. cit.*, p. 31. The change of title was announced in the House of Commons on 26th November 1940 by Anthony Eden, Secretary of State for War: Parliamentary Debates, 5th Series, House of Commons (= HC). HC, vol. 367, col. 131.

"Sappers", were "of course, the jacks-of-all trades".[18] It was regarded as "the dumping ground of the British army; all human dross, it was once unkindly said, was there. It was the natural home of illiterates and former criminals".[19] But not always. Arthur Koestler, the influential writer, was once a Pioneer, while other writers, musicians, actors and intellectuals – as well as representatives of virtually every profession imaginable[20] – helped to mark out the Corps as something different in the annals of the British army.[21] Even the former soup chef of the *Hotel Kaiserhof* in Berlin, frequented by Adolf Hitler before he became *Reichskanzler*, became a member of 88 Company AMPC.[22]

Of the five Training and Reception Centres (TRCs) for the AMPC, one TRC for special "Alien Companies" (ACs), No. 3 Centre, was established at a well-known transit camp for (mainly) Jewish refugees from Germany and Austria at Richborough on the Kent coast adjoining Sandwich (although it actually consisted of two camps, Kitchener and Haig).[23] On 25th October 1939, when the Marquis of Reading assumed command of No. 3 TRC at Richborough, and 16th November, when the first alien was enlisted, it could be said that German- and Austrian-Jewish refugees resident in the United Kingdom were at last taking up "the fight" against the enemy, albeit in unarmed units popularly known as the "King's Own Enemy Aliens".[24] This, however, merely increased the frustration many professional alien refugees felt at being forced to serve in a unit which, by any standards, undoubtedly wasted much ability and intelligence.[25] By 6th January 1940, some 905 aliens had been accepted for service in the British army,[26] while by the summer of 1940 about 2,400 foreigners were to be found in the Alien Companies of the Pioneer Corps,[27] although what proportion of these were alien Jewish refugees is difficult to ascertain precisely.

About half of Richborough's some 3,000–4,000 inmates eventually signed up. Yet many felt misgivings about wearing uniform, fearful for the safety of relatives still in Germany and Austria if this should become known to the German

[18] [Major] E.H. Rhodes-Wood, *A War History of the Royal Pioneer Corps 1939–1945*, Aldershot 1960, pp. 9, 86.
[19] Peter and Leni Gillman, *"Collar the Lot!" How Britain Interned and Expelled Its Wartime Refugees*, London 1980, p. 257; Rhodes-Wood, *op. cit.*, pp. 17–19, 83–84.
[20] Fred Warner, *Don't You Know There Is A War On? A Very Personal Account*, private typescript, p. 11. I am extremely grateful to Mr. Fred Warner for lending me a copy of this account of his life and experiences during the Second World War and for his permission to quote from it.
[21] Bentwich, *Risks, op. cit.*, pp. 52–62, esp. p. 56 for Koestler. See also J.M. Ritchie, 'Germans and Austrians in Exile in Great Britain. Inaugural Lecture delivered on 31st October 1988', in *Aberdeen University Review*, 181 (1989), pp. 18–29, esp. p. 23. I am extremely grateful to Professor Ritchie, Director of the Research Centre for Germans and Austrians in Exile in Great Britain of the University of Aberdeen, for sending me a copy of his inaugural lecture.
[22] Warner, *A Very Personal Account, op. cit.*, p. 19.
[23] Bentwich, *Risks, op. cit.*, pp. 26–34. On the Richborough Camp, see also Norman Bentwich, *They Found Refuge. An Account of British Jewry's Work for Victims of Nazi Oppression*, London 1956, pp. 102–110; and Judith Tydor-Baumel, 'The Kitchener Transmigration Camp at Richborough', in *Yad Vashem Studies*, 14 (1981), pp. 233–246.
[24] Bentwich, *They found Refuge, op. cit.*, p. 108.
[25] Rhodes-Wood, *op. cit.*, pp. 21–22, 66.
[26] HC, vol. 356, cols. 8–9, 16th January 1940, statement by Mr. Oliver Stanley, Secretary of State for War.
[27] Dokumentationsarchiv des österreichischen Widerstandes/Wolfgang Muchitsch (eds.), *Österreicher im Exil. Großbritannien 1938–1945. Eine Dokumentation*, Vienna 1992, p. 494. I am grateful to Dr. Arnold Paucker for drawing my attention to this publication.

authorities or their informants. Nor did British bureaucratic tactlessness help matters. Recruitment posters in the camp embellished the message, "England expects every man to do his duty", with the equivalent of a slap in the face by adding the rider: "You are not Englishmen, but you should do your duty."[28] Others held back from enlisting at that time because they still hoped to emigrate to the United States of America and elsewhere, while yet others applied for, and obtained, civilian employment.[29] At Richborough, those who did not volunteer for the Pioneers still took some part in the war effort by providing services (cooking, tailoring, cobbling) for those who enlisted. About 150 men were employed on special work for the Army, recording broadcasts day and night from German radio stations.[30] In addition, volunteers from the camp had already helped local Kent bodies in preparing coastal defences.[31] Many of the early 1939–1940 volunteers were undoubtedly motivated by "the need to repay the country which had granted them asylum and at the same time to aid the war effort against the Nazis".[32] Even service in the Pioneer Corps did wonders for the morale of those concerned, especially since it appeared to offer the opportunity of facing the Nazis on equal terms, i.e. with "Waffe in der Hand" as one former refugee puts it.[33]

Others, however, joined up in those early days of the war simply to escape the sheer institutionalised tedium of the transit camps. Certainly neither the Jewish refugee volunteers nor their "Tommy" comrades thought in heroic terms of "glory" and "adventure" as had the millions of young men throughout Europe in the heady (and innocent) days of August 1914. But even when some volunteers thought that by enlisting they would be contributing to the war effort against Nazism, there was not a great deal to encourage them. The AMPC and its Alien Companies were an unknown, untried, unarmed raggle-taggle collection of heterogeneous and disparate elements, formed during the static "phoney war" in the West when the larger question appeared to be whether there would be a war at all, rather than how long such a war would last. Doubts and frustrations were intensified by constant rumours of a compromise peace deal with Germany.

Many refugee volunteers perhaps still thought of returning one day to a non-Nazi Germany. Others, especially those who left Germany as early as 1933, had for a long time vowed never to return, so that the United Kingdom's war with Germany was not seen as being one with "my homeland".[34] At the same time, probably few of these early volunteers bore within them the deep feelings of revenge and revulsion that undoubtedly motivated those who joined or were active later – for obvious reasons from 1942 onwards. For many refugees, this later information about Nazi genocide simply confirmed previous thoughts about the nature of German society after January 1933. Herbert Goldsmith,

[28]Barry Turner, *The Long Horizon. 60 Years of CBF World Jewish Relief*, London, n.d., p. 33.
[29]Bentwich, *Risks, op. cit.*, p. 31.
[30]*Ibid.*, p. 32; Tydor-Baumel, *op. cit.*, p. 243.
[31]Tydor-Baumel, *op. cit.*, p. 243.
[32]*Ibid.*
[33]Communication from Paul Yogi Mayer to the author.
[34]Imperial War Museum, Department of Sound Records. Interview with Professor Hans Grüneberg. 004478/03. R02. Transcript, p. 14. At the end of the war, Grüneberg was offered a chair in Berlin, as well as the directorship of the *Max-Planck-Institut*, but he rejected both. On the other hand, he did holiday in Germany, as well as accepting invitations to lecture and attend scientific meetings there.

whose father had been interned in Sachsenhausen concentration camp after the *"Reichskristallnacht"* and who himself came to Britain in 1939 on a *Kindertransport*, recalled: "I think, even then, as today, one can't think of Germany as one's own country after the way the Jews were treated."[35] Generally, the earlier volunteers were under far less practical and psychological pressure to join the British army than those who joined after mid-1940.

Of the first six Alien Companies formed early in 1940, five – Numbers 69, 74, 77, 87 and 88 – were dispatched after a few weeks training to be an integral part of the British Expeditionary Force in France,[36] and later in other arenas of war. Whilst their main function was indeed that of unarmed "labourers" (employed on camp, road and railway construction), in the heat of battle in May 1940 members of the fourth and fifth Companies, Numbers 87 and 88, were given rifles and fifty rounds per man by their Commander, Colonel Arthur Evans, MP, to help defend Le Havre. Within a short time, they were also manning machine-guns and anti-tank rifles. But just as the Duke of Wellington at Waterloo in 1815 expressed himself more nervous about the common soldier under his command than about the opposing French, so some British naval officers at Le Havre were more fearful about these newly armed aliens in the British army than perhaps the *Wehrmacht*. One alien sentry with his newly-acquired rifle was asked by the Commanding Officer what he would do if a German appeared. He said he would call "Halt", and if the man still came on would further say: "Advance, and produce your AB (Army Book) 64, Part 2."[37] Nor could the sharp-eyed French locals have had much confidence in the ability of the Pioneer Corps to defend them against the advancing Germans. When members of 88 Company AMPC were first given their rifles and underwent essential weaponry drill, it was more a case of "rifles . . . falling all over the place" than a display of military efficiency guaranteed to instil confidence in soldiers and civilians alike.[38]

On 10th June 1940, war experience in Europe for 87 Company AMPC ended temporarily when it was withdrawn from St. Malo to Weymouth.[39] Almost a fortnight later, 88 Company AMPC also withdrew through St. Malo on 21st June, arriving at Southampton the following day.[40] The Pioneers brought with them every weapon they could carry, but were forced to hand them over to the authorities upon landing at Southampton or later in the TRCs. The pervasive doubts about the political reliability of the men of the Alien Companies was compounded by irrational fears of them handling arms.[41] Insult appeared to be added to injury when, on 30th July 1940, Anthony Eden, Secretary of State for

---

[35]Imperial War Museum, Department of Sound Records. Interview with Herbert Goldsmith. 003970/05. R01.

[36]Bentwich, *Risks, op. cit.*, pp. 35–36; Rhodes-Wood, *op. cit.*, p. 21.

[37]Bentwich, *Risks, op. cit.*, pp. 35–37; Rhodes-Wood, *op. cit.*, pp. 45–46. On the role of the AMPC in France and Belgium, see also [Major] L.F. Ellis, *The War In France and Flanders 1939–1940. History of the Second World War*, ed. by J.R.M. Butler, London 1953 (United Kingdom Military Series), pp. 21, 79, 153, 263.

[38]Warner, *A Very Personal Account, op. cit.*, p. 13.

[39]Communication from a former member of Twelve Force. A.W. Freud, in his private typescript, *Before the Anticlimax*, p. 23, gives the date of withdrawal as 18th June 1940. I am extremely grateful to Mr. Freud for kindly lending me his typescript and for permission to quote from it.

[40]Warner, *A Very Personal Account, op. cit.*, p. 16.

[41]Rhodes-Wood, *op. cit.*, p. 65.

War, announced that only British members of the Corps would be permitted to carry arms.[42] Thereafter, the Alien Companies – which between 1940 and 1943 were expanded to fifteen in all – were employed in various home defence and fortification projects in England and Wales, mainly assisting the Engineers and the Ordnance and Army Service Corps. During the summer of 1940 when invasion was daily expected, some were engaged in constructing pill-boxes and tank-traps and in digging trenches. When the Blitz began later in the year, many worked in London and other major cities on clearance and rescue tasks.[43]

However, the summer of 1940 proved to be yet another decisive turning-point for all Jewish refugees in the United Kingdom not yet granted British citizenship. The Allied withdrawal from Europe was immediately succeeded by the spy and invasion scare. This led to Britain's notorious policy of interning and deporting enemy aliens resident in the United Kingdom – including those most ardent anti-Nazis of all, the Jewish refugees from Germany and Austria.[44] Evidently, news about the policy of internment produced "a near riot" in the returning 88 Company AMPC, serious trouble only being avoided by a special visit from a War Office official who promised that all internees with relatives serving in the British Army would be released at once.[45] The spy mania which helped to bring about the policy of internment was probably responsible for one interned refugee being told by a policeman: "In wartime there are worse criminals than thieves or murderers."[46] Yet had Hitler succeeded in invading Britain in 1940, the United Kingdom's policy of deporting these Jews would have saved their lives.[47] Despite being interned on the Isle of Man, Herbert Sulzbach, who fled in 1937 from Nazi antisemitism in Frankfurt and joined the Pioneer Corps in 1940, realistically concluded that "internment, in the circumstances of the time, was a must for the British government. They couldn't have known who was who."[48] Other former refugees are more critical, considering the policy to have been a "serious infringement of our liberty, inflicted on us, who were totally devoted allies, by the British Government".[49] The concomitant of the internment and deportation policies was an immediate stop to the enlistment of enemy aliens in the British army.

In the event, opposition in Britain to internment, and other developments in Europe, caused yet more twists and turns in official policy towards the Jewish refugees resident in British territories, besides further influencing the refugees' own perceptions of their ambivalent position in British society. Following his conquests in Western Europe in 1940, Hitler made it plain for all to see how deadly serious his war in Europe was, when, on 22nd June 1941, he "snatched defeat from the claws of certain victory" by his onslaught on the Soviet Union.[50]

From the summer of 1940, then, the British government was not only forced to

[42]François Lafitte, *The Internment of Aliens*, London 1988, p. 243.
[43]Bentwich, *Risks, op. cit.*, pp. 38–39; Warner, *A Very Personal Account, op. cit.*, p. 17.
[44]See the studies by Gillman, *op. cit.*, and Lafitte, *op. cit.*
[45]Warner, *A Very Personal Account, op. cit.*, p. 17.
[46]Freud, *Anticlimax, op. cit.*, p. 12.
[47]*Ibid.*, pp. 13, 20.
[48]Imperial War Museum, Department of Sound Records. Interview with Herbert Sulzbach. 004338/03. R03.
[49]Dale, *Spanglet, op. cit.*, pp. 63, 71.
[50]Freud, *Anticlimax, op. cit.*, p. 18.

retreat from its internment policy, but also to allow once more the recruitment of foreigners into the British forces. Such recruitment was permitted to resume under categories 11 and 12 of the White Paper of 31st July 1940 dealing specifically with German and Austrian civilian internees, which allowed for the release of particular categories of internees.[51] For some time to come, however, such recruitment only meant service in the perceived dead-end of the British army, the Pioneer Corps. Posters explaining and encouraging enlistment in the Corps were soon displayed in all the male internment camps, although the poor reputation of the Corps led to disappointing results for the War Office and the government in terms of volunteers not forthcoming. Another likely reason for the poor response was the same fear – accentuated because of the spy scares of 1940 – of repercussions on relatives still in Germany and Austria, as had influenced many in Richborough Camp earlier in 1940.

However, as 1940 progressed and the enlistment of enemy aliens failed to improve significantly, British military and government authorities increasingly resorted to warning internees to enlist or else to face internment for the duration of the war. British officials were even sent to internment camps in Australia[52] and Canada[53] to press this point. Internees were told, in no uncertain terms, not to desist from enlisting in the hope of obtaining civilian employment, because it would not be theirs for the asking. Nor was the carrot of eventual British citizenship ever held out to these people.[54] Finally, in the House of Commons on 26th November 1940, Herbert Morrison, the Home Secretary, warned that the government regarded enlistment in the Pioneer Corps as the appropriate method of obtaining release for men between the ages of eighteen and fifty. It was, he declared, "an opportunity clearly to demonstrate their friendliness to the Allied cause by offering their services to this Corps".[55] Not that friendliness was always the sentiment first encountered by recently released internees in their first dealings with minor British officialdom upon their return to the United Kingdom.[56]

Gradually, though, more interned Jewish refugees enlisted. Some regarded the step as a chance to "do one's bit" for the war effort against Nazism,[57] especially

---

[51] Fox, *loc. cit.*, pp. 424–425; Kochan, *op. cit.*, pp. 123–124.

[52] For one brief account of the internees' journey out to Australia on the infamous *Dunera* and their reception and experiences in Australia, see Dale, *Spanglet, op. cit.*, pp. 64–72. One of Dale's fellow-internees in Australia was Franz Stampfel, who later trained Roger Bannister and his three companions for the breaking of the four-minute record for the mile in 1954; *ibid.*, p. 69. Another account of life on board the *Dunera* and internment in Australia is given in Freud, *Anticlimax, op. cit.*, pp. 12–19. The British official sent to the Australian camps was Major Julian Layton, an English-born Jew, whose job it was to "sort out the sheep from the goats"; *ibid.*, p. 19. Layton is also mentioned in Bentwich, *Risks, op. cit.*, p. 84.

[53] Imperial War Museum, Department of Sound Records. Interview with Clive Teddern. 003839/06. RO5. Transcript, pp. 41–42, 50. Teddern was interviewed by Alec Paterson (later Sir Alec), a Home Office official and a Prison Commissioner who evidently had "a great reputation for humanity"; Bentwich, *Risks, op. cit.*, p. 14; Ian Dear, *Ten Commando 1942–1945*, London 1987, p. 42.

[54] Imperial War Museum, Department of Sound Records. Interview with Herbert Goldsmith. 003970/05. R04; *ibid.*, Interview with Clive Teddern. 003839/06. R06. Transcript, p. 57.

[55] HC, vol. 367, cols. 79–81, 26th November 1940; Kochan, *op. cit.*, p. 165.

[56] Freud, *Anticlimax, op. cit.*, p. 20.

[57] Imperial War Museum, Department of Sound Records. Interview with Professor Hans Grüneberg. 004478/03. RO2. Transcript, p. 15; *ibid.*, Interview with Clive Teddern, 003839/06. R06. Transcript, p. 55.

since, as Herbert Goldsmith recalled, "other people were [also] being conscripted". Goldsmith emphasises, in contrast to other evidence, how "no direct pressure" was brought to bear upon refugees to volunteer. On the contrary, he felt the whole process was "very voluntary".[58] For many refugees, then, a sense of duty and responsibility increasingly prevailed, if not to Britain itself at least to the seriousness of the wider anti-Nazi cause. As it was, the Battle of Britain and the Blitz of 1940, and even Field-Marshal Rommel's threat to the British army in North Africa in 1942,[59] underlined the precariousness of Britain's position in the war. If the United Kingdom should ever succumb to a victorious Nazi Third *Reich*, the fate of Jewish refugees from Germany and Austria within its shores was a foregone conclusion. By helping to defend the United Kingdom and contributing to the ultimate defeat of Nazi Germany, the alien Jews would help to secure their own position. For others, especially younger recruits whose perception of the stark realities of the world was obviously less acute than that of their elders, enlistment appeared to offer adventure or excitement.[60] The reaction of one young non-Jewish German refugee was probably shared by many of his Jewish countrymen: "we were absolutely too young simply to sit around doing nothing [in the internment camps]".[61] Yet others eventually bowed to the direct and persistent official pressure either to enlist or to remain interned. But as one experienced author of the internment policy has commented, "this is not the way to win recruits among refugees".[62]

Ultimately, when the decision to enlist had finally been taken, most alien Jewish refugees, like their Gentile British comrades, found that service life was what they made it: hell if the official system was bucked, but not if it could be made to work for them, as long as the right fiddle was found in co-operation with sympathetic comrades; the immediate common enemy being not the distant German, but tedious and often petty army discipline, army food and the officer corps – that perfect mirror of the British class system. Moreover, as the war progressed, the position of the foreign enlistees *vis-à-vis* the British people vastly improved. Civilian communities responded well to the Alien Companies[63] when they were employed locally on such unspectacular but essential work as operating military depots and installations, fire-watching, construction work[64] and even when guarding Free French Forces who had surrendered in North Africa.[65] At the same time, Jewish members of the Alien Companies – in which non-Jews constituted anything between one-third to one-tenth of the strength[66] –

[58]Imperial War Museum, Department of Sound Records. Interview with Herbert Goldsmith. 003970/05. R04.
[59]Imperial War Museum, Department of Sound Records. Interview with Professor Hans Grüneberg. 004478/03. RO2. Transcript, p. 15.
[60]Imperial War Museum, Department of Sound Records. Interview with Clive Teddern. 003839/06. R06. Transcript, p. 55.
[61]Imperial War Museum, Department of Sound Records. Interview with Walter Horst Nessler. 003993/04. R03.
[62]Lafitte, *op. cit.*, p. 244.
[63]Imperial War Museum, Department of Sound Records. Interview with Herbert Goldsmith. 003970/05. R05.
[64]Rhodes-Wood, *op. cit.*, p. 217.
[65]Imperial War Museum, Department of Sound Records. Interview with Peter Midgley. 003941/05. RO4.
[66]Bentwich, *Risks, op. cit.*, p. 46.

generally found their religious requirements were fully met by their Gentile officers and comrades. In one Company, the CO secured a complete outfit of new cutlery, crockery, cooking utensils and an oven, so that the Jewish members could observe the Passover in its scrupulous detail. In another Company, the pay-day for three years was a Thursday instead of the usual Friday, because the religious Jews were unwilling to handle money on the eve of their Sabbath.[67]

During 1941, the War Office finally agreed to the granting of commissions to alien refugees in the Pioneer Corps, although this has been described as "a niggardly concession" since the aliens could be officers only in that Corps and not more than one alien officer could be posted to a Company. However, the self-esteem of many serving alien Jews grew enormously when, from 1941, they were consulted by Intelligence personnel in preparation for the Royal Air Force's early raids on Germany's industrial centres. Nevertheless, it was not until the end of 1941 that arms were issued to the men of the Alien Companies, and another year before many alien Pioneers actually received a modicum of regular weapon training.[68] By 2nd May 1941, the number of aliens in the Pioneer Corps with medical qualifications was 65 – 39 doctors and 26 dental surgeons.[69]

Gradually, other restrictions were lifted, *pari passu* with an intensification of the British war effort towards final victory. Transfer to other Army technical units, except signal formations (seen as particularly sensitive from an intelligence standpoint), was finally permitted from 2nd March 1943,[70] as was alien employment in skilled tradesmen's posts. From March 1943 as well, the War Office agreed to permit alien recruits with special qualifications to bypass the Pioneer Corps and be posted direct to units needing their special skills.[71] In the House of Commons on 22nd April 1943, Sir James Grigg announced that, from 1st May, aliens of enemy origin would be considered for direct enlistment into any corps of the armed services, other than the Royal Corps of Signals. That restriction was still to apply.[72] As of 2nd June 1943, it was established that there were approximately 4,760 aliens of enemy origin in the Pioneer Corps, of whom 112 had already been transferred to more actively combatant units while applications for transfer from a further 218 were then under consideration.[73] These developments undoubtedly helped to assuage some of the frustrations felt by many volunteer refugees at being forced simply to "stand by" – because of the length and nature of their training programmes, the enforced delay of an Allied

---

[67]*Ibid.*, pp. 44–45.
[68]*Ibid.*, pp. 69–70; Rhodes-Wood, *op. cit.*, pp. 138–139.
[69]HC, vol. 371, col. 716, 6th May 1941.
[70]HC, vol. 369, col. 789, 4th March 1941; *ibid.*, vol. 370, cols. 9–10, 18th March 1941; *ibid.*, vol. 372, col. 1183, 1st July 1941; *ibid.*, vol. 374, col. 855, 7th October 1941; *ibid.*, vol. 382, col. 1206, 6th August 1942; *ibid.*, vol. 387, cols. 477–478, 2nd March 1943.
[71]HC, vol. 387, cols. 1046–1047, 16th March 1943.
[72]HC, vol. 388, col. 1837, 22nd April 1943.
[73]Public Record Office, Kew. War Office Papers (= WO). WO 32/10676. 27/GEN/2884. Note of 2nd June 1943: 'Direct Enlistment of Aliens into Arms other than the Pioneer Corps'. Bentwich, *Risks, op. cit.*, pp. 81–82, lists the numbers of those transferred between 1941 and 1943 from the Pioneer Corps to elsewhere in the British armed forces: 800 to technical units; 450 to specialist units and the Intelligence Corps; 650 to the combatant units of the Infantry, Armoured Corps and the Artillery; 300 to the Commandos, the Airborne Troops, and the Special Forces; and over 100 to the Royal Navy and the Royal Air Force. How many of these transferees were Jewish refugees is, however, difficult to tell.

invasion of Europe, and their often being employed on duties far beneath their intelligence and abilities, instead of getting into action somewhere.[74]

The former hewers of wood and drawers of water could now be fighting soldiers in the true sense, or even use their technical skills and brains in army units other than the Alien Companies. Even when refugees remained in Alien Companies, other positive changes could be seen. For example, members of the senior Alien Pioneer Corps Company, 69A Company with its Headquarters at Darlington, were employed in helping the local Royal Engineers and the Royal Ordnance Corps, demanding and fulfilling work in its own right.[75] Other Companies worked under the general direction of the Royal Army Service Corps.[76] Accompanying these changes were others, as important psychologically as practically. Diffusing their numbers more widely throughout Britain's armed forces, with the attendant probability that they would become involved in combat – and the risks of combat were fully accepted[77] – the authorities decreed the compulsory Anglicisation of German-Jewish names. This was designed to protect any who were captured by the German from being singled out for special treatment as Jews.[78] As Herbert Goldsmith recalled, consequently, in the worst scenario of capture, British soldiers "very successfully shielded" their disguised German-Jewish comrades-in-arms – although Norman Bentwich records one case where one Jew captured by the Germans was nearly deliberately betrayed by his non-Jewish comrades.[79] Goldsmith approves of this decision by the British government.[80] Clive Teddern, on the other hand, records the resentment felt at military service without naturalisation: "without citizenship you had very little protection". Nor did he think that many Germans would have been fooled by the name-change policy.[81]

Increasingly, army experience for the alien Jewish refugee enlistees covered the kaleidoscopic highways and byways of military service confronted also by the British soldiers, beginning for most at the Huyton training camp for the Pioneer Corps, near Liverpool. Yet until "fortress Europe" was breached in 1943 and 1944, most service life also consisted of routine and boredom, except that by then the enlisted refugees were free men. Yet for some, army life had its moments of light relief. One Jewish enlistee, the grandson of Sigmund Freud, categorised the

---

[74]Communications from Peter A. Block and Paul Yogi Mayer to the author. See also Bentwich, *Risks*, *op. cit.*, chap. 5, 'The Years of Frustration, 1940–43', which includes references to those people within and without Parliament who fought long, and with a great deal of frustration, for "the right to fight" of members of the Alien Pioneer Corps. The greatest frustration was, of course, felt by the "enemy aliens" who felt doubly ill-treated when they saw "friendly aliens" from Belgium, France, Holland and Poland accepted more or less without question into British combatant units; *ibid.*, p. 78.
[75]Imperial War Museum, Department of Sound Records. Interview with Herbert Goldsmith. 003970/05. R05.
[76]Bentwich, *Risks*, *op. cit.*, pp. 48–51.
[77]Communication from Paul Yogi Mayer to the author.
[78]Bentwich, *Risks*, *op. cit.*, pp. 46–47.
[79]*Ibid.*, pp. 100–101.
[80]Imperial War Museum, Department of Sound Records. Interview with Herbert Goldsmith. 003970/05. R05.
[81]Imperial War Museum, Department of Sound Records. Interview with Clive Teddern. 003839/06. R06. Transcript, p. 58.

British officers in the Pioneer Corps as having been "flung out of every other unit in the British Army for total incompetence, madness or political unreliability".[82] He also recalls a one-armed officer who persisted in driving his own vehicle in camp – at a time when automatic gear-boxes were hardly standard issue in the British army. But there was more to note about this officer: not only did he insist on being saluted by all and sundry whilst driving, he returned those salutes throughout his particular form of military manoeuvres.[83] Yet another Jewish refugee, Herbert Sulzbach from Frankfurt and obviously a fluent German speaker, was trained as an interpreter. But, in the grand old tradition of British army bureaucratic muddle, his first posting was to a camp in England for Russians – of which language he spoke not a word. He was forced to remain there for at least a fortnight before the mistake was discovered and rectified.[84] Fred Warner, another refugee from Hamburg, recalls how, being laid low by a 'flu epidemic when his 88 Company AMPC was stationed at Lanvaches in Wales, he and other convalescents at Abergavenny were "honoured" in the summer of 1941 by having that other erstwhile refugee, Rudolf Hess, billeted in a small house in the grounds of their convalescent home. There was, however, more interest shown in the beautifully polished riding boots worn by Hess, who was guarded by a detachment from the Welsh Guards, than in the man himself.[85]

The wide range of military service experienced by the alien Jewish refugees from 1943 was indicative of the complexity and seriousness of the British war effort against the Nazi enemy. Some refugees put their scientific expertise to good effect in surprising directions. One distinguished geneticist and pathologist, Professor Hans Grüneberg, who came to Britain in 1933 from Freiburg University, volunteered for the Royal Army Medical Corps in 1942. Except that he then worked in a ballistics unit under the guidance of Solly Zuckerman, a senior and influential scientific government adviser, investigating the fragmentation pattern of bursting projectiles and the consequences for people hit by such fragments of red-hot metal. Through his contacts with Lieutenant-Colonel Nigel Balchin (the popular writer) in the War Office, Grüneberg was later instrumental in persuading the authorities to reject fantastic proposals from other quarters

---

[82]Bentwich, *Risks, op. cit.*, p. 71, also observes that in the stress of events after Dunkirk in 1940, some Commanding Officers of the Alien Companies were "temperamentally unfitted. They made no secret of their suspicion of all aliens, or their contempt for intellect and culture . . . The frequency of the change of command in several of the Companies is an indication of internal trouble." On the other hand, "some British officers had a most sympathetic understanding of 'their aliens', and won their lasting affection".

[83]Freud, *Anticlimax, op. cit.*, p. 24. It would just be too much of a coincidence if the one-armed officer described by Freud was the very same who responded to Stephen Dale's request for a transfer out of the Pioneer Corps with the following words: "You, a foreigner! There are plenty of British boys who want a crack at the enemy. Their needs are greater than yours. Dismiss." Dale, *Spanglet, op. cit.*, p. 78.

[84]Imperial War Museum, Department of Sound Records. Interview with Herbert Sulzbach. 004338/03. R02. For comments about Sulzbach's work in Haltwhistle Camp for German prisoners of war, where he tried to "lay the foundation amongst the prisoners of a new democratic way of life and a new philosophy", see Bentwich, *Risks, op. cit.*, pp. 132–134.

[85]Warner, *A Very Personal Account, op. cit.*, pp. 19–20.

for equipping the eventual Allied invasion force with complicated body armour.[86]

Others put their special intellectual and linguistic skills to good use in the field of intelligence and analysis, psychological warfare against the enemy, and, under the auspices of the Political Warfare Executive, the writing of such essential tools for the imminent Allied victors as the volume, *Germany. A Basic Handbook*.[87] They also had a special role to play – compounded by their own motives after news was received in 1942 of the Nazi genocide programme – in prisoner-of-war camps for Germans where it was part of their duty to re-educate the prisoners away from Nazi ideology.[88] After all, these prisoners would constitute the citizenry of a future Germany.

Jewish refugees thus came to play an increasingly important part in Britain's variegated preparations for the invasion of Europe. In 1944, for example, Herbert Goldsmith was attached to a Field Company of the Royal Engineers, part of a Corps which included a Guards Armoured Division for the invasion of Europe. Other work that year involved learning how to load and unload ships under the expert tuition of Hull dockers. Around the time of the Normandy invasions on 6th June 1944, Goldsmith's Company was moved to St. Leonard's in Sussex where it built emplacements for heavy anti-aircraft gun batteries trying to deal with the V-1 rocket bombs. On D-Day plus 60, in early August 1944, he landed on the invasion front at Arromanches-les-Bains – "Gold Beach" in the British sector on 6th June 1944 – thereafter serving in Cannes, Bruges and Antwerp, where, indirectly, employed "as labourers", he and his colleagues worked "on a secret ultra-violet fixture to binoculars". Finally, he was transferred to the interpreter's pool at Bruxelles where "we worked a fiddle, very successfully", which was "okay, so long as it was not against the law".[89] Other refugees also played important roles in pre-invasion commando, infantry, armoured formations and in actual operations in Sicily, Italy and Normandy from 1943 and 1944.[90] A few Jews even managed to enter that bastion of Britishness, the Royal Navy.[91] Within one highly secret commando unit known as 10 (Inter-Allied) Commando, comprising several nationality groups, German- and Austrian-Jewish refugees constituted the bulk of X-Troop, more

---

[86] Imperial War Museum, Department of Sound Records. Interview with Professor Hans Grüneberg. 004478/03. RO2. Transcript, pp. 17–18. Grüneberg also spent a year with the Army Blood Supply Depot near Bristol, which collected 15,000 pints of blood for blood transfusions, presumably in preparation for the casualties expected during the forthcoming Allied invasion of Europe. Later, he spent time in Italy as an army pathologist in a military hospital where his work was essentially bacteriology. That also led him to becoming something else quite unexpected in his civilian or even military career: "And also I was in essence a coroner for a large part of Italy so far as the Army was concerned in that unexplained deaths tended to land up on my post mortem table, and I had to learn things pretty damn quick, which as a student I never thought I would have to do myself." *Ibid.*, Transcript, pp. 18–19. Grüneberg is briefly mentioned in Bentwich, *Risks, op. cit.*, p. 152.

[87] Imperial War Museum, Department of Sound Records. Interview with Professor F.L. Carsten. 004483/R03.

[88] Bentwich, *Risks, op. cit.*, p. 132.

[89] Imperial War Museum, Department of Sound Records. Interview with Herbert Goldsmith. 003970/05. R05.

[90] *Ibid.* See also Bentwich, *Risks, op. cit.*, chap. 7, 'Airborne Troops, Commandos and Special Services'; and *ibid.*, chap. 8, 'The Army: Infantry, Armoured Formations, Royal Artillery'.

[91] Bentwich, *Risks, op. cit.*, p. 120.

formally known as No. 3 (Miscellaneous) Troop (X-Troop). It appears that the idea of X-Troop – classified as "the British" troop[92] – actually came from Admiral Lord Louis Mountbatten, Chief of Combined Operations 1941–1943, and then Supreme Allied Commander Southeast Asia Command 1943–1945. In October 1946, he not only revealed the unit's existence, but stated that "it is to men like these we must look for the building of a new Germany".[93]

A vague hint about the existence of this secret X-Troop had previously been revealed on 8th December 1945, in an article in the British Army magazine *Soldier* by Major-General Robert Laycock,[94] who succeeded Mountbatten as Chief of Combined Operations in September 1943.[95] Yet more tantalising hints about the unit were dropped in the London *News Chronicle* of 25th October 1946 when the then Lieutenant-Colonel Peter Laycock, who had commanded X-Troop for two years, told something of its story. He acknowledged that its formation and operations were "a top secret of the most vital order". Members of X-Troop were therefore ordered to destroy their Army papers with their German names, which were replaced by War Office forgeries complete with new Anglicised names – some of which were wildly imaginative – chosen by the men themselves.[96]

Given their specialised local knowledge of Europe and their linguistic skills, many Jewish refugee members of X-Troop were attached to other Commando units as interrogators, interpreters, military intelligence experts and occasionally even for work behind the German lines.[97] Unlike the French section of 10-Commando in the run-up to and following the Normandy landings in June 1944, X-Troop did not fight as a unit. Its members were divided into small detachments of between two and five men each, and attached to the Commando and the two Brigade Headquarters which took part in the D-Day landings and the fighting thereafter.[98] One of them, Erich Nathan (renamed Howarth for security reasons), whose father had been a Jewish lawyer in Ulm, was dropped in Normandy near the beaches on D-Day itself by the Caen canal, but was seriously wounded and immediately evacuated back to Britain. In January 1945, Nathan was again in action, this time with the Commandos in Holland, and in April 1945 in the attack on Osnabrück. There, however, he was mortally wounded.[99]

[92]*Ibid.*, p. 101.
[93]*Ibid.*, p. 107; Dear, *Ten Commando, op. cit.*, pp. 6, 36.
[94]Major-General Robert Edward Laycock, DSO, 'Farewell Commandos', in *Soldier. The British Army Magazine* (8th December 1945), pp. 4–5.
[95]Dear, *Ten Commando, op. cit.*, p. 14.
[96]'George, the man who deceived Rommel', in *News Chronicle* (25th October 1946). I am extremely grateful to a former member of this group, Arthur F. Lowy, who forwarded copies of *Soldier* and the *News Chronicle* to the Leo Baeck Institute in New York. In turn, I received them from Dr. Arnold Paucker of the London Leo Baeck Institute. Warner, *A Very Personal Account, op. cit.*, pp. 20–21, gives several examples of the imaginative names proposed by refugees, as well as the story of the unfortunate Orderly Room Sergeant, one Samuel Buck, who commented sarcastically on the names proposed and declared he then wished to change his name to Oppenheimer. Inevitably, and following in the grand traditions of British service life, thereafter he was forever known as "Sergeant Oppenheimer".
[97]Dear, *Ten Commando, op. cit.*, pp. 92, 163.
[98]*Ibid.*, p. 126.
[99]Bentwich, *Risks, op. cit.*, pp. 15–16. On pp. 101ff., Bentwich recounts some of the actions in which members of No. 3 Troop were involved, but without specifying which of the individuals he mentions were Jewish.

Other Jewish refugees from Germany and Austria were specially selected for secret commando operations by the equally secret Special Operations Executive (SOE). Established on 22nd July 1940 by the War Cabinet, SOE's brief was "to co-ordinate all action, by way of subversion and sabotage, against the enemy overseas", i.e. to stir up opposition against Nazism in Occupied Europe by sending in combatant citizens or former citizens of the countries in question.[100] The intention was to force the Germans to employ their military forces to maintain internal discipline in their European empire rather than being able to send them to the fighting fronts. SOE's German section, known as X-Section, covered Austria as well.[101] The Austrian sub-section, under the charge of a Miss Graham-Stamper, was designated X/AUS.[102]

About X-Section of SOE, it has been written that its activities are "still shrouded in mystery and very little has been written about it".[103] It has also been observed that "SOE had no inclination to send agents into Germany because there was so little they could do", in a country under such tight police control.[104] SOE seemed predetermined to believe there was little chance of "successful guerrilla action" in the German *Reich* because "so large a slice of the public took the opposite side". Resignedly, therefore, it has been concluded that "it was hardly SOE's fault that its German section did so badly".[105] Partly, this was due to the fact that the essential back-up facility of agents on the spot in Germany and Austria for in-coming agents and saboteurs had long been abandoned by the Secret Intelligence Service (SIS). Instead, and according to Nigel West, "X-Section limited its activities to offering support to the OSS [the American Office of Strategic Services] operation, centred on 70 Grosvenor Street in Mayfair". West also writes that:

> "SOE's assistance was translated into the provision of sixteen recruits, most being members of the Pioneer Corps, with Leftist political leanings, and all of Austro-German origin. These were the initial candidates for OSS's ambitious plan to infiltrate agents either by air from Italy, or overland through Switzerland and Yugoslavia."

In the event, "none of OSS's other missions into Austria and Germany accomplished anything of significance".[106]

Today, SOE's dwindling band of survivors from X-Section call themselves Twelve Force, largely because "12" was the prefix of several training courses at Special Training Schools they all attended.[107] Most members of X-Section were Jewish – a point not mentioned by West – although not all were. Some were *Mischlinge*, and others were Gentiles of the Socialist persuasion. Twelve Force

---

[100]M.R.D. Foot, *SOE. An Outline History of the Special Operations Executive 1940–46*, London 1993, p. 21; Nigel West, *Secret War. The Story of SOE, Britain's Wartime Sabotage Organisation*, London 1993, pp. 24–27.
[101]Foot, *SOE, op. cit.*, pp. 290–291.
[102]West, *Secret War, op. cit.*, p. 312.
[103]*Ibid.*, p. 312.
[104]*Ibid.*, p. 314.
[105]Foot, *SOE, op. cit.*, p. 288.
[106]West, *Secret War, op. cit.*, p. 314.
[107]Bentwich, *Risks, op. cit.*, pp. 108–112, recounts some of the actions undertaken by alien members of the Pioneer Corps for the SOE, again without detailing which of those he mentions were Jewish.

itself has been described as "a child without [a] name until after the war".[108] Not that entry into the various SOE sub-units was a foregone conclusion for all those refugees who responded to official, but sometimes roundabout, approaches from SOE "recruiting officers", followed by rigorous interviews at the War Office in London. Only twenty out of seventy-five applicants from the Pioneer Corps were accepted into a special pathfinder unit called the 21st Independent Parachute Company, whose organiser was especially keen on recruiting linguists into his group. It was intended that members of this Company should drop before the main invasion force for Europe, to mark drop zones and landing zones for gliders, as well as bringing Allied aircraft in on the somewhat new and still secret Rebecca/Eureka beacons.[109] While not all of those selected for training from 1942 were used, some of the survivors consider that even if they were actually sent on operations, they were not used properly.[110] Of the original 1943 group, about eighteen were dropped into enemy territory, two of whom went in twice, and one was killed. Two of this group were captured by the Germans.[111] Nevertheless, the military training undertaken by these Jewish refugees in the Special Training Schools of the SOE, usually situated in large country houses standing in their own grounds and not easily accessible from outside,[112] was "both thorough and intensive" – in other words, "really tough" – given that the final (ideal) objective was dangerous operational duty behind enemy lines in Nazi-occupied Europe as "highly specialised saboteurs".[113] It included training in wireless communications and code work, field-craft exercises – known as "schemes" when the trainees were dropped "blind" anywhere in the United Kingdom without maps or money and told to return to base as quickly as possible – parachute jumping, the use of explosives, exploitation of enemy weapons, supervision of subversive operations, methods of evading and countering police operations abroad and the planning of operations and selection of targets, all designed at creating the maximum amount of damage to the enemy and its prestige in occupied countries. Some training included learning how to drive locomotives, the basic (and logical) premise being that trainees should first learn how to handle such vehicles before being capable of sabotaging enemy rolling stock, above all the important turn-tables in locomotive sheds.[114] Fortuitously, the training also included instruction on how to counter *Gestapo* interrogation techniques, something which became of prime importance to some members of this special group who were captured on operational service.[115] SOE even made available to its trainees the services of professional lock and safe

[108]Communication from a former member of Twelve Force to the author. Paul Yogi Mayer also states that the term Twelve Force was only used "well after the war".
[109]Communication from Peter A. Block to the author; Warner, *A Very Personal Account, op. cit.*, p. 40.
[110]I am grateful to Mr. Stephen Dale for these points of information.
[111]Dale, *Spanglet, op. cit.*, p. 85.
[112]For a list of the "dozens" of these STS, see West, *Secret War, op. cit.*, pp. 397–398.
[113]Warner, *A Very Personal Account, op. cit.*, p. 24.
[114]*Ibid.*, pp. 24–25.
[115]There are accounts of such training for SOE operations in Dale, *Spanglet, op. cit.*, pp. 79–84; Freud, *Anticlimax, op. cit.*, pp. 29–35; Warner, *A Very Personal Account, op. cit.*, pp. 24–33. See also chap. 4, 'Recruiting and Training', pp. 64–91, in Foot, *SOE, op. cit.*

Julius Carlebach

Werner E. Mosse

Arnold Paucker

Members of the London Leo Baeck Institute
Executive in the British Forces

Fred M. Warner and comrade, Weapon Training Course in Tenby

By courtesy of Fred M. Warner

Paul Yogi Mayer in uniform of Pioneer Corps

By courtesy of Paul Y. Mayer

Captain Edward "Teddy" Lees, Special Operations Executive
with partisans in Italy, 1944

By courtesy of Stephen Dale

WALES AND THE WORLD

Singing the praises of a hero . . .

ONE OF the unsung heroes of World Ward II, Captain Edward "Teddy" Lees, of Westernmoor Road, Neath, has died, aged 64.

A native of Germany, Mr Lees left the country when he was 13 after the sudden disappearance of his Jewish stepmother and his father. Mr Lees came to England by boat and lived with a Jewish family in Manchester.

When war broke out he was too young to enlist but the following year, at the age of 17, he joined the Pioneer Corps. Picked out by a general selection committee, he joined the Special Operations Executive — one of its youngest members.

One of his most daring exploits was in 1944. Already a commissioned officer, he was parachuted into Italy one dark night, the valley was under German control and the whole Tramontina Valley in the north was riddled with Germans.

Gathering up their parachutes and digging them in, they set out to link up with the partisans. Time and time again, Mr Lees and his two companions, also members of the SAE, raided the Germans from the hillsides — their mission was to blow up bridges and disrupt transport.

They were then ordered to rescue three top Americans who had crashed in the mountains near Trieste in Yugoslavia. It took three months hand-to-pmouth living, fighting and intrigue, to get the Americans to safety.

Mr Lees ended the war as interpreter and intelligence officer at Island Farm prisoner-of-war camp, Bridgend. Senior German officers were in custody there and had to be interrogated.

In 1949, Mr Lees joined the Glamorgan Fire Service at Bridgend and ended up as Station Officer. For many years he was the official German interpreter to Glamorgan County Council. He leaves a widow, Peggy, and a daughter, Judith.

Article on Lees in the Western Mail, 17th June 1985

Reproduced from, and by courtesy of, the Western Mail, Cardiff

Stephen Dale

POW Identity Card. The British Army changed the names
of German refugees to English ones (here "Turner"), to hide their identity

By courtesy of Stephen Dale

Section 6 of 220 Company Royal Pioneer Corps, building a sawmill in the Forest of Dean in 1942. The section included a member trained at Krupps. His advice was ignored by the Royal Engineers and all the labour building the sawmill was wasted when it collapsed

By courtesy of Peter W. Johnson

Sections 5 and 6 of 220 Company Royal Pioneer Corps in April 1944, waiting to be sent to France with the 21st Army Group. The members were mainly German, Austrian and Czech refugees, not all of them Jewish

By courtesy of Peter W. Johnson

breakers, at that time seeing out the war in several of His Majesty's Prisons. From such specialists in their chosen craft, the SOE trainees soon learnt how useful the spokes of bicycle wheels could be for opening locks of all descriptions.[116] Despite its strenuousness – and as with all such enterprises, there was an inevitable failure rate – one young Jewish trainee in 1942 (who broke an ankle on his second parachute jump) remembered having "enjoyed every minute of it . . . I was very young and had to settle a score with the Germans".[117] In his case and others of a similar nature, internment in 1940 was nothing compared to the chance to get back at the Nazi regime in Germany.

Naturally, the training programmes could be extremely dangerous and uncomfortable. Broken bones, scraped shins and getting soaking wet were the order of the day on most field exercises. More serious was the occurrence at Pembroke Dock camp, the base of 87 Company, Pioneer Corps. Whilst the Company's third-successive commanding officer lectured on the techniques for handling and laying land-mines, the problem was that for demonstration purposes, he used live mines. One day the inevitable happened, there was an explosion, and at least fifty people were killed. For days afterwards, the rest of the Company had to collect the shattered bodies.[118]

Certain unforeseen hazards also had to be dealt with. In Italy, for example, thieves often stole trainees' unfurled parachutes on the way back to base so as to provide their girlfriends and wives with extremely desirable dress- and lingerie-material, such essential aids to seduction and marital harmony being otherwise unobtainable in wartime Italy.[119] In yet other cases, the hazards were provided by the trainees for other people – *pace* the Admiral who lost "his port" because of the efficiency with which one group penetrated the supposedly tight security arrangements at Portland Harbour, and even the Navy Command Centre at Portland.[120] Likewise, it was fortunate for Sir Oswald Mosley, leader of the British Union of Fascists, that the superior officers of one group of trainees vetoed their plan – proposed, of course, simply as "an excellent exercise" in training – to enter his home and abduct him, just after his release from prison in November 1943, where he had been placed in May 1940 under regulation 18B (1A).[121] At times, however, the tables were turned on the trainees, although such experiences still helped to equip them for their future role as secret agents in Occupied Europe. One Jewish refugee soon learnt how dangerous it was to fall

[116]Freud, *Anticlimax*, op. cit., p. 30; Warner, *A Very Personal Account*, op. cit., p. 29.
[117]Communication from Eric F. Bowes to the author. Bowes's parents – his original name was Erich Franz Brauer of Breslau – were interned in Theresienstadt during the war. His father was later sent to Auschwitz, but was able to escape, an exploit highlighted by the Earl of Lytton in the House of Lords in 1947. Both parents survived the war. However, despite Bowes's own war record in the British armed forces, he was unable to bring his parents to England from a Displaced Persons' Camp at Deggendorf, Bavaria.
[118]Freud, *Anticlimax*, op. cit., pp. 24–25.
[119]*Ibid.*, pp. 31–32.
[120]Communication from Paul Yogi Mayer to the author. The Portland episode is also mentioned in Dale, *Spanglet*, op. cit., p. 83; Freud, *Anticlimax*, op. cit., p. 34; Warner, *A Very Personal Account*, op. cit., pp. 29–30.
[121]Warner, *A Very Personal Account*, op. cit., p. 29. For Mosley's own account of his wartime internment and political career, see Sir Oswald Mosley, *My Life*, London 1968.

seriously ill in the Pioneer Corps. Admitted to army hospital, ill with pneumonia and high fever, and for a while unconscious, he was subjected to long and intense efforts by a Catholic Army Chaplain to "save his soul".[122] Then there is the story of one group, "sent in" during April 1944 as "agents" to destroy the bridges and railway yards of the city of Birmingham, a city none of them knew. Only the Birmingham Chief of Police had been told of the exercise in any detail, while CID officers only knew they had to look out for four "suspected enemy agents". Two of the group were arrested in the street, while another, Fred Warner, was arrested and intensively interrogated in his lodging house in Hagley Road – much to the chagrin of his loudly furious and night-gowned landlady. Warner considers that he and his CID captors were lucky to leave the house "without being bodily attacked" – although that is what happened to him during further interrogations at Winson Green Prison. Upon release, however, he received the best breakfast he had had in a long time.[123] One trainee member of what was to become Twelve Force eventually asked for a transfer. He ended up in a small, very secret group of four who never knew each other's identity and who worked separately under the direction of Professor Lindemann, science adviser to Winston Churchill. In this group, he was trained for the destruction of the key German ball-bearing factories at Schweinfurt.[124] Another member of the group was trained to attack transformer factories, and another to destroy railway turn-tables at major rail crossings.[125] Yet another Jewish refugee from Austria – another "escapee" from the Pioneer Corps – worked during 1943 and 1944 in a highly secret statistical unit established within Headquarters Home Forces and thereafter at the HQ of 21st Army Group. This involved drawing up a monthly return on the distribution and efficiency of tanks, including those on the secret list whose tests showed what modifications were required. The confidential analyses of this "enemy alien" then went by special dispatch riders to the War Office, and thence to the government for distribution only to officers of the rank of Major-General and above. Had it become known to outsiders what information passed through this individual's hands during the spring of 1944, he would have become a prime target of German intelligence. Given his work on the statistics of army vehicles and their movements to the south of England, which also indicated troop movements, he became *au fait* at an early stage with the detailed Allied order of battle for the invasion of Europe. Thirty-seven days after D-Day, he also landed in France, becoming responsible towards the end of the war for highly significant analyses of German transport statistics.[126]

Such training under SOE auspices was, of course, accompanied by unceasing strictures about the need for total secrecy – although that did not extend to the London cockney taxi driver who, in 1944, clearly knew the address of the supposedly secret "Spy Shop" (as he put it) at 64 Baker Street, i.e. SOE

[122] Freud, *Anticlimax*, op. cit., p. 22.
[123] Warner, *A Very Personal Account*, op. cit., pp. 30–32.
[124] For Schweinfurt as a potential and actual target of Bomber Command, see Anthony Verrier, *The Bomber Offensive*, London 1968, pp. 91, 171–172, 174, 181, 188, 192, 206, 218, 284, 291.
[125] Communication from Eric F. Bowes to the author.
[126] Private information.

Headquarters.[127] So far did official concern about secrecy go that one former member of Twelve Force observes that the term Special Operations Executive was not even known to him and other colleagues. Instead, their special training units (of SOE) were made to appear part of the regular British Army, by being "attached" to regiments such as the Royal Fusiliers.[128] Not that they ever "got anywhere near the Regiment at any time". When these SOE trainees were eventually commissioned, supposedly in the Royal Fusiliers, that fine body of men protested loudly that they "had no establishment for extra officers". This meant the SOE trainees being commissioned instead in the Army "General List".[129] The notion of secrecy might also be extended to the fact that when these trainees were finally sent out on "ops", they were issued with lethal pills, "if we wished", as Fred Warner remembers it.[130] As to some of the secret "ops" in which a few of the Jewish refugees took part, further details have recently been helpfully provided by the participants, although here of course their telling has necessarily been compressed.

As early as May 1943, one group of parachutists was sent to Oran in Algeria and Tunisia, where they stayed until September when the Allies invaded Italy. On 12th September 1943, when landing from the cruiser *Aurora* at Taranto on the south-eastern coast of Italy in the Gulf of Taranto, three days after the port was taken intact by a convoy of five cruisers and a mine-layer in Operation Slapstick,[131] they became the first British troops to land on that side of Italy. Against negligible opposition from retreating German troops, principally depleted units of the German 1st Parachute Division,[132] the group eventually advanced to beyond Foggia, 120 miles north of Taranto. Before being withdrawn, the group suffered several casualties. Thereafter, members of the group were moved to Sicily for attachment to the United States Air Force Transport Command, training their pilots how to drop troops in the right place and at the right time, a vital procedure for the future success of Allied invasion plans.

In November 1943, however, two-thirds of the company left for Britain, leaving behind a platoon which then became the 1st Independent Parachute Platoon, part of the 2nd Parachute Brigade. Those that left for the United Kingdom subsequently fought with distinction – and many died – in the actions at Arnhem in mid-September 1944, part of Operation Market Garden.[133] Other

[127]Warner, *A Very Personal Account, op. cit.*, p. 33. Foot, *SOE, op. cit.*, pp. 24–25, describes how, by the winter of 1943–1944, most of the west side of Baker Street, through to Gloucester Place, had been requisitioned by SOE under one or another of its cover names in order to house the various sub-offices of SOE.

[128]Communication from a former member of Twelve Force. The information about the Royal Fusiliers is confirmed by the army record of another former refugee, whose record also shows him as belonging to the Intelligence Corps after being in the Royal Fusiliers. Information communicated to the author by Mrs. Dora Blake. See also Dale, *Spanglet, op. cit.*, p. 84.

[129] Warner, *A Very Personal Account, op. cit.*, p. 27.

[130]*Ibid.*, p. 39.

[131]Basil Henry Liddell Hart, *History of the Second World War*, London 1973, pp. 466–467. See also C.R.S. Harris, *Allied Military Administration of Italy, 1943–1945. History of the Second World War*, ed. by J.R.M. Butler, London 1957 (United Kingdom Military Series), pp. 73ff.

[132]Hart, *Second World War, op. cit.*, p. 467.

[133]Among them was Walter Lewy-Lingen (renamed Landon), the son of a Jewish Judge of the German Supreme Court; Bentwich, *Risks, op. cit.*, pp. 16–17.

members of the Ist Independent Parachute Platoon continued to serve in an active sense in Italy behind German lines, before becoming involved, on 15th August 1944, in Operation Dragoon, the Allied invasion of southern France between Toulon and Cannes.[134] Action there also involved being dropped behind enemy lines, as "pathfinders" for the gliders bringing in the Allied invasion force. Nor was that the finish of war experience for this particular group of Jewish refugees. Following the landing at Patras in Greece on 4th October 1944 of other British parachute troops in Operation Manna,[135] on 12th October they were dropped near Athens to spearhead an Allied presence in Greece at the time of the German withdrawal. Thereafter, they found themselves in the thick of fighting around Athens between Greek government forces and ELAS, the military arm of EAM, the Communist-dominated Popular Front organisation. Some casualties were also suffered through sniper fire.[136]

Italy was also the first "drop" in the summer of 1944 for yet another special group from the SOE training mill. The plan was to land behind German lines in northern Italy, some 180 miles north of the front line on the Rimini-Forli axis, near to the Austrian and Yugoslavian borders. The main objectives were: to support the partisans; guide back escaped Allied prisoners of war; and hinder the retreat of the Germans once they had retired northwards over the River Po. However, contrary to the assurances of their "conducting Officer" when departing from La Selva di Fasano near Monopoli between Bari and Brindisi, that the "very good Polish crew" who had done "some excellent work over Warsaw" would drop them accurately, the group was landed in the wrong place behind German lines. One member of the group reckoned he landed in the valley running north from Tolmezzo to the Plöcken Pass, about fifteen miles to the east from Tramonte where he should have been. On 13th October 1944 he was captured by members of a mixed German-Cossack unit. Thereafter, he was imprisoned and interrogated by the *Gestapo* at the Coroneo prison in Trieste. In January 1945, he was handed over to the German Army and transferred to the Kaisersteinbruch camp in Austria containing at least 50,000 other prisoners from throughout Europe. The following month he was moved to Oflag 79 near Brunswick, where he remained until the American army liberated the camp on 12th April 1945. In a form of poetic justice, he found himself involved in the de-Nazification process in Germany at the war's end as part of his work in the RZA (*Reichsbahn-Zentralamt*).[137]

Another German-Jewish refugee by the name of Lindenbaum – who had changed his name to Priestley – was also dropped in the wrong place behind enemy lines in northern Italy where he was supposed to reinforce a party of Italian guerrillas. These should have helped guide in the plane and act as his reception committee upon landing. Unfortunately, the pilot who dropped

---

[134]John Ehrman, *Grand Strategy*, vol. V, *August 1943–September 1944. History of the Second World War*, ed. by J.R.M. Butler, London 1956 (United Kingdom Military Series), pp. 377ff.; Martin Gilbert, *Second World War*, London 1989, p. 568.
[135]Gilbert, *Second World War, op. cit.*, p. 598.
[136]Communication from Peter A. Block to the author.
[137]Dale, *Spanglet, op. cit.*, pp. 88–109, 118–120.

Priestley mistook the lights from a badly blacked-out German army camp for those of his supposed reception committee. Alternatively, it is suggested that these Italian guerrillas may have been penetrated by the *Gestapo*, as happened in Holland, and that it was a well-prepared trap. In any case, Priestley was taken prisoner, also by a mixed group of Russian or Ukrainian volunteers. Fortunately, northern Italy was still under a form of Italian jurisdiction. Although the Italians condemned Priestley to death and placed him in solitary confinement in a prison in Trieste, the death sentence was never carried out and he survived the war.[138]

Polish pilots were not the only ones to miss predetermined DZs (Dropping Zones). A.W. Freud was a member of a group of two, and Fred Warner one of a group of four, in a joint "op" dropped over Austria in April 1945 by American pilots, who also missed their target. At that time the key question about Austria was less the final outcome of the battles between the *Wehrmacht* in the region and the apparently unstoppable Red Army – Russian forces under Marshals Tolbukhin and Malinovsky had crossed the Austrian frontier at the end of March, while by 13th April 1945 Tolbukhin's Third Ukraine Front and Malinovsky's forces had captured Vienna[139] – than the extent and nature of the Soviet occupation of Austria.[140] The two groups had several key objectives to fulfil: to contact the Austrian underground, if any; contact and help Allied prisoners-of-war; sabotage road and rail transport facilities; report troop movements and the exact positions of ammunition and supply dumps; prevent the Germans from blowing up the facilities at the aerodrome of Zeltweg, about eight kilometres east of Judenburg, itself approximately fifty-five kilometres north-west of Graz in Styria; and to establish a British presence in the area, especially at Zeltweg. Both Freud and Warner, in their separate flights down to *terra firma*, landed way off target near small out-of-the-way villages: Freud near Oberzeiring and at least twenty kilometres north-east of Judenburg, and Warner near to Weißenbach. Although the first priority had to be physical survival in adverse conditions, both men set out to achieve what they could of their mission.

Insofar as contact with Austrian resistance was concerned, Freud's experience of encountering mainly women and old men in the countryside – to whom he would often give a cheerful "Heil Hitler" salute – ruled this out for him. Warner at least was introduced to an Austrian Army Captain in Weißenbach, responsible for the anti-Nazi activities of the area – collecting together as many anti-Nazis in the village as possible, listening to BBC news programmes every evening and making lists of known Nazis in the local area. Nevertheless, both Freud's and Warner's main objective was to secure Zeltweg aerodrome for the British, a tall order for two individual agents in enemy-occupied territory. In the event, Freud arrived at Zeltweg first, having "persuaded" the Mayor of the small town of Scheifling to drive him there, in the town's fire engine. However, Freud's blustering tactics with the Mayor of Scheifling did not work with the Commanding Officer at Zeltweg, from whom he demanded the aerodrome on behalf of

[138]Freud, *Anticlimax, op. cit.*, p. 9.
[139]Ehrman, *op. cit.*, pp. 156–157; Peter Young (ed.), *The Almanac of World War II*, London 1981, p. 339.
[140]Herbert Feis, *Churchill. Roosevelt. Stalin. The War They Waged and the Peace They Sought*, Princeton, NJ 1957, pp. 621ff.

General Bernard Montgomery and the British army.[141] Not that the CO was in an easy situation, with nearby SS units breathing down his neck. But neither could he delay too long because of the advancing Russians. Unable to obtain from Freud any authoritative credentials, and with Freud likewise unable to raise his HQ through Zeltweg's wireless transmitters, the German CO finally agreed to arrange a meeting the following day with local Nazi leaders and other officials to discuss the matter. In the meantime, would Herr Freud please be the guest of the Zeltweg aerodrome Officers' Mess? Food and drink there was in plenty, after which Freud was given a comfortable room in which to sleep – on one wall of which was a large picture of Hitler. As Freud nonchalantly remembers, "we did not disturb each other". At the meeting the following day with at least twenty to twenty-five Nazi officers and officials, Freud bluntly stated that either the British occupied Zeltweg, and it would remain in the future British zone of Austria, or the Russians would. Freud believes that if he had been of more senior rank and accompanied by colleagues, he might have got away with it and personally "occupied" Zeltweg. Instead, the assembled officials hedged their bets by sending Freud to higher authorities for a decision, to Linz and the HQ of the Commander of the German Southern Front, General Dr. Lothar Rendulic.[142] If the General approved Freud's plans, they would accede to such superior instructions. Revealingly, throughout the meeting Freud was approached by about half the company who assured him of their positive feelings for the Jews, hoping this would "be taken into consideration after the war". Although Freud was unable to see General Rendulic at Linz, other officers who received him told him he was welcome to Zeltweg aerodrome because of their wish to block the territorial aims of the Russians in Austria. But Freud never made it back to Zeltweg. Indeed, being strafed by Russian aircraft, held up by mutinous units of the Austrian army and threatened with shooting by a nervous German army officer at the front line with the Americans, Freud was lucky to get out of Austria – courtesy of the Americans – in one piece. But his cool reception from diplomats in the British Embassy in Paris and authorities in the United

---

[141] For Montgomery's role in the critical end-phase of the Second World War, see the most recent study by Alistair Horne with David Montgomery, *The Lonely Leader. Monty, 1944–1945*, London 1994.

[142] Rendulic came from an old Austrian family of soldiers and had been a member of the Austrian General Staff. While military attaché in Paris, he had been expelled from the Austrian Army for National-Socialist activities. It has been written of him that, as a soldier, "his nature showed a curious dualism. He took his National Socialism deadly seriously, and yet [he] affected a most elegant style of life." See Walter Görlitz, *The German General Staff. Its History and Structure 1657–1945*, London 1953, pp. 443–444. Not surprisingly, General Rendulic was one of the few Generals in the German Army in whom Hitler had some faith during the early desperate months of 1945, moving him around the eastern command structure of the *Wehrmacht* much as one would move a knight on a chess board, and with the same degree of effectiveness. Generally known for his "absolute nervelessness", Rendulic replaced Staff Officers peremptorily dismissed by Hitler for their perceived failures in the last desperate struggles against the inexorable advance of the Russian Red Army, beyond and within the frontiers of the *Reich*. On 16th January 1945, Rendulic was placed in command of Army Group North (Courland); on 27th January in command of Army Group North (East Prussia); and on 3rd April 1945 in command of Army Group South (Ostmark). See Earl F. Ziemke, *Stalingrad to Berlin. The German Defeat in the East*, Washington, DC 1968, pp. 422, 432–433, 455. See also Walter Warlimont, *Inside Hitler's Headquarters 1939–1945*, London 1964, p. 384, notes.

Kingdom, where he landed on VE Day, 8th May 1945, brought home to him once more the realities of being an alien Jewish refugee in Britain.[143]

Warner, too, eventually arrived at Zeltweg aerodrome – after Freud's departure, and having experienced several "adventures" en route – to find not only the other members of his group of four, but also the Russians. Like Freud, Warner's companions had had their own somewhat "positive" encounters with the increasingly worried German occupation forces. By circuitous means, they became almost honoured guests of General Rendolitsch[144] and his Staff Officers at their Headquarters in Schloß Thalheim, near Judenburg, because of their eagerness to surrender to British forces and not to the Russians. One of the group even borrowed a German officer's uniform and travelled with two officers of the *Abwehr* to the town of Murau, fifty kilometres west of Judenburg, so as to retrieve the group's equipment and vital transmitting and receiving wireless set. Eventually, messages were sent to the group's HQ requesting instructions concerning the surrender to the western Allies of the Army Groups of General Rendolitsch (Rendulic) and Colonel-General Alexander Löhr. The latter was Commander of Army Group E, and from January 1945 had been fighting rearguard actions against the Russians, beginning in Yugoslavia.[145] During the two days when nothing was transmitted back to the group, they decided to try to capture Zeltweg aerodrome from the *Luftwaffe*. Fortunately, they were again protected by their new "friends", the *Abwehr* officers, since the *Luftwaffe* Colonel in charge of Zeltweg was distinctly unfriendly, refused to hand over the aerodrome and demanded that the *Abwehr* officers arrest the agents. This they refused to do. Again during the same few days, another member of that group – also dressed as a German captain and accompanied by *Abwehr* officers – was driven to Klagenfurt, some one hundred kilometres south-west of Graz, to interview the infamous *SS-Obergruppenführer* Odilo Globocnik, who had fled to Carinthia in Austria. Globocnik is well known for having been *SS- und Polizeiführer Distrikt Lublin* where he was responsible for the mass extermination of Polish Jews in the operation *Aktion Reinhard*.[146] In front of the British agent, Globocnik made a rousing propaganda speech, but then begged him to emphasise to his superiors how urgent it was that the western Allies and the remnants of the German army join forces to fight the approaching "Russian hordes". Later, another of the group returned to arrest Globocnik, but he had already taken poison. Eventually, the group's superior officers at the Headquarters of Field Marshal Sir Harold Alexander, Supreme Allied Commander in the Mediterranean, informed them that the Army Groups of Generals Rendo-

---

[143]Freud, *Anticlimax, op. cit.*, pp. 46–65; Bentwich, *Risks, op. cit.*, pp. 111–112, briefly mentions Freud and the Zeltweg aerodrome incident.

[144]It may well be that Warner, from whom this account is taken, in using the name "Rendolitsch" in reality means "Rendulic".

[145]Christian Zentner and Friedemann Bedürftig (eds.), *Das Große Lexikon des Dritten Reiches*, Munich 1985, p. 361; Ziemke, *op. cit.*, pp. 365, 371, 373–375, 377, 497. See also The Institute for Contemporary History and Narodna Knjiga (eds.), *The Third Reich and Yugoslavia 1933–1945*, Belgrade 1977, pp. 480–482, 487, 587, 681, 693, 754.

[146]See for example, Yitzhak Arad, *Belzec, Sobibor, Treblinka. The Operation Reinhard Death Camps*, Bloomington–Indianapolis 1987.

litsch (Rendulic) and Löhr should surrender to those forces against whom they fought last, the Russians and the Yugoslavs. The Generals refused this pointblank, and instead withdrew with all their forces westwards to surrender to the Americans.[147] With the two German Army Groups withdrawn, the CO of Zeltweg aerodrome immediately became more co-operative. He ordered the lifting of all mines on the aerodrome, besides providing lists of aircraft, stores and equipment. These were passed on to RAF authorities, which promised to occupy the place soon. They did not, the only planes showing interest in Zeltweg being those of the Red Air Force, which bombed it, and an American pilot who landed there in his Mosquito aircraft. He told of delays in the British advance – SS troops were holding out for better surrender terms – and of the unchecked Russian advance into Austria. The American advised the *Luftwaffe* personnel to save themselves and their aircraft by flying to Linz, to surrender to American forces there. This advice was complied with expeditiously. Shortly afterwards, an advance guard of Russians arrived, followed by their main force. Around then Warner arrived, just in time to join his group in having to abandon their own "occupation" of Zeltweg aerodrome as a consequence of negotiations between British and Russian forces in the vicinity concerning which Austrian territory should be earmarked for which side.

However, that was not an end to the group's war service in that area. They continued to help maintain a British presence until the main British forces arrived. Moreover, they helped local civilians deal with the inevitable problems caused by the presence of often unruly Russian soldiers, including advising women raped by the latter. When the 2/5 Leicester Regiment arrived in mid-May 1945, the group liaised with it. This was one of the regiments to be involved in the forcible rounding up of remnants of the Cossack Corps under General von Pannwitz, then running wild in that part of Styria and terrorising the local population.[148]

Towards the end of hostilities in Europe and afterwards, Jewish refugees serving in the British army often had a key role to play in the hunting down of suspected Nazi war criminals,[149] the investigation of Nazi war crimes and assisting in the preparation of the post-war trials of Nazi war criminals through the work of the British War Crimes Executive.[150] A Pioneer of 137 Company became Principal Investigator of outrages in concentration camps and later, as Prosecutor, conducted the trial of SS men charged with crimes at Ravensbrück Camp. He was also Assistant Prosecutor at the trial of the leaders of Belsen Camp. Another, Fred Warner, commanded a team of sixty officers and sergeants, largely Pioneers, which arrested some of the most notorious German

---

[147]On 16th February 1947, Löhr was hanged in Belgrade after being tried and found guilty of war crimes against the Yugoslavs, in particular for having directed the aerial bombing of Belgrade on 6th April 1941; Zentner and Bedürftig, *Lexikon, op. cit.*, p. 361.

[148]Warner, *A Very Personal Account, op. cit.*, pp. 56–88. On the contentious subject of the United Kingdom and the return of the Cossacks in Austria to the Russian authorities at the end of the war, see Nikolai Tolstoy, *The Minister and the Massacres*, London 1986.

[149]Dear, *Ten Commando, op. cit.*, pp. 185–186.

[150]Bentwich, *Risks, op. cit.*, pp. 136, 165.

war criminals, including Rudolf Höss, the former commandant of Auschwitz,[151] and Oswald Pohl, who had been second to Himmler in the SS.[152] Pohl, from 31st December 1942 Head of the *SS-Wirtschafts- und Verwaltungshauptamt* and therefore overlord of the vast Nazi concentration camp system,[153] was in fact arrested by a former member of Twelve Force, Lieutenant Harry Schweiger, who died some years ago.[154] A.W. Freud helped to hunt down Dr. Bruno Tesch who prepared the poison gas for the extermination chambers at Auschwitz.[155] Yet others found new employment in various units of the Military Government and Control Commissions in Germany and Austria,[156] and even in the preparation and translation of the many tons of German records which were recovered upon the total defeat and occupation of the German *Reich*.[157] Some ended up in Norway, interrogating German prisoners of war in order to group them according to the extent of their Nazi sympathies.[158]

For some German-Jewish refugees involved in war crimes work in Germany at the end of the war, there was undoubtedly an element of poetic justice at work, even though revenge was not always uppermost in their thoughts. This was particularly true for the former Manfred Werner from Hamburg, who returned to Germany in the autumn of 1945 as Captain Frederick Michael Warner of the victorious British army attached to the War Crimes Group (North-West Europe), with its HQ at Bad Oeynhausen, Rhine Army HQ.[159] Before this posting, which lasted three years and which involved travel all over Germany and to Denmark, he was informed by Colonel Gerald Draper of the Judge Advocate General's Branch, who appointed him to the War Crimes Group, that in 1944 his parents and young sister had been sent to the Auschwitz-Birkenau extermination camp.[160] Later, Warner heard that distant relatives of his, a family by the name of Rosenthal and their daughter who had emigrated to

---

[151]For Höss's role in the Nazi *Endlösung* during the Second World War, see his interesting and informative memoirs published by Martin Broszat, *Rudolf Höss. Kommandant in Auschwitz. Autobiographische Aufzeichnungen*, Munich 1958. The 14th edition of the paperback, published by DTV Munich since 1963, appeared in January 1994.
[152]Bentwich, *Risks, op. cit.*, p. 135.
[153]Zentner and Bedürftig, *Lexikon, op. cit.*, p. 447.
[154]I am grateful to Mr. Stephen Dale for this information.
[155]Bentwich, *Risks, op. cit.*, pp. 136–137; Dear, *Ten Commando, op. cit.*, pp. 185–186; Rhodes-Wood, *op. cit.*, pp. 287–288. Bruno Tesch was the director of the firm of Tesch and Stabenow, an "international pest control company" in Hamburg, one of several which supplied Zyklon B to the Nazi extermination camps. On this subject, see the important study edited by Eugen Kogon, Hermann Langbein and Adalbert Rückerl (now available in an English translation), *Nazi Mass Murder. A Documentary History of the Use of Poison Gas*, New Haven–London 1993. See also Jean-Claude Pressac, *Les crématoires d'Auschwitz. La machinerie du meurtre de masse*, Paris 1993.
[156]Warner, *A Very Personal Account, op. cit.*, p. 88.
[157]Bentwich, *Risks, op. cit.*, pp. 130–131, 160–168; communication from Erich Saunders to the author.
[158]Communication to the author from Mrs. Dora Blake.
[159]It is a well-known phenomenon that, particularly when abroad, Britons usually try to marry something local with that perennial mystery to all foreigners, the peculiar British sense of humour. At Bad Oeynhausen, only the entrenched British military personnel must have found the following sign highly amusing, placed on a nearby road by the British Military Police: "Bad Road, Bad Bends, Bad Oeynhausen". It was probably incomprehensible to the local Germans. Warner, *A Very Personal Account, op. cit.*, p. 96.
[160]*Ibid.*, p. 93.

Holland from Germany, had been sent to Bergen-Belsen by the Nazi occupation authorities in the Netherlands. Although Herr Rosenthal died at the camp, his wife and daughter survived.[161] During his work with the NWE War Crimes Group, Warner's chief functions were looking after witnesses and transporting suspects from one prison to another, or from interrogation centres to trial courts. Among those he came into contact with were the British agent, Odette Churchill, née Sansom, who had been held in the Ravensbrück concentration camp; von Bassewitz-Behr, who had to be delivered to the British War Crimes Liaison Officer in West Berlin for immediate delivery to the Russians because of war crimes he had committed in Russia; and Dr. Alfred Schweder, a one-time colleague of Reinhard Heydrich and former head of the Bremen *Gestapo*.[162] At Nuremberg, Warner also had to interview the infamous Otto Ohlendorf, former leader of *Einsatzgruppe D*, which had operated in southern Russia and had executed tens of thousands of Russian Jews and other civilians. Not surprisingly, Warner found him to be a thoroughly unpleasant and arrogant character.[163]

Jewish refugees from Germany and Austria who served in Britain's armed forces during the Second World War thus played a more than active role in the wider European resistance and opposition to the Nazi Third *Reich*. There was, however, one storm cloud which loomed over all their achievements in the fight against the common enemy. Throughout the war, a protracted legal and political struggle ensued within and without Parliament on behalf of the serving alien Jewish refugees. It concerned three aspects of the same problem. First, especially in the case of those enlistees likely to be dropped behind enemy lines, whether they could be granted immediate naturalisation as British subjects so as to provide them with the internationally protective status of prisoners of war, instead of their more likely treatment by the Germans as Jewish traitors to the Fatherland. Second, whether the serving alien Jewish refugees could not be assured of British nationality at war's end. And third, whether they would face repatriation, even against their will, to Germany and Austria after the war. Throughout and to the end of the war, the British government set its face firmly against all concessions, although at approximately two minutes to midnight, it finally yielded in important aspects.[164]

Such official attitudes obviously affected the perceptions held by many serving alien Jewish refugees about British Gentile society and their place within it during war and peacetime. Yet by war's end, those perceptions were also influenced by the changes wrought in the refugees' perceptions of their former

---

[161] *Ibid.*, p. 99.

[162] For brief references to Schweder, see Günther Deschner, *Reinhard Heydrich. Statthalter der totalen Macht*, Munich 1986, p. 94; Heinz Höhne, *The Order of the Death's Head. The Story of Hitler's SS*, London 1972, pp. 158, 168.

[163] Warner, *A Very Personal Account, op. cit.*, pp. 100–101. For Ohlendorf, see the accounts by Raul Hilberg, *The Destruction of the European Jews*, London 1961; and Helmut Krausnick and Hans-Heinrich Wilhelm, *Die Truppe des Weltanschauungskrieges. Die Einsatzgruppen der Sicherheitspolizei und des SD 1938–1942*, Stuttgart 1981.

[164] See Fox, *loc.cit., passim*. On the other hand, that these policies could be abandoned for specific official purposes has been shown to be the case in particular instances by Dear, *Ten Commando, op. cit.*, p. 47.

homelands. How many would have actually returned "home" after the war, had its entire course, duration, and nature been different, is, of course, the crucial, but unanswerable question. Early on, some thought they might return to Germany when the war was over.[165] Yet confirmation at war's end of what many people had previously regarded as unproven rumour – Nazi Germany's programme of racial genocide against the Jews and other ethnic groups of Russia and Europe – decided most of these Jewish refugees that their homes and lives were to be found in Britain, and Britain alone. In many cases, the Nazi policy of genocide directly affected the German and Austrian refugees discussed here. Families and friends left behind were destroyed physically, or at least psychologically scarred for life if they survived any of the Nazi concentration and extermination camps. Some relatives committed suicide, as did the mother of one serving refugee, following the death of her husband after detention, when she was not even allowed to attend his funeral. She gassed herself the day before she was due to report with all her possessions in one small suitcase[166] – report, that is, obviously for deportation to, and extermination in the East.

And yet – as the wife of one of them recalls – great bitterness and disappointment rankled for years to come that such men, having faithfully served "King and Country", and having put life and limb at risk in the process, were told the day after demobilisation in 1945 and 1946 to report to the police upon arrival at their home towns because they were aliens.[167] Yet when some of these "enemy aliens" appeared at police stations to register, taking with them their war record books and especially if appearing in military uniform complete with medals, the awkwardness was more generally felt by the English "bobby" on duty.[168]

Fortunately, in most cases, this difficult and fraught story had a somewhat positive ending. Much against its will, or rather against the entrenched and hard-fought Home Office fortress mentality, the British government relented on the nationality issue, and from the end of 1945 procedures were set in train enabling those alien Jewish refugees discussed here to apply for, and obtain, that prized possession, British nationality. At the relevant ceremonies, there must have been quite a number of Commissioners of Oaths who were "amazed" to find that the British Army had contained many officers who were not only *not* British citizens, but had actually then been classified as enemy aliens.[169]

For almost all, life in Britain in pursuit of asylum from the threat of Nazi persecution – and on behalf of the United Kingdom as members of the British armed forces during the Second World War – had been far from easy. On the contrary, in the conditions of war and in the midst of a Gentile society, the constant themes of their experience had been uncertainty, ambiguity and ultimately danger – resulting in, as one refugee put it in 1942, "a certain

---

[165]Imperial War Museum, Department of Sound Records. Interview with Clive Teddern. 003839/R06. Transcript, pp. 55–56.
[166]Private communication to the author.
[167]I am grateful to Mrs. Dora Blake, the wife of a former refugee, for this information.
[168]Communication from Peter A. Block to the author.
[169]Communication from a former member of Twelve Force to the author.

disillusionment with England".[170] But at least from 1945 and 1946, once the nationality issue had been resolved, most could then concentrate on the task of normal daily life in Britain, even though some of the ambiguities of life for foreign Jews within such a Gentile society remained after the war. As it was, the "foreign" aspects of the cases discussed here were often compounded by the original German or Austrian nationality of the Jewish refugees. Some, once back in civvies, experienced elements of the anti-German sentiment prevalent in British society during the war and after VE Day in May 1945. Inevitably, the practitioners of such anti-German hostility drew no fine distinctions between obvious anti-Nazis and the Nazi regime in Berlin, much to the emotional and intellectual frustration of the Jews in question. However, given their decision to remain in Britain after the war, such frustrations were seen simply as yet another hurdle in the post-Nazi Europe which lay before them.

[170]Berghahn, *op. cit.*, p. 155.

The Jewish Exiles in the Service of US Intelligence
The Post-War Years

BY GUY STERN

Chronicling the participation in the Second World War of Jews from Germany and Austria continues now as before to be a scholarly desideratum,* especially of the London Leo Baeck Institute and their *Year Book*.[1] Even my far more modest topic, the exiles' contributions to the US intelligence services, has not significantly progressed beyond initial investigations.[2] Also, the beginnings and endings of their involvement have not been fully clarified. So-called enemy aliens were inducted as conscripts or volunteers in significant numbers into the US Armed Forces only after 1943, often ending up in one of the branches of the intelligence services. Why as late as 1943? Nor has it been explained why they were suddenly and massively dismissed from military or civilian service in 1947. Answers to these questions emerge from recently declassified materials at the National Archives in Washington, DC and Suitland, MD, one of the primary sources for this article.

The operative authorisation for "Acceptability of Aliens for Service in the Army of the United States" is contained in a letter of the Adjutant Generals Office War Department of 1st October 1942, which also issued the awesome DSS Form 304 "Alien's Personal History and Statement", eliciting information as sweeping as a potential inductee's family history, affiliations, political beliefs and police records.[3] None the less, induction of aliens tended to be at first sporadic

---

*In the preparation of this article I received valuable help from Drs. Diane Spielmann and Frank Mecklenburg of the Leo Baeck Institute, New York; Dr. Arnold Paucker, LBI, London; Dr. Robert Wolf of the National Archives, Washington, DC; and Hans Weinmann of the Holocaust Memorial Center, Detroit, MI.

[1] In pointing out the magnitude of the task, Arnold Paucker observes: "In such a work [i.e. a history of the Jews fighting in the war against Nazi Germany] many chapters would have to be devoted to the part played by the Jews from Germany who joined the Allied Armies." See his "Preface/Introduction" to *LBI Year Book XXXVII* (1992), p. XV.

[2] The few previous and largely sporadic secondary sources are cited in my two previous articles on the subject. See Guy Stern, 'The Exiles and the War of the Minds', in Helmut Pfanner (ed.), *Der Zweite Weltkrieg und die Exilanten. Eine literarische Antwort*, Bonn–Berlin 1991 (Studien zur Literatur der Moderne 13), pp. 311–324; and idem, 'In the Service of American Intelligence. German-Jewish Exiles in the War Against Hitler', in *LBI Year Book XXXVII* (1992), pp. 461–477.

[3] National Archives, Washington, DC, PG 407, Army Adjutant General Decimal File, 1940–1945, Box No. 2561, File 341.

and conditional on the attitudes of local draft boards as well as on a waiver of alien status from the Adjutant Generals Office.

In all likelihood the impetus to accept enemy aliens as volunteers came from that most unconventional of all warriors, William J. ("Wild Bill") Donovan. Taking straight aim at the Armed Forces' apparently still largely persisting exclusionary policy *vis-à-vis* non-citizens, he addressed a memorandum to the Assistant Chief of Staff, G-1, US Army on 17th April 1943 arguing that there existed a need "for certain specially qualified personnel from civilian life". Among other waivers, such as age limitations, Donovan specifically requested the acceptance into the Office of Strategic Services (OSS) of aliens:

> "3. It is further requested the current regulations prohibiting the enlistment of non-citizens be waived in connection with this procurement authorization, due to the specialized qualifications involved and the urgent need."

As early as ten days later, the Adjutant General, under "orders of the Secretary of War", acceded to Donovan's request, but stipulated that aliens must demonstrate certain physical and other qualifications, receive a waiver from the Adjutant General and be cleared by military intelligence.[4] But after this concession, coupled with an earlier if vaguer memorandum by the General Staff Office, the "piecemeal requests" yielded to a more elastic open-door policy.

Once accepted, the exiles proved their value in virtually all branches of the war-time Army and Navy Intelligence Services, as argued in the second of my previous articles on the subject. I further maintained that their post-war accomplishments, no less variegated, might also fill volumes. "An appreciable number applied their rare talents, honed during the war, to the war crime trials and to such tasks as the supervision of the reviving German media, to military government, or to temporary new assignments."[5] This paper, by drawing upon widely varying examples, will try to draft a contour map of their activities.

The primary sources for such a study are sparse. Also, the previous outpourings of secondary works on the US intelligence services have dwindled down to a trickle and some, such as William B. Breuer's *The Secret War with Germany*, appear so far removed from intelligence field operations that one is reminded of one of Bertolt Brecht's justified demurrals against a history viewed from the top. Brecht asked: "Young Alexander conquered India – all by himself?"[6] Breuer's celebrated military brass could not have fought its secret war without the activities of far lesser ranks, exiles prominent among them. Aside from military histories, the ever more accessible files of the National Archives remain a significant source. But the memoirs of the Jewish exiles themselves, written or elicited by oral history, constitute a valuable, often under-explored, resource. This paper has drawn on representative examples of all of these primary and secondary sources, including some of my own experiences.

[4]*Ibid.*
[5]Stern, 'In the Service', *loc. cit.*, p. 472.
[6]William B. Breuer, *The Secret War with Germany. Deception, Espionage and Dirty Tricks, 1939–1945*, Shrewsbury 1988. The Brecht quotation is from 'Fragen eines lesenden Arbeiters', in Bertolt Brecht, *Gesammelte Werke*, vol. IX, Frankfurt 1967, pp. 656f.

Before launching into a discussion of post-bellum intelligence work, a retraction is in order. My conclusion in a previous article was that *war-time* intelligence personnel did not themselves militarily intervene on information obtained from prisoners. They might help, by capturing POWs or through psychological warfare, to convince enemy soldiers to desert. But to act like a reconnaissance patrol? That was invariably left to infantry units. Yet this was wrong. Viennese-born George Chuz, who after the war became a nationally-known lighting engineer for public buildings, recalled just such an incident during a recent interview. Attached to a regiment of the 36th Infantry Division, Ninth Army, during its participation in the invasion of Southern France, he and his interrogation team were charged with pinpointing the position of enemy artillery pieces shelling the regiment. Aerial reconnaissance had proved unavailing: When the Piper Cubs were overhead, the camouflaged German howitzers simply stopped firing, thus thwarting US aerial reconnaissance. Chuz's chance came with the capture of three German artillery soldiers by an infantry patrol. On the basis of their flashes and paybooks, he quickly identified them as members of the opposing artillery unit. But when asked to pinpoint the position of the various gun emplacements on a map, they displayed, or simulated, an unfamiliarity with map-reading. In his frustration, Chuz chivvied them into pointing out the actual emplacements on the battlefield by crawling with them towards the German lines, with his gun trained on them. The frightened prisoners decided to co-operate. Chuz then entered the positions on a map, delivered it to the regimental S-2 and within minutes US bombers had obliterated the emplacements. For this exploit Chuz received the Bronze Star for bravery.[7] This heroic act gives yet another example of the exiles' highly individual mode of warfare within the seemingly regimented procedures of military intelligence.

Returning now to the post-war intelligence activities of the exiles, their effectiveness in four areas should be exemplified. While mere examples and anecdotes appear suspect to some military historians, such as John Gaddis,[8] this author unabashedly joins the post-moderns, such as Walter Laqueur. "I can tell you", writes Laqueur, "it sits better than the other history".[9] Only the assembling of the widely divergent war-time activities of the Jewish exiles can fill in the as-yet uncompleted mosaic.

As is well known, many exiles, some of them while still in service with Military Intelligence, were recruited as interpreters, aides and informants during the Nuremberg War Crimes Trials. Writes Telford Taylor: "[Many] who had fled the Nazi regime, some naturalised in Britain or the United States, some not, were used in linguistic and research capacities, and one, Dr. Robert Kempner, appeared as counsel before the tribunal."[10] None rose as high or made as great an

---

[7]Interview with George Chuz of Southfield, MI, 4th December 1993.
[8]John Gaddis in Walter T. Hitchcock (ed.), *The Intelligence Revolution. A Historical Perspective*, US Air Force Academy, Colorado Springs, CO 1988 and Office of Air Force History, Washington, DC 1991 (Proceedings of the Thirteenth Military History Symposium), pp. 265–266.
[9]Walter Laqueur, 'The Legacy Comments', in *ibid.*, p. 297.
[10]Telford Taylor, *The Anatomy of the Nuremberg Trials. A Personal Memoir*, New York 1992, p. 218.

impact on the emerging war crime justice system as the aforementioned Robert K.W. Kempner. Born in Freiburg i. Br., Kempner attained the civil service rank of *Justitiar* in the Prussian Ministry of the Interior before being dismissed immediately after the Nazis' accession to power. As an expert on the German civil service code he became invaluable, first as an adviser to the US Department of Justice and OSS, then at Nuremberg. Even before the trial he joined the US War Crimes Commission in Washington and prepared the briefs against the accused for the Chief US Prosecutor, Robert H. Jackson. Jackson also delegated the opening speech of the prosecution against Wilhelm Frick, Nazi Minister of the Interior, to his deputy.[11] In subsequent trials against Nazi diplomats, Kempner assumed the position of chief prosecutor. He himself has described his role in the war crimes trials and the principles guiding his investigation:

> "As a member of the Staff of Justice Robert H. Jackson, the chief US prosecutor before the International Tribunal, and later as deputy chief prosecutor of the 12 further court cases directed by Gen. Telford Taylor, I championed a principle I deemed important, to listen myself to the persons, whom I had to recommend to be future defendants, or not to be arraigned or to be witnesses. According to this *modus operandi* I discussed at length the personal and factual background and experiences of potential defendants and witnesses, of their friends and opponents. Only in this manner was I able to form a clear picture of the perpetrators and their deeds. The psychological contact, so important for investigations, was quickly established through a common language, my knowledge of the German Civil Service and my former residence in the capital city Berlin. For someone acquainted with the atmosphere in Nuremberg it will not be surprising that elements of a professional chief prosecutor, historian, and father-confessor blended into one."[12]

Naturally some of the unreconstructed Germans, among them a Protestant bishop, the *bête noire* of General Clay, expressed resentment at having a refugee prosecute Germany's fallen rulers.[13] But a German scholar redressed the balance. As Werner Maser put it: "Kempner had been a Prussian civil servant (deprived of all civil rights by Hitler . . .). He was naturally particularly well informed on all details and circumstances."[14] Erich Maria Remarque put it even more tersely: "Kempner was possessed by a passion for justice."[15]

While Kempner achieved a great deal of recognition both for his work for OSS,

---

[11]*Ibid.*, p. 267.
[12]Robert W. Kempner, 'Vorwort', in *idem, Das dritte Reich im Kreuzverhör. Aus den unveröffentlichten Vernehmungsprotokollen des Anklägers,*Munich–Esslingen 1969, pp. 9f. (author's translation).
[13]See Hans Habe, *Our Love Affair with Germany,* New York 1953, p. 8: "We also committed the mistake of entrusting a most important part of the prosecution to a lawyer from Philadelphia, Robert Kempner. The former Prussian *Regierungsrat,* a Jewish refugee and new American citizen, did his very best in carrying out his arduous task. It wasn't his fault that from the beginning he was suspected of bias by all Germans and that by now his name has become a symbol of anti-Americanism and anti-Semitism in Germany." Bishop Wurm's attack on the War Crimes Trials, partially through letters to Kempner, is summarised by Frank Buscher, *The U.S. War Crime Trial Program,* New York–Westport, CN–London 1989 (Contributions in Military Studies 86), p. 99.
[14]Werner Maser, *Nuremberg. A Nation on Trial,* transl. by Richard Barry, New York 1979, p. 58.
[15]Quoted in (Henry Marx), 'Robert Kempner zum Neunzigsten', in *Aufbau* (13th October 1989), p. 4. For a succinct summary of Kempner's life and work, including his research leading to the finding of the Wannsee Protocols, see Eric Pace's obituary, 'Robert Kempner, 93, a Prosecutor at Nuremberg', in *New York Times* (17th August 1993), p. 27.

Three American soldiers interrogating four Germans
Normandy, 1944, shortly after D-Day. Guy Stern in forefront

Guy Stern interrogating a German soldier after the
repulsion of the Ardennes offensive, January 1945

By courtesy of Guy Stern

Master Sergeant W.T. Angress,
(Board member of the London Leo Baeck Institute)
82nd Airborne Division,
Ludwigslust, Mecklenburg, May 1945

Group picture prior to jump, Nijmwegen, 17th September 1944,
508th Parachute Infantry Regiment
(Next to Angress, 2nd row at the outside, Master Sgt. Brodsky,
a Jewish refugee from Liegnitz)

By courtesy of Werner T. Angress

as a prosecutor and later as a champion of restitution, his fellow member of the US prosecution team, John H.E. Fried, has commanded less public and scholarly attention. Yet the collection of manuscripts at the Leo Baeck Institute in New York of the Viennese-born John Fried, documenting his contributions to the Nuremberg Trials, is likewise impressive. They include the briefs prepared by him as legal consultant to the trials as well as his contributions to the trial of Erhard Milch, Inspector General of the German Airforce under Göring.[16]

Several other German-Jewish refugees played significant roles at Nuremberg, among them John Herz as interpreter, researcher, and investigator of Wilhelm Frick, and Robert K. Wilhelm, who helped interrogate both Hermann Göring and Joachim von Ribbentrop.[17] Herz's voluminous correspondence also provides a whole series of snapshots of the proceedings at Nuremberg, not sparing its shortcomings. While castigating the ahistorical and provincial outlook of many of the American-born lawyers at Nuremberg, he also deplores, in a letter of 28th November 1945, the less-than-full employment of the exiled experts:

> "Here in Nuremberg our intention to depart at an early date has caused some resentment, especially among people who only now, quite belatedly, have come to notice that in court cases, which up to 80% concern German events, institutions and laws, some experts on German questions might be needed."[18]

An almost exhaustive activity report of exiled lawyers at Nuremberg and elsewhere in Germany, including the evidentiary intelligence work of the OSS's Research and Analysis Division, can be found in Ernst Stiefel's and Frank Mecklenburg's superb study of German refugee lawyers.[19] The investigative team work before and during the trials constituted, in Robert Kempner's words, "the world's greatest research institute".[20]

Further clues as to the extent of these investigations continue to emerge. One of my informants, Werner Stark, was among the first to interrogate Joseph Mengele, when the Auschwitz doctor was still imprisoned in the American compound in Grafenbroich in the winter of 1944–1945. As Stark remembers it, Mengele claimed, when asked about his inhumane experiments at Auschwitz, to have conducted them "only upon criminals and volunteers". Viennese-born Ernest Drucker, a CIC agent trained at Camp Ritchie and a combatant since the Normandy invasion, joined the hunt for Martin Bormann after the war, while Hitler's deputy was being tried at Nuremberg *in absentia*.[21] But the most unusual assignment came to the aforementioned Staff Sgt. Werner Stark, trained in

---

[16] See John H.E. Fried Collection in LBI Archives, New York, Accession Number AR7262, Box 2.
[17] John Herz, who was dispatched to Nuremberg at the insistence of Bill Donovan, recalls his interrogation of Frick in his memoirs, *Vom Überleben. Wie ein Weltbild entstand. Autobiographie*, Düsseldorf 1984, p. 142. See also Robert K. Wilhelm, 'Memoir of Service in the U.S. Army during World War II', Manuscript, 15 pp., in LBI Archives, New York, Accession Number ME 214.
[18] See the Herz-Aschaffenburg File, LBI Archives, New York, Accession Number AR 5753, folder 6.
[19] See Ernst C. Stiefel and Frank Mecklenburg, *Deutsche Juristen im amerikanischen Exil. 1933–1950*, Tübingen 1991.
[20] Robert W. Kempner, 'The Nuremberg Trials as Sources of Recent German Political and Historical Materials', in *American Political Science Review*, vol. XLIV, No. 44 (June 1950), p. 447.
[21] See Carla Jean Schwartz, 'Profile Ernest Drucker', in *Detroit Jewish News* (23rd October 1992), p. 12.

Camp Ritchie as a teletype operator and subsequently attached, during the war, to the 22nd Corps of the Third Army. At the end of the war he was assigned to the International Tribunal as an interpreter. Shielded from the Nazi defendants by a screen when serving as a two-way interpreter and hence remaining incognito, he was given a second task almost from the beginning. Donning civilian clothes in lieu of his army uniform and pretending to be a German, he was installed as assistant manager of the Grand Hotel, the billet of Allied military and civilian personnel at Nuremberg. The managerial assignment, while real enough, also served as camouflage for his role in internal security, observing suspected Germans: for example Ernst Kaltenbrunner's former mistress, who at that time became romantically attached to an American officer, and the comings and goings of personnel from the Soviet Union, whose government was already pursuing a Cold War agenda.[22]

Beyond their participation in the war crimes trials, the exiles took part in all activities of the US Military Government, including the attendant intelligence work. These activities ranged from the clearance of prospective new teachers, university professors and curricula to the re-zoning of districts of the US zone, and from licensing and staffing newspapers to the complex tasks of denazification, but their accomplishments have often been slighted.[23] Hence, in this instance as well, memoirs, written and oral, must enlarge our knowledge of the exiles' contributions. No memoir comes more readily to mind than that of Felix Gilbert, the first recipient of the American Historical Association's "Award for Scholarly Distinction". His reminiscences fit the definition he himself places upon the genre "memoirs". "When drawing distinctions between it and a historical book", he argues, "the writer of memoirs is less concerned with what actually happened than with the emotions, the thoughts, perhaps even the actions that an event inspired."[24] Stationed in Wiesbaden as a member of the

[22]Interview with Werner Stark at his firm, Stark & Company, Farmington Hills, MI, on 8th December 1993.
[23]Some of the early accounts of US Military Government may have set the tone for the slighting of the exiles. See Harold Zink, *American Military Government in Germany*, New York 1947, pp. 242–243:

"The American attitude toward refugee Germans has been generally sympathetic as long as the latter remained in the United States or outside of Germany. However, American military government has looked with suspicion on the return of these refugees to make use of certain of these German refugees for planning purposes. One project involved the preparation of textbooks for use in German schools by refugees in the United States. But virtually all of these were turned down for one reason or another. Objection was made that the German refugees were not reliable and could not always be depended upon to support American interests. In the case of the refugees who offered to prepare textbooks and certain other instances it was argued that they had lost touch with psychology in Germany and would be so resented by the German people that they could serve no useful purpose. After V-E Day some German refugees were brought back to the *Reich* to assist in the labor program. Certain others were occasionally made use of for other purposes, but there was no widespread authorization of their return. It is probable that this policy in general has substantial foundation to support it, though it may have been carried to an extreme. There are individual German refugees in the United States and elsewhere whose experience has been such that they should be able to make a considerable contribution to American efforts in Germany; inasmuch as they have passed tests indicating their anti-Nazi records it would seem that they might be safely employed."

[24]Felix Gilbert, *A European Past. Memoirs, 1905–1945*, New York–London 1988, pp. 221f.

Research and Analysis (R and A Division) of OSS, Gilbert's primary activities were only tangentially of an intelligence nature. "I had my hand . . . in two issues that loomed quite large on the agenda of these first months in occupied Germany: the reopening of the universities and the revival of political life."[25] But for a brief period Gilbert was detached from OSS and temporarily assigned to a State Department mission under DeWitt Poole, charged with investigating Soviet-German relations immediately prior to the Second World War. Gilbert discharged his quasi-historical assignment by enlisting the help of Heinz Trützschler von Falkenstein, a pre-war acquaintance in the German diplomatic corps.[26]

Another revealing memoir is a volume by Joachim von Elbe, *Witness to History. A Refugee from the Third Reich Remembers*. A non-Jew by any reasonable definition, von Elbe was none the less categorised as a non-Aryan by the Nazis and left Germany in 1934. After graduating from the Fourth Military Intelligence Class at Camp Ritchie, von Elbe eventually joined the G-2 Division of SHAEF (Allied Supreme Headquarters), charged with "the evaluation of German military documents".[27] The assignment, frequently productive of outstanding intelligence information and of statistics on German officer casualties, took him from London to Paris to Frankfurt. After the war, von Elbe secured a position "with the Legal Division of OMGUS",[28] the Office of Military Government in the US zone. One of his tasks returned von Elbe – or nearly so – to his war-time intelligence activities. But now, instead of poring over German military and occupational documents, von Elbe "was to identify Nazi provisions in German legislation" and "to prepare for their repeal through Control Council Legislation . . . There were the large [legal] codes that had to be scrutinised, such as the codes of civil and criminal procedures."[29] By von Elbe's account even marriage laws were filled with political ballast.

Occasionally, as told to me in interviews, the intelligence work carried out by exiles during the war continued into the early post-war period. Max Sheldon, before the Second World War a renowned athlete – he competed successfully in the 1938 *Makkabiade* as a sprinter – was assigned to censor the mail of German prisoners-of-war and to cull it for material suitable for psychological warfare. He continued this task after the surrender, but at that time it was for the purpose of assessing potentially dangerous anti-American activities in occupied Germany.[30]

"Johannes Werner", whose war-time exploits in the OSS have been described in Anthony Cave Brown's *The Last Hero. Wild Bill Donovan*, but who is now a successful author and businessman, was pressed into clandestine service once more in Munich. Rumours of an uprising among high-ranking SS officers, confined in the former Dachau concentration camp, and of other rumours about

---

[25]*Ibid.*, pp. 204f.
[26]*Ibid.*, pp. 215 and 216.
[27]Joachim von Elbe, *Witness to History. A Refugee from the Third Reich Remembers*, Madison, WI 1988, pp. 263 and 270f.
[28]*Ibid.*, p. 294.
[29]*Ibid.*, pp. 305 and 306.
[30]Telephone interview with Max Sheldon of Boca Raton, FL, of 3rd December 1993.

planned *Werwolf* sabotage, dispatched him, appropriately disguised, first to Dachau, then to taverns frequented by unreconstructed adolescents. Each time the rumours fortunately proved false. Vern Leopold, during the war a decorated member of an I & R platoon of the 99th Infantry Division, was transferred after the war to an entirely new intelligence unit. In 1945 General Carl Spaatz, then Commanding General of the US Strategic Air Forces, called into being the Air Technical Intelligence with a sub-unit called "Air Document Center". In its service Leopold recovered secret German technical publications and documents dealing with rocketry and missiles and identified their inventors. Many of the latter were subsequently shipped to the US.[31]

John Kirsners, a prisoner-of-war interrogator, was posted to Vienna after the war because of his facility in Slavic languages. As an interpreter with the US Military Government in Vienna, he was asked to investigate the deterioration of the American-Russian relationship in Vienna even in the negotiation of routine matters. His investigation did not take long: American Military government was using, as simultaneous translator, a Russian national who during the war had joined the so-called army of the renegade Colonel Vlassov, a traitor to the Soviet Union.[32] No wonder the Russians had bristled!

One of the most frequent, dramatic, and mostly frustrating if occasionally rewarding, intelligence tasks was the process known as denazification. That it should be attacked by unreconstructed Germans holds no surprises; Ernst von Salomon's purportedly documentary novel, *Der Fragebogen* (The Questionnaire), is perhaps the most pernicious example of such broadsides.[33] But some of the exiles, if for entirely opposite reasons, were also highly critical; the title of John Herz's article 'The Fiasco of Denazification in Germany' speaks volumes.[34] Yet despite errors in concept and catastrophes in execution, the system occasionally meted out justice and caused disquiet to some of the Nazi criminals.

Denazification, the ferreting out of high Nazi officials, their removal from office and/or arrest, was carried out at several levels. During my own brief postwar service I was involved, never at a policy-making level, in three of these stages. The first happened at a prisoner-of-war enclosure in Koblenz. We, as members of Military Intelligence, were charged with clearing POW's for dismissal from US confinement. This involved the examination of thousands of paybooks, interrogation of their owners, and such rough-and-ready verifications as checking for the blood type tattooed under the armpit of *Waffen*-SS personnel. About two per cent of our charges proved to be arrestable and were dispatched to prison. But our success – even if we ignore our oversights – was marred by an egregious error of judgement. We were beguiled by a confidence trickster in *Wehrmacht*-uniform whom we had made a trusty on the strength of his past

[31] Anthony Cave Brown, *The Last Hero. Wild Bill Donovan*, New York 1982, pp. 767, 768, 770. "Johannes Werner" is the cover name given the former officer by OSS, which he retains when telling of his clandestine activities. I interviewed him in New York on 31st January 1994. My telephone interview with Vern Leopold, now a Michigan lawyer, took place on 9th February 1994.
[32] Information gathered during my long years of friendship with the late John Kirsners.
[33] Ernst von Salomon, *Der Fragebogen*, Hamburg 1953.
[34] John Herz, 'The Fiasco of Denazification in Germany', in *Political Science Quarterly*, 63 (1948), pp. 569–594.

incarceration in a Nazi army prison. One day, after we had segregated an unusually large group of Nazi bigwigs, we returned to the enclosure only to find out that all of them had disappeared – together with the trusty. An all-out alarm returned less than half of the fifty escapees. Under interrogation, they told us that for a reward, the trusty had stolen standard release forms from our HQ tent, forged our signatures, and escorted the Nazis past the MPs, finally releasing himself.

If less dramatic, the experience of Henry Weinsaft, recently interviewed by me, was equally frustrating. After serving with distinction with the Tenth Mountain Division in Italy, then as a translator in the headquarters of General Mark Clark, Weinsaft was given the post-war assignment of denazifying the Austrian *Kreditbank*. After sifting out the guilty, he learned at a later date that every single one of the rejects had been reinstalled in his or her previous position. By that time, however, Weinsaft had taken full advantage of his intelligence training, albeit in an entirely different capacity. He had become the Security Officer on the Palestine-bound rescue ship *Exodus*.[35]

My own experience, when attached first to a CIC unit, then to the military government of the City of Karlsruhe, brought similar frustrations together with the success of seeing a *Kreisleiter* jailed. But some of my arrestees, especially several men and one woman deemed irreplaceable in their profession, were set free again within hours. I later learned that such contradictions became commonplace. Others, slated for arrest, proved completely elusive. Some fled abroad or, an evasive manoeuvre almost as effective, took up residence in another occupation zone. Perhaps one of my thwarted arrests may symbolise our everyday obstacles. I was given the address of a high-ranking Nazi in Karlsruhe, went to an apartment building and rang his bell. Receiving no answer, I rang, detective-fashion, all the bells of the dwelling. No one responded. I stepped back from the building. Then I realised that only the façade had been left standing.

The literature on the final post-war activity of the exiles is not voluminous, but does give at least nodding recognition of the lasting value of their accomplishments.[36] The investigations prior to the staffing of a non-Fascist German press and broadcasting stations have even been recreated in works of fiction.[37] Felix Gilbert, ever the objective historian, recounts his success in getting Theodor Heuss installed as editor of the *Rhein-Main Zeitung* despite the initial opposition of his superior.[38] This type of clearance, of course, involved a considerable amount of intelligence work, often under-appreciated. A particularly well-documented

---

[35] Interview with Henry Weinsaft of Detroit, MI, of 4th December 1993. His subsequent service on the rescue ship *Exodus* is described in Leonard Slater, *The Pledge*, New York 1970, pp. 114, 115, 197; and in Chaim Herzog, *Heroes of Israel. Profiles of Jewish Courage*, Boston 1983, p. 183.

[36] The plethora of information accumulated during the war and post-war years seems to have had a long-range effect on American intellectual life. See Robin W. Winks, *Cloak and Gown, 1939–1961. Scholars in the Secret War*, New York 1987, p. 111, where he attributes the predominance of American scholarship in the fifties, including the humanities and the social sciences, to the reorganisation of knowledge begun by the Research and Analysis Section of OSS. All this was "aided enormously by refugee scholars".

[37] David Davidson, *The Steeper Cliff*, New York 1947.

[38] Gilbert, *op. cit.*, pp. 210–212.

example of the military intelligence work that a position in Information Control entailed is provided by the service records of Gustave Mathieu, before his return to university life a civilian employee in the western sector of occupied Berlin.

Mathieu, after the surrender chief political reporter for the Information Control Office in Bad Godesberg, was leap-frogged to the much higher position of Radio Control Officer in West Berlin at the special request of General Robert A. McClure, the Director of Information Control. With the establishment of an American radio station in Berlin, partly in competition to the previous Soviet radio monopoly, the staffing of the new station had become urgent; RIAS was to be operative within three weeks. Mathieu, after his arrival in Berlin, was "appointed News Chief... and [to him was] delegated the specific responsibility of setting up a new department [and] ... the creation of other political broadcasts such as a daily Berlin press review, etc."[39] The "etc." alluded to Mathieu's introduction to the German air waves of political round tables as a means of electioneering, involving the four competing parties in Berlin.

Equally telling are passages of the commendation that allude to his investigative work, a skill acquired, in part, during his war-time service with the Office of War Information in New York and Paris. Both the vetting of German personnel and the re-education towards democracy had been war-time activities of various US intelligence services; both this selection process and re-education now became key tasks of Information Control, entrusted not infrequently to exiles like Gustave Mathieu:

> "It was Mr. Mathieu's responsibility to make a proper selection of personnel qualified politically to carry out the mission of editing and writing news as desired by the Americans. The selection of the news personnel which today number more than 25 has proven successful.
> *Political training*: the main task of Mr. Mathieu was, however, the training of the German staff to write and edit news according to the principles that news are to be broadcast in an objective way."[40]

One of Mathieu's German recruits and trainees, who subsequently achieved prominence in German television, echoed the above encomiums in his volume of memoirs. Gerhard Löwenthal called him a "particularly empathetic partner".[41]

Laudatory comments came also to various exile intelligence servicemen and civilians, especially from OSS.[42] But the reaction of the commanding general of OMGUS, General Lucius D. Clay, was quite otherwise. It was reminiscent of a

---

[39] All of the above information is contained in a memorandum of 28th November 1946 by the Office of Military Government, Berlin Sector, Information Control Branch, entitled: "Gustave Mathieu. Recommendation for Award." A copy was kindly furnished to me by Professor Mathieu of Laguna Beach, CA, who, to the best of his recollection, attributes the communication to Lt. Col. F.N. Leonard, Chief of the Division. An earlier, if terser, appreciation came from Brig. Gen. Robert A. McClure, Director, Information Control Service. Dated 8th February 1946, it congratulated Mathieu upon his opening broadcast for RIAS.

[40] *Ibid.* Further information obtained in a telephone interview with Professor Mathieu, 10th December 1993.

[41] Gerhard Löwenthal, *Ich bin geblieben*, Munich 1987, p. 125. See also pp. 135 and 136.

[42] As reported by Ladislav Farago, *Burn After Reading. The Espionage History of World War II*, New York 1961, p. 219.

much-quoted citation from Schiller's play *Die Verschwörung des Fiesco zu Genua*: "The Moor has done his duty. The Moor can go." In 1947 General Clay issued a directive, intentionally never codified into an order which, reeking of ingratitude and duplicity, was only recently discovered by me in the Suitland Annex of the National Archives.

The memorandum, dated 7th April 1947 and classified "confidential", was issued from Frank L. Keating, Major General, USA, Deputy Military Governor and is addressed to the Director of Military Government of Greater Hessia, with simultaneous mailings going to the directors of Bavaria, Würtemberg-Badem (*sic*), Bremen and to General Taylor. The peremptoriness of its contents and the callousness of its style deserve to be preserved by reproducing the text in full.

> "1. I discussed the matter of employment and renewal of contracts of civilian employees who have been naturalized American citizens for less than fifteen years with General Clay. He has decided we shall not employ anyone or renew any contracts of anyone who has been naturalized since 1933.
>
> 2. It is recognized that a certain degree of flexibility must be applied to this order as there are a number of such individuals employed by Military Government in very technical capacities whom we may have to retain; for example, an individual thoroughly acquainted with German law. Even in cases like this, we should try to find a way out.
>
> 3. It is therefore directed that you take necessary action to implement this directive and in so doing will refrain from general discussion of the subject or issuance of any orders. It is not necessary for us to indicate why we do not intend to rehire anyone, and it is up to you to see that diplomacy is used in handling each case. It is also desired that you accept this letter as being highly confidential and not reveal its contents to your staff except to those who must be informed of its provisions."[43]

To be sure, a pencilled one-word notation over initials that appear to be those of General Clay read "Recalled", but in the meantime the damage had been done. The same box of documents at the National Archives contains, next to such trivia as minor motor vehicle violations by American personnel, also the indignant protests of those suddenly dismissed. None of the protestations, however, drew forth as much publicity as the case of Frankfurt-born Walter Pulitzer, who had fought during the war in France, Luxembourg and Germany and had become a Special Branch Investigator for Denazification in Bavaria. His dismissal was covered by the United Press, apparently because Pulitzer had also alerted Senator Wagner (Democrat, NY) to the new and less-than-totally hidden policy change and because he was a distant relative of the famous publishing family.

Pulitzer, speaking for "hundreds of other veterans now working in Germany", called the rumoured new order undemocratic, a poor model for the re-education of Germans and an indignity to those who had fought for the US cause during the war. Both he and the UP dispatches pointed to the disastrous results for the US Military Government of this new policy. Its responsibilities for counter-intelligence, denazification and media reform would be crippled by replacing

---

[43] In National Archives, Suitland, MD, RG 260, US Occupation HQ, World War II, Box 581, File AG 49, B43.

experienced, language-proficient, foreign-born Americans by monolingual new arrivals, though born in America.[44]

The refugees' expertise as Nazi hunters were, one may assume, no longer wanted at the onset of the Cold War; their frequent sympathies with liberal causes had become suspect during the paranoia about Communists. And General Lucius Dubignon Clay, as even an admirer conceded, "is destined to remain a controversial figure . . . democrat and autocrat".[45]

Hence, my additional exploration of the subject comes to a rather sad conclusion. But the sorry action of America's proconsul should not diminish the sense of fulfilment, even of exhilaration, that so many of us felt while fighting, even after the cessation of hostilities, for a better future according to our lights. Nor should the cavalier treatment dissuade us from further research. The Jewish exiles performed tasks in war-time and post-war intelligence work which even until now have gone unrecorded.[46] For example, a recent article documents the involvement of the Library of Congress, under Archibald MacLeish, in intelligence gathering and in the reshaping of German libraries after the war.[47] To this purpose, MacLeish gathered together the foremost historians, economists and geographers in the US, undoubtedly many Jewish exiles among them.

In May 1994, fifty years have elapsed since many Jewish exiles once more left their American asylum and returned to Europe courtesy of the US Intelligence Services. Let it be said of them that they earned a small, but not insignificant, commemoration in the annals of history.

---

[44]The UP Dispatch is dated 1947; it is included in the files because it was sent (and prefaced) by a transmittal note from Sprowl, PRD EUCOM, to Grey, PRO OMGUS, Berlin.

[45]Don D. Humphrey, 'Epilogue', in John H. Backer's *Winds of History. The German Years of Lucius Dubignon Clay*, New York–Cincinnati etc. 1983, p. 392. The theory that Clay's non-renewal of foreign-born citizens came about because of his new anti-Communist stance of 1947 is lent support by Daniel E. Rogers, 'Transforming the German Party System. The United States and the Origins of Political Moderation, 1945–1949', in *Journal of Modern History*, 65 (1993), p. 515: "After 1947 . . . U.S. occupation director General Lucius D. Clay climbed aboard the bandwagon of containment [of the Left]."

[46]After the completion of my article a remarkable book of memoirs appeared in Israel which buttresses my contention that the extent of the exiles' war-time and post-war activities has been less than fully explored. Latvian-born, Heidelberg-educated Alex Rafaeli had been dispatched to the US from Palestine by the *Irgun* in 1940; two years later he received organisational permission to join the US Army. He details his adventurous army career in his *Dream and Action. The Story of My Life*, Jerusalem 1993. With his unit assigned to the Ruhr Valley, Rafaeli became the principal investigator of Alfried Krupp, the manager of the Krupp concern, after his father's bout with paralysis. Rafaeli's interrogations of Alfried Krupp and his painstaking analysis of incriminating papers led to Krupp being sentenced to twelve years imprisonment at the Nuremberg trials (pp. 126–128). Rafaeli also managed to ferret out and arrest the former *Gauleiter* Leo Schlessmann, who had gone underground in a hospital (p. 127), and three weapon engineers at Krupp's sought by the US Army Corps of Engineers (pp. 128 and 134). Once more an observation about one of the exiles, i.e. that Rafaeli's activities in the CIC "called for courage" (as Harold Blumberg put it in a *Jerusalem Post* review of 31st December 1993), applies equally to many of these members of America's intelligence units.

[47]See Frederick J. Stielow, 'Librarian Warriors and Rapprochement. Carl Milam, Archibald MacLeish, and World War II', in *Library and Culture*, 23 (1990), pp. 513–533.

Jewish Conversion from the Seventeenth to the Nineteenth Century

Converts and their Narratives in Early Modern Germany
The Case of Friedrich Albrecht Christiani*

BY ELISHEVA CARLEBACH

Friedrich Albrecht Christiani began his life (c.1647) as Baruch, son of Rabbi Moses and Sara, in the Moravian town of Proßnitz. At the age of eighteen, he took a position as cantor in the tiny nascent Jewish community of Bruchsal. A decade later, he converted to Christianity and embarked upon a successful career as an academic Hebraist. Like so many other converts of his age, Christiani wrote an autobiographical account of his conversion published first in 1676, then a second time in 1713.[1] While the texts of both editions are virtually identical, they were produced under very different circumstances. The earlier edition was published in the first blush of enthusiasm after Christiani's conversion; the latter after he had reverted to Judaism. They serve as the points of demarcation for everything we know about his life.

In the years between the emergence of Protestantism in the early sixteenth century and the Jewish Enlightenment in the mid-eighteenth, untold numbers of Jews in German lands converted to Christianity and told their tales.[2] Converts,

---

*The Klau Library at the Hebrew Union College, Cincinnati, has been my richest source of conversion narratives to date and I thank the entire staff for putting the sources at my disposal. I acknowledge with gratitude travel and research support from the Memorial Foundation for Jewish Culture and a grant from the PSC/CUNY Research Award Program. I thank my colleague Professor Marion Kaplan for her helpful comments.

[1] The work was first published with Christiani's Hebrew translation of *Epistle to the Hebrews* with an introduction by Johann Benedict Carpzov, as *Sippur Mahalakh ha-Hayim . . . Das ist: Lebens=Lauff Eines bekehrten Jüden/darinnen seine Ankunfft/ bishero geführtes Leben und Wandel/ auch die Ursach seiner Bekehrung . . .* Leipzig 1676, pp. 50–70. The *Lebens=Lauff* was published a second time as part of the foreword by Christian Reineccius (dated 1705) to Christiani's *Der Juden Glaube und Aberglaube*, Leipzig 1713.

[2] For Jewish converts in sixteenth-century Germany see Georg Hammann, 'Konversionen deutscher und ungarischer Juden in der frühen Reformationszeit', in *Zeitschrift für Bayerische Kirchengeschichte*, 39 (1970), pp. 207–237; Hava Fraenkel-Goldschmidt, 'On the Periphery of Jewish Society. Jewish Converts to Christianity in the Age of the Reformation', in Menahem Ben-Sasson et al. (eds.), *Culture and Society in Medieval Jewry. Studies Dedicated to the Memory of Hayim Hillel Ben-Sasson*, Jerusalem 1989, pp. 623–654 (in Hebrew). For the eighteenth century, see Benjamin Zev Kedar, 'Continuity and Change in Jewish Conversion to Christianity in Eighteenth Century Germany', in E. Etkes and Y. Salmon (eds.), *Studies in the History of Jewish Society in the Middle Ages and in the Modern Period. Presented to Jacob Katz*, Jerusalem 1980, pp. 154–170 (in Hebrew); Christian Hermann Kalkar, *Israel und die Kirche. Geschichtlicher Überblick der Bekehrungen der Juden zum Christenthume in allen Jahrhunderten*, Hamburg 1869; Johann Jacob Schudt, *Jüdische Merckwürdigkeiten*, 4 vols., Frankfurt a. Main–Leipzig 1714–1718, vol. II, chap. 29, pp. 83ff. For nineteenth-century Berlin see Guido Kisch, *Judentaufen. Eine historisch-biographisch-psychologisch-soziologische Studie besonders für Berlin und Königsberg*, Berlin 1973. The most comprehensive study of Protestant converts is Johannes F.A. de le Roi, *Die Evangelische Christenheit und die Juden*, 3 vols., Karlsruhe–Leipzig 1884.

both male and female, spanned the socio-economic spectrum from *Hofjuden* to *Betteljuden*. Most tended to be in their twenties or early thirties, although every age was represented.[3] Their conversion narratives constitute a treasure-trove of autobiographical writing in which Jewish lives are illuminated, albeit for brief moments. Written with transparently ulterior motives, limited in scope and artificial in construction, the hermeneutic of scepticism with which any autobiography must be approached is compounded by the particular problems and circumstances that shaped the stories told by the converts.[4] Despite the limitations inherent in narratives shaped to theological expectations, they form a chapter within the histories of early modern European and Jewish autobiographical writing, and should be considered within their multiple contexts.[5] While the conversion experience is the matrix for one of the oldest and strongest traditions of autobiographical writing, it is also one of the most problematic because the real subject of these narratives is the new religion; everything subserves this didactic purpose.[6]

In some cases it is unclear whether the words we are reading are those of the

---

[3] For female converts in this period, see the questions raised by Deborah Hertz in her 'Women at the edge of Judaism. Female converts in Germany, 1600–1750', in Menachem Mor (ed.), *Jewish Assimilation, Acculturation and Accommodation*, Lanham, MD 1990.

[4] Many of these issues have been raised in the abundant literary and scholarly studies of autobiography in the past decades. Particularly relevant are Roy Pascal, *Design and Truth in Autobiography*, Cambridge, MA–London 1960; and Geoffrey Galt Harpham, 'Conversion and the Language of Autobiography', in James Olney (ed.), *Studies in Autobiography*, Oxford 1988, pp. 42–50. Karl F. Morrison, *Conversion and Text*, Charlottesville, VA 1992.

[5] The sixteenth and seventeenth century witnessed a flowering of autobiographical writing. While Renaissance Italian-Jewish autobiographies such as those of Isaac min Halevi'im, Abraham Y(J)agel and Leon da Modena might seem the least relevant to our works, even their influence cannot be discounted. Christiani published a translation of Modena's *Sur me-Ra=Der Belehrte und Bekehrte Spieler*, Leipzig 1683, a treatise on gambling (sometimes published as *Eldad u-Medad*, which refers to the names of the disputants). He may well have taken an interest in other aspects of Modena's career. On Modena's autobiography see Natalie Zemon Davis, 'Fame and Secrecy. Leon Modena's *Life* as an Early Modern Autobiography', in Mark R. Cohen (ed.), *The Autobiography of a Seventeenth-Century Venetian Rabbi*, Princeton 1988, pp. 50–70. On Protestant autobiographies of the early decades of the Reformation, see note 20. More importantly, there is an independent or overlapping tradition of German-Jewish autobiography which remains virtually unexplored for this period. These include the journals of Josel of Rosheim, ed. by J. (Isidor) Kracauer, in *Revue des Etudes Juives*, 16 (1888), pp. 85 ff.; Yomtov Lipmann Heller, *Megillat Eiva*, Breslau 1818; Ascher b. Eliezer Halevi (Ascher Levi), *Die Memoiren des Ascher Levy aus Reichshofen im Elsaß (1598–1635)*, ed., transl. and annotated by M. Ginsburger, Berlin 1913; *The Memoirs of Glückel of Hameln*, transl. by Marvin Lowenthal, New York 1977; the anonymous Bohemian Jew in Alexander Marx, 'A Seventeenth Century Autobiography', in *Jewish Quarterly Review*, N.S., 8 (1917–1918), pp. 269–304; and Jacob Emden's *Megillat Sefer*, ed. by David Kahana, Warsaw 1896; up to the autobiography of Salomon Maimon, ed. by Moses Hadas, New York 1947.

[6] See the remarks of Israel Jacob Yuval, 'A German Jewish Autobiography from the Fourteenth Century', in *Tarbiz*, vol. LV, No. 4 (1986), p. 543 (in Hebrew).

convert or of a ghost-writer who was more fluent in the vernacular.[7] Christian Reineccius praised Christiani's "Teutsche Mutter=Sprache" as "gantz accurat, nett und zierlich (welches bey den Jüden etwas seltzames . . . ist)".[8] The close filiation of printed conversion autobiographies from the sermon preached at the baptismal ceremony is also worth noting. The sermons usually contained brief biographical sketches of the converts, based on information which could only have been provided by the convert, and were sometimes published exactly as they were preached.[9] To present the conversion narratives in the first person autobiographical voice required relatively little editorial revision. The narratives are a unique layering of material shaped both by the converts and those who converted them, mirroring two obverse and complementary sets of expectations.

The literary paradigm for conversion narratives from Judaism to Christianity remains the Pauline, in which a mystical experience was the catalyst for conversion.[10] Medieval conversion narratives tended to emphasise, in addition to the standard theological justifications, an experiential component. The famous medieval convert, known as "Hermannus quondam Judaeus" is associated with a classical autobiographical essay in which his conversion from Judaism was presented as the fulfilment of a dream.[11] In the early sixteenth century, Johannes Pfefferkorn still wrote of himself as, "vormals ein Jude, nun

---

[7] For a discussion of translations of works by converts, see Fraenkel-Goldschmidt, 'Jewish Converts', *loc. cit.*, p. 625, note 11, on the translation of Victor von Carben's *Juden Büchlein* from German into Latin (*Opus Aureum*) by Ortwin Gratius; and *ibid.*, p. 626, on the second edition of Anthonius Margaritha's *Der Gantz Jüdisch Glaub*, first published in Augsburg 1530. The second edition of Leipzig 1531 was "corrected and improved" by the author himself, indicating that Margaritha was not the original author-editor. On the degree to which Johannes Pfefferkorn wrote his own work, see the discussion in Hans-Martin Kirn, *Das Bild vom Juden im Deutschland des frühen 16. Jahrhunderts, dargestellt an den Schriften Johannes Pfefferkorns*, Tübingen 1989, pp. 4–5; and Jacob Goldberg, *Converted Jews in the Polish Commonwealth*, Jerusalem 1985, p. 14, note 4 (in Hebrew), on a purportedly autobiographical letter of the convert Michael, dated 1584. Goldberg casts doubt over its authenticity because the letter is written in fluent Polish only a year after the conversion. More candid than most, the *Lebens=Geschichte und Glaubens=Bekenntnis* of Gütgen Steinhardin (b. Bintzwang near Dillingen 1752) admitted on the title page that the work was "größtentheils selbst gefertigt", but that it had actually been prepared for publication by the converter (Nuremberg n.d. – probably shortly after her conversion in 1775). Perhaps the admission of editorial shaping was less compromising in the case of a female author.

[8] Reineccius, intro. to Christiani, *Der Juden Glaube, op. cit.*, p. 84.

[9] See for example the sermon published by Johann Conrad Spoerl 'Kurze Betrachtung ueber die in der Heil. Schrifft oeffters vorkommende Worte: Ich bin der Gott Abrahams und der Gott Isaac, und der Gott Jacobs. In einer oeffentlichen Rede bey feyerlicher Tauf-Handlung zweyer gebohrner Juden, Vater und Sohns, nemlich Lazarus Wolfs, nunmehro Wilhelm Christian Christlieb und Samuel Lazari oder Laezers nunmehro Carl Hector Christlieb genannt. Den 2. Dezember 1733 in der Kirche zu Burg-Farrenbach vorgelegt', Nuremberg; Theodore John, *An Account of the Conversion of Theodore John, a late teacher among the Jews . . . which he delivered before he was baptised in the presence of the Lutheran congregation, 31 October 1692*, transl. from German, London 1693.

[10] On Paul's conversion, see Alan F. Segal, *Paul the Convert. The Apostolate and Apostasy of Saul the Pharisee*, New Haven–London 1990, esp. pp. 285–300.

[11] On Hermannus's autobiography, see Georg Misch, *Geschichte der Autobiographie*, vol. III, section 2, Frankfurt a. Main 1959, pp. 505–522; Bernhard Blumenkranz, 'Jüdische und christliche Konvertiten im jüdisch-christlichen Religionsgespräch des Mittelalters', in *Judentum im Mittelalter*, ed. by Paul Wilpert, Berlin 1966, pp. 264–282, esp. pp. 275–279; Avrom Saltman, 'Hermann's Opusculum de Conversione Sua. Truth or Fiction?', in *Revue des Etudes Juives*, 147 (1988), pp. 31–56; Morrison, *op. cit.*, p. 113.

ein Christ in dem dritten Jahr meiner Geburt", signifying his decisive break with his past and spiritual rebirth as a Christian.[12] The spiritual experience, whether an illumination, revelation, or ecstatic-mystical sensation, affirmed for the convert, and for his audience, that a deep structural change had occurred. It facilitated the extreme reversal of identities, from persecuted to persecutor, from apostate to zealous apostle; a change dramatised in medieval writing such as the convert Petrus Alfonsi's *Dialogus Petri et Moysi Judæi*, a polemic against his former self.[13] Such extreme reversals are much less frequent in the conversion accounts under consideration, and are absent from Christiani's and most of his contemporaries'. Unlike their medieval predecessors, early modern converts offered no pretence that revelations, dreams or other spiritual events precipitated their journey to the baptismal font. Lack of the affective component of conversion was a sign that inner identity structures had not changed suddenly and profoundly, as the case of Christiani illustrates. By the seventeenth and eighteenth centuries, conversion narratives integrated the Jewish past into the Christian persona of the convert. Instead of trying to present themselves as models of Christian learning or piety, the converts of the seventeenth and eighteenth centuries emphasised their Jewish pasts as their most valuable commodity. Christiani represents converts in an age of transition, who had broken from the medieval model of conversion, but not yet embraced the path that would characterise conversions in the nineteenth century.

> "I was so zealous for my Jewishness that had someone told me then of my prospective conversion, it would have appeared as strange to me as it seems incredible to others, that in these last days apparently considerable numbers of Jews would, through the grace of God, be converted."[14]

Christiani's assertion that he had no inkling that he would have been amenable to conversion even a short while prior to its occurrence is an element in many contemporary conversion narratives. Some describe complete ignorance, others parental cultivation of an active hatred of the Christian world prior to a decisive

---

[12] Cited from *Judenspiegel*, 1507, col. 13v, in Hans-Martin Kirn, *Das Bild vom Juden, op. cit.*, p. 9.

[13] On Petrus Alfonsi see, *Dialogus Petri et Moysi Judæi*, in Jacques-Paul Migne, *Patrologia latina*, vol. CLVII (1844–1864), cols. 535–672; and the discussion in Jeremy Cohen, 'The Mentality of the Medieval Jewish Apostate. Peter Alfonsi, Hermann of Cologne, and Pablo Christiani', in Todd M. Endelman (ed.), *Jewish Apostasy in the Modern World. Converts and Missionaries in Historical Perspective*, New York–London 1987, pp. 20–47.

[14] Christiani, *Lebens=Lauff* (1713), *op. cit.*, p. 66. ". . . war ich so eiffrig in meinem Juedenthum, daß, wenn mir dazumahl jemand von meiner nunmehro geschehenen Bekehrung gesaget haette, solches mir eben so wunderlich vorkommen, als ist manchem dieses unglaeublich und wunderlich scheinet, nehmlich daß *in denen letzten Tagen* eine ziemliche Anzahl derer Jueden durch Gottes Gnade bekehret werden sollen." (Author's emphasis.) Christiani's reference to "letzten Tagen" carried an eschatological meaning. I thank Professor Jean Jofen for alerting me to this. Cf. Johannes Elias Dupré, *Die in denen letzten Tagen Neuen Testaments anzuhoffende Bekehrung des Judischen Volcks wurde bei Gelegenheit der Tauffe eines Israelitischen Junglings ehemahlen Solomon David anjetzo Phillip Heinrich Christian genannt* . . . Mannheim 1755; and Johann Christoph Gottfried, *Yeshu'a Mashiach ha-Amiti ba-nigleh u-va-nistar, Das ist: Jesus der wahre Messias* . . . Regensburg 1721, intro: "Jews, my brothers in the flesh, know that these days are the last days of the six thousand years of the world's existence." (Author's translation from the Hebrew.)

encounter.[15] Taken at face value, the statements depict a sudden conversion, brought on neither by inner illumination nor by the process of "drift and defection". This multi-generational process, the product of a gradual drift away from Jewish tradition into the upper levels of society-at-large, has been vividly analysed for English Jews by Todd Endelman.[16] Many nineteenth-century German Jews followed a similar trajectory. In the case of Christiani and his contemporaries, the reversal occurred within a single generation, sometimes to more than one family member. A chance meeting with a Christian or a momentous historical event, such as the messianic movement of Sabbatai Zvi, prompted the convert to conclude that Judaism had erred in its interpretation of Scripture and history.[17] The converts' insistence on the abrupt nature of the transformation, contrary to the facts,[18] was intended to refute the deeply held conviction within the Jewish communities that the souls lost to conversion had been tainted from the start, that conversion was the fulfilment of a destiny that was first manifested by earlier acts of betrayal of the community or rebellion against its standards.[19]

It is precisely because these conversions do not fit easily into the medieval or modern patterns that their stories merit closer attention. By the late eighteenth century, conversion was becoming a more common choice for Jews. Many of the lifelong inner conflicts that accompanied modern conversions were already faced

---

[15]Joachim Christian Franck, *Das von dem Stamm Juds* . . . Leipzig 1724, p. 5, recalled that long before his Bar Mitzvah, he had been taught to hate Christians. He converted to the Lutheran Evangelical church in Lübeck in 1696. Joseph Samuel C.F. Frey, *Narrative of Joseph Samuel C.F. Frey with an address to Christians, of all denominations* . . . 2nd edn., London 1812, p. 3, wrote that his tutors "took every opportunity to inspire us with prejudices and hatred against the Christian religion", while his mother "was a most inveterate enemy to Christianity, because her brother had embraced the Christian religion".

[16]Todd M. Endelman, *Radical Assimilation in English Jewish History, 1656–1945*, Bloomington 1990.

[17]Christiani cited the messianic movement as a prime motive for his decision to convert. On the impact of this movement on individual converts, see Elisheva Carlebach, 'Sabbatianism and the Jewish-Christian Polemic', in *Proceedings of the Tenth World Congress of Jewish Studies*, Division C (Jewish Thought and Literature), vol. II, Jerusalem 1990, pp. 1–7.

[18]See the patterns in the list of converts from eighteenth-century Nuremberg in Azriel Shohet, *Beginnings of the Haskalah among German Jewry*, Jerusalem 1960, p. 316, note 10 (in Hebrew), in which family members contemplate conversion with apparent openness. Similarly Frey, *Narrative, op. cit.*, related a chance meeting with a Scripture-quoting fellow passenger as having opened his eyes, p. 11, when he had earlier stated that his uncle had converted to Christianity, p. 3.

[19]Nowhere is the doctrine of the inevitability of conversion for *mosrim* (informers) or other sinners stated with greater conviction than in the writings of the sixteenth-century Jewish leader, Josel of Rosheim. Josel cited numerous examples of the trajectory that led directly from betrayal to conversion. He maintained that this destiny of tainted souls affected individuals regardless of their family's prominence. If not fulfilled immediately, the inevitable destiny would be deferred to a later generation – if the marked person did not convert, his children would. See Hava Fraenkel-Goldschmidt (ed.), intro. to Josel of Rosheim, *Sefer HaMiknah*, Jerusalem 1970, pp. xxii-xxxiii. In his journal, Josel wrote of an oral tradition he received from his father that is a striking example of this doctrine. Of the eighty Jewish victims of the blood libel at Ensheim, seventy-four were martyred and six were forcibly converted. Of the six who were baptised, all managed to revert to Judaism, except for one man, named Raphael, who died in Colmar before he had a chance to escape and revert to Judaism. Josel repeated the tradition that this man's end was already manifest while he was Jewish, because he had his wife immerse herself, contrary to Jewish Law, during the days of her menstruation. "Surely for this reason he did not merit repentance, for sin had long ago taken root in his soul." Kracauer (ed.), 'Josel of Rosheim', *loc. cit.*, p. 86.

by converts in the age of transition. The narratives invoke the familiar parallel to a triptych in which the convert stands at the centre, his Jewish past on one side and Christian expectations on the other. Each component contained many layers of ambivalence and ambiguity, mutual attraction and repulsion. The large number of conversion narratives that were written in German in the early modern period attest to the fact that in some cultural environments, these programmatic statements had become *de rigueur* for the convert, part of the rite of passage out of the old life and passport to the new.[20] These texts, along with other material by the converts, constitute a unique testimony to this otherwise obscure chapter in Jewish and German history. Did the converts have a historical consciousness of their role within German-Jewish history? A close reading of their narratives remains our only means of touching upon some aspects of this critical juncture in their individual and communal lives.

It is not the distinctive personal shape of their childhoods, which every autobiography seeks to retrieve and incorporate into the mature life, that the converts chose to tell, but precisely the elements that made it a Jewish childhood – their experiences of Jewish education, worship, or ritual training. It is significant that most seventeenth-century autobiographical essays contain at least a cursory statement concerning the convert's Jewish education. Christiani wrote:

> ". . . haben mich auch von Jugend auff in dem Juedenthum erzogen/ in den Juedischen Gesetzen und Gebraeuchen unterrichtet/ und zu dem *Studio Rabbinico* dergestalt angehalten/ daß/ nachdem ich allbereit zu Hause ziemliche *Fundamenda* in demselbigen geleget / sie mich in die Synagoge nach Posen verschicket/ da ich endlichen so weit kommen/ daß ich nicht allein die Schrifft Altes Testamentes in Hebraeischer Sprache verstehen/ sondern auch die Rabbinischen *Commentatores* fertig lesen koennen/ und in den Talmudischen Buechern wohl bekandt worden."[21]

Ludwig Compiègne de Veil, born Daniel in 1637, wrote that he had studied Hebrew to the age of sixteen and only then began to study Talmud, continuing through to his nineteenth year.[22] John Xeres, who converted in 1709, recalled: "I was Born there to a Father so Zealous for his Religion, that, being able to support the Charge of such an Education, he designed to make me a Rabbin. Accordingly, I have been brought up under the most famous of our Doctors, and

---

[20]Protestant autobiographies proliferated in the early decades of the Reformation. On the role of the Reformation in reviving religious individualism and the tendency to autobiography, see Arthur M. Clark, *Autobiography. Its Genesis and Phases*, Folcroft, PA 1935, repr. 1969, p. 31. Some were modelled on Luther's own conversion account, and were characterised by declarations of independence from the shackles of Papism. See Walter Muschg's introduction to Thomas Platter, *Lebensbeschreibung*, Basel 1944. On Luther's *Turmerlebnis* see Marilyn J. Harran, *Luther on Conversion. The Early Years*, Ithaca–London 1983, pp. 174–193. Endelman, *Radical Assimilation, op. cit.*, p. 43, notes the relative paucity of autobiographical material for English converts compared to the abundance of such materials for German Jews. This may not simply be a reflection of one group's innate reticence versus another's volubility, but the very different contexts and expectations that accompanied conversions in each setting.

[21]Christiani, *Lebens=Lauff* (1713), *op. cit.*, p. 65.

[22]Cited in Gerardus Johannes de Weille and Gustaaf Alexander de Weille Jr., *Het Geslacht de Weille. (Weil, Weill, de Veille, de Veil)*, Weesp 1936, p. 58; from foreword to de Veil's translation of Maimonides's *Yad Hachazaka*.

tho' I have not yet been raised to that Degree . . .".²³ In many cases their education led the converts to be qualified for some position as functionary within the Jewish community as teacher, rabbi, or preacher.²⁴

The autobiographies of male converts tended to boast of a solid Jewish education and some of their later efforts at scholarly Hebraism support these claims. The course described by Christiani appears to be rather standard fare for Jewish boys. That he persisted to the age of sixteen meant that he had shown some promise, as his parents did not force him to end his studies earlier to seek his livelihood; had his talents displayed more stellar qualities, he would have continued his studies at a larger *yeshiva*.

By emphasising that their Jewish education defined their youth, the converts were tapping into existing traditions of Jewish autobiography which were generally influenced by "chain of tradition" literature, and German-Jewish autobiography in particular.²⁵ Unlike the *Haskalah* autobiographies of a later century, these do not complain about the short-comings of the system or of their teachers.²⁶ Their conversions are presented as occurring at the apex of perfect Jewish educations, not out of disgust for inadequate ones. This idealisation of their Jewish education may have been influenced by very pragmatic considerations. A significant number of converts entered university careers as teachers of Hebrew, rabbinics and cognate subjects, for which their own claims of proficiency often constituted the sole employment criteria.²⁷ Where no possibility of such a career existed, as in the case of female converts, Jewish education was evaluated more harshly. Gütgen Steinhardin wrote that her parents did not neglect her intellectual development; they sent her to the house of a teacher (*Praeceptor*) of Hebrew. She complained that she learned how to read without any comprehension, and was taught nothing of the religion because it was not the custom among Jews to teach their daughters anything about religion. Joseph Samuel C.F. Frey wrote of the sharp discrepancy between the education of Jewish boys and girls in almost identical words: "My sisters were taught to read

---

²³John Xeres, *An address to the Jews . . . containing his reasons for leaving the Jewish and embracing the Christian religion*, London 1710, pp. 2–3. Xeres, from Saphia in North Africa, may have been of Sephardic descent. See the testimony about him appended to his *Address* by Peter Fleuriot et al., and Xeres's own description of his search for religious truth.
²⁴See numerous additional examples in Shohet, *Beginnings of the Haskalah, op. cit.*, pp. 182–185.
²⁵See the nearly contemporary full-length autobiography of Halevi, *Die Memoiren des Ascher Levy, op. cit.*
²⁶The experience of a *kefira*, an apostasy from the ancestral religion to a religion ostensibly of reason, was central to autobiography from the Enlightenment age. The autobiographies often used the educational system as a symbol for everything that ailed the traditional Jewish society they rejected. See Alan Mintz, *"Banished from their Father's Table". Loss of Faith and Hebrew Autobiography*, Bloomington 1989, p. 4. In conversion autobiographies which preceded the Enlightenment, the defining moment was an actual, rather than metaphorical, abandonment of the father's religion.
²⁷The second half of the seventeenth century saw many Protestant universities in Germany struggling to rebuild in the aftermath of the Thirty Years' War. Many now included departments of Oriental Languages, Rabbinics and other subjects for which converts were in demand. Lewis White Beck, *Early German Philosophy. Kant and his Predecessors*, Cambridge, MA 1969, p. 85; see the mid-sixteenth-century letter of convert Paul Altdorfer to the Bishop of Würzburg seeking employment in the new university. Franz Xavier von Wegele, *Geschichte der Universität Würzburg*. Würzburg 1882, repr. Aalen 1969, vol. II, pp. 42–43.

the prayer book in the Hebrew language, i.e. to pronounce the words without understanding even the literal meaning of a single sentence. This, alas! is usually all the education which the females receive." Frey then called upon Christian women to support his missionary endeavours which made no such discrimination between the sexes.[28] Already in the sixteenth century, converts and missionaries castigated Jews for not providing their daughters with equal religious status and education.[29] Nevertheless, the educational experience of Jewish boys in early modern Germany may have contained the roots of some of these later defections. Young children were taught either by their fathers or by very junior students. As soon as they were old enough, they were sent from home to study in larger cities.[30] The combination of poverty and peripatetic life-style rendered students vulnerable to promises of income, shelter and stability.

With the exception of Karl Anton, who made much of the fact that he had studied under Rabbi Jonathan Eybeschuetz (Eibenschütz), most do not mention the names of their teachers. How reliable are the testimonies of the converts concerning their Jewish education? Often even the rudiments of their personal histories are so selectively arranged that we have no choice but to question all statements that cannot be confirmed by other evidence. One eighteenth-century convert was challenged concerning his credentials shortly after he published his account. Friedrich Albrecht Augusti (formerly Joshua ben Abraham Herschel), who converted in Dessau in 1720, claimed that he had been a rabbi in Sondershausen. His critic countered that he had only been a schoolmaster and possibly a *shohet* as well.[31] The title page of Johann Christoph Gottfried's (born in Breslau, 1684) work claimed that he had been "Vormahlig Jüdischem[r] Rabbi".[32] Moses Marcus referred in his autobiography to his father who at a tender age had left him for ten-year intervals. He did not mention his father's

---

[28] Steinhardin, *Lebens=Geschichte, op. cit.*, p. 4: "weil es nicht Sitte ist bey den Juden die Mädgen etwas von der religion beyzubringen". The main source of this unmerciful attitude "gegen die armen Mädgen" was the Talmud. Frey, *Narrative, op. cit.*, p. 2. While there is no way to test the truth of these individual statements, contrast the overall picture to the presence of women in the world of Jewish scholarship and particularly those employed in the Hebrew publishing industry. See Menahem Schmelzer, 'Hebrew Printing and Publishing in Germany, 1650–1750. On Jewish Book Culture and the Emergence of Modern Jewry', in *LBI Year Book XXXIII* (1988), p. 381.

[29] Victor von Carben, *Juden Büchlein*, vol. I, n.p. (Strasbourg) 1550, p. 97.

[30] The fourteenth-century German-Jewish autobiography published by Yuval, *loc. cit.*, p. 564, begins with the moment that the author/subject left his father's home in Düren to study in Mainz. The anonymous author in Marx, 'Seventeenth Century Autobiography', *loc. cit.*, delivered a scathing critique of the vacuum in the educational system that left him at the mercy of his inept father, pp. 269–270. Excerpted in Jacob Marcus, *The Jew in the Medieval World. A Source Book, 315–1791*, Cincinnati 1938, pp. 431–435.

[31] Anonymous, *Merckwürdige Lebens-Geschichte Fr. A. Augusti . . . die Stelle eines Jüdischen Rabbi in Sondershausen bekleidet . . .* Erfurt 1751. The biography, ostensibly written by a friend, was undoubtedly inspired by Augusti himself, a reversal of the more usual pattern. See the early criticism of Augusti's Jewish expertise by S.J. Baumgarten, *Nachrichten von Merkwürdigen Büchern*, vol. I, Halle 1752, pp. 341–351; entry on 'Augusti, Friedrich Albrecht' in *Jewish Encyclopaedia*, vol. II, cols. 311–312, New York-London 1925ff.; and de le Roi, *Die Evangelische Christenheit, op. cit.*, pp. 381–386.

[32] Johann Christoph Gottfried, *Jesus der wahre Messias, op. cit.*

excommunication by the Jewish community as the reason for the forced departures.[33]

A considerable number of converts claimed to have been second-rank religious functionaries prior to their conversions. Jacob Melamed from Cornitz in Podolia was a schoolteacher in the Ashkenazic community in Hamburg. Phillip Christfells taught at the *yeshiva* in Fürth. Christiani wrote that after his education ended at age sixteen, he returned to his parents' home where he remained for two years. Then he left to become cantor in the Jewish community at Bruchsal: ". . . wurde ich von dannen nacher Bruchsal am Rhein gefodert/ und zu einen *Chasan* oder Vorsinger in der Synagoge daselbsten auffgenommen".[34] The profession of cantor is noteworthy in several respects. In communities too small to sustain a rabbi, the cantor often served as the repository of tradition and performed many rabbinical functions. A parallel position existed among Catholics of Central Europe, in that a cantor, i.e. school choirmaster, could head the services by leading the singing of hymns when no parish priest was available.[35] Such positions within the community were consistent with the converts' fair, but not outstanding, academic training. They formed a class of individuals who worked often at great distances from the communities that nurtured them, separated not only from parents, but from wives and children as well, isolated, indigent and generally treated with disrespect.[36] In a later period, these individuals might have fled the bleakness of their destinies by emigrating or advancing socially and economically as new opportunities for Jewish entry into society became available. In the seventeenth century there were precious few ways out. In an age when even the most prominent rabbis complained of penurious salaries, it is no coincidence that members of these ranks were vulnerable to the blandishments of the missionaries.[37] Johann Adam Gottfried, born in Altona as Nathan, admitted that after his family's money had been lost and he proved to be a business failure in his own right, he became a private tutor

---

[33] On the excommunication, see David Kaufmann, 'Rabbi Zevi Ashkenazi and his Family in London', in *Transactions of the Jewish Historical Society of England*, 3 (1896–1898), pp. 102–125. Reference to Glückel's family on pp. 112ff. For a similar case in which a wealthy and influential individual was stripped of his honour by the Jewish community and had offspring who converted, see Alexander Scheiber, 'Mendel of Buda in Nuremberg', in *Journal of Jewish Studies*, vol. XXIII, No. 2 (1972), pp. 191–195. The one offspring of the Mendel family whose traces can be found after his conversion, Christoff Mendel, used all his influence to land a position teaching Hebrew at Ansbach, *ibid.*, p. 194.

[34] Christiani, *Lebens=Lauff* (1713), *op. cit.*, p. 66.

[35] Marie-Elisabeth Ducreux, 'Reading unto Death. Readers in Eighteenth-Century Bohemia', in *The Culture of Print*, ed. by Roger Chartier, transl. by Lydia Cochrane, Princeton 1989, pp. 191–197.

[36] On the position of cantors in late-medieval Ashkenaz, see Bernard Rosensweig, *Ashkenazic Jewry in Transition*, Ontario 1975, p. 67; Leo Landman, *The Cantor. An Historic Perspective*, New York 1972, pp. 20–27. For descriptions of the plight of late seventeenth- and early eighteenth-century cantors, see Yehudah Leib of Zelechow, *Shire Yehudah*, Amsterdam 1697 (in Hebrew); Solomon Lipschütz, *Teudat Shlomoh*, Offenbach 1718 (in Hebrew).

[37] Yomtov Lipmann Heller recorded his exchange with an Imperial official in Vienna, through whom he channelled his request to be reinstated as Chief Rabbi of Prague after he was exonerated of the false charges brought against him. When the Imperial councillor remonstrated that surely he could have any rabbinic post in Germany, Heller replied that there was not even one that would support his family. Yomtov Lipmann Heller, *Megillat Ebah [A Chronicle of Hardship and Hope]*, transl. by CIS publ., New York 1991, p. 46.

to Jews in Anspach and Sulzbach, and then converted.[38] Shalome ben Shalomon wrote of being orphaned in Eastern Europe at the age of twelve, entering the army of the Duke (of Brandenburg?) and converting in Berlin shortly before the turn of the century.[39]

While opportunism was surely not absent from conversions like Christiani's, this does not exhaust the complicated personal and communal factors that led to his conversion, better classified as historical-pragmatic. Of course, some converts embellished upon their plight as destitute martyrs thrust into social and economic limbo in order to appeal to Christian charity. The entire phenomenon of conversion narratives *cum* appeals for sympathy was greatly facilitated by the ready availability of inexpensive printing.[40]

The very act of writing a conversion narrative invites emulation and promotes the convert as a model. The life story of the convert is not told for its own sake; it is transcended by its larger inspirational meaning. This is the only way we can understand how Reineccius republished Christiani's *Lebens=Lauff* years after his reversion to Judaism.[41] He believed that even the author's "relapse" did not invalidate the fundamental message of the autobiography: its call to Jews to convert. The autobiographies mirrored the Christian expectation that a convert ought not be content with his personal salvation, but must strive to serve as something more. Some of the works contain explicit addresses to former co-religionists, inviting them to follow their example. John Xeres expressed "a tender Affection . . . and an ardent Desire of procuring your Salvation" to his former co-religionists.[42] Just as every Jew was regarded as a potential convert, every convert was a potential bridge to other Jews, a possible Paul, a keystone and instrument for the future mass conversion.[43]

The attribution of special responsibilities and powers to the converts meshed with and reinforced their own difficult personal passage into the new social and religious worlds that awaited them. The converts developed an ideology of themselves as a bridge between the two religious communities, modelling themselves on other converts rather than directly on Christian personalities. They saw themselves as apostles to the Jews, and at the same time as defenders of the Jews against some of the worst calumnies and misconceptions held by Christians. Like children of divorced parents, they dreamed that they could bring about the ultimate reconciliation. Jews would come to recognise the truth

---

[38] Johann Adam J.A.C.K. Gottfried, *Wahrhafter Bericht von M. Johann Adam Gottfrieds sonderbaren Bekehrung* . . . n.p. 1776, pp. 7–9.

[39] Shalome ben Shalomon, *A true narrative of God's gracious dealings with the soul of . . . A Jew. With an account of his conversion,* London 1700, pp. 2–3.

[40] See for example Christian Gottleb Hirschlein, *Nachricht von einem . . . von . . . Jesu Christo auf den rechten Weg . . . gebracht . . . Schaafe des Hauses Israels,* Zürich 1746. The convert Friedrich August Constans published his *Das vertraute Gespräch des Herrn mit seinem . . . Knecht . . .* Rothenburg o.d. Tauber 1745, "auf eigene Kosten des autoris", and he hoped to recover his costs through the sale of the book.

[41] Reineccius brought the *Lebens=Lauff* to press almost a decade after Christiani's reversion. See Reineccius's introduction dated 1705, pp. 81ff., in Christiani, *Der Juden Glaube, op. cit.*

[42] Xeres, *An Address, op. cit.,* p. 1.

[43] See for example Johann Christoph Wagenseil, *Hofnung der Erlösung Israelis,* Nuremberg–Altdorf 1707.

embedded in their own Scriptures, while Christians would abandon their deeply held negative stereotypes and acknowledge the role of the Jews. Many converts believed that there was an important role for their work in the interim.[44]

During his life as a convert, Christiani published three works on Jewish ritual: a treatise on the observance of Passover,[45] another on Purim[46] and the more comprehensive *Der Juden Glaube und Aberglaube*.[47] These works by Christiani are representative of the contribution of converts to a body of literature about Jews intended for Christian readers. All three fit comfortably into a genre which we can call "*Jüdisches Zeremoniell*".[48] With its genesis in the writings of sixteenth-century converts, it represented a significant innovation in the literature of the Jewish-Christian discourse and Jewish converts played a special role throughout its development.

Convert literature symbolised the effort to mediate between two different religious cultures; it also created a literal corpus of translations of the religious canons. Converts rendered parts of the Christian Bible into Hebrew, and Hebrew biblical and rabbinic works into Latin, in an attempt to bridge the gulf between two mutually inaccessible sets of texts. Christiani was noted for his translation of *Epistle to the Hebrews* into Hebrew which went through many editions, and his translation into Latin of the Book of Jonah as an aid to Christian scholars learning Hebrew.[49] Moses Marcus, the grandson of Glückel von Hameln, who converted in the first quarter of the eighteenth century and established himself in London, articulated his position as defender of the Jews

---

[44]Even in the nineteenth century converts of widely disparate backgrounds were clustered together as a distinct historical entity, often by scholars who were converts themselves: Alexander Fürst, *Christen und Juden. Licht- und Schattenbilder aus Kirche und Synagoge*, Strasbourg 1892; Kalkar, *Israel und die Kirche, op. cit.*; Jacob August Hausmeister, *Merkwürdige Lebens- und Bekehrungsgeschichten nebst interessanten Äusserungen bekehrter Israeliten*, Basel 1835; Aaron Bernstein, *Some Jewish Witnesses for Christ*, London 1909. I thank Dr. Benny Ogorek for bringing the latter work to my attention.

[45]*Zebach Pesach. Das ist: kurze jedoch voellige Beschreibung des Oster-Festes . . . allen rechtschaffenen Christen zu sonderbarer Nachricht auffgezeichnet*, Leipzig 1677.

[46]*Seudas Purim. Das ist: kurtze Beschreibung von den Jüdischen Fast=Nachten/ Wie sie sich dabey so wol in ihren vermeynten Fasten/ und Beten/ als auch Fressen und Sauffen verhalten: Allen rechtschaffenen Christen zu Nachricht auffgezeichnet*, Leipzig 1677.

[47]Published in Leipzig 1713.

[48]For some useful rubrics and definitions see Burton Leiser, *Custom, Law and Morality. Conflict and Continuity in Social Behaviour*, New York 1969. Some of the converts' works bore "Jewish Ceremonial" as their actual title. See for example Christian Gottlieb Seeligman, *Jüdische Ceremonien, von der Jüden Hochzeiten, Fest- und Feyer-Tagen durchs gantze Jahr; nebst ihrem dabey habenden Aberglauben zum Dienst der Warheit vorgestellt*, Stockholm 1725.

[49]On the earliest impulses towards Hebraica of early sixteenth-century converts and theologians, see Jerome Friedman, *The Most Ancient Testimony. Sixteenth Century Christian Hebraica in the Age of Renaissance Nostalgia*, Athens, OH 1983; Frank E. Manuel, *The Broken Staff. Judaism through Christian Eyes*, Cambridge, MA 1992, pp. 66–107. On Pfefferkorn's simultaneous Hebrew and Latin credos, see Kirn, *Das Bild vom Juden, op. cit.*, pp. 20–22. The sixteenth century saw a reawakening of concern over the discrepancies between the Masoretic Hebrew Bible and the Vulgate. Many of the converts, including Pfefferkorn, endeavoured to refute the charge that the Jews had corrupted the Hebrew text. Others translated the Christian Scriptures into Hebrew. See Pinchas Lapide, *Hebrew in the Church. The Foundations of Jewish-Christian Dialogue*, transl. by Erroll Rhodes, Grand Rapids 1984; Friedrich Albrecht Christiani's *Epistle to the Hebrews*, Leipzig 1673, Halle 1734 and Florence 1766; his Latin translation of Jonah, *Jonas illustratus sive Hebraicè et Chaldaicè*, Leipzig 1683.

and their texts against the Christian calumnies that Jews had deliberately distorted the Scriptures:

> "If any Man be curious enough to ask, why I, in particular, have engaged in this Affair . . . I had a particular Ambition to vindicate the *Jews*, my own Brethren and Countreymen, from so heavy and heinous a Charge, as that of maliciously and sacrilegiously corrupting and depraving the *sacred Text* . . . having been ever most religiously scrupulous in regard to the *sacred Text*, and not at all less conscientious, in that respect, than even the most pious *Christians*. Their Infidelity, and Opposition to *Christ Jesus* my Saviour, (owing to the unconquerable Prejudices of Education) I heartily condemn: And I thank my God, every Day of my Life, for giving me a Sight and Sense of my Errors . . . But still I retain, and ever shall retain that Regard for my Brethren, whom I have left for the sake of *Christ*, as to do them all reasonable Justice, and to defend their Reputation against downright Calumny. Such was the Part that Johan. Isaac a converted *Jew*, long ago [*A.D. 1559][50] acted against the Papist *Lindanus*, who had slanderously charged the *Jews* with corrupting the *Hebrew* Scriptures . . . As he defended his Countreymen, and the Word of God at the same Time, so do I in like circumstances."[51]

There are several noteworthy elements in Marcus's statement. It conveyed no sense of the convert's zeal to justify his defection by extreme repudiation of Judaism and Jews. While a few converts continued to spew venom against their former religion and its bearers,[52] Marcus communicated the sense of a living bond to the Jewish people, although he employed the common metaphor of his conversion as a granting of new sight. This matter-of-fact acceptance of their links to their Jewish past and its central place in their works is characteristic of converts such as Marcus and his contemporaries. As his model he cited another convert, Johannes Isaac, who defended Jews against similar charges.[53] Theologian August Pfeiffer compared Christiani to other learned Jewish converts: Paul of Burgos (Salomo Halevi), Nicholas Lyra, Johannes Isaac, Paul Weidner,

---

[50] This appears on the page as a footnote.

[51] This passage appears in Marcus's preface to his translation from Latin into English of Johann Gottlob Carpzov's *A Defence of the Hebrew Bible, in answer to the charge of Corruption brought against it by Mr. Whiston, in his essay towards restoring the true text of the Old Testament, etc. Wherein Mr. Whiston's pretenses are . . . examined and confuted by Dr. Carpzov*, London 1729, p. ix. On the title page, Marcus is identified as "Moses Marcus, A Converted *Jew*, and Teacher of the *Oriental* Languages". He does not appear to have adopted a Christian baptismal name, and it is rather unusual for a convert to keep a name like Moses. The full story of Marcus's life remains to be told. See the somewhat contradictory testimonials: Cecil Roth (ed.), *Anglo-Jewish Letters (1158–1917)*, London 1938, pp. 97-98, cites a letter of May 1724, shortly after his conversion, in which Marcus purportedly confessed to have converted as a means of extracting money from his parents; and the excerpt from the diaries of Augustus Arthur Perceval, Earl of Egmont in R.A. Roberts (ed.), *Report on the Manuscripts of the Earl of Egmont. Diary of the First Earl of Egmont (Viscount Perceval)*, vol. II (1734–1738), London 1923, pp. 276ff. Both sources are in Abraham Cohen, *An Anglo-Jewish Scrapbook 1600–1840. The Jew through English eyes*, London 1943, p. 222.

[52] As in the work of convert Friedrich Christian Meyer, addressed on the title page to "Jewish sinners, presented for their conversion and improvement". See *Der abscheuliche und höchstraffbare Mord Christi . . .* Hamburg 1719.

[53] On Johannes Isaac and his son Stephan, see Fraenkel-Goldschmidt, 'Jewish Converts', *loc. cit.*, pp. 627–635.

Christian Gerson and Julius Conrad Otto (Naftali Margalita).[54] Some converts took pride in families that had produced noted converts from Judaism. Johann Christoph Gottfried boasted of being from the notable German-Jewish family Margalioth that had produced the sixteenth-century convert Anthonius Margaritha.[55] Members of the de Veil family listed many converts among their ranks. Others, like the eighteenth-century Karl Anton, gloried in their distinguished rabbinic pedigrees, perhaps to counter the assertion that converts must have descended from tainted families.[56] Johannes Pfefferkorn claimed that his uncle who tutored him, Meir Pfefferkorn, was the most learned rabbi of his age.[57] Paul of Burgos (1350–1435) provides a parallel among medieval Iberian *conversos*. In the dedication of his book *Additiones ad postillam Magistri Lyra* (1429) to his son Alonso, he reminded his son of his Jewish, Levitic ancestry, and urged him to continue in the priestly tradition.[58] Iberian *conversos* saw themselves as theologically central to the apocalyptic conciliation of Jews and Christians, perhaps best exemplified by the thought of Isaac de la Peyrère (Pereira), and some regarded themselves as superior to "Old Christians" because of their Jewish ancestry.[59] In the work of early nineteenth-century convert Isaak da Costa of Amsterdam, *Israel and the Gentiles. Contributions to the History of the Jews from the Earliest Times to the Present Day*,[60] the entire history of Jews is recounted from the perspective of the converts. Abetted by solicitous missionaries like those in Halle, converts were encouraged to create a sense of community, history and identity that was distinct from the larger Christian community. The designation *"Judaeus Convertendus"*, which appeared after the name of converted authors, was emblematic of the special status of the convert who straddled two worlds but fully inhabited neither, parallel to the Iberian terms *conversos* or *Christãos Novos* (New Christians). These terms conveyed the message that there was something about them that the baptismal chrism could not reconfigure. Jewish mental structures and social habits would persist despite attempts by wider society to end Judaism historically. Charles Leslie argued that the most effective way to encourage converts

---

[54] Pfeiffer, intro. to Christiani, *Belehrte und Bekehrte Spieler, op. cit.*, p. 9. While there is no evidence that Lyra was a convert, Pfeiffer believed him to have been one, a belief widespread since the fifteenth century.

[55] Georg Serpilius, intro. to Johann Christoph Gottfried, *Jesus der wahre Messias, op. cit.*

[56] Ernst August Bertling, intro. to Karl Anton, *Kurzer Entwurf der Erklärung jüdischer Gebräuche*, vol. I, Brunswick 1751, n.p. He claimed that Anton's father, Gershon Moses Cohen, was descended from the author of *Matnot Kehuna* and from Obadiah Bertinoro; on his mother's side from rabbis Hayim Vital and Lipman Heller. In his introduction to Johann Gottfried, see note 55, Serpilius listed the notable rabbis of the Margalith family including Jacob Margalith, "head of the Jewish community here in Regensburg" and correspondant of Johannes Reuchlin; Isaac Margolith, c. 1530, head of the *yeshiva* in Prague; Moses Mordechai who annotated *Zohar Hadash* and commented on Psalms 72; Samuel Margolith, moralist, and others still living. On the belief that converts descended from impure families, see Schudt, *Jüdische Merckwürdigkeiten*, vol. II, *op. cit.*, p. 85.

[57] *A Hebrew Chronicle from Prague*, ed. by Abraham David, transl. by L. Weinberger with D. Ordan, Tuscaloosa 1993, p. 23.

[58] Américo Castro, *La Realidad Histórica de España*, Porrua 1993, p. 49.

[59] Richard Popkin, *Isaac La Peyrère (1596–1676). His Life, Work and Influence*, Leiden 1987, and *idem*, 'Jewish-Christian Relations in the Sixteenth and Seventeenth Centuries', in *Jewish History*, vol. VI, Nos. 1–2 (1992), pp. 163–177.

[60] London 1850, transl. by Mary Kennedy. On da Costa, see Johannes F.A. de le Roi, 'Isaak da Costa. Der Holländische Christ und Dichter aus Israel', Leipzig 1899. (Special offprint from *Nathanael*).

was to reassure them that even if all Jews were to convert, their identity would not be fully submerged; some vestiges of Judaism would persist eternally: "The conversion of the Jews will [be of] . . . no hindrance to the perpetuating of their name and mention."[61] The converts' inability to eradicate a sense of their origins from their work and sensibilities was partly due to the perception that their Jewishness was such an essential part of their nature that it could not be erased by any ceremony. As the popular medieval epigram advised: "So wahr die Maus die Katz nit frisst/ wird der Jud kein wahrer Christ."[62]

Each successive attempt to reinvent Christianity in Germany, especially the Lutheran and Pietist movements, revived millennial expectations that Jews would convert in large numbers. The tension between the ideal of mass conversion of Jews to Christianity and the meagre results gave rise to a literature of frustration on "Das schwer zu bekehrende Juden-Hertz".[63] Over a millennium of Christian preaching concerning Jewish obduracy was reinforced by the relative difficulty of sustaining even small numbers of conversions. The doctrine of Jewish obduracy followed the converts into their new faith. Their motives for converting were constantly deemed suspect and their validity as good socio-economic "material" was brought into question. As Joseph Justus Scaliger (1540–1609), the sixteenth-century Orientalist asserted, most Jews who converted were inherently inferior: "Rarement un juif converti au Christianisme est homme de bien; les convertis sont généralement mauvaises gens."[64]

In 1695 Christiani and his daughter reverted to Judaism, a decision that was far from unique among converts. Unfortunately, we do not know how Christiani viewed his conversion after all those years, or what caused him to revert. It seems that in his somewhat fluid approach we are really witnessing a historical turning point in the attitude of Ashkenazic Jews towards this sacrament. Throughout the medieval period, Ashkenazic Jews appear to have internalised Christian faith in the magical-sacral power of baptismal waters. Jewish victims of the Crusaders believed that the baptismal waters, sprinkled over them under threat of death or against their will, had profoundly violated them in a manner which only death could expiate. This was demonstrated in several notable episodes during the Crusades, including the one in which a man who had been forcibly baptised later killed himself and his entire family as an atonement.[65] Rashi's insistence that forcible converts be restored to their prior status within the Jewish community was already then a polemic against opposing voices within the community.[66]

---

[61]Charles Leslie, *A Short and Easy Method with the Jews*, 1st edn. 1698; repr. London 1878, pp. 103–104.
[62]From an inscription under the depiction of the "*Judensau*" in the cathedral at Freising. Oskar Frankl, *Der Jude in den Deutschen Dichtungen des 15, 16 und 17. Jahrhunderts*, Leipzig 1905, p. 56, note 1.
[63]Sigismund Hosmann, *Das Schwer zu bekehrende Juden-Hertz, nebst einigen Vorbereitungs-Mitteln zu der Juden Bekehrung*, Zelle 1699. The edition consulted was Helmstedt 1701.
[64]Cited in Jonathan I. Israel, *European Jewry in the Age of Mercantilism, 1550–1750*, London–Oxford 1985, p. 55. Scaliger was concerned that Christians who intended to convert Jews had no knowledge of their post-biblical literature. He advocated the study of Talmud and Jewish literature to aid conversionary efforts.
[65]*The Jews and the Crusaders. The Hebrew chronicles of the First and Second Crusades*, ed. and transl. by Shlomo Eidelberg, Madison 1977, pp. 40–41.
[66]See the illuminating discussion in Jacob Katz, 'Although he has sinned, he remains a Jew', in *Tarbiz*, 27 (1958), pp. 203–217 (in Hebrew).

When two brothers in one family converted to Christianity, their apostasy was "traced" to the forced conversion of their ancestor during the Crusade period, generations earlier.[67] The attitude of Josel of Rosheim, alluded to above, proves that this belief in the magical efficacy of baptism continued among German Jews throughout the sixteenth century. This Ashkenazic attitude stands in sharp contrast to attitudes in the Sephardic world. Marranism could not have existed if Iberian Jews, under less direct coercion, had not rejected baptism as an ineradicable alteration of their Jewish souls.

It is difficult to pinpoint exactly when a change occurred in German-Jewish attitudes towards baptism. The re-evaluation of the sacraments that accompanied Luther's Reformation, and Luther's insistence on inward conversion, may have served as the catalysts for eventual change. Under the influence of Pietism in the latter part of the seventeenth century, Protestant missionaries in Germany abandoned negative conversion tactics that could even be loosely construed as coercive. The confessionalisation of German society after the Reformation[68] provided Jewish converts with a further choice between denominations. Statements by Christiani and other converts to the effect that they had weighed more than one Christian denomination before making a final choice demonstrated the converts' awareness of the arbitrary nature of confessional choice. When Benedictus Sebastian Sperling, member of a Lutheran family of Hamburg, justified his conversion to Judaism in a letter of January 1682, he wrote: "I have recently discovered that I am myself descended from the Jewish race . . . my father's ancestors, in order to save their lives during the ill fortunes of war, became Christians."[69] While his genealogy contributes nothing to understanding the motives for Benedictus's conversion, he used the information to justify his act on technical grounds. Since his ancestors' conversion was coerced, it was invalid; becoming Jewish was more the exercise of a birthright than a radical break from his past.

Where could a penitent convert like Christiani have found a congenial refuge? One possibility was Amsterdam, whose Sephardic community had long played this role for returning Iberian Marranos. From the late seventeenth century, Amsterdam became the centre for the return to Judaism of Ashkenazic converts. Benedictus Sperling, the letter writer cited above, now Israel Benedeti, asked that his mail be addressed care of Rabbi Chaim Lubliner, on the Eulenborg in Amsterdam.[70] In 1715, on the verge of his conversion to Christianity in Frankfurt, Leib Alexander, son-in-law of Rabbi David Grünhut, suddenly ended up in Amsterdam with his plans changed. When convert Johannes Zacharias Heilwort began fomenting trouble among his former co-religionists in Frankfurt a. Main in 1708, they spirited him to Amsterdam, but their efforts to change his mind came to no avail. Conrad Jacob Hang was baptised in Frankfurt a. Main

---

[67]Cited in Robert Chazan, *European Jewry and the First Crusade*, Berkeley 1987, p. 147, from *Sefer Hasidim*, ed. by J. Wistinetzki, Berlin 1891, No. 1922.
[68]R. Po-Chia Hsia, *Social Discipline in the Reformation*, London 1989.
[69]Gerald Strauss, 'A Seventeenth-Century Conversion to Judaism. Two Letters from Benedictus Sperling to His Mother, 1682', in *Jewish Social Studies*, vol. XXXVI, No. 2 (1974), p. 171.
[70]*Ibid.*, p. 170.

and reverted in Amsterdam.⁷¹ Christian Glaubtreu, the former Michael David, left for Holland after his conversion in 1724, and ultimately reverted to Judaism and returned to Mannheim as a Jewish schoolteacher.⁷² One Jew told Johann Heinrich Callenberg that he was wasting his time dealing with converts from Judaism, "as there are currently in Amsterdam some two hundred Jews who had been baptised, and have returned to Judaism there".⁷³ Amsterdam's role as a centre for reversion of Ashkenazic converts has yet to be studied; its printing presses even began publishing Yiddish refutations of Christianity in the late seventeenth century.⁷⁴ Not only could Jewish communities accept those converts who reverted of their own will, in some cases they made active efforts to detain the potential convert and prevent the conversion, an endeavour which would have been conducted at the greatest risk in the medieval world.⁷⁵ While Christiani's traces disappear after his reversion, Amsterdam represents one path he could have taken back.

Relapses from Christianity reinforced the stereotype which denied that Jews had been sincere in their conversion, and raised questions about the extent to which the inner identities of the converts could be transformed.⁷⁶ At the same time that converts served as a bridge between the Jewish and Christian worlds, they were also a wedge, affirming some of the most negative assumptions Christians made about the Jewish character. Missionaries, including some former Jews, noted with chagrin that no conversion to Christianity was ever final.⁷⁷ Georg Serpilius of Regensburg wrote a *Catalogum getauffter Juden nach allen saeculis aufgesetzt* (Catalogue of converts from Judaism listed by centuries). He divided them into two categories: "der beständigen und der wieder abgefallenen bekehrten Juden". Schudt's very substantial section on conversions opened with

---

⁷¹Shohet, *Beginnings of the Haskalah, op. cit.*, pp. 184–185.
⁷²*Ibid.*, p. 192.
⁷³*Ibid.*, p. 193, and note 204.
⁷⁴*Bukh der Farzaykhnung*, a compendium of Biblical verses needed to refute Christian polemicists, was published there in 1696. For reference see L. Fuks and R.G. Fuks-Mansfeld, *Hebrew Typography in the Northern Netherlands, 1585–1815*, vol. II, Leiden 1987, p. 399, No. 524; Isaac Troki's classical anti-Christian polemic *Hizzuk Emunah* was translated into Yiddish, and published in Amsterdam in 1717.
⁷⁵On efforts to prevent baptisms, see the cases cited in Shohet, *Beginnings of the Haskalah, op. cit.*, such as that in Kursachsen in which the Jews detained a youth on the brink of conversion, p. 181. In Berlin, the community tried to withhold the minor children of a convert from the baptismal font, but the intervention of Jablonski prevented them from success, p. 179. See also the case of Jacob Melamed who was attacked by thugs allegedly hired by the Berlin Jewish community, p. 176.
⁷⁶On the medieval German stage, whether in the *Fastnachtsspiel*, *Weihnachtsspiel* or Passion play, Jews were always assigned the most objectionable roles and characters; only through conversion could they escape their fates. Even then, in some cases, their intractable natures outlived their conversions: "ein jud ward Christ, verdarb, und ward wieder reich", i.e. returned to his original avaricious nature; J. Kürschner, *Deutsche Nationalliteratur*, vol. XXIV, p. 214, cited in Frankl, *Der Jude in den Deutschen Dichtungen*, op. cit. p. 56, note 2.
⁷⁷Paul Wilhelm Hirsch, *Sefer Megalleh Tekuphot, Entdeckung derer Tekuphot*, Berlin 1717, intro., wrote of the difficulty of converting Jews and of several converted Jews who had reverted to Judaism. See also Johannes Joachimo Zengravio (Zengraf), *Disputatio Theologica de Conversione secunda Relapsorum*. (The copy in the Rare Book Collection of the Columbia University Library carried neither place nor date.)

a long discussion of the prevailing prejudices against the possibility of successful conversions.[78]

Statistical data for reversions are even less likely to exist than for conversions. Some converts were motivated by the most shallow pecuniary interest – the *Taufgeschenk* up to 100 *Reichsthaler*.[79] This prompted some missionaries to call for the publication of conversion narratives for the purpose of discouraging multiple baptisms and abuses of the system, a complete inversion of their original purpose. But for most converts, the effects of the passage into another religious and social world may have had unforeseen consequences. Once the pomp and ceremony of baptism receded,[80] converts often suffered from lack of a social life. Those who did not become faculty members in schools or departments of theology were not easily integrated into Christian society, and were subject to bouts of loneliness, depression and regret over their choice. As Perceval, Earl of Egmont recorded in his diary concerning Glückel's converted descendant in 1736:

> "In the evening I went to the Wood Street Counter to relieve Moses Marcus, a converted Jew, whom Smith the engraver had cast into prison for 8*l*. because he was not paid for the copper plates of the book Marcus is publishing. Moses said five guineas would get him out, which I gave him. The poor man has a family to subsist, and nothing to live on, but teaching languages and composing books relating to the Jewish religion, which he is well qualified for, understanding his own Hebrew, Latin, Italian, and English."[81]

Clearly, the converts occupied a more important place in the theological vocation of the missionaries than in the social world of their parishioners.

Christiani created the impression that his conversion initiated a break so extreme that his former co-religionists spurned him and cut off ties to him

---

[78]Schudt, *Jüdische Merckwürdigkeiten*, vol. II, *op. cit.*, chap. 29, "Von der Bekehrung einiger Franckfurter und anderer Juden", pp. 83–85. Johann Riederer introduced vol. IV of Schudt by citing the anomalous case of two brothers named Bleibtreu (converted in Frankfurt 1681), who were, true to their name, loyal Christians to the end.

[79]The practice of rewarding conversions appears as ecclesiastical compensation for the confiscation of the convert's estate by medieval kings who did not want to lose the income from their former Jews. See Louis Rabinowitz, *The Social Life of the Jews in Northern France in the XII-XIV Centuries*, London 1938, p. 103. Marianne Calmann, *The Carrière of Carpentras*, Oxford 1984, p. 185, lists the expenses related to a conversion. The substantial gift to the neophyte, 130 *livres*, was a possible motivation for the poorest converts.

[80]There are many descriptions of the extravagant nature of baptismal ceremonies. Godparents of the convert were the highest-ranking aristocracy or royalty. See for example the description of the baptism of Metz-born Ludwig Compiègne de Veil on 12th June 1655:
> "Il eut pour Parrain et Marraine
> Le Roy, nôtre Sire, et la Reine;
> Ce fur l'Evesque de Soissons
> Qui le baptiza sur les Fonts;
> De Gens, une troupe infinie,
> Voyans cette cérémonie . . ."

Cited from Jean Loret, *La Muze Historique*, Paris 1857, vol. I, p. 543, in G.J. de Weille and G.A. de Weille Jr., *Het Geslacht, op. cit.*, p. 59.

[81]*Report on the Manuscripts of the Earl of Egmont, op. cit.*, vol. II, pp. 276ff.

altogether. This picture accords completely with the ideal treatment of apostates in Jewish law, as well as the strictures of the Church.[82] Christiani's patent motive for his depiction of the rupture as final and complete was his need to appeal to Christian charity as an orphan from the community that nurtured him. He appealed for financial generosity as well as social acceptance. But his depiction could not have been further from the truth. Every party to this ideal vision of the reborn convert had practical and ideological motives for maintaining it, but while it might justifiably remain a religious goal, it cannot be sustained as an historical construct for understanding the relationship between the convert, his former community and his new one. Although apostates were routinely excluded from all public communal functions, and indeed church law may have made such participation impossible, there were many areas of congruence and continuity. In several important domains, the conflicting visions of the apostate demanded a practical resolution. Queries concerning the status of an apostate married to a Jewish woman pervaded *halakhic* literature. By the seventeenth century, a vast body of Sephardic rabbinic literature dealt with this issue in relation to the Jewishness of the Marranos and their marriages and divorces.[83] *Responsa* literature from German lands, which is replete with examples of this interaction, has never been similarly analysed. While converts were relegated to the periphery of Jewish society, they could never be completely banished.

The Pietist movement of the seventeenth century opened the door for practical changes in the way German missionaries and theologians approached Jews. The movement's emphasis on the regeneration of each individual made a lasting contribution to the German ideal of *Bildung* and permanently changed the approach towards Jews as potential converts.[84] The trust of Jews was to be won through an empathetic understanding of Jewish life, rather than proclamations of Jewish blindness and obduracy. Two practitioners of the Pietist method were very successful: Esdras Edzard, a colleague of Pietist-founder Philipp Jacob Spener, established a fund for proselytes in the latter half of the seventeenth century in Hamburg (which was dissolved by the Nazis in 1942). He and his son

---

[82]On the status of apostates in medieval Jewish society see Jacob Katz, 'Although he has sinned', *loc. cit.*, pp. 203–217; idem, *Exclusiveness and Tolerance. Studies in Jewish-Gentile Relations in Medieval and Modern Times*, London 1961, chap. 6. For a discussion of medieval Jewish rituals for receiving apostates back into the Jewish fold, see Yosef Hayim Yerushalmi, 'The Inquisition and the Jews of France in the Time of Bernard Gui', in *Harvard Theological Review*, 63 (1970), pp. 363–374.

[83]See Benzion Netanyahu, *The Marranos of Spain from the Late XIVth to the Early XVIth Century. According to Contemporary Hebrew Sources*, New York 1966; Simcha Assaf, 'Ha-Anusim . . .', in *Be-Oholey Ya'akov*, Jerusalem 1943, pp. 145–180; Yosef Hayim Yerushalmi, *From Spanish Court to Italian Ghetto. Isaac Cardoso. A Study in Seventeenth Century Marranism and Jewish Apologetics*, New York 1971, pp. 22–31.

[84]Koppel S. Pinson, 'German Pietism and the Jews', in *Freedom and Reason. Studies in Philosophy and Jewish Culture in Memory of Morris Raphael Cohen*, ed. by Salo Baron, Ernest Nagel and Koppel S. Pinson, Illinois 1951; idem, *Pietism as a Factor in the Rise of German Nationalism*, New York 1934; F.E. Stoeffler, *German Pietism During the Eighteenth Century*, Leiden 1973; Martin Friedrich, *Zwischen Abwehr und Bekehrung. Die Stellung der deutschen evangelischen Theologie zum Judentum im 17. Jahrhundert*, Tübingen 1988 (Beiträge zur historischen Theologie 72).

reportedly baptised hundreds of Jews, including Christiani.[85] In 1728, Johann Callenberg established the *Institutum Judaicum* in Halle to train missionaries. The institute published the journals of the emissaries which constitute a primary source of great importance for their missionary activities, as well as other manuals to aid their work.[86] They identified poor or uprooted Jews and Jews who were sympathetic to Sabbatianism[87] as particularly vulnerable to the Christian mission, and rejected the notion of unconvertible Jews.[88]

The belief and behaviour patterns of German Jewry for the period before the age of Mendelssohn remain largely unexplored. This small, widely dispersed community was augmented in the seventeenth century by East-European refugees. As a result of their distinctive and fragmented settlement pattern, these Jews were highly visible, vulnerable and very self-conscious within the Christian world that enveloped them.[89] In the quest for the roots of Jewish modernity, their contribution has not been sufficiently considered. This terrain has been mapped out extensively for Sephardic Jews, ironically first by German-Jewish historians who idealised the Sephardic model.* Yet for German Jewry, which underwent the most tortuous passage to modernity, Mendelssohn appears on the scene virtually *ex nihilo*. There are few antecedents. The early modern converts open a partial and tentative aperture into the entanglements of early modern Jewish-German-Christian relations.

---

[85]Heinz M. Graupe, *The Rise of Modern Judaism. An Intellectual History of Germany Jewry, 1650–1942*, transl. by John Robinson, New York 1978, pp. 54–55. Edzard was not an apostate from Judaism, as some had originally thought, but a pupil of Johannes Buxtorf senior who had studied rabbinics in Hamburg. On Edzard, see Carl Wilhelm Gleiss, *Esdras Edzardus, ein alter Hamburger Judenfreund*, 2nd edn., Hamburg 1871. In addition to being credited by Christiani for his conversion, Edzard is mentioned prominently by many others. See for example the elaborate paean to Edzard in David Hieronymus (Jacob Melamed), *Christliche Glaubens=Bekäntniss*, Neustadt 1677, intro.

[86]The journals were published as *Bericht an einige christliche Freunde von einem Versuch das arme juedische Volk zur Erkenntniss und Annehmung der christlichen Wahrheit anzuleiten*, 2nd edn., Halle 1730. Successive volumes were published every year until 1791. A digest of this material was translated and published in English: John Henry Callenberg, *His Short Account of an Essay to bring the Jewish Nation to the Knowledge and practice of the truth of the Gospel and his endeavour to promote the conversion of the Mahommedans to Christianity* (dated Halle 1732, transl. made in 1734, printed in 1751). Among Callenberg's missionary manuals were two of particular interest: his *Juedischteutsches Woerterbuechlein. Die Christliche Wahrheit unter den Juden so wohl muendlich als schriftlich bekant machen helfen wollen*, Halle 1736, attempted to teach key Yiddish phrases to the missionaries; for the converts, he translated the Gospels into Yiddish, Halle 1730.

[87]G. Scholem, 'Information on Sabbatians in the works of Eighteenth Century Missionaries', in *Zion*, 9 (1944), pp. 27–38, 84–88 (in Hebrew). Yehudah Liebes, 'On a Secret Jewish-Christian Sect that Originated in Sabbatianism', in *Tarbiz*, vol. LVII, No. 3 (1988), pp. 349–384 (in Hebrew); Shohet, *The Beginnings of the Haskalah, op. cit.*, pp. 174–197.

[88]At the end of the eighteenth century this zeal was transplanted to London which became another centre for conversion of Jews. See the works of Joseph Samuel C.F. Frey, the German Jewish convert who moved to London and helped found the London Society for the Promotion of Christianity among the Jews. See also Mel Scult, 'English Missions to the Jews. Conversion in the Age of Emancipation', in *Jewish Social Studies*, vol. XXXV, No. 1 (1973), p. 4.

[89]On the tenuous and scattered nature of most German-Jewish communities in this period see Meir Hildesheimer, *German Jewry in the Seventeenth Century in Light of the Responsa Literature*, M.A. diss., Bar Ilan University 1972, pp. 191ff. (in Hebrew).

*On the idealisation of Sephardic Jewry see Ismar Schorsch, 'The Myth of Sephardic Supremacy', in *LBI Year Book XXXIV* (1989), pp. 47–66 – (Ed.).

Figure 1
Contemporary engraving of the *Hep! Hep!* riot in Frankfurt a. Main, 1819

Why Did the Christian Gentleman Assault the Jüdischer Elegant? Four Conversion Stories from Berlin, 1816–1825*

BY DEBORAH HERTZ

I

When we look at the 1819 engraving of the *Hep! Hep!* riot[1] in Frankfurt a. Main (Figure 1), we see two large muscular women on the left, one with a broom poised above her head, and one about to hit an escaping victim with her pitchfork. They, and their victim, fit the story that has come down to us about who joined in these antisemitic riots. The first riot broke out on 2nd August 1819 in Würzburg, Bavaria. Soon parallel disturbances occurred in Bamberg, Frankfurt a. Main, Darmstadt, Karlsruhe, Heidelberg and several smaller towns as well.

In trying to explain the riots, historians point to the famine which hit very hard in 1816. Bread prices remained high for years afterwards due to continuing bad harvests. British-manufactured goods, which had been kept out of Germany during the Continental System imposed by Napoleon, now flooded the German market. Artisans were thrown out of work by the thousands. The victim of the women in Figure I could well have been a Jewish moneylender or a shopkeeper who was blamed for profiteering from the high prices.[2]

When, however, one examines the right side of the lithograph another beating is clearly about to take place. Here both the attacker and the victim are of a higher social position. But who are they? Perhaps the Christian attacker is a university student. This would fit well into the story of the 1819 riots, for university students did take an active part in these disturbances. Indeed the entire decade culminating in these riots was marked by intense student political

---

*I am grateful to Professor Todd M. Endelman of the University of Michigan and to my mother, Lorraine Blumenfeld Hertz, for their useful comments on earlier versions of this essay.

[1]There is no consensus among scholars on the meaning contemporaries had in mind when they used the phrase *Hep! Hep!*. Eleonore O. Sterling, in her 'Anti-Jewish Riots in Germany in 1819. A Displacement of Social Protest', in *Historia Judaica*, vol. XXII, No. 2 (1950), pp. 105–142, here p. 121, note 7, lists several possible meanings. One was derived from the Crusades (the initials from "Hierosolyma est perdita", or "Jerusalem is lost"). A second meaning is derived from the calls of Franconian goatherds, with Jews standing in for the goats because of their beards. A third derivation is from three great enemies of the Jews: Haman, Esau and Pharaoh. See also the short article on the *Hep! Hep!* riots in the *Jüdisches Lexikon*, vol. II, Berlin 1927, cols. 1546–1548; and Christian Anton Krollmann, *Warum gab es im Jahre 1819 eine "Judenhetze"?*, Berlin 1899.

[2]See Sterling, 'Anti-Jewish Riots', *loc. cit.*, p. 108; and August Sartorius von Waltershausen, *Deutsche Wirtschaftsgeschichte 1815–1914*, Jena 1920, pp. 31–34.

activity. Many students had become ardent Nationalists during the French occupation, and had fought in the Wars of Liberation against Napoleon of 1813–1814. University students later created a national network of activist fraternities, based on the ideas of progressive professors like Johann Fichte, Friedrich Rühs and Jakob Fries. The students tended to include antisemitism with their populism, their Pan-German Nationalism and their Romantic Christianity. Student radicals seem to have labelled Jews as the "domestic Other", strongly linking the Jews with the French, who had become the hated "foreign Other" during the years of occupation.[3]

But let us return to the identity of the well-dressed assailant. If we look carefully, the attacker wearing the six-button waistcoat seems more distinguished than a student. Perhaps our unknown artist imagined him as a professor, a government official, perhaps even a leisured noble landowner. In this essay he will be called the "Christian gentleman". None of the historical accounts of the 1819 riots explain what so prominent a person would be doing in the street hitting a Jew. How is his presence in the lithograph to be explained? Not that we cannot imagine a Christian gentlemen harbouring antisemitic feelings in early nineteenth-century Germany. We know, for instance, that aristocrats who visited Jewish salons in Berlin in the years before the Napoleonic occupation were known to have made snide antisemitic comments behind the backs of their Jewish friends.[4] But why give expression to such feelings in the street, alongside humble artisans?

And what about the Christian gentleman's victim? The answer seems clear. His victim was the *jüdischer Elegant*,[5] an image which survives from an anonymous caricature drawn in the same era. What was his profession? Perhaps financier, physician, writer, perhaps even professor or official, if our top-hatted *Elegant* had converted to Protestantism. The essence of the satire on this poor man is that his body cries out from under his clothes: "I don't fit in here!" His sheer physical difference from the Christian gentleman's shape is supposed to make us laugh. That he would have the funds and the good taste to cover *this* body with gentlemanly clothing is understood to be problematic, touchy, somehow offensive. In short, the *jüdischer Elegant* is suffering from anti-assimilationist antisemitism, a kind of antisemitism which was just starting to arise as polished acculturated Jews began appearing on promenades, in coffee houses and in salons.

Jewish men trying to make their way in the world must have lived through frequent daily humiliations which were but pale versions of the moment of

---

[3]My analysis here is sharply different from other Jewish historians in that I try to preserve the significance of these men's Left-wing radicalism, even if they were also antisemitic. Jacob Katz, in his *From Prejudice to Destruction. Antisemitism, 1700–1933*, vol. II, Cambridge, MA 1980, is not concerned with other issues that Fries and Rühs fought for. Paul Lawrence Rose, in his *Revolutionary Antisemitism in Germany from Kant to Wagner*, Princeton 1990, chap. 8, argues that in this era and indeed throughout German history, Left-wing antisemitism was essentially similar to Right-wing antisemitism.

[4]See Deborah Hertz, *Jewish High Society in Old Regime Berlin*, New Haven–London 1988, pp. 257–259.

[5]This label comes from Wilhelm Grattenauer, pamphlet three, 'Erklärung an das Publikum über meine Schrift: Wider die Juden', published under the title *Wider die Juden*, Berlin 1803, p. 8.

Figure II
Contemporary caricature of a salon Jew

violence captured in Figure I. This essay reconstructs these humiliations in the lives of four Jewish men in the years around 1819; men who tried so hard to become the equal, the colleague, the friend of the Christian gentleman. The four are Felix Mendelssohn the composer, David Koreff the physician and Eduard Gans and Friedrich Julius Stahl, both law professors. All four were born to wealth and privilege, but decided that their fathers' successes within the Jewish world were not enough for them, and consequently left Judaism. All four lived most or all of their lives in Berlin, the city with the wealthiest, most intellectually exciting and elegant Jewish community in Germany at that time.

It is imperative to examine their turn towards Christianity in close detail because in the eighteen-tens men, and not women, filled the ranks of the converts. Women, many of them wealthy, had predominated among adult converts in the late Enlightenment and early Romantic decades, beginning in 1770, until the era of the Napoleonic wars in 1810. Women also took the lead in intermarriage rates in these decades.[6] These higher female conversion and intermarriage rates stimulated public discussion, among Jews and Christians alike, of female salon-hosting, dress styles and education. Women then were notorious pioneers in assimilation.[7]

---

[6] See Hertz, *Jewish High Society*, *op. cit.*, chap. 7, for details. For more recently analysed data, see *idem*, 'Leaving Judaism for a Man. Female Conversion and Intermarriage in Germany 1812–1819', in Julius Carlebach (ed.), *Zur Geschichte der jüdischen Frau in Deutschland*, Berlin 1993, pp. 113–146.

[7] One example of negative attention given to Jewish women's assimilation in these years can be found in Grattenauer, *Wider die Juden*, *op. cit.*, especially in pamphlet four, 'Erster Nachtrag zu meiner Erklärung', pp. 50–51.

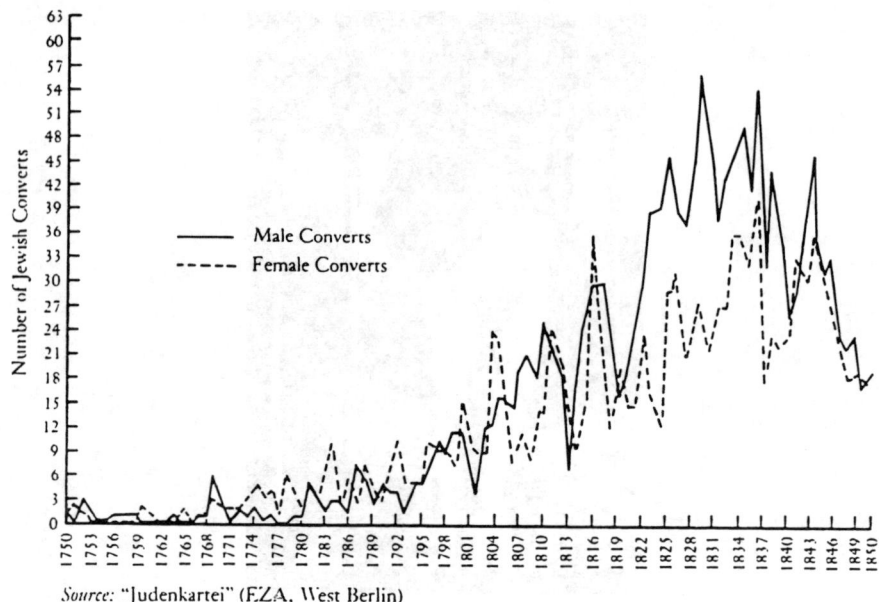

Source: "Judenkartei" (EZA, West Berlin)

Figure III
Male and Female Jewish Converts in Berlin, 1750–1850

Gender patterns among converts returned to the more typical pattern of men converting more than women after the Napoleonic years. In fact, in the 1820s and 1830s the surge of male converts was remarkably high in the overall nineteenth-century context. Just who these men were and why they converted are important questions. If any era deserves the label "conversion wave", it is this one, not the latter years of the previous century.[8]

Here the life stories of four prominent, well-documented converts are reconstructed so that we can become more clear about their precise motives for changing their faith. To be sure these four stories cannot possibly be representative of the hundreds of other men who made the same religious decision during these years.[9] Fame itself, and leaving a record behind for posterity, already indicate a special fate. Further study of the *Judenkartei* records will reveal whether

---

[8] For the references to historians who identified the "wave" of conversions as an eighteenth-century event, see Hertz, *Jewish High Society, op. cit.*, p. 224, note 32. Since that book was published, other historians who identify "the" or "a" wave of conversions in the period described in this essay have come to my attention. See David Sorkin, *The Transformation of German Jewry 1780–1840*, Oxford–New York 1987, p. 111; and Julius Carlebach, *Karl Marx and the Radical Critique of Judaism*, London 1978, p. 32.

[9] In future publications, especially my *Goodbye to Jewishness. Radical Assimilation in Nineteenth-Century Berlin* (in progress), I will further explore the relationship between famous converts such as these four and the anonymous converts listed in my central quantifiable source, the *Judenkartei*. The *Judenkartei* is a collated card file assembled by church and party workers during the Third *Reich* from primary source baptismal records in Berlin's Protestant and Catholic parishes, covering the years 1645–1933, now housed at the *Evangelisches Zentralarchiv* in Berlin.

the level of wealth of these four men and their eventual place in the social structure were or were not typical of the more obscure converts. This rather challenging issue is yet to be addressed. For now, the four stories will simply help to clear away some outdated models.

Even to take the complexity of the converts' stories seriously is a departure. Missionaries, who wrote histories of conversion obviously assumed that converts' motives were sincerely religious.[10] Historians of Judaism, contrariwise, have tended either to ignore converts altogether or to dismiss their motives as opportunistic. The aim here is to avoid both errors; not to idealise converts and not to dismiss them either. This essay shows just why it was that these four men found conversion attractive and possibly essential. Close study of individual converts' lives reveals how misleading it can be to make easy, polarised judgements about motives.[11] It is simplistic to divide converts into just two simple groups of those who had "authentic spiritual" motives and others who acted from "inauthentic opportunist" motives.

By expanding the level of detail of individual lives, the subtle mixes of external pressure and internal desire that converts experienced can be explored. What is so crucial is that neither the external pressures nor their internal desires were necessarily religious in character, at least in any traditional way. The measure of what precisely it was that defined membership to the mainstream was gradually shifting from Christianity to Germanness. Thus the problem with polarised models of conversion motives is not just that such models are simplistic. More to the point is that for this era such models are especially inadequate in capturing the shift to Germanness that pulled Jews away from Judaism.

These four lives show how burning ambition, the ambition felt by the "best and the brightest", complicated the picture considerably. What these men wanted, sometimes what their families wanted for them, were not just any appointments, not just any friends and not just any patrons. Since they were all born into wealthy families, they could have easily enjoyed life at the summit of the Jewish world. But what they could not enjoy even at the top of that world, or what they thought they could not enjoy there, were careers in high culture.

Their stories show that the drive to escape from Jewishness and propel oneself and one's children immediately to the top levels of the secular world created particular tensions. By aiming so high, the four risked becoming the target of the new anti-assimilationist antisemitism which was emerging in response to their own changes in language, dress, values, friends and social habits. Did the four men's conversions spare them the beating by the Christian gentleman, be that

---

[10] The richest collection of missionary stories about converts is by Johannes F.A. de le Roi, *Die evangelische Christenheit und die Juden unter dem Gesichtspunkte der Mission betrachtet*, vols. I and II, Karlsruhe–Leipzig 1884.

[11] For example, see Carlebach, *Karl Marx, op. cit.*, p. 32: "Most Jews who now converted to Christianity did so simply as a mode of qualifying for social and professional positions in society, with little interest in Christianity *per se* and, as often as not, without really relinquishing their family and social ties with the Jewish community." Jacob Katz, in his essay 'Judaism and Christianity Against Modern Secularism', notes three kinds of converts in this era, with the assumption that the three types were mutually exclusive. This discussion appears on pp. 36–38 of the essay, which is included in idem, *Jewish Emancipation and Self-Emancipation*, Philadelphia 1986.

beating with a stick, with words, with a look, or with a social snub? Was their new Protestantism like the *Elegant*'s top-hat, a decoration he thought would make him more like the Christian gentleman, but actually, in its very imitation, enraged him?

The inherent paradoxes of conversion were especially vivid in the tumultuous setting of Berlin during the eighteen-tens. By definition, converts were somewhat adrift, removed from Judaism, but not fully Christian; religious insiders, but still ethnically outsiders. One could leave Judaism behind more easily than one could leave Jewishness behind. And now, in post-Napoleonic Berlin, there was much confusion. The glitter and success of the men's new opportunities must be seen against a dark, disturbing side of life in the eighteen-tens. After Napoleon, it became less and less fashionable for intellectuals to favour Jewish emancipation.[12] Before Napoleon, there had been a number of Christian intellectuals in Germany who argued the cause of Jewish political emancipation. Even in the fairly religious German setting, deism grew so strong that some intellectuals actually expected the differences between Judaism and the various versions of Christianity to disappear in the future. Friedrich Schleiermacher, a prominent Liberal minister and friend of several Jewish salon women, publicly doubted whether Judaism would survive as a religion. To be sure, the end of religious differences imagined by Schleiermacher and his colleagues was not quite as neutral as it initially sounds. Schleiermacher was hoping for Judaism's kind willingness to disappear first. The hierarchy between the faiths was striking here, as it was so often in this setting.[13]

Beyond the world of books and pamphlets, too, antisemitism grew stronger and became more diverse in these years. Anti-assimilationist antisemitism was now expressed because there were many more Jewish dandies and fine ladies in German cities who made it harder and harder to tell who was Jewish. The new student movement which emerged in the struggle against Napoleon was decisive. A variety of political impulses and psychological associations stimulated the students to become antisemitic. The case of Jewish civic emancipation, once one of the centrepieces of the Liberal programme, was less frequently pleaded by those opposed to the *status quo*. The Left-wing radicals, so new on the German scene, were now increasingly indifferent to the Jewish cause, or even opposed it. In these ways life in the eighteen-tens was full of promise. But achievement, at this particular moment, stimulated hostility.

In the heightened mood of national awakening, during and after the Wars of Liberation in 1813–1814, Jewish wealth and its uses came under greater scrutiny. The very existence of Jewish associations whose aim was to hire proxies

---

[12] An excellent review of these themes is given in Rainer Erb and Werner Bergmann, *Die Nachtseite der Judenemanzipation. Der Widerstand gegen die Integration der Juden in Deutschland 1780–1860*, Berlin 1989.
[13] Here is a quote from Schleiermacher: "Judaism is long since dead", although some "yet wear its livery but sit lamenting beside the imperishable mummy, bewailing its departure and its sad legacy". Idem, *On Religion. Speeches to its Cultured Despisers*, repr., New York 1958, p. 238.

for military service must have been troubling to many.[14] Hungry, out-of-work artisans were angry when Jewish importers flooded the domestic market with cheap British-manufactured goods.[15] And populist patriots were irked when wealthy Jewish families put their banking firms at the service of Prince Klemens von Metternich of Austria, arch-Conservative and foe of German unification.[16]

Jewish aspirations during this period, at least in Prussia, seemed condemned to a cruel, vicious circle. Back in 1812 Prussia had enacted the very forward-looking Edict of Emancipation. The lawmakers saw their work as a granting of partial civic rights to Jews who had already achieved much in the economic and cultural worlds. One goal of that law was to encourage wider Jewish distribution across the occupations, and thereby to decrease the antisemitism presumably caused by extreme concentrations of Jews in certain jobs. Our four men wanted to realise this aim too, by reaching high-ranking cultural positions in the state service, if the new law would permit it. Thus at least in Prussia, the new law seemed useful in allowing a wider distribution of Jews across the social structure. But the details of the 1812 Edict were vague. They would have to be tested by ambitious Jews and ex-Jews hammering on doors. After the Vienna Congress of 1815, as the spirit of the new era evolved, no one, least of all the ambitious men themselves, knew just how difficult it would be to earn a living by mastering some kind of high culture. And so painful personal career struggles became central to the fight for a certain kind of élite male emancipation in these years.

II

The youngest of the four men, the first to convert, and by far the most fortunate of them, was Felix Mendelssohn. Mendelssohn was born into a family that was at the pinnacle of Jewish wealth and intellect, and he arrived in the Protestant world more or less alongside his siblings and parents. Thus he was in an ideal position to integrate past and future, Judaism and Christianity, kin and non-kin.

Both of Felix's parents had been born to extraordinary wealth and talent. Each belonged to one of the most prominent families in Berlin. Leah was Daniel Itzig's grand-daughter, and the name Itzig stood then for great wealth and unusual

---

[14]David Sorkin notes the existence of such associations in his 'The Impact of Emancipation on German Jewry. A Reconsideration', in *Assimilation and Community. The Jews in Nineteenth-Century Europe*, ed. by Jonathan Frankel and Steven Zipperstein, Cambridge 1992, pp. 177–198, here p. 191. Sorkin does not note that the sheer existence of such associations might contribute to antisemitism.

[15]See Sterling, 'Anti-Jewish Riots', *loc. cit.*, p. 418.

[16]On the Rothschild-Metternich connection, see Heinrich von Treitschke, *Deutsche Geschichte im neunzehnten Jahrhundert*, pt. 2, repr., Düsseldorf 1981, p. 418. Treitschke obviously himself had antisemitic views, but I take this one statement to be factual. My point in the entire paragraph is not to exonerate antisemitic critics of Jewish business practices, but to establish the facts of the matter.

political privileges.[17] Abraham was Moses Mendelssohn's son, and one could not be more intellectually illustrious than that. When Leah and Abraham married in 1804, Abraham was in business with his brother Joseph in Hamburg. In 1811, the couple and their three children fled from Hamburg and returned to Berlin. Their patriotic business practices had landed them in trouble with the French occupation authorities, who made it clear they should leave Hamburg at once.[18] After they returned to Berlin, Abraham and Leah and their by then four children were happily settled in a grand home, at the centre of a lively social circle of prominent, cultured ex-Jews and Christians.

Every Sunday the Mendelssohn-Bartholdys hosted a concert and reception in their home. Close family friends included Wilhelm von Humboldt and Karl Friedrich Zelter, then Director of the *Singakademie*, Berlin's musical conservatory.[19] The family was also close to other converted and Reform-minded Jews who shared their ambiguous status. One family with a parallel fate – save the conversion – were the Herz Beers. Amalia Beer, the mother, was a well-known salon host and the son, Giacomo Meyerbeer, was, like Felix Mendelssohn, a composer.[20] Law students Heinrich Heine and his friend Eduard Gans were also in the Mendelssohn-Bartholdy circle. Both men, so it seems, proposed marriage to Felix's sister, Rebecca, and she turned down both of them.[21]

At almost every stage in their life together, conversion seems to have been a complex issue for Leah and Abraham. There were clear models within their own families for the various choices on the intricate spectrum between traditional Judaism and absorption into the Christian world. Leah's parents, Bella (Bilke) and Levin Jacob Salomon, remained quite religious, although all five of their children seem to have converted.[22] Leah also had two influential aunts who, like

[17]See the very useful essay by Steven M. Lowenstein, 'Jewish Upper Crust and Berlin Jewish Enlightenment. The Family of Daniel Itzig', in *From East and West. Jews in a Changing Europe, 1750–1870*, ed. by Frances Malino and David Sorkin, Oxford 1990, pp. 182–201. Lowenstein's new monograph, *The Berlin Jewish Community. Enlightenment, Family and Crisis*, New York–Oxford 1994, has been long awaited by scholars in the field.

[18]See Sebastian Hensel, *Die Familie Mendelssohn, 1729 bis 1847*, vol. I, Berlin 1904, p. 84. According to Hensel, Abraham did not enter this era a patriot, but did indeed become one, eventually funding volunteers for the Wars of Liberation, as well as paying for nursing expenses for wounded soldiers. See Hertz, 'Leaving Judaism for a Man', *loc. cit.*, p. 120, for discussion of Rahel Varnhagen's financial relationship with Abraham in Prague in 1813, during the months when she organised a nursing campaign using his funds.

[19]Good descriptions of the family's various homes and the concerts can be found in Ernst Wolff, *Felix Mendelssohn Bartholdy*, Berlin 1909, pp. 12–14 and pp. 18–24; and also in Jacques Petitpierre, *The Romance of the Mendelssohns*, London 1947, p. 103.

[20]I intend to develop the comparison between Meyerbeer and Mendelssohn in the hope of discovering how the former could succeed without the conversion that the latter's parents found so necessary. See Julius Kapp, *Meyerbeer*, Berlin 1920. I am grateful to Count L.F. Chodkiewicz Chudzikiewicz of New York City for sending me the manuscript of his unpublished article 'Felix Mendelssohn Bartholdy and Giacomo Meyerbeer'.

[21]Berlin, Nationalgalerie, *Preussische Bildnisse des 19. Jahrhunderts. Zeichnungen von Wilhelm Hensel*, exhibition catalogue, ed. by Cécile Lowenthal-Hensel, Lucius Grisebach and Horst Ludwig, Berlin 1981, p. 75.

[22]The four other siblings were Jacob Salomon Bartholdy, Marianne Saaling, Julie Heyse and Rebecca Friedländer. The circumstances of Rebecca Friedländer's conversion are discussed in the letters Rahel Levin Varnhagen wrote to her. See Hertz (ed.), *Briefe an eine Freundin. Rahel Varnhagen an Rebecca Friedländer*, Cologne 1988.

her parents, refused to convert. One was Sara Levy, an accomplished pianist and *salonnière*, married but childless, who never divorced her Jewish husband and never converted.[23] Another of Leah's "loyalist" aunts was Fanny von Arnstein of Vienna, wife of an ennobled, but still Jewish, banker, hostess of supreme influence and a real and cherished friend of many Viennese nobles. Fanny von Arnstein took a public stand against conversion, and she justified this refusal by reference to Moses Mendelssohn's legacy.[24] The issue of just what Mendelssohn's legacy was on this question was certainly a charged, touchy point for this generation.

So Leah was undoubtedly counselled against conversion by her parents and these two aunts. But she was also much in the orbit of her brother, Jacob Salomon Bartholdy, who was a passionate enthusiast for all aspects of radical assimilation. When he was twenty-six, in 1805, Jacob became a Protestant. This led to a sharp, bitter estrangement from his mother.[25] When he changed his faith, Jacob took on a new last name, Bartholdy. This choice was ironic indeed. The name belonged originally to the Christian owner of a large estate on the edge of Berlin, in Neukölln, which Jacob and Leah's grandfather, Daniel Itzig, had purchased some decades earlier. Jacob inherited the property and passed its name on to his sister's family. Eventually settling in Rome with a position as a Prussian diplomat, he became a major art patron. He never married. Jacob seems to have consistently pressured Leah to cover over and depart Jewishness. Because he had no heirs, but did have a large inheritance, Leah may have been not-so-subtly motivated to please her brother. His role in her life illustrates well that conversion could result from conformity to the lifestyle and values of one's relatives as well as from rebellion against family. Leah's cousin Julius Eduard Itzig was another prominent convert whose life course may have coloured her decision to convert. Itzig converted in 1799, and enjoyed quite a central role in Berlin literary society as a publisher and host of regular gatherings of leading intellectuals in his home. All of this was accomplished under the very slightly altered name of Hitzig.[26] So were Leah to convert, she would hardly have lost contact with her family, since several close relations were already Christians.

On Abraham's side, three siblings besides himself eventually converted. This meant that four of Moses Mendelssohn's six children left Judaism. Abraham's older sister Dorothea lived out a particularly complicated story. She became a Protestant when she married the writer Friedrich Schlegel in 1804, and together they both became Catholics in 1808. Her exit from Judaism and from her extended family was apparently so stormy that she became a kind of pariah even

---

[23]For a short description of Levy, see Hertz, *Jewish High Society*, op. cit., pp. 102–103.
[24]See Hilde Spiel, *Fanny von Arnstein. A Daughter of the Enlightenment, 1758–1818*, New York–Oxford 1991, pp. 91–95.
[25]On Bartholdy, see *Preussische Bildnisse*, op. cit., pp. 77–78, and Petitpierre, *Romance*, op. cit., p. 97, note 1.
[26]See Petra Wilhelmy, *Der Berliner Salon im 19. Jahrhundert (1780–1914)*, Berlin–New York 1989, pp. 704, 855, as well as Spiel, *Fanny von Arnstein*, op. cit., p. 221.

within this *avant-garde* family.²⁷ So Jacob Salomon Bartholdy, Julius Hitzig and Abraham's sister Dorothea were converted role models for the couple.

Ultimately, Leah and Abraham began the process by converting their four children first, in Berlin in 1816. Felix was seven. For reasons that are not entirely clear, Leah and Abraham waited another six years before they too left Judaism. Their time came in October 1822, while away from Berlin, in Frankfurt a. Main. Leah's mother, Bella Salomon, was still alive at this point, so preventing her unhappiness cannot have been paramount in their minds.

For years afterwards, Abraham seemed to spend considerable energy defending "the decision" to his children. Several letters on the theme survive from the late 1820s, when Felix was in his early twenties and was beginning to be quite successful across Europe as a composer and performer. Abraham's main aim in these letters seems to have been to convince his children that he was not betraying his own father's moral legacy by converting his family. That was obviously not a simple task. Abraham was surely aware that others, including his wife's aunts, were convinced that they were fulfilling Mendelssohn's legacy by *not* converting. Abraham always discussed the adoption of his brother-in-law's last name Bartholdy as part of the conversion process. He frequently compared the new name with his own father's decision to give up his original name, Moshe ben Mendel Dessau. In an 1829 letter, Abraham recounted how he had raised his children as "neutral", so long as the government did not enforce "religious requirements". Once that situation apparently changed, in 1816 by his account, Abraham chose the religious form "accepted by the majority of civilised people". Precisely what change in government policy took place in 1816 is unclear. As for the old name of Mendelssohn, Abraham urged his son to use the name "Felix M. Bartholdy" on his concert programmes. He summed up the connection between religion and name by reminding his son that "a Christian Mendelssohn is an impossibility. A Christian Mendelssohn the world would never recognise. 'Mendelssohn' does and always will stand for a Judaism in transition . . .".²⁸

As it happened, their children did not always agree with Abraham's complex, nuanced version of the family's exit from Jewishness. Felix's youngest sister, Rebecca, refused to use "Bartholdy" at all, and Felix also resisted his father's entreaty not to be a "Christian Mendelssohn". Felix refused to drop Mendelssohn or to reduce it to the mere initial "M". In a variety of ways, he seems to have at least tried to integrate his Jewish origins and his Christian affiliation more than his father did; perhaps because Abraham rejected Judaism and apparently had no feeling for Christianity, whereas Felix, as a believing Christian, found more room, at least in his heart, for the Jewish religion. In his music, Felix synthesised Jewish and Christian themes. He had a reputation for being a truly

---

²⁷The most recent biography of Dorothea Mendelssohn Veit Schlegel is by Carola Stern, *"Ich möchte mir Flügel wünschen." Das Leben der Dorothea Schlegel*, Hamburg 1990.

²⁸Eric Werner, *Mendelssohn. A New Image of the Composer and His Age*, transl. by D. Newlin, London–New York 1963, pp. 36–38, reproduces in full a translated version of Abraham's letter of 8th July 1829.

spiritual person, known for having a "more positive feeling for the fate of Jewry" than his father supposedly had.[29]

But even the cherished, talented prodigy Felix Mendelssohn could only watch in shock when the identity so precariously constructed for him was shattered by sharp attack out in the "real world". At the age of ten, just months before the *Hep! Hep!* riots in 1819, no less than a "royal prince" stopped Felix on the street, spat at his feet, and called out "Hep! Hep! Jew-boy!" This is reminiscent of the scene portrayed in Figure I, with the "royal prince" as the Christian gentleman, and Felix Mendelssohn as the *jüdischer Elegant*. And again, some five years later, in 1824, when he was fifteen, while his family was vacationing at a Baltic resort, two "street urchins" stoned Felix and his sister Fanny, and called him a "Jew-boy". Felix was apparently brave and angry on the scene, but collapsed later at home.[30]

Even having converted their children, Abraham and Leah obviously could not protect them from the real antisemitism that surrounded their charmed circle. But inside that special world, neither the necessity nor the precise motives of the family conversion are entirely clear. Composing and performing music, even an affiliation with the Berlin *Singakademie*, did not require conversion in the same way that academia or state service did. If Meyerbeer could be a composer without converting, and his brother Michael Beer could be a prominent writer without converting, why exactly did Abraham and Leah insist on it for their children? In short, the "professional advancement" interpretation is not entirely convincing. What about religious motives? Abraham himself showed no signs of Christian spirituality, whether "authentic" or possibly "constructed". No, Abraham's rationale for his children's conversions were not religious at all. He seems to have viewed conversion as a secular issue, at least to the degree one could in early nineteenth-century Germany. For how were these souls, trapped in a past not ready for their modernity, to escape the religious vocabulary, the status hierarchy of Judaism and Protestantism so fixed by the wider world? Abraham positioned himself a step beyond where his own father stood, beyond a "Judaism in transition". The problem for Abraham and Leah was that there was no truly secular space "beyond" this. They were really premature "Ethical Culturalists", with no institutional umbrella except Christianity. That, at least, is a charitable interpretation of Abraham's written legacy. The darker versions of their religious identities, the possibly painful splits within themselves, remain elusive to us now. But surely life for Abraham as Moses Mendelssohn's son, and life for Leah as Daniel Itzig's grand-daughter, cannot have been quite so harmonious as Abraham's carefully constructed letters to their son Felix at first suggest.

III

In 1816, the year that seven-year-old Felix Mendelssohn was baptised by his parents, another talented, wealthy, ambitious Jewish man also left his faith. That

---

[29] *Ibid.*, p. 42.
[30] For a discussion of the 1819 and 1824 episodes, see *ibid.*, pp. 28, 40 respectively.

man was David Ferdinand Koreff, then a 33-year-old physician. If the Mendelssohn-Bartholdy family's motives for conversion were so nuanced as to be somewhat baffling, Koreff's motive was absolutely simple: in 1816, he needed to convert to become a professor, and he complied. His predicament was probably well-known to the Mendelssohn-Bartholdy family. Although they do not seem to have been particularly close, Koreff surely knew them, for he lived out much of his social life in the same circle to which the Mendelssohn-Bartholdys belonged. Koreff had long been close to Wilhelm von Humboldt, who was a frequent visitor to the Mendelssohn-Bartholdy home.[31] One of Koreff's closest friends from the days before Napoleon came to Prussia was Karl August Varnhagen, a roving military journalist and soldier in the Austrian and Russian armies. Later in the eighteen-tens Varnhagen was a troublesome, politically quite radical diplomat. Back in 1814, he had married Rahel Levin, who had grown up with Abraham's sister Dorothea. Rahel was also close friends with Abraham and Leah.

David Koreff was at the peak of his life, personally and professionally, in 1816. He had just been appointed a professor of medicine at the new University of Berlin, which had opened in 1810. Prince Karl August von Hardenberg, the reformist Chancellor of Prussia and Koreff's important patron and loyal patient, had promised him a clinic to run as well. Koreff's road to the top was eased by financial means and abundant talent. He was born into a distinguished family. Unlike the other three converts discussed here, whose fathers were in finance, Koreff's father had broken out of the business world and was a physician. An uncle on his mother's side was the Hebrew poet Ephraim Moses Kuh. Koreff himself attended medical school at the University of Halle. In 1803 he came to Berlin to live for a time before returning to Halle to graduate, and it was at this time that Koreff began to attract the prominent patients who would so greatly aid his advancement in life.[32]

Throughout these years, Koreff apparently never rested and was a whirlwind of productive activity in a variety of fields. In addition to his medical practice and a most active social life, he composed operas and published poetry and musical reviews. He also penned scientific articles defending mesmerism, the *avant-garde* medical practice of the day, involving hypnotism and beliefs about "animal magnetism".[33]

During the ensuing decade of Napoleonic turmoil, Koreff lived in Paris, with a full roster of prominent patients and numerous personal intrigues. His father died in 1805, leaving him a wealthy man. Thus he could select his patients and treat them *gratis*, leaving time for other pursuits. Subtle exchanges evolved. His free, yet sophisticated, medical services and his charismatic personality may well have compensated for his Jewishness. Patients often became intimate friends.

---

[31] A most useful volume on Humboldt and his Jewish friends is Wilhelm Grau, *Wilhelm von Humboldt und die Juden*, Hamburg 1935 – in spite of Grau's odious ideology.

[32] The most thorough source on Koreff is Friedrich von Oppeln-Bronikowski, *David Ferdinand Koreff. Serapionsbruder, Magnetiseur, Geheimrat und Dichter*, Berlin 1928. See also the article on Koreff by Hans Johni in the *Neue Deutsche Biographie*, Berlin–Leipzig 1980, vol. XXII, pp. 582–583.

[33] See Robert Darnton, *Mesmerism and the End of the Enlightenment in France*, Cambridge, MA 1968.

Koreff remained single in these years, but seemed always to be deep into a flirtation or two, sometimes with single women, and sometimes, surprisingly enough, with the wives of his noble patrons. One of these dalliances was apparently with none other than Wilhelm von Humboldt's wife, Karoline, one of the leading intellects among Prussian aristocrats at the time. This despite the fact that it was precisely in these years that Karoline began snubbing previously intimate Jewish women friends, especially Rahel Levin Varnhagen.[34]

At the close of the Wars of Liberation in the spring of 1814, Koreff left Paris. He went first to Vienna, where he served as an aid to Hardenberg during the Vienna Congress in the years 1814–1815. Hardenberg made many promises that year to ambitious men, Koreff among them. Finally, a year after the Congress had ended, in June 1816, Koreff received his long-awaited position at the University of Berlin.

It was at this juncture that Koreff became a Lutheran. His path towards baptism seems to have been anything but calculated and planned. After the cabinet order appointing Koreff to the professorship had already been announced, Hardenberg apparently asked Koreff if he was still Jewish. Since his answer was "yes", Koreff was told he must change that religious label. Koreff converted in Meißen, near Dresden, in August 1816.[35] Like Leah and Abraham Mendelssohn-Bartholdy, the home town was apparently not always the locale of choice for the conversion ritual. Perhaps conversion was best dealt with away from prying eyes, like an abortion or elopement,[36] or pastors in other cities had different standards for assessing the religious sincerity of would-be converts.

It is difficult to explain Hardenberg's ignorance about Koreff's faith in 1816. He and Koreff had been unusually close for years. Koreff was Hardenberg's private physician and cared for him on a daily basis. Perhaps Hardenberg's query to Koreff was not reported accurately. Perhaps we lack key contextual information. As the story goes, Hardenberg's question does suggest that baptism may not have been the public turning point, the external marker, that it looks to us from across a distance of almost two centuries.

During the entire six years that Koreff taught at the university, from 1816 until 1822, he encountered difficulties. Hardenberg had obviously muddied the waters at the outset by not consulting with the medical faculty before he made the appointment. Students humiliated Koreff by smoking in class.[37] Koreff seems to have had plenty of enemies among his new colleagues. Some disagreed with his mesmerist medical practices. Some were no doubt antisemitic. His

---

[34]Sometime before her marriage to Wilhelm von Humboldt in 1792, Karoline von Dacheröden admitted that her admiration of her Jewish women friends was tinged with just a bit of jealousy of their intellectual skills. On this admission, see Hannah Arendt, *Rahel Varnhagen. The Life of a Jewess*, London 1957, p. 17. Beginning in 1803, Karoline broke off her long-standing friendship with Rahel Levin, and in 1811 wounded Levin deeply by addressing her as *Sie*, rather than *du*. On this event, see Grau, *Wilhelm von Humboldt, op. cit.*, pp. 57ff., 81.

[35]See Oppeln-Bronikowski, *Koreff, op. cit.*, p. 56. Later in the volume he notes that in January 1820 Koreff's friend Friedrich von Stägemann inquired in a letter to Karl Varnhagen whether he knew whether Koreff had converted by then, p. 161.

[36]I am grateful to Paul Lawrence Rose for suggesting this idea to me in 1988, in conversation.

[37]See Oppeln-Bronikowski, *Koreff, op. cit.*, p. 61.

whirlwind personal lifestyle probably alienated others, but probably not Hardenberg himself, who was by then married to his third wife, with at least one mistress on the side.[38] Berlin in these years was definitely not Victorian in terms of public sexual mores.

Koreff never did obtain the promised clinic. Still, in spite of his university troubles, Johann Koreff – David was replaced by Johann when he converted – had consolations during these years. Hardenberg chose him to play a major role in the founding of the University of Bonn in 1818. He spent a good deal of time with his intimate men friends in a literary club called the *Serapionsbrüder*. He lived in an elegant home in the centre of town. As for his all-important love life, it gave plenty of material for gossip. The real truth about his intrigues still remains difficult to pin down. By the early 1820s, Koreff was reportedly involved indeed with none other than Hardenberg's then (third) wife. She defended Koreff to Hardenberg when he was attacked from various quarters.[39]

These six years, while he was in his late thirties, were the peak of Koreff's career. His descent from power was a very steep, rapid fall indeed. By 1819, Hardenberg was no longer in favour with Friedrich Wilhelm III, who was increasingly sympathetic to Prince Metternich's conservative politics. That development in itself spelled doom for Liberals like Koreff and for the political fate of Prussia and Germany in the nineteenth century. As the king became more and more disgruntled with Hardenberg's liberal policies, Hardenberg gradually lost influence. Koreff found himself excluded from Hardenberg's favour at the same time. Thus he experienced the consequences of a parallel double fall from favour: his own from Hardenberg, and Hardenberg's from the king. Koreff came to have money troubles as well.[40] Then Hardenberg and his third wife decided to separate. Koreff, apparently still quite intimate with her, thus lost his defender with Hardenberg. (Although it is hard to imagine that her defence of her lover Koreff was terribly effective with her soon-to-be ex-husband.) By 1821 Koreff had lost his professorship. His position on Hardenberg's staff in the government had disappeared the previous year.[41] Johann Koreff left Berlin for Paris, in poor health, in April 1823.

During Koreff's first years of exile, he lived with Hardenberg's estranged wife for some time in Paris. Over a decade later, in 1836, he married a German-Jewish woman. During his last years in Paris, Koreff continued to practise medicine and to attract prominent patients. He also composed new operas, and after he married, he and his wife entertained frequently. But his last years were difficult. He lost his remaining funds during the financial upsets of the 1848 revolution,

---

[38]See Hartmann Freiherr von Richthofen, *Hardenberg. Bilder aus dem bewegten Leben eines großen Staatsmannes*, Berlin 1933.

[39]See Oppeln-Bronikowski, *Koreff, op. cit.*, p. 61. A fuller account can be found in Richthofen, *Hardenberg, op. cit.*

[40]See Oppeln-Bronikowski, *Koreff, op. cit.*, p. 110 regarding Koreff's financial situation, and p. 115 regarding his dismissal.

[41]The article on Koreff in the *Jüdisches Lexikon*, Berlin 1929, vol. III, col. 867, includes a claim that Koreff lost his post because of antisemitism. Neither Oppeln-Bronikowski nor Richthofen stress this motive for Koreff's dismissal.

and his humiliation deepened when he lost a controversial lawsuit against two English dukes.[42] Koreff died at sixty-four, lonely and poor.

IV

Three years after 1816, the year that David Koreff and Felix Mendelssohn became Lutherans, Julius Jolson, an 18-year-old university student, also entered the Christian world. Let us enter Jolson's life on an August evening in the decisive *Hep! Hep!* summer of 1819, the evening when Jolson walked into a *Wirtshaus* in Erlangen.[43] He was a *Gymnasium* graduate from Munich, who had moved to Erlangen to begin his university studies. Apparently the students who were eating and drinking that night in the *Wirtshaus* somehow knew that Jolson was planning to convert later that summer to become a Lutheran. They loudly mocked his intentions, insulting him terribly. Jolson, who was dark, of slight build, and reportedly very Jewish in appearance, puzzled about how to "defend his honour without humiliation".[44]

He must have been deeply wounded. Jolson had been involved in patriotic student politics for the past several years, while he was a teenage *Gymnasium* student in Munich. He had wrestled during these years with his deepening spiritual identification with Protestantism; this in Catholic Munich. Jolson was by no means indifferent to the pull of Judaism, convinced as he was that the heart-felt rituals of Jewish practice had no counterpart in Protestant life.[45] In his adolescent years, as Jolson found himself increasingly drawn to Protestantism, debates were raging among Nationalist students about the political status of Jewish would-be patriots. Religion was taking on a political meaning, and Jolson's fate was centrally entangled in the new civic interpretations of Christian identity.

These debates had obvious personal significance for Jolson and like-minded patriotic Jewish students. Eventually, most fraternities decided that unconverted Jews would be allowed to join the fraternities.[46] It was obviously on these terms

---

[42]See the article on Koreff in the *Große Jüdische National-Biographie*, ed. by S. Wininger, Cernauti 1928, pp. 510–511.

[43]For introductions to Stahl see the short articles in the *Encyclopaedia Judaica*, Jerusalem 1971, vol. XV, col. 326; in the *Biographisches Wörterbuch zur deutschen Geschichte*, ed. by K. Bosl, G. Franz and H.H. Hofmann, Munich 1975, vol. III, cols. 2725–2727; and the longer essay in the *Allgemeine Deutsche Biographie*, Munich 1971, vol. XXXV, pp. 392–400. See also Robert H. Kann, 'Friedrich Julius Stahl. A Re-examination of his Conservatism', in *LBI Year Book XII* (1967), pp. 55–74.

[44]See Gerhard Masur, *Friedrich Julius Stahl. Geschichte seines Lebens. Aufstieg und Entfaltung 1802–1840*, Berlin 1930, pp. 42–43.

[45]According to Kann, 'Stahl', *loc. cit.*, p. 55, Stahl's mother's family tended to be Reform in their religious orientation, and it was his father who represented Orthodoxy. It was according to Orthodox practices that Stahl was raised.

[46]For discussion of this issue, see Oskar Scheuer, *Burschenschaft und Judenfrage. Der Rassenantisemitismus in der deutschen Studentenschaft*, Berlin 1927, pp. 32–35. A recent volume on the theme, published in the German Democratic Republic shortly before its demise, is Günter Steiger, *Urburschenschaft und Wartburgfest. Aufbruch nach Deutschland*, Leipzig–Jena–Berlin 1991. Another publication which appeared in the same year in the GDR, which is of particular interest to students of Jewish history, is the four-volume collection (including primary source reprints) ed. by Peter Hacks, *Ascher gegen Jahn. Ein Freiheitskrieg*, Berlin 1991.

that Jolson had been involved in *Gymnasium* student politics in Munich, since he had not converted then. A second, less tolerant decision would be to allow only converted Jews into the fraternities.[47] This was the classic solution of religious antisemites: a change of religion would allow escape from the Jewish label. The third and harshest option was to allow neither converted nor unconverted Jews into the fraternities. This was what we would now call the racist choice. Change of religion would not alter the problematic status of Jews. This option was not actively under consideration at this juncture. Racially antisemitic views along these lines were, to be sure, present in the marketplace of ideas in early nineteenth-century Germany. This was Wilhelm Grattenauer's novel theme in his *Wider die Juden* (1803). Individual fraternity members may have looked at Jews this way, but this explicitly ethnic exclusion even of unconverted Jews does not seem to have been considered by the Nationalist fraternity students during this period.

Yet if racially exclusivist politics were not fraternity policy, why did the students in the *Wirtshaus* mock Jolson's planned conversion? Conversion should, logically, have been seen as Jolson's surrendering of "national" separateness, a decision to make himself German in religion as well as in patriotic conviction and action. As the story goes, Jolson was saved by a fortuitous event: the arrival of Hermann von Rotenhan, a well-situated aristocratic student who had abandoned the task of running his family estates to attend university at Erlangen. According to legend, as soon as Rotenhan opened the door of the inn, Jolson sensed an "instinctive affinity" with him, a feeling that he could "hope for protection" from Rotenhan. And sure enough, Rotenhan did indeed intervene on behalf of Jolson "in a chivalrous manner". After a short time, the students' mockery ended. Jolson and Rotenhan became close friends.[48] Jolson re-named himself Friedrich Julius Stahl and became a Protestant. Several years later, his parents dropped their previous opposition to conversion and followed their son into the Protestant church. Stahl went on to become a professor of law, a prolific writer in his field. As his political thinking matured, he became increasingly conservative. In the 1850s, he was a leading representative in the Prussian Upper House of the Right-wing *Evangelischer Oberkirchenrat* and he was also active in the lay leadership of the Lutheran Church. His special focus in policy was the Christian character of the Prussian state. Stahl argued that unconverted Jews should not be allowed to hold government posts. He was not shutting the door that was directly behind him, since according to his lights other converted Jews were free to follow his climb out of Jewishness. But his was obviously a touchy position.

Thus, the paradoxes of his life were many. When Stahl made a name for himself in advocating exclusion of unconverted Jews from the insider position he had achieved, he moved about as far as one could from his former faith, and

---

[47]Often historians note that some or all of the fraternities "excluded Jews". What they usually seem to mean in the terms I have outlined here is that unconverted Jews were excluded. See, for example, Kann's remark in 'Stahl', *loc. cit.*, p. 56, that the fraternity in Heidelberg "banned" Jews from membership.

[48]See Masur, *Stahl, op. cit.*, p. 42–43

surely from many relatives and early friends. It was inevitably a painful, and at times nostalgic, life. Apparently Stahl used to like to walk in the Jewish neighbourhoods on Friday evenings, to watch the candles in the windows. Protestantism offered much, but not the magic of ritual.[49]

V

The pivotal summer of 1819, the summer that Julius Jolson re-created himself as Friedrich Julius Stahl, found 21-year-old Eduard Gans much closer to Judaism than Stahl had been for many a year. In 1819, Gans was a student of law at the new university in Berlin, active in study circles with other Jewish students. Like the three other ambitious young Jewish men described here who had already made their way across the religious divide, Gans had been born to wealth and privilege. His grandfather had been a court financier in Hanover, and his mother was from a wealthy Berlin family.[50] But in 1813, just as the Prussian War of Liberation was beginning, life became very difficult. During the French occupation of Prussia, his father had helped arrange the payment of Prussian war taxes to France. As Nationalist sentiment spread, involvement in any kind of profitable dealings with the French enemy became problematic. Unfortunately for his son, whatever profits the elder Gans made from the tax payments did not survive his death in 1813. Gans's mother's family insisted that young Eduard become a banker so as to pay off his father's debts and restore the honour of the family name.

But Gans refused to do this. Like the other three converts in this article, Gans intended to use the financial achievements of parents and grandparents to help make his own name in cultured society. Educated Jewish men in this setting tended to despise the world of commerce which had made their education possible. Perhaps it was not only the work itself which they disdained but also the homogeneous, possibly claustrophobic, atmosphere of small family banking firms. Gans therefore spent the next decade struggling to make a career as a professor of legal history. Obtaining the degree and writing respected articles and books were not a problem. Obtaining the teaching position was, very much so. In the early 1820s, while he pursued this elusive goal, Gans was living in Berlin, publishing learned volumes on Roman legal history, and gradually assuming an ever more important place in Hegelian intellectual circles. He lived in an apartment in the home of a prominent state official, Friedrich August von Stägemann.[51] His domestic setting reveals a rather good placement in the Christian social world, quite a bit higher than that of others with the same social ambitions. Apparently during the 1820s Rahel and Karl August Varnhagen

---

[49]*Ibid.*, p. 24.
[50]Gans's family background is noted briefly in John Toews, *Hegelianism. The Path Toward Dialectical Humanism, 1805–1841*, Cambridge 1980, pp. 108–109. See also Hanns G. Reissner, 'Felix Mendelssohn-Bartholdy und Eduard Gans', in *LBI Year Book IV* (1959), pp. 92–110.
[51]This telling detail is noted in A.W. Ward, G.W. Prothero and Stanley Leathes (eds.), *The Cambridge Modern History*, vol. IX, *Napoleon*, planned by the late Lord Acton, Cambridge 1906, p. 227.

were "rarely" invited to visit at the Stägemann household. This was rather grim for them since the von Stägemanns were centrally placed in Christian high society. The Varnhagens' banishment was especially humiliating because Karl August and Friedrich von Stägemann had worked closely together in national causes during the Wars of Liberation.[52]

Like Koreff, Gans looked to Chancellor von Hardenberg to be his patron within the government. But in the early 1820s Hardenberg had less power to help Gans than he had been able to offer Koreff in 1816. As for Gans, he was publicly resisting conversion, the price that Koreff had apparently paid quite readily back in 1816. Gans seems to have felt himself surrounded by enemies as he pounded at the doors of the University of Berlin demanding a professorship. Friedrich Rühs explicitly attacked Gans's father's past business connections with France as unpatriotic.[53] Rühs's attack, coming as it did from a staunch Democrat, must have pained Gans, himself a Democrat, who had argued in his legal scholarship against the conservatism of the Historical School of law.[54] Gans fought Romantic conservatism in the name of liberal, rational Hegelianism.

Unlike any of the previous three converts, at this point in his journey Gans was also passionate about reforming Judaism. He was the dynamic organiser of the *Verein für Cultur und Wissenschaft der Juden* (*Culturverein*) which came into existence in Berlin just after the *Hep! Hep!* riots.[55] Jewish students in Gans's social circle reacted to the sharp new negativity about Jewish emancipation by planning a wide-ranging reform of Judaism on every front. So many of the projects which would become central for later reformers began in the minds of the *Culturverein* members at this time. They wanted scholars to examine Jewish history and literature with modern methods and ask modern questions. They called for major changes in ritual practice. *Culturverein* members also aimed at popularising new versions of Judaism among poor Jews and educating them in secular subjects as well. *Culturverein* activists planned a broad, ambitious reform programme.

In 1820 and 1821, while Gans was busy with his academic publications and organising the *Culturverein*, he sincerely believed that he had the law on his side in his struggle to become a professor of legal history at the University. Paragraph eight of the 1812 Edict stipulated that "qualified Jews could hold academic teaching and municipal positions".[56] Actually, the problem was not paragraph eight, but paragraph nine, in which the king reserved the right to "issue regulations as to the eligibility of Jews for other public services". There was a rather blatant contradiction here.

In 1821 Gans presented a long brief for his case. His thesis was: Do not require

---

[52] See Wilhelmy, *Der Berliner Salon, op. cit.*, p. 849.
[53] See Johann Brau, 'Die "Lex Gans". Ein Kapital aus der Geschichte der Judenemanzipation in Preussen', in *Zeitschrift der Savigny-Stiftung für Rechtsgeschichte, Germanistische Abteilung*, 102 (1985), pp. 60–98, here p. 71, note 50.
[54] Toews, *Hegelianism, op. cit.*, pp. 81–87, is particularly useful in clarifying these debates.
[55] A useful recent essay on the *Culturverein* is by Rachel Livné-Freudenthal, 'Der "Verein für Cultur und Wissenschaft der Juden" (1819–1824). Zwischen Staatskonformismus und Staatskritik', in *Tel Aviver Jahrbuch für deutsche Geschichte*, 20 (1991), pp. 103–125.
[56] See Kann, 'Stahl', *loc. cit.*, p. 181.

me to convert, or that sacred ritual will become a farce.[57] This was obviously a crucial moment in Gans's life, and equally momentous in the larger story. Unlike Stahl, Gans had not experienced an authentic spiritual rebirth as a Protestant, nor did he claim that he had experienced such a rebirth. Unlike Abraham and Leah Mendelssohn-Bartholdy, Gans did not discuss Christianity in cultural or national terms. Rather, Gans's plea was based on the traditional assumption that Christianity was to be viewed mainly as a religion, however central it was in defining the character of the Prussian state. His lack of Christian conviction therefore mattered to him. Gans argued that this should also matter to government officials who defined the state in Christian terms. Unlike Koreff, he would not, at least in 1821, convert to get the post.[58]

Finally, on 18th August 1822, a Royal Cabinet Order was issued to settle the Gans case. It implied that paragraph eight of the 1812 Edict was not to be taken seriously, at least for the time being. So Gans, as a Jew, could not become a professor. Only converted Jewish professors would be allowed. Gans's compensation was a travel grant to research a new book on the history of law, with the unspoken proviso that he remain abroad. Exile, usually to Paris, was soon to become a frequent choice for ambitious Jewish intellectuals in Germany. This was of course a solution eminently suitable to state authorities.

In the end, in 1822, Gans accepted the grant, although in doing so he feared that he had compromised himself. He was giving up hope that he could become an unconverted professor, at least for the time being. While in Paris on his government grant, Gans does seem to have seriously considered converting. In May 1823, Gans resigned from the presidency of the *Culturverein*. But he was still Jewish. As late as 1825 he promised his friend Heinrich Heine, who was also active in the *Culturverein* and also an aspiring law professor, that he, Gans, would not "crawl to the cross".[59]

But later that same year, Gans did convert, as did his friend Heine. In defence of his decision, Gans wrote to a friend that: "If the state is so stupid as to forbid me to serve it in a capacity which suits my particular talents unless I profess something I do not believe – and something which the responsible minister *knows* I do not believe: all right then, it shall have its wish."[60] Gans's conversion did ease his way to gaining a university post. Afterwards, he distanced himself almost completely from Jewish concerns. He was a prolific writer and effective as a liberal academic. He never married. His death in 1839, when he was only forty-one, was attributed to obesity and high blood pressure.

And who should replace Gans as professor of law at the University of Berlin but Friedrich Julius Stahl? Stahl had converted back in 1819, but he was actually a few years younger than Gans. It was an obvious joke at the time to observe that

---

[57]The petition is reprinted in Brau, 'Die "Lex Gans" ', *loc. cit.*, pp. 77–88.

[58]For a fascinating series of comparisons between Gans and his friend Heinrich Heine on this issue of spiritual authenticity, see S.S. Prawer, *Heine's Jewish Comedy. A Study of his Portraits of Jews and Judaism*, Oxford 1983, pp. 10–26.

[59]This quote is cited by Toews, *Hegelianism, op. cit.*, p. 129.

[60]Prawer, *Heine, op. cit.*, p. 12, quotes Gans; his source is Hanns G. Reissner, *Eduard Gans. Ein Leben im Vormärz*, Tübingen 1965 (Schriftenreihe wissenschaftlicher Abhandlungen des Leo Baeck Instituts 14), p. 36.

here was a slot reserved for converted Jews. Conversion was not the only issue here. Much was at stake intellectually and politically. The loss of the liberal Gans, and his replacement by the conservative Stahl was a very significant switch indeed.

Gans's conversion is especially poignant in the light of his early passion for reforming Judaism to meet the needs of sophisticated Jews like himself and his friends. Neither his fate while he lived nor his early death are at all enviable. Perhaps Gans would have been happier as a banker.

VI

When Stahl moved away from the Left-wing politics of the student movement, he remained committed to the notion that the Prussian state should have an essentially Christian character. In this setting, Left- and Right-wing intellectuals seem to have shared the notion that the state should be Christian. The separation of Church and State which had already emerged in France would take decades to take hold among German intellectuals and policy makers. Historians of Germany have often lamented that so many intellectuals across the political spectrum envisaged the state from a religious point of view. This failure to separate State and Church has been seen as yet another way that Germany followed a separate path (*Sonderweg*) from France and England during the nineteenth century.[61]

As we have seen, it was during the eighteen-tens that intellectuals began to define Jewishness as being outside the emerging national consensus. This discovery fits neatly into the *Sonderweg* interpretation of the German past. Because Jewish religious and ethnic marginality was made explicit in theory and was enforced in policy, individual Jews were compelled to make painful decisions that affected every aspect of their lives. This is yet another example of how many kinds of social, religious and ethnic differences were stigmatised in the German setting.

Since the Holocaust, historians of Jewry have written their own version of the *Sonderweg* interpretation. Their implicit, sometimes explicit, assumption has been that Jewish life in Germany was different, usually worse, than Jewish life in other Western and Central-European countries. According to these histories, the Left- and Right-wing intellectuals' failure to properly separate Church and State was unfortunate. One consequence of the Christian definition of the state in Germany was the requirement that Jewish professionals give up their faith, thereby deserting their families and betraying their community. The conversion requirement was, in this view, retrograde and unfair. There is factual, if not interpretative truth in this line of reasoning. Surely forced career conversions were unfair. Life was very hard for Jews in Germany in other ways too. Racially antisemitic parties appeared in the 1890s. Although the parties did dissolve

---

[61] For a summary and critique of this model, see Geoff Eley and David Blackbourn, *The Peculiarities of German History*, New York 1983.

within a short time, the issue remained politically topical thereafter. Participants in upper-class society remained intensely antisemitic into the twentieth century. Because of the conversion clause and also because of antisemitism against even those Jews who did convert, both Jews and ex-Jews were under-represented at the highest levels of government, in the military and in the universities.

In spite of these frustrations and obstacles, however, over the decades Germany turned out to be a positive setting for many Jews. And this is where we must be careful before accepting a *Sonderweg* interpretation for the German-Jewish past. Reform Judaism, Liberal Judaism, modern Orthodoxy, academic Jewish studies and "post-assimilation" Zionism were all founded in Germany. Jewish and ex-Jewish participation in the arts was considerable. Controversial as they might be for us today, Germany's comparatively high intermarriage rates were, in practice, signs of successful assimilation. East-European Jewish intellectuals looked to Germany as a model of Jewish renewal and sophisticated acculturation. These positive dimensions to the Jewish legacy in Germany should make us pause before assuming a Jewish version of the *Sonderweg* model.

It is difficult to make a sober judgement on these matters. The *Sonderweg* interpretation does seem to fit all too neatly with the tragic way that Nazi state officials chose to terminate the history of German Jewry. But parallels between the *Sonderweg* interpretation and the Holocaust do not mean that this interpretation is correct for the nineteenth century. Just how to properly interpret the nineteenth-century experience requires more research, both as regards the Jewish subculture and society-at-large. Thus we cannot assume, at least not yet, that the *Sonderweg* model best explains the German-Jewish past. Whether or not intellectuals and state officials in Germany were acting in a particularly discriminatory way when they required conversion for high-power careers must be discovered, rather than assumed.

A fresher, better way of viewing conversion is as a policy mechanism that had the function of restricting the supply of candidates for top positions. To investigate this model, we would need to discover the comparative number of educated Jewish men qualified for state positions, a vast list which included professors, lawyers, local municipal functionaries, judges, diplomats and career army officers. Perhaps government élites in other lands would have imposed conversion, or other onerous requirements, had the comparative ranks of ambitious Jewish men been larger in those countries. In short, we need to know the supply and demand patterns in the top ranks of civil service in the nineteenth century. This knowledge may help us understand why conversion was a requirement for so many careers in nineteenth-century Germany. That many intellectuals defined the German State as a Christian institution may well have been a decisive factor in the rate of conversion and the kinds of people who converted. But it would surely be better to study the role of ideology in the wider context of education and employment patterns than to rest the case with ideology alone.

There is also a need to explore how plausible it is to explain the conversion requirement as at least in part a functional way to limit Jewish entry into top positions. When such a study is completed, then perhaps the inventive, still loyalist subculture within Judaism that David Sorkin sees in this past can find its place beside the radical assimilation charted in this essay. What is meant here by "finding its place" is that we will stop trying to decide whether "loyalist acculturation" or "radical assimilation" best describes German-Jewish life in the nineteenth century. Rather, we may be able to sketch a picture in which widespread acculturation, initially loyalist, resulted in a large supply of educated Jewish men, which in turn may have stimulated state officials to require career conversions. That requirement, in turn, may have led to widespread radical assimilation, sometimes of the "best and brightest". In this polarity between loyalist acculturation and departure by conversion, as in so many other polarities, Germany proved to be the land of extremes and of conflict, conflict which was sometimes creative, and at other times quite treacherous.

The Conversionary Impulse in Fin De Siècle Germany

BY ALAN LEVENSON

The word "conversion" has a variety of meanings. In his 1901/1902 Gifford Lectures, philosopher of religion William James described conversion as a healing process, "by which a self hitherto divided . . . becomes unified and consciously right, superior and happy".[1] For historians of Jewry, conversion usually means apostasy, a radical severing of the bonds which tie an individual Jew to the Jewish people.[2] I want to problematise the term conversion in order to grapple with the fact that while approximately 10,000 German Jews converted to Christianity during the *Kaiserreich*, a figure that more than doubles if we include Jews in the German *Kulturbereich*, we have no way of knowing how many more Jews contemplated this step and desisted.[3] It should be obvious, however, that the same forces which drove some German Jews *over* the edge drove others *to* that edge. While this dividing line remains critical, focusing on the border between apostasy and continued Jewish affiliation indicates a surprisingly permeable boundary. A range of quantifiable, objective factors, such as changing legal status and gender, affected apostasy and intermarriage rates profoundly.[4]

---

[1] William James, *The Varieties of Religious Experience*, New York 1958, p. 157.
[2] Rabbinic tradition generally splits the word, and thus the phenomenon, in two. One is either a convert to Judaism, a proselyte (*ger, ger tzedek*) and therefore praiseworthy; or one is a convert out of Judaism, an apostate (*meshumad, mumar*) and therefore despised. James's primary definition of conversion as spiritual renewal within the confines of a given religion is probably closer to the rabbinic concept of *teshuva* than any of the above.
[3] There is general agreement concerning the number of baptised Jews. Arthur Ruppin, quoting Johannes de le Roi in *The Jewish Fate and Future*, transl. by E.W. Dickes, London 1940, p. 284, estimated the number of Jewish converts to Christianity in Germany during the nineteenth century at 23,000; Jacob Toury, *Soziale und politische Geschichte der Juden in Deutschland 1847–1871. Zwischen Revolution, Reaktion und Emanzipation*, Düsseldorf 1977, p. 51, comes close to that figure, and further estimates that 11,500 were baptised between 1871–1900 (p. 60). The rising number of apostates after 1880 is well documented. Monika Richarz (ed.), *Jüdisches Leben in Deutschland*, vol. II, *Selbstzeugnisse zur Sozialgeschichte im Kaiserreich*, Stuttgart 1979. Veröffentlichung des Leo Baeck Instituts, p. 16, estimates that between 1871–1919 approximately 23,000 German Jews converted. These numbers, of course, do not reflect the extreme infrequency of apostasy in rural areas, nor the relative prevalence of apostasy in cities such as Berlin, which, in the years 1889–1903, saw approximately 200 Jews per year leave the community. For a recent assessment of the sometimes varying figures on baptism, see Usiel O. Schmelz, 'Die demographische Entwicklung der Juden in Deutschland von der Mitte des 19. Jahrhunderts bis 1933', in *Bulletin des Leo Baeck Instituts*, No. 83 (1989), pp. 39–41.
[4] Deborah Hertz, *Jewish High Society in Old Regime Berlin*, New Haven–London 1988, has shown the influence of gender on conversion and intermarriage rates. Peter Honigmann, 'Jewish Conversions – A Measure of Assimilation? A Discussion of the Berlin Secession Statistics of 1770–1941', in *LBI Year Book XXXIV* (1989), pp. 3–39, demonstrates the impact of the legal situation on the various conversion and intermarriage rates in turn of the century Vienna and Berlin respectively.

Nevertheless, a willingness to sever one's ties with the Jewish community, the prerequisite to radical assimilation, also deserves examination. This paper will explore the subjective dimensions that led individuals to sever, contemplate severing, or radically redefine the terms of their Jewish identity – what will be called here the "conversionary impulse".

Why was switching to Christianity – accomplished or contemplated – a "live option" for a considerable number of German Jews?[5] Alienation from Judaism and the forms of external hostility distinguish modern Jewish apostates from their medieval predecessors, but these two factors also varied according to time and place. In the hope of being more specific with respect to forces that led German Jews towards apostasy, two well-known "conversionary experiences" shall be described here that ended with dramatic assertions of Jewish identity: those of Theodor Herzl and Franz Rosenzweig.

As a boy growing up in Budapest, Herzl must have been aware of the antisemitic debates raging in the Hungarian Parliament.[6] On at least two occasions, in Vienna and Mainz, Herzl was subjected to antisemitic insults, and in Salzburg he suffered occupational discrimination.[7] While Herzl spent his formative years in Budapest and Vienna, his Paris years (1891–1895) marked a turning point in his conception of the "Jewish Question".[8] In Paris, Herzl could travel "unrecognised" as a Jew, if not as a native German-speaker, and it was here where he attained what he later misconstrued as "a more disinterested" view of antisemitism. Herzl's early diaries proposed several solutions to the "Jewish Question". In one of these, Herzl, among other "leading Jews", would chaperon Austria's assimilated Jews to St. Stephen's Church in broad daylight. While eschewing baptism for themselves, these leaders would effect "with proud gestures" a mass conversion and make the shameful apostasies of individual Jews unnecessary in the future. The cardinal importance of "proud gestures" also surfaced in Herzl's fascination with duels as a refutation of antisemitic smears and a proof of Jewish character; in the two-dimensional aristocratic heroes of his early plays; and in his contemplating having his only son, Hans, baptised – in his view a dishonourable course of action for a mature adult, but not for a mere lad.[9]

---

[5] Todd M. Endelman, 'The Social and Political Context of Conversion in Germany and England, 1870–1914', in idem (ed.), *Jewish Apostasy in the Modern World. Missionaries and Converts in Historical Perspective*, New York–London 1987, p. 84. I borrow the phrase "live option" from William James, *op. cit.*, whose view of conversion informs this essay. For a recent discussion of conversion as an analytic concept, see Alan F. Segal, *Paul the Convert. The Apostolate and Apostasy of Saul the Pharisee*, New Haven–London 1990.

[6] On the influence of Herzl's Hungarian upbringing, see Andrew Handler, *Dori. The Life and Times of Theodor Herzl in Budapest, 1860–1878*, Tuscaloosa 1983.

[7] Theodor Herzl, 'An Autobiographical Sketch', in *The Jewish Chronicle*, (14th January 1898). Herzl's differing accounts of early encounters with antisemitism recommend scepticism. On their general untrustworthiness, I side with Jacques Kornberg, 'Theodor Herzl. A Reevaluation', in *Journal of Modern History*, 52 (1980), pp. 226–251. See also Peter Loewenberg, 'Theodor Herzl. A Psychoanalytic Study in Charismatic Political Leadership', in Benjamin B. Wolman (ed.), *The Psychoanalytic Interpretation of History*, New York–London 1971, pp. 150–191.

[8] *The Complete Diaries of Theodor Herzl*, ed. by Raphael Patai, transl. by H. Zohn, New York–London 1960, pp. 3–13. I do not maintain that Dreyfus's trial and the ensuing public reaction sparked this "conversion", nor do I think that it eradicated a lifetime's accumulation of antisemitic stereotypes.

[9] Alex Bein, *Theodore Herzl*, Philadelphia 1941, pp. 90–91.

This obsession with interpreting the "Jewish Question" as one of honour, reflected in his confession that he would have liked to have been born a Prussian nobleman,[10] is epitomised in Herzl's reaction to the Kishinev pogrom of 1903:

> "Wann erscheint mir als gelungen
> Mein Bemüh'n auf dieser Erden?
> Wenn aus armen Judenjungen
> Stolze junge Juden werden!"

Certainly it was not the Dreyfus Affair alone, but rather a lifelong dilemma, which preceded Herzl's discovering the key to turning *Judenjungen* into "proud young Jews".[11] As Jacques Kornberg noted, Herzl's play *Das neue Ghetto* (The New Ghetto), written in the autumn of 1894, evidences the inability to find honour as a Jew – except through death – and thus represents a dead-end in solving the Jewish problem. How was one to enter honourable, in other words, Gentile, society, when the only path, apostasy, was dishonourable?[12] This "catch-22", in Peter Loewenberg's judgement, drove Herzl, in early 1895, "almost to the point of a psychotic breakdown".[13]

Herzl's Zionist epiphany solved this problem. Both the spiritual struggle beforehand and the sense of relief and mission afterwards justify our calling this experience "conversionary".[14] Nobility and European culture, previously accessible only through the medium of Christianity, became an alternate mode of existence for the Jews. William James characterised the psychology of the convert as "consciously right and superior",[15] and this factor, as Chaim Weizmann acutely observed, not Herzl's profundity or Judaic commitment, electrified Zionism.[16] Additionally, Eastern Jews sensed his commitment to a national solution. While Herzl could imagine solving the Jewish problem for Jews in general without solving it for himself, he could not imagine the converse. Even before his mass baptism fantasy, Herzl had entertained a vision of mass Jewish-Christian intermarriage:

> "Only the encouragement of such a general improvement of the figurative and actual profile could and will solve the Jewish question satisfactorily. Cross-breeding of the occidental races with the so-called oriental one on the basis of a common state-religion – this is the desirable great solution!"[17]

---

[10]Loewenberg, *loc. cit.*, p. 159. Herzl's best friend, Heinrich Kana, had committed suicide in 1891, in part as a result of financial disaster. Kana's refusal to accept monetary help probably led Herzl to glamorise characters like him as models of Jewish financial integrity.
[11]Quoted in Alex Bein, 'Herzls sittlich-soziales Wollen', in Tulo Nussenblatt (ed.), *Theodor Herzl Jahrbuch*, Vienna 1937, pp. 224–231.
[12]Herzl's refusal to change his name to something less Jewish replicates this same dilemma in miniature. See also the story of Herzl's resignation from the *Albia* fraternity in Amos Elon, *Herzl*, New York 1975, pp. 60–63.
[13]Loewenberg, *loc. cit.*, p. 181. In a well-known letter to Bismarck, Herzl concluded, "And now I shall finally risk it: I believe I have found the solution to the Jewish Question. Not *a* solution, but *the* solution, the only one." Quoted in David Vital, *The Origins of Zionism*, Oxford 1975, p. 245.
[14]See the appendix in Segal, *op. cit.*, pp. 285–300.
[15]James, *op. cit.*, pp. 157–206.
[16]Chaim Weizmann, *Trial and Error*, New York 1940, pp. 43–44.
[17]Raphael Patai (ed.), 'From Herzl's Early Diary', in *Herzl Year Book*, 1 (1958), p. 331.

Herzl accepted a solution of the "Jewish Question" through biological means as a scientific and value-neutral one. But he refused to have himself baptised precisely because the lack of Jewish honour was the crux of his personal *Judenfrage* and because he accepted the judgement of his Jewish subculture that apostasy was dishonourable.[18] For Herzl, a political "conversion" propelled him from one mode of Jewish existence to another. Zionism met this existential need, although Herzl's solution was far less "disinterested" than he thought.[19]

Herzl's "conversion" occurred in 1895. Moving to the end of the *fin de siècle*, we confront the religious conversionary experience of Franz Rosenzweig, whose letters and diaries frequently discussed his spiritual longings.[20] Christianity, a "live option" for Rosenzweig in a religious as well as in a socio-cultural sense, seemed like the logical end of that journey. Despite biographers' references to Adam Rosenzweig's Jewish influence on his nephew, Franz Rosenzweig's circle of friends as a teenager and in his twenties – if his *Tagebücher* and *Briefe* are representative – consisted mostly of Christians and "New Christians". Rosenzweig's reading list reflected his tenuous Jewish loyalties. His *Tagebuch* records Schleiermacher's description, "Judaism: nowadays a Mummy";[21] praises the antisemite Houston Stewart Chamberlain as the best expositor of Kant; and shows how he devoured books recommended by his relatives, the Ehrenbergs, and Eugen Rosenstock-Huessy: books replete with anti-Jewish sentiment.[22] The two Jews in Rosenzweig's circle of regular correspondents were Gertrud Oppenheim, who considered Franz the family's (Jewish) fanatic for expressing a mild enthusiasm for Hebrew and a mild antipathy towards Christmas trees;[23] and Rosenzweig's mother Adele, whose personality he respected much more than her Judaism. Oppenheim considered her family more assimilated than the

---

[18] While some Christians voiced the opinion that baptism without conviction was dishonourable, the public debate centred around the question of whether or not baptism was effective in removing Jewish elements.

[19] Herzl warned Jacob De Haas about a "Herzlian" club: "Let us beware of turning a national movement into a personal one." Herzl to Haas, 12th May 1897, cited in Elon, *Herzl, op. cit.*, p. 222.

[20] Rosenzweig referred often to his "uncompleted journey", "journey with no certain destination" and the like. See Nahum N. Glatzer, *Franz Rosenzweig. His Life and Thought*, New York 1953. The theme of incompleteness operated in Rosenzweig's youthful comparisons of Germany and America, Jews and Christians, Goethe and Nietzsche – in each case Rosenzweig associated himself with the placid and motionless dyad, but admired the dynamic "other". Ultimately, of course, Rosenzweig's *Der Stern der Erlösung* (1921) reconciled dynamic, ever-expanding, ever-incomplete Christianity with an eternal, realised Israel. See Eliezer Berkowitz, *Major Themes in Modern Philosophies of Judaism*, New York 1973.

[21] Franz Rosenzweig, *Briefe und Tagebücher*, ed. by Rachel Rosenzweig and Edith Rosenzweig-Scheinmann with the assistance of Bernhard Casper, vol. I, *1900–1918*, The Hague 1979, entry No. 179 (20.9.1910), pp. 109–110.

[22] Considering the books recommended to Rosenzweig by Hans Ehrenberg and Eugen Rosenstock-Huessy (e.g. Paul de Lagarde, Arthur Gobineau, Eduard Meyer, Houston Stewart Chamberlain) it becomes clear why Rosenzweig felt intellectually besieged by Jew-hostile formulations of Christianity.

[23] Christmas, of course, was a much beloved holiday in many German-Jewish homes. Adele Rosenzweig recalls her mother's (Kantian) dictum that the purpose of religion was, "Tu du, was Du für am Besten hältst!" Quoted on p. 140 in Rivka Horwitz (ed.), 'Adele Rosenzweigs Jugenderinnerungen', in *Bulletin des Leo Baeck Instituts*, Nos. 53–54 (1977/1978), pp. 133–146. For an evaluation of religion comparable to Adele Rosenzweig's, see Eduard Bernstein, 'Wie ich als Jude in der Diaspora aufwuchs', in *Der Jude*, 2 (1917/1918), pp. 186–195.

Rosenzweigs, yet Adele had come close to marrying a non-Jew, and raised no objection when her younger brother, Adolf Alsberg, declared that he intended to baptise his children. Franz considered himself "dogmatically entirely estranged from the Judaism of today: I believe in sin and the necessity of an intermediary".[24] With withering sarcasm Rosenzweig wrote to his assimilationist parents about Emil Cohen's oratory, noting: "How unfortunate . . . that one must be a Zionist in order to be able to speak so truly and not dishonestly (*so unverlogen*)."[25] Socially, as well, Rosenzweig considered Jewry inferior, different from the norm, yet unlike the superior caste, the German aristocracy.[26] Rosenzweig's refusal to condemn Hans Ehrenberg's baptism testifies to his assessment of Judaism and Christianity prior to his own "conversion":

> "We are Christian in everything. We live in a Christian state, attend Christian schools, read Christian books, in short, our whole 'culture' rests entirely on a Christian foundation; consequently a man who has nothing holding him back needs only a very slight push . . . to make him accept Christianity. In Germany today the Jewish religion cannot be 'accepted', it has to be grafted on by circumcision, dietary observances, and Bar Mitzvah . . . it would have been entirely out of the question for Hans to become a Jew; a Christian, however, he can become."[27]

Rosenzweig never abandoned his view that "one could never become a Jew"; he only side-stepped it by declaring himself a Jew, in a state of "being", not that of "becoming".[28] Reflecting on Ehrenberg's situation, Rosenzweig mused, in a Nietzschean vein, that someone who had the courage of total commitment to the individual, at the expense of the Jewish collective, could overcome the stigma attached to the baptismal act. And Rosenzweig, like Herzl, considered child baptism acceptable.[29] Despite Rosenzweig's sense of Christianity's superiority, he delayed four more years before contemplating the same step his cousin Hans took. One could easily imagine Rosenzweig entering a synagogue and suddenly intoning the Lord's Prayer: this happened during Hanukkah to Karl Jakob Hirsch, the expressionist painter.[30] Instead, on Yom Kippur 1913/1914, having declared his intention to become a Christian through Judaism, Rosenzweig became a believing Jew, ending his "spiritual longing", and within a few years composed both a practical (*Zeit Ist's*) and a theoretical (*Der Stern der Erlösung*)

---

[24]Rosenzweig, *Briefe und Tagebücher*, vol. I, *op. cit.*, entry No. 172 (1.9.1910), p. 107.
[25]*Ibid.*, entry No. 186 (3.3.1911), p. 117. Rosenzweig's German text reads: "Schade . . . daß einer Zionist sein muß, um so echt und unverlogen sprechen zu können."
[26]*Ibid.*, entry No. 173 (5.9.1910), pp. 106–107.
[27]Glatzer, *op. cit.*, p. 19.
[28]*Ibid.*, p. 28. Rosenzweig conceded all sorts of antisemitic canards regarding Judaism in his debate with Rosenstock-Huessy. Yet he rejected the latter's claim to speak as a Jew as well as a Christian. Eugen Rosenstock-Huessy (ed.), *Judaism Despite Christianity*, transl. by Dorothy M. Emmet, Alabama 1969, p. 97.
[29]Glatzer, *op. cit.*, pp. 10–11.
[30]Quoted in Guido Kisch, *Judentaufen. Eine historisch-biographisch-psychologisch-soziologische Studie besonders für Berlin und Königsberg*, Berlin 1973, pp. 91–92.

programme for Jewish renaissance.³¹ Despite the intensely personal nature of his conversion, Rosenzweig devoted his greatest energies guiding the German-Jewish collective "into life".

Herzl and Rosenzweig sought a conversion out of Jewishness, yet felt bound by their connections to Jewry. Only by overcoming a Jewish situation both perceived as unbearable did Herzl and Rosenzweig launch their brief but creative careers. Conversion offered both men a road out. But not everybody who looked for this road found it. Take the case of Adolf Weißler, a jurist, author and notary from the university town of Halle a.d. Saale. Weißler's mainstream career profile suggests the sort of Jew whom we might have expected to join the *Centralverein deutscher Staatsbürger jüdischen Glaubens*. Instead of this, however, the forty-five-year-old Weißler published an article in the prestigious *Preußische Jahrbücher* under the pseudonym Benedictus Levita, entitled 'Die Erlösung des Judentums'.³² In this, Weißler bemoaned the growing exclusion of Jews from state service, army and university life; conceded the ethical superiority of Christianity; and lamented the fact that honour precluded conversion to a church still clinging to outmoded dogma. But a solution existed for those who felt "overripe" for liberation from Judaism: to baptise one's children. In this way, Weißler concluded, "The eternal Jew will die. Our children will become Christians." In the words of a man trying to convince himself, Weißler opined: "We are no longer Jews, so we have no right to educate our children to be Jews. We have recognised in Christianity the right religion, so we must educate our children in that religion." Weißler's piece struck a raw nerve. Parents who baptised their children at birth saved them the legal requirement of declaring their estrangement from the Jewish community later on.³³ A dozen replies in the German-Jewish press savaged Weißler's article. The notion that childhood baptism presented an "honourable" avenue of escaping Jewishness came under special attack in the works of Nathan Samter, Fritz Wittels and Gustav

---

³¹Rosenzweig's crisis began in 1909, to be resolved in his "conversionary experience" of 1913. The chronological link between Rosenzweig's religious progress and his academic career deserves mention. In 1907–1908 Rosenzweig abandoned the study of medicine for history and philosophy. His father regarded this switch as a desertion from bourgeois goals; which, for Rosenzweig, seemed indistinguishable from his father's Judaism. In 1909 Rosenzweig urged child baptism and wrote the letter concerning Hans Ehrenberg cited above. In 1912, having previously conceded the superiority of Christianity, he completed his dissertation on Hegel and the State. In October 1913 Rosenzweig experienced his "conversion". Liberated from his sense of Jewish inferiority, he made his greatest academic discovery: in 1914 he revealed Hegel's debt to Schelling as the founder of German Idealism. Finally, liberated from the historical inevitability of Christianity, Rosenzweig in 1917 began writing his ahistorical classic, *Der Stern der Erlösung*. See Stefan Meinecke, 'A Life of Contradiction. The Philosopher Franz Rosenzweig and his Relationship to History and Politics', in *LBI Year Book XXXVI* (1991), pp. 461–489. I do not, however, accept Rosenzweig's early relationship with Judaism as "nothing more than a statistical entry", p. 462.

³²Benedictus Levita, 'Die Erlösung des Judentums', in *Preußische Jahrbücher*, 102 (1900), pp. 131–140. Both the pseudonym and the article title deserve notice. The "Blessed Levite" is here the Jew who feels estranged from his Jewish co-religionists. "Erlösung" translates as "freeing" or "redeeming"; "Der Erlöser", however, is also a name for Jesus Christ.

³³In Berlin, this practice occurred frequently enough to account for a statistical discrepancy between the loss counted by the Jewish community and the gain registered by the Protestant Church.

Levinstein, a trio of anti-apostasy authors.[34] The number and the vituperation of these attacks reflected more than the statistical dimensions of child baptisms; it also reflected a dangerous and seductive line of thought the authors wished to quash.

Ironically, Weißler's solution not only failed to convince many Jews, he even failed to convince himself. Twelve years later, Weißler revived the pseudonym Benedictus Levita to present a rambling novel entitled *Der König von Juda*.[35] He conceived a balkanised Palestine ultimately united by the force of arms, wielded mostly by Jewish expatriates forced out of Germany by antisemitism. "Juda" would become a peaceful, tolerant kingdom under the hegemony of the *Kaiser*. The temple in "Juda" portrayed Moses and Jesus hand-in-hand under the sole dogma of "freedom of belief within religious community". Weißler's *Der König von Juda* offered a photo-negative of Theodor Herzl's *Altneuland*, despite the elements common to both fantasies – including intolerant rabbis and effusive paeans to tolerance. Whatever its merits as literature or as a Judaic utopia, *Altneuland* presents a clear before and after picture of a liberated, accomplished, yet dignified Jewry. David Litwak, *Altneuland*'s newly-elected President, represents the condition of *schlemihldom* cured: "What a fine man the little beggar Jew boy had become! Grave and free, healthy and cultured, a man who could stand up for himself."[36] Weißler's imaginary Jews, on the other hand, remain conflicted and enmeshed in Europe; they attained no peace, and neither did their creator.[37] In December 1919 the *Centralverein*'s newspaper carried Weißler's last statement on the "Jewish Question": his suicide note. The text of his epitaph read, "He did not wish to survive the humiliation of his people." In the end, Weißler failed to integrate his German and Jewish identities. He had remained a member of the Halle Jewish community, and we do not even know whether he followed his own advice with regard to his children.[38] Weißler exhibited the intense need for conversion, and the price one paid for failing to achieve it.[39]

THE NEXUS OF SUBCULTURE AND APOSTASY

Most Jews in the German *Kulturbereich* remained satisfied and protected by their subculture. This subculture, though largely composed of German culture, remained distinctly Jewish by dint of residential concentration, social networks,

---

[34]Nathan Samter, *Was tun?*, Berlin 1900; Franz (Fritz) Wittels, *Der Taufjude*, Vienna 1904; Gustav Levinstein, *Zur Ehre des Judentums*, Berlin 1911.

[35]Benedictus Levita, *Der König von Juda. Eine Geschichte die einmal Wahr werden könnte*, Leipzig 1912.

[36]Theodor Herzl, *Old-Newland*, transl. by Lotta Levensohn, New York 1941, p. 69. See pp. 40–41 and 252–253 on the theme of Jewish honour.

[37]However devoid of Judaic content, however contrived the plot, Herzl's Jewish characters are at least happy and filled with purpose. Weißler's conclusion, by contrast, seems forced and unconvincing.

[38]*C.V. Zeitung. Im deutschen Reich*, vol. XXV, No. 12 (December 1919), p. 537. Friedrich Weißler, a lawyer in Halle, possibly Adolf Weißler's son, was killed in Sachsenhausen in 1937.

[39]I am not suggesting that baptism would have solved Weißler's Jewish problem. Baptism guaranteed neither an end to Jewish anxieties nor acceptance by the non-Jewish environment.

employment patterns, a pronounced preference for endogamy, and a commitment to an Enlightenment variety of *Bildung* increasingly out of fashion in Germany at large.[40] It both retarded the assimilation of Jews and provided a new structural basis for the Jewish community. Jewish identity would be retained, yet often compartmentalised and privatised. Nevertheless, an examination of the conversionary impulse at the *fin de siècle* indicates significant differences between a Jewish culture and a German-Jewish subculture. To put it bluntly, many Jews susceptible to baptism (converts and would-be converts) often found themselves too estranged from a Jewish *Weltanschauung* to conceive of a Judaism independent of Christianity. Whether one viewed Judaism as the broken staff left on the roadside of history, the Hegelian perspective of the young Rosenzweig; or as the religion in which one beat the thick bushes of law for a few berries of moral enlightenment, an attitude Weißler adopted from Adolf von Harnack; or as the source of the *"Nicht-Satisfactionsfähigkeit"* which tormented Herzl; none of the three could envision Judaism with a reasonable degree of independence from the surrounding Christian culture. Medieval and modern apostates could certainly detail elements within Judaism deserving of praise and blame.[41] At the beginning of the nineteenth century Rahel Varnhagen and David Friedländer had a clear idea of what pulled them towards Christian culture, but also of who would remain loyal to Judaism and why.[42] One generation later, Gabriel Riesser (1806–1863), whose own rejection of baptism became part of the mythology of the ensuing subculture, grew up in the home of a very traditional mother and the *maskil* Lazarus Jakob Riesser.[43] Their successors, a couple of generations removed from an intense Jewish life, had a much fuzzier background to draw on when challenged to explain why their particular subculture deserved loyalty. A functioning subculture may prove an inadequate spiritual and intellectual construct in times of personal crisis, crises not infrequent at a time when German youth revolted against the values of their parents and when German culture increasingly repudiated its Jewish offspring.

The testimonies of the following converts to Christianity begin to indicate how easily estrangement from Judaism and the breakdown of the subculture may lead to outright apostasy. One woman (anonymous), who described herself as coming from "a good Jewish house", only vaguely recollected the dreary dullness of the synagogue, but clearly recalled the (favourable) impact made by Christian worship – a dichotomy that many subscribed to.[44] Kurt Waldmann, who grew up in Berlin in the early years of this century, spent his school years singing in a

---

[40]For a trenchant use of this concept, see David Sorkin, *The Transformation of German Jewry, 1780–1840*, Oxford–New York 1987.
[41]See Elisheva Carlebach's essay in this volume of the *LBI Year Book*.
[42]Hertz, *op. cit.*, pp. 156–203.
[43]Moshe Rinott, 'Gabriel Riesser. Fighter for Jewish Emancipation', in *LBI Year Book VII* (1962), pp. 11–38.
[44]Occasionally hostile recollections of Judaic religious practices which do not explicitly compare Judaism with Christianity nevertheless echo a liberal Protestant conception of what religion ought to be. See 'Philippine Landau, née Fulda', in Monika Richarz (ed.), *Jewish Life in Germany. Memoirs from Three Centuries*, transl. by P. Rosenfeld and S. Rosenfeld, Bloomington–Indianapolis 1991, p. 249; Charlotte Wolff, *Hindsight*, London 1980, pp. 7–8.

Christian choir, learning in Evangelical study groups and attending Evangelical services during his army years.⁴⁵ Ernst Ginsburg, like Waldmann a child of Berlin in the *fin de siècle*, remembered that his father preferred no Judaism to a watered-down Judaism. Ginsburg's father refused baptism, but the substance of his Jewish upbringing was this warning: "You are Jews and must behave more decently than others."⁴⁶ Karl Jacob Hirsch, whose dramatic Hanukkah conversion is mentioned above, had been led to the baptismal font by a close companionship with a Protestant pastor. Hirsch's earliest account of his conversion, "I believe that I was never a better Jew than today", expressed a classically Christian view of "the economy of salvation", no doubt learned through his friend Pastor Forell.⁴⁷ These conversionary testimonies indicate a view of Judaism (exhausted, dreary, primitive, legalistic) that reflected the caricatures of the "Higher Critics" and Christian theology in general. To adopt a phrase used to describe pragmatic conversions, the converts mentioned above were simply acknowledging the distance which they had already travelled, albeit in a very dramatic fashion.

Children of the Imperial era, whose conversions occurred later in life, offer additional evidence of the failures of this subculture to instil a spiritual dimension to their children's Jewish identity. Edith Stein (1891–1942), whose apostasy provokes controversy even today, grew up in a distinctly Jewish family which still sought relatives for marriage partners and banished its one intermarried member – a severe sanction by the standards of the time. Yet her memoirs display little comprehension or empathy for the practices she observed. Stein's one opportunity to question a relative better versed in the Judaic tradition, an observant journalist named Eduard Metis, ended in disappointment. Asking whether Metis believed in a personal God, Stein recalled his answer and her response, " 'God is spirit; nothing more can be said about it.' To me, it was like receiving a stone instead of bread."⁴⁸

Karl Stern grew up in rural Bavarian village whose Jewish population declined from 205 in 1871 to 19 in 1933.⁴⁹ Stern's grandfather, one of Floss's more learned Jews, expected his descendants to abandon strict Orthodoxy and raised no objection when Karl became the first Jewish child sent to a Catholic kindergarten.⁵⁰ One may dismiss as exaggeration Stern's verdict that, "The

---

⁴⁵Theo Bergthaler, 'Das Taufmotiv in der Judentaufe', in *Judaica*, vol. VII, No. 1 (1951). *Judaica* was a missionary journal and I treat its conversion reports accordingly - with suspicion. Students of radical assimilation face particular difficulties in assessing the subjective factors that led a Jew to cut his or her ties with the Jewish community. With the exception of devout Christians, most Jews who left the fold only left a small paper trail attesting to their motives. The sincere convert presents another set of interpretative problems since earlier experiences are filtered through the lens of subsequent Christian faith.

⁴⁶Kisch, *Judentaufen, op. cit.*, p. 97.

⁴⁷*Ibid.*, p. 95. In later memoirs, Hirsch recognised his conversion as a repudiation, rather than as a fulfilment of Judaism. Karl Jacob Hirsch, *Quintessenz meines Lebens*, Mainz 1990, pp. 238–242.

⁴⁸Edith Stein, *Aus dem Leben einer jüdischen Familie*, ed. by Lucy Gelber and Romaeus Leuven, *Werke*, vol. VII, Louvain–Freiburg i. Br 1965, p. 142. The only discussions of Stein's 1922 conversion I have come across are found in hagiographies.

⁴⁹See entry on 'Floss', in *Encyclopaedia Judaica*, vol. VI, Jerusalem 1972, col. 1364.

⁵⁰Karl Stern, *Pillar of Fire*, New York 1951, p. 19.

people of my parents' generation were almost entirely cut off from Jewish tradition." Nevertheless, in comparison to Floss's Christian maids, who led lives of "humility and charity", Stern may well have considered Judaism formalistic and lacking in a spiritual dimension.[51] Time and again, these conversionary testimonies indicate that those individuals who still possessed strong Jewish loyalties failed to inculcate other Jews with the substance which supported these sentiments.[52] Though an entire generation older than Stein and Stern, Philippine Landau (1869–1964) described the waning orthopraxy of her parental home in familiar terms: "Lacking were the prerequisites that allowed things to become truly alive and necessary: true belief and genuine piety."[53]

The inability to construct a plausible Jewish identity also led to baptism without any apparent emotional or religious turmoil. These "pragmatic" conversions were far more numerous than the religious conversions described above. Fritz Haber, the noted chemist, saw Christianity as a part of a German identity, as did the journalist Maximilian Harden.[54] Werner E. Mosse has assembled an impressive number of examples that demonstrate that the third generation of the German-Jewish economic élite ("the heirs") exhibited a considerable tendency towards apostasy.[55] While the decisive moments of these pragmatic conversions lacked drama, they emerged from subculture alienation and an inability to balance Jewish values against the tangible and intangible benefits of belonging to the non-Jewish environment.

"Pragmatic" converts, for obvious reasons, rarely detailed their departures from the Jewish fold; but those Jews who remained in the community of their birth after wrestling with the temptations of baptism shed some light on the conversionary process. Willy Ritter Liebermann von Wahlendorf (1863–1939) described the path which led his brother to apostasy: intense animosity towards the merchant class, mixed with Prussian militarism.[56] That Liebermann himself affirmed his Jewish identity seems no more self-evident than his brother's apostasy – there was little in the wealthy von Wahlendorf family's religious practices or social relations (which included Jews, baptised Jews and Christians) which would have encouraged fidelity to Judaism. Liebermann's angry description of the effects of antisemitism offers unwitting testimony to the fragility of the Judaic element of the German-Jewish subculture:

---

[51]*Ibid.*, pp. 16, 273–274.
[52]Heinrich Kronstein (1897–1972) recalled his father's love of Jewish practices and his affinity for "lernen". Yet Kronstein never reflected any of that affection, describing, for example, the Jewish funeral service as empty, crass and nihilistic. Kronstein, *Briefe an einen jungen Deutschen*, Munich 1967, pp. 48–49, 163. The classic representation of this theme is Franz Kafka's *Brief an den Vater*.
[53]Quoted in Richarz, *Jewish Life in Germany, op. cit.*, p. 249.
[54]Fritz Stern, *Dreams and Delusions. The Drama of German History*, New York 1987, pp. 51–76; Rudolph A. Stern, 'Fritz Haber. Personal Recollections', in *LBI Year Book VIII* (1963), pp. 70–110; Harry F. Young, *Maximilian Harden. Censor Germaniae. The Critic in Opposition from Bismarck to the Rise of Nazism*, The Hague 1959. See the discussion in Endelman, 'The Social and Political Context of Conversion in Germany and England, 1870–1914', *loc. cit.*
[55]Werner E. Mosse, *The German-Jewish Economic Elite, 1820–1935. A Socio-Cultural Profile*, Oxford 1989, pp. 46–92 and *passim*.
[56]Willy Ritter Liebermann von Wahlendorf, *Erinnerungen eines deutschen Juden, 1863–1936*, ed. by Ernst Reinhard Piper, Munich 1988.

"Wilhelminian antisemitism – with its principle of baptism: that any Jew, one day after his conversion, to put it crudely, could achieve what was still closed to him the day before – destroyed the bases of Jewish morale, pride, self-awareness and the elements of Jewish ethics, i.e. the teachings of Jewish values."[57]

Can one imagine a medieval apostate conceding to antisemitism the power to destroy Jewish honour, self-awareness, ethics and self-worth? Liebermann's memoirs testify to the *Gymnasien*, the army and academia as settings where baptism represented a choice actively forwarded by empowered individuals, not merely a background temptation. Liebermann resisted this pressure, but recalled that "most of my friends allowed either themselves or their children to be baptised".[58] The structures of the subculture succeeded in retaining Liebermann's Jewish loyalties; we cannot conclusively answer why in his brother's case they failed.

Richard Lichtheim (1885–1963), a good example of the generation of Zionists termed "post-emancipatory" by Kurt Blumenfeld, grew up in a family that had numbered apostates within its ranks for three generations, child baptism being the preferred method of escaping Jewish identity. This "family tradition", as Richard Lichtheim described it, led Lichtheim's own father, George, to propose baptism to Richard – a suggestion the latter rejected.[59] Lichtheim's mother Clara, who died when Richard was eleven, preserved a deep animosity towards apostates. While her strong feelings against apostasy and his father's rejection of baptism for himself presumably influenced Richard to refuse this proposal, nothing indicates that George and Clara instilled a specifically Jewish identity in any of the usual familiar settings. 'Geschichte einer Bekehrung', as Lichtheim described his eventual embrace of Zionism, portrayed a Jewish subculture gradually being absorbed into its surroundings.[60] The passage of years and his subsequent career probably caused Lichtheim to exaggerate the starkness of his youthful rejection of the German-Jewish subculture, but there is no reason to doubt either that Lichtheim found the solutions of his parents' generation unsatisfactory, or that he experienced Zionism as a dramatic redefinition of his own Jewish identity.

The renunciation of an impoverished German-Jewish subculture could play itself out through the familial drama of generational conflict.[61] For the jurist

---

[57]*Ibid.*, p. 107. The original reads: "Denn der Wilhelminische Antisemitismus zerstörte durch das Prinzip der Taufe und dadurch, daß jeder Jude am Tage nach seine Übertritt, kraß gesprochen, all das erreichen konnte, was ihm am Tage vorher noch verschlossen war, die Grundlage der jüdischen Moral, des jüdischen Stolzes, seines Selbstbewußtseins und die Elemente der jüdischen Ethik, der Lehre des jüdischen Wertes."

[58]*Ibid.*, p. 107.

[59]Richard Lichtheim, *Rückkehr. Lebenserinnerungen aus der Frühzeit des deutschen Zionismus*, Stuttgart 1970. Veröffentlichung des Leo Baeck Instituts, p. 31.

[60]Lichtheim's memoirs are certainly tendentious with respect to German Jewry. I am inclined, however, to trust Lichtheim's memories as to which family members were baptised, the differing attitudes of his parents towards apostasy and the religious practices of his own household.

[61]Generational conflict was pronounced and explicit in the memoirs of Rosenzweig, Lichtheim, Blumenfeld and Wolff as well as in many memoirs from this period which do not come under purview here. See also Gershom Scholem, *From Berlin to Jerusalem. Memories of My Youth*, transl. by Harry Zohn, New York 1980, pp. 41–43; and 'Philipp Löwenfeld', in Richarz, *Jewish Life in Germany*, *op. cit.*, pp. 234–246.

Ludwig Bendix (1877–1954), the family's move from Dorstfeld to Berlin initiated a five-year period of estrangement from Judaism. Under the influence of his *Gymnasium* teacher Rudolf Lehmann (born Jewish, baptised as a child), Ludwig and his two closest friends immersed themselves in German high culture and male bonding. Ludwig's Bar Mitzvah ceremony and some remnants of orthopraxy proved no match against the blandishments of Max Koehler's rationalism and Bernhard Schmiedler's individualistic Protestant piety. In his first year at the University of Berlin, Ludwig wrote to his father, Gustav Bendix, declaring his abandonment of all Jewish observances. His father's reply casts a bad light on Ludwig's maturity, but also on the shortcomings of the older generation:

> "[Your] confession was neither asked for nor indicated, but it reveals in any case that you were in a great hurry to throw something overboard which perhaps was very valuable, to disdain something which you had never yet examined as to its true value, which you are also quite incapable of examining."[62]

Despite the advantages to a young man planning for a career in law, Ludwig Bendix did not have himself baptised. Neither did Paul Mühsam (1876–1960), who grew up in a distinctly Jewish household, yet disavowed any appreciation of Judaism's religious significance and expressed considerable animosity towards his parents ethnic Jewishness and frequent Yiddishisms.[63] Bendix and Mühsam, like most German Jews, resisted the temptation of baptism, "for reasons of filial love", out of an abhorrence of a public renunciation of "family and virtue", out of a refusal to participate in "an unprincipled and servile act", or simply out of a sense that, "one does not abandon a besieged fortress".[64] Yet the very frequency with which this option is dismissed in the memoirs of middle-class German Jews, and their numerous recollections of friends and family members who accepted this option but did not write about it, indicates that contemplating apostasy was not so exceptional.

The German-Jewish subculture successfully transmitted its antipathy towards apostasy in the home and in the synagogue, in the Jewish press and in the propaganda and public demonstrations sponsored by the *Centralverein*. While the members of the German-Jewish subculture succeeded in convincing their children that being Jewish was important, it often failed to transmit very much to the children coming to maturity in the *fin de siècle* in the way of positive Judaic content. Even the argument for Jewish loyalty, as George Mosse once observed, based itself not on inherently Judaic values, but on the premises of a universalist

---

[62]Reinhard Bendix, *From Berlin to Berkeley. German-Jewish Identities*, New Brunswick, NJ 1985, p. 22.

[63]Mühsam attended service once a year at his father's behest, lit *yahrzeit* candles and was aware of his mother's habit of intoning Friday night prayers. None of this seems to have made a positive impression and Mühsam could write, "I lacked absolutely all of the inner and external qualifications for pursuing the path to the Jewish community. I knew nothing about Judaism. It offered me nothing whatsoever." Quoted in Richarz, *Jewish Life in Germany, op. cit.*, p. 258.

[64]The quotes belong to the following authors: "aus Gründen der Pietät gegen meine Eltern" (Paul Mühsam in Monika Richarz, *Jüdisches Leben, op. cit.*, p. 363); abhorrence of a public renunciation "of family and virtue" (Enoch Heinrich Kisch, *Erlebtes und Erstrebtes. Erinnerungen*, cited in Kisch, *Judentaufen, op. cit.*, p. 112); "a servile and unprincipled act" (Gershom Scholem, *op. cit.*); "daß man aus einer belagerten Festung nicht entweicht" (Philipp Löwenfeld's father in Richarz, *Jüdisches Leben, op. cit.*, p. 312).

humanism.⁶⁵ To quote Ruppin's observation, borne out by many memoirs: "If numbers of men and women cannot decide to be baptised, it is not so much because of their love of Judaism as because of their unwillingness to face the reproach of cowardice and treachery by deserting a minority which is in danger, and being attacked on all sides."⁶⁶

THE NEXUS OF APOSTASY AND THE "JEWISH QUESTION"

Conversion to Christianity posed a "live option" not only because of the limitations of the subculture in fostering Jewish identity, a criticism which could be made of many modern Jewries, but also because the pressures to leave that subculture were subtle and pervasive.⁶⁷ These pressures cannot be reduced to expressions of antisemitism and to the anti-Jewish discrimination practiced in so many areas of German public life. As Marion Kaplan noted, these challenges Jews "took for granted and overcame".⁶⁸ Moreover, the values of the subculture (tolerance, progress, the *Rechtsstaat*) provided the proper intellectual ammunition to respond to this blatant illiberalism. But it was not only the Jews' enemies, but also their friends, who inculcated in them a sense of Jewish religious and cultural inferiority. The ambivalent nature of German philosemitism and its impact on Jewish identity formation has been largely neglected; the following comments point to some areas worthy of further investigation.

The process by which German Jews saw their Judaism through Christian eyes could begin at an early age. Kurt Blumenfeld recalled a Christian maid who considered it a sin to work for Christ-crucifying Jews.⁶⁹ But probably more common were the maids who taught their young charges to say their prayers, praised their "Christian" hearts, and impressed them with a piety usually unmatched by their own (Jewish) parents.⁷⁰ Charlotte Wolff, who envied the physical skills of the father of one of her Christian friends, a blacksmith, also took to secretly worshipping Jesus as the "Personal Saviour" who loved children – a striking contrast to the impersonal tedium of her Jewish Sunday school.⁷¹ Eduard Bernstein's parents, who belonged to the Berlin *Reformgenossenschaft*,

---

⁶⁵George L. Mosse, *German Jews Beyond Judaism*, Bloomington–Cincinnati 1985, pp. 18–19. Anti-apostasy rhetoric also drew from the values of the German *Bürgertum*. This is particularly clear in the writings of the industrialist Gustav Levinstein, *Zur Ehre des Judentums* (1911).
⁶⁶Arthur Ruppin, *The Jews of Today*, transl. by Margery Bentwich, New York 1913, p. 194.
⁶⁷The model of subculture which informs some of the best German-Jewish historiography was initially developed by American sociologists and describes a Jewish community (America's) relatively unaffected by antisemitism. The subculture operates against a neutral background, assuming freely a variety of configurations and competing only with effects of voluntary assimilation and religious indifference. The differences between the American and German situations counsel caution.
⁶⁸Marion A. Kaplan, *The Making of the Jewish Middle-Class. Women, Family and Identity in Imperial Germany*, New York–Oxford 1991, p. 14.
⁶⁹Kurt Blumenfeld, *Erlebte Judenfrage. Ein Vierteljahrhundert deutscher Zionismus*, Stuttgart 1962, p. 27.
⁷⁰Jakob Wassermann, *My Life As A German And Jew*, New York 1933, pp. 20–22; Stern, *Pillar of Fire*, *op. cit.*, p. 274.
⁷¹Wolff, *op. cit.*, pp. 7–8.

allowed him to attend Christian religious instruction in school and encouraged him to socialise with non-Jews – hardly unique circumstances. How many Jewish families heard the praise accorded the Bernsteins that they were not "really" Jews?[72] How often was it recognised that the "better" dance clubs and health spas were the "mixed" ones?[73] The intellectual sparring which emerged from friendships cemented during *Gymnasium* days – and later at university – could lead directly to disenchantment with the Judaism of their subculture. In a society which afforded ample opportunity for male bonding, Jakob Wassermann's recollection of a friendship soured by the gradual revelation that he was considered an exception – the one "good Jew" – takes on a new poignancy. In the case of converts, a relatively uncultivated sense of Jewish self-esteem, a depreciation of Jewishness imbibed from philosemitic friends, and the ever-present desire to fully identify with German-Christian culture developed concurrently. Thus, all assessments of apostasy which neatly distinguish between "push" and "pull" factors, in other words, what pushed apostates to leave Judaism and what pulled them towards Christianity, underrate the complex seductiveness of leaving the Jewish fold in the German *Kulturbereich*.[74]

While German Jews recognised and rejected antisemitism in its more obvious forms, the anti-Jewish animus of declared philosemites was another matter. In the 1890s (earlier in Austria), a new wave of social, intellectual and cultural antisemitism intensified the debate over the "Jewish Question".[75] While this essay hardly allows for a survey of this debate, one telling body of evidence is especially worth citing: the collections of short essays, perhaps best categorised as *Rundfragen*, which offered the ruminations of a wide sample of the German intelligentsia on the "Jewish Question".[76] These volumes featured Jewish and non-Jewish spokespersons and provided a unique forum for discussion. Those non-Jewish Germans who felt that the "Jewish Question" could be solved at all agreed that a) the Jews were less willing to assimilate than they admitted, and b) only the disappearance of German Jewry through apostasy and intermarriage could offer a possible solution for the "Jewish Question".

As proof of the first contention, Herbert Eulenberg asserted that the Jews' devotion to endogamy – fitting for the nineteenth but not the twentieth century – precluded their final acceptance. That Christian reluctance might bear some of the responsibility did not seem to enter into Eulenberg's thinking. Richard

---

[72]Bernstein, *loc. cit.*, p. 189.

[73]Alex Bein (ed.), *Arthur Ruppin. Memoirs, Diaries, Letters*, New York 1982, p. 28; Stern, 'Fritz Haber', *loc. cit.*, pp. 70–102.

[74]See Jonathan Helfand, 'Passports and Piety. Apostasy in Nineteenth-Century France', in *Jewish History*, vol. III, No. 2 (1988), pp. 59–81; and the ensuing discussion in *Jewish History*, vol. V, No. 2 (1991), pp. 47–71.

[75]Peter Pulzer has pointed out that the persistence of both the "Jewish Question" and antisemitism had a mutually reinforcing effect; Pulzer, 'Why was there a "Jewish Question" in Imperial Germany?', in *LBI Year Book XXV* (1980), pp. 133–146.

[76]Hermann Bahr, *Der Antisemitismus. Ein internationales Interview* (1894), ed. by Hermann Greive, Königstein 1979; Arthur Landsberger, *Diskussion Kultur-Parlement*, Berlin–Leipzig 1912; Julius Moses, *Die Lösung der Judenfrage. Eine Rundfrage*, Berlin–Leipzig 1907. Also relevant to this discourse was the famous *Kunstwart-Debatte* prompted by Moritz Goldstein's provocative essay 'Deutsch-jüdischer Parnass', in *Kunstwart*, vol. XXV, No. 11 (1912) and subsequent issues.

Nordhausen, reversing the Bismarckian image of crossing "the German stallion with the Jewish mare", considered how some excitable Jewish blood would invigorate the sleepy Germans. In Professor Otto Caspari's view, the Jews ought to be willing to convert to Christianity if it would make intermarriage easier. Typical of the "philosemitic" camp, the poet Richard Dehmel invited Jews and Christians to become dissidents together.[77] The anti-antisemitic *Verein zur Abwehr des Antisemitismus*, certainly a philosemitic organisation by Wilhelminian standards, articulated their view that intermarriage and baptism presented, the "best means . . . of closing religious differences".[78] Some Christians, who took their sacraments more seriously, recognised that insincere baptism should not be encouraged. "Most desirable, however, is that the Jew enter into intermarriage and bring up his children in the Christian religion."[79] The terms *Amalgamation* and *Aufgehen*, synonymous with complete eradication of distinctive Jewish elements, surfaced continually in these discussions. The Bible scholar Hermann Gunkel undoubtedly spoke for the majority when he stated: "The 'Jewish Question' in Germany will disappear only with the disappearance of the Jews."[80] In no period before the *fin de siècle* were so many Jews so deeply involved in a discourse that called for their own disappearance. One hundred years after Dohm, the Jews had "improved" their appearance, their language, their education, their occupations and their religion – but obviously not enough. One did not need to be a self-hating Jew or a subscriber to *Semi-Gotha* to feel at one's wit's end. Looking back forty-five years to his provocative 1912 essay 'Deutschjüdischer Parnass', which had called for the voluntary Jewish disengagement from German culture, Moritz Goldstein correctly observed: "It was not a programme . . . it was a confession."[81]

CONCLUSIONS

Few scholars have investigated the contours of identity formation in the generation of German Jews who came to maturity in the post-emancipatory community. Fewer still have analysed the impact of Germany's thoroughly ambivalent philosemitism on German-Jewish self-perceptions. These conclusions, then, are offered principally as a springboard for further reflection.

---

[77] Richard Dehmel, 'Mischehen', in Landsberger, *op. cit.* Dehmel presented his two marriages to Jewesses as the credentials of a philosemite; Wilhelm Marr could have made the same claim.
[78] 'Von den christlich-jüdischen Mischehen', in *Mitteilungen aus dem Verein zur Abwehr des Antisemitismus*, vol. III, No. 44 (29th October 1893), pp. 402–403. Albrecht Weber, an *Abwehrverein* activist, called intermarriage "the best kind of *Judenmission*". See also Barbara Suchy, 'The *Verein zur Abwehr des Antisemitismus*. (I) From its Beginnings to the First World War', in *LBI Year Book XXVIII* (1983), pp. 205–239.
[79] Hermann Gunkel, in Moses, *op. cit.*, pp. 231–232. Matthias Erzberger, quoted in Kisch, *Judentaufen*, *op. cit.*, pp. 30–33, expressed a similar view.
[80] Gunkel, *loc. cit.*, pp. 231–232. This viewpoint was also propounded by (Jewish) radical assimilationists (e.g. Adolf Weißler, Jacob Stern, Martin Maass, Friedrich Blach) who were vilified by mainstream Jewry.
[81] Moritz Goldstein, 'German Jewry's Dilemma. The Story of A Provocative Essay', in *LBI Year Book II* (1957), p. 245.

Beginning in the 1880s, the majority of Jewry began displaying many signs of renewed vitality.[82] Concurrently, a growing number of German-speaking Jews apostatised. These developments should be seen as dialectical rather than as contradictory. Both accelerated vitality and accelerated defection indicate the limitations of a German-Jewish subculture to provide what a Jewish culture once provided: both developments indicate a need for viable post-emancipatory Jewish identities. The institutional features of this new identity have been well researched. But the ways in which individuals developed their own set of values, and the ways in which they related these values to the larger group, have been largely assumed from the institutional perspective; or, to put it another way, from the silent majority. This essay has tried to demonstrate that apostasy lay at one end of a continuum of options. Whether actual apostates represented the tip of the iceberg, or only the tip of an ice cube, may be debated.

This cursory glance at individual identity formation does suggest a particular *fin de siècle* German context. Rosenzweig, Herzl and Weißler felt the distinctive pull of the Jewish collective – this is evidenced by the nature of their suggestions for general solutions to the "Jewish Question" as well as by their residual Jewish loyalties, a value which surely emerged from the Jewish subculture, not German culture at large. Initially, however, they could only visualise that Jewish collective through the hostile eyes of the majority; this was the burden of their common historical circumstances. Their conversionary experiences mediated – or failed to mediate – a transformation to a new Jewish identity. Weißler became an ideologue for radical assimilation, Herzl and Rosenzweig carried banners for a Jewish renaissance. Their struggle with the conversionary impulse demonstrates in a dramatic fashion the brinkmanship that other, less well-known German Jews experienced as they, too, sought to integrate the German and the Jewish components of their personalities.

---

[82]This vitality, this "dissimilation", was manifested initially in student organisations such as the *Akademischer Verein für jüdische Geschichte und Literatur* (1883) and *Viadrina* (1886); subsequently in the creation of the *Centralverein* (1893), the *Zionistische Vereinigung für Deutschland* (1897), the *Jüdischer Frauenbund* (1904), as well as in the intellectual and cultural efflorescence that would last through the Weimar period.

Leaving the Jewish Fold in Germany
Comments on the Papers of Elisheva Carlebach, Deborah Hertz and Alan Levenson

BY TODD M. ENDELMAN

Professors Carlebach, Hertz and Levenson reveal once again the burden of being Jewish in Germany, both before and after emancipation. Each describes the material and mental pressures that turned Jewish status and consciousness into matters of public concern, leaving Jews vulnerable to the temptation to turn Christian. None of them addresses head-on the issue whether this burden was more acutely felt in Germany than elsewhere in the West, whether there was a Jewish *Sonderweg*; but it is present none the less, as a kind of subtext, an issue that weaves its way in and out of their presentations. Certainly, the pre-emancipation conversion of Baruch ben Moshe of Proßnitz (Friedrich Albrecht Christiani), the subject of Elisheva Carlebach's study, was paralleled in other lands in the early modern period. Although there is little statistical information on this period, non-quantitative "anecdotal" evidence suggests that baptisms were as common in Italy and Poland as in Germany.[1] Indeed, in the case of some Italian communities (for example Rome), the number of converts was sufficient to exact a demographic toll,[2] which was not the case in seventeenth- or eighteenth-century Germany. This suggests that whatever made conversion a prominent feature of German-Jewish life from the *Haskalah* period on was not a permanent feature of the German landscape, but a product of the specific contours of the emancipation experience there.

What we do not know, given the state of current research, is whether the circumstances that led Jews to convert in early modern Germany were the same as in other lands. But Professor Carlebach is clear about the changed character of conversions in this period in comparison to earlier centuries. The converts she has studied were less eager than their medieval counterparts to declare themselves new men, spiritually transformed beyond recognition, with no links to their Jewish past. Rather, she notes, they used their Jewish background, especially their education, as spiritual and pragmatic credentials in claiming a

---

[1]Jacob Goldberg, *Ha-mumarim be-mamlekhet Polin-Lita* (Converts in the Kingdom of Poland-Lithuania), Jerusalem 1985; Luciano Allegra, 'L'ospizio dei catecumeni di Torino', in *Bollettino Storico-Bibliografico Subalpino*, 88 (1990), pp. 513–573.
[2]In Rome, 788 Jews converted to Christianity between 1634 and 1700, and 873 between 1700, and 1790. Attilio Milano, 'Battesimi di ebrei a Roma dal cinquecento all'ottocento', in Daniel Carpi, Attilio Milano and Umberto Nahon (eds.), *Scritti im memoria di Enzo Sereni. Saggi sull'ebraismo romano*, Jerusalem 1970, p. 140.

place for themselves in Christian society. One pattern in particular which she has identified continued to be common in the nineteenth and early twentieth centuries throughout Europe and North America: the employment of converts, because of their expertise in Jewish texts and first-hand knowledge of Jewish customs, as missionaries and teachers of Hebrew and Judaica in universities and seminaries. Without them, the London Society for the Promotion of Christianity among the Jews, the most active conversionist group in Europe, would have been hard-pressed to staff its worldwide network of missionary stations.[3] For their part, converts were eager to exploit their credentials as "learned" Jews, since their baptism cut them off from their previous sources of livelihood. Many "rabbis" whose conversions were celebrated in print as triumphs of Christian faith were, in fact, minor religious functionaries – *melamdim*, *chasanim* and *shohetim* – whose low status and pay and often peripatetic lifestyle contributed to their decision to become Christians. This was true in both early modern Germany and in later centuries among immigrants from Central and Eastern Europe who were converted by missionaries in Western Europe.

The motives that led Jews to convert were complex. Disentangling this web, and the social circumstances that created it, is a central concern of the three papers, which all seek to transcend an older historiographical tradition, rooted in both ideology and folk wisdom, that attributed base or opportunistic reasons alone to Jews who embraced Christianity. In dozens of Jewish jokes about converts, which circulated at the turn of the century and reflect this popular construction of conversion, a prominent theme is the insincerity of converts and their efforts to portray their change of faith as high-minded and disinterested. One well-known Eastern European story, collected by Alter Druyanov (1870–1938) and first published in Frankfurt a. Main in 1922, will have to suffice here to illustrate this point.[4] The story concerns four converts who gathered for drinks in a tavern. As the alcohol began to loosen their tongues, the oldest one said, "I admit it – the desire for wealth, for a good life, made me convert." The second said, "I was a great philosopher. I denied everything. And since all is vanity, there is no law or justice. If so, I reasoned, why should I suffer for nothing?" The third man lowered his head and confessed, "I converted because of a woman." The fourth convert remained quiet. Then the old one asked him, "And you?" Standing up straight, he replied, "I didn't do it for the reasons you did. I believed with all my heart" – to which the old man responded, "Save that for the *goyim*, my friend."

The papers under discussion suggest that the question of motive is more complex than this folk tradition allows. To be sure, pure opportunism loomed large in most decisions to convert. As Professors Hertz and Levenson indicate, it was difficult, if not impossible, for Jews to feel comfortable with their inherited

---

[3]Todd M. Endelman, *Radical Assimilation in English Jewish History, 1656–1945*, Bloomington 1990, pp. 159–165.
[4]Avraham Alter Druyanov, *Sefer ha-bedihah ve-ha-hiddud* (The Book of Jokes and Witticisms), 3 vols., Tel-Aviv 1980, vol. II, pp. 134–135. The story of the four converts in the tavern is long-lived; it is told in a Jewish response to the publication of the convert Karl Stern's autobiography *Pillar of Fire*. See Bernard Heller, *Epistle to an Apostate*, New York 1951, pp. 46–47.

identity and at the same time still participate in public life. The pressures to merge completely, to shed all vestiges of Jewishness, were strong and hard to resist; not for all Jews equally, of course, but for those who wished to move in non-Jewish social and cultural circles or, in the case of men, to make careers for themselves outside commerce and finance. What is remarkable, Professor Levenson tells us, is that even otherwise well-disposed intellectuals in the quarter-century before the First World War could not imagine any effective solution to the *Judenfrage* short of the Jews' gradual disappearance through mass intermarriage and conversion. In other words, both antisemites and anti-antisemites in Germany devalued Jewishness and the survival of the Jews as a distinct group; where they differed was in their solution – voluntary or coerced – to bring about the Jews' disappearance from the German scene. In this regard, the German-Jewish experience was unusual, perhaps even unique, for in most western states liberals, even if incapable of valuing Jewish particularism, did not urge Jews to liquidate themselves as a group. This suggests, at the very least, a higher level of anxiety about questions of national identity in Germany than elsewhere in the West.

But even when hostility to Jewishness in all its manifestations is taken into account, opportunism alone is insufficient to illustrate the complex conversion process. The case of Abraham Mendelssohn, which Professor Hertz describes, demonstrates beyond question that opportunistic and intellectual motives could operate in tandem. Indeed, in cases like this, it is fruitless to ask which motive was dominant. Moreover, even for those who saw conversion as a pragmatic social or career strategy, the actual decision to convert was conditioned by constraints of a psychological nature: parental bonds, for example, or, in the *Kaiserreich*, concern about being stigmatised as a dishonourable opportunist, willing to desert the sinking Jewish ship in order to save one's own skin. To convert under these circumstances would confirm the antisemitic construction of the Jew as manipulative, ambitious, shallow and dishonest. Professor Levenson makes the important observation that more Jews considered baptism, viewing it as a serious option, than actually went through with it. The memoir literature from this period abounds with references to what he terms "the conversionary impulse" – a felicitous phrase that should become part of the historian's vocabulary. To cite two instances: the Nobel prize winner and chemist Richard Willstätter (1872–1942) was repeatedly urged to convert by his mentor and teacher Adolf von Baeyer (1835–1917), himself of part-Jewish origin, but always refused, believing that baptism for personal advantage was improper. Professor Levenson gives, as an example, the lawyer Paul Mühsam (1876–1960), son of a shopkeeper, who grew up in total ignorance of Judaism, regarding it as "eine Hülle ohne Inhalt" and "eine lästige Fessel", and considered, but in the end rejected, baptism because it would upset his parents and because without "innere Notwendigkeit" it would be "feige, charakterlos und verächtlich".[5]

---

[5]Richard Willstätter, *From My Life. The Memoirs of Richard Willstätter*, transl. by Lilli S. Hornig, ed. by Arthur Stoll, New York 1965, pp. 83–84; Monika Richarz (ed.), *Jüdisches Leben in Deutschland*, vol. II, *Selbstzeugnisse zur Sozialgeschichte im Kaiserreich*, Stuttgart 1979. Veröffentlichung des Leo Baeck Instituts, p. 363.

Neither Mühsam nor Willstätter, nor the individuals cited by Levenson who weighed the merits and demerits of baptism, were attached in any positive sense to Judaism. Secularisation and German representations of Judaism as primitive and unspiritual, which had become part and parcel of the Jews' own outlook, left them hostile or indifferent to Jewish customs, worship and learning. However successful it was in preserving ethnic boundaries, the Jewish subculture failed to transmit from one generation to the next an attachment to the Jewish religion. By stressing that the experience of alienation was common to both those who became Christians and those who stopped short of the baptismal font, Levenson moves the history of conversion from the periphery of the historiographical stage to its centre. He provides a response to those historians who dispute the fruitfulness of studying the subject or who dismiss it as an exercise in the marginal, the exotic and the deviant.[6] For implicit in his treatment is the fundamental insight that conversion reflected stresses and strains which operated throughout Jewish society and the impact of which were more profound than the number of persons who formally renounced their ties to Judaism would suggest. Conversion, in other words, was the tip of an iceberg of religious indifference, self-hatred and communal alienation.

In addition to the question of motives, all three authors also address what can be called the aftermath of conversion – the success or failure of converts to find material success, social acceptance and inner contentment as new Christians. The conclusion that emerges is that neither before nor after 1812 did conversion guarantee integration into Gentile society. Professor Carlebach notes that even in the early modern period, when conversion meant the severing of both social and religious ties with the Jewish community, when there was no neutral, secularised space between the two groups, baptised Jews were not easily integrated and suffered from a lack of social life. The fund for proselytes established by Esdras Edzard in Hamburg in the second half of the seventeenth century was the first of scores of institutions in Europe and North America, including schools, hostels and workshops, designed to ease the difficult social and material passage from Judaism to Christianity. The high proportion of converted Jews in the early modern period who became clergymen and then teachers in theological faculties is attributable, in part, to the fact that doing so resolved for them the problem of finding a social niche once they had cut their ties to Jewry. It should be added that joining the clergy performed an important psychological function as well. For converts who suffered from guilt for having abandoned the faith of their fathers, becoming exponents and defenders of the Christian faith provided reassurance of the correctness of their decision, helping to silence whatever doubts remained.

Some of the difficulty in gaining a foothold in Christian society in the early modern period was due to the suspicion that the converts' Jewishness was an essential part of their nature, an ineradicable element that persisted after

---

[6]This is certainly the tone of some earlier studies like Isaac Remba, *Banim akhlu boser* (The Sons Have Eaten Sour Grapes), ed. by Joseph Nedava, n.p. 1973; and Shmuel Leib Tsitron, *Mei-ahorei ha-pargod. Mumarim, bogedim, mitkahshim* (From Behind the Screen. Converts, Traitors, Deniers), 2 vols., Vilna 1923–1925.

baptism. Referring to formerly-Jewish Christians as "converted Jews", Professor Carlebach notes, embodies this feeling. The importance of this insight cannot be exaggerated, for it suggests that racial constructions of Jewishness were not restricted to the Iberian Peninsula in the early modern period, but were found in Central Europe as well, if in a less virulent form. Of course, these constructions did not employ the biological language of modern racial discourse, but their conclusion was the same: baptism could not wash away the taint of Jewishness. In the nineteenth century, even before the ascendance of "scientific" racial categories, it was common to think of Jewishness in non-religious, essentialist terms.[7] In Heinrich Heine's oft-quoted words of 1826, "Isn't it ridiculous that I am no sooner baptised than I am upbraided as a Jew?"[8] It would seem, then, that there was an unbroken tradition, a more or less continuous line of inchoate sentiment, questioning the power of baptism to alter the inner nature of Jews, that stretched from the seventeenth century, perhaps earlier, to the twentieth.

In Heine's time, as well as in later periods, essentialist perceptions of Jewishness acted as a brake on the social integration of converts. While such sentiments were to be found in most European states, they tended to be less effective in preventing social acceptance in Western than in Central Europe. In other words, in those states where baptism was most "needed" for social and career reasons, it was less efficacious than in those states where it was less "needed" and hence less common. In Georgian and Victorian England, for example, converted Jews encountered few obstacles to their occupational and social ascent.[9] Benjamin Disraeli, who flaunted his Jewishness but none the less rose to the top of the political heap, could not have had a German counterpart. Nor could Frances, Countess of Waldegrave (1821–1879), daughter of the famous tenor John Braham (1774–1856) and one of the great political hostesses of the mid-Victorian years.

Before the modern period, conversion meant automatic exclusion from the Jewish community. Not so in the nineteenth century. The loss of communal autonomy and weakening of religious sureties opened up neutral space. In the social circles inhabited by Heinrich Heine and Abraham Mendelssohn, for example, Jews, converted Jews and non-Jews mixed with apparent ease. In this sense, conversion represented less of a radical break than in the early modern period, when the lines between Christian and Jew were firmly drawn. This, in turn, suggests several questions. Did converts continue to mix with their former co-religionists because access to purely Christian circles was blocked? In those cases where conversion was intended to achieve immediate, short-term goals, such as appointment to a university or civil service post (rather than full absorption into Christian society), did converts keep up old ties once their goal was accomplished, because it was easier than cultivating new ones, which

---

[7]Jacob Katz, *From Prejudice to Destruction. Anti-Semitism, 1700–1933*, Cambridge, MA 1980; Paul Lawrence Rose, *Revolutionary Antisemitism in Germany from Kant to Wagner*, Princeton 1990.
[8]Heinrich Heine to Moses Moser, 9th January 1826, in Hugo Bieber (ed.), *Heinrich Heine. A Biographical Anthology*, Philadelphia 1956, p. 205.
[9]Endelman, *op. cit., passim*.

required the dismantling of social barriers often more durable than legal ones? For, as noted earlier, the taint of Jewishness lingered long after conversion.

Interestingly, Jewish humour shared the widespread German perception that baptism was a charade, with little impact on the Jewishness of the Jew. Druyanov's collection includes over a dozen illustrations of this point, of which the following is typical. A Catholic priest converted a Jew on a Thursday. The next day – a Friday, when Catholics were forbidden to eat meat – he found him eating roast goose. The convert looked at the priest and, seeing that he was furious, said, "Don't worry, dear priest, this is fish." This made the priest even angrier. "It's not enough that you are a transgressor but you are also a liar." The convert replied: "God forbid, dear priest. I have simply done as you have done. You threw pure water on me and said, 'Until now you were a Jew; from now on, you are a Catholic.' I threw pure water on the goose and said to it, 'Until now you were a goose; from now on, you are a fish.' "[10]

Professor Hertz also reminds us that, however efficacious conversion was in occupational and social terms, some converts failed to break with their past at the psychological level. Like Heinrich Heine, they were unable to forget their Jewish origins and feel comfortable, at home, so to speak, in their new identity. In part, this was because the Gentile world would not allow them to do so; in part, because their own mental constitution refused to let go of earlier attachments. However, as the Jewish past receded, it became easier to enter the Christian world. Professor Hertz illustrates this point with reference to Abraham and Felix Mendelssohn. Abraham, the son of Moses Mendelssohn, experienced inner turmoil in having to repudiate his famous father's heritage, as the tortuous explanation for becoming Christian that he offered to his children testifies. His son Felix, on the other hand, was spared this kind of problem. He was not distressed by the presence of Jews in the family tree and rejected his father's entreaty to drop "Mendelssohn" from his surname. In Germany, it would seem, radical assimilation required two generations at a minimum to succeed. Its rewards were available in full only to the children and grandchildren of converts, not to the converts themselves.

If this – and other conclusions about the conversion experience made in these papers – are to be accepted, however, the range of evidence supporting them must be broadened. All three focus on the lives of a handful of educated, articulate Jews who moved in more or less privileged circles. Whether their experiences were representative of broader numbers of converts is an issue that remains unaddressed. In her work on the Jewish salons of old regime Berlin, Professor Hertz found, on the basis of quantitative evidence, how untypical the baptisms of salon-visiting Jews were. Of the 249 Jews who left the fold in Berlin in the three decades 1770–1799, two-thirds were children aged five years or younger; of the 134 whose fathers' occupations were indicated in the records she analysed, sixty per cent were from middle- to low-income families.[11] In nineteenth-century Warsaw, for which quantitative evidence is also available, the social origins of converts were equally diverse: forty-seven per cent of those

[10]Druyanov, *op. cit.*, vol. II, p. 138.
[11]Deborah Hertz, *Jewish High Society in Old Regime Berlin*, New Haven–London 1988, pp. 232–234.

whose occupation was recorded at the time of their baptism were artisans, shopkeepers, petty traders and unskilled workers.[12] This then leaves us to wonder whether the insights and observations of Professors Carlebach, Hertz and Levenson would have been different if they had examined a broader range of lives and careers.

---

[12]Todd M. Endelman, with the assistance of Magdalena Sekutowska, 'Jewish Converts in Nineteenth-Century Warsaw. A Quantitative Analysis' (in progress).

German Jews in the Age of Emancipation

Mendelssohn and "Mendelssohn's Disciples"
A Re-examination

BY SHMUEL FEINER

In the fifth chapter of his impressive biography of Mendelssohn, the most comprehensive to date, Alexander Altmann introduces Mendelssohn's disciples, who in his view became a cohesive group from the 1770s onwards. Altmann describes them in order of their arrival at Mendelssohn's Berlin "court". They were the physician Marcus Herz (1747–1803), a student of Kant and husband of the famous *salonnière* Henriette; David Friedländer (1750–1834), a wealthy member of the Jewish élite; Isaak Satanow (1732–1805), a teacher, printer and writer from Poland; and Salomon Dubno (1738–1813), who was the Hebrew teacher of Mendelssohn's son, Joseph, and who encouraged Mendelssohn to publish his German translation of the Pentateuch. Later arrivals were the Hebrew poet Naphtali Herz Wessely (1725–1805); Baruch Schik of Shklov (1740–1812), a member (*dayan*) of the rabbinic court in Minsk; Naphtali Herz Homberg (1749–1841), also a private teacher in the Mendelssohn household; Aaron Zechariah Friedenthal of Jaroslav, a participant in the *Biur* enterprise, who was to return to Galicia to teach in the new Jewish schools; the physician Isaac Joel from Halberstadt (1747–1813), who apparently had hoped that Mendelssohn would help him find work in Berlin; the Lithuanian-German philosopher Salomon Maimon (1754–1800); Joel Brill-Loewe (1760–1802) and Isaac Abraham Euchel (1758–1804), private teachers and editors of the Hebrew journal *Hame'asef*.[1]

The historical reconstruction based on this model of a master and twelve faithful disciples, who spread his word among the people, assumes the unmediated attachment of these disciples to their teacher as the sole binding criterion between them. In the eyes of the historian, it is this relationship that turns them into a group and circle of *maskilim*. Consequently, Altmann thought it pertinent to present them according to the sequence of their first meeting with Mendelssohn. He eventually concedes that the group was not homogeneous and that their historical association is mainly based on their having visited Mendelssohn on a regular basis. But although without this connection there would be no clear common denominator among them, Altmann states that Mendelssohn became

---

[1]Alexander Altmann, *Moses Mendelssohn. A Biographical Study*, Philadelphia 1973, chap. 5. Altmann added the Vilna physician and writer Jehuda Hurwitz (a typical early Eastern European *Haskalah* figure) and Avigdor Levi of Glogau, who lived in Prague and corresponded with Mendelssohn.

the acknowledged leader of a group of *maskilim* who became the proponents of the *Haskalah*.

In this manner, Mendelssohn's most eminent biographer follows a long historiographical tradition which is also part of the Jewish collective memory of the modern era, identifying the *Haskalah* in general, and that of the eighteenth century in particular, as the product of the leadership of the "Jewish Socrates". According to this tradition, Mendelssohn founded and led the movement, raising a phalanx of followers – "Mendelssohn's disciples" – who continued in his footsteps and disseminated his teachings. This concept of Mendelssohn is based on the generalised assumption that the *Haskalah* as an historical movement in the history of the Jewish people can, or even should, focus upon the distinguished and mythological figure of the philosopher Moses Mendelssohn. Hence, the thoughts and activities of the "disciples" exist only by virtue of Mendelssohn's dominant personality, are overshadowed by him and therefore are only of marginal significance; they do not stand independently in the historical reconstruction, but are contingent on their relation to the teacher. Were the disciples faithful followers? How did they spread his teachings? Did any of them deviate from these teachings, and if so, why? These are the central questions as long as the focus is on the figure of the teacher, the "father of the *Haskalah*".

Another conclusion which can be derived from the historical model of "Mendelssohn's disciples" is to identify his circle as both the creators and the progeny of the *Haskalah* movement in Germany in the eighteenth century. The well-known Enlightenment historian Peter Gay defined the members of the eighteenth-century European Enlightenment as a "little flock of philosophs" with common goals, and he tried to reconstruct their "family ties" and relations. At the same time Gay broadened its scope considerably. He portrayed the Enlightenment movement as an army arrayed under a common flag: a hard core of philosophers, organised into different brigades, and a reading public which together constituted "the literary republic" of the Enlightenment.[2] On the other hand, the Jewish Enlightenment was depicted as a *beit midrash* for *maskilim* with a curriculum of studies that deviated from the traditional religious curriculum, as a kind of *yeshiva* or *Hasidic* court assembled around a rabbi or a *zaddik* – in this case a *maskil* philosopher – with students, thirsting for knowledge, sitting at his feet.

The model of "Mendelssohn's disciples" gave rise to a number of historical conclusions about the nature of the *Haskalah*. The first attributes the entire *Haskalah* enterprise and its ideas to a single source of inspiration and guidance. "The first pioneers of the *Haskalah*", wrote Simon Dubnow, "came mainly from Mendelssohn's circle."[3] Simon Bernfeld was even able to describe, without

---

[2]Peter Gay, *The Enlightenment. An Interpretation*, vol. I, *The Rise of Modern Paganism*, New York 1966, pp. 3–19.
[3]Simon Dubnow, *History of the Jews*, 4 vols., transl. by M. Spiegel, vol. IV, New York 1971, p. 343.

attempting to hide the analogy with a *Hasidic* court, exactly how "Mendelssohn would usually sit on his chair, with his young companions gathered about hanging on his every word. They considered each sound uttered from his mouth as [one would] a prophecy . . . seeking his advice as one would from an oracle."[4] In order to overcome the biographical hurdle (as it is known that some of those in Mendelssohn's circle were his age or older, it would be difficult to classify them as his "disciples"), sometimes a distinction was made between a "disciple-colleague", like Wessely, and "disciples", like the younger *maskilim*.[5]

Another implication of the model of "Mendelssohn and his disciples" was the development of a picture of historical continuity: the *Haskalah* was recorded as a movement established by Mendelssohn, which after his death passed into the hands of David Friedländer. This "disciple" maintained the direction of the movement, though with quite a few changes, helped by a number of young *maskilim*. Together they transmitted the Mendelssohnian *Haskalah* tradition to the following generations.[6]

Beginning with Perez Smolenskin – Mendelssohn's most formidable critic deriving from his national anti-*Haskalah* stance – and ranging from the more moderate Bernfeld to the Mendelssohn-revering Heinrich Graetz, and even to twentieth-century historians, the *Haskalah*, identified with the teachings of Mendelssohn, was perceived as playing a crucial role in most of the modernisation processes in nineteenth-century Ashkenazic Jewry in Germany, and to a certain extent also in Eastern Europe.[7] The Reform movement, acculturation to the Gentile environment, emancipation, the disregard of *Halakhah* and the *mitzvot*, assimilation and the blurring of Jewish national uniqueness were all seen, for better or worse, as stemming directly from Mendelssohn's teachings. In this regard there is general agreement, but opinions are divided over the consequences. Some see these developments as Mendelssohn's "rotten fruit", an attitude which, paradoxically, secular Nationalists and the Orthodox – both

---

[4]Simon Bernfeld, *Dor Tahapuchot*, vol. I, Warsaw 1914, p. 11. See also Tsemah Tsamriyon, *Moshe Mendelssohn Vehaidiologia shel Hahaskalah*, Tel Aviv 1985, pp. 104–105; David Sorkin, 'From Context to Comparison. The German *Haskalah* and Reform Catholicism', in *Tel Aviver Jahrbuch für deutsche Geschichte*, 20 (1991), p. 33.
[5]Heinz M. Graupe, *The Rise of Modern Judaism. An Intellectual History of German Jewry, 1650–1942*, New York 1978, chap. 10.
[6]Simon Bernfeld, *Toledot ha-Reformatsyon ha-Datit Be-Yisrael*, Cracow 1900, p. 31: "After the Rambeman's [Rabbi Moses son of Menahem] death David Friedländer was the leader of a small community of *maskilim* in Berlin and all the Prussian cities." See also Michael A. Meyer, *The Origins of the Modern Jew*, Detroit 1979, chap. 3; David Sorkin, *The Transformation of German Jewry, 1780–1840*, New York–Oxford 1987, pp. 73–78.
[7]Shmuel Feiner, 'Kfirato shel Smolenskin Bahaskalah Veshorshei Hahistoriographia Hayehudit Haleumit', in *Zionism*, 16 (1991), pp. 9–31; Joseph Klausner, *Historia shel Hasifrut Haivrit Hahadasha*, vol. V, Jerusalem 1959, pp. 101–124; Isaac Eisenstein-Barzilay, 'Smolenskin's Polemic Against Mendelssohn in Historical Perspective', in *Proceedings of the American Academy for Jewish Research*, 53 (1986), pp. 11–48; Bernfeld, *Dor Tahapuchot*, vol. I, *op. cit.*, p. 127; Heinrich Graetz, *Geschichte der Juden von den ältesten Zeiten bis auf die Gegenwart*, 11 vols., 2nd edn., Leipzig 1863–1900, vol. XI, pp. 1–92.

mitnagdim and *hasidim* – could share.⁸ Others praise the Mendelssohnian heritage, believing that his teachings have brought about the development of self-awareness and a positive rejection of tradition and the ghetto.

Other conclusions, derived from the concept of "Mendelssohn's disciples", were used to overcome the apparent contradiction between Mendelssohn's adherence to Jewish religious precepts and his unswerving loyalty to Jewish society on the one hand, and on the other the patterns of social and cultural assimilation, calls for religious reforms and deism of some of his "disciples". One way of solving the problem is the *"Haskalah* conspiracy" theory, according to which Mendelssohn was actually a good deal more radical than he displayed in public. Graetz, for example, believed that his disciples "completed openly and in a high-handed manner what Ben-Menahem had worked for slowly and quietly".⁹ From here it can be inferred that Mendelssohn's Berlin circle had been engaged in contriving a clandestine plan, the radical disciples had learned the hidden agenda and had the courage to put it into practice.¹⁰ Another possible solution is what may be referred to as the "second step" theory, whereby "his disciples only had to draw the later conclusions and eliminate the apparent duplicity".¹¹ After Mendelssohn had concluded in his philosophical distinctions that reason was superior to revealed religion, disciples such as Friedländer, Lazarus Bendavid or Saul Ascher could relatively easily – even if they were critical of their master's teachings as was Ascher – take an extra step and eliminate the obligation to fulfil the practical *mitzvot*. Historians who accept the "second step" theory assume that even if Friedländer, for instance, deviated from the path of his great teacher, as is obvious in his well-known 1799 letter to Probst Wilhelm Teller, he none the less acted in a way consistent with the essence of Mendelssohn's teachings. In Friedländer, "the logic of Mendelssohn came to its

---

⁸In contrast to the admiration of Graetz see the hostile attitude of Rabbi Baruch Halevi Epstein of Pinsk: "And so it is, such is the teaching of Mendelssohn and this is its fruit! Crisis, destruction and censure of the transmitted Torah and all of Judaism! . . . Ah, how many souls have been torn away from us and how many families uprooted from within us by the teachings of this awful teacher." Baruch Halevi Epstein, *Mekor Baruch*, pt. 2, Vilna 1928, p. 1050, see also pp. 1028–1033 (in Hebrew). The same negative attitude is to be found in the hasidic tradition. According to Rabbi Yosef Yitzhak Schneersohn, the founder of hasidism, Rabbi Israel ben Eliezer said of Mendelssohn and his disciples: "And the Satan nourishes him and lets him be successful, for he chose him to divert Israel with false beliefs." *Divrei Hayamim Hahem. As copied from the notes of Yosef Schneersohn of Lubavitch*, Jerusalem 1964, pp. 9–10 (in Hebrew). See also Israel Bartal, 'Shimon ha-Kofer. A Chapter in Orthodox Historiography', in *idem*, C. Turniansky and E. Mendelssohn (eds.), *Studies in Jewish Culture in Honour of Chone Shmeruk*, Jerusalem 1993, pp. 243–268 (in Hebrew).

⁹The quotation is based on the Hebrew translation of Graetz, *Divrei Yemei Ha-Yehudim*, transl. by Y.A. Trivash, vol. IX, Warsaw 1914, facs. Jerusalem 1972, p. 95. Compare with Graetz, *Geschichte der Juden, op. cit.*, vol. XI, p. 119.

¹⁰The "conspiracy" theory had already appeared in the fourth volume of Perez Smolenskin's 1876 Hebrew novel, *Hato'e Bedarkei Ha-Hayim*, vol. IV, Warsaw 1910, pp. 60–61: "But he sowed his seed clandestinely and he knew how to hide it and it struck a fertile root and a wormwood shoot . . . all his sons and all his daughters . . . were the greatest enemies of our people". Compare with the positive attitude towards Mendelssohn in Meir Hildesheimer, 'Moses Mendelssohn in Nineteenth-Century Rabbinical Literature', in *Proceedings of the American Academy for Jewish Research*, 55 (1988), pp. 79–133. See also Zeew Jawitz, the Orthodox historian and moderate *maskil*, who argued that there was a total break between Mendelssohn and those "dishonest disciples" who "overcooked his fine stew", *Knesset Yisrael*, vol. I, *Migdal Hameah*, Warsaw 1886, pp. 100–101.

¹¹Raphael Mahler, *Divrei yemei Yisrael dorot Haronim*, vol. I, Merhavia 1954, pp. 150–151.

necessary conclusion once the attachment to the ceremonial law was lost". In the case of Saul Ascher, in his 1792 work *Leviathan*, the "second step" led him to conclude, through a critical-philosophical discussion developed from Kantian concepts, on the dualism he had discovered in Mendelssohn's teachings.[12]

The roots of the term "Mendelssohn's disciples" go well beyond historiography. They developed in the concepts and self-image of the *maskilim* themselves, who traced their spiritual lineage to Mendelssohn and praised him abundantly. As Moshe Pelli has shown, the *maskilim*, in the pages of the Hebrew journal *Hame'asef*, constructed a model of Mendelssohn and his disciples that paralleled that of the Torah rabbi. They lamented his death as one would that of a *zaddik*; they perceived themselves as Mendelssohn's followers and were therefore obliged to preserve his teachings and follow his lead.[13] Mendelssohn was the source of their inspiration and they nurtured the myth of him as "the great light", God's emissary and the saviour of his people.[14] A marble bust of Mendelssohn was sculpted as early as 1785 by Jean Pierre Antoine Tassaert and placed in the board room of the Jewish *Freischule* in Berlin by the *Hevrat Hinuch Ne'arim* (Society for Youth Education).[15] David Friedländer, who constantly described himself as *the* disciple, probably went further than anyone else when he put in his will that this sentiment be engraved on his tombstone.[16] The last editors of *Hame'asef*, Aaron Wolfsohn and Joel Brill-Loewe, accepted Friedländer's charge willingly, and in a paean of praise composed in 1794 they described him as the defender of Mendelssohn's heritage, his successor and faithful follower:

"He sat in his shadow . . . there he gathered the treasures of wisdom . . . as the suckler of nectar from the breast, you sucked from his wisdom, there you learned

---

[12]Meyer, *op. cit.*, p. 73; Michael Graetz, 'Toda'a Yehudit Hadasha Bereshit Hitgabshuta Bedor Talmidei Mendelssohn - Saul Ascher', in *Mehkarim Betoldot Am Yisrael Ve'eretz Yisrael*, vol. IV, Haifa 1976, pp. 219–237 (in Hebrew): "Ascher did not reject Mendelssohn's distinction [between 'law' and 'eternal truths'] but tried to combine them in a consistent manner in the conceptual system of a mainly Kantian general philosophy, while employing the historical-dynamical dimension that was absent in Mendelssohn." (p. 222).

[13]Moshe Pelli, 'Demuto shel Mendelssohn Kefi Shehi Mishtakefet Bereshita shel Sifrut Hahaskalah Begermania', in *Proceedings of the Fifth World Congress for Jewish Studies*, vol. III, Jerusalem 1972, pp. 269–282.

[14]A *maskil* who called himself "Amitai the Samaritan" spoke of his conversion to *Haskalah* as follows: "Indeed, I became a different person after the light of the great lights of the wise of the generation, the scholar R' Moses of Dessau, may his light shine, and the patron R' Naphtali Herz Wessely shone upon me." *Hame'asef*, III (1786), p. 87. Euchel's biography of Mendelssohn, published shortly after his death, served for many years as the *maskilim*'s canon and was a kind of hagiography for a "secular saint". Isaac Euchel, *Toldot Rabbenu he-Hakham Moshe Ben Menahem* (1788), Vienna 1814.

[15]*Hame'asef*, V (1789), p. 51. On the Mendelssohn myth in German Jewry see Max Freudenthal, *Zum Zweihundertjährigen Geburtstag Moses Mendelssohns*, Berlin 1929; Alexander Altmann, 'Moses Mendelssohn as the Archetypal German Jew', in Jehuda Reinharz and Walter Schatzberg (eds.), *The Jewish Response to German Culture. From the Enlightenment to the Second World War*, Hanover–London 1985, pp. 17–31.

[16]The epitaph on the tombstone in the Jewish cemetery in Schönhauser Allee, as quoted in Immanuel Ritter, *David Friedländer. Sein Leben und Wirken*, vol. II, Berlin 1861, p. 174: "Grabstätte David Friedländers, geb. in Königsberg, 6. Dezbr. 5511, Des edlen Joachim Moses Friedländers Sohn, treuer Schüler und Freund des weltweisen Moses Mendelssohn, gest. Berlin 25. Dezbr. 5595."

well, happy are you, David, that you kept his precepts, pleased are we with you, his picture is before us."[17]

This self-image of "Mendelssohn's disciples" penetrated into Eastern Europe in the nineteenth century, and a hundred years after his death the *maskil* Abraham Bär Gottlober declared that all *maskilim* were Mendelssohn's disciples, and "if not for the Rambeman [Rabbi Moses the son of Menahem] of blessed memory . . . none of us would be".[18]

The dominant colours of this historical picture of the *Haskalah* in Germany are those of Moses Mendelssohn, his personality and teachings determining its nature and ideas, while the image of the other *maskilim* is rather blurred. They seem to confirm and sustain the myth of Mendelssohn as the patron of modern German Jewry, and perhaps of the entire Modern Era of Jewish history.[19] Be that as it may, attributing the founding and leadership of an ideology and an historical movement to Mendelssohn in terms reminiscent of the Polish-Lithuanian "disciples" of the Ba'al Shem Tov, the Maggid, and of the Vilna Gaon, is out of place in the case of the *Haskalah*. The issue needs to be re-examined in a manner not influenced by historical tradition and the Mendelssohnian myth. In addition the contemporary historiographical pattern of giving more weight than hitherto to secondary figures should be followed. This is especially applicable to the *Haskalah*, where they played an important, even crucial, role. This pattern liberates us from the all-embracing model of "Mendelssohn's disciples" and allows us to reconsider the hegemony of the "father of the *Haskalah*".[20] By doing so, a number of relatively anonymous secondary characters come to the fore and a complete reconstruction of the *Haskalah* can be undertaken.

I

The twelve members of Mendelssohn's circle mentioned above constitute only a small part of the *maskilim* of the last third of the eighteenth century. Some of them had only a passing acquaintance with Mendelssohn, were neither permanent residents of Berlin nor of any of the German states, and can be defined only with

---

[17] Aaron Wolfsohn, 'Shirim al Yom Huledet Hahakham R' David Friedländer', in *Hame'asef*, VII, Booklet I (1794), pp. 14–19.
[18] Abraham Bär Gottlober, 'Et La'akor Natua', in *Haboker Or*, 1 (1876), pp. 232–233. See also Shmuel Feiner, *Hahaskalah Beyahasa Lahistoria – Hakarat He'avar Vetifkudo Betnuat Hahaskalah Hayehudit, 1782–1881*, Ph.D. diss., Hebrew University Jerusalem 1990, p. 270.
[19] Altmann, 'Moses Mendelssohn as the Archetypal German Jew', *loc. cit.*
[20] On this pattern in Enlightenment historiography see Roy Porter, *The Enlightenment*, New Hampshire–London 1990, chap. 5; Robert Darnton, 'In Search of the Enlightenment. Recent Attempts to Create a Social History of Ideas', in *Journal of Modern History*, 43 (1973), pp. 113–132. As to the attempts to estimate the dimensions and social characteristics of the "carrier stratum" (*Trägerschicht*) of the *Aufklärung* in Germany see Franklin Kopitzsch, *Aufklärung, Absolutismus und Bürgertum in Deutschland*, Munich 1976, pp. 59–60; and Shmuel Feiner, 'Isaac Euchel, "Entrepreneur" of the Haskalah Movement in Germany', in *Zion*, vol. LII, No. 4 (1987), pp. 427–469 (in Hebrew).

difficulty as *maskilim*. The attempt to portray them as a united group of disciples is largely artificial. The "group" included members of two generations such as Naphtali Herz Wessely, who was fifty-five in 1780 and therefore four years older than the master, and Joel Brill-Loewe, who was only twenty-eight. Baruch Schik of Shklov, for instance, did not belong to the group at all because he was only in Berlin for a few months in 1777, when he published his Hebrew scientific essays.[21] Isaac Euchel, even though he had lived in Berlin for a number of years in his youth, arrived at Mendelssohn's "court" only as a visitor on his way from Königsberg to the city of his birth, Copenhagen, in 1784. Euchel was an active *maskil* without any "disciple" connection to Mendelssohn. By the time he arrived in Berlin he was already well-known in *maskil* circles and was an accomplished writer and *Haskalah* organiser. Hence his warm reception, the accolades of Mendelssohn, Wessely and others and the poems of praise that were transcribed in his travel journal.[22] The physician Isaac Joel from Halberstadt, armed with a letter of recommendation from Immanuel Kant, paid a visit to Mendelssohn but returned to his position as the Königsberg community's burial-society doctor. He is not known to have contributed to the Jewish *Haskalah*.[23] Neither from their world view nor from the character of their writings could Salomon Dubno or Baruch Schik be called *maskilim*. At most they were representatives of an early *Haskalah*, learned in Jewish sources, with a knowledge of the Hebrew language and science. Yet they lacked the outlook that would give their endeavours that new quality of *Haskalah*.[24] Salomon Maimon passed through the Berlin *maskil* circle and Mendelssohn's home, but went from there to the wider world of philosophy. By the 1790s he was far removed from the *maskilim* and Jewish society.[25]

None of them met all the others for the simple reason that they were never at Mendelssohn's home at the same time. The most significant encounter apparently happened in the *Biur* enterprise when Dubno, Wessely, Homberg and Friedenthal came together. But it is by no means clear if the meetings were coordinated or if each wrote the section of the *Biur* apportioned to him by Dubno and Mendelssohn.[26] Among the twelve "disciples" only four, Friedländer, Herz, Satanow and Wessely, lived consistently in Berlin in proximity to the Mendelssohnian "court". Moreover, it is somewhat unlikely that anything more than a

---

[21]David Fishman, 'A Polish Rabbi meets the Berlin *Haskalah*. The Case of R. Baruch Schick', in *Association for Jewish Studies Review*, 12 (1987), pp. 95–121.

[22]Feiner, 'Isaac Euchel', *loc. cit.*, pp. 444–445. See the letter of recommendation Mendelssohn wrote for Euchel to his brothers-in-law Moses Fürst and Joseph Gugenheim in Copenhagen on 15th June 1784, in Moses Mendelssohn, *Gesammelte Schriften*, Jubiläumsausgabe (*JubA*), vol. XIX, Stuttgart 1974, p. 294.

[23]Details about him may be found in Hans-Jürgen Krüger, *Die Judenschaft von Königsberg in Preussen, 1700–1812*, Marburg 1966 (Wissenschaftliche Beiträge zur Geschichte und Landeskunde Ost- und Mitteleuropas 76), p. 93.

[24]For another way of examining them and their identification as representatives of an "orthodox *Haskalah*" see the studies of David Sorkin, especially 'From Context to Comparison', *loc. cit.*, p. 29–33.

[25]*Salomon Maimons Lebensgeschichte. Von ihm selbst geschrieben (1792–1793)*, ed. by Octavia Winkler, Berlin 1988.

[26]Peretz Sandler, *Ha-Biur la-Torah shel Moshe Mendelssohn ve-Siato*, Jerusalem 1984.

patron-like relationship developed between such figures as the wealthy and famous Dr. Herz, a disciple of Kant, frequenter of the salons of Berlin high society, author of articles for important contemporary German journals, who gave courses at his home in physics and philosophy, and the destitute and ascetic Podolian *maskil* Satanow, whose life was dedicated to writing and printing Hebrew essays.

So much for the twelve "disciples" mentioned by Altmann. But who were the other *maskilim*? Who really constituted the eighteenth-century *Haskalah* movement? These questions have been asked about the European Enlightenment, but have hardly been dealt with in the context of the Jewish Enlightenment.[27] The fact is that apart from about twenty relatively well-known figures, our information about the *maskilim* is rather sketchy. Usually, two factors are applied to gauge the strength, scope and geographical extent of the *Haskalah*: the number of subscribers to the *Biur* and to *Hame'asef*.[28] However, of the 492 *Biur* subscribers, 172 lived outside the German states and 21 were Christians. These were the adherents of the *Haskalah*, described by the *maskilim* as "contributors", who were meant to render financial support. The *maskilim* distinguished between them and the scholars who actually developed and spread the *Haskalah*.[29] The merchants, bankers, industrialists and doctors of the Jewish élite and their families comprised the *Bildungsbürgertum* or *aufgeklärtes Bürgertum*, the target audience of the *Hochdeutsch* translation of the Pentateuch; but they were not necessarily those who had initiated or were the "creators" of the *Haskalah*. Nor were the eight rabbis who subscribed to the *Biur* among the *maskilim* or "Mendelssohn's disciples".[30] The same holds for the 295 *Hame'asef* subscribers in the years 1785 to 1788, who ordered a total of 318 copies, though some *maskilim* were part of this group as members of the *Hevrat Doreshei Leshon 'Ever* (Society for the Promotion of the Hebrew Language), which included writers who contributed articles. The editors contended that the number of subscribers was greater since the published subscription list was incomplete.[31] This was certainly the case with Euchel's translation of the *siddur*, published in Königsberg in 1786. Euchel's Latin-

[27] Porter, *op. cit.*, pp. 42–50.
[28] For an excellent study analysing the *Biur*'s subscribers see Steven M. Lowenstein, 'The Readership of Mendelssohn's Bible Translation', in *Hebrew Union College Annual*, 52 (1982), pp. 170–213.
[29] A clear distinction between the supporters and the *maskilim* was made by the *Hevrat Shoharei Hatov Vehatushia* (Society for the Propagation of Goodness and Virtue), in *Tavnit Hevrat Shoharei Hatov Vehatushia*, Königsberg–Berlin 1787. Compare also Lowenstein's clear distinction: "On the whole, the wealthy were the protectors and patrons of the Enlightenment rather than the creative spirits." Steven M. Lowenstein, 'Jewish Upper Crust and the Berlin Jewish Enlightenment. The Family of Daniel Itzig', in Francis Malino and David Sorkin (eds.), *From East and West. Jews in a Changing Europe, 1750–1870*, Oxford 1991, p. 187. See also *idem*, *The Berlin Jewish Community. Enlightenment, Family and Crisis, 1770–1830*, Oxford 1994.
[30] Hildesheimer, *loc. cit.*, pp. 102–103.
[31] The data is based on the lists of subscribers that appeared in *Hame'asef* between 1785–1788. Compare Walter Röll, 'The Kassel *Hame'asef* of 1799', in Reinharz and Schatzberg (eds.), *op. cit.*, pp. 32–50, esp. pp. 34–37. The German journals of that time had a distribution of 1,000–2,000 copies or more. See also Horst Möller, *Aufklärung in Preussen. Der Verleger, Publizist und Geschichtsschreiber Christoph Friedrich Nicolai*, Berlin 1974, pp. 203–204. Compare the data on the *Encyclopédie* subscribers in France in Robert Darnton, *The Business of Enlightenment*, Cambridge–London 1979, pp. 287–294.

character translation had a pre-publication subscription list of 188 men and women, while Friedländer's Hebrew-character translation had 416 subscribers. About ten per cent of the subscribers of both editions were women whose education and degree of acculturation convinced the translators that it was necessary to prepare a proper translation of the *siddur*. The German translation, in Hebrew characters, of the five *megillot*, published by Aaron Wolfsohn and Joel Brill-Loewe in 1789, had 384 subscribers, but the best-seller was Mendelssohn's translation of the *Psalms*, printed in 1791 with Brill-Loewe's commentary. It had a pre-publication list of 705 subscribers who ordered a total of 1,013 copies. These subscribers, and even the *Hame'asef* subscribers, benefited from the creativity and literary initiative of the *maskilim*, but at most they were no more than supporters of the *Haskalah*.[32]

The group of *maskilim* one encounters when entering the inner circle of "the family of *maskilim*" – writers, initiators, agents – was relatively small, yet much greater than that portrayed by the model of "Mendelssohn's disciples". A collective portrait has yet to be painted, but even at this stage some of its "unknown sons" can be depicted. In the main, they were far removed from Mendelssohn's "court" and were not direct "disciples"; but they were the true proponents and activists of the *Haskalah*.

Simon BaRaZ of Königsberg was one of the most diligent and enthusiastic members of the *Hevrat Doreshei Leshon 'Ever* and he took part in *Hame'asef* until his untimely death in 1787.[33] David Hannover was a faithful reader of this journal while still in his teens. He yearned to join the *Hevrat Shoharei Hatov Vehatushia* (Society for the Propagation of Goodness and Virtue) and bypass the hurdles placed in his path by teachers and relatives who tried to prevent his deviating from the traditional religious curriculum. Meanwhile, he was forced to content himself with writing commentaries on particularly difficult scriptural passages and poems that he sent from Hanover to the editorial board in Berlin.[34] David Theodore, a native of Altschottland near Danzig, who began studying medicine in 1779 at the University of Königsberg, was a member of the *Hevrat Shoharei Hatov Vehatushia*, participated in *Hame'asef* and was an agent and bookseller for the printing house of the *Hevrat Hinuch Ne'arim*, the *Orientalische Buchdruckerei*.[35] At the end of the 1780s Gedaliah Moshe, the son of the rabbi of Obrasitzka in western Poland, continued the *Biur* project by translating and writing a commentary on the weekly portion of the Prophets (*haftara*) for the *Hevrat Shoharei*

---

[32]Isaac Euchel, *Gebete der hochdeutschen und polnischen Juden*, Königsberg 1786; David Friedländer, *Gebete der Juden auf das ganze Jahr*, Berlin 1786 (Hebrew letters); *Hamesh Megilot im Tirgum Ashkenazi Ubiur. Hevi'um Ledfus al yedei Aharon Ben-Wolf Umerehu Yoel Brill, Haverim Lehevrat Shoharei Hatov Vehatushia*, Berlin 1789; Joel Brill-Loewe, *Sefer Tehilim. Zmirot Yisrael*, Berlin 1791. As to the intention that the prayerbooks were meant for women, compare Chone Shmeruk, *Sifrut Yiddish. Prakim Letoldoteha*, Tel Aviv 1978, pp. 149–152.

[33]*Hame'asef*, IV (1788), p. 43.

[34]1782 letter of David Hannover, *Hame'asef*, VII, Booklet 1 (1794), pp. 9–14: "It has been three years since I tore the ropes that bound my arms; I broke down the heavy doors that were placed over my heart . . . and sought out the scholars of science and the seekers of justice, lovers of wisdom; towards the lovers of honesty ran I; I plucked ripe ears of corn from the gardens that they planted; I said I will lie in their shadow, and I found peace!"

[35]Krüger, *op. cit.*, pp. 95–96.

Hatov Vehatushia. He served as a teacher in Stockholm and in 1805 became headmaster of the school in Copenhagen modelled after the Berlin *Freischule*. None the less, it is by no means clear if he ever set foot in Berlin.[36] Judah Loeb Ben-Ze'ev, who served an important role as writer and proof-reader in printing houses in a number of *Haskalah* centres, arrived in Berlin only after Mendelssohn's death. He later worked in Potsdam and Breslau before settling in Vienna.[37] Menahem Mendel Breslau, who was one of the founders of the *Hevrat Doreshei Leshon 'Ever* in Königsberg and the joint chief editor of *Hame'asef* along with Euchel, as well as a teacher and educator whose main literary output was of a didactic nature (for example Hebrew language textbooks), returned to Breslau in 1796. As far as we know, he never reached Mendelssohn's "court".[38] On the other hand, the twenty-four-year-old Baruch Lindau did join the *maskilim* in response to the call of their 1783 manifesto 'Nahal Habesor'. He moved to Berlin from his native Hanover, worked as a private tutor, occasionally wrote poems and Hebrew-language articles on science and in 1789 served as the secretary of the *Hevrat Shoharei Hatov Vehatushia*.[39] Hayim Keslin, a Berlin-born teacher whose main vocation was the Hebrew language, lived in Hamburg and Stettin.[40] Josel Pick of Reichenau in Bohemia was employed by Mendelssohn as his children's private tutor after Homberg resigned in 1782. Pick later left Berlin for Breslau, where he was also employed as a private tutor. In both cities Pick was a member of the *Hevrat Doreshei Leshon 'Ever* and the *Hevrat Shoharei Hatov Vehatushia* and served as an agent for the books of the *maskilim*.[41] Shabbetai of Yanov was the administrative director of the *Orientalische Buchdruckerei*.[42] Dr. Shlomo Schönemann, Isaak Satanow's son, was a physician in Driesen. He wrote popular science articles on chemistry and published a new edition of Rabbi Moses Hajim Luzzatto's (Ramhal) *Praise unto the Righteous*.[43] Joseph BaRaN, a central figure

---

[36] Moses Shulvass, *From East and West. The Westward Migration of Jews from Eastern Europe during the Seventeenth and Eighteenth Centuries*, Detroit 1972; M. Rosenmann, *Isak Noa Mannheimer*, Vienna–Berlin 1922, pp. 24–25. The Copenhagen *Freischule* was established in 1805 on the initiative of Mendel Levin Nathanson. A similar proposal had already been raised in 1786 by Gottlob Euchel, *ibid.*, pp. 23–24.

[37] See Klausner, *op. cit.*, vol. I, pp. 178–190 and the bibliography.

[38] G. Kressel, *Lexicon Hasifrut Haivrit Badorot Ha'aharonim*, vol. I, Tel Aviv 1967, pp. 376–378; Moshe Pelli, *Bema'avakei Tmura. Iyunim Bahaskalah Haivrit Begermania Beshalhei Hamea Hayod het*, Tel Aviv 1988, pp. 167–174.

[39] Klausner, *op. cit.*, vol. I, pp. 191–192. See also his letter 'Igeret Lehabahur Hayakar R' Baruch Lindau Behanover Lehevrat Doreshei Leshon Ever', that appeared in *Hame'asef*, I (1784), pp. 75–76.

[40] Kressel, *op. cit.*, vol. II, pp. 784–785; and Hayim Keslin, *Maslul Bedikduk Lashon Hakodesh*, Hamburg 1788, which was published in about 20 more editions over a hundred years; *Kriyat HaTorah*, Berlin 1814 (in Hebrew).

[41] Altmann, *Moses Mendelssohn, op. cit.*, p. 724.

[42] Among other books he also published Naphtali Herz Wessely's *Ma'amar Hikkur Din*, Berlin 1788.

[43] *Hame'asef*, IV (1788), p. 84. See Pelli, *Bema'avakei Tmura, op. cit.*, pp. 90–91. Among the essays were: Dr. Shlomo Schönemann, *Khimiya. Oder Scheidkunst*, Berlin 1795; and Moses Hajim Luzzatto, *Layesharim Tehila. Shir Yedidut . . . Nidpas Bapa'am Hashlishit al yedei Harofe hamumhe Harabbani Hamufla Hahacham Schönemann Doktor*, Berlin 1799.

among the Berlin *maskilim*, a scholar, writer and translator, died at the age of twenty-four.[44]

II

The information currently available shows that there were about two hundred maskilim who in one way or another were affiliated with or active in the *Haskalah* either in a "productive" capacity or as agents, rather than as "supporters". About two-thirds lived in Germany, or at least had lived there for part of their lives, while the others lived elsewhere in Europe. The main centres were of course in Prussia – Berlin, Königsberg, Frankfurt a.d. Oder and Breslau – but there was also a *maskil* presence in Hamburg, Dessau, Hanover, Mainz, Cassel, Fürth, Frankfurt a. Main, Copenhagen, Prague, Vienna, Metz, Strasbourg, Amsterdam, Shklov and even Vilna.[45]

Mendelssohn's home was indeed a place of pilgrimage and a point of orientation for the admiring *maskilim*. It seems, however, that the young "*Haskalah* family" found its organisational framework and its direction without Mendelssohn's guidance. David Friedrichsfeld, for instance, who was sent to Berlin as a youth to study in one of its *batei hamidrash*, and in the 1770s was a protégé of Friedländer, Daniel Itzig and Veitel Heine Ephraim (who supported him financially), was indeed presented to Mendelssohn; but the circle Friedrichsfeld was closest to was that of Wessely. Thus Wessely, too, maintained a kind of *maskil* "court" where young men would visit on the Sabbath and Holidays to discuss language and literature. The first *maskil* society, the *Hevrat Doreshei Leshon 'Ever* (Society for the Promotion of the Hebrew Language) was actually organised in Königsberg in 1783, and not in Mendelssohn's Berlin. A few months later the society published the first issue of *Hame'asef*. Its initiators, foremost

---

[44]*Hame'asef*, VII, Booklet III (1796), pp. 274–275.
[45]The data is based on the collective biography composed by the author, using the criterion of active participation in *Haskalah* projects – members in the *maskil* societies, the *Hevrat Doreshei Leshon 'Ever* and the *Hevrat Shoharei Hatov Vehatushia*, authors of books and articles, especially active participants in *Hame'asef*, as well as agents and distributors of *Haskalah* books. Graetz, *Geschichte der Juden, op. cit.*, vol. XI, p. 140, estimated that after Mendelssohn's death there were about 100 young *maskilim* in Berlin alone, but this figure was based on the members of the *Gesellschaft der Freunde*, only some of whom were *maskilim*. On the *Haskalah* in Scandinavia see D. Simonsen, 'Mendelssohniana aus Dänemark', in *Festschrift zum siebzigsten Geburtstag Martin Philippsons*, Leipzig 1916, pp. 213–224; Kurt Wilhelm, 'The Influence of German Jewry on Jewish Communities in Scandinavia', in *LBI Year Book III* (1958), pp. 313–332. On the *Haskalah* in France see Jonathan I. Helfand, 'The Symbolic Relationship between French and German Jewry in the Age of Enlightenment', in *LBI Year Book XXIX* (1984), pp. 331–350; and Jay R. Berkovitz, *The Shaping of Jewish Identity in Nineteenth-Century France*, Detroit 1989, chap. 3. Cf. the data on the number of writers in France and Germany in the Enlightenment period: for Paris in the year 1750 434 writers, in Robert Darnton, *The Great Cat Massacre and other episodes in French cultural history*, London 1984, pp. 141–183, and according to Kopitzsch, *op. cit.*, pp. 60–61, about 5,000 writers in the German-speaking countries. See also Horst Möller, 'Wie aufgeklärt war Preussen?', in H.J. Puhle and H.U. Wehler (eds.), *Preussen im Rückblick*, Göttingen 1980, pp. 176–201.

among them Euchel, decided to establish a kind of Jewish reading society and a medium for publicising and communicating among the *maskilim*. The auspices and imprimatur they sought, however, were Wessely's, since they considered him to be their patron.[46] Nor was Mendelssohn actually involved in the initiative to establish the *Freischule* in Berlin and it is not known whether he belonged to that society.[47] One hundred and forty-five people, among them the wealthy as well as *maskilim*, responded to Isaak Satanow's 1786 call and established the *Hevrat Mazdike HaRabim* (Society of Righteousness to the Many), with the purpose of financing Hebrew book printing at the *Orientalische Buchdruckerei* for the *Hevrat Hinuch Ne'arim*. Friedländer and Isaac Daniel Itzig headed the new society. Only shortly before his death did Mendelssohn join this society.[48] The *Hevrat Mazdike HaRabim* merged with the *Hevrat Doreshei Leshon 'Ever* a year later and, again at Euchel's initiative, formed the *Hevrat Shoharei Hatov Vehatushia* as the umbrella organisation of the *maskilim*. The purpose of the new society was to foster various *Haskalah* enterprises, give monetary grants to writers and provide liaison among *maskilim* everywhere. They were called upon to organise local associations subordinate to the dual directorship in Berlin and Königsberg. The various associations appointed agents in many communities to promote the sale of books, most of which were printed at the *Orientalische Buchdruckerei*, and to solicit pre-publication subscriptions. A relatively large literary project was promoted from 1788–1791 when fifteen *maskilim* in different cities banded together to translate *Haftarot*, the weekly Sabbath readings from the Prophets.[49] Furthermore, there were local organisational initiatives: the *Gesellschaft der Brüder* in Breslau; the society that established the *Herzogliche Franzschule* in Dessau; a small group of seven men in Cassel at the end of the eighteenth century who published a kind of continuation of *Hame'asef* in manuscript form; a Jewish students' circle in Königsberg; and a group of wealthy Jews in Shklov with government connections, which supported a number of *maskil* scholars. There was also a circle of *maskilim* in Lemberg, composed of a group of teachers, during the years that Naphtali Herz Homberg was implementing the Austrian monarchy's enforced *Haskalah* programme in Galicia. The Prague *maskilim*, a number of whom maintained close ties with Berlin in the 1780s and 1790s,

---

[46]David Friedrichsfeld, *Zekher Tsadik*, Amsterdam 1809, introduction and p. 20; 'Nahal Habesor', published at the head of *Hame'asef*, I (1784). Josel Pick of Reichenau is mentioned there as living in Wessely's home.

[47]Compare Mordechai Eliav, *Ha-Hinukh Ha-Yehudi Be-Germanya Bi-Mei Ha-Haskalah Ve-ha-Emantsi-patsiya*, Jerusalem 1960, pp. 71–79.

[48]*Pinkas Ukhtav Hadat. Beyn Adat Havurat Matsdikei Harabim Asher Nadva Ruham Otam Latet Kesef Motsa, Lehadpis Sefarim Hadashim Im Yeshanim*, Berlin 1786. See also Feiner, 'Isaac Euchel', *loc. cit.*, p. 465.

[49]*Haftarot Mikol Hashana. Im Tirgum Ashkenazi Ubiur, Huva Lidfus al yedei Hevrat Shoharei Hatov Vehatushiya*, Berlin 1790–1791. David Friedländer's translation of the Yom Kippur morning service *Haftara* was published in 1788. The following *maskilim* took part in the project: Joel Brill-Loewe, Baruch Lindau, David Friedländer, Bunem Friedländer, Moses Friedländer, Joseph Abraham Friedländer, Abraham Ben David Friedländer, Elhanan Brill, Gottlob Euchel, David Theodore, Josel Pick, Gedaliah Moshe of Obrasitzka, Isaac Euchel, Aaron Wolfsohn and Jacob Z.B.

organised the short-lived *Gesellschaft der jungen Hebräer*.⁵⁰ The *maskilim* who belonged to these circles were far removed, in the main, from "neutral" frameworks such as the cafés frequented by scholars, the Berlin or Vienna high society salons, or other associations of German *maskilim*. Deborah Hertz, in her study of the salons, located only eight male Jews among the salon *habitués*; of these only Mendelssohn, Friedländer and Marcus Herz belonged to the *Haskalah*.⁵¹ Ten Jews participated in the German journal *Berlinische Monatschrift* between 1783–1796, forming three per cent of the contributors, who included Mendelssohn, Friedländer and Herz, the physicians Michal Friedländer, Oppenheimer, and Marcus Eliezer Bloch; and Salomon Maimon, Lazarus Bendavid, Saul Ascher and Moshe Wessely, the Hamburg merchant and brother of Naphtali Herz Wessely.⁵² The list of Jewish participants in the journal *Berlinisches Archiv der Zeit und ihres Geschmacks* in the last five years of the century shows a similar picture. Again we find Herz, Bendavid and Maimon, together with a Jewish musician, a designer of medals at the royal court, an apostate physician, and a man and woman who were representatives of salon society.⁵³ These *maskilim* sought to demonstrate their writing talents and earn their fame among the non-Jewish German public.

This fact leads to an interim conclusion concerning the character of the *Haskalah*: it was a broader and more varied phenomenon than implied by the term "Mendelssohn's disciples". Indeed, a society such as the *Gesellschaft der Freunde*, which emblazoned in its programme Mendelssohn's well known slogan, "Nach Wahrheit forschen, Schönheit lieben, Gutes wollen, das Beste tun", was not established to spread *Haskalah*. It gave social support to the bachelors in the Berlin and Königsberg Jewish communities and its main struggles were on the early burials issue. It was one of the first voluntary Jewish societies, which eventually became very common in German Jewry. It appears that Isaac Euchel, and for a few months Aaron Wolfsohn, were the only *maskil* writers in that society. Others such as Nathan Oppenheimer, Joseph Mendelssohn and Aaron Neo were merchants, bankers and businessmen who were not interested in

---

⁵⁰See Eliav, *op. cit.*, pp. 88–89; Feiner, 'Isaac Euchel', *loc. cit.*, pp. 464–465; M. Brann, *Geschichte der Gesellschaft der Brüder*, Breslau 1880; Ludwig Horowitz, 'Ein Bildungsverein an Ausgang des vorigen Jahrhunderts', in *Allgemeine Zeitung des Judentums* (1897), pp. 32–50; Röll, 'The Kassel *Hame'asef*', *loc. cit.*, pp. 439–441; *Hame'asef* of summer 1799, Manuscript Photocopies Department of the National and University Library in Jerusalem, No. 3092 (Strasbourg MSS 4040); Hillel J. Kieval, 'Caution's Progress. The Modernization of Jewish Life in Prague 1780–1830', in Jacob Katz (ed.), *Toward Modernity. The European Jewish Model*, New Brunswick–Oxford 1987, pp. 71–105; R. Kestenberg-Gladstein, *Neuere Geschichte der Juden in den böhmischen Ländern*, pt. 1, *Das Zeitalter der Aufklärung 1780–1830*, Tübingen 1969 (Schriftenreihe wissenschaftlicher Abhandlungen des Leo Baeck Instituts 18/1), pp. 191–195, 200–201; David E. Fishman, *Science, Enlightenment and Rabbinic Culture in Belorussian Jewry 1772–1804*, Ph.D. diss., Harvard University 1985, pp. 53–65; Mahler, *op. cit.*, vol. IV, pp. 150–151; Winkler (ed.), *Salomon Maimons Lebensgeschichte, op. cit.*, pp. 118–119; N.M. Gelber, 'Lvov', in *Encyclopedia shel Galuyot*, vol. IV, Jerusalem–Tel Aviv 1956, p. 188.

⁵¹Deborah Hertz, *Jewish High Society in Old Regime Berlin*, New Haven–London 1988, pp. 147–150.

⁵²Ursula Schulz, *Die Berlinische Monatsschrift 1783–1796. Eine Bibliographie*, Bremen 1968; Horst Möller, *Vernunft und Kritik. Deutsche Aufklärung im 17. und 18. Jahrhundert*, Frankfurt a. Main 1986, pp. 295–296; idem, *Aufklärung in Preussen, op. cit.*, pp. 246–254.

⁵³Günther and Ursula Schulz, *Das Berlinische Archiv der Zeit*, Bremen 1967; Jacob Toury, *Kavim Leheker Knisat Hayehudim Lahayim Haezrahiim Begarmania*, Tel Aviv 1972, p. 68.

fostering Hebrew literature.⁵⁴ Thus at the end of the century there were two sectors in the *Haskalah*. Members of the first group were active in neutral environments where they sought to make their mark. They were German-language writers who wrote for a non-Jewish audience with radical and deistic religious beliefs. Prominent among them were physicians and graduates of German universities, enlightened merchants who had received a modern education at the hands of private tutors, and members of the free professions. Virtually all of them were German-born and acculturated in German language and culture. The second group, on the other hand, engaged in *maskil* activities that were meant for Jews alone. Its members hardly ever appeared in the general German public and were active mainly in the Hebrew language – even if they advocated learning the language and culture of their country – and their attitude towards religion was moderate. If they were critical of religion, their appraisals were usually limited to superstitions, the rabbinic leadership (especially that of Poland), and to protesting against the emphasis on Torah study at the virtual exclusion of general knowledge and culture. Otherwise most of them hardly dealt with religious principles and *Halakhah*. Prominent in this category were the Hebrew writers and poets who served as private tutors in the homes of the wealthy.

The *Haskalah* connection of the first group was not in doubt. But they soon tried to push it into a new and radical stage, towards religious reforms and the swift acquisition of political rights. The abandonment of the Hebrew language and its readership were soon to follow. Their degree of acculturation to the German environment in the end led some of the members of this group to a break with the *maskilim*. A prominent example of this pattern is Salomon Maimon, who by the 1790s, the last decade of his life, was no longer involved in the Jewish sphere and in his philosophical essays no longer dealt with Jewish themes. Bendavid and Friedländer also shifted their attention to problems in the Jewish religion. Their target audience was no longer Jewish society, but mainly beyond, although it included Jews like themselves who had become acculturated enough to be recipients of German literature.

Others whose degree of acculturation was rather weak and whose culture was still embedded in Torah and the Jewish scholarly tradition, fostered the *Haskalah* – even if they had tried and partly succeeded in making their way into European culture. *Maskilim* of this second group were usually in their twenties and thirties. Mendelssohn, who was fifty-four and Wessely, who was fifty-eight when the *Hevrat Doreshei Leshon 'Ever* was established, were a generation older than the other society members, whose average age was about twenty-seven. Most of them were born in the 1750s and 1760s, but some were still in their teens when they joined the society. "For we are young", they said of themselves, "and many of us are preoccupied with our vocations in order to make a living, some engaged

---

⁵⁴L. Lesser, *Chronik der Gesellschaft der Freunde in Berlin*, Berlin 1842; Feiner, 'Isaac Euchel', *loc. cit.*, pp. 464–465; Henry Wasserman, *Yehudim, Burganut Ve 'Hevra Burganit' Beidan Liberali Begermania 1840–1880*, Ph.D. diss., The Hebrew University Jerusalem 1978, pp. 75–80.

in educating the youth and others in business."[55] Only a few were married, but official permission to marry was often connected to occupational and legal status. Only half of them were German-born, the others were immigrants from Poland who, like the Jewish *melamdim*, began leaving Poland well before the period of the *Haskalah*. Among these immigrants, even among the German-born, was a substantial number who for one reason or another had not been raised by their biological families. Joel Brill-Loewe apparently was born in Berlin and from the age of nine lived in the home of the wealthy banker Aaron Meyer Joresch, son-in-law of Veitel Heine Ephraim. At the age of thirteen, Euchel had been sent from Copenhagen to Berlin after his father's death to study Talmud under his uncle's supervision. Wolf Dessau also came to Berlin at the age of fifteen after his father's death, and David Friedrichsfeld was sent there to study after his father became impoverished. Others left home when they became dissatisfied with the traditional curriculum; they wanted to broaden their horizons and even to study at university. Such was the case not only of Salomon Maimon, but also of Moses Ensheim of Metz, Judah Loeb Ben-Ze'ev of Cracow and Aaron Friedenthal of Jaroslav.[56] This group belonged to the same stratum of society that produced the traditional scholarly élite. However, emigration to Germany, the acquisition of the German language (usually acquired autodidactically) and exposure to European culture altered their fate. Their youth and separation from their families led them to seek patrons who would employ them. Since they were intellectuals, though usually without a formal education, they worked as private tutors in German-Jewish homes. They were a new type of *melammed*, versed in Hebrew as well as in the traditional literature, but also in European languages and science. Euchel was a teacher in the households of the David family in Hanover and the Friedländer family in Königsberg, Ensheim taught mathematics to Mendelssohn's children, Homberg taught them Hebrew and Josel Pick succeeded him; Brill-Loewe also made his living as a teacher in David Friedländer's home. Some of the *maskilim* found work in the Hebrew printing houses of Berlin, Breslau, Vienna and Prague. Others changed their status from teacher to clerk in their patrons' businesses. In all cases, their employment earned them the right of residence in Germany, a limited right difficult to obtain for those not born into the rich élite families – even then the right of residence and marriage were subject to supervision and limitations. The *maskilim* entreated parents to hire these youths as tutors for their children and give them a place to live. But they also demanded that their importance be

---

[55]The quotation is from Euchel's introduction to *Hame'asef*, IV (1788), n.p. On the biographies of the *maskilim* see also Feiner, 'Isaac Euchel', *loc. cit.*; and Sorkin, 'From Context to Comparison', *loc. cit.*, p. 33. Cf. the emotional call of "A Young Man of the Society for the Promotion of the Hebrew Language" in the first issue of *Hame'asef*: "My brothers and friends who foster the language of Ever! If before you there stands as a man an inexperienced youth such as myself, do not be incensed or judge in anger . . .", *Hame'asef*, I (1784), p. 2, and the letter of the young Baruch Lindau of Hanover in the same issue, pp. 75–76. As to the *maskilim* from Poland, see Shulvass, *op. cit.*: the non-Jewish *Aufklärer* were mostly born in the 1730s and 1740s, and were therefore about a generation older than the *maskilim* and closer to the generation of Mendelssohn and Wessely. See also Möller, *Vernunft und Kritik*, *op. cit.*, pp. 295–296 and the note on p. 344.

[56]The details are based on the author's card index of collective biography, see note 45.

recognised and that they should not be treated in the demeaning manner of servants as was apparently often the case. Josel Pick expressed the frustration the tutors often felt:

> "It is thus seemly that a father able to do so should seek out a learned and intelligent and upright man and take him into his home; he should not, however, consider him as one would a lowly domestic servant, but enter into a covenant with him, and respect him for the sake of the children in his charge, for in this way the love of the teacher for them will increase, he will guard over them benevolently and treat them pleasantly."[57]

Theirs was a marginal position in German-Jewish society, with an uncertain legal status often contingent on employment in the homes of the wealthy. Their teaching occupation, their tendency towards literary endeavours and their association with families that showed at least outward acculturation to the German environment motivated them to seek outlets for self-expression as well as supportive social frameworks. It also led them to a critique of traditional Jewish society which still included the great majority of German Jews, even in Berlin, the centre of the *Haskalah*. They also advocated and launched new initiatives, especially in the areas of education and literature; they blended the old and the new, the Jewish and the universal and as such offered alternative values for the future of Jewish society. Among the first to engage in these activities was Joseph Levin, a teacher from Potsdam, in a 1772 proposal on educational reform. The initiative was emulated by the founders of the *Hevrat Hinuch Ne'arim* and simultaneously in Kiel and in Königsberg by Isaac Euchel. Wessely, of course, was the most prominent figure in this endeavour with the detailed programme for a *maskil* Jewish education that he drew up for the Jews of the Austrian Empire in the tolerant spirit of Joseph II.[58] The concepts of "covenant" and the "men of the covenant" (*anshei beritenu*) that frequently appear among this group which even called itself "the community" or "the association of *maskilim*" testifies to their self-image as a special group with close ties and common goals. They also saw themselves as having a mission towards society as a whole and a responsibility for its fate.[59]

One might justifiably apply to these two secondary groups Anthony Smith's distinction between an assimilationist intelligentsia and a reformist one. The first group, represented by Friedländer, Bendavid and Maimon in the 1790s invested most of its energies into an attempt to penetrate the modern world and acquire the status of members of universal society while abandoning Jewish particularism. The second group of *maskilim* endeavoured to renovate Jewish culture,

[57] *Hame'asef*, V (1789), pp. 180–181.

[58] Moritz Stern, 'Jugendunterricht in der Berliner Gemeinde während des 18. Jahrhunderts', in *Jahrbuch der jüdisch-literarischen Gesellschaft*, 19 (1928), pp. 39–68 and 20 (1929), p. 379; Eliav, *op. cit.*, pp. 23ff.

[59] See *Hame'asef*, II (1785), p. 174; Meir Gillon, 'Hasatira Haivrit Betkufat Hahaskalah Begermania -Anatomia shel Mehkar', in *Zion*, 52 (1987), pp. 213–217, emphasises the importance of the development of a type of secular writer-preacher seeking for the first time to seize the public stage and appeal to Jewish public opinion: "The salient novelty of the Berlin *Haskalah* . . . is the appearance of a previously unknown social figure, the writer as preacher and teacher, instead of the rabbi or the traditional preacher . . .".

society, customs, morals and education by removing all the impurities they perceived. To a certain extent this division is very similar to that made years ago by Ben-Zion Dinur. He distinguished between *maskilim* "connectors" on the one hand, who entered German Enlightenment society and for whom the *Haskalah* was a "bridge and passage to Christian society", and the "uplifters" on the other, *maskilim* for whom the *Haskalah* was a "project of healing the people". The latter were Jewish writers who in the 1780s and 1790s were active as a reforming and "rehabilitating" intelligentsia. They were not only intellectuals, but conscious disseminators of a new knowledge which would ensure harmony between tradition and modernity, expunge ignorance, and create new values which would fashion a moral society. They were the planners and initiators of programmes that would transform Jewish society as well as those who implemented them.[60] The *maskil*, in Dinur's words, was "the new man who remained within the walls", for whom the new was bound up with and integrated into Jewish life. Both as a secular writer, who had assumed the role of the traditional preacher, and as a teacher with a sense of mission and responsibility, the *maskil* strived to reshape Jewish society and repair it from within. He drew his self-confidence from his wealthy patrons and from the societies he founded. But more than anything else his confidence came from the belief that he embodied the new path of European history for Jewish society; that he alone knew how to decipher the historical map and identify the positive shift taking place in a humanistic era ruled by benevolent kings.[61]

III

Was Moses Mendelssohn truly a party to these goals of the *maskilim*? Was he really the teacher who paved their way ideologically and organisationally? Is it possible to classify him with this type of *maskil*, and was he a member or a leader of their circle? The answer given here to these questions challenges or even totally negates accepted ideas. Mendelssohn was neither the teacher who invested his energy and time in shaping and guiding a group of *maskilim*, nor did he consider it his destiny to do so. Only a few, like Friedländer, Maimon, Wessely, Homberg, Brill-Loewe, Euchel and to a certain extent Isaak Satanow, were regularly or even only once directly privy to his views and thoughts on different subjects. Many others, not only those who would be numbered among the *maskilim*, turned to him for advice. Mendelssohn for example referred the young Benjamin Ephraim, son of Veitel Heine Ephraim, to a Jewish teacher to learn mathematics and recommended that he read the works of Montesquieu

---

[60]Anthony D. Smith, *Theories of Nationalism*, London 1971, pp. 133–138; Ben-Zion Dinur, 'She'elat Ha-geula Vedrakeha Biymei Reshit Ha-haskalah Upulmus Ha-emantsipatsia Harishona', in *idem*, *Be-Mifne Ha-Dorot*, Jerusalem 1972, pp. 239–250.

[61]On historical turning points as a fundamental concept in the *maskil* consciousness see Feiner, *Ha-Haskalah Beyahasa Lahistoria*, *op. cit.*, chap. 1.

and Hume. Benjamin, however, a scion of the wealthy Ephraim family, never became a *maskil*, but engaged in business and politics.[62]

It is true that Mendelssohn's home at 68 Spandaustraße served as a "court" for many people who wished to enjoy the company of the famous and admired philosopher. It was, however, open to Jews and Gentiles, wealthy merchants of the Berlin élite, occasional visitors, Polish Talmud scholars, German professors, wealthy physicians, educated women and others. Virtually every foreign scholar and every respectable tourist who passed through Berlin took the opportunity to visit Mendelssohn. According to the testimony of Henriette Herz, a regular visitor and friend of his daughters, they came without invitation. Herz stressed the distinction between the open house of the learned man and the closed exclusive "salon", where the dominant presence was that of women, such as the salon she herself held after her marriage to the physician Marcus Herz.[63] Lengthy discussions on literature and the main philosophical issues that interested Mendelssohn were held at his home, among them natural religion, human perfection, moral principles and the immortality of the soul.[64] Friends and disciples who heard him, Euchel testified – and as noted he only saw Mendelssohn when he visited Berlin in 1784 – sat around Mendelssohn. He was gregarious by nature and welcomed everyone who visited him. The more famous he became, the greater the number of visitors. Every day many came as guests and as "pilgrims". "The person who saw him and heard his word only one time", Euchel wrote in an attempt to fathom Mendelssohn's great attraction, "was captured by his love and heartened by his admonitions and teaching." Social life was exceptionally important to the Mendelssohn family. Mendelssohn himself was invited to many parties, where he was generally considered the guest of honour.[65] Maimon, who had lengthy conversations with Mendelssohn on their differing philosophical views during their walks in Berlin, spoke of him as a master of the art of conversation, blessed with the ability to fathom every person's soul, enter his thoughts and to tailor his conversation accordingly. He was very patient and treated everyone cordially.[66] Friedländer has left a detailed and vivid description of life at the Mendelssohnian "court". He recounts a heated argument between Wessely and Euchel at Mendelssohn's home in the summer of 1784. The topic was the creation of the world as described in *Genesis*.

---

[62]On a visit of Isaak Satanow's to Mendelssohn see Isaac Euchel, *Toldot Rabbenu he-Hakham, op. cit.*, pp. 138–140. Cf. Altmann, *Moses Mendelssohn, op. cit.*, p. 430. On Benjamin Veitel Ephraim's relations with Mendelssohn see his autobiography, *Über meine Verhaftung und einige andere Vorfälle meines Lebens*, Berlin 1807, pp. 86–88; and Dolf Michaelis, 'The Ephraim Family', in *LBI Year Book XXI* (1976), pp. 218–219.

[63]See Euchel's testimony: "All those who arrived in Berlin honoured him. Nobles and high officials who travelled from their lands to see new things and were attentive to everything dear, were not in Berlin long before they visited him at his home." *Hame'asef*, V (1789), p. 73. See also Henriette Herz's report in Ulrich Janetzki (ed.), *Henriette Herz in Erinnerungen, Briefen und Zeugnissen*, Frankfurt a. Main 1984, pp. 61–62; and Hertz, *op. cit.*, p. 98.

[64]Winkler (ed.), *Salomon Maimons Lebensgeschichte, op. cit.*, pp. 150–151.

[65]*Hame'asef*, V (1789), p. 71; Winkler (ed.), *Salomon Maimons Lebensgeschichte, op. cit.*, pp. 150–151, Frumet's letter of 18th July 1777 in *JubA*, vol. XIX, pp. 217–218; Janetzki (ed.), *Henriette Herz, op. cit.*, p. 48.

[66]Winkler (ed.), *Salomon Maimons Lebensgeschichte, op. cit.*, pp. 144–155.

Mendelssohn listened to the argument without interfering or expressing his opinion, even though it was clear to all that the polemicists were directing their arguments towards the admired philosopher. Friday evenings and Holidays were apparently dedicated to Jewish guests and Jewish topics: aspects of morality and education, Hebrew linguistics, literature and religion. Mendelssohn, Friedländer stressed, never lectured on the subjects raised (as did Marcus Herz in the courses he held at his home), but was content with the role of the congenial, encouraging host presiding over the gathering. He usually sat in an armchair in the corner of the salon, eyes lowered. The topics discussed were chosen by the guests and his response was expressed by a slight nod, smile or encouraging word. None the less, sometimes he would introduce a young guest and praise his wisdom publicly before the visitor was given leave to speak.

Even Friedländer, the "foremost disciple", was forced to admit that Mendelssohn had no disciples in the usual sense: "Schüler, im gewöhnlichen Sinn des Wortes, hat mein unsterblicher Lehrer nicht gehabt. Öffentliche Vorlesungen hat er nie gehalten."[67] This is consistent with Mendelssohn's own testimony. In a digression in *Jerusalem, oder über religiöse Macht und Judentum* he defended the scholar whose public demands that he write and publish his thoughts. Pining for days past, Mendelssohn harked back to the old model of the teacher-student relationship that existed before the invention of the printing press placed the book, the written word, between them:

> "Man was more necessary to man; teaching was more closely connected with life, contemplation was more intimately bound up with action. The inexperienced man had to follow in the footsteps of the experienced, the student in those of his teacher; he had to seek his company, to observe him, and as it were, sound him out, if he wanted to satisfy his thirst for knowledge."[68]

If Mendelssohn did act as teacher, then, according to Friedländer, he followed the Socratic model by encouraging debate and participating in discussions. The young men who visited Mendelssohn loved wisdom and science and sought "sich zu bilden und zu belehren" just by seeing with their own eyes this famous person. Thus Mendelssohn did have a great influence – "Er hat einen weit größeren Antheil an der Aufklärung und Bildung seiner Religionsgenossen."[69] These very guests, Friedländer argued, were Mendelssohn's "disciples" and it was they who spread the *Haskalah* in the spirit of "Mendelssohn's school" throughout the Jewish world.[70] Friedländer's description, however, only strengthens the impression that this circle of visitors at Mendelssohn's home, this *Abendgesellschaft*, consisted of random visitors of all levels of Berlin Jewish society. It was an

---

[67]David Friedländer, *Moses Mendelssohn. Fragmente von ihm und über ihn*, Berlin 1819, pp. 31f. See also Meir Gillon, *Kohelet Musar LeMendelssohn al Reka Tkufato*, Jerusalem 1979, pp. 18–19.
[68]Moses Mendelssohn, *Jerusalem or On Religious Power and Judaism*, transl. by Allan Arkush, Hanover–London 1983, p. 104. Original German quote in *JubA*, vol. VIII, p. 170.
[69]Friedländer, *Moses Mendelssohn, op. cit.*, pp. 32–38.
[70]Friedländer, however, admitted that Mendelssohn's main influence was through the *Biur*, which was indeed the major agent of the German *Haskalah* in Eastern Europe. Cf. the testimony of two nineteenth-century Russian *maskilim*, Shmuel Yosef Fuenn, *Safa Lene'emanim*, Vilna 1881, pp. 92–94; and Abraham Bär Gottlober, *Zikhronot Umasaot*, Jerusalem 1976, pp. 58 and 234.

open "court" of curiosity seekers and admirers, not a consolidated framework of teacher and disciples with goals and a programme. It bore no relation to a true association of *maskilim* like the *Hevrat Doreshei Leshon 'Ever* in Königsberg, whose members were bound by an idea, an enterprise and the consciousness of a common destiny and mission.

It should not be forgotten that Mendelssohn also belonged to other circles and societies. From the mid-1750s he was member of a number of "neutral" societies of enlightened Germans, where he was usually the only Jew or perhaps one of two or three. Mendelssohn belonged to the *Gelehrtes Kaffeehaus*; on Sunday evenings he visited the home of Christoph Friedrich Nicolai, a kind of open house for scholars, where the Berlin enlightened met; and in 1783 he was appointed an honorary member of the *Mittwochsgesellschaft*, a society of senior government officials, clerics, physicians and writers.[71]

In Mendelssohn's prolific correspondence the *maskilim* and their affairs were only marginal. Most of those he exchanged letters with were Christians and apart from corresponding with Wessely, before he settled in Berlin, and with Friedländer, Mendelssohn's only lengthy letters were to Homberg after the latter left Berlin in 1782. No letters to other *maskilim* appear in the volumes of Mendelssohn's correspondence. Especially noteworthy is the absence of letters to members of *maskil* societies, which are never even mentioned in the letters he wrote to others. As is known, most of his essays were written for German literary and scientific journals. The personal bonds of friendship, mutual visits, membership in learned societies and correspondence were the warp and woof of the German Enlightenment movement in which Mendelssohn played an active and particularly prominent role. Most of the *maskilim*, in contrast, had no access to these forums. Consequently, Mendelssohn's areas of activity spread into much broader cultural regions than his "court", and the attention he was able to devote to his followers was limited.

The admiration for Mendelssohn's unique personality, which after his death reached legendary proportions, was not enough to create the Jewish *Haskalah* movement. But it did give the *maskilim* a kind of reference point: Mendelssohn could serve as a cultural hero, a successful example of a Jewish man of the European Enlightenment, whose "glory among the nations" raised the Jews' image in the eyes of the Christian world and provided a source of self-respect and security for his disciples. The *maskilim* could also benefit from Mendelssohn's unique status. A case in point is that of the private tutor Mendel of Strasbourg: armed with a letter of recommendation from Mendelssohn, he applied to the Prussian authorities for a Berlin residence permit. Salomon Maimon also enjoyed Mendelssohn's protection: he recommended to the city's wealthy Jews that they should provide for his needs. In this way Maimon had support and

---

[71] Altmann, *Moses Mendelssohn, op. cit.*, pp. 74–76; Möller, *Aufklärung in Preussen, op. cit.*, pp. 226–232; Hertz, *op. cit.*, pp. 96–98; Heinrich Meisner, 'Die Freunde der Aufklärung', in *Festschrift zur Fünfzigjährigen Doctorjubelfeier Karl Weinholds*, Strasbourg 1896, pp. 43–54. In an invitation sent to Mendelssohn by Johann Erich Biester in 1783, he defined the society as a "gelehrte Gesellschaft", in *JubA*, vol. XIII, pp. 96–97.

access to their rich private libraries. Furthermore, when he left Berlin he was armed with a warm letter of recommendation from Mendelssohn.

However, there was a glaring social chasm between Mendelssohn and most of the *maskilim*. Maimon was so apprehensive about his first visit to him that he almost ran away in fright:

> "The manners and lifestyle of the *Berliner* were so new to me that I was frightened and bewildered before entering the home of one of the pillars of the community. And when I opened the door of Mendelssohn's home and saw him and other respectable people of the same class, and the well-appointed rooms and aesthetic furnishings, I stepped back and closed the door and did not want to go in."[72]

Aware of the fact that the company of most of Mendelssohn's visitors was above his social standing, Maimon for a while sought out what he called the "middle society" of Jewish private teachers in Berlin. They were also drawn to Mendelssohn, but did not have sufficient standing to visit him often, and as a matter of course sought the company of other young bachelors. Maimon was disdainful of their inability to grasp his philosophy, soon squabbled with them and parted company with them. At any rate, he apparently felt more comfortable among those who did not expect him to observe the finer points of etiquette. Mendelssohn at one point reproached Maimon after someone told him about the latter's licentious and heretical lifestyle.

In Mendelssohn, Maimon found someone with whom he could discuss philosophy, as well as a patron and anchor in a relatively alien and hostile world, whose culture he was attempting to absorb. Generally, however, Mendelssohn did not have answers to practical questions relating to the Jewish *Haskalah*. When the question of *maskil* projects was raised, Mendelssohn was rather apathetic. Salomon Maimon took it upon himself to translate "books of science to the Hebrew language for the purpose of the enlightenment of the Polish Jews who were mired in the darkness of ignorance".[73] The society of *maskilim* in Berlin initiated the project and even guaranteed funding for printing the essay. At Mendelssohn's home, but without his direct intervention, a discussion took place on whether it was preferable to translate a book on Jewish history or, following Friedländer's suggestion, a book outlining the principles of morality and natural religion. Maimon himself preferred to write a mathematics textbook. When Mendelssohn was asked, according to Maimon "he declined to express his opinion, believing that every such project would do no harm, but would not bring any noticeable benefit."[74] When the *maskilim* failed to provide the necessary funds for the project and it seemed that it would never get off the ground, Maimon complained to Mendelssohn. The latter offered no real solution, however, but only suggested that Maimon seek funding through subscriptions.[75] There is other proof that Mendelssohn declined an active role in

---

[72] *Hame'asef*, V (1789), pp. 57–58; Winkler (ed.), *Salomon Maimons Lebensgeschichte*, *op. cit.*, pp. 140–143.
[73] *Ibid.*, pp. 177–178.
[74] *Ibid.*, p. 178: "Mendelssohn hielt seine Meinung zurück, weil er glaubte, daß alles, was man von dieser Art unternähme, zwar nichts schaden, aber auch nicht viel nützen würde."
[75] *Ibid.*, pp. 180–181.

the *Haskalah* and its projects, despite his ties with the movement and some of its important representatives, and despite his standing among the *maskilim* – even if such an active involvement was later attributed to him. The first proposal to set up a modern school in Berlin as an alternative to the traditional *heder*, where German, arithmetic and other general subjects would be taught, was put forward by the Berlin community leaders Ephraim and Daniel Itzig in 1761. In 1772, as noted, the Moravian-born Joseph Levin, who served as a private tutor in Potsdam, in a memorandum to King Frederick the Great proposed a wide-ranging plan for fundamental changes in the Jewish educational system in Prussia, and the printing and import of Hebrew books. The proposal followed Enlightenment principles and appealed to the interests of the absolutist state.[76] Both these proposals were in areas where *maskilim* invested most of their energy and hung their hopes for a reform of Jewish society; Mendelssohn was involved in neither of them. Nor did he, as far as we know, take part in the initiative that eventually came to fruition: the *Hevrat Hinuch Ne'arim* was organised in 1778, and due to the activities of the brothers-in-law David Friedländer and Daniel Itzig, the first modern Jewish school officially opened its doors in Germany in 1781. The two also served as directors of the educational institute that was meant mainly for the children of poor Jews. Even though a *Hame'asef* article contended that Mendelssohn, as Daniel Itzig's teacher, was the indirect source of inspiration for the school, he had no involvement in its founding.[77] Only when public examinations were held there in 1784 was Mendelssohn invited to join the learned panel of examination judges as an honoured guest.[78] It was Friedländer who headed the project of compiling the first reader for the new school, *Ein Lesebuch für jüdische Kinder*, in 1779. All Mendelssohn was asked to contribute were some selections, including the translation (still in manuscript form) of the Ten Commandments from his Torah translation and the German translation of Maimonides's *Thirteen Principles*.[79]

The *Orientalische Buchdruckerei*, founded in 1784, was in effect the first modern Hebrew printing house, publishing the literature of the Hebrew *Haskalah* until the beginning of the nineteenth century. Behind this enterprise, too, were Friedländer and Itzig, the directors of the *Hevrat Hinuch Ne'arim*. The printing house served mainly the *maskilim*. Isaak Satanow, its long-time director, guided it mainly towards publishing books funded by the *Hevrat Mazdike HaRabim*, including not a few of his own. The heads of the *Hevrat Shoharei Hatov Vehatushia* required that its members print their essays only there. The *Orientalische Buchdruckerei* also published some of Mendelssohn's essays, including the *Biur Sefer Milot Hahigayon*, a Hebrew translation of *Phaedon*, the German translation

---

[76] Eliav, *op. cit.*, pp. 23–24; Stern, *loc. cit.*

[77] *Hame'asef*, I (1784), p. 43. It seems more likely that the article was written by a *maskil* and not, as indicated, by an anonymous Christian.

[78] *Hame'asef*, I (1784), p. 62.

[79] For a reprint of the original edition of the *Lesebuch* and a detailed discussion of its contents and historical context see David Friedländer, *Lesebuch für jüdische Kinder*, ed. by Zohar Shavit, Frankfurt a. Main 1989. In a letter of 25th December 1778 Mendelssohn recommended that Friedländer have his reader printed at the same printing house as the *Biur* and attributed it to him alone (*"Ihr Lesebüchlein . . ."*), in *JubA*, vol. XIX, p. 245.

(in Hebrew characters) of the *Psalms* and *Sefer Hanefesh*, which was prepared for printing by Friedländer. The bibliographer Steinschneider considered this printing house the expression of the "Mendelssohn school". Be that as it may, an examination of the more than 200 books published in the forty years of its existence shows that those who influenced *Hame'asef* were writers and *maskilim* such as Wessely, Euchel and Satanow rather than Mendelssohn.[80]

When the leaders of the Trieste community in Northern Italy, at the recommendation of the Austrian governor von Zinzendorf, asked Mendelssohn to suggest school textbooks in the spirit of Joseph II's *Toleranzedikt*, Mendelssohn sent them a list of his essays and referred them to Naphtali Herz Wessely, as the latter was much better qualified to help them. This was the beginning of Wessely's ties to the North Italian communities, connections he used when grappling with the opponents of the educational programme he proposed in *Divrei Shalom Ve'Emeth* (Words of Peace and Truth).[81] In 1780, when Herz Cerfbeer, in the name of the Alsatian Jews, asked Mendelssohn to write an *apologia* in their struggle against Christian enmity and restrictive legislation, Mendelssohn referred them to his *Mittwochsgesellschaft* colleague Christian Wilhelm von Dohm, a Prussian civil servant and journalist. Dohm's subsequent book, *Über die bürgerliche Verbesserung der Juden*, became the major essay on the status of the Jews; its line of thought and interpretation of the Jewish people's fate were not only adopted by the Enlightenment, but also by the *maskilim*. Mendelssohn may well have believed that a scholarly defence by a Christian would be more effective,[82] but this way of acting was typical of him in another way: he avoided public debate on matters of principle as well as current political and religious issues. He had, in fact, acted in the same manner in his polemic with Lavater.

Mendelssohn, on his own initiative, would not have set about formulating a comprehensive exposition of his Jewish philosophy. But the anonymous publication in 1782 of August Friedrich Cranz's essay "Das Forschen nach Licht und Recht in einem Schreiben an den Herrn Moses Mendelssohn . . ." catalysed the formulations of the last section of his 1783 book, *Jerusalem*. But it was neither intended to provide a conceptual framework for the *Haskalah*, nor did it contain a definite programme. All it intended was to answer the question of how Mendelssohn could continue to hold on to the religion of his forebears, while at the same time maintaining a general rational philosophy opposed to religious coercion and based on tolerance.

None the less, in a number of cases Mendelssohn did not decline to exploit his reputation and influence in favour of a distressed Jewish community. His intervention against the expulsion order issued against the Dresden community in 1777 is an example of this.[83] Mendelssohn also intervened in the polemic that

---

[80]About the printing house see Moritz Steinschneider, 'Hebräische Drucke in Deutschland', in *Zeitschrift für die Geschichte der Juden in Deutschland*, 5 (1892), pp. 166–182.
[81]Naphtali Herz Wessely, *Mikhtav Shlishi. Ein Mishpat*, Berlin 1784, pp. 7–8; and also Lois C. Dubin, 'Trieste and Berlin. The Italian Role in the Cultural Politics of the *Haskalah*', in Katz (ed.), *Toward Modernity, op. cit.*, pp. 189–224.
[82]Meyer, *op. cit.*, pp. 46–47; Altmann, *Moses Mendelssohn, op. cit.*, pp. 449–461.
[83]Altmann, *ibid.*, pp. 427–429.

erupted after the 1782 publication of Wessely's *Divrei Shalom Ve'Emeth*. Prussian Education Minister von Zedlitz heard that plans were afoot to expel Wessely from the community and asked its leaders to keep him informed of developments. As a result, Mendelssohn encouraged the community leaders Friedländer, Daniel Itzig and Isaak Daniel Itzig to pre-empt Rabbi Zevi Hirschel Lewin's intentions. Lewin was under great pressure from rabbis of other communities, especially from Ezekiel Landau of Prague, to take forceful action against Wessely because of his provocative essay.[84] Mendelssohn did not, however, take the offensive for the sake of the *Haskalah* programme, but because of matters of principle: the freedom of thought and speech and the problem of the Jews' image in the eyes of enlightened Christians. "I am not interested in examining who is right on the issue", Mendelssohn wrote to Friedländer, "I am, however, concerned over what Christians might think and say of us upon learning that we are preventing a writer from publishing his views in a book." Mendelssohn suggested demanding that the rabbi not speak out against Wessely in the synagogue. But he preferred that someone else personally approach the rabbi so that he, Mendelssohn, would not be placed in a situation where he had to argue with Lewin about the issues raised by Wessely.[85] Freedom of expression and publication were paramount to Mendelssohn, but even though he undoubtedly supported Wessely and his programme, he did not express these views in public. Mendelssohn was content with writing personal letters censuring the opponents of the Austrian programme to establish modern schools for the Jews, and he expressed gratification that Wessely had succeeded in assuaging the rabbis of Poland and Germany without a protracted struggle.[86] It may be added that Mendelssohn did not become a member of the *Hevrat Doreshei Leshon 'Ever* and was not among the initiators of *Hame'asef*, even though there were those who saw him as their source of inspiration. These were initiatives of young Königsberg *maskilim* who won supporters in Berlin and other communities. The initiative for both endeavours came mainly from Isaac Euchel and, as noted, the *maskil* sought the patronage of Wessely. Mendelssohn was among the fifty-three Berlin subscribers of *Hame'asef*, and his name was prominently displayed in the subscription list published in 1785, but soliciting his articles for the journal was not an easy task. At a 1784 Berlin visit, Euchel did succeed in getting one of Mendelssohn's poems for publication – but without his signature.[87] At that time, apparently through the intervention of Joel Brill-Loewe, Euchel received a copy of Mendelssohn's 1755 Hebrew journal, *Kohelet Musar*, from which he published

---

[84]Moshe Samet, 'Mendelssohn, N. H. Wessely Verabbanei Doram', in *Mehkarim Betoldot Am Yisrael Ve'eretz Yisrael*, Haifa 1970, pp. 233–257.

[85]Letter to Friedländer of 17th April 1782, in *JubA*, vol. XIII, p. 34.

[86]Letter to Wolf Dessau, *ibid.*, pp. 69–70. In the letter to Joseph Gallico (7th May 1782), Mendelssohn enquired about the progress of the establishment of normal schools and asked whether the composition of textbooks for religion and morals had begun. He defended Wessely and praised his desire to repair the faults of Jewish society: "he had arisen to strengthen weak hands and awaken those asleep in lazy slumber", *JubA*, vol. XIX, pp. 281–282.

[87]'Zikhron Yedidyt Legever Maskil Began Re'o', in *Hame'asef*, I (1784), pp. 130–132. Mendelssohn also signed the manifesto of the *Hevrat Mazdike HaRabim*, whose goal was to support Isaak Satanow's Hebrew book publishing initiative. See *Pinkas Ukhtav Hadat*, *op. cit.*

Mendelssohn and his "Disciples"

three essays.[88] More significant than his actual contribution was the adulation Mendelssohn received during *Hame'asef*'s first three years. These sentiments grew, especially after his death.

His relative apathy towards *maskilim* projects and his unwillingness to adopt a clear position in their favour is evidence of Mendelssohn's true status in the circle of *maskilim*. If Mendelssohn had any real influence beyond his revered image, it was through his essays. It would appear that only in the short-lived *Kohelet Musar* of the 1750s, in *Biur Sefer Milot Hahigayon*, the commentary on Maimonides's *Logical Terms* of the 1760s, and in the *Biur* did Mendelssohn display *Haskalah* interests, with the aim of attaining cultural and social objectives in Jewish society by literary means. But it should be noted that Mendelssohn composed *Kohelet Musar* together with the unknown Rabbi Tuvya (Tobias), and there is no way of knowing who was really behind the journal. *Biur Sefer Milot Hahigayon* was devised as an aid to logical thinking for rabbinical scholars, and Mendelssohn took pains in the foreword to emphasise that "external wisdom" was not involved here, since it was a legitimate "inquiry" – Maimonides, "the minister [master] of Torah", presented to the Jews after sifting out the Aristotelianism. Moreover, according to Mendelssohn's own clear testimony, the initial and main motivation behind the *Biur* enterprise was that of Salomon Dubno, his son's private tutor, who later left the project.[89] The *Biur* was to become the basic book of the *maskilim*. Wessely had already recommended it in *Divrei Shalom Ve'Emeth*, and it was to become the visiting card of the Berlin *Haskalah* to *Haskalah* centres beyond Germany in the nineteenth century, especially in Eastern Europe. *Phaedon*, Mendelssohn's only essay translated fully into Hebrew and published by the *maskilim*, was translated by Isaiah Beer-Bing of Metz only twenty years after its 1767 publication, and it was quoted frequently in *Hame'asef* articles.[90] *Jerusalem* was another evidence of Mendelssohn's teaching and the Jewish reader was able to read excerpts in Mendelssohn's biography.[91]

A close examination of the *maskilim*'s reliance on Mendelssohn's writings shows that while they identified with his general ideas about the perfection of human beings, the immortality of the soul, the moral ideal etc., in everything concerning *Haskalah* in general and its objectives in particular, they diverged from his conceptions. It is possible that this difference explains why Mendelssohn did not actually take part in the practical shaping of the *Haskalah*.

IV

David Sorkin has recently convincingly shown that a more precise understanding of Mendelssohn is possible, not just by examining the historical context in

---

[88] Gillon, *Kohelet Musar, op. cit.*, pp. 20–21.
[89] Gillon, *ibid.*; Moses Mendelssohn, *Biur Milot Higayon Larambam*, 3rd edn., Berlin 1784, Foreword, pp. 368–420.
[90] Moses Mendelssohn, *Phaedon. Hu Sefer Hash'arat Hanefesh* . . . Berlin 1787.
[91] See the foreword of *Hame'asef*, IV (1788); and Euchel's introduction to *Gebete der hochdeutschen und polnischen Juden, op. cit.*, p. XVII.

which he lived, but also by comparing him to the early eighteenth-century Protestant and Catholic Enlightenment in Europe.[92] The early Enlightenment, with Mendelssohn as its most prominent Jewish representative, sought to reconcile through philosophy religious belief and reason by seeking the support of the new sciences and philosophy and adapting them to religious faith. Mendelssohn's well-known contention that church and state should be separate, because religion should be founded on a free association of believers, complies, as Sorkin has shown, with the "collegial theory" of the early Enlightenment. According to this theory, natural law can be reconciled with religion when the church is perceived as a voluntary association of individuals with the right to liberty of conscience and tolerance.[93]

Mendelssohn was truly a figure of the early Enlightenment. From the standpoint of the *Haskalah* as it developed in the 1780s, he stood virtually alone as a philosopher among the *maskilim*, with the exceptions of Herz, Maimon and Naftali Hirz Ulmann of Holland. He interpreted reality in terms of all-inclusive, abstract principles and usually tended towards a pessimistic, or at least a very cautious, approach in everything concerning the possibility of influencing and changing reality. In 1768, when Basedow sought his assistance in spreading the idea of philanthropic education and in recruiting Jewish subscribers for a book he had written, Mendelssohn replied that it was better not to arouse exaggerated expectations in a people with no foreseeable opportunity of gaining freedom from political oppression and winning the rights of citizens. As long as Jewish youth could not benefit from "philanthropic freedom", he considered it unfair to present them with "the fruits of Enlightenment in their perfect and glorious beauty". "Must I teach them", Mendelssohn asked, "the pleasures of human society that have been denied them by the law of the state, so that they feel their absence even more keenly and be even more wretched?"[94]

In the Lavater polemic Mendelssohn had argued with the Zurich pastor that his civic state prevented him from engaging in an open religious argument, and from a personal standpoint he avoided public contentions.[95] In *Jerusalem*, Mendelssohn negated one of the Enlightenment's optimistic beliefs, that of the progress of human society. He criticised his friend Lessing's *Die Erziehung des Menschengeschlechts* (1777), rejecting his scheme of human progress out of hand. For Mendelssohn there was no progress and perfection except that of the individual; humankind in general never advanced without later slipping back.[96] Similar pessimism about the possibility of a fundamental historical change is also evident in his 1770 letter "to a man of exalted status", who asked his opinion

---

[92] David Sorkin, 'The Case for Comparison. Moses Mendelssohn and the Religious Enlightenment', in *Modern Judaism*, 14 (1994), pp. 121–138.
[93] Sorkin, *ibid*.
[94] Letter to Basedow of April (?) 1768, in *JubA*, vol. XII/1, pp. 159–160; Azriel Shohet, *Im Hilufei Tekufot. Reshit ha-Haskalah be-Yahadut Germanya*, Jerusalem 1960, p. 252.
[95] Mendelssohn, 'A letter to Lavater', in *JubA*, vol. VII, pp. 7–17.
[96] "Humanity in general is always wavering, ascending and descending in its different endeavours, and usually maintaining a certain level of morality, a level of religiosity or lack of religiosity, of justice and injustice, of wealth and poverty." Mendelssohn, *Jerusalem*, in *JubA*, vol. VIII, pp. 162–163.

Mendelssohn and his "Disciples"

about the possibility of the Jewish people returning to its land. After apologising for his meagre knowledge of politics and statistics and for being a theoretician incapable of taking on great projects, Mendelssohn answered that such an enterprise would require a basic change in the Jewish people's pessimistic nature which seemed unlikely: "The natural urge for liberty lost its vitality within us. It has been turned into the charity of monks, and expressed in prayer and suffering, not action."[97] As an early representative of a later orthodoxy, Mendelssohn pointed to the prohibitions of the "three oaths" as proof of the Jews' inability to display activism on the national plane.[98]

This pattern of "escape" from historical reality can also be seen in Mendelssohn's attitude towards history, which he classified as one of the "civic sciences" and therefore as irrelevant for Jews as long as they were excluded from matters of the state.[99] Even the hopes that he had originally pinned on the policies of Joseph II of Austria soon gave room to suspicions of a "Jesuit plot", the hidden objective of which was supposedly a religious unity based on conversion.[100] When Dohm proposed changes in the occupational structure of Jewish society in his reform programme, suggesting the abandonment of commercial occupations in favour of skilled trades and even agriculture, Mendelssohn defended the existing situation. By praising free market economy, competition and the "hidden hand", Mendelssohn objected to what was presented as turning the Jews towards more productive endeavours. He argued that the Jewish merchant and itinerant pedlar were of great benefit to the state and that there was no justification in the demand for the Jews to change their way of making a living as a precondition for human and civic rights.[101] Mendelssohn was willing to admit, if cautiously and hesitantly, that positive processes leading to a better future were taking place in his day. Even if superstition and barbarism had not yet passed from the world, one could not deny "the fortunate hour where human rights in all their correct implications were being considered". None the less, Mendelssohn immediately hedged and said that he was so far removed from cabinets and decision-making centres, living a private life uninvolved in the practical world, that he could only observe from a distance "in bated childish breath" and wonder what would come at the end of this historical process.[102]

This characteristic image and even self-assessment of Mendelssohn as the intellectual, the philosopher, the pessimistic thinker far removed from the enthusiasm of the *Haskalah*'s reformist intelligentsia and its ideology did not pass unnoticed by the *maskilim*, his "disciples". Even though they discussed their ideas with him and at times asked him to subscribe to and support books about to be published, they did not expect him to take *Haskalah* initiatives, formulate

---

[97] Letter of 26th January 1770, in *JubA*, vol. XII/1, pp. 211–212.
[98] See Aviezer Ravitzky, *Messianism, Zionism and Jewish Religious Radicalism*, Tel Aviv 1993, pp. 24–26 (in Hebrew).
[99] Feiner, *Hahaskalah Beyahasa Lahistoria, op. cit.*, p. 20.
[100] *JubA*, vol. XIII, pp. 132–134 and 177–181. See also Jacob Katz, 'To whom was Mendelssohn Replying in "Jerusalem"?', in *Zion*, 29 (1964), pp. 112–132 (in Hebrew).
[101] Menasseh Ben-Israel, *Rettung der Juden . . . Nebst einer Vorrede von Moses Mendelssohn . . .* in *JubA*, vol. VIII, pp. 11–16.
[102] *Ibid.*, pp. 3–5.

ideological platforms, or support manifestos and programmes meant to change Jewish society. Out of Mendelssohn's earshot they even said so, as did Euchel, his great admirer and future biographer, who was responsible for the loyalty of generations to come to Mendelssohn as teacher. When proposing a detailed programme of modern Jewish education to the King of Denmark in 1784, Euchel spoke of Mendelssohn's character. He is truly a man every *maskil* (*aufgeklärter Jude*) should respect, Euchel wrote of him, but he follows the wise maxim not to touch publicly on matters rooted in a religious party, as long as there is no hope of changing them; and is therefore tolerably respectful towards the rabbis in his public writings. Indeed, as a theoretician (*theoretischer Schriftsteller*) one cannot fault him for this, but he who thinks about the facts and seeks to relate to the real situation, cannot help but expose the great deficiencies of Jewish society, its rabbis and its educational methods. Euchel thus assumes the task himself, with implicit reservations about Mendelssohn's refraining from doing so.[103]

Indeed, the *maskilim* were not content with theories and ideas, but formulated programmes, criticism and objectives for the transformation and reform of Jewish society. They optimistically believed in the possibility of changing traditional society now that the world was advancing towards greater tolerance, humanism and rationalism. Therefore the *maskilim* can be identified with the ideology and world view of the later *Haskalah* more than with the early *Haskalah* of their teacher.[104] They believed in progress, were enthused by the new opportunities opened to the Jews of Austria by Joseph II's *Toleranzedikt* and saw it as further justification of their belief that the current era was superseding the previous and that it was possible to look optimistically towards the future. In practical terms, the *maskilim* adopted most of Dohm's reform programme. Mendelssohn, on the other hand, demanded rights for Jews regardless of reform and without prior conditions, on the basis of a recognition of universal human rights as set down in natural law.[105]

In the biography written after Mendelssohn's death, Euchel tried to present his ideas as no different from those of the *maskilim*. Thus he omitted translating sections of Mendelssohn's introduction to a book by Menasseh Ben-Israel, where he objected to Dohm's suggestions concerning a diversification of the Jews' occupational structure. Instead, Euchel attributed to Mendelssohn a stance which he had not actually held, namely that he was disdainful of commerce.[106]

---

[103]Euchel's letter of 21st October 1784 to the King of Denmark, photocopy in the General Archive of Jewish History in Jerusalem (HM2/1062a), p. 16: "Herr Moses Mendelssohn, ein Mann, dem jeder aufgeklärte Jude viel Achtung schuldig ist, befolgt die weise Maxime, Dinge, die seit vielen Jahren bei einer Religionsparthey eingewurzelt sind, nicht öffentlich anzutasten, solange nicht Hoffnung da ist, sie aufheben zu können, und begegnet aus diesem Grunde den Rabbinen in seinen öffentlichen Schriften einigermassen mit Achtung. Als theoretischer Schriftsteller ist ihm diese Politesse nicht zu verdenken. Allein wer an die Thatsachen denkt, kann unmöglich umhin, diesen großen Verderb freymüthig darzustellen."

[104]Only *ex post facto* did they try to attribute a reform tendency to him. Thus, for instance, Euchel when writing about Mendelssohn's contribution to educational reform in *Hame'asef*, V (1789), pp. 57–58.

[105]As to the *maskilim*'s understanding of Dohm's programme see Feiner, *Hahaskalah Beyahasa Lahistoria, op. cit.*, chap. 1.

[106]*Hameasef*, IV (1788), pp. 119, 179–184.

Another example is Euchel's representation of Mendelssohn as a *maskil* who placed great importance on the study of history, and was even learned in it. This is diametrically opposite to what Mendelssohn testified about himself, but it suited Euchel's view of the great didactic and moral importance of history.[107]

Contrary to Mendelssohn's suspicions, the *maskilim* believed that historical change was indeed occurring, a belief on which they based their calls to Jewish society, especially its youth. In the manner of a manifesto and with the consciousness of an avant-garde seeking to draw the masses, the *maskilim* called:

> "Hearken, Oh enlightened youth, lovers of morality and knowledge, incline your ear to us. Know that this comes from your brothers who love you . . . for your sakes, Oh dear ones! At this time wisdom sings outside, calls in the streets. Hurry call her, quickly bring her home . . . yes, the time of science for all peoples has arrived . . . and why should we sit idly by and do nothing! Please, brothers, let us rise and revive stones from mounds of dust!"[108]

As is well-known, Mendelssohn advocated the model of the tolerant state, the ideal of the perfection of the rational, moral and cultural person (*Bildung*) and of voluntary religious communities whose rabbis did not have the right to excommunicate. He also recommended the adoption of the German language and the abandonment of Yiddish, which he believed was morally detrimental to the Jews. The later *maskilim* tried to transfer these ideals from theory to practice and considerably expanded his objectives. They did not refrain from casting sarcastic criticism at the values of traditional Jewish society: its superstitions, corrupt education and the figures of the ignorant Polish rabbi and *melammed*. On the other hand, they drew a picture of a future reformed Jewish society.[109] If the Enlightenment was based, in the words of the German Enlightenment scholar Horst Möller, on the two central elements of *Vernunft* and *Kritik*, then Mendelssohn, as the representative of the early Enlightenment, held more to the element of rationalism than criticism, while the *maskilim* attempted to apply the principle of rationalism and translate it into criticism.[110]

Mendelssohn, it would seem, was hardly a partner in the aim of the *maskilim* to disseminate *Haskalah*, with the possible exception of that oft-quoted sentence where he says that the *Biur*, in the future, would serve as the "first step towards culture, from which to my sorrow my people is so far removed that one might despair of the possibility of improvement".[111] The *maskilim*, on the other hand, considered the spread of *Haskalah* as the reason for maintaining a united circle of writers. The editors of *Hame'asef* said as much in a call to their readers: "Da der

---

[107]Isaac Euchel, 'Davar el Hakore Mitoelet Hayamim Hakadmonim Vehayediot Hamehubarot Lahem', in *Hame'asef*, I (1784), pp. 9–14, 25–30.
[108]'Nahal Habesor', *loc. cit.*, pp. 11–13.
[109]See among others the *maskil* utopian outline in Isaak Satanow's *Divrei Rivot*, Berlin 1793 (?); and in Isaac Euchel's 'Igeret Meshullam Haeshtamoai', in Yehuda Friedlander (ed.), *Perakim Basitira Haivrit*, Tel Aviv 1979, pp. 41–59.
[110]Möller, *Vernunft und Kritik*, *op. cit.*, pp. 11–19.
[111]Letter of Mendelssohn to Hennings of 29th June 1779 in *JubA*, vol. XII/2, pp. 147–150: "Dies ist der erste Schritt zur Cultur, von welcher meine Nation leider! in einer solchen Entfernung gehalten wird, daß man an der Möglichkeit einer Verbesserung beynahe verzweifeln möchte." See also Shohet, *op. cit.*, p. 253; Sorkin, *The Transformation of German Jewry*, *op. cit.*, pp. 71–72.

Wunsch der Herausgeber bloß zur Beförderung der Aufklärung der Nation abzielt."[112] The goal was "to give the youth knowledge and a stratagem . . . to spread the treasures of our holy language of Israel . . .", wrote the members of the *Hevrat Doreshei Leshon 'Ever* in their manifesto, while the *Hevrat Shoharei Hatov Vehatushia* declared its goal to be the dissemination of *Haskalah*.[113] They knew that the *maskilim*'s aims would not be attained without criticising and struggling against the opponents of *Haskalah*. They encouraged one another and called for an opening of the people's eyes "to improve others like them, to sow the seed of reason in the heart of chaos, to give the ignorant cunning . . .". When, in the words of Simon BaRaZ's optimistic poem, "those who have gone astray" would learn understanding, and the "impetuous" would become enlightened, the earth would be full of knowledge like water.[114]

Mendelssohn's reply to the question "What is Enlightenment?", that was raised at the *Mittwochsgesellschaft*, appeared in the September 1784 issue of the *Berlinische Monatsschrift*. A comparison of Mendelssohn's understanding of Enlightenment with Euchel's detailed lecture on the objectives of the *Haskalah* (written in October of that year as an accompanying letter to his educational programme for the Jews of Denmark, mentioned above), proves the difference between Mendelssohn as a philosopher and theoretician and the reform-minded, visionary *maskil*. It would appear that the latter was actually closer to the concept of Enlightenment as expressed by Immanuel Kant in his well-known answer of December 1784 to the same question.[115] Mendelssohn grappled with finding a precise definition of a new term like *Aufklärung* and warned against the exaggerated use and misuse of the term that could lead to social anarchy and religious and moral breakdown. He set limits on its use, taking into consideration the possibility of a conflict between the demands it made on the individual, those made upon him as a citizen of the state and the damage it could cause to those who lived in a country not yet ripe for "Enlightenment". In the end, however, Mendelssohn left the reader with many question marks and no direction or real guidance.[116] He found that "Enlightenment" was one branch of the self-education of the individual and of society (*Bildung*), with *Kultur* constituting the other branch. Whereas Enlightenment relates to the theoretical realm as the knowledge, consciousness and rational thought each person needs as a human being, culture relates to the practical social dimension – the arts, aesthetics,

---

[112] A message to the readers at the end of the German appendix of *Hame'asef*, I (1784), p. 20.

[113] *Tavnit Hevrat Shoharei Hatov Vehatushia*, op. cit. In 1785 an anonymous *maskil* suggested establishing in Königsberg a society called *Hevrat Hinuch Ne'arim* (Society for Youth Education), where the *maskilim* of the *Hevrat Doreshei Leshon 'Ever* would volunteer to teach an hour a day. He thought that this example would draw many others to the *Haskalah*; in *Hame'asef*, II (1785), pp. 40–43.

[114] Simon BaRaZ, *Ma'arkhei Lev. Letkufat Hayamim asher Nityasda Hevrat Doreshei Leshon 'Ever*, Königsberg 1785.

[115] *"Was ist Aufklärung?" Thesen und Definitionen*, ed. by Erhard Bahr, Stuttgart 1974. See Altmann, *Moses Mendelssohn*, op. cit., pp. 653f.

[116] See N. Rotenstreich, 'Enlightenment. Between Mendelssohn and Kant', in Siegfried Stein and Raphael Loewe (eds.), *Studies in Jewish Religious and Intellectual History*, Alabama 1979, pp. 279–363; J. Schmidt, 'The Question of Enlightenment. Kant, Mendelssohn and the *Mittwochsgesellschaft*', in *Journal of the History of Ideas*, 50 (1989), pp. 269–291. Cf. Uzi Shavit, 'Haskalah Mahi. Levirur Musag Hahaskalah Basifrut Haivrit', in *Mehkarei Yerushalayim Besifrut Ivrit*, 12 (1990), pp. 51–83.

social manners and everything concerning social conduct. Once again he displays the same sense of impotence of a Jew aware of his special situation in the state. Hence Mendelssohn attempts to restrict the demands the Enlightenment makes of the individual. A state which does not know how to co-ordinate culture and Enlightenment and prevents it from spreading throughout all its groups is a hapless state, but even so one may not transgress its laws.[117]

Kant, on the other hand, has a much more inclusive concept of Enlightenment. For him it was bound up with liberty, human respect, criticism of traditional institutions and values as well as their reform. It not only related to theory, but also to practice: to politics and religion. Kant's essay was daring and activist, a cry for human emancipation. Kant's enlightened person is required to express criticism, even if restrained by the harsh demands of total obedience to the law of the state and the official requirements of the public functions he fulfils.[118]

It seems that Euchel, who criticised Mendelssohn as a theoretician removed from practical work, was espousing the Enlightenment conception of Kant, who had been his teacher at the University of Königsberg, rather than Mendelssohn's. The problem he had to confront was that of the Jews' ignorance and superstitious beliefs. The solution proposed by Euchel was a reform of Jewish society through educational change. The way to rehabilitate a people that was degenerating was not, according to Euchel, through the political means of the state, as Dohm had proposed and as Mendelssohn had hoped, but through change in Jewish society itself. The Jews themselves, under the aegis of the *maskilim*, would extricate themselves and correct their imperfections. He called for the rabbis' true face to be exposed, for shaking off prejudice and opening dauntless criticism. Lessing, too, was one of Euchel's guides and it was from him that he had learned that obstacles could be removed only after a long, gradual process of education. But for him there was no longer time for restraint in a situation where the tone of Jewish society and culture were set by ignorant Polish *melamdim* and rabbis. This should no longer be possible, Euchel said, "in unserem aufgeklärten Jahrhundert".[119] Euchel had a pragmatic plan that was based on substituting those in key positions so that the whole society and culture could be reshaped – he recommended replacing the teachers and rabbis with *maskilim*. Euchel looked towards the future with a measure of optimism, towards that happy time when the first graduates would leave modern Jewish educational institutions:

> "Within 10 years there will be enlightened Jews who will not only be engaged in their personal happiness, but will also serve the entire people as teachers, rabbis and adjudicators. Oh, how glorious will it be in the future, how wonderful will be the fruits that grow from this good action . . ."[120]

---

[117]See Sorkin, *The Transformation of German Jewry, op. cit.*, pp. 71–73.
[118]Rotenstreich, *loc. cit.*
[119]Euchel's letter to the King of Denmark, see note 103, p. 14.
[120]*Ibid.*, p. 23: "Oh, wie glänzend ist diese Aussicht in die Zukunft, wie glücklich werden die Früchte dieser Wohlthat treiben."

It seems that this type of active, enterprising, critical *maskil*, an ideological secular preacher imbued with a sense of mission, was far from Mendelssohn's concept of the *Haskalah*. Neither does it seem that this was a development of Mendelssohn's teachings nor a response to his hopes. More than being a disciple of Mendelssohn, Euchel was the disciple of Kant and other men of the Enlightenment.

V

In 1808, when Shalom Ha-Cohen tried to renew *Hame'asef* and set up a new society of *maskilim* different from the patterns that had developed in German Jewry at the beginning of the nineteenth century, he published a poem of praise to Naphtali Herz Wessely in the imprint and published his biography in the first volume. Twenty-two years had passed since Mendelssohn's death and fourteen years since the previous editors of *Hame'asef* in its original form had declared that David Friedländer was Mendelssohn's true heir. But this heir, the apparently natural participant in the renewal of the *Haskalah* in Germany, was not part of the new enterprise. Shalom Ha-Cohen and his colleagues in the *Hevrat Oharei Lashon Ivrit* (Lovers of the Hebrew Language) chose Wessely's legacy because for them this offered a relevant model for a group of *maskilim* seeking to renew the *Haskalah*, especially through Hebrew literature. "Among the members of our group", Ha-Cohen wrote, there were "Torah scholars, physicians, scientists and linguists . . . all of us love God and his true Torah, and we have no part in those who turn their backs on every word of the living God". It should be emphasised that Mendelssohn was not missing from the renewed *Hame'asef*. Even the Hebrew translation of a chapter of *Morning Hours* was undoubtedly meant as an attempt to convey Mendelssohn's thought to Hebrew readers, most of whom did not live in Berlin but, as the subscription list shows, in communities such as Prague, Glogau, Dresden, Breslau, Brunswick, Posen, Cassel, Brody and Mitau.[121]

For David Friedländer, who more than anyone else fostered the term "Mendelssohn's disciples", as well as for the representatives of the new religious trends and schools of thought in nineteenth-century German Jewry, Mendelssohn's heritage had great prestige and value. They cultivated the myth of Mendelssohn as the first modern German Jew, the spiritual father of every liberal Jewish trend and the author of the social and cultural integration of the Jews in the modern era. Friedländer, who had long abandoned the *Haskalah* in its original sense, took over Mendelssohn's heritage and did with it as he pleased. It was he who had implied that in Mendelssohn's teaching the observation of the religious precepts was not essential. Hence the "second step" or the final

[121] According to the subscribers' list of the new *Hame'asef*: "An Offering of Remembrance, in Honour of the Spirit within Us, the Delicate Soul, The Revered Master, the Torah Scholar, the Great and Praised Mediator, the Late Naphtali Herz Wessely. May the Memory of the Righteous Be Blessed", *Hame'asef* (1809), pp. 5–8; see also the biography by David Friedrichsfeld, *ibid.*, pp. 38, 230–234, 263–271; Moses Mendelssohn, Hebrew translation of the fifth chapter of *Morgenstunden*, in *Hame'asef* (1809), pp. 24–30.

inference of the pattern of freeing oneself from *Halakhah* was not, according to this line of thinking, a contradiction to Mendelssohn's thought. For Friedländer, Mendelssohn was the intermediary who facilitated the maintenance of a system of social relations between Jews and Gentiles. As he wrote in his memoirs of Mendelssohn: "Das gesellige Verhältnis zwischen Nichtjuden und Juden in unseren Gegenden ist ganz sein Werk."[122]

The myth that enveloped Mendelssohn for German Jewry and Eastern European *maskilim* throughout the nineteenth century must not be allowed to blur our view of the *Haskalah*. An examination of the nature of their relations and the guidance Mendelssohn gave those *maskilim* who sought it shows that he was not the *Haskalah*'s direct source of inspiration, certainly not when it came to providing guidance or clear goals and plans. Neither did a centre for the *maskilim* or a place where they could convene develop at his "court", which was open to all. Mendelssohn, it would appear, remained in the early stage of the Enlightenment and was content with intellectual endeavours that were meant to demonstrate that religion and reason were compatible from the Jewish standpoint. It was, however, difficult for him to serve as a teacher for the *maskilim* who saw the *Haskalah* as a programme of social and cultural reform and criticism geared towards bringing about change. Neither was Mendelssohn the type of person to set about establishing institutions and organisations to foster and spread the *Haskalah*. Unlike those *maskilim* who kept their finger on the pulse of Jewish society, Mendelssohn remained a theoretician and a philosopher. At a time when a *maskil* such as Euchel went from community to community gauging the extent of the *Haskalah*'s progress or drawing up detailed plans for a transformation of the rabbinic leadership and the educational system, Mendelssohn was worrying about the possible pitfalls of unsupervised Enlightenment and tried to define it conceptually in relation to the term culture. While the *maskilim* were investing their energy in the rehabilitation of Jewish society and culture from within, Mendelssohn was preoccupied with long-term changes in the state, the triumph of reason and natural law, and the external political forces that would guarantee the future existence of the Jewish people. Meanwhile, he also cautioned against any illusions and had great doubts and suspicions about the politics of rulers such as Joseph II. If dealing with change, to his mind it was preferable to concentrate on culture and on the practical outward aspect of *Bildung*. The other *maskilim* read the historical map differently. They, too, considered change in the political regime of great importance, but they believed that the time of Enlightenment had already come. According to them, the progressive direction of the modern era was not in doubt.

Finally, was a "Mendelssohnian school" established? His legacy is complex and needs to be examined. It comprised at least three aspects: his philosophy, his historical image and the Jewish Enlightenment movement attributed to him. There is no doubt that Mendelssohn's contribution to Jewish thought served as a reference point, focus and challenge to later thinkers. From the standpoint of the history of modern Jewish philosophy, or the history of biblical translation and

[122]Friedländer, *Moses Mendelssohn, op. cit.*, p. 14.

exegesis, Mendelssohn's concepts on issues relevant to the age of emancipation and secularisation are of great importance. Thus on topics such as the place of the Jewish community in the modern state, the validity of *Halakhah*, the belief in divine revelation, the relations between religion and community, the question of coercion in religious matters and the status of the *mitzvot*, Mendelssohn not only asked questions, but also proposed answers that were of great significance for modern Jewish thought.[123] However, this philosophical legacy did not necessarily lead to the establishment of the *Haskalah* movement or the creation of a school of *maskilim*. Both the figure and image of Mendelssohn and his thought did influence the representatives of the different religious movements in nineteenth-century Germany, and his faithful followers could be found even among the new Orthodoxy; certainly as pertains to the concept of the *mitzvot* and their relationship to life. Even though Rabbi Samson Raphael Hirsch, for example, had many reservations about Mendelssohn's thought, the scholar of German Orthodoxy, Professor Mordechai Breuer, can argue that "as a religious rationalist Hirsch was a disciple of Mendelssohn".[124]

The other component – Mendelssohn's historical image, the halo of an historical hero – had great force. It helped to avoid having to relate directly and specifically to his thought. Whether deists, salon women, fighters for emancipation, *maskilim*, religious reformers, ideologues or scholars of the new *Wissenschaft des Judentums*, a variety of different groups could relate to Mendelssohn. His place of honour in the pantheon of German cultural heroes gratified their Jewish honour, without his thought necessarily having any significant influence on them at all.[125]

A *Haskalah* school was indeed established, but it related much more to figures such as Wessely, Euchel, Brill-Loewe, Satanow, Wolfsohn and others, to the *Hame'asef* circle, the critical satirical works of the 1790s, the programmes for Jewish educational reform, and to the *maskilim's* picture of the future, than to Mendelssohn's philosophy. They all cultivated the image of Mendelssohn, but it was in fact his "disciples" who were the true founders of the *Haskalah*. It was they who provided the model to be emulated by the *Haskalah* movement that developed in Eastern Europe after its centres in Germany declined at the turn of the century. Thus the *Haskalah* did not have just one progenitor, but rather a number of initiators and activists. Mendelssohn, who was generally content with giving the moral support of a distant observer, was not numbered among them. Only a few maskilim enjoyed a close relationship with him; whereas associating with the *maskilim* was only a marginal part of Mendelssohn's extensive social life. Most of the meetings at his "court" were random encounters and the great majority of those engaged in *Haskalah* did not have direct contact with him, they did not even correspond with him. The non-Jewish sources that relate to Mendelssohn and his associates are limited to those German-language writers who had gained distinction in the "neutral" societies: Friedländer, Bendavid,

[123]See Eliezer Schweid, *Toldot ha-Hagut ha-Yehudit ba-Eit ha-Hadasha*, Jerusalem 1977, chap. 3.
[124]Mordechai Breuer, *Jüdische Orthodoxie im Deutschen Reich, 1871–1918. Die Sozialgeschichte einer religiösen Minderheit*, Frankfurt a. Main 1986. Veröffentlichung des Leo Baeck Instituts, chap. 3.
[125]*Ibid.*, chap. 2; Altmann, 'Moses Mendelssohn as the Archetypal German Jew', *loc. cit.*

Herz and Bloch. Hardly any of the other *maskilim* were mentioned by the non-Jewish Germans who described Jewish Berlin and the patterns of renewal and modernisation they discerned there.[126]

VI

The *maskilim* saw in Mendelssohn everything they themselves lacked. In essence they "drafted" him into their ranks as a person worthy of serving as their teacher and leader. But in reality, they went about their projects without him. If that was the way they behaved in his lifetime, it was even more the case after his death. They continued to nurture their adulation and anointed Mendelssohn as the teacher, father and founder of their movement. The relatively few who fully fathomed his philosophy of Judaism could, of course, adopt and develop a few useful concepts. It seems, however, that by the end of the eighteenth century his thought was used mainly by the radical *maskilim* who found in Mendelssohn a reference point for their deistic beliefs or their plans for religious reform. The Hebrew readers among the nineteenth-century *maskilim*, mainly concentrated in Eastern Europe, were rather restricted in what they could learn about Mendelssohn's thought. The fact that the *maskilim* hardly bothered to translate Mendelssohn's philosophical works into Hebrew (*Jerusalem* first appeared in Hebrew translation in 1867) shows that for the admirers Mendelssohn was first of all a unique personality. Only later, if at all, did they relate to his thought, which apart from the *Biur* did not play a central role in the nineteenth-century Eastern European *Haskalah*.[127]

The picture that evolves from the historical perspective presented here, one that assesses the parameters of the *Haskalah*, the identity of the *maskilim* and the many and significant differences between them and Mendelssohn, shows that their connection to him was one of admiration more than of discipleship. The distinction between the *maskilim* and "Mendelssohn's disciples" lets us examine the *maskilim*, their programme and the extent of their influence without identifying the *Haskalah* as a historical phenomenon almost totally subservient to the giant shadow cast by the German-Jewish philosopher Mendelssohn. There were, indeed, areas of common contact between Mendelssohn and the *maskilim*. However, the *Haskalah* as an historical ideological movement goes well beyond Mendelssohn and was not totally dependent on him.

---

[126]Stefi Jersch-Wenzel, 'Die Juden im gesellschaftlichen Gefüge Berlins um 1800', in *Bild und Selbstbild der Juden Berlins zwischen Aufklärung und Romantik*, ed. by Marianne Awerbuch and Stefi Jersch-Wenzel, Berlin 1992, pp. 139–154.
[127]See Feiner, *Hahaskalah Beyahasa Lahistoria, op. cit.*, pp. 263–270.

Religious Reforms and Secular Trends in German-Jewish Life
An Agenda for Research

BY DAVID SORKIN

Perhaps the single most important factor in considering religious reform and secular trends in German-Jewish history is that the scholarship has until recently been dominated by *Geistesgeschichte*. Based on the work of a handful of intellectual élites, scholars have time and again presented the history of religious and secular thought as if it were the history of religious reform and secular trends. Only in the past decade or two have studies begun to appear that alter our understanding by conceiving these topics not as narrow issues of religious and intellectual history, but rather as broader social and cultural processes.*

In surveying what we know about religious reform and secular trends, as well as indicating the areas that future scholarship might try to address, it is important to keep in mind that the two subjects cannot be isolated from the larger issue of German Jewry's transformation from a quasi-corporation on the margins of estate society to a minority in bourgeois society.[1] That historic transition can be said to have entailed a threefold revolution: political, ideological and social. These three revolutions were intimately linked and, to a large degree, inextricable. Since they shaped German-Jewish history, they will also serve to structure our analysis.

I. RELIGIOUS REFORM

Germany was the incontrovertible home of religious reform in Europe. Most of the forms of Jewish religious thought and practice normally identified as being distinctly modern (*Haskalah*, Reform, *Wissenschaft des Judentums*, Neo-Orthodoxy, Positive-Historical Judaism), and which largely provided the foundations for the various "movements" which have dominated Jewish religious life until the late

---

*An abbreviated version of this paper was delivered at the conference "Integration and Identity. The Jewish Experience in Germany and Italy from Enlightenment to Fascism" (Rome, 15th-18th November 1993), sponsored by the Leo Baeck Institute, London; The Goethe Institute, Rome; and the University of Rome "La Sapienza".

[1]Trude Maurer makes this same point in the introduction to her excellent survey of recent literature on German-Jewish history. See *Die Entwicklung der jüdischen Minderheit in Deutschland (1780–1933). Neuere Forschungen und offene Fragen*, Tübingen 1992 (Internationales Archiv für Sozialgeschichte der deutschen Literatur 4), pp. 7–11.

twentieth century, originated in Germany in the closing decades of the eighteenth and the first half of the nineteenth century. This irreducible fact accounts for the Germanocentric view of much of the scholarship on the modern history of the Jews: German Jewry has been deemed the "mirror of modernity" or the locus for the "origins of the modern Jew". Yet the scholarship has gone beyond merely focusing on Germany to treating it as a virtual model or paradigm, asking the extent to which it influenced, or was followed by, Jews in other countries.[2]

The question we need to ask now is not why other Jewries followed a different path, but why German Jewry followed its path? Not why Germany was the rule, but why it was the exception? For if one looks around Europe in the same period there is simply nothing comparable to its fundamental ideological ferment: English Jewry created a refined "High-Church" Orthodoxy with mild reform in synagogues in London (West End) and Manchester; French Jewry never went beyond minor reforms of aesthetics and decorum; while *minhag Wien* was a decorous Orthodoxy entirely within the bounds of *Halakhah*.[3] We need to identify those factors which differentiated German from other Jewries and created the preconditions for religious ferment.

The first factor was the intensity and duration of German Jewry's political revolution. It was in the German states that an autonomous Ashkenazic community collided with enlightened absolutism and remained engaged with the tutelary state. Ashkenazic Jews from Alsace in the west to the Polish-Lithuanian Kingdom in the east were organised as autonomous communities in which, in exchange for the remission of taxes and other revenues, the Jews exercised considerable control over numerous aspects of their collective lives, e.g. religion, education and social welfare (there were significant regional variations in the structure of the autonomous communities – the supra-community "Council of Four Lands" in Poland, the *Landjudenschaft* in many German states – yet these did not alter the basic pattern). All of these communities had

---

[2]Gerson D. Cohen, 'German Jewry as Mirror of Modernity', in *LBI Year Book XX* (1975), pp. IX-XXXI; and Michael A. Meyer, *The Origins of the Modern Jew. Jewish Identity and European Culture in Germany, 1749–1824*, Detroit 1967. For German Jewry and other Jewries see Jacob Katz (ed.), *Toward Modernity. The European Jewish Model*, New Brunswick–Oxford 1987, in which there is a discernible tension between the question the editor posed and the responses of many of the contributors. The "Germanocentric" view of modern Jewish history can be seen in the predominance of German material in the religio-intellectual sections of what has become the standard documentary reader in modern Jewish history in the United States, Paul R. Mendes-Flohr and Jehuda Reinharz (eds.), *The Jew in the Modern World. A Documentary History*, New York 1980.

[3]For England see Todd M. Endelman, *The Jews of Georgian England, 1714–1830. Tradition and Change in a Liberal Society*, Philadelphia 1979; and *idem*, 'The Englishness of Jewish Modernity in England', in Katz (ed.), *Toward Modernity, op. cit.*, pp. 225–246. For Manchester see Bill Williams, *The Making of Manchester Jewry, 1740–1875*, Manchester 1976, pp. 221–267. For France see Jay Berkovitz, *The Shaping of Jewish Identity in 19th-Century France*, Detroit 1989. For Vienna see Marsha L. Rozenblit, 'The Struggle over Religious Reform in Nineteenth-Century Vienna', in *Association for Jewish Studies Review*, vol. XIV, No. 2 (1989), pp. 179–221; and *idem*, 'Jewish Identity and the Modern Rabbi. The Cases of Isak Noa Mannheimer, Adolf Jellinek and Moritz Güdemann in Nineteenth-Century Vienna', in *LBI Year Book XXXV* (1990), pp. 103–131; and Robert S. Wistrich, 'The Modernization of Viennese Jewry. The Impact of German Culture in a Multi-Ethnic State', in Katz (ed.), *Toward Modernity, op. cit.*, pp. 43–70. For a masterful overview of reform throughout Europe see Michael A. Meyer, *Response to Modernity. A History of the Reform Movement in Judaism*, New York–Oxford 1988.

institutionalised an insular version of Judaism which rested on the study of Talmud, Kabbalah and homily to the virtual exclusion of the Hebrew language and independent study of the Bible, and the rejection of practically all secular subjects such as mathematics, science and philosophy.[4] Only in the German states did such a community encounter enlightened despotism head on. In the Habsburg lands Joseph II's reforms of the 1780s were short-lived; the discussion of the Jews' status in that same decade in France resulted in only the most tentative legislation (1787); and the partitions of the Polish-Lithuanian Kingdom prevented the discussions there from leading to actual legislation.

The encounter in Germany began from the very readmission of the Jews during and after the Thirty Years' War. From the start a peculiar tension was at work. Cameralist policies recommended the admission of Jews (and other dissident groups such as the Huguenots) to stimulate trade and rebuild shattered economies in the name of dynastic consolidation, yet without altering the Jews' status as segregated inferiors living on sufferance. Yet that same policy of consolidation included an administrative centralisation which, by gradually depriving the Jewish communities of their autonomy, increasingly integrated them into the mechanism of the bureaucratic state.[5] Such administrative integration paved the way for emancipation: once the Jews' quasi-corporate status had been levelled – as part of a general levelling of corporate privilege – *raison d'état* militated against the maintenance of inferior status. Legislation and life none the less resisted logic: the process of political integration was to be neither quick nor painless.

The *Haskalah* is thought to have resulted from this peculiar tension, since it emerged at the very moment when corporate society was showing signs of its impending demise but had not yet given birth to a new order. The *Haskalah* is normally seen as the first in the series of religious reforms, for it introduced a new set of general human or secular criteria into Judaism on the basis of which its adherents claimed the right to exercise authority and leadership. It is usually dated to the 1770s and 1780s when it emerged publicly and began to form a distinct subgroup in the Jewish community.[6]

This view ignores the *Haskalah*'s internal origins. It had originated as an effort to renew Judaism by restoring neglected elements of the textual tradition, especially the cognate disciplines of Jewish biblical exegesis and philosophy, as well as making available the secular knowledge (languages, mathematics,

---

[4]For the most comprehensive description see Jacob Elbaum, *Petihut ve-Histagrut. Ha-Yetsira ha-Ruhanit ha-Sifrutit be-Polin ube-Artsot Ashkenaz be-Shalhei ha-Meah ha-Sheish Esrei*, Jerusalem 1990. For a brief discussion of baroque Judaism see David Sorkin, 'From Context to Comparison. The German Haskalah and Reform Catholicism', in *Tel Aviver Jahrbuch für deutsche Geschichte*, 20 (1991), pp. 23–28.
[5]For this process see the now classic work of Selma Stern, *Der Preussische Staat und die Juden* (4 parts), Tübingen 1962–1975 (Schriftenreihe wissenschaftlicher Abhandlungen des Leo Baeck Instituts 7/1,2; 8/1,2; 24/1, 24/2, I and II; 32); and the more recent work of Albert A. Bruer, *Geschichte der Juden in Preußen (1750–1820)*, Frankfurt a. Main 1991.
[6]A comprehensive historical study of the *Haskalah* is a major desideratum. For aspects of the *Haskalah* see, for example, Jacob Katz, *Tradition and Crisis. Jewish Society at the End of the Middle Ages*, New York 1961, pp. 245–274 (I have not had access to the new edition of this classic work); Meyer, *The Origins of the Modern Jew, op. cit.*; David Sorkin, *The Transformation of German Jewry, 1780–1840*, New York 1987, pp. 41–78.

science, philosophy) needed to support them. Early figures were drawn from three groups: university-trained physicians (Tobias Cohen, 1652–1729; Aaron Salomon Gumpertz, 1723–1769; Abraham Kisch, b. 1728); autodidacts (Raphael Levi of Hanover, 1685–1779; Israel Samocz (Zamosc), 1700–1772; Moses Mendelssohn, 1729–1786); and sympathetic rabbis (David Fraenkel, 1707–1762). In its early decades (*circa* 1720–1770) the *Haskalah* was a tendency within mainstream Judaism, a situation confirmed by the fact that Hebrew works on science, grammar and philosophy came off the same presses as casuistic, kabbalistic and ethical ones.[7] At least one scholar has attempted to show that the *Haskalah* represented an internal effort to stem the tide of acculturation of Jews to the larger society which had been under way since the end of the seventeenth century.[8] Be that as it may, only in the 1770s and 1780s did the *Haskalah* turn from the renewal of Judaism to the reform of the Jews and of Judaism. It now advocated not just a revamping of the educational curriculum, but also a restructuring of Jewish occupations and the Jewish community, going so far as to attempt to create alternative institutions to implement its programme.[9]

This turn belonged to the politicisation characteristic of the late Enlightenment in general and the German *Aufklärung* in particular, of which the discussion of Jewish emancipation (e.g. Christian Wilhelm von Dohm) was an integral part. There was also an incontrovertible internal dynamic at play: younger *maskilim* (Isaac Euchel, Joel Brill-Loewe), figures on the periphery of the movement (Salomon Maimon), or a wealthy and increasingly radical leader such as David Friedländer, did not hesitate to provoke, indeed often desired, a rift with the rabbis and their insular Judaism. Yet the acceleration of external events set the pace: Naphtali Herz Wessely's pamphlet advocating educational reform, *Divrei Shalom Ve' Emeth* (Words of Peace and Truth), which has often been called the manifesto of the *Haskalah*, was a direct response to Joseph II's edict, whereas the major Jewish defence of emancipation, Mendelssohn's *Jerusalem, oder über religiöse Macht und Judentum*, was part of the public debate.

The relationship of the *Haskalah* to subsequent reforms on the one side and to German Jewry's continuing political revolution on the other, has been a focus of controversy. Reformers of various persuasions consistently invoked the *Haskalah*'s and especially Moses Mendelssohn's authority, and an older scholarship favourable to reform did the same. The latter also appealed to political events and the *Zeitgeist* to justify reforms.[10] Reforms in fact kept pace with the politics of emancipation: emancipation was conceived as a *quid pro quo* predicated on an exchange of rights for regeneration. Making Judaism an "ethical", aesthetic and edifying religion rather than a ritualistic one was also part of the contract. This is neither to deny nor to deprecate the genuine religious and intellectual impulses

---

[7]On this point see Sorkin, 'From Context to Comparison', *loc. cit.*, pp. 30–32.
[8]Azriel Shohet, *Im Hilufei Tekufot. Reshit ha-Haskalah be-Yahadut Germanya*, Jerusalem 1960.
[9]Shmuel Feiner, 'Isaac Euchel, "Entrepreneur" of the Haskalah Movement in Germany', in *Zion*, vol. LII, No. 4 (1987), pp. 427–469 (in Hebrew); Sorkin, 'From Context to Comparison', *loc. cit.*, pp. 36–41.
[10]For a striking example see David Philipson, *The Reform Movement in Judaism*, 2nd edn., New York 1931.

which motivated many of the reformers, but rather to delineate the larger context in which they functioned.[11] Thus the political and ideological revolutions were so closely linked as to be inseparable. The continuing pressure for emancipation from the tutelary state which monitored, supervised and in many cases also legislated reform of all aspects of Jewish life penetrated to the very heart of Jewish religious self-understanding and expression. There were other factors that also differentiated the Jews' situation in the German states: for example the religious and intellectual ferment in *Vormärz* Protestantism, which served as an impetus and model (France and England had no equivalent), and the exclusion of Jewish university graduates from civil service positions, which kept them in the Jewish community and provided a radical leadership (French Jews were appointed to civil service positions). These were only necessary causes; emancipation was both necessary and sufficient.

The chronology of Reform is easily summarised. Pamphlets and articles advocating reform appeared in the 1790s.[12] The first efforts at actual reform, albeit extremely limited, appeared in the first decade of the nineteenth century under the auspices of the Kingdom of Westphalia which, following Napoleon's model, appointed a central *consistoire* that was empowered to introduce changes. Significant changes (omission of *piyutim*; the *kol nidre* on Yom Kippur and the prayer for the ingathering of exiles; shift to Sephardic pronunciation; German sermons) were introduced in a private synagogue in Berlin during the period of liberation and in the years immediately following the Congress of Vienna, yet were suppressed by a conservative Prussian government opposed to all political or religious innovation. In 1818–1819 Hamburg became the site of the first Reform Temple and also the first major religious controversy over reform (the changes here included such innovations as a German sermon, alteration or omission of passages in the liturgy dealing with the re-institution of sacrifices and the return to Zion, omission of the particularist *aleinu* prayer except on the High Holidays and elimination of the readings from the prophetic books – *Haftorah* – on the Sabbath).[13] The 1830s witnessed struggles over the appointments of rabbis in major communities (Breslau, Hamburg) and the emergence of Neo-Orthodoxy. The 1840s saw the emergence of lay groups (Berlin, Frankfurt a. Main) which attempted to become the vanguard of Reform; and in that same decade a number of rabbinical conferences convened which endeavoured to assert the leadership of a new group of rabbis. In the 1850s the first modern rabbinical seminary opened its doors in Breslau, establishing Zacharias Frankel's "Positive-Historical Judaism" midway between Reform and Orthodoxy.

---

[11]The relationship of reform to emancipation is a delicate subject. Michael Meyer's sophisticated treatment is somewhat ambiguous on this point. See Meyer, *Response to Modernity, op. cit.*, pp. 17, 144, 193, 194–195, 225. For an analysis that sees the politics of the German states as totally determinant, see Calvin Goldscheider and Alan S. Zuckerman, *The Transformation of the Jews*, Chicago 1984, pp. 63–75. For a recent masterful review of the literature on reform see Michael A. Meyer, 'Recent Historiography on the Jewish Religion in Modern Germany', in *LBI Year Book XXXV* (1990), pp. 3–16.

[12]See, for example, Lazarus Bendavid, *Etwas zur Charakteristik der Juden*, Leipzig 1793; Saul Ascher, *Leviathan, oder Über Religion in Rücksicht des Judentums*, Berlin 1792.

[13]Meyer, *Response to Modernity, op. cit.*, pp. 57–61.

Additional synods were held in the 1860s. In the 1870s Liberal and Orthodox seminaries were established in Berlin that institutionalised the religious divisions.

This summary merits elucidation. The chronological high point of Reform as an ideology was in the *Vormärz*, when the political pressures of emancipation were most intense. The notion that regeneration was the price of emancipation pervaded the public debates and legislation of the period. After the Revolution of 1848 Jewish emancipation became part of the political agenda of Liberalism, for German liberals realised that curtailing the Jews' freedom was injurious to the greater cause of establishing a constitutional monarchy.[14] The idea of a *quid pro quo* of rights for regeneration that held sway in the *Vormärz* gradually faded, and so, too, did the sense of urgency in the process of religious reform. The conferences of the 1860s seemed tame, if not routine, in comparison with those of the 1840s.[15] The religious revolution had largely spent itself by the time emancipation was achieved (1871). Subsequent changes were largely embellishments on an already established structure.

The entire religious landscape of German Jewry was altered. The emergence of reforms or Reform belonged to an overall restructuring of Jewish religious life to fit the new circumstances of the political revolution.[16] Orthodoxy only emerged in response to Reform; it appeared at the time of the Hamburg Temple controversy, when its first programmatic statement proclaimed its existence.[17] From that point onwards it was engaged with the opposition, often fighting "fire with fire" by adapting Reform methods to Orthodox ends.[18] The same holds for Positive-Historical Judaism and Neo-Orthodoxy, only more so. In retrospect the areas of agreement between them and Reform far outweighed the points of contention: the acceptance of the emancipation contract, the confessionalisation of Judaism, the idea of the Jews' "mission", the centrality of *Bildung* and *Wissenschaft*, the figure of the *Rabbiner-Doktor* (modern Rabbi). This underlying consensus was the clearest evidence for the ideological revolution: all these versions of Judaism belonged to the subculture – the amalgam of subtly

---

[14]For this point see Reinhard Rürup, 'Jewish Emancipation and Bourgeois Society', in *LBI Year Book XIV* (1969), pp. 67–91.

[15]Meyer, *Response to Modernity, op. cit.*, pp. 187–191.

[16]Max Wiener, *Jüdische Religion im Zeitalter der Emanzipation*, Berlin 1933.

[17]Moshe Samet, 'The Beginnings of Orthodoxy', in *Modern Judaism*, vol. VIII, No. 3 (1988), pp. 249–269; Jacob Katz, 'Orthodoxy in Historical Perspective', in *Studies in Contemporary Jewry*, 2 (1986), pp. 3–17. This is also borne out by the biography of one of the major figures of modern German Orthodoxy. See David Ellenson, *Rabbi Esriel Hildesheimer and the Creation of a Modern Jewish Orthodoxy*, Tuscaloosa 1990.

[18]The German-language press, German-language sermons and the use of *Wissenschaft* are some of the most obvious examples. On these points see Judith Bleich, 'The Emergence of an Orthodox Press in Nineteenth-Century Germany', in *Jewish Social Studies*, vol. XLII, No. 3–4 (1980), pp. 323–344; idem, *Jacob Ettlinger. His Life and Times*, unpublished Ph.D. diss., New York University 1974; Ellenson, *Rabbi Esriel Hildesheimer, op. cit.*; and, for a later period, Mordechai Breuer, *Jüdische Orthodoxie im deutschen Reich, 1871–1918. Die Sozialgeschichte einer religiösen Minderheit*, Frankfurt a. Main 1986. Veröffentlichung des Leo Baeck Instituts.

transformed German culture and Judaism created in response to the emancipation process.[19]

The *Gemeinde* structure intensified the conflict. Jews in virtually all German states were part of an obligatory unified community with powers of taxation until the Law of Secession (*Austrittsgesetz*) was adopted in 1876. The conflicts over Reform affected the interests of the entire community; they involved the allocation of shared resources. The Reformers' initial hope was to gain the allegiance of the majority and make its version the Judaism of the entire community. When they realised the failure of that hope, they settled for the status of a denomination – the *Gemeinde* remained united for matters of social welfare but divided in religious observance – and the communities institutionalised toleration and intra-confessional pluralism by supporting "temples" as well as "synagogues". The contrast with other countries is significant. In England affiliation to a synagogue was entirely voluntary, and the Chief Rabbi's authority was more *de facto* than *de jure*. The centralised *consistoire* in France vested authority in Paris, and thus the conflicts in France were often between the provinces and the capital.[20]

The extent to which these reforms were disseminated remains something of an open question. Considerable research has been carried out on the leaders and thinkers of the movements: Abraham Geiger and Zacharias Frankel, Samson Raphael Hirsch and Jakob Ettlinger, Esriel Hildesheimer and Heinrich Graetz, though even here much work remains to be done.[21] We can therefore trace the development of ideas among these figures with some precision. We are less able to trace the diffusion of Reform or even to say whether there was a process of diffusion with discernible directions. It does seem to be the case that Reform developed first as an ideology and then as a movement.[22] Whereas most of the major ideas of Reform were already in circulation in the 1830s, it was only from the late 1830s that a new cohort of university-educated rabbis (*Rabbiner-Doktoren*) brought the practice of reform to the communities. In fact, the rabbinical conferences of the 1840s were as much an instrument for the diffusion of Reform as the result of prior achievements: many of the delegates to the conferences (the maximum attendance was thirty-one) returned to their communities and

---

[19]Sorkin, *The Transformation of German Jewry*, *op. cit*.; Maurer, *Die Entwicklung der jüdischen Minderheit*, *op. cit*., p. 22. Shulamit Volkov has recently made a similar argument, asserting that German Jewry "created" a "modern tradition". See her *Die Erfindung einer Tradition. Zur Entstehung des modernen Judentums in Deutschland*, Munich 1992. For Orthodox attitudes to emancipation see the little-known but important article by Mordechai Breuer, 'Emancipation and the Rabbis', in *Niv Hamidrashia*, 13 (1978–1979), pp. 26–51.

[20]For the structure of the consistory see Phyllis Cohen Albert, *The Modernisation of French Jewry. Consistory and Community in the Nineteenth Century*, Hanover, NH 1977; for conflicts between one province and the centre see Paula E. Hyman, *The Emancipation of the Jews of Alsace. Acculturation and Tradition in the Nineteenth Century*, New Haven 1991.

[21]For an English-speaking audience there is, however, a dearth of primary material in translation. A series of classics of German-Jewish thought, on the model of *Heinrich Graetz. The Structure of Jewish History and Other Essays*, ed., transl. by Ismar Schorsch, New York 1975, would be highly desirable.

[22]I rely here on the excellent study of Steven M. Lowenstein, 'The 1840s and the Creation of the German-Jewish Religious Reform Movement', in Werner E. Mosse, Arnold Paucker and Reinhard Rürup (eds.), *Revolution and Evolution. 1848 in German-Jewish History*, Tübingen 1981 (Schriftenreihe wissenschaftlicher Abhandlungen des Leo Baeck Instituts 39), pp. 255–297.

introduced Reform for the first time.[23] The movement continued to spread and consolidate during the 1850s and 1860s.[24] Diffusion depended to a large extent on the emancipation process: those governments which favoured emancipation (particularly in the south and southwest, e.g. Baden and Württemberg) either allowed or often required reform, whereas conservative governments which opposed emancipation often opposed or banned it (Prussia from 1823 to 1840; Bavaria reversed its policy: after favouring reform, it became an opponent in the 1840s). No strict urban-rural distinction existed. While the reforms in the first two decades of the century were decidedly urban, the participants at the rabbinical conferences of the 1840s were as likely as their Orthodox opponents to hail from small towns. Only in the second half, and especially in the last third of the century was there a discernible concentration of Orthodoxy in rural areas. This was the flip side of urbanisation: as migration to urban areas emptied the rural areas of Jews favouring Reform, the proportion of Orthodox among those who remained in the hamlets and villages increased.

The social basis of Reform remains shrouded in mystery. In Frankfurt a. Main, for example, it was largely championed by a group of relative "newcomers" to the city whose secular educations and professions set them off from the "native" banking and commercial groups, who supported Orthodoxy and eventually became the leaders of the *Israelitische Religionsgesellschaft* which appointed Samson Raphael Hirsch its spiritual leader (1851).[25] The Hamburg Reform Temple was probably established by younger men from the middle of the economic spectrum who, because of commercial pursuits, had more contact with non-Jews than wealthier, older and more established members of the community.[26] For other communities we lack such an analysis. In consequence, the political and ideological revolutions have yet to be connected with the social one.[27] We suspect that the growth of an urban middle class promoted the spread of Reform; we lack the hard evidence to prove it. At this point we should examine what we do know about secular trends within German Jewry.

II. SECULAR TRENDS

The history of secular trends has often been presented by turning the thoughts and lives of the most prominent individuals from the late eighteenth century

---

[23] Meyer, *Response to Modernity, op. cit.*, pp. 134–138.

[24] Jacob Toury would argue that the decisive battle between Reform and Orthodoxy was fought between 1848 and 1858. See his *Der Eintritt der Juden ins deutsche Bürgertum. Eine Dokumentation*, Tel Aviv 1972, p. 318, and ' "Deutsche Juden" im Vormärz', in *Bulletin des Leo Baeck Instituts*, Nos. 29–32 (1965), pp. 65f.

[25] Robert Liberles, *Religious Conflict in Social Context. The Resurgence of Orthodox Judaism in Frankfurt am Main, 1838–1877*, Westport, CT 1985.

[26] Michael A. Meyer, 'The Establishment of the Hamburg Temple', in E. Etkes and Y. Salomon (eds.), *Perakim be-Toldot ha-Hevra ha-Yehudit*, Jerusalem 1980, pp. 218–224 (in Hebrew).

[27] Jacob Toury has recently argued that Reform Judaism failed to deliver the revolution in Jewish life it promised – the ideological revolution did not result in a social revolution – and thus became a form of "shallow denominationalism". See 'The Revolution that Did Not Happen', in *Zeitschrift für Religions- und Geistesgeschichte*, vol. XXXIV, No. 3 (1984), pp. 193–203.

onwards into representative biographies, and of later organisations into representative movements. At the risk of caricature, as well as doing a disservice to colleagues past and present, that view could be summarised as follows: secular trends began with Moses Mendelssohn, who bridged between the atrophied Judaism of the ghetto and German culture. A minor figure, such as the physician and popular philosophical lecturer Marcus Herz, added additional spans to the bridge (Kant thought him to be one of the best interpreters of his philosophy). The Jewish *salonnières* of the 1790s and the next decade (Dorothea Mendelssohn, Henriette Herz, Rahel Varnhagen) added to the intellectual and cultural connection an erotic dimension and a religious fervour which took them beyond Judaism.[28] In the *Vormärz* Jews, or former Jews, such as Eduard Gans, Heinrich Heine and Ludwig Börne were at the centre of German intellectual life, whereas the writer Berthold Auerbach was equally important for German popular culture. Prior to their conversions, Gans and Heine were members of the student group in Berlin which established the academic study of Judaism (*Wissenschaft des Judentums*), thus contributing to the emergence of a secular, or secularising, method of study. Also in the *Vormärz* one begins to find Jews (Moses Hess) or former Jews (Karl Marx) among the early Socialists who pioneered radically secular doctrines.[29] The dialectical complement to the flight from Judaism was a return to Jewish identity: such a return found literary expression in the poetry and prose of Heine, and historio-philosophical expression in the work of Moses Hess.[30] In the 1850s and 1860s the torch of representative biography perhaps passed to such political figures as Eduard Lasker and Ludwig Bamberger who symbolised the emergence of secular liberal politics.[31] It was then carried on by a figure such as Hermann Cohen, who reformulated the ideology of emancipation in the face of the new antisemitism during the infamous debate with Treitschke, yet then went on to rediscover Judaism and reshape his philosophy in the closing period of his life.[32]

In the last decades of the century representative individuals gave way to representative institutions and movements. The *Centralverein deutscher Staatsbürger jüdischen Glaubens* and the *Zionistische Vereinigung für Deutschland* symbolised the poles of Jewish self-understanding and, in their common adherence to things

---

[28]On the *salonnières* see most recently, Deborah Hertz, *Jewish High Society in Old Regime Berlin*, New Haven–London 1988.

[29]For a sophisticated version for the *Vormärz* see Hanns G. Reissner, 'Begegnung zwischen Deutschen und Juden im Zeichen der Romantik', in Hans Liebeschütz and Arnold Paucker (eds.), *Das Judentum in der Deutschen Umwelt 1800–1850*, Tübingen 1977 (Schriftenreihe wissenschaftlicher Abhandlungen des Leo Baeck Instituts 35), pp. 325–357.

[30]In the enormous literature on Heine see for example, Siegfried Prawer, *Heine's Jewish Comedy. A Study of his Portraits of Jews and Judaism*, Oxford 1983; the biography by Jeffrey L. Sammons, *Heinrich Heine. A Modern Biography*, Princeton 1979; and the introduction by Ritchie Robertson, *Heine*, London 1988. For Hess see Shlomo Avineri, *Moses Hess. Prophet of Zionism and of Communism*, New York 1985.

[31]For the most recent and informative study see Peter Pulzer, *Jews and the German State. The Political History of a Minority 1848–1933*, Oxford 1992, pp. 85–96.

[32]Pinchas E. Rosenblüth, 'Die geistigen und religiösen Strömungen in der deutschen Judenheit', in *Juden im Wilhelminischen Deutschland 1890–1914*, hrsg. von Werner E. Mosse unter Mitwirkung von Arnold Paucker, Tübingen 1976 (Schriftenreihe wissenschaftlicher Abhandlungen des Leo Baeck Instituts 33), pp. 559–567.

German, the march of secularisation. The association of Jews with modernist culture as producers, consumers and patrons would further add to the picture.[33] The early twentieth century would have its returnees to Judaism as well, beginning with Cohen and continuing with Buber and Rosenzweig.

While the brevity and superficiality of this summary obviously does an injustice to the subject, it does indicate that the study of a few representative figures or organisations does not equal an analysis of Germany Jewry's social revolution, namely, the larger institutional and socio-cultural changes by which an urban middle class emerged and became dominant.[34]

This third revolution took place in relationship to the larger society and specifically the German *Bildungsbürgertum*, which served German Jewry as both a model for emulation and as a target for integration.[35] The *Bildungsbürgertum* was not defined by economic standing or assigned status – it was neither an estate nor a class – but, rather, constituted a culture.[36] Entrance to this culture to be sure presupposed certain means or income, but even more required the acquisition of a set of attributes ranging from language and education to moral attitudes and forms of sociability. For German Jews these attributes were in fact the very ones stipulated by the emancipation contract of regeneration for rights.[37] In consequence, the social revolution was rooted in the political one, and German Jewry's secularisation was a function of its *embourgeoisement*: the secular trends it exhibited were, by and large, what made it part of the middle class. The key question is

---

[33] Peter Gay, *Freud, Jews and Other Germans. Masters and Victims in Modernist Culture*, chap. 'Encounter with Modernism. German Jews in Wilhelminian Culture', New York 1978, pp. 93–169. On Jews in German culture see also Jacob Katz, 'German Culture and the Jews', in Jehuda Reinharz and Walter Schatzberg (eds.), *The Jewish Response to German Culture. From the Enlightenment to the Second World War*, Hanover, NH 1985, pp. 85–99.

[34] Jacob Toury would estimate that 80% of German Jewry qualified as bourgeois by 1870. See *Soziale und politische Geschichte der Juden in Deutschland, 1848–1871. Zwischen Revolution, Reaktion und Emanzipation*, Düsseldorf 1977, p. 277. Shulamit Volkov has criticised the narrow notion of "culture" that informs much of the scholarship. See her *Jüdisches Leben und Antisemitismus im 19. und 20. Jahrhundert. Zehn Essays*, Munich 1990, chap. 'Jüdische Assimilation und Eigenart im Kaiserreich', p. 137. The persistence of the lower classes has only recently begun to receive attention. For the eighteenth century see Rudolf Glanz, *Geschichte des niederen jüdischen Volkes in Deutschland. Eine Studie über historisches Gaunertum, Bettelwesen und Vagantentum*, New York 1968. For the nineteenth century see the recent works of Claudia Prestel, 'Jüdische Unterschichten im Zeitalter der Emanzipation, dargestellt anhand der Gemeinde Fürth, 1826–1870', in *Aschkenas*, 1 (1991), pp. 95–134; and Aharon Bornstein, *HaKabtsanim. Perek Be-Toldot Yehudei Germanya*, Jerusalem 1992.

[35] This was first argued by Jacob Katz, in *Die Entstehung der Judenassimilation und deren Ideologie*, Frankfurt 1935. See also Jacob Toury, 'Der Eintritt der Juden ins deutsche Bürgertum', in Liebeschütz and Paucker (eds.), *Judentum in der deutschen Umwelt, op. cit.*, pp. 139–242; David Sorkin, *The Transformation of German Jewry, op. cit., passim*; and Shulamit Volkov, chap. 'Die Verbürgerlichung der Juden in Deutschland als Paradigma', in *Jüdisches Leben und Antisemitismus, op. cit.*, pp. 111–131. On *Bildung* as the civil religion of German Jewry see George L. Mosse, *German Jews Beyond Judaism*, Bloomington 1985.

[36] Jürgen Kocka, 'Bürgertum und Bürgerlichkeit als Probleme der deutschen Geschichte vom späten 18. zum frühen 20. Jahrhundert', in idem (ed.), *Bürger und Bürgerlichkeit im 19. Jahrhundert*, Göttingen 1987, pp. 42–48; and Volkov, 'Die Verbürgerlichung der Juden in Deutschland', *loc. cit.*, pp. 113–114.

[37] George L. Mosse, 'Jewish Emancipation. Between *Bildung* and Respectability', in Reinharz and Schatzberg (eds.), *The Jewish Response to German Culture, op. cit.*, pp. 1–16. Mosse would see religious reform as a result of the social revolution (pp. 6–7), as would Volkov, in 'Die Verbürgerlichung der Juden in Deutschland', *loc. cit.*, pp. 121–123.

whether such *embourgeoisement*/secularisation distanced German Jews from Judaism and/or Jewish identification. Did the third revolution entail "assimilation"?[38] The representative biographies and institutions suggest a picture of increasing "assimilation". But the scholarship on this third revolution is still incomplete. What is known about three central institutions is surveyed in what follows.

Schooling was at the heart of the process of *embourgeoisement*. Education figured prominently from the inception of the emancipation process, e.g. Dohm's tract *Über die bürgerliche Verbesserung der Juden* and Joseph II's legislation. Detailed studies exist on the shift in curriculum from the *heder*, with its exclusive concentration on Jewish texts, to schools that included secular subjects, and/or taught Jewish subjects in a new spirit, as well as the Orthodox schools which were reshaped to accommodate secular education.[39] The *maskilim* created the first of these schools, yet in the period from 1778 to 1815 the schools did not enrol more than 20% of the eligible students; moreover, at least half of these students came from the poorest families. Whether this spelled achievement or failure, whether the cup of *maskilic* education was half empty or half full, is difficult to assess. Whatever their direct impact, these schools also had an indirect impact in that they served as models for the numerous schools founded during the *Vormärz* as a result of compulsory education legislation. This type of Jewish school reached its apogee in the mid-century. In 1847 in Prussia half of the eligible Jewish students attended Jewish elementary schools. The proportions declined steadily thereafter: 1886, 37%; 1901, 29% – as the appearance of the *Simultanschule*, which accommodated students of various confessions, removed many of the remaining obstacles for attendance at state schools.[40]

The extant studies have emphasised the institution of the school: the curriculum, the communal politics involved in the establishment and maintenance of the school and attendance figures. In contrast, we know precious little about the students: what impact did the schools have on them, whether on their Jewish self-understanding or, for that matter, on their occupations and economic success? Was there any correlation in the first half of the nineteenth century between education and social mobility? What about the relationship between education and Jewish allegiance or secularisation, or, for that matter, between mobility and secularisation? Studies which traced the careers and beliefs of the graduates of the various sorts of schools would contribute to our understanding

---

[38]For the term "assimilation" and a survey of the scholarship see David Sorkin, 'Emancipation and Assimilation. Two Concepts and their Application to German-Jewish History', in *LBI Year Book* XXXV (1990), pp. 17–33. For the use of the term in France see Phyllis Cohen Albert, 'Israelite and Jew. How did nineteenth-century French Jews understand assimilation?', in Jonathan Frankel and Steven J. Zipperstein (eds.), *Assimilation and Community. The Jews in Nineteenth-Century Europe*, Cambridge etc. 1992, pp. 88–109.

[39]The prime work here remains Mordechai Eliav, *Ha-Hinukh ha-Yehudi be-Germanya bi-Mei ha-Haskalah ve-ha-Emanzipatsiya*, Jerusalem 1960. For a more recent study in one region see, for example, Claudia Prestel, *Jüdisches Schul- und Erziehungswesen in Bayern 1804–1933. Tradition und Modernisierung im Zeitalter der Emanzipation*, Göttingen 1989.

[40]Prestel, *Jüdisches Schul-und Erziehungswesen, op. cit.*; Eliav, *Ha-Hinukh Ha-Yehudi, op. cit., passim*. For a survey of our present understanding of education see Maurer, *Die Entwicklung der jüdischen Minderheit, op. cit.*, pp. 34–35.

of the role these schools played in the process of *embourgeoisement* and secularisation.⁴¹

One scholar has recently tried to shift focus for the period of the *Kaiserreich*, arguing that if one looks at all of the "agents of socialisation" rather than just at educational institutions, Jewish and German institutions played paradoxically opposed roles: whereas Jewish institutions socialised Jews to be Germans, German institutions, through forms of discrimination ranging from the subtle and unwitting to the overt and deliberate, taught them that they remained Jews no matter how German they might become. He termed this a process of "reverse socialisation".⁴² This provocative thesis is a step in the right direction, though it does seem to simplify unduly the complex interplay of German culture and Judaism characteristic of Jewish institutions.

Language was at the heart of schooling and *embourgeoisement*, and for German Jews "language" signified the transition from Yiddish to German. While all the emancipation edicts legislated this transition, it did not occur in one stroke but, like the larger revolution to which it belonged, was a prolonged process stretching over a number of generations. Some of the literary evidence for this linguistic shift has been categorised. Books in old literary Yiddish continued to appear into the 1830s, but these were solely reprints of older works (e.g. prayer book translations, women's prayer books, collections of religious customs). The last such work was printed in 1836. A number of transitional stages existed between written Yiddish and written German. Yiddish works in Hebrew script appeared until the 1820s, yet these were almost exclusively dialogues in dramatic works whose purpose was to bring the message of the *Haskalah* to a Jewish audience. German works in Hebrew script (*Jüdisch-deutsch*) were also of two sorts. The first were works of the *Haskalah* which began to appear in the second half of the eighteenth century, with Mendelssohn's Bible translation being the most famous. *Maskilim* continued to write German in Hebrew script into the early decades of the nineteenth century, and a few schools taught it until the closing decades of that century. From the 1830s such *Jüdisch-deutsch* works became the province of Orthodox Jews, and religious works in this form issued from the presses until the 1870s and 1880s.⁴³ The duration of the process can be seen from the fact that as late as 1844 Anton Rée published a tract in which he applied Dohm's "environmental" thesis to the issue of language: since language peculiarities (i.e. Yiddish) were a result of the environment rather than of innate

---

⁴¹An interesting contribution on teacher training is Wolfgang Marienfeld, 'Jüdische Lehrerbildung in Hannover, 1848–1923', in *Hannoversche Geschichtsblätter*, vol. XXXVI, Nos. 1–2 (1982), pp. 1–107.

⁴²Chaim Schatzker, *Jüdische Jugend im zweiten Kaiserreich. Sozialisations- und Erziehungsprozesse der jüdischen Jugend in Deutschland, 1870–1917*, Frankfurt a. Main 1988 (Studien zur Erziehungswissenschaft 24).

⁴³Steven M. Lowenstein, 'The Yiddish Written Word in Nineteenth-Century Germany', in *LBI Year Book XXIV* (1979), pp. 179–192. See also Jacob Toury, 'Die Sprache als Problem der jüdischen Einordnung in den deutschen Kulturraum', in Walter Grab (ed.), *Gegenseitige Einflüsse deutscher und jüdischer Kultur. Von der Epoche der Aufklärung bis zur Weimarer Republik*, Tel-Aviv 1982 (Jahrbuch des Instituts für deutsche Geschichte, Beiheft 4), pp. 75–95.

national characteristics, they were subject to change. He advocated the adoption of High German as necessary to the achievement of emancipation.[44]

How long did Jews continue to speak Yiddish? At what point did generational differences in language usage in families cease? To what extent did Yiddish survive in phrases or intonations within High German, and among which speakers? The literary sources suggest that the point of no return may have been in the 1870s and 1880s. For example, at this point Jews began to write Yiddish in Latin script for Jewish audiences, using the language either as a joke or as a way to evoke a lost or disappearing way of life.[45] For the other uses of Yiddish we lack answers.[46] Literacy rates might, however, be helpful in this regard. What were the rates of literacy among Jews in the various German states? At what point in time were most Jews sufficiently literate to be culturally German or to claim membership in the *Bildungsbürgertum*? A number of scholars have suggested, for example, that Jewish emigration from Germany to the United States, which rose dramatically after mid-century, was a by-product of literacy (coupled with the growing social awareness aroused by the emancipation process).[47] Most of the published state censuses include information on literacy – as well as listing Jews separately, which makes the data accessible – and might provide information useful for answering these questions.

University attendance has probably received more attention, largely because it provides the background to the élites and representative figures. These studies show that the number of Jews attending universities jumped noticeably after 1815 and again in the early 1820s and early 1830s. The numbers continued to rise after mid-century, with a massive influx of Jews into the universities during the *Kaiserreich*.[48] The almost clichéd three-generational pattern of the grandfather who founded a business, the son who made it successful and the grandson who, after receiving a university education, spurned it for the arts or a profession, came to fruition in the *Kaiserreich*. The third generation was decidedly Wilhelminian. In making its way, that generation encountered considerable opposition. While the first appointment to a university professorship of an unconverted Jew

---

[44]Anton Rée, *Die Sprachverhältnisse der heutigen Juden, im Interesse der Gegenwart und mit besonderer Rücksicht auf Volkserziehung*, Hamburg 1844. For a discussion of Rée's work see Peter Freimark, 'Language Behaviour and Assimilation. The Situation of the Jews in Northern Germany in the First Half of the Nineteenth Century', in *LBI Year Book XXIV* (1979), pp. 157–177.

[45]Lowenstein, 'The Yiddish Written Word', *loc. cit.* Non-Jews used Latin script for Yiddish in the first half of the century in works which expressed opposition to emancipation or animosity towards Jews through linguistic condescension, i.e. mockery of Yiddish.

[46]For one preliminary attempt see *idem*, 'Results of Atlas Investigations among Jews of Germany', in *Field of Yiddish*, 3 (1969), pp. 16–35.

[47]Hanns G. Reissner, 'The German-American Jews (1800–1850)', in *LBI Year Book X* (1965), p. 69. For a more recent discussion see Günter Moltmann, 'Auf dem Auswandererschiff. Zur jüdischen Komponente der deutschen Amerikawanderung im 19. Jahrhundert', in Peter Freimark, Alice Jankowski and Ina S. Lorenz (eds.), *Juden in Deutschland. Emanzipation, Integration, Verfolgung und Vernichtung*, Hamburg 1991 (Hamburger Beiträge zur Geschichte der Juden 17), pp. 286–288.

[48]Monika Richarz, *Der Eintritt der Juden in die akademischen Berufe. Jüdische Studenten und Akademiker in Deutschland 1678–1848*, Tübingen 1974 (Schriftenreihe wissenschaftlicher Abhandlungen des Leo Baeck Instituts 28); Norbert Kampe, 'Jews and Antisemites at Universities in Imperial Germany (I). Jewish Students. Social History and Social Conflict', in *LBI Year Book XXX* (1985), pp. 357–394.

occurred in 1858 (Moritz Stern, in the discipline of mathematics), Jews continued to find their careers stymied because of their religion.[49] One scholar has suggested that the source of individual Jews' success can be found in the long years in which these aspiring academics, languishing as *Privatdozenten*, found their way into unknown or marginal areas of science and had the opportunity to specialise and discover or develop new fields of knowledge: discrimination, in other words, also had its "advantages". Moreover, these individuals were not secularised by the university, but tended to come from families already in possession of both *Bildung* and *Besitz*: they desired not social mobility but complete social acceptance.[50] The question that remains to be answered is: did the university merely give expression to already extant secular patterns rather than serving as an agent of secularisation? Or was this the case only from the *Kaiserreich* onwards, whereas earlier in the century the university did serve to secularise students?[51*]

Secondary associations (*Vereine*) were integral to the emergence of the *Bildungsbürgertum* and German Jewry's effort to integrate into it.[52] From the end of the eighteenth century German Jews either created new associations or transformed existing ones – namely, the *hevrot* of the autonomous community – to demonstrate their regeneration and meet the needs of emancipation. These associations helped to institutionalise German Jewry's ideology of emancipation and qualify it for inclusion in the *Bildungsbürgertum*. While these associations often introduced secular motives into previously religious undertakings, for example the ideal of philanthropy appearing alongside the commandment of charity, or established new ones on entirely secular foundations, their actual social function departed from their founders' intentions: they often served to create a form of "parallel sociability" in which the minority group had an associational life of its own patterned after that of the majority society. Integration could thus take the

---

[49]Jacob Toury, *Soziale und politische Geschichte der Juden in Deutschland, 1847–1871*, Düsseldorf 1977, p. 95.
[50]Volkov, 'Soziale Ursachen des jüdischen Erfolgs in der Wissenschaft', in *Jüdisches Leben und Antisemitismus*, op. cit., pp. 146–165.
[51]The extant literature focuses narrowly on Jewish student organisations – emphasising the response to antisemitism and the struggle between Liberalism and Zionism – and is therefore unable to provide answers to these larger questions. For a representative sample of this literature see Moshe Zimmermann, 'Jewish Nationalism and Zionism in German-Jewish Students' Organisations', in *LBI Year Book XXVII* (1982), pp. 129–153; Adolph Asch, *Geschichte des K.C. (Kartellverband jüdischer Studenten) im Lichte der deutschen kulturellen und politischen Entwicklung*, London 1964; Adolph Asch and Johanna Philippson, 'Self-Defence at the Turn of the Century. The Emergence of the K.C.', in *LBI Year Book III* (1958), pp. 122–139; Thomas Schindler, *Studentischer Antisemitismus und jüdische Studentenverbindungen 1880–1933*, Giessen 1988. For a recent, promising effort to address the broader question of identity, see Keith H. Pickus, *Jewish University Students in Germany and the Construction of a Post-Emancipatory Identity, 1815–1914*, unpublished Ph.D. diss., University of Washington 1993.
*See now *idem*, 'Jewish University Students in Germany and the Construction of a Post-Emancipatory Jewish Identity. The Model of the Freie Wissenschaftliche Vereinigung', in *LBI Year Book XXXIX* (1994), pp. 65–81 – (Ed.).
[52]Thomas Nipperdey, 'Verein als soziale Struktur in Deutschland im späten 18. und frühen 19. Jahrhundert', in Hartmut Boockmann (ed.), *Geschichtswissenschaft und Vereinswesen im 19. Jahrhundert*, Göttingen 1972; Henry Wassermann, *Jews, Bürgertum and "Bürgerliche Gesellschaft" in a Liberal Era in Germany, 1840–1880*, unpublished Ph.D. diss., Hebrew University 1979; Sorkin, *The Transformation of German Jewry*, op. cit., pp. 112–123.

form of a distinct German-Jewish bourgeois life alongside that of the German *Bildungsbürgertum*. The chronological development of that associational life would seem to reflect the development of the German-Jewish bourgeoisie and the growth of German associational life in general. The re-fashioning of older religious organisations took place primarily from the 1780s to 1848. In contrast, new associations were founded throughout the nineteenth century. Perhaps one in five appeared during the *Vormärz* and well over two or three in five during the later half of the century and especially during the *Kaiserreich*, when associational life in general grew dramatically.[53]

What role did these associations play in secularisation? While they often exhibited secular elements, for example the use of German and German culture (poems, songs), they just as frequently contained distinct Jewish ones as well. In other words, here is another example of the way in which the subculture was an amalgam of Jewish and secular German elements. Moreover, the associations could often be devoted to specifically Jewish purposes. The purpose of the *Verein für jüdische Geschichte und Literatur* (started in a number of towns in 1883), for example, was "to disseminate knowledge of Jewish history and literature in all circles . . ." through lectures and the formation of local libraries. Arising in response to antisemitism – and founded in the same year as the *Centralverein* – the organisation took on a life of its own: the various *Vereine* united in one *Verband der Vereine für jüdische Geschichte und Literatur* with some 48 chapters in 1893, and reached its high point on the eve of the First World War when some 229 chapters existed throughout the *Kaiserreich*. In Westphalia some six per cent of the adult Jewish population belonged to it.[54] What was the relationship in this organisation between the Jewish and the secular? While the purpose and contents were specifically Jewish, the form had all of the hallmarks of German *Bildung*. Yet to what extent was *Bildung* also a specifically German-Jewish characteristic by this time? How then does one distinguish?

These issues become even more ambiguous when one looks at the family – an institution whose socio-cultural importance is beyond doubt. Did the Jewish family introduce secular trends or did it preserve Judaism? Recent studies would suggest that the Jewish family in the *Kaiserreich* did both, with considerable success and without contradiction, by creating a new sort of secular "Jewishness". An emphasis on *Bildung* and respectability (manners, decorum, gentility) were the foundation on which an "intimate culture" of family life and tradition were erected: "The family functioned to maintain religious practice, religion functioned to affirm family connectedness."[55] While public religious observance was infrequent and the level of religious education relatively low (the *Verein für jüdische Geschichte und Literatur* was, after all, intended to correct that situation), a

---

[53]Sorkin, *The Transformation of German Jewry*, op. cit.

[54]Diethard Aschoff, 'Die westfälischen Vereine für jüdische Geschichte und Literatur im Spiegel ihrer Jahrbücher (1899–1920)', in Peter Freimark and Helmut Richtering (eds.), *Gedenkschrift für Bernhard Brilling*, Hamburg 1988, pp. 218–245.

[55]Marion Kaplan, *The Making of the Jewish Middle Class. Women, Family, and Identity in Imperial Germany*, New York–Oxford 1991, p. 75. The term "intimate culture" comes from Volkov, 'Jüdische Assimilation und Eigenart im Kaiserreich', *loc. cit.*, p. 137.

sense of "Jewishness" or "domestic Judaism" pervaded, and was reproduced in, the family.[56] Low birth rates and a marked emphasis on education were the social hallmarks of this new, bourgeois German-Jewish family, which emerged at least a generation earlier than its counterpart in the larger society.[57] In this respect Jews pioneered an aspect of bourgeois life, yet their version of it proclaimed both Jewishness and Germanness.[58]

This brief survey of only some aspects of German Jewry's social revolution suggests that an equation of *embourgeoisement* or secularisation with "assimilation" cannot be sustained. Once one looks beyond representative figures and representative institutions it becomes unmistakably clear that German Jewry's third revolution did not lead inevitably to the loss of belief and identification, but instead resulted in a complex pattern of integration which could also include the creation of new forms of identity and solidarity. Yet such a conclusion remains preliminary; further research is essential. Some of the subjects that need to be studied have already been noted; one additional subject deserves mention. A German-language public sphere (*Öffentlichkeit*) of newspapers, journals, magazines, sermons, pamphlets and books was central to German Jewry's experience and self-understanding. Besides some preliminary studies for the early part of the century, we lack detailed studies of the individual constituents of that public sphere as well as of its overall structure and social function.[59] As our knowledge of secular trends as a socio-cultural process develops, we will no doubt wish to refine our concepts and perhaps even to redefine our basic theses. Whatever form those new concepts and theses take, one thing seems almost certain: they will not produce the same picture of secular trends that has been limned for so long through the use of representative biographies and institutions.

---

[56]Kaplan, *The Making of the Jewish Middle Class*, op. cit., pp. 41–83. For evidence of the decline in public observance see the interesting article on the disappearance of the *eruv* from the major German cities. Peter Freimark, 'Eruw/"Judentore". Zur Geschichte einer rituellen Institution im Hamburger Raum (und anderswo)', in Peter Freimark *et al.* (eds.), *Judentore, Kuggel, Steuerkonten. Untersuchungen zur Geschichte der deutschen Juden, vornehmlich im Hamburger Raum*, Hamburg 1983, pp. 10–69. For a study of changing patterns in burial practice see Michael Edward Panitz, *Modernity and Mortality. The Transformation of Central European Jewish Responses to Death*, unpublished Ph.D. diss., Jewish Theological Seminary, New York 1989.

[57]Volkov, 'Jüdische Assimilation und Eigenart', *loc. cit.*, pp. 138–145. The role of dowries has recently been a subject of debate. See Kaplan, *The Making of the Jewish Middle Class*, op. cit., pp. 85–116; Werner E. Mosse, 'Jewish Marriage Strategies. The German Jewish Economic Elite', in *Studia Rosenthaliana*, vol. XIX, No. 2 (1985), pp. 188–202; Trude Maurer, 'Partnersuche und Lebensplanung. Heiratsannoncen als Quelle für die Sozial- und Mentalitätsgeschichte der Juden in Deutschland', in Freimark *et al.* (eds.), *Juden in Deutschland*, op. cit., pp. 344–374.

[58]Kaplan, *The Making of the Jewish Middle Class*, op. cit., p. 83; Volkov, 'Jüdische Assimilation und Eigenart im Kaiserreich', *loc. cit.*, pp. 144–145. Julius Carlebach has made a case for the continuities between Jewish life in the autonomous community and during the emancipation process. See 'Deutsche Juden und der Säkularisierungsprozess in der Erziehung. Kritische Bemerkungen zu einem Problemkreis der jüdischen Emanzipation', in Liebeschütz and Paucker (eds.), *Das Judentum in der deutschen Umwelt*, op. cit., pp. 55–93.

[59]Trude Maurer has pointed to our lack of understanding of the German-Jewish *Öffentlichkeit* in *Die Entwicklung der jüdischen Minderheit*, op. cit., pp. 51–56. For the early period see Sorkin, *The Transformation of German Jewry*, op. cit., pp. 79–104.

The Rise of the Religious Right and the Recasting of the "Jewish Question" Baden in the 1840s

BY DAGMAR HERZOG

Although some scholars who have investigated the relationship between German liberalism and Jewish emancipation have noted the phenomenon of liberal ambivalence about emancipation, the prevailing view in German history and Jewish studies circles is that liberals were the most important and dependable political allies of the Jews.[1] What has not been explained is precisely *how* reluctant liberals became the staunch defenders of emancipation they were subsequently celebrated to be. By analysing debates over Jewish rights in Baden, well-known as nineteenth-century Germany's most liberal state, this essay explores this apparent contradiction.

The contention here is that debates over Jewish rights can be more fully understood when we grasp how these debates were interwoven in complex ways with a variety of intra-Christian conflicts over sex, love and marriage, and over the relationship between individual subjectivity and religious authority. For Baden, in the 1830s and 1840s, was not only home to some of Germany's greatest liberal luminaries, but was also the seedbed for politically effective conservative Catholicism. Disputes over priestly celibacy, over mixed marriages between Protestants and Catholics, and over the rights of Christian dissenters increasingly pitted political liberals against this rising religious Right led by ultramontanes. It was really, at base, a longstanding fight over male sexual and romantic rights that ultimately caused the most admired and respected of German liberals to become the defenders of Jewish rights which most historians have assumed they were all along. This was so because the intensification of conflict over the content and meaning of Christianity caused a fundamental recasting of the terms in which the "Jewish Question" was understood and debated.

---

[1]Groundbreaking early efforts to document liberal ambivalence and/or hostility towards Jews can be found in Eleonore Sterling, *Judenhaß. Die Anfänge des politischen Antisemitismus in Deutschland, 1815–1850*, Frankfurt a. Main 1969; Reinhard Rürup, 'German Liberalism and the Emancipation of the Jews', in *LBI Year Book XX* (1975), pp. 59–68. But in a recent collection of essays on the relationship between German liberalism and Jewish emancipation, although various authors mention the problems in liberals' attitudes, the overall message once again reflects the scholarly consensus that "Liberals were the staunchest, indeed the only allies of Jews in their struggle for emancipation and equal rights", and "Liberals regarded Jewish emancipation as an integral part of their political programme." Werner E. Mosse, 'Introduction. German Jewry and Liberalism', in Friedrich-Naumann-Stiftung (ed.), *Das deutsche Judentum und der Liberalismus – German Jewry and Liberalism*, Sankt Augustin 1986, pp. 22–23.

The Grand Duchy of Baden was formed between 1803 and 1806 as part of the Napoleonic reorganisation of Europe. A Protestant monarch ruled over a population that was two-thirds Catholic and only one-third Protestant. None the less, there were initially few conflicts between the state and the Catholic leadership, for in the early decades of the nineteenth century, much of Baden's Catholic hierarchy and clergy was Enlightenment-inspired and sought out reconciliation with Protestants and distance from Rome. The great drama of the 1830s and 1840s involved the displacement of these more reformist Catholics with activist ultramontanes. Contemporaneous with the rise of ultramontanism came the rise of self-conscious, self-confident political liberalism. Although the Baden Diet had been established in 1819, it was only after the accession to the throne in 1830 of Grand Duke Leopold, more open-minded than his predecessor, that the Lower Chamber of the Diet acquired the freedom to discuss any and all political matters that made it the envy of the rest of Germany, and the leading forum for the airing of liberal views in the pre-1848 era.

1831 was considered a year of triumph for liberal agendas such as free elections, a freer press and expanded communal self-government, but when discussion turned to the issue of Jewish emancipation, liberals joined conservatives in rejecting the Jewish community's petitions for full equality. Thus, in 1831, the 18,000 Jews in a population of more than one million Badeners (by 1846 there would be approximately 21,000 Jews in a population of 1.3 million Badeners) were still denied four fundamental rights: the right to be a delegate to the Lower Chamber, the right to all military and state offices, the right to be a mayor or town councillor, and the right to move from one community into another, where no Jews had as yet lived, without permission from that community.

On the issue of Jewish emancipation, the self-identified liberals in Baden's Lower Chamber tended to divide into two general camps. A majority of liberals (and herein they concurred with the majority of those who saw themselves as government loyalists) insisted that emancipation could not be granted until Jews had proved themselves worthy by becoming more assimilated into Christian society. None the less, except for a dogged few who expressed doubt that Jews were capable of, or interested in, such moral self-improvement, this group continually averred that it favoured emancipation as an ultimate goal. A minority of liberals, by contrast, pressed for immediate emancipation, arguing that only the granting of emancipation would cause Jews to assimilate in the desired ways.

The majority resistant to emancipation included some of the most illustrious liberals in Baden; men roundly esteemed for their consistent commitment to securing all manner of free institutions and expansions of civic rights; men like Karl von Rotteck, Adam von Itzstein, Adolf Sander, Ignaz Rindeschwender and Friedrich Hecker. They perceived Jews to be the ones who were peculiarly illiberal, resistant to modernity, uncompromising towards Christians. Sander even went so far as to declare that "if we were to change positions, and to trade places with them, if we 18,000 Christians placed ourselves *vis-à-vis* one million Jews, I ask you, would they emancipate us? No, they would devour us, as the hated children of Noab [sic], with fire and the sword. Don't think that these are empty words."[2]

The majority of liberals found three dimensions of Jewish distinctiveness objectionable – they referred to them as religious, national and social peculiarities – and tended to see these three dimensions as inextricably fused with one another. Thus, for example, in response to those leaders of the Jewish community who stressed that it was unconscionable for the delegates to demand that Jews change any of their religious practices – that no human being should be asked to trade his faith for political advantage – these delegates vehemently denied that they had any religious prejudice against Jews, even as they continually referred to Baden as a Christian state. But because they saw the three dimensions of Jewish difference as interconnected, they then typically proceeded either to argue that the problem with the Jewish religion was that it was "theocratic": that the longing of the Jews for their Messiah made them incapable of genuine obedience to the laws of a non-Jewish state, and/or that rabbinical teachings caused Jews to behave in socially offensive ways, and thus that it was the national or social difference of Jews that was the "real" problem.

Within this circular method of argumentation, the national dimension of Jewish difference was also emphasised by constant reference to the notion that Jews constituted a separate nation, that they were foreigners, not Germans, not Badeners: a homeless, displaced people that refused to mingle with any other peoples, that clung rigidly to the faith of its fathers. Arguments about the social dimension also circled back to religious matters. Here the two main complaints had to do with Jewish self-segregation – believed to be expressed in such elements of Jewish religious practice as dietary laws or the observation of the Sabbath on Saturdays – and with the perception that Jews were dishonest in their economic dealings with non-Jews: that the petty trading and money-lending on which the majority of Baden's Jewish community subsisted was necessarily usurious and exploitative, and that this "unproductive" behaviour took its justification from the Talmud.

In short, despite the disclaimers about religious prejudice, these liberal delegates tended to portray Judaism as a religion vastly inferior to Christianity, and to stress a causal connection between this religion and the Jews' much-maligned economic roles. As self-perceived representatives of "the people", the majority of liberals used popular hostility towards Jews as the justification for their own hesitancy to extend emancipation. They did so without bothering to analyse how the transition from a feudal to a market economy had forced rural Christians into a dependent relationship with Jews as the social group responsible for exporting and importing goods out of and into the rural economy, and the group most willing to offer small credit. They also failed to consider how the ongoing restrictions on Jews' residence rights limited the feasibility for Jews of taking up their only recently acquired right to enter the trades or agriculture, for in most villages all occupational niches were filled.

The more progressive minority of liberals sought to counter these arguments

[2]Adolf Sander, in *Verhandlungen der Stände-Versammlung des Grossherzogthums Baden* (hereafter *Verhandlungen*) (II. Kammer), 27th September 1833, 14. Protokollheft, p. 305.

in a variety of ways. They tended to emphasise that the major difference between Jews and Christians was a religious one, and that religious difference should be no excuse for political inequality. But they also stressed the ways Baden's Jews were modernising their religion: how they were replacing the Hebrew language with German in their synagogue services; or how the new books for religious education of their children contained only the purest moral principles. They insisted that Baden's Jews were indeed Germans and Badeners, that they had lived in the land for centuries, that they were loyal to the monarch and that they had fought impressively in the recent Wars of Liberation. They reeled off statistics about the number of Jews who were taking up respectable trades and entering the professions. They reminded their colleagues that there were Christian usurers as well as Jewish ones; that by no means all Jewish moneylenders were usurious; that the operative moral distinction should be between usurers and non-usurers, not between Jews and Christians. Finally, they stressed that they, too, were faith-filled Christians, and many (though not all) also said they valued the notion of a Christian state, but they pointed out that Christianity was a religion based on love and equality, not hatred and hierarchy.

Yet these counter-arguments were almost invariably embedded in a more problematic line of reasoning, which turned on the notion that the granting of equality would lead to the dilution of difference, and that such dilution was eminently desirable. No matter how militant their defence of the principle that "by nature every human being has equal rights", they routinely coupled this insight with the notion that "emancipation should not be . . . the *reward* for enlightenment, but rather the means by which that enlightenment will be achieved".[3] As one avid pro-emancipationist put it in a classic formulation: "It is my conviction that nothing remains but to throw the Israelites, with equal rights, into the mass of the Christian population, so that, ripped along by the torrent, they will, like the pebbles rolling along in a riverbed, round themselves off and fit themselves in."[4] Another fervent pro-emancipationist declared:

> "I want to give them freedom . . . because I want to better them, and because I am convinced that only in freedom . . . can one truly thrive . . . We should seek justice, and *then* all else will be given unto us. *Then* also the Jews will be given unto us, that means they will no longer hesitate . . . to accommodate themselves more fully to our conditions."[5]

Although (in response to petitions submitted by leaders of Baden's Jewish community) Jewish emancipation was debated in Baden's Lower Chamber in 1831, 1833, 1835, 1837, 1840, 1842 and 1845, nothing much changed either in the terms of debate or in the proportion of delegates supporting equality. From a high of nineteen men (out of a total of sixty-three) in 1835, the number of pro-emancipationists in the chamber tumbled back down to fifteen in February 1845, even as the number of self-identified liberals in the chamber had climbed in the

---

[3]Johann Baptist Bekk, *ibid.*, p. 293; cf. also p. 295. Emphasis, here as elsewhere in this essay, was in the original quote.
[4]Josef Merk, *ibid.*, p. 281.
[5]Karl Christian Mez, in *Verhandlungen* (II. Kammer), 18th February 1845, 12. Protokollheft, p. 78.

1840s to more than half the delegates. However, only a brief eighteen months later, in August 1846, there was a dramatic reversal of opinion: fully two-thirds of the delegates, in a triumphant landslide, voted in favour of full Jewish emancipation. This sudden shift in liberal attitudes cannot be understood until we see that the 1830s and 1840s were times of intensifying ideological polarisation in Baden, in which the liberal majority in the Lower Chamber became increasingly distressed about the growth of a religious Right outside the chamber.

The polarisation first took shape in the late 1820s and early 1830s around a conflict over priestly celibacy. In two widely-publicised campaigns, reform-minded Catholic laypeople and priests (led by prominent professors at Freiburg's Catholic university) solicited the Lower Chamber's assistance in convincing the Grand Duke to induce the archbishop to abolish enforced priestly celibacy within Baden's borders. The reformers called celibacy "unnatural, illegal and immoral", an "unnecessary coercion", which robbed the individual of his "personal freedom" and of the "enjoyment" of "one of the most essential natural rights".[6] Because of the enlightened tendencies of much of Baden's Catholic clergy in the early nineteenth century; because in the wake of the French Revolution Rome's power was at a nadir; and especially because of the Baden state government's commitment to keeping the Catholic Church in check with the principle of *Staatskirchentum*, the anti-celibacy activists' hope of success was actually plausible.

Although the intimidated chamber of 1828 did not feel competent to take a stand on religious matters, the famous liberal chamber of 1831 enthusiastically supported the reformers' demands. Calling celibacy "unnatural" and "inhumane", and decrying the "exclusion of a whole class from the greatest of life's pleasures", one delegate after another voted in favour of urging the Grand Duke to plan for a Catholic synod at which the matter of priestly celibacy could be discussed and appropriately resolved.[7] The reformers had miscalculated, however, when they tried to play two authorities off against each other; for despite its resistance to Catholic autonomy, the state felt itself far too dependent on the Catholic Church as a guardian of order and morality even to consider intervening in the Church's handling of celibacy, and therefore rejected the reformers' request out of hand. The reformers had clearly failed to achieve the desired result.

More significantly, the long-term effect of the anti-celibacy campaign was that the leaders of the campaign lost their jobs. Though initially the state government was reluctant to accede to Rome's wishes, eventually all the progressive Catholic professors at Freiburg were replaced by men who had, as one historian put it, "overcome . . . the Enlightenment".[8] Young men studying for the priesthood in

[6]See the oft-repeated slogan of Professor Heinrich Schreiber, cited in Heinrich Maas, *Geschichte der katholischen Kirche im Grossherzogthum Baden*, Freiburg i. Br. 1891, p. 52; and the petition by Professors Heinrich Amann and Karl Zell, signed by twenty-three Catholic laypeople, reprinted in *Verhandlungen* (II. Kammer), 9th May 1828, 4. Protokollheft, pp. 59–75, especially pp. 64 and 69.
[7]Johann Sebastian Bader, *Verhandlungen* (II. Kammer), 16th December 1831, 35. Protokollheft, p. 22.
[8]Josef Becker, *Liberaler Staat und Kirche in der Ära von Reichsgründung und Kulturkampf. Geschichte und Strukturen ihres Verhältnisses in Baden, 1860–1876*, Mainz 1973, p. 20.

Baden were now exposed primarily to conservative teachers, and this tremendously alarmed political liberals. From this point on, men's rights to sexual expression and freedom from Church coercion would be a major plank in the liberal platform and liberals would identify the now increasingly confident ultramontanes as their most formidable ideological opponents. The liberals' sense of threat intensified in the 1840s as a conservative renewal indisputably took place within Badenese Catholicism. A group of leading laypeople, with the immensely influential professor and publicist Franz Josef Buß foremost among them, had founded a new Catholic newspaper, the *Süddeutsche Zeitung für Kirche und Staat*, which tried to spread ultramontane ideas and soon established itself as the most conservative newspaper in Baden. It succeeded dramatically in expanding the terms of debate on a wide range of issues and continually forced papers of all other persuasions to engage with its perspectives. Another prominent conservative and director of the *Collegium Theologicum* in Freiburg, Alban Stolz, had begun to produce the *Kalender für Zeit und Ewigkeit*, an annual almanac with explicitly ultramontane tendencies, written in an accessible, earthy style, which rapidly became one of the few texts typically read in Baden's impoverished rural areas. The new archbishop Hermann von Vicari also contributed to the conservative revival through his many travels and visits to parishes throughout Baden, and through his establishment of new church-run seminaries. Liberals were especially worried about these new educational institutions, in which they feared that young boys would be trained in obscurantist anti-rationalism.

Just how much the hostility between liberals and conservative Catholics had grown became apparent particularly when a growing conflict over mixed marriages between Catholics and Protestants came to a head early in 1845. The conflict had already been initiated by Rome in 1836, but for a while it remained largely confined to negotiations between representatives of the state and the Church. In Baden at that time, many hundreds of couples lived in mixed marriages – more, in proportion to the size of the population, than in any other German state.

The state government, deeply concerned to maintain confessional peace and believing mixed marriages to be the major site at which the Catholic and Protestant populations of the Grand Duchy could be harmoniously unified, strenuously sought to protect the rights of mixed couples to choose each other and to choose how to raise their children. Thus, for example, Baden's liberal Minister of the Interior, Karl Friedrich Nebenius, earnestly discoursed on "the reconciling power of marriage", and elaborated that mixed marriages had helped to "overcome the damaging mutual prejudices, antipathies and hesitations, interweave the physical and spiritual interests of families of different confessions in the most intimate way, and therefore in all these ways like almost no other thing worked towards the inner unity and strengthening of the life of the state and the life of the *Volk*".[9] The state therefore insisted on maintaining the long-established practice (which was also ensconced in the law of the land) that both

[9] [Karl Friedrich Nebenius], *Der Streit über gemischte Ehen und das Kirchenhoheitsrecht im Grossherzogthum Baden*, Karlsruhe 1847, p. xvii.

the Catholic and the Protestant clergyman should refrain from pressuring mixed couples in any way and that both should participate in blessing the marriage.

However, the state once again also felt itself to be dependent on the churches, for it wanted marriage to be not just a civil act, but rather for "its higher nature also to be brought to light through the consecration of the church".[10] In short, it was precisely because of this ambivalence on the part of the state that Catholic conservatives could promote their own perspectives ever more successfully. This became apparent in January 1845, when the new archbishop Vicari, with Rome's support, circumvented the state authorities and secretly circulated a directive to his clergymen with the goal of encouraging them either to dissuade mixed couples from marrying at all or at least to insist on the Catholic upbringing of their children. Baden's Catholic clergymen were now faced with two competing authorities: the state demanding that they maintain the old and more relaxed practice, and the Church hierarchy insisting that they initiate a stricter practice.

This state-Church stand-off (which, incidentally, the Church would win) was soon publicised and rapidly spiralled into a much larger public debate with far-reaching effects.[11] From the pulpit, in the daily press, in polemical tracts and in scholarly reference works, mixed marriages became the subject of the most heated outpourings. Liberals in the Lower Chamber and the press, wielding the slogan "Love unites what faith divided", continually stressed individual freedom of choice and the socially transformative power of love, and pounced on every countervailing perspective presented by the conservatives. For liberals, the controversy over mixed marriages was another incarnation of the earlier controversy over celibacy. In both, their anti-authoritarianism and preoccupation with individual freedom of choice was conjoined with a programmatic insistence on the joys of married life, in which they continually conflated insistence on every man's right to sexual expression with paeans to domestic bliss.[12]

Conservative Catholics, by contrast, voiced a deep distrust of love and sexual attraction as the basis for a marriage: "What?", a member of the archbishop's staff had asked, "The conscience of the couple . . . bribed by the most powerful

[10] *Ibid.*, p. xxix.
[11] The prospect of priests suddenly refusing to play their dual role as servants of both church and state – in other words, the spectre of potentially massive civil disobedience from a sector of its employees – finally forced the state to promulgate a new law in November 1846; a law which provided for the possibility of secular civil marriage in the event of the non-cooperation of religious authorities. Thus it seemed as though the liberal premise of equality between the confessions and every individual's right to marry whomever he or she chose, had emerged victorious. However, the outcome of the dispute was far more ambiguous. Not until 1862 did the first couple in Baden get married in a purely civil ceremony, so the promulgation of the new law had nothing to do with actually opening up new freedom for mixed couples. Rather, the real and immediate effect of the November 1846 law was that the state had implicitly given up its legal right to intervene in the Catholic Church's handling of marriage; and, with very few exceptions, priests immediately began to follow Vicari's directives and thus to intervene more forcefully in the private lives of their parishioners.
[12] For a classic articulation of this combination of views, see Karl Theodor Welcker's opening statement in 'Verbotene Ehen, insbesondere Priester-Cölibat', in Welcker and Karl von Rotteck (eds.), *Das Staats-Lexikon*, 1st edn., vol. XV, Altona 1843, p. 665.

sensual attraction, should *decide* – decide in . . . their own case?! What? The defendant should also be the judge?"¹³ Similarly, the *Süddeutsche Zeitung für Kirche und Staat* asserted that "in marriage a brutal, powerful sensuality must be combated. If marriage becomes debased, then the spouses, the children, the family, and the state . . . are *all* endangered."¹⁴ And one of the newly-installed conservative Freiburg professors declared that it was (Catholic) Christianity that saved sexual relations within marriage from being purely "animalistic".¹⁵ In mixed marriages, on the other hand, as one conservative priest intoned, there was "only love of the flesh".¹⁶

It was right in the midst of this battle, in the summer of 1845, that the religious landscape of Baden changed. Just as elsewhere across the German lands, so also in Baden, a protest movement emerged specifically in reaction to the rise of Catholic ultramontanism in general and Rome's new authoritarianism in marital matters in particular (although the most immediate catalyst was outrage over a mass pilgrimage organised in 1844 to the Holy Robe of Trier, supposedly worn by Jesus at his death). The Catholic dissenters, led by Johannes Ronge, a former Catholic chaplain from Silesia who had been excommunicated because of a letter of dissent he wrote about the Robe, were joined by Protestants disaffected by neo-orthodox trends in their own church. Together, they split from the established churches and founded democratically-run congregations, dedicated to individual freedom of belief and the separation of church and state. In Baden, there were ten congregations, encompassing 700 official members, though there were many more sympathisers.

The dissenters particularly welcomed priests who wanted to marry as their spiritual leaders, and especially encouraged mixed Protestant-Catholic couples to join their fold, thus directly snubbing the Catholic hierarchy in its stances on sex and marriage. The dissenters developed the liberal defence of sex even further, insisting that sex was not only natural, but also divine – a "sacred yearning" – and they rhapsodised about "sexual love, that divine and deifying love between man and woman".¹⁷ The dissenters called themselves *Deutschkatholiken*, as opposed to Roman Catholics. Though a number of historians have analysed the nationalist, anti-Rome impulses reflected in the movement's chosen name, and others have studied its important role in launching the first organised German women's movement, the movement's central preoccupation with men's sexual and romantic rights has received no attention.¹⁸ Yet because of the

¹³Ludwig Buchegger's memorandum of 1839, repr. in [Adolf Strehle], *Die gemischten Ehen in der Erzdiöcese Freiburg*, Regensburg 1846, p. 79.
¹⁴*Süddeutsche Zeitung für Kirche und Staat*, Freiburg (29th November 1846), p. 1077.
¹⁵See Johann Baptist Hirscher, *Die Christliche Moral als Lehre von der Verwirklichung des göttlichen Reiches in der Menschheit*, 5th edn., vol. III, Tübingen 1851, pp. 513 and 516.
¹⁶Anon., *Die Musterehe und die Nothwendigkeit einer Wiederherstellung der Ehe nach der Musterehe*, Freiburg i. Br. 1850, p. 17.
¹⁷'Die Ehe, vom bürgerlichen und kirchlichen Standpunkte aus betrachtet', in *Katholische Kirchenreform*, Berlin (June 1845), p. 165; and J. Kinorhc, 'Über die Ehe zwischen Juden und Christen', in *Kirchliche Reform*, Halle (October 1846), p. 1.
¹⁸See especially Sylvia Paletschek, *Frauen und Dissens. Frauen im Deutschkatholizismus und in den freien Gemeinden, 1841–1852*, Göttingen 1990; and Catherine M. Prelinger, *Charity, Challenge and Change. Religious Dimensions of the Mid-Nineteenth-Century Women's Movement in Germany*, New York 1987.

evolving tension between liberals and ultramontanes over these rights, it was precisely this element of the movement's vision that was to have important consequences for how liberals came to reconceptualise the "Jewish Question". Because of their own indignation at conservative Catholic views on individual freedom and on sex and marriage, political liberals were thrilled with the emergence of dissent and rushed vociferously to the dissenters' defence when these dissenters, by stepping out of the traditional Christian churches, lost the political rights they had previously held and became similar in status to Jews. Simultaneously, livid about how brazenly the dissenters were taking on the Catholic hierarchy, Catholic conservatives vied with each other to defame them in the most lurid terms.

It was in this context of liberal delight in dissent and concern about rising ultramontanism that liberal delegate Karl Zittel, on 15th December 1845, advanced before his colleagues in the Lower Chamber the principle that every citizen in Baden ought to be able to profess his faith without thereby forfeiting any rights of citizenship. He introduced a motion that would implement this principle, yet he also included a clause that would limit it to avowed Christians. Although the realisation of complete religious freedom was his genuine goal (Zittel, a recent convert to emancipation, had already expressed strong support for it in the last debate on that topic ten months earlier), he added this limiting clause because his most immediate goal was to secure the right of the *Deutschkatholiken* to organise themselves as a church. He was well aware that his motion could face severe objections even with this clause, but given the continuing hostility to Jewish emancipation among the majority of his colleagues, the motion had almost no chance of passing without it.

Therefore, in the speech introducing his motion for universal religious freedom, Zittel went to great lengths not to mention Jews by name, in an obvious attempt to strengthen the motion's chances. He did, however, albeit in a convoluted fashion, refer to the implications the motion inevitably held for Baden's Jews:

> "I would be unfaithful to my own principles if I were to limit my motion from the outset through the exclusion of any one religious party. But – I cannot say this without a certain shame – I cannot insist on this, for I can have no hope that my motion, phrased so generally, will receive the approval of the House. The majority of you feels itself more accountable to the general antipathy against a religious party which lives among us, an antipathy which it has of course primarily incurred through the way of life of its lower classes, than to justice . . . In order therefore not to cause the motion for religious freedom itself to fail, [a freedom] which has recently become so very important because of the movement in the *Christian* population, I at this point of course see myself forced *possibly* to limit the motion in the second instance to those who profess the Christian religion."[19]

Recognising that this willingness to limit the motion only to Christians necessarily called attention to the question of whether the dissenters were in fact Christians, Zittel knew he had to counter the new strict definitions of Christia-

---

[19]Karl Zittel, *Verhandlungen* (II. Kammer), 15th December 1845, 6. Beilagenheft, p. 42.

nity increasingly being advanced by conservative Catholics in the contentious debates surrounding priestly celibacy and mixed marriages. These conservatives insisted that the Catholic Church, under the guidance of Rome, was the only true expression of Christianity. They continually asserted that without obedience to the Church hierarchy and uniformity of belief within the Church, disintegration of the social fabric and the spread of immorality were inevitable.

Against this conception, Zittel stressed the sacred inviolability of the individual's understanding of spiritual matters. He also argued that the drive for community was fundamental to human nature, and that each individual should be free to join with others of like mind to satisfy his or her spiritual needs; and he insisted that society as a whole benefited from such freedom of spiritual expression. In summary, Zittel wished to "let truth everywhere cut its own path, and give the spirit freedom; true religiosity is rooted only in this freedom. Even if this may seem problematic for the church, religion is more important than the church; better no church than no religion."[20]

It was clear that it was the growth of ultramontanism that was motivating Zittel to attempt to ensconce religious freedom in the law of the land, for he offered his colleagues an extended summary of the whole rise of the religious Right over the preceding years, replete with references to the battles over mixed marriages in Prussia and Baden, and to the Trier pilgrimage that had been the catalyst for the dissenting movement. "Worse things yet are being silently planned", he warned, "the dark spirit of fanaticism has almost everywhere moved in to the educational institutions for future religious teachers . . . A dark mysterious force has arisen from the grave and has spread itself over our fatherland . . . Jesuitism is marching forwards with giant steps, trampling under its feet our century's budding seeds of freedom and Enlightenment."[21]

Acutely aware that the *Deutschkatholiken* were not considered Christians by conservative Catholics, Zittel addressed this point directly:

> "Gentlemen, recognise well what question lies here before us: Are the *Deutschkatholiken* Christians? Is their statement of faith Christian? Is their church Christian? Now, who will answer? Who should decide? . . . Look around, gentlemen, in the whole realm of the state you find no tribunal of faith; the nineteenth century no longer tolerates one. For the state, it must be enough that a religious corporation declares, *that it wants* to be *Christian*. The *deutschkatholisch* community has done this; it has declared that it wants to develop a community in the sense and the spirit of Jesus the Christ, and that it seeks nourishment in His gospel for its religious meaning and life. The state must see to it that the spirit of immorality does not gain ground within it and that it does not nurture principles dangerous to the state; but as long as that is not the case, the state cannot deny it the label and recognition as a *Christian* community."[22]

In his concluding remarks, Zittel reiterated the Christian identity of the dissenters when he stressed that the movement for religious freedom they

---

[20] *Ibid.*, p. 39.
[21] *Ibid.*, p. 37.
[22] *Ibid.*, p. 43.

represented would lead to the reconciliation of all Christian Germans that had for so painfully long eluded the German people.

Similar tendencies appeared in the remarks made by other liberal delegates in the brief discussion following Zittel's statement. Liberals who favoured Jewish emancipation extolled the virtues of dissent, continually reinforced the idea that dissenters were Christians, and made only indirect gestures in favour of Jewish equality by applauding the inclusion of "all religions" in Zittel's motion.[23] The fervently pro-dissent but anti-emancipationist Friedrich Hecker, prominent liberal and later revolutionary, however, made the distinction he saw between dissenters and Jews explicit. Hecker, who hated ultramontanes – "nobody lusts for power like the priest", he wrote in a book defending dissent – also here in the chamber described in glowing terms the "great moment in our history" signalled by the emergence of dissent, and declared that it would be "blasphemy", "slander of that which is most sacred, if one were to try to prevent a human being from worshipping the Eternal in his own way".[24] Yet he failed to connect such sentiments with his attitudes towards Jews; the allusion was indirect, but Hecker's meaning was unmistakable: "In the interest of freedom, I do not support the motion for one part of the population of this land. I do not want the priests' state, and I also do not want the theocratic state."[25]

Less liberal delegates lamented the assaults on Catholicism and/or indicated that they were not in agreement with Zittel on all points, but they acknowledged that the motion was "maybe the most important matter that will be discussed in this session of the Diet", and they were willing to let the motion be debated further at a later date.[26] In fact, the discussion that day was only supposed to decide one thing: whether Zittel's motion should be printed and sent to committee, so that a report could be prepared and then the matter could be discussed substantively at a future point by the full house. At the end of the discussion, the sixty delegates present unanimously decided that this would indeed happen.

The relaxed attitude of the conservatives in the Lower Chamber incensed conservatives elsewhere in Baden. While the *Süddeutsche Zeitung für Kirche und Staat* had been fiercely criticising the *Deutschkatholiken* since their emergence, it was specifically the unanimous vote to send Zittel's motion to committee that turned its single-handed effort into a broad-based protest.[27] A rash of tracts censuring the *Deutschkatholiken* appeared, stirring up public opinion, alerting Grand Duke

---

[23]Friedrich Daniel Bassermann, *Verhandlungen* (II. Kammer), 15th December 1845, 1. Protokollheft, p. 140; cf. Welcker's call for "the whole motion", followed by a "general bravo", *ibid.*, p. 145.
[24]Karl Friedrich Hecker, *Die staatsrechtlichen Verhältnisse der Deutschkatholiken mit besonderem Hinblick auf Baden*, Heidelberg 1845, p. 28; and *idem*, *Verhandlungen* (II. Kammer), 15th December 1845, 1. Protokollheft, p. 147.
[25]Hecker, *Verhandlungen* (II. Kammer), 15th December 1845, 1. Protokollheft, p. 147.
[26]Cf. Franz Christoph Trefurt, *ibid.*, p. 143; Bader and Christian Friedrich Platz, *ibid.*, p. 146; Friedrich Theodor Schaaff, *ibid.*, p. 148.
[27]For an overview of its attacks on the *Deutschkatholiken*, see Wilhelm Hubert Ganser, *Die Süddeutsche Zeitung für Kirche und Staat*, Berlin 1936, pp. 24–46.

Leopold's government to the dangers of religious freedom, and castigating the conservative delegates for their inattention.[28]

In stark contrast to the vague allusions to Jews made by Zittel and his liberal supporters in their endorsement of the dissenters, critics of the motion for religious freedom constantly worked to link dissenters and Jews. The pamphleteer Ludwig Castorph, for instance, articulated clearly what he saw as the logical implication of granting full equality to the dissenters: "The requested religious freedom, in the way *they* mean it, is unacceptable, because then, to be fair, the *other sects* and *the Jews* would also have to be granted equal rights and privileges."[29] The prominent conservative Catholic professor Johann Baptist Hirscher similarly warned that "immorality . . . is decisively encouraged when good and bad are treated equally in social life. Thereby the worth of morality sinks in the eyes of the public. Likewise, the worth of religion must sink in the eyes of the people, when the law . . . treats Christians, Jews and pagans as equals".[30] Franz Josef Buß, in his *Das Rongethum in der badischen Abgeordnetenkammer* (1846), exposed the implications of Zittel's reasoning most pointedly:

> "But you, Mr Friend of Light, believe that as long as the spirit of morality finds its place in your protégé congregation, and as long as no principles are nurtured there that threaten the state, then the state could not refuse it recognition as a *Christian* community. But according to this logic, a Jew, a pagan, and a Turk would also be a Christian."[31]

Aside from Buß, the other most influential anti-dissent activist was Alban Stolz, who wrote three tracts against the dissenters. His *Landwehr gegen den badischen Landstand* (1845) was sent into every Catholic community in Baden and was read aloud to the townspeople by priests and mayors.[32] It explicitly urged the readers and listeners both to pray daily that God might rescue Baden from the dissenting movement and the faithlessness, sin and sexual corruption it represented, and to send petitions to the Grand Duke requesting that the Lower Chamber be dissolved for having let Zittel's motion go to committee. (This dissolution of the chamber had been Buß's express goal as well.)

Furthermore, in a striking parallel with the way religious and economic arguments had long been intertwined in attacks on Jews, Stolz used a similar

---

[28] Aside from the ones to be quoted below, typical examples include Wilhelm Stern, *Antrag auf Glaubensfreiheit*, Karlsruhe 1846; Franz Anton Staudenmaier, *Das Wesen der katholischen Kirche. Mit Rücksicht auf ihre Gegner dargestellt*, Freiburg i. Br. 1845, esp. pp. 177–193; and Franz Josef Mone, *Beleuchtung der Zittelschen Motion über Religionsfreiheit*, Bonn 1846.

[29] Ludwig Castorph, *Sendschreiben als unterthänigste Petition an die Allerhöchste Badische Staatsregierung und Hohe Badische Ständekammer. Hervorgerufen durch die Motion des Herrn Abgeordneten Zittel*, Baden-Baden 1846, p. 30.

[30] Johann Baptist Hirscher, *Beleuchtung der Motion des Abgeordneten Zittel*, Freiburg i. Br. 1846, p. 21.

[31] Franz Joseph Buß, *Das Rongethum in der badischen Abgeordnetenkammer*, Freiburg i. Br. 1846, p. 70. "Friends of Light" (*Lichtfreunde*) was the sarcastic term formerly applied to Protestant dissenters by their opponents. Soon, however, dissenters proudly adopted the term to describe themselves. "Rongethum" was a reference to Johannes Ronge, the founder of the *deutschkatholisch* movement.

[32] Alban Stolz, *Landwehr gegen den badischen Landstand* (1845), repr. in Alban Stolz, *Gesammelte Werke*, ed. by Julius Mayer, 3rd. edn., vol. VIII, Freiburg i. Br. 1913/1914, pp. 7–14. The information about the public readings comes from editor Julius Mayer's introduction (p. vii) and his editorial footnote on p. 14.

combination of arguments against dissenters. He accused the Diet delegates of using the dissenting movement to destroy Catholicism, and he claimed that if Zittel's motion was passed, the townspeople would be forced to pay heavily for dissenters' churches, pastors and schoolteachers. Like other pamphleteers, Stolz stressed that the dissenters were just as un-Christian as Jews or Turks.[33]

Stolz's two other anti-*Deutschkatholiken* tracts, also consciously geared to an illiterate rural audience, were even more graphic in the way they both sexualised and "judaised" the dissenters. Both these tactics served to undermine dissenters' claims to be Christians. The sexualisation was a logical rhetorical tactic because of the genuine significance of sexual matters for the movement and its supporters – sex was very much at the heart of liberal-ultramontane hostilities – but it also served as a more general signifier of the all-too-human and thus not properly spiritual concerns of the dissenters. The "judaising" of dissenters was obviously a way to undermine their self-perception as Christians; throwing in references to Turks for good measure served to exoticise both Jews and dissenters, reinforcing the implication that these were foreign elements. In *Amulett gegen die jungkatholische Sucht* (1845), Stolz repeatedly associated dissent with lust and adultery, and slyly suggested that dissenters were offering Catholic priests a trade: the "priests of the flesh" could have women, if the parishioners no longer had to go to confession.[34] Furthermore, after having established that "God destroyed the Jews' temple and rejected their worship", he declared that "now the *Rongeaner* want to become like the Jews, they want . . . only rabbis who will sing for them and make pretty speeches".[35] In criticising the dissenters' rationalist rejection of the notion that Christ was literally present in the communion wafer, he declared that "if Christ were not in the Host, then we Catholics would be idol-worshippers, we would thus be more wicked than Jews and Turks".[36]

Merging these two rhetorical manoeuvres in *Der neue Kometstern mit seinem Schweif, oder Johannes Ronge und seine Briefträger* (1846), Stolz described those Catholics who would be attracted to such a "religion of the flesh" as he claimed the dissenters were promoting: those who "grew up lasciviously in arrogance and licentiousness, whose synagogue is the tavern, whose gospel is newspapers with rotten principles".[37] Among the dangerous newspapers he named was also "that Jew-paper, the *Frankfurter Journal*".[38] Equating Christianity with Catholicism, he also argued that "the most precious thing the human being can possess is the Christian religion, the secure, solid Catholic faith, the Holy Sacraments. But now there are peddling Jews [*Schacherjuden*] at the door, traders in souls . . . who

---

[33]"In many towns two churches would have to be built . . . For the *Rongeaner* fit just as poorly into a Catholic church as Jews or Turks, probably because the majority of them, and especially their main founders, believe just as little in Jesus Christ, the Son of God, even though they won't admit it." Stolz, *Landwehr*, op. cit., p. 9.

[34]Alban Stolz, *Amulett gegen die jungkatholische Sucht* (1845), repr. in *Gesammelte Werke*, op. cit., pp. 30 and 43.

[35]*Ibid.*, pp. 32–33.

[36]*Ibid.*, p. 30.

[37]Alban Stolz, *Der neue Kometstern mit seinem Schweif, oder Johannes Ronge und seine Briefträger* (1846), repr. in *Gesammelte Werke*, op. cit., pp. 56 and 60.

[38]*Ibid.*, p. 58

want to swindle you, Catholic folk, out of your precious faith . . . Whoever has good sense and love of religion will be filled with nausea at . . . this carnal lust and haughtiness."[39]

Buß made similar connections between sex, dissent and Jews. For example, this is how Buß described the entry of the *Deutschkatholiken* into the Lower Chamber's agenda:

> "A few dissolute chaplains begin the business. A debauched press, usually led by Jews, seizes upon the inflammatory subject-matter. Political radicalism, having exhausted its formal constitutional questions, throws the material onto its dying embers."[40]

Buß mocked the concessions to anti-Judaism evident in Zittel's willingness to limit his motion solely to the dissenters – "because you fear the consequences of Jew-hatred in the chamber and among the people for your miserable little bit of popular appeal"[41] – but also contributed to anti-Jewish sentiments with his own remarks, taking swipes at "Young Israel's" role in the "crusade against Catholicism", and telling Zittel that his comments in his speech about the archbishop's handling of mixed marriages showed the speech could just as well have been delivered by "a Jew, a Turk".[42] Buß also called dissenting groups "these untested suddenly-surfacing sects, germinated in the lasciviousness of radical rabble-rousing", and declared that "it is not rationalism which confronts us here, it is a disgraceful sensualism, the wretchedness of which is glued together with a few rags of humanitarianism of the sort which all lewd people appeal to, bedizened with a few glitters of nationalism . . . They have done all frivolous and sensuous people a favour by offering them a religion of convenience, because it is still somewhat a part of good manners to be religious."[43]

Banking on popular animosity towards Jews (but obviously also dignifying it as an article of faith); casting aspersions on the dissenters' characters and motivations; playing on the economic fears of a predominantly agricultural population whose financial security was frequently shaky, the anti-dissent activists successfully convinced thousands of Baden Catholics that dissent was a mortal danger. Archbishop von Vicari, too, had thrown his weight behind the anti-dissent campaign, releasing an "emergency call" to his flock that "they are trying to steal your faith!"[44] Already in January 1846, petitions against Zittel's motion started arriving in the Lower Chamber and, in keeping with Stolz's suggestions, the petitions stressed the religious and economic dangers dissent

---

[39] *Ibid.*, pp. 57–58.
[40] Buß, *Rongethum, op. cit.*, p. 75.
[41] *Ibid.*
[42] *Ibid.*, pp. 8–9, 63.
[43] *Ibid.*, pp. 21 and 72.
[44] Quoted in Karl Zittel, 'Die politischen Partheiungen in Baden', in *Jahrbücher der Gegenwart*, ed. by Albert Schwegler, Tübingen 1847, p. 358.

presented.⁴⁵ Defenders of the motion tried to organise petitions as well, but the opponents were in the overwhelming majority.

The Right was not only more in touch with grassroots sentiment on religious and economic matters than the Left, but also in a better position to organise petitions. Priests across the Catholic areas of Baden announced from the pulpit that their parishioners should sign petitions against the motion and these were laid out for signing immediately after church. Liberals had no forum like the church in which to display petitions or solicit signatures, with the exception of newspapers, and (according to liberal delegates) censors saw to it that every announcement about petitions in the newspapers was excised.

Already by the middle of January 1846, liberal delegates were becoming worried by the preponderance of anti-*Deutschkatholiken* petitions. This was so not least because the petitions often demanded that the Lower Chamber be dissolved by the Grand Duke for having allowed Zittel's motion to go to committee in the first place. But it was also because the liberals saw whatever hopes they had had for religious liberalisation in Baden slip away under the impact of an unforeseen radicalisation and organisation of the Right.

Also within the chamber, conservatives now started to mobilise. Countering demands for religious freedom became a matter of principle for conservative delegates, who had been silent only a few weeks earlier, and had voted with the liberals to send Zittel's motion to committee. The same tracts detailing the dangers of *Deutschkatholizismus* that had convinced local priests to organise petition drives, had also persuaded them. Now conservative delegates began to argue, as Johann Baptist Karl Junghanns did, that passage of the motion would lead to "the disintegration of Christianity in the Grand Duchy of Baden".⁴⁶

Conservatives took the pamphleteers' cue to expose how the liberals' humanist redefinition of Christianity, taken to its logical conclusion, made religious differences uncomfortably difficult to pinpoint. Gideon Weizel expressed the conservative view clearly when he said:

> "How can you hold it against a Catholic if he resists with all his strength this motion, which in its first sentence requests that *every* religious association, no matter of what name, whether it is a *Christian* one *or not*, should be granted already through the *fact* of its emergence alone *full* and *equal rights* with both of the existing Christian churches in our land, whereby the delegate who made the motion sets up no other precondition except that the members of that society should only fulfil the *state-citizen* duties, for the rest it could be Christian or Mohammedan. Gentlemen, against such a motion I would vote as a *Christian*, not as a Catholic or Protestant . . . After all, they are not

---

⁴⁵The petition from the city of Konstanz, for example, argued that the *Deutschkatholiken*'s "divergence in matters of faith will logically not encourage the unity of the German people, but rather will paralyse its strength through internal divisiveness, because it consumes its life-marrow, which is the Christian principle". See Generallandesarchiv Karlsruhe, 231/1436, petition of 8th January 1846. The petition from the town of Wiesloch, however, was most concerned that the *Deutschkatholiken* should be denied "those same state-citizen rights which the members of the Roman Catholic and Evangelical Protestant church are allowed, that they should thereby not be granted . . . the right to state financial support of their potential future parsonages and schools etc.". Quoted by Johann Baptist Karl Junghanns in *Verhandlungen* (II. Kammer), 23rd January 1846, 2. Protokollheft, p. 74.

⁴⁶*Ibid.*, p. 75.

only requesting religious freedom for Christian associations, but also for *un-Christian* ones."[47]

Ultimately, the "petition storm" organised by conservatives brought 347 petitions (with close to 50,000 signatures) against the *Deutschkatholiken* into the Lower Chamber. (Only thirty-one petitions had been sent in support of Zittel's motion.)[48] It was the first mass petitioning campaign in German history, and the moment historians rightly cite as the birthdate of political Catholicism in Germany.[49] The general state of uproar in the land convinced Grand Duke Leopold's ministerial advisers that the Lower Chamber should indeed be dissolved, and the Grand Duke did so on 9th February 1846.

Thinking that the petition storm also reflected a politically conservative trend in the population, the Grand Duke and his advisors assumed that in the new elections set for 3rd April 1846, a majority of conservative candidates would win. But confessional tensions within the conservative camp hampered campaigning – traditional Protestant government loyalists, for example, were quite uncomfortable making common cause with upstart ultramontane Catholics; meanwhile, the emerging tension between radical and moderate liberals was temporarily put aside in the interests of combating the religious Right. Furthermore, as liberals later analysed it, it is also likely that although rural Catholics would mobilise to defend their faith and economic interests in a petition campaign, they saw their political interests best guaranteed by liberals, who were not so tainted by association with the often detested local government administrators as the conservatives were. Conservative observers, by contrast, called attention to the peculiarities of Baden's indirect voting system, which favoured the persistence of a "politics of notables", in which well-known individuals routinely got voted into public office regardless of their ideological affiliation. For all these reasons, an even larger liberal majority was returned to the Lower Chamber than before.[50] Thirty-six liberals faced twenty-seven conservatives when the Lower Chamber reopened on 1st May. In fact, the only new conservative to win a seat was Franz Josef Buß himself.

On 26th June 1846, the liberal delegate Ignaz Rindeschwender delivered the report of the petition committee on the *Deutschkatholiken*'s request for revocation of the Grand Duke's decree, which had deprived them of political rights and restricted their ability to worship and organise. The committee was very favourably disposed to the petitioners. The major thrust of Rindeschwender's argument was that:

---

[47]Franz Gideon Weizel, *Verhandlungen* (II. Kammer), 3rd February 1846, 2. Protokollheft, pp. 207–208.

[48]See Generallandesarchiv Karlsruhe, 231/1436.

[49]Becker, *Liberaler Staat, op. cit.*, p. 21; Kurt Kluxen, 'Religion und Nationalstaat im 19. Jahrhundert', in Julius H. Schoeps (ed.), *Religion und Zeitgeist im 19. Jahrhundert*, Stuttgart–Bonn 1982, p. 41.

[50]Cf. Norbert Deuchert, *Vom Hambacher Fest zur badischen Revolution. Politische Presse und Anfänge deutscher Demokratie, 1832–1848/49*, Stuttgart 1983, p. 201; and Manfred Hörner, *Die Wahlen zur badischen zweiten Kammer im Vormärz, 1819–1847*, Göttingen 1987, pp. 454–468. For the contemporaries' contrasting views, see Zittel, 'Die politischen Partheiungen', *loc. cit.*, pp. 352–353 and 358–361; and *Süddeutsche Zeitung für Kirche und Staat* (9th April 1846), p. 292; *ibid.* (15th April 1846), p. 308; *ibid.* (24th June 1846), pp. 542–543.

> "It would offend healthy common sense and moral feeling alike, if a citizen who previously enjoyed *all* state-citizen rights, should now find himself . . . robbed of . . . the most important of these, because on a few points he is changing his religious opinion – to be more exact, because he is honest enough to speak openly, that which thousands and thousands think of as he does, but do not profess loudly."[51]

Thus Rindeschwender not only placed the *Deutschkatholiken* firmly among the Christians from whom they had emerged, but also portrayed them as even better Christians than those who remained in the traditional churches.

Rindeschwender, who as a longstanding fierce opponent of Jewish emancipation had once been a pioneering articulator of the "Christian state" concept, now also used arguments which fundamentally undermined that ideal. He noted that many feared "an atomistic disintegration of the existing great churches"; but he said that this was not the concern of the state, whose only purpose was to guarantee justice (which included full freedom of conscience) and whose justification only derived from its capacity for "satisfaction of the general needs of human nature".[52] He further redefined both Christianity and the purpose of the state when he argued:

> "If it lies in the course of the development of humanity that from time to time the Christian religion creates other forms for itself . . . if periodically there emerges . . . a dissatisfaction with the old structure, *the state should let it be*; the movement will either, in league with the *truth*, safely break ground for itself and bear good fruit, or it will – if its foundation is *frivolous* – silently seep into the sand like undammed water, without leaving a trace . . . A government . . . does not comprehend its position, its well-being, if it, with intensified heart-pounding, tightens the reins of domination ever more, instead of letting go freely that which has outgrown its minority and can control itself in a manly, prudent manner. Let religious life take care of itself."[53]

It was a fact not lost on any of the men in the liberal majority that it was the issue of religious freedom that had caused the Chamber to be dissolved in the first place, and that religious conservatism was their most immediate enemy. As one newly-elected liberal put it, "let's admit it, the Chamber was dissolved . . . as a result of a *monstrous priestly lie*, the petition storm, or if you prefer, as a result of the religious upheaval in the land".[54] Buß and Stolz and their cohorts had made opposition to the *Deutschkatholiken* a matter of principle for the Right; in response, the *Deutschkatholiken* became even more of a *cause célèbre* for the Left. No longer was it only the promise of national unity and an end to the religious divisions which rent Germany; no longer was it only the appeal of a democratic experiment in brotherly love that inspired the *Deutschkatholiken*'s defenders. Despite their electoral triumph, they had also had to confront the political effectuality of conservative Catholicism; its ability to expose the liberals' distance from "the people", in whose name they pronounced their views on matters great and small; its ability, indeed, to rob them (however temporarily) of their exalted status and

---

[51]Ignaz Rindeschwender, *Verhandlungen* (II. Kammer), 26th June 1846, 7. Beilagenheft, p. 135.
[52]*Ibid.*, p. 149.
[53]*Ibid.*, p. 150.
[54]Johann Georg Christian Kapp, *Verhandlungen* (II. Kammer), 13th August 1846, 8. Protokollheft, p. 63.

identity as members of a Diet which had the eyes of all Germany on it. Religious freedom, once a matter of ambivalence for liberals, became their rallying cry. And – especially given the comparisons between dissenters and Jews their opponents were pressing – this could not help but affect their stand on the "Jewish Question" as well.

The liberal delegates' overriding concern, however, was to resist the ways in which the religious Right was trying to define the content of Christianity. In the two days of debates about Rindeschwender's report, on 12th and 13th August 1846, liberal after liberal certainly called for religious freedom, but the bulk of most liberals' statements was given over to an elaborate defence of the *Deutschkatholiken*'s identity as Christians. Some delegates even went so far as to compare the dissenters with the early disciples of Christ, taunting those who opposed dissent that if they had lived 1,800 years earlier, they would have, "in the name of peace, order, unity", opposed Christ himself.[55] As the Grand Duke's decree limiting dissenters' rights had implicitly acknowledged that the dissenters were Christians, giving liberals a wedge with which to argue that the decree itself was unconstitutional, the focus on the dissenters' Christian identity was a logical strategy to pursue.[56]

Yet the insistence on the dissenters' Christianity was not purely strategic, but also the result of a deeply-felt revulsion at those who would arrogate to themselves the right to determine the value of another person's faith. As Friedrich Hecker put it to those of his colleagues who denigrated dissent: "How can you be so presumptuous as to present yourself, as it were, as identical with God and say: these alone are the true paths that lead to temporal and eternal happiness?"[57] Others criticised Buß and everything he stood for directly, either declaring that "not one Badener out of a thousand wants a Catholicism like Buß", or trying to point out that "we all stand on the ground of subjectivity, Representative Buß just as much as we".[58] The general message of most of the liberals' statements was that Baden was in grave danger because of "jesuitical" and "ultramontane" machinations, and that supporting dissenters' rights was an excellent way to resist such trends.[59] Thus, given the preponderance of liberals in the Chamber, it was no great surprise that when the vote was held on whether the dissenters' petitions should be forwarded to the Grand Duke's government with the "urgent recommendation" that the petitioners' requests be satisfied, this recommendation passed by a vote of thirty-six to twenty-six.[60]

Significantly, in this debate on the dissenters it had been left to the Lower

---

[55]Rindeschwender, *ibid.*, p. 155; cf. Karl Mathy, *ibid.*, p. 118; and Bassermann, *Verhandlungen* (II. Kammer), 12th August 1846, 8. Protokollheft, p. 50.

[56]The Evangelical-Reformed and Lutheran churches in Baden were not united with each other until 1821, and thus in 1818, when the constitution was formulated, it had been necessary to say that members of all three Christian churches in the state (the two Protestant ones and the Catholic church) would be guaranteed equal political rights. The original recognition that there were three fully legitimate forms of Christianity gave liberals the opening for arguing that newly emergent forms of Christianity should also be legitimated.

[57]Hecker, *Verhandlungen* (II. Kammer), 13th August 1846, 8. Protokollheft, p. 103.

[58]Welcker, *ibid.*, p. 139; Zittel, *ibid.*, p. 148.

[59]For example, cf. Kapp, *ibid.*, pp. 74–75; and Ludwig Weller, *ibid.*, p. 141.

[60]*Ibid.*, p. 160.

Chamber's conservatives to point out that liberals had caught themselves in a contradiction when they demanded freedom of religion for those who left the Christian churches, even though they had not been particularly eager to work for the equality of non-Christians. Franz Christoph Trefurt, one of the very few pro-emancipationists who was also a government loyalist, specifically asked Hecker how he could reconcile his previous opposition to equality of Jewish rights with his indignant demands for an equal status for the *Deutschkatholiken*. It was this challenge which prompted Hecker to declare:

> "I must admit that this religious persecution, this repression for the sake of faith, makes quite clear to me what sort of oppression has weighed on the Jews, and from the moment I saw the oppression of our *Deutschkatholiken*, I vowed to vote for the emancipation of the Jews. (Many voices cry bravo.) . . . I was caught in the prejudice of youth, of custom, and now I have returned to freedom . . . I would not be able to justify it before God and the people to put someone in a worse or lower position, because he cannot worship God as I do, but rather wants to serve Him in his own way."[61]

Both the liberal and the conservative press recognised the significance of Hecker's public change of heart, because of the important leadership role he played among his fellow liberals. The progressive *Mannheimer Abendzeitung* notified its readers that:

> "Many previous opponents of emancipation among our delegates have changed their opinion on this matter, and particularly the delegate Hecker has publicly declared in the midst of the debates on the *Deutschkatholiken* that with respect to Jewish emancipation he has changed his previous views; and so it cannot be doubted that an imposing majority will be for emancipation."[62]

The conservative *Mannheimer Morgenblatt*, however mockingly, conveyed the same message: "Now various of the most bitter opponents of emancipation have converted; Mr. Hecker has transformed himself from a Christian Paul into a Jewish Saul; without fail, the great man will carry away the little ones with him."[63]

And indeed, so it was. One week after the debate on the dissenters, on 21st August 1846, when debates were reopened on Jewish emancipation, it quickly became evident that the terms in which the debates had for so long been cast had been fundamentally transformed. Previously, the debate had centred on whether equality would cause the dilution of difference or whether it should be the reward for such dilution. In the most recent debate on the subject in February 1845, for example, one anti-emancipationist had summarised the delegates' choices thus:

> "The giving-up of nationality is either the prerequisite or the result of so-called emancipation . . . We, and all Diet decisions since 1831, demand certain concessions, the clearing-away of the obstacles inhibiting equalisation; we attach to emancipation *conditions that must be fulfilled beforehand*, but the petitioners and their Christian friends

---

[61]Hecker, *ibid.*, p. 106.
[62]*Mannheimer Abendzeitung* (20th August 1846), p. 898.
[63]*Mannheimer Morgenblatt* (14th April 1847), p. 491.

say: emancipate us *first*, and then the fulfilment of your demands will come of its own accord; for this is the necessary effect of emancipation."[64]

In August 1846, the operative question had changed entirely. Now, what was at stake was deciding between the realisation of the principle of religious freedom on the one hand, or the maintenance of a Christian state on the other. As the pro-emancipationist Anton Christ put it:

"Choose one or the other of the two opposing possibilities, either take a stand for emancipation or against it. In both cases, what is at stake is the principle of religious freedom; and here everyone is consistent if he says, I demand sameness [*Gleichheit*] of religion in a state, or if he says, in relation to the state it is not necessary for all members to have the same religion . . . If one starts from the principle [that the religion of the individual should be irrelevant to the state], then one can with respect to the Jews no longer be in doubt even for a moment, that one must also declare them to have equal rights in relation to the state."[65]

In short, Christ urged consistency from those who a week earlier had propounded the notion that there was more than one acceptable way to be a person of faith. Newly fervent for the cause of emancipation, Friedrich Hecker similarly called attention to the way the emergence of dissent and the conservative attack on it had changed the ways Jewish emancipation needed to be conceptualised. He, too, as his colleagues well knew, had once been ambivalent about Jewish rights. "But in the meantime", he said, "an event has intervened, that challenged everyone to think more closely about persecution for the sake of faith."[66]

Other liberal pro-emancipationists sought to provoke those liberals who were still reluctant in similar ways, particularly by focusing on the concept of the "Christian state", which had in previous years so successfully been used to justify the maintenance of the Jews' political inequality. Some pro-emancipationist liberals had already in earlier debates argued that a truly Christian state was one in which everyone was treated in accordance with the Christian values of love and justice, not one in which everyone had to be Christian, and this kind of argument recurred in 1846 as well. But now that religious conservatives had given the idea of the Christian state a new, and for most liberals, quite frightening meaning, there was a greater pugnacity in liberal comments on the term. One expressed gratitude that his opponents' concept of a Christian state did not exist, for, he charged, "it would necessarily lead to an inquisition or to hypocrisy".[67] Another delegate compared the idea of the Christian state to the Ottoman Islamic state – where Christians were being persecuted.[68] Yet others provocatively equated the Christian state with the notion of the "theocratic state" more typically evoked in standard criticisms of the Jews, pleading instead for a "state of law" (*Rechtsstaat*) in which the state "has no right to demand of its citizens . . . that they belong to a particular faith".[69]

[64]Franz Burckhard Fauth, *Verhandlungen* (II. Kammer), 19th February 1845, 13. Beilagenheft, p. 362.
[65]Anton Christ, *Verhandlungen* (II. Kammer), 21st August 1846, 9. Protokollheft, pp. 47–48.
[66]Hecker, *ibid.*, p. 63.
[67]Lorenz Peter Brentano, in his report to the Chamber, in *Verhandlungen* (II. Kammer), 7th August 1846, 7. Beilagenheft, p. 341. This report served as the basis for the 21st August discussion.
[68]Bassermann, *Verhandlungen* (II. Kammer), 21st August 1846, 9. Protokollheft, p. 61.
[69]Alexander von Soiron, *ibid.*, p. 62.

A newly elected radical liberal delegate, Johann Georg Christian Kapp, played out the comparison between the new conservative Roman Catholicism and the old stereotypes against Judaism with particular wit and rage. Reminding his listeners that German Jews had modernised their faith over the centuries just as most German Christians had, Kapp responded to the venomously anti-emancipationist liberal Ludwig Weller – who had just warmed up all the hoary clichés about the Jews' rigidity, self-segregation and arrogance *vis-à-vis* Christians – by contending that the Roman Catholic Church was just as separatist as Weller claimed the Jews were, and that conservative Catholics also thought themselves to be the chosen people of God. "According to this theory of exclusivism the state government would, to be *consistent*, finally also have to take away the rights of all who belong to the Roman Church, insofar as it wants to be exclusive." But Kapp went on to note that "the humorous side of such consistency harbours a tragic seriousness".[70]

Another effect of the reconfiguration of Baden's religious landscape was that liberals came to feel differently about "public opinion". The petition storm had driven home for the liberals their distance from "the people", and this had clearly created an awkwardness for many liberals about the old tactic of wrapping themselves in the cloak of "public opinion" when they sought to justify their resistance to Jewish emancipation. Furthermore, the entire conservative mobilisation against dissent had revealed that the strategic deployment of anti-Jewish rhetoric in general was a gambit that was now being used more effectively by the Right – not just against dissent, but also against liberalism itself, and the issues dear to its heart. (Typical devices designed to excite public opinion against liberalism and its values, for example, were to call liberal newspapers "Jew-papers", and to portray mixed Catholic-Protestant marriages as just as "unacceptable" as a Christian-Jewish marriage.)[71]

As a result, liberals were suddenly theorising the gaps in their relationship to the populace as never before, and commenting on the phenomenon of mass politics and its vulnerability to demagogic manipulation. Alexander von Soiron, for example, suggested that "there is also a sort of public opinion that one shouldn't really recognise".[72] Lorenz Brentano called on his colleagues to "have the courage to resist public opinion when it wants something unjust ... especially when public opinion has been led astray. For who represents public opinion? Surely not those who consider themselves justified when they persecute another because of his faith."[73] And Kapp announced that Jews "are almost only hated in those places where one *fanaticises the people against them*", and reported that the conservatives were already plotting how to use the pro-emancipationist

---

[70]Kapp, *ibid.*, p. 67.
[71]For examples, see notes 38 and 40; Franz Josef Buß, 'Aufgabe der Zeitschrift', in *Capistran. Zeitschrift für die Rechte und Interessen des katholischen Teutschlands*, vol. I, No. 1, Schaffhausen 1847, pp. 15–16; and Franz Rosshirt, *Beleuchtung und actenmässige Ergänzung der Karlsruher Schrift "Der Streit über gemischte Ehen und das Kirchenhoheitsrecht im Grossherzogthum Baden"*, Schaffhausen 1847, p. 19. Also cf. Amts-Assessor Herterich, 'Die Judenemancipation und ihre beiden Geschwister, der Deutschkatholicismus und der Radikalismus', in *Mannheimer Morgenblatt* (26th February 1847), p. 269.
[72]Soiron, *Verhandlungen* (II. Kammer), 21st August 1846, 9. Protokollheft, p. 62.
[73]Brentano, *Verhandlungen* (II. Kammer), 7th August 1846, 7. Beilagenheft, p. 342.

stand the Chamber was to take that day to embitter public opinion against the liberals.[74]

In the end, it was the way in which the "Jewish Question" had been recast that caused the answer to that question to be new and different as well. Characteristically, it was again the conservative Catholic Buß who articulated more clearly than any other the new division between defenders and opponents of emancipation: The choice no longer revolved around whether *"Gleichheit"* (sameness, equality) would be the precondition or the reward for overcoming difference. Now the choice was: support for complete religious freedom *or* support for the hierarchical Christian state. Thus the anti-emancipationist Buß echoed the pro-emancipationist Christ's remarks, but from the opposite perspective. Both sides were aware how much the terms of debate had shifted. Buß said:

> "The question of emancipation, which is a source of embarrassment for many a political character, is not so for me. Someone who starts from the principle that our states are Christian states, and that Baden, too, is still a Christian state; who strives to restore the quality of a Christian state, which has in recent times become completely weakened under the impact of legal religious indifference, cannot be for emancipation. But all who are for this religious indifference, all who advocated the civic recognition of *Rongethum*, must, if they are to be consistent, vote for the emancipation of the Jews."[75]

Though they disagreed with Buß, many delegates agreed with his summary of the choices facing them. A number of previous opponents of equal rights for Baden's Jewish community indicated clearly that – although they retained deep ambivalence about Jews – the changed context was leading them to support emancipation for the first time. Other longstanding anti-emancipationists simply voted quietly in favour of it, without making any speech at all. Thus, for the first time in its history, on 21st August 1846, the Lower Chamber voted for Jewish emancipation by a margin of thirty-six to eighteen.[76]

Jewish observers across the German lands were absolutely delighted, and expected that Jewish emancipation would soon become law in Baden.[77] But as it

---

[74]Kapp, *Verhandlungen* (II. Kammer), 21st August 1846, 9. Protokollheft, pp. 66 and 69.
[75]Buß, *ibid.*, pp. 69–70.
[76]The Lower Chamber protocols only listed thirty-five proponents of emancipation. See *ibid.*, p. 74. But contemporary newspaper reports said the vote was thirty-six to eighteen; see, for example, *Seeblätter*, Konstanz (25th August 1846) – apparently Trefurt belatedly added his name to the pro-emancipation side. *Die Reform des Judenthums*, Mannheim (26th August 1846), p. 176, reported that of the delegates missing on the day of the vote, "five as well as the president of the Chamber had already earlier expressed their support for [Jewish] equalisation; thus, forty-two members, i.e. exactly two-thirds of the Chamber, have voted for emancipation, surely a happy outcome".
[77]For example, see the *Allgemeine Zeitung des Judenthums*, Leipzig (14th September 1846), p. 549, which argued that "it is true that the vote has as yet no immediate practical result; . . . [and] that until its realisation it must still pass through three authorities . . . But let us not forget, that in Baden it is *usually* a matter of *principle* rights, less of material [rights] . . . Restrictions, reservations, clauses may therefore become popular, but the principle has been decided, it has conquered, and after a short time it will also conquer them." Also compare *Die Reform des Judenthums* (26th August 1846), p. 176; *Zeitschrift für die religiösen Interessen des Judenthums*, Leipzig 1846, p. 389; *Reform-Zeitung*, Berlin (April 1847), p. 30; and the enthusiastic report on the Baden vote squeezed into the index of Isaak Markus Jost's about-to-be-published *Culturgeschichte zur neueren Geschichte der Israeliten von 1815 bis 1845*, Berlin 1847, p. 283.

turned out, these observers were wrong, for precisely at this moment when Baden's famed liberals were most visionary, their hands were tied. The Grand Duke, his ministers and the Upper Chamber stalled and failed to accept the Lower Chamber's recommendation.[78] Although emancipation was partially implemented in the revolutionary year of 1849 (indicatively, it was understood as part of a larger move to make political rights independent of religious affiliation and to ensure that churches should have no influence on the state), there were many post-revolutionary set-backs and it was not until 1862 that Jews were given complete equality with Christians in Baden. Indeed, the most immediate effect of the vote was to inspire outbreaks of anti-Jewish violence in a number of Baden communities.[79] And, as Kapp had predicted, conservative Catholics tried to turn this popular hostility to their own advantage. The *Süddeutsche Zeitung für Kirche und Staat* reported smugly that "the vote on the issue of Jewish emancipation has generated a great deal of hostility among the people, something that can be excused by anyone who is familiar with the situation in places where Christians and Jews live beside each other and therefore knows how much the domestic welfare of the latter is ever increasing at the expense of the former".[80] The paper noted with glee how in the wake of the vote, "the popular halo of certain people has been severely tarnished" and how "every now and then one of our parliamentary men-of-the-people trembles in fear of losing his popular glory".[81] Increasingly, liberals returned the favour – comments about how conservative or "jesuitical" forces were fanaticising the masses against Jews became standard elements in liberals' arguments.[82]

Thus essentially it was not the emergence of the *Deutschkatholiken* themselves that made religious freedom a matter of principle for liberals and led them to change their minds about Jewish rights. Rather, it was the conservative counter-attack on liberalising tendencies within Christianity; the conservative assault on free choice in matters of faith and love, culminating in the stricter handling of mixed marriages and in the petition storm; and the rhetoric in and around the dissolution of the Chamber, that had confronted liberals with the reality of conservative Catholicism's increasing political effectiveness. It was this that

---

[78]On the Ministry of State's and the Upper Chamber's deliberate obstructionism, see the detailed report in Berthold Rosenthal, *Heimatgeschichte der badischen Juden seit ihrem geschichtlichen Auftreten bis zur Gegenwart*, Bühl/Baden 1927, pp. 285–288.
[79]See Franz Hundsnurscher and Gerhard Taddey, *Die jüdischen Gemeinden in Baden. Denkmale. Geschichte. Schicksale*, Stuttgart 1968, p. 16; and Adolf Lewin, *Geschichte der badischen Juden seit der Regierung Karl Friedrichs, 1738–1909*, Karlsruhe 1909, p. 277.
[80]*Süddeutsche Zeitung für Kirche und Staat* (16th September 1846), p. 822.
[81]*Süddeutsche Zeitung für Kirche und Staat* (13th September 1846), p. 815; *ibid.* (16th September 1846), p. 822.
[82]For examples, see *Mannheimer Abendzeitung* (25th December 1846), p. 1405; *ibid.* (8th March 1847), p. 259; *ibid.* (14th October 1847), pp. 1118–1119; *ibid.* (9th March 1848), p. 271; Brentano, in *Verhandlungen* (II. Kammer), 9th March 1848, 3. Protokollheft, p. 108; Hecker, in *Verhandlungen* (II. Kammer), 7th April 1848, 4. Protokollheft, p. 45; and *Deutschkatholisches Sonntags-Blatt*, Wiesbaden (7th August 1853), p. 125.

provoked Baden's leading liberals into taking an emancipatory stand. In short, it was above all liberals' hatred of conservative Catholicism, and not a commitment to universal equality, that led them to reframe how they understood the "Jewish Question", and to revise their previous stance on it.

*Responses to Persecution in the 1930s
Two New Perspectives*

The Persecution of the Heine Family in Germany 1933–1939

BY EDITH RAIM

The subject of this essay is the persecution of a family of part-Jewish origin and their expulsion from their home in a small village on the shores of the Ammersee in Upper Bavaria during the Third *Reich*. The family is that of the artist and caricaturist Thomas Theodor Heine. Heine was, according to Nazi criteria, "racially" clearly classified as a "Volljude",[1] although he had no affiliation to Judaism. Magdalena, his wife, was Protestant and their daughter was therefore defined as half-Jewish. The history of their expulsion represents the fate of many others within National-Socialist Germany. It is singled out here because of the abundance of material on their case, which is lacking for less prominent victims. Another noteworthy aspect is that despite the harassment and intimidation the family suffered from local Nazis, they were able to get some legal protection through "Aryan" German lawyers, which enabled them to keep their property until 1939. State offices also helped the family at first, but slowly withdrew their support until the Heine family finally left.

The first section of this essay, dealing with Heine's expulsion, is largely biographical and rests on his own testimony through his letters and cartoons, as well as letters addressed to Heine from the painter Max Liebermann.[2] The second section, which deals with the persecution of his family, relies on the letters exchanged between various offices of the district of Upper Bavaria.[3]

Thomas Theodor Heine, born in Leipzig on 28th February 1867, studied at the art colleges of Düsseldorf and Munich. In 1896 he and the publisher Albert Langen founded the illustrated satirical weekly *Simplicissimus*, whose emblem, the red bulldog, was Heine's own creation. During his time with *Simplicissimus*, which lasted nearly forty years, Heine published countless cartoons. At the same

---

[1]Wassermann and Schoenberner claim that Heine was of mixed parentage and had been raised as a Christian. See Henry Wassermann, 'Jews in Jugendstil. The Simplicissimus 1896–1914', in *LBI Year Book XXXI* (1986), pp. 71–104, here p. 85; and Franz Schoenberner, *Confessions of a European Intellectual*, New York 1946, pp. 1–15, here p. 4, who describes Heine as son of a Jewish father and an English mother. The mother, however, was also from a Jewish family.
[2]See Thomas Theodor Heine Collection, File AR 841, 'Letters' and File AR 1671, 'Cartoons'; and Max Liebermann Collection, File AR 847, Leo Baeck Institute Archives (hereafter LBIA), New York.
[3]The file is titled 'Akten des Bezirksamtes Landsberg. Betreff Enteignung/Spezialia', and is housed in the Staatsarchiv (StA) München, LRA 45921.

time he illustrated books, including Thomas Mann's *Wälsungenblut*.[4] A letter written by perhaps the most famous German Impressionist painter, Max Liebermann, reveals the high regard colleagues had for Heine's artistic work. In this letter he thanks Heine for his willingness to draw a *Signet* free of charge for an unnamed society:

> "Jung-Stilling sagte von Göthe [*sic*]: sein Herz, das nur wenige kannten, war so groß, wie sein Genie, das alle kannten. Da jeder Strich Ihrer Hand den Stempel Ihrer Persönlichkeit trägt – wie denn in der Kunst die Ausführung der Gedanke ist – wird uns freuen, was Sie für uns're Gesellschaft machen wollen und – last not least – uns'rem Maxim förderlich sein."[5]

It was Heine's profession, as a cartoonist, to criticise human failings and social conditions through humour and mockery. The possibility of causing offence has always been the occupational hazard of an artist. In 1899 he was imprisoned for six months in a fortress in Königstein, Saxony. The reason: *lèse-majesté*, in a cartoon of Wilhelm II.[6] Even as a schoolboy Heine had caused consternation with cartoons of his teachers; in the sixth year he was expelled from his *Gymnasium* because of his secret work for the magazine *Leipziger Pikante Blätter*. Even if *Simplicissimus* countenanced nationalist and antisemitic attacks, its overall political tendencies could not please the emerging National-Socialist Party. It is true that *Simplicissimus* – and with it Heine – approved of the war in 1914; it is also true that even Heine had published antisemitic cartoons contributing to the perverted image of Jews.[7] None the less, he had often opposed the pillars of a complacent society: the military, judiciary, police, bureaucracy and also the abuses by the *Burschenschaften* and the petits bourgeois. Despite occasional lapses of judgement, Heine had devoted his life to fighting authoritarian regimes and their wrongdoings, whether public opinion supported him or not. Many of the other cartoonists at *Simplicissimus* lacked the courage to attack National Socialism the way he did, even after Hitler's *Machtübernahme*. In 1932 Heine depicted Hitler as a frog prince – with characteristic lock of hair, moustache and swastika armband – with the caption: "Es war einmal ein Froschkönig, der lebte in einem braunen Sumpf. Er hatte nichts als ein großes

---

[4]Heine's work as an illustrator is acknowledged in Justin Howes and Pauline Paucker, 'German Jews and the Graphic Arts', in *LBI Year Book XXXIV* (1989), p. 450.
[5]Letter by Max Liebermann to Th.Th. Heine, Berlin, 1st December 1930, in Max Liebermann Collection, LBIA, New York, File AR 847.
[6]As well as incarceration for Heine, the skit (which included a poem by Frank Wedekind) resulted in the publisher, Albert Langen, having to leave the country and only being able to return in 1903 after paying a 30,000 *Mark* fine. Wedekind first fled to Austria and later met Langen in Zürich. However, when he returned to Germany he was condemned to seven months imprisonment. See Eugen Roth, *Simplicissimus. Ein Rückblick auf die satirische Zeitschrift*, Hanover 1954, p. 18; and Corona Hepp, *Avantgarde. Moderne Kunst, Kulturkritik und Reformbewegungen nach der Jahrhundertwende*, Munich 1987, pp. 43–46. Funnily enough, Heine and Wedekind met during their imprisonment in Königstein. Heine in a letter: "Vorigen Donnerstag ist Wedekind hier eingetroffen. Er ist doch ein interessanter Mensch. Ich unterhalte mich gut mit ihm." Heine to (the unidentified) Lisl, Königstein, 25th September 1899, in Franz Schoenberner Collection, Box No. 3, Folder 'Correspondence Th. Th. Heine', Hoover Institution on War, Revolution and Peace, Archives, Stanford, CA.
[7]Wassermann, 'Jews in Jugendstil', *loc. cit.*, pp. 85ff., deals with Heine's mockery of Jews and his amibivalent position towards them.

Maul und war weder gut anzusehen noch gut anzuhören."[8] In another cartoon a mother refers her hungry child to the Nazis' Four Year Plan: "Du Lausejunge wirst wohl noch die vier Jährchen warten können!"[9] On the occasion of the March elections in 1933, Heine emphasised the violent tendencies of National Socialism: he drew the burning *Reichstag*, with people fighting, while in the foreground people sing merrily on their way to the polling station, ignoring the violence. The caption, with altered lines from a popular folk song, reads: "Der März ist gekommen, die Knüppel schlagen aus . . ."[10] He also expressed his antipathy towards the National Socialists in the cartoon 'Die Unpolitischen', which could well be an illustration of Max Liebermann's famous remark about the emergence of National Socialism: "Man kann nicht soviel fressen, wie man kotzen möchte!": one man is vomiting, another is holding his stomach and covering his mouth with his hand. The text reads: "Politik macht zwar nicht satt, aber sie nimmt einem wenigstens den Appetit."[11]

Heine had prophesised that 1933 would be a "year of new humanity": "Ein Jahr der neuen Humanität: die Zunahme des Okkultismus wird wieder zu Hexenverbrennungen führen . . .",[12] probably not suspecting just how right he was and how soon he himself would fall among the victims.

I. THE EXPULSION OF THOMAS THEODOR HEINE FROM GERMANY

With Hitler's *Machtübernahme*, it soon became clear that Heine's life as an artist and cartoonist was no longer possible. Heine was aware of his precarious situation, as is clear from Liebermann's response to a – probably no longer extant – letter from Heine. This letter describes the position of the Jewish artist in the first months of the Third *Reich*. Liebermann first expresses reservations about a proclamation in support of cultural freedom published in February 1933, signed by Käthe Kollwitz, Heinrich Mann and many other artists and significant cultural figures, on which Heine seems to have solicited Liebermann's opinion. Liebermann assumes a stance of cautious restraint:

> "Das Natürlichste wäre, [aus der Preußischen Akademie der Künste] auszutreten. Aber mir, als Juden, würde das als Feigheit ausgelegt werden, wie mir schon mein Rücktritt von der Präsidentschaft als Feigheit ausgelegt worden ist.[13]
> Nochmehr aber verhindert mich daran die Erwägung, durch meinen Austritt gerade das zu tun, was die Gegner wünschen. Ich möchte nicht denselben Fehler

---

[8]*Simplicissimus*, 37, No. 33 (13th November 1932).
[9]*Simplicissimus*, 37, No. 48 (26th February 1933).
[10]*Simplicissimus*, 37, No. 49 (5th March 1933).
[11]*Simplicissimus*, 37, No. 51 (19th March 1933).
[12]*Simplicissimus*, 37, No. 40 (1st January 1933).
[13]Liebermann, who had been the president of the Prussian Academy of Fine Arts since 1920, stepped down in 1932, after which he became honorary president.

machen, den ich vor 20 Jahren begangen habe, als ich den Andern die Secession aushändigte."¹⁴

Ich möchte, daß die Gegenpartei das tut. Allerdings kommt Alles [sic] darauf an, ob ich Gefolgschaft finde (was mehr als zweifelhaft, doch will ich Nichts [sic] unversucht lassen). Also abwarten bitte. Bis dahin mit bestem Dank für Ihren Brief und mit freundlichen Grüßen auch an Gulbrans[s]on Ihr sehr ergebener Max Liebermann."¹⁵

However, the Nazi authorities did not leave either artist much time: in 1933, Liebermann was forced to give up membership and the honorary presidency of the Academy, and Heine was expelled from the editorial board of *Simplicissimus*.¹⁶ Any further artistic activity in Germany was forbidden to him. In a letter to Rudolf Grossmann, a draughtsman and painter from Freiburg, written in Munich on 26th March 1933, Heine describes the course of events:

"Wir hatten eine Gesellschafter-Versammlung. Irgendeiner von uns [vielleicht Olaf (Gulbransson) und Thöny zusammen] hatten es dem Ministerium des Inneren mitgeteilt. Es erschienen daraufhin bei uns 2 Abgesandte des Ministeriums mit dem Auftrag[,] mich zu verhaften und ins Konzentrationslager nach Dachau zu bringen, wenn ich nicht sofort ein mir vorgelegtes Schriftstück unterschreibe. Darin stand[,] daß ich einsehe, daß ich mit meiner Stellungnahme¹⁷ im Unrecht war und daß ich auf jede Redaktionstätigkeit verzichte. Natürlich mußte ich es unterschreiben und ich kümmere mich nun um nichts mehr. Das Blatt geht sowieso schnell kaput [sic]. Es ist immer noch verboten. Man hätte es längst freibekommen können, wenn nicht jeder etwas anderes unternehmen würde, einer gegen den anderen arbeitete und besonders die Weiber sich in der übelsten Weise hervortäten. So sind wir erledigt und ich kann schauen, wo ich ein paar Pfennige verdienen kann."¹⁸

Heine miscalculated if he thought that ultimate responsibility for the journals would fall upon the editorial board. The purge of *Simplicissimus* focused on him, because he, classified as a Jew and an anti-Nazi cartoonist, embodied the Nazi

---

¹⁴In 1898, Liebermann founded the *Berliner Sezession* with Walter Leistikow; he was its first president from 1899 to 1911. In 1910 the young modern artists separated and organised the *Neue Sezession*. In 1913 Liebermann, along with other artists, left the *Berliner Sezession* which was now led by Lovis Corinth and created the *Freie Sezession*.

¹⁵Letter of Max Liebermann to Th.Th. Heine, Berlin, 23rd February 1933, in Max Liebermann Collection, LBIA, New York, File AR 847.

¹⁶Authors often rely on Eugen Roth's account of this event. See *idem*, *Simplicissimus*, *op. cit.*, pp. 103ff. A more knowledgeable portrayal of the situation can be found in the Franz Schoenberner Collection, Box No. 2, Folder Writings 'Life and Death of *Simplicissimus*', Hoover Institution, Archives, Stanford, CA, or in Franz Schoenberner, *Confessions of a European Intellectual*, *op. cit.*, pp. 1–15.

¹⁷It is not clear to what statement Heine is referring to here, since the majority of the articles in *Simplicissimus* were short satires, trenchant stories about everyday occurrences or jokes. Only one article in the issue of 12th March 1933 might qualify as overtly political. It reads: "Sie erinnern sich noch, mit welcher Entschiedenheit Hitler, eben Reichskanzler geworden, den Vertretern der Presse erklärte, die Meinungs- und Pressefreiheit grundsätzlich nicht antasten zu wollen. Inzwischen haben wir nun auf diesem Gebiet auch allerhand erlebt: die Meldungen über Zeitungsverbote füllen beinahe jeden Tag eine Spalte." The text goes on: "Und was wir jetzt unter Herrn Hitlers Kanzlerschaft erleben, ist nur die Erfüllung alter revolutionärer deutscher Sehnsucht. Preßfreiheit und Zensur: die Nationalsozialisten haben auch hier die Synthese gefunden." *Simplicissimus*, 37, No. 50 (12th March 1933).

¹⁸Letter from Th.Th. Heine to Rudolf Grossmann, Munich, 26th March 1933, in Thomas Theodor Heine Collection, LBIA, New York, File AR 841, 'Letters'.

concept of the enemy. Heine's colleagues of many years preferred to keep in with the new regime. He describes their opportunism with hurt and anger:

> "Die Situation ist wie bei einem Schiffbruch. Schiffbrüchige auf einer Planke [gerettet (crossed out)] leiden Hunger, überlegen, wen sie verzehren wollen. So haben sie mich geschlachtet. Aber sie werden sich doch nicht retten können. Olaf hat einen Brief an das braune Haus geschrieben: er sei ja immer national gesinnt gewesen und nur vergewaltigt worden. Er ist der Partei beigetreten. Thöny ist schon lange Mitglied. Auch Schilling hat entdeckt, daß er schon immer streng national war und nur von Schoenberner und mir genotzüchtigt worden ist. Es kommt mir vor, wie das Mädchen, das neun Kinder hatte und angeblich jedesmal vergewaltigt worden war. Es wird Liebermann sicher interessieren zu hören, wie es bei uns zugegangen ist. Was jetzt aus mir wird, weiß ich gar nicht. Sie sehen, daß Sie nicht der Einzige sind, der gegenüber dem visàvis du rien steht.[19] Hoffentlich geht es bei Ihnen besser aus. Mit den besten Grüßen Ihr TTH."[20]

On the surface, the *Gleichschaltung* of *Simplicissimus* happened discreetly: only one issue was dropped during this time. In No. 51 Schoenberner is identified as the responsible editor. The new year's issue appeared under the editorial responsibility of Anton Rath. A paper band around this issue announced: "Das zeitweilige Verbot des 'Simplicissimus' ist aufgehoben. Redaktion und Verlag." In the issue a note explained the price paid for the lifting of censorship: "Der Verlautbarung auf der Titelseite dieser Nummer haben wir noch anzufügen, daß die Zurücknahme des zeitweiligen Verbots unseres Blattes erfolgt ist, nachdem wir der Regierung gegenüber loyales Verhalten in nationaler Beziehung in bindender Form zugesagt haben. Hand in Hand mit dieser Zusage ging eine Umstellung der Redaktion. Redaktion, Verlag und Druckerei des Simplicissimus."[21] The cover of this issue already revealed the new line: it shows Johann Strauß playing the violin, while black jazz musicians fall into an abyss. The text says: "Der Jazzmusik wird heimgegeigt – der Walzer erwacht – die Neger entfliehen." The last Heine cartoon in *Simplicissimus* is found in this issue entitled – certainly not by chance – 'Epilogue'.[22]

---

[19]Grossmann had asked Heine about the publication of his portrait caricatures, which had not been accepted by *Simplicissimus*. In subsequent 1933 issues, portrait caricatures by Grossmann can be found.

[20]See note 18.

[21]*Simplicissimus*, 38, No. 1 (1st April 1933). In the Franz Schoenberner Collection, Box No. 4, Folder 'Personal correspondence' in the Hoover Institution, I found a leaflet also commenting on the *Gleichschaltung* of *Simplicissimus*. It is dated 27th March 1933 and reads: " 'Simplicissimus'. Begründet von Albert Langen. [Th.Th. Heine is of course no longer mentioned.] An unsere Abnehmer. Das zeitweilige Verbot des Erscheinens unseres Blattes wurde nach vollzogenem Wechsel in der Redaktion aufgehoben. Wir werden nun den Versand der Nr. 1 in den nächsten Tagen vornehmen, ebenso hoffen wir, auch Nr. 52 in dieser Woche noch frei zu bekommen, so daß wir auch diese Nummer nachzuliefern vermögen. Wir bitten unsere Freunde, dem *Simplicissimus* auch fernerhin die Treue zu halten, der er heute mehr denn je bedarf, sollen nicht unersetzliche Kulturwerte ernstlich gefährdet werden. Redaktion, Verlag und Versandstelle des *Simplicissimus*." As the following issues of *Simplicissimus* show, the new editorial board fully carried out its promise in regard to cultural values.

[22]An old couple is walking through a park in spring surrounded by young people hugging and kissing. Despite this display the old lady remarks to her companion: "Das mit dem Frühling wird doch eigentlich stark überschätzt . . .".

The changes in the magazine, which led Heine to forecast its imminent demise, can be gauged by comparing its covers for two Christian holidays – reliable litmus tests for a satirical magazine. The cover cartoon for the 1932 Christmas issue is called 'Germanias Weihnachtsbescherung' and refers to the fast changes of chancellors and the instability of the *Reich* in the last years of the Weimar Republic. Heine's cartoon shows the *Reichskanzler* General Kurt von Schleicher under a Christmas tree. *Reichspräsident* Hindenburg leads his blushing daughter Germania to him with the words: "Und hier, mein liebes Kind, das schönste Weihnachtsgeschenk: ein lebendiger General! Hoffentlich gefällt er dir. Ein Umtausch kommt zunächst nicht in Betracht."[23] The Easter issue, with text and drawings by Wilhelm Schulz is, however, an unabashed German idyll: a wayfarer walks through a small village. Under this drawing one reads:

> "Ostern.
> Wie sind heut voller Sonnenschein
> Die Berge und die Täler
> Wehn auch noch kühle Winde drein
> Die Lust wird drum nicht schmäler.
> Was lange wie gestorben lag
> Beginnt sich froh zu regen
> Die Vögel singen laut im Hag
> Es blüht an allen Wegen.
> Ein Wunder sich dem andern paart:
> Aus Ketten und aus Banden
> Ist deutscher Sinn und deutsche Art
> Auch wieder auferstanden."[24]

Simplicissimus, once the top satirical magazine of the *Kaiserreich* and the Weimar Republic, had been reduced within a few weeks to the intellectual level of the *Gartenlaube*.

Heine, co-founder and decade-long staff member of the journal, had not only lost all opportunities to work and earn money; his liberty was also threatened. The postscript of the March letter to Grossmann reads: "Seit drei Wochen bin ich nicht mehr draußen [Dießen am Ammersee] gewesen, weil fortwährend Leute kommen, mich wegzuschleppen. Meine Frau oder Tochter besucht mich manchmal hierin [Heine's studio in Munich], wo ich mich verbergen muß."[25]

Heine, who had considered the Third *Reich* a farce; who, despite the repeated warnings of his friends, considered his lawyer sufficient defence against the Nazi terror,[26] now fled to Prague. At the beginning of 1936 he left Prague for Brno. His letter to Mrs. Keller, the wife of the publishing director of the *Prager Tageblatt*, Dr. Rudolf Keller, thanked her for the friendship and kindness with which he had been received: "Es war eine schöne Zeit in Prag und ich werde immer gern daran zurückdenken, nicht ganz ohne die Hoffnung, daß sich doch einmal die

---

[23] *Simplicissimus* cover by Th.Th. Heine, 37, No. 39 (25th December 1932).
[24] *Simplicissimus* cover by W. Schulz, 38, No. 3 (16th April 1933).
[25] See note 18.
[26] See Schoenberner, *Confessions of a European Intellectual, op. cit.*, pp. 12ff., and Roth, *Simplicissimus, op. cit.*, p. 104.

Möglichkeit ergibt, wieder dort zu leben."²⁷ But his letter also reflects the difficulties and hardship of exile: "Hier lebe ich ja sehr bequem und habe auch liebe Freunde gefunden, die bemüht sind, mir das Leben zu erleichtern. Aber ein klein wenig komme ich mir doch wie der alte Casanova vor, der auf ähnliche Art seine alten Tage in der Tschechoslowakei verlebte.²⁸ Allerdings, wenn es damals schon Equilibrin gegeben hätte, wäre er vielleicht zufriedener gewesen. Bitte sagen Sie Ihrem Herrn Gemahl, daß ich tatsächlich eine gute Wirkung des Mittels verspürt habe, so daß ich meinen Umzug ohne die geringste Nervosität bewerkstelligen konnte und hier eine leichte Depression erfolgreich damit bekämpft habe."²⁹

Heine fled to Oslo in 1938, then in 1942 from occupied Norway to Sweden. He died in Stockholm, on 26th January 1948, as an honoured artist. Heine's non-Jewish wife and daughter stayed in Dießen am Ammersee, where the family owned an estate of 14 *Tagwerk* (5 hectares).³⁰ This property became a bone of contention shortly after the National Socialists came to power.³¹

II. THE PLANNED "DEJUDAISATION" OF AN ESTATE

The first attempt to "dejudaise" the estate was made by the *Königlich Privilegierte Feuerschützengesellschaft*, a local shooting association in Dießen. It had placed its shooting range close by, for the use of the local SA. The *Königlich Privilegierte Feuerschützengesellschaft* had problems with the neighbouring Heine who owned the land they had leased. They believed he had bought the adjacent property in order to disrupt their shooting. Since 1929 they had been exposed to Heine's constant harassment; Heine's lawyer had even demanded the firing range be demolished. The club, however, had worked for years to "toughen up the young" and quite a few of the SA members owed their shooting skills to it.³²

The local branch of the NSDAP supported the concerns of the *Feuerschützengesellschaft* with a plea to the temporary Minister of the Interior in Bavaria, Adolf Wagner, to allow the young storm troopers shooting practice on the Heine estate. In their eyes this was justified by *raison d'état*. The local branch leader of the Nazi Party, Gebhardt, wrote to the Minister of the Interior about the *Simplicissimus* "owner" Heine as follows: "Heine, um dessen Verhaftungserlaubnis wir erst

---

²⁷Letter from Th.Th. Heine to Mrs. Keller, Brno, 28th February 1936, in Thomas Theodor Heine Collection, LBIA, New York, File AR 841, 'Letters'.
²⁸Heine's parallel to Casanova's life is interesting and apt: when Count Waldstein invited him to the castle of Dux in Bohemia as a librarian, Casanova was 58 years old. He lived his last 15 years unhappily, a relic of a past time, on Dux. When Heine was forced to leave Germany in 1933, he was 66 and had 15 years of exile until his death, many of which were spent outside Czechoslovakia.
²⁹See note 27.
³⁰It could not be clarified whether Heine and his wife owned the house jointly or whether it became her sole property after he left the country.
³¹A painting of the house (which was demolished after the war) by Th.Th. Heine can be found in the *Lenbach-Haus* in Munich.
³²All documents quoted in this section belong to the file 'Akten des Bezirksamtes Landsberg. Betreff Enteignung/Spezialia' mentioned in note 3.

nachgesucht haben, ist jener Jude [*sic*], der während seiner ganzen 'künstlerischen' Tätigkeit nichts unterließ, was geeignet gewesen wäre, alles, was dem deutschen Volke hoch und heilig war, in den Dreck zu zerren."[33] The *Bezirksamt* Landsberg – since 1938 *Landratsamt* – took no action and noted on 12th April 1933 that Heine had only forbidden the use of his land, having been repeatedly attacked by members of the *Feuerschützengesellschaft*. The *Bezirksamt* expressed its confidence that Heine would not demand an injunction against the *Feuerschützengesellschaft* and storm troopers, if he was left unmolested and his property kept safe. The *Marktgemeinderat* (local council) Dießen was told by the *Bezirksamt* that Heine, as landowner, had the right to forbid the use of the firing ranges; but, if all parties behaved themselves, Heine would not object to shooting practice. The affair seemed settled, but the *Feuerschützengesellschaft* kept a greedy eye on Heine's property.

On 18th June 1933, they demanded proceedings for the expropriation of Heine's estate from the *Bezirksamt* Landsberg. Their justification lay in the recent law of 8th June 1933, which allowed the dispossession of "unpatriotic" land. It was claimed that Heine had forbidden shooting practice on 30th September 1932; had impeded repairs to the targets on his land and increased his harassment of the *Feuerschützengesellschaft*. The land – so they said – was a wilderness without any value for Heine. Recalling their 600 years of tradition, they lamented: "Es wäre doch das traurigste Zeichen der heutigen Zeit, wenn einem solchen schikanösen Nachbarn sein Ziel in Erfüllung gehen würde."[34] It also would be unpatriotic if the activities of such a "national corporation" as the *Feuerschützengesellschaft* were prevented from carrying on. In the original version this reads: "Die kgl. priv. Feuerschützengesellschaft ist vollkommen auf nationalen [*sic*] Basis umgestellt und betreibt ganz im Sinne unseres großen Führers Adolf Hitler seinen Schießsport, dagegen ist bekannt, daß Herr Th.Th. Heine ein ausgesprochener Gegner der nationalen Bewegung war, und infolge seiner unlauteren Gesinnung zur nationalen Sache seit April heurigen Jahres aus Dießen verschwunden ist. Wir haben nur noch als letzte Rettung das Enteignungsgesetz vom 8.6.1933 zur Verfügung und ersuchen dieses in diesem Fall zur Durchführung zu bringen."[35] Even the local council in Dießen supported the wish of the *Feuerschützengesellschaft* in a letter which emphasised the importance of unobstructed shooting as a contribution to the toughening up of young people.[36] The *Bezirksamt* Landsberg, to which the letters were addressed, consulted Heine's lawyer in Landsberg. He, quite courageously defending the property of Heine, explained that Heine had demanded the injunction only because the *Feuerschützengesellschaft* had completely disregarded his property rights and refused to renew the lease. Heine had bought the land for 700 *Reichsmark* and was willing to sell it to the shooting club, but not for the 150 *Reichsmark* they offered.

---

[33]Letter of NSDAP *Ortsgruppe* Dießen, signed by *Ortsgruppenleiter* Gebhardt, to Adolf Wagner, Minister of the Interior in Bavaria, 18th March 1933, in the above-mentioned file.
[34]Letter of the *Königlich Privilegierte Feuerschützengesellschaft* to the *Bezirksamt* Landsberg, 18th June 1933.
[35]See note 30.
[36]Letter of the *Marktgemeinderat* Dießen to the *Bezirksamt* Landsberg, 21st June 1933.

On 6th July 1933 the Dießen local council learnt from the *Bezirksamt* that this request for confiscation should be made to the State Ministry of the Interior. Such an act would only be possible if the use of the land were fundamentally opposed to national aims and the will of the people. In Heine's case neither prerequisite was fulfilled; an expropriation of the land was thus impossible. The *Feuerschützengesellschaft* was told to renew the lease with Heine or his family if they wanted to keep shooting.

However, the club was defiant; they even began to use heavier guns. Support came from a Beauftragter des Sonderkommissars der SA-Führung beim Bezirksamt Fürstenfeldbruck. This person demanded the confiscation of the Heine estate. His demand was supported by the Sonderkommissar der Obersten SA-Führung bei der Regierung von Oberbayern. The shooting ban, he argued, was directed not only against the *Feuerschützengesellschaft*, but also against the storm troopers. The personnel of the SA and the club had come to overlap a great deal.[37] The *Bezirksamt* Landsberg was not impressed by this new confiscation attempt by the SA. Their reasons were not sufficient: Heine had only intended to end the non-contractual situation by banning the shooting; and it was not the task of the *Bezirksamt* to judge the question merely on the grounds of Heine's work for *Simplicissimus*. The *Bezirksamt* Landsberg informed the *Beauftragter des Sonderkommissars*, Wolkersdorfer, that a commission of the ministerial council would decide the question; until then the shooting could go on as normal.

On 11th August 1933, the legal adviser of the *Oberste SA-Führung* stated simply in a letter to the *SA-Standarte 2 M-O* in Munich that the view of the *Bezirksamt* Landsberg was wrong. The plot was unsuitable for any use. Only the *Feuerschützengesellschaft*, which trained its members there, and the SA could make proper use of Heine's land. It was clear to the SA's legal adviser, "daß dem jüdischen Pacifisten Heine auch dieses kleine Stück Wehrhafterhaltung und Wehrhaftmachung ein Dorn im Auge sein mußte". He went on to say, "daß Heine das Grundstück nur kaufte, um die Schützen in der Erreichung des vaterländischen Zweckes zu hemmen und zu schikanieren".[38]

Especially remarkable is the view of the role of law and justice in the early Third *Reich* expressed in this letter from the *Feuerschützengesellschaft* to the *Bezirksamt* Landsberg: "Es ist nun auch nicht mehr die Zeit, daß man Gesetze nach der alten verknöcherten Art zu einem leblosen Gebilde herabdrückt und lediglich juristische Düftelei [sic] und juristischen Scharfsinn spielen läßt, sondern es ist Hauptgebot und hehrste Aufgabe des Juristen, dem Gesetz zu dem Erfolg zu verhelfen, den der Gesetzgeber erreicht wissen will. Es sind daher m.E. die Voraussetzungen für eine Enteignung gegeben, zumal der vaterlandslose Geselle und Schmierfink Heine deutschen Boden verlassen hat und nur aus dem einen Grund, weil er eben ein gerüttelt Maß von Schuld gegen die Interessen des deutschen Volkes auf sich geladen hat."[39] Finally the letter threatened Heine's

---

[37]Letter of the *Beauftragter des Sonderkommissars der SA-Führung beim Bezirksamt Fürstenfeldbruck* to the *Bezirksamt* Landsberg, 25th July 1933.

[38]Letter of the legal adviser of the *Oberster SA-Führer* to the *SA-Standarte 2 M-O* in Munich, 11th August 1933.

[39]See note 34.

lawyer Meyding in Landsberg: "Die Vertretung des Volksfeindes Heine ist als Nationalsozialist und SA-Mann schärfstens zu verurteilen. Weitere diesbezügliche Schritte werden noch folgen."

The Bavarian Interior Ministry then exercised its authority when, on 22nd August 1933, it informed the *Bezirksamt* Landsberg that no immediate reason existed to expropriate Heine's land. Its use was considered compatible with the national goals of the state and the will of the German people. Surprisingly enough, state institutions and a lawyer had defended Heine's rights against the shooting club and their Nazi allies.

However, the Heines had won the battle, not the war. It was only a temporary victory for Heine's wife and daughter: he had already turned his back on Germany. Because it lacked a legal basis, the argument in favour of confiscation was founded on ideology. In reviewing the stereotypical accusations made, we see that Heine was a ready-made victim, combining, as he did, the characteristics most hated by the Nazis: an artist (in Nazi terminology a *Schmierfink*), a pacifist (*vaterlandsloser Geselle, Volksverräter*) and – most intolerable – of Jewish descent. When, in 1937, the next attempt was made to bring the Heine estate into the "right" hands, Nazi ideology would again play a major role.

III. THE BLOOD AND SOIL ARGUMENT APPLIED TO THE HEINE ESTATE

The local Nazi Party leader in Dießen, who had already made himself spokesman of the *Feuerschützengesellschaft*, described his troubles to the Nazi Party leadership in Landsberg:

> "Zu Beginn der Frühjahrszeit fühle ich mich veranlaßt, auf einen besonderen Mißstand in unserer Gemeinde hinzuweisen. Das Anwesen des im Jahre 1933 emigrierten Juden Th.Th. Heine wird heute noch von dessen Frau bewohnt, während der ca. 20 Tagwerk große Garten, welcher zum Teil bestes Gartenland und Wiesen darstellt, vollkommen verlotert [*sic*]. Ich glaube, daß es in der heutigen Zeit, in der man die Bauern immer wieder auffordert, jedes Stückchen Boden zu verbessern und auszunutzen, unverantwortlich ist, wenn hier nicht eingeschritten wird. Es wurde die letzten Jahre versucht, den Grund pachtweise wenigstens teilweise auszunutzen, was aber fast nicht möglich ist, weil sich niemand mit der Frau Heine einlaßen [*sic*] will, weil diese als unverschämte Person bekannt ist. Ein alter Pg. [Parteigenosse] mit 70 Jahren, dessen beide Söhne im Krieg gefallen sind, der mit seiner Frau hier ein kleines Anwesen bewirtschaftet, hat voriges Jahr dort Pachtland übernommen. Ein Teil dieses war schon zwei Jahre nicht mehr gemäht & konnte nur mehr als Streu Verwendung finden. Mit vieler Mühe hat der alte Mann dieses gemäht, konnte aber durch die Ungunst der Witterung das Material im Vorjahre nicht mehr einbringen. Jetzt im Frühjahr wollte er die Streu trocknen, nun hat aber Frau Heine dieselbe vernichten laßen [*sic*] mit der Begründung, die Pacht wäre 1936 gewesen und der Mann hätte 1937 in ihrem Garten nichts mehr zu suchen.
> Heil Hitler
> NSDAP PG Dießen, gez. Gebhardt"[40]

[40]Letter of NSDAP *Ortsgruppe* Dießen to the *Kreisleitung der NSDAP* in Landsberg, 16th March 1937.

The Persecution of the Heine Family, 1933–1939

The letter was given to the *Bezirksamt* Landsberg, which sent it to the *Kreisbauernschaft* Weilheim, asking them to make a statement. Some days after, the *Kreisbauernschaft* replied that by the decree that safeguarded farmland, the *Bezirksamt* could proceed against Heine's wife and end her unpatriotic behaviour. Finally, they recommended: "Im vorliegenden Fall wäre Schutzhaft sehr angebracht."[41]

At this point, Dr. Linn, the Mayor of Landsberg from 1936 to 1945, joined the witchhunt. It is unclear how he became involved as the town of Landsberg had nothing to do with the administration of the county. But the Third *Reich* did not bother about such formalities. It also seemed to be unnecessary for the mayor to question the claims of the leader of the local Nazi Party in Dießen: the accusation reappears – orthographically corrected – word for word in his letter addressed to Mrs. Heine:

> "Den Berichten nach lassen Sie Ihren ungefähr 20 Tagwerk großen Garten vollkommen verlottern. Es scheint Ihnen noch nicht zum Bewußtsein gekommen zu sein, daß im heutigen Staat jedes Eigentum von Grund und Boden auch die Verpflichtung in sich birgt, den Boden entsprechend zu bewirtschaften. Die Verordnung zur Sicherung der Landbewirtschaftung vom 23.3.1937 bietet die Möglichkeit, die Bewirtschaftung Ihres Gartens, wie sie im Interesse des deutschen Volkes gefordert werden muß, unter allen Umständen sicherzustellen. Sie werden vorerst verwarnt und aufgefordert, Ihr Gartenland und die Wiesenflächen entweder selbst ordnungsgemäß zu nutzen, zu verpachten oder zu verkaufen. Bis längstens 1. Mai wollen Sie dem Bezirksamt bindende Mitteilung machen, in welcher Weise Sie sich die künftige Bewirtschaftung denken. Von dieser Mitteilung muß ich mein weiteres Vorgehen abhängig machen."[42]

The Heine family's lawyers, Valentin Heins and Walter Buhmann, both in Munich, answered on 10th April 1937 that ill-disposed inhabitants of Dießen had made false accusations. They constructed a countercase for every point: they corrected the size of the land downwards and stated that most parts were wasteland and marshland. The cultivation of useful plants was ruled out because drainage was inadequate. The meadow had been cut and the hay had been sold as long as a gardener had been there. It was now leased out or harvested by the Heines. The orchard had been fertilised with liquid manure bought from a local farmer; the vegetable garden had been improved with three loads of fertiliser from a local farmer called Schmid in 1936. Vegetable and flower seeds had been bought and used. The garden hedge had been cut to the proper height, of which inspector Stürz of the Dießen police had been reassured after an unfounded report. Besides, the Heines wanted to sell the estate and so were interested in keeping the land well-tended.

An inspection by the *Landwirtschaftsamt* initiated by the *Bezirksamt* Landsberg confirmed the account of the lawyers. In 1935, Magdalena Heine had even sold 120 hundredweight of fruit to buyers in Munich. The report further stated that the garden was well cultivated, and that the cultivation of arable land was guaranteed, though a large proportion of the land was only fit for timber. The

---

[41] Letter of the *Kreisbauernschaft* Weilheim to the *Bezirksamt* Landsberg, 26th March 1937.
[42] Letter from Dr. Linn to Magdalena Heine, 2nd April 1937.

Bezirksamt Landsberg sent this report – together with receipts for fertiliser and seeds – to the *Kreisbauernschaft* Weilheim. Although all their accusations had been proven wrong, the *Kreisbauernschaft* insisted that the complaints had been justified.

The contradictory arguments used to acquire the Heine estate are interesting: in 1933 it was military strength, in 1937 it was blood and soil. In 1933 the soil was without any value, in 1937 it was of high quality. Interesting, too, is the speed with which the bureaucracy worked on the Heine affair. The letters of the various institutions were exchanged in a few days. *Schutzhaft* was demanded in a casual way. Because Heine had escaped protective custody in 1933, the resentment and vengeance focused on his wife and daughter. Though it is doubtful there were many *Simplicissimus* readers in Dießen who would have been in a position to judge Heine's work, people were willing to join in the persecution of the wife and daughter of an emigrant who was hated by the Nazi regime. Their means were unfounded reports and false charges; they also saw a chance to further their private interests. The only inconvenience was that different groups and offices coveted the estate.

IV. THE EXPULSION OF HEINE'S WIFE AND DAUGHTER FROM THE COMMUNITY

Heine's daughter, Johanna, decided to leave Germany shortly after the *"Kristallnacht"*. The local newspaper had commented on the events of that night:

> "Der Kreis Landsberg judenrein
> Die hinterlistige Mordtat des Judenjungen Grünspan [sic] hat auch die Bevölkerung unseres Kreises in flammende Empörung versetzt. Überall wurde die Forderung nach schleunigster Entfernung der noch im Kreis Landsberg befindlichen Juden laut. Es zeugt von der vorbildlichen Disziplin der Volksgenossen, daß diese Forderung verwirklicht werden konnte, ohne daß einem Juden ein Haar gekrümmt wurde. Die noch im Kreis Landsberg ansässigen Juden wurden veranlaßt, ihre Wohnsitze sofort aufzugeben, und seit gestern ist unser Gebiet vollkommen judenrein. Es wird jedoch darauf aufmerksam gemacht, daß eine spätere Rückkehr von Juden in den Kreis Landsberg unter keinen Umständen geduldet werden kann."[43]

This frightening atmosphere must have driven Johanna Heine to make plans for leaving Germany. This is reflected in a letter of the Mayor of Dießen, who asked the *Landratsamt* Landsberg whether they had any objections to Johanna Heine's intention to visit the United States. He also provided a possible reason: "Johanna Heine ist Halbjüdin".[44] The proposed visit, however, made the *Landratsamt* suspicious. In a letter addressed to the *Finanzamt* Landsberg, dated 17th December 1938, "betreffs vorbereitender Maßnahmen zur Verlegung des Wohnsitzes ins Ausland ... der berufslosen, ledigen Johanna Heine, geb. am

---

[43]*Landsberger Zeitung* (11th November 1938).
[44]Letter of Mayor Trahner of Dießen to the *Bezirksamt* Landsberg, 10th December 1938.

26.4.1896 in München, nicht arisch", it was questioned in the column "Verdachtsgründe" whether she really only wanted to visit the United States. On 3rd January 1939, the *Gestapo Staatspolizeileitstelle* München tersely informed the *Landratsamt* Landsberg that the minister of the interior's decree of 16th November 1937, "Pol.SV62252/37–453–12",[45] refused the "Jüdin Heine" a passport. She could only obtain one if she left Germany forever. The Heines' lawyer, Heins, realised that in the meantime his client's passport had been changed into a *Judenpaß* and had the incriminating second name Sara added. He requested this name be removed: her mother was "Aryan" and Johanna Heine therefore "half-Aryan". He also asked for a re-entry stamp in the passport.[46]

The *Landrat* asked the *Gestapo* in Munich on 10th March 1939 whether there were still objections to handing back the passport. On 17th March 1939 the *Gestapo* answered that the matter rested with the resolution of 3rd January 1939, although Heine was half-Jewish and not, as assumed, fully Jewish. Johanna Heine tried to end the war of nerves by declaring that she would emigrate to England. The *Landratsamt* Landsberg asked for new instructions from the Munich *Gestapo*, which would not have pleased the Nazis in Dießen. The local *Kreisleiter* of the National-Socialist Party, von Moltke, wrote to the *Landratsamt* on 14th April 1939:

> "Soviel mir bekannt wurde, stößt die Ausstellung eines Reisepasses an die Halbjüdin Heine auf Schwierigkeiten. Die Geheime Staatspolizei soll der Ansicht sein, daß nur bei Dauerverzug aus Deutschland ein Paß ausgestellt werden darf. Nun sind aber die Verhältnisse in Dießen so gelagert, daß das Anwesen der Heine, welches die Marktgemeinde Dießen erworben hat [!], für diese nur nutzbringend verwendet werden kann, wenn das Anwesen Heine durch die Mutter und Tochter geräumt wird. Sollte nun die junge Heine einen Auslandspaß bekommen, so würde auch die alte Heine aus dem Hause sofort herausgehen. Ich ersuche daher im Interesse der wirtschaftlichen Belange der Marktgemeinde Dießen, nochmals bei der Geh. Staatspolizei vorstellig zu werden, der Johanna Heine einen Paß ausstellen zu dürfen, wenn diese nur vorübergehend nach London gehen würde.
> Heil Hitler! von Moltke, Kreisleiter"[47]

The *Gestapo* gave way, consenting to a passport for the "Mischling Heine". Finally they referred to a new decree by which Jews might be removed from their flats and houses. Although there was no legal device to deprive the Heines, the decrees against Jews were easily applied also to half-Jewish or non-Jewish family members. After the "devisenrechtliche Unbedenklichkeitserklärung des Oberfinanzpräsidenten von München" and the "steuerliche Unbedenklichkeitsbescheinigung" of the *Finanzamt* Landsberg had been given to the *Landratsamt* Landsberg, Johanna Heine received her passport on 20th May 1939. When the Heines left Dießen, they had capitulated to the heavy-handed harassment of petty Nazis in a small Bavarian village. However, neither Johanna Heine nor her

---

[45]Letter of *Gestapo Staatspolizeileitstelle* München to *Bezirksamt* Landsberg, 3rd January 1939: "mitgeteilt durch Entschließung vom 29.12.37 B. Nr. 89977 II B3".
[46]Letter of Valentin Heins to the *Landratsamt* Landsberg, 7th March 1939.
[47]Letter of NSDAP *Kreisleiter* von Moltke to *Landratsamt* Landsberg, 14th April 1939.

mother were able to leave Germany. Magdalena Heine died in Munich in a small hotel in October 1939, Johanna Heine three years later also in Munich.[48]

Is it worth dealing with the case of the Heine family? Was theirs not the fate of hundreds and thousands of others in Nazi Germany? Was not the withdrawal of employment and the "Aryanisation" of land belonging to a prominent political opponent a common practice during the Third *Reich*? The example of the Heine family shows how step by step the life of Jews or people who were perceived by the National Socialists as Jews (and also their non-Jewish family members) was made impossible in Germany and how the principle of *Sippenhaft* was consequently applied. In all three stages of persecution and expulsion, one member of the Heine family was the focus of "official" attention, first Heine himself, then his wife and finally their daughter. It was not enough for the local officials that Heine himself had left Germany as fast as possible – his family was also unwanted.

With Hitler's *Machtübernahme*, the field was open to opportunistic Nazis: they took great pains to confiscate the property of a hated "Jew" and emigrant as fast as possible. Every new decree or law, however abused, was employed to this end, be it the confiscation of "unpatriotically" used property, the safe-guarding of agriculture or the removal of Jews, and by extension families with members of Jewish origin, from their homes: all were used in the name of military virtue and sustaining the nation. Private interests played their part too. It was the many small-time Nazis who made life hard for both real as well as putative opponents of the regime and who went beyond the official measures of persecution. Resentment and hatred of Jews and dissenters did not have to be ordered from above. Every bout of the Heines' persecution began with the action of a local Nazi leader or official. Depending upon the Nazi presence in state or public institutions, expulsion and confiscation might be impeded or promoted. "Jew" was casually used, whereas the Heine family's lawyer tried to oppose the official term "half-Jew" with "half-Aryan". The municipality of Dießen was not really bothered: having acquired the Heines' property, it let both Heine's wife and daughter leave the community. As for Thomas Heine, who had foreseen Germany's fate under Nazi rule in many of his cartoons, he was deprived of his work, persecuted and separated from his family by the Nazis of a small village.

---

[48]See AG München, Nr.1939/4226, StA München, for Magdalena Heine's death on 13th October 1939 and her last will.

Lambeth Palace, the Church of England and the Jews of Germany and Austria in 1938

BY ANDREW CHANDLER

Before it came to power, the National-Socialist movement persecuted Jews with vicious speeches, defamatory literature and brutal acts of physical violence. After 30th January 1933, when Hitler became Chancellor, these works inevitably proliferated and were formalised, for instance in the boycott of Jewish businesses on 1st April 1933 and the Nuremberg Laws of September 1935. All of these measures arose in the midst of an ongoing popular and civic persecution of Jewish families across the country. By 1938, therefore, the world had long been familiar with the antisemitism of National-Socialist Germany. Unhappy observers judged that the government of that country was based on a fanatical and wicked system, and that Germany itself stood degraded before the world. Others, meanwhile, remarked that the National-Socialist Party state was the powerful expression of a national movement of great stature. They only regretted the persecution of minorities as an unfortunate, excessive answer to a genuine social anxiety. Both of these contrasting interpretations were apparent in Britain. Although the accusers were by far the majority, the sympathisers were by no means insignificant in number, and they included a good many who were eminent and respected citizens. The churches of Britain provided much criticism of the Hitler regime, and little sympathy for it. God was not thanked for Hitler, as he was in Germany. Instead, his victims were remembered in prayer. To the minds of most British Christians, a regime which sent Communists, Socialists and Pacifists to concentration camps could not be just. A state which disrupted the life and corrupted the religion of churches could hardly be Christian. A society which humiliated, harassed and attacked Jews must appear medieval and barbarous. But there were occasional sympathisers, even here.

The purpose of this article is to describe the views and efforts of those who led one British church, the Church of England, in one particular year, 1938.[1] For the historian, the unique significance of the Church of England may be said to lie in its position as the Established Church, for it enjoyed a legal place within the political state and was a religious body theoretically represented in every community of the country. The importance of the year 1938 is clearly marked by

---

[1] The author would like to express his thanks to Professor John Grenville of the University of Birmingham, Dr. David M. Thompson, Fitzwilliam College Cambridge, Professor John Conway of the University of British Columbia and Mr. Richard Gutteridge of Cambridge. He also thanks Lambeth Palace Library and, in particular, its archivist Miss Melanie Barber.

three episodes, each declaring an ever deepening intensification of the plight of the Jews of Central Europe: the *Anschluß* with Austria in March; the *Sudeten* crisis and the ensuing Munich Pact in September; and the devastating pogrom, immediately dubbed the *"Kristallnacht"*, against the Jews of Germany and Austria in November. If, at the onset of 1938, the world found Germany uncongenial but settled, twelve months later it stood breathless in the wake of these shocks, bleakly contemplating the appalling probability of war.

How sensitive was the Church of England as a Christian community to the position and rights of Jewish people abroad?* Did those who led the church exploit their peculiar position as archbishops and bishops of the Established Church on behalf of the persecuted? And what do these things suggest about the ability of that church to function in a political world? Historically, churches have rarely contested the policies of secular authority, and for centuries Christians were themselves the persecutors of Jews.

The crises of 1938 presented those in public office outside Germany with ghastly dilemmas. Few would suggest that they were firmly resolved. At the same time, those who led Christian opinion viewed events in Germany with particular anxiety and struggled to frame an effective moral response. Nazism might be loathsome, and they must, as Christians, protest against its cruelties, but if they condemned the policies of a tyrannous government would that save its victims, or only antagonise the persecutors and provoke more violence? In 1938 a second dilemma arose. People across Europe feared for peace. They might not much wish for friendship with National-Socialist Germany, but they could only think that friendly relations between nations must make war less likely. Would this be a betrayal of their sympathy for those who were the victims of the regime? These difficulties were turned over and over. Some argued that co-operation between Britain and Germany could never ensue until Germany ceased to persecute its Jews, and others that only by friendship might the Hitler regime be led to better ways. Yet, as "Septuagenarian" observed in the correspondence columns of the Evangelical Anglican newspaper *The Record* in February 1938: "How is it possible for us to cultivate friendship with those who treat this people so cruelly?"[2] For most, perhaps, it was unhappy necessity. War would destroy them all. For Bishop Henson of Durham, advancing reluctantly towards old age and retirement, it was a "surrender of moral principle to political expediency". How could they pass these matters by – the very things which above all they must uphold, the very ethics of their faith and, they hoped, of their civilisation, without being themselves complicit and thereby demeaned? It was a humiliation – for Henson, an intolerable one. If they were unmoved there must be something grievously awry. If they were moved, but did nothing, who was to know or care?[3] The editor of the *Church Times*, Sidney Dark, also reviled the complacent doctrine that good relations between governments, and so peace between nations, alone

---
*In this connection see also the essay on an earlier period by Andrew Chandler, 'A Question of Fundamental Principles. The Church of England and the Jews of Germany 1933–1937', in *LBI Year Book XXXVIII* (1993), pp. 221–261–(Ed.).

[2] *The Record* (11th February 1938), p. 90b.

[3] *Journal of Bishop Henson*, vol. 66, p. 206, 11th May 1936.

counted. In 1935 he had considered the kind of diplomacy which might be appropriate with the National-Socialist state, and recalled the words of Shylock to Bassanio in *The Merchant of Venice*: "I will buy with you, sell with you, talk with you, walk with you, and so following; but I will not eat with you, drink with you, nor pray with you."[4] But Dark was not as consistent a judge as Henson. As 1938 unfolded, few proved to be.

The Church Mission to the Jews was an Anglican body, by now much in decline, largely engaged in the centre of Europe. In March 1938 the Secretary of the movement, A.R. Penn, arranged a brief visit to Vienna on his return home from Poland and Romania. He arrived at mid-day on 11th March to find the country bustling with excitement. In only a few days a plebiscite on Austrian independence from Germany would take place. The campaign between the Schuschnigg and Hitler parties was in full swing. Youths marched noisily up and down the streets; Schuschnigg's portrait was much paraded, his name and symbol painted in large white characters across the pavements. Penn's hosts at the British Jews' Society and the Swedish Mission predicted a substantial majority for him. Yet only hours later President Schuschnigg himself was broadcasting a sombre farewell to the nation, and within minutes wireless reports spoke of German forces sweeping across the Austrian border. When Penn arose the next morning he found himself in a Vienna that was quite different. The posters of Schuschnigg had all but disappeared; only here and there a few disfigured portraits and painted inscriptions which could not be scrubbed away caught his eye. But the same streets were swirling with excitement and noise, and cries of "Heil Hitler!". Overnight, Nazi flags had been hoisted from buildings. "Everyone", Penn observed, "had apparently gone Nazi." Even now German officers and officials were arriving in motor cars as squadrons of twin-engined bombers off-loaded thousands of leaflets over the city. At mid-day on 12th March, as Penn sat talking to the British embassy chaplain, he heard Hitler proclaim the *Anschluß* of Germany and Austria. Later he saw the fear and despair, but also the dignity, of his Jewish friends:

> "Before leaving for England, I drove up on one of the hills overlooking Vienna, which is surely the most beautifully situated capital in Europe; a Jewish friend was acting as my guide. As we gazed down on the city, with its splendid buildings, its encircling hills, and the Danube flowing majestically away to the East, she said to me, 'I feel as if I were looking at my beloved Vienna for the last time.' "[5]

Later, reports of hundreds of suicides in Vienna jolted and shocked Christian opinion in Britain. "I am told", wrote the President of the ecumenical "Life and Work" movement, Bishop Bell of Chichester, to the Swiss ecumenist, Professor Adolf Keller, "that the suicides which have been so sensationally numerous, are really, in many cases, murders. I wonder if that is your impression?"[6]

The British government came under pressure to lend what assistance it could. Surely, refugees from such tyranny could be offered sanctuary? Some were

---

[4]*Church Times* (26th July 1935), p. 93a.
[5]*The Record* (8th April 1938), p. 214d.
[6]Bell to Keller, 1st April 1938, London, Lambeth Palace Library, *Bell Papers*, vol. IX, fol. 219.

doubtful that the authorities were rising to the issue. On 22nd March the Archbishop of Canterbury, Cosmo Lang wrote a letter, a combination of diffident phrases and firm language, to the Home Secretary, Samuel Hoare:

> "I have received information from Vienna of the miserable plight of the Jews in that city and in Austria and of their apprehension and even terror. I am told that those who may succeed in getting out of Austria would not be allowed to enter England. I have been told that one or two Austrian Jews who arrived at Croydon were not allowed to land but were sent back. No one knows better than I do the difficulties which might be created if any large number of Austrian Jews were permitted to enter this country. But it seems lamentable that there should be no place of refuge for these unhappy people. Would you be so kind as to direct some information to be sent to me as to their position? I am sure you have been giving it your personal consideration. Forgive me for troubling you."[7]

In the House of Commons, too, Hoare and the Prime Minister, Neville Chamberlain, faced questions about the entry of Austrian refugees. The Home Secretary assured the House that the issue had received "careful and sympathetic consideration" by the government. Britain would maintain its tradition of offering asylum to the victims of persecution abroad. But the government could not allow indiscriminate admission: "Such a policy would not only create difficulties from the police point of view but would have grave economic results in aggravating the unemployment problem, the housing problem and other social problems." He did not think that "the special circumstances created by the present situation afford any grounds for an alteration of the laws". Every individual case would be sympathetically considered on its own merits.[8]

On 29th March Archbishop Lang addressed the House of Lords. A frequent speaker there, he now ventured into Parliament with some hesitation. Even so, his words were curiously confident. He acknowledged the shock the *Anschluß* had caused in the international community, but there were, he thought "some considerations which make for calmness and balance of judgement". The separation of Austria from Germany was the product of a treaty which was "vindictive and arbitrary, and could not possibly be permanent". He continued: "The union of Austria and Germany sooner or later was inevitable. If the division had continued much longer it might have been a continuing sore which would have spread infection to other nations. However reprehensible may be the manner in which the thing was done, the fact that the thing was done, and done finally, may bring some measure of stability to Europe." And Lang thought it popular with the Austrians. A "very prominent artist" in Austria had told him so, had spoken of "joy without parallel", and even "sudden salvation". This may well be exaggerated, but if the artist was right – and, as he claimed to have no connection with any political party, why should he be doubted? – they might all feel at peace. The Roman Catholic hierarchy in Austria endorsed the union; Cardinal Innitzer had written a public letter to be read in all the churches accepting the new state. This, thought Lang, might mitigate the oppression that

---

[7]Lang to Hoare, 22nd March 1938, London, Lambeth Palace Library, *Lang Papers*, vol. 38, fol. 152.
[8]*Parliamentary Debates*, House of Commons, 5th Series, vol. 333, cols. 990–996, 22nd March 1938.

Christians, both Roman Catholic and Protestant, endured under National Socialism. If the union was inevitable, "it is something for which to be thankful that it took place without any bloodshed whatever". Within hours these words would be lastingly committed to paper.[9]

How had it been possible for the Archbishop of Canterbury, so long a vocal friend of the Jews in Germany, to overlook the suicides of Viennese Jews? He must have known of them. Other speakers did. Before him, Lord Snell had seen a "gay, cultured, kindly people being subdued and merged into the savage tribalism of the Nazi regime". It was "our shame that *civilised* Europe has remained passive in relation to their fate".[10] Another peer, Lord Crewe, observed a "sinister system of persecution and confiscation".[11] After Lang's contribution his fellow Anglican, Lord Cecil, condemned the *Anschluß* as a challenge flung at international authority and order. Cecil did not wish to criticise his old friend the Archbishop. But such a speech unsettled him: "I will only make this one observation. If he happened to be a Liberal or a Jew or a Roman Catholic in Austria I doubt very much whether he would talk about a bloodless operation."[12]

But Lord Strabolgi was bitter against Lang:

> "It has been said that there has been no bloodshed in Austria, but there have been 1,700 suicides. Suicide may be wrong, but I think it is even more wrong to drive people to suicide... The right reverend Primate is, however, silent on these matters today. I cannot help thinking of the thousands of the clergy of our Church with whom I have had the honour of pleading for great causes in the country, and I must again express regret on behalf of my noble friends that that speech was made."[13]

In his haste to deprecate international disruption and press the claims of peace, Lang had doubtless perceived that he was doing his moral duty. But he had left unsaid those things which he ought to have said. At once he knew his mistake. His chaplain, Alan Don, remarked that the Archbishop had given the impression of "whitewashing Hitler... This is unfortunate and C.C. [Cosmo Cantuar] frankly admits that he was foolish in saying as much as he did and in omitting certain qualifying sentences which he had intended to insert."[14]

Evidently, Christian opinion in the country was perturbed by the speech. It did not help that the *Daily Mirror* reported the debate with the banner headline "Primate backs *Anschluß*", as Alan Don observed the day after.[15] *The Record* chided Lang sternly, "Everybody knows that the Archbishop views with utter distaste and horror the treatment which has been meted out to Jews and other opponents of the Nazi regime. It is the more to be regretted that... he did not take the occasion to protest in the name of Christ against race discrimination, and persecution of other kinds."[16] The Bishop of Winchester, Cyril Forster

[9]*Parliamentary Debates*, House of Lords, 5th Series, vol. 108, cols. 448–449, 29th March 1938.
[10]*Ibid.*, col. 129.
[11]*Ibid.*, col. 168.
[12]*Ibid.*, col. 452.
[13]*Ibid.*, col. 474.
[14]*Journal of Alan C. Don*, M.S. 2866, p. 27, 30th March 1938.
[15]*Ibid.*
[16]*The Record* (8th April 1938), p. 209a.

Garbett, had by then deplored "the insults and outrages committed upon men and women of the Jewish race, and expressed the loathing with which the great mass of decent people throughout the Anglo-Saxon world regarded such conduct".[17]

Other church leaders were by now busy. An appeal meeting for refugees took place at the Friends' Meeting House in London at the end of April. Archbishop Lang, Cardinal Hinsley and the President of the Free Church Council, Dr. Griffiths Jones, sent their own messages of support to the gathering. The Bishop of Chelmsford attended, and subjected the German government to "scathing denunciations".[18] As April passed the refugee crisis swelled. On 3rd May 1938 a Czechoslovakian rabbi, Michael Dov Weissmandl, secretly visited Lambeth Palace, instructed by the rabbis of Vienna to plead for help on behalf of the Orthodox Jews of the Burgenland. He was furnished with a letter of introduction, signed by Isaiah Porritt, senior Orthodox Rabbi in Vienna, and Samuel Epp, the most prominent rabbi in Burgenland. This Don duly sent off to Oxford for translation. Weissmandl asked him if there was a safe place to which the Orthodox Jews of Burgenland might migrate? Don felt hopeless. He remarked to his translator, "The plight of these wretched people is utterly pitiable and there is so little that can be done. I understand that Professor Norman Bentwich tried to get into Austria the other day on his way home from Palestine and was refused admission. So what can anybody do?"[19] In the privacy of his diary he wrote bitterly, "The anti-semitism of the Nazis is of the devil and stamps them as ruthless brutes devoid of pity and glorying in cruelty for its own sake."[20]

But Don met Weissmandl a second time. On 9th May he wrote a confidential letter to Samuel Hoare at the Home Office:

> "I am instructed by the Archbishop of Canterbury to bring to your notice the desperate plight in which the Jews of the Burgenland find themselves.
>
> A Jewish Rabbi from Czechoslovakia called last week at Lambeth Palace bringing with him a pathetic appeal for assistance from the leading Burgenland Rabbis. These people appear to be a compact body of some 3,000 Orthodox Jews who have already been forcibly ejected from their homes and who are at a loss to know where to go. There are of course multitudes of Jews in a somewhat similar plight, but the Archbishop wonders whether it might be possible to give some special consideration to the particular group of the Austrian Jews whose lot would appear to be even more desperate than that of the Jews in general."[21]

On 13th May the *Church Times* printed a letter on behalf of an Austrian woman seeking a record of the birth of her grandparents, so that she might prove her non-Jewish descent.[22] Churchpeople who had themselves rescued small numbers of Jews and "non-Aryans" wrote to the press requesting assistance and

---

[17] *Ibid.*
[18] *Ibid.* (29th April 1938), p. 266.
[19] Don to Danby, 5th May 1938, *Lang Papers*, vol. 38, fol. 158. Norman Bentwich was Director of the High Commission for Refugees from Germany.
[20] *Journal of Alan C. Don*, M.S. 2866, p. 36, 4th May 1938.
[21] Don to Hoare, 9th May 1938, *Lang Papers*, vol. 38, fol. 159.
[22] *Church Times* (13th May 1938), p. 537c.

employment for their new charges. On 20th May *The Record* warmly endorsed a plea by Bishop Perowne of Worcester that the persecution be placed at the very top of the agenda whenever British and German politicians met. The heart of Christian England, he said, had not been so moved since the Bulgarian atrocities of the last century.[23] On 31st May Hoare's secretary, Hutchinson, replied to Lambeth Palace. The Home Secretary knew of the position of the Burgenland Jews, and understood that their situation had been discussed by the League of Nations High Commissioner for German refugees, and the Liaison Committee for the refugee organisations of the different countries, "although technically, as they are still in Austria, they do not strictly fall within the High Commissioner's jurisdiction". The Home Secretary did not think it likely that they could be accommodated in Britain, but hoped that the efforts of the High Commissioner and the voluntary groups would secure their resettlement overseas.[24] So Lang proceeded to approach the High Commissioner himself, General Sir Neill Malcolm. The consequences of this approach are unrecorded.

The Jewish Board of Deputies was growing restive. After an impatient meeting on 20th June 1938 two of the leading lights of British Jewry, Neville Laski and Louis Gluckstein, met Alan Don to discuss a joint response to the crisis. They found him nervous that firm protests might only undermine the efforts the British government made for peace. But during their conversation Laski and Gluckstein suggested that the Church might pray for the persecuted. That evening Don talked of the idea with both Lang and William Temple, the Archbishop of York. They suggested that international peace be attached to racial persecution, and were "most ready" to announce special prayers on Sunday, 17th July. Laski replied that the intercessions would "greatly hearten, not merely the Jews of this country but Jews in those countries on behalf of whom our services of intercession are to be held. Indeed, this truly Christian gesture will obviously have a profound meaning for the very many who will hear of it, and, we feel sure, take pride in it."[25] The Chief Rabbi, J. H. Hertz, had been informed, and was grateful. A formal letter to which he could reply was all that was needed, and these would be released to the Press. Gluckstein wrote to Don:

> "At our interview, and in your letter, you showed a sympathy and an understanding of the plight of my co-religionists which deeply impressed and heartened me. I feel sure that you will understand me when I say that, in the situation in which the Jewish community finds itself, it is immeasurably helpful to know that men like yourself are feeling for it and willing to aid it by their prayers."[26]

Lang's public letter did not mention Germany by name, but contained, nevertheless, an explicit reference to the German crisis:

> "When I was informed that you had asked your own people to intercede with Almighty God on Sunday, July 17th, on behalf of all members of your race who are suffering oppression and persecution it seemed to me that it would be right that

---

[23] *The Record* (20th May 1938), p. 313c.
[24] Hutchinson to Don, 31st May 1938, *Lang Papers*, vol. 38, fol. 161.
[25] Laski to Don, 27th June 1938, *ibid.*, fol. 167.
[26] Gluckstein to Don, 23rd June 1938, *ibid.*, fol. 171.

> Christian people should join in these intercessions. I have therefore in my own Diocesan Gazette (which is often quoted in the Press generally) asked that in all our churches so far as possible remembrance should be made on the same Sunday of the multitudes of Jews who are undergoing this sore ordeal. I can only hope that this request will meet with a general response. I need not assure you of my own deep and real sympathy."

Hertz replied on 1st July that Jews across the world would hear of the Archbishop's call to prayer with "deep emotion".[27] He asked the synagogues of the Empire to hold intercessions at five o'clock on the same day. Jew and Christian were to stand side by side.

Lang appeared quite sure at this time that public meetings were a dangerous form of dissent. On 22nd June the Honorary Secretary of the British Section of the World Jewish Congress had written to him of a new protest meeting at the central Friends' Meeting House in London. Might the Archbishop send a message of support "to demonstrate your solidarity with the Jewish people in their hour of trial"?[28] Don was not drawn. He referred to the day of intercessions:

> "The Archbishop is of the opinion that the sympathy of Christian people for the Jewish sufferers in all parts of the world can most fruitfully be shown in that particular way. That being so, he does not think that anything would be gained by his sending any special message to be read at the meeting... He was interested to notice that you have secured a really strong platform of speakers."[29]

They could pray, but not protest, without offending the sensitive authorities in Germany and undermining the delicate international situation. But, whatever their dilemmas, they must still work for the victims. Bishop Bell, who had laboured assiduously since 1933 to co-ordinate a Christian response to the refugee crisis, now made a further appeal to his own church community. On 23rd June he went to the Church Assembly to move that it record its deep distress at the sufferings of the Jews and "non-Aryans" of Germany and Austria, urging Christians everywhere to express their sympathy in prayer and by "material gifts", and appealing to the government to do "everything possible" to assist the resettlement of refugees abroad. Bell had long tried to rouse the conscience of what he believed was a slumbering Church. Now he told the Assembly that their response to the issue was a test of their very Christianity. It was a particularly effective speech. Bell observed the great efforts of the British Jewish community and remarked, "the bond of race was strong: was the bond of the Christian religion to be no bond at all?". He pressed upon his audience the long apparent truth that no more could the persecution be regarded as "a sudden irrational burst of hatred", but "the working out of a fundamental article of a creed, a creed first announced in 1920". He carefully explained its methods. He refrained from illustrations, though he said he could give many, and sought instead to emphasise "the hard reality which underlay everything" – that there was no future in Germany and Austria for those who were Jewish, or partly so.[30]

[27] Exchange of letters between Lang and Hertz, 28th June and 1st July 1938, *ibid.*, fols. 175–176.
[28] Barou to Lang, 22nd June 1938, *ibid.*, fol. 166.
[29] Don to Barou, 25th June 1938, *ibid.*, fol. 172.
[30] *Proceedings of the Church Assembly*, vol. XVII, London 1938, 23rd June 1938, pp. 389–394.

The publication of Lang's diocesan message, and of the letters exchanged between the Archbishop and the Chief Rabbi, inspired a serious response in some quarters. A week before the day of joint intercession a vicar in Kent, H. Hammond, wrote to Lambeth Palace to enquire whether a Jewish friend of his, a fellow member of the Society of Jews and Christians, might talk to his congregation in Rucking Church itself, or in the Mission Room at Upper Rucking. Lang's secretary and chaplain, A.E. Sargent, replied on behalf of the Archbishop that such a use of the parish hall should raise no objection. Hammond proposed that after the morning service the congregation should slip across the road to the hall and listen to Mr. Marks there: "I do feel that a Jew is the correct person to tell of the sufferings of the Jews." In the evening Hammond would close the altar doors of the mission room, and Marks would give another talk. The vicar was confident that this would do; once the altar had been shut off the mission room was often used for whist drives, socials and dances. Might he have a line to confirm that his plans were in order? Further, might Marks read the Old Testament lesson at morning and evening prayer? Sargent duly assured his correspondent that the arrangements for the two speeches were entirely proper, but that it would not be quite wise to allow his friend to read the two lessons. It is interesting to observe where the lines of propriety were drawn.

So Mr. Marks addressed a Christian congregation, uprooted though it might have been. Moved and indignant at what they heard, they recorded a resolution expressing their "horror at the treatment of the Jews in Germany and Austria". Hammond wrote a final letter to ask if the Archbishop might have a use for it; he was willing to seek signatures for it if so.[31]

On the appointed day in Birmingham, Canon Guy Rogers and Dr. Aaron Cohen, the Chief Minister of the city's Hebrew Congregation, led a crowded service for German Christians and Jews; the rabbi praying for the imprisoned Pastor Martin Niemöller, and the clergyman for the suffering Jews.[32] Special intercessions were held in Germany itself at the Anglican church in Berlin. To avoid political disorder they occurred, unannounced, in the form of a simple prayer for the persecuted. At the end of the service the congregation waited silently to think of individuals known to them personally. Bishop Batty had discussed the service with Archbishop Lang at some length, and sent a full report.[33] In this way were the Jews, in the heart of National-Socialist Germany, formally remembered in an Anglican church. Denominational leaders thought the joint intercessions a success. Hertz wrote to Lang of his "deepfelt thanks": "It was a wonderful manifestation of spiritual unity among men of goodwill of all creeds."[34] But the public was increasingly conscious that the Jewish crisis was deepening. The next day the *Church Times* printed an editorial condemning the persecution: "Murder Must Advertise". It declared, "the only prospect that

---

[31] The correspondence of Hammond and Sargent, 10th–21st July 1938, *Lang Papers*, vol. 164, fols. 307–313.
[32] Recalled by Canon Guy Rogers in his speech to the Church Assembly, in *Proceedings of the Church Assembly*, vol. XIX, London 1938, 16th November 1938, p. 543.
[33] Batty to Lang, 21st July 1938, *Lang Papers*, vol. 38, fol. 178.
[34] Hertz to Lang, 21st July 1938, *ibid.*, fol. 179.

opens for the bulk of victims seems to be extinction in circumstances of unspeakable degradation and misery". In the face of its new assault on the territorial arrangement of Europe, how odd that the German government, "so profoundly excited by the comparatively light afflictions suffered by the Sudeten minority in Czechoslovakia, is determined to exterminate its own Jewish or fractionally Jewish minority".[35]

On 27th July 1938 Bell made his maiden speech in the House of Lords. He used the most important national stage available to him as a bishop of the Established Church to move a motion on behalf of the refugees. The time for diplomacy was past; it was difficult to imagine how things might decline further. To the Church Assembly he had merely described Nazi racialism as "extraordinary"; now he dismissed it as "a pure fantasy for which there is no scientific justification whatever". Bell let that lunacy speak for itself: "for some posts it is required that a man be possessed of full German blood back to 1800". He knew many Germans, but sadly confessed himself at a loss to understand how their own kinsmen could so lower themselves to such dishonour and cowardice:

> "I know and have seen those who have lately lived in Vienna as well as those who have been there as visitors, and the situation is so cruel that it is commonly said, not by S.S. and S.A. men but by Governors and Ministers of State . . . that if non-Aryans cannot find a country that will receive them there is always the Danube, and there are plenty of cemeteries to be filled by December."[36]

The refugee situation must be met with clearer strategies. On 16th September Sir Wyndham Deedes, the distinguished public servant and Anglican layman, wrote to Lang of the creation of a Christian council to assist refugees from Germany and Austria. Its chairman was to be the authoritative Sir John Hope Simpson, and it would meet for the first time at the Jerusalem Chamber in Westminster on 6th October 1938. Deedes asked if the Archbishop would serve as a patron?[37] In reply, Alan Don confessed his confusion. Was this new body an amalgamation of existing organisations? "There are", he remarked, "so many refugee agencies that it is difficult to bear them all in mind."[38] Deedes replied that there were presently four separate bodies: the Inter-Aid Committee for Children from Germany, of which he himself was Chairman; the Friends' Emergency Committee for Jews and non-Jews; the Bishop of Chichester's Committee devoted to emergency "non-Aryan" victims; and the Academic Assistance Council, now renamed the Society for the Protection of Science and Learning. These were all voluntary bodies, and had "practically no resources". He believed that the Archbishops' Appeal for £50,000 two years before had largely failed because these societies had failed to combine to promote it, and observed that no new appeal had been issued since. After the *Anschluß* the number of "non-Aryan" refugees had grown "enormously", but the organisations together were no better placed to help them. The new Christian Council would represent all denomi-

---

[35] *Church Times* (22nd July 1938), p. 92c–d.
[36] *Parliamentary Debates*, House of Lords, 5th Series, vol. 110, cols. 1206–1216, 27th July 1938.
[37] Deedes to Lang, 16th September 1938, *Lang Papers*, vol. 38, fol. 181.
[38] Don to Deedes, 21st September 1938, *ibid.*, fol. 187.

The Church of England and the Jews of Germany and Austria   235

nations, but not the Roman Catholics who had their own appeal. Its functions would be to raise and distribute funds for these groups, to assist the Inter-Aid Committee for Children, and to press the governments of the Dominions to receive emigrants.[39] This was sufficient for Lang. "Permit me", he replied on 29th September, "therefore to send through you a message of cordial interest and goodwill to the Council, of my hopes that it may even in the midst of the present turmoil keep alive the conscience of Christian people in this country, and that God's blessing may be given to its endeavours".[40]

The "present turmoil" was by then being confronted by the statesmen of Europe at Munich. How might the territorial integrity of Czechoslovakia be preserved in the shadow of another Great War? Rabbi Weissmandl had written to Lambeth Palace, "This republic has remained an island of freedom and respect for humanity in the middle of a sea of hate and intolerance. Moreover the Jews, the most oppressed section of humanity in so many lands, are in this free country the most ardent testimony to the nobility of mind of the Czechoslovak people." He added, "Perhaps one day a future method of writing history will determine the value of each nation by the way it has treated its Jews."[41] It was sent away for translation to Miss Wallace, secretary of the Council on Foreign Relations. By the time Wallace had completed her work, the crisis was past, and Czechoslovakia in disarray.

On 1st October most of the Church of England thanked God for the Munich settlement.[42] They had prayed for deliverance, and had been saved at the eleventh hour. Services of thanksgiving resounded across the parishes of the country. What could be less Christian than war, and more Christian than peace? Christians agonised about the justice of the peace that had been won, but most were reassured that it had been right. Czechoslovakia had been saved by peace, for it could only have been destroyed by war. But many were soon unsettled. The *Church Times* had expected that the settlement would make some arrangement for those who were vulnerable to the persecution of the Hitler regime. It did not. Bishop Bell wrote to Downing Street of them, and received the reply: "You may be sure that the question of aid for the Czech refugees is not being overlooked. I do not think anyone is yet in a position to say what the needs may be."[43]

But Jews and Christians abroad continued to debate the question of how best to respond. On 3rd October 1938 Neville Laski sent to Lambeth Palace copies of an exchange of letters between the Duke of Buccleugh and his own father, Nathan Laski. He suggested that they were representative of "responsible Jewish opinion, which I feel his Grace will think is in accord with the views held by him". Buccleuch had written that public "abuse" of the German government for its antisemitism "only seems to stimulate them to provoke worse measures. It

[39] Deedes to Don, 22nd September 1938, *ibid.*, fols. 183–184.
[40] Lang to Deedes, 29th September 1938, *ibid.*, fol. 185.
[41] Weissmandl to Lang, 22nd September 1938, *ibid.*, fols. 204–206.
[42] See Alan Wilkinson, *Dissent or Conform? War, Peace and the English Churches 1900–1945*, London 1986, pp. 171–189; Adrian Hastings, *A History of English Christianity 1920–1985*, London 1986, pp. 346–352; and Andrew Chandler, 'Munich and Morality. The Bishops of the Church of England and Appeasement', in *Twentieth-Century British History*, vol. V, No. 1 (1994), pp. 77–99.
[43] Wilson to Bell, 3rd October 1938, *Bell Papers*, vol. LXV, fol. 90.

seems a wiser policy for Britain to take more active steps to secure more friendly relations with Germany, unless other nations intend to fight and crush Germany and the Nazi movement now." Friendliness created the conditions for humane influence. But Laski was unpersuaded. Men like Lord Londonderry, who had written sympathetically of Hitler, might well claim that he could be trusted: "But the Jews have found from their own experience that it is a myth." Nazism was considered another, more dangerous, form of Bolshevism. It was not realistic to hope for conciliation and trust if they did not know what the ambitions of the German government were. *Mein Kampf* stated them to be "German overlordship of the European continent". It was too late for warm relations to protect and assist German Jews, who had all lost their jobs. Laski declared: "I do not believe in the policy of keeping silent while there are inhumanities being committed which cry to heaven."[44] Alan Don replied that the Archbishop would "keep this carefully as being a considered statement of the Jewish position".[45]

Jewish refugees were once again discussed on 19th–20th October, when the bishops of the Church of England met in conference in London. Their perceived moral obligations, to appease and to condemn, still appeared in conflict. The pacifist Bishop Barnes of Birmingham hoped that a new appeal for refugees would not appear to imply any criticism of Germany, "with whom of all things they wanted peace". Archbishop Temple disagreed. The German government would, he thought, be impressed by "a really strong body of public opinion in this country".[46] But Barnes was not alone. Another example of caution was offered shortly afterwards by *The Record*. Preferring not even to mention the name of Germany at all, on 28th October it pronounced, "With regard to the persecution in Central Europe we have every desire to preserve a discreet and helpful reticence."[47] On 2nd November 1938 the General Secretary of the British Section of the ecumenical body, the World's Evangelical Alliance, sent to Lambeth Palace a "preliminary statement on the consequences of the dismemberment of Czechoslovakia for the Evangelical Church of Czech Brethren". The report was compiled by the Czech Protestant Churches Refugee Fund. "Břeclav", it observed, "is a city in the south of Moravia with some 11,000 inhabitants, only 1,500 of whom are Germans. Still it has been occupied by Germany . . . In Southern Moravia two other congregations, Miroslav (Misslitz) and Hustopeče (Auspitz) have been ceded to Germany; only a few villages belonging to these congregations remain in Czechoslovakia. In both places the German majority is very slight, nay, if you deduct the German-speaking Jews, the majority is really Czech." Other anomalies were listed in Eastern Moravia and Eastern Bohemia. A donation slip to the fund was attached. The letter also informed Lang of a protest meeting, possibly to take place at the Queen's Hall, and asked if the

---

[44] Correspondence between Buccleuch and Nathan Laski, 27th August–12th September 1938, sent by Neville Laski, 3rd October 1938, *Lang Papers*, fols. 188–199.

[45] Don to Laski, 6th October 1938, *ibid.*, fol. 200.

[46] Record of Bishops' Meetings, 19th–20th October 1938, London, Lambeth Palace Library, B.M. 10, fols. 406–409.

[47] *The Record* (28th October 1938), p. 680b.

Archbishop would take part?[48] But Lambeth Palace still refrained from public condemnation. Alan Don replied that Lang was unsure that such a gesture would prove successful. It might only "irritate and annoy with unfortunate results for the Jews themselves. In these matters it is unfortunately necessary to consider what are likely to be the psychological reactions of people who are obsessed with anti-semitic prejudices." Lang thought he could do more "by private efforts behind the scenes".[49] In contrast, he was prepared to contest the efforts of racialist movements in Britain itself. Two days later he lent his name to a declaration deploring antisemitism, at the invitation of Toynbee Hall in East London.[50] His cautious approach was vulnerable, however, and could stand little pressure. Only five weeks after the Munich settlement it was shattered at once when, on the night of 9th–10th November, a savage pogrom exploded across Germany and Austria. The British people wished to think the best of the German government; they had hoped that Hitler had mended his ways after the near catastrophe of a war with Britain and France. But this appalling attack appeared to demonstrate that he had not. Opinion in the Church of England was outraged. After Munich they had preached that only a change of heart in Europe, within nations and between them, could mean peace between peoples. But there could be no peace under these grotesque circumstances. Caution was overthrown. Not even for the peace of Europe could the Church be silent. Lang was bitter. He dispatched a dismayed and powerful letter to *The Times*: "A Black Day for Germany", quite unadvised and of his own initiative, but expressly assuming the approval of every British church. "Whatever provocation may have been given by the deplorable act of a single irresponsible Jewish youth, reprisals on such a scale, so fierce, cruel and vindictive, cannot possibly be justified. A sinister significance is added to them by the fact that the police seem either to have acquiesced in them or to have been powerless to restrain them." They in Britain wished for peace: "Would that the rulers of the *Reich* could realise that such excesses of hatred and malice put upon the friendship which we are so ready to offer an almost intolerable strain!"[51] So far the Established Church had endorsed the policy of the state, but the "*Kristallnacht*" was a watershed for the leaders of the Church of England. From now on Lang, Temple and their bishops looked to the British government to frame an assertive response to Hitler. Nazism had for ever placed itself beyond the pale. Lang met Cardinal Hinsley and agreed that the German government could not be trusted with the protection of those it perceived to be racially inferior. If the British government suggested that, in the appeasement of Hitler, former German colonies should return to their old authorities, the churches would oppose the policy firmly. Alan Don thought the pogrom "disgusting and brutal". On 13th November he preached at Rugby Memorial Chapel:

---

[48]Gooch to Lang, 2nd November 1938, with 'Preliminary Statement on the Consequences of the Dismemberment of Czechoslovakia, for the Evangelical Church of Czech Brethren', published by the World's Evangelical Alliance, *Lang Papers*, vol. 38, fols. 207–211.

[49]Don to Gooch, 5th November 1938, *ibid.*, fol. 214.

[50]Don to Mallon, 7th November 1938, *ibid.*, fol. 215.

[51]*The Times* (12th November 1938), p. 13e.

> "I had spoken of... Love... as the only power that could produce conditions that made for peace and goodwill – and at the back of one's mind all the time was the thought of the Satanic persecution of the Jews in Germany – I had almost decided to abandon what I intended to say, so hollow did it seem to plead for goodwill towards people capable of such barbarities."[52]

On 14th November George Bell sent a copy of a new inter-denominational appeal for Christian refugees to Lambeth Palace. He added, "I am delighted you wrote to the *The Times*".[53] Lang agreed to sign it, but he was still cautious that it should not appear to ask the government to grant entry to "all and sundry". Would it be better to plead for a "generous" policy, rather than a seemingly arbitrary one?[54] His suggestion was adopted. On 17th November 1938 the statement was published in *The Times*. It combined pressure on the government with an appeal to the public conscience. Over 200,000 Christians, it declared, had been driven from Germany:

> "The ultimate solution of this tragic problem rests with the Governments of the countries of settlement to adopt a more liberal emigration policy. We appeal to our own Government to give a lead to the world in this matter. We beg them in the name both of our Christian faith and of common humanity to open their doors generously to refugees before it is too late. They will have their reward in the skill and labour of devoted new citizens and in the gratitude of posterity. Above all they will have the satisfaction of the knowledge that they have done right."

Congregations were invited to adopt individual refugees, and to give to the Christian Council for Refugees from Germany and Central Europe: "Let Christians prove themselves to be Christians and give liberally at once."[55]

Lang's indignation was echoed in the speeches of his bishops and clergy. The Church Assembly formally associated itself with his letter of 11th November and pronounced that the Archbishop had expressed "the feelings of indignation felt by Christian people of this country". In moving that motion, Canon Rogers of Birmingham thanked Lang for "the witness he had given to fundamental principles".[56] Lang, who was present at the Assembly (his attendance was expected, and usually he came reluctantly), answered for himself by condemning for a third time the "almost unprecedented manifestation of injustice and hatred", which had occasioned his protest.[57] Bishop Bell, so long a friend of the German people, stressed that millions of Germans had no part whatever in the outrage. On that day he appeared a sad man at the Church Assembly, speaking to welcome the long overdue foundation of a united Christian Council for Refugees. Characteristically still disclaiming any wish to arouse or condemn, he appealed to the pity of his audience:

> "Imagine the intensity of the misery – old men of 75 turned out of their homes, refused a lodging and forced night after night to find shelter under the bridges in

---

[52] *Journal of Alan C. Don*, 11th and 13th November 1938, M.S. 2866, pp. 80–81.
[53] Bell to Lang, 14th November 1938, *Lang Papers*, vol. 38, fol. 218.
[54] Lang to Bell, 14th November 1938, *ibid.*, fol. 221.
[55] *The Times* (17th November 1938), p. 10d.
[56] *Proceedings of the Church Assembly*, vol. XIX, 16th November 1938, p. 543.
[57] *Ibid.*, p. 545.

Vienna; children terrified and clinging to their mothers as they tried to hide; young men taken to the concentration camp and ordered to leave Germany if they would leave the concentration camp, and no country would have them, and offered the escape of suicide [sic] . . .".[58]

In Liverpool the Central Hall was packed as Bishop David attacked the "vile and brutish" pogrom and emphasised that he too could not be silent.[59] At a meeting of the League of Nations Union in Leeds, Canon Thompson Elliott declared:

> "I am sure that no right-thinking man can have anything but a feeling of horror and detestation for the policy of brutal persecution which is being carried on in Germany at the present time. The last effrontery is the statement that if there is any hostile reaction . . . in other countries, Germany may adopt a less merciful policy. That is a piece of blackmail, nothing more or less . . . I cannot see the Jews in Germany have anything to lose by protests from other countries, and it is to be hoped that they have something to gain."[60]

At a service at Weymouth, Bishop Lovett of Salisbury spoke out:

> "These outbreaks against the Jews in Germany . . . are done on a miserable pretext. The thing itself is bad enough, but what makes it infinitely worse is that civilised people are doing this . . . I take it as an indication of the way the mentality of mankind is sagging back into barbarism."[61]

On Remembrance Sunday, the congregation at Westminster Abbey paused in silent prayer for "the Jewish people in their hour of trouble".[62] Prayers were offered on their behalf in Southwark Cathedral. Bishop Henson and Bishop Whittingham of St. Edmundsbury and Ipswich also registered their own disapprobation. On 24th November the two congregations of Edgware parish church and synagogue in London gathered inside the church hall, 350 crammed together, an overflow of 100, and still more turned away. The rector, the Rev. R.A.H. Lea, declared that in their union the hope of a year had been realised. A collection was taken, and the meeting "produced a remarkable feeling of sympathy and understanding between the two sections of the community".[63] The Anglican press chorused its disapproval of the pogrom. *The Guardian* pronounced, "The Nazis have not merely surpassed what one would have set as the limits of calculated savagery, but to have become fantastic; the lust of cruelty seems to have become maniacal."[64] *The Record* observed that their patience with the German government was almost exhausted:

> "A heavy responsibility rests upon the Christian Churches, who should with one accord make continued progress against all forms of anti-semitism as being completely contrary to the teaching of the message of Jesus Christ. Churches

---

[58] *Ibid.*, p. 503.
[59] *Church Times* (25th November 1938), p. 587d.
[60] *The Guardian* (18th November 1938), p. 754a.
[61] *Ibid.*
[62] *Ibid.*
[63] *The Record* (2nd December 1938), p. 769a.
[64] *The Guardian* (18th November 1938), p. 747a.

speaking with one voice could do more than is generally believed to rally those elements in Germany which look with horror upon such hooliganism."[65]

Protest was crucial, but material support for the Jews must be forthcoming. Never before had this seemed so clear to Christian opinion. On 16th November Bishop Bell asked the Church Assembly to give a lead to dioceses and parishes across the country by requesting the Central Board of Finance to make a grant of £5,000 to a new appeal for refugees. It was passed forthwith. £1,748 had been subscribed in the hall itself by the end of the day. The next day the new appeal was formally announced in *The Times*. The target was £50,000.

Existing restrictions were overruled or bypassed. Earl Grey wrote to Lang that the legal committee of the church had found that the Church Assembly could not, within the existing regulations governing their relationship, direct the Central Board of Finance to donate £5,000 to the fund for refugees. Nor was the Central Board competent under those regulations to collect the sum. It would be "absurd" to appoint another Special Committee to consider the impasse. However, if the present members of the Central Board could assume the functions of such a committee, any technical objections could be resisted. Not that Grey thought such objections likely. The problem need not, he thought, become public.[66]

"Can you tell me anything about this appeal for £50,000 for non-Aryan Christians?" wrote the Bishop of Dover to Lambeth Palace, evidently thinking of something very remote indeed. "What are we going to do about it in this Diocese? Am I supposed to be doing anything at all?"[67] Evidently, however, such a response was unusual. The diocesan magazines reveal a vigorous surge of concern and activity. At his diocesan conference in Liverpool Bishop David said: "Let us speak out as strongly as we feel, but let us not be content until we have translated our feelings into action."[68]

Correspondence at Lambeth Palace mounted. A second appeal, led by the former Prime Minister, Lord Baldwin, was being prepared. On 25th November Wyndham Deedes wrote to Don that Baldwin must surely stress that, until now, "practically all the money" had been raised by a Jewish community of 300,000 – and £250,000 on one day alone, for an appeal for Austrian Jews – and "practically nothing" by a "Christian" public of 40 million.[69] On the same day Robert Stopford of the British Legation in Prague wrote to him that in granting £10 million to the Czech government the British government had made clear its hope that refugees should have "first claim" on the fund. The Czech Ministry of Social Welfare would now oversee the work of a new Refugee Institute.[70] On 30th November 1938, Don again complained: "The multiplicity of Committees and Appeals relating to refugees is becoming very confusing."[71]

[65] *The Record* (25th November 1938), p. 737c.
[66] Grey to Lang, 22nd November 1938, *Lang Papers*, vol. 38, fol. 228.
[67] Dover to Sargent, 29th November 1938, *ibid.*, fol. 251.
[68] *The Guardian* (2nd December 1938), p. 795b.
[69] Deedes to Don, 25th November 1938, *Lang Papers*, vol. 38, fols. 231–232.
[70] Stopford to Don, 25th November 1938, *ibid.*, fols. 236–237.
[71] Don to Grey, 30th November 1938, *ibid.*, fol. 253.

The Jewish Board of Deputies had organised a new protest meeting, and enlisted Archbishop Temple, Cardinal Hinsley and the Moderator of the Free Churches, Robert Bond, to speak at the Royal Albert Hall on 1st December. It was the eminent and popular Temple who dominated the report to be found the next day in *The Times*. "Protest Against Persecution", it read. "Moral Principles: Dr. Temple's Appeal to the German People". The Archbishop of York declared Britain's own share of responsibility for the plight of the Jews in Germany and Austria, for their own treatment of Germany after the Great War had prepared the way for this "reaction" against the Jews there: "We are told that a recognition of this should keep us silent. I say that it should make us speak out, lest we become accomplices in the effect, as well as in the cause." He observed the danger that the world might instead "sink into moral numbness and lethargy", and continued:

> "The most dreadful element in the persecution of Jews and of many Christians in Germany was that it was proclaimed as a kind of justice. The horrifying fact was that the Nazi Government preached what it practised. It was against that, even more than against the practice itself, that we were bound to protest, less moral principles went altogether by default."[72]

Temple's speech was reported fully. Beneath it brief mention was made of the contributions of other speakers. It was not admired by everyone. In a letter to Don the day after, Earl Grey scribbled, "I think Temple made a bad speech at the Albert Hall. I quite agree that what he said is worth saying at the proper time and place, but last night it was most unsuitable and, as normal, it is the only thing reported!"[73]

The refugees had become at last a public preoccupation. Lord Baldwin, never more respected by the broad public than at this time and a politician much admired in church life, announced the opening of the new fund in a radio broadcast on 8th December. The organising committee of the appeal included Lord Rothschild, the Member of Parliament Godfrey Nicholson and the Methodist Reverend William Simpson. A day of collection was set for 7th January 1939. Plans were hatched for a four-minute broadcast appeal for the cinemas on that date. Film distributors arranged to contribute a tenth of the day's taking to the fund. On 7th December Bell wrote to Lang, "The Baldwin Broadcast Appeal for Jews and Non-Aryans (to be made tomorrow, Thursday) is going very strongly indeed, and is likely to secure in its various departments a very big response." Simpson's Jewish secretary, Philip Voss, thought £100,000 very possible. Bell commended to Lang a request from both Jews and Christians on the Baldwin Committee that the Archbishop should feature in the film. He added: "I do very much hope you may say 'yes'. It would be an immense help to the whole cause."[74] Don put the request to Lang, and the next day replied,

> "My reading of your letter of December 7th was accompanied by a variety of snorts and protestations from His Grace of Canterbury who hitherto has stubbornly refused

---

[72] *The Times* (2nd December 1938), p. 16d.
[73] Grey to Don, 2nd December 1938, *Lang Papers*, vol. 38, fol. 259.
[74] Bell to Lang, 7th December 1938, *ibid.*, fol. 268.

to utilise the talkie-film for the purpose of propaganda. By the exercise of a certain amount of patience and persuasion I brought His Grace to the point of agreeing to subject himself to the ordeal provided that arrangements can be made for the recording to be made before he goes to Canterbury on the 15th December."[75]

Evidently, Lang proved a rather graceless performer. "I hope he *looked* benign", wrote Alan Don after the film-makers had visited the Palace, "but I doubt it."[76]

The Record published a report by the director of the Barbican Mission to the Jews, C.E. Davidson. Davidson had returned from a harrowing visit to a mission in Czechoslovakia. In the unclaimed regions which lay between that country and the newly refashioned German border he had found clusters of beleaguered refugees; many of them starving, shattered, pitiable, some crazed with fear, others bewildered and lost. Behind them their synagogues had been burnt down and their cemeteries desecrated, their property plundered and destroyed, their families scattered. Some had been beaten, many more were still to be shot by German soldiers as they strayed in and out of the vague frontiers. "Only the heart of a Nazi would not be moved by their tears" Davidson wrote bitterly.[77]

On 9th December Lang moved more firmly into the public forum when he stepped on to the platform at the Mansion House, alongside Cardinal Hinsley; the leader of the Labour Party, Clement Attlee; Lords Rothschild, Samuel, Dawson, Bearsted and Reading; Neville Laski and the Dean of St. Paul's Cathedral, W.R. Matthews. Messages from Cardinal Pacelli, on behalf of Pope Pius XI, and General Evangeline Booth of the Salvation Army were read out to the gathering. Lang's own doubts and anxieties were still apparent, but he declared them resolved. *The Times* reported his speech fully. "It was difficult", he observed, "for those who knew only the statistics that had been published to realise the character of the persecution to which more than half a million of their fellow creatures were now being exposed. Only those who, like himself, had seen and talked to the individual sufferers could realise what it meant. He hoped that he would speak with the needed moderation, but it was very difficult." Lang deplored "an ingenious and elaborate system of persecution, of mental and moral torture, which would be incredible unless it were known that it was actually happening". He wondered what it all meant for their belief in the progress of "just and humane government", for the accumulated barbarities of medieval times offered no comparison. They were right to protest: "It would have been impossible to keep silent. Silence might have seemed to be acquiescence. It might have increased the atrophy of heart and conscience which was the real danger in a world like ours when miseries were being inflicted in all parts of the world which completely baffled our imagination." This was a world problem which must be confronted with international measures and a "long-term policy". Lang declared his admiration for the voluntary organisations and the generosity of the Jewish community. But he also observed, "the very variety of these efforts constituted a special difficulty. The ordinary man was in the difficulty of not knowing, in the midst of all these different movements, how he could best help. It

[75]Don to Bell, 8th December 1938, *ibid.*, fol. 270.
[76]*Journal of Alan C. Don*, 14th December 1938, M.S. 2866, p. 90.
[77]*The Record* (9th December 1938), p. 92c–d.

was here that the Lord Baldwin Fund filled a very timely need."[78] Later that month all three church leaders signed, at Godfrey Nicholson's request, a letter to *The Times* refuting any sense that this was solely a Jewish issue, and a concern for Jews alone.[79]

The Church's own appeal was receiving powerful support in the dioceses. Since October 1938 a hostel for Jewish-Christian students had been supervised by the Jewish Christian Union at Holy Trinity Church, Shoreditch, in London.[80] Others followed elsewhere; one in Kilburn was furnished and equipped by the congregation of St. Augustine's parish church.[81] In December, Bishop Kirk of Oxford wrote firmly in his pastoral letter: "I wish to secure that no part of our Diocese shall be untouched by these various appeals . . . every parish which has not already had a church collection for these Refugee Funds should have one at the earliest possible moment . . . If there is a collection in your parish, give to it; if not, find out why it has been omitted."[82] Little wonder, perhaps, that by the following March he could announce that Oxford had raised £3,071, more than any other diocese; more even than Bell's Chichester, which had managed £2 less. A month before, the *York Diocesan Gazette* reported the raising of £1,800 – £600 above the most optimistic expectations – and contributions from a hundred more parishes were still awaited. In January Bishop Lovett proudly remarked: "I am very happy to perceive that however obnoxious the blood of Jewish people may be to a Teutonic Government, there is a strong element of the Good Samaritan in British Christianity, and that it has shown itself as a generous stream in the Diocese of Salisbury."[83] By February Salisbury had managed to produce a sum of £1,916 19s. 8d. Lovett offered guidance to those who might house the new refugees, invoking the words, "I was a stranger and ye took me in."[84] On 12th January 1939 Earl Grey reported to Lambeth Palace, "there is over £40,000 in the bank".[85] By 8th March the figure stood at £60,173 1s. 6d. In February 1939 the Dean and Chapter of Ely offered to accommodate a number of refugees in the empty house of the fifth canonry; after their troubles the house, situated by the quiet college parks, was thought ideal.[86]

But the despairing letters to Lambeth Palace grew daily. Alan Don forwarded many of them to the secretary of the Archbishop's Council on Foreign Relations, Miss Wallace, and she, in turn, sent them to the appropriate agencies. Between 26th and 29th December alone, eight names were forwarded to her. Wallace's position was not altogether easy. Without a guarantee from a body or an individual, no Jew could migrate to Britain. A number of these cases had no such assurance. Could they not appeal publicly for volunteers, or establish a guarantee fund with a proportion of the money raised by the Baldwin Fund? She

---

[78]*The Times* (10th December 1938), p. 14b.
[79]Lang to Nicholson, 24th December 1938, *Lang Papers*, vol. 38, fol. 287.
[80]Letter from Dr. Paul Levetoff, *Church Times* (3rd February 1939), p. 100b.
[81]Letter from W.P.T. Atkinson, *ibid.* (10th February 1939), p. 125a.
[82]*Oxford Diocesan Magazine*, Bishop's letter, December 1938.
[83]*Salisbury Diocesan Gazette*, Bishop's letter, January 1939.
[84]*Ibid.*, Bishop's letter, February 1939.
[85]Grey to Lang, 12th January 1939, *Lang Papers*, vol. 38, fol. 310.
[86]*Church Times* (17th February 1939), p. 159d.

suspected that the refugee organisations themselves were ignorant of the nature of the guarantee. She was working with one committee which offered hospitality, but could find no refugees for it.[87]

On 9th December Don himself had interviewed Rabbi Chaim Bloch from Vienna. Bloch had written against the Nazis and now sought to escape them. He showed Don sympathetic affidavits from Cardinal Innitzer and other churchmen and explained that he was seeking to travel to America, where a post had been offered to him. But his family was trapped in Vienna, and he feared that they might be interned as hostages. Bloch was born a Czech, and was covered by Czech arrangements. But his wife and daughter were born in Poland and had to comply with different, restrictive, regulations. He asked if the Archbishop might write to the American Embassy in London to enquire if his family could be transferred to the Czech quota. Meanwhile, his other daughter and her family were seeking to migrate to Palestine. Could the Archbishop approach the British Colonial Office on their behalf? Lang asked Don to write these letters. On 19th December Alan Don wrote in his diary of a meeting with a rabbi from Vienna who burst into tears before him. It is probable that this was Bloch. "And he", Don reflected bleakly, "is but one among hundreds for whom life has been made unendurable."[88] On 30th December Don learnt from the Colonial Office that these decisions were not for them, but for the Palestinian Government. Bloch was thwarted. On 4th January 1939 he pleaded with Don to write to the British passport control officer in Vienna for "a certificate for Palestine" for his daughter and son-in-law.[89] Don wrote at once, but warned him not to hope for too much. On 11th January Bloch asked Don to write on his behalf to the Emigration Department of the Jewish Agency in Great Russell Street, London. On 14th January Don did so. The next day Bloch wrote to him, "I have just received news from my dear wife and daughter that they have now obtained their visas for the United States. They write to me that this was solely due to the kind intervention of His Eminence the Archbishop of Canterbury."[90]

Abroad, the chaplaincies of the church had long faced intolerable pressures. As 1938 unfolded rumours spread that Jews were being baptised *en masse* at the British legation in Vienna. Bishop Batty, suffragan Bishop of Fulham and Bishop of North and Central Europe, visited Austria to investigate. The suspicions continued. On 30th November 1938 Bishop Bell had sent to Lambeth a letter from a Mrs. Baker, who, in turn, had received a letter from the Church of Scotland chaplain in Budapest, G.A.F. Knight. Knight complained that "all through the summer" the Anglican chaplain in Vienna had "accepted Jews and baptised them, without any preparation whatsoever, and baptised them in batches of some 50 [*sic*] a day. Several eye witnesses have told me as much."[91] Don wrote to Batty, anxious about scandal. Batty replied promptly. "The matter to which you refer", he said, "was first brought to my notice by an article in a

[87] Wallace to Don, 31st December 1938, *Lang Papers*, vol. 38, fols. 293–294.
[88] *Journal of Alan C. Don*, 19th December 1938, M.S. 2866, p. 89.
[89] Bloch to Don, 4th January 1939, *Lang Papers*, vol. 38, fol. 297.
[90] Bloch to Don, 15th January 1939, *ibid.*, fol. 318.
[91] Don to Batty, 5th December 1938, *ibid.*, fol. 260.

The Church of England and the Jews of Germany and Austria 245

German paper which attacks all Christian institutions and leaders." The charge of baptism without preparation was "absolutely untrue":

> "We have our missions to the Jews and it is difficult for a priest to refuse to deal with a Jew who wishes to become a Christian but at the moment on political grounds the greatest care is necessary and instructions were issued to the Chaplain in Vienna to this effect.
>
> The Chaplain responsible in the summer when this occurred was the Revd. C.H.D. Grimes a scholar and a gentleman in whom I have confidence. I think it must be admitted that his intense sympathy with these poor people in their terrible sufferings led him to a greater belief in their sincerity than an outsider would have had.
>
> Mr. Grimes resigned the Chaplaincy and left over three months ago. He has been succeeded temporarily by the Revd. F.A. Evelyn who is an experienced priest. He has been instructed that the greatest care must be taken in these cases and long preparation given. Also that if there is the slightest ground for believing that Baptism is wanted on political grounds, it must be refused."[92]

But the story continued to circulate into the new year. A book by one George Pitt-Rivers called *The Czech Conspiracy* was published, and there the report was repeated in print and enlarged extravagantly.[93] On 12th January 1939 a correspondent who had read the work wrote to Lambeth Palace of its claim that 900 baptisms into the Anglican Church had occurred every day in Vienna and demanded "a categorical denial that this scandalous imputation is true".[94] Alan Don reassured her that it was "grotesquely untrue . . . fantastic". He attributed the rumour to "enemies of the Jewish race".[95] Don wrote again to Batty to ask if any action might be taken against the author. Batty replied again that the allegation was "absurd". He would write to the author once he had heard from Grimes. In the meantime, he added, "I have just dealt with a complaint from Prague where a German Lutheran minister has baptised a very large number with 'Baptist (Church of England)'. His excuse being that he used our Prayer Book."[96]

The ensuing months were increasingly disfigured by pessimism and hopelessness. As thousands more refugees struggled across the face of the continent, Europe descended irretrievably into chaos. The church press saw the coming of war. The bishops' pastoral letters spoke of the duty of reason to contest the claims of brute force. The voluntary organisations worked frantically. The politicians debated whether or not to appease further. On 3rd September 1939 Britain declared war on Germany, and many spoke of it as a crusade against evil.

The turbulent passage of 1938 revealed many aspects of the character and work of the Church of England as a religious body, as an "Established" institution and as a denomination of public opinion. It offered significant, and often impressive, evidence of the moral concern its members felt for the

---

[92] Batty to Don, 6th December 1938, *ibid.*, fol. 264.
[93] George Lane Fox Pitt-Rivers, *The Czech Conspiracy. A Phase in the World-War Plot*, London 1938. It is interesting to note that the author was imprisoned by the Home Secretary from 1940–1942.
[94] Ludovici to Don, 12th January 1938, *Lang Papers*, vol. 38, fol. 311.
[95] Don to Ludovici, 13th January 1939, *ibid.*, fols. 313–314.
[96] Batty to Don (undated), *ibid.*, fol. 324.

persecuted. It saw a deepening of the mutual awareness and friendship of Christians and Jews in England, and brought together representatives of both communities in a sporadic, but earnest, working relationship on behalf of Jews abroad. In time, the consequences of these sympathetic expressions would prove genuinely significant, not least in the foundation of the Council of Christians and Jews in 1942. These things suggest much about the religious identity and principles of an important fraction of the European Church. Meanwhile, the National-Socialist persecution of the Jews illustrated both the strengths and limitations of the Establishment of the Church of England. The leaders of the church certainly sought to use the peculiar privileges of their relationship with the British State on behalf of the Jews of Europe. The Establishment of the church placed bishops in the House of Lords: in 1938 Bishop Bell grasped the potential value of this right, using Parliament to subject the policies of the government to moral scrutiny. It also offered the church prestige. When Lang or Temple made a speech, the newspapers reported it at length. Cardinal Hinsley or the Moderator of the Free Churches enjoyed little such favour. This too was exploited. Meanwhile, discreet efforts were made to intercede behind the scenes on behalf of Jews and their families. It was possible that an Established Church was better able to sustain the moral character of the state than one which was not Established. Yet it was also evident that the privileges and apparent opportunities enjoyed by the Church of England rarely influenced government policy much. Sometimes the private intercessions which were made on behalf of particular communities or individuals were fruitless.

Contemporary observers could hardly doubt that the anti-Jewish policies of the Hitler regime were condemned by the Church of England. But the church did not see itself as a pressure group, and its leaders did not seek to frame policies on behalf of the whole Christian community. Anglican culture encouraged archbishops and bishops to speak out as they themselves saw fit. This was valuable, but it was insufficient. Too often it meant that they faced the dilemmas attending protest alone. Accordingly, they were all the more likely to be inconsistent with each other, and even, over time, with themselves. The troubles of Archbishop Lang symbolised this most obviously and significantly. If a church is to address political questions it must, as a body, take that responsibility seriously. That seriousness could only be expressed successfully by the creation of permanent councils at the very heart of the institution and throughout the dioceses. In the National-Socialist era the improvisation of small committees on the fringe could not prove sufficient. Before 1938 Bell feared that Christians in Britain had failed to rise to the moral and practical demands of the refugee crisis. Although he could see far more evidence of charitable activity across the dioceses and parishes of the country by the end of the year, he must have seen that this was still marked by too weak a sense of overall direction. Meanwhile, there was too little in the fabric of the Church of England to guide its archbishops systematically, and too little to involve the broad Church community in political matters. Beyond the announcement of intercessions and the raising of money, collective action was not considered. It would never have occurred to Lang, or even to Temple or Bell, to lead a Christian boycott of German businesses. It was not the sort of thing that the Church did. Possibly it was too "political". It might appear authoritarian, for reasonable and humane churchpeople would be sure to disagree, and they must not be coerced or marginalised. At all events, instead of developing collective strategies, the bishops of the Church of England perpetuated a culture of political individualism. There was nothing wrong about it, and in many ways it was truly wise. But the expressions of such a culture could never be adequate in the midst of a world *in extremis*. The story of the Church of England and the Jews of Germany and Austria from 1933 to 1939 is one of genuine and humane, but occasional and irregular, vision and effort. There are many examples of the moral goodness which the Church represented institutionally and encouraged socially. Equally evident, however, was the genuine failure of the Church to recognise fully the moral demands which the political world made upon it.

Judaica

A Disputed Precedent
The Prague Organ in Nineteenth-Century Central-European Legal Literature and Polemics

BY DAVID ELLENSON

When the Hamburg Reform temple was dedicated on 18th October 1818, the employment of an organ during worship was among the central innovations the Reformers proposed in order to enhance the aesthetics of the contemporary Jewish service. This innovation, as well as other changes the Reform temple had introduced, aroused the fierce opposition of the Orthodox and, in 1819, a pamphlet issued by the Orthodox Rabbinic Court of Hamburg under the title *Eileh Divrei Habrit* collected twenty-two opinions signed by forty rabbis asserting that the "work of the 'innovators' stood outside the pale of Judaism".[1] The authors of this pamphlet were particularly anxious to respond to and counter claims supporting Reform innovations that had been made two years earlier in Berlin. These warrants on behalf of Reform had been collected and issued in two volumes, *Nogah Ha-Zedek* and *Or Nogah*, by Eliezer Liebermann, a teacher and itinerant preacher, in 1818 in Dessau.[2] The Orthodox rabbis of *Eileh Divrei Habrit* were aware that the arguments contained in these Reform pamphlets drew upon classical rabbinic sources and practices that could mislead the unsuspecting into believing that the employment of instrumental music, among other things, was justified in religious devotions. In this way, the two Reform writings came to play a central role in the struggle over Reform in Hamburg in 1818 to 1819.

Rabbi David Zvi Hoffmann, Professor of Talmud and Codes, and since 1899 head of the *Rabbinerseminar für das orthodoxe Judentum* in Berlin, testified almost eighty years later to the significance this event and these writings held for the history of modern Jewish religious denominationalism. It was there, "in the city of Hamburg", he wrote, that "the evil [of Reform] first burst forth". Despite the protests of the Hamburg rabbinate, "the destroyers" insisted on unleashing their "destructive innovations" on Judaism and the Jewish public. Chief among these innovations was the organ.[3] Debate over the employment of an organ in Jewish worship remained the single most significant point of boundary demarcation

---

[1] *Eileh Divrei Habrit*, Altona 1819, repr. Farnborough 1969 (in Hebrew); see Michael A. Meyer, *Response to Modernity. A History of the Reform Movement in Judaism*, New York–Oxford 1988, p. 58.
[2] *Ibid.*, pp. 50–51; Eliezer Liebermann, *Nogah Ha-Zedek*, Dessau 1818 (in Hebrew); idem, *Or Nogah*, Dessau 1818 (in Hebrew).
[3] David Hoffmann, *Melammed L'Hoyil, Orah Hayim*, No. 16. At the end of this *responsum*, Hoffmann reveals its date to be 1897.

between Liberal and Orthodox Judaism in Germany throughout the nineteenth century.[4] Disputes over its use abound in Central-European legal literature of this age.[5] Its importance was such, Hoffmann observed, that a codicil was "issued to each student of our seminary here in Berlin along with his certificate of ordination stipulating that the organ was forbidden on account of the biblical injunction 'Thou shalt not walk in their ways' (*Leviticus* XVIII:3)".[6] If a student, in later years, elected to serve a community that employed the organ either on the Sabbath or during the week, then, the codicil stated, the ordination certificate that had been issued to the student was to be considered, "completely cancelled, null and void" (*bteilin u'm'vutalin, la sharirin v'la kayamin*).[7]

In view of the importance assigned to the issue of the organ, it is particularly noteworthy to view the role ascribed by each side in this controversy to the precedent of an organ that had been played during worship in the Maisel Synagogue in Prague. At the onset of the struggle between the Reform and Orthodox factions in early nineteenth-century Germany, the Reformers, Hoffmann noted, had in *Or Nogah* and *Nogah Ha-Zedek* drawn legal justification for this practice from "the organ that existed in the Holy Community of Prague".[8] Testimony to the employment of this organ can be found in a 1679 Prague *siddur*.[9]

---

[4] See David Ellenson, *Tradition in Transition. Orthodoxy, Halakha and the Boundaries of Modern Jewish Identity*, Lanham, MD 1989, pp. 34–46.

[5] For a bibliography of much of this literature, see the article by Abraham Berliner, 'Literargeschichtliche Belege über die christliche Orgel im jüdischen Gottesdienste', in *idem* (ed.), *Zur Lehr' und zur Wehr. Über und gegen die kirchliche Orgel im jüdischen Gottesdienste*, Berlin 1904.

[6] Hoffmann, *op. cit.*, No. 16. See also Berliner's discussion of this codicil, *loc. cit.*, p. 58. A full translation and discussion of the text of this codicil can be found in David Ellenson, 'The Rabbiner-Seminar Codicil. An Instrument of Boundary Maintenance', in *Festschrift for Rabbi Jerome Malino* (forthcoming).

[7] The language of the codicil is taken from the text given to Jacob Lauterbach upon his ordination from the Seminary. Lauterbach's student, Professor Lou Silberman, kindly provided me with this document.

[8] Hoffmann, *op. cit.*, No. 16.

[9] This *siddur* is contained as an appendix in Shabbetai Bass, *Siftei Yeshenim*, Amsterdam 1680 (in Hebrew). The use of an organ in the liturgical and ceremonial life of the Prague Jewish community prior to the nineteenth century is attested to and described in other sources as well. Johann Jakob Schudt, *Jüdische Merckwürdigkeiten*, 4 vols., Frankfurt a. Main–Leipzig 1714–1718, makes several references to the employment of the organ in the synagogue life of Prague. For example, in vol. I, p. 218, Schudt writes "daß die Juden zu Prag in der Alt-Neuen Synagog . . . eine Orgel haben/ die sie aber zum GOttes=Dienst weiter nicht brauchen/ als nur/ wann sie Freytags Abends das Bewillkommungs-Lied des *Schabbes* singen". On that same page Schudt adds that the organ which accompanied this service welcoming the Sabbath was also played by a Jew. See also vol. IV, p. 366. Dr. Alexander Putik of the Jewish Museum in Prague, in a personal letter dated 6th May 1994, asserts that "in the baroque period", as these sources indicate, there is reference to the organ in both "the Old-New and Mayzl Synagogues" and he does not preclude the possibility that the organ was also used in the liturgical rites of other contemporaneous Prague synagogues. He adds, "I assume that both [the organs employed at the Old-New and Mayzl Synagogues] were portable." Dr. Putik makes this assumption because there appears to be no place designated for the permanent placement of an organ in either of these synagogues and as a 1716 copperplate engraving (reproduced as *Procession of Prague Jews, marking the birth of Prince Leopold, successor to the throne* in this article) reveals, portable organs were played in public processions marking the arrival of rulers and coronations. Furthermore, a circular which illuminates a 1741 copperplate engraving depicting a celebratory procession of Prague Jews at a similar occasion makes reference to a "*Positiv oder Orgel=Fliegel*", a portable organ. It is printed in Milada Vilimkova, *The Prague Ghetto*, Prague 1993, p. 48.

There, prior to the recitation of the hymn *L'cha Dodi* in the service welcoming the Sabbath, the following instruction is found: "A pleasant song by Rabbi Solomon Singer, played in the Maisel Synagogue of the Holy Community of Prague, on the organ (*'ugav*) and lyre prior to *L'cha Dodi*." The Reformers cited this custom as a legitimate precedent for their employment of the organ. In contrast, the Orthodox proclaimed it inapposite as a justification. A description and analysis of the dispute that initially raged about the Prague organ, as well as the ongoing debate this precedent evoked in Orthodox legal literature during the middle and again at the end of the century, comprises an interesting and overlooked chapter in the history of Reform-Orthodox disputations of the nineteenth century.

I. THE REFORM POSITION

Rabbi Aaron Chorin of Arad, Hungary, writing in *Nogah Ha-Zedek*, pointed out that most Jewish legal authorities forbade the organ in Jewish worship on the grounds that the employment of this instrument during worship violated the biblical injunction "Thou shalt not walk in their ways". This, Chorin contended, was true only if a particular practice or custom current in Gentile usage fell under a category labelled "ways of the Amorites". Such a custom, inasmuch as it was either idolatrous in and of itself, or facilitated or contributed to idolatry, was strictly forbidden. A Jew could not "walk in such ways". If, on the other hand, a Gentile practice enhanced the glory of God, then such a custom would not constitute an instance of this category. The organ, in Chorin's view, was an instance of the latter type of custom, one designed to enhance the honour and respect due to God, and not an example of the former that would foster idolatry. Consequently, the custom of employing a musical instrument during worship was not one that Jews were forbidden to adopt or imitate. Rather, it was one that they could and ought to adopt. Chorin supported this position by observing that Christians, after all, were not idolaters. Upon this there was an *halakhic* consensus. They, like Jews, "recognise the Creator and His attributes" (*midot*). Hence the organ, admittedly employed by Christians during their worship, cannot be considered an instrument of idolatry or the use of an organ during prayer as an "imitation of the Amorites". Rather, it is a "sweet practice", and its pleasant tones aim at and promote "the uplifting of the soul" (*hitorerut hanefesh*). The Polish rabbi and Talmudic scholar Moses Isserles (1510/20–1572), Chorin implied, had recognised this. Therefore, in *Orah Hayim*, 560:3, Isserles wrote that musical accompaniment was permitted for the sake of observing a commandment. Chorin felt, as the act of public prayer was such a commandment, it was permissible to employ the organ during worship. He further argued, in a point particularly germane to our concerns, that actual Jewish custom and usage legitimated this understanding of Jewish law. "Even today", Chorin observed, "holy communities are accustomed to employing musical instruments when singing *L'cha Dodi* at the reception of the Sabbath." The practice of the Jewish people during worship indicated that Jewish law countenanced musical accompaniment as a valid element in the choreography of public prayer.[10]

Chorin, to be sure, did not mention the Prague precedent explicitly, though he no doubt had it in mind. It was left to Eliezer Liebermann, in his *Or Nogah*, to make precise reference to the custom of Prague. Liebermann, after producing extensive classical textual sources and arguments calling for the employment of music during prayer, added the following observation:

> "I have also not forgotten that which several elders related to me at the time I was in Prague. They remember the organ that was in the *Altneuschul*. There, on every Sabbath, Rosh Chodesh, and Holiday eve they would play it, and even today they receive the Sabbath in the *Altschul* with musical instruments. The music continues for a half hour into the night, and those who perform it are Jews."

Liebermann's account of the Prague rite, as we shall see, would not go undisputed. However, it was sufficient to allow him to conclude that there was no Jewish legal prohibition against employing the organ or any other musical instrument during worship. "On the contrary", Liebermann concluded, "the honour of God [demands that we] laud him with song and praise, in joy and mirth, with every musical instrument."[11] Liebermann's argument obviously paralleled that of Chorin. The actual practice of the Prague community validated a particular understanding of Jewish law on the question of whether musical instruments could be used during prayer. It testified to the manner in which observant Jews had comprehended and applied the law, and provided a powerful precedent for the Reformers in their quest to warrant their employment of the organ in Hamburg and elsewhere. In view of the *halakhic* dictum, "The custom of the people of Israel is Torah", the case of Prague was too significant for the Orthodox to ignore. Their attempt to grapple with this precedent, and to dispute its Reform interpretation and application, was immediate and strong.

II. THE RESPONSE OF CONTEMPORANEOUS ORTHODOXY

Rabbi Hirtz Scheur of Mainz, writing at the outset of *Eileh Divrei Habrit*, underscored that the issue of the organ was critical for establishing Orthodox boundaries against Reform practices. Scheur conceded that there was some traditional legal justification for permitting the organ to be employed in a synagogue, as well as for joyous occasions such as weddings or the celebration of the King's birthday. However, "in our generation", he wrote, "where the lawless among our people have publicly increased . . . and where many publicly profane the Sabbath, we have no right at all to permit such a thing". Instead, the rabbis of this generation should be as stringent in condemning the use of the organ as the authorities in the generation of Elisha ben Avuyah had been when they stoned him for riding his horse on the Sabbath. Rabbi Scheur implored his colleagues, "on account of the needs of the hour", to be unyielding in their

---

[10] Liebermann, *Nogah Ha-Zedek, op. cit.*, p. 21.
[11] Liebermann, *Or Nogah, op. cit.*, pt. 1, p. 17.

opposition to musical instruments in the synagogue. There was no matter of "lawlessness" more pressing than this, Scheur concluded, "against which you must erect a barrier".

In the course of his argument, Scheur explicitly addressed the challenge presented to his position by the precedent of the organ employed in Prague. He noted that there were nine synagogues in Prague, and observed that in the largest of them, "the Sabbath has been ushered in with song and musical instrument". However, unlike Liebermann, Scheur would not concede that the organ was played there "for a half hour into the night". Instead, he reported that the instrument was employed only "up to *Bo'i B'shalom* [i.e. before the Sabbath actually begins] and it never occurred to anyone to do so [employ a musical instrument] on the Sabbath or a Holiday". Scheur argued in effect that Liebermann had misrepresented the facts of the Prague precedent. The Prague organ had not been used, and therefore could not be employed, to justify the use of a musical instrument as an accompaniment to prayers on the Sabbath or Holidays. Scheur also reiterated his earlier observation that the organ was employed in only one synagogue in Prague. The refusal of the other eight synagogues to do so indicated that the single precedent of the one synagogue hardly constituted what the law would consider "custom and usage". Scheur, in this way, hoped to emphasise how limited the use of the organ had been in Prague. His argument called into question whether the isolated case of a single organ even constituted a precedent. Scheur's efforts were intended to limit the scope and application of the Prague precedent and, in light of the Reformers' emphasis upon the importance of the organ, to argue against its contemporary use altogether.[12]

Scheur's arguments, as well as an explicit assault against the Reformers' attempts to employ the precedent of Prague as a warrant for their use of the organ, are echoed in a letter sent to the Hamburg Rabbinical Court by the members of the Orthodox Rabbinical Court in Prague. Rabbis Eleazar Fleckeles, Samuel Segal Landau and Leib Melish began their letter to the Hamburg rabbis by asserting that what was happening in the Hamburg temple, "sickens and pains the heart of the listener. Woe to the generation where such a thing has occurred". The Hamburg Reformers were for them persons of no religion, neither Jews nor Gentiles. Particularly disturbing to the Prague rabbis was the use the Reformers had made of the Prague rite in justifying their employment of the organ. Immediately after their introductory words of lament, they turned to the Reformers' claims and addressed the issue directly. The honour of Prague was clearly at stake! "It is an absolute prohibition" (*issur gamur*), they wrote, to play any type of musical instrument on the Sabbath or Holidays. They acknowledged that there were "those in our community who play instruments to welcome the Sabbath". However, "the custom here is that the musicians must put their instruments away a half hour before the *Barchu*" [i.e. the prayer that marks the onset of the Sabbath itself]. Consequently, what was "printed in that invalid book (*sefer pasul*) in Dessau" should be recognised for the lie it is. "Called

---

[12]Scheur's position is stated in Letter 2 of *Eileh Divrei Habrit, op. cit.*

Nogah Ha-Zedek, it is evil darkness and should not be relied on at all . . . Everything in it is a devilish lie (*tahbulot shaker*) [designed] to blind the eyes of the Jews and lead them astray." The Prague organ was irrelevant as a precedent for the playing of the organ in a synagogue on either Holidays or the Sabbath. The Reformers had misinformed and misled the public in their citation of it.[13]

Rabbi Moses Sofer (Schreiber) of Preßburg, the *Chatam* Sofer, also dealt directly with the Prague precedent in his arguments against the employment of the organ during prayer and expanded the parameters of the ban that Rabbi Scheur and the members of the Prague Rabbinic Court had issued. Like the others, Rabbi Sofer had read *Nogah Ha-Zedek*. Its authors were the "wicked of the earth" (*rishei aretz*). The organ itself, even in antiquity, "was placed in the temples of ancient idol worship, and it was not used for any other purpose". The organ, he claimed, was therefore the only musical instrument prohibited in the ancient Temple. It was banned on account of *Leviticus* XVIII:3, "Thou shalt not walk in their ways". Sofer's attempt to ban the organ on the basis of this biblical commandment compelled him to confront the precedent of the Prague organ in a way which his colleagues in *Eileh Divrei Habrit* had not. For the latter, it was sufficient to refute the claim that the organ was used on either the Sabbath or Holidays. These men simply had to argue that Liebermann was incorrect in *Or Nogah* when he reported that the organ had been used in the Prague synagogue after the Sabbath had already begun. This alone would demonstrate that the Prague precedent could not be used to justify musical accompaniment for the prayers on the Sabbath or Holidays. Sofer, in contrast, desired much more. The prohibition against the organ was a *din torah*, a law derived from the Torah itself, and, in his view, had been enacted prior to the destruction of the Temple. It was, and continued to be, designed to separate the Jewish people from the idolatrous ways of the pagans.

Sofer's understanding of this issue placed him on the horns of a dilemma. The Jews of the Prague synagogue were traditionally observant, as was the ritual conducted within its walls. If this was so, then how could one understand that the organ had been employed for so long in even this one Orthodox synagogue? Sofer needed to explain, in light of his claim that the ban against the use of the organ stemmed from the days of the Temple itself, how it was that the traditional Prague community had come to employ the organ even in a circumscribed way. Furthermore, he desired to demonstrate why even this limited precedent did not constitute an appropriate justification for those who wanted to defend the use of the organ in a synagogue at times other than the Sabbath or Holidays.

At the outset, Rabbi Sofer stated, "Our fathers told us that in earlier days there was an organ in the *Altneuschul* in Prague and this is cited in the book *A've'n* ["Wickedness", an acronym for *Or Nogah*]. However, [the author] testified falsely that a Jew plays there on the Sabbath eve until a half hour into the night, God deliver us . . . We have reliable testimony that they ceased their playing in Prague before the recitation of Psalm 92 [well before the Sabbath actually begins]." Sofer, in these few lines, essentially repeated the same arguments that

---
[13]*Ibid.*, Letter 5.

his allies had put forth earlier. He, like the other authors, disputed the claims advanced by the Reformers concerning the use of the organ during worship in Prague. Liebermann had "testified falsely" and reliable testimony contravened the assertion that the organ was used to accompany prayers on the Sabbath. The Prague precedent, in this reading, had no bearing on the question of whether musical instruments could be employed in prayer on the Sabbath or Holidays. The instance of Prague did not even address, much less justify, that practice. The Reformers were therefore wrong to cite it. Up to this juncture, the *Chatam* Sofer's position simply echoes that of his colleagues. Yet, as we have seen, his claim was that the organ was banned on the basis of *Leviticus* XVIII:3 even during the time that the Temple stood. This caused him to expand his arguments beyond those of his contemporaries. "It is true", Sofer conceded, "that in Prague they did employ the organ in song [in the *Altneuschul*] . . . but not in any of the other synagogues in this great city of God." His observation once more parallels that of Scheur. However, he immediately went on to assert: "In addition, even here, when it broke, they did not repair it." This fact was of supreme importance to Sofer. He construed this decision as an acknowledgment on the part of the Prague Jews that the entire custom was based on an error (*ta'ut*). They had mistakenly assumed that the organ (*'ugav*) had been played in the Temple. Consequently, they were not aware of the prohibition against it and believed their use of the organ to be legitimate and countenanced by Jewish law. When they realised that this practice constituted an erroneous custom (*minhag ta'ut*), they ceased employing the organ altogether.

The *Chatam* Sofer clearly felt he had succeeded in doing more than narrowing the potential conclusions to be drawn from the Prague precedent. The Prague congregation's decision to discontinue its previous custom bore witness to their acceptance of his understanding of the rule. It reflected a universal Orthodox recognition of the correctness of his position and refuted Reform claims to the contrary. This, in effect, allowed Sofer to contend that the precedent was in fact no precedent at all! He had, to his own satisfaction, demonstrated that the Prague organ could not be cited as a precedent for employing an organ in a synagogue even during weekdays.[14]

A variant of the *Chatam* Sofer's position concerning Prague also appears in Rabbi Abraham Levy Löwenstamm of Emden's *Tseror Hahayim*, which was published in Amsterdam in 1820. Meyer has identified this work as, "the most extensive polemic against religious reform" published at that time.[15] Löwenstamm labelled the first *responsum* in his collection 'Kol Hashir' (Sound of the Song), and devoted it to the issue of the organ. On the title page he declared, "In this [*responsum*] it is explained that it is forbidden to pray in a synagogue accompanied by the musical instrument called an organ (*Orgel*)." On the first page of his ruling, Löwenstamm quoted the by now familiar passage from Liebermann which asserted that the organ was played in Prague by Jews on the

---

[14]*Ibid.*, Letter 12.
[15]Meyer, *Response to Modernity, op. cit.*, p. 59.

Sabbath itself. He concluded his citation of this precedent with the query, "May one depend upon these words to permit the organ or not?" Not surprisingly, Löwenstamm, in response to his own question, proceeded to marshall, quite apart from the precedent of Prague, an impressive array of classical rabbinic sources to refute the Reformers' reading of the sources and to support his own contention that it was not permissible to play an organ in a synagogue. Like Sofer, he forbade the organ altogether on the basis of *Leviticus* XVIII:3. Ultimately he came to the case of Prague itself. Löwenstamm, as had his other colleagues, acknowledged "that there was an organ in Prague in earlier times". Unlike Sofer, however, he did not argue that the organ had been banned from the time of the Temple itself. Instead, he hypothesised:

> ". . . perhaps the synagogue [in Prague] was constructed with this organ at a time when this custom [of playing the organ] was not part of their [Christian or pagan] worship. In truth, according to what we have heard, this synagogue has been standing since the time of the Second Temple. Consequently, [the organ] was installed legally (*nitkanah b'heter*). The prohibition against imitating the ways of the Gentiles did not apply in this instance, and [the organ] was therefore not moved from its place. However, when it broke, they did not repair it or erect another, because at the time of its destruction, the Gentiles already employed this musical instrument, i.e. the organ, in their houses of worship for the specific purpose of idol worship. [Hence] it is forbidden."[16]

Löwenstamm's view of the case of the Prague organ was identical to the ruling of Sofer. Both banned the organ altogether as "an imitation of the Gentiles". The differences in their dating of the prohibition of organs during Jewish worship should not obscure this fundamental point of legal agreement between them. Indeed, the genuine distinction marking Löwenstamm's treatment of the Prague precedent is his seeming lack of concern with the fact that an organ was played at all in Prague. Unlike his other Orthodox colleagues, including the *Chatam* Sofer, Löwenstamm did not, at this juncture, even bother to brand Liebermann's report about the playing of the organ in the Prague synagogue after the beginning of the Sabbath as a lie. It was sufficient for him to assert that the playing of the organ constituted "an imitation of the Gentiles". The historical conditions which obtained at the moment of the synagogue's construction accounted for the previous practice. An awareness of these conditions indicated why the practice did not comprise a precedent for the playing of the organ in either the present era or the future. The Prague precedent, for Löwenstamm as for Sofer, was no precedent at all. The decision to neither repair nor replace the organ once it was broken indicated that all traditional Jewry recognised the reason for, and universality of, the prohibition. The organ could not be employed in a Jewish house of worship on either a Holiday or a weekday. The custom of Prague, in the end, supported this ruling.

---

[16]Abraham Levy Löwenstamm, *Tseror Hahayim*, Amsterdam 1820, p. 6b.

III. MID-CENTURY DISCUSSIONS

The struggle over the organ in the *responsa* literature of the nineteenth century did not end with *Eileh Divrei Habrit* or with *Tseror Hahayim*. Many prominent nineteenth-century Central-European rabbinical authorities – including Esriel Hildesheimer and Samson Raphael Hirsch among the Orthodox, and Ludwig Philippson and Abraham Geiger among the Reformers – addressed the issue of the organ in their legal writings.[17] However, these writings, in their discussion of the matter, focused exclusively on the literary precedents in the Jewish legal tradition. They did not mention the precedent of the Prague organ.

A major exception to this was Rabbi Zevi Hirsch Chajes of Zolkiew. In his *Minhat Kenaot* (1845), Chajes, in the course of his arguments against the Reformers, cited the case of Prague. In arguing against the organ, he reiterated the positions enumerated by his Orthodox colleagues two decades earlier. He repeated Liebermann's claim that "there was an organ in the *Altneuschul* in an earlier period". However, like Löwenstamm, he contended that "perhaps they established this [practice] before the Gentiles were accustomed to doing this in their houses of worship". He therefore concluded that this precedent was inapposite for the same reason as Löwenstamm, and forbade the organ on the same biblical grounds that his senior colleagues had put forth in their fight against Reform in 1819.[18]

In the 1860s another dispute over the organ erupted in Berlin. Reform members of the community urged that an organ be installed in a synagogue then being constructed in Oranienburgerstraße in the Prussian capital. The governing board of the community sought out rabbinic opinions on the matter.[19] Among them two, written by Michael Sachs of Berlin and David Oppenheim of Nagy-Becskerek, cited disputes over an organ in Prague in their *responsa*. Sachs, a traditionalist sympathetic to the Positive-Historical Judaism of Zacharias Frankel, had served in Prague during the early part of his career. He asserted that an organ had been played there "in the so-called *Neuer Tempel*". However, it had not been used on the Sabbath or Holidays. While the bulk of his *responsum* was primarily devoted to aesthetic objections to the employment of an organ, Sachs, in his discussion of the Prague case, was careful to note that there were "ritual-legal limits" (*ritualgesetzliche Grenzen*) that even the Reformers in the Prague community had been careful to observe. Hence, the employment of the

---

[17]For Hildesheimer, see the *Responsa of Rabbi Esriel*, 'Yoreh Deah', No. 187; and 'Novellae to Yoreh Deah', p. 362. Hirsch's views are contained in his *Shemesh M'rapei*, *Orah Hayim*, No. 2, section 3. Geiger's views, issued on 30th October 1861, were published under the title, 'Gutachten über die rituale Statthaftigkeit der Orgel bei dem synagogalen Gottesdienste', and can be found in his *Nachgelassene Schriften*, ed. by Ludwig Geiger, 5 vols., Berlin 1875–1878, vol. I, pp. 283–295. Philippson's opinion was published as the leading article in his *Allgemeine Zeitung des Judenthums*, No. 48 (17th November 1861).
[18]*Minhat Kenaot*, in *Kol Kitvei Maharatz Hayot*, vol. II, p. 990.
[19]Berliner, 'Literargeschichtliche Belege', *loc. cit.*, p. 48.

organ, even in this one liberal Prague synagogue,[20] was confined to weddings, services for the New Month and Half-Holidays (*Halbfeiertage*), and the service welcoming the Sabbath.[21] As for Oppenheim, he branded the type of claims put forward in *Or Nogah* concerning the organ in Prague as belonging to "the realm of fantasy" (*das Reich der Phantasie*). The organ was not played on the Sabbath or Holidays. In reality, it was only the hymn *L'cha Dodi* which was regularly accompanied by instrumental music, and this was done, in accordance with Jewish law, so that the entry of the Sabbath bride could be appropriately marked and celebrated.[22] Sachs and Oppenheim, like Scheur and others forty years earlier, were not concerned with banning the organ altogether on the grounds that the employment of an organ during worship constituted a violation of *Leviticus* XVIII:3. Instead, their aim was to ban the use of the organ on Sabbaths and Holidays. As their goals were less broad than those of Sofer and others, they were content to demonstrate that Prague could not be employed as a precedent to justify the usage of an organ on those days. Their arguments allowed them to assert, like earlier opponents of the organ, that the case of the Prague organ – whether found in a traditional or a Reform synagogue – constituted no precedent whatsoever.

The "Prague precedent" remained dormant for the next thirty-five years. It was to be revived in the writings of Rabbi David Zvi Hoffmann at the end of the century.

IV. FINAL ECHOES

The problem presented by the use of an organ during worship continued to plague German Orthodox rabbis operating within the context of *Einheitsgemeinden* (unified communities of Orthodox and Liberal Jews) during the last decade of the nineteenth century. In the latter part of that decade, an Orthodox rabbi serving in such a community approached Rabbi David Zvi Hoffmann with the following dilemma. The rabbi, a former student of the *Rabbinerseminar*, reported that his congregation had installed an organ against his wishes. He clearly would not countenance its use on the Sabbath or Holidays. However, the problem, as this rabbi saw it, was whether he could remain in the congregation even if the use

---

[20]Vilimkova, *The Prague Ghetto, op. cit.*, pp. 107–110, has a general discussion of the history of this synagogue building. She notes that the synagogue, known both as "The Temple" and "The Old Shul", was completely demolished in 1867 and subsequently rebuilt as "The Spanish Synagogue". In 1837 it became "the first synagogue in Prague to introduce the reformed rite". As it "allowed for the use of music . . . an organ was installed". See the illustration *Engraving of the Old Synagogue, 1855* reproduced in this article. Meyer, *Response to Modernity, op. cit.*, p. 154, comments that Sachs officiated at this synagogue at the inaugural service in April 1837, and that he "presided over a service that included German sermons, a few German prayers and songs, a choir and organ accompaniment, though in the Prague tradition the instrument was not played on the Sabbath itself".

[21]Sachs's *responsum*, dated 13th November 1861, is found under the title, 'Gutachten des Dr. Michael Sachs gegen die Orgel', in Berliner (ed.), *Zur Lehr' und zur Wehr, op. cit.*, p. 21.

[22]David Oppenheim, 'Die Synagoge und die Musik. Eine antiquarisch-historische Studie', *ibid.*, p. 37.

of the organ was limited to weekday occasions such as weddings. The rabbi, in conclusion, observed that if he did leave the community as a result of this reform, the rabbi selected as his replacement would undoubtedly not only permit the organ on weekdays, but would introduce and embrace other reforms as well. The rabbi wanted to know, in light of all this, what Jewish law required of him.[23]

Hoffmann's response was lengthy, and reflected his command of the issue. At the outset, he noted that this question had been a focal point of contention between Orthodoxy and Reform in the struggle that had ensued between both sides between 1817 and 1821. Hoffmann observed, among many other points, that those who defended the use of the organ did so, in large measure, on the basis of the precedent provided by the organ in Prague. There was no doubt, Hoffmann conceded, that the organ had indeed been employed in Prague as a musical accompaniment to worship in the service immediately prior to the onset of the Sabbath. Inasmuch as Hoffmann, like the *Chatam* Sofer, wanted to ban it altogether on the basis of *Leviticus* XVIII:3, he had to address this precedent and abrogate the seeming justification it offered for this practice for the same reason as several of his Orthodox predecessors seventy years earlier.

In his discussion of the precedent, Hoffmann initially noted that the organ, as his Orthodox colleague in Hamburg had pointed out to him, had actually been employed in Prague's Maisel Synagogue, not the *Altneuschul* as Rabbi Sofer and other respondents in *Eileh Divrei Habrit* had incorrectly asserted.[24] The observation of his Hamburg contemporary was corroborated, Hoffmann reported, by Jakob Wagner, "an expert in Hebrew literature", as well as by his student (and later son-in-law) Alexander Marx. Marx had shown Hoffmann a copy of Shabbatai Bass's *Siftei Yeshenim* which included, as reported above, the 1679 Prague *siddur* with Rabbi Singer's poem prior to *L'cha Dodi*. The content of the poem, Hoffmann felt, contained the key to understanding why this traditional synagogue in Prague had employed the organ in its service welcoming the Sabbath. The relevant lines in the poem, that accounted for the seeming paradox of a traditional congregation's sanctioning even this limited use of the organ, compared the Sabbath and its reception by the community of Israel to the union between a bride and groom. Rabbi Singer's composition, preceded by the instruction that the words should be sung accompanied by an organ and a lyre, clearly drew upon Jewish mystical themes. The lines stated,

> "The Sabbath bride with the groom, in splendour and greatness; if we observe the two of them according to proper rite, law and custom, we will immediately merit redemption; and then God will send a redeemer, in joy he will surely come. This is the day that God has made, the joy of his heart; we will rejoice and be glad in it."

Rabbi Hoffmann therefore reasoned "that because they [were accustomed] and permitted the organ to be played to honour a bride and groom, they also permitted it [to be played] to honour the union of the Sabbath Queen and Israel, for they are to be likened to a bride and groom".

Hoffmann was compelled to concede that the employment of the organ was

---

[23]See Berliner, 'Literargeschichtliche Belege', *loc. cit.*, pp. 58–59.
[24]See note 9 above.

historically part of the accepted "custom and usage" of the Maisel Synagogue. This was because, as the *Chatam* Sofer had maintained, the members of the congregation had mistakenly believed that the organ was among the musical instruments that had been sanctioned for use in the ancient Temple. Furthermore, as Rabbi Löwenstamm had argued, the organ was not associated with Gentile worship at the time the Maisel Synagogue was constructed. Indeed, Hoffmann stated, "it is well known that in earlier times the organ was not so commonly employed in their [the Christians] houses of worship". In a later era, when this was the case, the practice, as both Sofer and Löwenstamm had testified, was "abolished" by the congregation. "As they later abrogated the practice", Hoffmann concluded, "the end proves its beginning. They erred [in employing the organ altogether]." As a "postscript" to this section of his *responsum*, Hoffmann, like Scheur in *Eileh Divrei Habrit*, added that even in past centuries the Maisel Synagogue was alone among all the congregations in Prague in employing the organ. It was the practice of a single congregation and ran counter to accepted custom in every other synagogue among the people of Israel "until the time when the hand of the destroyers grew". The organ in the Maisel Synagogue could not be deemed a sufficient warrant for Jewish custom and practice. The precedent of the Prague organ, for Hoffmann, as for his Orthodox predecessors two generations earlier, was in the end no precedent at all. Hoffmann, in effect, distilled the arguments of these rabbis and reasserted the correctness of their stance seven decades later. Like Sofer, he labelled the use of the organ as both "an imitation of the Gentiles" and "an imitation of the heretics" and forbade its employment in the synagogue on the basis of *Leviticus* XVIII:3.[25]

Precisely because he viewed this issue as critical to Orthodox identity in Germany, Hoffmann was not content to express a lone opinion on the matter. He wrote to several Orthodox colleagues asking them to respond to his writing on the subject. Hoffmann undoubtedly wanted to enlist their support. Among the replies was that of Rabbi Marcus Horovitz of Frankfurt a. Main. Horovitz, in responding to his close friend from student days, addressed the issue of the precedent created by the organ in Prague. He began by asserting that because their teacher, Rabbi Esriel Hildesheimer, had already ruled negatively on the matter of the organ, he would not disagree. However, he felt compelled to dissent from the notion that the organ was forbidden on account of *Leviticus* XVIII:3, basing this dissension, in part, on the precedent of the Prague organ. Horovitz wrote: "On weekdays, it is clear that they [played the organ] in the holy congregation of Prague with the sanction of the greatest authorities of earlier times. And who will come after them and contend that it is forbidden on account of *Leviticus* XVIII:3." The rabbis, not the Bible, had prohibited the use of the organ on Sabbath and Holidays and for the "faithful", those committed to Orthodox Judaism, this was sufficient reason. Horovitz did not countenance the use of the organ in the synagogue. His *responsum* makes clear his unalterable opposition, at least as far as far as Sabbaths and Holidays were concerned. However, the precedent of the Prague organ caused him to disagree with the

---

[25]Hoffmann, *op. cit.*, No. 16.

Procession of Prague Jews in 1716, marking the birth of Prince Leopold, successor to the throne
Under number 19 in the illustration can be seen the portable organ used on that occasion

Engraving of the Old Synagogue in Prague, 1855

By courtesy of the Jewish Museum, Prague

reasoning his friend and colleague Hoffmann offered for the ban. Prague, in Rabbi Horovitz's opinion, demonstrated that *Leviticus* XVIII:3 could not be cited as a justification for the prohibition.[26]

Horovitz's opinion closed this nineteenth-century chapter in the ongoing struggle over the use of the organ in Central-European communal worship. He ultimately came to assume the same position which the Prague Rabbinic Court and Rabbi Scheur had put forth on this issue in *Eileh Divrei Habrit*, and which Rabbis Sachs and Oppenheim had advanced later in the century. Rabbi Hoffmann, in contrast, took the same stance that Sofer and Löwenstamm had adopted. The disagreement between these two Orthodox colleagues provided a fitting conclusion to the debate the precedent of the Prague organ had engendered in nineteenth-century Jewish legal writings.

V. CONCLUSION AND FINAL CONSIDERATIONS

The dispute over the Prague organ at the beginning of the nineteenth century between warring Reform and Orthodox camps reflects a community engaged in the nascent stages of denominational struggles. Liebermann and Chorin, no less than Sofer or Löwenstamm, were enmeshed in tradition. They were, therefore, committed to debating the issue of the organ within the framework of a traditional Jewish legal system that ascribed an authoritative role to the legal convention of precedent. Consequently, the precedent provided by Prague was crucial to them. Their attention to it reflects a Reform Judaism that saw itself as part of the historical community of rabbinic Judaism. The lack of interdenominational debate over this precedent in Central Europe by the end of the nineteenth century reflects a Reform Judaism that no longer defined itself in legal categories, employing other arguments to defend and justify Reform practices. The evolution and direction of Reform Judaism in the course of that century are foreshadowed in the legal literature of 1818 and its use of the precedent of the Prague organ. The absence of such literature by the 1890s reveals that Reform Judaism ultimately came to abjure law as a defining characteristic of the movement and marks its departure from the classical legal canon of rabbinic civilisation. This study of the Prague organ in nineteenth-century Jewish legal literature thus helps to illuminate the course of Reform Judaism during that century. It was a Reform, as Gerald Blidstein has observed, that was no longer tied to "the authority of precedent" to sanction its actions.[27]

Conversely, the Orthodox reliance upon precedent as a source for Jewish law compelled them to respond to Reform claims concerning the Prague organ as soon as they were put forth. The continuing debate Prague engendered at the end of the century between Hoffmann and Horovitz testified not only to the vital and authoritative role that precedent occupied for both these men, but to the continuing commitment they both held as Orthodox rabbis to this legal

---

[26]Marcus Horovitz, *Matte Levi*, Orah Hayim, No. 6.
[27]Gerald Blidstein, 'Early Reform and Its Approach', in *Tradition*, vol. XI, No. 3 (1970), p. 85.

convention. Indeed, the continuing vitality of precedent in Jewish law in general, as well as the relevance of the Prague precedent in particular, are evidenced in the continued citation of the Prague organ in twentieth-century rabbinic discussions of the issue.[28] Should the issue arise in the future, others may undoubtedly have occasion to employ it.

Accepted custom and usage, in Jewish law as in other legal systems, remains a principal source of law. However, as has been demonstrated here, precedent can seldom be applied in a direct and uncontroversial way. Different rabbis, whether in identical or in distinct denominational camps, depending upon their own goals and convictions, understand and affirm the validity of a precedent in disparate ways. This study of the precedent of the Prague organ and the dispute surrounding it in the nineteenth century indicates that precedent gives rise to judicial disagreement. The unresolved nature of that debate as well as the conflict over the meaning of the precedent only underscores the role that judicial interpretation plays in the legal process. An analysis of the dispute over the Prague organ in nineteenth-century legal literature provides insights into the character and evolution of Jewish religious denominationalism in Central Europe during that period. It also casts light on the commitments of these movements and illuminates something of the character and directions of Jewish law in the modern period.

---

[28]See for example, Rabbi Jechiel Ya'akov Weinberg, *Seridei Eish, Orah Hayim*, No. 12; and Rabbi Aharon Epstein's 1933 volume of *responsa, Kapei Aharon, Orah Hayim*, No. 20:1. I would like to thank Marc Shapiro for pointing out this latter source to me.

Jewish Ceremonial Silver from Germany in the Jewish Historical Museum, Amsterdam

BY EDWARD VAN VOOLEN, IRENE FABER AND ANNETTE WEBER

The following contribution is the result of a project initiated by Edward van Voolen in close co-operation with colleagues at the Jewish Museums in Amsterdam and Frankfurt a. Main. Authorship has been the joint responsibility of all three authors cited.

The Jewish ceremonial silver, presently comprising 385 objects, is one of the most important treasures in the collections of the Jewish Historical Museum in Amsterdam.[1] A small catalogue published on the occasion of the opening of the Museum in 1932 lists a number of silver ritual objects dating from the seventeenth and eighteenth centuries, including several that were made in Germany.[2] An inventory book, which was used until the German occupation of the Netherlands in May 1940 and reappeared only in 1987, mentions in total 785 objects.[3] The collection, with the exception of a number of private loans, was seized shortly after the capitulation of the Netherlands and taken to Germany. Only a fraction – approximately a quarter – was later recovered and returned. Not until 1955 was the Museum reopened in its original home, the former city-gate of Amsterdam, later 'De Waag', on Nieuwmarkt.

Since 1987 the Museum has been housed in the four monumental, completely renovated former Ashkenazic Synagogues dating from the seventeenth and eighteenth centuries, opposite the famous Sephardic Synagogue (1672–1675) which is still in use today. The collection is presented in these original surroundings and some of the objects are still used occasionally in religious services.

The Republic of the Seven United Provinces, with Amsterdam for centuries its leading city, was justly famed far beyond its borders as a centre for goldsmiths and silversmiths, whose output was considerable in terms of quantity and quality alike. In this centre of world trade, products and treasures from abroad were also prized. The first Spanish-Portuguese Jews settled in Amsterdam shortly before 1600, attracted by the economic prospects available to them there. They were valued by the authorities for their knowledge of languages and their economic

---

[1] On the history of the collection see Edward van Voolen, 'Das Jüdische Historische Museum in Amsterdam', in *Anzeiger des Germanischen Nationalmuseums* (1989), pp. 27–34; idem, *Guide to the Jewish Historical Museum Amsterdam*, The Hague 1988.
[2] *Joods Historisch Museum Amsterdam*, Amsterdam 1932. A total of 177 objects were listed.
[3] *Inventaris Joods Historisch Museum Amsterdam*, Amsterdam 1937.

links with relatives in the Iberian peninsula and the other centres of European trade such as Bordeaux, Venice, Byzantium, Antwerp and Hamburg and later also London, Brazil and New Amsterdam (New York). From about 1630 on, the relatively favourable living conditions in Amsterdam – no compulsory wearing of distinguishing marks such as yellow patches, and no restriction to certain residential areas such as the Jewish quarters in Germany and the ghettos in Italy – also attracted Jews from Central Europe. They came particularly from Germany, ravaged by the Thirty Years' War, and from Poland, devastated by the Ukrainian army leader Bogdan Chmelnicki during the years 1645 to 1648. A very few were able to bring their money with them; they included the donor of the marble Torah ark in the Great Synagogue (1671), Abraham bar Isaak Auerbach, a scholar and court Jew from Coesfeld near Münster.[4] Most, however, arrived as poor as they had been in their country of origin. Among the most important restrictions on the Jews, which affected the poor most of all, was a law of 1632 which forbade them from becoming members of the guilds. Ceremonial silver objects were therefore made by non-Jewish silversmiths on behalf of the Jews.

As suppliers of victuals to nobility and princes at home and abroad, Sephardic Jews in particular had trade links with relatives and Jewish colleagues throughout Europe. The records thus contain well-known names such as Gompertz, Oppenheimer and Wertheimer. Ashkenazic Jews visited the fairs in Frankfurt and Leipzig as agents because of their mastery of languages.[5] It is likely that this was the route by which the superb Augsburg plate and goblet came into the possession of the wealthy Sephardic community in Amsterdam.[6]

Another important reason explaining the presence of German silver in Jewish communities in the Dutch provinces was the fact that until the nineteenth century not only community members, but also religious leaders, came to the Netherlands from the German-speaking lands. A Silesian ewer and basin were for instance brought to the Netherlands by a German-Jewish refugee family in the 1930s. In 1734 it had been presented by grateful students to their teacher in Glogau and had remained in the possession of the family in Germany. The teacher of the students, Aryeh Loeb, later became Chief Rabbi of Amsterdam. Thus, an early connection with the Netherlands was later re-established.[7] Rabbi Samuel Berish Berenstein, who came to Holland in 1802, received from his home community a beautiful eighteenth-century Augsburg cup as a gift.[8]

We do not know how most of the other silverwork in the museum's collection came here. Emigration, pogroms and flight have surely been the most important reasons over the last three centuries. Besides the Torah scrolls, ceremonial silver comprises the most valuable items, guarded carefully by pious community

---

[4]Edward van Voolen, *A Golden Trail. Dutch Jewish Culture in the Golden Age*, Amsterdam 1993, p. 13. A book with his prayers of repentance and thanksgiving was produced by Joseph Athias in 1677. See Leo Fuks and Renate G. Fuks-Mansfeld, *Hebrew Typography in the Northern Netherlands*, vol. II, Leiden 1987, No. 397.
[5]Jonathan I. Israel, *European Jewry in the Age of Mercantilism 1550–1750*, London–Oxford 1985, p. 173.
[6]Inv. No. *JHM* B 95 and B 96, see in text.
[7]Inv. No. *JHM* 734, see in text.
[8]Inv. No. *JHM* 537, see in text.

members and indeed the whole community. Jewish family names as well as the historical sources reveal the influential role played by Central-European Jews in the Netherlands to the present day.[9]

The objects are listed in chronological order.

JHM 121 Torah shield
Master: Daniel Michael (?); Augsburg, *c.* 1675.
Silver, embossed, chased, engraved, partial gilt; height: 16.5 cm/width: 15.5 cm.
Hall-marks: maker's mark DM = Daniel Michael (?) (Augsburg, born *c.* 1641, master 1671, died 1718; No. 1709 in Seling[10]), city mark Augsburg (unclear).
Hebrew inscription on plates: Shavuot / Pesach / Hanukkah / Purim / Sukkoth / 17 Tammuz / Rosh Hashanah / Yom Kippur.

The cartouche-shaped shield contains three rectangular apertures placed one above the other, surrounded by delicately embossed leaf and flower ornamentation in relief. The largest of the three rectangles in the centre contains four interchangeable plaques engraved with the Hebrew names of eight Holidays. In the topmost rectangle there is, abbreviated, the inscription "Crown of the Torah" which shows the intended use of the shield. The lowest rectangle has only two narrow, vertical apertures.

The decoration is typical of Augsburg silver of the period. It is similar to that on shield *JHM* 562, also made in Augsburg in *c.* 1675. On the latter, a non-Jewish iconography of three putti can be seen.[11]

The shields originally served as wall calendars giving the days, months and years.[12] The secular piece was made in a Christian silver-workshop and became a ritual object only with the additions which the Jewish owner ordered to be carried out.

JHM B 95 Ewer
Master: David Bessmann; Augsburg, 1652–1653.
Silver, embossed, chased, partial gilt; height: 43.5 cm / width: 28 cm.
Hall-marks: maker's mark DB = David Bessmann (Augsburg, master about 1640, died 1677; Seling, No. 1502), city mark Augsburg 1652–1653 (Seling, No. 79).
Loan: *Portugees-Israelietische Gemeente*, Amsterdam.

---

[9]See J. Michman, H. Beem and D. Michman, *Pinkas Geschiedenis van de joodse gemeenschap in Nederland*, Ede 1992.

[10]H. Seling, *Die Kunst der Augsburger Goldschmiede 1529–1868*, vols. I-III, Munich 1980. Hereafter referred to in text as Seling.

[11]*JHM* 562, Torah shield, master unidentified, Augsburg, *c.* 1675; silver, brass (plate), embossed, chased, partial gilt (height: 26 cm / width: 20 cm); hall-marks: maker's mark and city mark Augsburg (?) unclear. For further description and illustration see Irene Faber, Edward van Voolen and Annette Weber, 'Judaica deutscher Gold- und Silberschmiede', in *Kunst und Antiquitäten*, 10 (1993), p. 34.

[12]Yerahmiel Cohen, 'Torah Breastplates from Augsburg in the Israel Museum', in *Israel Museum News*, 14 (1978), pp. 74–85.

JHM B 96 Basin
Master: Abraham Warnberger II; Augsburg, 1665–1670.
Silver, embossed, chased, partial gilt; length: 84 cm / width: 74 cm / depth: 8 cm.
Hall-marks: maker's mark AW = Abraham II Warnberger (born in Augsburg 1632, master 1664, died 1704; Seling, No. 1659), city mark Augsburg 1665–1670 (Seling, No. 102 or No. 103).
Inscription: initials CEMZB on the back.
Loan: *Portugees-Israelietische Gemeente*, Amsterdam.

In the centre section of the oval plate there is an embossed relief showing the judgement of Paris. The broad rim is formed in auricular style with shells and has a scalloped edge. The picture tells in vivid fashion the story of the choice made by Paris – shown in the centre – which falls on Aphrodite.

In terms of style this superb Augsburg plate can be classified as Augsburg baroque (1630–1660). The style can be compared to a presentation plate by Jakob II Plank, dated around 1650, in the Kremlin Museum in Moscow, which also depicts a scene from mythology (probably Orpheus and the nereids).[13] Seling identifies the mark AW (set one above the other) as an early mark of Abraham Warnberger II.[14] Warnberger was married to the daughter of David Bessmann, the silversmith of ewer *JHM* B 95.

The ewer has an embossed base consisting of two levels decorated with small, embossed waves. A nereid with a double fish-tail emerges from the base as if lifting herself out of the sea. Above her head she is carrying the shell-shaped ewer, decorated in auricular style with shells and punched shell ornamentation. The highly arched lid has a scalloped edge and contains a shell in the middle. A thin, twisting serpent, with its head resting on the lid, serves as a handle. The ewer fits in well with Bessmann's work in around 1650. He produced a number of ewers and basins.[15]

The basin and ewer are on loan from the Portuguese-Jewish congregation in Amsterdam and are used in the synagogue liturgy for the washing of hands of the *kohanim*. The initials CEMZB probably refer to a previous, non-Jewish owner. However, we do not know the identity of the donor, or when the ewer and basin were given to the community. Until now, no reference to Sephardic families with contacts to Ashkenazic court Jews, who might have served as intermediaries, has been found in the documents. It is probable that the objects were given as a donation on the occasion of the inauguration of the synagogue in Amsterdam in 1675.[16] In any event, it happened at a time when the depiction of antique mythology did not meet with objections from within the Jewish community.

[13] Inv. No. 19138; Seling, *op. cit.*, illustration 501.
[14] Seling, *op. cit.*, Supplement to vol. III, No. 1659a; letter from Seling to JHM, 13th July 1994.
[15] For example, basin by David Bessmann in Wadsworth Atheneum, Hartford, CT, 'Alexander and Darius', dated Augsburg around 1652. Discussed and illustrated in L. Horvitz Roth (ed.), *J. Pierpont Morgan Collector*, New York 1987, Cat. No. 17, illustration p. 87 (Inv. No. 1917.255, 66 x 56 cm). Some ewers by Bessmann can be found in the Kremlin Museum, Moscow (Inv. Nos. 2244, 1474, 1473, 1472). See Seling, *op. cit.*, No. 1502 and Supplement No. 1502a.
[16] Israel, *European Jews*, *op. cit.*, p. 178, refers to the role of Ashkenazic traders in precious metals. Perhaps they supplied this ewer and basin to the wealthy Sephardic merchant, who donated it in turn to the synagogue. See van Voolen, *A Golden Trail*, *op. cit.*, p. 29.

JHM 102 Kiddush cup

Master: Johann Beckert III; Augsburg, 1690–1694.
Silver, embossed, stippled, engraved, interior gilt; height: 8 cm / diameter: 6.5 cm.
Hall-marks: maker's mark IB = Johann Beckert III (born 1654, master 1684, died 1704; Seling, Suppl., No. 1799^b), city mark Augsburg 1690–1694 (Seling, No. 145).
Dutch and Hebrew inscription: "In memory of long years of friendly neighbourly relations between the esteemed gentlemen J.M. Chumaceiro (long may he live) and Jacob Meyer Jacobson (may he rest in peace) / Donation by the son of the deceased, I.J. Jacobson Jr., on Friday evening the 14th Teweth 5637, when the Torah section Vayechi [*Genesis* XLVII:28–L:26] was read" (= 29th December 1876).

The round, slightly conical and straight-sided cup has a double-chased line running round the lower edge. Up to the smooth rim near the top, the side is supplied with a thick, fine-grained punching which classifies the cup as a snakeskin or fishskin cup. The smooth rim beneath the lip, which is also separated from the punched area by a double-chased line, contains the Dutch and Hebrew inscriptions.

The inscription refers to the banker Jacob Meyer Jacobson (Rotterdam 1807 – Amsterdam 1876), teacher of the banker Georg Rosenthal (1828–1909), who was born in Hanover and founded the Amsterdam *Lipmann-Rosenthal-Bank* (1859) and the *Bibliotheca Rosenthaliana* in 1880.[17] His son Isaac Jacob Jacobson (1839 – Amsterdam 1907) was administrator of the Jewish Association Talmud Torah in Amsterdam from 1879. Josef Mendes Chumaceiro (1818–Amsterdam 1887) was *chasan* of the Portuguese community between 1846 and 1885, and lived near Jacobson on Jonas Daniel Meijerplein in Amsterdam (numbers 7 and 11 respectively).[18]

This type of fishskin cup was a popular model in Augsburg during the seventeenth and eighteenth centuries. A similar cup, of equal size, with the Hebrew inscription *Pesach* and made by the same master IB, is to be found in the Israel Museum, Jerusalem, Feuchtwanger Collection.[19] Seling identifies IB as Johann Beckert III and mentions two fishskin cups by him.

JHM B 742 Torah shield

Master: AH; Halle a.d. Saale, 1716.
Silver, partial gilt, embossed, engraved, stippled, precious stone/rock-crystal trimming, reverse with red velvet lining; height: 39 cm / width: 34 cm.

---

[17]N.P. van den Berg, 'Een geschenk aan de stad Amsterdam. Achtergronden van de Bibliotheca Rosenthaliana', in *Jaarboek Amstelodamum*, 84 (1987), pp. 131–158.

[18]References kindly provided by Dr. Jelka Kröger, City Archives, Amsterdam.

[19]Description and illustration in I. Schachar, *Jewish Tradition in Art. The Feuchtwanger Collection of Judaica. The Israel Museum*, Jerusalem 1981, Cat. No. 452.

Hall-marks: master's mark AH (Rosenberg[20] 2324), city mark Halle (R 2307), year mark I = 1716 (cf. R 2308 – 2312), inspection mark 1728–1769 (R 2313).
Loan: *Nederlands Israelietische Hoofdsynagoge*, Arnhem.

The shield, which is almost quadratic, has a dramatically curved outline embellished with small flowers. The large box in the centre of the shield, adorned with precious stones, once held the plaques which showed on which Holidays the Torah scrolls were to be read. Directly above the box are three crowns of foliage also decorated with precious stones. The box is flanked by the figures of Moses and Aaron, who are standing in front of large pillars on which lions are seated. The lions hold volutes bearing a shell as the upper end of the shield. Originally three medallions hung on the shield, probably indicating the donor, the date and the occasion for the gift.[21]

This Torah shield, similar in type to the Hamburg shields of the first half of the eighteenth century,[22] is a work of very high quality produced by the Halle master AH, for whom Rosenberg provides evidence of twenty-two works on behalf of the Saxonian court. According to the year mark the shield was made in 1716, and the inspection mark reveals that it remained in Halle until 1728, suggesting that the client came from among the well-to-do Jews of that town.

The Jewish community in Halle comprised no more than twenty families in the first half of the eighteenth century.[23] However, it included such significant and wealthy members as Assur Marx, who supplied metal to the mint of Elector August II of Saxony (1670–1733). Assur Marx also dealt in silver and jewels. From 1700 until his death in 1730 he was head of the Jewish Community of Halle, and in 1700 he successfully organised the purchase of a house in which to establish a synagogue. It seems reasonable to assume that the Torah shield was ordered for this synagogue. The illustration of Moses and Aaron on the shield may be a reference to Assur Marx, since these two figures are frequently found on the title pages of Hebrew books, and Assur Marx not only possessed one of the biggest collections of Jewish books in the German-speaking area, but also supported Hebrew printing in Halle.[24]

JHM 537 *Kiddush* cup
Master: Albrecht Biller; Augsburg, 1717–1718.
Silver, embossed, engraved; height: 20 cm / diameter: 11 cm.
Hall-marks: master's mark AB = Albrecht Biller (born 1663, master about 1681, died 1720; Seling, No. 1777), city mark Augsburg 1717–1718 (Seling, No. 177 or No. 178).

---

[20]M. Rosenberg, *Der Goldschmiede Merkzeichen*, 3rd extended and illustrated edn., vols. I-IV, Frankfurt a. Main–Berlin 1922–1928. Hereafter referred to in text as R.
[21]See illustration in the journal *Menorah*, 3 (1925), p. 101.
[22]See E. Schliemann, *Die Goldschmiede Hamburgs*, vols. I-III, Hamburg 1985, illustrations 842 and 845 (referred to hereafter in text as Schliemann).
[23]Guido Kisch, *Rechts- und Sozialgeschichte der Juden in Halle 1686–1730*, Berlin 1970, pp. 28–30, on the synagogue pp. 104f.
[24]Kisch, *op. cit.*, pp. 61f.

Hebrew inscription: "Gift from the Jewish Community Hanover to Rabbi Samuel Berenstein/Rabbi in Groningen/15 Ellul 5564" (Wednesday 22nd August 1804).

The round, slightly conical ball-foot cup with lid stands on three ball-feet. Above the foot, under the lip and on the lid it carries a border decoration of embossed leaf and strapwork in the style known as *Bérain*, which was popular in Augsburg about 1710. Like many *kiddush* cups made in Augsburg, it has a lid with several ridges which decrease in size from bottom to top. It is crowned with a ball on a narrow neck. The Hebrew inscription is engraved around the cup in the smooth middle section.

Samuel Berish Berenstein, born in Hanover in 1767, became Rabbi of Groningen in 1802. In 1812, during the French occupation, he was called to Amsterdam as *Grandrabbin de l'Arrondissement Consistorial Zuiderzee*. In 1815 he followed his father-in-law Jacob Moses Löwenstamm as Chief Rabbi in Amsterdam, where he lived until his death in 1838.[25] Hanover presented Berenstein with a *kiddush* cup in 1804 as well as 1819 (see *JHM* 153 below).

JHM B 155 *Havdalah* candleholder and drawer for spices
Master: unknown; Frankfurt a. Main, *c.* 1725.
Silver, cast, embossed; height: 29.8 cm / diameter: 8 cm.
Hall-marks: unmarked.
Loan: *Gemeentemuseum*, The Hague.

On a round-cast, stepped and lobed base, a small bearded Jewish manikin stands as atlante for a *havdalah* holder and drawer for spices. It wears the costume of the Frankfurt Jews in the seventeenth and eighteenth centuries. In its right hand it holds the plaited *havdalah* candle which is lit at the end of Sabbath; in the left it holds the cup for the blessing of the wine at this ceremony. The drawer section on its head carries the four supporting rods which rise from the corners. They are surrounded by a fleur-de-lis balustrade worked *à jour*. A *repoussé* mascaron forms the end of each rod. Fitted over the rods is the actual, movable candle holder, also surrounded by a fleur-de-lis balustrade worked *à jour*.

In construction and ornamentation the *havdalah* candleholder resembles the Frankfurt candleholders of Jeremias Zobel (1670–1741) and Röttger Herfurth (1722–1776) in the Jewish Museum, New York.[26] A holder attributed to Johann Adam Boller (1679–1732) in the Israel Museum in Jerusalem has an almost identical Jewish manikin with a *kiddush* cup and spice box as attributes, as well as

---

[25]His portrait is reproduced by M.H. Gans, *Memorbook. History of Dutch Jewry from the Renaissance to 1940*, Baarn 1971, p. 314.

[26]Stephen S. Kayser and Guido Schoenberger, *Jewish Ceremonial Art*, Philadelphia 1959, Cat. 96 (Inv. Nos. jm 36–52). For the Herfurth example see also Frankfurt a. Main, Jüdisches Museum, *Was übrig blieb. Das Museum Jüdischer Altertümer in Frankfurt 1922–1938*, exhibition catalogue, Frankfurt a. Main 1988, Cat. No. 27 with other references. Added to this list should be Herfurth's *havdalah* candleholder in the Victoria and Albert Museum; see Michael E. Keen, *Jewish Ritual Art*, London 1991, Cat. No. 55.

the same balustrades and mascarons on the rods.[27] In the place of the spice drawer, Boller has four further manikins at each corner of the lower plate; these function as atlante figures for the lid plate with the rods. In stylistic terms the two Jewish manikins are so closely related as to make it probable that both were made from the same mould. The drawer for spices for this delicate holder in the *Joods Historisch Museum* is unusually solid. Its simple, cast form with large silver knob belongs stylistically more to the beginning of the nineteenth century. Most probably it was introduced during a later repair, since the soldering is irregular and the remnants of a border worked *à jour* can still be seen on the inside.

JHM B24 Case for Megillat Esther
Master: Christian Beyl; Breslau, 1727–1737.
Silver, embossed, engraved, stamped; height: 34 cm / diameter: 5 cm.
Hall-marks: maker's mark CB = Christian Beyl (master 1725–1778),[28] St. John's head = Breslau, year mark C = 1727–1737.
Hebrew inscription: "This scroll was left by Isaak Abraham Zvi son of Abraham Moses Lehren for our community in the year 5679" (=1919).
Loan: *Nederlands Israelietische Hoofdsynagoge*, Amsterdam.

The cylindrical silver case with relief illustrations contains a parchment scroll with the handwritten text of the Book of Esther, which has no illustrations. The case is divided into two pictorial fields by a wreath running around the centre. Both above and below, these fields end with a border strip consisting of several ridges. The upper one shows two striding stags and above them two flying putti with a basket of flowers and a garland. Beneath them stands Haman in Hussar's uniform with the scales for the lots before the Persian King Ahasverus, who is enthroned beneath an enormous canopy.

The stag motif is probably a reference to the person who placed the order: of the few Jews who had the right of residence in Breslau in the first half of the eighteenth century, the name Hirsch appears in the case of two families in the 1725 register.[29] The client may have been either Philipp Lazarus Hirschel, imperial court Jew, who had the right of residence in Breslau and who lived there with a large household which included a scribe; or Benedikt Hirschel from Glogau, imperially privileged Jew and plenipotentiary of the imperial *Oberfaktor* Emanuel Oppenheimer (d. 1721) of Vienna, who also kept a large household.[30]

Isaac, son of Abraham Moses Lehren, was born on 9th September 1859. His sixtieth birthday in 1919 was surely the occasion for his gift to the Jewish community in Amsterdam. He was a grandson of Jacob Meier Lehren (1793–1861) who, together with his brothers Akiba (1795–1876) and Zvi Hirsch

---

[27] Inv. No. 124/396. See Jerusalem, Israel Museum, *Towers of Spice*, exhibition catalogue, Jerusalem 1982, p. 56; and C. Benjamin, *The Stieglitz Collection. The Israel Museum*, Jerusalem 1987, Cat. No. 67/II.
[28] E. Hintze, *Die Breslauer Goldschmiede*, Breslau 1906, table II and IV.
[29] Bernhard Brilling, 'Regesten zur Geschichte der Juden in Breslau vom 16.-18. Jahrhundert (1555–1749)', in *Hamburger Mittel- und Ostdeutsche Forschungen*, 7 (1970), pp. 129–152, 114.
[30] *Ibid.*, pp. 114f.

(1784–1853), originated from Lehrensteinfeld in Württemberg. They founded a banking house in Amsterdam in 1822, and played an important role as benefactors for Palestine and other religious causes.[31]

JHM 734 Ewer and Basin
Master: unknown; Glogau/Silesia, 1734–1735.
Silver, embossed, chased, engraved, stamped; ewer: height: 23.5 cm / width: 17.5 cm / diameter: 10.5 cm; basin: diameter: 38.5 cm.
Hall-marks: unmarked (Jewish silversmith?).
Hebrew inscription on basin: "To our schoolmaster and rabbi, learned head of Golat Ariel, Aryeh 'of noble family', our teacher, the Rabbi Aryeh Loeb, head of the Rabbinical Court and leader of the *Yeshivah* of the holy community. Groß-Glogau, according to the short system [of chronology] 'may his life increase in pleasantness' " (= chronogram 494 = 1734).
Inscription on the back: AEG VK (unidentified).
Hebrew inscription on ewer: "From prominent youths studying at the *Yeshiva* of Glogau, a double gift, according to the short system" (= chronogram 495 = 1735).

The set consists of a round, shallow basin with a rim and a conical ewer. Both pieces are richly decorated: the foot-ring of the basin consists of a wreath of twisted *repoussé* pipes and bead work, the motif being repeated on the ewer. The centre has delicately engraved acanthus foliage. The base of the ewer with its scalloped edge and pipe-shaped decoration repeats the ornamentation of the foot-ring, making it appear as though the ewer is actually growing out of the basin. The baluster shaft with engraved acanthus leaves is separated from the base of the ewer by means of a foot-ring; the nodus has an engraved scale pattern. The scale pattern and acanthus leaves appear again on the corpus of the ewer, the shoulder area of which is marked with a ridged ring. Above it the rim begins which is engraved with acanthus foliage and has a smooth extended spout. The smooth, S-shaped handle is mounted on an equally curved abutment.

During the making of the set, a place was apparently reserved for the current inscription on the rim of the basin, so that we can be certain of the client and the date. The inscription reveals that the piece was a gift from the *yeshiva* students of Glogau to the Rabbi Aryeh Loeb in Glogau in 1734–1735. Aryeh Loeb ben Saul (1690–1755) was the leader of the *yeshiva* and also Chief Rabbi of Groß-Glogau between 1734 and 1739. In 1740 he was chosen as Chief Rabbi of Amsterdam.[32]

The first article of the new statutes of the Glogau community, confirmed by the Royal Office in 1688, stated that "the community commits itself to finance the study of twelve students, eight gifted foreigners and four native inhabitants without means".[33] This was presumably a reference to the *yeshiva* mentioned in

---

[31] Van den Berg, 'Een geschenk', *loc. cit.*, pp. 131–158, esp. p. 137.
[32] Franz D. Lucas and Margret Heitmann, *Stadt des Glaubens. Geschichte und Kultur der Juden in Glogau*, Hildesheim 1991, pp. 233–237.
[33] *Ibid.*, p. 191.

the inscription. The Jewish community had obtained its first privileges as far back as the thirteenth century, and since then the Jews had enjoyed over six hundred years of unbroken rights of residence. Between 1526 and 1740 Glogau was part of the Austrian Habsburg Empire. In 1636 the synagogue on Bailstraße was established, being renovated in 1676 and 1714.[34] In 1725, 278 Jewish families lived in the thirty-six houses of the Jewish quarter, with a total of 1,564 Jewish inhabitants. At the end of the eighteenth century, Groß-Glogau was one of the most respected communities in Central Europe.[35] Since the items bear neither a maker's mark nor a city mark, but were made for a Jewish client from Glogau, it is possible that, after the Silesian Toleration Edict of 1628, they were made by a Jewish goldsmith. This edict permitted the work of Jewish goldsmiths for Jewish clients, though the works were not allowed to be marked. In Glogau we have proof that there were Jewish goldsmiths since 1686.[36] Stylistically and typologically the piece belongs to Silesia, since the pipe-shaped decoration is typical of this region and there was once a comparable set in the Breslau *Landschul*.[37] Another comparable set, made in 1702 by the German master Johann Georg Lux, is in the possession of the Prague Pinkas synagogue.[38]

The Levite ewer and basin were presented to the *Joods Historisch Museum* by friends in memory of Sigmund Seligsberger (born in Würzburg in 1855) and Sara Seligsberger-Wolf (born in Zell a. Main in 1885), who emigrated from Germany to Holland in the 1930s and were murdered in Sobibor in 1943. Surviving family retain their right to reclaim these objects.

JHM 565 Torah finials
Master: Hans Hinrich Krumstroh; Hamburg, 1740–1767.
Silver, embossed, stippled, cast, engraved; height: 41 cm / width: 18 cm.
Hall-marks: master's mark HHK = Hans Hinrich Krumstroh (Hamburg, active 1730–1770, Schliemann, No. F394),[39] city mark Hamburg 1740–1767 (Schliemann, p. 11).
Hebrew inscription: "This is a gift from the eminent Isaac/son of Jacob Gans z.l. in the Synagogue/of the community of Celle."

The spherical finials are situated on a smooth and straight shaft, one of which bears an inscription. The spherical shape stands on a round base, and is decorated with open-work rocaille shapes which alternately surround a heart, a

---

[34]*Ibid.*, p. 266.
[35]Thus Joseph Heller in *Encyclopaedia Judaica*, vol. VII, Berlin 1931, cols. 440–441.
[36]Bernhard Brilling, 'Geschichte des jüdischen Goldschmiedegewerbes in Schlesien', in *Hamburger Mittel- und Ostdeutsche Forschungen*, 6 (1967), pp. 163–221.
[37]Nuremberg, Germanisches Nationalmuseum, *Schlesische Goldschmiedearbeiten im Germanischen Nationalmuseum*, exhibition catalogue, ed. by Karl Pechstein, Nuremberg 1990, Cat. Nos. 31, 34 (Inv. Nos. GNM HG 12586, HG 10469). On the Breslau *Landsynagoge* see Alfred Grotte, 'Jüdische Sakralkunst in Schlesien', in *Menorah*, 4 (1926), p. 277 (with illustration).
[38]K. Pechstein, in Berthold Roland (ed.), *Judaica aus dem staatlichen Jüdischen Museum in Prag*, Mainz 1991, Cat. No. 49.
[39]Schliemann, *op. cit.*, p. 350. Also made by Krumstroh and with a similar form are finials in the possession of the museum with the Hamburg city mark 1760–1784 (*JHM* 564).

ewer and a basin. Little bells hang from the volutes which project all around. On the narrowing neck sits a crown, adorned with little bells and coloured imitation gemstones. Four high bows come together in the centre of the crown and encircle a bell there. Atop the bell in the centre is a pine-cone with leaf motifs. The neck has been reworked during restoration.

The Hebrew inscription ascribes these finials with a particular historical significance relating to the Jewish community in Celle close to Hanover. It was there that the court agent Isaac Jacob Gans lived (1728–1797). The progenitor of the Gans family was Salomon Gans (*c.* 1674–1733), who had lived in Celle since 1689 as one of the ten so-called *Schutzjuden* who were given rights of residence there. He was the father of Jacob Gans (1702–1770) and the grandfather of court agent Isaac Jacob Gans (1728–1797). Isaac's daughter Madel (1747–1825) was married to Abraham Herz Cohen, son of the Hanoverian court agent Herz Leffman Cohen and Serchen Wertheimer. Isaac Jacob Gans's grandson was the famous Berlin jurist and historian Eduard Gans (1798–1839).

The Jewish cemetery in Celle contains a number of richly decorated gravestones belonging to members of this family of court Jews, even including one with a coat of arms bearing a goose.[40] Isaac's will (1797) provides evidence of his wealth, with capital of more than 100,000 *Reichstaler*. In addition to his economic activities – he was the owner of the *Fortuna* tobacco factory – he was also active in social affairs. We know that in 1825 the contents of the synagogue included "a number of silver vessels for religious purposes and thirteen Torahs" provided by the Gans family.[41] It is possible that the above-mentioned Torah finials were among the synagogue articles given by the Gans family. According to Angie von Gans, surviving descendant of the family, the family in Celle was the origin of the 'von Gans' family which established the important chemical firm *IG Farben*.

JHM 568 Torah shield
Master: Hans Hinrich Brahmfeld; Hamburg, 1760–1765.
Silver, embossed, chased, engraved, partial gilt; height: 41 cm / width: 33 cm.
Hall-marks: master's mark HB = Hinrich Brahmfeld (Hamburg, born 1703, master 1743, died 1782; Schliemann, No. 426), city mark Hamburg 1760–1784 (Schliemann, p. 11).
Hebrew inscription: "This is donated by Isaac son of Jacob Gans to the Synagogue of the Celle community [5]525" (=1765).

A gilt turban-shaped baldachin with symmetrically drawn curtains forms the upper end of the shield. In its centre two lions rampant in *repoussé* hold the Tables of the Law over a protruding rectangular casket. It contains three interchangeable plates, on the front and back of each of which is engraved the name of a Holiday in Hebrew square script: Sukkoth/Shemini Azeret/Sabbath/Sabbath

---

[40]Nicolaus Heutger, *Niedersächsische Juden*, Hildesheim 1978, p. 33.
[41]John Busch and Jürgen Ricklefs (eds.), *Zur Geschichte der Juden in Celle. Festschrift zur Wiederherstellung der Synagoge*, Celle 1974, p. 27.

Rosh Chodesh/Pesach/Shavuot. The centre of the shield is flanked by two embossed, gilt columns on high pedestals; the columns are wound with vines and crowned by a pine-cone. Between the columns embossed rocailles decorated with agate glass mark the interior field between the upper and lower sections. Vividly curved rocaille volutes form the end of the shield at each side.

The Hebrew inscription regarding the donor is engraved on the column pedestals. Like *JHM* 565 (the aforementioned Torah finials by Krumstroh) this bears the name of Isaac Gans of the Jewish community in Celle, who donated the shield in 1765. It can be assumed that this shield was among the synagogue objects of the Gans family listed in 1825 and forms an ensemble with the Torah finials of *JHM* 565. Today the Baroque synagogue in Celle, built in 1740, is among the oldest surviving Jewish religious houses in Germany.[42] Schliemann has reported another shield by Hinrich Brahmfeld, once mentioned to be in the possession of the Hamburg Synagogue, and made between 1760 and 1774.[43]

JHM B729 Torah finials
Master: unknown; Hamburg(?) /Rendsburg(?), 1750–1800.
Silver, embossed, chased, cast, partial gilt (crown); height: 48.1 cm / width: 19 cm.
Hall-marks: master's mark ISH or HSI.
Loan: *Nederlands Israelietische Hoofdsynagoge*, Arnhem.

In these Torah finials the shaft, furnished with a double edge on the base, is straight until it narrows shortly before meeting the spherical finial. On the finial are six vertical panels, adorned with open-work rocaille shapes and flower ornamentation. Three of these panels contain cartouches with illustrations of an embossed basin and ewer. The bulged finial narrows gently towards the top and carries a round crown bearing little bells and coloured imitation gemstones. On the crown are four bows which enclose a bell. This is crowned by a finial decorated with embossed flower motifs.

The lack of any city mark and the unidentified master's mark make it difficult to determine its origin with any certainty. However, a comparison of the shape and ornamentation with *JHM* 564 and *JHM* 565 makes it probable that it originated in the vicinity of Hamburg. Possibly we are dealing here with a master from Rendsburg in Schleswig-Holstein. The Rendsburg city mark showed the city gate, which in this case would have been linked with the master's mark. Rendsburg had one of the largest and most important Jewish rural communities in Schleswig-Holstein.[44]

JHM 567 Torah shield
Master: Hans Hinrich Krumstroh; Hamburg, 1760–1770.

---

[42]Heutger, *op. cit.*, pp. 29–30; Carol H. Krinsky, *Synagogues of Europe. Architecture, History, Meaning*, Cambridge, MA 1985, p. 343, fig. 7.
[43]Schliemann, *op. cit.*, vol. II, No. 426:25.
[44]Ole Harck (ed.), *Julius Magnus-Ausstellung. Zur Geschichte der jüdischen Gemeinden in Schleswig-Holstein*, Rendsburg 1985.

Silver, embossed, chased, engraved; height: 45 cm / width: 24.5 cm.
Hall-marks: master's mark HHK = Hans Hinrich Krumstroh (Hamburg, active 1730–1770; Schliemann, No. F394).
Hebrew inscription on shields, on chains: "Belongs to the eminent Sir/Jacob son of /Israel/ from Tarchdorf in the year [5]525 [=1765] and his wife/the eminent good Lady Jerocham/daughter of the eminent Itsik/Katz/from Ostrowo"(?).

The almost rectangular shield has, on both sides, semi-circular embossed columns covered with vines. The upper and lower parts of the shield have embossed and chased rocailles with leaf- and shell-work motifs. On the smooth central section are a round half-crown and a rectangle surrounded by leaf and rocaille ornamentation. Plates with the Jewish Holidays can be inserted into this rectangle by turns on Pesach, Shavuot, Sukkoth, Sabbath, Rosh Hashanah and Yom Kippur. On the lower side of the shield hang three small cartouche-shaped signs, attached to chains, on which inscriptions are engraved in Hebrew.

It is not certain whether the reference is to the Ostrowo community in Poznań, Poland, one of the oldest and biggest Jewish communities in the eighteenth and nineteenth centuries, or to Osterode near Göttingen. It is not known where the Tarchdorf community was situated.

Works by Hans Hinrich Krumstroh for both Jewish and non-Jewish clients have survived.[45] Schliemann mentions a Torah shield, formerly in the possession of the synagogue in Hamburg, in an almost identical style and with a rectangular shape like the *JHM* shield.[46] The museum in Altona has the pattern or model book of the family of Frantz Peter Krumstroh, which he left to a nephew in 1784.[47] The rococo forms and types in this book show that our shield has a decoration characteristic for Hamburg towards the end of its heyday of gold and silversmith work; a skilled craft working mainly from patterns.

JHM 100 Hanukkah lamp
Master: HS; West Prussia(?), *c.* 1780.
Silver, embossed, stippled; height: 13.5 cm / width: 14 cm / depth: 6.5 cm.
Hall-marks: master's mark HS (unidentified), German silver mark 13.

The simple rectangular, bench-shaped candleholder has projecting, lancet-shaped wick snouts, and closes with a hinged lid. This base rests on simple legs, the ends of which have been flattened and widened as well as turned at the ends to form feet. The back plate is decorated with an oval medallion in relief with the nine-branched Hanukkah lamp as a tree of lights. This medallion is framed by two heavy garlands and crowned with an undulating ribbon. Two tongue-shaped ornaments, turning into twisted bands, support the medallion. On the back, the *shammash* is placed on a high stand to the right. The strictly symmetrical arrangement of the back and the broadening heavy garlands are typical features

---

[45] See *JHM* 565.
[46] Schliemann, *op. cit.*, illustration 845.
[47] *Ibid.*, vol. I, p. 41.

of the *Zopfstil* which developed at the end of the eighteenth century during the transition period from rococo to classicism.

JHM 745 Kiddush cup
Master: Johann Friedrich Ehe; Nuremberg, 1787–1790.
Silver, embossed, engraved, chased; height: 6.5 cm / diameter: 6 cm.
Hall-marks: IFE in trefoil = Johann Friedrich Ehe (Nuremberg, master 1773, died 1808, R 4304), city mark Nuremberg, year mark G: 1787–1790 (R 3778).

The small, ball-foot cup stands on three ball-feet. The side is slightly conical and is decorated with five rows of semicircular rings arranged one above the other and embossed in a scale pattern. Directly above the ball-feet on the base is a straight chased line. Here the master achieved an increase in three-dimensional quality by placing another row of embossed semicircles behind the upper row. According to tradition this cup was used as a *kiddush* cup.[48]

Further evidence that Johann Friedrich Ehe's workshop produced a significant number of Jewish ritual objects is provided by a Hanukkah lamp in bench form in the Jewish Museum of Switzerland,[49] a Torah shield in Cologne,[50] five *kiddush* cups of the chalice type on a highly arched base[51] and a Sabbath lamp.[52]

JHM 142 Kiddush cup
Master: VT (?); Nuremberg, 1790–1794.
Silver, embossed, cast, engraved; height: 12.5 cm / diameter: 6 cm.
Hall-marks: master's mark VT (?), city mark Nuremberg 1790–1794 (R 3779, R 3767).
Hebrew inscription: "Blow the trumpet at the new moon, at the full moon, on our feast day" (*Psalms* LXXXI:3).

The baluster-shaped, eight-sided shaft rises from a highly arched, stepped base furnished with stylised leaf decoration and stepped into eight panels. The chalice-shaped cup also has eight sides and is chased with rococo ornaments such as flowers and rocailles. Below the lip is an engraved Hebrew inscription –

---

[48] Also *kiddush* cups, according to tradition and from Nuremberg, are a conical cup by Johann Höffler (*JHM* 141) and a ball-foot cup by Sigmund Bierfreund (*JHM* 2193). Both are adorned with embossed decoration of leaves and calyxes and date from 1655–1700.

[49] Inv. No. F 308. See Nuremberg, Germanisches Nationalmuseum, *Siehe der Stein schreit aus der Mauer. Geschichte und Kultur der Juden in Bayern*, exhibition catalogue, ed. by Bernward Deneke, Nuremberg 1988, Cat. No. 3/118, with year mark F.

[50] Illustration in Liesel Franzheim, *Judaica. Kölnisches Stadtmuseum*, Cologne 1980, Cat. No. 39 (Inv. No. RM 1929–1223).

[51] Deneke (ed.), *Siehe der Stein schreit, op. cit.*, Cat. No. 3/60 (from Tüchersfeld, Fränkische Schweiz-Museum, Inv. No. E 1708, with same year mark G), 3/61 (Speyer, Historisches Museum der Pfalz, Inv. No. HM 1964/38b), 3/106 (ibid., Inv. No. HM 1964/38a); *The Leon J. and Julia S. Obermeyer Collection at Congregation Rodeph Shalom*, Philadelphia 1988, Cat. No. 1; Vienna, Kunsthistorisches Museum, *Thora und Krone. Kultgeräte der jüdischen Diaspora in der Ukraine*, exhibition catalogue, ed. by W. Seipel, Vienna 1993, Cat. No. 89 (also with year mark G).

[52] Star-shaped pendant lamp with chandelier, around 1780: Hanover, Jüdisches Kulturzentrum, *Jüdisches Kultgerät im Lande Niedersachsen*, exhibition catalogue, Hanover 1969, Cat. No. 27.

JHM B96 Basin
Master: Abraham Warnberger II; Augsburg, 1665–1670
Silver, embossed, chased, partial gilt
Length: 84 cm / width: 74 cm / depth: 8 cm

JHM B95 Ewer
Master: David Bessmann; Augsburg, 1652–1653
Silver, embossed, chased, partial gilt
Height: 43.5 cm / width: 28 cm

All photographs by courtesy of the Jewish Historical Musuem, Amsterdam

JHM 121 Torah shield
Master: Daniel Michael (?); Augsburg, *c.* 1675
Silver, embossed, chased, engraved, partial gilt; height: 16.5 cm / width: 15.5 cm

JHM 102 *Kiddush* cup
Master: Johann Beckert III; Augsburg, 1690–1694
Silver, embossed, stippled, engraved, interior gilt
Height: 8 cm / diameter: 6.5 cm

JHM B742 Torah shield
Master: AH; Halle a.d. Saale, 1716
Silver, partial gilt, embossed, engraved, stippled, precious stone/rock-crystal trimming,
reverse with red velvet lining
Height: 39 cm / width: 34 cm

JHM 537 *Kiddush* cup
Master: Albrecht Biller; Augsburg, 1717–1718
Silver, embossed, engraved; height: 20 cm / diameter: 11 cm

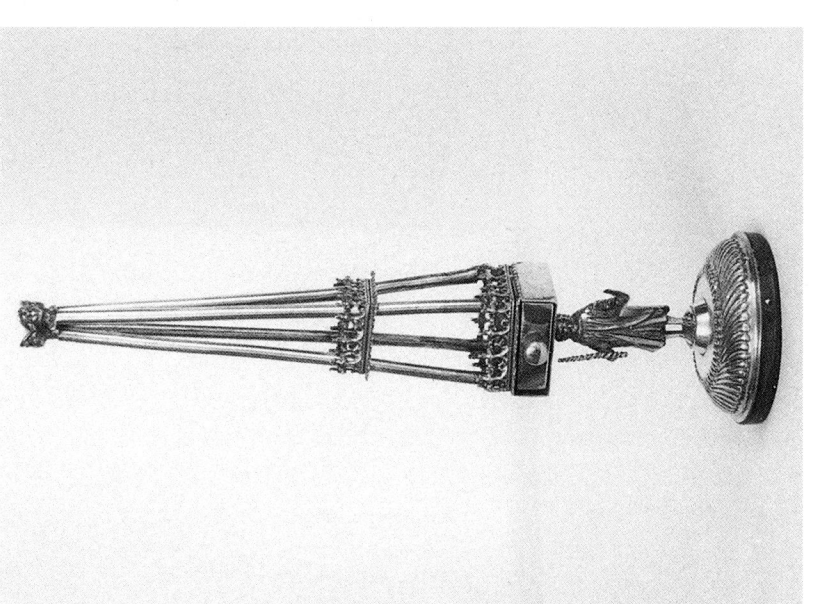

JHM B24 Case for Megillat Esther
Master: Christian Beyl; Breslau, 1727–1737
Silver, embossed, engraved, stamped; height: 34 cm / diameter: 5 cm

JHM B155 *Havdalah* candleholder and drawer for spices
Master: unknown; Frankfurt a. Main, *c.* 1725
Silver, cast, embossed; height: 29.8 cm / diameter: 8 cm

JHM 734 Ewer and Basin
Master: unknown; Glogau/Silesia, 1734–1735
Silver, embossed, chased, engraved, stamped
Ewer: height: 23.5 cm / width: 17.5 cm / diameter: 10.5 cm; basin: diameter: 38.5 cm

JHM 565 Torah finials
Master: Hans Hinrich Krumstroh; Hamburg, 1740–1767
Silver, embossed, stippled, cast, engraved; height: 41 cm / width: 18 cm

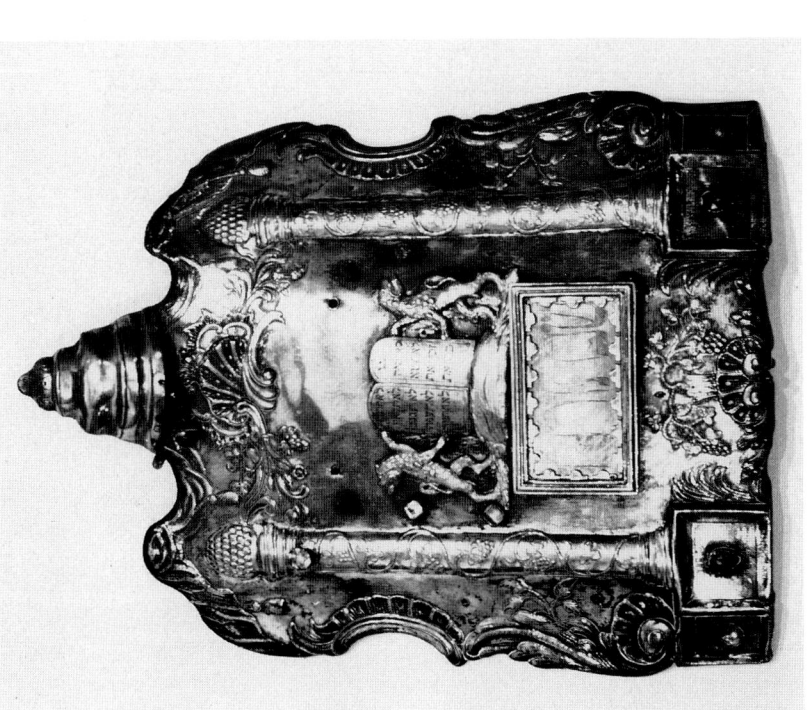

JHM 568 Torah shield
Master: Hans Hinrich Brahmfeld; Hamburg, 1760–1765
Silver, embossed, chased, engraved, partial gilt; height: 41 cm / width: 33 cm

JHM 567 Torah shield
Master: Hans Hinrich Krumstroh; Hamburg, 1760–1770
Silver, embossed, chased, engraved; height: 45 cm / width: 24.5 cm

JHM B729 Torah finials
Master: unknown; Hamburg (?)/Rendsburg (?), 1750–1800
Silver, embossed, chased, cast, partial gilt (crown); height: 48.1 cm / width: 19 cm

JHM 100 Hanukkah lamp
Master: HS; West Prussia (?), *c.* 1780
Silver, embossed, stippled; height: 13.5 cm / width: 14 cm / depth: 6.5 cm

JHM 745 *Kiddush* cup
Master: Johann Friedrich Ehe
Nuremberg, 1787–1790
Silver, embossed, engraved, chased
Height: 6.5 cm / diameter: 6 cm

JHM 142 *Kiddush* cup
Master: VT (?); Nuremberg, 1790–1794
Silver, embossed, cast, engraved; height: 12.5 cm / diameter: 6 cm

JHM B735 Torah finials
Master: Franz Anton Gutwein; Augsburg, 1803
Silver, embossed, engraved, partial gilt, carved; height: 35 cm / width: 13 cm

JHM 101 Hanukkah lamp
Master: Carl Friedrich Huebner; Berlin, late eighteenth century
Silver, embossed, stippled, engraved; height: 15.5 cm / width: 17 cm / depth: 6 cm

JHM 170 Hanukkah lamp
Master: Johann Friedrich Wilhelm Borcke; Berlin, 1817
Silver, embossed, engraved; height: 11 cm / width: 11 cm

JHM B889 Hanukkah lamp
Master: Georg Christian Friedrich Sick; Stuttgart, *c.* 1830
Silver, cast, embossed; height: 31 cm / width: 33.5 cm / depth: 13 cm

JHM 128 *Kiddush* cup
Master: unknown; Germany, *c.* 1850
Silver, embossed, engraved; height: 22 cm / diameter: 10 cm

JHM 153 *Kiddush* cup
Master: EB; Germany, before 1819
Silver, stippled, cast, engraved, gilt; height: 30 cm / diameter: 13 cm

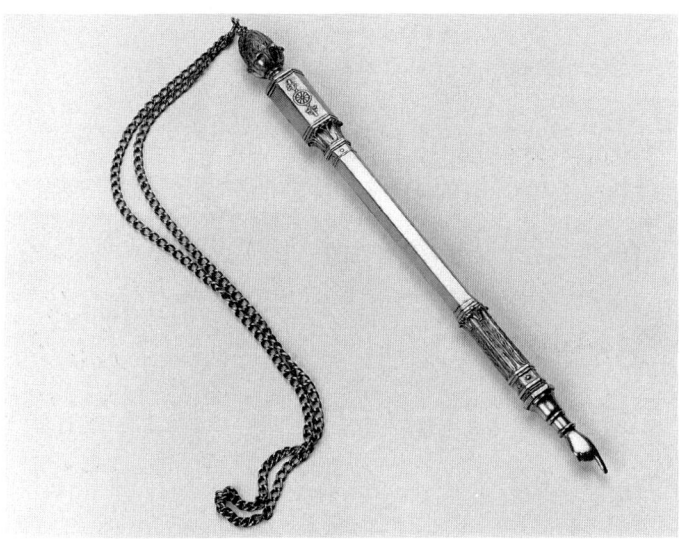

JHM 119 Torah pointer
Maker: Silberwarenfirma Lazarus Posen Witwe; Berlin or Frankfurt a. Main, *c.* 1900
Silver, cast, stippled, chased; length: 30.5 cm / diameter: 2.5 cm

JHM 167 Spice tower
Master: unknown
Germany, late nineteenth century
Silver, cast, stippled, chased, engraved
Height: 20 cm / diameter: 10 cm

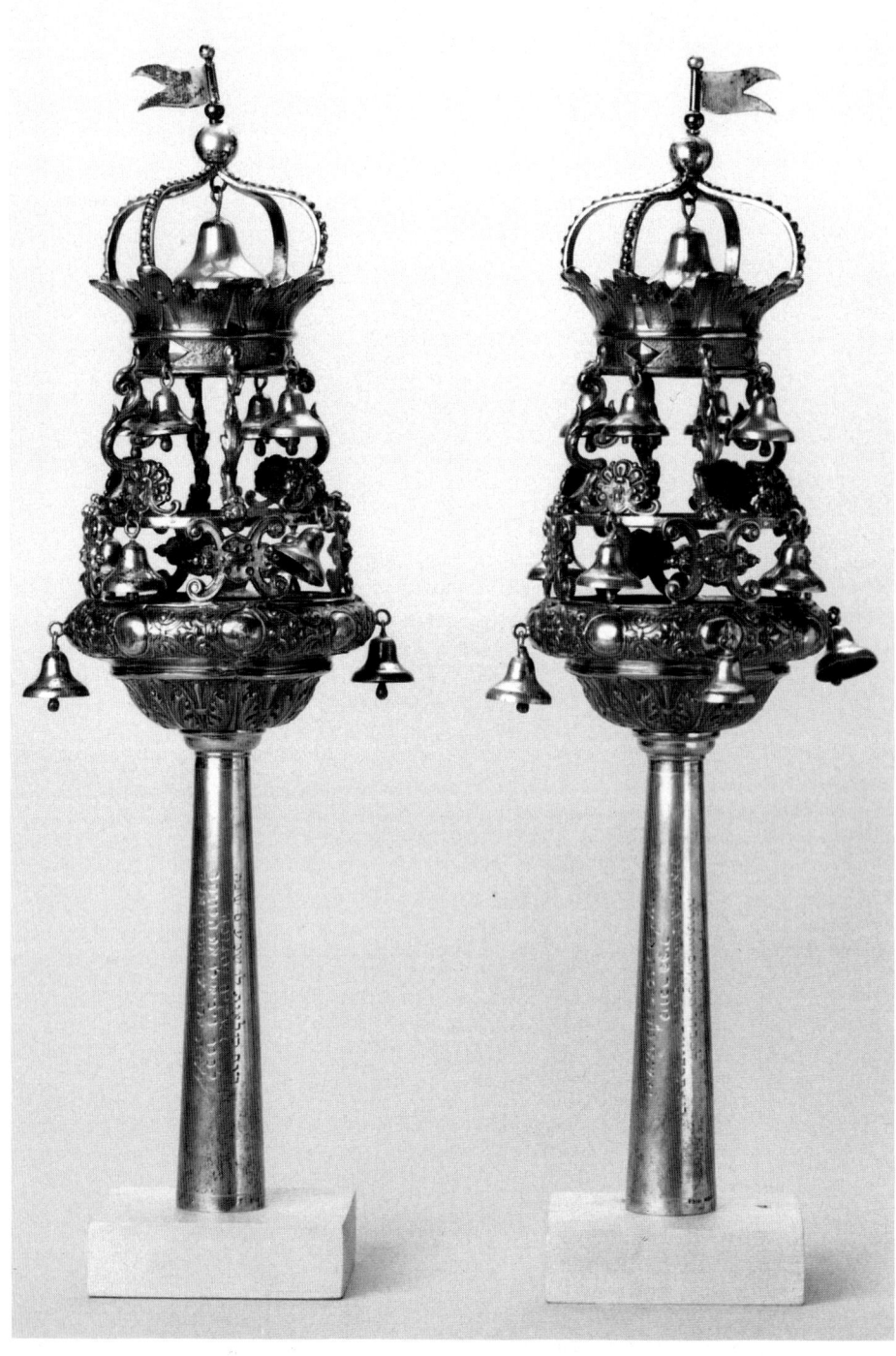

JHM B734 Torah finials
Maker: Silberwarenfirma Lazarus Posen Witwe; Frankfurt a. Main or Berlin, *c.* 1900
Silver, cast, stippled, chased, engraved; height: 44 cm / diameter: 15 cm

JHM 132 Torah crown
Master: unknown; Germany, *c.* 1900
Silver, cast, stippled, engraved, chased; height: 25 cm / diameter: 26 cm

JHM 222 Seder plate
Maker: Silberwarenfirma Gebrüder Gutgesell; Hanau, 1922–1926
Silver, cast, stippled, chased; diameter: 47 cm

JHM 3861 *Havdalah* plate
Maker: Silberwarenfirma Gebrüder Gutgesell; Hanau, *c.* 1920
Silver, stippled, cast, engraved; diameter: 22.5 cm

JHM 4115 Hanukkah lamp
Maker: Silberwarenfirma Gebrüder Gutgesell; Hanau, *c.* 1920
Silver, stippled, chased; height: 23.2 cm / width: 26 cm / depth: 10 cm

referring to the New Year liturgy – between which is appropriately depicted a man blowing a *shofar* horn.

The nature of the shape and decoration was popular for use as *kiddush* cups in Augsburg and Nuremberg in the eighteenth century. In such cups, the inscription below the lip generally gives the designation for the Sabbath.[53] Occasionally some other Holiday is specified by means of inscriptions and engraved decorations, for example Sukkoth and Pesach.[54] The *Hessisches Landesmuseum* in Kassel formerly possessed a Nuremberg cup of the same size and with the same rococo decoration and city mark; also like this cup, it showed a man blowing a horn.[55]

JHM 101 Hanukkah lamp
Master: Carl Friedrich Huebner; Berlin, late eighteenth century.
Silver, embossed, stippled, engraved; height: 15.5 cm / width: 17 cm / depth: 6 cm.
Hall-marks: master's mark CFH = Carl Friedrich Huebner (born in Berlin 1746, died 1816; No. 1178 in Scheffler[56]), city mark: bear = Berlin, year mark deformed.

The simple rectangular bench-shaped candleholder covered with lid and eight protruding lancet-shaped wick snouts rests on four legs with ball-feet. Palmettes have been soldered to both the right and left sides of the bank as handles. The backplate, embossed with a lattice pattern, is bordered with vividly curved, partially embossed rocailles. At the top to the right is placed the dish for the server light, the *shammash*.

The goldsmith C.F. Huebner used the same engraved lattice pattern with the four dots punched on the intersections on his Torah shield in the Berlin Museum.[57] It is a typical decorative element in Prussian rococo which, as is documented by other examples in the *Berlin Museum*, recurs on many Berlin Torah shields from the late eighteenth century.[58]

JHM B 735 Torah finials
Master: Franz Anton Gutwein; Augsburg, 1803.

---

[53]Schachar, *Jewish Tradition in Art, op. cit.*, Cat. No. 222, with illustration, has as inscription (*Exodus* XX:8) and dates from the early eighteenth century. Cat. No. 223, *ibid.*, also comes from Nuremberg (1761) and has the same inscription. Such *kiddush* cups can also be found in the Jewish Museum London, two of them made by Hieronymus Mittnacht in Augsburg in 1761–1763: London, The Jewish Museum, *Catalogue of the Permanent and Loan Collections of the Jewish Museum London*, ed. by R.D. Barnett, London–New York 1974, Cat. Nos. 394 and 395.
[54]Franzheim, *op. cit.*, Cat. No. 143: a Nuremberg cup, eighteenth-century, with the inscription on both sides of a bunch of grapes referring to Pesach: "Unleavened bread shall be eaten seven days" (*Exodus* XIII:7). The inscription on the 1763 Augsburg cup by F.C. Mederle refers to all three pilgrimage festivals (*Leviticus* XXIII:44), see M.E. Keen, *op. cit.*, Cat. No. 46.
[55]Rudolf Hallo, *Jüdische Kunst aus Hessen und Nassau*, Berlin 1933, p. 21, Cat. No. 66, with illustration. For further literature and examples of this type of chalice, see *JHM* 745 and note 51.
[56]Wolfgang Scheffler, *Berliner Goldschmiede*, Berlin 1968. Hereafter referred to in text as Scheffler Berlin.
[57]V. Bendt, *Judaica des Berlin Museums*, Berlin 1989, Cat. No. 102 (Inv. No. KGM 80/2).
[58]*Ibid.*, Cat. No. 101 (Inv. No. KGM 83/18).

Silver, embossed, engraved, partial gilt, carved; height: 35 cm / width: 13 cm.
Hall-marks: master's mark AG in contour = Franz Anton Gutwein (Augsburg, born about 1729, master 1759, died 1805; Seling, No. 2455), city mark Augsburg 1803 (Seling, No. 287).
Loan: *Nederlands Israelietische Hoofdsynagoge*, Arnhem.

A smooth shaft, furnished at both ends with a bulged ring, carries the arched base with embossed leaf decoration. Two friezes running round it show an openwork cubic motif with rosettes. A wider frieze in the middle is adorned with stylised flower motifs, and has ten apertures which contain five little bells. Above it is a frieze decorated with four projecting dragons' heads, each of which carries a little bell on a ring. The open-work, convex transition to the crown is provided by four flat columns, between each of which are sited lambrequins. The round crown with beaded edge and leaf motifs is arched and topped by a gilt lion rampant holding an oval shield.

There are several Torah finials dating from the early nineteenth century which are constructed of friezes with open-work motifs. These Gutwein *rimmonim* from 1803 appear to have been an early pair of this type. The Furman collection contains a pair made in 1810 by Balthasar Friedrich Stenglin (Seling, No. 2648),[59] and there is a comparable pair, made in 1818, in the Stieglitz collection in Jerusalem.[60] The Jewish Museum in New York has two pairs with the master's mark CB. According to Braunstein, this must be Karl Bitzel (Seling, No. 2608), who made them in 1802–1803 (Seling, Nos. 286–287).[61] In Kempten there is another pair of *rimmonim* by Gutwein, with bow crown on a fluted shaft, made in 1801 (Seling, No. 291).[62] A Torah shield by his hand, with the year letter I for 1797–1799 (Seling, Nos. 281–282) is to be found in Jerusalem.[63] A second shield, from 1801, is in Washington.[64] The *Joods Historisch Museum* also has eight small *kiddush* cups by Franz Anton Gutwein.[65]

JHM 170 Hanukkah lamp
Master: Johann Friedrich Wilhelm Borcke; Berlin, 1817.
Silver, embossed, engraved; height: 11 cm / width: 11 cm.
Hall-marks: master's mark WB = Johann Friedrich Wilhelm Borcke (born in Berlin 1789, master in 1816, died in 1839; Scheffler Berlin, No. 1702), city mark Berlin = bear with Year mark I (Scheffler Berlin, No. 13).

---

[59]New York, The Jewish Museum, *Personal Vision. The Furman Collection of Jewish Ceremonial Art*, exhibition catalogue, ed. by Susan L. Braunstein, New York 1985, Cat. No. 6 (Inv. No. JF 125).
[60]Benjamin, *The Stieglitz Collection, op. cit.*, Cat. No. 14 (Inv. No. 147/331).
[61]Jewish Museum, Inv. Nos. F 3919 and F 3920; Braunstein (ed.), *Personal Vision, op. cit.*, Cat. No. 6, note 1.
[62]*Museen und Sammlungen der Stadt Kempten*, Kempten (Inv. No. 4897/2 and 3); see Deneke (ed.), *Siehe der Stein schreit, op. cit.*, Cat. No. 3/14.
[63]The Israel Museum (Inv. No. 14 8/42); see Deneke (ed.), *Siehe der Stein schreit, op. cit.*, Cat. No. 3/28.
[64]L. Altshuler, *In the Spirit of Tradition*, B'nai Brith Klutznick Museum, Washington 1988, Cat. Nos. 112 and p. 53 (illustration).
[65]*JHM* 746: Augsburg 1799 and 1800 (Seling, *op. cit.*, Nos. 283 and 284), with scale decoration and three ball-feet.

The simple rectangular bench-shaped candleholder, with lid and spouts for the wick snouts, stands on square-turned volute feet. The *repoussé* backplate shows a symmetrically arranged bound nosegay of leaves, the individual branches of which end in volutes. In the upper corners are blossoms. The *shammash* is missing. The foliage, which imitates antique acanthus leaves, shows strict symmetry, clearly following the development of Berlin classicism from the *Zopfstil*.

The master J.F.W. Borcke also produced, in addition to the Hanukkah lamp, a Torah shield,[66] a Torah crown,[67] a pair of *rimmonim* and an alms dish.[68]

JHM B 889 Hanukkah lamp
Master: Georg Christian Friedrich Sick; Stuttgart, c. 1830.
Silver, cast, embossed; height: 31 cm / width: 33.5 cm / depth: 13 cm.
Hall-marks: master's mark SICK = Georg Christian Friedrich Sick (Stuttgart 1794–1863, master about 1816), city mark Stuttgart: jumping horse with year mark Q in oval, c. 1830 (R 4629).
Loan: A.D. Heilbut-Frankfort and D.A. Frankfort, Amsterdam.

The lamp, in the shape of a ship, rests on a shaft which is adorned with acanthus leaves and set on an oval base. The ship is borne on the wings of a bird which sits above the shaft. At both ends the ship culminates in beaked heads which carry the bank of candles, hung by chains so that it is suspended freely in the middle.

The shape, in the form of a ship, is highly unusual and unique.[69] Perhaps it was the result of an individual flight of the imagination on the part of the silversmith, or the deliberate choice of the client. Sick came from a family of goldsmiths which was particularly important in Stuttgart in the first half of the nineteenth century. The imitations of classical antiquity in his style are also revealed in other works, such as a lamp of 1835 and a cup. They can be traced back to designs by the architect Karl Friedrich Schinkel.[70]

JHM 153 *Kiddush* cup
Master: EB; Germany, before 1819.
Silver, stippled, cast, engraved, gilt; height: 30 cm / diameter: 13 cm.
Hall-marks: master's mark EB, German silver mark 12.
Hebrew inscription: "Presented as a memento to Samuel, Rabbi of Amsterdam, by the Hanover community which came there in the year [5]579" (= 1819).

---

[66]Scheffler, *Berliner Goldschmiede*, op. cit., Nr. 1702: Märkisches Museum Berlin (Inv. No. 3933).
[67]Jewish Museum, New York (Inv. No. F 1649), see New York, Jewish Museum, *A Tale of Two Cities. Jewish Life in Frankfurt and Istanbul 1750–1870*, exhibition catalogue, ed. by Vivian B. Mann, New York 1982, Cat. No. 70.
[68]Jewish Museum, New York (Inv. Nos. D 170 and D 226), see New York, Jewish Museum, *Danzig 1939. Treasures of a Destroyed City*, exhibition catalogue, New York 1980, Cat. Nos. 218 and 274.
[69]Deneke (ed.), *Siehe der Stein schreit*, op. cit., Cat. No. 3/130 with illustration.
[70]Nuremberg, Germanisches Nationalmuseum, *Deutsche Goldschmiedekunst*, exhibition catalogue, ed. by K. Pechstein, Berlin 1987, Cat. No. 130: lamp, No. 132: ewer.

The large *kiddush* cup, standing on four ball-feet, has a rectangular base with stylised leaf decoration. Upon it stands a round foot with baluster shaft, which is adorned with flower motifs and two rows of bead-work. The highly conical, smooth chalice – with the Hebrew inscription on the front – has a lid which is slightly raised in the middle and is crowned with a pine-cone on a rosette of flowers.

Samuel Berish Berenstein (see also *JHM* 537 in connection with the *kiddush* cup presented to him in 1804) came from a famous rabbinical family. His grandfather Levi Josua (also called Aryeh Loeb) was *Landesrabbiner* in Hanover from 1761 to 1789. Samuel's father Berend Josua (also called Isachar Berish) held office in Hanover until his death in 1802.[71] According to the inscription, his former Hanover community visited Samuel Berenstein, Chief Rabbi of Amsterdam since 1815, in 1819 and presented him with this cup.

JHM 128 *Kiddush* cup
Master: unknown; Germany, *c*. 1850.
Silver, embossed, engraved; height: 22 cm / diameter: 10 cm.
Hall-marks: German silver mark 13.
Hebrew inscriptions: "To commemorate our esteemed teacher (Rabbi) Isachar Beer Berenstein, chairman of the Rabbinical Court of the holy community The Hague" and "To commemorate the consecration of the Synagogue at Den Helder 25 years ago. Weekly passage *Ki Tetse* [*Deuteronomy* XXI:10 – XXV:19], [5]622" (= Saturday 7th September 1862).

The round, stepped foot has buckle decoration running round it and delicate bead-work. It carries a baluster shaft engraved with rose blossoms, lobed in four sections. On it sits a chalice-shaped cup with an extended lip and a bulged lower part arranged in eight lobed sections. The relief garland of oak leaves carries the engraved Hebrew dedication for Isachar Beer Berenstein.

There is a *kiddush* cup with a very similar shape, made in Berlin about 1840, in the possession of the Berlin Museum.[72] The shape was widely used in the German *Biedermeier*; such cups were already being manufactured in series and only became objects with individual application after a dedication was added.

Isachar Beer (= Berish Samuel) Berenstein (1808–1893) was the son of Chief Rabbi Samuel Berish Berenstein of Amsterdam[73] and Rebecca Roesle Löwenstamm, daughter of the Amsterdam Rabbi Jacob Moses Löwenstamm. He was trained at the *Nederlands Israelitisch Seminarium*, where he later taught. From 1838 he was rabbi in Amsterdam and, from 1848 until his death, Chief Rabbi in The Hague, as well as being an outstanding scholar who promoted Jewish literature and history.[74]

The town of Den Helder, north of Amsterdam, had 25,434 inhabitants in 1840,

---

[71]Peter Schulze (ed.), ". . . *daß die Juden in unsern Landen einen Rabbinen erwehlen*. . ." Hanover 1987, pp. 18–20.
[72]*Judaica des Berlin Museums, op. cit.*, Cat. No. 145 (Inv. No. KGM 81/110).
[73]See *JHM* Inv. No. 153 and *JHM* Inv. No. 537, *kiddush* cup Augsburg 1717–1718.
[74]His portrait is reproduced by Gans, *Memorbook, op. cit.*, p. 429.

including 256 members of the Jewish community. The Den Helder community had made available the building ground for the synagogue. A Jewish school was also established in 1837, financed with assistance from the families Rothschild in Paris and Wolf de Rothschild from Frankfurt.[75]

JHM 167 Spice tower
Master: unknown; Germany, late nineteenth century.
Silver, cast, stippled, chased, engraved; height: 20 cm / diameter: 10 cm.
Hall-marks: unmarked.

The two-storey tower rises from a square base on a sloping pedestal, this latter being carried by four ball-feet. The pyramid-shaped spire, slightly set back, is enclosed by a protruding, open-work balustrade. Each of the four corners of the balustrade has a small round tower with a flag. The top of the spire also has a small flag on a baluster shaft. Both storeys have large round arch windows with rich tracery alongside engraved masonry. The four upper windows have three sections; the three lower ones have only two sections and have simpler tracery. On the lower storey, the fourth side has a heavily barred door. A simple stamped ridge separates the storeys.

The *Musée de Cluny* has a spice tower from the Strauss collection which is very similar, but for the spire with its *à jour* work; this has been placed by Klagsbald as German and from the nineteenth century.[76] The similarity of the work permits us to conclude that here we have silver cast from moulds – that is, manufactured products dating from the late nineteenth century. The little towers on the corners of the balustrade and the medieval tracery windows reveal the adoption of motifs from the oldest known German spice towers from Kassel[77] and the Friedberg synagogue, which date from the sixteenth century.[78] These two towers were among the famous Jewish works of art which received publicity at an early stage and were thereby destined to be copied in manufactured goods.

JHM 119 Torah pointer
Maker: Silberwarenfirma Lazarus Posen Witwe; Berlin or Frankfurt a. Main, c. 1900.
Silver, cast, stippled, chased; length: 30.5 cm / diameter: 2.5 cm.
Hall-marks: master's mark Posen = Silberwarenfirma Lazarus Posen Witwe, Frankfurt a. Main & Berlin, German imperial silver mark.

---

[75]Michman, Beem and Michman, *Pinkas Geschiedenis, op. cit.*, pp. 328f.
[76]Inv. No. Cl. 12319; V. Klagsbald, *Catalogue raisonné de la collection juive du Musée de Cluny*, Paris 1981, Cat. No. 97. The spice tower in the Victoria and Albert Museum (Inv. No. 408–1956), now attributed to the seventeenth-century Netherlands, is probably also nineteenth-century. See Keen, *Jewish Ritual Art, op. cit.*, Cat. No. 51.
[77]Spice tower (or table decoration?), formerly Hessisches Landsmuseum Kassel, cf. Hallo, *op. cit.*, No. 74, now in the Floersheim collection Zürich.
[78]Jewish Museum (Inv. Nos. 23–52), description and illustration in N.L. Kleeblatt and Vivian B. Mann, *Treasures of the Jewish Museum*, New York 1986, pp. 34–35.

The hexagonal pointer, which has several sections, has a pine-cone as knob; the chain is fastened to it. The short, protruding transition piece is decorated with a *repoussé* blossom between two palmettes in classical style in relief. This gives way to the long, slim grip, which is constructed as a pillar with Egyptian-style leaf capital and a base with several ridges. This base stands on a form of pedestal which is clothed in large lancet-shaped scalloped leaves and has a high profiled base. The round double cuff is attached directly to this pedestal, and on it sits the delicate hand with stretched index finger.

The mark Posen was established in Frankfurt a. Main in 1869 with the aid of Baron Wilhelm von Rothschild. Subsequently the founder's widow and her sons continued the business as the *Silberwarenfirma Lazarus Posen Witwe* with such success that a branch was established in Berlin in 1890.[79] The business specialised in tableware and also in Judaica, as is demonstrated in the 1897 catalogue of the company, which by then was accorded the title of *Hofsilberschmied*.[80] The model of this pointer was offered as a design in the catalogue under the No. 7592. A variation of it, offered under No. 7593, has a baluster-shaped shaft. A Torah shield in the same style as the pointer was offered under No. 7588 with similar classical ornamentation. The pointer and Torah shield were evidently designed as an ensemble.

JHM B 734 Torah finials
Maker: Silberwarenfirma Lazarus Posen Witwe; Frankfurt a. Main or Berlin, c. 1900.
Silver, cast, stippled, chased, engraved; height: 44 cm / diameter: 15 cm.
Hall-marks: master's mark Posen = Silberwarenfirma Lazarus Posen Witwe, German imperial silver mark.
Hebrew inscription: "Gift of thanks in honour of the Lord and the Torah of Jakob ben Moses Frankfort, paper-seller, and his wife Reische bat Elias Spier. On the occasion of his 70th birthday at Sabbat Rosh Chodesh and Hanukkah, after the passage 'they brought into the house to him the present' [*Genesis* XLIII:26] for the famous community of Arnhem in the year [5]682" (= 31st December 1921).
Loan: *Nederlands Israelietische Hoofdsynagoge*, Arnhem.

The long conical shafts with the inscription each bear a chalice-shaped ridged base on which sits a broad convex ring. This gives way to two *à jour*-worked tower storeys culminating in a bow crown. The *repoussé* decor consists of a garland of acanthus leaves on the base and scrollwork and embossed strapwork on the ring. On this ring, from which two bells hang, stand four scrollwork cartouches which carry the second storey circle. This circle carries four volutes on lion's feet, alternating with four palmettes hung with bells. The volutes bear the crown, which is itself also hung with little bells.

Like the pointer (see *JHM* 119 above), the model of these *rimmonim* was also

---

[79] J. Michael, *The Silver Company Lazarus Posen Wwe. 1869–1938*, M.A. diss., Parsons School of Design, New York 1990, pp. 8ff.
[80] *Catalog der Silberwarenfirma Lazarus Posen Wwe. Hofsilberschmied*, Frankfurt a. Main–Berlin 1897.

offered as a design in the 1897 catalogue of the Posen firm, under No. 3217. Several variations on this type were available (Nos. 3216 and 6828). The individual decorations modify the forms of the famous Frankfurt *rimmonim* of Jeremias Zobel dating from the first quarter of the eighteenth century, which can now be found in New York[81] and Frankfurt a. Main,[82] and were originally in the possession of the Frankfurt Jewish community. These *rimmonim*, evidently already well-known by the end of the nineteenth century, were also on offer by *Lazarus Posen Witwe*, as reproductions cast from moulds, under No. 3274.

The subject of the inscription is Jakob ben Moses Frankfort (1852–1934) and his wife Reische Spier, two members of the Arnhem Jewish community. This provincial capital counted in 1930 1,389 Jews out of a total population of 94,457 citizens.

JHM 132 Torah crown
Master: unknown; Germany, *c*. 1900.
Silver, cast, stippled, engraved, chased; height: 25 cm / diameter: 26 cm.
Hall-marks: unmarked.
Inscription on the shield: initial words of the Ten Commandments.

The spherical crown, gently flattened towards the top, is composed of two half bowls cast from moulds; the lower bowl sits on a bulged ring adorned with engraved zigzag bands and dots. The top takes the shape of a hilltop, signifying Mount Sinai, on which the Tables of the Law are standing. These are held on each side by two fully three-dimensional lions rampant. The initial words of the Ten Commandments are inscribed in relief on each tablet. Eight resonance apertures have been cut into each half-bowl; the ones above are round and those below have six lobes. The apertures are surrounded by an engraved and stippled ornamentation of acanthus leaves and blossoms. The upper semi-sphere has one bell inside it, the lower one a bell in each aperture. For placing the crown on the Torah scroll, two strips with moveable cuffs have been mounted on the bulged ring.

There are numerous examples and variations of this type of crown, including one in the *Joods Historisch Museum*.[83] Another example, with an inscription dating from 1912 and dated by Vera Bendt to about 1910, is to be found in the Berlin Museum.[84] According to the German text the piece probably comes from Tuchel in West Prussia. The crown in the Jewish Museum in New York comes from the Danzig community and was made in about 1870.[85] A similar piece in the *Stadtgeschichtliches Museum* of Altona is reputed to be from Berlin.[86] A variation on

---

[81] Jewish Museum (Inv. No. F 3685); description and illustration in Kayser and Schoenberger, *op. cit.*, No. 29; and Mann, *Treasures, op. cit.*, pp. 84, 85.
[82] Historisches Museum, Frankfurt a. Main (Inv. No. x 51:11 v-w); description and illustration in Cologne, Kölnisches Stadtmuseum, *Monumenta Judaica*, exhibition catalogue, Cologne 1963, E 330, illustration 93.
[83] Inv. No. 133, unmarked, can be dated from the Hebrew inscription to 1896.
[84] Inv. No. KGM 80/5, illustration: *Judaica des Berlin Museums, op. cit.*, Cat. No. 119 and illustration 15.
[85] Inv. No. D 62, see *Danzig 1939, op. cit.*, Cat. No. 75, where further examples are mentioned.
[86] Inv. No. 1913/68, cited in *Judaica des Berlin Museums, op. cit.*, Cat. No. 119; see *Danzig 1939, op. cit.*, Cat. No. 75; illustration in *Monumenta Judaica, op. cit.*, E 343, illustration 92.

this type of crown was made by the Berlin silverware firm of *H. Meyen & Co.* for the synagogue in Berlin-Charlottenburg, which was dedicated in 1912.[87] It can therefore be assumed that what we have here is a type of Torah crown made by Berlin silverware firms in the last quarter of the nineteenth century.

JHM 222 Seder plate
Maker: Silberwarenfirma Gebrüder Gutgesell; Hanau, 1922–1926.
Silver, cast, stippled, chased; diameter: 47 cm.
Hall-marks: master's mark rose = Silberwarenfirma Gutgesell Hanau (Wolfgang Scheffler, *Die Goldschmiede Hessens*, Berlin 1976, No. 477),[88] city mark N = Nuremberg, standard mark 13.
Hebrew inscriptions: 15 mnemonic words indicating the order of the Passover meal and *Psalms* CXXVIII, 2–6.

The round, flat plate has a broad rim with a scalloped edge and a centre surface in bold *repoussé*. The centre shows the fifteen catchwords for the order of Seder service in large Hebrew square script and Psalm 128, verses 2–6, in small script, with the first word "kaddesh" from the order of Seder set in a garland above the text. On the rim four oval medallions alternate with four small cartouches against a background decorated with leaves and flowers in *repoussé*. The medallions above and below the script show the sacrifice of Isaac, and the five Rabbis of Bnei Brak in discussion on Seder night, each with the description in Hebrew. The medallions to the side contain bunches of fruit, and the cartouches show Moses, Aaron, David and Jonathan, each with the name inscribed in Hebrew.

This Seder plate exists in numerous examples; one is to be found in the Jewish Museum in London,[89] one in Amsterdam,[90] and yet another in the E. Feinberg collection in Detroit.[91] In addition, we know of variants with different inscriptions in the centre and diverse figurative scenes in the oval medallions. The plates frequently are stamped with the Nuremberg city mark. Cecil Roth has pointed out that the plates were produced by silverware firms in Hanau or Pforzheim at the end of the nineteenth century and later, and were not works made in Nuremberg.[92] This can be confirmed by our Seder plate, which in addition to the Nuremberg mark is stamped with a rose with two leaves on a short stem: the mark of the Hanau silverware firm *Gebrüder Gutgesell*. This firm made tableware and Judaica in the style of antique silver, with the Nuremberg

---

[87] K. Bayer, 'Die neue Synagoge in Charlottenburg', in *Ost und West*, 12 (1912), pp. 929f.; illustration p. 936 – another example is mentioned by Hallo, *op. cit.*, Cat. No. 15, Table 5, in the Hessisches Landesmuseum, Kassel, apparently from Tula (now Keila) in Estonia.

[88] Hereafter referred to in text as Scheffler Hessen.

[89] Barnett (ed.), *Catalogue of the Jewish Museum London, op. cit.*, Cat. No. 360.

[90] Joods Historisch Museum, Inv. No. B 1596, from the workshop of Emil Freund, a metal and silverware factory in Hanau.

[91] Detroit, The Institute of Arts, *Exhibition of Jewish Ceremonial Art*, exhibition catalogue, Detroit 1951, Cat. No. 107.

[92] Cecil Roth, 'Majolica Passover Plates of the Seventeenth - Eighteenth Centuries', in *Eretz Israel*, 7 (1963), p. 111.

city mark, the Standard mark "13" and sometimes the rose mark or "GG". Its products date mainly from the first twenty years of this century and were all cast from moulds.

For this Seder plate, the model was taken from an Italian type of Seder plate of majolica. According to Roth this was a type of plate whose manufacture we can first trace to Padua in the sixteenth century, and which was made by the families Cohen and Azulai in Pesaro and Ancona well into the eighteenth century.[93] However, Vivian Mann has shown that the majolica Seder plates are not originals dating from the sixteenth to the eighteenth centuries, but works produced in the potteries of Savona and Albisola at the end of the nineteenth century in historical style and with illustrations derived from the Trieste *Haggadah* of 1864.[94] These plates, adorned with the forged signatures of Jewish potters from the sixteenth to the eighteenth centuries, were already being shown at exhibitions from the end of the nineteenth century, and were among the most coveted collectors' pieces among Judaica.[95] These forgeries in their turn served as the model for the series production of the Hanau silverware firm of *Gebrüder Gutgesell*, which made their pieces look "genuine" – that is, like sixteenth- to eighteenth-century silver – by adding the forged Nuremberg city mark!

JHM 3861 *Havdalah* plate
Maker: Silberwarenfirma Gebrüder Gutgesell; Hanau, c. 1920.
Silver, stippled, cast, engraved; height: 2.5 cm / diameter: 22.5 cm.
Hall-marks: master's mark rose = Silberwarenfabrik Gebrüder Gutgesell, Hanau (Scheffler Hessen, No. 477), city mark N = Nuremberg, German silver mark 13.
Hebrew inscription on rim: "The commandment of the Lord is pure, enlightening the eyes" (*Psalms* XIX:8); centre: "Good week and good year".

The round shallow plate with scalloped edge stands on four cast volute feet. Two curved grotesques serve as handles. On the broad rim is embossed the inscription from Psalm 19, verse 8, in large *repoussé* letters, subdivided rhythmically by bunches of grapes. In the slightly sunken centre is the Star of David in flat relief with engraved rays. In the middle of the star is the second inscription in Yiddish in delicate *repoussé* letters.

There are numerous further examples of this plate, previously attributed – because of the city mark – to Nuremberg in the second half of the nineteenth

---

[93] *Ibid.*, pp. 106–111, see Barnett (ed.), *Catalogue of the Jewish Museum London, op. cit.*, Cat. Nos. 339 and 340.
[94] Vivian B. Mann, 'Forging Judaica. The Case of the Italian Majolica Seder Plates', in E. Mendelsohn (ed.), *Art and its Visual Uses. Studies in Contemporary Jewry*, vol. VI, Oxford 1990, pp. 201–224.
[95] Such a plate was exhibited at the Anglo-Jewish Exhibition in London in 1887, see Roth, *J. Pierpont Morgan Collector, op. cit.*

century.[96] However, the combination of the Nuremberg city mark with the German silver mark "13" and the rose – sometimes combined with a "GG" – clearly indicates the Hanau silverware firm *Gebrüder Gutgesell*, which was active in the first third of this century.[97]

JHM 4115 Hanukkah lamp
Maker: Silberwarenfirma Gebrüder Gutgesell; Hanau, *c.* 1920.
Silver, stippled, chased; height: 23.2 cm / width: 26 cm / depth: 10 cm.
Hall-marks: master's mark rose with GG = Silberwarenfirma Gebrüder Gutgesell, Hanau (Scheffler Hessen, No. 477), city mark N = Nuremberg, German silver mark 13.

The trapezium-shaped bench of this lamp has eight detachable dishes in the form of ships, equipped with spike and wick snouts and able to function both as candleholders and as oil dishes. At the front in the middle the bench is held up by a rocaille cartouche from which further rocailles emerge to the sides; these end in dolphin heads which support the bench at its front corners. At the rear, volute feet flank the box for the mechanism of a musical box. The open-work backplate consists of two opposed lions rampant in *repoussé* holding a central shield topped by a crown. The shield shows a nine-armed stylised tree of lights as the symbol of the Holiday. The *shammash* is sited in the centre.

The lamp is a further example of the production of Judaica by the silverware firm *Gebrüder Gutgesell* of Hanau and its "antique silver style", which is dominated by the forms of the second Rococo.[98]

---

[96]Most recently C. Grossmann in *A Temple Treasury. The Judaica Collection of the Congregation Emanu-El of the City of New York*, New York 1989, Cat. No. 95; Cat No. 94 appears to be a variant of the same plate, also by the *Gebrüder Gutgesell* company. A further example can be found in the Israel Museum (Inv. No. 125/4; see Schachar, *Jewish Tradition in Art, op. cit.*, Cat. No. 233, with illustration). In her article 'Forging Judaica', *loc. cit.*, Mann has already pointed to the problem of dating and classifying these plates.
[97]Scheffler, *Die Goldschmiede Hessens, op. cit.*, No. 477; see Seder plate (Inv. No. 222) and Hanukkah lamp (Inv. No. 4115) of the Joods Historisch Museum Amsterdam.
[98]See Seder plate (Inv. No. 222) and *havdalah* plate (Inv. No. 3861) of the Joods Historisch Museum Amsterdam.

Historiographical Review

Persecution and the Holocaust
A Provisional Review of GDR Historiography

BY KURT PÄTZOLD

I

In the East German state a new history, with representatives who described themselves as Marxists or Marxist-Leninists, was created only at the end of the 1950s and the beginning of the 1960s. This period saw the emergence of young historians who had begun their studies after the end of the Second World War, often at the *Arbeiter- und Bauern* faculties, before completing their doctorates and starting work in the universities. This generation of historians exerted an enormous influence on the writing of history in the GDR until its fall, and occupied key positions on the committees of the "guild" (the *Historikergesellschaft*, the *Rat für Geschichtswissenschaft*, etc.). They had been profoundly affected by the experience of Nazism. The older members had themselves been soldiers in the *Wehrmacht*, while the younger ones – either voluntarily or under compulsion – had belonged to the youth organisations of the NSDAP. Some of them had an anti-Nazi background, usually in Social Democratic or Communist families which had never accepted the Nazi regime. Their attitudes towards the East German state were greatly affected by the fact that in the old Germany – the Nazi state as well as the Weimar Republic – many of these young academics would not have been given the chance to finish secondary school and go on to university. The doors of higher education had been opened for them by the far-reaching changes made after 1945. During their education they were constantly reminded that they were studying at the expense of the workers and peasants and that, as academics, they must repay their benefactors by championing the interests of the workers.

Some of the teachers of these young historians had also taught during the years of Nazi rule, but had not adopted or transmitted the inhuman ideas of the regime. In addition, especially in Berlin and Leipzig, returning exiles[1] and former inmates of Nazi prisons and concentration camps[2] began to work as

---

[1] Among those to return from exile in Britain were the economic historian Jürgen Kuczynski and the historian Alfred Meusel. Both played a significant role in teaching at Berlin's Humboldt University.

[2] Among them were Walter Bartel, who fell into the hands of the Nazis in Czechoslovakia in 1939 and was held in Buchenwald concentration camp, where he was on the illegal international camp committee. After serving as Wilhelm Pieck's secretary, Bartel taught at university in Leipzig and later in Berlin. Erich Paterna, who also worked at the Humboldt University, had been incarcerated in Brandenburg prison. Another former prisoner was Walter Markov, who later established an internationally renowned centre of comparative research in revolution at Leipzig University.

teachers; they enjoyed particularly great authority despite the fact that many of them lacked formal "academic" qualifications.

Significant numbers of the rising generation of historians were persuaded by their own experiences and their encounters with anti-Nazis to study the history of Germany in the twentieth century. These historians sought answers to the questions life had "drummed" into them during their childhood and youth. They participated in the endeavour to create "another" Germany because, though most of them were not personally guilty of participating in German crimes, they wished to accept their share of responsibility before history. In their investigations of the history of the twentieth century, especially the period after the German military defeat of 1918, most of the young historians were self-taught. The period had been virtually ignored in lectures and seminars while they were university students; in Jena, for example, the latest year studied was 1888, the "Year of the Three Kaisers". This was still the case in 1953.

This group, which came to be known as the "younger generation of academics", concentrated its research on two main themes. The first concerned the rise and triumph of Nazism in Germany, concentrating on the Weimar Republic and its final phase, and included the controversial issue of the character of the Nazi system. The second theme dealt with the immediate prelude to, and the history of, the Second World War. One of its main aims was to expose the crimes committed by the Nazi regime against the peoples of Europe.[3] The earlier years of peace in the Third *Reich*, which enabled its leaders to create a mass basis of support for the regime, were not studied in anything like the same depth.[4]

As part of their work on the second theme, East German historians began to study the history of the Nazi persecution of the Jews and the genocide of European Jewry. The first result, which dealt with the subject in general, was a volume of photographs and texts which appeared in 1966 and was primarily the achievement of Helmut Eschwege.[5] His colleagues on the project were Rudi Goguel and Klaus Drobisch, a historian who worked at the *Institut für Geschichte* at the East German *Akademie der Wissenschaften zu Berlin* and a member of the younger generation. Eschwege gave his own view of the background to this manuscript in his memoirs, which appeared shortly before his death.[6] A second

---

[3]The special volumes of the *Zeitschrift für Geschichtswissenschaft* (Berlin), appearing at ten-year intervals on the occasion of the International Historians' Congress (1960, 1970, 1980), give a survey of GDR historiography, though unfortunately with scarcely any critical commentary. The manuscript of the fourth volume, due to appear at the Madrid Congress of 1990, was not published. A critical survey, of the type which would have been both possible and necessary, was never produced in the period after November 1989. Even today the majority of GDR historians are reluctant to make any public assessment of their own works.

[4]Following the appearance of the multi-volume work by a collective under Wolfgang Schumann, *Deutschland im zweiten Weltkrieg*, 6 vols., Berlin 1974–1985, which for over a decade had linked workers from the *Zentralinstitut für deutsche Geschichte* at the *Akademie der Wissenschaften* in Berlin and the *Institut für Militärgeschichte der DDR* in Potsdam, this lack was due to be remedied by a reorganisation in the *Akademie-Institut*. This never took place and the institute has now been disbanded.

[5]*Kennzeichen J. Bilder, Dokumente, Berichte zur Geschichte der Verbrechen des Hitlerfaschismus an den deutschen Juden 1933–1945*, ed. by Helmut Eschwege, with a foreword by Arnold Zweig, Berlin 1966.

[6]Helmut Eschwege, *Fremd unter meinesgleichen. Erinnerungen eines Dresdner Juden*, Berlin 1991, pp. 184ff.

edition of the book appeared only in 1981, long after it had become unavailable in the shops.[7] The book did not achieve the impact it deserved, owing to the isolation of the GDR internationally, but it is no exaggeration to say that it is among the most important documentary volumes on the history and pre-history of the Holocaust.[*] Arnold Zweig, who had returned to Germany in 1948 and made his home in East Berlin, prefaced the book with a word of thanks to Eschwege and added his hope that it would "inspire coming generations of German readers with the courage . . . to place themselves with all their strength on the Left of our creative development".[8]

Not until twelve years later was an overall history of the persecution and destruction of the Jews published in East Germany. Once again Helmut Eschwege played a role, more significant than is apparent from the brief remarks at the beginning of the work.[9] The authors were Klaus Drobisch and Rudi Goguel, the historian and journalist Werner Müller and the historian Horst Dohle, who was a long-standing member of the East German government's *Staatssekretariat für Kirchenfragen*. The first chapter gave a survey of the history of antisemitism from German unification in 1871 to 1933. A short time before, this had also been the subject of a dissertation by Walter Mohrmann, supervised by Joachim Streisand at the Humboldt University in Berlin.[10] The subtitle of Mohrmann's subsequent book, which translates as *Ideology and History in Imperial Germany and in the Weimar Republic*, was something of an exaggeration, since the author ended with the early days of the NSDAP and did not investigate the history of antisemitism throughout the Weimar Republic. The comparatively muted response to the work can be seen as evidence that the public's own questions began just where Mohrmann had ended.

II

Intellectual analysis in East Germany of the hatred and murder of the Jews has a long history, stretching back beyond the belated participation of historians in examining its most terrible outcome. The analysis began immediately after the defeat of Hitler's state, in the newspapers and journals of the Soviet occupation zone, as well as during early political training in the infant political parties and other political organisations. These first attempts at self-understanding were encouraged by a wide range of pamphlets (at a time when paper was extremely

---

[7]In most cases the failure to issue subsequent editions should not be regarded as evidence of a desire to suppress the book. They were more likely not to appear owing to a shortage of printing capacity in the GDR and the permanent scarcity of paper.

[*]See also Helmut Eschwege, 'The Churches and the Jews in the German Democratic Republic', in *LBI Year Book XXXVII* (1992), pp. 497–513; and *idem*, 'Resistance of German Jews against the Nazi Regime', in *LBI Year Book XV* (1970), pp. 143–180 – (Ed.).

[8]Eschwege (ed.), *Kennzeichen J, op. cit.*, p. 5.

[9]Klaus Drobisch et al., *Juden unterm Hakenkreuz. Verfolgung und Ausrottung der deutschen Juden 1933–1945*, Berlin 1973.

[10]Walter Mohrmann, *Antisemitismus. Ideologie und Geschichte im Kaiserreich und in der Weimarer Republik*, Berlin 1972.

scarce, proper means of printing were lacking and the occupying power was operating a system of licenses). Today these pamphlets are very rare specimens. Historians have yet to analyse the content and effects of this early literature opposing racism, racial antisemitism and hatred of the Jews. Without anticipating such studies, we can say that the press reporting of the Nuremberg Trials of the major war criminals made the greatest contribution to an early and irrefutable documentation of the crimes against the Jews and other European peoples, nations and groups.

After the war, the first East German book to have a lasting and profound influence on large numbers of young Germans at school and university – a minority, but one which was preparing to take responsible posts in society – was written by the philologist and scholar of Romance languages and literature, Victor Klemperer. It was rooted in his own bitter experiences as a Jew in a "mixed marriage" who survived the Nazi years in Dresden and eventually escaped death near the end of the war by "going underground". His book *LTI. Notizbuch eines Philologen* (for *Lingua Tertii Imperii* – the language of the Third Reich)[11] helped thousands who had been born or who had grown up in a society where "Nazified" language was written and spoken, to recognise the basic characteristics of this system and its often hidden modes of operation. For Germans born between 1920 and 1930 the book deciphered the ways in which Nazi terminology had drawn them intellectually under the spell of the regime. Furthermore, and most important of all, it showed them that they still had to liberate themselves by their own continuous efforts.

Klemperer's was an authentic account of the everyday life of a human being in Germany who was excluded, defamed and ultimately threatened with death. Crucially, by describing numerous incidents between 1933 and 1945, it also revealed how deeply anti-Jewish ideas and an anti-Jewish mentality had taken root even among Germans who could say that they had not been active supporters of the Nazis. It thus showed that the fight against antisemitism could not be restricted to Nazi activists alone, but was truly a task for society as a whole. In this respect, Klemperer's *LTI* was effective for only a limited period and on a limited readership; otherwise, more attention would have been devoted in the later years of the GDR to the tenacity of antisemitic ideas and sentiment.

Notwithstanding this fact, Klemperer's book was reissued many times in East Germany, with the cheap paperback editions of the Leipzig *Reclam Verlag* gaining a particularly wide readership. It was also used in seminars by university students who could recognise the vocabulary of *LTI* in conversations with their parents and grandparents and even from their own mouths, and who were also aware that the words so misused by the Nazis were appearing again in their own society. Klemperer thought these tainted words should remain buried for some time. However, he also hoped that they would be recovered one day: the philologist did not wish to allow the Nazi regime the retrospective triumph of forever robbing the German language of the real words beneath the Nazi connotations.

[11] Victor Klemperer, *LTI. Notizbuch eines Philologen*, Halle 1947.

Victor Klemperer worked as a teacher at the Technical University of Dresden and as an executive member of the *Kulturbund zur demokratischen Erneuerung Deutschlands*. He gave many lectures on *LTI*, mainly to young Germans who filled the lecture halls. In addition to Klemperer, two works by young Jewish Communists[12] did most to encourage intellectual attempts in the Soviet zone to come to terms with antisemitism. Both were published in 1948 by the *Dietz Verlag* of the *Sozialistische Einheitspartei Deutschlands* (SED). Beyond their actual subject – and the effect of these books is difficult to grasp today – they became important study texts for students who sought alternatives to the vast quantities of historical-idealist teaching they received in lectures and libraries.

The life histories of the two authors, Stefan Heymann[13] and Siegbert Kahn, reveal why they were able to contribute so greatly to the intellectual endeavour to come to terms with the recent German past. Stefan Heymann, who had worked as a newspaper reporter before 1933, was among those anti-Nazis who had spent almost the entire twelve years of Nazi rule in prisons or concentration camps, surviving both Buchenwald and Auschwitz. After 1945 he undertook political work in the cultural section of the KPD/SED apparatus in Thuringia before transferring to Berlin and then to the diplomatic service.

Siegbert Kahn, after being imprisoned in Brandenburg/Görden, had escaped to Czechoslovakia and then travelled to Britain, where he worked in the Communist organisation and in the *Freie Deutsche Bewegung*. He returned to East Germany in 1946 and, at the time of writing his book, held an administrative post in Berlin where he worked on economic issues. Subsequently he became director of the *Deutsches Wirtschaftsinstitut* in the GDR.

Heymann and Kahn both emphasised the links between racism, antisemitism and the drive for expansion, preparation for war and war itself – the intention to enslave Europe and the European peoples and create a "new order" on the continent in line with the requirements of German imperialism. They indicated the historical place and specific social and political functions of the deliberate incitement of millions of Germans of all classes against the Jews as the universal scapegoat. At the same time, they described the central position of racism in the structure of Nazi ideology (a recognition which was later to be abandoned in many cases in favour of a concentration on Nazi anti-Communism). Heymann and Kahn showed how the spread of antisemitism helped the masters of the Third *Reich* to "justify" racism in general. In fact, incitement of hatred against the Jews resembled the administration of a drug which was to enable the German "race warriors" to fall on any group of people, to persecute, expel and murder them. Much of what Heymann and Kahn wrote about the connection between the material interest in expansion and its ideological clothing appears oversimplified in the light of our current research knowledge. Yet it was not their intention to simplify these complex issues into a matter of vulgar materialism.

---

[12]Stefan Heymann, *Marxismus und Rassenfrage*, Berlin 1948; Siegbert Kahn, *Antisemitismus und Rassenhetze. Eine Übersicht über ihre Entwicklung in Deutschland*, Berlin 1948.

[13]In the 1980s a new state school at Gotha in Thuringia was named after Stefan Heymann and contained an informative permanent exhibition with documents recording the life of this anti-Fascist. The name has now been changed.

They knew of the power that a reactionary ideology could attain if it gained a hold over the minds of millions; they inquired into the originators of this ideology, into the processes which encouraged its spread and into those who benefited from it.

On one particular subject – the attitude towards racism taken by the majority of Germans during the Nazi dictatorship – Heymann and Kahn took a cautious approach.[14] This fact can be regarded as an expression of the dilemma facing the anti-Nazi minority throughout Germany after the end of the war. On the one hand, it was their job to tell the majority some highly unpleasant truths about their role in the Nazi state and, where necessary, to make moral and political accusations. On the other hand, they also wanted to persuade the majority and gain its support for their own ideas and plans. Yet despite their concern and caution, Heymann and Kahn left no doubt about the extent to which this antihumanist ideology had spread among the people. Antisemitism had been a "mass phenomenon" even before Hitler. This fact enabled the NSDAP to draw on, as well as expand, the anti-Jewish ideas and sentiments of millions in their efforts to "win over the German petits bourgeois, the farmers and even the workers".[15] Eventually the Germans had followed the "racial rat catchers" and been tricked by their "swindle". The wording of these arguments was so chosen that the personal responsibility of the Nazi followers was clear to see. In subsequent accounts, however, this important aspect frequently receded into the background. Thereafter the Germans tended to be portrayed as the dupes of the "rat catchers", thus putting the majority itself into the category of victims – of a special sort, but victims nevertheless – and building a linguistic bridge, at least, to the victims in the prisons and concentration camps. As we will see later, with the passage of time the role of the majority of Germans as instruments of the criminal regime was given less and less attention in everyday political discourse, although not in literature and art.

Some of the most important arguments of Heymann and Kahn have been repeated here because they had more influence on later research into the persecution of the Jews than the resolutions and directives of the SED Political Bureau, which gave guidelines – never put together in a coherent form – for handling the legacy of what, despite reservations, was increasingly referred to as the Holocaust. Both Heymann and Kahn concluded with a direct demand for racism and antisemitism to be torn up at the roots. Kahn also called, "within the framework of economic circumstances, for reparations to be made for the crimes committed against the Jews", at least to the extent that reparation was conceivable.[16] In this, as we now know, he was unsuccessful.

Kahn had stressed the implacable opposition to antisemitism and the persecution of the Jews within the German workers' movement, though he also

---

[14]The only comment was that "the majority of the German people tolerated the barbarity of the Nazis without mounting any widely perceptible resistance", Kahn, *op. cit.*, p. 86. Even this was almost too mild, since in the case of the majority there had been no resistance at all.

[15]Heymann, *op. cit.*, p. 43.

[16]Kahn, *op. cit.*, p. 90.

pointed out that it had neglected to mount "a direct struggle against antisemitism" or to undertake "wide-ranging work to enlighten the masses of the population".[17] He made it clear that this comment related to a period when Nazi mass-murder had yet to be experienced – and, indeed, lay outside the limits of human imagination. Nevertheless, although he aimed at an historically-based judgement, this did not lessen the challenge contained in his self-critical arguments.

Heymann and Kahn were convinced that racism and antisemitism could not be permanently overcome without profound socio-economic changes in German society. Yet neither regarded the economy of capitalist society and the intellectual and moral constitution of the people as a simplistic relationship of cause and effect. There is nothing in their writings to indicate any belief that the tasks ahead would be easy or would be quickly completed. Nevertheless, only twelve years later – Eichmann had been captured in Argentina and was on trial in Israel – many official and unofficial publications were asserting that the problem in East Germany had been virtually solved. According to this view, the actual tasks of "national education" had been completed at the end of the 1950s and the beginning of the 1960s, even before the emergence of a school of history trained in East Germany itself. The academic world thus needed only to deepen and round off what politics, journalism and propaganda had already achieved. Such assertions, it must be said, were not based on actual social analysis.

Even with these reservations, it is also true that in the first fifteen years after the liberation from Nazi rule much was achieved in the analysis of racial antisemitism and hostility to the Jews. Much of the credit for this must go to those men and women who worked in the cultural arena, especially in theatre and film. A significant contribution was also made by writers. It would require studies by specialists in the history of these artistic disciplines to assess their achievements properly, but a few facts deserve brief mention here. On 7th September 1945 the *Deutsches Theater* in the Soviet sector of Berlin re-opened with its first post-war production of Lessing's *Nathan der Weise*. The same piece was staged by other theatres, including the *Nationaltheater* in Weimar, as they began work again after the war.

One of the first feature films produced by the *Deutsche Film AG* (DEFA), founded in Potsdam in 1946, was *Ehe im Schatten*, directed by Kurt Maetzig; by means of the artistic interpretation of actual events, this showed how the Nazis' merciless hatred of Jews had driven human beings to their death. The DEFA remained true to these beginnings throughout its existence. Under its auspices, in 1958–1959, Konrad Wolf produced the film *Sterne*, which was based on the transformation of a *Wehrmacht* soldier in the face of the deportation of Greek Jews to Auschwitz. Among the outstanding films to deal with the fate of the Jews under the scourge of the swastika was the film version of Jurek Becker's 1968

---

[17] *Ibid.*, p. 71.

novel *Jakob, der Lügner*. All these films were shown outside East Germany as well as to a home audience. *Sterne* was awarded a prize at the International Film Festival in Cannes, while others were worthy of similar recognition.

Attempts by East German poets to analyse the antisemitism of the Nazis are also worthy of mention. Some idea of these works can be obtained from a volume which appeared in 1968 containing poems collected by Heinz Seydel: *Welch Wort in die Kälte gerufen? Die Judenverfolgung des Dritten Reiches im Deutschen Gedicht*. This anthology brought together German poems which had been written and published before, during and after the Nazi dictatorship. Alongside the work of well-known poets, many of whom had opposed the persecutions and mass-murder from exile, it included many younger writers, who tended to concentrate on the themes of "Auschwitz" and "Theresienstadt" and to deal with questions of responsibility and guilt, of mourning and of the steps which must be taken to prevent the recurrence of barbarism. Some of the poems had clearly been written in response to the 1960s trials of both individual perpetrators and whole groups. These younger poets included Günther Deicke (b. 1922), Karl Heinz Jacobs (b. 1929), Jens Gerlach (b. 1926), Rainer Kirsch (b. 1934), Sarah Kirsch (b. 1935), Armin Müller (b. 1928) and Günter Kunert (b. 1929). Many of them expressed their opposition to the tendency to forget or to suppress the past. Johannes Robert Becher, taking up the theme of the 1944 poem *Die Kinderschuhe von Lublin*, which had become well-known in East Germany, wrote *Der Lagerraum (Auschwitz)* and asked in the last verse: "Sagt, wem ist noch ein Mahnmal; solch ein Lager?" Stephan Hermlin's poem *Die Asche von Birkenau*, written after a visit to Poland and first published in 1948, contains the following lines: "Doch die sich entsinnen, sind da, sind viele, werden mehr. Kein Mörder wird entrinnen, kein Nebel fällt um ihn her." The poetry which appeared in the GDR contained a mixture of deep concern, demand and programmatic intent. As this anthology shows, it was infused with both a commitment to tradition and a sense of responsibility for the future.

There are two reasons for recalling the contribution of literature and art in coming to terms with the Nazi legacy in general, and antisemitism in particular. First, because these masters of words and images played a part – not measurable, but none the less greater than historians could achieve – in the development of anti-Nazi thinking and sentiment across the generations in East Germany. And second, because current claims that in East Germany there was only an "anti-Fascism by decree", rather than a genuine, voluntarily adopted anti-Fascism of the heart, is likely to result in the neglect or belittling of works which continue to be worthy of political and artistic respect and attention even today.

This, however, is a digression from our main focus of interest, historiography. It is impossible to provide a complete list or examination of the books and essays which dealt with the persecution and genocide of the European Jews. A general assessment, therefore, requires an investigation of the standard general histories of the years 1933–1945 for the way in which they covered the topic. Our survey will be limited to those works most used in universities, by teachers in state schools, and for the political training system which was developed in the parties and mass organisations.

In 1966 the eight-volume *Geschichte der deutschen Arbeiterbewegung*[18] was published. This official party publication, on which Walter Ulbricht had significant influence and which he submitted to the SED Central Committee "for approval" before publication, contained the most important facts about the persecution and expulsion of the Jews before the war. An account was given of the Nazis' aim not only to win over non-Jewish Germans to their racial policy and to corrupt them, but also to intimidate them. The description of the attitude of the majority was outlined much less clearly, as is revealed, for example, in the following comments: "there was . . . no extensive protest movement"; the "passivity shown by significant parts of the German people" in the face of Nazi conduct was regarded as evidence of the fact that "fascist ideology had gained increasing influence". On the other hand, the book argued that the "class-conscious core of the . . . working class" had offered persecuted Jewish citizens "whatever help was possible", while "Christian citizens, too," had "given active help in numerous cases". Specific problems and difficulties, such as the general limitedness of all these expressions of solidarity, were suggested rather than given detailed treatment. Three years later a textbook was issued for the training of historians at universities and institutes of higher education,[19] and was subsequently used by many other East Germans with an interest in the subject. This volume dealt with the theme in more detail: with the uncertain fate of the majority of Jews who had been deprived of their posts in 1933; with the corruption of the Nazis' own supporters and fellow-travellers as a result of the direct advantages they gained from the persecutions; with the role of the anti-Jewish terror in keeping non-Jews in line; and with its significance as the barbaric prelude to the ruthless treatment of other races. In this textbook it was pointed out that the Nuremberg Laws were put into practice without protest from "millions of members of the same people" – the non-Jewish majority. The theft of Jewish property in the "Aryanisation" campaign was described, attention was concentrated on its perpetrators and beneficiaries, and Nazi lies about a "spontaneous outburst of popular anger" were exposed. However, the authors tended to see the conduct of the majority as the result of intimidation rather than as the reflection of the indoctrination of millions with racism and antisemitism. Mention was made of those people who tried to help the Jews in secret. A direct link was made between the preparation of "economic death" for the Jews and their subsequent physical liquidation; this would probably have been revised in later editions of the volume, but none were ever published.

In 1967 there appeared the twelfth and final volume of the textbook written by members of the *Institut für Geschichte* of the *Deutsche Akademie der Wissenschaften zu Berlin* and the *Institut für Militärgeschichte der DDR* (Potsdam). A second, revised

---

[18] *Geschichte der deutschen Arbeiterbewegung in acht Bänden*, herausgegeben vom Institut für Marxismus-Leninismus beim Zentralkomitee der Sozialistischen Einheitspartei Deutschlands, Berlin 1966, esp. vol. V, from which the extracts are taken. See esp. pp. 214–215.

[19] *Deutschland von 1933 bis 1939. Von der Machtübertragung an den Faschismus bis zur Entfesselung des zweiten Weltkrieges*, by Erich Paterna et al., Berlin 1969. (It was part of the twelve-volume *Lehrbuch-Reihe zur deutschen Geschichte*, ed. by Joachim Streisand.)

edition was published in 1975.[20] The authors investigated the intensification of Jewish persecutions in Germany and the conquered territories of Poland after the outbreak of war, the beginning of expulsions and ghettoisation and the development of a separate apparatus to organise and co-ordinate these measures in the *Reichssicherheitshauptamt* under Eichmann. They provided details about the Madagascar Plan, the murders committed by the *Einsatzgruppen* and described the Wannsee Conference. The last murder action against half a million Hungarian Jews, conducted under the direct command of Eichmann, was outlined. The authors also gave a figure for the total number of Jewish victims in the extermination camps; this reflected the extent of knowledge at that time on this subject and has since been revised.[21] Overall it is necessary to point out that this volume pays insufficient attention to the groups of perpetrators or to an analysis of the complicity of millions of Germans. Its description of the terror waged by the Nazis against their own population might also have encouraged the impression that there was greater opposition on principle to the Nazi war effort than was in fact the case.

This brief, inevitably incomplete survey of the standard works of GDR historiography is sufficient to disprove current claims that East German citizens were given no way of finding out about the Jews and their persecution and murder. This is just one part of a more general tendency among former citizens of the GDR to avoid any recognition of personal failings or omissions by blaming them on the East German *Unrechtsstaat*. Yet the matter cannot be left there. An examination of these standard works also shows which themes were given preferential treatment in research and which were neglected. In other words, it reveals an imbalance and a failure to do justice to the subject.

Before we investigate further, and also in order to make this imbalance clear, it is useful to glance at the treatment of the subject in schools. In East Germany there was *one* school text which was approved by the Ministry of Education for each discipline and each school year; teachers usually worked with these on the basis of compulsory teaching plans and with the aid of a methodological handbook. It should be stated from the start that a more detailed analysis of the teaching plans, teachers' handbooks and school texts is necessary than there is space for here. Equally, it would be illuminating to observe the amendments made to each new edition of school history books, rather than simply looking at

---

[20] *Deutschland von 1939 bis 1945. (Deutschland während des zweiten Weltkriegs)*, by Wolfgang Bleyer et al., Berlin 1967 and 1975. The first edition was also published in Russian (Moscow 1971). During its preparation there was an inconclusive debate between historians from the GDR and the Soviet Union. The translated version was not faithful to the original text. In the Moscow edition passages referring to Jews, Jewish resistance and the murder of the Jews were omitted. See esp. pp. 40–41 of the German version and p. 37 of the Russian edition. The author would like to thank Professor Gerhart Hass (Rangsdorf, Berlin), who took part in the discussions in Moscow, for these references. It was typical of the nature of co-operation at the time that, in the foreword to the second edition (1975), the German authors expressed their gratitude for the "considerable assistance" of their Soviet partners (see p. 12), though they retained the comments made in the first edition.

[21] Wolfgang Bleyer et al., *Deutschland von 1939 bis 1945, op. cit.*, pp. 43, 205, 210–211, 213ff., 352.

the last edition to be published in the GDR as done here.[22] This last edition, introduced in 1988, was the work of the *Zentralinstitut für Geschichte* of the *Akademie der Wissenschaften der DDR*, a fact which makes clear the extensive intellectual influence of the members of the *Akademie*. On the other hand, it could also be regarded as a somewhat wasteful use of the labour of academics whose real task was to undertake basic research.

In East German schools the Nazi era was covered in Year 9; that is, by fourteen- to fifteen-year-old children. Throughout the school year their subject of study was world history (with the main emphasis on German history) between 1917 and 1949. Like the university texts we have studied, the school book provided details of the most important anti-Jewish measures and the attempts to justify them on the basis of racism and antisemitism: the boycott of 1933, the Nuremberg Laws, the Pogrom of 1938 and subsequent legislation, the "Aryanisation" programme, the increase in persecution after the attack on Poland with the expulsion and ghettoisation of the Jews, the Wannsee Conference, the establishment of the extermination camps and sites. The book included photographs showing the boycott appeal, the removal of Jewish men to concentration camps in 1938, the arrival of victims in Auschwitz-Birkenau and a map showing the sites of the "death factories" of Auschwitz, Belzec, Sobibor, Treblinka, Majdanek and Kulmhof. Anyone wishing to know whether East German school pupils were able to find out about the persecution and murder of the Jews must also examine, in addition to history lessons, the teaching of German literature and the history of art. The teaching plan for Year 7 (thirteen-year-olds) thus required the study of the work *Die Geschwister von Ravensbrück*, by F.C. Weiskopf, which tells the remarkable story of Jewish orphans who escaped the murderers. In Year 9 the play by Friedrich Wolf, *Professor Mamlock*, written in exile in the Soviet Union, was compulsory reading; a film and a radio version were available for inclusion in the teaching programme. During the same Year 9, Lessing's *Nathan der Weise* was read in extracts which emphasised the parable of the ring – a plea for religious tolerance. Furthermore, the reader for the teaching of German in Year 9 included two poems by Johannes R. Becher. The text of the above-mentioned *Kinderschuhe aus Lublin* (here Lublin meant Majdanek concentration and extermination camp) was preceded by a short extract of the report written in 1944 by Konstantin Simonov following the liberation of the camp by Soviet troops. Detailed treatment was also given to the *Ballade von den dreien*, which Becher wrote in 1941 and which expressed the hope that Germans would refuse to kill Russians, Jews and fellow Germans who opposed these crimes. Though the poem ends by observing that the Germans did choose to kill, there was considerable room for teachers to interpret the poem as they saw fit: the focus could have been on the Germans who resisted, or on the majority who committed murder. In Year 10, the last year of compulsory schooling, pupils read extracts from Heinrich Mann's novel *Der Untertan*. The teaching plan

---

[22] *Geschichte. Lehrbuch für Klasse 9*, ed. by the Zentralinstitut für Geschichte an der Akademie der Wissenschaften der DDR, Berlin 1988, esp. pp. 129, 142, 150, 168f., 172, 192. The coverage of the Second World War ends by observing that 270,000 Jews had been driven from Germany and approximately 240,000 of those who remained had been murdered (p. 200).

specifically demanded a discussion of the way in which Diederich Heßling's Prussian-German school had developed his craving for power over others, and of the fact that one result was his "ruthless conduct" towards his Jewish fellow pupils. In short, the material gave both teachers and pupils the opportunity to examine antisemitism and the persecution of the Jews in a variety of ways.

As in every country and at all times, there were undoubted failings in certain aspects of the East German school texts. On this subject there is room for argument. Vital, however, was the failure to place the history of the Jews and their persecutors between 1933 and 1945 in their historical context from the Jewish point of view, thus leaving the topic more or less "in mid-air". East German children were taught next to nothing about the origins of the Jews, their religion, their arrival in Germany, the changes in their lives and their position in state and society after emancipation, their role in the sciences, the arts, in culture and the emerging capitalist economy. Even the teachers knew little. It was difficult for them to fill these gaps in information without turning to specialist publications or to older material in academic libraries. In any case, which teachers had the time and opportunity for such study? Omissions in research and publishing thus had a serious effect on popular education in the broadest sense. Of course there were well-read teachers who made use of East German books from various genres and taught themselves about the history of the Jewish people. Yet they could not hope to gain adequate information from their own resources. With few exceptions, school teaching on the subject of the Nazi persecution of the Jews mirrored the state of academic research, its strengths and weaknesses, its achievements as well as its omissions and failures.[23]

III

Throughout the whole history of the GDR no research institute or centre was established to deal specifically with the history of the Jews and their persecution in Germany – neither in the seven universities nor in any of the history research centres of the *Akademie der Wissenschaften*. When a few researchers did turn to the subject, it was as the result of a personal decision. The lack of an institutional centre or focus (quite unlike the history of the German workers' movement, for example) inevitably had a negative effect on the regional and local activities of historians, especially those in medium- and small-sized towns.

Only in 1988 did East German historians, teachers and archivists engaged with the history of the Jews and their persecution come together for the first (and only) time in order to exchange information and to provide details of their work.

---

[23]The theme was the subject of one of the few controversies (see also note 3) in which historians of the former GDR engaged in over their work. It was carried on in the pages of the journal *Konkret*, which appeared in Hamburg, and involved Olaf Groehler, latterly deputy director of the *Zentralinstitut für deutsche Geschichte* at the *Akademie der Wissenschaften zu Berlin*, Jürgen Kuczynski, Kurt Gossweiler, retired veteran member of the *Institut*, and the author of this article, who was a professor at the Humboldt University until 1992. Contributions can be found in Nos. 5 (1992), 8 (1992) and 3 (1993).

Though this had not been forbidden before, it had never been encouraged either. It was a reflection of the ossified East German political system that, unless things were actually demanded by the central authorities, they were rarely encouraged at middle and lower levels of the state. When researchers wanted to produce small publications on the local history of the Jews, for which they needed help with printing costs or other assistance from state agencies, they faced many obstacles – and sometimes failed to overcome them.[24] Given these facts, which are beyond dispute, it is easy to resort to accusations of disguised antisemitism. Yet in reality, they are more an indication of submissiveness to authority and its unavoidable corollary, a self-imposed withdrawal from all initiatives "from below", however reasonable. On a larger scale, such attitudes were part of the sickness which ultimately brought down the GDR itself. There were no institutions – and not a single periodical – dealing with the history of the Jews. For this situation the historians themselves must bear a high degree of responsibility: even in 1988, when the chances of success were relatively good, there was no attempt to remedy this entirely unsatisfactory state of affairs.

Marxist historians in the GDR concentrated their efforts on the study of two main themes within the vast subject of the persecution and murder of Jews under the swastika. The first related to the functions of antisemitism in the 1930s and 1940s. Several studies were written about the needs which were served by the spread of antisemitism before and after the establishment of the Nazi dictatorship. These will be briefly described here. In line with its traditional course, antisemitism was seen to have steered social protest against the Jews, thus diverting it away from the true originators of German misfortunes. To an extent previously unknown in German history, it served to rally masses of people around an extreme reactionary leadership group advocating the most inhumane programme to be pursued both inside and outside Germany. During the establishment and consolidation of the Nazi dictatorship antisemitism acted as a substitute for the failure to introduce those fundamental changes in society which had been trumpeted as "National Socialism". During the initially insidious and then runaway "Aryanisation" programme it served as a justification for the enrichment of members of all classes of the non-Jewish population, following the state-regulated principle of "to him who hath, shall be given". It helped Germany's rulers to corrupt a section of its followers – a number difficult to quantify, but not only active Nazis in the NSDAP, the SA and SS: first, they were corrupted materially with jobs made vacant by the dismissal and expulsion of the Jews, with homes that Jews had been forced to leave and with promotion prospects; second, they were corrupted spiritually by the ludicrous claim that they – in reality degraded followers – were members of the "master race". Long before the outbreak of war, antisemitism served to incite the population to racial chauvinism against the Soviet Union ("Jewish Bolshevism") and against the bourgeois democracies of the West ("Jewish plutocracy"). Subsequently, it was used in order to depict the war as a crime launched by a two-pronged "international Jewry" in its alleged desire to destroy Germany. In these ways,

[24]Works of varying quality were produced on Jewish local history in Rostock, Görlitz, Leipzig, Plauen and other towns in East Germany.

though East German historians did not discover these functions of antisemitism, they helped to define its role in the system.

The second complex of themes studied by East German academics, which can be mentioned only briefly here, related to the criminal consequences of antisemitism, especially in the war years. At a time when West German historiography was still reticent, to say the least, historians from the GDR did much to prove that not all murderers wore black or brown uniforms, but that large numbers of men in field grey and in civilian clothes took part in the "Final Solution" actively or from their desks. This line of research bore fruit with the documentary collection *Europa unterm Hakenkreuz*, published in several volumes and edited by the late Wolfgang Schumann and Ludwig Nestler.[25] This work neither left out, nor glossed over information, brought recognition both to its authors as individuals and to the historical profession in the GDR, and led to invitations to national and international conferences following its publication.

Compared to these two major themes others, as we have seen, were unjustifiably neglected. A number of philosophers and literary scholars produced more important studies of the structure, history and pre-history of Nazi ideology and its antisemitic core than did historians. The works of Joachim Petzold in the 1970s and 1980s deserve particular attention.[26] The most important early analysis, however, was produced by the philosopher Wolfgang Heise in his book *Aufbruch in die Illusion*, which appeared in 1964[27] and was never reprinted. This work investigated the relationship of antisemitism and racial theory to other elements of Nazi ideology. In an argument which bore marked similarities to those of Heymann and Kahn, Heise wrote that the "proclamation of Germanic-Aryan racial supremacy in association with the practice of antisemitism was – on the basis of the terror waged against all anti-Fascist forces – the decisive ideological-political means of intimidation, corruption and bestialisation".[28]

As in the case of the gaps in the school texts, historians in the GDR significantly failed to produce an analysis of the way in which millions of people became prejudiced against the Jews, allowed themselves to be incited against them or – as in the case of the majority – watched their sufferings with indifference and a lack of sympathy, either from mental and spiritual inertia or because they regarded at least some of the treatment of the Jews as justified. The fact that no monograph appeared on this subject is the responsibility of the historians. Their failure, however, is indirectly linked with an attitude within the East German leadership élite, which began to develop alongside the socio-

---

[25] *Europa unterm Hakenkreuz. Die Okkupationspolitik des deutschen Faschismus (1938–1945)*, ed. by Wolfgang Schumann, Ludwig Nestler *et al.* Seven of the eight volumes appeared between 1988 and 1993, organised according to countries or groups of countries. The last two were edited by the *Bundesarchiv*, Koblenz. The series was the only unfinished work in several volumes dating from GDR times not to fall victim to the changed political conditions.

[26] Joachim Petzold, *Die Demagogie des Hitlerfaschismus. Die politische Funktion der Naziideologie auf dem Wege zur faschistischen Diktatur*, Berlin 1982.

[27] Wolfgang Heise, *Aufbruch in die Illusion. Zur Kritik der bürgerlichen Philosophie in Deutschland*, Berlin 1964.

[28] *Ibid.*, p. 323.

economic changes introduced by the East German state and which was reinforced by the Cold War. It regarded participation in the building of an alternative society as the best (and soon as the only), form of practical reparation which could be demanded from the followers of Nazism as expiation for the crimes of the regime. Such participation would stand as proof that each individual was coming to terms with the Nazi past. Influential forces in the state leadership saw any discussion of the role of older Germans in the criminal Nazi regime, with a few laudable exceptions, as likely to hinder the development of solidarity for new programmes and objectives. Whether this assumption was based on conjecture or reality cannot be decided with hindsight. In East Germany, under the impact of internal conditions and external influences, there was thus an "indulgent" treatment of the former citizens of the Third *Reich*. Their lives and work had altered fundamentally after 1945, initially without most of them doing anything to bring this about. Today it is impossible to know whether, and to what extent, these objective changes were linked with a subjective change in the form of the emergence of a new world of ideas and feelings. Though there was undoubtedly opportunism on a massive scale, there was also evidence of a genuine search for a new direction. The indulgent treatment of people who had supported the Nazis only a few years before cannot be adequately explained without reference to events in the western zones of occupation at the same time. In the new Federal Republic a number of tainted Nazis were rising to leading positions in state and society. In consequence, not a few former Nazi functionaries in the Soviet Zone were drawn to the West, either because they hoped to return to their old posts, or because they could at least expect to have their pension and insurance claims recognised (which they were not in the East).

What have these facts to do with historiography? One significant result was a marked chronological dislocation. In the very early post-war years, when only a few anti-Fascists were writing and speaking challengingly of the masses' co-responsibility and guilt for the Nazi regime and its crimes – and this debate was *essential* to explain and justify the profound effects involved in the changes to the eastern borders and the reparations payments – there was as yet no historiography of Nazism in the East. By the time new generations of historians could have described these years, the theme was regarded politically not only as "untopical", but also as an unwelcome revival of the question of guilt. It was on this soil that the "seeds of Socialist development" were to grow.

From the end of the 1950s until the collapse of the GDR, a number of younger East German historians took as a central theme the complex relationship between the theory and practice of antisemitism, the interests of big corporations and the role of the upper and middle classes in the various stages of the persecutions. They thus investigated a sequence of events beginning with the "Aryanisation" of boards of trustees and executives, company meetings and management, proceeding to the "Aryanisation" of Jewish wealth in banks and industrial concerns and ending with the process of mass-extermination itself. At an early stage Kahn had drawn up a brief list of firms which had enriched themselves. However, he had left open some very important questions. Were the main beneficiaries also the initiators of, or at least accomplices in, the assaults on the banking and industrial wealth and landed property of German, Austrian and other Jews? Had they been well-organised thieves operating according to a set plan, or "merely" opportunists? In their shameless driving of Jewish workers to death (*Vernichtung durch Arbeit*) had they followed the orders of state authorities, or had they themselves issued these orders by virtue of their influence within the machinery of Nazi rule? During this period, West German historiography and journalism singularly failed to take account of the research by American groups into the role of non-Jewish corporations in the "Aryanisation business",[29] and there was a widespread and growing ignorance of the judgements reached at Nuremberg. At the same time, and in response, historians in East Germany felt an even greater duty to bring new information to light and to prevent well-known facts being forgotten. This happened in a situation where the mass of relevant sources was not accessible to researchers and restrictive measures had been imposed (a fact which tends to be forgotten today).[30]

For several decades, the web of relations encompassing capital interests – state policy, ideology and the persecution and murder of the Jews – was one of the most important themes of debate between the advocates of various theories about Fascism. This was obviously about more than the answer to a partial question, since the response had implications for the entire system and its depiction. It is not unreasonable to ask what place material and, especially, economic facts and processes would have occupied in West German historiography if there had been no such challenge from the GDR. East German works of academic history and journalism contained a number of more or less striking simplifications in the description of the connections between economic interests and the laws, decrees, measures and actions of the state. However, attempts to explain these inadequacies fall short when they refer solely to Georgi Dimitrov's "doctrine of Fascism"; indeed, those who write of this formula seek to create the impression that the Marxist understanding of Fascism consisted of one definition only, which made the debate easier and even appear superfluous. In reality, simplifications and false abstractions from reality were more often the result of the authors' inadequate mastery of their "own" theory and their inability to think in terms of complex contexts and processes. On occasion, slavish adherence to the idea that "the main thing is to strike a blow against imperialism" also seduced East German historians and worked against their original intent. Although it cannot be denied that there were simplifications in the writing produced, these were not as numerous, and in their content not as trite, as the constant assertions of Federal Republican publications that the aforementioned connections were supposedly a dogmatic construction removed from reality. Even more misconceived – and opposed by East German historians – were those West German

[29]Verbatim details of the Office of Military Government for Germany (OMGIS). Reports with their findings against *IG-Farben*, the *Dresdner Bank* and the *Deutsche Bank* were only made available to a wider public in 1985 and 1986 through the German editions published by a small company in the old Federal Republic.

[30]Among these practices was one whereby users of GDR archives were asked to pay the cost of copying documents not in cash but, if they came from Western countries, to pay the equivalent in the form of microfilms which were not available to GDR purchasers.

attempts to reduce the Nazi state to the person of Hitler and to claim that he alone was responsible for the transition to the mass murder of the Jews.[31]

Historians in the GDR also took part in the still highly topical international historical debate about the place of the murder of European Jewry within the overall concept of German imperialism. Here they opposed the view that it was possible to separate this crime from the other misdeeds of the Nazi conquerors in their struggle for world supremacy because it was a self-standing goal – and ultimately became a substitute for unattainable final military victory. Specialists in World War history pointed out that the new "Europe under the swastika" was to be a continent without a single Jew, but that in the "Greater Germanic world empire" there was to be no room for other German and non-German groups of people either. A glance at the total plan, especially the *Generalplan Ost* which the Nazis produced and began to put into practice, takes nothing away from the specific character of the genocide of the Jews, which both links it with the crimes against the gypsies (Sinti and Roma), Slavs, Asians and others and also distinguishes it from them. The Jews occupied the first place in the racist hierarchy of human beings to be persecuted. Until May 1945 they were hounded and exterminated to a degree which far exceeded the fate meted out to other groups, with the exception of the gypsies. Their merciless and soulless torturers placed the Jews in the category of animals, judged them as worthless, and also deemed them to be the most dangerous of all the opponents of their plans for world mastery. Various "Final Solution programmes", in more or less clear form, existed for the period following final military victory: against homosexuals and against groups of the supposedly or actually incurably sick, for example. The "Final Solution of the Jewish problem", however, was to take place during the course of the war itself; where the Jews were concerned there was no argument for even a temporary postponement of the murderous onslaught. This fact did not preclude the discovery of the Jewish capacity for work, especially when workers began to grow scarce.

Within the historiography of the persecution and murder of the Jews there is one specific line of argument which sees their fate as irrefutable proof that the Nazi state had detached itself completely from the interests it had originally represented and which had once spoon-fed Hitler and his followers within the NSDAP, launched them to power and financed their establishment. According to this theory, the Nazi state in its relations with these interests had moved from a position of relative independence to one of complete autonomy. The mass murder of the Jews was thus seen as evidence in support of a history which presented Nazi rule as increasingly, and in the end totally, determined by ideology and by Hitler. From its capitalist beginnings and foundation – insofar as these were actually recognised as a factor in the early stages of the regime – the Nazi state had so-to-speak reached astronomic heights. The murder of the Jews was regarded as proof that capital interests and political rule had ultimately

---

[31] For example, the subtitle of Gerald Reitlinger's famous book on the "Final Solution", which in the English edition was *The Attempt to Exterminate the Jews of Europe, 1939–1945*, was changed in the German version and its subsequent editions to *Hitlers Versuch der Ausrottung der Juden Europas 1939–1945*.

broken apart altogether and become as incompatible as fire and water: the one required the retention of potential workers, the other exterminated them in millions. Historians in the GDR did not give these arguments in favour of a theory of "anti-capitalist Fascism" the attention which might have been expected from advocates of a historical-materialist conception of history. In many cases the theoretical implications of this interpretation of the genocide of the Jews were not even perceived. The assertion that the mass murder of people who were in many cases capable of work was incompatible in principle with the profit-interests of capital was clearly unhistorical. Throughout its history capitalism had not been interested in an absolute surplus of workers, as was proven by the history of colonialism from beginning to end. Capitalism recognised the need to have workers available only within the limits of its momentary and foreseeable demand. When the German rulers began the extermination of the Jews in 1941, they had at their disposal a seemingly inexhaustible potential supply of human beings whom they could use as forced labour. They still believed this to be the case the following year, when their plan for the swift defeat of the Soviet Union had failed. Apart from certain exceptions, Jewish labour was generally regarded as easy to replace. While the Jews were murdered in their tens and hundreds of thousands, the conquerors supplied their war industries with slave labourers from nearly all the conquered territories; they directed men and women wherever they saw a need for them, they sent Yugoslav workers to Norway to labour for the "Final Victory".

Beyond doubt, detailed investigation had revealed the history of the persecution and murder of the Jews to be a field in which theories of Fascism were able to prove themselves indispensable or be shown as untenable. Given this fact, East German researchers into Nazism generally failed to take sufficient part in the various international debates. This was especially true of the *Historikerstreit* which excited attention and argument far beyond the confines of the historical profession and the borders of Germany.[32] This must be seen as a loss of tradition, as in the theoretical work done on the history of the German workers' movement since its beginnings, preference had often been given to polemical forms of describing individual positions. Among East German historians there was never any dispute which resembled that waged between the "intentionalists" and the "functionalists" in the Federal Republic and among historians engaged on the study of the Holocaust in general. Part of the reason may lie in the fact that there were few researchers in this comparatively narrow field inside the smaller and less densely populated East German state. Second – and much more significant – was the fact that differences of opinion, though they existed, were seldom expressed in public. The outward image of a unified Marxist-Leninist view of history, and the solidarity of its representatives, was not even to be questioned,

---

[32] The author, however, took part in these debates in two West German journals. Though several West German publishers documented the controversy in paperback editions, there was no publication giving the opinions of participants from outside Germany.

let alone shaken or destroyed. Of course some controversial issues did arise and were debated among East German historians. They arose from differences of methodological approach or directly from the contradictory nature of the subject of research. Before the terms "intentionalist" and "functionalist" had been coined, this author took the view – contrary to that developed by Rudi Goguel – that it was both possible and necessary to distinguish between the murderous anti-Jewish thinking of the German National Socialists, which was evident from the beginning of their activity, and the step-by-step approach and transition to actual mass murder; that the anti-Jewish policy of the leaders around Hitler was not simply derived from a concept that was unalterable once laid down, but was itself the subject of development. Controversies of this nature, however, were carried out on the periphery of historical work and were barely perceived outside the profession. This fact itself was not without negative effects on general awareness of the issue, including that of students.

This brings us to an issue which is now highly topical: how much did the SED leadership and the state influence academic life? We live in a time when many people in Eastern Germany are inclined to see themselves as the victims of the former state, perhaps to help them make a start in the new one, or simply to modify their life stories so as to make them more livable. In these circumstances it should be stressed that historians in the GDR themselves bore the main responsibility for what they wrote. This is not to deny that there were powerful non-academic and politically significant influences on research and publication; on many occasions, academic historians were expected to take their own political direction from politically loaded concepts such as the *"nationale Grundkonzeption"* (Basic National Concept) and later *"Erbe und Tradition"* (Heritage and Tradition).

Nevertheless, across wide areas of their discipline – with the exception of the history of the workers' movement in the twentieth century and the history of the GDR – historians themselves could decide what to research and how to present their findings. This was certainly the case with the history of the persecution and murder of the Jews. No historian can justifiably offer the excuse that certain things were prescribed and others forbidden. State policy undeniably exerted an indirect influence: as a result of its enduring contention that there was no particular value in researching this subject, in contrast to the history of the workers' movement, it failed to offer any sort of appropriate encouragement. Even so, as we have seen, historians could at least have demanded a more positive approach from the state. Not until the resolution calling for the establishment of the *Centrum Judaicum* in Berlin, with its site next to the partially reconstructed synagogue in Oranienburgerstraße, was there any prospect of a research centre concentrating on the history of the Jews, of persecution and of antisemitism. By the end of the GDR these plans had made little progress and had yet to be put into practice. Now that Berlin is no longer partitioned, the *Zentrum für Antisemitismusforschung* at the *Technische Universität* has become the focus for research, including that undertaken outside the university.

On this subject too there were potential and actual areas of conflict between politics and academic life. While it is true that East German historiography was unaffected by the wild anti-Zionist campaigns of the late 1940s and early 1950s, which also reached the GDR,[33] this was only because no such research was yet being done. Only now, with the release of archival material, is it clear that these internal Communist arguments, carried out under the false flag of a struggle against the alleged "Zionist-imperialist world conspiracy", gave overt antisemites the opportunity to act with the state security apparatus.

Partisan support of the Arabs during the long Arab-Israeli struggle did not influence the historical research of the 1960s, which was very limited in scope. It had much more effect on political journalism and, to an extent which is difficult to define, served to encourage and revive old anti-Jewish ideas. A part was played here by the coarse depiction of the origins and driving forces of the conflict despite the fact that the Soviet thesis of "blue and white Fascism" was not adopted.[34] The historical profession in the GDR had no specialists who could have given truthful accounts to counter the clichés being spread about Zionism. Even a brief examination of the history of the *Zionistische Vereinigung für Deutschland* in Germany during the 1920s and early 1930s is, of course, sufficient to reveal the variety of positions adopted by the Zionists. In the last years of the East German state, political interests began to dictate a change of policy when *Staatsratvorsitzender* Erich Honecker was seeking an official visit to the United States. Part of the attempt to arrange such a visit involved ostentatious assertions that the small Jewish minority in the GDR was protected and able to live according to its own norms and standards, and that the East German state recognised a duty to encourage popular remembrance of the millions of Jewish victims of the Nazis. The fiftieth anniversary of the November Pogrom in 1938 was marked by a series of publications and announcements by the state and its various organs and institutions. These showed that much could be achieved once the state authorities had pointed the way. Regional and local initiatives now had more chance to make progress. Yet in many ways this campaign made little impact on the academic world, which could not produce in-depth research and publications in response to recent short-term orders. As regards the growth of general awareness, it was significant that in 1988 the Jews were not depicted solely as a group with a special historical and ethnic past, but also as a religious minority. Nevertheless, information regarding the nature and attributes of this religious belief remained meagre.

It is pointless to ask what effects the campaign of 1988 might have had on the society of the GDR and its historical profession in the long term. The political and economic crisis was already coming to a head. Attempts to end the paralysis and seek a new understanding between the members of society, to which the

[33] Research has begun on this theme and its results are voiced mainly in newspapers and journals. This has revealed that the anti-Zionist campaign left its ugly traces in the GDR, though not to the extent found in the Soviet Union and some other "people's democracies" (especially Czechoslovakia with the Slansky trial). See for example Wilfriede Otto, 'Genossen, ich verstehe nicht', in *Neues Deutschland* (23rd March 1993), p. 14. This shows the fate of the Communist Hans Schrecker, who was arrested after false accusations in 1952 and subjected to antisemitic abuse from his investigators; they were not brought to account even after his release in 1956.
[34] Recently two historians from the former GDR have made critical and self-critical assessments of the view of Israel which was disseminated for decades. See for example Johannes Glasneck and Angelika Timm, *Israel. Die Geschichte des Staates seit seiner Gründung*, Bonn–Berlin 1992.

remembrance of the events of 1938 can to some extent be added, were no more than half-hearted. They came much too late and were doomed to failure.

This article was written at a time when the public in Berlin and the new federal states, as elsewhere, were commemorating the fiftieth anniversary of the Warsaw Ghetto rising. Now is an appropriate time to ask how East German historiography dealt with the theme of Jewish resistance and the resistance of Jews (while the two are not identical, the difference between them is so fine as to be almost purely academic). It is worth pointing out that Eschwege ended his volume with a chapter entitled 'Resistance', which concentrated on the minority of survivors and those who helped them. In *Juden unterm Hakenkreuz* the authors mentioned the resistance in several sections and ended their account with an assessment of 'Resistance and help in the last phase of mass murder'. However, just as historians in general gave an inadequate account of the life and everyday experiences of non-Jewish Germans under the Nazi regime, so their failure to explain what it meant to live as a Jew in Germany at that time was even greater. Because attention was concentrated on dramatic events – 1st April 1933, 15th September 1933, 9th-10th November 1938 – the majority of the population, which was born after the war, could gain no real idea of the permanent drama of life in a society ruled by Jew-haters, nor of the defence mounted by the persecuted, their acts of self-assertion and their resistance and survival. In discussions and meetings with young citizens, historians were regularly asked why the Jews had not defended themselves. At one of these meetings, in East Berlin in 1984, the question was turned around: "Do you have any idea what you are talking about?" In order to understand the behaviour of the persecuted, it was and is essential for us to acquire and to disseminate knowledge about the history of the Jews and their organisations, about the development of their position and attitudes, about the prospects for and limits on independent action. These details were – and are – largely lacking. It must be said that this situation was not unique to the popular consciousness of the GDR.

In East Germany, however, there was for a long time an additional obstacle. Not immediately after the war, but with increasing force thereafter, the concept of resistance came to be subjected to a narrow and dogmatic framework. The limits and levels which existed within the resistance, the differences between its supporters, participants, methods, means and ends, were subjected to a schematic classification. The anti-imperialist goal increasingly became the yardstick for evaluating actions against the Nazi regime. Unquestionably this had consequences for the judgement of the conduct of the Jews. The classification of individuals into resistance fighters on the one hand, and victims who were not resistance fighters on the other, did not permit any understanding of the specific situation facing the German Jews. They could not develop their own strategy and tactics of self-assertion until they had begun to be aware of their common fate and had to decide whether to accept it or to devise means of thwarting, or at least limiting, the plans of their persecutors.

To categorise the underestimation of Jewish efforts at self-assertion under conditions of increasing persecution as "antisemitism" means another use of the framework employed to distinguish between "fighters" and "victims". This narrowing of the concept of resistance had specific *political* roots. It was designed to ensure the leadership élite of the GDR, which included genuine opponents of the Nazis who had suffered for many years – Erich Honecker in prison, Horst Sindermann in Mauthausen, and many others – an extraordinary and undisputed authority. This increased as they came to rank among the last survivors of the underground struggle against the Nazi regime.

In terms of organisation a form of supervisory role was assumed by the *Komittee der Widerstandskämpfer der DDR*, and especially its leaders. This committee did much to ensure the Communist monopoly of the concept of resistance – against all better judgement. Since the committee and its subordinate bodies exerted the major influence on resistance memorials – especially the National Memorials on the sites of the former big camps (Buchenwald, Sachsenhausen, Ravensbrück) – its attitudes were also expressed in the exhibitions and publications of these institutions. The few historians who worked in them, members of later generations, worked on the basis of directives from above. This situation ensured that only in isolated cases, for example in Ravensbrück, studies were made of the fate of the Jews in these camps. Though the 1980s saw the beginning of a shift in the traditional attitude and a move towards a wider perspective, there were no fundamental changes in GDR times. Here it must be noted that a significant number of the resistance fighters themselves disagreed with the dogmatisation of the concept and image of resistance, but were unable to alter it. Today these individuals not only agree with the changes – for example in the memorials – but are also taking part in implementing them as far as possibilities allow.

Overall, this provisional account, in my opinion, justifies the assertion that East German historians did discharge their duty to describe the crimes of the Nazis against the Jews and to keep the memory alive. For the reasons explained above, they neglected to present an unvarnished account of the role of non-Jewish Germans in the Nazi regime and their attitude towards the persecution of the Jews. Historians made little response to a call by Professor Moshe Zimmermann at a meeting of the Stuttgart International Historians' Congress in 1985, to the effect that German historians had a duty to write the history of the Jews during the Nazi dictatorship, not because they were the next generation after the persecutors, but because the few remaining Jews in Germany could not do this for themselves.

Looking back on my own work, I am aware at a certain point of a feeling of inhibition. Is it possible to write objectively about this subject – especially given that history is necessarily written from a critical perspective? This is a point every historian has to come to terms with, especially if he or she has been born a German.

Publications on German-speaking Jewry

A Selected and Annotated Bibliography of Books and Articles 1994

Compiled by

BARBARA SUCHY and ANNETTE PRINGLE

Leo Baeck Institute
4 Devonshire Street
London W1N 2BH

CONTENTS

		Page
I.	HISTORY	
	A. General	315
	Linguistics/Western Yiddish	320
	B. Communal and Regional History	322
	1. Germany	322
	1a. Alsace	334
	2. Austria	334
	3. Central Europe	337
	4. Switzerland	338
	C. German-speaking Jews in Various Countries	339
II.	RESEARCH AND BIBLIOGRAPHY	
	A. Libraries and Institutes	342
	B. Bibliographies, Catalogues and Reference Books	344
III.	THE NAZI PERIOD	
	A. General	346
	B. Jewish Resistance	363
IV.	POST WAR	
	A. General	364
	B. Education and Teaching. Memorials	369
V.	JUDAISM	
	A. Jewish Learning and Scholars	371
	B. The Jewish Problem	376
	C. Jewish Life and Organisations	377
	D. Jewish Art and Music	380
VI.	ZIONISM AND ISRAEL	380
VII.	PARTICIPATION IN CULTURAL AND PUBLIC LIFE	
	A. General	382
	B. Individual	389
VIII.	AUTOBIOGRAPHY, MEMOIRS, LETTERS, GENEALOGY	406
IX.	GERMAN-JEWISH RELATIONS	
	A. General	410
	B. Church and Synagogue	412
	C. Antisemitism	413
	D. Noted Germans and Jews	416
X.	FICTION AND POETRY	418
	INDEX	421

BIBLIOGRAPHY 1995

I. HISTORY

A. General

31384. BATTENBERG, FRIEDRICH: *Die Juden Mitteleuropas und das Reichskammergericht.* [In]: Recht und Verfassung in Hessen. Vom Reichskammergericht zur Landesverfassung. Hrsg.: Hess. Landeszentrale für polit. Bildung, Wiesbaden, 1994. Pp. 28–38, notes, illus.

31385. BATTENBERG, FRIEDRICH: *Juden in Europa. Zur tausendjährigen Geschichte einer Minderheit.* [In]: Kulturen in Europa. Hrsg.: Forschungsstelle Migration und Integration. H. 1/2/3, Freiburg: Forschungsstelle Migration und Integration, 1993. Pp. 105–126, footnotes.(Interkulturell.)

31386. BATTENBERG, FRIEDRICH: *Juden vor dem Reichskammergericht.* [In]: Frieden durch Recht. Das Reichskammergericht 1495 bis 1806. Hrsg. von Ingrid Scheurmann. Mit Beiträgen von Heinz Durchhardt [et al.]. Mainz: Philipp v. Zabern, 1994. Pp. 322–327, notes.

31387. BURGHARTZ, SUSANNE [et al.], Hrsg.: *Spannungen und Widersprüche.* Gedenkschrift für Frantisek Graus. Sigmaringen: Thorbecke, 1992. 324 pp. [Incl. four essays dealing with Jewish history: Juden – eine Minderheit vor Gericht, Zürich 1378–1436 (Susanne Burghartz, 229–244). La question des images dans les débats entre juifs et chrétiens au XIIe siècle (Jean-Claude Schmitt, 245–254). Der Tag von Benfeld im Januar 1349: Sie kamen zusammen und kamen überein, die Juden zu vernichten (Reinhard Schneider, 255–272). Königtum und Juden im deutschen Spätmittelalter (Peter Aufgebauer/Ernst Schubert, 273–314.]

31388. BURMEISTER, KARL HEINZ: *Der Würfelzoll, eine Variante des Leibzolls.* [In]: Aschkenas, Jg. 3, Wien, 1993. Pp. 49–64, footnotes. [Corrected name of journal in entry No. 30086/YB XXXIX.]

31389. COHEN, RICHARD I.: *'And your eyes shall see your teachers'; the rabbi as icon.* [In]: Zion, Vol. 58, No. 4, Jerusalem, 1993. Pp. 407–452. [In Hebrew, with English summary.] [On portraits of rabbis from Central and Western Europe (Germany, Hungary, Poland, and Holland) from 18th until 19th cent., and their popularity in Orthodox Jewish homes. Incl. the reactions of R. Jacob Emden to the subject, the portraits of R. Akiva Eger, and of R. Seckel Leib Wormser of Michelstadt; also on printing placards in 19th cent. Breslau.]

31390. FEINER, SHMUEL: *The modern Jewish woman; a test-case in the relationship between Haskalah and modernity.* [In Hebrew, with English summary.] [In]: Zion, Vol. 58, No. 4, Jerusalem, 1993. Pp. 452–499. [On Maskilim in Germany and Russia and their attitudes towards the emancipation of Jewish women. Deals with Jewish women in 18th- and 19th-century Germany (pp. 453–467).]

31391. GAMM, HANS-JOCHEN: *Das Judentum: eine Einführung.* Überarb. Neuausgabe. Frankfurt am Main; New York: Campus, 1994. 190 pp., bibl. (185–188). (Reihe Campus, Bd. 1031.) [First publ. in 1961 under the title 'Judentumskunde; eine Einführung'.]

31392. *Geschichte und Kultur der Juden in Schwaben.* Wissenschaftliche Tagung der Heimatpflege des Bezirks Schwaben in Zusammenarbeit mit der Schwabenakademie Irsee am 14./15. Oktober 1989 in Irsee. Hrsg. von Peter Fassl. Sigmaringen: Thorbecke, 1994. 186 pp., illus., footnotes. (Irseer Schriften, Bd. 2.) [Incl. (titles partly abbr.): Quellen zur Geschichte der Juden in Schwaben (Doris Pfister, 9–18). Zur Topographie der älteren Judengemeinden in Augsburg und Lauingen (Reinhard H. Seitz, 19–36). Mobilität und Migration der Juden in

Bayern und angrenzenden Gebieten (Johannes Litzel, 37–44). Zur Bildungsgeschichte der Juden in Schwaben vor Moses Mendelssohn (Reinhard Jakob, 45–62). Die baugeschichtliche Bedeutung der Synagogen in Schwaben (Bernd Vollmar, 63–72). Die Beteiligung von Juden an der politischen Willensbildung in Schwaben 1818–1871 (Gerhard Hetzer, 73–92). Die Geschichte der jüdischen Gemeinde Altenstadt (Karin Sommer, 93–104). Zur jüngeren Geschichte der Juden in Kempten (Karl Filser, 105–116). Die Einbindung der Juden in das öffentliche Leben in der Gemeinde Hürben/Krumbach (Herbert Auer, 117–128). Die wirtschaftliche und soziale Stellung der Juden in Augsburg im 19. und beginnenden 20. Jahrhundert (Peter Fassl, 129–146). Die wirtschaftliche Verdrängung der Juden in Augsburg (Hans K. Hirsch, 147–156). Judenmägd' in Ichenhausen. Christliche Angestellte in jüdischen Haushalten (Silvester Lechner, 157–170). Judenverfolgung in Schwaben: das Beispiel Ichenhausen (Zdenek Zofka, 171–176). Das Ende der jüdischen Gemeinden in Schwaben (Gernot Römer, 177–186).]

31393. *Geschichte der Frauen*. Band 3: *Frühe Neuzeit*. Hrsg. von Arlette Farge und Natalie Zemon Davis. Band 4: *19. Jahrhundert*. Hrsg. von Geneviève Fraisse und Michelle Perrot. Editorische Betreuung der deutschen Gesamtausgabe: Heike Wunder. Frankfurt am Main; New York: Campus, 1994. 2 vols. [Bd. 3 incl.: Glückel von Hameln. Jüdische Händlerin, Hamburg - Metz, 17. Jahrhundert (529–533; excerpts from her memoirs). Bd. 4 incl.: Die jüdische Frau: Variationen und Transformationen (Nancy Green, 237–252, notes (653–655); compares the Jewess of the Berlin salons with the Russian 'traditional' Jewess and emigrant women in the USA.]

31394. GRABMEYER, JOHANNES: *Rudolf von Schlettstadt und das aschkenasische Judentum um 1300*. [In]: Aschkenas, Jg. 4,/1994, H. 2, Wien, 1995. Pp. 301–336.

31395. HARTMANN, STEFAN: *Die Bedeutung des Hardenbergschen Edikts von 1812 für den Emanzipationsprozeß der preußischen Juden im 19. Jahrhundert*. [In]: Forschungen zur brandenburgischen und preußischen Geschichte, N.F., Beiheft 2: Gemeingeist und Bürgersinn; die preußischen Reformen. Hrsg. von Bernd Sösemann. Berlin: Duncker & Humblot, 1993. Pp. 247–260.

31396. HERZIG, ARNO: *Die Judischheit teutscher Nation. Zur Krise der deutschen Judenheit im Reich im 16. und 17. Jahrhundert*. [In]: Aschkenas, Jg. 4, H. 1, Wien, 1994. Pp. 127–132, footnotes.

31397. HOROWITZ, ELLIOTT: *Visages du judaisme: de la barbe en monde juif et de l'élaboration de ses significations*. [In]: Annales, Vol. 49, No. 5, Paris, Sept.- Oct. 1994. Pp. 1065–1090. [With Engl. summary, p. 1276; deals with the range of meanings associated with the Jewish beard in medieval Europe and elsewhere.]

31398. HORTZITZ, NICOLINE: *'Der Judenarzt'*. Historische und sprachliche Untersuchungen zur Diskriminierung eines Berufsstandes in der frühen Neuzeit. Heidelberg: Univers.-Verl, C. Winter, 1994. 162 pp.

31399. *Jewish intellectual history in the Middle Ages*. Ed. by Joseph Dan. Westport, Ct.; London: Praeger, 1994. XIII, 197 pp. (Binah: Studies in Jewish history, culture, and thought, No. 3.) [Incl. chaps.: A German-Jewish autobiography of the fourteenth century (Israel J. Yuval, 79–100; deals with Simon of Siegburg, 1377). The image of God as the source of man's evil, according to the Maharal of Prague (Yoram Jacobson, 135–158).]

31400. *Juden in Deutschland. Lebenswelten und Einzelschicksale*. Ringvorlesung der Philosophischen Fakultät der Universität des Saarlandes im Wintersemester 1988/89. Hrsg. von Reinhard Schneider. St. Ingbert: Röhrig, 1994. 331 pp., footnotes. (Annales Universitatis Saraviensis, Bd. 1.) [Incl.: Judenschutz – eine mittelalterliche Königstugend? (Kurt-Ulrich Jäschke, 35–149). Wirtschaftlicher Aufstieg und partielle gesellschaftliche Integration: zur wirtschaftlichen, sozialen und politischen Rolle der deutschen Juden im 19. Jahrhundert (Hans-Werner Hahn, 203–236). Die 'Judenrepublik' und ihre Literatur. Die Schriftsteller und ihr Staat von 1918 bis 1933 (Gerhard Schmidt-Henkel, 237–270). Further contribs. are listed according to subject.]

Bibliography

31401. *Juden in Deutschland. Von der Aufkärung bis zur Gegenwart.* Ein Lesebuch. Hrsg. von Ludger Heid und Julius H. Schoeps. München: Piper, 1994. 369 pp., notes. [Cont. Jewish testimonies taken from memoirs, letters, articles, speeches, addresses and petitions reflecting Jewish attitudes and opinions. Incl.: Mußte die Emanzipation mißlingen? Zur Geschichte des deutsch-jüdischen Verhältnisses (Julius H. Schoeps, 11–23). Editorische Nachbemerkung (365–369).]

31402. KASPER-HOLTKOTTE, CILLI: *'Jud, gib dein Geld her oder du bist des Todes!' Die Banditengruppe des Schinderhannes und die Juden.* [In]: Aschkenas, Jg. 3, Wien, 1993. Pp. 113–188, footnotes. [On the robber bands in the Hunsrück-Moselle district between 1797 and 1802 and the fact that Jews were especially marked to be victims of the bands.] [Corrected name of journal in entry No. 30106/YB XXXIX.]

31403. KATZ, JACOB: *Das Ende einer Zwangsgemeinschaft. Zur Geschichte eines Ghettos.* [In]: Tribüne, Jg. 33, H. 130, Frankfurt am Main, 1994. Pp. 181–187. [Dealing mainly with the Frankfurt ghetto.]

31404. KATZ, JACOB: *Tradition and crisis: Jewish society at the end of the Middle Ages.* Transl. and with an afterword and bibl. by Bernard Dov Cooperman. New York: New York Univ. Press, 1993. XV, 392 pp., notes (255–359), bibl. (361–381). [Incl. Jews in the German Empire, Court Jews, Moses Mendelssohn. For earlier Hebrew and English edns. see No. 1922/YB VI.]

31405. KIEßLING, ROLF, Hrsg.: *Judengemeinden in Schwaben im Kontext des Alten Reiches.* Hrsg. von Rolf Kießling. Red.: Sabine Ullmann. Berlin: Akademie-Verl., 1994. 335 pp., illus., tabs., footnotes, index (325–334), map [inside back cover]. (Colloquia Augustana, Bd. 2.) [Cont. the sections: Einführung (Rolf Kießling, 11–19). I.: Städtisches Judentum im Mittelalter, pp. 23–50; incl.: Christen und Juden im Augsburg des Mittelalters (Bernhard Schimmelpfennig, 23–38). Zur wirtschaftlichen Lage und Tätigkeit der Juden im deutschen Sprachraum des Spätmittelalters (Michael Toch, 39–50). II.: Landjudentum in der Frühen Neuzeit, pp. 53–180; incl.: rechtliche Rahmenbedingungen jüdischer Existenz in der Frühneuzeit zwischen Reich und Territorium (Friedrich Battenberg, 53–79). Medinat Schwaben. Jüdisches Leben in einer süddeutschen Landschaft in der Frühneuzeit (Stefan Rohrbacher, 80–109). Zwischen Vertreibung und Wiederansiedlung. Die Reichstadt Augsburg und die Juden vom 15. bis zum 18. Jahrhundert (Wolfram Baer, 110–127). Die Judenpolitik der geistlichen Territorien Schwabens während der Frühen Neuzeit (Wolfgang Wüst, 128–153). Zwischen Vertreibung und Emanzipation – Judendörfer in Ostschwaben während der Frühen Neuzeit (Rolf Kießling, 154–180). III.: Mechanismen der Diskriminierung, pp. 183–245; incl.: Linguistik der Diskriminierung; über die Agitation gegen Juden in Flugblättern der Frühen Neuzeit (Hans Wellmann, 183–193). Verfahrensweisen sprachlicher Diskriminierung in antijüdischen Texten der Frühen Neuzeit; aufgezeigt am Beispiel der Metaphorik (Nicoline Hortzitz, 194–216). Persistenz und Wandel antijüdischer Vorurteile im 18. und frühen 19. Jahrhundert (Rainer Erb, 217–245). IV.: Emanzipation und Assimilation, pp. 249–323; incl.: '. . . weil es gefährlich wäre, die Kette des groß gewachsenen Sklaven zu lösen'; Lokalstudie zur Effektivität bayerischer Judenpolitik in der ersten Hälfte des 19. Jahrhunderts (Karl Filser, 249–281). Finanznot und Domizilrecht. Zur Aufnahme jüdischer Wechselhäuser in Augsburg 1803 (Volker Dotterweich & Beate Reißner, 282–305). Zur Situation der Juden in Augsburg während der Emanzipationszeit (Hans K. Hirsch, 306–323).]

31406. KRAUTHEIMER, RICHARD: *Synagogues in the middle ages.* [In Hebrew, title transl.] Jerusalem: Mossad Bialik, 1994. 232 pp., illus., facsims. [Translated from German into Hebrew by Amos Goren; orig. edn. published in 1927 under the title 'Mittelalterliche Synagogen'. Incl. an introd. by Moshe Badash.]

31407. LINDEMANN, ALBERT S.: *Jews and the German state: the political history of a minority, 1848–1933.* [In]: Central European History, Vol. 26, No. 3, Riverside, Ca., 1994. Pp. 349–351. [Review essay on Peter Pulzer's 'Jews and the German state', see No. 29033/YB XXXVIII.]

31408. LIXL-PURCELL, ANDREAS: *Memoirs as history*. [In]: Leo Baeck Institute Year Book XXXIX, London, 1994. Pp. 227–238, footnotes. [On the specific importance of Jewish women's memoirs for historiography.]

31409. LOTTER, FRIEDRICH: *Die Juden in ihrer mittelalterlichen Umwelt*. Veröffentlichungen der Jahre 1991/2. [In]: Aschkenas, Jg. 4, Wien, 1994. Pp. 175–190, footnotes. [Review article.]

31410. LOWENSTEIN, STEVEN M.: *Ashkenazic Jewry and the European marriage pattern: a preliminary survey of Jewish marriage age*. [In]: Jewish History, Vol. 8, Nos. 1–2, Haifa 1994. Pp. 155–175, tabs. [Incl. statistics for German-Jewish marriage patterns from many different regions of Germany.]

31411. MARCUS, IVAN G.: *Une communauté pieuse et le doute: mourir pour la sanctification du nom (qiddouch ha-chem) en Achkenaz (Europe du Nord) et l'histoire de rabbi Amnon de Mayence*. [In]: Annales, Vol. 49, No. 5, Paris, Sept.- Oct. 1994. Pp. 1031–1048. [With English summary, p. 1275.]

31412. MEHLHAUSEN, JOACHIM: *Assimilation – Integration – Taufe*. Hoffnungen und enttäuschte Erwartungen deutscher Staatsbürger jüdischen Glaubens von der Romantik bis zum Jahre 1933. [In]: Evangelische Theologie, Jg. 54, H. 1, Gütersloh, 1994. Pp. 23–44, footnotes. [Opening lecture held in the Evang. Akademie Mülheim/Ruhr, April 2, 1993 at a conference dealing with the fate of Protestant Christians of Jewish descent in Germany.]

31413. MEYER, MICHAEL A.: *Von Moses Mendelssohn zu Leopold Zunz. Jüdische Identität in Deutschland 1749–1824*. Aus dem Englischen von Ernst-Peter Wieckenberg. München: Beck, 1994. 284 pp. [Transl. of 'The origins of the modern Jew', publ. in 1967; see No. 6416/YB XIII.] [Cf.: Signal nach innen (Hans-Joachim Neubauer [in]: Die Zeit, Nr. 36, Hamburg, 2. Sept. 1994, p. 63. Besprechung (Avraham Barkai) [in]: 'MB', Jg. 63, Nr. 105, Tel Aviv, Jan. 1995, pp. 7–8. In zwei Welten (Thomas Sparr) [in]: 'NZZ', Nr. 137, Zürich, 15. Juni, 1994, p. 47.]

31414. MOSSE, GEORGE L.: *Confronting the nation: Jewish and western nationalism*. Hanover, NH.: Univ. of New England; Waltham, Ma.: Brandeis Univ. Press, 1993. 220 pp., notes (195–211). (The Tauber Institute for the Study of European Jewry, 16.) [Examines the rise of nationalism in the last two centuries, especially in Germany, and argues that although Jews incl. German Jews were not immune to nationalism they preserved a stronger liberal tradition. Also incl. Zionist nationalism.] [Incl. chaps.: Jewish emancipation: between Bildung and respectability; German Jews and liberalism in retrospect; Max Nordau: liberalism and the new Jew; Gershom Scholem as a German Jew.]

31415. PATAI, RAPHAEL: *The Jewish alchemists: a history and source book*. Princeton, N.J.: Princeton Univ. Press, 1994. XIV, 617 pp., illus. [Incl. Jacob Emden, Hamburg, 1697–1776.]

31416. REICH, RONNY: *A tourist in Ashkenaz*. [In]: Eretz. The Geographic Magazine from Israel, No. 33, Jerusalem, Jan.-Feb. 1994. Pp. 35–50. [A pictorial account of the author's visits to sites of medieval Jewish communities in Germany: Speyer, Worms, Mainz, and Rothenburg o.d. Tauber.]

31417. RICHARZ, MONIKA: *Bürger auf Widerruf. Lebenszeugnisse deutscher Juden 1780–1945*. Hrsg. von Monika Richarz. Translated into Hebrew by Abraham Kadima. [Publ. by the Leo Baeck Institute and the Bialik Institute, Jerusalem]: 1993. 517 pp., footnotes, index (495–517). [For orig. German edn. publ. in 1989 see No. 25958/YB XXXV; for English translation publ. in 1991 see No. 27972/YB XXXVII.]

31418. ROECK, BERND: *Aussenseiter, Randgruppen, Minderheiten: Fremde im Deutschland der frühen Neuzeit*. Göttingen: Vandenhoeck und Ruprecht, 1993. 195 pp., notes, bibl. (170–191), index. (Kleine Vandenhoeck-Reihe.) [Incl. chap.: Die Juden im frühneuzeitlichen Reich (23–41); also passim references to Jews in other chaps.]

31419. SCHORSCH, ISMAR: *From text to context: the turn to history in modern Judaism.* Hanover, N.H.: Univ. Press of New England; Waltham, Ma.: Brandeis Univ. Press, 1994. XV, 403 pp., tabs., notes, index. (Tauber Institute for the Study of European Jewry series, 19.) [Deals mainly with German-Jewish history; also on German-Jewish historiography, Wissenschaft des Judentums, the Leo Baeck Institute.]

31420. SCHRECKENBERG, WILHELM: *Das Judentum in Geschichte und Gegenwart.* Teil I – IV. [In]: Geschichte in Wissenschaft und Unterricht, Nr. 9 (pp. 592–604) & Nr. 10 (pp. 645–660) & Nr. 11 (pp. 715–724) & Nr. 12 (pp. 772–781), Stuttgart, 1994. [Review articles.]

31421. SEIDEL, ESTHER: *Is there a German-Jewish legacy?* [In]: European Judaism, Vol. 27, No. 2, London, Autumn 1994. Pp. 57–67, notes. [Given as a lecture on Oct. 13, 1994 at the Leo Baeck College in London.]

31422. SIMON, HEINRICH: *Die Vielen im Schatten der Hofjuden.* [In]: Kairos, N.F., Jg. 34/35, Salzburg, 1992/93. Pp. 132–147, notes. [On Jewish servants, artisans, beggars and criminals in eighteenth-century Germany.]

31423. TIMMS, EDWARD: *Between Holocaustism and symbiotics: new approaches to German-Jewish studies.* [In]: Jewish Quarterly, Vol. 41, No. 2, London, Summer 1994. Pp. 55–60, illus. [Review essays of (a.o.) Ruth Gay's 'The Jews of Germany', see No. 29004/YB XXXVIII and Peter Pulzer's 'Jews and the German state', see No. 29033/YB XXXVIII.]

31424. TRAVERSO, ENZIO: *Les juifs et l'Allemagne. De la 'symbiose judéo-allemande à la mémoire d'Auschwitz.* Paris: Ed. La Découverte, 1993. 260 pp. (Textes à l'appui: série histoire contemporaine.)

31425. VOLKOV, SHULAMIT, ed.: *Deutsche Juden und die Moderne.* Hrsg. von Shulamit Volkov unter Mitarbeit von Elisabeth Müller-Luckner. München: Oldenbourg, 1994. XXIV, 170 pp., footnotes, index. (Schriften des Historischen Kollegs: Kolloquien, 25.) [Cont. the following essays.: Zur Einführung (Shulamit Volkov, VII-XXIII). Reform und Geschichte: Die Modernisierung des deutschen Judentums (Amos Funkenstein, 1–8). Juden und Katholiken: deutsch-jüdische Kultur im Vergleich 1750–1850). Why music? Jews and the commitment to modernity (Ruth Katz, 31–38). Schrittmacher der Moderne? Der Beitrag des Judentums zum deutschen Theater zwischen 1848 und 1933 (39–56). Women and the shaping of modern Jewish identity in Imperial Germany (Marion A. Kaplan, 57–74). Die Innenwelt der Außenwelt. Modernitätserfahrung von Frauen zwischen Gleichheit und Differenz (Ute Frevert, 75–94). Die westfälischen Juden im Modernitätsprozess (Arno Herzig, 95–118). Amerikawanderung, Sozialprofil und Identitätsproblematik der deutschen Juden 1830–1914 (Avraham Barkai, 119–128). Wilna und die Entstehung eines ostjüdischen Sozialismus 1870–1900 (Gottfried Schramm, 129–140). Division and cohesion in the process of modernization: a comparison of the Jewish communities of Vienna and Warsaw during the 1920s (Alan S. Zuckerman, 141–164).]

31426. VOLKOV, SHULAMIT: *Die Juden in Deutschland 1780–1918.* Aus dem Englischen übersetzt von Simone Gundi. München: Oldenbourg, 1994. 162 pp., bibl. 131–153), indexes (155–162). (Enzyklopädie deutscher Geschichte, Bd. 16.)

31427. YUVAL, ISRAEL JACOB: *Vengeance and damnation, blood and defamation. From Jewish martyrdom to blood libel accusations.* [See No. 30124/YB XXXIX.] [Responses to this article in]: Zion, Vol. 59, No. 2–3, Jerusalem, 1994. [In Hebrew.]: The 'persecutions of 1096' – from martyrdom to martyrology: the sociocultural context of the Hebrew crusade chronicles (Jeremy Cohen, 169–208). Kiddush-ha-Shem in German Christian eyes in the middle ages (Mary Minty, 209–266). Christian-Jewish relations in the middle ages distorted (Ezra Fleischer, 267–316). The historian's imagination and the historical truth (Mordechai Breuer, 317–324). 'Redemption by conversion' in the teachings of early Ashkenazi sages (Abraham Grossman, 325–342). The origins of the blood libel (Gerd Mentgen, 343–349). 'The Lord will take vengeance, vengeance for His temple' – history sine ira et studio (Israel J. Yuval, 351–414; a response to the above articles).] [Also, on this discussion: Lieber tot als christlich. Warum

Juden im Mittelalter als blutdürstig galten (Joseph Croitoru) [in]: 'FAZ', Nr. 136, Frankfurt am Main, 14. Juni 1994, p. N 5.] [See also Nos. 32397–32402.]

Linguistics/Western Yiddish

31428. APTROOT, MARION: *'In galkhes they do not say so, but the taytsh is as it stands her'. Notes on the Amsterdam Yiddish Bible translations by Blitz and Witzenhausen.* Studia Rosentaliana, Vol. 27, Nr. 27, Assen, 1993. Pp. 136–160.

31429. BAUMGARTEN, JEAN: *Introduction à la littérature yiddish ancienne.* Paris: Ed. du Cerf, 1993. 530 pp. [Cf.: compte rendu (Delphine Bechtel) [in]: Annales, Vol. 49, No. 5, Paris, Sept.- Oct. 1994. Pp. 1260–1262.]

31430. DACHLIKA, SASSONA [formerly SIGRID RIEDEL]: *'Brantspigel'. Ethik im alten Aschkenas.* [In]: Jüdischer Almanach 1995 des Leo Baeck Instituts. Frankfurt am Main, 1994. Pp. 60–68.

31431. *The field of Yiddish: studies in language, folklore, and literature: fifth collection.* Ed. by David Goldberg. Evanston, Ill.: Northwestern Univ. Press; New York: YIVO Institute for Jewish Research, 1993. VIII, 327 pp., illus.

31432. GROSSMAN, JEFFREY ALAN: *The space of Yiddish in the German and German-Jewish discourse.* Ann Arbor: Univ. Microfilms International 1993. 262 pp., bibl. (242–263). (Austin, Univ. of Texas, Diss., 1992.)

31433. GUTH, WERNER MAXIMO: *Sabiduria popular judia. Refranero idish de Europa Occidental.* Buenos Aires: Grupo editorial Shalom, 1992. 1 vol.

31434. HILGERT, WILFRIED: *Mores, Zores un Maschores: Jiddisch-Hebräisch in unserer Mundart.* Ill. von Erhard Hütz. 2. Aufl. Horrweiler: Hilgert, 1994. 143 pp., illus.

31435. *Jiddistik-Mitteilungen: Jiddistik in deutschsprachigen Ländern.* Nr. 11 & 12. Hrsg. von der Jiddistik im Fachbreich Sprach- und Literaturwissenschaften der Universität Trier (FB II/Jiddistik, 54286 Trier). Red.: Jiddistik der Univ. Trier. Trier, April & Nov. 1994. 2 issues, notes, bibl. [Nr. 11 incl.: Altjiddische Drucke in der Universitätsbibliothek Rostock (Heike Tröger, 14–16; on the collection of Oluf Gerhard Tychsen). Another contrib. listed according to subject. Nr. 12 incl.: Eine unbekannte Prager Ausgabe des altjiddischen Romans 'Paris un Wine' (Thomas Soxberger, 1–7).]

31436. KLAYMAN-COHEN, ISRAELA: *Die hebräische Komponente im Westjiddischen am Beispiel der Memoiren der Glückel von Hameln.* Hamburg: Buske, 1994. VIII, 205 pp. (jidische schtudies, Bd. 4.)

31437. NEUBERG, SIMON: *Zur Geschichte des jiddischen Wortes makeinen.* [In]: Aschkenas, Jg. 4/1994, H. 2, Wien, 1995. Pp. 469–474.

31438. RIEDEL, SIGRID, ed.: *Moses Henochs Altschul-Jeruschalmi 'Brantspigel'.* Transkribiert und ediert nach der Erstausgabe Krakau 1596. Frankfurt am Main: Lang, 1993. 1 vol. [Judaeo-German moral compendium written by the author in 16th century Prague.]

31439. STARCK, ASTRID: *A nineteenth-century Yiddish newspaper 'Israels Stimme: hakol kol yaakov'.* [In]: Leo Baeck Institute Year Book XXXIX, London, 1994. Pp. 53–63, footnotes. [On Yiddish newspapers in Alsace-Lorraine.]

31440. STARCK, ASTRID: *Das elsässer-jiddische Theater in interkultureller Perspektive.* [In]: Praxis interkultureller Germanistik. Forschung – Bildung – Politik. Hrsg. von Bernd Thum und Gonthier-Louis Fink. München: Iudicium Verl., 1993. (Beiträge zum internationalen

Kongress der Gesellschaft für Interkulturelle Germanistik, 2) (Publikationen der Gesellschaft für Interkulturelle Germanistik, 4.)[No pp. given.]

31441. STARCK, ASTRID: *Introduction au théâtre yidich alsacien.* [In]: Domaine Yiddish. YOD, Nos. 31/ 32, Paris, 1992. Pp. 145–157.

31442. STARCK, ASTRID: *Le yidich alsacien.* [In]: Association des professeurs de langue vivante. Bulletin régional, No. 42, 1991. Pp. 20–22.

31443. STARCK, ASTRID: *Le yidich occidental (Alsacien) dans l'oeuvre de Claude Vigée.* [In]: La terre et le souffle. Rencontre autour de Claude Vigée. Colloque de Cerisy-la-Salle. Paris: Albin Michel, 1992. Pp. 83–84.

31444. STARCK, ASTRID: *Jiddische Lebensbeschreibung.* Ein Dokument aus dem Jüdischen Museum der Schweiz. [In]: Juden im Elsass. Begleitpublikation des Museums für Völkerkunde und des Schweizerischen Museums für Volkskunde. Basel: Schweizerisches Museum f. Volkskunde; Jüd. Museum der Schweiz, 1992. Pp. 16–19. [See No. 30285/YBXXXIX.]

31445. STARCK, ASTRID [ed.]: *Westjiddisch. Mündlichkeit und Schriftlichkeit.* Le Yiddish occidental. Actes du Colloque de Mulhouse. Aarau: Sauerländer, 1994. 184 pp., notes. (Reihe Sprachlandschaft, Bd. II,) [Papers given at a colloquium at Mulhouse Jan. 16 – 17, 1989. Cont.: Introduction (Astrid Starck, 7–8). Ernest-Henri Lévy et le 'Dukus Horant' (Jean Fourquet, 9–14). Florence Guggenheim-Grünberg: ihr Beitrag zur Erforschung des Westjiddischen (Robert Schläpfer, 15–19). Das Surbtaler Jiddisch (Dieter Thommen, 20–27). Reste des Jiddischen in Hessen (Hans-Peter Althaus, 28–42). Jiddisch in Ungarn (Claus Jürgen Hutterer, 43–60). Le yidich dans les 'Pinkasim' de Metz et d'Odratzheim et dans les 'Piskedinim' de Metz (Samuel Kerner, 61–69). Wörtlichkeit als Quelle sprachlicher Kreativität (Erika Timm, 70–77). Les rapports du yidich occidental et de la littérature yidich ancienne (Alexandre Derczansky, 78–83). Wigalois – Widuwilt. Wandlungen des Artusromans im Jiddischen (Wulf-Otto Dreessen, 84–98). L'étude de la langue yiddish à la Renaissance (XVIe et XVIIe siécle) (Jean Baumgarten, 99–111). West- und Ostjiddisch auf Amsterdamer Bühnen gegen Ende des achtzehnten Jahrhunderts (Renate Fuks-Mansfeld, 112–118). La littérature orale yiddish alsacienne (Astrid Starck, 119–127). Josouillet Rabat-Joie (Freddy Raphael, 128–156). Le Yidich occidental (alsacien) dans l'oevre de Claude Vigée (Astrid Starck, 157–166). A Peissach Brief/Une Epître Pascale/ Chadüschem aus baris im Tsarfess (Claude Vigée, 167–172). Bibliographie du yidich alsacien (Astrid Starck, 173–184).]

31446. *Territoires du Yiddish: de la création vivante à la désolation.* Paris Cédex: Éd. du Cerf, 1992. 264 pp. (Pardès, 15.) [A collection of essays.]

31447. TIMM, ERIKA: *Zwei neuaufgefundene jiddische Briefe von 1602 und ihre Bedeutung für die Sozial- und Sprachgeschichte.* [In]: Aschkenas, Jg. 4/1994, H. 2, Wien, 1995. Pp. 449–468.

31448. *Verzeichnis der jiddischen Drucke: Bestände der Sondersammelgebietsbibliothek Frankfurt am Main.* Frankfurt am Main: Stadt- und Univ.-Bibliothek, 1993. 378 cols. [This collection is considered the second largest in Europe, cont. ca. 600 (Western) Yiddish titles publ. before 1900, the oldest dating back to 1560. Among later 19th cent. publications national Jewish fiction and poetry from Eastern Europe preponderate.]

31449. WEINBERG, WERNER: *Lexikon zum religiösen Wortschatz und Brauchtum der deutschen Juden.* Hrsg. von Walter Röll. Stuttgart-Bad Cannstadt: Frommann-Holzboog, 1994. 356 pp., indexes, bibl. (313–319). [Cf.: Besprechung (Walter Röll) [in]: Jiddistik-Mitteilungen, Nr. 12, Trier, Nov. 1994, pp. 18–23.] [The author, b. May 30, 1915 in Rheda, educated at the Würzburg Lehrerseminar, emigr. to Netherlands in 1939, 1943–1945 imprisoned in Westerbork and Bergen-Belsen. Returned to Netherlands until 1948. Now Prof.em. for Hebrew Literature at the Hebrew Union College, Cincinnati.]

Bibliography

B. Communal and Regional History

1. Germany

31450. AHRWEILER. LOHMILLER, ASTRID/MÜLLER-FELDMANN, ANNEMARIE: *Der jüdische Friedhof in Ahrweiler.* [In]: Beiträge zur jüdischen Geschichte in Rheinland-Pfalz, Jg. 4, Ausgabe 1, Bad Kreuznach, 1994. Pp. 28–37. (Heft Nr. 6.)

31451. AHRWEILER. WARNECKE, HANS: *Die Synagoge in Ahrweiler.* Bad-Neuenahr-Ahrweiler: ARE-Verl., 1994. 43 pp., illus. [Incl. chap. on the history of the Ahrweiler Jews.]

31452. ANRÖCHTE. BLANKE, FRANZ: *Juden in Anröchte.* Eine Zusammenfassung unseres heutigen Wissens. Anröchte: Heimatverein Anröchte e.V., 1991. 271 pp., illus., facsims., list of names.

31453. ASCHAFFENBURG. KÖRNER, PETER: *Biographisches Handbuch der Juden in Stadt und Altkreis Aschaffenburg.* Hrsg.: Geschichts- und Kunstverein Aschaffenburg e.V. Aschaffenburg: Geschichts- und Kunstverein, 1993. 287 pp., illus., graphs. (Veröffentlichungen des Geschichts- und Kunstvereins Aschaffenburg e.V.; 39.)

— AUGSBURG. [See No. 31405.]

31454. BAD OEYNHAUSEN. *Juden in Bad Oeynhausen.* Einzelschicksale, Personenlisten, Dokumentation der 'Tage der Begegnung mit Ehemaligen Jüdischen Bürgern Bad Oeynhausens'. Hrsg.: Stadt Bad Oeynhausen – Volkshochschule. Bad Oeynhausen: Volkshochsch. der Stadt, 1994. 96 pp., illus. (Schriftenreihe der Volkshochschule, Jg. 7, Nr. 7.)

31455. BADEN-WÜRTTEMBERG. HONIGMANN, PETER: *Dokumentation jüdischer Grabinschriften in der BRD.* Ein kurzer Überblick anhand der Erfahrungen in Baden-Württemberg. [In]: Aschkenas, Jg. 3, Wien, 1993. Pp. 267–273, footnotes. [Corrected name of journal in entry No. 30138/YB XXXIX.]

31456. BADEN-WÜRTTEMBERG. KULLEN, SIEGFRIED: *Spurensuche. Jüdische Gemeinden im nördlichen Oberschwaben.* Blaubeurer Geographische Hefte 5. Blaubeuren: Denkhaus, 1994. 79 pp., maps, illus., notes,

31457. BAVARIA. HARRIS, JAMES F.: *The people speak!: anti-Semitism and emancipation in nineteenth-century Bavaria.* Ann Arbor: Univ. of Michigan Press, 1994. XII, 290 pp., illus., tabs., map., appendixes, notes, bibl. (263–280). (Social history, popular culture, and politics in Germany.) [Discusses the popular outcry against a proposed bill by the Bavarian government to give Jews the same rights as Christians. The bill was defeated in 1850.]

31458. BERLIN. *Jüdisches Adressbuch für Gross-Berlin.* Berlin: Arani-Verl., 1994. 108; 448; 39 pp. [Reprint of the 1931 edn.]

— BERLIN. LICHTBLAU, ALBERT: *Antisemitismus und soziale Spannung in Berlin und Wien 1867–1914.* [See No. 32415.]

31459. BERLIN. LINDNER, ERIK: *Britannia, Borussia, sie reichen sich die Hände. Über den Journalisten Elias Samter und die Berliner Polizei im Jahre 1858.* [In]: Gerhard Hentrich – der Verleger. Eine Festschrift zum 70. Geburtstag für Gerhard Hentrich. Hrsg. von Werner Buchwald und Hermann Simon. Berlin: Ed. Hentrich, 1994. Pp. 80–89. [Incl. a patriotic poem, written on the occasion of the marriage of the later Friedrich III. and the English Princess Victoria, the parents of Wilhelm II.]

31460. BERLIN. LOWENSTEIN, STEVEN M.: *The Berlin Jewish community: enlightenment, family and crisis, 1770–1830.* London; New York: Oxford Univ. Press, 1994. XII, 300 pp., illus., tabs., geneal. tabs., maps, notes, bibl. (277–283), index.

31461. BERLIN. Pracht, Elfi: *M. Kempinski & Co.* Hrsg. von der Historischen Kommission zu Berlin. Berlin: Nicolai, 1994. 179 pp., illus., bibl. [On the history of the Berlin wine and gastronomy company, famous above all for its Hotel Kempinski, 'aryanised' in 1937.]

31462. BERLIN. Read, Anthony/Fischer, David: *Berlin: the biography of a city.* London: Hutchinson, 1994. 341 pp., illus., map, bibl. (320–324). [Incl. Nazi period and persecution of Jews; Berlin Jewish community past and present.]

31463. BERLIN-CHARLOTTENBURG. Herzfeld, Erika: *Levi und Moses Ulff aus Wesel, Seidenbandmanufakturunternehmer in Charlottenburg.* [In]: Kairos, N.F., Jg. 34/35, Salzburg, 1992/93. Pp. 148–167, notes. [Deals with the beginning of silk ribbon manufacture in Wesel and Emmerich at the end of the 17th cent., and, after much trouble, its subsequent relocation in Charlottenburg.]

31464. BERLIN-SPANDAU. Brocke, Michael: *Die mittelalterlichen jüdischen Grabmale in Spandau 1244–1474.* In Zusammenarbeit mit Nathanja Hüttenmeister, Birgit Klein, Gesine Palmer und Aubrey Pomerance. [In]: Ausgrabungen in Berlin, 9/1994, Berlin: Volker Spiess, 1994. Pp. 8–116, illus., footnotes, lists. [A complete documentation of all gravestones excavated in Spandau fortress since 1957. Incl. photos and description of gravestones, Hebrew inscriptions, German translation and annotations. Also on the medieval history of the Spandau and Berlin Jews.]

31465. BERLIN-WEISSENSEE. *Juden in Weissensee.* 'Ich hatte einst ein schönes Vaterland'. Hrsg.: Kulturamt Weissensee und Stadtgeschichtliches Museum. Berlin: Hentrich, 1994. 272 pp., illus., facsims., notes, bibl., index (persons). (Reihe Deutsche Vergangenheit, Stätten der Geschichte Berlins, Bd. 107.) [Incl. Nazi period, cemeteries.]

31466. BERNBURG. *Spurensuche: was wurde aus den Juden der Stadt Bernburg?* Zum Gedenken an den 50. Jahrestag der Pogromnacht am 9. November 1938. Von einem Arbeitskreis der Martinsgemeinde unter Leitung von Dietrich Bungeroth. [Hrsg.: Verein der Freunde und Förderer der Kulturstiftung Bernburg] 3., völlig neu gestaltete und erw. Aufl. Bernburg: Verein der Freunde und Förderer der Kulturstiftung Bernburg, 1993. 101 pp., illus., graphs, map.

31467. BOTTROP. Lück, Manfred: *Juden in Bottrop.* Band 2: Biographische Notizen und Erinnerungen. Beiträge zur Bottroper Geschichte, Nr. 20, Bottrop, Nov. 1993. 206 pp. [Part 1 cont. biographical data of ca. 1,600 Jews, who lived in Bottrop between the beginning of the 19th cent. and 1945. Part 2 cont. 9 personal recollections based on interviews.]

31468. BRAUNSCHWEIG. *Braunschweigisches Landesmuseum. Abteilung Jüdisches Museum.* 3. Aufl., Hrsg. von Gerd Biegel. Braunschweig: Joh. Heinr. Meyer, 1993. 20 pp., illus. (Veröffentlichungen des Braunschweigischen Landesmuseums 71.) [Catalogue. Deals also with the synagogue of Hornburg.]

31469. BRESLAU. Walk, Joseph: *'Almemor und Gitter'. Ein Kapitel zur Geschichte der Storch-Synagoge in Breslau.* [In]: Menora 5, München, 1994. Pp. 349–365, notes.

31470. Brocke, Michael/Ruthenberg, Eckehart/Schulenburg, Kai Uwe: *Stein und Name. Die jüdischen Friedhöfe in Ostdeutschland (Neue Bundesländer/DDR und Berlin).* Berlin: Institut Kirche und Judentum, 1994. 720 pp., illus., facsims., maps, tabs., bibl., indexes, glossary. (Veröffentlichungen aus dem Institut Kirche und Judentum, Bd. 22.) [Cont. in alphabetical order the description of ca. 300 cemeteries. Incl: Jüdische Friedhöfe. Zur ersten Orientierung (28–56).]

31471. BURRWEILER. Kukatzki, Bernhard: *Juden in Burrweiler.* Landkreis Südliche Weinstraße. (67099) Schifferstadt (Postfach 1133), 1994. 38 pp., illus., facsims. [Private print.]

31472. BUTTENHAUSEN. *Juden in Buttenhausen.* Ständige Ausstellung in der Bernheimer'schen Realschule. [Hrsg.: Stadt Münsingen, Bearb.: Roland Deigendesch, Texte Religion: Annemarie Mayer]. Münsingen: Stadtarchiv, 1994. 97 pp., illus. (Schriftenreihe/Stadtarchiv Münsingen, Bd. 3.)

31473. BUTTENHAUSEN. RENZ, ULRICH: *Der kleine Rabbi von Buttenhausen.* [In]: Tribüne, Jg. 33, H. 131, Frankfurt am Main, 1994. Pp. 161–165. [On the history of the Swabian village of Buttenhausen, which had a majority of Jewish inhabitants at the end of the 19th cent.]

31474. COLOGNE. NIEMÖLLER, WOLFGANG: *Kölner Musikleben und jüdisches Mäzenatentum bis 1933.* [In]: Die Moderne im Rheinland. Ihre Förderung und Durchsetzung in Literatur, Theater, Musik, Architektur, angewandter und bildender Kunst 1900–1933. Vorträge des Interdisziplinären Arbeitskreises zur Erforschung der Moderne im Rheinland. Hrsg. von Dieter Breuer. Köln/Bonn: Rheinland-Verl./Habelt Verl., 1994. Pp. 225–241, facsims., notes.

31475. DESSAU. GROSSERT, WERNER: *Chronik: Geschichte der Juden in Dessau.* Dessau: Moses-Mendelssohn-Gesellschaft e.V., 1993. 32 pp., facsims. (Schriftenreihe der Moses-Mendelssohn-Gesellschaft e.V., Nr. 1.) [Incl. Nazi period and post-war history.]

31476. DRENSTEINFURT (Westphalia). GABRIEL, PETER: *Wer wies den Wernern den Weg? Die Synagoge in Drensteinfurt – Lehrhaus der Geschichte.* [In]: Jahrbuch Westfalen '94, Münster, 1994. Pp. 47–52, illus. [On the November Pogrom in Drensteinfurt and the participation of SS-men and SA-men from Werne; also on the efforts to restore the former synagogue as a place of memory and education.]

31477. EAST FRIESLAND. VAHLENKAMP, WERNER: *Juden in Ostfriesland.* Zum Ende einer alten Geschichte. [In]: Tribüne, Jg. 33, H. 130, Frankfurt am Main, 1994. Pp. 156–161.

31478. EBERSWALDE. ARENDT, LUDWIG: *Zur Geschichte der Eberswalder Synagogen-Gemeinde.* Begleitheft zur Sonderausstellung im Stadt- und Kreismuseum 'Schicksale jüdischer Bürger aus Eberswalde'. Red. Bearb.: Ingrid Fischer, Karin Friese. Hrsg.: Stadt- und Kreismuseum, 16225 Eberswalde, 1993. 130 pp., illus., facsims. (Heimatkundliche Beiträge, H. 2, 1993.)

31479. ESCHWEGE. HELLWEG, FRAUKE: *Der Putsch gegen den Gemeindevorsteher. Die Entwicklung einer jüdischen Gemeinde am Beispiel Eschwege im Jahr 1819.* [In]: Zeitschrift des Vereins für hess. Geschichte und Landeskunde. Bd. 99, Kassel, 1994. 71–86, notes.

31480. ESENS. ROKAHR, GERD: *Die Juden in Esens: die Geschichte der jüdischen Gemeinde in Esens von den Anfängen im 17. Jahrhundert bis zu ihrem Ende in nationalsozialistischer Zeit.* 2., durchges. Aufl. Aurich: Ostfriesische Landschaft, 1994. 288 pp., illus., graphs, bibl. (246–249). (Abhandlungen und Vorträge zur Geschichte Ostfrieslands, Bd. 65.)

31481. ESSEN. SCHREIBER, HANS-JÜRGEN: *Die Familie Steinberg/Kaufmann.* [In]: Das Münster am Hellweg, Jg. 46, Essen 1993. Pp. 76–90, illus., notes. [On two families in Altenessen.]

31482. ESSEN-STEELE. NIEMANN, INGRID/HÜLSKEMPER-NIEMANN, LUDGER: *Vom Geleitbrief zum gelben Stern: 450 Jahre jüdisches Leben in Steele.* Essen-Klartext, 1994. 224 pp., illus. (Studienreihe der alten Synagoge, Bd. 3.) [Incl. many testimonies of Jews from Steele.]

31483. ESSINGEN. DÖHRER, ANDREA [et al.]: *Jüdischer Friedhof in Essingen.* Wissenschaftliche Erfassung. [In]: Jiddistik-Mitteilungen, Nr. 11, Trier, April 1994. Pp. 17–20.

—— ESSLINGEN. [See also Nos. 31892, 31896 and 31998.]

31484. ESSLINGEN. HAHN, JOACHIM: *Jüdisches Leben in Esslingen.* Geschichte, Quellen und Dokumentation. [Hrsg.:] Stadtarchiv Esslingen am Neckar. Esslingen, 1994. 543 pp. [& 60 pp. unpag.], illustr., bibl., index. (Esslinger Studien; Schriftenreihe Bd. 14.) [Incl. the Nazi period.]

31485. FRANCONIA. GROISS-LAU, EVA: *Jüdisches Kulturgut auf dem Lande: Synagogen, Tauchbäder und Realien in Oberfranken*. Hrsg. von Klaus Guth. München: Dt. Kunstverl., 1994. 240 pp. (Landjudentum in Oberfranken, Bd. 2.)

31486. FRANCONIA. KREUTZ, WILHELM: *Les juifs du Palatinat au XIXe siècle: démographie – statut juridique – structure socio-professionelle*. [In]: Francia, Bd. 20/3 (1993), Sigmaringen, 1994. Pp. 1–17, tabs., footnotes.

31487. FRANKFURT am Main. DÜLMEN, RICHARD VAN: *Das Frankfurter Ghetto. Zur Lebensweise und Kultur der Juden in der frühen Neuzeit.* [In]: Juden in Deutschland. Lebenswelten und Einzelschicksale. Hrsg. von Reinhard Schneider [see No. 31400]. Pp. 151–178.

31488. FRANKFURT am Main. *German roots.* [In]: The Economist, Vol. 333, No. 7890, London, Nov. 19, 1994. Pp. 98–99. [On the exhibition about the Rothschilds at the Jewish Museum in Frankfurt am Main.]

31489. FRANKFURT am Main. HESCHEL, YISRAEL NATAN: *On the way of the author of Hafla'ah [Phinehas Horowitz] in Frankfurt am Main and the Frankfurt community regulations regarding Rabbi Nathan Adler*. [In Hebrew, title transl.] [In]: Kovetz Bais Aharon v'Yisrael, Vol 9, No. 3, Jerusalem, Shvat-Adar 5754 [= Jan./Feb. 1994]. Pp. 129–150.

31490. FRANKFURT am Main. *Jüdische Stiftungen in Frankfurt am Main.* M. J. Kirchheim'sche Stiftung Frankfurt a. M. Hrsg. von Arno Lustiger. Biogr. Teil mit Kurzbiographien jüdischer Stifter, Politiker und Mäzene mit Beiträgen von Hans Achinger [et al.]. Sachteil mit der Beschreibung von Stiftungen, Organisationen, Vereinen und Schenkungen dargest. von Gerhard Schiebler. Sigmaringen: Thorbecke, 1994. 422 pp., notes (225–288), index of foundations (415–422), bibl. [Reprint of the 1988 edn.; for full listing of contribs. see No. 25024/YB XXXIX.]

—— FRANKFURT am Main. *Die Rothschilds.* Bd. 1: Eine europäische Familie; Bd. 2: Die Rothschilds. Beiträge zur Geschichte einer europäischen Familie. [See No. 32115.] [For further books and articles on the Rothschild family see Nos.32113, 32114–32116.]

—— FRANKFURT am Main. SARKOWICZ, HANS, Hrsg.: *Die großen Frankfurter.* [See No. 32117.]

31491. FRANKFURT am Main. THIEL, HANS: *Die jüdischen Lehrer und Schüler der Frankfurter Helmholtzschule 1912–1936.* Hrsg.: Verein ehemaliger Helmholtzschüler e.V. [Postfach 60 08 65, 60338 Frankfurt a. M.] und Verein der Freunde und Förderer der Helmholtzschule e.V. Frankfurt am Main, 1994. 107 pp., illus., facsims., lists.

31492. FRANKFURT am Main. UNRUH, ILSE: *Wissenschaft und Volksbildung: Die Rothschild'sche Bibliothek in Frankfurt am Main.* [In]: Aus dem Antiquariat 11 [Beilage zum] Börsenblatt für den Deutschen Buchhandel, Nr. 95, Frankfurt am Main, 29. Nov., 1994, pp. A 432–A434.

31493. FÜRTH. ROSENFELD, JITZCHAK: *Das Schas des Fürther Drucker R' David Zirndorfer.* [In]: Nachrichten für den jüdischen Bürger Fürths. Fürth, 1993. Pp. 38–43.

31494. FÜRTH. ROSENFELD, MOSCHE N.: *Der Fürther Talmuddruck. Geschichte und Bibliographie.* [In]: Nachrichten für den jüdischen Bürger Fürths. Fürth, 1993. Pp. 29–37.

31495. GAILINGEN. BAR-GIORA BAMBERGER, NAFTALI: *Der jüdische Friedhof in Gailingen.* Memor-Buch. Erster Band. Gailingen: Gemeinde Gailingen/Verein für die Erhaltung des Jüdischen Friedhofes in Gailingen, 1994. 329, 27 [unpag.] pp., illus., footnotes, facsims., docs., plans. [Photographic documentation of the cemetery, the Hebrew inscriptions with German transl. and annotations; incl.: history of the cemetery; index of names with biographical data; 4 maps: 'Lageplanregister', chronol. register; birth register 1739–1811 (facsim.).]

31496. GEHRDEN (Hanover). WILHELM, HANS-ERICH: *Die Gehrdener israelitische Synagogengemeinde: Leben und Leiden jüdischer Mitbürger.* [Hrsg.: Deutsch-Israelische Gesellschaft, Arbeitsgemeinschaft Hannover]. Hannover: Dt.-Israel. Ges., Arbeitsgemeinschaft Hannover, 1992. 112pp., illus.

31497. GOSLAR. LANGE, HORST-GÜNTHER: *Die Geschichte der Juden in Goslar von den Anfängen bis 1933.* Goslar: Selbstverl. des Geschichts- und Heimatschutzvereins Goslar e.V., 1994. 233 pp., illus., bibl., index.

31498. GROSS-GERAU. *Der jüdische Friedhof Groß-Gerau.* Ein Beitrag zur Geschichte der Landjuden in Südhessen. Von Angelika Schleindl unter Mitarbeit von Hanna Salomon. Hrsg.: Magistrat der Kreisstadt Groß-Gerau. Darmstadt: Justus von Liebig Verl., 1993. 158 pp., illus., facsims., docs., map.

31499. GRÜNSTADT. KUKATZKI, BERNHARD: *Der jüdische Friedhof in Grünstadt.* Schifferstadt und Neuleiningen, 1994. 24 pp., illus. [Private print.]

31500. HALBERSTADT. HARTMANN, WERNER, Hrsg.: *Juden in Halberstadt: Geschichte, Ende und Spuren einer ausgelieferten Minderheit.* Belege und Beiträge. Bd. 3. Hrsg.: Synagogengemeinde Magdeburg. Ges. und hrsg. von Werner Hartmann. Magdeburg: Synagogengemeinde, 1992. 25 pp.

31501. HAMBURG. HERZIG, ARNO: *Die Hamburger Sephardim und ihr Taktieren um Niederlassungsrechte im Reich zu Beginn des 17. Jahrhunderts.* [In]: Aschkenas, Jg. 4, H. 1, Wien, 1994. Pp. 133–140, footnotes.

31502. HAMBURG. KNAPPE, SABINE: *The role of women's associations in the Jewish comunity. The example of the Israelitsch-humanitärer Frauenverein in Hamburg at the turn of the century.* [In]: Leo Baeck Institute Year Book XXXIX, London 1994. Pp. 153–178, ports., illus., footnotes. [Incl. Sidonie Werner and Gustav Tuch, the president of the Hamburg Henry-Jones Lodge, who initiated the founding of the Isr.-human. Frauenverein.]

31503. HAMBURG. LORENZ, INA S.: *Der jüdische Friedhof in Ottensen (Hamburg).* Ein Projektbericht. [In]: Aschkenas, Jg. 3, Wien, 1993. Pp. 282–290, footnotes. [Corrected name of journal in entry No. 30187.]

31504. HAMBURG. MARWEDEL, GÜNTER/ZÜRN, GABY: *Das Friedhofs- und Grabinschriftenprojekt des Instituts für die Geschichte der deutschen Juden (Hamburg).* [In]: Aschkenas, Jg. 3, Wien, 1993. Pp. 274–281, footnotes. [Corrected name of journal in entry No. 30188/YB XXXIX.]

31505. HAMBURG. PRENZEL, ARNDT: *Menschenliebe ist die Krone aller Tugenden. 155 Jahre Israelitisches Krankenhaus Hamburg.* [In]: Tribüne, Jg. 33, H. 132, Frankfurt am Main, 1994. Pp. 82–87.

31506. HAMBURG. STUDEMUND-HALÉVY, MICHAEL, Hrsg.: *Die Sefarden in Hamburg. Zur Geschichte einer Minderheit.* Erster Teil. Hrsg. von Michael Studemund-Halévy in Verbindung mit Peter Koj. Hamburg: Buske, 1994. XII, 502 pp., illus., facsims. (Romanistik in Geschichte und Gegenwart, Bd. 29.) [Incl.: Die Portugiesische Gemeinde in Hamburg und ihre Führung (Ben-Zion Ornan Pinkus, 3–36). Dokumentation Kahal Kadosh Bet Israel (Michael Studemund-Halévy, 37–62). The place of herem in the Sefardic community of Hamburg (Yosef Kaplan, 63–88). Antijüdische Ressentiments gegenüber den Sefardim im 17. Jahrhundert (Günter Böhm, 89–102). Der Friedhof der Portugiesisch-Jüdischen Gemeinden in Altona (1611–1902) (Gaby Zürn, 103–124). Friedhofandachten nach sephardischem Ritus (Isaac Cassuto, 125–134). Die Synagogen der Sefardim in Hamburg und Altona. Eine Spurensuche (Saskia Rohde, 141–152). Shabtai Zvi und Hamburg (Gershom Scholem, 201–224). Dokumentation: Affaire Shabtai Zvi (Uri R. Kaufmann/Michael Studemund Halévy, 225–266). Duarte Nunes da Costa alias Jacob Curie aus Hamburg (1585–1664) (Jonathan I. Israel, 267–292). Sefarden als Händler von Fayencen in Hamburg und Nordeuropa (Ulrich Bauche, 293–306). Moshe Gideon Abudiente et son oeuvre littéraire (Zvi Maleakhi, 307–316). Abudiente's Hebrew Grammar (Anthony J. Klijnsmit, 319–376). Sobre Abraham

Meldola e a sua Nova Grammatica Portugueza de 1785 (Karl-Hermann Körner, 375–382). 'Wie Sie sicher durch Fräulein de Castro wissen . . .' (Jutta Dick, 383–414). Die Cassutos und ihre Bibliothek (Margreet Mirande de Boer, 415–440). 'Os Cassutos teem sempre sorte' (Jehuda Leon Cassuto, 441–454). Sefardim contra Ashkenazim. Der späte Streit um das Grabdenkmal Gabriel Riesser (1937–1938) (Ina S. Lorenz, 455–488).]

31507. HAMM. HILSCHER, ELKE: '. . . die Liebe kann nicht untergehen . . .'. Jüdischer Friedhof in Hamm. Eine Dokumentation in Bildern. Photographie: Heinz Feussner. Hrsg.: Der Oberstadtdirektor der Stadt Hamm et al. 328 pp., illus., map, list of gravestones, index, bibl.

31508. HANAU. BURNETT, STEPHEN G.: *Hebrew censorship in Hanau*. A mirror of Jewish-Christian coexistence in seventeenth century Germany. [In]: The expulsion of the Jews 1492 and after. Ed. by Raymond B. Waddington and Arthur H. Williamson. New York; London: Garland, 1994. Pp. 199–122.

31509. HANAU. CANTHAL, FRITZ: *Lebenserinnerungen eines jüdischen Unternehmers aus Hanau/Main*. Bürgertum zwischen zwei Revolutionen (1848–1918). Dokumente, Illustrationen u. Beiträge zur Epoche. Hrsg.: Ruth Dröse. Hanau: Cocon, 1994. 205 pp., illus., docs., facsim., bibl.

—— HANOVER. HOMEYER, FRIEDEL: *100 Jahre israelitische Erziehungsanstalt; Israelitische Gartenbauschule 1893–1993*. [See No. 32032.]

31510. HECHINGEN. VEES, ADOLF: *Hechingen in New York. Zum 94. Geburtstag von Alfred Weil*. [In]: Hohenzollerische Heimat, Jg. 44, Nr. 2, Juni 1994. Pp. 19–20.

31511. HECHTSHEIM. KEIM, ANTON MARIA: *Von Süssel Hechtsheim bis David Kapp. Die Hechtsheimer Juden*. Schriftenreihe des Vereins Hechtsheimer Ortsgeschichte, Heft IV, Mainz-Hechtsheim, Mai 1994. 78 pp., illus., docs., facsims. [Incl. Nazi period.]

31512. HESSE. *Jüdische Geschichte in Hessen erforschen*. Ein Wegweiser zu Archiven, Forschungsstätten und Hilfsmitteln. Bearbeitet von Bernhard Post. Wiesbaden: Kommission für die Geschichte der Juden in Hessen, 1994. IX, 78 pp. (Schriften der Kommission für die Geschichte der Juden in Hessen XIV.)

31513. HESSE. SCHIMPF, DOROTHEE: *Emanzipation und Bildungswesen der Juden im Kurfürstentum Hessen 1807–1866. Jüdische Identität zwischen Selbstbehauptung und Assimilationsdruck*. Wiesbaden: Kommission für die Geschichte der Juden in Hessen. VII, 219 pp. (Schriften der Kommission für die Geschichte der Juden in Hessen, 13.) [On Jewish education and the reform of Jewish schools; incl also a chap. on the education of Jewish teachers.] [Cf.: Eberhard Mey (Besprechung) [in]: Zeitschrift des Vereins für hess. Geschichte und Landeskunde, Bd. 99, Wiesbaden, 1994. Pp. 285–286.]

31514. WIRTHWEIN, HEIKE: *Landjuden in Hessen im Vormärz. Juden zwischen Emanzipation, Assimilation und religiösem Traditionalismus*. [In]: Hessisches Jahrbuch für Landesgeschichte, Bd. 44, Marburg, 1994. Pp. 71–90.

31515. HÖCHBERG. BAR-GIORA BAMBERGER, NAFTALI: *Der jüdische Friedhof in Höchberg*. Memorbuch. Mit einem Beitrag von Hans-Peter Baum. Würzburg: Schöningh, 1991. 455 pp., illus. (Schriften des Stadtarchivs Würzburg, H. 8.) [Title also in Hebrew.]

31516. HÖXTER. WÜRZBURGER, ERNST: *Höxter: verdrängte Geschichte*. Zur Geschichte des Nationalsozialismus in einer ostwestfälischen Kreisstadt. Höxter: Villa Huxori e.V., 1990. 284 pp., illus. [Incl. the chap.: Die Ausgrenzung und Vernichtung der Juden (156–204); also list of deportees.]

31517. INGENHEIM. KUKATZKI, BERNHARD, Hrsg.: *Zwölf Bittschriften Ingenheimer Juden an die Freiherren von Gemmingen in den Jahren 1787 – 1790*. Landau in der Pfalz, 1994. 28 pp., notes, illus., facsims. [Printed privately.]

31518. KASSEL. *Die Kasseler Sammlung Alexander Fiorino.* Katalog zur Ausstellung in der Neuen Galerie 12. Juni – 11. September 1994. Hrsg.: Ulrich Schmidt. Kassel: Staatliche Museen Kassel, 1994. 168 pp., illus., bibl. [Alexander Fiorino, 1842 Kassel – 1940 Kassel, banker (Fiorino & Sichel, founded 1885), nephew of the miniature painter Jeremias David Alexander Fiorino. Part of his art collection was given to the city of Kassel before World War I; he was forced to sell the remainder in 1939.]

31519. KLEVE. KREBS, WOLFGANG: *Juden in Kleve. Spuren einer verlorenen Vergangenheit.* [Cover subtitle: Eine chronologische Bildfolge] Mit einem Nachwort von Werner Steinecke. Kleve: Verlag für Kultur und Technik, 1993. 88 pp., illus., facsims. [Based on an exhibition held in Kleve in 1992 on the occasion of the 750th jubilee of Kleve.]

31520. KORBACH. BEHR, HANS-JOACHIM: *Bischof Franz von Münster und die Korbacher Juden.* [In]: Westfälische Zeitschrift, Bd. 144, Paderborn, 1994. Pp. 89–95, footnotes. [On 16th. century 'Judenschutz' matters.]

31521. KORBACH. *Die Geschichte der jüdischen Gemeinde Korbach.* Bearb.: Karl Wilke. Hrsg.: Kreisstadt Korbach, Stadtarchiv. (34497) Korbach, 1993. 307 pp., illus., facsims. [Incl.: Nazi period.]

31522. KREFELD. *Steinerne Zeugen. Jüdische Grabstätten in Krefeld.* Red.: Ingrid Schupetta. Fotos: Andreas Hemstege. Hrsg.: Der Oberstadtdirektor der Stadt Krefeld, Stadtarchiv; NS-Dokumentations- und Begegnungszentrum. Krefeld: Stadtarchiv, 1991. 47 pp., illus. (Edition Billstein, Bd. 1.)

31523. LAMBSHEIM. KUKATZKI, BERNHARD/JACOBY, MARIO: *Der jüdische Friedhof in Lambsheim.* Ludwigshafen am Rhein: [Selbstverlag] 1994. 53 pp., illus.

31524. LEIPZIG. *Festschrift zum 75jährigen Bestehen der Leipziger Gemeindesynagoge 1855–1930.* Mit einem Vorwort von Fred Grubel, New York. Hrsg. von der Ephraim Carlebach Stiftung. Berlin: Arani, 1994. 88 pp., illus. [Reprint; orig. title: 'Aus der Geschichte und Leben der Juden in Leipzig. Festschrift zum 75jährigen Bestehen der Leipziger Gemeinde-Synagoge. Herausgegeben vom Vorstand der israelitischen Religionsgemeinde'. Cont. 8 articles on the history and present institutions of the Gemeinde. Incl.: Juden als Meßgäste in Leipzig (Max Freudenthal, 16–26).

31525. LEIPZIG. *Judaica Lipsiensia. Zur Geschichte der Juden in Leipzig.* Hrsg. von der Ephraim Carlebach Stiftung. Red.: Manfred Unger. Leipzig: Edition Leipzig, 1994. 322 pp., illus., ports., tabs., maps, footnotes, bibl., index of persons. [Incl. (titles partly abbr.): Jüdischer Messebesuch und Wiederansiedlung von Juden in Leipzig im 18. und frühen 19. Jahrhundert (Josef Reinhold, 12–27). Das Gutachten der Leipziger Theologischen Fakultät von 1714 gegen die jahrhundertealte Blutschuldlüge (Arno Herzig, 28–32). Henriette Goldschmidt. Vom Frauenrecht zur Kindererziehung (Annerose Kemp, 33–53). Jüdische Musikkultur und jüdische Musiker 1855–1933 (Thomas Schinköth, 54–69). Rafael Frank und seine hebräischen Druckschriften (Ittai Joseph Tamari, 70–78). Die jüdische Gemeinde auf dem Höhepunkt ihrer Existenz. Zur Berufs- und Sozialstruktur um das Jahr 1925 (Kerstin Plowinski, 79–91). C.F. Peters. – Ein deutscher Musikverlag im Leipziger Kulturleben. Zum Wirken von Max Abraham und Henri Hinrichsen (Irene Lawford-Hinrichsen/Norbert Molkenbur, 92–109). Jüdische Mediziner in Leipzig (Susanne Hahn, 110–122). Lazar Gulkowitsch an den Universitäten Leipzig und Dorpat (Siegfried Hoyer, 123–131). Die jüdischen sozialen Vereine Leipzigs 1929–1939 (André Bach, 132–143). Zur Demographie der jüdisch verfolgten Bürger 1933–1945 (Thomas Kübler, 144–154). Juden im Leipziger Widerstand 1933/34 (Solvejg Höppner, 155–166). Der Zionismus in Leipzig im Dritten Reich (Francis Nicosia, 167–178). Der Jüdische Kulturbund in Leipzig 1934–1938 (Manfred Unger, 179–193). Der Novemberpogrom in Leipzig (Steffen Heid, 194–206). Leipziger Juden in der Sowjetunion nach 1933 und in der DDR bis 1953 (Günter Fippel, 207–216). Die Juden in der SBZ (Siegfried Hollitzer, 217–227). Die Auswirkungen des Prager Slansky-Prozesses auf die Leipziger Juden 1952/53 (Esther Ludwig, 228–244). Der

Alte Israelitische Friedhof im Leipziger Johannisthal (Henning Steinführer, 246–258). Incl. also texts from previous publications and short biographies of Leipzig Jews.]

31526. LEIPZIG. *Jüdisches Jahrbuch für Sachsen und Adreßbuch der Gemeindebehörden, Organisationen und Vereine 1931/32. Ausgabe Leipzig.* Mit einem Vorwort von Hardy Fraenle, Ra'anama. Hrsg. von der Ephraim Carlebach Stiftung. Berlin: Arani, 1994. [Reprint.] [Incl.: I. Der sächsische Israelitische Gemeindeverband (Paul Salinger, 9–13). II. Aus dem jüdischen Leben Leipzigs. Vergangenheit (pp. 14–40; contribs. by Gustav Cohn and Saul Lilienthal). Gegenwart (on Jewish artists; Die soziale Struktur der Leipziger Judenheit (Felix Goldmann, 50–55). Die jüdische Schule (Ephraim Carlebach, 56–62). Das Leipziger Gemeindeblatt (Gustav Cohn, 63–74). III. Zur Arbeit der jüdischen Organisationen (5 articles by Felix Goldmann, Gustav Cohn, Oskar Dzialowski, Benno Sehr, Hans Oesterreicher and Fritz Grübel, pp. 75–103.]

31527. LEIPZIG. *Leipziger Jüdisches Jahr- und Adressbuch 1933.* Mit einem Vorwort von Rolf Kralovitz, Köln. Hrsg. von der Ephraim Carlebach Stiftung. Berlin: Arani, 1994. 90 pp. [Reprint].

31528. LEMGO. POHLMANN, HANNE/SCHEFFLER, JÜRGEN, Hrsg.: *Die jüdische Familie Katz.* Erinnerungsarbeit in Lemgo. Detmold: Ges. für Christl.-Jüd. Zusammenarbeit, 1991. 91 pp., illus. (Panu derech, Bd. 4.)

31529. LIPPE. FAASSEN, DINA VAN: *Die lippischen Juden zur Zeit Simons VI. und Simons VII.* Teil 1 [&] 2. [In]: AKK. Architektur, Kunst- und Kulturgeschichte in Nord- und Westdeutschland. Jg. 5, Nr. 1 [&] 2, Marburg, Feb. & Mai 1994. Pp. 3–13 [&] 43–50, notes.

31530. LIPPE. FAASSEN, DINA VAN: *Vom Schächten der jüdischen Metzgerei in Lippe. Die Entwicklung der jüdischen Metzgerei in Lippe.* [In]: Lippische Mitteilungen aus Geschichte und Landeskunde, Bd. 63, Detmold, 1994. Pp. 85–129, illus., facsims., footnotes.

31531. LOWER SAXONY. RIES, ROTRAUD: *Jüdisches Leben in Niedersachsen im 15. und 16. Jahrhundert.* Hannover: Verl. Hahnsche Buchhandlung, 1994. 614 pp., charts, tabs., bibl. (549–602), index (603–614). (Veröffentlichungen der Historischen Kommission für Niedersachsen und Bremen XXXV: Quellen und Untersuchungen zur allgemeinen Geschichte Niedersachsens in der Neuzeit, Bd. 13.)

31532. LOWER SAXONY. RIES, ROTRAUD: *Literatur zur Geschichte der Juden in Niedersachsen seit 1945.* Eine kommentierte Bibliographie, Teil 1. [In]: Aschkenas, Jg. 3, Wien, 1993. Pp. 239–266. [Lists 400 publications.] [Corrected name of journal in entry No. 30210/YB XXXIX.]

31533. LOWER SAXONY. RIES, ROTRAUD: *Literatur zur Geschichte der Juden in Niedersachsen seit 1945.* (Teil 2). [In]: Aschkenas, Jg. 4/1994, H. 2, Wien, 1995. Pp. 489–518. [Review essay.]

31534. LOWER SAXONY. SABELLECK, RAINER, Hrsg.: *Juden in Südniedersachsen. Geschichte – Lebensverhältnisse – Denkmäler.* Beiträge zu einer Tagung am 10. November 1990 in Göttingen. Hannover: Verl. Hahnsche Buchhandl. Hannover, 1994. 227 pp., tabs., facsims. (Schriftenreihe des Landschaftsverbandes Südniedersachsen, Bd. 2.) [Cont.: Einleitung (Rainer Sabelleck, 9–10). Strukturen frühneuzeitlicher Judenpolitik in Braunschweig-Calenberg (Rotraud Ries, 11–56). Das Judenrecht im Kurfürstentum und Königreich Hannover (Siegfried Schütz, 57–82). Aufenthalt auf Abruf; zur Praxis der Schutzbriefgewährung im Kurfürstentum und im Königreich Hannover (Rainer Sabelleck, 83–100). Hessische Judenpolitik in ihren Auswirkungen auf Südniedersachsen (Eike Dietert, 101–136). Die Juden in Duderstadt im Zeitalter der Emanzipation 1850–1918 (Hans-Heinrich Ebeling, 137–170). Lebensbedingungen des letzten Göttinger Rabbiners und seiner Gemeinde. Die Erinnerungen von Zvi Hermon (Peter Aufgebauer, 171–178). Probleme und Ergebnisse der Erforschung jüdischer Friedhöfe und ihrer Grabinschriften. Bericht aus der Arbeit im Göttinger Umfeld (Berndt Schaller, 179–184). Judenbäder in Hedemünden und Münden (Heinrich Hampe, 185–190). Mahnmaltexte in Südniedersachsen (Ulrike Haß-Zumkehr, 191–204). Auf den Spuren ehemaliger jüdischer Einwohner in Uslar (Bericht über ein

Schülerprojekt während der Projektwoche 1989 an der Orientierungsstufe Uslar) (Detlev Herbst, 205–208). Bibliographie zur Geschichte der Juden im Gebiet des heutigen Südniedersachsen (Rainer Sabelleck, 209–224).]

31535. LÜBECK. GUTTKUHN, PETER: *Von Zähnen, Warzen und Leichdörnern. Aus der Praxis des Lübecker Zahnarztes Jacob Levy (1784–1840).* [In]: Schleswig-Holsteinisches Ärzteblatt, Jg. 47, Nr. 1, Bad Segeberg, Jan. 1994. Pp. 7–9, notes.

31536. LÜDENSCHEID. KANN, ERICH/WAGNER, MATTHIAS: *Lüdenscheider Jüdinnen und Juden 1690–1945.* Hagen: Padligur, 1994. 260 pp., illus., notes, bibl. (Beiträge zur Förderung des christlich-jüdischen Dialogs, Bd. 12.) [Incl. list of Lüdenscheid Jews from 1933–1945.]

31537. MAINZ. LINK, HELMUT/SCHERF, FERDINAND,: *Begegnung mit dem Judentum am Rabanus-Maurus-Gymnasium Mainz.* Folgeband. Mainz, 1993. [Private print.] 166 pp., illus., facsims. [Incl. memoirs by Jews from Mainz, contribs. on the history of the Mainz community and its present situation.]

31538. MALCHOW (Mecklenburg). *Aus der jüdischen Gemeinde in Malchow (Meckl.)* Hrsg.: Stadt Malchow (Meckl.), 1994. Text: Karl-Heinz Oelke. 77 pp., illus., facsims.

31539. MEDEBACH. KLUETING, HARM, Hrsg.: *Geschichte von Amt und Stadt Medebach (Hochsauerland).* Hrsg. im Auftrag der Stadt Medebach. Medebach, 1994. 742 pp., illus., maps. [Incl. a chapt. on the Jews of Medebach.]

31540. MEISENHEIM. LAMB, ANNI/SCHLRAB, KLÄRE: *Jüdische Mitbürger in den 20er und 30er Jahren.* Zeitzeugen berichten. Meisenheimer Hefte, Jg. 14, Nr. 39, Meisenheim, 1992. 24 pp., illus.

31541. MÜLHEIM an der RUHR. BENNERTZ, GERHARD: *Jüdische Schicksale und Namen.* [In]: 900 Jahre Mülheim an der Ruhr, 1093–1993. Zeitschrift des Geschichtsvereins Mülheim a.d. Ruhr, Nr. 66, Mülheim a.d. Ruhr, 1993. [Special issue.] Pp. 547–568, illus., notes. [Incl. lists of names detailing the fate of Mülheim Jews during the Nazi period.]

31542. MUNICH. *Stieftöchter der Alma Mater? 90 Jahre Frauenstudium in Bayern – am Beispiel der Universität München.* Katalog zur Ausstellung. Hrsg. von Hadumod Bussmann. München: Kunstmann, 1993. 185 pp., illus., tabs. [Catalogue of an exhibition held at the Univ. of Munich Nov. 11, 1993 – Feb. 20, 1994. Incl. Jewish students. See also Aktenvermerk 'abgelehnt'. Jüdische Studenten an der Universität München und was aus ihnen wurde (Hiltrud Häntzschel) [in]: Süddeutsche Zeitung, Nr. 292, München, 18./19. Dez. 1993, p. V.] [See also No. 32176.]

31543. MUNICH. *Versagte Heimat. Jüdisches Leben in Münchens Isarvorstadt 1914–1945.* Hrsg. von Douglas Bokovoy und Stefan Meining. München: Verl. Peter Glas, 1994. 508 pp., illus., ports., facsims., docs. (Eine Veröffentlichung der Forschungsstelle deutsch-jüdische Zeitgeschichte e.V.) [Incl.: Teil 1: Lebensbedingungen (7–260); cont. essays by the eds. & Andreas Toscano del Banner, Reiner Pommerin and Stephan Heiß on Jews in the First World War, antisemitism, Eastern Jews, Jewish institutions and organisations, and persecution during the Nazi era). Teil 2: Lebenswege (261–508; cont. essays on Jewish personalities by Barbara Picht and Anja Siegemund; also contribs. and memoirs by Benjamin Mordechai (Benno) Engelhard, Inge Sadan née Engelhard, Jakob Kra-Os, Alexander Holthaus, Oskar Gröbel, Rudi Rosenfelder, Zita Kober née Landau, Nachum Tim Gidal and Ritta Bachenheimer née Bender.]

31544. MUTTERSTADT. KUKATZKI, BERNHARD: *Der jüdische Friedhof in Mutterstadt.* [In]: Beiträge zur jüdischen Geschichte in Rheinland-Pfalz. Jg. 4, Ausgabe 1, Bad Kreuznach, 1994, Heft Nr. 6. Pp. 5–15.

31545. NEU-ISENBURG. HEUBACH, HELGA, Hrsg: *'Das unsichtbare Isenburg': über das Heim des Jüdischen Frauenbundes in Neu-Isenburg, 1907 bis 1942.* Neu-Isenburg. Bertha Pappenheim u.a. Hrsg.: Kulturamt der Stadt Neu-Isenburg. Neu-Isenburg: Kulturamt, 1994. 218 pp., illus.

Bibliography

31546. NEUWIED. GONDORF, BERNHARD: *Die Wiedereinweihung der Synagoge von Neuwied 1844*. [In]: Heimatjahrbuch des Landkreises Neuwied 1994. Neuwied, 1994. Pp. 67–68.

31547. NIEDERBREISIG. KLEINPASS, HANS: *Synagogenbau in Niederbreisig blieb ein Wunschtraum – geplante Hauskollekte 1854 von der Regierung abgelehnt*. [In]: Kreis Ahrweiler: Heimat-Jahrbuch 1994. Jg. 51, Ahrweiler, 1994. Pp. 92–93.

31548. NIEDERZISSEN. ESTEN, STEPHAN: *Die Grabstätte des Leopold Kahn auf dem jüdischen Friedhof in Niederzissen*. [In]: Kreis Ahrweiler. Heimat-Jahrbuch 1994. Jg. 51, Ahrweiler, 1994. Pp. 103–105.

31549. NÜRNBERG. *Juden in Nürnberg. Geschichte der jüdischen Mitbürger vom Mittelalter bis zur Gegenwart*. Hrsg.: Stadt Nürnberg, Presse- und Informationsamt, 1993. Nürnberg: W. Tümmels, 1993. 76 pp., illus., facsims. [Incl.: Juden in Nürnberg (Herbert Lehnert, 4–55). Die israelitische Kultusgemeinde Nürnberg nach 1945 (Arno Hamburger, 56–70). Freundschaftsvertrag mit Hadera (Liane Zettl, 71–74).]

31550. ODENBACH. KUKATZKI, BERNHARD, Hrsg.: *Die Restaurierung der Synagoge in Odenbach*. Eine Dokumentation. (67099) Schifferstadt (Postfach 1133), 1994. 89 pp., illus., facsims., docs., bibl. [Private print.]

31551. OFFENBACH. *Zur Geschichte der Juden in Offenbach am Main*. Band 3. Werden und Vergehen: Aufstieg, Buchdruck, Friedhöfe, Erinnerungen. Hrsg.: Magistrat der Stadt Offenbach am Main. Offenbach: Magistrat der Stadt Offenbach am Main, 1994. XII, 180 pp., illus., map.

31552. OTTERSBERG (nr. BREMEN). KLUGE, HEIDELORE: *Wir haben immer gut zusammengelebt! Die Juden in Ottersberg*. Mit Zeichnungen von Gundula Dangschat und einem Geleitwort von Lea Rosh. Bremen: Donat, 1994. 93 pp., illus.

31553. PALATINATE. KUKATZKI, BERNHARD, Hrsg.: *Erinnerungen jüdischer Pfälzer*. (67099) Schifferstadt (Postfach 1133), 1994. 68 pp., illus., facsims., docs. [Incl. 19 memoirs.]

31554. PALATINATE. KUKATZKI, BERNHARD: *Jüdisches Leben in den Rheindörfern Roxheim und Bobenheim*. [In]; Beiträge zur jüdischen Geschichte in Rheinland-Pfalz, Jg. 4, Ausgabe 1, Bad Kreuznach, 1994. pp. 16–24. (Heft Nr. 6.) [Also, by same author: Juden in Bobenheim-Roxheim. Schifferstadt, 1994. 38 pp., bibl., illus., facsims., notes, bibl. (Private print).]

—— RHINELAND. BUNYAN, ANITA: *Rhenish Liberalism and the Jewish Question in the Vormärz. The case of the Kölnische Zeitung 1841–1847*. [See No. 32358.]

31555. RHINELAND. HEYNE, MAREN: *Stille Gärten – beredte Steine. Jüdische Friedhöfe im Rheinland*. Fotografien. Mit einer Einleitung von Ludger Heid. Bonn: Dietz, 1994. 153 [5] pp., illus., bibl. [Incl.: Jüdische Friedhöfe (Ludger Heid, 9–15).]

31556. RÖDELSEE (Franconia). REUTHER, CHRISTIAN/SCHNEEBERGER, MICHAEL: *Nichts mehr zu sagen und nichts zu beweinen. Ein jüdischer Friedhof in Deutschland*. [Lehrstück und Lesarten zum Jüdischen Friedhof Rödelsee, seiner Geschichte und seinen Menschen.] Hrsg.: Arbeitsgruppe Pädagogisches Museum e.V., Berlin. Berlin: Ed. Hentrich [1994]. 159 pp. illus. (Schriftenreihe AnDenken 3.) [Incl. texts by Henryk M. Broder, Hans-Joachim Langer and Klaus Kreimeier.]

31557. RÜLZHEIM. KUKATZKI, BERNHARD: *. . . das einzige Hotel in der ganzen Gegend, das koscher geführt wurde. Das Hotel Victoria in Rülzheim*. (67099) Schifferstadt: B. Kukatzki (Postfach 1133), 1994. 30 pp., illus., facsims., notes.

31558. SAARLOUIS. MÜLLER, WERNER: *Die jüdische Minderheit im Kreis Saarlouis: politische, sozialökonomische und kulturelle Aspekte ihrer Lebenssituation vom Ancien Régime bis zum Nationalsozialismus.* St. Ingbert: Röhrig, 1993. 173 pp., illus., bibl. (167–173). (Schriften des Landkreises Saarlouis, Bd. 1.)

31559. SAUERLAND. *Jüdisches Leben im Hochsauerland.* Hrsg.: Hochsauerlandkreis: Der Oberstadtdirektor. Red.: Rudolf Brüschke, Norbert Föckeler. Fredeburg: Grobbel, 1994. 588; II, 96 pp., illus., maps, graphs. (Hochsauerlandkreis – Schriftenreihe, 3.) [Incl.: Jüdische Kindheit im Altkreis Brilon zur Zeit des Nationalsozialismus (Katrin Frenzl, II, 96 pp., bound in at end of book).]

31560. SAXONY. *Juden in Sachsen: ihr Leben und Leiden.* [Hrsg.]: Gesellschaft für Christlich-Jüdische Zusammenarbeit Dresden e.V. Leipzig: Evang. Verl.-Anstalt, 1994. 120 pp., illus., map. [Incl. Nazi period.]

31561. SCHLESWIG-HOLSTEIN. *Ausgegrenzt – verachtet – vernichtet. Zur Geschichte der Juden in Schleswig-Holstein.* Mit Beiträgen von Wolfgang Benz [et al.] Hrsg.: Landeszentrale für Politische Bildung Schleswig-Holstein. Kiel, 1994. 109 pp., notes. [Incl. (titles partly abbr.): Die ersten jüdischen Gemeinden in Schleswig-Holstein im 17. Jahrhundert (Manfred Jakubowski-Tiessen, 9–26). Juden in Schleswig-Holstein im späten 18. und 19. Jahrhundert (Franklin Kopitzsch, 27–42). Bürgerliche Rechte für die Juden in Schleswig-Holstein (Ulrich Lange, 43–70). Antisemitismus in Schleswig-Holstein in der Zeit der Weimarer Republik (Peter Wulf, 71–82). Geschichte der Juden in Deutschland in der nationalsozialistischen Zeit (Wolfgang Benz, 83–94).]

—— SCHWABEN. *Geschichte und Kultur der Juden in Schwaben.* Hrsg. von Peter Fassl. [See No. 31392.]

31562. SCHWABEN. JAKOB, REINHARD: *Frühneuzeitliche Erwerbs- und Sozialstrukturen der schwäbischen Judenschaft. Dargestellt vornehmlich am Beispiel der oettingischen Stadt Harburg an der Wörnitz.* [In]: Aschkenas, Jg. 3, Wien, 1993. Pp. 65–84, footnotes. [Corrected name of journal in entry No. 30254/YB XXXIX.]

—— SCHWABEN. KIEßLING, ROLF, Hrsg.: *Judengemeinden in Schwaben im Kontext des Alten Reiches.* [See No. 31405.]

31563. SILESIA. FUCHS, KONRAD: *Jüdisches Unternehmertum in Schlesien.* [In]: Menora 5, München, 1994. Pp. 71–94, notes.

31564. SOEST. BUSS, WILFRIED: *Sosatia Judaica: ein Beitrag zur Geschichte der Juden in Soest.* Dortmund: Pädagogische Hochschule, 1994. 484 pp., illus., ports., facsims., tabs., bibl. (469–484). (Typescript) [Available at the LBI London.]

31565. SOLINGEN. BRAMANN, WILHELM: *Coppel. Geschichte einer jüdischen Familie in Solingen 1770–1942.* Hrsg.: Stadt Solingen, der Oberstadtdirektor. Solingen: Selbstverl. Stadtarchiv Solingen, 1994. 256 pp., illus., facsims., footnotes, names index (246–252), bibl., family tree [extra insert]. (Anker und Schwert, Bd. 13.) [On the Coppel family and their factories: Alexander Coppel, Stahlwaren- und Waffenfabrik Solingen, founded in 1821 and Alexander Coppel, Stahlrohrwerk Hilden.]

31566. STAUDERNHEIM. KUKATZKI, BERNHARD: *Die Staudernheimer Synagoge – ein Projekt des Museumsvereins Synagoge Staudernheim e.V., Landkreis Bad Kreuznach.* (67099) Schifferstadt: B. Kukatzki (Postfach 1133), 1994. 18 pp., illus., facsims.

31567. STUTTGART. LANGNER, BERND: *Gemeinnütziger Wohnungsbau um 1900. Karl Hengerers Bauten für den Stuttgarter Verein für das Wohl der arbeitenden Klassen.* Stuttgart: Klett-Cotta, 1994. 283 pp., illus., plans, notes, indexes, bibl. (263–274). Zugl.: Stuttgart, Univ., Diss., 1994. (Veröff. des Archivs der Stadt Stuttgart, Bd. 65.) [Incl. a chapter on Eduard Pfeiffer (1835–1921), social reformer, founder of the Verein für das Wohl der arbeitenden Klassen.]

31568. UNKEL. VOLLMER, RUDOLF: *Die ehemalige jüdische Gemeinde der Bürgermeisterei Unkel*. [In]: Heimat-Jahrbuch des Landkreises Neuwied 1994. Neuwied, 1994. Pp. 74–79.

31569. VOGELSBERG (Hesse). *Fragmente jüdischen Lebens im Vogelsberg*. Hrsg.: Kulturverein Lauterbach e.V. Lauterbach. Kulturverein, 1994. 145 pp., illus., graphs.

31570. WALDNIEL. ZÖHREN, PETER: *Zwei Besitzzeugnisse für Alex Levy aus Waldniel gefunden*. [In]: Heimatjahrbuch des Kreises Viersen 1994. 45. Folge, Viersen, 1994. Pp. 78–80, illus.

—— WARBURG. HERZ, EMIL: *Denk ich an Deutschland in der Nacht*. [See No. 32336.]

31571. WESTPHALIA. BRUNS, ALFRED, Bearb.: *Die Juden im Herzogtum Westfalen*. Dokumentation der zentralen Quellen. Bearb. von Alfred Bruns. Hrsg.: Hochsauerlandkreis: Der Oberkreisdirektor. Fredeburg: Grobbel, 1994. 397 pp., map, facsims., index (361–396). (Hochsauerlandkreis Schriftenreihe, Bd. II.) [Incl. 253 documents from 1255 until 1803.]

31572. WESTPHALIA. HEID, LUDGER: *'Ist die Beteiligung . . . russischer Juden festgestellt?' Ostjüdische Revolutionäre – revolutionäre Ostjuden im Ruhrgebiet*. [In]: Duisburger Forschungen, Band 41. Duisburg, 1994. Pp. 147–166

—— WESTPHALIA. HERZIG, ARNO: *Die westfälischen Juden im Modernitätsprozess*. [In]: Deutsche Juden und die Moderne. [See in No.31425.]

31573. WITTEN. *'Um Spott und Hohn der Wittener loszuwerden . . .'. Erinnerungen des jüdischen Lehrers und Kantors Jacob Ostwald 1863–1910*. Hrsg. von der Stadt Witten. Witten, 1994. 105 pp., notes. [Incl.: Einleitung. Die Memoiren des Jacob Ostwald (Martina Kliner-Fruck, 7–14).]

31574. WORMS. EIDELBERG, SHLOMO: *The Jews of Worms during the French conquest (1688–1697)*. [In]: Proceedings of the American Academy for Jewish Research, Vol. 60, Jerusalem, 1994. Pp. 71–100, illus., facsims., appendixes, footnotes.

31575. WÜRTTEMBERG. BURMEISTER, KARL HEINZ: *Medinat bodase. Zur Geschichte der Juden am Bodensee 1200–1349*. Bd. 1. Konstanz: UVK, Univers.-Verl. Konstanz, 1994. 181 pp., illus., map. (UVK-Geschichte.)

31576. WÜRTTEMBERG. BURMEISTER, KARL HEINZ: *Spuren jüdischer Geschichte und Kultur in der Grafschaft Montfort. Die Region Tettnang, Langenargen, Wasserburg*. Hrsg. von Eduard Hindelang. [Hrsg.:] Museum Langenargen am Bodensee. Sigmaringen: Thorbecke, 1994. 192 pp., illus., notes, bibl., indexes. (Veröffentlichungen des Museums Langenargen.)

31577. WÜRTTEMBERG. KUSTERMANN, ABRAHAM P./BAUER, DIETER R., Hrsg.: *Jüdisches Leben im Bodenseeraum. Zur Geschichte des alemannischen Judentums mit Thesen zum christlich-jüdischen Gespräch*. Ostfildern: Schwabenverlag, 1994. 299 pp., illus., notes. (Reihe Analaysen und Impulse in Zusammenarbeit mit der Akademie der Diözese Rottenburg-Stuttgart.) [Incl.: Juden im Bodenseeraum bis 1349 (Karl Heinz Burmeister, 19–36). Die Judengemeinden im nördlichen Bodenseeraum (Paul Sauer, 37–58). Laupheim – einst eine große und angesehene Judengemeinde (Ernst Schäll, 59–90). Religiosität und Bildung in jüdischen Landgemeinden (Gisela Roming, 91–108). Ein schweizerisch-jüdisches Leben für moderne Bildung und Emanzipation: Marcus Getsch Dreifus (1812–1877) aus Endingen (Uri R. Kaufmann, 109–132). 'Zur Anstellung als Rabbine . . . wird erfordert . . .'. Württemberg und der Umbruch von Rabbinat und Rabbinerausbildung im 19. Jahrhundert (Abraham Peter Kustermann, 133–158). Der jüdische Erzähler Jacob Picard (Manfred Bosch, 159–168). Das Los (Jacob Picard, 169–180). Das Jüdische Museum in Hohenems. Geschichte und Konzept eines Stadtmuseums der besonderen Art (Eva Grabherr, 181–192). 'Schweigend spricht der Stein'. Jüdische Architektur und Baukunst in der Bodensee-Region und in Oberschwaben (Joachim Hahn, 193–212). Zur regionalen Geschichte von Verfolgung und Vernichtung der Juden des Bodenseeraums 1933–1945 am Beispiel der Stadt Konstanz (Erhard Roy Wiehn, 213–240). Two further contribs. on Christian-Jewish dialogue (Rupert Feneberg & Joel Berger, 241–296).]

31578. ZIRNDORF. MAHR, HELMUT: *Die erste statistische Erfassung der jüdischen Gemeinde Zirndorf im Jahre 1911.* [In]: Nachrichten für den jüdischen Bürger Fürths, Fürth, 1994. Pp. 15 ff.

1a. Alsace

31579. ALSACE. WEYL, ROBERT: *Les tabatières aux trois juifs prétendues Alsaciennes ou les avatars d'une gravure.* [In]: Revue des Etudes Juives, Vol. 152, Nos. 1–2, Paris, Jan.-Juin 1993. Pp. 201–203, illus.

31580. *Archives Juives,* No. 27/2 [with the issue title]: *Dossier: Les juifs de Lorraine.* 2e semestre 1994. 1 issue. [Incl.: Un survol historique (Pierre-André Meyer, 4–24). La présence juive en Lorraine au moyen age. Continuités et ruptures (Jean-Luc Fray, 25–38). Un example original de réimplantation des juifs: Maggino Gabrieli, consul de la nation hébraique et levantine au service du duc de Lorraine Charles III (Martine Lemalet, 39–50). Le registre de correspondence des juifs de Lorraine (1789–1791) (Simon Schwarzfuchs, 51–61). Les juifs de Toul (1789–1850) (Jean-Paul Aubé, 62–77). Les juifs de Nancy pendant la guerre de 1939–1945 (Françoise Job, 78–88). Introduction à l'inventaire des archives de la communauté israélite de Nancy (Elisabeth Couteau, 89–91).]

—— BENFELD. SCHNEIDER, REINHARD: *Der Tag von Benfeld im Januar 1349: Sie kamen zusammen und kamen überein, die Juden zu vernichten.* [See in No. 31387.]

31581. METZ. MEYER, PIERRE-ANDRÉ: *La communauté juive de Metz au XVIIIe siécle.* Histoire et démographie. Nancy: Presses Universitaires de Nancy/Ed. Serpenoise, 1993. 325 pp., tabs., graphs, footnotes, bibl. (311–322). (Coll. Les Juifs de Lorraine.)

31582. MÜHLHAUSEN. FLEISCHMANN, JOHANN: *Das Protokollbuch der jüdischen Gemeinde von Mühlhausen 1880–1938.* [In]: Heimatbote aus dem Reichen Ebrachgrund 6, 1993. Pp. 92–113.

31583. NIEDERVISSE. DALTROFF, JEAN: *Les juifs de Niedervisse. Naissance, épanouissement et déclin d'une communauté.* Strasbourg: J. Daltroff (F-6700 Strasbourg, 20A, rue de Verdun), 1992. 215 pp., illus. [Incl. children's stories in the local Yiddish dialect with translation.]

—— STARCK, ASTRID: *A nineteenth-century Yiddish newspaper 'Israels Stimme: hakol kol yaakov'.* [See No. 31439.]

31584. STARCK, ASTRID [ed.]: *Westjiddisch. Mündlichkeit und Schriftlichkeit.* Le Yiddish occidental. Actes du Colloque de Mulhouse. [See No. 31445.]

2. Austria

31585. BURGENLAND. GENÉE, PIERRE: *Die Synagogen im Burgenland und deren Schicksal.* [In]: David, Jg. 6, Nr. 22, Wien, Sept. 1994. Pp. 10–19.

31586. EISENSTADT. Jüdisches Museum. *Spharadim-Spaniolen.* [Hrsg.: Österreichisches Jüdisches Museum in Eisenstadt]. Hrsg. von Felicitas Heimann-Jelinek und Kurt Schubert. Eisenstadt: Österr. Jüdisches Museum, 1992. 241 pp., illus., bibl. (239–242). [Studia Judaica Austriaca, Bd. 13.)

31587. EISENSTADT. Jüdisches Museum. *Die österreichischen Hofjuden und ihre Zeit.* Koord. und hrsg. von Kurt Schubert. Hrsg.: Österreichisches Jüdisches Museum in Eisenstadt. Eisenstadt: Österr. Jüdisches Museum, 1991. 120 [44] pp., illus. (Studia Judaica Austriaca, Bd.12.)

31588. FRIEDMANN, ALEXANDER/HOFSTÄTTER, MARIA/KNAPP, ILAN: *Eine neue Heimat? Jüdische Emigrantinnen und Emigranten aus der Sowjetunion.* Wien: Verl. für Gesellschaftskritik, 1994. 211 pp., tabs., bibl. (189–194). [A sociological survey of the Jewish immigrants from the former Soviet Union in Austria.]

31589. GRAZ. PHILIPPSOHN-LANG, TRUDE: *Eine Grazer Familie im Holocaust.* Eine Rekonstruktion aus Briefen und Meldungen des Roten Kreuzes. [In]: Geschichte und Gegenwart, Jg. 13, H. 4, Graz, Dez. 1994. Pp. 237–245.

31590. *The Habsburg legacy: national identity in historical perspective.* Ed. by Ritchie Robertson and Edward Timms. Edinburgh: Edinburgh University Press, 1994. X, 242 pp., illus., facsims., map, notes. (Austrian studies 5.) [Incl. the essays: 'Auf Fluch und Lüge baut sich kein Glück auf': Karl Emil Franzos's novel 'Judith Trachtenberg' and the question of Jewish assimilation (Florian Krobb, 84–93); Hugo von Hofmannsthal and the Austrian idea of Central Europe (Jacques Le Rider, transl. by Rosemary Morris, 121–135); The dilemma of identity: the impact of the First World War on Habsburg Jewry (Marsha L. Rozenblit, 144–157).]

31591. HOHENEMS. Jüdisches Museum. *Geschichten von Gegenständen. Judaica aus dem Beziehungsraum der Hohenemser Juden/Jewish ritual objects and the stories they tell. Artefacts in the Gross Family Collection, Tel Aviv, pertaining to the cultural world of the Jews of Hohenems.* The Gross Family Collection, Tel Aviv. Hrsg.: Eva Grabherr. Hohenems, Jüdisches Museum Hohenems, 1994. 183 pp., illus. [Catalogue of an exhibition held in the Jüdisches Museum Hohenems, June 17 – August 15, 1994; all texts in German and English.]

31592. KEIL, MARTHA/LOHRMANN, KLAUS, Hrsg.: *Studien zur Geschichte der Juden in Österreich.* Herwig Wolfram zum 60. Geburtstag. Wien: Böhlau, 1994. 191 pp., footnotes. (Handbuch zur Geschichte der Juden in Österreich, Reihe B, Bd. 2.) [Book publ. on the occasion of the 5th jubilee of the Institut für Geschichte der Juden in Österreich (St. Pölten).] [Cont.: Vorwort des Herausgebers (9–10). Überlegungen zur vermögensrechtlichen Stellung der Juden im Mittelalter (11–40). Der Liber Judeorum von Wr. Neustadt (1453–1500) – Edition (Martha Keil, 41–99). Hetschel von Herzogenburg und seine Familie (Hannelore Grahammer, 100–120). Die Juden in Vorarlberg und die süddeutsche Judenheit im 17. und 18. Jahrhundert (Bernhard Purin, 121–129). Die Blut- und Rassenschandeprozesse im Kontext der nationalsozialistischen Heilstheologie (Michael Ley, 130–139). Ungarisch-jüdische Zwangsarbeiter in Wien 1944/45 (Eleonore Lappin, 140–165). Jüdische Unternehmer in Österreich nach 1945. Oral History und ihre Forschungsperspektiven für die postfaschistische jüdische Geschichte (Michael John/Albert Lichtblau, 166–191).]

—— KLÜGER, RUTH: *Antisemitismus im Werk jüdisch-österreichischer Autoren.* [See No. 32369.]

31593. LANDER, KATJA: *Josef Samuel Bloch und die Österreichisch-Israelitische Union.* Initiativen zur Begründung einer jüdischen Politik im späten 19. Jahrhundert in Wien. Saarbrücken, Univ., Diss., 1993. 339 pp.

31594. LINZ. AIGNER, MANFRED: *Die Juden in Linz.* Frühe Zeugnisse. [In]: David, Jg. 6, Nr. 23, Wien, Dez. 1994. Pp. 5–12, illus., bibl.

31595. LORENZ, DAGMAR C.G.: *Austrian Jewish history and identity after 1945.* [In]: Modern Austrian Literature, Vol. 27, Nos. 3–4, Riverside, Ca., 1994. Pp. 1–18. [Discusses the still significant contribution made by Austrian Jews to post-war Austrian culture.]

31596. MITTENZWEI, INGRID: *Aus dem Alltagsleben des Wiener Grosskaufmanns Adam Albert Hönig am Ende des 18. Jahrhunderts.* [In]: Kairos, N.F., Jg. 34/35, Salzburg, 1992/93. Pp. 168–180.

31597. MOSES, LEOPOLD: *Spaziergänge. Studien und Skizzen zur Geschichte der Juden in Österreich.* Hrsg.: Patricia Steines. Wien: Löcker, 1994. 311 pp., facsims., bibl., indexes. [Incl.: Leopold Moses (1888–1943). Die innige Verbundenheit von Tradition, Wissenschaft und essayistischem Können (Patricia Steines, 9–21). 250 Jahre jüdisches Leben und jüdische Lehre im

Burgenland (Shlomo Spitzer, 22–36). Book contains further 38 texts of Moses, written between 1938 and 1943.] [Leopold Moses, April 24, 1888 Mödling – Dec. 1943, Auschwitz, historian, archivist.]

31598. SENEKOWITSCH, MARTIN: *Gleichberechtigte in einer grossen Armee. Zur Geschichte des Bundes Jüdischer Frontsoldaten Österreichs 1932–38.* Hrsg.: Militärkommando Wien, Abt. für Öffentlichkeitsarbeit, 1994. 18 pp., illus., docs. (10 pp., unpag.).

31599. SENEKOWITSCH, MARTIN: *Gleichberechtigte in einer großen Armee. Zur Geschichte des Bundes Jüdischer Frontsoldaten Österreichs 1932–1938.* [In]: David, Jg. 6, Nr. 22, Wien, Sept. 1994. Pp. 24–31.

31600. SIMMERING. EXENBERGER, HERBERT: *Die Geschichte der Juden in Simmering.* [In]: David, Jg. 6, Nr. 21, Wien, Juni/Juli 1994. Pp. 6–19. [Incl. Nazi period.] [An extended version of article incl. bibl. was publ. Sept. 1988 in: Simmeringer Museumsblätter.]

31601. STIEGNITZ, PETER: *Geschichte und Gegenwart der Juden in Österreich.* [In]: Tribüne, Jg. 33, H. 130, Frankfurt am Main, 1994. Pp. 126–142.

31602. TRIESTE. DUBIN, LOIS C.: *Les liaisons dangereuses. Mariage juif et état moderne à Trieste au XVIIIe siècle.* [In]: Annales, Vol. 49, No. 5, Paris, Sept.- Oct. 1994. Pp. 1139–1170. [With Engl. summary, p. 1277; deals with a struggle between the Jewish community and the state over which marriage law – Habsburg or Jewish – should prevail in late 18th cent. Trieste.]

31603. VIENNA. BERGER, HEINRICH: *'Unehrliche Gesellen'? Eine vergleichende Untersuchung zur Sozialstruktur von Juden und Nichtjuden während der Phase des Liberalismus – mit dem Hauptaugenmerk auf dem Handwerk, und unter Berücksichtigung des Antisemitismus.* Wien, Univ., Diplomarb., 1992. 152 pp.

31604. VIENNA. BERGER, HEINRICH: *Jüdische Handwerker und ihr sozialer Hintergrund in Wien während des Liberalismus.* [In]: Aschkenas, Jg. 4/1994, H. 2, Wien, 1995. Pp. 337–364.

31605. VIENNA. BURSTYN, RUTH: *Aus den Jugendjahren des Zionismus in Wien – die Ursachen für die Entstehung.* [In]: David, Jg. 6, Nr. 20, Wien, März, 1994. Pp. 28–30.

31606. VIENNA. CZEIKE, FELIX: *Historisches Lexikon Wien.* Band 1. Wien: Kremayr & Scheriau, 1992. 632 pp. [First vol. of 5. Cont. topographical, biographical and subject entries referring also to Jewish history and personalities and antisemitism.]

31607. VIENNA. FEICHTENSCHLAGER, NORBERT: *Der Novemberpogrom in Wien.* [In]: Zeitgeschichte, Jg. 21, H. 11/12, Wien, Nov./Dez. 1994. Pp. 363–387, notes.

31608. VIENNA. HÖDL, KLAUS: *Als Bettler in die Leopoldstadt. Galizische Juden auf dem Weg nach Wien.* Wien: Böhlau, 1993. 331 pp., illus., bibl. (323–331). (Böhlaus zeitgeschichtliche Bibliothek, Bd. 27.)

31609. VIENNA. *Juden im mittelalterlichen Wien.* Kleinausstellung des Wiener Stadt- und Landesarchivs. Hrsg.: Wiener Stadt- und Landesarchiv. [Autor]: Klaus Lohrmann. Wien: Wiener Stadt- und Landesarchiv, Magistratsabt. 8, 1994. 13 pp. (Veröffentlichungen des Wiener Stadt- und Landesarchivs: Reihe B, Ausstellungskataloge, H. 41.)

31610. VIENNA. KURTULAN, BANU: *Zur Geschichte der jüdischen Schüler des RG 18 1938.* Fachbereichsarbeit aus Geschichte BRG 18, 1994. Wien: Absolventenverein des Schopenhauergymnasiums (BRG 18, 1180 Wien, Schopenhauerstr. 49), 1994. 42 pp.

—— VIENNA. LICHTBLAU, ALBERT: *Antisemitismus und soziale Spannung in Berlin und Wien 1867–1914.* [See No. 32415.]

31611. VIENNA. LOHRMANN, KLAUS: *Juden im mittelalterlichen Wien.* Kleinausstellung des Wiener Stadt- und Landesarchivs. Hrsg.: Wiener Stadt- und Landesarchiv. Wien, 1994. 13 pp. (Veröffentlichungen des Wiener Stadt- und Landesarchivs, Reihe B: Ausstellungskataloge, Heft 41.)

31612. VIENNA. SENEKOWITSCH, MARTIN: *Ein ungewöhnliches Kriegerdenkmal. Das jüdische Heldendenkmal am Wiener Zentralfriedhof.* Hrsg.: Militärkommando Wien, Abt. für Öffentlichkeitsarbeit. Wien, 1994. [14 pp.], illus.

——— VIENNA. ZUCKERMAN, ALAN S.: *Division and cohesion in the process of modernization: a comparison of the Jewish communities of Vienna and Warsaw during the 1920s.* [See in No.31425.]

31613. VIENNA, Jüdisches Museum. *Jüdisches Wien, einst und jetzt.* Stadtplan. [Hrsg.: Jüdisches Museum Wien]. Wien: Freytag-Berndt, 1993. 77 pp., folded map. [In English and German.]

31614. VIENNA, Jüdisches Museum. *Wiener Jahrbuch für jüdische Geschichte, Kultur & Museumswesen.* Band 1, 1994/1995 – 5755. *Jüdische Kultur in Museen und Ausstellungen bis 1938.* Hrsg. vom Jüdischen Museum der Stadt Wien. Wien: Brandstätter, 1994. 199 pp., illus., notes. [Cont.: Jüdische Kultur in Museen und Ausstellungen bis 1938 – Einleitung (7–10). Vom Kultus zur Kultur. Jüdisches auf Weltausstellungen (Barbara Kirshenblatt-Gimblett, 11–38). Die Welt in der Vitrine und die Welt außerhalb: die soziale Konstruktion jüdischer Museumsexponate (Jeffrey David Feldman, 39–54). Jüdische Museologie. Entwicklungen der jüdischen Museumsarbeit im deutsch-jüdischen Kulturraum (Margrethe Brock-Nannestad, 55–70). Die 'Anglo-Jewish Historical Exhibition' und die Judaicasammlung des Victoria & Albert Museums (Michael E. Keen, 71–88). Dr. Max (Meir) Grunwald, Rabbiner, Volkskundler, Vergessener. Splitter aus der Geschichte des jüdischen Wiens und seines Museums (Christoph Daxelmüller, 89–106). Das Jüdische Zentralmuseum für Mähren-Schlesien in Nikolsburg (Falk Wiesemann, 107–132). Judaica-Sammlungen zwischen Galizien und Wien. Das Jüdische Museum in Lemberg und die Sammlung Maximilian Goldstein (Gabriele Kohlbauer-Fritz, 133–146). Geschichte hinter Geschichten. Kultobjekte aus Wiens Bethäusern und Synagogen (Felicitas Heimann-Jelinek, 147–154). Bilder für eine Ausstellung: Berlin – Tel Aviv (Joachim Schlör, 155–160). Jüdische Geschichte und Kultur in österreichischen Museen und Ausstellungen. Eine Bibliographie (Bernhard Purin, 161–186). Das Jüdische Museum der Stadt Wien 1993/94; Chronik (187–194).]

31615. WISTRICH, ROBERT S.: *Die Juden und die nationalen Konflikte in Ostmitteleuropa (in der Zeit von 1867 bis 1918).* [In]: Neue Literatur. Zeitschrift für Querverbindungen. N.F., Jg. 3, H. 4, Bonn, 1993. Pp. 96–111.

31616. WISTRICH, ROBERT S.: *The Jews and nationality conflicts in the Habsburg lands.* [In]: Nationalities Papers, Vol. 22, No. 1, Abingdon, UK, Spring 1994. Pp. 119–139, notes. [Initially given as an Inaugural Lecture for the Jewish Chronicle Chair of Jewish Studies, delivered at University College, London, November 13, 1991.]

3. Central Europe

31617. BOHEMIA. ZONIS, MARK/STERNER, GREGOR: *Juden in Karlsbad.* Ein Kapitel aus der wechselvollen Geschichte des böhmischen Judentums. [In]: Tribüne, Jg. 33, H. 131, Frankfurt am Main, 1994. Pp. 166–169.

31618. CZECHOSLOVAKIA. BRANDES, DETLEF/KURAL, VÁKLAV: *Der Weg in die Katastrophe. Deutsch-tschechoslowakische Beziehungen 1938-1947.* Hrsg. von Detlef Brandes und Václav Kural. (Veröffentlichungen des Instituts für Kultur und Geschichte der Deutschen im östlichen Europa, Bd.3.) 255 pp., footnotes. [Incl.: Zuflucht in der Tschechoslowakei. Die Situation deutscher Literaten in Prag und Brünn von 1933 bis 1939 (Thomas Kraft, 27–37.). Verdrängung und Verharmlosung: das Ende der jüdischen Bevölkerungsgruppe in den böhmischen Ländern nach ausgewählten tschechischen und sudetendeutschen Publikationen (Eva Hahn, 135–150). Die tschechoslowakischen Opfer der deutschen Okkupation (Miroslav Kárny, 151–160; incl. German-speaking Jews). Probleme bei der Berechnung der Zahl der tschechoslowakischen Todesopfer des nationalsozialistischen Deutschlands (Pavel Skorpil, 161–164).]

31619. DEAGLIO, ENRICO: *Die Banalität des Guten. Die Geschichte des Hochstaplers Giorgio Perlasca, der 5200 Juden das Leben rettete.* Aus dem Italienischen von Michaela Wunderle. Frankfurt am Main: Eichborn, 1994. 203 pp. [The story of an Italian businessman, who in 1944 in Budapest pretended to be a diplomat in order to save thousands of Jews from deportation.]

31620. GRUBER, RUTH ELLEN: *Upon the doorposts of thy house: Jewish life in East-Central Europe, yesterday and today.* New York: J. Wiley, 1994. IX, 310 pp., illus., glossary, notes, bibl. (301–304). [American-Jewish journalist and photographer searches for evidence of Jewish life in countries such as Hungary, Czechoslovakia, Poland; incl. visits to the Jewish quarter in Prague and to Auschwitz.]

31621. *Judaica Bohemiae.* Vol. 29. Praha, Státni Zidovské Muzeum, 1993 (1994). 111 pp., [16 pp. illus. at end of book]. [Incl.: The origin of the symbols of the Prague Jewish town. The banner of the Old-New Synagogue. David's Shield and the 'Swedish Hat' (Alexandr Putík, 4–37). Discovery of an unknown list of Prague Jews who died between 1749 and 1759 (Jirí Kudela, 38–53). Systematic collection of memories organised by the Jewish Museum in Prague [part] II (Anna Hyndráková/Anna Lorencová, 67–75; for part I see in No. 29217/YB XXXVIII.) Further articles are listed according to subject.]

31622. KÁRNY, MIROSLAV: *Die Protektoratsregierung und die Verordnungen des Reichsprotektors über das jüdische Vermögen.* [In]: Judaica Bohemiae, Vol. 29, Praha, 1993. Pp. 54–66, footnotes.

31623. PRAGUE. CHARNEY, ANN: *Holocaust holiday.* [In]: Utne Reader, No. 61, Minneapolis, Mn. 1994. Pp. 136–138. [Prague's large and historic collection of Jewish relics has became one of the country's main tourist attractions. Author sees an irony in this in the light of the country's history of antisemitism.]

31624. PRAGUE. *Geschichten aus dem alten Prag: Sippurim,* Hrsg., mit Anm. und einem Nachwort versehen von Peter Demetz. Frankfurt am Main: Insel, 1994. 375 pp., illus. Orig.-Ausgabe. (Insel-Taschenbuch.) [Most of these stories and legends were orig. published during the first half of the 19th century by Wolf Pascheles. They reflect Jewish life in Prague.]

31625. PRAGUE, Jewish Museum. VOLAVKOVÁ, HANA: *I have not seen a butterfly around here.* Children's drawings and poems from Terezin. Prague: The Jewish Museum, 1993. 90 pp., illus. [Based on previous edns. publ. in German in 1959, in English 1965.]

31626. RADEFF, ANNE/KAUFMANN, URI R.: *De la tolérance à l'ostracisme: la politique des États confédérés envers les Juifs, 1750 – 1798.* [In]: Schweizerische Zeitschrift für Geschichte, Vol. 44, Nr. 1, Basel, 1994. Pp. 2–13.

31627. VARGA, PÉTER: *Herz Homberg und Josef Perl. Jüdischdeutsche Bildung in Osteuropa.* [In]: Jahrbuch der ungarischen Germanistik 1992, Budapest, 1993. Pp. 417–428. [On Jewish-German schools during the last two decades of the 18th cent. in Galicia.]

4. Switzerland

31628. BASLE. STAUFFER, BEAT/POL, ANDRI: *Juden in Basel.* [In]: Basler Magazin Nr. 47, [Politisch-kulturelle Beilage der] Basler Zeitung, Nr. 277, Basel, 26. Nov. 1994. Pp. 1–5, illus.

31629. ENDINGEN-LENGNAU. *Der Judenfriedhof Endingen-Lengnau*. Gräberverzeichnis. Erster Band. Hrsg.: Verein für die Erhaltung der Synagogen und des Friedhofs Endingen-Lengnau (Baden, Aargau). Baden: Menes Verl., 1993. 159 pp., illus., facsims., docs. [Incl. history of the Jews in Endingen and Lengnau.]

31630. *GrenzWege: Widerstand an der Schweizer Grenze 1933–1945*. Ausstellung in Singen vom 21. Juni bis 25. Sept. 1994. [Haus der Geschichte Baden-Württemberg in Zusammenarbeit mit der Stadt Singen]. Hrsg. von Paula Lutum-Lenger. Mit Beitr. von Walter Hochreiter [et al.] und mit Zeichnungen von Peter Tucholski. Stuttgart: Haus der Geschichte Baden-Württemberg, 1994. 112 pp., illus., bibl. (106–110). [Incl.: Jewish refugees.]

——— KAUFMANN, URI R.: *Ein schweizerisch-jüdisches Leben für moderne Bildung und Emanzipation. Marcus Getsch Dreifus (1812–1877) aus Endingen*. [In]: Jüdisches Leben im Bodenseeraum [See in No. 31577.]

31631. PICARD, JACQUES: *Das Vermögen rassisch, religiös und politisch Verfolgter in der Schweiz und ihre Ablösung von 1946 bis 1973*. Gutachten, erstellt von Jacques Picard. Bern: J. Picard, 1993. 38 pp.

31632. PICARD, JACQUES: *Die Schweiz und die Juden 1933–1945. Schweizerischer Antisemitismus, jüdische Abwehr und internationale Migrations- und Flüchtlingspolitk*. Zürich: Chronos, 1994. 559 pp., notes, tabs., (463–518), bibl. (519–544), name index (547–559) [Cf.: Äußerst diskret. Anpassung nach außen, Beschwichtigung nach innen: die Schweiz und die Juden in den Jahren 1933 bis 1945 (Wolfgang Benz) [in]: Die Zeit, Nr. 13, Hamburg, 24. März 1995, p. 47. Kleiner als die Geschichte (Hg.) [in]: 'NZZ', Nr. 120, Zürich, 26. Mai 1994, p. 25.]

31633. ROSCHEWSKI, HEINZ: *Auf dem Weg zu einem neuen jüdischen Selbstbewußtsein? Geschichte der Juden in der Schweiz 1945–1994*. Hrsg.: Schweizerischer israelitischer Gemeindebund. Basel: Helbing & Lichtenhahn, 1994. 122 pp. (Beiträge zur Geschichte und Kultur der Juden in der Schweiz, Vol. 5.)

31634. WEBER, CHARLOTTE: *Gegen den Strom der Finsternis. Als Betreuerin in Schweizer Flüchtlingsheimen 1942–1945*. Zürich: Chronos, 1994. 285 pp., illus., facsims. [Memoirs of a Swiss journalist; worked during the war in refugee hostels, after the war for the youth aliyah in France.] [Cf.: Buchenwald-Kinder hinter Schweizer Stacheldraht (Heinz Moll) [in]: 'Allgemeine', Nr. 1, Bonn, 12. Jan. 1995, p. 15.]

——— ZURICH. BURGHARTZ, SUSANNE: *Juden – eine Minderheit vor Gericht, Zürich 1378–1436*. [See in No. 31387.]

C. Various Countries

31635. ARONSFELD, C.C.: *Uncle Gustavo in Lima: a 19th-century German-Jewish immigrant*. [In]: American Jewish Archives, Vol. 46, No. 1, Cincinnati, Spring-Summer 1994. Pp. 12–25. [On the author's great uncle Gustav Badt (1849–1914), who went from his native town of Exin to Peru in 1865.]

31636. AUFBAU, New York. BAUER-HACK, SUSANNE: *Die jüdische Wochenzeitung AUFBAU und die Wiedergutmachung*. Düsseldorf: Droste, 1994. 324 pp., illus., facsims., ports., notes, bibl. (295–308), index.

31637. AUFBAU, New York. KAUFMAN, MICHAEL T.: *Exiles sustain culture*. [In]: The New York Times, Vol. 144, New York, Dec. 3, 1994. Pp. 16; 27 (16 cols.) [On the 'Aufbau', New York.]

31638. AUFBAU, New York. *Zeitzeuge Aufbau. Texte aus sechs Jahrzehnten*. Hrsg. von Will Schaber. Mit einem Vorwort von Henry Marx und Zeichnungen von B.F. Dolbin. Gerlingen: Bleicher, 1994. 440 pp., illus. [On the occasion of the 60th anniversary of the German-language Jewish weekly in New York, founded by German-Jewish refugees.] [Cf.:In memoriam Henry Marx (various authors) [in]: Aufbau, Vol. 60, Nos. 14 & 17, New York, July 8 & Aug. 19, 1994, pp. 1–2, 10; & 20.] [Henry Marx, Nov. 3, 1911 Brussels – June 22, 1994 Frutigen, Switzerland, author, editor-in-chief of 'Aufbau' since 1985, emigr. 1937 via Cuba to the USA.]

31639. AUFBAU, New York. *Aufbau* [With the issue title]: *Jubiläumsausgabe. 60 Jahre Aufbau*. Vol. 60, No. 21, New York, Oct. 14, 1994. 48 pp. [Incl. numerous personal recollections of German-Jewish émigrés.]

31640. BARKAI, AVRAHAM: *Branching out: German-Jewish immigration to the United States 1820–1914*. New York; London: Holmes & Meier, 1994. XIII, 269 pp., illus., ports., tabs., map, notes (235–251), bibl. (253–261).

31641. BERGMANN, GÜNTHER J.: *Auslandsdeutsche in Paraguay, Brasilien, Argentinien*. Bad Münstereifel: Westkreuz, 1994. 256 pp., illus. (Zugl.: Mainz, Univ., Diss., 1992 u.d.T.: Das Deutschtum im paraguayisch-brasilianisch-argentinischen Dreiländerbereich des oberen Paraná.)

31642. BEVEGE, MARGARET: *Behind barbed wire: internment in Australia during World War II*. St. Lucia, Qld.: Univ. of Queensland Press, 1993. XXI, 314 pp., illus., bibl. (287–305). [Incl. German-Jewish internees from the 'Dunera'; mainly deals with official Australian internment policy.]

31643. CESARANI, DAVID: *The Jewish Chronicle and Anglo-Jewry, 1841–1991*. Cambridge; New York: Cambridge University Press, 1994. XIV, 329 pp., illus., ports., map, notes (254–298), bibl. (299–314). [Incl. the newspaper's coverage of the plight of German Jewry during the Nazi period; the influx of Jewish refugees from Germany and other Central European countries. Paper also published some of the earliest and most accurate reports on Nazi atrocities and the Holocaust.]

31644. *Codebreakers: the inside story of Bletchley Park*. Ed. by F.H. Hinsley and Alan Stripp. Oxford; New York: Oxford Univ. Press, 1994. XXI, 321 pp., illus. [Incl. participation of German- and Austrian-Jewish refugees in the British war effort.]

31645. DOHRN, VERENA: *Baltische Reise. Vielvölkerlandschaft des alten Europas*. Frankfurt am Main: Fischer, 1994. 284 pp., illus. [Deals also with German-speaking Jews; the ghettos of Riga and Vilna.]

31646. EXILE. ALTNER, MANFRED: *Eine Frau allein. Auguste Wieghardt-Lazar im englischen Exil* [In]: Mit der Ziehharmonika, Jg. 11, Nr. 2, Wien, Sept. 1994. Pp. 22–24, port., notes. [A.W.-L., Sept. 12, 1887 Vienna – April 7, 1970, Dresden, teacher, author of children's books, supported illegal Communist activities during Nazi period, emigr. to the U.K. in 1939, returned to Germany (East) 1949.]

31647. EXILE. BENZ, WOLFGANG/NEISS, MARION, Hrsg.: *Deutsch-jüdisches Exil: das Ende der Assimilation? Identitätsprobleme deutscher Juden in der Emigration*. Berlin: Metropol, 1994. 196 pp., footnotes. (Reihe Dokumente, Texte, Materialien, Bd. 14.) [Cont. (titles partly abbr.): Von der Emanzipation zur Emigration (Wolfgang Benz, 7–14). Walter Mehring und Hertha Pauli im Exil (Barbara Bauer/Renate Dürmeyer, 15–44). Identitätsprobleme Siegfried Kracauers (1889–1966) (Ingrid Belke, 45–66). Alfred Kerrs Einstellung zum Judentum vor und im Exil (Deborah Vietor-Engländer, 67–76). Kurt Tucholsky und das Judentum (Beate Schmeichel-Falkenberg, 79–94). Else Lasker-Schüler in Jerusalem (Sonja M. Hedgepeth, 95–104). Vera Lachmann – Lyrikerin und Pädagogin im Exil (Helga Gläser, 105–114). Die religiösen Filme von Hermann/Henry Koster(litz) (Helmut G. Asper, 115–124). Der deutsche Jude Hugo Simon (1880–1950) – Bankier, Mäzen, Bildungsbürger (Izabela Maria Furtado Kestler, 125–150). Hans Habe als Herausgeber der 'Neuen Zeitung' (Reinhard K. Zachau, 151–164). Das 'Pariser Tageblatt' und seine Palästina-Berichterstattung im Jahr 1935 (Thomas Stephan, 165–182). Das deutsch-jüdische Exil in der niederländischen Literatur 1933–1940 (Hanz Würzner, 183–194).]

31648. EXILE. *Modernisierung oder Überfremdung? Zur Wirkung deutscher Exilanten in der Germanistik der Aufnahmeländer*. Hrsg. von Walter Schmitz. Stuttgart: Metzler, 1994. 271 pp., footnotes, index (263–271). [Cont. papers and documentation of comment and discussion at a colloquium held in Marbach, Sept. 2–4, 1991 and arranged under the sections: Germanistik und Exil in Frankreich (contribs. by Richard Thieberger & Michel Espagne, 3–24). Germanistik und Exil in Neuseeland (contribs. by Paul Hoffmann & Christoph König, 25–54). Germanistik und Exil in Grossbritannien und Irland (Hans Reiss & Konrad Feilchenfeldt, 55–84). Germanistik und Exil in den USA und Kanada (Guy Stern & Frank Trommler, 85–108).]

31649. EXILE. MUCHITSCH, WOLFGANG: *Österreichische Flüchtlinge in Irland 1938–1945*. [In]: Dokumentationsarchiv des österreichischen Widerstandes. Jahrbuch 1994. Wien, 1994. Pp. 33–45.

31650. EXILE. RITCHIE, J.M.: *Women in exile in Great Britain*. [In]: German Life and Letters, Vol. 72, No. 1, Oxford, Jan. 1994. Pp. 51–66. [Incl. Grete Fischer, Henriette Hardenberg, Judith Kerr, Eva Reichmann, Hilde Spiel, Gabriele Tergit a.o.]

31651. EXILE. WOJAK, IRMTRUD: *Exil in Chile. Die deutsch-jüdische und politische Emigration während des Nationalsozialismus 1933–1945*. Berlin: Metropol, 1994. 304 pp., illus., tabs., bibl. (275–292), indexes. (Reihe Dokumente, Texte, Materialien, Bd. 16). Zugl.: Bochum, Univ., Diss., 1994.

31652. EXILE. *Exil in Brasilien. Die deutschsprachige Emigration 1933–1945*. Eine Ausstellung des deutschen Exilarchivs 1933–1945 der deutschen Bibliothek Frankfurt am Main/Die Deutsche Bibliothek. Bearb. von Christine Hohnschopp unter Mitwirkung von Frank Wendel. Leipzig: Die Deutsche Bibliothek, 1994. 173 pp., illus. (Sonderveröffentlichung der Deutschen Bibliothek, 21.)

31653. FELDMAN, DAVID: *Englishmen and Jews: social relations and political culture 1840–1914*. New Haven; London: Yale Univ. Press, 1994. XIV, 401 pp., tabs., notes. [Incl. immigration of German Jews.]

31654. FRANKAU FAMILY. ENDELMAN, TODD, M.: *The Frankaus of London: a study in radical assimilation, 1837–1967*. [In]: Jewish History, Vol. 8, Nos. 1–2, Haifa 1994. Pp. 117–154, notes. [Family of German-Jewish ancestry who came orig. from Franconia. The first member to settle in England was Joseph Frankau (1813–1857), who was a relative of Abraham Geiger.]

31655. GENIZI, HAIM: *America's fair share: the admission and resettlement of displaced persons, 1945–1952*. Detroit: Wayne State Univ. Press, 1994. XI, 273 pp., notes (212–251), bibl. (252–260). [Discusses the impact of the Displaced Persons Act, 1946–1948; the government policy favoured Christian refugees as well as Nazi collaborators and opposed the liberalisation of the immigrations laws for Jews, often fuelled by anti-Communist sentiments.]

31656. GUTWEIN, DANIEL: *Jewish financiers and industry, 1890–1914: England and Germany*. [In]: Jewish History, Vol. 8, Nos 1–2, Leiden, Haifa Univ. 1994. Pp. 177–204, notes. [Incl. the financier Felix Schuster, 1854–1936. Also discusses the role of German Jews in English banking.]

31657. HIRSCHFELD, GERHARD: *Deutsche Emigranten in Großbritannien und ihr Widerstand gegen den Nationalsozialismus*. [In]: Großbritannien und der deutsche Widerstand 1933–1944. Hrsg.: Klaus-Jürgen Müller/David N. Dilks. Paderborn, Schöningh, 1994. Pp. 107–122.

31658. *Hoffnung Amerika. Europäische Auswanderung in die Neue Welt*. Herausgegeben und zusammengestellt von Karin Schulz. Bremerhaven: NWD-Verl., 1994. 291 pp., illus., facsims. [Incl.: Jüdische Auswanderung aus Deutschland in die USA während der NS-Zeit (Juliane Wetzel, 175–186). Auswanderer, Emigrant, Exilant, Refugee: was bin ich? (Henry Marx, 187–192). Auf der Suche nach einem neuen Zuhause; Nachkriegsauswanderung von jüdischen 'Displaced Persons' in die USA (Hannah Levinsky-Koevary, 193–208).]

31659. JACOBS, JACK: *Ein Freund in Not. Das Jüdische Arbeiterkomitee in New York und die Flüchtlinge aus den deutschsprachigen Ländern, 1933–1945.* Hrsg.: Dieter Dowe, Forschungsinstitut der Friedrich-Ebert-Stiftung, Bonn. Bonn: Friedrich-Ebert-Stiftung, 1993. 38 pp., footnotes.

31660. *London calling: Deutsche im britischen Film der dreissiger Jahre.* Red.: Jörg Schöning [red. Mitarbeit, Übers.: Tim Bergfelder]. München: Ed. Text und Kritik, 1993. 172 pp. (Ein Cine-Graph-Buch.) [Incl. German Jews.]

31661. MATSDORF, WOLFGANG SIMON: *No time to grow. The story of the Gross-Breeseners in Australia.* Sidney: Univ. of Sidney, Archive of Australian Judaica, 1994. VI, 144 pp., bibl. (137–142). [Author, b. Aug. 9, 1907 in Berlin, lawyer, educator, emigr. to Australia in 1938.]

31662. *Pinkas. Geschiedenis van de joodse gemeenschap in Nederland.* [Eds.:] Jozeph Michmann, Hartog Beem, Dan Michman. Vertaald uit het Hebreeuw door Ruben Verhasselt. Amsterdam: Kluwer Algemene Boeken, 1992. 617 pp., illus., bibl, index. [Transl. of Pinkas ha-kehillot Holland, publ. in 1985 in Jerusalem. Incl. a section on Jewish refugees from Nazi Germany (pp. 165–209).]

— *Die Rothschilds.* [See No. 32115.]

31663. SAIDEL, ROCHELLE G./PLONSKI, GUILHERME ARY: *Shaping modern science and technology in Brazil. The contribution of refugees from National Socialism after 1933.* [In]: Leo Baeck Institute Year Book XXXIX, London, 1994. Pp. 257–270, illus., footnotes.

31664. SCHERKE, KATHARINA: *Die Society for the Protection of Science and Learning* [In]: Dokumentationsarchiv des österreichischen Widerstandes. Jahrbuch 1994. Wien, 1994. Pp. 46–57.

31666. SCHWARCZ, ALFREDO JOSÉ: *Trotz allem . . . ; die deutschsprachigen Juden in Argentinien.* Aus dem Spanischen von Bernardo und Inge Schwarcz. Wien: Böhlau, 1995. 328 pp., illus., footnotes.

31667. SHANGHAI. PRESSER, ELLEN: *Fluchtpunkt Shanghai.* [In]: Frankfurter Jüdische Nachrichten, Nr. 86, Frankfurt am Main, Sept. 1994. Pp. 47–48.

31668. SHANGHAI. ROSS, JAMES R.: *Escape to Shanghai. A Jewish community in China.* New York: The Free Press, 1994. XVI, 298 pp., illus., notes, index (285–298). [Covers the history of the Shanghai refugee community from 1938 til 1950.]

31669. SHANGHAI. RUBIN, EVELYN PIKE: *Ghetto Shanghai.* New York: Shengold, 1994. 199 pp., illus. [Author tells of her childhood experiences fleeing the Nazis and finding a refuge in the Shanghai ghetto; she now lives in the USA.]

31670. SHERMAN, A.J.: *Island refuge: Britain and refugees from the Third Reich 1933–1939.* London: Frank Cass, 1994. 239 pp., illus., tabs., bibls. (275–282; 283–284). [Second edn., with new introd. For orig. edn. publ. in 1973 see No. 11148/YB XIX.]

31671. VOLKMANN, MICHAEL: *Neuorientierung in Palästina. Erwachsenenbildung deutschsprachiger jüdischer Einwanderer 1933 bis 1948.* Köln: Böhlau, 1994. XVI, 342 pp., footnotes, bibl. (315–330). glossary, index. (Studien zur internationalen Erwachsenenbildung, Bd. 9; zugl. Tübingen, Univ., Diss.)

31672. ZAGGIA, STEFANO: *Die deutsche Synagoge in Padua 1603 – 1779.* [In]: Zeitschrift für Religions- und Geistesgeschichte, Jg. 46, H. 1, Leiden, 1994. Pp. 44–58, illus., footnotes.

II. RESEARCH AND BIBLIOGRAPHY

A. Libraries and Institutes

31673. ANNE-FRANK-SHOAH-BIBLIOTHEK, Leipzig: *Bestandsverzeichnis der Anne-Frank-Shoah-Bibliothek/Die Deutsche Bibliothek, Deutsche Bücherei Leipzig.* Leipzig: Anne-Frank-Shoah-Bibliothek, 1993. 96 pp. [Stand: 31. März 1993.]

31674. BERLIN DOCUMENT CENTER. POSNER, GERALD: *Secrets of the files*. [In]: The New Yorker, Vol. 70, No. 4, New York, March 14, 1994. Pp. 39–48. [On the handing over by the U.S. to Germany in 1994 of the archive of Nazi personnel records. Historians and war crime investigators may lose access to important records because Germany's public access laws are stricter than those of the US.]

31675. DOKUMENTATONSARCHIV DES ÖSTERREICHISCHEN WIDERSTANDES. SCHALLHARDT, VERONIKA/ GANGLMAIR, SIEGWALD: *Der Schwerpunkt Exil im Dokumentationsarchiv des österreichischen Widerstandes seit 1986*. [In]: Dokumentationsarchiv des österreichischen Widerstandes. Jahrbuch 1994. Wien, 1994. Pp. 138–142. [Also in this issue: Dokumentation, Datenbank und Handbuch der österreichischen Exilzeitschriften in Europa (1933/34–1945) (Fritz Hausjell/Andreas Ulrich, 143–146).]

31676. HOCHSCHULE FÜR JÜDISCHE STUDIEN, Heidelberg: *Trumah 4. Zeitschrift der Hochschule für Jüdische Studien, Heidelberg*. Hrsg. von der Hochschule für Jüdische Studien, Heidelberg. Red.: Carl S. Ehrlich, Daniel Krochmalnik. Koord.: Ursula Beitz. Berlin: Metropol, 1994. 146 pp., illus., footnotes, tabs. [Incl.: Vorwort (Julius Carlebach, 7). Contribs. pertinent to German-Jewish history are listed according to subject.]

31677. INSTITUTE OF CONTEMPORARY JEWRY, The Hebrew University: *Studies in Contemporary Jewry. An Annual. 10. Reshaping the past: Jewish history and the historians*. Ed. by Jonathan Frankel. New York; Oxford: Oxford Univ. Press, 1994. 439 pp., notes. [Cont. the sections: Symposium: Reshaping the past: Jewish history and the historians (3–194). Essays (195–258). Review essays & book reviews (259–439). Articles referring to German-Jewish scholars and German-Jewish history are listed according to subject.]

31678. INSTITUT FÜR DEUTSCHE GESCHICHTE, Universität Tel-Aviv: *Tel Aviver Jahrbuch für deutsche Geschichte*. Hrsg. im Auftrag des Instituts für Deutsche Geschichte von Dan Diner und Frank Stern. Bd. XXIII [with the title]: Nationalsozialismus aus heutiger Perspektive. Gerlingen: Bleicher, 1994. 493 pp., footnotes. [Articles referring to German-Jewish history are listed according to subject.]

31679. INSTITUT FÜR GESCHICHTE DER JUDEN IN ÖSTERREICH, St. Pölten [in Verbindung mit dem Deutschen Koordinierungsrat der Gesellschaften für Christl.-Jüd. Zusammenarbeit]. *Aschkenas 4. Zeitschrift für Geschichte und Kultur der Juden*. Hrsg.: Friedrich Battenberg und Markus J. Wenninger. Wien: Böhlau, 1994/1995. H.1 & 2, 300; 616 pp., footnotes, index (names, subjects, 593–611). *Beiheft 1*, 350 pp., footnotes. [H. 1 (1994) cont.: Editorische Vorbemerkung (eds., Friedrich Battenberger/Markus J. Wenninger, 1–4). Aufsätze (13–126). Kleinere Beiträge (127–174). Forschungs- und Literaturberichte (175–200). Rezensionen und Buchanzeigen (201–300). H. 2 (publ. 1995) cont.: Aufsätze (301–404). Kleinere Beiträge (405–488). Forschungs- und Literaturberichte (489–588). Projektberichte und Veranstaltungshinweise (589–593). Verzeichnisse (593–616).] [Contribs. pertinent to German-Jewish history are listed according to subject. *Beiheft 1* (1994) see No. 31946.]

—— INSTITUT FÜR GESCHICHTE DER JUDEN IN ÖSTERREICH, St. Pölten: *Studien zur Geschichte der Juden in Österreich*. Handbuch zur Geschichte der Juden in Österreich, Reihe B, Band 2. [See No. 31592.]

31680. LEO BAECK INSTITUTE. *LBI Information*. Nachrichten aus den Leo Baeck Instituten in Jerusalem, London, New York und der Wissenschaftlichen Arbeitsgemeinschaft des LBI in Deutschland. Hrsg. von den Freunden und Förderern des LBI e.V. in Frankfurt am Main. Red.: Georg Heuberger, Mitarbeit: Ursula Thürich. Nr. 4, 1994. Frankfurt am Main (Liebigstraße 24): Freunde und Förderer des LBI e.V., 1994. 78 pp., port. [Incl.: Obituary: Walter Hesselbach 1915–1993 (Ignatz Bubis, 4–5). Berichte aus den Arbeitszentren des Leo Baeck Instituts. Leo Baeck Institute New York: Der Gründungsvorstand [&] Die Entwicklung des Instituts (Fred Grubel, 13–21). Jenseits und dieseits des Abgrundes. Die Aufgaben des Leo Baeck Instituts (Michael A. Meyer, 6–12). Integration und Identität. Die jüdische Erfahrung in Deutschland und Italien von der Aufklärung bis zum Faschismus

(Barbara Suchy, 29–41; on the conference organised by the LBI in co-operation with the Goethe-Institut, the Centro Sistema Bibliotecario and the Unione Comunità Ebraiche Italiane in Rome, Nov. 15–18, 1993). Also reports on publications and projects of the LBI Jerusalem and activities of the Wissenschaftliche Arbeitsgemeinschaft des LBI. Further contribs. listed according to subject.]

31681. LEO BAECK INSTITUTE. *Jüdischer Almanach 1995 des Leo Baeck Instituts.* Hrsg. von Jakob Hessing. Frankfurt am Main: Jüdischer Verlag, 1994. 186 [2] pp., illus. [Incl.: Zu diesem Almanach (Jakob Hessing,., 7–8). Denk dir. Paul Celan in Jerusalem (Ilana Schmueli (9–36). Zeit der Zäsur. Über Don Pagis und Paul Celan (Amir Eshel, 37–4). Dan Pagis übersetzen (Anne Birkenhauer, 49–54). Fünf Gedichte (Sarah Kirsch, 55–59). Vom verlorenen Sohn (Wilhelm Bruner, 170–176). 'Sieht wie einer von uns aus'. Anton Schammas' Arabesken (Jürgen Nieraad (177–186). An der Zeitenwende. Achad Ha'Am in historischer Persepktive (Jossi Goldstein, 81–90). Further articles are listed according to subject.]

31682. LEO BAECK INSTITUTE. *Leo Baeck Institute Year Book XXXIX.* Ed.: J.A.S. Grenville, assoc. ed.: Julius Carlebach, assist. eds. Sylvia Gilchrist, Emma Morgan. London: Secker & Warburg, 1994. IV, 484 pp., illus., footnotes, bibl. (332–454), general index (468–484). [Cont.: Preface (John Grenville/Julius Carlebach, IV). Essays are arranged under the sections 1. Identity and emancipation. II. Some Jewish responses to National Socialism. III. Jews in welfare. IV. Gender and history. V. Emigration. VI. Memoir. Individual contribs. are listed according to subject.] [Cf.: Besprechung (Antje C. Naujoks) [in]: 'MB', Jg. 63, Nr. 107, Tel Aviv, März, 1995, p. 4.]

31683. LEO BAECK INSTITUTE, LBI New York: *Library & Archive News.* Ed. Gabrielle Bamberger with the assistance of Frank Mecklenburg. No. 33. New York: Leo Baeck Institute, Summer, 1994. [8] pp.

31684. SALOMON LUDWIG STEINHEIM INSTITUT FÜR DEUTSCH-JÜDISCHE GESCHICHTE, Universität Duisburg/MOSES MENDELSSOHN-ZENTRUM FÜR EUROPÄISCH-JÜDISCHE STUDIEN, Potsdam: *Menora 5.* Jahrbuch für deutsch-jüdische Geschichte 1994. Bd. 5. Im Auftrag des Salomon Ludwig Steinheim-Instituts für deutsch-jüdische Geschichte und des Moses Mendelssohn-Zentrums für europäisch-jüdische Studien hrsg. von Julius H. Schoeps, Karl E. Grözinger, Ludger Heid, Gerd Mattenklott. München: Piper, 1994. 455 pp., notes, index. (Serie Piper 1917.) [Cont. the sections: Einführung (pp. 9–11). I. Wirtschaft, Industrie und Politik, (25–94). II. Deutsch-jüdische Kultur: Literatur, Publizistik, Musik (97–194). III. Reisen – zwischen Berlin und Tel Aviv (197–285). IV. Jugendbewegung und Sport (287–347). V. Beiträge zur Lokal- und Regionalgeschichte: Schlesien (349–433). Individual contribs. are listed according to subject.]

31685. ZENTRUM FÜR ANTISEMITISMUSFORSCHUNG, Berlin: *Jahrbuch für Antisemitismusforschung 3.* Hrsg. von Wolfgang Benz für das Zentrum für Antisemitismusforschung der Technischen Universität Berlin. Red.: Werner Bergmann, Rainer Erb, Christhard Hoffmann. Geschäftsführende Redakteurin: Juliane Wetzel. Frankfurt am Main; New York: Campus, 1994. 371 pp., notes. [Incl.: Vorwort (Wolfgang Benz, 9–12). Individual contributions relevant to antisemitism and the history of German-speaking Jewry are listed according to subject.]

B. Bibliographies, Catalogues and Reference Books

31686. COHEN, SUSAN SARAH, ed.: *Antisemitism: an annotated bibliography.* Vol. 3: 1987–1988. [Publ. by] The Vidal Sassoon International Center for the Study of Antisemitism [of] the Hebrew University of Jerusalem. New York; London: Garland, 1994. XXXIV, 544 pp., author and subject indexes. [Incl. Austria and Germany.] [For Vol. 1 see No. 24162/YB XXXIII; for Vol. 2 see No. 29261/YB XXXVIII.]

— CZEIKE, FELIX: *Historisches Lexikon Wien.* [See No. 31606.]

31687. DREW, MARGARET A.: *Annotated bibliography*. Washington: U.S. Holocaust Memorial Museum, [1994]. 32 pp. [Bibliography on 'Holocaust' literature.]

31688. *Enzyklopädie des Märchens*. Handwörterbuch zur historischen und vergleichenden Erzählforschung. Bd. 7. Begr. von Kurt Ranke. Mit Unterstützung der Akad. der Wiss. zu Göttingen hrsg. von Wilhelm Brednich [et al.]. Göttingen: de Gruyter, 1993. 1446 cols. [Incl.: Jude, Judenlegenden (Rainer Erb, 676–686); Juden aus dem Himmel gelockt (Ulrich Manzolph, 686–687); Jüdisches Erzählgut (numerous authors, 688–749).]

—— FARNETTI, DAVID: *A Kurt Weill bibliography*. [See in No. 32308.]

31689. HOLOCAUST. EDELHEIT, ABRAHAM J./EDELHEIT, HERSHEL: *History of the Holocaust: a handbook and dictionary*. Boulder, Co.: Westview Press, 1994. 524 pp., illus., facsims., tabs., bibl. [Part 1 is an historical perspective of the Holocaust, incl. a brief survey of the Jews of Europe before the war. Part 2 is a dictionary of the Holocaust.]

—— HYNDRÁKOVÁ, ANNA/LORENCOVÁ, ANNA: *Systematic collection of memories organised by the Jewish Museum in Prague* [part] II. [See in No. 31621.]

31690. *The 'Jewish question' in German-speaking countries, 1848–1914: a bibliography*. Ed. by Rena R. Auerbach. New York: Garland, 1994. XXV, 385 pp., author index, subject index. (Garland reference library of the humanities, vol. 1571; a special publ. of the Felix Posen bibliographic project on antisemitism.) [Incl.: Introduction (Otto D. Kulka, IX-XI). Continues the 'Bibliographie zur Geschichte der Judenfrage' by Volkmar Eichstädt, publ. in 1938 and reprinted in 1969. Lists the literature both of and about the period. Incl.: Appendix: newspapers and periodicals (322–332).]

—— *Jüdische Geschichte in Hessen erforschen. Ein Wegweiser zu Archiven, Forschungsstätten und Hilfsmitteln*. [See No. 31512.]

31691. *Post-war publications on German-speaking Jewry; a selected bibliography of books and articles 1993*. Compiled by Barbara Suchy and Annette Pringle. [In]: Leo Baeck Institute Year Book XXXIX, London, 1994. Pp. 331–454, index (433–464).

—— PURIN, BERNHARD: *Jüdische Geschichte und Kultur in österreichischen Museen und Ausstellungen. Eine Bibliographie*. [See in No. 31614.]

31692. *Quellen zur deutschen politischen Emigration 1933–1945: Inventar von Nachlässen, nichtstaatlichen Akten und Sammlungen in Archiven und Bibliotheken der Bundesrepublik Deutschland*. Hrsg. im Auftrag der Herbert- und Elsbeth-Weichmann-Stiftung von Heinz Boberach [et al.]. Bearb. von Ingrid Schulze-Bidlingmaier unter Mitwirkung von Ursula Adam [et al.]. München; New Providence: Saur, 1994. XII, 368 pp., bibl. (291–293). (Nachlassverzeichnisse zur deutschsprachigen Emigration; Schriften der Herbert-und-Elsbeth-Weichmann-Stiftung).

—— SCHEFFLER, WOLFGANG: *Holocaustforschung am Wendepunkt. Kritische Anmerkungen zur deutschen Ausgabe der 'Enzyklopädie des Holocaust'*. [See No. 31777.]

31693. SPALEK, JOHN M.: *Deutschsprachige Exilliteratur seit 1933*. Band 4: Bibliographien. Schriftsteller, Publizisten und Literaturwissenschaftler in den USA. Teil 1–3. Hrsg. von John M. Spalek, Konrad Feilchenfeld und Sandra H. Hawrylchak. Bern: Saur, 1994. [Bd.1, Teil 1–3] 2110 pp. [For previous vols. see No. 13701/YB XXII & 27591/YBXXXVI.] [Cf.: Bibliograph Spalek (Will Schaber) [in]: Aufbau, Vol. 61, No. 2, New York, Jan. 20, 1995, p. 6.]

—— STARCK, ASTRID: *Bibliographie du yidich alsacien*. [See in No. 31445.]

31694. STUDEMUND-HALÉVY, MICHAEL: *Bibliographie zur Geschichte der Juden in Hamburg*. München; New Providence: Saur, 1994. 256 pp., indexes (231–254).

―― *Verzeichnis der jiddischen Drucke: Bestände der Sondersammelgebietsbibliothek.* Stadt- und Universitätsbibliothek Frankfurt am Main. [See No. 31448.]

―― WEGENER, BEATE: *Bibliographie Ernst Heilborn.* [See No. 32194.]

―― WEINBERG, WERNER: *Lexikon zum religiösen Wortschatz und Brauchtum der deutschen Juden.* [See No. 31449.]

31695. *Zeitschriftenverzeichnis Judaica: Bestände der Sondersammelgebietsbibliothek Frankfurt am Main.* Stand: 27.2.1992. Frankfurt am Main: Stadt- und Univ.-Bibliothek, 1992. 277 pp. [Lists 2750 periodicals.]

III. THE NAZI PERIOD

A. General

31696. AHLFELD-HEYMANN, MARIANNE: *Und trotzdem überlebt. Ein jüdisches Schicksal aus Köln durch Frankreich nach Israel 1905–1955 mit Erinnerungen an Paul Klee.* Hrsg. von Erhard Roy Wiehn. Konstanz: Hartung-Gorre, 1994. 122 pp., illus. [Author, b. 1905 in Cologne, studied woodcarving at the Weimar Bauhaus, 1933 emigr. to France, interned at Gurs from where she escaped and survived in hiding. Lives in Haifa.]

31697. ALY, GÖTZ: *Cleansing the fatherland: Nazi medicine and racial hygiene.* By Götz Aly, Peter Chroust, and Christian Pross. Transl. by Belinda Cooper. Foreword by Michael H. Kater. Baltimore: Johns Hopkins Univ. Press, 1994. XVI, 295 pp., illus. [Incl. Nazi race laws; medical experiments; Nazi eugenics.]

31698. AUSCHWITZ. *Anatomy of the Auschwitz death camp.* Ed. by Yisrael Gutman and Michael Berenbaum; editorial board: Yehuda Bauer, Raul Hilberg, and Franciszek Piper. Bloomington: Indiana Univ. Press, in association with the United States Holocaust Memorial Museum, Washington, D.C., 1994. XVI, 638 pp., illus., graphs, maps, tabs., footnotes. [Scholars from three continents collaborate on the first comprehensive account of the operation of the Auschwitz death camp. Incl.diaries of 'Sonderkommandos'; essays on the postwar trials; also abridged English transl. of a Holocaust denier's thesis.]

31699. AUSCHWITZ. BROD, TOMAN/KÁRNÝ, MIROSLAV/KÁRNÁ, MARGITA, eds.: *Terezínskrodinn– tábor v Osvetimi-Birkenau.* [Ed.]: Terezínská Iniciativa. Prague: Nadace Terezínská Iniciativa, 1994. 203 [2] pp., illus., notes, index. [14 contribs. on the 'Theresienstädter Familienlager' in Auschwitz-Birkenau and other related topics; to be published in German in 1995.]

31700. AUSCHWITZ. FREUND, FLORIAN [et al.]: *Der Bau des Vernichtungslagers Auschwitz-Birkenau. Die Aktenmappen der Zentralbauleitung Auschwitz 'Vorhaben: Kriegsgefangenenlager Auschwitz (Durchführung der Sonderbehandlung)' im Militärhistorischen Archiv Prag.* [In]: Zeitgeschichte, Jg. 2, H. 5/6, Wien, Mai/Juni 1993. Pp. 187–214, notes, facsims. [Incl. facsim. reprint of the document (13 pp.).]

31701. AUSCHWITZ. FRIEDRICH, OTTO: *The kingdom of Auschwitz.* New York; London: Harper Collins, 1994. XIV, 110 pp., map. [This short history of Auschwitz was first publ. in 1982 as an essay in 'Atlantic Monthly' and has been updated by the author.]

31702. AUSCHWITZ. GREIF, GIDEON: *Wir weinten tränenlos . . . Augenzeugenberichte der jüdischen 'Sonderkommandos' in Auschwitz.* Köln: Böhlau, 1994. LI, 307 pp., illus.

31703. AUSCHWITZ. PIPER, FRANCISZEK: *Die Zahl der Opfer von Auschwitz. Aufgrund der Quellen und der Erträge der Forschung 1945 bis 1990.* Übers. aus dem Polnischen ins Deutsche von Jochen August. Oswiecim: Verl. d. Staatlichen Museum in Oswiecim, 1993. 248 pp., illus., bibl. (228–234).

Bibliography 347

31704. AUSCHWITZ. SCHWALBOVÁ, MARGITA: *Elf Frauen: Leben in Wahrheit;* Eine Ärztin berichtet aus Auschwitz-Birkenau. [Abb.: Leo Haas] Annweiler: Plöger, 1994. 116 pp., illus. (Zeugen der Zeitgeschichte, 7.)

31705. AUSCHWITZ. SPRITZER, JENNY: *Ich war Nr. 10291. Als Sekretärin in Auschwitz.* Stäfa [CH 8712]: Rothenhäusler Verl., 1994. 158 pp. [Author was deported to Auschwitz in July 1942; publ. her recollections in 1946; lives in Zurich.]

31706. AUSTRIA. WOHNOUT, HELMUT: *Die Janusköpfigkeit des autoritären Österreich. Katholischer Antisemitismus in den Jahren vor 1938.* [In]: Geschichte und Gegenwart, Jg. 13, H. 1, Graz, März, 1994. Pp. 1–16 [with Engl. abstract]. [A discussion note on this article by Heinz Hürten under the title 'Katholischer Antisemitismus' was publ. in H. 4 (Dez. 1994) of the same journal (246–247).]

31707. BAD SODEN (Taunus). HEBAUF, RENATE: *Der jüdische Friedhof von Bad Soden in den Jahren 1938–1945.* Die Geschichte einer Zerstörung. Hrsg. vom Arbeitskreis für Bad Sodener Geschichte. [Bad Soden]: Arbeitskreis für Bad Sodener Geschichte, 1994. 71 pp. (Materialien zur Bad Sodener Geschichte, H. 15.)

31708. BAILEY, BRENDA: *A Quaker couple in Nazi Germany.* London: William Sessions, 1994. VIII, 300 pp., illus. [Author tells the story of her German father and English mother who were persecuted as Quakers in Nazi Germany and who helped countless Jews escape.]

31709. BAISINGEN. BECKER, FRANZISKA: *Gewalt und Gedächtnis: Erinnerungen an die nationalsozialistische Verfolgung einer jüdischen Landgemeinde.* Mit einem Vorwort von Hermann Bausinger. Göttingen: Schmerse, 1994. 156 pp., illus., graphs., bibl. (151–156). (Göttinger Beiträge zur Politik und Zeitgeschichte, 2.)

31710. BAUER, YEHUDA: *Jews for sale?: Nazi-Jewish negotiations, 1933–1945.* New Haven: Yale Univ. Press, 1994. XIII, 306 pp., notes (261–290), bibl. (291–295). [Examines the many different attempts to negotiate with the Nazis for the release of Jews in exchange for money, goods, or political benefit.]

31711. BERLIN. ELKIN, RIVKA: *Kinder zur Aufbewahrung im Jüdischen Krankenhaus zu Berlin in den Jahren 1943–1945.* [In]: Tel Aviver Jahrbuch für deutsche Geschichte, Bd. 23, Gerlingen, 1994. Pp. 247–274.

31712. BERLIN. JOCHHEIM, GERNOT: *Das Leben der Juden in Berlin in den Jahren 1940–1943.* Ein bislang unveröffentlichtes Dokument. [In]: Gerhard Hentrich – der Verleger. Eine Festschrift zum 70. Geburtstag für Gerhard Hentrich. Hrsg. von Werner Buchwald und Hermann Simon. Berlin: Ed. Hentrich, 1994. Pp. 40–67. [Incl. also: Von Tempelhof nach Auschwitz. Die Deportationen im Spiegel des Tätigkeitsbuches eines Polizeireviers (Kurt Schilde, 184–192.]

31713. BERLIN. KRÜGER, MAREN: *Herbert Sonnenfeld. Ein jüdischer Fotograf in Berlin 1933–1938.* [Katalog:] Berlin Museum, Abteilung Jüdisches Museum. Berlin: Nicolai, 1990. 146 pp., illus., facsims. [H.S., 1906 Berlin – 1972 New York, photographer, worked for Jewish newspapers and organisations during the Nazi period. Emigr. to the USA in Nov. 1939.]

31714. BERLIN. MEYHÖFER, RITA [et al.]: *Berliner Gedenkbuch für die jüdischen Opfer des Nationalsozialismus.* [In]: Berlin in Geschichte und Gegenwart, Berlin, 1993. Pp. 509–528.

—— BERLIN. SCHÖNFELD, MARTIN: *Gedenktafeln in West-Berlin.* [See No. 31951.]

31715. BRANDENBURG. *Verfolgung – Alltag – Widerstand. Brandenburg in der NS-Zeit.* Studien und Dokumente. Hrsg. von Dietrich Eichholtz unter Mitarbeit von Almuth Püschel im Auftrag der Brandenburgischen Landeszentrale für politische Bildung. Mit einem Geleitwort von Manfred Stolpe. Berlin: Volk & Welt, 1994. 440 [7] pp., illus., docs., facsims., tabs., lists, notes. [Incl.: Überfall auf jüdische Jungen im Juni 1933, Dokumente (Klaus Drobisch, 168–

206; on the Jewish Jugend- und Lehrheim Wolzig in Beeskow-Storkow and its inmates. Incl. list of the boys imprisoned in Oranienburg June until July 1933.). Boykott – Entrechtung – Pogrom – Deportation. Die 'Arisierung' jüdischen Eigentums während der NS-Diktatur. Untersucht und dargestellt an Beispielen aus der Provinz Mark Brandenburg (Irene Diekmann, 207–229). Brandenburgische Heil- und Pflegeanstalten in der NS-Zeit. Sterilisation und 'Vernichtung lebensunwerten Lebens' (Kristina Hübener, 230–246; also deals with the murder of Jewish patients).]

31716. BRANDT, MARION: *Gertrud Kolmar an Jacob Picard. Briefe aus den Jahren 1937–1939.* [In]: Jüdischer Almanach 1995. Frankfurt am Main, 1994. Pp. 136–149.

31717. BRECHER, ELINOR J.: *Schindler's legacy: true stories of the list survivors.* New York: Dutton, 1994. XXXVII, 442 pp., illus.

31718. BREMEN. RÜBSAM, ROLF: *Die Brombergers – Schicksal einer Künstlerfamilie.* Mit einem Vorwort von Heinrich Albertz. Bremen: Donat, 1992. 165 pp., illus., bibl. [On a family from Bremen, which was deported to Minsk.]

31719. BRENTZEL, MARIANNE: *Nesthäkchen kommt in KZ: eine Annäherung an Else Ury, 1877–1943.* Mit Photos, Briefen und mit einer Bibliographie der Werke Else Urys von Barbara Asper. Zürich: Ed. Ebersbach, 1992. 253 pp., illus. [E.U., author of once highly popular books for girls.]

31720. BRENDLER, KONRAD: *Die Holocaustrezeption der Enkelgeneration im Spannungsfeld von Abwehr und Traumatisierungen.* [In]: Jahrbuch für Antisemitismusforschung 3. Frankfurt am Main; New York, 1994. Pp. 303–340.

31721. BRESLAU. REINKE, ANDREAS: *Stufen der Zerstörung: das Breslauer Jüdische Krankenhaus während des Nationalsozialismus.* [In]: Menora 5. München, 1994. Pp. 379–413, notes.

31722. BRÜHL. THRAMS, PETER: *Brühl im Nationalsozialismus.* Bd. 2: Wirtschaft und Zweiter Weltkrieg. Köln: Wienand, 1993. 235 pp., illus., graphs. (Schriftenreihe zur Brühler Geschichte, Bd. 18.) [Incl. chap.: Juden in Brühl (Barbara Becker-Jákli, 123–140).]

31723. BUCHENWALD. *Der gesäuberte Antifaschismus. Die SED und die roten Kapos von Buchenwald. Dokumente.* Hrsg. von Lutz Niethammer unter Mitarbeit von Karin Hartewig [et. al.], eingeleitet von Karin Hartewig und Lutz Niethammer. Berlin: Akademie-Verlag, 1994. 566 pp. [Cf.: Im Dschungel der Wolfsgesellschaft (Hermann Weber) [in]: Die Zeit, Nr. 45, Hamburg, 4. Nov. 1994, p. 19.]

31724. CARPI, DANIEL: *Between Mussolini and Hitler: the Jews and the Italian authorities in France and Tunisia.* Hanover, N.H.: University of New England Press; Waltham, Ma.: Brandeis Univ. Press, 1994. IX, 341 pp., maps, notes (251–322), bibl. (323–332). (Tauber Institute for the study of European Jewry series, 17.) [Incl. the deportation of German-Jewish refugees from Tunisia.]

31725. *Children during the Nazi reign: psychological perspective on the interview process.* Ed. by Judith S. Kestenberg and Eva Fogelman. Westport, Ct.: Praeger, 1994. XXI, 221 pp. [Describes how psychological interviews are helpful in the healing process of Jewish child survivors.]

31726. CHURCH. ERICKSEN, ROBERT P./HESCHEL, SUSANNAH: *The German churches face Hitler. Assessment of the historiography.* [In]: Tel Aviver Jahrbuch für deutsche Geschichte, Bd. 23, Gerlingen, 1994. Pp. 433–459. [Review essay; incl. the section: The question of Christians and Jews.]

31727. CHURCH. SIEGELE-WENSCHKEWITZ, LEONORE, Hrsg.: *Christlicher Antijudaismus und Antisemitismus. Theologische und kirchliche Programme Deutscher Christen.* Frankfurt am Main: Haag + Herchen, 1994. XXI, 320 pp., notes. (Arnoldshainer Texte, Bd. 85.) [A collection of essays, some previously publ. Incl.: Vorwort (ed., I-XXI). Mitverantwortung und Schuld der

Christen am Holocaust (ed., 1–26). Adolf Schlatters Sicht des Judentums im politischen Kontext. Die Schrift 'Wird der Jude über uns siegen?' von 1935 (ed., 95–110). Spuren im Warschauer Ghetto (Hans-Joachim Barkenings, 111–124; on Ernst Flatow, 'non-Aryan' pastor, who died in the Warsaw ghetto in 1942). Theologen für Hitler. Walter Grundmann und das 'Institut zur Erforschung und Beseitigung des jüdischen Einflusses auf das deutsche kirchliche Leben' (Susannah Heschel, 125–170). Der theologische Werdegang Walter Grundmanns bis zum Erscheinen der '28 Thesen der sächsischen Volkskirche zum inneren Aufbau der Deutschen Evangelischen Kirche' Ende 1933 (Klaus-Peter Adam, 171–200). Wie wurde das Neue Testament zu einem sogenannten Volkstestament 'entjudet'? Aus der Arbeit des Eisenacher 'Instituts zur Erforschung und Beseitigung des jüdischen Einflusses auf das deutsche kirchliche Leben' (Birgit Jerke, 201–234). 'Und die Jünger wunderten sich . . .'. Christlicher Antijudaismus in der Auslegung von Joh. 4,27 (Martina S. Gnadt, 235–260; on Johannes Leipoldt). Further contribs. are listed according to subject.]

31728. COLOGNE. *Versteckte Vergangenheit. Über den Umgang mit der NS-Zeit in Köln.* Aufsätze und Essays hrsg. von Horst Matzerath, Harald Buhlan und Barbara Becker-Jákli. Köln: Emons, 1994. 338 pp., illus., notes. [Incl.: Zur 'Arisierung' und den Versuchen der 'Wiedergutmachung' in Köln (Britta Bopf, 163–194). Denunziationen und Denunziationsopfer – Auseinandersetzungen in der Nachkriegszeit (Katrin Dördelmann, 195–232). Verdunkelungsgefahr! – Die Kölner Justiz und die Verfolgung der NS-Verbrechen (Heiner Lichtenstein, 233–242).]

31729. CRETZMEYER, STACY: *Your name is Renée: Ruth's story as a hidden child.* The wartime experiences of Ruth Kapp Hartz. Brunswick, Me.: Biddle, (P.O. Box 1305 £ 103) 1994. 175 pp., illus., ports., map, bibl. [R.K. Hartz came from a German-Jewish family and survived the war hidden in various places in Vichy France, including a convent; went to the US in 1958.]

31730. CREW, DAVID F., ed.: *Nazism and German society, 1933–1945.* Introd. by David F. Crew. London; New York: Routledge, 1994. XI, 316 pp., tabs., notes. [Collection of 9 essays. Incl.: The genesis of the 'Final Solution' from the spirit of science (Detlev J.K. Peukert, 274–299).]

——— CZECHOSLOVAKIA. KRAFT, THOMAS: *Zuflucht in der Tschechoslowakei. Die Situation deutscher Literaten in Prag und Brünn von 1933 bis 1939.* [See in No. 31618.]

31731. DACHAU. *Dachauer Hefte.* Hrsg.: Wolfgang Benz und Barbara Distel, Dachau: Verlag Dachauer Hefte, 1994. Jg. 10, H. 10 (November 1994): Täter und Opfer. 1989. 242 pp., footnotes. Incl.: Editorial (eds., 1–2). Die Kommandanten des Konzentrationslagers Dachau (Johannes Tuchel, 69–90). Gnadengesuche und Gnadenerlasse. Kriegsverbrecher in der amerikanischen Besatzungszone (Robert Sigel, 214–224). Das Opfer als Täter? Die Lebensgeschichte des Erwin Goldmann (Wolfgang Benz, 225–242; see No. 31853).]

31732. DARMSTADT. *Das zweite Leben. Darmstädter Juden in der Emigration.* Ein Lesebuch. Im Auftrag des Magistrats der Stadt Darmstadt und der Jüdischen Gemeinde hrsg. von Moritz Neumann und Eva Reinhold-Postina. Darmstadt: Roether, 1993. 233 pp., illus.

31733. DELPARD, RAPHAEL: *Überleben im Versteck. Jüdische Kinder 1940–1944.* Aus dem Französischen von Bettina Schäfer. Bonn: Dietz Nachf., 1994. 236 pp., illus. [Orig. French edn. publ. in 1993 in Paris under the title 'Les enfants cachés'.] [Based on interviews with persons, who had survived in hiding, most of them in France. Incl. German-Jewish children.]

31734. DENMARK. HERBERT, ULRICH: *Die deutsche Besatzungspolitik in Dänemark im Zweiten Weltkrieg und die Rettung der dänischen Juden.* [In]: Tel Aviver Jahrbuch für deutsche Geschichte, Bd. 23, Gerlingen, 1994. Pp. 93–114.

31735. DÜSSELDORF. LEHMKUHL, GUNHILD: *Wo ist dein Bruder Abel? Jüdische Bürger in Eller, Lierenfeld und Vennhausen 1933–45.* Düsseldorf: Grupello, 1994. 126 pp., illus., facsims., notes. [Documents the author's attempts to find traces of Jewish families in three southern districts of Düsseldorf.]

31736. DURLACHER, GERHARD L.: *Streifen am Himmel. Vom Anfang und Ende einer Reise.* Aus dem Niederländischen übers. von Maria Csollány. Hamburg: Europ. Verlagsanstalt, 1994. 100 pp. [G. L. Durlacher, sociologist, born in Baden-Baden, emigr. to the Netherlands in 1937, deported from Westerbork to Theresienstadt in 1942 and from there to Auschwitz; while his family was murdered in Auschwitz, the 14-year-old was liberated at Groß-Rosen and returned to Amsterdam.]

31737. DWORK, DEBÓRAH: *Kinder mit dem gelben Stern.* Europa 1933–1945. Aus dem Englischen von Gabriele Krüger-Wirrer. München: Beck, 1994. 384 pp., illus., map., notes (311–348), bibl. (349–366), glossary, index (371–384). [For orig. edn., publ. 1991, see No. 28262/YB XXXVII.]

31738. EICHENGREEN, LUCILLE (WITH HARRIET HYMAN CHAMBERLAIN): *From ashes to life: my memories of the Holocaust.* San Francisco: Mercury House, 1994. IX, 217 pp., illus. [For orig. German edn. and data see No. 30481/YB XXXIX.]

31739. ESSEN. ALTE SYNAGOGE, HRSG.: *Entrechtung und Selbsthilfe. Zur Geschichte der Juden in Essen unter dem Nationalsozialismus.* Studienreihe der Alten Synagoge – Band 4. Essen. Klartext, 1994. 119 pp., illus., facsims., notes. [Incl.: Zur Einführung (Michael Zimmermann, 7–11). Die 'Entjudung' der Essener Wirtschaft von 1933 bis 1941 (Dirk van Laak, 12–30). Die Gründung der Reichsvertretung (Hugo Hahn, 31–42). Der Jüdische Kulturbund Rhein-Ruhr 1933–1938 (Dorothea Bessen, 43–65). Die 'Reichskristallnacht' 1938 in Essen (Michael Zimmermann, 66–97). Walter Rohr – 1938 aus Essen vertrieben, 1945 als US-Soldat zurückgekehrt (Ernst Schmidt, 98–117).]

31740. EXILE. *Exil in Dänemark. Deutschsprachige Wissenschaftler, Künstler und Schriftsteller im dänischen Exil nach 1933.* Hrsg. von Willy Dähnhardt und Birgit S. Nielsen. Heide: Boyens, 1993. 731 pp., illus., ports., facsims., notes, index (persons, 709–731).

31741. FELSTINER LOWENTHAL, MARY: *To paint her life: Charlotte Salomon in the Nazi era.* New York: Harper Collins, 1994. XIV, 290 pp., illus., notes (239–276). [Ch.S, April 16, 1917 Berlin – 1943 Auschwitz, artist, during her exile in the South of France she painted her life story in 769 pictures which are now housed in the Jewish Historical Museum in Amsterdam. Author juxtaposes the Salomon story with the story of the SS commander Alois Brunner who was responsible for Charlotte's deportation and who was never brought to justice. For earlier publs. on Ch. S. see No. 4222/YB IX and No. 18690/YB XXVII.]

31742. FINAL SOLUTION. BENZ, WOLFGANG: *Endlösung. Zur Geschichte des Begriffs.* [In]: Tribüne, Jg. 33, H. 132, Frankfurt am Main, 1994. Pp. 96–109.

31743. FINAL SOLUTION. BURRIN, PHILIPPE: *Hitler and the Jews: the genesis of the Holocaust.* Transl. by Patsy Southgate. Introd. by Saul Friedlander. London; New York: Edward Arnold, 1994. 177 pp., notes (155–174). [For orig. French edn. see No. 27275/YB XXXVI.]

31744. FINAL SOLUTION. COHEN, RAYA: *Das Riegner-Telegramm – Text, Kontext und Zwischentext.* [In]: Tel Aviver Jahrbuch für deutsche Geschichte, Bd. 23, Gerlingen. 1994. Pp. 301–324. [Gerhart R. Riegner, representative of World Jewish Congress, sent this telegram from Switzerland in Aug. 1942. First confirmation to the western Allies of the Nazi extermination plan.]

31745. FINAL SOLUTION. *The Final solution: origins and implementation.* Ed. and introd. by David Cesarani. London; New York: Routledge, 1994. X, 318 pp., notes. [Collection of 18 essays, product of a conference held in London on the 50th anniversary of the Wannsee-Conference in 1942. Incl.: Volksgemeinschaft, 'Aryanization' and the Holocaust (Avraham Barkai, 33–50). Euthanasia and the Final Solution (Henry Friedlander, 51–61). The idea of the Final Solution and the role of experts (Benno Müller-Hill, 62–72). Operation Barbarossa and the origins of the Final Solution (Omer Bartov, 119–136). Hitler and the euphoria of victory: the path to the Final Solution (Christopher R. Browning, 137–150). German public awareness of the Final Solution (David Bankier, 215–227). Documents on the Holocaust from the archives of the former Soviet Union (Shmuel Krakowski, 291–299). Conclusion: the significance of the Final Solution (Yehuda Bauer, 300–309).]

31746. FINAL SOLUTION. KAISER, WOLF: *Die Wannsee-Konferenz. Zur Bedeutung eines Protokolls.* [In]: Tribüne, Jg. 33, H. 132, Frankfurt am Main, 1994. Pp. 110–124, footnotes.

31747. FINAL SOLUTION. LAQUEUR, WALTER/BREITMAN, RICHARD: *Breaking the silence: the German who exposed the Final Solution.* Hanover, N.H.: University of New England Press; Waltham, Ma.: Brandeis Univ. Press, 1994. 328 pp., illus., notes. (Tauber Institute for the Study of European Jewry series, 18.) [This paperback edn. contains a new foreword and afterword by the authors. For orig. edn. see No. 23318/YB XXXII.]

31748. FINAL SOLUTION. *The Nazi decision to commit mass murder: three interpretations.* [In]: German Studies Review, Vol. 17, No. 3, Tempe, Az., Oct. 1994. Pp. 473–512, notes. [Incl.: The euphoria of victory and the Final Solution (Christopher R. Browning, 473–481). Plans for the Final Solution in early 1941 (Richard Breitman, 483–493). Step by step: the expansion of murder (Henry Friedlander, 495–509). Comments on the papers by Friedlander, Breitman and Browning (Gerhard L. Weinberg, 509–512).]

31749. FRANCE. GILZMER, MECHTILD: *Fraueninternierungslager in Südfrankreich. Rieucros und Brens 1939–1944.* Berlin: Orlanda Frauenverl., 1994. 240 pp., illus. (Der andere Blick.) [Incl. also Jewish refugees from Germany.]

31750. FRANCE. OBSCHERNITZKI, DORIS: *Deutsch-französische Vergangenheit. Das Internierungslager Les-Milles bei Aix-en-Provence.* [In]: Gerhard Hentrich – der Verleger. Eine Festschrift zum 70. Geburtstag für Gerhard Hentrich. Hrsg. von Werner Buchwald und Hermann Simon. Berlin: Ed. Hentrich, 1994. Pp. 120–127.

31751. FRANKFURT am Main. *Berichte gegen Vergessen und Verdrängen von 100 überlebenden jüdischen Schülerinnen und Schülern über die NS-Zeit in Frankfurt am Main.* Hrsg.: Benjamin Ortmeyer. Witterschlick/Bonn: Wehle, 1994. 179 pp., illus. (Eine Veröff. der Arbeitsgemeinschaft gegen Antisemitismus (Holbeinschule) in Koop. mit der Gesellschaft für Christl.-Jüd. Zusammenarbeit, Frankfurt am Main.)

31752. *Frauen in Konzentrationslagern: Bergen-Belsen, Ravensbrück.* Hrsg. von Claus Füllberg-Stolberg [et al.]. Bremen: Ed. Temmen, 1994. 347 pp., illus., facsims., bibl. [Cont. 29 essays on various aspects of Bergen-Belsen and Ravensbrück and their different groups of inmates arranged under the sections: I. Lagergeschichte (pp. 13–42); II. Lageralltag (43–220); III. Täterinnen und Täter (pp. 221–240): IV. Lebensgeschichten (pp. 259–339). Incl.: Kultur im KZ. Musik, Literatur und Kunst in Bergen-Belsen (Thomas Rahe, 193–206). 'Ein Symbol der menschlichen Würde'. Kunst und Kultur im KZ Ravensbrück (Susanne Minhoff, 207–220.]

31753. FREIBURG. OTT, HUGO: *Laubhüttenfest 1940. Warum Therese Loewy einsam sterben mußte.* Freiburg: Herder, 1994. 124 pp., notes. [On the widow of the mathematician Alfred Loewy, who committed suicide to avoid deportation to Gurs in Oct. 1940. Also on the role of Heidegger, a former student of Alfred Loewy.]

31754. GARBE, DETLEV: *'Sendboten des jüdischen Bolschewismus'. Antisemitismus als Motiv nationalsozialistischer Verfolgung der Zeugen Jehovas.* [In]: Tel Aviver Jahrbuch für deutsche Geschichte, Bd. 23, Gerlingen, 1994. Pp. 145–172.

31755. GERLACH, WOLFGANG: *Document: Armin T. Wegner's letter to German chancellor Adolf Hitler, Berlin, Easter Monday, April 11, 1933.* [In]: Holocaust and Genocide Studies, Vol. 8, No. 3, Oxford, Winter 1994. Pp. 395–409, notes. [Wegner, a non-Jew b. in Elberfeld in 1886, wrote a letter to Hitler warning him of the consequences of his anti-Jewish policies.]

31756. GERSHON, KAREN: *A lesser child*. An autobiography. London: Peter Owen, 1994. 198 pp., illus. [The recollections by K. G., née Löwenthal (1924–1993), the poet and writer, of her childhood in Bielefeld and her experiences under the Nazis, prior to coming to the U.K. with a 'Kindertransport'. For German edn. see No. 31198/YB XXXIX.]

31757. Jüdischer Alltag in Deutschland 1933–1945. Düsseldorf: Droste, 1994. 252 pp., illus., facsims., tabs., notes. (Fotografierte Zeitgeschichte.) (Sonderausgabe.) [Reprint of the 1985 edn., see No. 21093/YB XXX.]

31758. GIRTLER, ROLAND/OKLADEK, FRIEDERIKE: *Eine Wiener Jüdin im Chor der deutschen Wehrmacht. Die Geschichte einer Rebellin*. Wien: Ed. Wien/Dachs-Verlag, 1994. 200 pp. [Fr. Wilder-Okladek, b. 1921 in Vienna, emigr. 1938 to Holland, deported to Westerbork, escaped eventually via Paris to Spain. Emigr. later to Israel. Now lives in Vienna.]

31759. GÖPFERT, REBEKKA, Hrsg.: *Ich kam allein. Die Rettung von zehntausend jüdischen Kindern nach England 1938/39*. Hrsg. von Rebekka Göpfert. Aus dem Englischen von Susanne Röckel. München: Deutscher Taschenbuch Verlag, 1994. 177 pp. [Incl.: Der jüdische Kindertransport von Deutschland nach England 1938/39 (Rebekka Göpfert, 9–18). Selected edn. of 'I came alone. The Stories of the Kindertransports', publ. in 1990. For orig. edn. see No. 27302/YB XXXVI.]

31760. GÖPPINGEN. RUEß, KARL-HEINZ: *Die jüdische Gemeinde: verfolgt, vertrieben, vernichtet*. [In]: Göppingen unterm Hakenkreuz. Mit Beiträgen von Walter Bade [et al.]. Im Auftrag der Stadt Göppingen hrsg. von Karl-Heinz Rueß. Göppingen, Stadt Göppingen, 1994. Pp. 244–251, illus., notes.

31761. GROSS-ROSEN. SPRENGER, ISABELL: *'Der Judenblock bleibt stehen'. Jüdische Häftlinge in der ersten Kriegshälfte im Konzentrationslager Groß-Rosen in Schlesien*. [In]: Menora 5, München, 1994. Pp. 415–433, notes.

31762. GÜTERSLOH. GATZEN, HELMUT: *Novemberpogrom 1938 in Gütersloh. Nachts Orgie der Gewalt-tags organisierte Vernichtung*. Gütersloh: Flöttmann, 1994. 95 pp. [Cf.: Besprechung (Diethard Aschoff) [in]: Westfälische Forschungen, Jg. 44, Münster, 1994. Pp. 598–599.]

31763. HAGEN. ZABEL, HERMANN, HRSG.: *Mit Schimpf und Schande aus der Stadt, die ihnen Heimat war*. Beiträge zur Geschichte der jüdischen Gemeinde Hagen. Hrsg.: Gesellschaft für Christlich-Jüdische Zusammenarbeit Hagen und Umgebung e.V. Hagen: Padligur, 1994. 406 pp., illus., bibl. (385–404). (Beiträge zur Förderung des christlich-jüdischen Dialogs, Bd. 11.)

31764. HAMBURG. LIPPMANN, LEO: *'...dass ich wie ein guter Deutscher empfinde und handele': zur Geschichte der Deutsch-Israelitischen Gemeinde in der Zeit vom Herbst 1935 bis zum Ende 1942*. Zwei Berichte, hrsg. anläßlich des 50. Todestages von Staatsrat a.D. Dr. Leo Lippmann am 10. Juni 1993 von der Finanzbehörde Hamburg. Mit Beitr. von Wolfgang Curilla und Gabriele Fenyes und einer Einf. von Ina S. Lorenz. Hamburg: Dölling und Galitz, 1993. 127 pp.

31765. HAMBURG. ROMEY, STEFAN: *Ein KZ in Wandsbek. Zwangsarbeit im Hamburger Drägerwerk*. Hamburg: VSA-Verlag, 1994. 151 pp., illus., facsims, notes, bibl.

31766. HAMBURG. SCHWARBERG, GÜNTHER: *Der SS-Arzt und die Kinder vom Bullenhuser Damm*. Göttingen: Steidl, 1994. 174 pp. [The story of twenty Jewish children murdered in a Hamburg school on April 20, 1945.]

31767. HANOVER. BUCHHOLZ, MARLIS: *'... und hat unendlich viel Arbeit verursacht'. Hannovers Stadtverwaltung und die 'Judenhäuser'*. [In]: Rassismus in Deutschland. Beiträge zur Geschichte der nationalsozialistischen Verfolgung in Norddeutschland, Heft 1. Bremen: Temmen, 1994. Pp. 61–72, illus.

31768. HARTMAN, GEOFFREY H., ed.: *Holocaust remembrance: the shapes of memory.* Ed. by Geoffrey H. Hartman. Oxford; Cambridge, Ma.: Blackwell, 1994. XI, 306 pp., illus., notes (265–298). [A collection of 21 essays and texts, incl.: Jean Améry as witness (Alvin Rosenfeld, 59–69). The awakening (Aharaon Appelfeld, 149–152). German-Jewish memory and national consciousness (Michael Geyer/Miriam Hansen, 175–190). Trauma memory, and transference (Saul Friedlander, 252–263).]

31769. HAYES, PETER: *Big business and 'aryanisation' in Germany, 1993–1939.* [In]: Jahrbuch für Antisemitismusforschung 3, Frankfurt am Main; New York, 1994. Pp. 254–281.

31770. HEENEN-WOLFF, SUSANN: *Im Land der Täter. Gespräche mit überlebenden Juden.* Frankfurt am Main: Fischer-Taschenbuch-Verl., 1994. 306 pp. (Fischer Taschenbücher.) [Paperback edn. of No. 29518/YB XXXVIII.]

31771. HEIBER, HELMUT: *Universität unterm Hakenkreuz.* Teil II: Die Kapitulation der Hohen Schulen. Das Jahr 1933 und seine Themen. Band 2. München; New Providence, 1994: Saur, 1994. 858 pp., notes (737–828), indexes (831–858). [Incl. passim references to Jewish members of universities and their treatment by government officials, colleagues and students. For Part I see No. 38306/YB XXXVII.]

31772. HILDESHEIMER, ESRIEL: *Jüdische Selbstverwaltung unter dem NS-Regime.* Der Existenzkampf der Reichsvertretung und Reichsvereinigung der Juden in Deutschland. Tübingen: Mohr, 1994. XVI, 258 pp., glossary, bibl., index. (Schriftenreihe wissenschaftlicher Abhandlungen des Leo Baeck Instituts, 50.) [Cf.: Besprechung (Avraham Barkai) [in]: 'MB', Jg. 63, Nr. 109, Tel Aviv, Juni 1995, p. 6.]

31773. HISTORIOGRAPHY. ASCHHEIM, STEVEN E.: *Small forays, grand theories and deep origins: current trends in the historiography of the Holocaust.* [In]: Studies in Contemporary Jewry, 10, Oxford Univ. Press, 1994. Pp. 139–163. [Incl. historians' debate.]

31774. HISTORIOGRAPHY. BRAUN, R.: *The Holocaust and problems of historical representation.* [In]: History and Theory, Vol. 33, No. 2, Middletown, Ct., 1994. 172–197.

31775. HISTORIOGRAPHY. MAREK, MICHAEL: *Alltagsgeschichte und Holocaust.* '. . . war hier nicht so schlimm wie in anderen Orten!' [In]: Tribüne, Jg. 33, H. 130, Frankfurt am Main, 1994. Pp. 32–39, footnotes. [Critical review essay on local and regional studies of Jewish communities during the Nazi era.]

31776. HISTORIOGRAPHY. MARRUS, MICHAEL R.: *Reflections on the historiography of the Holocaust.* [In]: Journal of Modern History, Vol. 66, No. 1, Chicago, March 1994. Pp. 92–116.

31777. HISTORIOGRAPHY. SCHEFFLER, WOLFGANG: *Holocaustforschung am Wendepunkt. Kritische Anmerkungen zur deutschen Ausgabe der 'Enzyklopädie des Holocaust'.* [In]: Jahrbuch für Antisemitismusforschung 3, Frankfurt am Main; New York, 1994. Pp. 341–353. [Review essay on: 'Enzyklopädie des Holocaust. Die Verfolgung und Ermordung der europäischen Juden'. 3 vols. Berlin, 1993; see No. 30395/YB XXXIX.]

31778. HISTORIOGRAPHY & 'HISTORIANS' DEBATE'. LACAPRA, DOMINICK: *Representing the Holocaust: history, theory, trauma.* Ithaca: Cornell Univ. Press, 1994. XIII, 230 pp., bibl. [Incl. chaps. Reflections on the Historians' Debate; Historicizing the Holocaust; Heidegger's Nazi turn.]

31779. HISTORIOGRAPHY & HISTORIANS' DEBATE. BARNOUW, DAGMAR: *Politics, history and cultural memory: the historians' dispute.* [In]: Crisis and culture in post-enlightenment Germany. Essays in honour of Peter Heller [see No. 32119]. Pp. 469–482.

31780. HISTORIOGRAPHY & HISTORIANS' DEBATE. LOW, ALFRED D.: *The Third Reich and the Holocaust in German historiography: toward the Historikerstreit of the mid-1980s.* Boulder, Co.: East European Monographs; New York: Distr. by Columbia Univ. Press, 1994. XV, 255 pp., notes.

31781. HOLOCAUST. ALEXANDER, EDWARD: *The Holocaust: history and the war of ideas*. New Brunswick, N.J.: Transaction Books, 1994. IX, 242 pp., chronology, bibl. (277–231). [Incl. analysis of ancient and modern antisemitism as the primary cause of the Holocaust. Also discusses Holocaust literature; Holocaust denial.]

31782. HOLOCAUST. BIALAS, WOLFGANG: *Das Ende der Vernunft – der Holocaust und die Geschichte*. [In]: Geschichte, Erziehung, Politik, Jg. 5, H. 4, Berlin, April, 1994. Pp. 217 ff. [Article is discussed by Martin Koch [in]: H. 9 (Sept. 1994) of the same journal: Der Holocaust – einzigartig in der Geschichte (515–518).]

31783. HOLOCAUST. KATZ, STEVEN T.: *The Holocaust in historical context*. Vol. 1: The Holocaust and mass death before the modern age. New York; Oxford: Oxford Univ. Press, 1994. XV, 702 pp., bibl. (583–677). [In this first of three volumes author seeks to establish the uniqueness of the Holocaust comparing it to similar events in world history.] [Cf.: When is a genocide not a genocide? (David Cesarani) [in]: Jewish Chronicle, London, Oct. 21, 1994.]

31784. HOLOCAUST DENIAL. BASTIAN, TILL: *Auschwitz und die 'Auschwitzlüge'. Massenmord und Geschichtsfälschung*. München: Beck, 1994. 103 pp., illus., facsims., notes. (Beck'sche Reihe.) [Deals with Nazi concentration camps, the 'Final Solution', Auschwitz and especially with 'revivisionist' literature and propaganda about Auschwitz.]

31785. HOLOCAUST DENIAL. *Facets of Holocaust denial*. [In]: Dimensions: A Journal of Holocaust Studies, Vol. 8, No. 1, New York, 1994. [Cont.: History versus fiction (Dennis B. Klein, 2–3). Holocaust denial: an overview (Deborah Lipstadt, 3–7, notes, illus.). To combat denial (Richard Lourie, 9–12, illus.). Holocaust denial: the growing danger (Abraham H. Foxman, 13–16, illus.).] [Cf.: Holocaust denial research disclaimed (Alison Abbott) [in]: Nature, Vol. 368, No. 6471, London, April 7, 1994, p. 483.]

31786. HOLOCAUST DENIAL. FISCHEL, JACK: *Holocaust denial and the conspiracy theory of history*. [In]: Jewish Spectator, Vol. 59, No. 2, Calabasas, Ca., Fall 1994. Pp. 8–10. [Incl. the Protocols of the Elders of Zion.]

31787. HOLOCAUST DENIAL. HITCHENS, CHRISTOPHER: *Minority report*. [In]: The Nation, Vol. 259, No. 10, New York, Oct. 3, 1994, p. 335. [Discusses the views of Holocaust-denial historian Robert Faurisson, who came to the Holocaust Museum in Washington to air his ideas. His views are compared to David Irving's as well as those of other 'revisionist' historians'.]

31788. HOLOCAUST DENIAL. LIPSTADT, DEBORAH E.: *Betrifft: Leugnen des Holocaust*. Aus dem Amerikanischen von Gabriele Kosack. Zürich: Rio, 1994. 319 pp., notes, index (places, names, subjects). [For American edn. see No. 30553/YB XXXIX.] [Incl.: Der Vormarsch der Lügner (Erwin Leiser, 7–12).]

31789. HUNGARY. GANN, CHRISTOPH: *Lichter in der Finsternis. Raoul Wallenberg und die Rettung der Budapester Juden 1944/45*. Begleitheft zur gleichnamigen Ausstellung. Frankfurt am Main, 1994. [Private print.] 84 pp. [Exhibtion in Frankfurt, Jüdisches Gemeindezentrum, April 24 – May, 5 1994.]

31790. JACOBSON, KENNETH: *Embattled selves: an investigation into the nature of identity through oral histories of Holocaust survivours*. New York: Atlantic Monthly Press, 1994. X, 358 pp., bibl. [Recollections of 15 survivors, incl. German Jews; discusses how individual victims of Nazi persecution reacted to being confronted with their Jewish identity.]

—— JÄCKEL, EBERHARD: *Der Mord an den europäischen Juden*. [See in No. 31892.]

31791. JUREIT, ULRIKE/MEYER, BEATE: *Verletzungen. Lebensgeschichtliche Verarbeitung von Kriegserfahrungen*. Hrsg. von Ulrike Jureit und Beate Meyer für den Hamburger Arbeitskreis oral history unterstützt von der Kulturbehörde der Freien und Hansestadt Hamburg. Hamburg: Dölling und Galitz, 1994. 213 pp., illus. [Incl.: Auf dem Weg nach Palästina: in

Hamburg verhaftet – in Dänemark gerettet (Erika Hirsch, 156–174; recollections of six young people, on Hachshara in Hamburg in 1938). Die unerbittliche Vergangenheit. Bericht vom Bruch zwischen Trauma und 'Lebensnormalität'. (Reinhard Saloch/Dieter Thiele, 188–212; recollections of two men and one women, all from 'mixed marriages' living in Hamburg).]

31792. KAUFMANN, HANNE: *Die Nacht am Øresund. Ein jüdisches Schicksal.* Aus dem Dänischen übersetzt von Norbert Lochner. Gerlingen: Bleicher, 1994. 127 pp., illus., map. [Memoirs of a young German refugee girl from Frankfurt, who escaped with others in Oct. 1943 on a ship to Sweden from Nazi deportations.]

31793. KLEE, ERNST: *Vom Krankenmord zum Judenmord. Neue Forschungsergebnisse zur 'Euthanasie' im Nationalsozialismus.* [In]: Zeitgeschichte, Jg. 21, H. 5/6, Wien, Mai/Juni, 1994. Pp. 155–164, notes. [A.o. on the murder of ca. 200 Jewish psychiatric patients taken from Buch, nr. Berlin, to a former prison in the centre of Brandenburg and systematically gassed there in June 1940. 'Non-Aryan' patients were selected on the basis of their ability to work or not.]

31794. KLEINENBREMEN. GERNTRUP, WILHELM: *Das Schicksal der Kleinenbremer Einwohner jüdischen Glaubens in der Zeit der nationalsozialistischen Gewaltherrschaft 1933–1945.* Ein Beitrag zur Ortsgeschichte. Hrsg.: Heimatverein Kleinenbremen. Porta Westfalica, 1994. 134 pp., illus., facsims., docs.

31795. KLEVE. KREBS, WOLFGANG: *Klever Opfer des Holocaust.* Eine aktualisierte Zusammenstellung. [In]: Kalender für das Klever Land auf das Jahr 1994. Kleve, 1994. Pp. 36–39.

——— KONSTANZ. [See in No. 31577.]

31796. KRÜGER, ARND: *'Wenn die Olympiade vorbei, schlagen wir die Juden zu Brei!'. Das Verhältnis der Juden zu den Olympischen Spielen von 1936.* [In]: Menora 5, München, 1994. Pp. 331–347, notes.

31797. KÜHL, STEFAN: *The Nazi connection: Eugenics, American racism, and German National Socialism.* Oxford; New York: Oxford Univ. Press, 1994. XVIII, 166 pp., bibl. [Discusses the Nazi connection to American eugenicists in the 1930, also racial policies towards the Jews.]

31798. KUSHNER, TONY: *The Holocaust and the liberal imagination: a social and cultural history.* Oxford; Cambridge, Ma.: Blackwell, 1994. XIII, 366 pp., notes (279–343), bibl. (345–356). [Deals with the attitude of the liberal establishment in Britain and the USA to the Nazi persecution of the Jews; also discusses German-Jewish refugees in Britain.]

——— LEIPZIG. *Judaica Lipsiensia. Zur Geschichte der Juden in Leipzig.* [See No. 31525.]

31799. LEITNER, ISABELLA/LEITNER, IRVING A.: *Isabella: from Auschwitz to freedom.* New York: Anchor Books, 1994. 233 pp. [Memoirs of Hungarian author who survived Auschwitz and later emigr. to the USA. Previously published in two separate vols.: 'Fragments of Isabella' (1978) and 'Saving the fragments' (1985).]

31800. LEKEBUSCH, SIGRID: *Von der Zivilcourage bis zum Widerstand im Kreise der Christen jüdischer Herkunft.* Das Forschungsprojekt 'Die Verfolgung Christen jüdischer Herkunft'. [In]: Widerstandsforschung am Beispiel der rheinischen Kirche. Hrsg. vom Archiv der Evangelischen Kirche im Rheinland. Düsseldorf: Archiv der Evangelischen Kirche im Rheinland, 1994. (Arbeitshilfen des Archivs der Evangelischen Kirche im Rheinland, Nr. 2.) Pp. 15–35, footnotes.

31801. LEMMONS, RUSSEL: *Goebbels and 'Der Angriff'.* Lexington: Univ. Press of Kentucky, 1994. X, 172 pp., illus., bibl. (160–167). [Incl. the paper's antisemitism.]

31802. LENK, RUDOLF STEFAN/LENK, KARL: *The Mauritius affair: the boat people of 1940/41.* Privately published, 1994. 148 pp., illus. [Describes the experiences of Karl Lenk and some fellow Jews who left Vienna in 1939 by boat. Eventually they reached Haifa, were imprisoned by the British, then sent to Mauritius as prisoners, where Lenk died in 1941. Lenk's son, Dr. R.S. Lenk, transl. and ed. his father's original notes and wrote an up-to-date postcript.]

31803. LODZ [LITZMANNSTADT]. ROSENFELD, OSKAR: *Wozu noch Welt. Aufzeichnungen aus dem Ghetto Lodz.* Hrsg. von Hanno Loewy. Frankfurt am Main: Verl. Neue Kritik, 1994. 123 pp., illus., facsims., notes (299–320), glossary, map. [Fragments of a diary written between Feb. 1942 and July 1944 in the Ghetto of Lodz now in the archive of Yad Vashem.] [O.R., May 13, 1884 Korycany (Moravia) – 1944 Auschwitz, lived in Vienna as a journalist and author. Founder of the first Jewish theatre in Vienna. Emigr. in 1938 to Prague, in Nov. 1941 deported to Lodz, and to Auschwitz-Birkenau in July 1944.]

31804. MAIER, KARL-HEINZ: *. . . und höret niemals auf zu kämpfen.* Lebensbericht des Thomas A. Sharon. Berlin: Hentrich, 1994. 285 pp., illus. [Autobiographical story about the son of a non-Jewish mother and a Jewish father, who went into hiding to avoid slave labour in the Org. Todt ('OT'), later went to Israel to fight in the Israeli army, then returned to Berlin after 1956, where he lives as a journalist.]

31804. MAIER, DIETER: *Arbeitseinsatz und Deportation. Die Mitwirkung der Arbeitsverwaltung bei der nationalsozialistischen Judenverfolgung in den Jahren 1938–1945.* Berlin: Hentrich, 1994. 292 pp., illus., facsims., docs., notes, bibl. (Publikationen der Gedenkstätte Haus der Wannsee-Konferenz, Bd. 4.) [Incl. chaps. on forced labour of Hungarian Jews and Sinti and Roma.]

31806. MARKS, JANE: *Die versteckten Kinder.* Aus dem Amerikanischen übers. von Hildegard Doerr. Augsburg: Pattloch, 1994. 264 pp. [Orig. publ. in 1993 under the title: 'The hidden children; the secret survivors of the Holocaust'.]

31807. MATZNER, DAVID (with DAVID MARGOLIS): *The muselmann: the diary of a Jewish slave laborer.* Hoboken, N.J.: KTAV Publishing House, 1994. IX, 166 pp. [Author, 1894 Wiesbaden – 1986 USA, survived more than twenty prisons, slave-labour camps and concentration camps in France, Poland, and Germany.]

31808. MOERS. *Tatort Moers. Widerstand und Nationalsozialismus im südlichen Altkreis Moers.* [Autoren]: Bernhard Schmidt und Fritz Burger unter Mitarbeit von Kurt Jakob und Helmut Pitz [et al.]. Moers: Aragon, 1994. 538 pp., illus., facsims., docs., notes, index. [Incl. chap. on the persecution of the Jews (Kurt Jakob) and list of Jewish victims.]

31809. MORRIS, KATHERINE: *Balkan exile. The autobiography of Irene Gruenbaum.* [In]: Leo Baeck Institute Year Book XXXIX, London, 1994. Pp. 239, footnotes. [Irene Gruenbaum née Levi, b. 1909 Darmstadt – d. early 1980s, São Paulo.]

31810. MÜLLER-MADEJ, STELLA: *Das Mädchen von der Schindler-Liste.* Aus dem Polnischen von Bettina Thorn. Augsburg: Ölbaum, 1994. 278 pp. [Cf.: Eine Nacht im Totenhaus. Stella Müller-Madej ist die einzige der 'Schindler-Juden', die ihre Geschichte aufschrieb (Elke Schmitter) [in]: Die Zeit, Nr. 49, Hamburg, 2. Dez. 1994, p. 14.

31811. MÜNSTER. ZAHNOW, GREGOR: *Judenverfolgung in Münster.* Münster: Agenda, 1993. 155 pp., illus., notes, bibl. (148–155). (Agenda Geschichte, 1.)

31812. MÜNZ, CHRISTOPH: *Geschichtstheologie und jüdisches Gedächtnis nach Auschwitz.* Über den Versuch, den Schrecken der Geschichte zu bannen. Hrsg.: Stadt Frankfurt am Main, Dezernat für Kultur und Freizeit, Arbeitsstelle Fritz Bauer Institut – Studien-und Dokumentationszentrum zur Geschichte und Wirkung des Holocaust. 36 pp. (Materialien, Nr. 11.)

31813. MUNICH. *Die gefesselte Muse. Das Marionettentheater im Jüdischen Kulturbund München 1935–1937.* Text von Waldemar Bonard. Hrsg. vom Münchner Stadtmuseum. München: Buchendorfer, 1994. 96 pp., illus. [Catalogue of exhibition held under the same title in the Puppentheatermuseum of the Munich Stadtmuseum, April 29 – Oct. 3, 1994. Incl.: Ein

Münchner Künstlerkreis (Schalom Ben-Chorin, 8–10). Der Jüdische Kulturbund in Bayern, Ortsgruppe München, 1934–1938 (11–22). Also short biographies of 19 artists.]

31814. MUNICH. NEFZGER, CHRISTOPH: *Jüdische Unternehmen nach 1933 unter besonderer Berücksichtigung der Region München.* München, Univers., Diplomarbeit, 1993. 110 pp., tabs., bibl. (91–94). [Available at the LBI New York.]

31815. MUNICH. SELIG, WOLFRAM: *Judenverfolgung in München 1933–1941.* [In]: München – 'Hauptstadt der Bewegung'. Red.: Ulrike Haerendel. München: Münchner Stadtmuseum, 1993. Pp. 398–401. [Catalogue of exhibition of the same name in Munich, Oct. 22 1993 – March 27, 1994. Also in this catalogue: 'Aus dem Kapitel der Münchner Judenverfolgung (402–415).]

31816. *The Nazification of an academic discipline: folklore in the Third Reich.* Ed. and transl. by James R. Dow and Hannjost Lixfeld. Bloomington: Indiana Univ. Press, 1994. XX, 354 pp., illus., notes, bibl. (308–345). [A collection of essays on the use of folklore to support Nazi ideology and how it was employed as an academic discipline to isolate and denigrate Jews.]

31817. *Nazi mass murder: a documentary history of the use of poison gas.* Ed. by Eugen Kogon, Hermann Langbein, and Adalbert Rückerl. Editor's notes and foreword to the English-language edn. by Pierre Serge Choumoff. Transl. by Mary Scott and Caroline Lloyd-Morris. New Haven: Yale Univ. Press, 1993. XIII, 289 pp., illus., facsims., maps. chronol., appendixes, notes. [First publ. in German by S. Fischer in 1983.]

31818. NEUENGAMME. JUREIT, ULRIKE/ORTH, KARIN, Hrsg.: *Überlebensgeschichten. Gespräche mit Überlebenden des KZ Neuengamme.* Mit einem Beitrag von Detlef Garbe. Hrsg.: KZ-Gedenkstätte Neuengamme. Hamburg: Dölling und Galitz, 1994. 223 pp., bibl. (212–223).

31819. NICHOLAS, LYNN H.: *The rape of Europa: the fate of Europe's treasures in the Third Reich and the Second World War.* New York: Knopf (distrib. by Random House), 1994. X, 498 pp., illus., ports., maps, notes, bibl. (467–475). [Incl. anti-Jewish legislation affecting artists; the confiscation of Jewish art and works by Jewish artists all over Europe; Nazi purges of 'degenerate' art.]

31820. NORDHAUSEN. FEIST, CHANAN, ed.: *The odeyssey* [sic] *of my parents from the Nazis to freedom.* Edited and translated from German by Chanan Feist. Rehovot, 1991 [private print]. 49, 41 pp., illus., facsims. [Text in English and in Hebrew. Recollections of a family from Nordhausen.] [Available at the Bibliothek Germania Judaica, Cologne.]

31821. NORDHAUSEN. SCHRÖTER, MANFRED: *Die Verfolgung der Nordhäuser Juden 1933 bis 1945.* Bad Lauterbach im Harz: Kohlmann, 1992. 231 pp., illus.

31822. *Die Normalität des Verbrechens.* Bilanz und Perspektiven der Forschung zu den nationalsozialistischen Gewaltverbrechen. Festschrift für Wolfgang Scheffler zum 65. Geburtstag. Hrsg. von Helge Grabitz [et al.]. Berlin: Hentrich, 1994. 544 pp., notes, bibl. [Incl.: Ein Leben für die Zeitgeschichte (Alfred Streim, 9–12). Contribs. relevant to the persection of German Jewry: Umvolkungspläne des Nationalsozialismus und der Holocaust (Hans Mommsen, 68–84). Antisemitismus im Baltikum (Hans-Heinrich Wilhelm, 85–102). L'antisémitisme en tant que divertissement: illustré à l'exemple du film de Veit Harlan 'Le Juif Süss' (1940) (Friedrich Knilli, 103–119). Anmerkungen zu Rudolf Liepmann, einem Beteiligten an der Ermordung von Karl Liebknecht (Hermann Simon, 120–131). Die Deportation und Vernichtung der schlesischen Juden (Karol Jonca, 150–170).]

31823. NOVEMBER POGROM. HOFMANN, THOMAS/LOEWY, HANNO/STEIN, HARRY, Hrsg.: *Pogromnacht und Holocaust. Frankfurt, Weimar, Buchenwald . . . Die schwierige Erinnerung an die Stationen der Vernichtung.* Weimar: Böhlau, 1994. 199 pp., illus. (Schriftenreihe der Arbeitsstelle Fritz-Bauer-Institut, Studien- und Dokumentationszentrum zur Geschichte und Wirkung des Holocaust, Bd. 5.) [Incl.: Jeder Tag danach ein Geschenk. Ansprache zur Gedenkveranstaltung in Weimar am 12. November 1992 (Franz Ephraim Wagner, 9–19;

F.W., born 1919, in Nov. 1938 deported from Frankfurt am Main to Buchenwald, emigr. in 1939 to Palestine, now lives in Jerusalem). Von Weimar nach Buchenwald. Die Juden auf dem deutschen Sonderweg (Gert Mattenklott, 20–31). 'Reichskristallnacht' in Frankfurt am Main. Eine Skizze (Dieter Schiefelbein, 32–57). Von der 'Reichskristallnacht' zum 'Holocaust'. Der 9. November und das Ende des 'Radauantisemitismus' (Ulrich Herbert, 58–80). Juden im Konzentrationslager Buchenwald 1938–1942 (Harry Stein, 81–171). Erinnerungen an die 'Reichskristallnacht' in der SBZ und in der DDR (Olaf Groehler, 172–197).]

31824. NOVEMBER POGROM. HUDEMANN, RAINER: *Die 'Reichskristallnacht' in der Politik des 'Dritten Reiches'*. [In]: Juden in Deutschland. Lebenswelten und Einzelschicksale. Hrsg. von Reinhard Schneider [see No. 31400]. Pp. 9–34,

31825. NOVEMBER POGROM. KORN, SALOMON: *Die Aktualität der 'Reichskristallnacht'*. [In]: LBI Information, Nr. 4, Frankfurt am Main 1994.. Pp. 60–66.

——— NOVEMBER POGROM. Wacker, Ulrich: *Viermal neunter November: Gedenktage eines schwierigen Vaterlandes*. [See No. 31952.]

31826. NOVEMBER POGROM. WILLMS, JOHANNES, Hrsg.: *Der 9. November. 1918 – 1923 – 1938 – 1989*. Fünf Essays zur deutschen Geschichte. Von Peter Bender, Wolfgang Benz, Hans Mommsen, Fritz Stern und Heinrich August Winkler. Herausgegeben von Johannes Willms. München: Beck, 1994. 98 pp., notes (90–96). [Incl.: Vorwort: Der 9. November. Vier Zäsuren in der deutschen Geschichte (Johannes Willms, 7–10). Erziehung zur Unmenschlichkeit: der 9. November 1938 (Wolfgang Benz, 49–65). Vier Tage im November (Fritz Stern, 83–89).]

31827. ÖHRINGEN. *Jüdische Bürger in Öhringen*. Eine Dokumentation. [Hrsg.: Stadt Öhringen]. Öhringen. Stadt Öhringen, 1993. 128 pp., illus.

31828. OLDEN, RUDOLF & IKA: *'In tiefem Dunkel liegt Deutschland'. Von Hitler vertrieben – Ein Jahr deutsche Emigration*. Vorwort von Lion Feuchtwanger. Hrsg. und eingeleitet von Charmian Brinson und Marian Malet. Berlin: Metropol, 1994. 198 pp., notes (153–198). (Dokumente, Texte, Materialien, Bd. 11.) [R.O., 1885 Stettin – Sept. 1940, journalist, fled with his later wife Ika Halpern from Berlin via Prague and Paris to London; drowned after their boat was torpedoed on the way to the USA. Book was written in London between 1933 and 1934, but not publ.]

31829. PÄTZOLD, KURT/SCHWARZ, ERIKA: *'Auschwitz war für mich nur ein Bahnhof': Franz Noval, der Transportoffizier Adolf Eichmanns*. Berlin: Metropol, 1994. 240 pp. (Reihe Dokumente, Texte, Materialien, Bd. 13.) [Novak organised and registered deportation trains for Jews from many Nazi-occupied countries.]

31830. PSCHORR, ELIZABETH: *A privileged marriage*. The autobiography of Elizabeth Pschorr. Sausalito, Ca.: Windgate Press, 1994. IX, 368 pp., illus., tabs., genealogy. [E.P., née Holzer, b. Sept. 23, 1911 in Hamburg into an assimilated well-to-do family, describes her life in pre-war Germany, her marriage to F. Pschorr, a non-Jew, descendant of the brewery family; also her experiences during the Nazi era, the family's emigration to the U.S. and their subsequent life there.]

31831. RASTATT. *Rastatt 1933 bis 1945*. Katalog zur Ausstellung. Konzeption und Red.: Iris Baumgärtner [et al.], unter Mitarbeit von Anna-Ruth Löwenbrück [et al.]. Rastatt: Stadt Rastatt, Stadtarchiv/Stadtmuseum [1994?]. 166 pp., illus., facsims., maps, notes. [Incl.: Die Juden (Anna-Ruth Löwenbrück, 59–72).]

31832. REFUGEE POLICY. BARTROP, PAUL R.: *Australia and the Holocaust, 1933–45*. Melbourne: Australian Scholarly Pub., 1994. XVII, 304 pp., illus., ports., facsims., bibl. (289–299). [On Australia's restrictive refugee policy. Incl. the treatment of German, Austrian and other Central European Jews who went to Britain as refugees, and later were interned and sent to Australia on the 'Dunera' in 1940.]

31833. REFUGEE POLICY. BARTROP, PAUL R.: *From Lisbon to Jamaica: a study of British refugee rescue during the Second World War.* [In]: Immigrants & Minorities, Vol. 13, No. 1, London, March 1994. Pp. 48–64, notes. [Incl. German-Jewish refugees who had fled to Lisbon and one day before their expulsion were granted entry by Britain to Jamaica at British expense.]

31834. RENTSCHLER, ERIC: *Ministry of illusion: German film 1933–1945.* [In]: Film Comment, Vol. 30, No. 6, New York, Nov./Dec. 1994. Pp. 34–41., illus. [Incl. antisemitic films like 'Jud Süss'.]

31835. RESISTANCE BY NON-JEWS. DIPPER, CHRISTOF: *Der 20. Juli und die 'Judenfrage'.* [In]: Die Zeit, Nr. 27, Hamburg, 1. Juli 1994, p. 70. [On the antisemitic attitudes of some conservative members of the German resistance movement. A critical response: Sie erhoben sich, weil sie die Morde nicht dulden wollten; die Verfolgung der Juden als Motiv des 20. Juli (Peter Hoffmann) [in]: 'FAZ', Nr. 162, Frankfurt am Main, 15. Juli 1994, p. 6.]

31836. RESISTANCE BY NON-JEWS. FOGELMAN, EVA: *Conscience & courage: rescuers of Jews during the Holocaust.* New York; Anchor Books, 1994. XX, 393 pp., notes (323–354), bibl. (355–376). [Deals with gentile rescuers of Jews in several European countries, incl. Germany.] [Also by same author on this topic: *Rescuers of Jews during the Holocaust: a model for a caring community* [in]: Tikkun, Vol. 9, No. 2, Oakland, Ca., March-April 1994. Pp. 61–64, 90.]

31837. RESISTANCE BY NON-JEWS. GUSHEE, DAVID P.: *The righteous Gentiles of the Holocaust: a Christian interpretation.* Minneapolis, Mn.: Fortress Press, 1994. XIV, 258 pp. [Incl. Christian rescuers of Jews in Germany.]

31838. RESISTANCE BY NON-JEWS. GUSHEE, DAVID P.: *Why they helped the Jews: what we can learn from the religious Gentiles of the Holocaust.* [In]: Christianity Today, Vol. 38, No. 12, Carol Stream, Il., Oct. 24, 1994. Pp. 32–36. [Incl. Christian rescuers of Jews in Germany; also deals with Christian antisemitism throughout history.]

31839. ROTHSCHILD, RECHA: *Verschlungene Wege. Identitätssuche einer deutschen Jüdin.* Mit einem Nachwort vers. und bearb. von Karin Hartewig. 217 pp., port., facsims. Frankfurt am Main: Fischer Taschenbuch Verlag, 1994. (Originalausg.) [Incl.: Recha Rothschild – Mirjam Wolf. Ein Nachwort (Karin Hartewig, 207–218).] [Draft of an autobiographical novel found after the German reunification in the archives of the SED. Author, b. 1880 in Frankfurt am Main, was a teacher and Communist journalist, imprisoned 1933–1935, emigr. via Switzerland to France, interned at Gurs. Returned to Germany (East) in 1948 where she died in 1964.]

31840. RUHR. GLEISING, GÜNTER [et al.]: *Die Verfolgung der Juden in Bochum und Wattenscheid. Die Jahre 1933–1945 in Berichten, Bildern und Dokumenten.* Gewidmet den Opfern von Rassismus und Völkermord. Hrsg.: VVN-Bund der Antifaschisten, Kreisvereinigung Bochum. Bochum: Wurf, 1993. 72 pp., illus., facsims. (Schriften zur antifaschistischen Geschichte Bochums, Nr. 4.)

31841. SARFATTI, MICHELE: *Mussolini contro gli ebrei. Cronaca dell'elaborazione delle leggi del 1938.* Torino: Silvio Zamorani, 1994. 199 pp., illus., facsims., tabs., docs., notes. [On the introduction of the 'Nuremberg laws' in Italy, affecting Italian Jews and Jewish refugees.]

31842. SAXONY. *Medizin und Judentum.* Vorträge auf der Gedächtnisveranstaltung in Dresden aus Anlaß des Novemberpogroms 1938. Hrsg. von Nora Goldenbogen [et al.]. Dresden: Verein für regionale Geschichte und Politik Dresden e.V., 1994. 64 pp., illus., notes. (Historische Blätter, Sonderheft.) [Incl. (titles partly abbr.): Die Verfolgung, Vertreibung und Vernichtung jüdischer Ärzte nach 1933 in Deutschland, dargestellt am Beispiel der Stadt Leipzig (Susanne Hahn, 7–14). Zur Erinnerung an den Arzt und Parlamentarier Dr. Julius Moses (Kurt Nemitz, 15–26). Zur Rolle jüdischer Ärzte in der Dermatologie (Albrecht Scholz, 27–33). Das Schicksal der jüdischen Ärzte, Zahnärzte und Dentisten in Dresden nach 1933 (Antje & Matthias Koch, 34–41). Schicksale jüdischer Ärzte nach 1933 in Chemnitz (Mario Herrlich, 42–50). Jüdische Zahnärzte und Dentisten nach 1933 in Leipzig (47–50). Die deutsche Zahnärzteschaft im Umgang mit ihrer NS-Vergangenheit (Wolfgang Kirchhoff, 51–59). Juden in Dresden nach 1945 (Nora Goldenbogen, 60–64).]

31843. *Schindler's List.* Selected essays on the film 'Schindler's List' by Steven Spielberg (1994). Lebemann und Lebensretter (Janusz Tycner) [in]: Die Zeit, Nr. 6, Hamburg, 4. Feb. 1994, p. 18. Der Spieler (Hanno Loewy) [&] Fortsetzung der Lichterketten mit anderen Mitteln? Zur Bedeutung von 'Schindler's List' als Medien-Weltereignis (Detlev Claussen) [&] Deutsche Ausreden; über einige Lehren, die man hierzulande aus 'Schindlers Liste' ziehen kann – wenn man nur will [in]: Frankfurter Jüdische Nachrichten, Nr. 84, Frankfurt am Main, März/April 1994. Pp. 11–12 [&] 13–14 [&] 15–16. Anathema. Der Holocaust und das Bilderverbot (Siegfried Kohlhammer) [in]: Merkur, Jg. 48, H. 538–549, Stuttgart, 1994. Pp. 500–509. Bilder-Ballett mit Rune und Tod. Einspruch gegen Spielbergs Holocaust-Film 'Schindlers Liste' (Dietrich Kuhlbrodt) [in]: Lutherische Monatshefte, Jg. 33, Nr. 3, Hamburg, 1994. Pp. 33–35. Tränen und Zorn. Gegen den Verriß des Films 'Schindlers Liste' (Christoph Quarch) [&] Verbrechen und Spiel. Der Holocaust im Film und im jüdischen Theater (Matthias Morgenstern) [in]: Lutherische Monatshefte, Jg. 33, Nr.5, Hamburg, 1994. Pp.26–30.]

31844. SCHLÖR, JOACHIM: *Von Berlin nach Tel Aviv.* [In]: Menora 5, München, 1994. Pp. 231–259, notes. [On a lawyer from Berlin and his wife, who emigr. to Palestine in 1939. Based on documents found in a Tel Aviv antiquarian bookshop.]

31845. SCHMALLENBERG. *Der Weg in den Holocaust: mit Bildern aus dem Leben der jüdischen Gemeinde in Schmallenberg.* Texte zur Ausstellung im November 1994 anläßlich des 750jährigen Bestehens der Stadt Schmallenberg. [Verantw. für Bild und Text: Hannelore Schenk]. Schmallenberg: Glade, 1994. 60 pp., illus. [An addendum, a 'Dokumentationsmappe' under the same title, comp. by Hannelore Schenk, is publ. 1995.]

31846. *Der Schocken Verlag/Berlin. Jüdische Selbstbehauptung in Deutschland 1931–1938.* Essayband zur Ausstellung 'Dem suchenden Leser unserer Tage' der Nationalbibliothek Luxemburg. Hrsg. von Saskia Schreuder und Claude Weber in Verbindung mit Silke Schaeper und Frank Grunert. Berlin: Akademie Verlag, 1994. 406 pp., illus., bibl., index. [Incl. the following essays (titles partly abbr.): Salman Schocken (Volker Dahm, 15–38). Zur Programmatik des Schocken Verlags (Claude Weber, 39–54). Bubers Wiederherstellung der Gesprochenheit der Schrift (Emmanuel Bulz, 105–114). Rückführung zum Judentum (Klaus S. Davidowicz, 115–128). Geschichtliche Literatur im Schocken Verlag (Matthias Hambrock, 129–148). Schocken und Agnon (Ariel Hirschfeld, 191–202). Ludwig Strauß und der Schocken Verlag (Hans Otto Horch, 203–224). Das Forschungsinstitut für hebräische Dichtung (Peter S. Lehnardt, 299–320). Zur Buchgestaltung (Heinz-Hermann Hoppe, 321–320). Hebräische Typographie (Ittai J. Tamari, 327–346). Die Geschichte der Schocken Bibliothek bis 1939 (Silke Schaeper, 347–360). Der Schocken Verlag im Spiegel der jüdischen Kritik (Saskia Schreuder, 377–396).] [Cf.: Dienst an der Schrift, unerwidertes Geschenk an die Deutschen (Hans-Joachim Neubauer) [in]: 'FAZ', Nr. 98, Frankfurt am Main, 27. April 1995, p. 14.]

31847. SCHREIER, HELMUT/HEYL, MATTHIAS, Hrsg.: *Die Gegenwart der Schoah. Zur Aktualität des Mordes an den europäischen Juden.* Hamburg: Dr. R. Krämer, 1994. 287 pp., footnotes. [Incl. (titles partly abbr.): Von den Metaphern und der geteilten Erinnerung – Auschwitz, Holocaust, Schoah, Churban, 'Endlösung' [&] Generationen und Identitäten nach dem Mord an den europäischen Juden (Matthias Heyl, 1132; 51–92. Ruth Klügers 'Weiter leben' als weibliche Rekonstruktion der Holocaust-Erfahrung (Jennifer Taylor, 33–50). Über die seltsame Schuld der Ermordeten (Emanuel Hurwitz, 149–174). Abspaltung und Projektion: Zur Psychodynamik antisemitischer Strukturen (Dierk Juelich, 175–194). Die Affäre Auerbach. Zur Virulenz des Antisemitismus in den Gründerjahren der Bundesrepublik (Wolfgang Kraushaar, 195–218). Der Holocaust als Gegenstand der bundesdeutschen Strafjustiz (Gerhard Werle, 219–240). Möglichkeiten und Grenzen der Vermittlung jüdischer Geschichte im Unterricht (Gisela Schacht, 241–262). Didaktischer Vorschlag zum Projekt der Erziehung nach Auschwitz (Helmut Schreier, 263–284). Incl. also four essays under the heading of 'Aspekte des Umgangs mit der Erinnerung außerhalb Deutschlands'.]

31848. SCHWANDA-ARNBOM, MARIE-THERES,: *'Bürgerliche, allzu bürgerliche Begriffe . . .'; Lebenserfahrungen in der Emigration.* [In]: Zeitgeschichte, Jg. 20, H. 3/4, Wien, März/April, 1993. Pp. 113–129, notes. [Analyses the letters of Stefan Herz-Kestranek to his parents (written between 1938 and 1939) as an example of the continuation of bourgeois attitudes and life styles in the emigration, i. e. even after emigration and its attendant poverty.]

―――― SHANGHAI. [See Nos. 31667–31669.]

31849. SILVER, ERIC: *Sie waren stille Helden: Frauen und Männer, die Juden vor den Nazis retteten.* Aus dem Engl. von Verena Koch. München: Hanser, 1994. 252 pp., illus. [Orig. publ. in 1992 under the title 'The book of the just'; see No. 29458/YB XXXVIII.]

31850. SOMMER-LEFKOVITS, ELISABETH: *Ihr seid auch hier in dieser Hölle? Erinnerungen an die unheilvollen Zeiten 1944–1945.* Zürich: Chronos, 1994. 111 pp., illus., facsims. [Memoirs of a Hungarian Jewess, a pharmacist, b. 1904 in Dünaföldvar, deported 1944 from Presov to Ravensbrück, later to Bergen-Belsen, where she and her seven-year old son were liberated. Memoirs were written in Hungarian and translated by the author into German. The author died in 1994.]

31851. STEININGER, ROLF, ed.: *Der Umgang mit dem Holocaust. Europa – USA – Israel.* Hrsg. von Rolf Steininger unter Mitarbeit von Ingrid Böhler. Köln: Böhlau, 1994. 498 pp., footnotes, index (493–498). (Schriften des Instituts für Zeitgeschichte der Universität Innsbruck und des Jüdischen Museums Hohenems, Bd. 1.) [Cont. the sections (titles partly condensed): Einleitung. Nach dem Holocaust 1945–1994 (Rolf Steiniger, 11–30). 1. Vergangenheit und Gegenwart (pp. 31–118; cont. the essays): Die Durchführung der 'Endlösung' (Hermann Graml, 31–44). Ökonomische Aspekte der 'Endlösung' (Ulrich Herbert, 45–59). Zionismus und Antisemitismus im Dritten Reich. Folgen für die Zeit nach dem Holocaust (Francis R. Nicosia, 60–76). Der ewige Judenhaß – oder: Kein Ende der Geschichte? (Rolf Steiniger, 77–102). Die 'Auschwitz-Lüge' (Wolfgang Benz, 103–118). 2. Deutschland und Österreich (pp. 119–264; cont. the essays): Der Umgang der Kirche mit dem Holocaust nach 1945 (Ernst Klee, 119–136). Die katholische Kirche, der Vatikan und der Holocaust 1940–1965 (Michael Phayer, 137–146). Zur Aufrechterhaltung des österreichischen Opfermythos (Thomas Albrich, 147–166). Rehabilitierung der Juden oder materielle Wiedergutmachung – ein Vergleich (Frank Stern, 167–182). Die Behandlung von Opfern und Tätern des Nationalsozialismus durch die Republik Österreich (Brigitte Bailer, 183–197). Die Verfolgung von NS-Verbrechen in der Bundesrepublik Deutschland, der DDR und Österreich (Helge Grabitz, 198–220). Nationalsozialismus und Holocaust in westdeutschen Schulbüchern (Falk Pingel, 221–232). Der Umgang mit dem Holocaust in der DDR (Olaf Groehler, 233–245). Der 9. November 1938 in der politischen Kultur der DDR (Angelika Timm, 246–264). Sections 3 – 9 deal with Poland, Czchechoslovakia, France, Italy, USA, Israel and the Arabs. 10. Geschichte und Erinnerung (pp. 433–482; cont. essays on Holocaust memorials and general aspects of Holocaust remembering and trauma by Sybil Milton, Arno J. Mayer, John Bunzl and Dan Diner.]

31852. STROBL, INGRID: *Das Feld des Vergessens. Jüdischer Widerstand und deutsche 'Vergangenheitsbewältigung'.* Berlin: Ed. ID-Archiv, 1994. 140 pp. [Incl. an essay on the commandant of Treblinka, Kurt Franz, and a critical review of the Wannsee Conference memorial exhibition. Further essays are listed according to subject.]

31853. STUTTGART. BENZ, WOLFGANG: *Das Opfer als Täter? Die Lebensgeschichte des Erwin Goldmann.* [In]: Dachauer Hefte, Jg. 10, H. 10, Dachau, 1994. Pp. 225–242, footnotes. [Incl. documents and memoirs of the Stuttgart dentist E. G. (1891–1981), director of the Stuttgart dental hospitals until his dismissal in 1933. Baptised as a young man and married to a non-Jewish woman, G. displayed strong nationalist attitudes. Member of the Paulus-Bund until 1937. From 1940 until 1943 he co-operated with the 'SD', the 'SS' and the Gestapo, which led to his prosecution after the war.]

31854. TARRAB-MASLATON, MARTIN: *Rechtliche Strukturen der Diskriminierung der Juden im Dritten Reich*. Berlin: Duncker & Humblot, 1993. 281 pp., footnotes. (Zugl.: Bonn, Univ., Diss., 1991.) (Schriften zur Rechtsgeschichte, H. 61.)

31855. THERESIENSTADT. HERRMANNOVÁ, MARGIT: *Das Haupt der Medusa*. [In]: Judaica Bohemiae, Vol. 29, Praha, 1993. Pp. 76–80, notes. [Personal recollections of the transport from Theresienstadt to Auschwitz-Birkenau into the 'Familienlager'.]

31856. THERESIENSTADT. KÁRNÝ, MIROSLAV/KEMPER, RAIMUND/KÁRNÁ, MARGITA: *Theresienstädter Studien und Dokumente 1994*. Prag: Academia/Ed. Theresienstädter Initiative, 1994. 254 pp., illus., facsims., notes, index. [Cont.: Vorwort (7–10). Theresienstadt im Spiegel amerikanischer Dokumentation (Shlomo Aronson, 11–35). Deutsche Juden in Theresienstadt (Miroslav Kárný, 36–53). Eine Deportation nach Theresienstadt (Zur Rolle des Banalen bei der Durchsetzung des Monströsen) (Michael Zimmermann, 54–73; analyses the bureaucratic procedures of deportations from Essen to Theresienstadt, July 1942). Deportationen von Theresienstadt nach Majdanek (Miroslav Kryl, 74–89). Zur Geschichte der Produktionsstätten im Theresienstädter Ghetto (Rudolf Freiberger, 90–108). Ghetto Theresienstadt und Israel (Ruth Bondy, 109–121). Eine Reflektion der Erfahrungen aus Auschwitz (Tomás Radil, 122–127). Zur Problematik der deutschen Lyrik aus Theresienstadt 1941–1945 (Ludvík Váklavek (128–135). Aus der Tiefe der Vergangenheit (Anna Hyndráková/Anna Lorencová, 135–143; on an oral-history project organised by the Jewish Museum in Prague). . . . um Unmittelbares mitzuteilen (Pavel Stránsky, 144–148; deals with two novels by the Israeli writer O.B. Kraus about life in the Theresienstadt 'Familienlager' in Auschwitz-Birkenau, where he and the author were imprisoned). Die Eichmann-Männer (Winfried R. Garscha, 149–151; critical review of Hans Safrian's book Die Eichmann-Männer, see No. 30503/YB XXXIX). Jüdische Opfer des nationalsozialistischen Deutschland aus den böhmischen Ländern (Pavel Skorpil, 152–166). Dokumentation: Tagebuch (Oktober 1944 – Mai 1945 (Alisha Shek, 169–206). Über die Theresienstädter Kabarette (kommentiert von Eva Sormová) (Josef Taussig/Eva Sormová, 207–252).]

31857. THERESIENSTADT. MÜLLER-TUPATH, KARLA: *Das heimliche Leben des Anton Burger, Lagerkommandant von Theresienstadt*. Mit einem Vorwort von Simon Wiesenthal. Hamburg: Konkret Literatur Verlag, 1994. 199 pp., illus., notes. [On the life of the former 'Lagerkommandant' of the Theresienstadt ghetto (1943–1944) A.B., who lived as Anton Bauer undiscovered from 1961 until his death in 1991 in Essen.]

31858. *Truth and lamentation: poems and stories on the Holocaust*. Ed. by Milton Teichman and Sharon Leder. Urbana: Univ. of Illinois Press, 1994. 526 pp.

31859. TURNER, BARRY: *Kindertransport: eine beispiellose Rettungsaktion*. Mit einer Einleitung von Lucie Kaye. Übers. aus dem Engl. von Anna Kaiser. Gerlingen: Bleicher, 1994. 269 pp., illus. [For Engl. orig. edn., publ. in 1990, see No. 27404/YB XXXVI.]

31860. URBAN, SUSANNE: *Verbannung in ein Ghetto ohne Mauern. Jüdischer Verlag und Philo-Verlag 1933–1938*. [In]: Buchhandelsgeschichte. [Beilage zum] Börsenblatt für den deutschen Buchhandel, Jg. 161, Frankfurt am Main, 1994. B 12–29, illus., notes, bibl.

31861. WARBURG. HERMES, HERMANN: *Deportationsziel Riga: Schicksale Warburger Juden*. 2. Aufl. Warburg: Hermes, 1993. 148 pp., illus., map, bibl. (Warburger Schriften, 1.)

31862. WARENDORF. GERSTE, HANS-JÖRG: *Von der Pogromnacht zur Deportation*. Unveröffentlichtes Material zu Verfolgung und Schicksal der jüdischen Bürger von Oelde (1938–1945). Warendorf: Kreis Warendorf. Der Oberkreisdirektor, 1994. 82 pp., illus., facsims., docs., notes. (Veröffentlichungen aus dem Kreisarchiv Warendorf, Reihe 2, H. 6.) [Incl. personal memoirs of the deportation to the ghetto of Riga and the concentration camp Kaiserwald.]

31863. WASSENBERG. HEINRICHS, HERIBERT: *Betty Reis. Leben und Leiden eines jüdischen Mädchens aus Wassenberg*. [In]: Heimatkalender des Kreises Heinsberg 1994. Heinsberg, 1994. Pp. 167–183, illus., facsims., notes.

31864. WEISS, YFAAT: *'Ostjuden' in Deutschland als Freiwild. Die nationalsozialistische Außenpolitik zwischen Ideologie und Wirklichkeit.* [In]: Tel Aviver Jahrbuch für deutsche Geschichte, Bd. 23, Gerlingen, 1994. Pp. 215–232.

31865. WESTPHALIA. *Verdrängung und Vernichtung der Juden in Westfalen.* Hrsg. von Arno Herzig, Karl Teppe, Andreas Determann. Münster: Ardey, 1994. 262 pp., footnotes. (Forum Regionalgeschichte, 3.) [Incl.: Einleitung (Arno Herzig, 9–14). Die Verdrängung jüdischer Juristen aus dem Landgerichtsbezirk Bielefeld (Monika Minninger, 15–28). Die Ausweisungen von 'Ostjuden' aus dem Ruhrgebiet (Ludger Heid, 29–43). Katholizismus und Antisemitismus in Westfalen. Ein Desiderat (Wilhelm Damberg, 44–61). 'Nichtarische' Christen in der Westfälischen Provinzialkirche (Jochen-Christoph Kaiser, 62–75). Zwischen Verfolgung und Shoah. Die Zerstörung der Synagogen in Westfalen (Saskia Rohde, 76–90). Die 'Entjudung' der mittelständischen Wirtschaft im Regierungsbezirk Arnsberg (Gerhard Kratzsch, 91–114). Ausgrenzung und 'Arisierung' im Vorfeld der Endlösung (Avraham Barkai, 115–124). Vor der Deportation. Briefe Münsteraner Eltern an ihre Kinder in der Fremde [&] 'Versucht bitte alles, um zu erfahren, was aus mir geworden ist'. Der Brief von Lieselotte Rosenbaum aus dem Warschauer Ghetto (Gisela Möllenhoff, 125–142 & 156–168). Die Deportation Mindener Jüdinnen und Juden 1941 nach Riga (Marianne Nordsiek, 143–155). Autobiographische Zeugnisse westfälischer Juden über ihre Deportation und KZ-Haft (Diethard Aschoff, 169–214). Ausgegrenzt und verdrängt im 'Dritten Reich' – ungeliebt in der Bundesrepublik. Die jüdischen Rechtsanwälte (Eva Douma, 215–223). Rückkehr ohne Heimat. Jüdische EmigrantInnen und Bundesrepublik Deutschland (Joachim Meynert, 224–230). Das Kreuz mit dem Davidstern: Christen und Juden nach dem Holocaust (Josef Foschepoth, 231–244). Neue Quellen zur Geschichte der westfälischen und lippischen Juden in den Staatsarchiven (Wolfgang Müller, 245–262).]

31866. WOLFF, ANNI: *Schließlich waren wir alle jung und lebenslustig. Erinnerungen: von Berlin nach Israel.* Mit Beiträgen von Gerd E. Höhne und Herbert Scherer. Berlin: Mackensen, 1993. 59 pp., illus. [Author, née Gattel, b. 1913 in Berlin, emigr. 1936 to Palestine.]

31867. WOOD, E. THOMAS/JANKOWSKI, STANISLAW M.: *Karski. How one man tried to stop the Holocaust.* Foreword by Elie Wiesel. New York: John Wiley & Sons, 1994. VIII, 316 pp.

B. Jewish Resistance

31868. ADAM, URSULA: *'Die Generalsrevolte'. Deutsche Emigranten und der 20. Juli 1944.* Eine Dokumentation. Berlin: Aufbau Taschenbuch Verl., 1994. 234 pp. (AtV; Dokument und Essay.)

31869. CARTARIUS, ULRICH: *Opposition gegen Hitler.* Bilder, Texte, Dokumente. Mit einem Essay von Karl Otmar von Aretin. Berlin: Siedler, 1994. 315 pp., illus., ports. (Deutscher Widerstand 1933–1945. Zeitzeugnisse und Analysen.) [Incl. resistance by Jews.]

31870. COPPI, HANS/DANYEL, JÜRGEN/TUCHEL, JOHANNES, Hrsg.: *Die Rote Kapelle im Widerstand gegen den Nationalsozialismus.* Berlin: Hentrich, 1994. 307 pp., illus., facsims., docs., notes, bibl. (282–297), index.

—— GREBING, HELGA/WICKERT, CHRISTL, Hrsg.: *Das 'andere Deutschland' im Widerstand gegen den Nationalsozialismus.* Beiträge zur politischen Überwindung der nationalsozialistischen Diktatur im Exil und im Dritten Reich. [See No. 32088.]

31871. *Lexikon des deutschen Widerstandes.* Hrsg. von Wolfgang Benz und Walter H. Pehle. Frankfurt am Main: S. Fischer, 1994. 429 pp. [Incl. the following articles: Widerstand der Verfolgten (Barbara Distel, 113–127). Exil und Widerstand (Patrik von zur Mühlen, 128–140). Jüdischer Widerstand (Konrad Kwiet, 234–236); also entries on individual Jews, the Baum group, Zionist underground, hiding Jews, exile.]

31872. LUSTIGER, ARNO: *Zum Kampf auf Leben und Tod! Das Buch vom Widerstand der Juden 1933–1945*. Köln: Kiepenheuer und Witsch, 1994. 628 pp., illus., maps, bibl. (593–610), index (611–628). [Essays are arranged under the following sections: I. Zur Einführung, 15–40; incl.: Jüdischer Widerstand – eine historische Bewertung (Israel Gutmann, 26–34). Jüdischer und europäischer Widerstand (Nathan Eck, 35–40). II. Deutschland, 41–76; incl.: Zur Problematik des Widerstandes deutscher Juden (Werner Jochmann, 44–46). Jüdischer Widerstand in Deutschland (Arnold Paucker, 47–55). Die Herbert-Baum-Gruppe (K. Kwiet/H. Eschwege, 56–64). Werner Scharff und die Gemeinschaft für Frieden und Aufbau; Flugblatt Generalmobilmachung; Chug Chaluzi – eine zionistische Untergrundorganisation in Berlin; Hechaluz – eine zionistische Rettungsorganisation; Georg Hornstein – das Bekenntnis eines jüdischen Kämpfers (66–76). References to German-Jewish resistance fighters also in Parts III – XII.] [Cf.: Nicht nur passiv geblieben. Eine erste Gesamtdarstellung des jüdischen Widerstandes 1933–1945 (Willi Jasper) [in]: Die Zeit, Nr. 45, Hamburg, 4. Nov. 1994, p. 16. Ein argloses Lamm, zur Schlachtbank geführt? (Julius H. Schoeps) [in]: 'FAZ', Nr. 3, Frankfurt am Main, 4. Jan. 1995, p. 5. Kämpfer, nicht Lämmer (Miryam Gümbel) [in]: 'Allgemeine', Jg. 49, Nr. 22, Bonn, 3. Nov. 1994. Passiv bis zum Ende? Keineswegs! (Peter Tscherne) [in]: Aufbau, Vol. 61, No. 1, New York, Jan. 6, 1995, p. 6. Versuch einer Rehabilitation (Eva-Elisabeth Fischer) [in]: Süddeutsche Zeitung, Nr. 68, München, 22. März 1995.]

31873. RIES, MATTHIAS: *Jüdischer Widerstand im 'Dritten Reich'*. Trier: Kulturverein AphorismA (Jakobstr. 33, 54290 Trier), 1994. 28 pp., bibl.

31874. SCHABER, IRME: *Gerta Taro. Fotoreporterin im Spanischen Bürgerkrieg*. Eine Biografie. Marburg: Jonas, 255 pp., illus. [G.T., (orig. Pohorylle), b. 1911 in Lemberg (Lvov), grew up in Stuttgart and Leipzig, emigr. to Paris 1933, photo-journalist, friend of Robert Capa (André Friedmann), died at the age of 26 as a front line photo-reporter of the Spanish Civil War.]

31875. SEGAL, LILLI: *Vom Widerspruch zum Widerstand. Erinnerungen einer Tochter aus gutem Hause*. Essen: Neuer Weg, 1991. 254 pp., maps. [First publ. in 1986, see No. 24733/YB XXXIII.] [L.S., b. 1913 in Berlin, active in German and French Resistance, now lives in Berlin.] [For details see No. 24733/YB XXXIII.]

31876. STEINBACH, PETER/TUCHEL, JOHANNES: *Lexikon des Widerstandes 1933–1945*. München: Beck, 1994. 238 pp. [Incl. contribs. on German-speaking Jews and Jewish organisations.]

31877. STEINBACH, PETER: *Widerstand im Widerstreit. Der Widerstand gegen den Nationalsozialismus in der Erinnerung der Deutschen*. Ausgewählte Studien. Paderborn: Schöningh, 1994. 298 pp. [Incl.: Widerstand gegen den Nationalsozialismus aus dem Exil? Zur politischen und räumlichen Struktur der deutschen Emigration 1933–1945 (124–146). Selbstbehauptung als Widerstand: Widerstand von Juden als Thema deutsch-jüdischer Beziehungsgeschichte im 20. Jahrhundert (175–185).]

31878. *Widerstand gegen den Nationalsozialismus*. Hrsg. von Peter Steinbach und Johannes Tuchel. Berlin: Akademie-Verl., 1994. 672 pp., notes, bibl. (623–657), index (658–669). [Simultaneously publ. by Bundeszentrale für Politische Bildung, Bonn, 1994. (Schriftenreihe; Bundeszentrale für Politische Bildung, 323.).] [Incl.: Widerstand von Juden im Alltag und in nationalsozialistischen Lagern (Sylvia Rogge-Gau, 513–525). Auswahlbibliographie; incl. the sections: Exil; Hilfe für Verfolgte; Selbstbehauptung und Widerstand von Juden (649–652).]

IV. POSTWAR

A. General

31879. ABSE, LEO: *Wotan, my enemy: can Britain live with the Germans in the European Union?* London: Robson Books, 1994. XIV, 274 pp., bibl. [Author, of partly German-Jewish descent, discusses roots of Germany's troubled past and the way it is dealt with in Germany today;

also incl. the role assimilated Jews played in underestimating Nazism.] [Cf.: Forbidden territory (Anthony Howard) [in]: The Sunday Times, London, May 8, 1994. Attempting to discover what makes Teutons tick (Geoffrey Goodman) [in]: Jewish Chronicle, London, May 20, 1994.]

31880. *Antisemitism world report.* London: Institute of Jewish Affairs, 1994. 253 pp. [Incl.: Austria (2–12), Germany (34–42), Switzerland (80–84).]

31881. AUSTRIA. ADUNKA, EVELYN: *Friedrich Torberg und Hans Weigel – Zwei jüdische Schriftsteller im Nachkriegsösterreich.* [In]: Modern Austrian Literature, Vol. 27, Nos. 3–4, Riverside, Ca., 1994. Pp. 213–238. [Deals with the differing feelings these two authors have towards their Jewish background; Torberg, who saw his 'Jewishness' as a positive and enriching influence, and Weigel, who tried to deny his background and saw it as a burden.]

31882. AUSTRIA. *Contemporary Austrian Studies, Vol. 2* [with the issue title]: *The Kreisky era in Austria.* Ed. by Günter Bishof, Anton Pelinka, and Oliver Rathkolb. New Brunswick, N.J.: Transaction Books, 1994. 267 pp., illus., notes, biographical data. [Incl.: Kreisky and the Jews (Herbert Pierre Secher, 10–31). Bruno Kreisky's life as biography (review essay, 205–221). Austrian Jews from emancipation to Holocaust (John Haag, 222–237; review essay).]

31883. AUSTRIA. MICHAELS, JENNIFER E.: *Is Stein paranoid? Peter Henisch's reflections on the Jewish experience in Austria after the presidential election of 1986 in his novel 'Steins Paranoia'.* [In]: Modern Austrian Literature, Vol. 27, Nos. 3–4, Riverside, Ca., 1994. Pp. 107–126.

31884. AUSTRIA. MITTEN, RICHARD: *The eyes of the beholder: allied wartime attitudes and the delimiting of the 'Jewish Question' for post-war Austria.* [In]: Tel Aviver Jahrbuch für deutsche Geschichte, Bd. 23, Gerlingen, 1994. Pp. 345–370.

31885. AUSTRIA. WASSERMANN, HEINZ P.: *'Lange lebe Deutschland, lange lebe Argentinien, lange lebe Österreich . . .'. Der Prozess gegen Adolf Eichmann: eine Analyse historischer Bewußtseinsbildung durch die Tagespresse.* [In]: Zeitgeschichte, Jg. 20, H. 5/6, Wien, Mai/Juni 1993. Pp. 249–259, notes.

31886. BARZEL, NEIMA: *The Yishuv's call for punishment of Germany (1944–1947).* [In Hebrew, with English summary.] [In]: Cathedra for the History of Eretz Israel and its Yishuv, No. 73, Jerusalem, Sept. 1994. Pp. 158–180.

31887. BERGMANN, WERNER: *Medienöffentlichkeit und extremistisches Meinungsspektrum. Die Süddeutsche Zeitung und der Fall 'Adolf Bleibtreu'.* [In]: Jahrbuch für Antisemitismusforschung 3, Frankfurt am Main; New York, 1994. Pp. 51–67. [On a debate about antisemitism in 1949 and its implications for the present day.]

31888. BERLIN. NACHAMA, ANDREAS: *Zur Zurückdrängung des Rechtsextremismus in Deutschland. Die Öffentlichkeitsarbeit jüdischer Gemeinden am Beispiel Berlins.* [In]: Gerhard Hentrich – der Verleger. Eine Festschrift zum 70. Geburtstag für Gerhard Hentrich. Hrsg. von Werner Buchwald und Hermann Simon. Berlin: Ed. Hentrich, 1994. Pp. 108–119.

31889. BROCHHAGEN, ULRICH: *Nach Nürnberg. Vergangenheitsbewältigung und Westintegration in der Ära Adenauer.* Hamburg: Junius, 1994. 467 pp., notes (359–446), bibl. (447–464), index. (Schriftenreihe des Hamburger Instituts für Sozialforschung.) [Cont. chapts. on the prosecution of Nazi crimes, post-war antisemitism in Germany and the Eichmann Trial.]

31890. BROCKE, EDNA: *Jews in the new Germany: what has changed?* [In]: European Judaism, Vol. 27, No. 2, London, Autumn 1994. Pp. 73–78.

31891. COHN, MICHAEL: *The Jews in Germany, 1945–1993: the building of a minority.* Westport, Ct.: Praeger, 1994. XIV, 128 pp., bibl. (121–124).

31892. EHRLICH, ERNST LUDWIG, ed.: *Der Umgang mit der Shoah. Wie leben Juden der zweiten Generation mit dem Schicksal der Eltern?* Gerlingen: Schneider, 1993. 96 pp., notes. [A collection of essays, some of which were previously publ. Incl.: Der Mord an den europäischen Juden und die Geschichte (Eberhard Jäckel, 11–26). Die Bedeutung von Auschwitz für die Juden [&] Über jüdische Existenz in der Bundesrepublik Deutschland (Ernst Ludwig Ehrlich, 27–44 [&] 57–68). Die Bedeutung des Holocaust für das Selbstverständnis der israelischen Gesellschaft (Chaim Schatzker, 45–56). Zur Identität der Juden in der BRD (Micha Brumlik, 69–88).]

31893. ESSLINGEN. SCHORSCH, ISMAR: *Das Schwert und das Buch.* [In]: Aufbau, Jg. 60, New York, July 8, 1994. Pp. 16–19, port. [Personal recollections and general reflections on the occasion of a gathering held in Esslingen, July 3, 1994, to commemorate the 50th anniversary of the death of the author's grandfather, Theodor Rothschild, in Theresienstadt.] [See also Nos. 31896 and 31998.]

31894. FRANKFURT am Main. KUGELMANN, CILLY: *Die jüdische 'Stunde Null'. Ein Rückblick auf die ersten Nachkriegsjahre in Frankfurt am Main.* [In]: Frankfurter Jüdische Nachrichten, Nr. 84, Frankfurt am Main, März/April 1994. Pp. 3–4.

31895. GRODE, WALTER: *Judenhaß ohne Juden. Soziokultureller Antisemitismus und der Protest gegen die Moderne.* [In]: Lutherische Monatshefte, Nr. 5, Hamburg, 1994. Pp. 2–3. [Author comments on the arson attack on the Lübeck synagogue in May 1994.]

31896. GROEHLER, OLAF: *SED, VVN und Juden in der sowjetischen Besatzungszone Deutschlands (1945–1949).* [In]: Jahrbuch für Antisemitismusforschung 3, Frankfurt am Main; New York, 1994. Pp. 282–302.

31897. HANOVER. SCHORSCH, ISMAR: *Revisiting my father's synagogue.* [In]: Judaism, Vol. 43, No. 2, New York, Spring 1994. Pp. 205–211, notes. [Describes the Romanesque synagogue of Hanover for which the author's father served as rabbi and which was destroyed during the November Pogrom. Deals with the father's return visit to Hanover and his address at the opening of the new synagogue in Nov. of 1963.] [See also Nos. 31892 and 31998.]

31898. HERF, JEFFREY: *Antisemitismus in der SED.* Geheime Dokumente zum Fall Paul Merker aus SED- und MfS-Archiven. [In]: Vierteljahrshefte für Zeitgeschichte, Jg. 42, H. 4, München, Oktober 1994. Pp. 635–667, docs., footnotes. [P.M., until his denunciation and arrest leading Communist, principal target of a purge conducted by the East German regime in the aftermath of the Slansky Trial in Prague in 1952. P.M. (a non-Jew) had supported restitution payments to Jews and close relations with Israel.] [See also on the show trial against P.M. the author's article Der Geheimprozeß [in]: Die Zeit, Nr. 41, Hamburg, 7. Oktober 1994. Pp. 13, 14, 16, port.]

31899. HESSE. ALTARAS, THEA: *Das jüdische rituelle Tauchbad und: Synagogen in Hessen – was geschah seit 1945?* Teil II. Königstein im Ts.: Langewiesche, 1994. 180 pp., illus., graphs., map, bibl. (Die blauen Bücher.) [Deals with changes in the use of synagogues and other religious institutions between 1938 and 1988.]

31900. JACOBY, JESSICA [et al.], Hrsg.: *Nach der Shoa geboren. Jüdische Frauen in Deutschland.* Berlin: Elefanten Presse, 1994. 239 pp. [Cont. autobiographical texts, interviews and poems.]

31901. *Jewish voices, German words: growing up Jewish in postwar Germany and Austria.* Ed. and with an introd. by Elena Lappin. Transl. from the German by Krishna Winston. North Haven, Ct.: Catbird Press, 1994. 301 pp. [22 contributions in the form of stories, memoirs, and essays by German-Jewish and Austrian-Jewish writers, born during or after the war, who discuss their experience of growing up in Germany and Austria after World War II. Incl. both factual accounts and fiction.]

31902. *Jewish life in Germany today*. Ed. by Uri R. Kaufmann. Transl. by Susan Schwarz. Bonn: Inter Nationes, 1994. 215 pp., illus., ports., bibl. [Transl. of 'Jüdisches Leben heute in Deutschland'; for German edn. and table of contents see No. 30702/YB XXXIX.]

31903. KAPLAN, MARION: *Antisemitism in postwar Germany*. [In]: New German Critique, No. 58, Ithaca, N.Y., Winter 1993. Pp. 97–108.

—— KLÜGER, RUTH: *Gibt es ein 'Judenproblem' in der deutschen Nachkriegsliteratur?* [See in No. 32369.]

31904. KÖNIGSEDER, ANGELIKA/WETZEL, JULIANE: *Lebensmut im Wartesaal. Die jüdischen DPs (Displaced Persons) im Nachkriegsdeutschland*. Frankfurt am Main: Fischer Taschenbuch Verlag, 1994. 278 pp., illus., notes, bibl., indexes (names, subjects). [Incl. list of DP-camps.]

—— KRAUSHAAR, WOLFGANG: *Die Affäre Auerbach. Zur Virulenz des Antisemitismus in den Gründerjahren der Bundesrepublik*. [In]: Die Gegenwart der Schoah. Zur Aktualität des Mordes an den europäischen Juden. [See in No. 31849].

31905. LERNER, GERDA: *In the footsteps of the Cathars*. [In]: The Progressive, Vol. 58, No. 3, Madison, Wi., March 1994. Pp. 18–22. [Personal impressions by an American-Jewish academic while teaching in Germany. Author is disturbed by lingering antisemitism and a 'society cleansed of both Jews and guilt'.]

31906. MARKOVITS, ANDREI S.: *The politics of memory: the predicament of German-Jewish relations in the former Bundesrepublik and in post-wall Germany*. [In]: Brücken über dem Abgrund. Festschrift für Harry Zohn [see No. 32315]. Pp. 63–78.

—— *Markus Wolf. East Germany's Jewish master spy*. [See No. 32314.]

31907. NOLDEN, THOMAS: *Contemporary German-Jewish literature*. [In]: German Life and Letters, Vol. 47, No. 1, Oxford, Jan. 1994. Pp. 77–93, footnotes. [Incl. Maxim Biller, Irene Dische, Ester Dischereit, Barbara Honigmann, Ronnit Neumann, Jonathan Rubinstein, Raphael Seligmann.]

31908. NUREMBERG TRIALS. PERSICO, JOSEPH E.: *Nuremberg: infamy on trial*. New York: Viking, 1994. 520 pp., illus., notes, bibl.

31909. NUREMBERG TRIALS. TAYLOR, TELFORD: *Die Nürnberger Prozesse: Hintergründe, Analysen und Erkenntnisse aus heutiger Sicht*. Aus dem Amerikanischen von Michael Schmidt. München: Heyne, 1992. 799 pp., illus., bibl. (755–758). [For orig. edn. and details see No. 30708/YB XXXIX.]

31910. OBERLAENDER, FRANKLIN AHARON: *Zur Problematik der Identität christlicher Deutscher jüdischer Herkunft während und nach dem Nationalsozialismus und zur Identitätsentwicklung ihrer nach 1945 geborenen Kinder; eine sozial-psychologische empirische Forschungsarbeit auf fallkonstruktiver Grundlage*. Berlin, Freie Univ., Diss., 1993. 3 Mikrofiches.

31911. OSTOW, ROBIN: *From the Cold War through the Wende: history, belonging, and the self in East German Jewry*. [In]: The Oral History Review, Vol. 21, No. 2, Los Angeles, Winter 1993. Pp. 59–72.

31912. PROSECUTION OF NAZI CRIMES. ARENDT, HANNAH: *Eichmann in Jerusalem: a report on the banality of evil*. Rev. and enlarged edn. New York: Penguin Books, 1994. 312 pp. [For first edn. see No. 3790/YB IX.]

31913. PROSECUTION OF NAZI CRIMES. FREIWALD, AARON (with MARTIN MENDELSOHN): *The last Nazi: Josef Schwammberger and the Nazi past*. New York: Norton, 1994. 362 pp., notes (335–345); bibl. (346–349). [On the trial in 1992 in Germany of J. Schwammberger for crimes committed in Poland.]

31914. PROSECUTION OF NAZI CRIMES. LICHTENSTEIN, HEINER: *NS-Prozesse. Zum Ende eines Kapitels deutscher Justizgeschichte*. [In]: Tribüne, Jg. 33, H. 132, Frankfurt am Main, 1994. Pp. 146–156.

31915. PROSECUTION OF NAZI CRIMES. RENZ, ULRICH: *Zum Schutz der Mörder. NS-Verbrechen waren keine Kriegsverbrechen*. [In]: Tribüne, Jg. 33, H. 132, Frankfurt am Main, 1994. Pp. 158–168.

31916. PROSECUTION OF NAZI CRIMES. *Vereint vergessen? Justiz- und NS-Verbrechen in Deutschland*. Hrsg.: Landeszentrale für politische Bildung Nordrhein-Westfalen, Düsseldorf, 1994. 111 pp. [Cont.: Einführung; Nationalsozialismus und Justiz (Rolf Krumsiek, 11–16). Die Verfolgung von NS-Gewaltverbrechen in der Bundesrepublik Deutschland (Alfred Streim, 17–34). NS-Prozesse in der DDR (Kurt Pätzold, 35–50). Die Verfolgung von NS-Gewaltverbrechern in Österreich (Manfred Schausberger, 51–56). Die Verfolgung von NS-Gewaltverbrechen vor ausländischen Gerichten (Alfred Spieß, 57–68). NS-Prozesse und Öffentlichkeit (Heiner Lichtenstein, 69–76). Die zweite Schuld (Ralph Giordano, 77–92). Recht – nicht Rache. Kein Vergessen (Simon Wiesenthal, 93–102). NS-Vergangenheit als Aufgabe der politischen Bildung (Herbert Schnoor, 103–106).]

31917. PROSECUTION OF NAZI CRIMES. *Auschwitz – ein Prozess: Geschichte – Fragen – Wirkungen*. Hrsg. von Ulrich Schneider. Mit Beiträgen von Oskar Ansull [et al.]. Köln: PapyRossa, 1994. 156 pp. [Cont. 18 essays arranged under the sections: 1. Was war Auschwitz (11–66); 2. Der Prozeß (67–109); 3. Die Wirkungsgeschichte des Prozesses (110–155). Deals also with denial of the Holocaust, 'revisionism' and 'Vergangenheitsbewältigung'.]

31918. *Reemerging Jewish culture in Germany: life and literature since 1989*. Ed. and introd. by Sander L. Gilman and Karen Remmler. New York: New York Univ. Press, 1994. XII, 290 pp., index (283–290). [Incl. (titles partly abbr.): The contemporary German fascination for things Jewish: toward a Jewish minority culture (Jack Zippes, 15–45). A reemergence of German Jewry? (Y. Michael Bodemann, 46–61). Becoming strangers: Jews in Germany's five new provinces (Robin Ostow, 62–76). What is 'religion' among Jews in contemporary Germany? (Marion Kaplan, 77–112). Representation of Jews in the German media after 1989 (Katharina Ochse, 113–129). The 'ins' and 'outs' of the new Germany: Jews, foreigners, asylum seekers (Jeffrey M. Peck, 130–147). The Persian Gulf War and the Germans' 'Jewish Questions': transformation on the Left (Kizer Walker, 148–173). What keeps the Jews in Germany quiet? (Rafael Seligmann, 173–183). Tracing the genealogy of identity in the work of Esther Dischereit, Barbara Honigmann and Irene Dische (Karen Remmler, 184–209). Male sexuality and contemporary Jewish literature in German (Sander L. Gilman, 210–252). In defense of ambiguity (Susan Neiman, 253–265). No exit from this Jewry (Esther Dischereit, 266–282).]

31919. RESTITUTION. LUDWIG, JOHANNES: *Die doppelte Moral der Reprivatisierung: das jüdische Eigentum zwischen zweiter und dritter Enteignung*. [In]: Die Treuhand und die zweite Enteignung der Ostdeutschen. Hrsg. von Rüdiger Liedtke. München: Spangenberg, 1993. Pp. 114–135. [On restitution and indemnification claims in the former GDR.]

31920. RESTITUTION. PAWLITA, CORNELIUS: *'Wiedergutmachung' als Rechtsfrage? Die politische und juristische Auseinandersetzung um Entschädigung für die Opfer nationalsozialistischer Verfolgung (1945–1990)*. Frankfurt am Main; New York: Lang, 1994. 523 pp., footnotes, bibl. (472–514). (Europäische Hochschulschriften, Reihe II: Rechtswissenschaften; zugl.: Gießen, Univ., Diss., 1993.)

31921. ROSENFELD DE PRUSAK, KARIN MARIANA: *Identitätsprobleme bei jüdischen Jugendlichen in Deutschland und ihre Einflüsse auf den Verlauf der Adoleszenz*. Freiburg, Univ., Diss., 1993. [2], 79, [4] pp.

31922. SCHLESWIG-HOLSTEIN. *Rückkehr auf Zeit: Dokumentation zu den Besuchsreisen jüdischer ehemaliger Schleswig-Holsteiner in den Jahren 1986–1992*. Zusammengestellt von Gerd Stolz. Hrsg. von der Jüdischen Gemeinde in Hamburg. Heide: Boyens, 1992. 80 pp., illus., facsims., map, ports.

31923. SCHNEIDER, RICHARD CHAIM: *Zwischenwelten. Eine jüdische Jugend im heutigen Deutschland*. München: Kindler, 1994. 317 pp., bibl. (311–315). [About Jewish life in Germany; author, b. in Germany, belongs to the second generation of post-war Germany's Jews.]

—— SHAFIR, SHLOMO: *Goldmann and Adenauer*. [See No. 32426.]

31924. SHRIVASTAVA, ANJANA: *German neo-fascism and the politics of meaning*. [In]: Tikkun, Vol. 9, No. 4, Oakland, Ca., July/Aug. 1994. Pp. 9–12, 74, illus. [Incl. antisemitism.]

31925. STERN, FRANK: *From the liberation of the Jews to the unification of the Germans*. The discourse of antagonistic memories in Germany. [In]: Brücken über dem Abgrund. Festschrift für Harry Zohn [see in No. 323152]. Pp. 43–62.

31926. STERN, FRANK: *Jewish images in German films since 1945*. [In]: SICSA Report, No. 10, Jerusalem [The Hebrew University of Jerusalem], 1994. Pp. 2–4.

31927. STREIM, ALFRED: *Zur Legende von der 'zweiten Schuld'*. [In]: Tribüne, Jg. 33, H. 131, Frankfurt am Main, 1994. Pp. 129–142, footnotes. [Author is director of the Zentrale Stelle der Landesjustizverwaltungen zur Aufklärung von NS-Verbrechen, Ludwigsburg; his critical essay discusses 'Vergangenheitsbewältigung' and prosecution of Nazi crimes; esp. Ralph Giordano's book 'Die zweite Schuld' (see No. 24757/YB XXXIII) and Manfred Kittel's 'Die Legende von der zweiten Schuld' (see No. 31261/YB XXXIX).]

31928. TRAVERSO, ENZIO: *Allemagne: etre juif après Hitler*. [In]: Le Monde des Débats [Publication mensuelle de] Le Monde, Numéro 17, Paris, Mars 1994. Pp. 14–15.

31929. *Wie Fremdlinge im eigenen Land? Jüdische Identität in Deutschland*. Beiträge einer Tagung der Evangelischen Akademie Baden, 19. – 21. November 1993. Red.: Klaus Nagorni; Ralf Stieber. Mit Beitr. von Leonore Siegele-Wenschkewitz [et al.]. Hrsg.: Evangelische Akademie Baden. Karlsruhe: Evang. Akad. Baden, 1994. 74 pp., illus. (Herrenalber Protokolle, Bd. 100.)

B. Education and Teaching. Memorials

31930. ADLER, DAVID A.: *Hilde and Eli, children of the Holocaust*. Illustrated by Karen Ritz. New York: Holiday House, 1994. 1 vol. (unpag.), illus. [Biographies of two German-Jewish children and their experiences during the Holocaust, written for young people.]

31931. *Als eure Grosseltern jung waren: mit Kindern über den Holocaust sprechen*. Text von Judith S. Kestenberg, Bilder von Vivienne Koorland. Hamburg: Krämer, 1993. [72] pp., illus. [A book for children.]

31932. AUGUST, JOCHEN: *Annäherung an Auschwitz. Ein Versuch*. Analysen – Meinungen – Debatten. Polis, Nr. 10. Eine Schriftenreihe der Hessischen Landeszentrale für politische Bildung. Wiesbaden: Hess. Landeszentrale für pol. Bildung, 1994. 38 pp., bibl., map. [On the history of Auschwitz; also on the present situation. Incl. practical hints and addresses for visits and addresses of Polish Nazi memorial sites.]

31933. AUSCHWITZ. RYBACK, TIMOTHY W.: *Evidence of evil*. [In]: The New Yorker, New York, Nov. 15, 1994. Pp. 68–81. [On the Nazi's destruction of death camps at the end of the war. Discusses also the gradual disintegration of Auschwitz fifty years on.]

31934. BENZ, WOLFGANG: *Auschwitz and the Germans: the rememberance of the genocide*. [In]: Holocaust and Genocide Studies, Vol. 8, No. 1, Oxford, Spring 1994. Pp. 94–106, notes.

31935. BERGEN-BELSEN. RAHE, THOMAS: *Zur pädagogischen und wissenschaftlichen Arbeit der Gedenkstätte Bergen-Belsen*. [In]: Bulletin trimestriel de la Fondation Auschwitz. No. Special 42–43, Bruxelles, juillet – septembre 1994. Pp. 63–69.

31936. BERLIN. SCHITTENHELM, KARIN: *Mahnmal Putlitzbrücke: ein antisemitischer Bildersturm und seine Folgen.* [In]: Jahrbuch für Antisemitismusforschung 3, Frankfurt am Main; New York, 1994. Pp. 121–139. [On public reactions to a memorial in Berlin-Moabit, erected in 1987.]

31937. BRESHEET, HAIM/HOOD, STUART/JANSZ/LITZA: *The Holocaust for beginners* [sic]. Cambridge, Icon Books, 1994. 175 pp., illus. [Basic introduction to the history of antisemitism and Nazi annihilation of European Jewry.]

31938. BRUMLIK, MICHA: *Der Pogrom der 'Reichskristallnacht': Entwurf einer didaktischen Konzeption.* Frankfurt am Main: Arbeitsstelle zur Vorbereitung des Frankfurter Lern- und Dokumentationszentrums des Holocaust, [1993?]. 28 pp. (Materialien/ Arbeitsstelle zur Vorbereitung des Frankfurter Lern- und Dokumentationszentrum des Holocaust, Nr. 4.)

31939. BRUSTEN, MANFRED/WINKELMANN, BERND: *Wie denken deutsche Studenten in 'West' und 'Ost' nach der Wiedervereinigung über den Holocaust?* Erste empirische Ergebnisse zu den Auswirkungen unterschiedlicher 'politischer Sozialisation' und 'parteipolitischer Grundorientierung'. [In]: Tel Aviver Jahrbuch für deutsche Geschichte, Bd. 23, Gerlingen, 1994. Pp. 461–486, footnotes, tabs.

31940. BUCHENWALD. MONTEATH, PETER: *Buchenwald revisited: rewriting the history of a concentration camp.* [In]: The International History Review, Vol. XVI, No. 2, Toronto, May 1994. Pp. 221–440, footnotes. [On the attempts to transform Buchenwald's function as a memorial site after the collapse of the GDR.]

31941. *Didaktische Arbeit in KZ-Gedenkstätten. Erfahrungen und Perspektiven.* München: Bayerische Landeszentrale für politische Bildungsarbeit, 1993. 136 pp., illus. (Zeitfragen. Informationen, Meinungen, Dokumente.) [Incl. (titles abbr.): Erinnern als Verpflichtung (Wolfgang Benz, 11–21). Die KZ-Gedenkstätte Dachau (Barbara Distel, 22–28). Außenlager im Landkreis Mühldorf (Josef Wagner, 29–36). München-Berg am Laim (Erich Kasberger, 37–42). KZ-Außenlager in München (Ludwig Elber, 43–57). Der Dachauer KZ-Außenlagerkomplex Kaufering (Edith Raim, 76–88). Flossenbürg (Hans Simon-Pelanda, 89–99). Zur Pädagogik in Gedenkstätten für die Opfer des NS-Regimes (Thomas Lutz, 100–106). Haus der Wannsee-Konferenz (Wolf Kaiser, 107–112). Gedenkstätten zwischen Vergangenheits- und Zukunftsbewältigung (Detlef Garbe, 113–126). Theresienstadt (Miroslav Kárný, 127–130). Ravensbrück (Monika Herzog, 131–136).]

31942. GENGER, ANGELA: *Gedenkstätten in Deutschland.* Trauer – Dokumentation – Begegnung. [In]: Tribüne, Jg. 33, H. 132, Frankfurt am Main, 1994. Pp. 169–178, footnotes. [On the function of local memorial institutions and museums, esp. in North Rhine-Westphalia, where ten have been founded since 1980.]

31943. HÖLZER, STEFAN: *Dokumentation des Kongresses: 'Zukunft der Gedenkstätten zur Erinnerung an Verfolgung und Widerstand unter dem Nationalsozialismus': vom 6.- 8. November 1992 [in Braunschweig].* Red. und Hrsg.: Stefan Hölzer [et al.]. Braunschweig (Leopoldstr. 23): S. Hölzer c/o Antifaschistisches Kultur- und Informationszentrum Carl von Ossietzky, 1993.

31944. JANSEN, MECHTILD M./NORDMANN, INGEBORG: *Jüdische Frauen in Kultur, Politik und Wissenschaft.* Dokumentation einer Vortragsreihe. HLZ, Hessische Landeszentrale für Politische Bildung. Wiesbaden: HLZ, 1993. 256 pp., bibl.

31945. KRAUSE-VILMAR, DIETFRID: *Orte des Lernens. Zu den Empfehlungen für die Gedenkstätten in Buchenwald, Neuengamme und im Lande Brandenburg.* [In]: Rassismus in Deutschland. Beiträge zur Geschichte der nationalsozialistischen Verfolgung in Norddeutschland, Heft 1. Pp. 95–100.

31946. LANGE, THOMAS, Hrsg.: *Judentum und jüdische Geschichte im Schulunterricht nach 1945.* Bestandsaufnahmen, Erfahrungen und Analysen aus Deutschland, Österreich, Frankreich und Israel. Wien: Böhlau, 1994. 350 pp. (Aschkenas, Beiheft 1.) [Incl.: Einleitung: Judentum und jüdische Geschichte im Unterricht (Thomas Lange, 9–36). Jüdische Geschichte im

Schulbuch (37–141; contribs. by Georges Bensousson, Doron Niederland/Shlomo Fischer, Wolfgang Lassmann, Änne Rossow/Ulrich Wiegmann, Chaim Schatzker, Siegfried Wolf). Judentum in Lehrbüchern und Materialien zum Religionsunterricht (143–257; contribs. by Hans Erich Jung, Edgar Josef Korherr, Alfred Wittstock). Verunsicherte Annäherungen – Judentum und jüdische Geschichte im Unterricht (259–348; contribs. by Harald Freiling, Eckhard Glöckner, Frederic Gugelot, Gottfried Kössler, Markus Müller-Henning, Ursula Reck-Hog, Änne Rossow/Ulrich Wiegmann, Ingrid Schmidt/Helmut Ruppel, Gerd Steffens.]

31947. *Representing the Holocaust.* [In]: History and Theory, Vol. 33, No. 2, Middletown, Ct., May 1994. 127–197. [This special section incl. three contribs.: 'Never again' is now (Hans Kellner, 127–144). From exception to exemplum: the new approach to Nazism and the 'Final Solution' (Wulf Kansteiner, 145–171). The Holocaust and problems of historical representation (Robert Braun, 172–197).]

31948. ROTH, HARALD, Hrsg.: *Es tat weh, nicht mehr dazu zu gehören. Kindheit und Jugend im Exil.* Ravensburg: Maier, 1994. 298 pp., bibl. (Ravensburger Taschenbücher.) [A book for children.]

31949. SAMELY, ALEXANDER: *Nazis go to town: reflections on German-Jewish life today.* [In]: European Judaism, Vol. 27, No. 2, London, Autumn 1994. Pp. 67–73, notes.

―――― SCHACHT, GISELA: *Möglichkeiten und Grenzen der Vermittlung jüdischer Geschichte im Unterricht – Eine Stellungnahme aus der gegenwärtigen Schulpraxis.* [In]: Die Gegenwart der Schoah. Zur Aktualität des Mordes an den europäischen Juden. [See in No. 31847].

31950. SCHOEFER, CHRISTINE: *The politics of commemoration: the concentration camp memorial sites in the former GDR.* Berkeley, Ca.: Center for German and European Studies, Univ. of California, 1993. 28 pp.

31951. SCHÖNFELD, MARTIN: *Gedenktafeln in West-Berlin.* Hrsg.: Aktives Museum Faschismus und Widerstand in Berlin e.V. Berlin, 1993. 277 pp., illus., bibl., index. (Schriftenreihe Aktives Museum, Bd. 6.) [Incl. also Jewish memorials.]

―――― SCHREIER, HELMUT: *Einige schultheoretische Voraussetzungen und ein didaktischer Vorschlag zum Projekt der Erziehung nach Auschwitz.* [In]: Die Gegenwart der Schoah. Zur Aktualität des Mordes an den europäischen Juden. [See in No. 31847].

31952. WACKER, ULRICH: *Viermal neunter November: Gedenktage eines schwierigen Vaterlandes.* Hrsg.: Freie und Hansestadt Hamburg, Behörde für Schule, Jugend und Berufsbildung, Amt für Schule, Referat S 13/31. Hamburg: Amt für Schule, Jugend und Berufsbildung, Amt für Schule, 1994. 67 pp. (Geschichte – Zeitgeschehen – Politik: Aktuelles Zeitgeschehen.)

31953. YOUNG, JAMES E.: *Germany's vanishing Holocaust monuments.* [In]: Judaism, Vol. 43, No. 4, New York, Fall 1994. Pp. 412–418, notes.

31954. YOUNG, JAMES E., ed.: *Mahnmale des Holocaust. Motive, Rituale und Stätten des Gedenkens;* [Zur Ausstellung 'The Art of Memory: Holocaust memorials in History'; Begleitbuch zu der vom Jewish Museum in New York übernommenen Ausstellung im Historischen Museum in Berlin vom 8. Sept. bis 13. Nov. 1994, im Münchner Stadtmuseum vom 9. Dezember 1994 bis 5. März 1995 sowie in weiteren Museen Deutschlands] hrsg. von James E. Young. Mit Beiträgen von Matthew Baigell [et al.]. Übers. aus dem Englischen: Magda Moses [et al.]. München: Prestel, 1994. 171 pp., illus. [For orig. edn. publ. in 1993 see No. 30764/YB XXXIX.]

V. JUDAISM

A. Jewish Learning and Scholars

31955. BAECK, LEO. BAECK, LEO: *A Lehrhaus lecture of 30th May 1935.* Transl. by Curtis Cassel. [In]: European Judaism, Vol. 27, No. 1, London, Spring 1994. Pp. 11–17, notes.

31956. BAECK, LEO. *A letter to Leo Baeck from Claude G. Montefiore.* Introd. by Albert H. Friedlander. [In]: European Judaism, Vol. 27, No. 1, London, Spring 1994. Pp. 20–23. [This letter (one of twenty) is dated Sept. 1928, London and was found by Friedlander among the contents of L.B.'s Berlin desk, now housed at the Bundesarchiv branch in Coswig.]

—— BAECK, LEO. BOUREL, DOMINIQUE: *Judentum und Christentum bei Leo Baeck.* Jacob Taubes in memoriam. [See in No. 31717.]

31957. BAECK, LEO. HOMOLKA, WALTER: *Jüdische Identität in der modernen Welt. Leo Baeck und der deutsche Protestantismus.* Mit einer Einleitung von Albert H. Friedlander. Aus dem Englischen übersetzt von Sieglinde Denzel und Susanne Naumann. Gütersloh: Kaiser, 1994. 160 pp., bibl. (147–160). [Incl.: Einleitung: Leo Baeck in Theresienstadt (Albert H. Friedlander, 9–16).]

31958. BAECK, LEO. LICHARZ, WERNER: *Eine Leo Baeck-Werkausgabe?* [In]: LBI Information, Nr. 4, Frankfurt am Main, 1994. Pp. 56–59. [Recommends a complete edition of Baeck's writings.]

31959. BEUYS, BARBARA: *Ein Talmud aus deutscher Hand.* Der Judaist Peter Schäfer hat es schwer, seine Wissenschaft hier zu etablieren. [In]: Die Zeit, Nr. 47, Hamburg, 18. Nov. 1994, p. 48. [On the director of the 'Institut für Judaistik', Freie Univ. Berlin.]

31960. BIALE, DAVID: *Modern Jewish ideologies and the historiography of Jewish politics.* [In]: Studies in Contemporary Jewry, 10, Oxford Univ. Press, 1994. Pp. 3–14, notes. [Incl. H. Cohen, M. Mendelssohn, G. Scholem.]

31961. BUBER, MARTIN. TYLDESLY, MICHAEL: *Martin Buber and the Bruderhof communities.* [In]: Journal of Jewish Studies, Vol. 45, No. 2, Oxford, Autumn 1994. Pp. 258–272, footnotes, bibl. [Discusses Buber's interaction with members of the Christian 'Bruderhof' movement, whose first Kibbutz-like communities were near to Buber's home.]

31962. BUBER, MARTIN. VERMES, PAMELA: *Buber on God and the perfect man.* Oxford: Littman Library of Jewish Civilization, 1994. 320 pp. [For orig. edn. publ. in 1980 see No. 18221/YB XXVII.]

31963. BUBER, MARTIN. WERNER, HANS-JOACHIM: *Martin Buber.* Frankfurt am Main; New York: Campus, 1994. 207 pp., bibl. (195–207).

31964. BUBER, MARTIN. YARON, KALMAN/MENDES-FLOHR, PAUL, eds.: *Martin Buber in perspective.* [In Hebrew, title transl.] Jerusalem: Magnes Press, Hebrew Univ., 1992. 211 pp. [A collection of articles, divided into five sections: The Arab question as a Jewish problem; Paths to Utopia; Education as a dialogue; Buber and psychotherapy; Judaism.]

31965. COHEN, HERMANN. HACKESCHMIDT, JÖRG/SIEG, ULRICH: *Hermann Cohen, ein vergessener Kronzeuge liberaler Demokratie.* [In]: Jahrbuch zur Liberalismusforschung, Jg. 6, Baden-Baden, 1994. Pp. 159–166, footnotes.

31966. COHEN, HERMANN. HOLZHEY, HELMUT, Hrsg.: *Hermann Cohen.* Frankfurt am Main; New York: Lang, 1994. 362 pp., notes. (Auslegungen, Bd. 4.) [Cont.: 18 previously publ. texts documenting the reception and interpretation of Cohen and his work by Dieter Adelmann, Alexander Altmann, Hugo Bergmann, Ernst Cassirer, Julius Ebbinghaus, Nicolai Hartmann, Wilhelm Herrmann, Helmut Holzey, Benzion Kellermann, Hermann Lübbe, Paul Natorp, Hans-Ludwig Ollig, Ernst Reuter, Wolfgang Ritzel, Franz Rosenzweig, Steven S. Schwarzschild and Eggert Winter.]

31967. EGER, AKIVA. APFEL, YOSEF YEHOSHUA: *Our teacher Rabbi Akiva Eger.* [In Hebrew, title transl.] [In]: Sridim, Vol. 14, Jerusalem, April 1994. Pp. 13–21.

31968. ELIOR, RACHEL: *Nathan Adler and the Frankfurt pietists; Pietist groups in Eastern and Central Europe during the 18th century.* [In Hebrew, with English summary.] [In]: Zion, Vol. 59, No.1, Jerusalem, 1994. Pp. 31–64.

31969. ENGEL, EVA J.. *'Gedanck und Empfindung'. Ausgewählte Schriften von Eva J. Engel.* Festgabe zum 75. Geburtstag von Eva J. Engel am 18. August 1994. Auswahl und Redaktion: Oliver Schütze und Michael Albrecht. Stuttgart-Bad Cannstadt: Frommann-Holzboog, 1994. 366 pp., frontispiece. [Incl. Geleitwort [&] Vita Eva J. Engel (3–8). A collection of articles many of them dealing with Moses Mendelssohn.] [Engel (Holland), Eva J., b. 1919 in Dortmund, editor-general of Moses Mendelssohn Jubiläumsausgabe and author of books and numerous articles on German literature and philosophy.]

31970. FACKENHEIM, EMIL. FACKENHEIM, EMIL: *To mend the world: foundations of post-Holocaust Jewish thought.* Bloomington: Indiana Univ. Press, 1994. XLIX, 358 pp.

31971. FEINER, SHMUEL: *Nineteenth-century Jewish historiography: the second track.* [In]: Studies in Contemporary Jewry, 10, Oxford Univ. Press, 1994. Pp. 17–44, notes. [Incl. Wissenschaft des Judentums; Hermann Graetz.]

31972. FRANKEL, ZACHARIAS. BRÄMER, ANDREAS: *Lehrer der Jugend – Lehrer des Alters: Zacharias Frankel als Gemeinderabbiner in Teplitz und Dresden.* [In]: Trumah 4, Berlin, 1994. Pp. 63–90. [Z.F., 1801 Prague – 1875 Breslau, became 'Kreisrabbiner' of Leitmeritz in Teplitz in 1831, 'Oberrabbiner' in Dresden in 1836; in 1854 he became the first director of the newly founded Jüdisch-theologisches Seminar in Breslau.]

31973. *German essays on religion.* Ed. by Edward T. Oakes. New York: Continuum, 1994. XIV, 258 pp. (German library, Vol. 54.) [Incl. writings by Martin Buber, Sigmund Freud, Karl Marx, Franz Rosenzweig, Ludwig Wittgenstein.]

31974. GOTZMANN, ANDREAS: *Rabbiner und Bann. Zur Problematik der Analyse und Bewertung zweier Topoi des aufklärerischen Diskurses.* [In]: Aschkenas, Jg. 4, H. 1, Wien, 1994. Pp. 99–126, footnotes.

—— HEINEMANN, ISAAK. WIESE, CHRISTIAN: *Vom 'jüdischen Geist'. Isaak Heinemanns Auseinandersetzung mit dem akademischen Antisemitismus innerhalb der protestantischen Theologie in der Weimarer Republik.* [See No. 32422.]

31975. HIRSCH, SAMSON RAPHAEL. BREUER, MORDECHAI: *Rabbi Samson Raphael Hirsch and modern orthodoxy.* [In Hebrew, title transl.] [In]: Ha-Ma'yan, Vol. 34, No. 3, Jerusalem, Nissan 5754 [= March 1994]. Pp. 1–10.

31976. HOMOLKA, WALTER/FRIEDLANDER, ALBERT: *The gate to perfection: the ideal of peace in Jewish thought.* With a preface by Elie Wiesel. Providence, RI.: Berghahn Books, 1994. XV, 128 pp., appendix, bibl.

31977. IDEL, MOSHE: *Mystique juive et histoire juive.* [In]: Annales, Vol. 49, No. 5, Paris, Sept.- Oct. 1994. Pp. 1171–1182. [With Engl summary, p. 1278; deals mainly with Scholem's studies of Jewish mysticism.]

31978. *Das Judentum.* Hrsg. von Günter Mayer mit Beiträgen von Hermann Greive, Günter Mayer, Jakob J. Petuchowski, Phillip Segal, Leo Trepp. Stuttgart: Kohlhammer, 1994. 526 pp., footnotes, bibl (463–500), indexes (503–526). (Die Religionen der Menschheit, Bd. 27.) [Incl.: Geschichte des nachbiblischen Judentums in Grundzügen (Leo Trepp/Günter Mayer, 17–72; refers also to German Jewry). Halaka und Leben (Phillip Segal/Günter Mayer, 73–123; refers also to German Jewry). Jüdisches Denken im 20. Jahrhundert (Leo Trepp, 223–301; cont. a.o. essays on Martin Buber, Hermann Cohen, Emil Fackenheim, Franz Rosenzweig).]

31979. KAPLAN, EDWARD K.: *Sacred versus symbolic religion: Abraham Joshua Heschel and Martin Buber.* [In]: Modern Judaism, Vol. 14, No. 3, Baltimore, Oct. 1994. Pp. 213–231, notes.

31980. KLEINBERG, AVIAD M.: *Hermannus Judaeus opusculum: in defence of its authenticity*. [In]: Revue des études juives, Vol. 152, Paris, 1993. Pp. 337– 363.

31981. LIBERLES, ROBERT: *Postemancipation historiography and the Jewish historical societies of American and England*. [In]: Studies in Contemporary Jewry, 10, Oxford Univ. Press, 1994. Pp. 45–65, notes. [Incl. influence of German-Jewish historians and Wissenschaft des Judentums on these societies.]

31982. MALACHI, ZVI: *'Vikuach ha-shratsim' – an anti-Maskil allegory by Samson Friedburg of Hamburg*. [In Hebrew, title transl.] [In]: Mahut, No. 13, Lod, Summer 1994. Pp. 47–68.

31983. MEIR BEN BARUCH OF ROTHENBURG. METZGER, THÉRÈSE/METZGER, MENDEL: *Méir ben Baruch aus Rothenburg und die Streitfrage zu den Bildern bei den Juden im Mittelalter*. [In]: Aschkenas, Jg. 4, H. 1, Wien, 1994. Pp. 33–82, footnotes.

31984. MENDELSSOHN, MOSES. ARKUSH, ALLAN: *Moses Mendelssohn and the Enlightenment*. Albany: State Univ. of New York Press, 1994. XVI, 304 pp, notes, bibl. 293–299. (SUNY series in Judaica.)

31985. MENDELSSOHN, MOSES. HILDESHEIMER, MEIR: *The attitude of the Hatam Sofer toward Moses Mendelssohn*. [In]: Proceedings of the American Academy for Jewish Research, Vol. 60, Jerusalem, 1994. Pp. 141–187, tabs., footnotes. [Rabbi Moshe Sofer, known as Hatam Sofer, rabbi of Pressburg, 1763–1839.]

31986. MENDELSSOHN, MOSES. MENDELSSOHN, MOSES: *Briefwechsel (1761–1785)* In deutscher Umschrift und in Übersetzung aus dem Hebräischen. Bearbeitet von Reuven Michael. Gesammelte Schriften. Jubiläumsausgabe, Bd. 20,2. Stuttgart: Frommann-Holzboog, 1994. XXIII, 468 pp., notes, indexes. [Cont. the translation of 290 German letters written in Hebrew script, of 38 Hebrew letters and of the Judaeo-German letters of M.M. and his future wife Fromet Gugenheim.]

31987. MENDELSSOHN, MOSES. *Moses Mendelssohn und die Kreise seiner Wirksamkeit*. Herausgegeben von Michael Albrecht, Eva J. Engel und Norbert Hinske. Tübingen: Niemeyer, 1994. 445 pp., footnotes, index (434–445). (Wolfenbütteler Studien zur Aufklärung, Bd. 19.) [Incl. (titles partly condensed): Das Bild Moses Mendelssohns im deutschen Idealismus (Alexander Altmann, 1–24). Moses Mendelssohn und die Popularphilosophie (Rudolf Vierhaus, 25–42). Überlegungen zu einer Entwicklungsgeschichte der Ethik Mendelssohns (Michael Albrecht, 43–60). Mendelssohn und Iselin (Ulrich Im Hofe, 61–92). Moses Mendelssohn und die Berliner Mittwochsgesellschaft (Birgit Nehren, 93–112). Thomas Abbt und Moses Mendelssohn (Stefan Lorenz, 113–134). Das stillschweigende Gespräch (Norbert Hinske, 135–156; on Mendelssohn and Kant). Johann Jakob Engel und die Geschichtsphilosophie Mendelssohns (Christoph Böhr, 157–174). Hamann und Mendelssohn (Oswald Bayer, 175–190). Moses Mendelssohn and the right of toleration (Thomas Mautner, 191–214). Moses Mendelssohn und die Situation von Autor und Verleger im 18. Jahrhundert (Günther Holzboog, 215–248). Die Literaturbriefe 72 – 75 (13. und 20. Dezember 1759) (Eva J. Engel, 249–268). Lessing und Mendelssohn in ihrer Spätzeit (Ingrid Strohschneider-Kohrs, 269–290). Mendelssohn als Philosoph des Judentums (Friedrich Niewöhner, 291–314). Johann David Michaelis und Moses Mendelssohn. Judenfeindschaft im Zeit der Aufklärung (Anna-Ruth Löwenbrück, 315–332). The social dynamics of Jewish responses to Moses Mendelssohn (with special emphasis on the Mendelssohn Bible translation and on the Berlin Jewish community (Steven M. Lowenstein, 333–348). Moses Mendelssohns schwankendes Bild bei der jüdischen Nachwelt (Jacob Katz, 349–362). Eine Generation später: Lazarus Bendavid (1762–1832) (Dominique Bourel, 363–380). Adelbert von Chamisso, Moses Mendelssohn und Abba Glosk Leczeka (Chaim Shoham, 381–410). Moses Mendelssohn zwischen Heine und Marx (Siegbert S. Prawer, 411–430).]

31988. MENDELSSOHN, MOSES. NEHREN, BIRGIT: *Eine Dokumentation zum Streit über den Tod Moses Mendelssohns*. [In]: Aufklärung, Jg. 7, H. 1 [with the issue title]: Norbert Hinske, Hrsg.: Kant und die Aufklärung. Hamburg, 1992. Pp. 93–116, footnotes.

31989. MENDELSSOHN, MOSES. ROSENBERG, SHALOM/EVEN-CHEN, ALEXANDER: *An 18th-century dialogue: Moses Mendelssohn and Naftali Herz Ulmann.* [In Hebrew, with Engl. summary.] [In]: Iyyun, Vol. 43, Jerusalem, April 1994. Pp. 209–220.

31990. MENDELSSOHN, MOSES. SORKIN, DAVID: *The case for comparison: Moses Mendelssohn and the religious enlightenment.* [In]: Modern Judaism, Vol. 14, No. 2, Baltimore, May 1994. Pp. 121–138, notes.

31991. MÜLLER, ERNST. BRACKER, HANS-JÜRGEN: *Ernst Müller. Porträt eines Mitteleuropäers.* [In]: Novalis, Nr. 2/3, Schaffhausen, 1994. Pp. 16–20, notes, p. 82. [E.M., Nov. 21, 1880 Misslitz (Moravia) – Aug. 5, 1954 London, lived since 1898 in Vienna, librarian, adherent of Zionism and Anthroposophy, author of books and articles on Jewish mysticism and other esoteric topics. Translator of the Sohar. Emigr. 1939 to England.]

31992. ROSENHEIM, JAKOB. GREENBERG, GERSHON: *Sovereignty as catastrophe: Jakob Rosenheim's 'Hurban Weltanschauung'.* [In]: Holocaust and Genocide Studies, Vol. 8, No. 2, Oxford, Fall 1994. Pp. 202–224, notes. [J.R., 1870–1965, leader of Jewish Orthodoxy. Article deals with Rosenheim's interpretation of the Holocaust as expressed in his writings.]

31993. ROSENWALD, LAWRENCE: *On the reception of Buber and Rosenzweig's bible.* [In]: Prooftexts, Vol. 14, No. 2, Baltimore, May 1994. Pp. 141–165, notes.

31994. ROSENZWEIG, FRANZ. COHEN, RICHARD A.: *Elevations: the height of the good in Rosenzweig and Levinas.* Chicago: Univ. of Chicago Press, 1994. XXII, 342 pp., footnotes, bibl. (323–326). (Chicago studies in the history of Judaism.) [The philosophies of Buber, Husserl and Heidegger.]

31995. ROSENZWEIG, FRANZ. MEIR, EPHRAIM: *Star from Jacob; the life and work of Franz Rosenzweig.* [In Hebrew.] Jerusalem: Magnes Press, Hebrew Univ., 1994. 204 pp.

31996. SCHOLEM, GERSHOM. *Gershom Scholem's major trends in Jewish mysticism 50 years after: proceedings of the sixth international conference on the history of Jewish mysticism.* Ed. by Peter Schäfer and Joseph Dan. Tübingen: Mohr, 1993. IV, 336 pp. [This conference was held in Berlin in 1992.]

31997. SCHOLEM, GERSHOM. MENDES-FLOHR, PAUL, ed.: *Gershom Scholem: the man and his work.* Ed. by Paul Mendes-Flohr. Albany: State Univ. of New York Press; Jerusalem: Academy of Sciences and Humanities, 1994. 127 pp., frontispiece, illus. (SUNY series in Judaica.)

—— SCHOLEM, GERSHOM. SCHOLEM, GERSHOM: *Briefe I. 1914–1947.* Hrsg. von Itta Shedletzky. [See No. 32351.]

31998. SCHORSCH, ISMAR. ZIEGLER, MONIKA: *Dr. Ismar Schorsch auf den Spuren seiner Vorfahren.* [In]: Aufbau, Vol. 60, Nr. 16, New York, Aug. 5, 1994. Pp. 16–17, illus. [I. Sch., b. 1935 in Hanover, grandson of Theodor Rothschild (director of the Israelitisches Waisenhaus in Esslingen), historian, chancellor of the Jewish Theological Seminar, N.Y., president of the LBI, New York.] [See also Nos. 31892 and 31998.]

31999. SCHWEER, THOMAS: *Stichwort Judentum.* München: Heyne, 1994. 95 pp., graphs, tabs. Originalausgabe. (Heyne Sachbuch.) [Also on German Jewry, antisemitism and Holocaust.]

32000. SCHWEID, ELIEZER: *'Prophetic mysticism' in twentieth-century Jewish thought.* [In]: Modern Judaism, Vol. 14, No. 2, Baltimore, May 1994. Pp. 139–174, notes. [Incl. Leo Baeck, Isaac Breuer, Martin Buber, Joshua Heschel, Franz Rosenzweig, Gershom Scholem.]

32001. SCHWEID, ELIEZER: *Rethinking; new ways in Jewish religious and national thought in the 20th century.* [In Hebrew.] Jerusalem: Akademon, 1991. 306, 13 pp. [A collection of twelve previously publ. articles, dealing a.o. with Gershom Scholem, Franz Rosenzweig, Moses Mendelssohn and Isaac Breuer.]

32002. STEINHEIM, SALOMON LUDWIG. SHEAR-YASHUV, AHARON: *Steinheims Beziehung zur jüdischen Tradition.* [In]: Zeitschrift für Religions- und Geistesgeschichte, Jg. 46, H. 1, Leiden, 1994. Pp. 1–14, footnotes.

32003. STRAUSS, LEO. *Leo Strauss: political philosopher and Jewish thinker.* Ed. and with introd. by Kenneth L. Deutsch and Walter Nicgorski. Lanham, Md.: Rowman & Littlefield, 1994. IX, 396 pp, frontispiece., illus. notes. [Collection of essays in two parts under the headings: Strauss: Judaism, reason, and revelation; Strauss: classical political philosophy, modernity and the American regime.]

32004. TÄUBLER, EUGEN. TÄUBLER, EUGEN: *Inaugural lecture given to the 'Hochschule für die Wissenschaft des Judentums', Berlin in 1938.* Transl. and introd. by Albert H. Friedlander. [In]: European Judaism, Vol. 27, No. 1, London, Spring 1994. Pp. 17–20, notes.

32005. VOLKMANN, MICHAEL: *Eine andere Frankfurter Schul'. Das Freie Jüdische Lehrhaus 1920–1927.* Tübingen: TVT Medienverlag, 1994. 32 pp., footnotes. (Prophezey Schriften im TVT, Nr. 2.)

32006. WERSES, SHMUEL: *The expulsion from Spain as reflected in Haskalah literature.* [In Hebrew.] [In]: Pe'amim, No. 57, Jerusalem, Autumn 1993. Pp. 48–81. [Examines journalistic and historical works, mainly German, by Isaac Euchel, Salomon Hacohen, Salomon Loewisohn, J.M. Jost, Heinrich Graetz, Meyer Kayserling, and several others, incl. a few Russian writers.]

32007. WESSELY, HERZ NAPHTALY. HESCHEL, ISRAEL NATHAN: *The views of leading rabbis in their battle against the Maskil Naphtaly Herz Wessely.* [In Hebrew, title transl.] [In]: Kovetz Bais Aharon v'Yisrael, Vol. 8, No. 1, Jerusalem, Tishrei-Cheshvan 5753 [= Oct.- Nov. 1992]. Pp. 149–167. [Continued in the following issues: No. 2 (117–129); No. 3 (119–133); No. 4 (147–156); No. 5 (133–149).]

32008. ZUNZ, LEOPOLD. WAGNER, PETER: *Wir werden frei sein. Leopold Zunz 1794–1886.* Detmold: [Panu Derech], 1994. 137 pp., illus., footnotes. (Panu Derech, Schriften der Gesellschaft für Christlich-Jüdische Zusammenarbeit in Lippe e.V., Bd. 11.)

B. The Jewish Problem

32009. FINKIELKRAUT, ALAIN: *The imaginary Jew.* Transl. by Kevin O'Neill and David Suchoff with an introd. by David Suchoff. Lincoln: Univ. of Nebraska Press, 1994. XVIII, 201 pp., notes (181–191). [First publ. in French in 1980. On Jewish identity; incl. chap. on German Jews.]

32010. GILMAN, SANDER L.: *Sounding too Jewish: the dicourse of difference.* [In]: Brücken über dem Abgrund. Festschrift für Harry Zohn [see No. 32315]. Pp. 113–134.

32011. GRIJN SANTEN, W.B. VAN DER: *Die Weltbühne und das Judentum.* Eine Studie über das Verhältnis der Wochenschrift 'Die Weltbühne' zum Judentum, hauptsächlich die Jahre 1918 – 1926 betreffend. Würzburg: Königshausen & Neumann, 1994. 295 pp., notes, bibl. (273–282), index.

32012. HAMBURGER, MICHAEL: *Gedanken zur Identitätsfrage.* [In]: europäische ideen, Heft 88, Berlin, 1994. Pp. 19–24. [A critical approach by the author, who came to the U.K. at the age of nine, to the concepts of 'exile', 'Jewish author' and 'identity'.]

32013. JACOBS, JACK: *Sozialisten und die 'jüdische Frage' nach Marx*. Mit einem Vorwort von Susanne Miller. Aus dem Englischen von Cornelia Dieckmann. Mainz: Decaton, 1994. 239 pp., notes, bibl. 208–236), index (persons). (Jüdische Studien, Bd. 2.) [For American orig. edn. see No. 29622/YB XXXVIII.] [Cf.: 'Hi' auf beiden Seiten (Helmut Hirsch) [in]: 'FAZ', Nr. 95, Frankfurt am Main, 24. April, 1995, p. 13.

—— *The 'Jewish question' in German-speaking countries, 1848–1914: a bibliography*. Ed. by Rena R. Auerbach. [See No. 31690.]

32014. MENDELSOHN, EZRA: *Should we take notice of Berthe Weill? Reflections on the domain of Jewish history*. [In]: Jewish Social Studies, New Series, Vol. 1, No. 1, New York, Fall 1994. Pp. 22–39, notes. [Author discusses the questions how to define Jewish history and who is a Jew. Illustrates them by the careers of two German Jews: Felix Mendelssohn-Bartholdy, who was baptised as a child, and the anthropologist Franz Boas, 1852 Minden – 1942 New York.]

32015. SARTRE, JEAN PAUL: *Überlegungen zur Judenfrage*. Deutsch von Vincent von Wroblewski. Gesammelte Werke in Einzelausgaben. Politische Schriften, Bd. 2. Neuübersetzung. Reinbek b. Hamburg: Rowohlt, 1994. 281 pp., bibl. (269–272), index (273–281). [Orig. publ. 1954 under the title 'Réflexions sur la question juive'. Incl.: Nachwort: Sartres jüdisches Engagement – seine Vorgeschichte (Vincent von Wroblewsky, 249–268).]

32016. SCHOEPS, JULIUS H.: *Der Umgang mit dem Judesein. Zur Debatte um ein schwieriges Identitätsproblem*. [In]: Menora 5, München, 1994. Pp. 15–22, notes.

32017. STAV, SHIRA: *An Israeli playwright and the 'Jewish Soul', an interview with Yehoshua Sobol*. [In Hebrew.] [In]: Bamah; drama quarterly, No. 134, Jerusalem, 1993. Pp. 41–50. [Sobol relates the background of his play 'Soul of a Jew' to the life of Otto Weininger; discusses aspects of the text and the stage productions.]

C. Jewish Life and Organisations

32018. ADAM, JACOB: *Zeit zur Abreise: Lebensbericht eines jüdischen Händlers aus der Emanzipationszeit*. Bearb. und hrsg. von Jörg H. Fehrs und Margret Heitmann. Hildesheim; New York: Olms, 1993. 106 pp., illus. (Haskala, Bd. 5.) [Memoirs (1789–1830) of a Jewish merchant from Brandenburg, who lived in Berlin, Silesia, Poznán, West- and East Prussia from 1789 until some time after 1874.]

32019. ANDERL, GABRIELE. *Die 'Zentralstellen für jüdische Auswanderung' in Wien, Berlin und Prag – ein Vergleich*. [IN]: Tel Aviver Jahrbuch für deutsche Geschichte, Bd. 23, Gerlingen, 1994. Pp. 275–300.

32020. *Ariadne, Heft 23* [with the issue title]: *Jüdin – Deutsche – deutsche Jüdin? Auswirkungen des Antisemitismus in Deutschland*. Hrsg.: Archiv der deutschen Frauenbewegung, Kassel, 1994. 73 pp., illus. 1 issue. [Incl.: Die Stellung der Frau im Judentum (Rachel Heuberger, 5–8). Antisemitismus – Antifeminismus (Ilse Korotin, 9–16). 'Ich bin stolz, Jüdin zu sein'. Der Kampf des Jüdischen Frauenbundes gegen den Antisemitismus (Gudrun Maierhof, 17–22). Vertriebenes Wissen – jüdische Wissenschaftlerinnen in Deutschland (Silke Mehrwald/ Leonie Wagner, 23–27). '1933 wurde das anders. Da habe ich alles Jüdische betont'. Edith Wolff, genannt EWO. Eine Würdigung (Irmgard Klönne, 28–33). Hilde Lion zum 100. Geburtstag (1893–1970) (Monika Simmel-Joachim, 34–39). Tochter Zions, fürchte Dich! – Zur Auseinandersetzung jüdischer Frauen mit dem Antisemitismus (Sabine Hering, 40–44). Erscheinungsformen des Antisemitismus im Bund deutscher Frauenvereine (Marlis Dürkop, 45–52; previously publ. in 1984). Nationalsozialistinnen und Antisemitismus – Thesen und Anmerkungen (Leonie Wagner, 53–57). 'Was sie aus uns gemacht haben – wir waren keine Menschen mehr' – ein Interview mit Malka R. von Doris Fürstenberg (58–65; previously publ. in 1986). 'Von der Krankheit des Hasses'. Auszüge aus dem Vorwort: 'Die Flucht in den Haß' (Eva G. Reichmann, 66–67).]

32021. BAADER, MEIKE: *Jüdinnen in Deutschland*. Eine Sammelrezension. [In]: Babylon, H. 13–14, Frankfurt am Main, 1994. Pp. 177–182.

32022. BACKHAUSEN, MANFRED: *Hilfe zur Aufarbeitung jüdischer Schicksale im Rahmen von genealogischen Arbeiten*. [In]: Mitteilungen der westdeutschen Gesellschaft für Familienkunde, Bd. 36, Jg. 82, H. 8, Neustadt (Aisch), Okt.-Dez. 1994. Pp. 197–199, notes. [Cont. names of Nazi victims from Heiligenstadt, Mühlhausen (Thuringia), Duderstadt, Nordhausen and Coburg.]

32023. BARKAI, AVRAHAM: *Der CV im Jahre 1933: neu aufgefundene Dokumente im Moskauer 'Sonderarchiv'*. [In]: Tel Aviver Jahrbuch für deutsche Geschichte, Bd. 23, Gerlingen, 1994. Pp. 233–246.

32024. BOLZENIUS, RUPERT: *Beispielhafte Entwicklungsgeschichte jüdischer Krankenhäuser in Deutschland*. Aachen, Techn. Univ., Diss., 1994. III, 132 pp., illus.

32025. DAXELMÜLLER, CHRISTOPH: *Edle Ritter, fromme Rabbis, schöne Frauen. Alltagsvergnügen in der jüdischen Gesellschaft des 17. bis 20. Jahrhunderts*. [In]: Blick in die Wissenschaft. Forschungsmagazin der Univ. Regensburg 3, H. 4, Regensburg, 1994. Pp. 34–45. [Deals also with Western-Yiddish 'Ritterepik' and Purim plays.]

32026. DETTMER, FRAUKE: *Anmerkungen zu einer volkskundlichen jüdischen Quelle aus Schleswig-Holstein*. [In]: Volkskundliche Streifzüge. Festschrift für Kai Detlev Sievers zum 60. Geburtstag. Hrsg. von Silke Götsch [et al.]. Kiel: Mühlau, 1994. Pp. 25–29. [On an eighteenth-century mohel book from Rendsburg, sent to Theresienstadt to be translated there by Jacob Jacobson, the former archivist of the 'Gesamtarchiv'.]

32027. FRANK, JAKOB JOSEF. HOENSCH, JÖRG K.: *Der 'Polackenfürst von Offenbach'. Jakób Józef Frank und seine Sekte der Frankisten*. [In]: Juden in Deutschland. Lebenswelt und Einzelschicksale. Hrsg. von Reinhard Schneider [see No. 31400]. Pp. 179–202. [J.J.Frank, 18th-century pseudo-Messiah, founder of the Frankists.]

32028. GILBOA, MENUHA: *'Rimon=Milgroym'; an unusual arts magazine appeared in Berlin in Hebrew and Yiddish 70 years ago*. [In Hebrew, with English summary.] [In]: Qesher, No. 14, Tel-Aviv, Nov. 1993. Pp. 102–105.

32029. HERWEG, RACHEL MONIKA: *Die jüdische Mutter: das verborgene Matriarchat*. Darmstadt: Wiss. Buchgesellschaft, 1994. 252 pp., illus., footnotes, bibl. (Zugl.: Berlin, Freie Univ., Diss., 1993.) [Incl. references to traditions among German Jews.]

32030. HETKAMP, JUTTA: *Die jüdische Jugendbewegung in Deutschland von 1913–1933*. Mit einem Vorwort von Schalom Ben-Chorin. Band 1. Münster: LIT Verlag, 1994. 213 pp., illus., notes, bibl. (Anpassung – Selbstbehauptung – Widerstand, Bd. 4.) [Vol. 2 publ. in the same year under the title *Ausgewählte Interviews von Ehemaligen der Jüdischen Jugendbewegung in Deutschland von 1913–1933*. Band 2. 137 pp., illus. (Anpassung – Selbstbehauptung – Widerstand, Bd. 5.)]

32031. HETKAMP, JUTTA: *Sport als darstellendes Element einer Lebensphilosophie*. Ein Beitrag zum Stellenwert des Sports als Ausgleich von Minderwertigkeitsgefühlen bei Jungen in der Jüdischen Jugendbewegung Deutschlands. [In]: Menora 5, München, 1994. Pp. 313–329, notes.

32032. HOMEYER, FRIEDEL: *100 Jahre Israelitische Erziehungsanstalt, Israelitische Gartenbauschule 1893 – 1993*. Mahn- und Gedenkstätte des Landkreises Hannover in Ahlem. Hrsg.: Landkreis Hannover: der Oberkreisdirektor; Deutsch-Israelische Gesellschaft, Arbeitsgemeinschaft Hannover. Hannover, 1993. 97 pp., illus.

32033. KAUFMANN, IRENE: *Eine Frau im Amt des Rabbiners? Regina Jonas war die erste deutsche Rabbinerin*. [In]: Allgemeine Jüdische Wochenzeitung, Jg. 49, Nr. 19, Bonn, 22. Sept. 1994, p. 8. [On Regina Jonas, who became a rabbi in 1935. Murdered in Auschwitz in 1944.]

32034. KELLENBACH, KATHARINA VON: *'God does not oppress any human being'. The life and thought of rabbi Regina Jonas*. [In]: Leo Baeck Institute Year Book XXXIX, London, 1994. Pp. 213–225, footnotes.

32035. KÖNIG, HANS-JÜRGEN: *Zwischen Marginalisierung und Entfremdung; zum Nationalismus der jüdischen Turn- und Sportbewegung im Wilhelminischen Kaiserreich*. [In]: Stadion, Jg. 18, H. 1, St. Augustin, 1992. Pp. 106–125, notes.

32036. LAQUEUR, WALTER: *Family reunion*. [In]: Commentary, Vol. 98, No. 1, New York, July 1994. Pp. 43–46. [In 1993, 106 members of the Laqueur family met in Israel for a reunion and to share their life experiences in different countries and during the Nazi period. Family are descendants of Eliezer from the Silesian village of Staedtel.]

32037. LOWENTHAL, ERNST G.. *Obituaries Ernst G. Lowenthal.*: In memoriam (Herbert Freeden) [in]: 'MB' Jg. 62, Nr. 101, Tel Aviv, Aug.-Sept. 1994, p. 16. Prof. Dr. Ernst Gottfried Lowenthal zum Gedenken (Ernst Cramer) [in]: Bar-Ilan Universität, Zeitschrift der Repräsentanz für Deutschland [et al.], Nr. 7, Ramat-Gan, Winter 1994/95, p. 33. Dr. Ernst G. Lowenthal (E.G.L) [in]: 'AJR', Vol. 49, No. 9, London, Oct. 1994, p. 14. In memoriam Ernst Gottfried Lowenthal (R.A.) [in]: Aufbau, Vol. 60, New York, Aug. 19, 1994, p. 20. [E.G.L., Dec. 28, 1904 Cologne – 1994 Berlin, publicist, historian, senior staff member of the Central-Verein, Assistant editor of the C.-V.-Zeitung, co-founder of the AJR, board member of the LBI London, fled to England in 1939, returned to Germany in in 1946 as Field Director of the Jewish Relief Unit.]

32038. MAYER, PAUL YOGI: *Deutsche Juden und Sport. Ihre Leistungen – ihr Schicksal*. [In]: Menora 5, München, 1994. Pp. 287–311, illus., notes.

32039. MOSBERG, HELMUTH: *Schlemihls Schatten. Geschichte einer ostpreußischen Familie*. München: Universitas, 1993. 355 pp.

32040. NIEHOFF, MAREN R.: *Die Wiederentdeckung der Hagada im 19. Jahrhundert und die Suche nach einer modernen jüdischen Identität*. [In]: Jüdischer Almanach 1995 des Leo Baeck Instituts. Frankfurt am Main, 1994. Pp. 69–80.

32041. PAPPENHEIM, BERTHA. KEVAL, SUSANNA: *Bertha Pappenheim. Schon wieder oder immer noch aktuell?* [In]: Frankfurter Jüdische Nachrichten, Nr. 86, Frankfurt am Main, Sept. 1994. P. 13. [Author discusses the work and ideas of Pappenheim and their relevance and meaning for Jewish community work in Germany today.]

32042. PICKUS, KEITH H.: *Jewish university students in Germany and the construction of a post-emancipatory Jewish identity. The model of the Freie Wissenschaftliche Vereinigung*. [In]: Leo Baeck Institute Year Book XXXIX, London, 1994. Pp. 65–81, footnotes. [On the liberal, non-denominational students' organisation, founded in 1881 in Berlin.]

32043. PRESTEL, CLAUDIA: *Zur Stellung der Frau in jüdischen Organisationen und Gemeinden vor und nach dem Ersten Weltkrieg*. [In]: Jüdische Kultur und Weiblichkeit in der Moderne [see No. 32104]. Köln, 1994. Pp. 254–258.]

32044. SCHWERES-FICHTNER, MICHAEL: *Heute heißt das Martin-Buber-Haus Rommelvilla. Das Jüdische Landschulheim Herrlingen*. [In]: Süddeutsche Zeitung, Nr. 76, München, 2./3./4. April 1994, p. IV, illus. [On the history of the Landschulheim Herrlingen (new name commemorates General Erwin Rommel's stay and eventual suicide in Herrlingen in Oct. 1944).] [Also, by the same author on the history of the Landschulheim two contributions [in]: 'Allgemeine', Jg. 49, Nr. 15 & 17, Bonn, 20. Juli & 25. Aug. 1994. Pp. 15; 15.]

32045. SEEWANN, HARALD, Hrsg.: *Zirkel und Zionsstern. Bilder und Dokumente aus der versunkenen Welt des jüdisch-nationalen Korporationswesens. Ein Beitrag zur Geschichte des Zionismus auf akademischen Boden*. Bd. 4 (1994). Graz (Postfach 358): H. Seewann, 1994. 651 pp., illus., facsims., docs. (Historia Academica Judaica, Folge 4.)

32046. WANNER, HELMUT: *'Ist nicht Abraham ebenso schön wie Albert oder Adolf'*. [In]: 'Allgemeine', Jg. 49, Nr. 19, Bonn, 22. Sept. 1994, p. 9. [On the founder of 'Die Laubhütte', Seligmann Meyer, rabbi in Regensburg.]

32047. ZIMMERMANN, AKIVA: *'Ha'emet' ('The Truth'); the first Socialist journal in Hebrew*. [In Hebrew.] [In]: Our Press, No. 11, Tel-Aviv, 1993. Pp. 62–66. ['Ha'emet' was publ. in Vienna by Aaron Shmuel Liberman in 1877.] [Article was publ. simultaneously in the Hebrew and Yiddish edns. of the English 'Our Press'.]

D. Jewish Art and Music

32048. BLOCH, DAVID LUDWIG. *David Ludwig Bloch. Holzschnitte und Acrylbilder zum Holocaust*. [Hrsg.:] Jüdisches Regionalmuseum Fürth Schnaittach, [Fürth, 1994.] 18 pp., illus. [Exhibition of artist, b. 1910 in Floß; incl.: a contrib. on the artist's biography (Monika Berthold, 1–2). Die Anfangsjahre des 'Jüdischen Kulturbundes in Bayern/Ortsgruppe Nürnberg-Fürth' 1934 bis 1936 (Udo Sponsel/Helmut Steiner, 3–13).]

32049. HESKES, IRENE: *Passport to Jewish music: its history, traditions, and culture*. Westport, Con.: Greenwood Press, 1994. XII, 353 pp. (Contributions to the study of music and dance, No. 33.) [Incl. the musical legacy of the Holocaust; also deals with composers Bloch, Offenbach, Schönberg, Weill a.o.]

—— *Jüdische Kultur in Museen und Ausstellungen bis 1938*. [See No. 31614.]

32050. KRITTER, ULRICH VON/MILLER-BROMBACHER, JEANNE A.: *Literarische Bilderwelten des 20. Jahrhunderts. II. Teil: Jüdische und jiddische Literatur*. Hrsg. von Ulrich von Kritter und Jeanne A. Miller-Brombacher. Bad Homburg vor der Höhe: [Stiftung I. und U. von Kritter], 1993. 172 pp., illus. (Literarische Bilderwelten des 20. Jahrhunderts; Internationale Buchgraphik in Europa und Übersee aus der Sammlung v. Kritter; Wort und Bild als Medium zeitgenössischer Kulturen; Eine Dokumentation für die Stiftung I. und U. von Kritter 'Internationale Buchillustration'.) [Deals with the 'Jewish book', its definition, its topics and its illustrators. Incl.: Einleitung: das jüdische Buch; Illustration und Typographie (Ulrich von Kritter (9–11). Hebräische Themen und Illustratoren (Jeanne A. Miller-Brombacher, 12–14). Die Illustration zur ostjüdischen Literatur (Ulrich von Kritter, 81–84). Jüdische Künstler als Meister der Buchillustration in Berlin (D. Lemhoefer/X. Werner, 135–137). Kurzbiographien der Buchillustratoren [&] Bibliographie jüdischer Buchillustratoren, international (151–171).]

32051. MOSCHELES, IGNAZ. LABHART, WALTER: *Ein jüdischer Wegbereiter der Romantik: Ignaz Moscheles. Hinweise auf einen beinahe vergessenen Komponisten*. [In]: King David, Jg. 2, Nr. 9, 1994. Pp. 39–42.

32052. ROSENFELD, GAVRIEL D.: *Defining 'Jewish art' in Ost und West, 1901–1903. A study in the nationalisation of Jewish culture*. [In]: Leo Baeck Institute Year Book XXXIX, London, 1994. Pp. 83–110, illus., footnotes.

32053. SCHUBERT, URSULA: *Hebräische illustrierte Handschriften des 18. und 19. Jahrhunderts im Burgenland*. [In]: David, Jg. 6, Nr. 22, Wien, Sept. 1994. Pp. 6–8, illus.

VI. ZIONISM AND ISRAEL

32054. ALMOG, SHMUEL/REINHARZ, JEHUDA/SHAPIRA, ANITA: *Zionism and religion*. [In Hebrew.] Jerusalem: Zalman Shazar Center for Jewish History; Boston: Brandeis Univ., Tauber Inst., 1994. 416 pp. [Incl. articles in Hebrew (titles transl.): Liberal Judaism and Zionism in Germany (Michael A. Meyer, 11–126). Jewish Orthodoxy in Germany and its attitudes to Zionism (Ya'akob Tsur, 127–140). Zionism and its religious critics in Vienna at the end of the 19th century (Robert S. Wistrich, 167–188). The struggle with the question of religion in the Zionist youth movement in post-World War I Germany (Chaim Schatzker, 373–384).]

32055. BARZEL, NEIMA: *The attitude of Jews of German origin in Israel to Germany and Germans after the Holocaust 1945–1952.* [In]: Leo Baeck Institute Year Book XXXIX, London, 1994. Pp. 271–301, footnotes. [Deals particularly with attitudes reflected in the immigrant press.]

32056. COCHAVI, YEHOYAKIM: *Liberals and Zionists on the eve of the National-Socialist seizure of power.* [In]: Leo Baeck Institute Year Book XXXIX, London, 1994. Pp. 113–129, footnotes.

32057. ELBOIM-DROR, RACHEL: *Gender in Utopianism: the Zionist case.* [In]: History Workshop; a journal of socialist and feminist historians, Issue 37, Oxford, Spring, 1994. Pp. 99–116, notes. [Author examines five major Zionist utopias, incl. Herzl's 'Altneuland', Edmund Eisler's 'Ein Zukunftsbild' and Siegfried Bernfeld's 'Das Jüdische Volk und seine Jugend'.]

32058. FRIEDRICH, KARIN: *Wege ins Gelobte Land. Zehn Lebensgeschichten aus Israel.* Berlin: Metropol, 1994. 216 pp., illus., glossary. [Based on interviews with mostly former Germans and Austrians (Hannah & Benjamin Jeremias; Avital & Schalom Ben-Chorin; Margot & Dov Singer, Erica & Herbert Rosenkranz).]

32059. GREENBERG, GERSHON: *Ontic division and religious survival: wartime Palestinian orthodoxy and the Holocaust.* [In]: Modern Judaism, Vol. 14, No. 1, Baltimore, Feb. 1994. Pp. 21–61, footnotes, endnotes. [Incl. the Orthodox view on German-Jewish assimilation and its implied shared responsibility for the Holocaust.]

32060. HERZL, THEODOR. GIORA, ZVI: *On the 'conversion' of Herzl.* [In Hebrew.] [In]: Zmanim, No. 49, Tel-Aviv, Summer 1994. Pp. 79–85. [On Herzl's 'change of mind' from the idea of assimilation as solution to the 'Jewish Question' to that of national self-determination, claiming that this was brought about more by antisemitism in Vienna than by the Dreyfus affair.]

32061. HERZL, THEODOR. NICAULT, CATHERINE: *Theodor Herzl et l'affaire Dreyfus.* [In]: Archives Juives, No. 27/1, Paris, 1e semestre 1994. Pp. 15–25.

32062. HERZL, THEODOR. *90 years since the death of Dr. Theodor Herzl.* [In Hebrew, title transl.] [In]: Ha-Umma, No. 116, Tel-Aviv, Summer 1994. Pp. 441–459. [Incl. the following articles: Zionism as perpetual ideal; Herzl's socio-political viewpoint (Haya Harel, 441–451). Herzl's utopian view of the Land of Israel [= 'Altneuland'] (Dan Yahav, 452–456). Doctor Herzl (Ze'ev Jabotinsky, 457–459); relates to Vladimir Jabotinky's article of that title written in 1904).]

32063. *Das Jüdische Echo* [with the issue title]: *Theodor Herzl – Vision und Realität.* Vol. 43, Wien, Okt. 1994. 1 issue. [The first section cont. the following contribs. on Herzl (titles partly condensed): 'Wenn ihr wollt, ist es kein Märchen . . .' (Leon Zelman, 5–8). Herzls Diplomatie und sein Beitrag zum politischen Zionismus (Yosef Govrin, 15–18). Vom Dandy zum Messias (Paul Grosz, 19–20). Herzl und Oberrabbiner Güdemann (Paul Chaim Eisenberg, 21–22). Further articles on Herzl and Zionism are arranged under the following sections: Herzl und Wien: Zur Jahrhundertwende und danach (23–70; contribs. by Otto Schulmeister, Robert W. Rosner, Hubert Christian Ehalt, Evelyn Adunka, Steven Beller, Fred Hahn, Brigitte Hamann). Wien, Haupstadt der Zeitungen: Herzl und die 'Neue Freie Presse' (71–76; contribs. by Lucian O. Meysels, Thomas Chorherr). 'Eine Krone für Zion': Theodor Herzl und Karl Kraus (77–98; contribs. by Peter Loos, Gerald Krieghofer). Die Affaire Dreyfus (99–118; contribs. by Julius H. Schoeps, Robert S. Wistrich, Siegfried Loewe). Zionismus, alt & neu: das Jüdisch-Nationale und der Antisemitismus (119–144; contribs. by Harald Seewann, Klaus Hödl, John Bunzl, Alexander Steiner, Erika Weinzierl). Herzl und die Folgen: Zionismus und der Staat Israel (145–186; contribs. by David Ben Gurion, Abba Eban, Amos Oz, Anita Schapira, Mosche Meisels, Rita Koch, Bubi Zerwanitzer, Jossi Sarid, Amos Elon, Jizchak ben Aharon, Schimon Peres). Literatur,

Kunst, Wissenschaft (187–196, contribs. by Peter Dusek, Sylvia M. Patsch). Further articles are listed according to subject.]

32064. KAISER, WOLF: *Das 'heilende Bad der Seele' und das 'Wunder im Dünensand'. Jerusalem und Tel Aviv in deutschsprachigen Reisebeschreibungen.* [In]: Menora 5, München, 1994. Pp. 197–229, notes.

32065. KESSLER, MARIO: *Zionismus und internationale Arbeiterbewegung: 1897 bis 1933.* Berlin: Akad.-Verl., 1994. 210 pp. Zugl.:Berlin, Akad. d. Wiss. der DDR, Diss, 1990 u.d.T.: Sozialismus und Zionismus.

32066. KLINER-FRUCK, MARTINA: *Es ging ja ums Überleben: deutsch-jüdische Frauen unter nationalsozialistischer Verfolgung in der Emigration in Palästina, Israel und in der Remigration.* Dortmund, Univ., Diss., 1994. VII, 360 pp.

32067. MEYER-MARIL, EDINA: *Alexander Levy, architect in early Tel Aviv.* [In Hebrew, with Engl. summary.] [In]: Cathedra for the History of Eretz Israel and its Yishuv, No. 71, Jerusalem, March 1994. Pp. 61–73. [A.L., 1883 Berlin – 1942 Auschwitz. Lived in Palestine 1920–1927. After his return to Berlin in 1927 he changed his name to Alexander L. Lee. Emigr. to France in 1933.]

32068. PENKOWER, MONTY NOAM: *The Holocaust and Israel reborn: from catastrophe to sovereignty.* Urbana: Univ. Illinois Press, 1994. XIII, 361 pp.

32069. REINHARZ, JEHUDA: *Zionism and the Austrian Left before World War I.* [In]: Brücken über dem Abgrund. Festschrift für Harry Zohn [see No. 32315]. Pp. 79–94.

32070. SADMON, ZEEV W.: *Die Gründung des Technions in Haifa im Lichte deutscher Politik 1907–1920.* München: Sauer, 1994. 311 pp., illus., docs., foootnotes, bibl., index. (Einzelveröffentlichung der Historischen Kommission zu Berlin, Bd. 78; zugl. Trier, Univ., Diss.) [Incl. the role of the Hilfsverein der deutschen Juden, Paul Nathan, James Simon.]

32071. SASSON, AVI: *Rabbi Joseph Schwartz's map of Jerusalem.* [In Hebrew, title transl.] [In]: Sinai, Vol. 114, Jerusalem, Sivan-Tammuz 5754 [=May-June 1994]. Pp. 182–186. [J. Sch., born 1804 in Floss, studied geography and astronomy at the Univers. of Würzburg in the 1820s. Emigr. to Palestine in 1833 and settled in Jerusalem.]

32072. *60 Jahre 'Habonim' in Deutschland.* 60-jähriges Jubiläum der 'Habonim' Deutschland. Auszüge aus Ansprachen anläßlich des Treffens ehemaliger Mitglieder der 'Habonim – Noar Chaluzi' Deutschland am 4. Oktober 1993 im Kibbuz Givat Brenner, Israel. [Ed.]: Yad Tabenkin, Ramat Efal 52960, 1994. 70 pp., illus., tabs., docs.

32073. SELIGMANN, RAFAEL: *'Durch Hitler geboren'. Die deutschen Juden in Israel.* Teil 1 & 2. [In]: Der Spiegel, Nr. 43 & 44, Hamburg, 24. & 31. Okt. 1994. Pp. 130–142; 188–202, illus.

32074. WEITZ, YECHIAM: *Jewish refugees and Zionist policy during the Holocaust.* [In]: Middle Eastern Studies, Vol. 30, No. 2, London, April 1994. Pp. 351–368. [Discusses how the events of the Holocaust and the plight of European Jewry influenced Zionist policy with regard to the founding of the Jewish state.]

VII. PARTICIPATION IN CULTURAL AND PUBLIC LIFE

A. General

32075. ACHBERGER, FRIEDRICH: *Fluchtpunkt 1938.* Essays zur österreichischen Literatur zwischen 1918 und 1938. Hrsg. von Gerhard Scheit. Wien: Verl. für Gesellschaftskritik, 1994. 205 pp. [A collection of essays on Hermann Broch, Karl Kraus, Hugo von Hoffmannsthal et al.]

32076. BRAUN, GÜNTER & WALDTRAUT: *Mäzenatentum in Berlin.* Bürgersinn und kulturelle Kompetenz unter sich verändernden Bedingungen. Hrsg. von Günter und Waldtraut Braun. 258 pp., illus. [Incl. a section on Eduard Arnhold (Wolfgang Hardtwig, 43–46).]

32077. BRECHEISEN, CLAUDIA: *Literatur des Holocaust. Identität und Judentum bei Jakov Lind, Edgar Hilsenrath und Jurek Becker.* Augsburg, Univ., Diss., 1993. [2], 264 pp.

—— BREIDECKER, VOLKER: *Einige Fragmente einer intellektuellen Kollektivbiographie der kulturwissenschaftlichen Emigration.* [See in No. 32249.]

32078. DAHRENDORF, RALF: *Liberale und andere.* Porträts. Stuttgart: Deutsche Verlagsanstalt, 1994. 335 pp. [Incl. Karl R. Popper.]

32079. DEICHMANN, UTE: *Biologen unter Hitler: Vertreibung, Karrieren, Forschung.* Mit einem Vorwort von Benno Müller-Hill. Frankfurt am Main: Campus, 1992. 377 pp., footnotes, bibl. (322–341), index of persons (342–370). [Deals also with the fate of Jewish biologists (30–55).]

32080. DELF, HANNA/SCHOEPS, JULIUS H./WALTHER, MANFRED, Hrsg.: *Spinoza in der europäischen Geistesgeschichte.* Berlin: Hentrich, 1994. 464 pp., notes, index. [Cont. 19 papers given at a colloquium organised by the Moses Mendelssohn Zentrum für europäisch-jüdische Studien an der Universität Potsdam in spring 1993. Incl.: Engl. abstracts (444–451). Essays pertaining to German-speaking Jews: Mendelssohn zwischen Spinoza und Kant (Yirmiyahu Yovel, 12–25). Zwischen Kabbala und Kant. Salomon Maimons 'streifende' Spinoza-Rezeption (Achim Engstler, 162–192). Spielarten jüdischer Identitätsbestimmung im frühen 19. Jahrhundert; Berthold Auerbachs Spinoza-Roman (Gabriele von Glasenapp, 289–304). Spinozas Offenbarungslehre und der nachkantianische Idealismus in der jüdischen Religionsphilosophie Hermann Cohens (Eveline Goodman-Thau, 332–364). Jakob Stern – Sozialist und Spinozist; eine kleine Skizze zum 150. Geburtstag (Manfred Lauermann, 365–393).]

32081. ECKERT, MICHAEL: *Die Atomphysiker. Eine Geschichte der theoretischen Physik am Beispiel der Sommerfeld-Schule.* Wiesbaden: Vieweg, 1993. VIII, 300 pp., illus., notes, index. [Deals passim with Jewish colleagues and students of Arnold Sommerfeld and their fate, also on antisemitism. Incl. the chap.: Happy thirties? Physiker im Exil (147–172).]

32082. EFRON, JOHN M.: *Defenders of the race: Jewish doctors and race science in fin-de-siècle Europe.* New Haven; London: Yale Univ. Press, 1994. XII, 255 pp., illus., notes (181–214), bibl. (215–242). [Incl. racial antisemitism; also rejection of Jews by the medical establishment.]

32083. EIFERT, CHRISTIANE: *The forgotten members of the Arbeiterwohlfahrt. Jews in the Social Democratic Association.* [In]: Leo Baeck Institute Year Book XXXIX, London, 1994. Pp. 179–209.

32084. EXILE. CRITCHFIELD, RICHARD: *When Lucifer cometh: the autobiographical discourse of writers and intellectuals exiled during the Third Reich.* New York: Peter Lang, 1994. VII, 189 pp., notes (145–171), bibl. (173–186). (Literature and the sciences of man, Vol. 7.) [Incl. a.o. Alfred Döblin, Lion Feuchtwanger, Fritz Kortner, Ludwig Marcuse, Walter Mehring, Rober Neumann, Toni Sender, Hilde Spiel.]

32085. EXILE. *Exilforschung.* Ein internationales Jahrbuch. Bd. 12, 1994: *Aspekte der künstlerischen inneren Emigration 1933–1945.* Hrsg. im Auftrag der Gesellschaft für Exilforschung/Society for Exile Studies von Claus-Dieter Krohn [et al.]. München: Ed. Text + Kritik, 1994. 236 pp. (Exilforschung, Bd. 12.) [Incl.: Die Ausweglosigkeit der Nicht-Emigration. Jochen Klepper und die Verfolgung eines Patrioten (Wulf Koepke, 70–81). Die Ermordung Erich Mühsams. Stellungnahmen und Diskussionen deutscher Emigranten 1934–1935 (Hubert van den Berg, 174–190). Das Exil der deutschen Künstler in den dreißiger und vierziger Jahren. Zur Exilforschung (Jutta Held, 191–199).]

32086. EXILE. *Exil.* Forschung, Erkenntnisse, Ergebnisse. Jg. 14, Nr. 1 & 2. Red.: Edita Koch, Frithjof Trapp. Hrsg. von Edita Koch. Frankfurt am Main: E. Koch (Rheinstraße 20, 60325 Frankfurt am Main), 1994 & 1995. 109; 111 pp., illus., notes. [Jg. 14, Nr. 1 (1994) [on title page misprinted 'IX. Jahrgang'] incl.: 'Hier ist ein herrliches Land' – Otto Zareks Exil in Ungarn (René Geoffroy, 7–22). 'Vorläufiges Leben'. Emigrationsalltag in Prag 1933–1939 (Eva-Maria Siegel, 23–38). Exiltheater in der Tschechoslowakei (Hansjörg Schneider, 39–69). Theater zwischen 1933 und 1939 in der Freien Stadt Danzig (Boguslaw Drewniak, 70–76). Das Schicksal der Juden unter dem Vichy-Regime (Dieter Peter Meier-Lenz, 91–96). Also texts and poems by Ernest Bornemann, Karl Seemann, Birgit R. Erdle (on Hans Keilson), Christian Jacob (on Hans Sahl), Edita Koch (on Marie-Louise Motesiczky). Jg. 14, Nr 2 (1995) incl.: Schreiben nach Auschwitz: Hans Sahl (Momme Brodersen, 5–12). Apontamentos de Gurs (Elsbeth Weichmann, 13–24). Widersacher der Resignation: Albert O. Hirschmann (Michael Schornstheimer, 28–36). Gertrud Isolani und Heinrich Eduard Jacob: Korrespondenz über 'Stadt ohne Männer' (Anja Clarenbach, 37–50). Emigrantenhilfe von Emigranten – Die Notgemeinschaft Deutscher Wissenschaftler im Ausland (Regine Erichsen, 51–69). Ludwig Quiddes Prager 'Schützlinge' 1935–1938 (Karl Holl, 70–77). Bertha Dehn (1881–1953) – eine jüdische Musikerin in Hamburg (Ute Schomerus, 78–95). Musik im Exil (Gerhard Müller, 105–110).]

32087. EXILE. FRÜHWALD, WOLFGANG: *. . . meine Heimat ist die Erde, die Welt mein Vaterland'. Vergessene Exil-Traditionen in Deutschland.* [In]: Alexander-von-Humboldt-Magazin, Nr. 62, Bad Godesberg, 1993. Pp. 3–10, illus., facsims.

32088. EXILE. GREBING, HELGA/WICKERT, CHRISTL, Hrsg.: *Das 'andere Deutschland' im Widerstand gegen den Nationalsozialismus. Beiträge zur politischen Überwindung der nationalsozialistischen Diktatur im Exil und im Dritten Reich.* Hrsg. von Helga Grebing und Christl Wickert. Essen: Klartext, 1994. 226 pp. (Veröffentlichungen des Instituts zur Erforschung der europäischen Arbeiterbewegung, Schriftenreihe A: Darstellungen, Bd.6.) [Cont. (titles partly abbr.): Einleitung (Helga Grebing, 7–11). Das gescheiterte Projekt der sozialistischen Einigung im Pariser Exil 1938 (Gerhard Paul, 12–31). Zur Erfahrungsperspektive des Spanischen Bürgerkriegs (Klaus-Michael Mallmann, 32–55). Die Unabhängige Antifaschistische Gruppe 9. Kompanie im Lager Gurs (Dieter Nelles, 56–85). Zur Analyse der Exilpublizistik in Skandinavien (Frank Meyer, 86–116). Toni Sender; aus Amerika ein 'Blick nach Deutschland' (Anette Hild-Berg, 117–145). Fritz Lamm; Exil in Kuba (Detlev Brunner, 146–172). Die Vorbereitung politischer 999er in amerikanischer Kriegsgefangenschaft auf die Nachkriegszeit am Beispiel Fort Devens (Klaus Tulatz, 173–199). Frauen im Hintergrund; das Beispiel von Kommunistinnen und Bibelforscherinnen (Christl Wickert, 200–225).]

32089. EXILE. HAUSJELL, FRITZ/LANGENBUCHER, WOLFGANG R.: *Vertriebene Wahrheit: Journalismus aus dem Exil.* Wien: Ueberreuter, 1994. 430 pp.

32090. EXILE. KOCH, EDITA: *Das Exil als Dauerzustand. Nie wieder heimgeholt: Deutschland und seine vertriebenen jüdischen Schriftsteller.* [In]: 'Allgemeine', Jg. 49, Nr. 11, Bonn, 1. Juni 1994, p. 7. [Abbr. version of lecture given in honour of Hans Sahl, May 21, 1994 in Eisenach.]

32091. EXILE. KRAMER, THOMAS: *Film im Lauf der Zeit: 100 Jahre Kino in Deutschland.* Wien: Ueberreuter, 1994. 286 pp., illus. [Incl.: Emigrantenfilm in Österreich 1933–1936 (75–86).]

32092. EXILE. WEBER, HORST, Hrsg.: *Musik in der Emigration 1933–1945. Verfolgung – Vertreibung – Rückwirkung.* Symposium Essen, 10. bis 13. Juni 1992. Hrsg. von Horst Weber. Stuttgart: Metzler, 1994. 292 pp., illus., bibl. (273–282), index. [Incl. (titles condensed): Exilforschung (Horst Weber, 1–9). Die 'Säuberung' der Reichsmusikkammer (Gerhard Splitt, 10–55). Jüdische Musikwissenschaftler an den Universitäten der Weimarer Zeit (Pamela M. Potter, 56–68). Die Gleichschaltung der Berliner Musikhochschule ab 1933 (Albrecht Dümling, 69–107). Musik im Jüdischen Kulturbund 1933–1941 (Bernd Sponheuer (108–132). Die Emigranten und ihr Einfluß auf die Internationale Gesellschaft für Neue Musik (Anton Haefeli, 136–152). Prag als Asylstadt (Jaromír Paclt, 153–174). Zum Exil deutscher Dirigenten in der Sowjetunion 1933–1945 (Gregorij Pantielev, 175–182). Exilstation Paris

(Matthias Brzoska, 183–191). Im englischen Exil 1933–1945 (Erik Levi, 192–212). Der Fall Weill (Stephen Hinton, 213–227). Der lautlose Dissens der Musik im faschistischen Italien (Gianmario Borio, 228–240). Emigranten bei den Internationalen Ferienkursen für Neue Musik in Darmstadt (1946–1951) (Siegfried Mauser, 241–248). Remigranten in der DDR (Frank Schneider, 249–259). Jüdische Musiker nach der Gleichschaltung (Alexander L. Ringer, 260–272).]

32093. EXILE LITERATURE. BEER, FRITZ/WESTPHAL, UWE, eds.: *Exil ohne Ende. Das PEN-Zentrum deutschsprachiger Autoren im Ausland*. Essays, Biographien, Materialien. Gerlingen: Bleicher, 1994. 192 pp. [Incl. biographical and bibliographical list of members.]

32094. EXILE LITERATURE. *'Einmal Exil, immer Exil'*. [In]: Brücken über dem Abgrund. Festschrift für Harry Zohn [see No. 32315]. Pp. 239–298. [This section of book (= Teil zwei, I) cont. the following essays: God in exile: Abraham Joshua Heschel, translator of the spirit (Edward K. Kaplan, 239–254). Exile experience in Berthold Viertel's poetry (Eberhard Frey, 255–266). Joseph Roths politische Exilhaltung im Spiegel seiner Briefe (Joseph P. Strelka, 267–282). Österreichische Emigrantinnen schreiben in den USA (Lisa Kahn, 283–298).]

32095. EXILE LITERATURE. *Exil – Asyl. Tatort Deutschland*. Texte von 1933 bis heute – eine literarische Anthologie. Hrsg. von Henning Müller. Mit einem Nachwort von Wilhelm von Sternburg. Gerlingen: Schneider, 1994. 299 pp. [An anthology of texts and poems, many of them written by German-Jewish authors; cont. the sections: Vorwort (Henning Müller, 9–36). I. 'Werft Eure Hoffnung über neue Grenzen'. Texte des deutschen Exils (37–98). II. 'Ist dies Deutschland zu verstehen?!' Stimmen vor und nach 1945 – eine Zusammenschau (99–146). III: 'Sind wir Deutschen uns fremd geworden?' Stimmen heute (147–178). IV. 'Meine Ortschaft'. Unaussprechliches zu Auschwitz (179–220). Nachwort von Wilhelm von Sternburg (221–244). Anhang: Bio-bibliographische Angaben zu den Autoren (245–280). Quellenverzeichnis (281–299).]

32096. EXILE LITERATURE. *Literatur aus Exil und Widerstand: 1933–1948*. Ausstellung 13.12.93 bis 14.1.94; eine Auswahl aus den Beständen der Universitätsbibliothek Wuppertal. Katalog zur Ausstellung. Zusammengestellt von Benigna Gräfin von Rittberg. Wuppertal: Berg. Univ., Gesamthochschule, 1993. [101] pp.

32097. EXILE LITERATURE. THIELKING, SIGRID: *Die Grimasse des Caliban. Erklärungsmuster von Dekulturation bei deutschsprachig-jüdischen Autoren*. [In]: Jahrbuch für Antisemitismusforschung 3, Frankfurt am Main; New York, 1994. Pp. 165–177. [On Arnold Zweig and other exile authors.]

32098. EXILE LITERATURE. WALLACE, IAN, ed.: *Aliens – Uneingebürgerte. German and Austrian writers in exile*. Ed. by Ian Wallace. Amsterdam; Atlanta, GA: Rodopol, 1994. 251 pp., illus., footnotes. (Amsterdamer Beiträge zur neueren Germanistik, Bd. 37 – 1994.) [A collection of 14 essays, most of them dealing with German-speaking émigrés. Incl.: Arnold Zweigs Rückkehr nach Deutschland (Geoffrey V. Davis, 11–34). 'Andere Lösung Quatsch'; Anna Seghers and the film 'Die Toten bleiben jung' (Ian Wallace, 71–84). Jud Süß between art and politics: Veit Harlan and Lion Feuchtwanger (William Small, 85–100). Glaeser's cobwebbed gallery: 'der letzte Zivilist' as reminder (Geoffrey Butler, 135–144). 'Ein Experte des Überlebens': Robert Neumann in British exile (Richard Dove, 159–174). '. . . und wo die Synagogen brennen, erzittern auch schon die Kathedralen in ihren Grundfesten': kulturkritische Anmerkungen zu Heinz Carwins Tragikomödie 'Großmutter Himmelreich' (1944) (Jörg Thunecke, 195–206). Rehfisch in exile (Hamish Ritchie, 207–222). Rudolf Bernauer: 'Die leichtgeschürzte Muse' in London 1935–1955 (Jennifer Taylor, 223–236). Women only? The Feuilleton of 'Die Zeitung' (1941–45) (Donald McLaughlin, 237–242; bibl. of the prose and poetry publ. in the Feuilleton, 242–251).]

32099. FRANKFURT SCHOOL. VEAUTHIER, F. WERNER: *'Jüdisches' im Denken der Frankfurter Schule*. [In]: Juden in Deutschland. Lebenswelten und Einzelschicksale. Hrsg. von Reinhard Schneider [see No. 31400]. Pp. 271–308.

32100. FRANKFURT SCHOOL. WIGGERSHAUS, ROLF: *The Frankfurt School*. Transl. by Michael Robertson. Oxford: Polity; Cambridge, Ma.: MIT Press, 1994. IX, 787 pp., notes (660–714), bibl. (715–771). (Studies in contemporary German social thought.) [Incl. the exile years and the work at the New School for Social Research.]

32101. FRISCHENSCHLAGER, OSKAR, Hrsg.: *Wien, wo sonst! Die Entstehung der Psychoanalyse und ihrer Schulen*. Wien: Böhlau, 1994. 254 pp.

32102. HAHN, BARBARA: *Frauen in den Kulturwissenschaften*. Von Lou Andreas-Salomé bis Hannah Arendt. München: Beck, 1994. 163 pp., notes, bibl. Originalausgabe. (Beck'sche Reihe, 1043.) [Incl. essays on (titles abbr.): Rosa Luxemburg; Margarete Susman; Bertha Badt-Strauss (Barbara Hahn, 63–95; 152–165). Gertrud Kantorowicz (Barbara Paul, 96–109); Hedwig Hintze-Guggenheimer (Bernd Faulenbach, 136–151). Sabina Spielrein (Rike Felka, 166–188). Selma Stern (Michael Schmidt, 204–218). Melitta Gerhard (Gesa Dane, 219–234). Edith Stein (Hanna-Barbara Gerl, 235–249). Hannah Arendt (Ingeborg Nordmann, 262–277).]

32103. *In der Sprache der Mörder. Eine Literatur aus Czernowitz, Bukowina*. Ausstellungsbuch. Erarb. und hrsg. von Ernest Wichner und Herbert Wiesner. Berlin: Literaturhaus, 1993. 277 pp., illus. (Texte aus dem Literaturhaus Berlin, Bd. 9.) [Catalogue of an exhibition held in Berlin March 7 – April 12, 1993. Incl. many Jewish authors such as Rose Ausländer, Paul Celan, Alfred Kittner, Moses Rosenkranz, Alfred Margul-Sperber.] [Cf.: Grüne Mutter Bukowina. Eine deutsche Literatur aus Czernowitz (Matthias Rüb) [in]: 'FAZ', Nr. 133, Frankfurt am Main, 12. Juni 1993, Beilage.]

32104. *Jüdische Kultur und Weiblichkeit in der Moderne*. Hrsg. von Inge Stephan, Sabine Schilling und Sigrid Weigel. Köln: Böhlau, 1994. 351 pp., footnotes. [Incl. (titles abbr.): Einführung (Sigrid Weigel, 1–8). Sabina Spielrein (Inge Stephan, 51–72). Margarete Susman (Ingeborg Nordmann, 85–102). Charlotte Salomon (Gertrud Koch, 103–118 and Genia Schulz, 119–130). Charlotte Wolff (Marie Luise Gansberg, 159–172). Gertrud Kolmar (Marion Brandt, 173–186); Hannah Arendt (Dorothea Dornhof, 187–198). Schwierigkeiten mit dem Erinnern (Hannelore Scholz, 291–305; on Ruth Werner and Salomea Genin). Nichts wie zuhause (Leslie A. Adelson, 307–330; on Jeannette and Ronnith Neumann). Further essays are listed according to subject.]

32105. *Jüdische Porträts. Graphische Bildnisse prominenter Juden Mitteleuropas*. Mit einer Einleitung von Julius H. Schoeps. 72 pp., illus., bibl., index. [Catalogue of an exhibition held in the Stadtmuseum Münster Oct. 22, 1993 – Jan. 9, 1994, from a private collection. Incl. numerous German-Jewish personalities, also a section titled 'Münsteraner'.]

32106. KEßLER, MARIO: *Die kommunistische Linke und die Weimarer Republik*. [In]: Aus Politik und Zeitgeschichte. [Beilage zur Wochenzeitung] Das Parlament, B 32-33/94, Bonn, 12. Aug., 1994. Pp. 20–30. [Incl. many Jewish politicians and functionaries.]

32107. KNIESCHE, THOMAS W./BROCKMANN, STEPHEN: *Dancing on the volcano: essays on the culture of the Weimar Republic*. Ed. by Thomas W. Kniesche and Stephen Brockmann. Columbus, S.C.: Camden House, 1994. VII, 220 pp., illus., footnotes, bibl. [Incl. Theodor Adorno, Ernst Bloch, Sigmund Freud, Max Horkheimer, Fritz Lang, Ernst Toller.]

32108. LORENZ, DAGMAR C.G., WEINBERGER, GABRIELE, eds.: *Insiders and outsiders: Jewish and Gentile culture in Germany and Austria*. Ed. by Dagmar C.G. Lorenz and Gabriele Weinberger. Introd. by Dagmar C.G. Lorenz. Detroit: Wayne State Univ. Press, 1994. XII, 365 pp. [Incl.: Chicken soup; of the penalties of sounding too Jewish (Sander L. Gilman, 15–29). Residues of otherness: on Jewish emancipation during the age of German enlightenment (Barbara Fischer, 30–38). The Wandering Jew's Rhine journey: Heine's Lorelei (Jost Hermand, 39–46). Jews and antisemitism in fin-de-siècle Vienna (Egon Schwarz, 47–65). Historical visions: Anna Seghers on the revolutions in Haiti (Sima Kappeler, 66–72). Jean Améry and Austria (Ruth Beckermann, 73–86). Alsatian Yiddish theatre at the turn of the century (Astrid Starck, 100–108). Babylon or Jerusalem: Berlin as center of Jewish modernism in the 1920s (Delphine Bechtel, 116–123). Authors of German language in Israel (Margarita Pazi, 124–131). Thomas Mann's Wälsungenblut in the context of the intermarriage debate and the 'Jewish Question' (Alan Levenson, 135–143). The negative German-Jewish symbiosis (Jack Zipes, 144–154). Historical consciousness and Jewish identity: Stefan Zweig and Wilhelm Speyer on the way to themselves (Luke Springman, 155–174). Bezwingt des Herzens Bitterkeit: Hilde Burger's return from 'paradise'(Roslyn Abt Schindler, 175–185). 'You who live safe in your warm houses': your role in the production of Holocaust testimony (Irene Kacandes, 189–213). Social Darwinism in Edgar Hilsenrath's ghetto novel 'Nacht' [&] The case of Jacob Littner: authors, publishers, and Jewish history in unified Germany [&] The legacy of Jewish Vienna (Dagmar C.G. Lorenz, 214–223; 235–250; 293–300). Politics to pulp a novel: the fate of the first edition of Edgar Hilsenrath's novel 'Nacht' (Susann Moeller, 224–234). Beyond the bridges (Ruth Beckermann, 301–307). Lea Fleischmann and Wolf Biermann: like strangers in their own house (Peter Werres, 313–328). Barbara Honigmann: a preliminary assessment (Guy Stern, 329–346).]

32109. MAYER, HANS: *Der Widerruf. Über Deutsche und Juden.* Frankfurt am Main: Suhrkamp, 1994. 467 pp. [A collection of 17 essays; incl.: Felix Mendelssohn, Karl Kraus, Hugo von Hoffmannsthal, Otto Weininger, Arnold Schönberg, Walther Rathenau, Theodor Lessing, Ernst Bloch, Anna Seghers, Hanns Eisler, Max Brod, Franz Kafka, Albert Einstein, Walther Rathenau, Sigmund Freud, Arnold Zweig, Walter Benjamin, Gerhard/Gershom Scholem.] [Cf.: Haß und Selbsthaß. Hans Mayers große kulturhistorische Studie (Harro Zimmermann) [in]: Die Zeit, Nr. 12, Hamburg, 18. März 1994, p. 30.]

32110. *Messianismus zwischen Mythos und Macht: Jüdisches Denken in der europäischen Geistesgeschichte.* Hrsg. von Eveline Goodman-Thau und Wolfdietrich Schmied-Kowarzik. Berlin: Akademie Verl., 1994. 269 pp., footnotes, index. [Papers presented at a colloquium at the Univers. of Kassel, March 3 – 5, 1993. Cont. (titles partly abbr.): Einführende Bemerkungen (Wolfdietrich Schmied-Kowarzik, 13–19). Juden an der Universität (Michael Daxner, 19–28). Deutsche und Juden im 19. Jahrhundert (Yaakov Ben-Chanan, 29–48). Der Flavius Josephus Komplex (Jean-Luc Evard, 49–60). Cassirer und Levinas (Stéphane Weiss, 61–88). Tradition, Evolution, Erinnerung (Aleida Assmann, 89–100). Kabbala und neues Denken (Eveline Goodman-Thau, 101–126). In Rosenzweigs Seele – die Kabbala (Karl Erich Grözinger, 127–140). Vergil und Novalis (Richard Faber, 141–164). Der Zerfall des säkularisierten Messianismus (Michael Beintker, 165–178). Mythologie, Messianismus, Macht (Gert Mattenklott, 179–196). Messias und Identität (Christoph Schulte, 197–210): Max Brods Bewußtsein vom Judentum (Claus-E. Bärsch, 211–230). Theologie und Messianismus im Denken Adornos (Micha Brumlik, 231–252). Marc Rothko und Barnett Newman (Georg Syamken, 252–262).]

32111. NYE, ANDREA: *Philosophia: the thought of Rosa Luxemburg, Simone Weil, and Hannah Arendt.* New York; London: Routledge, 1994. XXI, 280 pp.

32112. REICH-RANICKI, MARCEL: *Die Anwälte der Literatur.* Stuttgart: Deutsche Verlags-Anstalt, 1994. 357 pp., notes (333–354), index. [Incl. a.o. essays on Ludwig Börne, Heinrich Heine, Alfred Kerr, Moritz Heimann, Alfred Polgar, Siegfried Jacobsohn, Kurt Tucholsky, Walter Benjamin, Robert Minder, Hans Mayer, Friedrich Luft and Hilde Spiel.] [The chap. on Ludwig Börne is reprinted in: Frankfurter Jüdische Nachrichten, Nr. 84, Frankfurt am Main, März/April, 1994. Pp. 7–9.]

32113. ROTHSCHILD FAMILY. HEUBERGER, GEORG: *Die Rothschilds. Eine jüdische Familie aus Frankfurt.* [In]: Tribüne, Jg. 33, H. 130, Frankfurt am Main, 1994. Pp. 176–180.

32114. ROTHSCHILD FAMILY. HEUBERGER, GEORG/URBAN, SUSANNE: *Die Rothschilds – der Weg einer europäischen Familie.* [In]: Tribüne, Jg. 33, H. 131, Frankfurt am Main, 1994. Pp. 151–160.

32115. ROTHSCHILD FAMILY. *Die Rothschilds.* Anläßlich der Ausstellung 'Die Rothschilds – eine europäische Familie', im Jüdischen Museum der Stadt Frankfurt am Main 11. Okt. 1994 – 27. Februar 1995, hrsg. von Georg Heuberger im Auftrag des Dezernats für Kultur und Freizeit, Amt für Wissenschaft und Kunst der Stadt Frankfurt am Main vom Jüdischen Museum der Stadt Frankfurt am Main. Sigmaringen: Thorbecke, 1994. 2 vols. *Bd. 1: Eine europäische Familie* [Begleitbuch]. Autoren: Fritz Backhaus, Lisbeth Ehlers, Ernst Karpf, Helga Krohn, Christine Lenger, Rainer Schlott, Annette Weber. 209 pp., illus., bibl. *Bd. 2: Die Rothschilds. Beiträge zur Geschichte einer europäischen Familie* [Essayband]. 423 pp., notes, illus. [Incl. (titles partly abbr.): Die Rothschilds – Familiengeschichte im Museum (Georg Heuberger, 15–20). Kurfürst Wilhelm I. von Hessen und Mayer Amschel Rothschild (Rainer von Hessen, 21–36). Die anderen Rothschilds: Frankfurter Privatbankiers im 18. und 19. Jahrhundert (Michael Jurk, 37–50). Der Aufstieg der Rothschilds (Manfred Pohl, 51–70). Die Etablierung der Rothschilds im englischen Bankgewerbe (Stanley Chapman, 71–86). Die Rothschilds, die Eisenbahn und die städtebauliche Entwicklung von Paris im 19. Jahrhundert (Karen Bowie, 89–100). Die 'Damaskus-Affäre' 1840 und die Bedeutung des Hauses Rothschild für die Mobilisierung der öffentlichen Meinung (Rainer Erb, 101–116). Lord Rothschild und seine armen Brüder: osteuropäische Juden in London 1880–1906 (Kerstin Warnke, 117–112). Edmond de Rothschild und Palästina (Yoram Mayorek, 113–150). Gedanken zur Familie Rothschild I: Die Männer [&] Gedanken über die Familie Rothschild II: Die Frauen (Miriam Rothschild, 141–170). Zur Soziologie der dynastischen Machtstellung der Rothschilds (Andreas Hansert, 171–184). Der Aufstieg der englischen Rothschilds in den Adel (Simone Mace, 185–200). Die Rothschilds und das Judentum (Robert Liberles, 201–210). Die wohltätigen Stiftungen der Rothschilds in Frankfurt am Main (Hans-Otto Schembs, 211–224). Über die Bauten der Familie Rothschild in Frankfurt am Main (Dieter Bartetzko, 225–246). Die Bauten der Rothschilds – England, Frankreich, Deutschland, Österreich und Italien (Pauline Prevost-Marcilhacy, 247–266). Die englischen Rothschilds als Sammler (Michael Hall, 267–290). Musik und Musiker bei den Rothschilds (Charlotte de Rothschild, 291–300). Der Mythos vom Bankier in Frankreich (Louis Bergeron, 301–310). Die Rothschilds in der Literatur (Thomas Sparr, 311–324). Die Rothschilds im 'Dritten Reich' (Christopher Kopper, 325–336). Eine Familie – zwei Filme (Régine Mihal Friedman, 337–354). Die 'Arisierung' der Rothschildschen Vermögen in Wien und ihre Restituierung in der Nachkriegszeit (Felicitas Heimann-Jelinek, 355–368). Ausstellungsdokumentation (377–412). [An Engl. edn. of Vol. 2 was publ. simultaneouly: *The Rothschilds*. Vol. 2: *Essays on the history of a European family*. Ed. by Georg Heuberger. Transl. from German into English: Jeremy Gaines, assisted by Paul Keast. Transl. from French into English: Steven Englund, Melissa Davidson, ed. by Jeremy Gaines. Transl. from Hebrew into English: Shlomo Ketko. Woodbridge, Suffolk: Boydell & Brewer, 1994. 419 pp., illus., facsims., ports., maps, lists, family trees.]

32116. ROTHSCHILD FAMILY. WILSON, DEREK: *Rothschild: a story of wealth and power*. Rev. edn. London: Mandarin Paperbacks, 1994. 511 pp., illus., genealogy, notes, bibl. (493–498). [First publ. in 1988 by André Deutsch. Incl. chaps. on the Frankfurt Rothschilds.]

32117. SARKOWICZ, HANS, Hrsg.: *Die großen Frankfurter*. Herausgegeben von Hans Sarkowicz. Frankfurt am Main: Insel, 1994. 287 pp., ports. [A collection of 26 essays. Incl. (titles abbr.): Mayer Amschel Rothschild (Johann Philipp Freiherr von Bethmann, 58–68). Ludwig Börne (Alfred Grosser, 126–132). Leopold Sonnemann (Walter Wallmann, 193–198). Paul Ehrlich und sein Georg-Speyer-Haus (Helga Rübsamen-Waigmann, 199–215). Theodor W. Adorno (Alfred Schmidt, 246–253). Ein Gespräch über Anne Frank (Ignatz Bubis, 254–266).]

32118. SCHÖNE, LOTHAR: *Neuigkeiten vom Mittelpunkt der Welt: der Kampf ums Theater in der Weimarer Republik*. Darmstadt: Wiss. Buchges. [Abt. Verl.], 1994. XI, 328 pp., illus. Zugl.: Diss. [Deals mainly with Alfred Kerr and Herbert Ihering.]

32119. SCHULTE, HANS/RICHARDS, DAVID: *Crisis and culture in post-enlightenment Germany*. Essays in honour of Peter Heller. Ed. by Hans Schulte and David Richards. Lanham, Md.: Univ. Press of America, 1993. 508 pp., bibl. [Cont. 23 essays, partly English, partly German. Incl.: Preface (an appraisal of Peter Heller and his work, 3 pp., unpag.). Arthur Schnitzler and Theodor Herzl: two roads into the open (Henry Lea, 319–342). Hugo Heller: bookseller and educator in Vienna (1870–1923) (Walter Grossmann, 377–394). Der 'Anschluß' in den Memoiren der 'Thirty-Eighters' (Harry Zohn, 433–452). Publications by Peter Heller (503–

508). Two further articles listed according to subject.] [Peter Heller, b. Jan. 11, 1920 Vienna, prof. of German and comparative literature, emigr. 1938 via Paris to London, interned in Canada, in 1944 went to the USA.]

32120. SHAKED, GERSHON: *Die Macht der Identität.* Essays über jüdische Schriftsteller. Aus dem Englischen von Ulrike Berger [et al.]. Frankfurt am Main: Jüdischer Verlag, 1992. 232 pp., index. (Eine Veröffentlichung des Leo Baeck Instituts.) [Incl. essays on Saul Friedländer, Franz Kafka, Joseph Roth and Stefan Zweig.] [Reprint of the 1986 edn.; see No. 23584/YB XXXII.]

32121. STOLLEIS, MICHAEL: *'Junges Deutschland', jüdische Emanzipation und liberale Staatsrechtslehre in Deutschland.* [In]: Sitzungsberichte der Wissenschaftlichen Gesellschaft an der Johann Wolfgang Goethe-Universität Frankfurt am Main, Band XXXII, Nr. 3. Stuttgart: Steiner, 1994. Pp. 5–25, footnotes. [Also on Jewish scholars of state and constitutional law.]

32122. *Turn-of-the-century Vienna and its legacy: essays in honor of Donald G. Daviau.* Ed. by Jeffrey B. Berlin, Jorun B. Johns, Richard H. Lawson. Edition Atelier, 1993. 546 pp., notes. [Incl. a.o. contribs. on Peter Altenberg, Felice Bauer, Max Brod, Hugo von Hofmannsthal, Richard Beer-Hofmann, Franz Kafka, Karl Kraus, Ludwig Wittgenstein, Arthur Schnitzler, Franz Werfel, Stefan Zweig; also the following articles: 'Some reflections on the image of woman in the works of Hofmannsthal and his Viennese contemporaries'; 'Theodor Herzl, Martin Buber, Berthold Feiwel, and the young-Jewish Viennese poets'.]

32123. ULBRICH, BERND GERHARD: *Gelehrte in Anhalt. Fünfzig Porträts.* Hrsg.: Anhaltischer Heimatbund e.V. Dessau: Anhaltische Verl.-Ges., 1994. 196 pp., illus., bibl. [Incl. Moses Mendelssohn, Gotthold Salomon, Ludwig Philippson, Heymann Steinthal, Hermann Cohen.]

32124. WARBURG FAMILY. CHERNOW, RON: *Die Warburgs. Odyssee einer Familie.* Aus dem Amerikanischen von Karl A. Klewer. Berlin: Siedler, 1994. 960 pp., illus. [For American edn. see No. 31240/YB XXXIX.] [Cf.: 'Nur durch Einigkeit werdet Ihr stark sein . . .' (Julius H. Schoeps) [in]: Die Zeit, Nr. 49, Hamburg, 2. Dez. 1994, p. 26. Die Warburgs (Andres Lepik) [in]: 'NZZ', Nr. 56, Zürich, 8. März 1995, p. 45. Die glorreichen Sieben (Ulrich Raulff) [in]: 'FAZ', Nr. 238, Frankfurt am Main, 6. Dez. 1994, p. 14.]

32125. WILCOCK, EVELYN: *Pacifism and the Jews.* Stroud, Glos., UK: Hawthorn Press, 1994. 248 pp., app., notes, index. [Incl. German-Jewish pacifists; also discusses pacifism in the face of the Holocaust.]

32126. WIRTH-NESHER, HANA, ed.: *What is Jewish literature?* Ed. with an introd. by Hana Wirth-Nesher. Philadelphia; Jerusalem: The Jewish Publication Society, 1994. X, 271 pp., notes, bibl. [Incl. chap. 'Shadows of identity': a comparative study of German Jewish and American Jewish literature (Gershon Shaked) (167–187); also chaps. on Yiddish language and literature; annotated list of authors.]

32127. WURM, CARSTEN: *150 Jahre Rütten & Loening. . . . mehr als eine Verlagsgeschichte.* Geleitwort von Alfred Grosser. Berlin: Rütten & Loening, 1994. 280 pp., illus. [Deals also with the Jewish co-founder Zacharias Löwenthal (later Loening) and other Jewish personalities associated with the publishing company, such as Martin Buber.] [Cf.: Im Labyrinth der Zeitgeschichte (Hans Altenhein) [in]: Börsenblatt für den Deutschen Buchhandel, Jg. 161, Nr. 57, Frankfurt am Main, 19. Juli 1994, p. 8.]

B. Individual

32128. AARON ISAAK. SIMON, MARIE: *Aaron Isaak, der erste Schutzjude in Schweden.* [In]: Kairos, N.F., Jg. 34/35, Salzburg, 1992/1993. Pp. 120–131, notes.

32129. AARON ISAAK. SIMON, BETTINA: *Isaak Aaron: Lebenserinnerungen.* Textfassung und Einleitung von Bettina Simon. Hrsg. Von Marie und Heinrich Simon. Berlin: Hentrich, 1994. 204 pp. [Incl.: Einleitung (Bettina Simon, 11–38).] [A.I., 1730 Treuenbrietzen nr.

Berlin – 1816 Stockholm, Jewish scholar, tradesman and engraver in Mecklenburg, went to Stockholm in 1774, where he became the first Swedish 'Schutzjude'. Founder of the Stockholm Jewish community. His memoirs were written in German/Judaeo-German with Hebrew letters.] [Cf.: Besprechung (Erika Timm) [in]: Jiddistik-Mitteilungen, Nr. 13, Trier, April 1995, p. 20–22.]

32130. ADLER, ALFRED. HOFFMAN, EDWARD: *The drive for self: Alfred Adler and the founding of individual psychology.* Reading, Mass.: Addison-Wesley, 1994. XIX, 390 pp., illus., notes.

32131. ADLER, FRIEDRICH. *Spurensuche: Friedrich Adler. Zwischen Jugendstil und Art déco.* Hrsg. und Red.: Brigitte Leonhardt und Dieter Zühlsdorff. Katalog-Autoren: Maike Bruhns [et al.]. Stuttgart: Arnold, 1994. 446 pp., illus., bibl. (428–435). [Catalogue book; exhibition with the same title first held in the Münchner Stadtmuseum, Feb. 2, 1994 – April 4, 1994.] [F.A., April 29, 1878 Laupheim – 1942 Auschwitz, designer, art educator, taught for 35 years at the Kunstgewerbeschule, Hamburg; dismissed in 1933, deported to Auschwitz July 11, 1942.]

32132. ADORNO, THEODOR. CLAUSSEN, DETLEV: *Nach Auschwitz kein Gedicht. Ist Adornos Diktum übertrieben, überholt und widerlegt?* [In]: Frankfurter Jüdische Nachrichten, Nr. 86, Frankfurt am Main, Sept. 1994. Pp. 37–38.

32133. AGNON, SHMUEL JOSEF. MIRON, DAN: *Ashkenaz; the Jewish-German experience in Agnon's writings.* [In Hebrew, title transl.] [In]: Zafon; literary periodical, Vol. 3, Haifa, 1994. Pp. 9–73.

32134. AGNON, SHMUEL JOSEF. *Tradition and trauma: studies in the fiction of S.J. Agnon.* Ed. by David Patterson and Glenda Abramson. Boulder, Co.: Westview Press, 1994. 226 pp., bibl., (213–218). [Incl. a personal statement by Aharon Appelfeld.]

32135. AMERY, JEAN. AMÉRY, JEAN: *On aging: revolt and resignation.* Transl. by John D. Barlow. Bloomington: Indiana Univ. Press, 1994. XXIII, 132 pp. [Five essays about the process of ageing.]

32136. APPELFELD, AHARON. APPELFELD, AHARON: *Beyond despair.* Three lectures and a talk with Philip Roth. Transl. by Jeffrey M. Green. New York: Fromm International, 1994. XV, 80 pp. (Radov lectures.) [Lectures deal with Appelfeld's confrontation of the Holocaust.]

32137. APPELFELD, AHARON. RAMRAS-RAUCH, GILA: *Aharon Appelfeld: the Holocaust and beyond.* Bloomington: Indiana Univ. Press, 1994. X, 211 pp., bibl. (Jewish literature and culture.) [Author discusses the effect the Holocaust had on Appelfeld's work.]

32138. ARENDT, HANNAH. D'ENTRÈVES, MAURIZIO PASSERIN: *The political philosophy of Hannah Arendt.* London; New York: Routledge, 1994. 217 pp., notes (167–197), bibl. (198–210).

32139. ARENDT, HANNAH. SCHINDLER, ROLAND W.: *Hannah Arendt und die [Historiker-]Kontroverse um die 'Rationalität' der Judenvernichtung.* [In]: Dialektik, H. 1, Hamburg, 1994. Pp. 147–160.

32140. ARNHEIM, RUDOLF. *Rudolf Arnheim. Zauber des Sehens.* Gespräch mit Ingo Hermann in der Reihe 'Zeugen des Jahrhunderts'. Hrsg. von Ingo Hermann, Göttingen: Lamuv, 1993. 105 pp. (Zeugen des Jahrhunderts.) [R.A., b. 1904, psychologist, film critic, assist. editor of 'Die Weltbühne', emigr. 1933 via Rome, London to the USA.]

32141. ARONSTEIN, PHILIPP. LEHBERGER, REINER: *'Wie aus dem Leben verdrängt'. Zum 50. Todestag von Philipp Aronstein.* [In]: Neusprachliche Mitteilungen aus Wissenschaft und Praxis, 4. Quartal, H. 4, Bielefeld, 1992. Pp. 220–225, notes. [Ph.A., philologist, for data see No. 25745/YB XXXIV.]

32142. BALL, HUGO: *Critique of the German intelligentsia.* Transl. by Brian B. Harris. New York: Columbia Univ. Press, 1993. XLII, 273 pp. (European perspectives.)

32143. BECK, ENRIQUE. Rudin-Bühlmann, Sibylle: *Enrique Beck. Ein Leben für Garcia Lorca.* Zürich: Pendo, 1993. 198 pp. [E.B., Feb. 12, 1904 Cologne – Sept. 16, 1974 Riehen (Switzerland), emigr. 1933 to Switzerland, 1934 to Spain, writer, translator.]

32144. BEER-HOFMANN, RICHARD. Mayer, Anton: *Richard Beer-Hofmann und das Wien des Fin de Siècle.* Biographie und Werkauswahl. [Wien]: Ed. Atelier, 1993. 178 pp.

32145. BENJAMIN, WALTER. Markner, Reinhard/Weber, Thomas: *Literatur über Walter Benjamin.* Kommentierte Bibliographie 1983–1992. Berlin: Argument-Verl., 1993. 310 pp. (Argument-Sonderband; N.F.)

32146. BENJAMIN, WALTER. Wolin, Richard: *Walter Benjamin: an aesthetic of redemption.* With a new introd. by the author. Berkeley: Univ. of California Press, 1994. LVIII, 316 pp., illus., notes, bibl. (Weimar and now, 7.) [For earlier edn. in 1982 see No. 19336/YB XXVIII.]

32147. BERG, JIMMY. Jarka, Horst: *'Vergriffen, vergessen usw.' Jimmy Berg (1908–1988) – Komponist und Textautor im New Yorker Exil.* [In]: Mit der Ziehharmonika, Jg. 11, Nr. 3, Wien, Nov. 1994. Pp. 3–7, port., notes.

32148. BERGNER, ELISABETH. *. . . unsere schwarze Rose Elisabeth Bergner.* [Hrsg.:] Astrid A. Gmeiner; Historisches Museum der Stadt Wien. Wien: Historisches Museum der Stadt Wien, 1993. 123 pp., illus. [Catalogue of exhibition, Vienna Jan. 21 – March 21, 1993. Incl. essays on life and work of E. Bergner: also hitherto unpubl. correspondence between E. Bergner and Boleslaw Barlog.]

32149. BERNSTEIN, EDUARD. Weisberger, Adam: *Utopia deferred: Eduard Bernstein and the messianic idea.* [In]: European Judaism, Vol. 27, No. 2, London, Autumn 1994. Pp. 28–46, notes, bibl.

32150. BETTAUER, HUGO. Krobb, Florian: *Vienna goes to pot without the Jews: Hugo Bettauer's novel 'Die Stadt ohne Juden' (the city without Jews).* [In]: Jewish Quarterly, Vol. 41, No. 2, London, Summer 1994. Pp. 17–20, illus. [Discusses both the author and the novel written in 1922.]

32151. BETTELHEIM, BRUNO. *Bruno Bettelheim. Erziehung zum Leben.* Gespräch mit Ingo Herrmann in der Reihe 'Zeugen des Jahrhunderts'. Hrsg. von Ingo Hermann. Göttingen: Lamuv, 1993. 154 pp. (Zeugen des Jahrhunderts.)

32152. BLOCH, ERNST. Franzke, Michael, Hrsg.: *Die ideologische Offensive. Ernst Bloch, SED und Universität.* Leipzig: Leipziger Univ.-Verl., 1994. 225 pp. [Incl. 40 documents from the archives of the SED.] [Cf.: Besprechung (Ruth Römer) [in]: 'FAZ', Nr. 61, Frankfurt am Main, 13. März, 1995, p. 10.

32153. BLOCH, ERNST. Herzberg, Guntolf: *Ernst Bloch in Leipzig: der operative Vorgang 'Wild'.* [In]: Zeitschrift für Geschichtswissenschaft, Jg. 42, Nr. 8, Berlin, 1994. Pp. 677–693, footnotes. [Deals with documents from the Ministerium für Staatssicherheit.]

32154. CANETTI, ELIAS. Canetti, Elias: *A false story which turns out to be true. Ten aphorisms.* [In]: Salmagundi, Nos. 104–105, Saratoga Springs, N.Y., Fall-Winter 1994/95. Pp. 204–205.

32155. CANETTI, ELIAS. Elbaz, Robert/Hadomi, Leah: *Text and metatext in Canetti's fictional world.* [In]: The German Quarterly, Vol. 67, No. 4, Riverside, Ca., Fall 1994. Pp. 521–533, notes.

32156. CANETTI, ELIAS. Potgieter, Johan: *Elias Canetti: Individuum versus Masse.* Eine sprachrealistische Veranschaulichung seiner Philosophie in 'Die Blendung'. [In]: Modern Austrian Literature, Vol. 27, Nos. 3–4, Riverside, Ca., 1994. Pp. 71–82.

32157. CANETTI, ELIAS. *Selected obituaries Elias Canetti.* Bildhaftigkeit des Denkens. Zum Tode von Elias Canetti (Hansres Jacobi) [in]: 'NZZ', Nr. 192, Zürich, 19. Aug. 1994, p. 41. Aus einem elementaren Vertrauen in die Sprache (Peter von Matt) [in]: 'NZZ', Nr. 230, Zürich, 3. Okt. 1994, p. 20. Der weise Komödiant. Zum Tod von Elias Canetti (Peter von Matt) [in]: Die Zeit, Nr. 35, Hamburg, 26. Aug. 1994, p. 44. Die Ohnmacht des Todes: Elias Canetti [in]: Das Jüdische Echo, Vol. 43, Wien, Okt. 1994, pp. 229–239; incl.: Ein Verneiner der Verneinung; Wiener Ausblicke auf Elias Canetti (Wolfgang Kraus, 229–234) [&] Von der Freiheit der Person; Überlegungen zu Elias Canetti (Friedrich Geyrhofer, 235–239). Das verworfene Paradies (Gustav Seibt) [in]: 'FAZ', Nr. 191, Frankfurt am Main, 18. Aug. 1994, p. 23. Obituary Elias Canetti [in]: 'AJR', Vol. 49, No. 9, London, Oct. 1994, p. 14. Obituary (Ronald Hyman) [in]: Jewish Quarterly, Vol. 41, No. 3, London, Fall 1994, pp. 70–71. Remembering Elias Canetti: memoirs by Roberto Calasso and Claudio Magris [in]: Salmagundi, Nos. 104–105, Saratoga Springs, N.Y., Fall-Winter 1994/95, pp. 199–203.] [Elias Canetti, writer, July 7, 1905 Ruschtschuk – Aug. 14, 1994 London.] [See also No. 32323.]

32158. CANETTI, VEZA. ENGELMAYER, ELFRIEDE: *'Denn der Mensch schreitet aufrecht, die erhabenen Zeichen der Seele ins Gesicht gebrannt'. Zu Veza Canettis 'Die gelbe Strasse'.* [In]: Mit der Ziehharmonika, Jg. 11, Nr. 2, Wien, Sept. 1994. Pp. 25–33, port., notes. [V.C., for data see No. 27903/YB XXXVI.]

32159. CASSIRER, ERNST. BRUNKHORST, HAUKE: *Gesetzesethik und demokratische Willensbildung – Ernst Cassirers Verteidigung der Republik.* [In]: Babylon, H. 13–14, Frankfurt am Main, 1994. Pp. 177–182.

32160. CASSIRER, ERNST. GRAESER, ANDREAS: *Ernst Cassirer.* München: Beck, 1994. 234 pp., illus., bibl. (214–227). (Beck'sche Reihe, 527: Denker.)

32161. CASSIRER, ERNST. KROIS, JOHN MICHAEL: *Ernst Cassirer 1874–1945.* [In]: Krois, John Michael [et al.]: Die Wissenschaftler. Ernst Cassirer – Bruno Snell – Siegfried Landshut. Hamburg: Verl. Verein für Hamburgische Geschichte, 1994. (Hamburgische Lebensbilder in Darstellungen und Selbstzeugnissen, Bd. 8.). Pp. 9–40, port., bibl.

—— CELAN, PAUL. ESHEL, AMIR: *Zeit der Zäsur. Über Dan Pagis und Paul Celan.* [See in No. 31681.]

32162. CELAN, PAUL. FELSTINER, JOHN: *Translation as reversion: Paul Celan's Jerusalem poems.* [In]: Judaism, Vol. 43, No. 4, New York, Fall 1994. Pp. 419–431, notes. [Author is translator of Celan's poetry. Also discusses Celan's life.]

—— CELAN, PAUL. SCHMUELI, ILANA: *Denk dir. Paul Celan in Jerusalem.* [See in No. 31681.]

32163. CELAN, PAUL. SILBERMANN, EDITH: *Begegnung mit Paul Celan.* Erinnerung und Interpretation. Aachen: Rimbaud, 1994. 93 pp., illus. [Author, born in Czernowitz, a friend of Celan since childhood, actress, lives in Düsseldorf.]

32164. COHEN, WALTER. SITT, MARTINA: *'Tief ist der Brunnen der Vergangenheit' – Walter Cohen – Wegbereiter der Moderne im Rheinland.* [In]: Kölner Museumsbulletin, Nr. 4, Köln, 1993. Pp. 18–27.

32165. COHEN, WALTER. SITT, MARTINA: *Auch ein Bild braucht einen Anwalt. Walter Cohen – Leben zwischen Kunst und Recht.* Mit einem Beitrag von Hans M. Schmidt. [Hrsg.:] Kunstmuseum Düsseldorf im Ehrenhof. München: Deutscher Kunstverl., 1994. 142 pp., illus., facsims., lists, notes, bibl. (Kunstgeschichte und Gegenwart.) [Incl. bibl. of W.C.'s publications.] [W.C., Feb. 18, 1880 Bonn – Oct. 8, 1942 Dachau, art historian, from 1922 custodian of the Düsseldorf Kunstmuseum until his dismissal in 1933.]

32166. COSSMANN, PAUL NICOLAUS. Pigge, Helmut: *Das Ende eines Wegbereiters.* [In]: Die Zeit, Nr. 29, Hamburg, 15. Juli 1994, p. 58. [P.N. Coßmann, 1869 Baden-Baden – 1942 Theresienstadt, publicist, editor of the 'Süddeutsche Monatshefte', converted to Catholicism 1905, as a nationalist involved in the 'Dolchstoß' trial 1925, imprisoned by the Nazis 1933-1934, deported to Theresienstadt in summer 1942.]

32167. DEUTSCHKRON, INGE. *Daffke . . . ! Die vier Leben der Inge Deutschkron.* 70 Jahre erlebte Politik. Hrsg. von Wolfgang Kolneder. Berlin: Ed. Hentrich, 1994. 237 pp., illus. [Incl. excerpts from I.D.'s books, a play about her and interviews from a film of the same title.]

32168. DOMIN, HILDE. Braun, Michael: *Exil und Engagement: Untersuchungen zur Lyrik und Poetik Hilde Domins.* Frankfurt am Main; New York: Lang, 1994. 273 pp. (Literarhistorische Untersuchungen, Bd. 23.) Zugl.: Aachen, Techn. Hochsch., Diss., 1993.

32169. DRACH, ALBERT. Auckenthaler, Karlheinz F.: *'Ich habe mich erst als Jude zu fühlen gehabt, als mich der Hitler als einen solchen erklärt hat.' Albert Drachs Beziehung zum Judentum in Leben und Werk.* [In]: Modern Austrian Literature, Vol. 27, Nos. 3–4, Riverside, Ca., 1994. Pp. 51–70. [Drach's relationship to his Jewish roots is explained in the context of his work, in particular his novel 'Das große Protokoll gegen Zwetschkenbaum'.]

32170. EHRENBERG, VICTOR. Franke, Peter Robert: *Victor Ehrenberg. Ein deutsches Gelehrtenschicksal 1891–1976.* [In]: Juden in Deutschland. Lebenswelten und Einzelschicksale. Hrsg. von Reinhard Schneider [see No. 31400]. Pp. 309–331. [V.E., historian, data see No. 12263/ YB XX.]

32171. EHRLICH, SIEGWART. Wolffram, Knud: *Erfolg in Berlin, Flucht nach Spanien, Tod in Mailand.* Erinnerungen an einen vergessenen Unterhaltungskünstler. [In]: Gerhard Hentrich – der Verleger. Eine Festschrift zum 70. Geburtstag für Gerhard Hentrich. Hrsg. von Werner Buchwald und Hermann Simon. Berlin: Ed. Hentrich, 1994. Pp. 284–297. [S. (orig. Siegbert) E., Dec. 17, 1881 Leipzig – Jan. 20, 1941 Milan, composer, author of numerous popular 'hits'.]

32172. EINSTEIN, ALBERT. Hermann, Armin: *Einstein: der Weltweise und sein Jahrhundert.* Eine Biographie. München: Piper, 1994. 635 pp., illus.

32173. EINSTEIN, ALBERT. Pais, Abraham: *Einstein lived here: essays for the layman.* Oxford: Clarendon Press; New York: Oxford Univ. Press, 1994. XVI, 282 pp., ports. [Collection of essays, some prev. publ., by author who was a collaborator of Einstein.]

32174. EISNER, KURT. Eisner, Freya: *Zwischen Kapitalismus und Kommunismus.* Oft verkannt, viel geschmäht – Kurt Eisner, Gründer und erster Ministerpräsident des Freistaates Bayern, wurde vor 75 Jahren ermordet. [In]: Die Zeit, Nr. 8, Hamburg, 18. Feb. 1994, p. 74.

32175. FEUCHTWANGER, LION. Sternburg, Wilhelm von: *Lion Feuchtwanger. Ein deutsches Schriftstellerleben.* Berlin: Aufbau, 1994. 566 pp., illus., index, bibl. (527–554).

32176. FIESEL, EVA. Häntzschel, Hiltrud: *Die Philologin Eva Fiesel (1891–1937).* Porträt einer Wissenschaftskarriere im Spannungsfeld von Weiblichkeit und Antisemitismus. [In]: Jahrbuch der Deutschen Schillergesellschaft, Bd. 38, Marbach am Neckar, 1994. Pp. 339–363, footnotes. [E. Fiesel née Lehmann, Dec. 23, 1891 Rostock – May 27, 1937 New York, linguist, Etruscanologist of international repute, taught at the University of Munich until her dismissal in 1933. Emigr. in 1933 via Italy to the USA, where she became 'research assistant' at Yale University, from 1936 professor at Bryn Mawr College.]

32177. FRANZOS, KARL EMIL. Lindemann, Karin: *Karl Emil Franzos: Die zweifache Wurzel.* [In]: Jüdischer Almanach 1995 des Leo Baeck Instituts. Frankfurt am Main, 1994. Pp. 91–103.

32178. FREUD, SIGMUND. APPIGNANESI, LISA/FORRESTER, JOHN: *Die Frauen Sigmund Freuds*. Aus dem Englischen von Brigitte Rapp und Uta Szyskowitz. München: List, 1994. 773 pp. [Cf.: Urvater und Schwesternhorde. Sigmund Freud im Schatten reifer Damenblüte (Rose-Maria Gropp) [in]: 'FAZ', Frankfurt am Main, 4. Okt. 1994, p. L 30.] [Orig. publ. in 1992, see No. 29755/YB XXXVIII.]

32179. FREUD, SIGMUND. GILMAN, SANDER: *Freud, race and gender*. Princeton: Princeton Univ. Press, 1993. XVI, 277 pp., illus., tabs., graphs, notes (201–265). [Incl. chaps.: Freud's Jewish identity and its interpretation; S. Freud and the epistemology of race; Jewish madness and gender.]

32180. FREUD, SIGMUND. GRESSER, MOSHE: *Dual allegiance: Freud as a modern Jew*. Albany: State Univ. of New York Press, 1994. XII, 337 pp., notes (253–289), index of letters, bibl. (291–302.) [Incl. Freud's Jewish education; also quotes his letters to a.o. Emil Fluss, Wilhelm Fliess, Martha Bernays.]

32181. FREUD, SIGMUND. GRUMAN, HARRISH: *Freud's 'forgetting of foreign words': the history of the Jews between parody and paranoia*. [In]: History and Memory, Vol. 6, No. 2, Tel-Aviv, Fall/Winter 1994. Pp. 125–151, notes. [Incl. Freud as a Jewish thinker.]

32182. FREUD, SIGMUND. KERR, JOHN: *Eine höchst gefährliche Methode. Freud, Jung und Sabina Spielrein*. Aus dem Amerikanischen von C. Broermann und U. Schäfer. München: Kindler, 1994. 687 pp.

32183. FREUD, SIGMUND. MINDER, BERNARD: *Jung an Freud 1905: ein Bericht über Sabina Spielrein*. [In]: Gesnerus – Schweizerische Zeitschrift für Geschichte der Medizin und der Naturwissenschaften, Jg. 50, H. 1/2, Aarau, 1993. Pp. 113–120.

32184. FREUD, SIGMUND. PINES, MALCOLM: *Sigmund Freud and Siegfried Heinrich Fuchs/Foulkes: Psychoanalysis and group analysis and German/Jewish relations*. [In]: European Judaism, Vol. 27, No. 2, London, Autumn 1994. Pp. 46–57, bibl. [S.H.F., b. Karlsruhe, analyst, left Germany in 1933.]

32185. FREUD, SIGMUND. SARTRE, JEAN PAUL: *Freud. Das Drehbuch*. Vorwort von J.B. Pontalis. Hrsg. von Vincent von Wroblewsky. Deutsch von Traugott König unter Mitarbeit von Judith Klein. Reinbek: Rowohlt, 1993. 631 pp. (Gesammelte Werke in Einzelausgaben. Drehbücher, Bd. 3.) [Cf.: Ein Abstieg in die Unterwelt. Jean-Paul Sartre – Sigmund Freud – ein kinematographischer Konflikt (Fritz Göttler) [in]: Süddeutsche Zeitung, Nr. 105, München, 8./9. Mai 1993, p. V.]

32186. FREUND, GISELE. *Gisèle Freund: Photographien*. Mit autobiographischen Texten und einem Vorwort von Christian Caujolle. Von Verena von der Heyden-Rynch [et al.] aus dem Franz. übertr. München: Schirmer-Mosel, 1993. 221 pp., illus.

32187. GOLDSCHMIDT, BERTHOLD. BÜNING, ELEONORE: *Später Lorbeer, süßer Wohlklang. In Konzerten und Opernpremieren nach Deutschland zurückgekehrt: der Komponist Berthold Goldschmidt*. [In]: Die Zeit, Nr. 39, Hamburg, 23. Sept. 1994, p. 74. [B.G., b. Jan. 18, 1903 in Hamburg, composer, conductor, emigr. to the U.K. in 1940, during World War II head of German music dept. of the BBC, lives in London.]

32188. GOLDSCHMIDT, BERTHOLD. DVORAK, CORDELIA: *Ein Leben mit dem absoluten Zeitgefühl. Die späte Wiederentdeckung des Komponisten Berthold Goldschmidt*. [In]: 'FAZ', Nr. 211, Frankfurt am Main, 10. Sept. 1994. Beilage.

32189. GOLDSCHMIDT, HERMANN LEVIN. GOETSCHEL, WILLI: *Perspektiven der Dialogik*. Zürcher Kolloquium zum 80. Geburtstag von Hermann Levin Goldschmidt. Wien: Passagen, 1994. 227 pp., notes. [Incl.: 'Gibt es eine jüdische Philosophie?'. Zur Problematik eines Topos (Willi Goetsche, 91–111; with reference to H.L.G.). Widersprüchliche Identität: Judentum und Postmoderne im Denken Hermann Levin Goldschmidts (David

Suchoff, 111–124).] [H.L.G., b. Berlin, April 11, 1914, philosopher, emigr. to Switzerland in 1938, founder of the Jüdisches Lehrhaus, Zurich.]

32190. GOMBRICH, ERNST H. WARNKE, MARTIN: *Aufklärung gegen Andacht. Der Kunsthistoriker Ernst H. Gombrich erhielt den Goethepreis der Stadt Frankfurt am Main.* [In]: Die Zeit, Nr. 36, Hamburg, 2. Sept. 1994, p. 48. [Laudatio, given at the Goethepreis award ceremony in Frankfurt am Main, Aug. 28, 1994. Deals with the life and work of Sir Ernest Gombrich.] [E.H.G., b. 1909 in Vienna, art historian, emigr. 1936 to London, director of the Warburg Institute 1959–1976.]

32191. GRANACH, ALEXANDER. KLEIN, ALBERT/KRUK, RAYA: *Alexander Granach. Fast verwehte Spuren*. Berlin: Ed. Hentrich, 1994. 219 pp., illus., notes, lists. [Incl. list of plays and films in which A.G. was acting.] [A.G., actor, data see No. 11798/YB XIX.]

32192. GUGGENHEIM, ALIS. *'Als ob ich selber nackt in Schnee und Regen stehe . . .'. Alis Guggenheim 1896–1958 – Jüdin, Kommunistin, Künstlerin*. Hrsg.: Aargauer Kunsthaus. Mit Beitr. von Hans Heinz Holz [et al.]. [Ennetbaden]: Müller, 1992. 199 pp., illus. [Catalogue of exhibition, Oct. 18 – Nov. 22, 1992 in Aargau.]

32193. HABER, FRITZ. STOLTZENBERG, DIETRICH: *Fritz Haber – Chemiker, Nobelpreisträger, Deutscher, Jude*. Weinheim; New York: VCH Verl., 1994. XIV, 669 pp., illus., graph., indexes (651–669). [Cf.: 'Im Frieden für die Menschheit – im Krieg für das Vaterland' (Michael Globig) [in]: MPG-Spiegel, Nr. 2, München, 1995, pp. 62–63. Der Vater des Gaskriegs (Ulla Fölsing) [in]: 'FAZ', Nr. 218, Frankfurt am Main, 19. Sept. 1994, p. 13.]

32194. HEILBORN, ERNST. WEGENER, BEATE: *Bibliographie Ernst Heilborn*. Opladen: Westdt. Verl., 1994. VII, 123 pp. (Forschungsberichte des Landes Nordrhein-Westfalen; Nr. 3250: Fachgruppe Geisteswissenschaften.) [E.H., literary critic, data see No. 26720/YB XXXV.]

32195. HEINE, HEINRICH. KROBB, FLORIAN: *'Mach die Augen zu, schöne Sara': zur Gestaltung der jüdischen Assimilationsproblematik in Heine's 'Der Rabbi von Bacherach'*. [In]: German Life and Letters, Vol. 72, No. 2, Oxford, April 1994. Pp. 167–181, notes.

32196. HEINE, HEINRICH. KRUSE, JOSEPH A.: *Heines Provinz Lüneburg. Heine als Theologe. Zwei Aufsätze*. Lüneburg: Literaturbüro [1994]. 38 pp. (Schriftenreihe: Literaturbüro im Heinrich-Heine-Haus Lüneburg, Bd. 4.)

32197. HEINE, HEINRICH. REEVES, NIGEL: *Heinrich Heine: poetry and politics*. London: Libris, 1994. XI, 209 pp. [First publ. in 1974, see No. 13068/YB XXI, this paperback edn. has a new preface.]

32198. HEINE, HEINRICH. ROBERTSON, RITCHIE: *Persona, race and gender in Heinrich Heine's Die Harzreise*. [In]: Brücken über dem Abgrund. Festschrift für Harry Zohn [see No. 32315]. Pp. 145–158.

32199. HEINE, HEINRICH. SONDEREGGER-RITTER, RUTH: *Heinrich Heine und die Brüder Grimm. Aspekte ihrer gegenseitigen Beziehungen*. [In]: Verborum amor. Studien zur Geschichte und Kunst der deutschen Sprache. Festschrift für Stefan Sonderegger zum 65. Geburtstag. Berlin; New York: de Gruyter, 1992.

32200. HEINE, HEINRICH. VOIGT, JÜRGEN: *O Deutschland, meine ferne Liebe . . . : der junge Heinrich Heine zwischen Nationalromantik und Judentum*. Bonn: Pahl-Rugenstein, 1993. 223 pp., bibl. (219–223). (Pahl-Rugenstein-Hochschulschriften, 283.)

32201. HEINE, SALOMON. WIBORG, SUSANNE: *Salomon Heine: Hamburgs Rothschild – Heinrichs Onkel*. Hamburg: Christians, 1994. 128 pp. [Cf.: Hamburg duckt sich: 'der falsche Heine' (Eckhart Kauntz) [in]: 'FAZ', Nr. 51, Frankfurt am Main, 1. März 1995, p. 10; article remarks on the book cover showing the portrait of Salomon Heine's associate Jacob Oppenheim. The same mistake is repeated on p. 12 of this edn.]

32202. HENSEL, FANNY [MENDELSSOHN]. TILLARD, FRANÇOISE: *Die verkannte Schwester: die späte Entdeckung der Komponistin Fanny Mendelssohn Bartholdy.* Aus dem Franz. von Ralf Stamm. München: Kindler, 1994. 400 [16] pp., illus., scores, bibl. [&] discogr. (379–391). [Cf.: Alles, nur nicht Komponistin (Eckart Klessmann) [in]: 'FAZ', Nr. 246, Frankfurt am Main, 22. Okt. 1994, Lit.]

32203. HILDESHEIMER, WOLFGANG. HILLRICHS, HANS HELMUT: *Ich werde nun schweigen.* Gespräch mit Hans Helmut Hillrichs in der Reihe 'Zeugen des Jahrhunderts'. Hrsg. von Ingo Hermann. Göttingen: Lamuv, 1993. 128 pp. (Zeugen des Jahrhunderts.) [Incl.: 'Werkverzeichnis' (112–121).]

32204. HIRSCH, ELLI. LORENZ, DETLEF: *Elli Hirsch – Aurelie Doepler. Spuren einer vergessenen Künstlerin.* [In]: Der Herold, Jg. 37, H. 7, 1994. Pp. 173–178, illus., notes. [On the second wife of the painter Emil Doepler the Younger, March 23, 1873 – Feb. 6, 1943, Theresienstadt.]

32205. HOFFNUNG, GERARD. HOFFNUNG, ANNETTA: *Gerard Hoffnung: his biography.* With a foreword by Peter Ustinov. London: Aurum Press; Portland, Or.: Amadeus Press, 1994. 176 pp., illus. [G.H., 1925 Berlin – 1959 London, humorist, cartoonist, went to England via Austria and Italy in 1939.]

32206. HORKHEIMER, MAX. SCHMIDT, AMOS: *Materialismus zwischen Metaphysik und Positivismus. Max Horkheimers Frühwerk, Darstellung und Kritik.* Opladen: Westdeutscher Verlag, 1993. 390 pp. [Incl. Horkheimer's biography.]

32207. JUNGK, ROBERT. Selected obituaries Robert Jungk. 'Mein Judentum ist auch ein Hoffnungsruf'. Eine Begegnung mit Martin Buber prägte ihn: zum Tod des Zukunftsforschers und Autors Robert Jungk (Evelyn Adunka) [in]: 'Allgemeine', Jg. 49, Nr. 15, Bonn, 28. Juli 1994, p. 8. Der aus der Zukunft kam; Brückenbauer zwischen Wissenschaft und Öffentlichkeit: zum Tode von Robert Jungk (Konrad Adam) [in]: 'FAZ', Nr. 162, Frankfurt am Main, 15. Juli 1994, p. 33. Obituary (bt.) [in]: 'NZZ', Nr. 163, Zürich, 15. Juli 1994, p. 18. [R.J., May 11, 1913 Berlin – July 14, 1994 Salzburg, author, futurologist.]

32208. KAFKA, FRANZ. BAIONI, GUILIANO: *Kafka: Literatur und Judentum.* Aus dem Ital. von Gertrud Billen und Josef Billen. Stuttgart: Metzler, 1994. 291 pp., bibl., index.

32209. KAFKA, FRANZ. BINDER, HARTMUT: *Vor dem Gesetz. Einführung in Kafkas Welt.* Stuttgart: Metzler, 1993. 288 pp.

32210. KAFKA, FRANZ. GRÖZINGER, KARL ERICH: *Kafka and Kabbalah.* Transl. by Susan Hecker Ray. New York: Continuum, 1994. 231 pp., appendix, notes (209–218), bibl. (219–222). [For German orig. edn. in 1992 see No. 29795/YB XXXVIII.]

32211. KAFKA, FRANZ. HEIDSIECK, ARNOLD: *The intellectual contexts of Kafka's fictions: philosophy, law, religion.* Columbia, S.C.: Camden House, 1994. XV, 214 pp. (Studies in German literature, linguistics, and culture.)

32212. KAFKA, FRANZ. MÖBUS, FRANK: *Sünden-Fälle. Die Geschlechtlichkeit in Erzählungen Franz Kafkas.* Göttingen: Wallstein, 1994. 182 pp., illus., footnotes, bibl. (158–181). (Zugl. Göttingen, Univ., Diss.)

32213. KAFKA, FRANZ. WAMBACH, LOVIS MAXIM: *Wer ein Verbot verletzt, erwirbt sich einen Ankläger: Die Umkehr als Schild gegen das göttliche Strafgericht. Bemerkungen zu Franz Kafkas 'Prozeß'.* [In]: Aschkenas, Jg. 3, Wien, 1993. Pp. 219–226, footnotes. [Corrected name of journal in entry No. 31060/YB XXXIX.]

32214. KAFKA, FRANZ. ZIMMERMANN, HANS DIETER: *Die endlose Suche nach dem Sinn. Kafka und die jiddische Moderne.* [In]: Nach erneuter Lektüre. Franz Kafkas Der Prozess. Hrsg. von Hans Dieter Zimmermann. Würzburg: Königshausen und Neumann, 1992.

32215. KANTOROWICZ, ERNST. LANDAUER, CARL: *Ernst Kantorowicz and the sacralization of the past.* [In]: Central European History, Vol. 27, No. 1, Riverside, Ca., 1994. Pp. 1–25, footnotes.

32216. KIRSCHSTEIN, SALLY. SIMON, HERMANN: *Ein leidenschaftlicher Judaica-Sammler: Sally Kirschstein.* [In]: Gerhard Hentrich – der Verleger. Eine Festschrift für Gerhard Hentrich. Hrsg. von Werner Buchwald und Hermann Simon. Berlin: Ed. Hentrich, 1994. Pp. 223–232. [S.K., July 26, 1869 Kolmar – Jan. 11, 1935 Berlin, sold his Judaica collection in 1926 to the Hebrew Union College in Cincinnati.]

32217. KISCH, EGON ERWIN. SCHÜTZ, ERHARD: *The poet-journalist from Prague.* [In Hebrew, with Engl. summary.] [In]: Qesher, No. 15, Tel-Aviv, May 1994. Pp. 45–55.

32218. KLINGER, RUTH. HEID, LUDGER: *Das Kabarett Kaftan unterwegs. Tourneen von Ruth Klinger (1930–1933).* [In]: Menora 5, München, 1994. Pp. 261–285, illus., notes.

32219. KLÜGER, RUTH. *Ruth Klüger in Deutschland.* Hrsg. von Stephan Braese und Holger Gehle. Bonn: Selbstverlag, 1994. 41 pp., bibl. (34–41). (Kassiber, 1.)

32220. KOBLER, FRANZ. ADUNKA, EVELYN: *Franz Kobler (1882–1965): Rechtsanwalt und Historiker.* [In]: Menora 5, München, 1994. Pp. 97–121, notes.

32221. KOLMAR, GERTRUD. COLIN, AMY: *Macht, Opfer, Selbstzerstörung. Jüdisches Schicksal in Gertrud Kolmars Nacht.* [In]: Brücken über dem Abgrund. Festschrift für Harry Zohn [see No. 32315]. Pp. 199–224.

32222. KRAUS, KARL. STIEG, GERALD: *Karl Kraus gegen Martin Heidegger.* [In]: Brücken über dem Abgrund. Festschrift für Harry Zohn [see No. 32315]. Pp. 159–184. [Also in this book: Karl Kraus and the struggle for rights (Edward Timms, 185–198).]

32223. LANDAUER, GUSTAV. SELIGMANN, CHAIM: *Gustav Landauer und die Französische Revolution.* [In]: Aschkenas, Jg. 3, Wien, 1993. Pp. 227–236, footnotes. [Corrected name of journal in entry No. 31075/YB XXXIX.]

32224. LANDAUER, GUSTAV. *Gustav Landauer. Von der Kaiserstraße nach Stadelheim (1870–1919).* Begleitbuch zur Ausstellung im Oberrheinischen Dichtermuseum Karlsruhe 10.6.1994 – 9.7.1994. Bearb. von Dörte Anders [et al.]. Karlsruhe: Ed. Isele, 1994. 84 pp., illus., facsims. (Rheinschrift, 2.) [Exhibition and catalogue produced by a group of students from the Univers. of Karlsruhe.]

32225. LANDAUER, GUSTAV. *Gustav Landauer [zum 75. Todestag].* [In]: Graswurzelrevolution, Nr. 188, Kassel, Mai, 1994. [8 pp.] [In this issue 8 extra pp., dedicated to Gustav Landauer, cont. texts by Bernhard Braun, Siegbert Wolf, Gustav Landauer; also on Hedwig Lachmann und Martin Buber.]

32226. LANDAUER, KARL. BRATH, KLAUS: *Zum Gedenken an Karl Landauer.* Der Initiator des Frankfurter Psychoanalytischen Instituts starb vor 50 Jahren im KZ Bergen-Belsen. [In]: Frankfurter Jüdische Nachrichten, Nr. 87, Frankfurt am Main, Dez., 1994, p. 9.

32227. LANDSHUT, SIEGFRIED. NICOLAYSEN, RAINER: *Siegfried Landshut 1897–1968.* [In]: Krois, John Michael [et al.]: Die Wissenschaftler Ernst Cassirer, Bruno Snell, Siegfried Landshut. Hamburg: Verl. Verein für Hamburgische Gesch., 1994. (Hamburgische Lebensbilder in Darstellungen und Selbstzeugnissen, Bd. 8.) Pp. 75–115, port., bibl. [Siegfried Salomon Landshut, Aug. 7, 1897 Strasbourg – Dec. 8, 1968 Hamburg, sociologist, economist, political scientist, 1933 dismissed from the Hamburg Institut für Auswärtige Politik, emigr. to Egypt, 1936 to Palestine, returned to Germany in 1950.]

32228. LASKER-SCHÜLER, ELSE. BODENHEIMER, ALFRED: *Vertreibung als Erlösung. Else Lasker-Schülers Zürcher Abschiedsvorlesung 1939.* [In]: 'NZZ', Nr. 54, Zürich, 5./6. März 1994, p. 69. [On an unpublished Ms. found in the Else Lasker-Schüler collection of the National Library, Hebrew University.]

32229. LASKER-SCHÜLER, Else. *Mein Herz – niemandem; ein Else-Lasker-Schüler-Almanach.* Hrsg. von Michael Schmid-Ospach. Gemeinsam hrsg. mit der Else-Lasker-Schüler-Gesellschaft und der Stadtbibliothek Wuppertal. Wuppertal: Hammer, 1993. 224 pp.

32230. LAZARUS, NAHIDA RUTH. KRATZ-RITTER, BETTINA: *Konversion als Antwort auf den Berliner Antisemitismusstreit?* Nahida Ruth Lazarus und ihr Weg zum Judentum. [In]: Zeitschrift für Religions- und Geistesgeschichte, Jg. 46, H. 1, Leiden, 1994. Pp. 15–30, footnotes. [Nahida (Ruth) Lazarus, née Sturmhoefel, Feb. 2, 1849 Berlin – Jan. 12, 1928 Merano, writer, married Moritz Lazarus after the death of her first husband (Max Remy), converted to Judaism, devoted herself to writing on Jewish themes.]

32231. LEMM, ALFRED. SENDTNER, FLORIAN: *Kämpfer gegen den Tod. Der unbekannte expressionistische Schriftsteller Alfred Lemm und eine allzu bekannte Debatte.* [In]: Die Zeit, Nr. 12, Hamburg, 18. März 1994, p. 64, port. [A. L. (orig. Lehmann), 1890 – Oct. 16, 1918 Berlin, author, pacifist; criticised Thomas Mann's 'unpolitical' attitudes in 1917.]

32232. LESSING, THEODOR. HUSS, AVRAHAM: *Criticism, satire, defamation.* [In Hebrew, title transl.] [In]: Iton 77, No. 170, Tel-Aviv, March 1994. Pp. 24–29. [On Lessing's acidly satirical review of the work of Shmuel Lublinsky, written in 1910, and the furor it aroused in literary cricles.]

32233. LEWALD, FANNY. SCHNEIDER, GABRIELE: *Fanny Lewald und Heine. Sein Einfluß und seine Bedeutung im Spiegel ihrer Schriften.* [In]: Heine Jahrbuch 1994. Jg. 33, Hamburg, 1994. pp. 202–216, notes.

32234. LICHTENSTEIN, KURT. ZUNDER, RAINER: *Erschossen in Zicherie. Vom Leben und Sterben des Journalisten Kurt Lichtenstein.* Berlin: Dietz, 1994. 263 pp. [K.L., Communist journalist, joined the International Brigades during the Spanish Civil War, returned to Western Germany after 1945, later expelled from the KPD and killed at the East-German border in Oct. 1961.]

32235. LIEBERMANN, MAX. HOWOLDT, JENNS E./BAUR, ANDREAS: *Max Liebermann in Hamburg: Landschaften zwischen Alster und Elbe 1890–1910.* Hrsg. von Uwe M. Schneede. Ostfildern-Ruit bei Stuttgart: Hatje, 1994. 71 pp., illus. [Catalogue of exhibition held in Hamburg, Feb. 25 – April 17, 1994.]

32236. LIEBERMANN, MAX. SCHMALHAUSEN, BERND: *'Ich bin doch nur ein Maler': Max und Martha Liebermann im Dritten Reich.* Hildesheim; New York: Olms, 1994. 214 pp., illus. (Haskala, Bd. 11.)

32237. LÖWITH, KARL. *My life in Germany before and after 1933: a report.* Transl. by Elizabeth King. London: Athlone Press, 1993; Urbana: Univ. of Illinois Press, 1994. XX, 175 pp., illus., ports. [These recollections were first written in exile in Japan and focus on the years 1914–39; also covered are the author's meetings with Heidegger and Husserl. For orig. German edn. see No. 23733/YB XXXII.]

32238. LÖWITH, KARL. SCHWENTKER, WOLFGANG: *Karl Löwith und Japan.* [In]: Archiv für Kulturgeschichte, Bd. 76, Heft 2, Köln, 1994. Pp. 415–450. [K.L., Jan. 9, 1897 Munich – May 23, 1973 Heidelberg, philosopher, emigr. in 1934 to Italy, to Japan in 1936, to the USA in 1941. Returned to the Univ. of Heidelberg in 1952.]

32239. LUXEMBURG, ROSA. WEITZ, ERIC D.: *'Rosa Luxemburg belongs to us!': German communism and the Luxemburg legacy.* [In]: Central European History, Vol. 27, No. 1, Riverside, Ca., 1994. Pp. 27–64, footnotes.

32240. MAHLER, GUSTAV. *Gustav Mahler: Leben und Werk in Zeugnissen der Zeit*. Gesammelt und hrsg. von Herta Blaukopf und Kurt Blaukopf. Mit Beitr. von Zoltan Roman. Stuttgart: Hatje, 1994. 255 pp., illus., music. [Incl. texts by and about Mahler.]

32241. MAHLER, GUSTAV. SHEDLETZKY, MOSCHE: *Zwischen 'Ahasver' und 'Leiermann' oder: Was ist jüdisch an Gustav Mahler?* [In]: Jüdischer Almanach 1995 des Leo Baeck Instituts. Frankfurt am Main: Jüdischer Verlag, 1994. Pp. 104–120.

32242. MEIDNER, LUDWIG. *Ludwig Meidner: 1884 Bernstadt – 1966 Darmstadt*. Zeichnungen, Radierungen. Red.: Bert Schlichtenmaier; wiss. Mitarb.: Christiane Luz, Christiane Rebmann. Grafenau: Ed. Schlichtenmaier, 1994. 59 pp., illus. [Exhibition catalogue.]

32243. MENDEL, EMANUEL. FLECKNER, UTA: *Emanuel Mendel (1839–1907)*. Leben und Werk eines Psychiaters im Deutschland der Jahrhundertwende. Berlin, Freie Univ., Diss., 1994. 207; 170 pp. (docs., facsims., reprints), bibl. [Available at the Bibliothek Germania Judaica, Cologne.][E.M., Oct. 28, 1839 Bunzlau – June 23, 1907 Berlin, neurologist, psychiatrist, Reichstag member of the Progressive Party 1877–1881.]

—— MORGENSTERN, SOMA. MORGENSTERN, SOMA: *Joseph Roths Flucht und Ende*. Erinnerungen. [See No. 22266.]

—— MOSES, JULIUS. NEMITZ, KURT: *Zur Erinnerung an den Arzt und Parlamentarier Dr. Julius Moses*. [See in No. 31842.]

32244. MOSSE, GEORGE L.. HERMAND, JOST: *Deutsche Juden jenseits des Judentums. Der Fall Gerhard, Israel, George L. Mosse*. [In]: Jahrbuch für Antisemitismusforschung 3, Frankfurt am Main; New York, 1994. Pp. 178–193.

32245. OPPENHEIMER, FRANZ. VOGT, BERNHARD: *Die Utopie als Tatsache? Judentum und Europa bei Franz Oppenheimer*. [In]: Menora 5, München, 1994. Pp. 123–141, notes. [On Franz Oppenheimer's utopian novel 'Sprung über ein Jahrhundert', publ. 1934 in Bern under the pseudonym Francis D. Pelton.] [F.O., March 30, 1864 Berlin – Sept. 30, 1943 Los Angeles, sociologist, economist, emigr. via Japan to the USA in 1938.]

32246. OPPENHEIMER, FRANZ. VOGT, BERNHARD: *Marktwirtschaft und Europa. Der erste Frankfurter Ordinarius für Soziologie*. [In]: Frankfurter Jüdische Nachrichten, Nr. 84, Frankfurt am Main, März/April 1994. Pp. 29–30.

32247. OPPENHEIMER, JOSEPH SÜSS. HAASIS, HELLMUT G.: *Joseph Süss Oppenheimers Rache*. Erzählung, biographischer Essay. Dokumente aus der Haft und dem Prozess. Mit Illus. von Jona Mach und historischen Stichen. Blieskastel: Gollenstein, 1994. 263 pp., illus. [Incl. a.o. docs. written in Judaeo-German.]

32248. OPPENHEIMER, MAX. MOPP. *Max Oppenheimer 1885–1954*. [Hrsg.:] Jüdisches Museum der Stadt Wien, Wien, 1994. 203 pp., illus. [Catalogue of first major M.O. retrospective, with the same title in the Jüdisches Museum der Stadt Wien, June 23 – Sept. 18, 1994.] [M.O., 1885 Vienna – 1954, New York, artist, illustrator, son of the writer Ludwig O., associated with the expressionist journal 'Die Aktion' in Berlin, emigr. in 1939 to the USA.]

32249. PANOFSKY, ERWIN. REUDENBACH, BRUNO, Hrsg.: *Erwin Panofsky*. Beiträge des Symposions Hamburg 1992. Herausgegeben von Bruno Reudenbach. Mit Beiträgen von H. Abels [et al.]. Berlin: Akademie-Verl., 1994. X, 235 pp., port., footnotes, index. (Schriften des Warburg-Archivs im Kunstgeschichtlichen Seminar der Universität Hamburg, Bd. 3.) [Following essays are relevant to Panofsky's biography and other art historians who were deprived of their posts: Das Kunsthistorische Seminar der Hamburgischen Universität (Heinrich Dilly, 1–14). Arkadien in Hamburg. Studierende und Lehrende am Kunsthistorischen Seminar der Hamburgischen Universität (Ulrike Wendland, 15–30). Ex nihilo: Panofskys Habilitation (Horst Bredekamp, 31–47). Einige Fragmente einer intellektuellen

Kollektivbiographie der kulturwissenschaftlichen Emigration (Volker Breidecker, 83–108). 'Barbari ad portas'. Panofsky in den fünfziger Jahren (Willibald Sauerländer, 123–138).]

32250. PERUTZ, LEO. EICHNER, HANS: *Leo Perutz, Meister des Erzählens: Bemerkungen aus Anlaß seiner Wiederentdeckung.* [In]: The German Quarterly, Vol. 67, No. 4, Riverside, Ca., Fall 1994. Pp. 493–499, notes.

32251. PHILIPPSON, ALFRED. MEHMEL, ASTRID: *Wie ich zum Geographen wurde – Aspekte zum Leben Alfred Philippsons.* [In]: Geographische Zeitschrift, Jg. 82, Heft 2, Stuttgart, 1994. Pp. 116–132, notes. [A.P., Jan. 1, 1864 – Bonn, March 3, 1953, Professor of Geography at the Univ. of Bonn, deported to Theresienstadt in 1942, where he wrote his memoirs.]

32252. PHILIPPSON, ALFRED. MEHMEL, ASTRID/HERMES, CLAUDIA: *Hinwegsehen über sein Judentum. Alfred Philippson – Lebenserinnerungen eines Geographen.* [In]: Aufbau, Vol. 60, No. 16, New York, 1994. Pp. 4–5, port.

32253. POLLAK, FELIX. MIEDER, WOLFGANG: *'Sprichwörter leuchten ein. Aphorismen leuchten auf': Zu den sprichwörtlichen Aphorismen von Felix Pollak.* [In]: The German Quarterly, Vol. 67, No. 4, Riverside, Ca., Fall 1994. Pp. 534–548. [F.P., 1909–1987, Austrian author.]

32254. POPPER, KARL. GEIER, MANFRED: *Karl Popper.* Reinbek: Rowohlt, 1994. 158 pp., illus., bibl. (146–155). Orig.-Ausg. (Rowohlts Monographien.) [Cf.: Die Krise ist der Normalzustand. Manfred Geiers sehr wohlwollende Karl-Popper-Biographie (Helmut Mayer) [in]: 'FAZ', Nr. 230, Frankfurt am Main, 4. Okt. 1994, p. L 83.]

32255. POPPER, KARL. *Selected obituaries Karl Popper.* Kritischer Rationalismus; zum Tode von Karl R. Popper (Hans Albert) [&] Poppers Vermächtnis (Martin Meyer) [in]: 'NZZ', Nr. 218, Zürich, 19. Sept. 1994, p. 17. Der öffentliche Professor (Ralf Dahrendorf) [&] Schulhaupt des Liberalismus (Eckhard Nordhofen) [in]: Die Zeit, Nr. 39, Hamburg, 23. Sept. 1994, pp. 70–71. Karl Popper und die Philosophie [in]: Das Jüdische Echo, Vol. 43, Wien, Okt. 1994, pp. 219–227; incl.: Probleme sind lösbar; Philosophien bleiben (Kurt Salamun, 223). Popper und die Assimilation (Michael Siegert, 221). Ein maßlos bescheidener Mensch (Franz Kreuzer, 225–227).] [K. Popper, July 28, 1902 Vienna – Sept. 17, 1994 Croydon nr. London, philosopher.]

32256. PRESSBURGER, EMERIC. MACDONALD, KEVIN: *Emeric Pressburger: the life and death of a screenwriter.* London: Faber, 1994. XIX, 467 pp., illus., filmography, notes, bibl. of E. P.'s works, bibl. [E.P, Dec. 5, 1902, Hungary – Feb. 5, 1988, England, screenwriter and filmmaker who worked for UFA in the 1920s and early 30s, moved to England after the Nazi takeover, where he collaborated with Michael Powell on many films.]

32257. PRINGSHEIM, ALFRED. KRUFT, HANNO WALTER, Hrsg.: *Alfred Pringsheim, Hans Thoma, Thomas Mann: eine Münchner Konstellation.* Mit Beiträgen von Roland Bulirsch und Horst Fuhrmann. Erw. Ausgabe. München: Verl. d. bayerischen Akademie der Wiss., 1993. 48, 39 pp., illus. (Abhandlungen/Bayerische Akademie der Wissenschaft, Philosophisch-Historische Klasse, 107.) [Article on Pringsheim by Horst Fuhrmann.] [A.P., Sept. 2, 1850 Ohlau (Silesia) – June 25, 1941 Zurich, mathematician, father-in-law of Thomas Mann.]

32258. RATHENAU, WALTER. KAPLAN, LOUIS: *Walter Rathenau's media technological turn as mediated through W. Hartenau's 'Die Resurrection Co.': an essay at resurrection.* [In]: new german critique, No. 62, Ithaca, N.Y., Spring-Summer 1994. Pp. 39–62, footnotes. ['W. Hartenau', pseudonym of W.R.]. Also in the same issue: Die Resurrection Co. (Hartenau, W., 63–69; this article, a parable on the American way of burial, was first publ. in 'Die Zukunft', Vol. 24, July 9, 1898.]

—— RATHENAU, WALTHER. GRUSON, PASCALE: *Die Krise der Moderne in europäischer Perspektive. Walther Rathenau, Ernst Troeltsch und die Weimarer Republik.* [See in No. 32417.]

——— RATHENAU, WALTHER. Sabrow, Martin: *Der Rathenaumord. Rekonstruktion einer Verschwörung gegen die Republik von Weimar.* [See No. 32418.]

32259. REICH, WILHELM. Sharaf, Myron: *Wilhelm Reich: der heilige Zorn des Lebendigen.* Die Biografie. Übers. und hrsg. von Jürgen Fischer. Bearb. von Ulrich Leutner. Berlin: Simon und Leutner, 1994. 637 pp., illus. [Orig. publ. under the title 'Fury on earth'.] [W.R., March 24, 1897 Dobrzcynia – Nov. 3, 1957 Lewisburg, Pa. (in prison), psychoanalyst, invented 'orgasm therapy'.] [Cf.: Ein Analytiker sucht die Physik der Liebe (Kuno Kruse) [in]: Die Zeit, Nr. 15, Hamburg, 7. April 1994, p. 54.

32260. ROTH, JOSEPH. Roth, Joseph: *Unter dem Bülowbogen.* Prosa zur Zeit. Hrsg. von Rainer-Joachim Siegel. Köln: Kiepenheuer und Witsch, 1994. 373 pp., notes. [Reports and other journalistic articles, republished here for the first time, ranging from 1919 (Vienna) up to Roth's exile in Paris.]

32261. ROTH, JOSEPH. Heller, André: *'Wahrscheinlich der größte unter den anständigen Menschen'. Vor hundert Jahren wurde Joseph Roth geboren.* [In]: 'FAZ', Nr. 205, Frankfurt am Main, 3. Sept. 1994. Beilage.

32262. ROTH, JOSEPH. Hundert: *Hundert Jahre: Joseph Roth.* [In]: Das Jüdische Echo, Vol. 43, Wien, Okt. 1994. [Incl. the following texts and articles: 'Ein Jude wider Willen?' Joseph Roth zum hundertsten Geburtstag (Victoria Lunzer-Talos/Heinz Lunzer, 197–202). Die Welt des Joseph Roth (Anton Mayer, 203–206). Begegnung mit dem jungen Joseph Roth (Soma Morgenstern, 207–218).]

32263. ROTH, JOSEPH. *Joseph Roth und Berlin.* [Katalog: Eberhard Siebert und Michael Bienert.] [Hrsg.]: Staatsbibliothek zu Berlin – Preussischer Kulturbesitz. Wiesbaden: Reichert, 1994. 56 pp., illus. (Ausstellungskataloge/Staatsbibliothek zu Berlin – Preussischer Kulturbesitz; N.F., 9.)

32264. ROTH, JOSEPH. Lunzer, Heinz/Lunzer-Talos, Victoria: *Joseph Roth: Leben und Werk in Bildern.* Köln: Kiepenhauer und Witsch. 279 pp., illus. [Cf.: '. . . zur Hälfte ein Wissender und zur Hälfte ein Weiser' (Eva Pfister) [in]: Börsenblatt für den Deutschen Buchhandel, Jg. 161, Nr. 68, Frankfurt am Main, 26. Aug. 1994, pp. 18–21; review essay, dealing also with other recent publications on Joseph Roth as well as editions of his works. Zum 100. Geburtstag Joseph Roths (Paul Proskauer) [in]: Aufbau, Vol. 60, No. 30, New York, Sept. 30, 1994, p. 6.]

32265. ROTH, JOSEPH. Melzer, Gerhard: *Die Wunder der Erzählens.* Zum 100. Geburtstag von Joseph Roth. [In]: 'NZZ', Nr. 205, Zürich, 3./4. Sept. 1994, p. 65.

32266. ROTH, JOSEPH. Morgenstern, Soma: *Joseph Roths Flucht und Ende.* Erinnerungen. Hrsg. und mit einem Nachwort von Ingolf Schulte. Lüneburg: zu Klampen, 1994. 328 [2] pp., footnotes. (Soma Morgenstern; Werke in Einzelbänden.) [Incl.: Soma Morgenstern – der Autor als Überlebender. Editorische Notiz (Ingolf Schulte, 301–326).] [Cf.: Ja, er trank. Soma Morgenstern erinnert sich an seinen Jugendfreund Joseph Roth (Fritz J. Raddatz) [in]: Die Zeit, Nr. 14, Hamburg, 31. März 1995, p. 72.] [Soma (orig. Salomon) Morgenstern, May 3, 1890 Budzanów, Galicia – April 17, 1976 New York, jurist, journalist, author, friend of Joseph Roth, Alban Berg. Emigr. after the 'Anschluß' to Paris, interned in Audierne, from where he escaped via Southern France, Morocco and Portugal to the USA in 1941.]

32267. ROTH, JOSEPH. Steierwald, Ulrike: *Leiden an der Geschichte; zur Geschichtsauffassung der Moderne in den Texten Joseph Roths.* Würzburg: Königshausen und Neumann, 1994. 198 pp. (Epistemata, Reihe Literaturwissenschaft, Bd. 121.) Zugl.: München, Univ., Diss., 1992.

32268. ROTH, JOSEPH. *Joseph Roth 1894–1939.* Ein Katalog der Dokumentationsstelle für Neuere Österreichische Literatur zur Ausstellung des Jüdischen Museums der Stadt Wien, 7. Oktober 1994 bis 12. Februar 1995. [Katalog: Heinz Lunzer und Victoria Lunzer-Talos.

Mitarb.: Angelika Eder.] Wien: Dokumentationsstelle für Neuere Österreich. Literatur, 1994. 180 pp., illus.

32269. RUBINSTEIN, HILDE: *'Ich wollte nichts als glücklich sein . . .'* Gefängnistagebücher unter Hitler und Stalin, Erzählungen, Gedichte, Essays. Hrsg. und mit einem Nachwort versehen von Maria Empting und Stefan Greif. Paderborn: Igel, 1994. 232 pp. [H.R., born Aug. 7, 1904 in Augsburg, writer, imprisoned under the Nazis as a member of the KPD, and during exile in the Soviet 1935/1936. Fled to Sweden in 1937, returned to Germany 1982, returned to Sweden in 1993.] [See also on H.R. in No. 30895/YB XXXIX.] [Cf.: Eine exilierte Dichterin (Hartmut Vollmer) [in]: 'NZZ', Nr. 80, Zürich, 7. April 1994, p. 30.]

32270. SACHS, NELLY. SOWA-BETTECKEN, BEATE: *Sprache der Hinterlassenschaft: jüdisch-christliche Überlieferung in der Lyrik von Nelly Sachs und Paul Celan.* Frankfurt am Main; New York: Lang, 1992. 311 pp. (Europäische Hochschulschriften: Reihe 1, Deutsche Sprache und Literatur, Bd. 1357.) Zugl.: Freiburg i. Br., Univ., Diss., 1991.

32271. SACHS, NELLY. STROBL, INGRID: *'Der Tod war mein Lehrmeister'. Die Lyrikerin Nelly Sachs.* [See in No. 31852]. Pp. 119–139.

32272. SAHL, HANS. *Hans Sahl: eine Würdigung.* Bearb.: Thomas Daum und Bernhard Spies. Hrsg.: Der Ministerpräsident des Landes Rheinland-Pfalz. Landau: Pfälz. Verl.- Anstalt, 1994. 76 pp., illus., bibl.

32273. SALOMON, ERICH. HUNTER-SALOMON, PETER: *Dr. Erich Salomon: Vater des modernen Bildjournalismus.* [In]: Deutschland, Nr. 5, Bonn, Okt. 1994. Pp. 60–63, illus. [E.S., 1886 Berlin – 1944 Auschwitz, jurist, photographer.]

32274. SCHLESINGER, PAUL. SÖSEMANN, BERND: *'Moabit's vigilant conscience'. Paul Schlesinger and his articles on court proceedings in the 'Vossische Zeitung'.* [In Hebrew, with Engl. summary.] [In]: Qesher, No. 15, Tel Aviv, May 1994. Pp. 61–64.

32275. SCHNITZLER, ARTHUR. WEINZIERL, ULRICH: *Arthur Schnitzler. Lieben, träumen, sterben.* Frankfurt am Main: S. Fischer, 1994. 288 pp., illus.

32276. SCHOCKEN, SALMAN. SCHAEPER, SILKE: *'Goldadern wertvollen jüdischen Lebens'. Salman Schocken und seine Hebraica-Sammlung.* [In]: Jüdischer Almanach 1995 des Leo Baeck Instituts. Frankfurt am Main, 1994. Pp. 121–135. [See also No. 31846.]

32277. SEGHERS, ANNA. BELLIN, KLAUS: *Die Wohnung mit Kajüte und Mastkorb.* [In]: Börsenblatt für den Deutschen Buchhandel, Jg. 161, Nr. 17, Frankfurt am Main, 1. März 1994. Pp. 10–12. [On Anna Segher's return from Mexico to Berlin from exile and the house where she lived from 1955 until her death in 1983; now a small museum, cont. an extensive library.]

32278. SEGHERS, ANNA. STEPHAN, ALEXANDER: *Anna Seghers im Exil.* Essays, Texte, Dokumente. Bonn: Bouvier, 1993. VI, 208 pp., bibl. (203–208). (Studien zur Literatur der Moderne, Bd. 23.)

32279. SEGHERS, ANNA. WALLACE, IAN: *'Andere Lösung Quatsch': Anna Seghers and the film of 'Die Toten bleiben jung'.* [In]: German Life and Letters, Vol. 72, No. 3, Oxford, July 1994. Pp. 313–324, notes. [Discusses A.S.'s novel 'Die Toten bleiben jung', her last major project in exile. Written in Mexico between 1944–47, the novel appeared in 1949 and was made into a film in the GDR 19 years later.] [See also in No. 32098.]

32280. SEGHERS, ANNA. *Anna Seghers.* Eine Biographie in Bildern. Mit einem Vorwort von Christa Wolf. Hrsg. von Frank Wagner [et al.]. Berlin: Aufbau, 1994. 264 pp., 252 photographs.

32281. SENDER, TONI. HILD-BERG, ANETTE: *Toni Sender (1888–1964)*. *Ein Leben im Namen der Freiheit und der sozialen Gerechtigkeit*. Mit einem Vorwort von Susanne Miller. Köln: Bund, 1994. 360 pp., footnotes, bibl. (333–360). [T.S., data see No. 29844/YB XXXVIII.]

32282. SILBERGLEIT, ARTHUR. *Arthur Silbergleit und Paul Mühsam. Zeugnisse einer Dichterfreundschaft*. Ein Zeitbild. Hrsg. und kommentiert von Else Levi-Mühsam. Würzburg: Bergstadt-Verl. Korn, 1994. 130 pp., ports., illus., facsims., notes, bibl. (Stiftung Kulturwerk Schlesien.) [Incl. biographies, letters and poems of both poets.] [P.M., July 17, 1876 Brandenburg – March 11, 1960 Jerusalem; A.S., May 26, 1881 Gleiwitz – March 1943 Auschwitz.]

32283. SILBERMANN, ALPHONS. *Alphons Silbermann: glücklich und bedeutsam*. Gespräch mit Hans Bünte in der Reihe 'Zeugen des Jahrhunderts'. Hrsg. von Ingo Hermann. Göttingen: Lamuv, 1994. 89 pp., illus. (Zeugen des Jahrhunderts.) [A.S., sociologist, data see No. 27796/YB XXXVI.]

32284. SIMMEL, GEORG. SELLERBERG, ANN-MARI: *A blend of contradictions: Georg Simmel in theory and practice*. New Brunswick, N.J.: Transaction Books, 1994. XVIII, 128 pp., bibl. (119–125).

32285. SOYFER, JURA. JARKA, HORST: *Drei Briefe von Helene Ultmann (Andis)*. *Vergebliche Hoffnung auf Jura Soyfers Freilassung. Erste Bemühungen um seinen Nachlass*. [In]: Mit der Ziehharmonika, Jg. 11, Nr. 2, Wien, Sept. 1994. Pp. 13–17, illus., notes.

32286. STAHL, HEINRICH. SIMON, HERMANN: *Heinrich Stahl (13. April 1886 – 4. November 1942.)* Vortrag, gehalten zur Gedenkfeier der Jüdischen Gemeinde zu Berlin am 22. April 1993. Berlin: Hentrich, 1993. 40 pp., illus., port., facsims., docs. (Schriften der Stiftung 'Neue Synagoge Berlin - Centrum Judaicum'.) [H.S., April 13, 1868 Berlin – Nov. 4, 1942 Theresienstadt, insurance executive, from 1933 President of the Berlin Jewish community, from 1939 President of the Reichsvertretung der Juden in Deutschland.] [Corrected name of author in entry No. 30852/YB XXXIX.]

32287. STEIN, ALEXANDER. PAPANEK, HANNA: *Alexander Stein (Pseudonym: Viator) 1881–1948, Socialist activist and writer in Russia, Germany and exile: biography and bibliography*. [In]: 'IKW', Int. wiss. Korrespondenz z. Gesch. der deutschen Arbeiterbewegung, Jg. 31, Nr. 3, Berlin, 1994. Pp. 343–379, notes, bibl. (371–379). [Incl.: Alexander Stein: Teilbibliographie (371–378; bibl. of books, articles and translations).] [A.St., orig. Alexander Rubinstein, 1881 Wolmar, Latvia – 1948 New York, political journalist, socialist, went to Berlin in 1906, joined the German Social Democrats, collaborated with Rudolf Hilferding, editor of the 'Vorwärts' and other Social-Democratic newspapers. Emigr. 1933 via Prague (until 1938) and Paris (until 1940) to the USA.]

32288. STEIN, EDITH. *The unnecessary problem of Edith Stein*. Ed. by Harry James Cargas. Lanham: Univ. Press of America, 1994. 105 pp., notes. (Studies in the Shoah, Vol. IV.) [Ten essays on various aspects of E.S.'s life and her role as a controversial figure in the Jewish-Catholic dialogue.]

32289. STERN, CLARA. DEUTSCH, WERNER: *Nicht nur Frau und Mutter. Clara Sterns Platz in der Geschichte der Psychologie*. [In]: Psychologie und Geschichte, Jg. 5, H. 3/4, Leverkusen, 1994. Pp. 171–182, notes, bibl., port. [C.St., 1878–1945, psychologist, wife of William Stern, mother of Hilde, Günther [Anders] and Eva St.]

32290. STRAUSS, OTTMAR. PRACHT, ELFI: *Ottmar Strauss: Industrieller, Staatsbeamter, Kunstsammler*. [In]: Menora 5, München, 1994. 39–70, notes. [Essay deals mainly with the 'Aryanisation' after 1933.] [O.St., May 19, 1878 Ludwigshafen – Aug. 25, 1941 Zurich, industrialist, co-owner of the Otto Wolff concern, Cologne, emigr. to Switzerland in 1936.]

32291. TÄUBLER, EUGEN. Myers, David N.: *Eugen Täubler. The personification of 'Judaism as tragic existence'*. [In]: Leo Baeck Institute Year Book XXXIX, London, 1994. Pp. 131–150, footnotes.

32292. TERGIT, GABRIELE. Tergit, Gabriele: *Atem einer anderen Welt*. Berliner Reportagen. Hrsg. und mit einem Nachwort versehen von Jens Brüning. Frankfurt am Main: Suhrkamp, 1994. 210 pp. (Erstausgabe.) [G. Tergit, orig. Elise Reifenberg née Hirschmann, 1894 Berlin – 1968 London, journalist, author, emigr. 1933 via Czechoslovakia to Palestine, 1938 to the U.K.]

32293. TOLLER, ERNST. Freeden, Herbert: *Ernst Toller – 100 Jahre*. [In]: europäische ideen, H. 86, London, 1994. Pp. 18–19.

32294. TOLLER, ERNST. Weisberger, Adam: *In memoriam Ernst Toller: jüdische und psychologische Aspekte in Leben und Werk*. [In]: Aschkenas, Jg. 4, H. 1, Wien, 1994. Pp. 163–174, footnotes.

32295. TORBERG, FRIEDRICH. Thunecke, Jörg: *'Man wird nicht Jude, man ist es': zur Funktion der jüdischen Moral in Friedrich Torbergs Novelle 'Mein ist die Rache' (1943)*. [In]: Modern Austrian Literature, Vol. 27, Nos. 3–4, Riverside, Ca., 1994. Pp. 19–36.

32296. TUCHOLSKY, KURT. Hepp, Michael: *Kurt Tucholsky*. Biographische Annäherungen. Reinbek: Rowohlt, 1993. 576 pp., port., bibl. (532–540). [Cf.: Opportunist? Polenhasser? Antisemit? Michael Hepp verteidigt Kurt Tucholsky gegen Marbach (Stephan Reinhardt) [in]: Süddeutsche Zeitung, Nr. 141, München, 23. Juni 1993, p. 14.]

32297. TUCHOLSKY, KURT. Soldenhoff, Richard von, Hrsg.: *Kurt Tucholsky: 1890–1935*. Ein Lebensbild; 'Erlebnis und Schreiben war ja immer – zweierlei'. Hrsg. von Richard von Soldenhoff. Neu ausgestattete Ausg. Weinheim: Beltz, Quadriga, 1994. 239 pp., illus.

32298. ULLMANN, VIKTOR. Schultz, Ingo: *Verlorene Werke Viktor Ullmanns im Spiegel zeitgenössischer Presseberichte*. Bibliographische Studien zum Prager Musikleben in den zwanziger Jahren. Hamburg: von Bockel, 1994. 103 pp. (Verdrängte Musik, Bd. 4.) [Incl.: Werkverzeichnis (95–100).]

32299. VARNHAGEN, RAHEL. Hundt, Irina: *Zur Biographie von Rahel Levin Varnhagen. Aufzeichnungen ihres Mannes Karl August Varnhagen von Ense*. [In]: Zeitschrift für Geschichtswissenschaft, Jg. 42, Heft 3, Berlin, 1994. Pp. 238–249, notes. [Incl. publication of documents found in the Biblioteka Jagiellonska Krakow.]

32300. VARNHAGEN, RAHEL. Söhn, Gerhart: *Rahel Varnhagen (1771–1833). Eine jüdische Frau in der Berliner Romantik*. [In]: Aus dem Antiquariat, 10, [Beilage zum] Börsenblatt für den Deutschen Buchhandel, Jg. 161, Nr. 86, Frankfurt am Main, 28. Okt. 1994. Pp. A384–A387, illus.

32301. VARNHAGEN, RAHEL. Stern, Carola: *Der Text meines Herzens. Das Leben der Rahel Varnhagen*. Reinbek: Rowohlt, 1994. 316 pp., illus.

32302. VARNHAGEN, RAHEL. Thomann Tewarson, Heidi: *German-Jewish identity in the correspondence between Rahel Levin Varnhagen and her brother, Ludwig Robert. Hopes and realities of emancipation 1780–1830*. [In]: Leo Baeck Institute Year Book XXXIX, London, 1994. Pp. 3–29, ports., footnotes.

32303. WARBURG FAMILY. Günther, Horst: *Aby Warburg und seine Brüder*. [In]: Deutsche Brüder. Zwölf Doppelporträts. Berlin: Rowohlt, 1994. Pp. 254–286, illus.

32304. WARBURG, ABY M.. Lerm, Christa-Maria: *Das jüdische Erbe bei Aby Warburg*. [In]: Menora 5, München, 1994. Pp. 143–171, notes.

32305. WASSERMANN, JAKOB. SCHNEIDER, ROLF: *Lochidisch braucht man nicht mehr. Mit Jakob Wassermann in der deutsch-jüdischen Vergangenheit.* [In]: Merkur, Jg. 48, Stuttgart, 1994. Pp. 49–61.

32306. WEIL, GRETE. AHRENDT, PETER: *'Eine schlechte Hasserin'. Über die jüdische Schriftstellerin Grete Weil.* [In]: Scriptum, Nr. 16, 1994. Pp. 4–7. [See also: Grete Weil: Warum ich trotzdem in Deutschland lebe. Ein Brief aus dem Jahr 1947 an Margarete Susman. Aufgefunden und zugänglich gemacht von Hiltrud Häntzschel [in]: Süddeutsche Zeitung, München, 16. Juli 1994, pp. V 3–5.]

32307. WEILL, KURT. HEYN, THOMAS: *Fünf Chorusse für Kurt Weill.* [In]: Menora 5, München, 1994. Pp. 173–195, notes, music notes. [An interpretation of Weill's music composed in Germany during the twenties and early thirties.]

32308. WEILL, KURT . *A stranger here myself. Kurt Weill Studien.* Hrsg. von Kim H. Kowalke und Horst Edler. Hildesheim; New York: Olms, 1993. 384 pp., illus., scores, bibl. (327–355), indexes. (Haskala, Bd. 8.) [A collection of essays, partly in German, partly in English, based on the 'Kurt-Weill-Festival' and 'Symposium' in Duisburg 1990. Essays of biographical relevance: Formerly German: Kurt Weill in America (Kim H. Kowalke, 35–57). 'Fremd bin ich eingezogen': Anmerkungen zu einer geteilten Biographie (Joachim Lucchesi, 58– 72). Der literarisch-kulturelle Horizont des jungen Weill: eine Analyse seiner ungedruckten frühen Briefe (Guy Stern, 73–106). Von der Provinz in die Stadt: die frühe musikalische Ausbildung Kurt Weills (Tamara Levitz, 107–142). Der 'alien American' Kurt Weill und seine Aktivitäten für den War Effort der USA 1940–1945 (Jürgen Schebera, 267–283). A Kurt Weill bibliography (David Farnetti, 327–358).]

32309. WERFEL, FRANZ. JUNGK, PETER STEPHAN: *Franz Werfel: eine Lebensgeschichte.* Frankfurt am Main: Fischer-Taschenbuch-Verl., 1994. 452 pp., illus. (Limitierte Sonderausgabe; Fischer-Taschenbücher.)

32310. WERFEL, FRANZ. STEINER, CARL: *Franz Werfels Jeremias-Roman 'Höret die Stimme'. Ein Bekenntnis zum Judentum.* [In]: Modern Austrian Literature, Vol. 27, Nos. 3–4, Riverside, Ca., 1994. Pp. 239–255, notes.

32311. WIESEL, ELIE. BOSCHKI, REINHOLD: *Der Schrei. Gott und Mensch im Werk von Elie Wiesel.* Mainz: Matthias-Grünewald-Verl., 1994. 260 pp. [Cf.: Besprechung (Herbert Winklehner) [in]: Freiburger Rundbrief, N.F., Jg. 2, Nr. 2, Freiburg, 1995, pp. 125–126.]

32312. WITTGENSTEIN FAMILY. KROSS, MATTHIAS: *Paul und Ludwig Wittgenstein.* [In]: Deutsche Brüder. Zwölf Doppelporträts. Berlin: Rowohlt, 1994. Pp. 287–329, illus. [Paul W., 5. Nov. 1887 Vienna – 3. March 1961 New York, pianist, after being injured in 1st World War developed repertoire for left-handed piano, emigr. 1938 via Switzerland to the USA.]

32313. WOLF, KONRAD. KOCH, GERTRUD: *On the disappearance of the dead among the living: the Holocaust and the confusion of identities in the films of Konrad Wolf.* [In]: new german critique, No. 60, Ithaca, N.Y., Fall 1993. Pp. 57–75, notes. [K.W., former East German filmmaker and brother of Markus Wolf, the former head of East German secret service.]

32314. WOLF, MARKUS. *Markus Wolf. East Germany's Jewish master spy.* Interview with Tikkun. [In]: Tikkun, Vol. 9, No. 1, Oakland, Ca., Jan./Feb. 1994. Pp. 51–52; 92–93. [M.W. reflects on his Jewish roots and the fact that as a Jew he was willing to join the Communist secret police in order to expose former Nazis.] [Cf.: A Wolf in sheep's clothing (Jeffrey Herf) [in]: Tikkun, Vol. 9, No. 4, Oakland, Ca., July/Aug. 1994, pp. 45–46; 70 (Herf seeks to set the record straight about antisemitic actions of the East German government of which W. was a member). I fought the revival of Nazism: Markus Wolf's reply (in same issue, pp. 70–73).]

32315. ZOHN, HARRY. COLIN, AMY/STRENGER, ELISABETH, eds.: *Brücken über dem Abgrund/ Bridging the abyss.* Auseinandersetzungen mit jüdischer Leidenserfahrung, Antisemitismus und Exil. Festschrift für Harry Zohn/Reflections on Jewish suffering, anti-semitism, and exile. Essays in honour of Harry Zohn. München: Fink, 1994. 428 pp., notes, bibl. (selected writings by Harry Zohn, 407–416), Tabula Gratulatoria (419–420), index (421–428). [Essays, poems and contribs. on translation, partly English, partly German, are arranged under the following sections: Vorwort (eds., in English and German, 9–26; deals with life and work of Harry Zohn). Teil eins: Macht, Rasse, Gender: von der politischen Wirklichkeit zur literarischen Metamorphose. I. Antisemitismus und kein Ende? (pp. 27–144). II. Worte als Waffen (pp. 145–238). Teil zwei: Exilerfahrungen. I. 'Einmal Exil, immer Exil' (pp. 239–298). II. Stefan Zweig und sein Freundeskreis (pp. 299–364). III. Brücken im Bau: Dichtung und Übersetzung als Vermittlungsversuch zwischen Kulturen (pp. 365–396). Essays of historical and biographical relevance are listed according to subject.] [H.Z., b. 1923 in Vienna, germanist and translator, emigr. with his family to England in 1939, to the USA in 1940. Since 1967 professor for modern German literature at Brandeis University.]

32316. ZWEIG, STEFAN. LESTER, DAVID: *Suicide and anti-semitism: the suicides of Stefan Zweig and Otto Weininger.* [In]: Journal of Psychology and Judaism, Vol. 18, No. 3, New York, Fall 1994. Pp. 249–258, notes.

32317. ZWEIG, STEFAN. *Stefan Zweig und sein Freundeskreis.* [In]: Brücken über dem Abgrund. Festschrift für Harry Zohn [see No. 32315]. Pp. 299–364. [This section of the book (=Teil zwei, II) cont. the following essays: Die letzten Zeugen der dritten großen Austreibung unserer sogenannten Rasse: Stefan Zweig im Exil (Donald G. Prater, 299–316). The friendship of Stefan Zweig and Felix Braun (Donald G. Daviau, 317–336). The unpublished correspondence between Albert Einstein and Stefan Zweig (Jeffrey B. Berlin, 337–363).]

VIII. AUTOBIOGRAPHIES, MEMOIRS, LETTERS, GENEALOGY

32318. ADORNO, THEODOR W./BENJAMIN, WALTER: *Briefwechsel 1928–1940.* Hrsg. von Henri Lonitz. Frankfurt am Main: Suhrkamp, 1994. 501 pp. [Cf.: Das Falsche im Eigenen (Jürgen Habermas) [in]: Die Zeit, Nr. 39, Hamburg, 23. Sept. 1994, pp. 77–78. 'Denn alle Verdinglichung ist ein Vergessen . . . (Martin Meyer) [in]; 'NZZ', Nr. 217, Zürich, 17./18. Sept. 1994, p. 65.]

—— BENDIX, REINHARD: *Assimiliertes Judentum in autobiographischer Perspektive.* [See in No. 32417.]

32319. BENJAMIN, WALTER. *The correspondence of Walter Benjamin, 1910–1940.* Ed. and annotated by Gershom Scholem and Theodor W. Adorno. Transl. by Manfred R. Jacobson and Evelyn M. Jacobson. Chicago: Univ. of Chicago Press, 1994. XXII, 651 pp., illus., notes, index of correspondents. [Incl. correspondence with a.o. Brecht, Hofmannsthal, Horkheimer, Scholem.]

32320. BERLIN, JEFFREY: *Der unveröffentlichte Briefwechsel zwischen Antoinette von Kahler und Hermann Broch unter Berücksichtigung einiger unveröffentlichter Briefe von Richard Beer-Hofmann, Albert Einstein und Thomas Mann.* [In]: Modern Austrian Literature, Vol. 27, No. 2, Riverside, Ca., 1994. Pp. 39–76, notes. [Based on unpubl. material from the archives of the Leo Baeck Institute, New York.]

32321. BERMANN FISCHER, GOTTFRIED. BERMANN FISCHER, GOTTFRIED: *Wanderer durch ein Jahrhundert.* Frankfurt am Main: Fischer Taschenbuch Verlag, 1994. 265 pp., illus., index. [G.B.F., orig. G. Bermann, b. 1897 Gleiwitz, studied medicine, married 1925 Brigitte Fischer and joined the S.Fischer Verlag, of which he became director in 1932. Emigr. 1936 via Vienna (until 1938) to Stockholm, 1942 to USA. Lives in Italy.]

32322. BUXBAUM, HENRY: *Scherben der Erinnerung.* Memoiren des Wetterauer Juden Henry Buxbaum. Bearb. von Hans-Helmut Hoos. Mit einem Nachwort von Richard Buxbaum. Friedberg (Hessen): Bindernagel, 1994. 246 pp., illus. (Wetterauer Geschichtsblätter; Sonderausgabe.) [For previous publ. and data see No. 26792/YB XXXV.]

32323. CANETTI, ELIAS. CANETTI, ELIAS: *Nachträge aus Hampstead.* Aufzeichnungen. München: Hanser, 1994. 206 pp. [Cf.: Zu alt, zu alt. Ein Tagebuch gegen den Tod: Elias Canettis 'Aufzeichnungen' 1954 bis 1971 (Dieter Hildebrandt) [in]: Die Zeit, Nr. 41, Hamburg, 7. Okt. 1994, p. 12. Das verlorene Herz der Dinge; Elias Canettis Aufzeichnungen als Poetik der Erlösung (Andreas Breitenstein) [in]: 'NZZ', Nr. 277, Zürich, 26./27. Nov. 1994, p. 67. Innere Wetterkunde (Henning Ritter) [in] 'FAZ', Nr. 281, Frankfurt am Main, 3. Dez. 1994, Beilage.] [For obits. see No. 32157.]

32324. EINSTEIN, ALBERT. *Am Sonntag küss' ich Dich mündlich: die Liebesbriefe 1897–1903. Albert Einstein – Mileva Maric.* Hrsg. und eingeleitet von Jürgen Renn und Robert Schulmann. [Hrsg. der deutschen Ausgabe: Armin Herrmann. Das Vorw., die Einl. und die Anm. wurden von Heike Nowotny und Armin Hermann aus dem Amerikan. übers.] München: Piper, 1994. 214 pp., illus., bibl. (205–210). [For American edn. see No. 29747/YB XXXVIII.]

32325. FREUD, ANNA. FREUD, ANNA: *Briefe an Eva Rosenfeld.* Hrsg. von Peter Heller. Übersetzung der Einführungen und Anmerkungen von Sabine Baumann. Basel: Stroemfeld, 1994. 324 pp., illus. [Cont. letters written between 1925 and 1932.]

32326. FREUD, SIGMUND. *The correspondence of Sigmund Freud and Sandor Ferenczi: Vol. 1: 1908–1914.* Ed. by Eva Brabant [et al.], transcribed by I. Meyer-Palmedo. Transl. by Peter T. Hoffer. Introd. by André Haynal. Cambridge, Ma.: Belknap Press of Harvard Univ. Press, 1993. 584 pp., bibl. (Freud's and Ferenczi's works, 565–571). [First volume of a three vol. edn.]

32327. FREUD, SIGMUND. *The Freud/Jung letters: the correspondence between Sigmund Freud and C.G. Jung.* Ed. with an introd. by William McGuire. Transl. by R.F.C. Hull and Ralph Manheim. Abridged by Alan McGlashan. Princeton: Princeton Univ. Press, 1994. XXIV, 283 pp., illus. (Bollingen series, XCIV.) [Abridged paperback edn. For orig. edn. see No. 12531/YB XX.]

32328. FÜRST, PETER: *Der Zigarrentöter. Don Quixote im Exil.* Aus dem Amerikanischen von Anna Blum. München: Hanser, 1994. 272 pp. [Memoirs, written in Engl., but first publ. in German.] [P.F., b. 1910 in Berlin, sports reporter of the 'Berliner Tageblatt', emigr. via several European countries to Dominica, later to the U.S., where he became director of the German dept. of the 'Voice of America' in New York.] [Cf.: Im Zeitwolf (Michael Skasa) [in]: Die Zeit, Nr. 19, Hamburg, 5. Mai 1995, p. 64. Romantische Memoiren: für Peter Fürst war das Exil eine Kette von Abenteuern (Will Schaber) [in]: Aufbau, Vol. 60, New York, Sept. 16, 1994, p. 6.]

32329. GLÜCKEL VON HAMELN. *Die Memoiren der Glückel von Hameln.* Aus dem Jüdisch-Deutschen von Bertha Pappenheim. Mit einem Vorwort von Viola Roggenkamp. Autoris. Übertragung nach der Ausg. von David Kaufmann, Wien 1910. Weinheim: Beltz Athenäum, 1994. XVII, 320 [7] pp.

32330. GORAL, ARIE: *An der Grenzscheide: kein Weg als Jude und Deutscher?* Münster: LIT Verlag, 1994. 200 pp. (Anpassung – Selbstbehauptung – Widerstand, Bd. 6.) [A.G., (orig. Walter L. Sternheim), author, b. Oct. 16, 1909 in Rheda, Westphalia, emigr. 1933 from Hamburg to France, since 1935 in Palestine, returned to Hamburg 1953.]

32331. GREVE, LUDWIG: *Wo gehörte ich hin? Geschichte einer Jugend.* Hrsg. und mit einem Nachbericht versehen von Reinhard Tgahrt. Frankfurt am Main: S. Fischer, 1994. 189 pp. [Cf.: '. . . fertig ist die Laube . . .'. Zu Ludwig Greves Erinnerungen (Werner Weber) [in]: 'NZZ', Nr. 156, Zürich, 7. Juli 1994, p. 39. Besprechung (Eva auf der Mauer) [in] Freiburger

Rundbrief, N.F., 2. Jg., Nr. 2, Freiburg, 1995, pp. 129–131.] [L.G., b. Berlin, date not known – July 12, 1991 (drowned nr. Amrum, North Sea), writer, director of the library of the Deutsches Literaturarchiv Marbach, fled in 1939 via France to Italy, where he was captured by the Nazis and deported to Auschwitz. Liberated in 1944, emigr. to Palestine 1945, returned to Germany 1950.]

32332. GRUBRICH-SIMITIS, ILSE: *'Kein großartigerer, reicherer, geheimnisvollerer Stoff [...] als das Seelenleben'*. Ein früher Briefaustausch zwischen Freud und Einstein. [In]: Neue Rundschau, Jg. 105, H. 1, Frankfurt am Main, 1994. Pp. 107–118. [Corrected year of publ. of No. 31203/YB XXXIX.] [On three letters discovered by the author in the Library of Congress in 1991.]

32333. HAMBURGER, KÄTE. SCHRÖTER, KLAUS, Hrsg.: *Um Thomas Mann: der Briefwechsel Käte Hamburger – Klaus Schröter 1964 – 1990*. In Zusammenarbeit mit Armin Huttenlocher hrsg. von Klaus Schröter. Hamburg: Europ. Verl.- Anstalt, 1994. 177 pp., illus.

32334. HEINEMANN FAMILY. HEINEMANN, MOSHE YOSEF: *Genealogical tree – fathers and sons of the Heinemann family*. [In Hebrew, title transl.] Benei-Brak: M.Y. Heinemann, 5754 [=1994]. 603 pp. [Most of the book consists of geneal. tables. Incl. short history of the family from the middle ages to the present. The first known Heinemann lived in Würzburg.]

32335. HERZ, JULIUS. KEYL, WERNER: *Nachtrag zu Julius Herz Ritter von Hertenried, Eisenbahningenieur, seine Familie und seine Vor- und Nachfahren*. [In]: Genealogie, Jg. 43, Bd. 22, H. 3/4, Neustadt/Aisch, März-April 1994. Pp. 84–105, illus., notes, family trees. [For previous articles on Julius Herz by the author and data see No. 25802/YB XXXIV.]

32336. HERZ, EMIL: *Denk ich an Deutschland in der Nacht*. Ergänzter und illustrierter Nachdruck, als Band 8 der Schriftenreihe des Museumsvereins Warburg e.V. hrsg. von Kurt Scheideler. Warburg: Hermann Hermes Verlag, 1994. 342 pp., illlus., port. (Warburger Schriften, Bd. 10). [Incl.: Von Warburg über Berlin nach Rochester: Emil Herz – Erinnerungen an sein Werk (Kurt Scheideler, 326–340, illus.).] [First publ. in 1951, see No. 755/YB I; American edn. in 1967 under the title 'Before the fury', see No. 6092/YB XII.] [Emanuel Emil H., April 5, 1877 Essen – July, 7, 1971 Rochester, N.Y., since 1880 in Warburg, later director of Ullstein books in Berlin, emigr. 1937 to Italy, in 1939 to Cuba, since 1940 Rochester, N.Y.]

32337. HILBERG, RAUL: *Unerbetene Erinnerung. Der Weg eines Holocaust-Forschers*. Aus dem Amerikanischen von Hans Günter Holl. Frankfurt am Main: S. Fischer, 1994. 175 pp., illus. [First publ. in German. Title of orig. manuscript: The politics of memory.] [Cf.: Kampf um die Wahrheit. Das bewegende Zeugnis eines großen Wissenschaftlers (Eberhard Jäckel) [in]: Die Zeit, Nr. 41, Hamburg, 7. Okt. 1994, p. 30. Chronist des Untergangs (Christian Meier) [in]: 'FAZ', Nr. 230, Frankfurt am Main, 4. Okt. 1994, p. L 27. Ein Leben mit der Vernichtung (Michael Marek) [in]: Das Parlament. Nr. 42, Bonn, 21. Okt. 1994, p. 15.]

32338. HIRSCH, HELMUT: *Onkel Sams Hütte. Autobiographisches Garn eines Asylanten in den USA*. Mit einem Geleitwort von Lew Kopelew. Leipzig: Leipziger Univ.- Verl., 1994. 382 pp., illus., facsims., index. [H.H., b. Sept. 2, 1907 in Barmen, prof. of history, fled to the Saar in 1933, to France in 1935, via Spain and Portugal to the USA in 1941, returned to Germany in 1961. Lives In Düsseldorf.]

32339. HOFMANNSTHAL, HUGO VON. HOFFMANNSTHAL, HUGO VON/PANNWITZ, RUDOLF: *Briefwechsel 1907–1926*. In Verbindung mit dem Deutschen Literaturarchiv herausgegeben von Gerhard Schuster. Mit einem Essay von Erwin Jaeckle. Frankfurt am Main: S. Fischer, 1994. 943 pp. [Cf.: Prophet der europäischen Krise (Paul Michael Lützeler) [in]: Die Zeit, Nr. 44, Hamburg, 28. Okt. 1994, p. 69.]

32340. JACOBY, H. [HANS]: *Ter herinnering. Memoires van een boekverkoper als ooggetuige van de twintigste eeuw*. Den Haag: Van Stockum, Belifante & Coebergh, 1992. 1 vol. [Memoirs of author, born 1904 in Salzburg; grew up in Austria, book-seller in Amsterdam.]

32341. KASHTI-KROCH, JUDITH: *Der Spuk geht vorüber. Behütete Kindheit – rauhes Exil – gelobtes Land.* Autobiographie 1924–1942. Leipzig: Sachsenbuch-Verl., 1993. 139 [4] pp., illus., familytree. [Memoirs and family recollections; author fled after the November Pogrom from Leipzig to Belgium, later to France and Switzerland. Lives in Israel.]

32342. KELLERMANN, HENRY J.: *From Imperial to National-Socialist Germany. Recollections of a German-Jewish youth leader.* [In]: Leo Baeck Institute Year Book XXXIX, London, 1994. Pp. 305–330, illus., facsim., footnotes. [H.J.K., b. Berlin 1910, formerly leader of the Bund deutschjüdischer Jugend, emigr. 1937 to the USA, where he became a career diplomat. Now lives in Washington DC.]

32343. KUCZYNSKI, JÜRGEN: *Ein hoffnungsloser Fall von Optimismus?* Memoiren 1989–1994. Berlin: Aufbau- Verl., 1994. 331 pp.

32344. KUCZYNSKI, JÜRGEN: *Ein Leben in der Wissenschaft der DDR.* Münster: Westfälisches Dampfboot, 1994. 163 pp. [Memoirs.]

32345. LANDAUER, GUSTAV/MAUTHNER, FRITZ. *Gustav Landauer – Fritz Mauthner: Briefwechsel 1890–1919.* Bearbeitet von Hanna Delf. [Gustav Landauer. Briefe. Im Auftrag des Moses Mendelssohn Zentrums für Europäisch-Jüdische Studien, Univ. Potsdam und des Salomon Ludwig Steinheim-Instituts für Deutsch-Jüdische Geschichte in Zusammenarbeit mit dem Internationaal Instituut voor Sociale Geschiedenis, Amsterdam hrsg. von Hanna Delf und Julius Schoeps.] München: Beck, 1994. 562 pp., illus., facsims., notes (369–478), bibl., index (549–562). [Cf.: Briefe von Stern zu Stern (Lorenz Jäger) [in]: 'FAZ', Frankfurt am Main, 4. Okt. 1994, p. L 26. Die unendliche Melodie zwischen den Zeilen (Barbara Hahn) [in]: Die Zeit, Nr. 49, 2. Dez. 1994, p. 19.]

32346. LIEBERMANN, MAX. *Max Liebermann – Briefe.* Auswahl von Franz Landsberger. Ergänzte Neuausgabe von Ernst Volker Braun. Stuttgart: Hatje, 1994. 88 pp., illus. (Korrespondenzen, 5.) [A collection of 70 letters first publ. in 1937 by Schocken-Verlag.]

32347. MÜHSAM, ERICH. *Tagebücher 1910–1924.* Hrsg. und mit einem Nachwort von Chris Hirte. München: Deutscher Taschenbuch-Verl., 1994. 418 pp. (Originalausgabe.) [Bohemien und Bürger. Erstmals in leider unvollständiger Edition: die Tagebücher Erich Mühsams aus den Jahren 1910–1924 (Volker Ullrich) [in]: Die Zeit, Nr. 39, Hamburg, 23. Sept. 1994, p. 83. Der gute Anarchist (Hermann Kurzke) [In]: 'FAZ', Nr. 287, Frankfurt am Main, 10. Dez. 1994, Beilage.]

32348. PHILIPPSOHN, KURT: *Zwischen Dresden und Tel Aviv.* [In]: Geschichte und Gegenwart, Jg. 12, H. 3, Graz, Sept. 1993. Pp. 179–183. [With Engl. summary.] [Memoirs of a young technician, who emigr. in 1933 via Prague to Palestine.]

32349. RUDEL, JOSEF N.: *Von Czernowitz bis Tel Aviv gab's immer was zum lachen.* Tel Aviv: Papyrus, 1994. 157 pp. [Incl.: Vorwort (Margarita Pazi). Personal memoirs and humorous sketches about life in Bukowina and Israel.] [Josef Norbert R., b. 1921 in Czernowitz, writer, journalist, went to Israel in 1972.]

32350. SCHMIDT, HELMUT. AUST, GERRIT/STEIN, IRMGARD: *Gumpel, Wenzel, Schmidt. Die unbekannten Vorfahren von Helmut Schmidt.* Hamburg: Dölling und Galitz, 1994. 49 [4] pp., illus., notes, family trees. [Incl. a letter by Wolfgang Schmidt. On H.Sch.'s grandfather Gustav Ludwig Sch., illegitimate son of Ludwig Gumpel of Bernburg.]

32351. SCHOLEM, GERSHOM. *Gershom Scholem: Briefe I. 1914–1947.* [Im Auftrag des Leo-Baeck-Instituts] hrsg. von Itta Shedletzky. München: Beck, 1994. XV, 525 pp., illus., facsims., notes (337–460), glossary (488–491), index (names, 503–525). [Incl.: Einleitung (Itta Shedletzky, VII-XV). Chronol. of Scholem's life, list of letters (499–501).] [Cf.: Ein Unfriedlicher (Walter Boehlich) [in]: Die Zeit, Nr. 8, Hamburg, 17. Feb. 1995, p. 21.]

32352. SCHOLEM, GERSHOM. SCHOLEM, GERSHOM: *Von Berlin nach Jerusalem*. Jugenderinnerungen. Erweiterte Fassung. Mit einem Glossar, Register und Nachwort. Aus dem Hebräischen von Michael Brocke und Andrea Schatz. Frankfurt am Main: Jüdischer Verl., 1994. 270 pp. [Cf.: Geschichte eines kulturellen Ortswechsels (Andreas Kilcher) [in]: 'NZZ', Nr. 253, Zürich, 29./30. Okt. 1994, p. 66. Das doppelte Gesicht (Jakob Hessing) [in]: 'FAZ', Nr. 202, Frankfurt am Main, 31. Aug. 1994, p. 31.]

32353. SCHROBSDORF, ANGELIKA: *Jerusalem war immer eine schwere Adresse*. München: Deutscher Tschenbuchverlag., 1991. 407 pp. [Memoirs, revised edn. of the author's 'Das Haus im Niemandsland', München, Bertelsmann, 1989.] [A. Sch., b. Dec. 24, 1928 in Freiburg i. Br., author, emigr. with her Jewish mother from Berlin to Sofia in 1939, returned to Germany in 1947, married to Claude Lanzmann in Jerusalem 1971, lived in Paris and Munich, finally settled in Israel in 1983.]

—— SEGAL, LILLI: *Vom Widerspruch zum Widerstand: Erinnerungen einer Tochter aus gutem Hause*. [See No. 31875.]

32354. STERN, WILLIAM. LÜCK, HELMUT E./LÖWISCH, DIETER-JÜRGEN: *William Stern: der Briefwechsel zwischen William Stern und Jonas Cohn*. Dokumente einer Freundschaft zwischen zwei Wissenschaftlern. Frankfurt am Main; New York, 1994. 216 pp., bibl. (209–211). (Beiträge zur Geschichte der Psychologie, Bd. 7.)

32355. WEIDENFELD, GEORGE: *Remembering my good friends: an autobiography*. London: Harper Collins, 1994. X, 483 pp., illus. [G.W., b. Vienna 1919, publisher, went to England in 1938.] [Cf.: Opening a new chapter (Valerie Monchi) [in]: Jewish Chronicle, London, Nov. 25, 1994, p. 24.]

32356. WEISS, RUTH: *Wege im harten Gras*. Erinnerungen an Deutschland, Südafrika und England. Mit einem Nachwort von Nadine Gordimer. Wuppertal: Hammer, 1994. 305 pp., illus.

IX. GERMAN-JEWISH RELATIONS

A. General

32357. BARKAI, AVRAHAM: *Judentum, Juden und Kapitalismus. Ökonomische Vorstellungen von Max Weber und Werner Sombart*. [In]: Menora 5, München, 1994. Pp. 25–38, notes.

32358. BUNYAN, ANITA: *Rhenish Liberalism and the Jewish Question in the Vormärz. The case of the Kölnische Zeitung 1841–1847*. [In]: Leo Baeck Institute Year Book XXXIX, London, 1994. Pp. 31–51, footnotes.

32359. DOMHARDT, YVONNE: *Juden in der deutschen und französischen Literatur zwischen 1870 und 1914 – eine Bibliographie*. [In]: Judaica, Jg. 50, H. 1–2, Basel, Sept. 1994. Pp. 141–150.

32360. FRIEDLANDER, ALBERT: *Riders towards the dawn: from ultimate suffering to tempered hope*. London: Constable, 1993. 328 pp. [Deals with the effect the Holocaust had on Judaism and Christian and Jewish theology.]

32361. FRIEDLANDER, ALBERT H.: *Meister Eckhardt and the Jewish tradition*. [In]: European Judaism, Vol. 27, No. 2, London, Autumn 1994. Pp. 78–90, notes.

32362. HEITMANN, MARGRET: *Flucht vor der Taufe. Der Übertritt von Marcus Joel aus Glogau und seine Folgen*. [In]: Menora 5, München, 1994. Pp. 349–365, notes. [Deals with conversions in the early 18th century.]

32363. HENKE, HANS-GERD: *Der 'Jude' als Kollektivsymbol in der deutschen Sozialdemokratie 1890–1914*. Mainz: decaton, 1994. 130 pp., notes, bibl.

32364. HIRSCH, HELMUT: *'Frauen, Franzosen, Philister und Juden'.* Zu den Ausschlußklauseln der Tischgesellschaft. [In]: Die Erfahrung anderer Länder. Beiträge eines Wiepersdorfer Kolloquiums zu Achim und Bettina von Arnim. Hrsg. von Heinz Härtl und Hartwig Schultz. Berlin; New York: de Gruyter, 1994. Pp. 153–164, footnotes.

32365. HOFFMANN-AXTHELM, DAGMAR: *Bach und die 'perfidia iudaica'. Zur Symmetrie der Judenchöre in der Johannespassion.* [In]: 'NZZ', Nr. 77, Zürich, 2./3. April 1994, p. 63. [Examines the influence of Luther's anti-Jewish attitudes on Bach.]

32366. HOLZTRÄGER, HANS: *Erinnerungslücken und Verschweigen. Das Bild der Juden und Zigeuner und die NS-Vergangenheit der Siebenbürger Sachsen und Banater Schwaben in den Südostdeutschen Vierteljahresblättern nach 1965.* [In]: Halbjahresschrift für südosteuropäische Geschichte, Literatur und Politk. Jg. 5, H. 2, Ippesheim, 1993. Pp. 30–38.

32367. KATZ, JACOB/RENGSTORF, KARL HEINRICH, Hrsg.: *Begegnungen von Deutschen und Juden in der Geistesgeschichte des 18. Jahrhunderts.* Hrsg. von Jacob Katz und Karl Heinrich Rengstorf. Tübingen: Niemeyer, 1994. VIII, 129 pp., notes, index. (Wolfenbütteler Studien zur Aufklärung, Bd. 10.) [Papers presented at a colloquium held by the Lessing-Akademie with the assistance of the Israel Academy of Sciences and Humanities in Jeruslaem, Sept. 1978.] [Cont.: Die deutschen Pietisten und ihr Bild des Judentums (Karl Heinrich Rengstorf, 1–16). Der Einfluß von Hermann Samuel Reimarus auf Moses Mendelssohn (Gerhard Alexander, 17–24). Johann David Michaelis und Moses Mendelssohn (Karlfried Gründer, 25–50). Salomon Maimons Position in der Entwicklung der Philosophie (Nathan Rotenstreich, 51–64). Zur Figur eines edlen Juden im Aufklärungsroman vor Lessing (Wolfgang Martens, 65–78). Frühantisemitismus in Deutschland (Jacob Katz, 79–90). Lazarus Bendavid an die Akademie der Wissenschaften in Berlin. Eine Miszelle (Dominique Bourel, 91–94). Die Lessinghandschriften der Familien Friedländer und Mendelssohn (Wolfgang Milde, 95–106). Christian Wilhelm Dohm. Ein politischer Schriftsteller der deutschen Aufklärung (Rudolf Vierhaus, 107–124).]

32368. KINZIG, WOLFRAM: *Philosemitismus.* Teil I: *Zur Geschichte des Begriffs* [&] Teil II: *Zur historiographischen Verwendung des Begriffs.* [In]: Zeitschrift für Kirchengeschichte, Bd. 105 (1994), 4. Folge XLIII, H. 1 [&] H. 2, Stuttgart, 1994. Pp. 202–228; 361–383, footnotes.

32369. KLÜGER, RUTH: *Katastropen. Über deutsche Literatur.* Göttingen: Wallstein, 1994. 229 pp., notes. [A collection of 8 essays; incl.: Gibt es ein 'Judenproblem' in der deutschen Nachkriegsliteratur? (9–38). Thomas Manns jüdische Gestalten (39–58). 'Die Ödnis des entlarvten Landes': Antisemitismus im Werk jüdisch-österreichischer Autoren (59–82). Die Leiche unterm Tisch: jüdische Gestalten aus der deutschen Literatur des neunzehnten Jahrhunderts (83–106). Kreuzzug und Kinderträume in Lessings 'Nathan der Weise' (189–227).]

32370. KULKE, CHRISTINE/LEDERER, GERDA, Hrsg.: *Der gewöhnliche Antisemitismus. Zur politischen Psychologie der Verachtung.* Pfaffenweiler: Centaurus, 1994. 193 pp., footnotes. (Studien und Materialien zum Rechtsextremismus, Bd. 2.) [Incl. (titles partly condensed): Antisemitismus und politische Kultur (Christine Kulke, 7–18). Wie antisemitisch sind die Deutschen? (Gerda Lederer, 19–39). Hitlers Enkel im Schatten der Vergangenheit (Sibylle Hübner-Funk, 40–52). The delegitimization of Jews in Germany, 1933–1945 (Daniel Bar-Tal, 53–69). Auschwitz und die Notwendigkeit der Erinnerung (Öjvind Larsen, 70–85). Die Wiederkehr des Verdrängten (Dirk Juelich, 86–102). Antisemitische Stereotype in Österreich (Hilde Weiss, 105–124). Stereotype über Juden als strukturelle Elemente religiös-politischer Überzeugungen (Volker Berbüsse, 125–139). Ignoranz, Solidarität und Nationalwahn zu Zeiten der DDR. Innensicht aus jüdischer Perspektive (Irene Runge, 159–170). Die deutsche Einheit und des Problem das Antisemitismus (Frank Stern, 171–189).]

32371. LANGER, MICHAEL: *Zwischen Vorurteil und Aggression. Zum Judenbild in der deutschsprachigen katholischen Volksbildung des 19. Jahrhunderts.* Freiburg: Herder, 1994. 587 pp., notes (314–519), bibl. (521–575), index (persons, 576–587). (Reihe 'Lernprozess Christen Juden' Bd. 9.)

32372. LEA, CHARLENE: *The 'Christlich-Deutsche Tischgesellschaft': Napoleonic hegemony engenders political anti-semitism.* [In]: Crisis and Culture in post-enlightenment Germany. Essays in honour of Peter Heller [see No. 32119]. Pp. 319–342.

32373. MAZURA, UWE: *Zentrumspartei und Judenfrage 1870/71–1933. Verfassungsstaat und Minderheitenschutz.* Mainz: Matthias-Grünewald-Verlag, 1994. LVII, 229 pp., footnotes, index. (Veröffentlichungen der Kommission für Zeitgeschichte, Reihe B: Forschungen, Bd. 62.)

32374. *'Mit dem Gebetsmantel zum Gegenangriff': Juden im Bild der Bundesrepublik.* Begleitbuch zur Ausstellung. Hrsg.: Alte Synagoge Essen. Konzeption: Edna Brocke [et al.]. Essen: Klartext, 1994. 115 pp., illus. (Studienreihe der Alten Synagoge, Bd. 2) [Cf.: Besprechung (Boike Jacobs) [in]: Frankfurter Jüdische Nachrichten, Nr. 85, Frankfurt am Main, Juni/Juli 1994, p. 10; a critical essay on the exhibition.]

32375. NEUBAUER, HANS-JOACHIM: *Judenfiguren: Drama und Theater im frühen 19. Jahrhundert.* Frankfurt am Main; New York: Campus, 1994. 206 pp., illus., footnotes, bibl. (182–205). (Schriftenreihe des Zentrums für Antisemitismusforschung Berlin, Bd. 2.)

—— NOWAK, KURT/RAULET, GÉRARD, eds.: *Protestantismus und Antisemitismus in der Weimarer Republik.* [See No. 32417.]

32376. OLSON, MICHAEL P.: *Playing it safe: historicizing Thomas Bernhard's Jews.* [In]: Modern Austrian Literature, Vol. 27, Nos. 3–4, Riverside, Ca., 1994. Pp. 37–50.

32377. SCHOENBERG, BARBARA ZEISL: *'Ich wollt immer nur ein anständiger Mensch sein': the Jewish presence in the works of Felix Mitterer, Hilde Spiel and Thomas Bernhard.* [In]: Modern Austrian Literature, Vol. 27, Nos. 3–4, Riverside, Ca., 1994. Pp. 127–142. [Discusses the presence of the Jew in German-language literature, and points out the differences in conception by Jewish and non-Jewish authors.]

32378. STERN, FRANK: *Berlin 1949. Lessings Nathan, Dickens' Fagin und Harlans Jud Süß zwischen Theater und Straßenschlacht.* [In]: Jüdischer Almanach 1995 des Leo Baeck Instituts. Frankfurt am Main, 1994. Pp. 150–159.

32379. TIMMS, EDWARD: *The Wandering Jew. A Leitmotiv in German literature and politics.* Professorial Lecture given at the University of Sussex on Tuesday, 26 April 1994. 40 [4] pp., illus., facsims. [Univ. of Sussex, 1994.] [Obtainable at the Bibliothek Germania Judaica, Cologne.]

32380. WEDEMEIER, KLAUS: *Mut zum Erinnern – gegen das Vergessen.* Reden und Texte zum Umgang mit deutscher Schuld und Verantwortung. Mit einem Geleitwort von Ignatz Bubis. Bremen: Donat, 1994. 184 pp. [A collection of articles dealing with Vergangenheitsbewältigung.]

B. Church and Synagogue

32381. ABRAMS, DANIEL: *The literary emergence of esotericism in German pietism.* [In]: Shofar, Vol. 12, No. 2, West Lafayette, Ind., Purdue Univ., Winter 1994. Pp. 67–85, notes. [Incl. kabbalists Judah the Pious (Juda ben Samuel, Regensburg), Eleazar of Worms.]

32382. ANONYMUS: *Tractatus adversus Judaeum (1122).* Hrsg. von Wolfgang Bunte. Frankfurt am Main: Lang, 1993. 192 pp. (Judentum und Umwelt, Bd. 40.)

32383. ARING, PAUL: *'Wage du, zu irren und zu träumen . . .'. Juden und Christen unterwegs.* Theologische Biographien – biographische Theologie im christlich-jüdischen Dialog der Barockzeit. Leipzig: Leipziger Univ.- Verl./Köln: Verlag Wissenschaft und Politik, 1992. 234 pp., docs., indexes, bibl. (226–233). [Incl.: Präsentation (Siegfried Hoyer, 12–14); mainly dealing with Johann Christoph Wagenseil; also on the Jewish community of Nuremberg,

Andreas Osiander, Nikolaus Kopernikus, Isaak Troki and Menasse Ben Israel and his friends and opponents.]

32384. BROCKE, EDNA: *Von der Aporie im Gespräch zwischen Christen und Juden. Eine persönliche Standortbestimmung.* [In]: Jüdischer Almanach 1995 des Leo Baeck Instituts. Frankfurt am Main, 1994. Pp. 160–169.

32385. *Jewish-Christian encounters over the centuries: symbiosis, prejudice, Holocaust, dialogue.* Ed. by Marvin Perry and Frederick M. Schweitzer. New York: Peter Lang, 1994. X, 436 pp. (American University Studies. Series IX, History, vol. 136.) [19 Essays, incl.: Medieval perceptions of Jews and Judaism (Frederick M. Schweitzer, 131–168). The Jews in Reformation theology (Eric W. Gritsch, 197–214). The image of Judaism in nineteenth-century Christian New Testament scholarship in Germany (Susannah Heschel, 215–240). Racial Nationalism and the rise of modern antisemitism (Marvin Perry, 241–268). The Vatican and the Holocaust: unresolved issues (John T. Pawlikowski, 293–312). Allied foreign policy and the Holocaust (Henry L. Feingold, 313–326). Martin Niemöller, activist as bystander; the oft-quoted reflection (Ruth Zerner, 327–340). The Holocaust and Christian thought (Alan Davies, 341–368).]

32386. MENTGEN, GERD: *Jüdische Proselyten im Oberrheingebiet während des Spätmittelalters. Schicksale und Probleme einer 'doppelten' Minderheit.* [In]: Zeitschrift für die Geschichte des Oberrheins. Bd. 142. Stuttgart, 1994. Pp. 116–139, footnotes.

32387. NEWMAN, AMY: *The death of Judaism in German Protestant thought from Luther to Hegel.* [In]: Journal of the American Academy of Religion, Vol. 61, No. 3, Atlanta, Ga., Fall 1993. Pp. 455–485.

32388. SAUERBIER, EDITH, Hrsg.: *Charlotte Klein – Pionierin der Verständigung.* Bendorf: Hedwig-Dransfeld-Haus, 1992. 141 pp. [Cf.: Besprechung (Ruth Ahl) [in]: Freiburger Rundbrief, N.F., 2. Jg., Nr. 2, 1995. Pp. 141–142.] [Ch. K., 1915 Berlin – 1985 London, born into an Orthodox Eastern-Jewish family, converted to Catholicism and became a nun, author of 'Theologie und Anti-Judaismus', publ. in 1975.]

32389. STEGEMANN, EKKEHARD W.: *Martin Buber and Karl Ludwig Schmidt: A Jewish-Christian dialogue on the eve of the Shoah.* [In]: European Judaism, Vol. 27, No. 1, London, Spring 1994. Pp. 3–11, notes. [This dialogue was first publ. in 'Theologische Blätter' 12, 1933, 257–274.]

32390. WARNECKE, HANS: *Von der Judenmission zu einem neuen Verhältnis zwischen Juden und Christen.* [In]: Kreis Ahrweiler. Heimat-Jahrbuch 1994. Jg. 51, Ahrweiler, 1994. Pp. 66–68.

32391. WIESE, CHRISTIAN: *Jahwe – ein Gott nur für Juden? Der Disput um das Gottesverständnis zwischen Wissenschaft des Judentums und protestantischer alttestamentlicher Wissenschaft im Kaiserreich.* [In]: Christlicher Antijudaismus und Antisemitismus. Theologische und kirchliche Programme Deutscher Christen. Hrsg. von Leonore Siegele-Wenschkewitz [see No. 31727]. Pp. 27–94, notes. [On the law trials C.V. versus Theodor Fritsch 1910–1914 and the role of Protestant theologians, esp. on Rudolf Kittel as expert witness and commentator.]

32392. WOLFSON, ELLIOT R.: *The mystical significance of Torah study in German pietism.* [In]: The Jewish Quarterly Review, Vol. 84, No. 1, Philadelphia, 1994. Pp. 43–78.

C. Antisemitism

32393. *Antisemitismus in Baden 1890–1914.* [In]: Zeitschrift für die Geschichte des Oberrheins, Bd. 141. Stuttgart, 1993. Pp. 279–335, footnotes. [Cont.: Alltag und politischer Antisemitismus in Baden, 1890–1900 (Helmut Walser Smith, 280–303). Aktivitäten antisemitischer Parteien im Großherzogtum Baden zwischen 1890 und 1914 (Stefan Scheil, 304–335).]

32394. AUSTRIA. GEHLER, MICHAEL: *Männer im Lebensbund. Studentenvereine im 19. und 20. Jahrhundert unter besonderer Berücksichtigung der österreichischen Entwicklung.* [In]: Zeitgeschichte, Jg. 21, H. 1, Wien, 1994. Pp. 45–66, notes. [Deals also passim with antisemitism.]

32395. AUSTRIA. HOFINGER, NIKO: *'Unsere Losung ist: Tirol den Tirolern!'. Antisemitismus in Tirol 1918–1938.* [In]: Zeitgeschichte, Jg. 21, H. 3/4, Wien, April 1994. Pp. 83–108, notes.

32396. BERGDOLT, KLAUS: *Der Schwarze Tod in Europa. Die grosse Pest und das Ende des Mittelalters.* München: Beck, 1994. 266 pp., illus., bibl. (249–258). [Incl. chapt. on the persecution of Jews.] [Cf.: Gesellschaft im Ausnahmezustand (Volker Ullrich) [in]: Die Zeit, Nr. 37, Hamburg, 9. Sept. 1994, p. 60.]

32397. BLOOD LIBEL. Battenberg, Friedrich: *Herrschaft und Verfahren. Politische Prozesse im mittelalterlichen Römisch-Deutschen Reich.* Darmstadt: Wiss. Buchgesellschaft, 1994. X, 254 pp. [Incl.: 'Minderheitenschutz' im Reich: der Prozeß um den Fuldaer Ritualmordvorwurf von 1236 (30–38, notes:179–184).]

32398. BLOOD LIBEL. BIALE, DAVID: *Blood libels and blood vengeance.* [In]: Tikkun, Vol. 9, No. 4, Oakland, Ca., July/Aug. 1994. Pp. 39–40, 75, illus. [Discusses the controversy in the Israeli press over an article by Israel Yuval about the Hebrew Chronicles of the First Crusade in 1096.]

32399. BLOOD LIBEL. HÄGLER, BRIGITTE: *Judenhaß und Ritualmordlegende: zur 'Rationalisierung' des Judenhasses im 16. Jahrhundert.* [In]: Aschkenas, Jg. 4/1994, H. 2, Wien, 1995. Pp. 425–448.

32400. BLOOD LIBEL. KIEVAL, HILLEL J.: *Antisémitisme ou savoir social? Sur la genèse du procès moderne pour meurtre rituel.* [In]: Annales, Vol. 49, No. 5, Paris, Sept.- Oct. 1994. Pp. 1091–1106. [With Engl summary, p. 1276; examines the reappearance of ritual murder trials involving Jews in modern Europe 1882–1914.]

32401. BLOOD LIBEL. KIEVAL, HILLEL J.: *Representation and knowledge in medieval and modern accounts of Jewish ritual murder.* [In]: Jewish Social Studies, New Series, Vol. 1, No. 1, New York, Fall 1994. Pp. 52–72, notes. [Discusses several accusations of blood libel in Germany and England, in particular a case in Fulda in 1235 and one in a Czech village in 1895.]

32402. BLOOD LIBEL. MENTGEN, GERD: *Über den Ursprung der Ritualmordfibel.* [In]: Aschkenas, Jg. 4/1994, H. 2, Wien, 1995. Pp. 405–416.

—— BLOOD LIBEL. YUVAL, ISRAEL JACOB: *Vengeance and damnation, blood and defamation. From Jewish martyrdom to blood libel accusations.* [See No. 31427.]

32403. BRAUN, CHRISTINA VON: *Zur Bedeutung der Sexualbilder im rassistischen Antisemitismus.* [In]: Jüdische Kultur und Weiblichkeit in der Moderne [see No. 32104]. Köln, 1994. Pp. 23–50.

32404. *Central European History, Vol. 27, No. 3* [with the issue title]: *Christian religion and anti-semitism in modern German history.* Riverside, Ca., 1994. 1 issue. [Incl.: Introduction to the theme (James F. Harris, 261–266). Anti-Judaism in intra-Christian conflict: Catholics and Liberals in Baden in the 1840s (Dagmar Herzog, 267–282). Religion and conflict: Protestants, Catholics, and anti-semitism in the state of Baden in the era of William II (Helmut Walser Smith, 283–314). The learned and the popular discourse of anti-semitism in the catholic milieu of the Kaiserreich (Helmut Walser Smith, 315–328). Catholics, Protestants, and antisemitism in Nazi Germany (Doris L. Bergen, 329–348). Commentary on Christians and anti-semitism (Jonathan Sperber, 349–354).]

32405. CLAUSSEN, DETLEV: *Grenzen der Aufklärung; die gesellschaftliche Genese des modernen Antisemitismus.* Überarbeitete Neuausgabe. Frankfurt am Main: Fischer-Taschenbuch-Verl., 1994. 264 pp., bibl. (257–262).

—— COHEN, SUSAN SARAH, ed.: *Antisemitism: an annotated bibliography. Vol. 3: 1987–1988.* [See No. 31686.]

32406. EHMANN, ANNEGRET: *Rassistische und antisemitische Traditionslinien in der deutschen Geschichte des 19. und 20. Jahrhunderts.* [In]: Sportmuseum Berlin, Hrsg.: Sportstadt Berlin in Geschichte und Gegenwart. Jahrbuch 1993 des Sportmuseums Berlin. In Zusammenarbeit mit der Gedenkstätte Haus der Wannsee-Konferenz und dem Forum für Sportgeschichte. Berlin, 1993. Pp. 131–145, notes.

—— ERB, RAINER: *Persistenz und Wandel antijüdischer Vorurteile im 18. und frühen 19. Jahrhundert.* [See in No. 31405.]

32407. ERDLE, BIRGIT R.: *Der ursprüngliche Schrecken. Zur Liaison von Antisemitismus und Kulturkritik.* [In]: Jüdische Kultur und Weiblichkeit in der Moderne [see No. 32104]. Pp. 11–22.

32408. HOFFMANN, CHRISTHARD: *Christlicher Antijudaismus und moderner Antisemitismus. Zusammenhänge und Differenzen als Problem der historischen Antisemitismusforschung.* [In]: Christlicher Antijudaismus und Antisemitismus. Theologische und kirchliche Programme Deutscher Christen. [see No. 31727]. Pp. 293–318, notes.

32409. HOFFMANN, CHRISTHARD: *Politische Kultur und Gewalt gegen Minderheiten. Die antisemitischen Ausschreitungen in Pommern und Westpreussen 1881.* [In]: Jahrbuch für Antisemitismusforschung 3, Frankfurt am Main; New York, 1994. Pp. 93–120.

32410. HORTZITZ, NICOLINE: *Der 'Judenarzt'. Zur Diskriminierung eines Berufsstandes in der Frühen Neuzeit.* [In]: Aschkenas, Jg. 3, Wien, 1993. Pp. 85–112, footnotes. [Corrected name of journal in entry No. 30103/YB XXXIX.]

—— HORTZITZ, NICOLINE: *Verfahrensweisen sprachlicher Diskriminierung in antijüdischen Texten der Frühen Neuzeit; aufgezeigt am Beispiel der Metaphorik.* [See in No. 31405.]

—— *The 'Jewish Question' in German-speaking countries 1848–1914. A Bibliography.* Ed. by Rena R. Auerbach. [See No. 31690.]

—— *Jüdin – deutsche – deutsche Jüdin? Auswirkungen des Antisemitismus in Deutschland.* [See No. 32020.]

32411. KAPLAN, MARION: *Schwesterlichkeit auf dem Prüfstand: Feminismus und Antisemitismus in Deutschland, 1904–1938.* [In]: Brücken über dem Abgrund. Festschrift für Harry Zohn [see No. 32315]. Pp. 95–112.

32412. KATZ, JACOB: *Die Hep-Hep-Verfolgungen des Jahres 1819.* Nachwort von Stefan Rohrbacher. Berlin: Metropol, 1994. 136 pp., footnotes, docs. (Reihe Dokumente, Texte, Materialien, Bd. 8.) [First publ. in Hebrew in 'Sion', Vol. 38, 1973. This German edn. is enlarged by ten documents compiled by Stefan Rohrbacher, who also added an essay (Nachwort, 122–136).]

32413. KINZIG, WOLFRAM: *'Ich kann gewiß nichts dafür . . .'. Der Skandal um Hofprediger Adolf Stoecker in London im November 1883.* [In]: Aschkenas, Jg. 4/1994, H. 2, Wien, 1995. Pp. 365–403.

32414. KOCH, GRIT: *Adolf Stoecker 1835 – 1909. Ein Leben zwischen Politik und Kirche.* Erlangen: Palm & Enke, 1993. 250 pp. (Erlanger Studien, Bd. 101.) Zugl.: Erlangen/Nürnberg, Univ., Diss., 1993.

—— KULKE, CHRISTINE/LEDERER, GERDA, Hrsg.: *Der gewöhnliche Antisemitismus. Zur politischen Psychologie der Verachtung.* [See No. 32370.]

32415. LICHTBLAU, ALBERT: *Antisemitismus und soziale Spannung in Berlin und Wien 1867–1914.* Berlin: Metropol, 1994. 282 pp., tabs., notes, bibl. 251–280). (Reihe Dokumente, Texte, Materialien, Bd. 8.)

32416. NEISS, MARION: *Schändungen jüdischer Friedhöfe im Deutschland des 18. und 19. Jahrhunderts.* [In]: Jahrbuch für Antisemitismusforschung 3, Frankfurt am Main; New York, 1994. Pp. 68–92.

32417. NOWAK, KURT/RAULET, GÉRARD, eds.: *Protestantismus und Antisemitismus in der Weimarer Republik.* Frankfurt am Main: Campus, 1994. 228 pp., footnotes. Assimiliertes Judentum in autobiographischer Perspektive (Reinhard Bendix, 17–32). Judentum und Christentum bei

Leo Baeck (Dominique Bourel, 33–42). Die Krise der Moderne in europäischer Perspektive. Walther Rathenau, Ernst Troeltsch und die Weimarer Republik (Pascale Gruson, 43–84). Das Wesen der Prophetie. Ernst Troeltschs Aufsatz 'Glaube und Ethos der hebräischen Propheten' (Annette Disselkamp, 85– 94). Von Strack zu Jeremias. Der Anteil der neutestamentlichen Wissenschaft an der Vorgeschichte der evangelischen Judaistik (Wolfgang Wiefel, 95–126). Die Konzepte einiger protestantischer deutscher Theologen zur 'Judenfrage' (Bernard Reymond, 127–146). Die Schwäche des Kulturprotestantismus bei der Bekämpfung des Antisemitismus (Rita R. Thalmann, 147–166). Der Kulturantisemitismus von Wilhelm Stapel (Louis Dupeux, 167–176). Der 'Bund für deutsche Kirche' und seine völkisch-antijudaistische Theologie (Kurt Meier, 177–198). Der deutsche Protestantismus und die 'Mission unter Israel' zwischen Weltkrieg und 'NS-Machtergreifung'. Antisemitismus und Wahlverhalten. Sozialhistorische Beobachtungen zur protestantischen Bevölkerung auf dem Lande und in den Mittelschichten (Alfred Wahl, 219–228).]

32418. SABROW, MARTIN: *Der Rathenaumord. Rekonstruktion einer Verschwörung gegen die Republik von Weimar.* München: Oldenbourg, 1994. 231 pp., footnotes, bibl. (216–226), index (228–231). Zugl. Freiburg (Breisgau), Univ., Diss., 1992. (Schriftenreihe der Vierteljahrshefte für Zeitgeschichte, Bd. 69.)

32419. SCHOEPS, JULIUS H.: *Vom Antijudaismus zum Antisemitismus: zur Struktur, Funktion und Wirkung eines Vorurteils.* [In]: Brücken über dem Abgrund. Festschrift für Harry Zohn [see No. 32315]. Pp. 27–42.

32420. STROBL, INGRID: *Das unbegriffene Erbe. Bemerkungen zum Antisemitismus der Linken.* [See in No. 31852]. Pp. 102–118.

32421. STROBL, INGRID: *Rechter Blutrausch. Antisemitismus in Tirol.* [See in No. 31852]. Pp. 65–70.

―――― WELLMANN, HANS: *Linguistik der Diskriminierung. Über die Agitation gegen Juden in Flugblättern der Frühen Neuzeit.* [See in No. 31405.]

32422. WIESE, CHRISTIAN: *Vom 'jüdischen Geist'.* Isaak Heinemanns Auseinandersetzung mit dem akademischen Antisemitismus innerhalb der protestantischen Theologie in der Weimarer Republik. [In]: Zeitschrift für Religions- und Geistesgeschichte, Jg. 46, H. 3, Leiden, 1994. Pp. 209–234, footnotes. [On Heinemann's 'Vom 'jüdischen Geist' – ein Wort an die Ehrlichen unter seinen Anklägern', publ. 1924, in which he discusses a.o. writings by Otto Procksch and Reinhold Seeberg, two professors of theology.]

32423. ZIEGE, EVA-MARIA: *Antisemitische Frauen und misogyne Bilder vom jüdischen 'Anderen'.* [In]: METIS, Zeitschrift für hist. Frauenforschung und feministische Praxis, Jg. 2, H. 2, Pfaffenweiler, 1993. Pp. 66–80. [A.o. on a debate between Eva Reichmann and an adherent of the NSDAP, Margarete Adam.]

32424. ZÖLLER, SONJA: *Judenfeindschaft in den Schwänken des 16. Jahrhunderts.* [In]: Daphnis, Bd. 23, H. 1–2, Amsterdam, 1994. Pp. 345–369.

32425. ZUMBINI, MASSIMO FERRARI: *Große Migration und Antislawismus: negative Ostjudenbilder im Kaiserreich.* [In]: Jahrbuch für Antisemitismusforschung 3, Frankfurt am Main; New York, 1994. Pp. 227–253.

D. Noted Germans and Jews

32426. ADENAUER, KONRAD. SHAFIR, SHLOMO: *Goldmann and Adenauer.* [In Hebrew, with English summary.] [In]: Gesher, No. 129, Jerusalem, Summer 1994. Pp. 59–83.

32427. BRAUN, KARL. KERN, BERND-RÜDIGER/BEDDIES, TOMKE: *Ein Beitrag Karl Brauns zur Judenemanzipation.* Einleitung und Edition. [In]: Aschkenas, Jg. 4, H. 1, Wien, 1994. Pp. 153–162, footnotes. [Reprint of an article by K.B., written in 1844, condemning antisemitism and speaking out in favour of emancipation of the Jews.]

32428. CURTIUS, ERNST ROBERT. Hoeges, Dirk: *Kontroverse am Abgrund: Ernst Robert Curtius und Karl Mannheim. Intellektuelle und 'freischwebende Intelligenz' in der Weimarer Republik.* Frankfurt am Main: Fischer-Taschenbuch-Verl., 1994. 270 pp., notes, bibl. (246–262), index. (Originalausgabe). [Cf.: Showdown in Weimar (Hugo Velarde) [in]: Die Zeit, Nr. 45, Hamburg, 4. Nov. 1994, p. 26.]

32429. DROSTE-HÜLSHOFF, ANNETTE. Doerr, Karin: *The specter of anti-semitism in and around Annette von Droste-Hülshoff's 'Judenbuche'.* [In]: German Studies Review, Vol. 17, No. 3, Tempe, Az., Oct. 1994. Pp. 447–472.

32430. FONTANE, THEODOR. *Theodor Fontane – Briefe an Georg Friedlaender.* Aufgrund der Edition von Kurt Schreinert und der Handschriften neu herausgegeben und mit einem Nachwort versehen von Walter Hettche. Mit einem Essay von Thomas Mann. Frankfurt am Main: Insel, 1994. 488 pp., index. (Insel Taschenbuch 1565.) [G.F., lawyer, country court judge in Schmiedeberg, great-grandson of David Friedlaender.]

32431. GOETHE, JOHANN WOLFGANG. Hartung, Günter: *Goethe und die Juden.* [In]: Weimarer Beiträge 40, Berlin, 1994. Pp. 398–416.

32432. HEIDEGGER, MARTIN. Wolzogen, Christoph von: *'Vertauschte Fronten'. Heidegger und Rosenzweig.* [In]: Zeitschrift für Religions- und Geistesgeschichte, Jg. 46, H. 2, Leiden, 1994. Pp. 107–125, footnotes.

32433. JUNG, CARL GUSTAV. Samuels, Andrew: *Jung and antisemitism.* [In]: Jewish Quarterly, Vol. 41, No. 1, London, Spring 1994. Pp. 59–63, illus., notes.

32434. JUNG, CARL GUSTAV. Samuels, A.: *New material concerning Jung, anti-semitism, and the Nazis.* [In]: Journal of Analytical Psychology, Vol. 38, No. 4, London, Oct. 1993. Pp. 463–470.

— LESSING, GOTTHOLD EPHRAIM. Klüger, Ruth: *Kreuzzug und Kinderträume in Lessings 'Nathan der Weise'.* [See in No. 32369.]

32435. MANN, THOMAS. Hermann, Armin: *Albert Einstein und Thomas Mann: Einig gegen das 'Geziefer'.* [In]: Damals, H. 2, 1993. Pp. 26–29, illus.

32436. NIEMÖLLER, MARTIN. Siegele-Wenschkewitz, Leonore: *Auseinandersetzungen mit einem Stereotyp. Die Judenfrage im Leben Martin Niemöllers.* [In]: Christlicher Antijudaismus und Antisemitismus. Theologische und kirchliche Programme Deutscher Christen. Hrsg. von Leonore Siegele-Wenschkewitz [see No. 31727]. Pp. 261–291, notes.

32437. NIETZSCHE, FRIEDRICH. Aschheim, Steven E.: *The Nietzsche legacy in Germany, 1890–1990.* Berkeley: University of California Press; UK distribution: Chichester: Wiley, 1993. XII, 337 pp., illus. [Incl. Nietzsche and antisemitism; attitude to Judaism; Hitler's and the Third Reich's use of N.'s philosophy.] [See also by same author: Nietzsche and the Nietzschean moment in Jewish life (1890–1939)[in]: LBI Year Book XXXVII, London, 1992. Pp. 189–212, footnotes.] [Cf.: Make your own Nietzsche (Jerry Z. Muller) [in]: TLS, London, June 17, 1994.]

32438. NIETZSCHE, FRIEDRICH. Santaniello, Weaver: *Nietzsche, God, and the Jews: his critique of Judeo-Christianity in relation to the Nazi myth.* Foreword by David Tracy. Albany: State Univ. of New York Press, 1994. XVI, 232 pp.

32439. SCHILLER, FRIEDRICH VON. Regensteiner, Henry: *Moses in the light of Schiller.* [In]: Judaism, Vol. 43, No. 1, New York, Winter 1994. Pp. 61–65, notes. [Discusses how Schiller planned to write a play on Moses; his references to Moses and the Jewish people in speeches and lectures; also his attitude to contemporary Jews.]

32440. SCHMITT, CARL. FABER, RICHARD: *Es gibt einen antijüdischen Affekt! Über Carl Schmitts 'Glossarium'.* [In]: Zeitschrift für Religions- und Geistesgeschichte, Jg. 46, H. 1, Leiden, 1994. Pp. 70–73

32441. SCHUMANN, ROBERT/SCHUMANN, CLARA. *The marriage diaries of Robert and Clara Schumann.* Ed. by Gerd Neuhaus. Transl. by Peter Ostwald. London: Robson Books, 1994. 256 pp., illus. [Also discusses attitude to Jews, incl. hostile and antisemitic comments about Felix Mendelssohn.]

32442. VINCKE, LUDWIG FREIHERR. ASCHOFF, DIETHARD/SCHLAUTMANN-OVERMEYER, RITA: *Vincke und die Juden.* [In]: Ludwig Freiherr Vincke. Ein westfälisches Profil zwischen Reform und Restauration in Preußen. Hrsg. von Hans-Joachim Behr und Jürgen Kloosterhuis. Münster: Selbstverl. d. Vereins f. Gesch. und Altertumskunde Westfalens, 1994. Pp. 289–308 [&] 680–686, footnotes. [Incl. the document: Oberpräsident Ludw. Frhr. Vincke, an Minister des Innern, Friedrich Frhr. v. Schuckmann: Integration der jüdischen Bevölkerung durch deren (Zwangs-)Bekehrung zum Christentum (680–686).]

32443. WAGNER, RICHARD. COHEN, MITCHELL: *Politics at the opera.* [In]: Dissent, Vol. 41, No. 3, New York, Summer 1994. Pp. 354–364. [Discusses how Wagner's antisemitism is reflected in his operas.]

32444. WEBER, MAX. AY, KARL-LUDWIG: *Max Weber und der Begriff der Rasse.* [In]: Aschkenas, Jg. 3, Wien, 1993. Pp. 189–218, footnotes. [On Weber's refusal to support the biological idea of race and racial antisemitism.] [Corrected name of journal in entry No. 31356/YB XXXIX.]

32445. WILHELM II. RÖHL, JOHN C.G.: *The Kaiser and his court: Wilhelm II and the government of Germany.* Transl. from the German by Terence F. Cole. Cambridge; New York: Cambridge University Press, 1994. XI, 275 pp., illus., notes (213–266). [Incl. chap. 'Kaiser Wilhelm II and German anti-semitism' (190–212). See also No. 31358/YB XXXIX.]

X. FICTION AND POETRY

32446. BEN-YITZHAQ, AVRAHAM: *Es entfernen sich die Dinge.* Gedichte und Fragmente. Hrsg. und aus dem Hebr. übers. von Efrat Gal-Ed und Christoph Meckel. München: Hanser, 1994. 111 pp. [Texts partly in Hebrew, partly in German.] [Cf.: 'Fern meinem Leben' (Joseph Croitoru) [in]: 'NZZ', Nr. 106, Zürich, 9. Mai 1994, p. 75.] [A. Ben Yitzhak, orig. Abraham Sonne, 1889 Galicia – 1950 Jerusalem, educationalist, Zionist, studied in Berlin and Vienna, emigr. 1938 to Palestine, publ. 11 poems.]

32447. BERADT, MARTIN: *Beide Seiten einer Strasse.* Roman aus dem Scheunenviertel. Mit einem Nachwort von Eike Geisel. Berlin: Mackensen, 1993. 274, XVIII pp. [New, slightly augmented edn. of 'Die Strasse der kleinen Ewigkeit', 1965.]

32448. CHOTJEWITZ, DAVID: *Das Abenteuer des Denkens. Roman über Albert Einstein.* Frankfurt am Main: Alibaba, 1994. 397 pp.

32449. COLIN, AMY/KITTNER, ALFRED, Hrsg.: *Versunkene Dichtung der Bukowina.* Eine Anthologie deutschsprachiger Lyrik. Hrsg. von Amy Colin und Alfred Kittner. München: Fink, 422 pp., index (421–422). [An anthology, incl. numerous Jewish authors. Cont.: Vorwort & Einleitung (Amy Colin, 9–24). I. Verzeichnis der Autorinnen, Autoren und ihrer Gedichte (Sammlung von Alfred Kittner) (25–37). II. Gedichte (Auswahl von Alfred Kittner unter Mitwirkung von Amy Colin) (39–344). III. Apparat: Biographien/Bibliographien (345–410); Nachwort (Alfred Kittner, 411–419).] [Alfred Kittner, Nov. 24, 1906 Czernowitz – Aug. 14, 1991 Düsseldorf, poet, writer. Together with Alfred Margul-Sperber started a collection of Bukovinian German literature in the 30s in Czernowitz. Most of the collection was confiscated and lost in Romania after World War II. Left in 1980 and went to live in Germany.]

32450. DRACH, ALBERT. DRACH, ALBERT: *Ironie vom Glück*. Kleine Protokolle und Erzählungen. München: Hanser, 1994. 237 pp. [Incl. autobiographical short stories.] [See also No. 32169.] [Cf.: Lehrstücke eines Misanthropen (Ulrich Weinzierl) [in]: 'FAZ', Nr. 282, Frankfurt am Main, 1994, p. 36.]

32451. HEBEL, JOHANN PETER: *The treasure chest*. Unexpected reunion and other stories, illustrated with contemporary woodcuts; introduced and translated by John Hibberd. London: Libris, 1994. XXIX, 175 pp., illus. [Cont. stories about rural Jews.]

32452. HEIMANN, MORITZ: *Märkische Novellen*. Eingeleitet von Günter de Bruyn. Frankfurt am Main: Fischer Taschenbuch Verl., 1993. 154 pp., frontisp. [Incl.: Im Schatten der eigenen Bedeutung; Moritz Heimann – ein jüdischer Autor der Mark (9–24). Cont. three stories, first publ. between 1905 and 1913: Wintergespinst; Die Tobias-Vase; Dr. Wislizenus.] [See also on Heimann in No. 32112.]

32453. HERNÁDI, MIKLÓS: *Weiningers Ende*. Ein Kriminalroman. Aus dem Ungarischen von Erika Bollweg. Frankfurt am Main: Eichborn, 1993. 382 pp., illus. [Cf.: Dokument und Fiktion. Miklós Hernádis Roman 'Weiningers Ende' (Eva Haldimann) [in]: 'NZZ', Nr. 73, Zürich, 29. März 1993, p. 16.] [See also No. 32316.]

32454. HILSENRATH, EDGAR: *Jossel Wassermanns Heimkehr*. Roman. München: Piper, 1993. 320 pp. [On Jewish life in a small town in Bukowina.] [E.H., b. 1926 in Leipzig, fled in 1938 to Romania, from there deported to the Ukraine, emigr. after liberation to Palestine, later to the USA, lives in Berlin.]

32455. HONIGMANN, BARBARA: *Damals, dann und danach*. Eine Erzählung. [In]: Frankfurter Jüdische Nachrichten, Nr. 84, Frankfurt am Main, März/April 1994. Pp. 37–39. [Autobiographical short story about the author's mother, a Hungarian Jewess who grew up in Vienna, emigr. to London and returned with her husband to East Germany after the war.]

32456. KATZ, HENRY WILLIAM: *Die Fischmanns*. Roman. Weinheim: Beltz, Quadriga, 1994. 263 pp. [Autobiographical novel about a Jewish family from Galicia before the First World War; written in 1934 in Lyon and publ. in 1938, also transl. into English and Polish. Republ. in 1985.] [H.W.K., orig. Hertz Wolff, 1906 Rudki – 1992 Florida, journalist, writer, emigr. to France in 1933, interned in 1940, escaped to the USA in 1941.]

32457. KATZ, HENRY WILLIAM: *Schlossgasse 21. In einer kleinen deutschen Stadt*. Roman. Weinheim: Beltz, Quadriga, 1994. 586 pp. [Continuation of 'Die Fischmanns', see above, depicting the life of a family from Galicia in a small Saxonian town from World War I to 1933. First publ. in English in 1940 in New York; first German edn. in 1986.] [Cf.: Die Exilgeschichte der Fischmanns – H.W. Katz' 'Tragödie der Heimatlosigkeit' – wiederentdeckt (Stefan Berkholtz) [in]: Die Zeit, Nr. 15, Hamburg, 7. April 1995, p. 16.]

32458. KENEALLY, THOMAS: *Schindlers Liste*. Roman. Aus dem Englischen von Günther Danehl. München: Goldmann, 1994. 345 pp., illus. [First German paperback edn. of documentary novel. For orig. edns. publ. in London and New York in 1982, see No. 19742/YB XXVIII. For first German edn. publ. in 1983, see No. 20802/YB XXIX.] [See also Nos. 31717 and 31843.]

32459. MALAMUD, BERNARD: *Der deutsche Flüchtling*. [In]: Frankfurter Jüdische Nachrichten, Nr. 86, Frankfurt am Main, Sept. 1994. Pp. 49–52. [On a German-Jewish refugee in New York, his language and pronounciation problems. Taken from a collection of short stories, 'Schwarz ist meine Lieblingsfarbe', and transl. into German by Annemarie Böll.]

32460. MANN, FRIDO: *Terezín oder Der Führer schenkt den Juden eine Stadt*. Eine Parabel. Münster: Lit, 1994. 278 pp., illus.

32461. MEGGED, AHARON: *Heinz, sein Sohn und der böse Geist.* Erzählung. Aus dem Hebräischen übers. von Barbara Linner. Gerlingen: Bleicher, 1994. 159 pp. [Tells the story of Heinz Hirsch, a typical 'yekke', engaged in a tragicomic struggle to cope with adjustment to a new life in Israel.]

32462. MORTON, FREDERIC: *Geschichten aus zwei Welten.* Wien: Deuticke, 1994. 160 pp. [Incl. 10 short stories, several of an autobiographical nature.] [F.M., orig. Fritz Mandelbaum, b. Vienna, Oct. 5, 1925, emigr. to the USA in 1940, returned to Europe in the eighties, novelist, essayist.] [Cf.: Zwei Welten (Karl-Markus Gauss) [in]: 'NZZ', Nr. 147, Zürich, 27. Juni 1994, p. 19.]

32463. PERUTZ, LEO. *The master of the day of judgment.* Transl. by Eric Mosbacher. London: Harvill; New York: Arcade Publishers, 1994. XXI, 147 pp. [First English and American edn.; orig. publ. in Germany, 1923.] [L.P., born in Prague in 1882, lived in Vienna, after the Anschluß emigrated to Israel where he died in 1957.]

32464. PICARD, JACOB: *Und war ihm leicht wie nie zuvor im Leben.* Die schönsten Erzählungen aus dem süddeutschen Landjudentum. Mit einem Nachwort von Manfred Bosch. Bottighofen: Libelle, 1993. 194 pp.

32465. SCHINDEL, ROBERT: *Ein Feuerchen im Hintennach.* Gedichte 1986–1991. Frankfurt am Main: Suhrkamp, 1992. 78 [4] pp. (Erstausgabe.) [Incl. poems dealing with Jewish themes.]

32466. WANDER, FRED: *Hotel Baalbek.* Roman. Frankfurt am Main: Fischer Taschenbuch-Verl., 1994. 222 pp. [Paperback edn., for orig. edn. and data F.W. see No. 28987/YB XXXVII.]

32467. WELSH, RENATE: *Das Lufthaus.* Roman. Graz: Styria, 1994. 384 pp. [Based on an extensive family correspondence, this novel depicts the life of a young Jewish woman from Karlsruhe who becomes involved with the 1848 revolution in Vienna and later flees to America.]

Index to Bibliography

Aargau, 31577, 31629
Aaron Isaak, 32128, 32129
Abbott, Alison, 31785
Abbt, Thomas, 31987
Abraham, Max, 31525
Abrams, Daniel, 32381
Abramson, Glenda, 32134
Abse, Leo, 31879
Abt Schindler, Roslyn, 32108
Abudiente, Moshe Gideon, 31506
Achberger, Friedrich, 32075
Adam, Jacob, 32018
Adam, Klaus-Peter, 31727
Adam, Konrad, 32207
Adam, Ursula, 31692, 31868
Adelmann, Dieter, 31966
Adenauer, Konrad, 32426
Adler, Alfred, 32130
Adler, David A., 31930
Adler, Friedrich, 32131
Adler, Nathan, 31968
Adler, Nathan ben Simeon ha-Kohen, 31489
Adorno, Theodor W., 32107, 32110, 32117, 32132, 32318, 32319
Adunka, Evelyn, 31881, 32063, 32207, 32220
Agnon, Shmuel Josef, 31846, 32133, 32134
Ahl, Ruth, 32388
Ahlem, 32032
Ahlfeld-Heymann, Marianne, 31696
Ahrendt, Peter, 32306
Ahrweiler, 31450, 31451, 31547
Aigner, Manfred, 31594
'AJR Information', 32037, 32157
'AKK', 31529
Albania, Nazi Period, 31809
Albert, Hans, 32255
Albrecht, Michael, 31969, 31987
Albrich, Thoma, 31851
Alexander, Edward, 31781
Alexander, Gerhard, 32367
'Alexander-von-Humboldt-Magazin', 32087
Aliens – Uneingebürgerte, 32098
'Allgemeine' Jüd. Wochenzeitung, 31634, 31872, 32033, 32044, 32090, 32207
Almog, Shmuel, 32054
Alsace, 31439, 31440, 31445, 31579, 31582, 32108, 32386
Altaras, Thea, 31899
Altenberg, Peter, 32122
Altenessen, 31481
Altenhein, Hans, 32127

Altenstadt, 31392
Althaus, Hans-Peter, 31445
Altmann, Alexander; 31966, 31987
Altner, Manfred, 31646
Altona, 31506
'American Jewish Archives', 31635
Améry, Jean, 31768, 32108, 32135
Amnon of Mainz, 31411
Amsterdam, 31445, 32383
Anderl, Gabriele, 32019
Anders, Dörte, 32223
Anhalt, 32123
'Annales', 31397, 31411, 31429, 31977, 32400
Anröchte, 31452
Anschluß, 32119
Anti-Judaism, 31427, 31727, 32371, 32385, 32408
Antisemitism, 31398, 31405, 31457, 31543, 31603, 31686, 31690, 31706, 31801, 31835, 31865, 31937, 31987, 32015, 32020, 32316, 32367, 32371, 32372, 32375, 32385, 32393–32425, 32443
Antisemitism, Christian, 31727, 31838, 32391, 32408, 32422
Antisemitism, Defence, 32391
Antisemitism, Imperial Germany, 32042, 32230, 32373, 32391, 32404, 32409, 32413, 32414
Antisemitism, Middle Ages (see also Anti-Judaism; Blood Libel), 31427
Antisemitism, Nazi, 31754, 31822, 32404
Antisemitism, Post War, 31880, 31885, 31887, 31889, 31895, 31898, 31903, 31924, 31936, 32370, 32378, 32420
Antisemitism, Weimar Republic, 32373, 32417, 32422
Antisemitism World Report, 31880
Apfel, Yosef Yehoshua, 31967
Appelfeld, Aharon, 31768, 32136, 32137
Appignanesi, Lisa, 32178
Aptroot, Marion, 31428
'Archiv für Kulturgeschichte', 32238
Archives, 31512
'Archives Juives', 31580, 32061
Arendt, Hannah, 31912, 32102, 32111, 32138, 32139
Arendt, Ludwig, 31478
Aretin, Karl Otmar von, 31869
Argentina, 31641, 31666
'Ariadne', 32020
Aring, Paul Gerhard, 32383
Arkush, Allan, 31984

Army, Jews in the (see also War and Jews), 31599
Arnheim, Rudolf, 32140
Arnhold, Eduard, 32076
Arnim, Achim von, 32364, 32372
Arnsberg, 31865
Aronsfeld, C.C., 31635
Aronson, Shlomo, 31856
Aronstein, Philipp, 32141
Art Collectors, 31518, 32115
Art Historians, 32165, 32190, 32249, 32304
Art, Jewish, 32050, 32052
Art, Jews in, 32131
Aryanisation, 31392, 31715, 31728, 31739, 31769, 31865, 32115, 32290
Aschaffenburg, 31453
Aschheim, Steven E., 31773, 32437
'Aschkenas', 31679; 31388, 31394, 31396, 31402, 31409, 31437, 31447, 31455, 31501, 31503, 31504, 31532, 31533, 31562, 31604, 31974, 31983, 32213, 32225, 32294, 32399, 32402, 32410, 32413, 32427, 32444
'Aschkenas' (Beiheft), 31946
Aschoff, Diethard, 31762, 31865, 32442
Asper, Barbara, 31719
Asper, Helmut G., 31647
Assimilation, Acculturation (see also Emancipation), 32417
Assmann, Aleida, 32110
Aubé, Jean-Paul, 31580
Auckenthaler, Karlheinz F., 32169
Auer, Herbert, 31392
Auerbach, Berthold, 32080
Auerbach, Rena R., 31690
Auf der Mauer, Eva, 32331
'Aufbau', New York, 31636–31638, 31639, 31693, 31872, 31893, 31998, 32037, 32252, 32328
Aufgebauer, Peter, 31387, 31534
'Aufklärung', 31988
Augsburg, 31392, 31405
August, Jochen, 31932
'Aus dem Antiquariat', 31492, 32300
'Aus Politik und Zeitgeschichte', 32106
Auschwitz, 31620, 31698–31705, 31784, 31799, 31829, 31855, 31856, 31892, 31913, 31932, 31933
Ausgrabungen in Berlin, 31464
Ausländer, Rose, 32103
Aust, Gerrit, 32350
Australia, Refugees, 31661, 31832
Austria (see also Vienna), 31587, 31596–31599, 31616, 31881–31883, 32069, 32108, 32115, 32122
Austria, Antisemitism, 31603, 31706, 31880, 32108, 32369, 32370, 32394, 32395, 32421
Austria, Emigration, 31649, 32094
Austria, Immigration, 31588
Austria, Nazi Period, 31597, 31610, 31851, 32091

Austria, Post War, 31588, 31592, 31595, 31601, 31851, 31884, 31901
Autobiographies, Memoirs, Diaries, Letters, 31417, 31923, 31986, 32058, 32129, 32318, 32319, 32321–32324, 32326, 32327, 32329, 32330, 32333, 32337–32340, 32342, 32343, 32345–32347, 32349, 32351–32353, 32356
Autobiographies, Memoirs, Nazi Period, 31408, 31696, 31736, 31756, 31758, 31804, 31839, 31848, 31866, 31875, 32322, 32328, 32341
Ay, Karl-Ludwig, 32444, 32444

Baader, Meike, 32021
'Babylon', 32021, 32159
Bach, André, 31525
Bach, Johann Sebastian, 32365
Bachenheimer, Ritta, 31543
Backhaus, Fritz, 32115
Backhausen, Manfred, 32022
Bad Oeynhausen, 31454
Bad Soden, 31707
Baden, 31387, 31445, 32393
Baden-Württemberg, 31455, 31456
Badt, Gustav, 31635
Badt-Strauss, Bertha, 32102
Baeck, Leo, 31955–31958, 31978, 32000, 32417
Baer, Wolfram, 31405
Bärsch, Claus-Ekkehard, 32110
Baigell, Matthew, 31954
Bailer, Brigitte, 31851
Bailey, Brenda, 31708
Baioni, Giuliano, 32208
Baisingen, 31709
Ball, Hugo, 32142
'Bamah – Drama Quarterly', 32017
Bamberger, Gabrielle, 31683
Bankier, David, 31745
Banking, Jews in (see also Court Jews, Financiers), 32115, 32124
Baptism see Conversion
Bar-Giora-Bamberger, Naftali, 31495, 31515
Bar-Tal, Daniel, 32370
Barkai, Avraham, 31413, 31640, 31745, 31772, 31865, 32023, 32357
Barkenings, Hans-Joachim, 31727
Barnouw, Dagmar, 31779
Bartetzko, Dieter, 32115
Bartov, Omer, 31745
Bartrop, Paul R., 31832, 31833
Barzel, Neima, 31886, 32055
Basle, 31628
'Basler Zeitung', 31628
Bastian, Till, 31784
Battenberg, Friedrich, 31384–31386, 31405, 31679, 32397
Bauche, Ulrich, 31506
Bauer, Barbara, 31647
Bauer, Dieter R., 31577

Index to Bibliography

Bauer, Felice, 32122
Bauer, Yehuda, 31710, 31745
Bauer-Hack, Susanne, 31636
Baumann, Sabine, 32325
Baumgarten, Jean, 31429, 31445
Baur, Andreas, 32235
Bavaria, 31405, 31457
Bayer, Oswald, 31987
Bechtel, Delphine, 31429
Beck, Enrique, 32143
Becker, Franziska, 31709
Becker, Jurek, 32077
Becker-Jákli, Barbara, 31722, 31728
Beckermann, Ruth, 32108
Beddies, Tomke, 32427
Beem, Hartog, 31662
Beer, Fritz, 32093
Beer-Hofmann, Richard, 32122, 32144, 32320
Behr, Hans-Joachim, 31520, 32442
Beintker, Michael, 32110
'Beiträge zur Bottroper Geschichte', 31467
'Beiträge zur jüd. Geschichte in Rheinland-Pfalz', 31450, 31544, 31554
Belke, Ingrid, 31647
Beller, Steven, 32063
Bellin, Klaus, 32278
Ben Gurion, David, 32063
Ben-Aharon, Yitzhak, 32063
Ben-Chanan, Yaacov, 32110
Ben-Chorin, Schalom, 31813
Ben-Yitzhah, Avraham, 32446
Bendavid, Lazarus, 31987, 32367
Bender, Peter, 31826
Bendix, Reinhard, 32417
Benfeld, 31387
Benjamin, Walter, 32109, 32112, 32145, 32146, 32318, 32319
Bennertz, Gerhard, 31541
Bensousson, Georges, 31946
Benz, Wolfgang, 31561, 31632, 31647, 31685, 31731, 31742, 31826, 31851, 31871, 31934, 31941
Beradt, Martin, 32447
Berbüsse, Volker, 32370
Berenbaum, Michael, 31698
Berg, Hubert van den, 32085
Berg, Jimmy, 32147
Bergdolt, Klaus, 32396
Bergen, Doris L., 32404
Bergen-Belsen, 31752, 31850, 31935
Berger, Heinrich, 31603, 31604
Berger, Joel, 31577
Bergeron, Louis, 32115
Bergfelder, Tim, 31660
Bergmann, Günther J., 31641
Bergmann, Hugo, 31966
Bergmann, Werner, 31685, 31887
Bergner, Elisabeth, 32148
Berkholtz, Stefan, 32457

Berlin, 31458, 31460–31462, 31470, 31711–31716, 31844, 31846, 31866, 31888, 31936, 31951, 31987, 32028, 32076, 32108, 32118, 32230, 32263, 32286, 32372, 32378, 32415
Berlin-Charlottenburg, 31463
Berlin-Spandau, 31464
Berlin-Weissensee, 31465
Berlin, Document Center, 31674
Berlin, Zentrum f. Antisemitismusforschung, 31685
Berlin, Jeffrey B., 32122, 32317, 32320
Bermann Fischer, Gottfried, 32321
Bernauer, Rudolf, 32098
Bernays, Martha, 32180
Bernburg, 31466, 32350
Bernfeld, Siegfried, 32057
Bernhard, Thomas, 32376, 32377
Bernstein, Eduard, 32149
Berthold, Monika, 32048
Bessen, Dorothea, 31739
Bethmann, Johann Philipp Freiherr von, 32117
Bettauer, Hugo, 32150
Bettelheim, Bruno, 32151
Beuys, Barbara, 31959
Bevege, Margaret, 31642
Bialas, Wolfgang, 31782
Biale, David, 31960, 32398
Bibliographies, Catalogues, Inventories, 31445, 31448, 31532, 31534, 31614, 31673, 31686, 31687, 31690, 31691, 31693, 31694, 31695
Bibliographies, Personal, 32194, 32308
Bielefeld, 31865
Bienert, Michael, 32263
Biermann, Wolf, 32108
Biller, Maxim, 31907
Binder, Hartmut, 32209
Birkenhauer, Anne, 31681
Bishof, Günter, 31882
Blanke, Franz, 31452
Blaukopf, Herta & Kurt, 32240
'Blick in die Wissenschaft' (Univ. Regensburg), 32025
Bloch, David Ludwig, 32048
Bloch, Ernst, 32107, 32109, 32152, 32153
Bloch, Josef Samuel, 31593
Blood Libel, 31427, 31525, 32115, 32397–32402
Boas, Franz, 32014
Bobenheim, 31554
Boberach, Heinz, 31692
Bochum, 31840
Bodemann, Y. Michal, 31918
Bodenheimer, Alfred, 32228
Bodensee (see also Württemberg; Vorarlberg; Switzerland), 31575
Böhler, Ingrid, 31851
Böhlich, Walter, 32351
Böhm, Günter, 31506
Böhr, Christoph, 31987
Börne, Ludwig, 32112, 32117

'Börsenblatt für den Deutschen Buchhandel', 32127, 32265, 32278
Bohemia, 31617
Bokovoy, Douglas, 31543
Bolzenius, Rupert, 32024
Bonard, Waldemar, 31813
Bondy, Ruth, 31856
Book Trade, Jews in, 32340
Bopf, Britta, 31728
Borio, Gianmario, 32092
Bornemann, Ernest, 32086
Bosch, Manfred, 31577
Boschki, Reinhold, 32311
Bottrop, 31467
Bourel, Dominique, 31987, 32367
Bowie, Karen, 32115
Brabant, Eva, 32326
Bracker, Hans-Jürgen, 31991
Brämer, Andreas, 31972
Bräse, Stephan, 32219
Bramann, Wilhelm, 31565
Brandenburg, 31470, 31715, 31793
Brandes, Detlef, 31618
Brandt, Marion, 31716
Brath, Klaus, 32226
Braun, Bernhard, 32224
Braun, Christina von, 32403
Braun, Ernst Volker, 32346
Braun, Felix, 32317
Braun, Günter & Waldtraut, 32076
Braun, Karl, 32427
Braun, Michael, 32168
Braun, R., 31774
Braun, Robert, 31947
Braunschweig, Jüdisches Museum, 31468
Braunschweig-Calenberg, 31534
Brazil, 31641, 31663
Brecheisen, Claudia, 32077
Brecher, Elinor J., 31717
Bredekamp, Horst, 32249
Brednich, Wilhelm, 31688
Breidecker, Volker, 32249
Breitenstein, Andreas, 32323
Breitman, Richard, 31747, 31748
Bremen, 31552, 31718
Brendler, Konrad, 31720
Brentzel, Marianne, 31719
Bresheeth, Haim, 31937
Breslau, 31721
Breuer, Isaac, 32000, 32001
Breuer, Mordechai, 31427, 31975
Brilon, 31559
Broch, Hermann, 32075, 32320
Brochhagen, Ulrich, 31889
Brocke, Edna, 31890, 32374, 32384
Brocke, Michael, 31464, 31470, 32352
Brockmann, Stephen, 32107
Brod, Max, 32109, 32110
Broder, Henryk M., 31556, 31843

Brodersen, Momme, 32086
Bromberger Family, 31718
Bromberger, David, 31718
Browning, Christopher R., 31745, 31748
Bruderhof Movement, 31961
Brücken über dem Abgrund. Festschrift für Harry Zohn, 32315; 31906, 31925, 32010, 32069, 32094, 32198, 32221, 32222, 32411, 32419
Brühl, 31722
Brüning, Jens, 32292
Brüschke, Rudolf, 31559
Bruhns, Maike, 32131
Brumlik, Micha, 31892, 31938, 32110
Bruners, Wilhelm, 31681
Brunkhorst, Hauke, 32159
Brunner, Detlev, 32088
Bruns, Alfred, 31571
Brusten, Manfred, 31939
Brzoska, Matthias, 32092
Buber, Martin, 31846, 31961–31964, 31973, 31978, 31993, 32000, 32122, 32224, 32389
Bubis, Ignatz, 31680, 32117, 32380
Buchenwald, 31723, 31823, 31940
'Buchhandelsgeschichte', 31860
Buchholz, Marlis, 31767
Budapest, 31619
Bühler, Michael see Volkmann, Michael
Büning, Eleonore, 32187
Bünte, Hans, 32283
Buhlan, Harald, 31728
Bukowina, 32103, 32449, 32454
Bulgaria, Nazi Period, 31809
Bulz, Emmanuel, 31846
Bund Jüdischer Frontsoldaten (Austria), 31598, 31599
Bungeroth, Dietrich, 31466
Bunte, Wolfgang, 32382
Bunyan, Anita, 32358
Bunzl, John, 31851, 32063
Burgenland, 31585, 31597
Burger, Anton, 31857
Burger, Fritz, 31808
Burger, Hilde, 32108
Burghartz, Susanne, 31387
Burmeister, Karl Heinz, 31388, 31575, 31576, 31577
Burnett, Stephen G., 31508
Burrin, Philippe, 31743
Burrweiler, 31471
Burstyn, Ruth, 31605
Buss, Wilfried, 31564
Bussmann, Hadumod, 31542
Butler, Geoffrey, 32098
Buttenhausen, 31472, 31473
Buxbaum, Heinrich (Henry), 32322
Buxbaum, Richard, 32322

Calasso, Elias, 32157
Canada, Refugees, 31648

Canetti, Elias, 32154–32157, 32323
Canetti, Veza, 32158
Canthal, Fritz, 31509
Cargas, Harry James, 32288
Carlebach, Ephraim, 31526
Carlebach, Julius, 31676, 31682
Carpi, Daniel, 31724
Cartarius, Ulrich, 31869
Carwin, Heinz, 32098
Cassirer, Ernst, 31966, 32110, 32159–32161
Cassuto, Isaac, 31506
Cassuto, Jehuda Leon, 31506
Catalogues, of Exhibitions, 31468, 31518, 31591, 31815, 32103, 32115, 32131, 32192, 32235, 32242, 32248, 32263
'Cathedra', 31886, 32067
Caujolle, Christian, 32186
Celan, Paul, 31681, 32103, 32162, 32163, 32270
Cemeteries, 31455, 31464, 31465, 31470, 31483, 31495, 31498, 31499, 31503, 31504, 31507, 31515, 31522, 31523, 31525, 31534, 31544, 31555, 31556, 31629, 31707, 32416
'Central European History', 31407, 32215, 32239, 32404
Centralverein dt. Staatsbürger jüd. Glaubens (C.V.), 32023, 32391
Cesarani, David, 31643, 31745, 31783
Chamberlain, Harriet Hyman, 31738
Chamisso, Adelbert von, 31987
Chapman, Stanley, 32115
Charlottenburg, 31463
Charney, Ann, 31623
Chemnitz, 31842
Chernow, Ron, 32124
Chile, 31651
China (see also Shanghai), 31668
Chorherr, Thomas, 32063
Chotjewitz, David, 32448
'Christianity Today', 31838
Christlicher Antijudaismus und Antisemitismus, 31727, 32391, 32408, 32436
Chug Chaluzi, 31872
Church, Christians and Jews, 31727, 32371, 32383, 32417
Church, Christians and Jews, Nazi Period, 31726, 31727, 31851, 31865, 32385
Church, Christians and Jews, Post War, 31577, 31865, 32384, 32390
Clarenbach, Anja, 32086
Claussen, Detlev, 31843, 32132, 32405
Coburg, 32022
Cochavi, Yehoyakim, 32056
Cohen, Hermann, 31960, 31965, 31966, 31978, 32080
Cohen, Jeremy, 31427
Cohen, Mitchell, 32443
Cohen, Raya, 31744
Cohen, Richard A., 31994
Cohen, Richard I., 31389

Cohen, Susan Sarah, 31686
Cohen, Walter, 32164, 32165
Cohn, Gustav, 31526
Cohn, Jonas, 32354
Cohn, Michael, 31891
Colin, Amy, 32221, 32315, 32449
Cologne, 31474, 31728, 32290
'Commentary', 32036
Communists, 31723, 31839, 31898, 32013, 32065, 32106, 32234, 32314
Concentration and Internment Camps, Ghettos see Auschwitz; Bergen-Belsen; Flossenbürg; Kaiserwald; Les Milles; Lodz; Neuengamme; Riga; Treblinka
Conversion from Judaism, Baptism, 31853, 32027, 32362, 32386
Coppel Family, 31565
Coppi, Hans, 31870
Cossmann, Paul Nicolaus, 32166
Court Jews, 31586, 32247
Couteau, Elisabeth, 31580
Cramer, Ernst, 32037
Cretzmeyer, Stacy, 31729
Crew, David F., 31730
Crisis and Culture in Post-Enlightenment Germany, 32119; 31779, 32372
Critchfield, Richard, 32084
Croitoru, Joseph, 31427, 32446
Crusades, 31427
Cuba, 32088
Curie, Jacob, 31506
Curilla, Wolfgang, 31764
Curtius, Ernst Robert, 32428
Customs, Folklore, 31397
Czechoslovakia, 31620
Czechoslovakia, Nazi Period, 31618, 31622, 31856, 32086
Czeike, Felix, 31606
Czernowitz, 32103, 32349

Dachau, 31731, 31941
'Dachauer Hefte', 31731, 31853
Dachlika, Sassona, 31430
Dähnhardt, Willy, 31740
Dahm, Volker, 31846
Dahrendorf, Ralf, 32078, 32255
Daltroff, Jean, 31583
'Damals', 32435
Damberg, Wilhelm, 31865
Dan, Joseph, 31399, 31996
Danyel, Jürgen, 31870
'Daphnis', 32424
Darmstadt, 31732
Daum, Thomas, 32272
Daviau, Donald G. (Festschrift), 32122
Daviau, Donald G., 32317
'David', 31585, 31594, 31599, 31600, 31605, 32053
Davidodowicz, Klaus S., 31846

Davies, Alan, 32385
Davis, Geoffrey V., 32098
Daxelmüller, Christoph, 32025
Daxner, Michael, 32110
De Bruyn, Günter, 32452
Deaglio, Enrico, 31619
Dehn, Bertha, 32086
Deichmann, Ute, 32079
Deigendesch, Roland, 31472
Delf, Hanna, 32080, 32345
Delpard, Raphael, 31733
Demetz, Peter, 31624
Demography, Statistics, 31410, 31486
Denazification, 31728
Denmark, Nazi Period, 31734
Denmark, Refugees, 31740, 31792
D'Entrèves, Maurizio Passerin, 32138
Deportations, 31712, 31829, 31856, 31865
Derczansky, Alexandre, 31445
Dessau, 31475, 32123
Determann, Andreas, 31865
Dettmer, Frauke, 32026
Deutsch, Kenneth L., 32003
Deutsch, Werner, 32289
Deutsche Juden und die Moderne, 31425
Deutscher Koordinierungsrat, 31679
Deutsches Exilarchiv, 31652
Deutschkron, Inge, 32167
'Deutschland', 32273
'Dialektik', 32139
Dick, Jutta, 31506
Diekmann, Irene, 31715
Dietert, Eike, 31534
Dilly, Heinrich, 32249
'Dimensions', 31785
Diner, Dan, 31678, 31851
Dipper, Christof, 31835
Dische, Irene, 31907, 31918
Dischereit, Esther, 31907, 31918
Displaced Persons, 31655, 31658, 31904
Disselkamp, Annette, 32417
'Dissent', 32443
Distel, Barbara, 31731, 31871, 31941
Döblin, Alfred, 32084
Döhrer, Andrea, 31483
Döpler, Aurelie see Hirsch, Elli
Dörr, Karin, 32429
Dohm, Christian Wilhelm von, 32367
Dohrn, Verena, 31645
Dokumentationsarchiv d. österr. Widerstandes, 'Jahrbuch', 31649, 31664, 31675
Dolbin, Benedikt Fred, 31638
Domhardt, Yvonne, 32359
Domin, Hilde, 32168
Dominican Republic, 32328
Dotterweich, Volker, 31405
Douma, Eva, 31865
Dove, Richard, 32098
Dow, James R., 31816

Drach, Albert, 32169, 32450
Dreessen, Wulf-Otto, 31445
Dreifus, Marcus Getsch, 31577
Drensteinfurt, 31476
Dresden, 31842, 31972, 32348
Drew, Margaret A., 31687
Drewniak, Boguslaw, 32086
Dreyfus Affair, 32063
Drobisch, Klaus, 31715
Dröse, Rith, 31509
Droste-Hülshoff, Annette von, 32429
Dubin, Lois C., 31602
Duby, Georges, 31393
Duderstadt, 31534, 32022
Dülmen, Richard van, 31487
Dümling, Albrecht, 32092
Dürkop, Marlis, 32020
Dürmeyer, Renate, 31647
Düsseldorf, 31735, 32165
'Duisburger Forschungen', 31572
Dunera, 31642, 31832
Dupeux, Louis, 32417
Durlacher, Gerhard L., 31736
Dusek, Peter, 32063
Dvorak, Cordelia, 32188
Dwork, Debórah, 31737
Dzialowski, Oskar, 31526

Early Modern Period (Pre-Enlightenment), 31396, 31398, 31405, 31447, 31531, 32383, 32410, 32424
East Friesland, 31477
East Prussia, 32039
Eastern Jewry, 31572, 31608, 31864, 31865, 32425
Eban, Abba, 32063
Ebbinghaus, Julius, 31966
Ebeling, Hans-Heinrich, 31534
Eberswalde, 31478
Eck, Nathan, 31872
Eckert, Michael, 32081
'(The) Economist', 31488
Edelheit, Abraham J, 31689
Edelheit, Hershel, 31689
Eder, Angelika, 32264
Edler, Horst, 32308
Education, 31392, 31610, 31627, 31671, 32005, 32032
Efron, John M., 32082
Eger, Akiva (Rabbi), 31967
Ehalt, Hubert Christian, 32063
Ehlers, Lisbeth, 32115
Ehmann, Annegret, 32406
Ehrenberg, Victor, 32170
Ehrlich, Carl S., 31676
Ehrlich, Ernst Ludwig, 31892
Ehrlich, Paul, 32117
Ehrlich, Siegwart, 32171
Eiber, Ludwig, 31941

Index to Bibliography

Eichengreen, Lucille, 31738
Eichholtz, Dietrich, 31715
Eichmann, Adolf, 31829, 31885, 31889, 31912
Eichner, Hans, 32250
Eidelberg, Shlomo, 31574
Eifert, Christiane, 32083
Einstein, Albert, 32109, 32172, 32173, 32317, 32320, 32324, 32332, 32448
Eisenberg, Paul Chaim, 32063
Eisenstadt, Jüd. Museum, 31586, 31587
Eisler, Edmund, 32057
Eisler, Hanns, 32109
Eisner, Kurt, 32174
Eisner, Freya, 32174
Elbaz, Robert, 32155
Elboim-Dror, Rachel, 32057
Eliesar ben Juda, Worms, 32381
Elior, Rachel, 31968
Elkin, Rivka, 31711
Elon, Amos, 32063
Emancipation, 31395, 31405, 31457, 31513, 31647, 32121, 32129, 32367, 32427, 32442
Emigration (see also Name of Country; Exile; Refugees), 31635, 31647, 31651, 31692, 31732, 31848, 32087, 32095
Empting, Maria, 32269
Endelman, Todd M., 31654
Endingen, 31577, 31629
Engel, Eva J., 31969 (Festschrift), 31987
Engel, Johann Jakob, 31987
Engelhard, Benjamin Mordechai, 31543
Engelmayer, Elfriede, 32158
Engstler, Achim, 32080
Enlightenment (see also Haskalah), 31413, 31987, 31990, 32007
Enzyklopädie des Holocaust, 31777
Enzyklopädie des Märchens, 31688
Ephraim, Meir, 31995
Erb, Rainer, 31405, 31685, 31688, 32115
Erdle, Birgit R., 32086, 32407
'Eretz', 31416
Erichsen, Regine, 32086
Ericksen, Robert P., 31726
Eschwege, 31479
Eschwege, Helmut, 31872
Esens, 31480
Eshel, Amir, 31681
Espagne, Michel, 31648
Essen, 31481, 31739
Essen-Steele, 31482
Essingen, 31483
Esslingen, 31484, 31893, 31998
Esten, Stephan, 31548
Euchel, Isaac, 32006
'Europäische Ideen', 32012, 32293
'European Judaism', 31421, 31890, 31949, 31955, 31956, 32004, 32149, 32184, 32361, 32389
Euthanasia, 31697, 31715, 31793

'Evangelische Theologie', 31412
Evard, Jean-Luc, 32110
Even-Chen, Alexander, 31989
Exenberger, Herbert, 31600
'Exil. Forschung, Erkenntnisse, Ergebnisse', 32086
Exile (see also Name of Country; Emigration; Refugees), 31637, 31650, 31675, 31692, 31877, 32087, 32089, 32090
Exile, Humanities, 32176
Exile, Journalism, 31828
Exile, Literature and Arts, 31675, 31693, 31740, 32012, 32084, 32085, 32093, 32095–32098, 32315
Exile, Music, 32092, 32147, 32187
Exile, Sciences, 32081
Exile, Social Sciences, 32100
'Exilforschung, Int. Jahrbuch', 32085

Faassen, Dina van, 31529, 31530
Faber, Richard, 32110, 32440
Fackenheim, Emil, 31970, 31978
Farge, Arlette, 31393
Fassl, Peter, 31392
Faulenbach, Bernd, 32102
Fehrs, Jörg H., 32018
Feichtenschlager, Norbert, 31607
Feilchenfeldt, Konrad, 31648
Feiner, Shmuel, 31390, 31971
Feingold, Henry L., 32385
Feist, Chanan, 31820
Feiwel, Berthold, 32122
Feldman, David, 31653
Felka, Rike, 32102
Felstiner, John, 32162
Felstiner Lowenthal, Mary 31741
Feneberg, Rupert, 31577
Fenyes, Gabriele, 31764
Ferenczi, Sandor, 32326
Festschrift, see Daviau, Donald G.; Engel, Eva J. Heller, Peter; Hentrich, Gerhard; Scheffler, Wolfgang; Sievers, Kai Detlev; Sonderegger, Stefan; Wolfram, Herwig; Zohn, Harry
Feuchtwanger, Lion, 32084, 32098, 32175
Fiesel, Eva, 32176
Film see Theatre
'Film Comment', 31834
Filser, Karl, 31392, 31405
Final Solution (see also Holocaust), 31730, 31742–31748, 31793, 31851, 32139
Financiers, 31656
Finkielkraut, Alain, 32009
Fiorino, Alexander, 31518
Fippel, Günter, 31525
Fischel, Jack, 31786
Fischer, Barbara, 32108
Fischer, David, 31462
Fischer, Eva-Elisabeth, 31872
Fischer, Grete, 31650

Fischer, Ingrid, 31478
Fischer, Shlomo, 31946
Flatow, Ernst, 31727
Fleckner, Uta, 32243
Fleischer, Ezra, 31427
Fleischmann, Johann, 31582
Fleischmann, Lea, 32108
Fliess, Emil, 32180
Fliess, Wilhelm, 32180
Floss, 32071
Flossenbürg, 31941
Föckeler, Norbert, 31559
Fölsing, Ulla, 32193
Fogelman, Eva, 31836
Fogelman, Eva., 31725
Fontane, Theodor, 32430
Forced Labour, 31592, 31761, 31765, 31805, 31856
Forrester, John, 32178
Foschepoth, Josef, 31865
Fourquet, Jean, 31445
Foxman, Abraham H., 31785
Fraisse, Geneviève, 31393
France, 32115
France, Nazi Period, 31733, 31749, 32086
France, Refugees, 31647, 31648, 31758, 32088
'Francia', 31486
Franconia, 31485, 31556, 31654
Frank, Anne, 32117
Frank, Jakob Josef (Leibowitz), 32027
Frank, Rafael, 31525
Frankau Family, 31654
Franke, Peter Robert, 32170
Frankel, Jonathan, 31677
Frankel, Zacharias, 31972
Frankfurt am Main, 31403, 31487–31492, 31751, 31823, 31968, 32005, 32113–32117
Frankfurt am Main, Jüdisches Museum, 32115
Frankfurt am Main, Stadt- und Universitätsbibliothek, 31448, 31695
Frankfurt School, 32099, 32100
'Frankfurter Allg. Zeitung' ('FAZ'), 31427, 31835, 31846, 31872, 32013, 32103, 32124, 32152, 32157, 32188, 32193, 32201, 32202, 32207, 32254, 32261, 32323, 32337, 32345, 32347, 32352, 32450
'Frankfurter Jüdische Nachrichten', 31667, 31843, 31894, 32041, 32112, 32132, 32226, 32246, 32374, 32455, 32459
Franzke, Michael, 32152
Franzos, Karl Emil, 32177
Fray, Jean-Luc, 31580
Freeden, Herbert, 32037, 32293
Freiberger, Rudolf, 31856
Freiburg, 31753
'Freiburger Rundbrief', 32311, 32331, 32388
Freie Wissenschaftliche Vereinigung, 32042
Freiling, Harald, 31946
Freiwald, Aaron, 31914

Frenzl, Katrin, 31559
Freud, Anna, 32325
Freud, Sigmund, 31973, 32107, 32109, 32178–32185, 32326, 32327, 32332
Freudenthal, Max, 31524
Freund, Florian, 31700
Freund, Gisèle, 32186
Frey, Eberhard, 32094
Friedburg, Samson, 31982
Friedländer Family, 32367
Friedländer, Georg, 32430
Friedländer, Saul, 31768, 32120
Friedlander, Albert H., 31956, 31957, 31976, 32360, 32361
Friedlander, Henry, 31745, 31748
Friedman, Régine Mihal, 32115
Friedmann, Alexander, 31588
Friedrich, Karin, 32058
Friedrich, Otto, 31701
Friese, Karin, 31478
Frischenschlager, Oskar, 32101
Fritsch, Theodor, 32391
Frühwald, Wolfgang, 32087
Fuchs, Konrad, 31563
Füllberg-Stolberg, Claus, 31752
Fürst, Peter, 32328
Fürstenberg, Doris, 32020
Fürth, 31493, 31494
Fuks-Mansfeld, Renate, 31445
Fulda, 32397
Funkenstein, Amos, 31425
Furtado Kestler, Izabela Maria, 31647

Gabriel, Peter, 31476
Gabrieli, Maggino, 31580
Gailingen, 31495
Gal-Ed, Efrat, 32446
Galicia, 31608, 31627, 32456
Gamm, Hans-Jochen, 31391
Ganglmair, Siegwald, 31675
Gann, Christoph, 31789
Garbe, Detlef, 31754, 31818, 31941
Garscha, Winfried R., 31856
Gauss, Karl-Markus, 32462
(Die) Gegenwart der Schoah, 31847
Gehle, Holger, 32219
Gehler, Michael, 32394
Gehrden, 31496
Geier, Manfred, 32254
Geisel, Eike, 32447
'Genealogie', 32335
Genealogy, 31654, 32022, 32039, 32334
Genée, Pierre, 31585
Genger, Angela, 31942
Genizi, Haim, 31655
Geoffroy, René, 32086
Gerhard, Melitta, 32102
Gerl, Hanna-Barbara, 32102
Gerlach, Wolfgang, 31755

German Democratic Republic, see Germany, Post War, GDR
'German Life and Letters', 31650, 31907, 32195, 32280
'(The) German Quarterly', 32250, 32253
'German Studies Review', 31748, 32429
Germany, Post War, 31549, 31894, 31896, 31900, 31917, 32374, 32426
Germany, Post War, GDR, 31525, 31851, 31898, 31917, 31950, 32153, 32314, 32344
Germany, Post War, Immigration, 31865
Gerntrup, Wilhelm, 31794
Gershon, Karen, 31756
Gerste, Hans-Jörg, 31862
'Geschichte in Wissenschaft und Unterricht', 31420
'Geschichte und Gegenwart', 31589, 31706, 32348
'Geschichte, Erziehung, Politik', 31782
'Gesher', 32426
'Gesnerus', 32183
Geyrhofer, Friedrich, 32157
Gidal, Nachum Tim, 31543
Gilboa, Menuha, 32028
Gilchrist, Sylvia, 31682
Gilman, Sander L., 31918, 32010, 32108, 32179
Gilzmer, Mechtild, 31749
Ginzel, Günther B. (Bernd), 31757
Giora, Zvi, 32060
Giordano, Ralph, 31917
Girtler, Roland, 31758
Gläser, Helga, 31647
Glaeser, Ernst, 32098
Glasenapp, Gabriele von, 32080
Gleising, Günter, 31840
Globig, Michael, 32193
Glöckner, Eckhard, 31946
Glogau, 32362
Glückel von Hameln, 31393, 31436, 32329
Gmeiner, Astrid A., 32148
Gnadt, Martina S., 31727
Goebbels, Joseph, 31801
Göpfert, Rebekka, 31759
Göppingen, 31760
Goethe, Johann Wolfgang von, 32431
Götschel, Willi, 32189
Göttingen, 31534
Göttler, Fritz, 32185
Götz, Aly, 31697
Goldberg, David, 31431
Goldenbogen, Nora, 31842
Goldmann, Erwin, 31853
Goldmann, Felix, 31526
Goldmann, Nahum, 32426
Goldschmidt, Berthold, 32187, 32188
Goldschmidt, Henriette, 31525
Goldschmidt, Hermann Levin, 32189
Goldstein, Jossi, 31681
Goldstein, Maximilian, 31614

Gombrich, Ernest H., 32190
Gondorf, Bernhard, 31546
Goodman, Geoffrey, 31879
Goodman-Thau, Eveline, 32080, 32110
Goral, Arie, 32330
Gordimer, Nadine, 32356
Goslar, 31497
Gotzmann, Andreas, 31974
Govrin, Yosef, 32063
Grabherr, Eva, 31577, 31591
Grabitz, Helge, 31822, 31851
Grabmayer, Johannes, 31394
Gräser, Andreas, 32160
Graetz, Heinrich, 32006
Grahammer, Hannelore, 31592
Graml, Hermann, 31851
Granach, Alexander, 32191
'Graswurzelrevolution', 32224
Graus, František (Gedenkschrift), 31387
Graz, 31589
Great Britain, 31656
Great Britain, Immigration, 32115
Great Britain, Nazi Period, 31660, 31798
Great Britain, Refugees, 31643, 31644, 31648, 31657, 31670, 31759, 31833, 31859, 32098
Grebing, Helga, 32088
Green, Nancy, 31393
Greenberg, Gershon, 31992, 32059
Greif, Gideon, 31702
Greif, Stefan, 32269
Greive, Hermann, 31978
Grenville, John A. S., 31682
Gresser, Moshe, 32180
Greve, Ludwig, 32331
Grijn Santen, W.B. van der, 32011
Grimm, Gebrüder, 32199
Gritsch, Eric W., 32385
Grode, Walter, 31895
Gröbel, Oskar, 31543
Groehler, Olaf, 31823, 31896
Grözinger, Karl Erich, 31684, 32110, 32210
Groiss-Lau, Eva, 31485
Gross-Breesen, 31661
Gross-Gerau, 31498
Gross-Rosen, 31761
Grosser, Alfred, 32117
Grossert, Werner, 31475
Grossman, Avraham, 31427
Grossman, Jeffrey Alan, 31432
Grossmann, Walter, 32119
Grubel, Fred, 31524, 31526, 31680
Gruber, Ruth Ellen, 31620
Grubrich-Simitis, Ilse, 32332
Grübel, Fritz see Grubel, Fred
Grünbaum, Irene, 31809
Gründer, Karlfried, 32367
Grünstadt, 31499
Gruman, Harrish, 32181
Grundmann, Walter, 31727

Grunert, Frank, 31846
Gruson, Pascale, 32417
Gümbel, Miryam, 31872
Günther, Horst, 32303
Gütersloh, 31762
Gugelot, Frederic, 31946
Gugenheim, Fromet, 31986
Guggenheim, Alis, 32192
Guggenheim-Grünberg, Florence, 31445
Gulkowitsch, Lazar, 31525
Gumpel Family, 32350
Gurs, 32086, 32088
Gushee, David P., 31837, 31838
Guth, Klaus, 31485
Guth, Werner Maximo, 31433
Gutman, Israel (Yisrael), 31698, 31872
Guttkuhn, Peter, 31535
Gutwein, Daniel, 31656

Haag, John, 31882
Ha'am, Achad, 31681
Haasis, Hellmut G., 32247
Habe, Hans, 31647
Haber, Fritz, 32193
Habermas, Jürgen, 32318
Habonim, 32072
Habsburg, 31615, 31616
Hackeschmidt, Jörg, 31965
Hacohen, Salomon, 32006
Hadomi, Lea, 32155
Häfeli, Anton, 32092
Hägler, Brigitte, 32399
Häntzschel, Hiltrud, 31542, 32176, 32306
Härendel, Ulrike, 31815
Hagen, 31763
Hahn, Barbara, 32102, 32345
Hahn, Eva, 31618
Hahn, Fred, 32063
Hahn, Hans-Werner, 31400
Hahn, Hugo, 31739
Hahn, Joachim, 31484, 31577
Hahn, Susanne, 31525, 31842
Halakha, 31978
Halberstadt, 31500
'Halbjahresschrift f. Südosteurop. Gesch., Lit. u. Politik', 32366
Haldimann, Eva, 32453
Hall, Michael, 32115
Hamann, Brigitte, 32063
Hamann, Johann Georg, 31987
'Ha-Ma'yan', 31975
Hambrock, Matthias, 31846
Hamburg, 31501–31506, 31694, 31764–31766, 31791, 32201, 32235, 32249, 32350, 32501
Hamburg-Ottensen, 31503
Hamburger, Arno, 31549
Hamburger, Käte, 32333
Hamburger, Michael, 32012
Hamm, 31507

Hampe, Heinrich, 31534
'Ha-Umma', 32062
Hanau, 31508, 31509
Hanover, 31496, 31534, 31767, 31897, 32032
Hansert, Andreas, 32115
Harburg an der Wörnitz, 31562
Hardenberg, Henriette, 31650
Hardtwig, Wolfgang, 32076
Harel, Haya, 32062
Harlan, Veit, 31822, 32098
Harris, James F., 31457, 32404
Hartewig, Karin, 31723, 31839
Hartman, Geoffrey H., 31768
Hartmann, Nicolai, 31966
Hartmann, Stefan, 31395
Hartmann, Werner, 31500
Hartung, Günter, 32431
Hartz, Ruth Kapp, 31729
Haskalah (see also Enlightenment), 31390, 31982, 32007
Hass-Zumkehr, Ulrike, 31534
Hausjell, Fritz, 31675, 32089
Hawrylchak, Sandra H., 31693
Hayes, Peter, 31769
Haynal, André, 32326
Hebauf, Renate, 31707
Hebel, Johann Peter, 32451
Hebrew Literature, 32028, 32047, 32053
Hechaluz, 31872
Hechingen, 31510
Hechtsheim, 31511
Hedemünden, 31534
Hedgepeth, Sonja M., 31647
Heenen-Wolff, Susann, 31770
Heiber, Helmut, 31771
Heid, Ludger, 31401, 31555, 31572, 31684, 31865, 32218
Heidegger, Martin, 31753, 32222, 32432
Heidsieck, Arnold, 32211
Heilborn, Ernst, 32194
Heimann, Moritz, 32112, 32452
Heimann-Jelinek, Felicitas, 31587, 31614, 32115
'Heimatbote aus d. Reichen Ebrachgrund', 31582
'Heimatbuch d. Kreises Viersen', 31570
'Heimatjahrbuch d. Kreises Neuwied', 31546, 31568
'Heimatjahrbuch Kreis Ahrweiler', 31547, 31548, 32390
'Heimatkalender d. Kreises Heinsberg', 31863
Heine, Heinrich, 31987, 32108, 32112, 32195–32201, 32233
Heine, Heinrich, 'Heine Jahrbuch', 32233
Heine, Salomon, 32201
Heinemann Family, 32334
Heinemann, Isaak, 32422
Heinemann, Moshe Yosef, 32334
Heinrichs, Heribert, 31863
Heiss, Stephan, 31543

Heitmann, Margret, 32018, 32362
Held, Jutta, 32085
Held, Steffen, 31525
Heller, André, 32261
Heller, Hugo, 32119
Heller, Peter, 32119, 32325
Hellwig, Frauke, 31479
Hemstege, Andreas, 31522
Hengerer, Karl, 31567
Henisch, Peter, 31883
Henke, Hans-Gerd, 32363
Henochs, Moses, 31430, 31438
Hensel, Fanny, 32202
Hentrich, Gerhard (Festschrift), 31459, 31712, 31750, 31888, 32171, 32216
Hepp, Michael, 32296
Herbert, Ulrich, 31734, 31823, 31851
Herbst, Detlev, 31534
Herf, Jeffrey, 31898, 32314
Hering, Sabine, 32020
Hermand, Jost, 32108, 32244
Hermann, Armin, 32172, 32435
Hermann, Ingo, 32140, 32151, 32203
Hermannus Quondam Judaeus, 31980
Hermes, Claudia, 32252
Hermes, Hermann, 31861
Hermon, Zvi, 31534
Hernádi, Miklós 32453
'(Der) Herold', 32204
Herrlich, Mario, 31842
Herrlingen, 32044
Herrmann, Wilhelm, 31966
Herrmannová, Margit, 31855
Herweg, Rachel Monika, 32029
Herz, Emil, 32336
Herz, Julius Ritter von Hertenried, 32335
Herz-Kestranek, Stefan, 31848
Herzberg, Guntolf, 32153
Herzig, Arno, 31396, 31501, 31525, 31865
Herzl, Theodor, 32057, 32060–32063, 32119, 32122
Herzog, Dagmar, 32404
Herzog, Monika, 31941
Herzogenburg, Hetschel von, 31592
Heschel, Abraham Joshua, 32000, 32094
Heschel, Israel Nathan, 32007
Heschel, Susannah, 31726, 31727, 32385
Heschel, Yisrael, 31489
Heskes, Irene, 32049
Hesse, 31498, 31512–31514, 31534, 31569, 31899
Hesselbach, Walter, 31680
Hessen, Rainer von, 32115
Hessing, Jakob, 31681, 32352
'Hessisches Jahrbuch für Landesgeschichte', 31514
Hetkamp, Jutta, 32030, 32031
Hettche, Walter, 32430
Hetzer, Gerhard, 31392

Heubach, Helga, 31545
Heuberger, Georg, 31680, 32113, 32114, 32115
Heuberger, Rachel, 32020
Heyl, Matthias, 31847
Heyn, Thomas, 32307
Heyne, Maren, 31555
Hibberd, John, 32451
Hilberg, Raul, 32337
Hild-Berg, Anette, 32088, 32281
Hildebrandt, Dieter, 32323
Hildesheimer, Esriel, 31772
Hildesheimer, Meir, 31985
Hildesheimer, Wolfgang, 32203
Hilfsverein d. dt. Juden, 32070
Hilgert, Wilfried, 31434
Hillrichs, Hans Helmut, 32203
Hilscher, Elke, 31507
Hilsenrath, Edgar, 32077, 32108, 32454
Hinrichsen, Henri, 31525
Hinske, Norbert, 31987, 31988
Hinsley, F. H., 31644
Hinton, Stephen, 32092
Hintze-Guggenheimer, Hedwig, 32102
Hirsch, Elli (Aurelie Döpler), 32204
Hirsch, Erika, 31791
Hirsch, Hans K., 31392, 31405
Hirsch, Helmut, 32013, 32338, 32364
Hirsch, Samson Raphael, 31975
Hirschfeld, Ariel, 31846
Hirschfeld, Gerhard, 31657
Hirschmann, Albert O., 32086
Hirte, Chris, 32347
Historians, 32170, 32220, 32291
Historians' Debate, 31773, 31779, 31780
Historiography, 31419, 31427, 31678, 31775
Historiography, Nazi Period (see also Holocaust, Historiography), 31726, 31745
Historiography, 'Revisionism' (see also Holocaust Denial), 31787
'History and Memory', 32181
'History and Theory', 31774, 31947
'History Workshop', 32057
Hitchens, Christopher, 31787
Hochschule für Jüdische Studien, Heidelberg, 31676
Hochschule f. d. Wissenschaft d. Judentums, Berlin, 32004
Höchberg, 31515
Hödl, Klaus, 31608, 32063
Höges, Dirk, 32428
Höhne, Gerd E., 31866
Hölzer, Stefan, 31943
Hönsch, Jörg K., 32027
Höppner, Solvejg, 31525
Höxter, 31516
Hoffman, Edward, 32130
Hoffmann, Christhard, 31685, 32408, 32409
Hoffmann, Paul, 31648
Hoffmann, Peter, 31835

Hoffmann-Axthelm, Dagmar, 32365
Hoffnung, Annetta, 32205
Hoffnung, Gerard, 32205
Hofinger, Niko, 32395
Hofmannsthal, Hugo von, 32075, 32109, 32122, 32339
Hofstätter, Maria, 31588
Hohenems, Jüd. Museum, 31577, 31591
'Hohenzollerische Heimat', 31510
Hohnschopp, Christine, 31652
Holl, Karl, 32086
Hollitzer, Siegfried, 31525
Holocaust (see also Final Solution), 31687, 31689, 31717, 31778, 31781, 31783, 31817, 31858, 31930, 32068
Holocaust, Art, 31625, 31752
Holocaust, Denial, 31784, 31785, 31786, 31787, 31788, 31851
Holocaust, Historiography, 31773, 31774, 31776, 31782, 31947
Holocaust, Knowledge, 31867
Holocaust, Reaction, 31643, 31744, 31747, 32385
Holocaust, Teaching, 31931, 31932, 31935, 31937, 31946
Holocaust, Theological and Philosophical Impact, 31812, 31892, 31970, 32311, 32360, 32385
Holocaust, Trauma, 31720, 31790, 31851
'Holocaust and Genocide Studies', 31755, 31934, 31992
Holthaus, Alexander, 31543
Holz, Hans Heinz, 32192
Holzboog, Günther, 31987
Holzhey, Helmut, 31966
Holzträger, Hans, 32366
Homberg, Herz, 31627
Homeyer, Friedel, 32032
Homolka, Walter, 31957, 31976
Honigmann, Barbara, 31907, 31918, 32108, 32455
Honigmann, Peter, 31455
Hood, Stuart, 31937
Hoos, Hans-Helmut, 32322
Hoppe, Heinz-Hermann, 31846
Horch, Hans Otto, 31846
Horkheimer, Max, 32107, 32206
Hornburg, 31468
Hornstein, Georg, 31872
Horowitz, Elliott, 31397
Horowitz, Phinehas ben Zevi Hirsch ha-Levi, 31489
Hortzitz, Nicoline, 31398, 31405, 32410
Howard, Anthony, 31879
Howoldt, Jenns E., 32235
Hoyer, Siegfried, 31525, 32383
Hudemann, Rainer, 31824
Hübener, Kristina, 31715
Hübner-Funk, Sibylle, 32370

Hülskemper-Niemann, Ludger, 31482
Hürben, 31392
Hürten, Heinz, 31706
Hüttenmeister, Nathanja, 31464
Hundt, Irina, 32299
Hungary, 31445, 31620
Hungary, Nazi Period, 31592, 31619, 31805, 31850
Hunter-Salomon, Peter, 32273
Hurwitz, Emanuel, 31847
Huss, Avraham, 32232
Hutterer, Claus Jürgen, 31445
Hyman, Ronald, 32157
Hyndráková, Anna, 31621, 31856

Ichenhausen, 31392
Idel, Moshe, 31977
Identity, Jewish, 31413, 31647, 31790, 31892, 31910, 31918, 31921, 31957, 32009, 32012, 32016, 32040, 32099, 32244, 32291, 32304
Ihering, Herbert, 32118
Im Hofe, Ulrich, 31987
'Immigrants & Minorities', 31833
Immigration see Name of Country; Refugees; Exile
Imperial Germany, 31502, 32035, 32042, 32391, 32393, 32415, 32425
Industrialists, 31563, 31565
Ingenheim, 31517
Institut f. d. Gesch. d. Juden in Deutschland, 31504
Institut f. Geschichte d. Juden in Österreich, 31679
'Interkulturell', 31385
'(The) International History Review', 31940
Internment Camps, 31749
Ireland, Refugees, 31649
'Iron 77', 32232
Irving, David, 31787
Isaak, Aaron see Aaron Isaak
Iselin, Isaak, 31987
Isolani, Gertrud, 32086
Israel, 31804, 31892, 32055, 32058, 32066
Israel, Immigration, 32461
Israel, Jonathan I., 31506
Israelitisch-Humanitärer Frauenverein, 31502
Italy, 31672
Italy, Nazi Period, 31724, 31841
'IWK, Int. Wiss. Korr. z. Gesch. d. dt. Arbeiterbewegung', 32287
'Iyyun', 31989

Jabotinsky, Vladimir S., 32062
Jabotinsky, Ze'ev, 32062
Jacob, Christian, 32086
Jacob, Heinrich Eduard, 32086
Jacobi, Hansres, 32157
Jacobs, Boike, 32374
Jacobs, Jack, 31659, 32013

Jacobsohn, Siegfried, 32112
Jacobson, Kenneth, 31790
Jacobson, Yoram, 31399
Jacoby, Hans, 32340
Jacoby, Jessica, 31900
Jacoby, Mario, 31523
Jäckel, Eberhard, 31892, 32337
Jäger, Lorenz, 32345
Jäschke, Kurt-Ulrich, 31400
'Jahrbuch f. Antisemitismusforschung', 31685; 31720, 31769, 31777, 31887, 31896, 31936, 32097, 32244, 32409, 32416
'Jahrbuch d. ungarischen Germanistik', 31627
'Jahrbuch z. Liberalismusforschung', 31965
'Jahrbuch d. deutschen Schillergesellschaft', 32176
'Jahrbuch Westfalen', 31476
Jakob, Kurt, 31808
Jakob, Reinhard, 31392, 31562
Jakubowski-Tiessen, Manfred, 31561
Jankowski, Stanislaw M., 31867
Jansen, Mechtild, 31944
Jansz, Litza, 31937
Jarka, Horst, 32147, 32285
Jasper, Willi, 31872
Jerke, Birgit, 31727
'Jewish Chronicle', 31643, 31783, 31879, 32355
'Jewish History', 31410, 31654, 31656
Jewish Problem (see also Identity, Jewish), 31647, 31690, 32015, 32016, 32017, 32031, 32099, 32108, 32291, 32363, 32417
'(The) Jewish Quarterly', 31423, 32150, 32157
'(The) Jewish Quarterly Review', 32392
Jewish Question (see also Antisemitism), 32013, 32358, 32373, 32417
'Jewish Social Studies', 32401
'Jewish Spectator', 31786
'Jiddistik-Mitteilungen', 31435, 31449, 31483, 32129
Job, Françoise, 31580
Jochheim, Gernot, 31712
Jochmann, Werner, 31872
Joel, Marcus, 32362
John, Michael, 31592
Joint (American Jewish Joint Distribution Committee), 31904
Jonas, Regina, 32033, 32034
Jonca, Karol, 31822
Jost, J. M., 32006
'Journal of the American Academy of Religion', 32387
'Journal of Analytical Psychology', 32434
'Journal of Jewish Studies', 31961
'Journal of Modern History', 31776
'Journal of Psychology and Judaism', 32316
Journalists, 31459, 32089, 32260
Juda ben Samuel (the Pious), 32381
'Judaica Bohemiae', 31621, 31855
'Judaica', 32359

Judaism, 31676, 31957, 31978
'Judaism', 31897, 31953, 32162, 32439
Judaism, Jewish History, in Teaching, 31946, 31959
Juden in Deutschland, 31401, 32027, 32099
Juden in Deutschland. Lebenswelt und Einzelschicksale, 31400, 31487, 31824, 32027, 32170
Judengemeinden in Schwaben im Kontext des Alten Reiches, 31405
'(Das) Jüdische Echo', 32063, 32262, 32157, 32255
Jüdische Kultur und Weiblichkeit in der Moderne, 32043, 32104, 32403, 32407
'Jüdischer Almanach' see Leo Baeck Institute, 'Jüdischer Almanach'
Jüdischer Frauenbund, 31545, 32020
Jüdischer Kulturbund, see Kulturbund, Jüdischer
Juelich, Dierk, 31847, 32370
Jung, Carl Gustav, 32182, 32183, 32327, 32433, 32434
Jung, Hans Erich, 31946
Jungk, Peter Stephan, 32309
Jungk, Robert, 32207
Jureit, Ulrike, 31791, 31818
Jurk, Michael, 32115

Kabbalah (see also Mysticism), 32110, 31991
Kacandes, Irene, 32108
Kafka, Frantisek, 32122
Kafka, Franz, 32109, 32120, 32208–32214
Kahler, Antoinette von, 32320
Kahn, Lisa, 32094
'Kairos', 31422, 31463, 31596, 32128
Kaiser, Jochen-Christoph, 31865, 32417
Kaiser, Wolf, 31746, 31941, 32064
Kaiserwald, 31862
'Kalender f. d. Klever Land', 31795
Kann, Erich, 31536
Kansteiner, Wulf, 31947
Kant, Immanuel, 31987
Kantorowicz, Ernst, 32215
Kantorowicz, Gertrud, 32102
Kaplan, Edward K., 31979, 32094
Kaplan, Louis, 32258
Kaplan, Marion, 31903, 31918, 32411
Kaplan, Yosef, 31506
Kappeler, Sima, 32108
Karlsbad, 31617
Karlsruhe, 32467
Kárná, Margita, 31699, 31856
Kárný, Miroslav, 31618, 31622, 31699, 31941
Karski, Jan, 31867
Kasberger, Erich, 31941
Kashti-Kroch, Judith, 32341
Kasper-Holtkotte, Cilli, 31402
Kassel, 31518
Katz Family, 31528
Katz, Henry W., 32456, 32457

Katz, Jacob, 31403, 31404, 31987, 32367, 32412
Katz, Steven T., 31783
Kaufering, 31941
Kaufman, Michael T., 31637
Kaufmann Family, 31481
Kaufmann, Hanne, 31792
Kaufmann, Irene, 32033
Kaufmann, Uri R., 31506, 31577, 31626, 31902
Kauntz, Eckhart, 32201, 32201
Kayserling, Meyer, 32006
Keil, Martha, 31592
Keilson, Hans, 32086
Keim, Anton Maria, 31511
Kellenbach, Katharina von, 32034
Kellermann, Benzion, 31966
Kellermann, Henry J., 32342
Kellner, Hans, 31947
Kemp, Annerose, 31525
Kempinski, M., 31461
Kempten (Bayerisch-Schwaben), 31392
Keneally, Thomas, 32458
Kern, Bernd-Rüdiger, 32427
Kerner, Samuel, 31445
Kerr, Alfred, 31647, 32112, 32118
Kerr, John, 32182
Kerr, Judith, 31650
Kessler, Mario, 32065, 32106
Kestenberg, Judith S., 31725, 31931
Keval, Susanna, 32041
Keyl, Werner, 32335
Kiessling, Rolf, 31405
Kieval, Hillel Josef, 32400, 32401
Kilcher, Andreas, 32352
'King David', 32051
Kindertransport, 31759, 31859
Kinzig, Wolfram, 32368, 32413
Kirchhoff, Wolfgang, 31842
Kirsch, Sarah, 31681
Kirschstein, Sally, 32216
Kisch, Egon Erwin, 32217
Kittner, Alfred, 32103, 32449
Klayman-Cohen, Israela, 31436
Klee, Ernst, 31793, 31851
Klein, Albert, 32191
Klein, Birgit, 31464
Klein, Charlotte, 32388
Klein, Dennis B., 31785
Kleinberg, Aviad M., 31980
Kleinenbremen, 31794
Kleinpass, Hans, 31547
Klepper, Jochen, 32085
Klessmann, Eckart, 32202
Kleve, 31463, 31519, 31795
Klijnsmit, Anthony J., 31506
Kliner-Fruck, Martina, 31573, 32066
Klinger, Ruth, 32218
Klönne, Irmgard, 32020
Kloosterhuis, Jürgen, 32442
Klüger, Ruth, 31847, 32219, 32369
Klüting, Harm, 31539
Kluge, Heidelore, 31552
Knapp, Ilan, 31588
Knappe, Sabine, 31502
Kniesche, Thomas W., 32107
Knilli, Friedrich, 31822
Kober, Zita, 31543
Kobler, Franz, 32220
Koch, Antje & Matthias, 31842
Koch, Edita, 32090
Koch, Gertrud, 32313
Koch, Grit, 32414
Koch, Martin, 31782
Koch, Rita, 32063
'Kölner Museumsbulletin', 32164
König, Christoph, 31648
König, Hans-Jürgen, 32035
Königseder, Angelika, 31904
Köpke, Wulf, 32085
Körner, Karl-Hermann, 31506
Körner, Peter, 31453
Kössler, Gottfried, 31946
Kogon, Eugen, 31817
Kohlbauer-Fritz, Gabriele, 31614
Kohlhammer, Siegfried, 31843
Koj, Peter, 31506
Kolmar, Gertrud, 31716, 32221
Kolneder, Wolfgang, 32167
Konstanz, 31577
Kopper, Christopher, 32115
Korbach, 31520, 31521
Korherr, Edgar Josef, 31946
Korn, Salomon, 31825
Korotin, Ilse, 32020
Kortner, Fritz, 32084
Kosterlitz, Hermann (Henry Koster), 31647
'Kovetz Bais Aharon v'Yisrael', 31489, 32007
Kowalke, Kim H., 32308
Kra-Os, Jakob, 31543
Kracauer, Siegfried, 31647
Kraft, Thomas, 31618
Krakowski, Shmuel, 31745
Kralovitz, Rolf, 31527
Kramer, Thomas, 32091
Krapf, Ernst, 32115
Kratz-Ritter, Bettina, 32230
Kratzsch, Gerhard, 31865
Kraus, Karl, 32075, 32109, 32122, 32222
Kraus, O. B., 31856
Kraus, Wolfgang, 32157
Krause-Vilmar, Dietfrid, 31945
Kraushaar, Wolfgang, 31847
Krautheimer, Richard,
Krebs, Wolfgang, 31519, 31795
Krefeld, 31522
Kreimeier, Klaus, 31556
Kreisky, Bruno, 31882
Kreutz, Wilhelm, 31486
Kreuzer, Franz, 32255

Index to Bibliography

Krieghofer, Gerald, 32063
Kritter, Ulrich von, 32050
Krobb, Florian, 32150, 32195
Krochmalnik, Daniel, 31676
Krohn, Claus-Dieter, 32085
Krohn, Helga, 32115
Krois, John Michael, 32161
Kross, Matthias, 32312
Krüger, Arnd, 31796
Krüger, Maren, 31713
Kruft, Hanno Walter, 32257
Kruk, Raya, 32191
Krumbach, 31392
Krumsiek, Rolf, 31917
Kruse, Joseph A., 32196
Kruse, Kuno, 32259
Kryl, Miroslav, 31856
Kuczynski, Jürgen, 32343, 32344
Kudela, Jirí, 31621
Kühl, Stefan, 31797
Kugelmann, Cilly, 31894
Kuhlbrodt, Dietrich, 31843
Kukatzki, Bernhard, 31471, 31499, 31517, 31523, 31544, 31550, 31553, 31554, 31557, 31566
Kulka, Otto Dov, 31690
Kulke, Christine, 32370
Kullen, Siegfried, 31456
Kulturbund, Jüdischer, 31525, 31739, 31813, 32092
Kural, Václav, 31618
Kurtulan, Banu, 31610
Kurzke, Hermann, 32347
Kushner, Tony, 31798
Kustermann, Abraham Peter, 31577
Kwiet, Konrad, 31871, 31872

Laak, Dirk van, 31739
Labhart, Walter, 32051
Lacapra, Dominick, 31778
Lachmann, Hedwig, 32224
Lachmann, Vera, 31647
Lake Constance (see also Württemberg; Vorarlberg; Switzerland), 31575
Lamb, Anni, 31540
Lambsheim, 31523
Lamm, Fritz, 32088
Landauer, Carl, 32215
Landauer, Gustav, 32223, 32224, 32225, 32345
Landauer, Karl, 32226
Lander, Katja, 31593
Landsberger, Franz, 32346
Landshut, Siegfried, 32227
Lang, Fritz, 32107
Langbein, Hermann, 31817
Lange, Horst-Günther, 31497
Lange, Thomas, 31946
Lange, Ulrich, 31561

Langenargen, 31576
Langenbucher, Wolfgang R., 32089
Langer, Hans-Joachim, 31556
Langer, Michael, 32371
Langner, Bernd, 31567
Lappin, Elena, 31901
Lappin, Eleonore, 31592
Laqueur, Walter, 31747, 32036
Larsen, Oejvind, 32370
Lasker-Schüler, Else, 31647, 32228, 32229
Lassmann, Wolfgang, 31946
'(Die) Laubhütte', 32046
Lauermann, Manfred, 32080
Lauingen (Donau), 31392
Laupheim, 31577
Lauterbach, 31569
Lawford-Hinrichsen, Irene, 31525
Lazarus, Moritz, 32230
Lazarus, Nahida Ruth, 32230
Lea, Henry, 32119, 32372
Lechner, Silvester, 31392
Leczeka, Abba Glosk, 31987
Leder, Sharon, 31858
Lederer, Gerda, 32370
Legal History, 31384, 31386, 31388, 31395, 31400, 31405, 31531, 31534, 31592, 31854, 32442
Legal Professions, Jews in, 31865
Lehberger, Reiner, 32141
Lehmkuhl, Gunhild, 31735
Lehnardt, Peter S., 31846
Lehnert, Herbert, 31549
Leibzoll, 31388
Leipoldt, Johannes, 31727
Leipzig, 31524–31527, 31842, 32341
Leipzig, Anne-Frank-Shoah-Bibliothek, 31673
Leiser, Erwin, 31788
Leitner, Irving A., 31799
Leitner, Isabella, 31799
Lekebusch, Sigrid, 31800
Lemalet, Martine, 31580
Lemberg (Lvov), 31614
Lemgo, 31528
Lemhöfer, D., 32050
Lemm, Alfred, 32231
Lemmons, Russel, 31801
Lenger, Christine, 32115
Lengnau, 31629
Lenk, Karl, 31802
Lenk, Rudolf Stefan, 31802
Leo Baeck Institute, 31419, 31680
Leo Baeck Institute, Jerusalem, 31680
Leo Baeck Institute, 'Jüdischer Almanach', 31681; 31430, 32040, 32177, 32241, 32378, 32384
Leo Baeck Institute, 'LBI Information. Nachrichten aus den Leo Baeck Instituten', 31680; 31825, 31958
Leo Baeck Institute, New York, 31680

Leo Baeck Institute, New York, 'Library and Archive News', 31683
Leo Baeck Institute, Schriftenreihe, 31772
Leo Baeck Institute, Veröffentlichung, 32120
Leo Baeck Institute, 'Year Book', 31682; 31408, 31439, 31502, 31663, 31691, 31809, 32034, 32042, 32052, 32055, 32056, 32083, 32291, 32302, 32342, 32358, 32437
Leonhardt, Brigitte, 32131
Lepik, Andres, 32124
Lerm, Christa-Maria, 32304
Lerner, Gerda, 31905
Les Milles, 31750
Lessing, Gotthold Ephraim, 31987, 32367, 32369
Lessing, Theodor, 32109, 32232
Lester, David, 32316
Levenson, Alan, 32108
Levi, Erik, 32092
Levi-Mühsam, Else, 32282
Levinas, Emmanuel, 31994, 32110
Levinsky-Koevary, Hannah, 31658
Levy (Lee), Alexander, 32067
Lévy, Ernest-Henri, 31445
Levy, Jacob, 31535
Lewald, Fanny, 32233
Lexikon zum religiösen Wortschatz und Brauchtum der deutschen Juden, 31449
Ley, Michael, 31592
Liberalism, 32054, 32056
Liberalism (pol.), 32042, 32121, 32358
Liberles, Robert, 31981, 32115
Liberman, Aaron Shmuel, 32047
Licharz, Werner, 31958
Lichtblau, Albert, 31592, 32415
Lichtenstein, Heiner, 31728, 31915, 31917
Lichtenstein, Kurt, 32234
Liebermann, Max, 32235, 32346
Liebermann, Max & Martha, 32236
Liepmann, Rudolf, 31822
Lilienthal, Saul, 31526
Lind, Jacov, 32077
Lindemann, Albert S., 31407
Lindemann, Karin, 32177
Lindner, Erik, 31459
Link, Helmut, 31537
Linz, 31594
Lion, Hilde, 32020
Lippe, 31529, 31530
'Lippische Mitteilungen', 31530
Lippmann, Leo, 31764
Lipstadt, Deborah E., 31785, 31788
Literary Studies, Jews in, 31693
Literature, Jews depicted in, 32115, 32359, 32367, 32369, 32371, 32374, 32375, 32379
Litzel, Johannes, 31392
Litzmannstadt see Lodz
Lixfeld, Hannjost, 31816
Lixl-Purcell, Andreas, 31408

Lodz, 31803
Loewe, Siegfried, 32063
Löwenbrück, Anna-Ruth, 31831, 31987
Löwisch, Dieter-Jürgen, 32354
Löwisohn, Salomon, 32006
Löwith, Karl, 32237, 32238
Loewy, Alfred & Therese, 31753
Loewy, Hanno, 31803
Lohrmann, Klaus, 31592, 31609, 31611
Lonitz, Henri, 32318
Loos, Peter, 32063
Lorencová, Anna, 31621, 31856
Lorenz, Dagmar C. G., 31595, 32108
Lorenz, Ina S., 31503, 31506, 31764
Lorenz, Stefan, 31987
Lorraine, 31445, 31580, 31581, 31583
Lotter, Friedrich, 31409
Lourie, Richard, 31785
Low, Alfred D., 31780
Lowenstein, Steven M., 31410, 31460, 31987
Lowenthal, Ernst G., 32037
Lower Saxony, 31531, 31532, 31533, 31534
Lublinsky, Shmuel, 32232
Ludwig, Esther, 31525
Ludwig, Johannes, 31919
Lübbe, Hermann, 31966
Lübeck, 31535
Lück, Helmut E., 32354
Lück, Manfred, 31467
Lüdenscheid, 31536
Lüneburg, 32196
Lützeler, Paul Michael, 32339
Luft, Friedrich, 32112
Lunzer, Heinz, 32262, 32265
Lunzer-Talos, Victoria, 32262, 32264, 32265
Lustiger, Arno, 31490, 31872
Luther, Martin, 32365
'Lutherische Monatshefte', 31843, 31895
Lutum-Lenger, Paula, 31630
Lutz, Thomas, 31941
Luxemburg, Rosa, 32102, 32111, 32239

Macdonald, Kevin, 32256
Mace, Simone, 32115
Magris, Claudio, 32157
Maharal, Rabbi Judah Loeb, 31399
Mahler, Gustav, 32240, 32241
Mahr, Helmut, 31578
'Mahut', 31982
Maier, Dieter, 31805
Maier, Karl-Heinz, 31804
Maierhof, Gudrun, 32020
Maimon, Salomon, 32080, 32367
Mainz, 31416, 31537
Malachi, Zvi, 31982
Malamud, Bernard, 32459
Malchow, 31538
Maleakhi, Zvi, 31506
Mallmann, Klaus Michael, 32088

Mann, Frido, 32460
Mann, Thomas, 32108, 32231, 32320, 32333, 32369, 32430, 32435
Mannheim, Karl, 32428
Manufacturers, 31463
Manzolph, Ulrich, 31688
Marcus, Ivan G., 31411
Marcuse, Ludwig, 32084
Marek, Michael, 31775, 32337
Margolis, David, 31807
Margul-Sperber, Alfred, 32103
Maric, Mileva, 32324
Markner, Reinhard, 32145
Markovits, Andrei S., 31906
Marks, Jane, 31806
Marrus, M.R., 31776
Martens, Wolfgang, 32367
Marwedel, Günter, 31504
Marx, Henry, 31638, 31658
Marx, Karl, 31973, 31987
Matsdorf, Wolfgang Simon, 31661
Matt, Peter von, 32157
Mattenklott, Gert, 31684, 31823, 32110
Matzerath, Horst, 31728
Matzner, David, 31807
Mauritius, 31802
Mauser, Siegfried, 32092
Mauthner, Fritz, 32345
Mautner, Thomas, 31987
Mayer, Annemarie, 31472
Mayer, Anton, 32144, 32262
Mayer, Arno J., 31851
Mayer, Günter, 31978
Mayer, Hans, 32109, 32112
Mayer, Helmut, 32254
Mayer, Paul Yogi, 32038
Mayorek, Yoram, 32115
Mazura, Uwe, 32373
'MB' Mitteilungsblatt des Irgun Olei Merkas Europa, 31413, 31682, 31772, 32037
McGuire, William, 32327
McLaughlin, Donal, 32098
Meckel, Christoph, 32446
Mecklenburg, 31470, 31538, 32129
Mecklenburg, Frank, 31683
Medebach, 31539
Medicine, Jews in, 31525, 31535, 32082, 32410
Megged, Aharon, 32461
Mehlhausen, Joachim, 31412
Mehmel, Astrid, 32251, 32252
Mehring, Walter, 31647, 32084
Mehrwald, Silke, 32020
Meidner, Ludwig, 32242
Meier, Christian, 32337
Meier, Kurt, 32417
Meier-Lenz, Dieter Peter, 32086
Meining, Stefan, 31543
Meir Ben Baruch of Rothenburg, 31983
Meisels, Mosche, 32063

Meisenheim, 31540
Melzer, Gerhard, 32266
Memorials, 31534, 31851, 31935, 31940–31943, 31945, 31950, 31951, 31953, 31954
Menasse ben Israel, 32383
Mendel, Emanuel, 32243
Mendelsohn, Ezra, 32014
Mendelssohn Family, 32367
Mendelssohn, Fanny see Hensel, Fanny
Mendelssohn, Felix, 32014, 32109, 32441
Mendelssohn, Moses, 31960, 31969, 31984–32001, 32080, 32123, 32367
Mendes-Flohr, Paul, 31964, 31997
'Menora', 31684; 31469, 31563, 31721, 31761, 31796, 31844, 32016, 32031, 32038, 32064, 32218, 32220, 32245, 32290, 32304, 32307, 32357, 32362
Mentgen, Gerd, 31427, 32386, 32402
Merchants, 31596
Merker, Paul, 31898
'Merkur', 31843, 32305
Messianism, 32027, 32110
'Metis', 32423
Metz, 31445, 31581
Metzger, Mendel, 31983
Metzger, Thérèse, 31983
Mey, Bernhard, 31513
Meyer, Beate, 31791
Meyer, Frank, 32088
Meyer, Martin, 32255, 32318
Meyer, Michael A., 31413, 31680, 32054
Meyer, Pierre-André, 31580, 31581
Meyer, Seligmann, 32046
Meyer-Maril, Edina, 32067
Meyhöfer, Rita, 31714
Meynert, Joachim, 31865
Meysels, Lucian O., 32063
Michael, Reuven, 31986
Michaelis, Johann David, 31987, 32367
Michaels, Jennifer, 31883
Michman, Dan, 31662
Michman, Jozeph, 31662
Middle Ages, 31387, 31388, 31394, 31397, 31399, 31400, 31405, 31427, 31464, 31577, 31592, 31609, 31611, 31983, 32382, 32385, 32386, 32396–32399, 32401, 32402,
'Middle Eastern Studies', 32074
Mieder, Wolfgang, 32253
Migration, 31392
Milde, Wolfgang, 32367
Miller, Susanne, 32013, 32281
Miller-Brombacher, Jeanne A., 32050
Milton, Sybil, 31851
Minden, 31865
Minder, Bernard, 32183
Minder, Robert, 32112
Minhoff, Susanne, 31752
Minninger, Monika, 31865
Minty, Mary, 31427

Mirande de Boer, Margreet, 31506
Miron, Dan, 32133
'Mit der Ziehharmonika', 31646, 32147, 32158, 32285
'Mitteilungen d. Westdt. Gesellschaft f. Familienkunde', 32022
Mitten, Richard, 31884
Mittenzwei, Ingrid, 31596
Mitterer, Felix, 32377
Mixed Marriages, 31830, 32108
Mixed Marriages, Children of, 31791
'Modern Austrian Literature', 31595, 31881, 31883, 32156, 32169, 32295, 32310, 32320, 32376, 32377
'Modern Judaism', 31979, 31990, 32000, 32059
Möbus, Frank, 32212
Möllenhoff, Gisela, 31865
Möller, Susann, 32108
Moers, 31808
Molkenbur, Norbert, 31525
Moll, Heinz, 31634
Mommsen, Hans, 31822, 31826
Monchi, Valerie, 32355
'(Le) Monde', 31928
Monteath, Peter, 31940
Montefiore, Claude G., 31956
Montfort, 31576
Morgan, Emma, 31682
Morgenstern, Matthias, 31843
Morgenstern, Soma, 32262, 32267
Morris, Katherine, 31809
Morton, Frederic, 32462
Mosberg, Helmuth, 32039
Moscheles, Ignaz, 32051
Moselle, 31402
Moses Mendelssohn und die Kreise seiner Wirksamkeit, 31987
Moses, Julius, 31842
Moses, Leopold, 31597
Mosse, George L., 31414, 32244
Motesiczky, Marie-Louise, 32086
'MPG-Spiegel', 32193
Muchitsch, Wolfgang, 31649
Mühldorf, 31941
Mühlhausen, 31582
Mühlhausen (Thuringia), 32022
Mühsam, Erich, 32085, 32347
Mühsam, Paul, 32282
Mülheim (Ruhr), 31541
Müller, Ernst, 31991
Müller, Gerhard, 32086
Müller, Henning, 32095
Müller, Werner, 31558
Müller, Wolfgang, 31865
Müller-Henning, Markus, 31946
Müller-Hill, Benno, 31745
Müller-Luckner, Elisabeth, 31425
Müller-Madej, Stella, 31810
Müller-Tupath, Karla, 31857

Münden, 31534
Münster, 31811, 31865, 32105
Münz, Christoph, 31812
Muller, Jerry Z., 32437
Munich, 31543, 31813–31815, 32176
Music, Jews in, 31525, 32051, 32147, 32187, 32202, 32240, 32298, 32308, 32312
Musicians, Composers, 32092, 32308
Mutterstadt, 31544
Myers, David N., 32291
Mysticism, 31977

Nachama, Andreas, 31888
'Nachrichten f. d. jüd. Bürger Fürths', 31493, 31494, 31578
Nagorni, Klaus, 31929
Nancy, 31580
Nathan, Paul, 32070
'(The) Nation', 31787
Nationalism, 31616, 32166
'Nationalities Papers', 31616
Natorp, Paul, 31966
Naujoks, Antje C., 31682
Nazi Crimes, 31817
Nazi Crimes, Prosecution of, 31728, 31731, 31857, 31885, 31886, 31889, 31908, 31909, 31912–31917, 31927
Nazi Ideology, 31592
Nazi Period, Jewish Life in Germany, 31713, 31757, 31764, 31813
Nazi Period, Survival in Hiding, 31836, 31849
Nazi Period, Teaching, 31851, 31932, 31937, 31939–31942, 31945, 31947, 31948
Nazi Politics and Propaganda, 31742, 31822, 31823, 31824, 31864
Nefzger, Christoph, 31814
Nehren, Birgit, 31987, 31988
Neiman, Susan, 31918
Neiss, Marion, 32416
Nemitz, Kurt, 31842
Netherlands, 32340
Netherlands, Refugees, 31647, 31662
Neu-Isenburg, 31545
Neubauer, Hans-Joachim, 31413, 31846, 32375
Neuberg, Simon, 31437
'Neue Literatur. Ztschr. f. Querverbindungen', 31615
'Neue Rundschau', 32332
'Neue Zürcher Zeitung' ('NZZ'), 31413, 31632, 32124, 32157, 32207, 32228, 32255, 32266, 32269, 32318, 32323, 32331, 32352, 32365, 32446, 32453, 32462
Neuengamme, 31818
Neuhaus, Gerd, 32441
Neumann, Moritz, 31732
Neumann, Robert, 32084, 32098
Neumann, Ronnit, 31907
'Neusprachliche Mitt. aus Wiss. und Praxis', 32141

Neuwied, 31546
'New German Critique', 31903, 32258, 32313
'(The) New York Times', 31637
'(The) New Yorker', 31674, 31933
New Zealand, Refugees, 31648
Newman, Amy, 32387
Newman, Barnett, 32110
Nicault, Catherine, 32061
Nicgorski, Walter, 32003
Nicholas, Lynn H., 31819
Nicolaysen, Rainer, 32227
Nicosia, Francis R., 31525, 31851
Niederland, Doron, 31946
Niedersachsen see Lower Saxony
Niedervisse, 31583
Niederzissen, 31548
Niehoff, Maren R., 32040
Nielsen, Birgit S., 31740
Niemann, Ingrid, 31482
Niemöller, Martin, 32385, 32436
Niemöller, Wolfgang, 31474
Nieraad, Jürgen, 31681
Niethammer, Lutz, 31723
Nietzsche, Friedrich, 32437, 32438
Niewöhner, Friedrich, 31987
Nikolsburg, Jüd. Museum für Mähren-Schlesien, 31614
Nolden, Thomas, 31907
'Non-Aryan' Christians (see also Mixed Marriages), 31800, 31865, 31910
Nordhausen, 31820, 31821, 32022
Nordhofen, Eckhard, 32255
Nordmann, Ingeborg, 31944, 32102
Nordsiek, Marianne, 31865
(Die) Normalität des Verbrechens, 31822
North Rhine-Westphalia, 31942
Notgemeinschaft deutscher Wissenschaftler im Ausland, 32086
Novak, Kurt, 31829
'Novalis', 31991
November Pogrom, 31476, 31525, 31607, 31739, 31762, 31823–31826, 31938, 31952
November Pogrom, in Teaching, 31851, 31938
Nowak, Kurt, 32417
Nuremberg, 31549, 32383
Nuremberg Laws, 31841
Nuremberg Trials, 31889, 31908, 31909
Nyc, Andrea, 32111

Oakes, Edward T., 31973
Oberländer, Franklin Aharon, 31910
Obschernitzki, Doris, 31750
Ochse, Katharina, 31918
Odenbach, 31550
Odratzheim, 31445
Öhringen, 31827
Oelke, Karl-Heinz, 31538
Oesterreicher, Hans, 31526
Österreichisch-Israelitische Union, 31593

Offenbach am Main, 31551, 32027
Okladek, Friederike, 31758
Olden, Ika, 31828
Olden, Rudolf, 31828
Ollig, Hans-Ludwig, 31966
Olson, Michael P., 32376
Oppenheimer, Franz, 32245, 32246
Oppenheimer, Joseph Süss, 32247
Oppenheimer, Max, 32248
'(The) Oral History Review', 31911
Organisations, 31490, 31502, 31524–31526, 31545, 31593, 32020, 32030, 32032, 32038, 32042, 32043, 32070, 32072
Organisations, Nazi Period, 31545, 31598, 31772, 32019, 32023
Orthodoxy, 31389, 32007, 32054
Ortmeyer, Benjamin, 31751
Osiander, Andreas, 32383
'Ost und West', 32052
Ostjuden see Eastern Jewry
Ostow, Robin, 31911, 31918
Ostwald, Jacob, 31573
Ott, Hugo, 31753
Ottersberg, 31552
'Our Press', 32047
Oz, Amos, 32063

Pacifism, 32125, 32231
Paclt, Jaromír, 32092
Padua, 31672
Pätzold, Kurt, 31829, 31917
Pagis, Dan, 31681
Pais, Abraham, 32173
Palatinate, 31486, 31499, 31523, 31544, 31550, 31553, 31554, 31557
Palestine, 31671, 32064, 32071, 32115
Palestine, Immigration, 32058, 32348
Palestine, Refugees, 31802, 31844, 32055, 32066
Palmer, Gesine, 31464
Pannwitz, Rudolf, 32339
Panofsky, Erwin, 32249
Pantielev, Gregorij, 32092
Papanek, Hanna, 32287
Pappenheim, Bertha, 31545, 32041, 32329
Paraguay, 31641
Paris, 32088
'Pariser Tageblatt', 31647
'(Das) Parlament', 32337
Pascheles, Wolf, 31624
Patai, Raphael, 31415
Patsch, Sylvia M., 32063
Patterson, David, 32134
Paucker, Arnold, 31872
Paul, Barbara, 32102
Paul, Gerhard, 32088
Pauli, Hertha, 31647
Paulus-Bund, 31853
Pawlikowski, John T., 32385
Pawlita, Cornelius, 31920

Pazi, Margarita, 32108
'Pe'amim', 32006
Peck, Jeffrey M., 31918
Penkower, Monty Noam, 32068
Peres, Schimon, 32063
Perl, Josef, 31627
Perrot, Michelle, 31393
Perry, Marvin, 32385
Persico, Joseph E., 31908
Peru, 31635
Perutz, Leo, 32250, 32463
Petuchowski, Jakob J., 31978
Peukert, Detlev, 31730
Pfalz see Palatinate
Pfeiffer, Eduard, 31567
Pfister, Doris, 31392
Pfister, Eva, 32265
Phayer, Michael, 31851
Philanthropists, 31474, 31490, 31492, 32076, 32115
Philippsohn, Kurt, 32348
Philippsohn-Lang, Trude, 31589
Philippson, Alfred, 32251, 32252
Philosemitism, 32368
Philosophy and Learning, Jews in, 32003, 32160, 32161, 32189, 32312
Philosophy, Jewish, 32189
Picard, Jacob, 31577, 31716, 32464
Picard, Jacques, 31631, 31632
Picht, Barbara, 31543
Pickus, Keith H., 32042
Pigge, Helmut, 32166
Pines, Malcolm,, 32184
Pingel, Falk, 31851
Pinkas Hakehillot, 31662
Pinkus, Ben-Zion Ornan, 31506
Piper, Franciszek, 31703
Plonski, Guilherme Ary, 31663
Plowinski, Kerstin, 31525
Poetry, 32282, 32449
Pohl, Manfred, 32115
Pohlmann, Hanne, 31528
Pol, Andri, 31628
Polgar, Alfred, 32112
Political Sciences, Jews in, 32227
Politics, Jews in, 31392, 32243
Pollak, Felix, 32253
Pomerance, Aubrey, 31464
Pomerania, 32409
Popper, Karl, 32078, 32254, 32255
Portugal, Nazi Period, 31833
Posner, Gerald, 31674
Post, Bernhard, 31512
Potgieter, Johan, 32156
Potter, Pamela M., 32092
Pracht, Elfi, 31461, 32290
Prague, 31618, 31620–31624, 32086, 32092
Prague, Jewish Museum, 31856
Prater, Donald A., 32317

Prawer, Siegbert S., 31987
Prenzel, Arndt, 31505
Press, Jewish, 32046, 32047
Pressburg, 31985
Pressburger, Emeric, 32256
Presser, Ellen, 31667
Prestel, Claudia, 32043
Prevost-Marcilhacy, Pauline, 32115
Pringle, Annette, 31691
Pringsheim, Alfred, 32257
Printers, Hebrew, 31493, 31508, 31525
'Proceedings of the American Academy for Jewish Research', 31574, 31985
Procksch, Otto, 32422
'(The) Progressive', 31905
'Prooftexts', 31993
Prosecution of Nazi Crimes see Nazi crimes, Prosecution of
Prussia, 31395, 32442
'Psychologie und Geschichte', 32289
Pschorr, Elizabeth, 31830
Psychoanalysts, Psychologists, 32101, 32226, 32243, 32289
Publicists, Journalists, 31693, 32166
Publishers, Printers, 31846, 31860, 32127, 32321, 32355
Püschel, Almuth, 31715
Pulzer, Peter, 31407
Purin, Bernhard, 31592, 31614
Putík, Alexandr, 31621

'Qesher', 32028, 32217, 32274
Quarch, Christoph, 31843
Quidde, Ludwig, 32086

Rabbis, 31389, 31577, 31972, 31974, 31985, 32033, 32034
Racism, 31592, 31697, 32082, 32385, 32406
Raddatz, Fritz J., 32267
Radeff, Anne, 31626
Radil, Thomás, 31856
Rahe, Thomas, 31752, 31935
Raim, Edith, 31941
Ramras-Rauch, Gila, 32137
Ranke, Kurt, 31688
Raphael, Freddy, 31445
Rastatt, 31831
Rathenau, Walther, 31822, 32109, 32258, 32417, 32418
Raulet, Gérard, 32417
Raulff, Ulrich, 32124
Ravensbrück, 31752, 31850, 31941
Read, Anthony, 31462
Reck-Hog, Ursula, 31946
Reemerging Jewish Culture in Germany, 31918
Reeves, Nigel, 32197
Reform Judaism, 31972
Refugee Policy, 31670, 31802, 31832, 31833
Regensteiner, Henry, 32439

Reich, Ronny, 31416
Reich, Wilhelm, 32259
Reich-Ranicki, Marcel, 32112
Reichmann, Eva, 31650, 32020, 32423
Reichsvereinigung d. Juden in Deutschland, 31772
Reichsvertretung d. Juden in Deutschland, 31739, 31772, 32286
Reimarus, Hermann Samuel, 32367
Reinhardt, Stephan, 32296
Reinharz, Jehuda, 32054, 32069
Reinhold, Josef, 31525
Reinhold-Postina, Eva, 31732
Reinke, Andreas, 31721
Reis, Betty, 31863
Reiss, Hans, 31648
Reissner, Beate, 31405
Remigration, 31865, 32066
Remmler, Karen, 31918
Remy, Nahida see Lazarus, Nahida Ruth
Rendsburg, 32026
Rengstorf, Karl Heinrich, 32367
Rentschler, Eric, 31834
Renz, Ulrich, 31473, 31916
Reshaping the Past, 31677, 31773, 31960, 31971, 31981
Resistance, Jewish, 31525, 31657, 31868–31878
Resistance, Non-Jewish, 31619, 31835–31838, 31849, 31876, 31877, 32458
Restitution, 31631, 31636, 31851, 31919, 31920
Reuter, Ernst, 31966
Reuther, Christian, 31556
Revolution and Jews, 32225
'Revue des Etudes Juives', 31579, 31980
Reymond, Bernard, 32417
Rhineland, 31555, 31565, 32358
Richards, David, 32119
Richarz, Monika, 31417
Riedel, Sigrid, 31438
Riegner, Gerhart R., 31744
Ries, Matthias, 31873
Ries, Rotraud, 31531, 31532–31534
Riesser, Gabriel, 31506
Riga, 31645, 31862, 31865
Ringer, Alexander L., 32092
Ritchie, James M., 32098
Rites and Ceremonies, 31397, 31438, 31530, 31577, 31602, 31624, 32025, 32026, 32029
Rittberg, Benigna Gräfin von, 32096
Ritter, Henning, 32323
Ritual Bath, 31485, 31534, 31899
Ritual Murder see Blood Libel
Ritzel, Wolfgang, 31966
Robert, Ludwig, 32302
Robertson, Ritchie, 31590, 32198
Röck, Bernd, 31418
Rödelsee, 31556
Röhl, John C.G., 32445
Röll, Walter, 31449

Römer, Gernot, 31392
Römer, Ruth, 32152
Rogge-Gau, Sylvia, 31878
Roggenkamp, Viola, 32329
Rohde, Saskia, 31506, 31865
Rohr, Walter, 31739
Rohrbacher, Stefan, 31405, 32412
Rokahr, Gerd, 31480
Roman, Zoltan, 32240
Romey, Stefan, 31765
Roming, Gisela, 31577
Roschewski, Heinz, 31633
Rosenbaum, Lieselotte, 31865
Rosenberg, Shalom, 31989
Rosenfeld de Prusak, Karin Mariana, 31921
Rosenfeld, Eva, 32325
Rosenfeld, Gavriel D., 32052
Rosenfeld, Jitzchak, 31493
Rosenfeld, Mosche N., 31494
Rosenfeld, Oskar, 31803
Rosenfelder, Rudi, 31543
Rosenheim, Jakob, 31992
Rosenkranz, Moses, 32103
Rosenzweig, Franz, 31966, 31973, 31978, 31993–31995, 32000, 32001, 32005, 32110, 32432
Rosner, Robert W., 32063
Ross, James R., 31668
Rossow, Änne, 31946
Rote Kapelle, 31870
Rotenstreich, Nathan, 32367
Roth, Harald, 31948
Roth, Joseph, 32094, 32120, 32260–32268
Roth, Philip, 32136
Rothenburg ob der Tauber, 31416
Rothko, Marc, 32110
Rothschild Family, 31488, 31492, 32113–32116
Rothschild, Charlotte de, 32115
Rothschild, Mayer Amschel, 32117
Rothschild, Miriam, 32115
Rothschild, Recha, 31839
Roxheim, 31554
Rubin, Evelyn Pike, 31669
Rubinstein, Hilde, 32269
Rubinstein, Jonathan, 31907
Rudel, Josef Norbert, 32349
Rudin-Bühlmann, Sibylle, 32143
Rüb, Matthias, 32103
Rübsam, Rolf, 31718
Rübsamen-Waigmann, Helga, 32117
Rückerl, Adalbert, 31817
Rülzheim, 31557
Rüss, Karl-Heinz, 31760
Ruhr, 31840
Runge, Irene, 32370
Ruppel, Helmut, 31946
Rural Jewry, 31405, 31514, 31577, 32464
Ruthenberg, Eckehart, 31470
Rybac, Timothy W., 31933

Index to Bibliography

Saarlouis, 31558
Sabelleck, Rainer, 31534
Sabrow, Martin, 32418
Sachs, Nelly, 32270, 32271
Sachsen-Anhalt, 31470
Sadan, Inge, 31543
Sadmon, Zeev W., 32070
Safrian, Hans, 31856
Sahl, Hans, 32086, 32090, 32272
Saidel, Rochelle G., 31663
Salamun, Kurt, 32255
Salinger, Paul, 31526
'Salmagundi', 32154, 32157
Saloch, Reinhard, 31791
Salomon, Charlotte, 31741
Salomon, Erich, 32273
Salomon, Gotthold, 32123
Salomon, Hanna, 31498
Samely, Alexander, 31949
Samter, Elias, 31459
Samuels, Andrew, 32433, 32434
Santaniello, Weaver, 32438
Sarfatti, Michele, 31841
Sarid, Jossi, 32063
Sarkowicz, Hans, 32117
Sartre, Jean-Paul, 32015, 32185
Sasson, Avi, 32071
Sauer, Paul, 31577
Sauerländer, Willibald, 32249
Sauerland, 31559
Saxony, 31470, 31526, 31560, 31842
Scandinavia, Refugees, 32088
Schaber, Irme, 31874
Schaber, Will, 31638, 31693, 32328
Schacht, Gisela, 31847
Schäfer, Peter, 31959, 31996
Schäll, Ernst, 31577
Schaeper, Silke, 31846, 32276
Schaller, Berndt, 31534
Schallhardt, Veronika, 31675
Schammas, Anton, 31681
Schapira, Anita, 32063
Schatz, Andrea, 32352
Schatzker, Chaim, 31892, 31946, 32054
Schausberger, Manfred, 31917
Schebera, Jürgen, 32308
Scheffler, Jürgen, 31528
Scheffler, Wolfgang, 31777, 31822 (Festschrift)
Scheideler, Kurt, 32336
Scheil, Stefan, 32393
Schembs, Hans-Otto, 32115
Schenk, Hannelore, 31845
Scherer, Herbert, 31866
Scherf, Ferdinand, 31537
Scherke, Katharina, 31664
Schiebler, Gerhard, 31490
Schiefelbein, Peter, 31823
Schilde, Kurt, 31712
Schiller, Friedrich von, 32439

Schilling, Sabine, 32104
Schimmelpfennig, Bernhard, 31405
Schimpf, Dorothee, 31513
Schindel, Robert, 32465
Schinderhannes (Johannes Bückler), 31402
Schindler, Oskar, 31717, 31843, 32458
Schindler, Roland W., 32139
Schinköth, Thomas, 31525
Schittenhelm, Karin, 31936
Schläpfer, Robert, 31445
Schlarb, Kläre, 31540
Schlatter, Adolf, 31727
Schlautmann-Overmeyer, Rita, 32442
Schleindl, Angelika, 31498
Schlesinger, Paul, 32274
Schleswig-Holstein, 31561, 31922
'Schleswig-Holsteinisches Ärzteblatt', 31535
Schlettstadt, Rudolf von, 31394
Schlichtenmaier, Gert, 32242
Schlör, Joachim, 31614, 31844
Schlott, Rainer, 32115
Schmalhausen, Bernd, 32236
Schmallenberg, 31845
Schmeichel-Falkenberg, Beate, 31647
Schmid-Ospach, Michael, 32229
Schmidt, Alfred, 32117
Schmidt, Amos, 32206
Schmidt, Bernhard, 31808
Schmidt, Ernst, 31739
Schmidt, Hans M., 32165
Schmidt, Helmut, 32350
Schmidt, Ingrid, 31946
Schmidt, Karl Ludwig, 32389
Schmidt, Michael, 32102
Schmidt-Henkel, Gerhard, 31400
Schmied-Kowarzik, Wolfdietrich, 32110
Schmitt, Carl, 32440
Schmitt, Jean-Claude, 31387
Schmitter, Elke, 31810
Schmitz, Walter, 31648
Schmueli, Ilana, 31681
Schneeberger, Michael, 31556
Schneider, Frank, 32092
Schneider, Gabriele, 32233
Schneider, Hansjörg, 32086
Schneider, Reinhard, 31387
Schneider, Reinhold, 31400
Schneider, Richard Chaim, 31923
Schneider, Rolf, 32305
Schneider, Ulrich, 31913
Schnitzler, Arthur, 32119, 32122, 32275
Schnoor, Herbert, 31917
Schocken Verlag, 31846
Schocken, Salman, 31846, 32276
Schoefer, Christine, 31950
Schönberg, Arnold, 32109
Schönberg Zeisl, Barbara, 32377
Schöne, Lothar, 32118
Schönfeld, Martin, 31951

Index to Bibliography 443

Schöning, Jörg, 31660
Schoeps, Julius H., 31401, 31684, 31872, 32016, 32063, 32080, 32105, 32124, 32345, 32419
Scholem, Gershom, 31506, 31960, 31977, 31996, 31997, 32000, 32001, 32109, 32319, 32351, 32352
Scholz, Albrecht, 31842
Schomerus, Ute, 32086
Schornstheimer, Michael, 32086
Schorsch, Ismar, 31419, 31893, 31897, 31998
Schreckenberg, Wilhelm, 31420
Schreiber, Hans-Jürgen, 31481
Schreier, Helmut, 31847
Schreuder, Saskia, 31846
Schrobsdorff, Angelika, 32353
Schröter, Klaus, 32333
Schröter, Manfred, 31821
Schubert, Ernst, 31387
Schubert, Kurt, 31586, 31587
Schubert, Ursula, 32053
Schütz, Erhard, 32217
Schütz, Siegfried, 31534
Schütze, Oliver, 31969
Schulenburg, Kai Uwe, 31470
Schulmeister, Otto, 32063
Schulte, Christoph, 32110
Schulte, Hans, 32119
Schulte, Ingolf, 32267
Schultz, Ingo, 32298
Schulz, Karin, 31658, 31665
Schulze-Bidlingmaier, 31692
Schumann, Clara, 32441
Schumann, Robert, 32441
Schuppetal, Ingrid, 31522
Schuster, Felix, 31656
Schutzjuden, 32128, 32129
Schwaben, 31392, 31405, 31473, 31562
Schwalbová, Margita, 31704
Schwammberger, Josef, 31914
Schwanda-Arnbom, Marie-Theres, 31848
Schwarberg, Günther, 31766
Schwarcz, Alfredo José, 31666
Schwartz, Joseph, 32071
Schwarz, Egon, 32108
Schwarz, Erika, 31829
Schwarzfuchs, Simon, 31580
Schwarzschild, Steven S., 31966
Schweer, Thomas, 31999
Schweid, Eliezer, 32000, 32001
Schweitzer, Frederick M., 32385
'Schweizerische Zeitschrift f. Geschichte', 31626
Schwentker, Wolfgang, 32238
Schweres-Fichtner, Michael, 32044
Science of Judaism see Wissenschaft des Judentums
Sciences and Mathematics, Jews in, 32079, 32081, 32257
'Scriptum', 32306
Secher, Herbert Pierre, 31882

Seeberg, Reinhold, 32422
Seemann, Karl, 32086
Seewann, Harald, 32045, 32063
(Die) Sefarden in Hamburg, 31506
Segal, Lilli, 31875
Segal, Phillip, 31978
Seghers, Anna, 32098, 32108, 32109, 32277–32280
Sehr, Benno, 31526
Seibt, Gustav, 32157
Seidel, Esther, 31421
Seitz, Reinhard H., 31392
Selig, Wolfram, 31815
Seligmann, Chaim, 32225
Seligmann, Rafael, 31907, 31918, 32073
Sellerberg, Ann-Mari, 32284
Sender, Toni, 32088, 32281
Sendtner, Florian, 32231
Senekowitsch, Martin, 31598, 31599, 31612
Sephardi Communities, 31501, 31506, 31587
Shafir, Shlomo, 32426
Shaked, Gershon, 32120
Shanghai, Refugees, 31667–31669
Shapira, Anita, 32054
Sharaf, Myron, 32259
Shear-Yashuv, Aharon, 32002
Shedletzky, Itta, 32351
Shedletzky, Mosche, 32241
Shek, Allisah, 31856
Sherman, A.J., 31670
'Shofar', 32381
Shoham, Chaim, 31987
Shrivastava, Anjana, 31924
'Sicsa Report', 31926
Siebert, Eberhard, 32263
Sieg, Ulrich, 31965
Siegel, Eva Maria, 32086
Siegel, Rainer-Joachim, 32260
Siegele-Wenschkewitz, Leonore, 31727, 31929, 32436
Siegemund, Anja, 31543
Siegert, Michael, 32255
Sievers, Kai Detlev (Festschrift), 32026
Sigel, Robert, 31731
Silbergleit, Arthur, 32282
Silbermann, Alphons, 32283
Silbermann, Edith, 32163
Silesia, 31563, 31761, 31822, 32036, 32362
Silver, Eric, 31849
Simmel, Georg, 32284
Simmel-Joachim, Monika, 32020
Simmering, 31600
Simon of Siegburg, 31399
Simon, Bettina, 32129
Simon, Heinrich, 31422, 32192
Simon, Hermann, 31822, 32216, 32286
Simon, Hugo, 31647
Simon, James, 32070
Simon, Marie, 32129

Simon-Pelanda, Hans, 31941
'Sinai', 32071
Sitt, Martina, 32164, 32165
Skorpil, Pavel, 31618, 31856
Slave Labour see Forced Labour
Small, William, 32098
Smith, Helmut Walser, 32393
Sobol, Yehoshua, 32017
Social and Economic Development, 31405, 31422, 31562, 31603, 31604
Social Sciences, Jews in, 32099, 32283
Social Welfare, Social Reform, 31505, 31567, 32024, 32083
Socialists, Social Democrats, 32013, 32065, 32083, 32287, 32363
(The) Society for the Protection of Science and Learning, 31664
Söhn, Gerhart, 32300
Sösemann, Bernd, 32274
Soest, 31564
Sofer, Moshe (Hatam), 31985
Soldenhoff, Richard von, 32297
Soldiers see Army; War
Solingen, 31565
Sombart, Werner, 32357
Sommer, Karin, 31392
Sommer-Lefkovits, Elisabeth, 31850
Sommerfeld, Arnold, 32081
Sonderegger, Stefan (Festschrift), 32199
Sonderegger-Ritter, Ruth, 32199
Sonnemann, Leopold, 32117
Sonnenfeld, Herbert, 31713
Sorkin, David, 31425, 31990
Sormova, Eva, 31856
Soviet Union, 31588
Sowa-Bettecken, Beate, 32270
Soxberger, Thomas, 31435
Soyfer, Jura, 32285
Spain, Nazi Period, 32088
Spalek, John M., 31693
Sparr, Thomas, 31413, 32115
Sperber, Jonathan, 32404
Speyer, 31416
Speyer, Georg, 32117
Speyer, Wilhelm, 32108
'(Der) Spiegel', 32073
Spiel, Hilde, 31650, 32084, 32112, 32377
Spielberg, Steven, 31843
Spielrein, Sabina, 32102, 32182, 32183
Spies, Bernhard, 32272
Spiess, Alfred, 31917
Spinoza, Baruch, 32080
Spitzer, Shlomo, 31597
Splitt, Gerhard, 32092
Sponheuer, Bernd, 32092
Sponsel, Udo, 32048
Sports, Jews in, 31796, 32031, 32035, 32038
Sprenger, Isabell, 31761
Springman, Luke, 32108

Spritzer, Jenny, 31705
'Sridim', 31967
'Stadion', 32035
Stahl, Heinrich, 32286
Stapel, Wilhelm, 32417
Starck, Astrid, 31439–31442, 31445, 32108,
Staudernheim, 31566
Stauffer, Beat, 31628
Stav, Shira, 32017
Steele see Essen-Steele
Steffens, Gerd, 31946
Stegemann, Ekkehard W., 32389
Steierwald, Ulrike, 32268
Stein, Alexander, 32287
Stein, Edith, 32102, 32288
Stein, Harry, 31823
Stein, Irmgard, 32350
Steinbach, Peter, 31876, 31877, 31878
Steinberg Family, 31481
Steiner, Alexander, 32063
Steiner, Carl, 32310
Steines, Patricia, 31597
Steinführer, Henning, 31525
Steinheim, Salomon Ludwig, 32002
Steinheim-Institut, 31684
Steininger, Rolf, 31851
Steinthal, Heymann, 32123
Stephan, Alexander, 32279
Stephan, Inge, 32104
Stephan, Thomas, 31647
Stern, Carola, 32301
Stern, Clara, 32289
Stern, Frank, 31678, 31851, 31925, 31926, 32370, 32378
Stern, Fritz, 31826
Stern, Guy, 31648, 32108
Stern, Jakob, 32080
Stern, Selma, 32102
Stern, William, 32354
Sternburg, Wilhelm von, 32095, 32175
Sterner, Gregor, 31617
Sternheim, Walter G. see Goral, Arie
Stieber, Ralf, 31929
Stieg, Gerald, 32222
Stiegnitz, Peter, 31601
Stoecker, Adolf, 32413, 32414
Stolleis, Michael, 32121
Stoltzenberg, Dietrich, 32193
Stolz, Gerd, 31922
Strack, Hermann, 32417
Stránský, Pavel, 31856
Strauss, Leo, 32003
Strauss, Ludwig, 31846
Strauss, Ottmar, 32290
Streim, Alfred, 31917, 31927
Strelka, Joseph P., 32094
Strenger, Elisabeth, 32315
Stripp, Alan, 31644
Strobl, Ingrid, 31852, 32271, 32420, 32421

Strohschneider-Kohrs, Ingrid, 31987
Studemund-Halévy, Michael, 31506, 31694
'Studia Rosenthaliana', 31428
'Studies in Contemporary Jewry', 31677, 31773, 31960, 31971, 31981
Stuttgart, 31567, 31853
Suchoff, David, 32189
Suchy, Barbara, 31680, 31691
'Süddeutsche Zeitung', 31542, 31872, 32044, 32185, 32296, 32306
'(The) Sunday Times', 31879
Survival in Hiding, 31733, 31758, 31806, 31849
Susman, Margarete, 32102, 32306
Sweden, 32129
Switzerland, 31387, 31577, 31626, 31631
Switzerland, Antisemitism, 31880
Switzerland, Nazi Period, 31632
Switzerland, Post War, 31633
Switzerland, Refugees, 31630, 31634
Syamken, Georg, 32110
Synagogues, 31392, 31451, 31469, 31485, 31506, 31550, 31566, 31577, 31585, 31672, 31865, 31899

Täubler, Eugen, 32004, 32291
Tamari, Ittai Joseph, 31525, 31846
Taro, Gerta, 31874
Tarrab-Maslaton, Martin, 31854
Taussig, Josef, 31856
Taylor, Jennifer A., 31847, 32098
Taylor, Telford, 31909
Teachers see Education
Technion, Haifa, 32070
Teichman, Milton, 31858
'Tel Aviver Jahrbuch für deutsche Geschichte', 31678; 31711, 31726, 31734, 31744, 31754, 31864, 31884, 31939, 32019, 32023
Teplitz, 31972
Teppe, Karl, 31865
Tergit, Gabriele, 31650, 32292
Territoires du Yiddish, 31446
Tettnang, 31576
Tgahrt, Reinhard, 32331
Thalmann, Rita, 32417
Theatre, Cabaret, Cinema, Jews in, 31660, 31813, 32091, 32148, 32218
Theatre, Film, Jews Depicted in, 31822, 31834, 31918, 31926, 32115, 32191, 32375, 32424
Theresienstadt, 31625, 31699, 31855–31857, 31941, 31957, 32026, 32460
Thieberger, Richard, 31648
Thiele, Dieter, 31791
Thielking, Sigrid, 32097
Thomann Tewarson, Heidi, 32302
Thommen, Dieter, 31445
Thrams, Peter, 31722
Thürich, Ursula, 31680
Thunecke, Jörg, 32098, 32295
Thuringia, 31470

'Tikkun', 31836, 31924, 32314, 32398
Tillard, Françoise, 32202
'Times Literary Supplement' ('TLS'), 32437
Timm, Angelika, 31851
Timm, Erika, 31445, 31447, 32129
Timms, Edward, 31423, 31590, 32222, 32379
Toch, Michael, 31405
Toller, Ernst, 32107, 32293, 32294
Torberg, Friedrich, 31881, 32295
Toscano del Banner, Andreas, 31543
Toul, 31580
Trapp, Frithjof, 32086
Traverso, Enzio, 31424, 31928
Treblinka, 31852
Trepp, Leo, 31978
'Tribüne', 31403, 31473, 31477, 31505, 31601, 31617, 31742, 31746, 31775, 31915, 31916, 31927, 31942, 32113, 32114
Trieste, 31602
Tröger, Heike, 31435
Troeltsch, Ernst, 32417
Troki, Isaak, 32383
Trommler, Frank, 31648
'Trumah', 31676; 31972
Tscherne, Peter, 31872
Tsur, Ya'akob, 32054
Tuch, Gustav, 31502
Tuchel, Johannes, 31731, 31870, 31876, 31878
Tucholsky, Kurt, 31647, 32112, 32296, 32297
Tulatz, Claus, 32088
Turn-of-the-Century Vienna and its Legacy, 32122
Turner, Barry, 31859
Tycner, Janusz, 31843
Tyldesly, Michael, 31961
Tyrol, 32395

Ulbrich, Bernd Gerhard, 32123
Ulff, Levi & Moses, 31463
Ullmann, Sabine, 31405
Ullmann, Viktor, 32298
Ullrich, Volker, 32347, 32396
Ulmann, Naftali Hirz ben Juda Loeb, 31989
Ulrich, Andreas, 31675
Ultmann (Andis), Helene, 32285
(Der) Umgang mit dem Holocaust, 31851
Unger, Manfred, 31525
Universities and Jews, 31542, 31771, 32042, 32045, 32110, 32161, 32227, 32249, 32394
Unkel, 31568
Unruh, Ilse, 31492
Urban, Susanne, 31860, 32114
Ury, Else, 31719
USA, Holocaust, Reaction, 31744, 31798
USA, Immigration, 31640, 31658, 31665
USA, Refugees, 31636, 31639, 31648, 31659, 31665, 32088, 32459
Uslar, 31534
'Utne Reader', 31623

Václavek, Ludvík, 31856
Vahlenkamp, Werner, 31477
Varga, Péter, 31627
Varnhagen, Rahel, 32299, 32300, 32301, 32302
Veauthier, F. Werner, 32099
Vees, Adolf, 31510
Vergangenheitsbewältigung, 31851, 31879, 31885, 31906, 31927, 31934, 31941, 32380
Vermes, Pamela, 31962
Vienna, 31592–31596, 31603–31614, 32047, 32054, 32063, 32101, 32115, 32119, 32415
Vienna, Jüdisches Museum, 31613, 31614, 32248
Vierhaus, Rudolf, 31987, 32367
Viertel, Berthold, 32094
'Vierteljahrshefte für Zeitgeschichte', 31898
Vietor-Engländer, Deborah, 31647
Vigée, Claude, 31442, 31445
Vilna, 31645
Vincke, Ludwig Freiherr, 32442
Vogelsberg, 31569
Vogt, Bernhard, 32245, 32246
Voigt, Jürgen, 32200
Volavková, Hana, 31625
Volkmann, Michael (formerly Bühler), 31671, 32005
Volkov, Shulamit, 31425, 31426
Vollmar, Bernd, 31392
Vollmer, Hartmut, 32269
Vollmer, Rudolf, 31568
Vorarlberg, 31592

Wacker, Ulrich, 31952
Waddington, Raymond B., 31508
Wagenseil, Johann Christoph, 32383
Wagner, Frank, 32277
Wagner, Franz Ephraim, 31823
Wagner, Josef, 31941
Wagner, Leonie, 32020
Wagner, Matthias, 31536
Wagner, Peter, 32008
Wagner, Richard, 32443
Wahl, Alfred, 32417
Waldniel, 31570
Walk, Joseph, 31469
Walker, Kizer, 31918
Wallace, Ian, 32098, 32280
Wallenberg, Raoul, 31789
Wallmann, Walter, 32117
Walser Smith, Helmut, 32404
Walther, Manfred, 32080
Wambach, Lovis Maxim, 32213
Wander, Fred, 32466
Wandsbek, 31765
Wanner, Helmut, 32046
Wannsee Conference, 31745, 31746
Wannsee-Konferenz, Haus der (Gedenkstätte), 31941, 31852

War and German Jews (see also Army, Jews in the), 31612, 32125
Warburg, 31861, 32336
Warburg Family, 32124, 32303
Warburg Institute, 32303
Warburg, Aby M., 32303, 32304
Warendorf, 31862
Warnecke, Hans, 31451, 32390
Warnke, Kerstin, 32115
Warnke, Martin, 32190
Warsaw, Ghetto, 31727, 31865
Wassenberg, 31863
Wasserburg, 31576
Wassermann, Heinz P., 31885
Wassermann, Jakob, 32305
Wattenscheid, 31840
Weber, Annette, 32115
Weber, Charlotte, 31634
Weber, Claude, 31846
Weber, Hermann, 31723
Weber, Horst, 32092
Weber, Max, 32357, 32444, 32444
Weber, Thomas, 32145
Weber, Werner, 32331
Wedemeier, Klaus, 32380
Wegener, Beate, 32194
Wegner, Armin T., 31755
Weichmann, Elsbeth, 32086
Weidenfeld, George, 32355
Weigel, Hans, 31881
Weigel, Sigrid, 32104
Weil, Alfred, 31510
Weil, Grete, 32306
Weil, Simone, 32111
Weill, Kurt, 32092, 32307, 32308
Weimar Republic, 31400, 32054, 32056, 32083, 32106
'Weimarer Beiträge', 32431
Weinberg, Gerhard L., 31748
Weinberg, Werner, 31449
Weinberger, Gabriele, 32108
Weininger, Otto, 32017, 32109, 32316, 32453
Weinzierl, Erika, 32063
Weinzierl, Ulrich, 32275, 32450
Weisberger, Adam, 32149
Weisberger, Adam M., 32294
Weiss, Hilde, 32370
Weiss, Ruth, 32356
Weiss, Stéphane, 32110
Weiss, Yfaat, 31864
Weitz, Eric D., 32239
Weitz, Yechiam, 32074
Wellmann, Hans, 31405
Welsh, Renate, 32467
'(Die) Weltbühne', 32011
Wendel, Frank, 31652
Wendland, Ulrike, 32249
Wenninger, Markus J., 31679
Werfel, Franz, 32122, 32309, 32310

Werle, Gerhard, 31847
Werner, Hans-Joachim, 31963
Werner, Sidonie, 31502
Werner, X., 32050
Werres, Peter, 32108
Werses, Shmuel, 32006
Wesel, 31463
Wessely, Naphtaly Herz, 32007
West Prussia, 32409
'Westfälische Zeitschrift', 31520
Westphal, Uwe, 32093
Westphalia, 31516, 31559, 31571, 31763, 31794, 32442
Wetterau, 32322
Wetzel, Juliane, 31658, 31685, 31904
Weyl, Robert, 31579
Wiborg, Susanne, 32201, 32201
Wichner, Ernest, 32103
Wickert, Christl, 32088
Wiefel, Wolfgang, 32417
Wieghardt-Lazar, Auguste, 31646
Wiegmann, Ulrich, 31946
Wiehn, Erhard Roy, 31577, 31696
'Wiener Jahrbuch f. jüd. Gesch., Kultur & Museumswesen', 31614
Wiese, Christian, 32391
Wiesel, Elie, 31976, 32311
Wiesemann, Falk, 31614
Wiesenthal, Simon, 31857, 31917
Wiesner, Herbert, 32103
Wiggershaus, Rolf, 32100
Wilcock, Evelyn, 32125
Wilhelm II, 32445
Wilhelm, Hans-Erich, 31496
Wilhelm, Hans-Heinrich, 31822
Wilke, Karl, 31521
Willms, Johannes, 31826
Wilson, Derek, 32116
Winkelmann, Bernd, 31939
Winkler, Heinrich August, 31826
Winter, Eggert, 31966
Wirth-Nesher, Hana, 32126
Wirthwein, Heike, 31514
Wissenschaft des Judentums, 31971, 31981
Wistrich, Robert S., 31615, 31616, 32054, 32063
Witten, 31573
Wittgenstein, Ludwig, 31973, 32312
Wittgenstein, Paul, 32312
Wittstock, Alfred, 31946
Wohnout, Helmut, 31706
Wojak, Irmtrud, 31651
Wolf, Christa, 32277
Wolf, Konrad, 32313
Wolf, Markus, 32314
Wolf, Siegbert, 32224
Wolf, Siegfried, 31946
Wolff, Anni, 31866
Wolff, Edith, 32020
Wolffram, Knud, 32171

Wolfram, Herwig (Festschrift), 31592
Wolfson, Elliot R., 32392
Wolin, Richard, 32146
Wolzig, Lehrheim, 31715
Wolzogen, Christoph von, 32432
Women, 31390, 31393, 31408, 31425, 31502, 31525, 31542, 31650, 31704, 31752, 31809, 31874, 31900, 31944, 32020, 32021, 32029, 32033, 32034, 32057, 32066, 32104, 32115, 32122, 32176, 32178, 32202, 32301, 32411, 32423
Wood, E. Thomas, 31867
Worms, 31416, 31574
Wroblewsky, Vincent von, 32015
Württemberg, 31456, 31576, 32247
Würzburger, Ernst, 31516
Würzner, Hans, 31647
Wüst, Wolfgang, 31405
Wunder, Heide, 31393
Wurm, Carsten, 32127

Yahav, Dan, 32062
Yaron, Kalman, 31964
Yiddish, 31428–31449, 32025, 32108, 32126, 32129, 32214, 32247
Young, James E., 31953, 31954
Youth Movement, 32030, 32031, 32054
Yovel, Yirmiyahu, 32080
Yugoslavia, Nazi Period, 31809
Yuval, Israel Jacob, 31399, 31427

Zabel, Hermann, 31763
Zachau, Reinhard K., 31647
'Zafon', 32133
Zaggia, Stefano, 31672
Zahnow, Gregor, 31811
Zarek, Otto, 32086
'(Die) Zeit', 31413, 31723, 31810, 31835, 31843, 31872, 31898, 31959, 32109, 32157, 32166, 32174, 32187, 32231, 32259, 32267, 32318, 32337, 32339, 32345, 32347, 32351, 32396, 32428, 32457
'Zeitgeschichte', 31607, 31700, 31793, 31848, 31885, 32394, 32395
'Zeitschrift f. d. Gesch. d. Oberrheins', 32386, 32393
'Zeitschrift d. Geschichtsvereins Mülheim a.d. Ruhr', 31541
'Zeitschrift f. Geschichtswissenschaft', 32153, 32299
'Zeitschrift f. Kirchengeschichte', 32368
'Zeitschrift f. Religions-und Geistesgeschichte', 31672, 32002, 32230, 32422, 32432, 32440
'Zeitschrift d. Vereins f. hess. Landeskunde', 31479
Zeitschriftenverzeichnis Judaica, 31695
Zelman, Leon, 32063

Zemon, Natalie, 31393
Zentrum f. Antisemitismusforschung, Berlin, 31685
Zerner, Ruth, 32385
Zerwanitzer, Bubi, 32063
Ziege, Eva-Maria, 32423
Ziegler, Monika, 31998
Zimmermann, Akiva, 32047
Zimmermann, Hans Dieter, 32214
Zimmermann, Harro, 32109
Zimmermann, Michael, 31739, 31856
'Zion', 31389, 31390, 31427, 31968
Zionism, 31525, 31605, 32045, 32052, 32054, 32056, 32057, 32060–32065, 32069, 32072, 32352
Zionism and Nazis, 31851, 32074
Zipes, Jack, 31918

Zirndorf, 31578
'Zmanim', 32060
Zöhren, Peter, 31570
Zöller, Sonja, 32424
Zofka, Zdenek, 31392
Zohn, Harry, 32119, 32315 (Festschrift)
Zonis, Mark, 31617
Zühlsdorff, Dieter, 32131
Zürich, 31387
Zürn, Gaby, 31504, 31506
Zumbini, Massimo Ferrari, 32425
Zunder, Rainer, 32234
Zunz, Leopold, 32008
Zvi, Shabtai, 31506
Zweig, Arnold, 32097, 32098, 32109
Zweig, Stefan, 32108, 32120, 32122, 32315–32317

List of Contributors

CARLEBACH, Elisheva, Ph.D., b. 1954 in New York. Formerly Director of the Center for Jewish Studies, Queens College, CUNY. Currently Associate Professor of History at Queens College. Author of *The Pursuit of Heresy* (^{2}1994).

CHANDLER, Andrew, Ph.D., b. 1965 in Nuneaton, England. Lecturer in Modern History, University of Birmingham. Author of i.a. 'The Church of England and the Obliteration Bombing of Germany in the Second World War', in *English Historical Review* (1993); 'Munich and Morality. The Bishops of the Church of England and Appeasement', in *Twentieth Century British History* (1994); 'The Death of Dietrich Bonhoeffer', in *Journal of Ecclesiastical History* (1994). (Contributor to Year Book XXXVIII.)

ELLENSON, David, Ph.D., b. 1947 in Brookline, MA. I.H. and Anna Grancell Professor of Jewish Religious Thought, Hebrew Union College/Jewish Institute of Religion, Los Angeles. Author of i.a. *Tradition in Transition. Orthodoxy, Halakha, and the Boundaries of Modern Jewish Identity* (1989); *Rabbi Esriel Hildesheimer and the Creation of a Modern Jewish Orthodoxy* (1990); *Between Tradition and Culture. The Dialectics of Modern Jewish Religion and Identity* (1994).

ENDELMAN, Todd M., Ph.D., b. 1946 in Fresno, CA. William Haber Professor of Modern Jewish History, University of Michigan. Author of i.a. *The Jews of Georgian England, 1714–1830. Tradition and Change in a Liberal Society* (1979); *Radical Assimilation in English Jewish History, 1656–1945* (1990). Editor of *Jewish Apostasy in the Modern World* (1987).

FABER, Irene, Dr., b. 1956 in Amstelveen. Formerly Assistant Curator for the exhibition "Jüdische Lebenswelten" in Berlin and at the Jewish Historical Museum, Amsterdam. Currently works as a freelance art historian. Author of 'Die Geschichte der Juden in den Niederlanden', in *Jüdische Lebenswelten. Katalog* (1991); co-author of 'Judaika deutscher Gold- und Silberschmiede', in *Kunst und Antiquitäten* (1993).

FEINER, Shmuel, Ph.D., b. 1955 in Tel Aviv. Lecturer in Modern Jewish History, Bar-Ilan University, Ramat-Gan. Co-ordinator of the Samuel Braun Chair for the History of the Jews in Prussia. Author of *Haskalah and History* (forthcoming, in Hebrew) as well as various articles on the *Haskalah* movement in eighteenth-century Germany and nineteenth-century Russia, including 'Isaac Euchel. "Entrepreneur" of the Haskalah Movement in Germany', in *Zion* (1987) (in Hebrew).

List of Contributors

Fox, John P., Ph.D., F.R.Hist.S., b. 1937 in London. Formerly British editor of *Akten zur deutschen auswärtigen Politik, 1918–1945*. Currently editor of *The British Journal of Holocaust Education*. Author of i.a. *Germany and the Far Eastern Crisis 1931–1938. A Study in Diplomacy and Ideology* (^{2}1985); 'Archive and Library Resources in England for Holocaust-Related Subjects. A Short Guide for Students', in *The British Journal of Holocaust Education* (1993); 'How Far Did Vichy France "Sabotage" the Imperatives of Wannsee?', in David Cesarani (ed.), *The Final Solution. Origins and Implementation* (1994). (Contributor to Year Book XXXVII.)

Hertz, Deborah, Ph.D., b. 1949 in St. Paul, MN. Associate Professor of History, State University of New York, Binghamton. Visiting Senior Lecturer, University of Haifa, 1993/1994. Author of i.a. *Jewish High Society in Old Regime Berlin* (1988); *Briefe an eine Freundin. Rahel Varnhagen an Rebecca Friedländer* (1988).

Herzog, Dagmar, Ph.D., b. 1961 in Durham, NC. Assistant Professor of European History at Michigan State University. Author of i.a. 'Liberalism, Religious Dissent and Women's Rights. Louise Dittmar's Writings from the 1840s', in Konrad Jarausch/Larry Jones (eds.), *In Search of a Liberal Germany. Studies in the History of German Liberalism from 1789 to the Present* (1990); 'Carl Scholl, Gustav Struve and the Problematics of Philosemitism in 1840s Germany. Radical Christian Dissent and the Reform Jewish Response', in *Jewish History* (forthcoming).

Levenson, Alan T., Ph.D., b. 1960 in New York. Assistant Professor of Jewish History at the Cleveland College of Jewish Studies. Author of various articles on modern Jewish history and thought, including 'German Zionism and Radical Assimilation Before 1914', in *Studies in Zionism* (1992); 'Theodor Herzl and Bertha von Suttner. Criticism, Collaboration and Utopianism', in *Journal of Israeli History* (1994); 'Joseph B. Soloveitchik's *The Halachic Mind*. A Liberal Critique and Appreciation', in *Journal of Reform Judaism* (1994).

Pätzold, Kurt, Ph.D., b. 1930 in Breslau. Formerly Professor of German History at the Humboldt University, Berlin. Author of various publications on the history of National Socialism, antisemitism and the persecution of the Jews 1933–1945; co-author of *Tagesordnung Judenmord. Die Wannsee-Konferenz am 20. Januar 1942* (1992); *"Auschwitz war für mich nur ein Bahnhof." Adolf Eichmanns Transportoffizier Franz Novak* (1994).

Paucker, Arnold, Dr.phil., b. 1921 in Berlin. Director of the Leo Baeck Institute, London. Editor of the Year Book of the Leo Baeck Institute 1970–1992. Author of i.a. *Der jüdische Abwehrkampf gegen Antisemitismus und Nationalsozialismus in den letzten Jahren der Weimarer Republik* (^{2}1969); and of many essays on historical and philological subjects. Co-editor and editor of eight symposium volumes and of other publications of the Leo Baeck Institute, i.a. *The Jews in Nazi Germany, 1933–1943* (1986). (Contributor to Year Books V, VIII, XI, XIII, XV, XVI, XIX, XX, XXXIII, XXXIV and XXXVII.)

List of Contributors

RAIM, Edith, Dr.phil., b. 1965 in Munich. Lecturer in German, University of Durham and part-time Lecturer in History, University of Liverpool. Author of i.a. *Die Dachauer KZ-Außenlager Kaufering und Mühldorf. Rüstungsbauten und Zwangsarbeit im letzten Kriegsjahr* (1992); *Augen haben und nicht sehen* (forthcoming).

SORKIN, David, Ph.D., b. 1953 in Chicago. Formerly Assistant Professor of Judaic Studies at Brown University and Fellow of St. Antony's College and the Oxford Centre for Hebrew and Jewish Studies. Currently Frances and Laurence Weinstein Professor of Jewish History and Thought, University of Wisconsin, Madison. Author of i.a. *The Transformation of German Jewry, 1780–1840* (1987); *Moses Mendelssohn. An Introduction to his Jewish Thought* (forthcoming); co-editor of *From East and West. Jews in a Changing Europe, 1750–1870* (1990). Member of the Board of the London LBI. (Contributor to Year Books XXXII, XXXV and XXXVII.)

STERN, Guy, Ph.D., b. 1922 in Hildesheim. Formerly Vice President of the University of Cincinnati and then of Wayne State University. Currently Distinguished Professor, Department of German and Slavic Studies at Wayne State University, Detroit. Author of i.a. *Alfred Neumann* (1979); *Literatur im Exil* (1989); *Nazi Book Burning and the American Response* (1991); *Echoes of Exile* (in progress); as well as numerous articles on eighteenth- to twentieth-century literature and exile authors. (Contributor to Year Books VI, XIX and XXXVII.)

VAN VOOLEN, Edward, Dr., b. 1948 in Utrecht. Formerly Guest Professor at Spertus College, Chicago and the University of Potsdam; Chief Academic Advisor for the exhibition "Jüdische Lebenswelten", Berlin. Currently Curator at the Jewish Historical Museum, Amsterdam. Co-author of *Synagogues in the Netherlands* (1988); *The Amsterdam Mahzor* (1989); co-editor of *Jüdische Lebenswelten. Essays* (1991); contributor to i.a. *Encyclopaedia Judaica Yearbook* (1989); *The Blackwell Companion to Jewish Culture* (1989); author of several articles on Judaica from the collection of the Jewish Historical Museum.

WEBER, Annette, Dr. phil., b. 1957 in Hamburg. Currently works as the Curator of Judaica at the Jewish Museum of Frankfurt a. Main and lectures on Jewish art at the Johann Wolfgang Goethe University in Frankfurt a. Main. Author of i.a. 'Rekonstruktion von Synagogenausstattungen des 18. Jahrhunderts anhand der Photosammlung Harburger', in *Artistic Exchange. Akten des Internationalen Kongresses für Kunstgeschichte* (1992); 'Splendid bridal gifts', in *Journal of Jewish Art* (1993/1994); 'Die Rothschilds als Kunstsammler', in *Die Rothschilds. Eine europäische Familie* (1994).

Abstracts of articles in this Year Book are included in *Historical Abstracts* and *America: History and Life*.

General Index to Year Book XL of the Leo Baeck Institute

Abwehrverein *see* Verein zur Abwehr des Antisemitismus
Academic Assistance Council, 234
Acculturation *see* Assimilation
Agriculture, Jews and, 159
AH (silversmith in Halle), 269–270
Aid to the Persecuted: children, 234; Church appeals for refugees, 230, 232, 234, 238–241, 243; in Germany, 14, 299, 311; Lord Baldwin's Appeal, 240, 241–242; protest meetings: Albert Hall, 241; Friends' Meeting House, 232; Liverpool, 239; Mansion House, 242; Queen's Hall, 236–237
[Deutsche] Akademie der Wissenschaften zu Berlin [der DDR]: [Zentral]institut für [deutsche] Geschichte, 292, 299, 301, 302n
Akademischer Verein für jüdische Geschichte und Literatur, 122n
Albert, Phyllis Cohen, 179n
Albia (fraternity), 109n
Alexander, Harold (British field-marshal), 45
Alexander, Leib (son-in-law of D. Grünhut), 79
Alfonsi, Petrus (medieval convert), 68
'Allgemeine Zeitung des Judenthums' (Leipzig), 206n
Allied forces, emigrants in, 18n; in British forces, 21–50; in post-WWII US Intelligence, 51–62; as secret agents, 35–46; in US armed forces, 51
Alonso (son of Paul of Burgos), 77
Alsatian Jewry, 155
Alsberg, Adolf (uncle of F. Rosenzweig), 111
Altdorfer, Paul (convert), 71n
Altmann, Alexander (rabbi, philosopher), 133–134, 140
Amann, Heinrich (Baden professor), 189
American Historical Association, 21n, 56
Amitai the Samaritan (maskil), 137n
Amsterdam Jewish community, 265–288; Ashkenazim, 80, 265, 266, 268n; Bibliotheca Rosenthaliana, 269; former converts in, 79–80; Hoofdsynagoge, 270; Jewish Historical Museum, 265–288; maskilim in, 143; Sephardim, 79, 265–266, 267, 268, 269
Andreasch, Otto Ernst "Monti" (Mischlingsliga leader), 19n
Antifaschistische Partei Österreichs, 18
Anti-Nazi propaganda, 5, 9, 13, 18, 19, 24n

Antisemitism, 5, 95, 104–105, 113, 116–117, 119, 120, 125; anti-assimilationist, 86, 89; anti-Zionism, 309–310; Baden, 198, 207; Bamberg, 85; Britain, 24, 237; Buß, 198; H. S. Chamberlain, 110; Czechoslovakia, 310; East Germans and, 293, 294–298, 299, 301, 302, 303–304, 305, 309–310, 311; Christian, 76, 197–198, 205; Darmstadt, 85; "deicide", 119; Frankfurt a. M., 84–85; Hep! Hep!, 84–85, 86, 95, 99, 102; Heidelberg, 85; Th.Th. Heine and, 212; and Herzl, 108–109; "international Jewry", 303; "Judensau", 78n; Karlsruhe, 85; and Koreff, 97, 98n; liberals, 185n, 205; Nazi indoctrination, 294–296, 299, 303–304; political parties, 104; racist, 100, 126–127; religious, 100; "ritual murder", 69n; Rosenzweig and, 110, 111n; "Semi-Gotha", 121; 'Simplicissimus', 212; Slánský trial, 310n; Spain, 15; on stage, 80n; students, 85–86, 90, 99–100; in Weimar Republic, 293. *See also* Nuremberg Laws, November Pogrom, Pogroms
Antisemitism, defence, 14, 121; Jewish, 182n
Anton, Karl (convert), 72, 77
Antwerp Jewish community, 266
Arabs, 310
Arnhem Jewish community, 272, 276, 280, 284, 285
Arnstein, Fanny [Franziska] von (Viennese salon hostess), 93
"Aryanisation", expropriation, 214, 217–224, 230, 299, 301, 303, 305, 306
Aryeh Loeb ben Saul (1690–1755) (Chief Rabbi of Groß-Glogau, later of Amsterdam), 266, 273
Ascher ben Eliezer Halevi [Ascher Levi] (Renaissance Alsatian memoirist), 66n
Ascher, Saul (author, translator), 136, 137, 145
Ashkenazim: in Amsterdam, 80; attitude to baptism, 78–79; community structure, 170; and Haskalah, 135
Assimilation, 86, 87, 105, 108, 110, 114, 120, 186; anti-assimilation, German, 86, 89; and Haskalah, 135, 136, 146, 172; radical assimilation, 106, 108, 115, 121n, 128. *See also* Conversion; women, 141
Athias, Joseph (publisher), 266n
Atkinson, W.P.T. (churchman), 243n

Attlee, Clement (British politician), 242
Auerbach, Abraham bar Isaak (scholar, Court Jew), 266
Auerbach, Berthold [Moses Baruch Auerbacher] (author), 177
August II (Elector of Saxony), 270
Augusti, Friedrich Albrecht [Joshua ben Abraham Herschel] (convert), 72
Auschwitz extermination camp, 39n, 47, 55, 295; in film and literature, 297–298; in history teaching, 301
Austria: Anschluß, 17, 227–229, 234; post-1945, 58
Austrian Freedom Battalion, 20n
Austrian Jewry: in Austrian Empire, 120, 148, 155, 156; emigrants, 18, 228; in British forces, 21–50 *passim*; under Nazi regime, 16–20, 227–231, 232, 238–239, 240, 241, 244–245
Auxiliary Military Pioneer Corps *see* Pioneer Corps
Avon, Earl of *see* Anthony Eden
Azulai family (majolica makers in Ancona), 287

Baal-Shem-Tov [Israel b. Eliezer] (founder of Hasidism), 136n, 138
Baden: liberals in, 185–208
Baden Jewry, 15, 176, 185–189, 193, 195, 196, 198, 202–208. *See also* Liberals (and Jews)
Baeck, Leo (rabbi, scholar, Reichsvertretung President), IX, 7, 8
Baeyer, Adolf von (teacher), 125
Balchin, Nigel, 34
Baldwin of Bewdley, Stanley (1st Earl, British politician), 240, 241
Bamberger, Ludwig (liberal politician), 177
Bankers, Jewish, 91, 93, 101, 145, 273
Bannister, Roger, 30n
Baptism *see* Conversion
BaRaN, Joseph (scholar, maskil), 142–143
BaRaZ, Simon (of Königsberg), 141, 162
Barber, Melanie, 225n
Barbican Mission to the Jews, 242
Barnes, Ernest William (Bishop of Birmingham, pacifist), 236
Barou, Noa (London representative of World Jewish Congress), 232n
Bartel, Walter (teacher), 291n
Bartholdy, Jacob Salomon (brother of L. Mendelssohn) 92n, 93, 94
Basedow, Johann Bernhard (educationalist), 158
Bass, Shabbetai (printer, rabbinic scholar), 252n, 261
Bassermann, Friedrich Daniel (liberal politician), 195n, 204
Bassewitz-Behr, von (war criminal), 48
Batty, Basil Staunton (Bishop of Fulham), 233, 244–245

Baum, Herbert (resistance leader), 9n, 11–12n; Baum Group, 9n, 11n, 12n, 17, 20n
Bavarian Jewry, 176. *See also* Th.Th. Heine
Bearsted, Walter Horace Samuel (2nd Viscount), 242
Becher, Johannes Robert (poet), 298, 301
Becker, Jurek (novelist), 297
Beckert, Johann [III] (silversmith), 269
Beer, Amalia (salon hostess, mother of G. Meyerbeer), 92
Beer, Michael (poet, dramatist), 95
Beer-Bing, Isaiah (of Metz), 157
Beggars, Jewish, 66
Bell, George Kennedy Allen (Bishop of Chichester), 227, 232, 234, 235, 238, 240, 241, 243, 244, 246
Belzec extermination camp, 301
Ben Ze'ev [Sew], Judah Loeb (Hebrew author, maskil), 142, 147
Bendavid, Lazarus (mathematician, headmaster, maskil), 136, 145, 146, 148, 166
Bendix, Gustav (father of Ludwig B.), 118
Bendix, Ludwig (jurist), 118
Bendt, Vera, 285
Bentwich, Norman (barrister, writer), 21n, 33, 230
Benz, Wolfgang, 12n
Berenstein family, 282
Berenstein, Berend Josua [Isachar Berish] (Hanover rabbi), 282
Berenstein, Isachar Beer [Berish Samuel] (Chief Rabbi, The Hague), 282
Berenstein, Levi Josua [Aryeh Loeb] (Hanover rabbi, fl. 1761–1789), 282
Berenstein, Rebecca Roesle (née Löwenstamm, wife of Samuel B. B.), 282
Berenstein, Samuel Berish (Chief Rabbi of Amsterdam), 266, 271, 281–282
Bergen-Belsen concentration camp, 46, 48
Bergthaler, Theo (writer), 115n
Berlin Jewish community, 21, 80n, 101, 133–167; Jüdische Freischule, 137, 142, 144; Reform in, 173, 259; Reformgenossenschaft, 119; seminaries, 174; synagogues, 173, 259. *See also* Rabbinerseminar, Salons
Berlin Universities, 97, 101, 102; Humboldt University, 291n, 293
'Berlinische Monatsschrift', 145, 162
'Berlinisches Archiv der Zeit und ihres Geschmacks', 145
Bernfeld, Simon (Berlin rabbi), 134–135
Bernstein family, 119–120
Bernstein, Eduard (Socialist politician), 110n, 119–120
Bertinoro, Obadiah (ancestor of K. Anton), 77n
Berting, Ernst August (writer), 77n
Bessmann, David (silversmith), 267, 268
Beyer, Helga (of resistance), 13
Beyl, Christian (silversmith), 272

Bible, 171: translations, 75–76, 144; M. Mendelssohn (Biur), 133, 139, 141, 151n, 154–155, 157, 161, 167, 180; Gedaliah Moshe, 141–142. *See also* Judaism (liturgy)
Bierfreund, Sigmund (silversmith), 278n
Biester, Johann Erich (associate of M. Mendelssohn), 152n
Biller, Albrecht (silversmith), 270
Bismarck, Otto Fürst von, Herzog von Lauenburg (German statesman), 109n, 121
Bitzel, Karl (silversmith), 280
Biur *see* Bible translations
Blach, Friedrich (author, assimilationist), 121n
Blake, Dora, 41n, 47n, 49n
Bleibtreu brothers (converts), 81
Blidstein, Gerald, 263
Bloch, Chaim (Vienna rabbi), 244
Bloch, Marcus Eliezer (physician), 145, 167
Block, Peter A., 33n, 38n, 42n, 49n
Blumenfeld, Kurt (Zionist leader), 117, 119
Board of Deputies of British Jews, 231, 241
Börne, Ludwig [Lob Baruch] (author, critic, "Young Germany" leader), 177
Boller, Johann Adam (silversmith), 271, 272
Bond, Robert (Moderator of the Free Churches), 241, 246
Bonn University, 98
Booth, Evangeline (Salvation Army general), 242
Borcke, Johann Friedrich Wilhelm (silversmith), 280–281
Bordeaux Jewish community, 266
Bormann, Martin (Nazi leader), 55
Borochov-Jugend, 5, 10n, 17
Bowes, Eric F. [Erich Franz Bauer], 39n, 40n
Boycotts: anti-Jewish, 225, 301; anti-Nazi, 246
Braham, John (singer), 127
Brahmfeld, Hans Hinrich (silversmith), 275, 276
Brandenburg (Nazi prison), 291n, 295
Braunstein, Susan L., 280
Brazilian Jewry, 266
Brecht, Bertolt (poet, playwright), 52
Brentano, Lorenz Peter (liberal, emancipationist), 204, 205
Breslau Jewish community, 173, 272; Gesellschaft der Brüder, 144; maskilim in, 142, 143, 144, 164; printing houses, 147; Rabbinical Seminary, 173
Breslau, Menahem Mendel (teacher, editor, maskil), 142
Breuer, Mordechai, 166, 175n
Breuer, William B., 52
Brill, Elhanan (maskil), 144n
Brill-Loewe, Joel (teacher, editor, maskil), 133, 137, 139, 141, 144n, 147, 149, 156, 166, 172
Britain, emigrants to: in Armed Forces, 21–50; Communist, 295; deportation to Commonwealth, 29, 30; "enemy aliens", 2, 25, 26, 33n, 40, 45, 49; internment, 29, 30, 31, 39; Isle of Man, 29; naturalisation, 22, 24–25, 30, 33, 48–50; return to Germany, 23, 27, 49
Britain, Jews in, 170, 175; Anglo-Jewish Exhibition (1887), 287n
British Empire, emigrants to, 235
British Jews' Society, 227
Brody Jewish community, 164
Brothers, Eric, 11n, 20n
Bruchsal Jewish community, 65, 73
Brunswick Jewish community, 164
Bry, Gerhard, 5n
Buber, Martin (philosopher), 178
Buccleugh and Queensberry, Walter John Montagu-Douglas-Scott (8th/10th Duke of), 235–236
Buchegger, Ludwig (writer), 191–192
Buchenwald concentration camp, 291n, 295, 312
Buck, Samuel (British sergeant), 36n
Buhmann, Walter (lawyer for Heine family), 221
Bund deutsch-jüdischer Jugend, 13
Bundesministerium des Innern, XI
Burgenland Jewry, 230, 231
Burschenschaften, 211
Buß, Franz Josef (professor, Catholic publicist), 190, 196, 198, 200, 201, 202, 206
Buxtorf, Johannes [sr] (Hebraist), 83n
Byzantium Jewish community, 266

Callenberg, Johann Heinrich (philosopher), 80, 83
Calmann, Marianne, 81n
Cantors, 73
Capitalism, 305–306, 307–308
Carben, Victor von (convert), 66n, 72n
Caricature *see* Th.Th. Heine
Carlebach, Elisheva, 123, 126–127, 129
Carlebach, Julius, 89n, 184n
Carpzov, Johann Benedict (editor), 65n
Carpzov, Johann Gottlob (defended Hebrew Bible), 76n
Casanova de Seingalt, Giovanni Giacomo (adventurer), 217
Caspari, Otto (assimilationist), 121
Cassel Jewish community, 143, 144, 164, 283
Castorph, Ludwig (pamphleteer), 196
Cave Brown, Anthony, 57
CB (silversmith) *see* K. Bitzel
Cecil of Chelwood, [Edgar Algernon] Robert Gascoyne (Viscount), 229
Celle Jewish community, 274–276
Centralverein deutscher Staatsbürger jüdischen Glaubens, XII, 111, 118, 122, 177, 183
Centrum Judaicum, Berlin, 309
Ceremonial art, 265–288
Cerfbeer, Herz Medelsheim (Alsatian Jewish politician), 155

General Index

Chajes, Zevi Hirsch (Zolkiew rabbi), 259
Chamberlain, [Arthur] Neville (British politician), 25, 228
Chamberlain, Houston Stewart (racist author), 110
Chelmno [Kulmhof] extermination camp, 301
Child immigrants, 47, 234, 235; Kindertransporte, 28
Chmelnicki, Bogdan (Ukrainian Cossack leader), 266
Chorin, Aaron (Hungarian rabbi), 253–254, 263
Christ, Anton (emancipationist), 204, 206
Christfells, Phillip (convert), 73
Christian Council for Refugees from Germany and Central Europe, 238
Christian, Phillip Heinrich [Solomon David] (convert), 68n
"Christian state", 104, 187, 188, 201, 204, 206
Christiani, Friedrich Albert [Baruch ben Moses] (Hebraist, convert), 65–83, 123; reversion to Judaism, 74, 78, 79, 80
Christians: and Austrian Anschluß, 228; Catholics, 185–208, 235; Catholic dissenters *see* Deutschkatholiken; Catholic-Protestant intermarriage, 185, 190–193, 194, 198, 205, 207; conservative Catholics, 185, 190, 191–193, 194, 196–207; inter-Christian conflict, 185, 189, 207; Jesuits, 159, 202; under Nazi regime, 228–229, 238; Protestants, 71n, 79, 185–186, 192, 196, 202. *See also* Church of England
Christians and Jews, X; Christian Hebraists, 75–76; Catholics *see* Emancipation; Christmas, 110; convert clergy, 126; converts' defence of Jews, 75–76; Jewish image, 156; Protestants, 173; refutations of Christianity, 80; social relations, 165. *See also* Aid to the Persecuted
Christlieb, Carl Hector [Samuel Lazarus] (convert), 67n
Christlieb, Wilhelm Christian [Lazarus Wolf] (convert), 67n
Chudzikiewicz, [Count] L.F. Chodkiewicz, 92n
Chumaceiro, Josef Mendes (chasan in Amsterdam), 269
Church Mission to the Jews, 227
Church of England, 225–247; Anglican Church Assembly, 232, 234, 238, 240; Bishop of Chichester's Committee, 234; Central Board of Finance, 240; Archbishop's Council on Foreign Relations, 235, 243. *See also* Aid to the Persecuted
'Church Times', 226, 230, 233–234
Churchill [Sansom], Odette (British agent), 48
Churchill, Winston Spencer (British statesman), 40
Chuz, George (lighting engineer, of US Intelligence), 53

Civil servants, German, 7, 54, 173
Clark, Mark (US general), 59
Clay, Lucius Dubignon (US Military Governor for Germany), 54, 60–61, 62
Cohen family (majolica makers in Pesaro), 287
Cohen, Aaron (Birmingham rabbi), 233
Cohen, Abraham Herz (son of Herz L. Cohen), 275
Cohen, Emil (German Zionist), 111
Cohen, Gershon Moses (father of K. Anton), 77n
Cohen, Hermann (philosopher), 177, 178
Cohen, Herz Leffman (Court Jew), 275
Cohen, Phyllis, 175n
Cohen, Tobias (physician), 172
Cohn, Bertha (bibliographer), X
Communism, Communists, 4, 5, 8–10, 11, 13, 16n, 225; anti-Communism, 295; and anti-Zionism, 8, 9; in Austria, 17, 18, 19; in Spain, 18n
Community structure, 114, 166, 170, 175
Concentration camps, 11, 13, 225, 239, 291, 295, 296, 300, 301. *See also* Persecution *and* individual camps
Conservatives: conservative Catholics, 185, 190, 191–193, 194, 196–207; and Jews, 7–8, 196, 197–198; National Conservatives, 6. *See also* Resistance (Right-wing)
Constans, Friedrich August (convert), 74n
Conversion, 65–83, 85–106, 107–122, 123–129; in Berlin, 80n, 84–105; biographical narratives, 65–78, 115; to Catholicism, 93; child baptism, 94, 95, 108, 111, 112–113, 117; East European Jews, 83; in England, 127; forced, 69n, 78–79; in Italy, 123; Jewish attitudes to, 80–82, 107, 112–113, 117, 118–119n, 121n, 127; Judenkartei, 89; mass baptism, 244–245; missionaries, 77, 79, 81, 82–83, 89, 115n, 124; in Poland, 123; prevention, 80n; to Protestantism, 93, 95, 97, 99, 100–101; refusal to convert, 110, 112, 113, 114, 115, 117, 118, 125; reversion, 69n, 74, 79–81; statistics, 107n, 128–129; Taufgeschenk, 81; women, 66n, 67n, 71, 87–88
Conway, John, 225n
Copenhagen Jewish community, 142, 143
Corbach, Dieter (writer), 12n
Corinth, Lovis (painter), 214n
Council of Christians and Jews, 246
Council of Four Lands, 170
Counter Intelligence Corps (CIC) (US organisation), 55
Court Jews, 66, 272, 275
Cranz, August Friedrich (writer), 155
Crewe, Robert Offley A. Crewe-Milnes (1st Marquess), 229
Crusaders and Jews, 78–79
'C.V. Zeitung', 113
Czech Protestant Churches Refugee Fund, 236

Czechoslovakia: emigrants from, 25, 235, 240; emigrants to, 216–217
Czechoslovakian Jewry, 235, 236, 242, 245. *See also* Prague

da Costa, Isaak (convert, of Amsterdam), 77
Dachau (post-1945 detention camp), 57
Dachau concentration camp, 214
'Daily Mirror', 229
Dale, Stephen, 21n, 24n, 34n, 38n, 47n
Danish Jewry, 142, 159, 162
Danzig Jewish community, 285
Dark, Sidney (editor), 226–227
David family (Hanover), 147
David, Albert Augustus (Bishop of Liverpool), 239, 240
Davidson, C.E. (of Barbican Mission), 242
Dawson of Penn, Bertrand Edward (1st Viscount, physician), 242
Deedes, [Sir] Wyndham (promoted refugee aid), 234–235, 240
Dehmel, Richard (poet, playwright), 121
Deicker, Günther (poet), 298
Deportation, 12, 13, 14, 15, 49, 297
Dessau Jewish community, 143, 144
Dessau, Wolf (maskil), 147, 156n
Deutsche Bank, 306n
Deutsche Film AG (DEFA), 297–298
Deutschkatholiken (dissident Catholics), 192–193, 194–203, 205n, 207
Dießen: Königlich Priviligierte Feuerschützengesellschaft, 217–220; local Nazi officials, 217–219, 220, 221, 222, 224
Dietz Verlag, 295
Dimitrov, Georgi (Bulgarian politician), 306
Dinaburg [Dinur], Ben Zion (Israeli historian), 149
Dipper, Christof, 8n
Disabilities, Jewish, 173, 186; right of residence, 147, 272, 274, 275; of goldsmiths, 266, 274; Schutzjuden, 275
Displaced Persons (DPs), 39n
Disraeli, Benjamin [Earl of Beaconsfield] (British statesman), 127
Dohle, Horst (historian), 293
Dohm, Christian Wilhelm von (Prussian civil servant, archivist), 121, 155, 158, 160, 163, 172, 179, 180
Dokumentationsarchiv des österreichischen Widerstandes (DÖW), 16
Don, Alan (chaplain), 229, 230, 231, 232, 234, 236, 237–238, 240, 241–242, 243, 244, 245
Donovan, William J. "Wild Bill" (US General, founder of OSS), 52, 55n, 57
Dov Baer [Maggid of Mezritch] (hasidic leader), 138
Draper, Gerald (of Judge Advocate General's Branch), 47
Dresden Jewish community, 155, 164

Dresdner Bank, 306n
Dreyfus Affair, 108n, 109
Drobisch, Klaus, 292, 293
Drucker, Ernest (CIC agent), 55
Druyanov, Avraham Alter (compiler of Jewish folk wit), 124, 128
Dubno, Salomon (teacher, maskil), 133, 139, 157
Dubnow, Simon (historian), 134
Duelling, 108
"Dunera" (ship), 30n
Dupré, Johannes Elias (writer), 68n

EAM (National Liberation Front, Greek Communist Resistance organisation), 42
East European Jewry, 7, 83, 105, 109; and Haskalah, 133n, 135, 157, 161, 166, 167. *See also* Polish Jewry
EB (silversmith), 281
Eden, Anthony [Earl of Avon] (British statesman), 25n, 28
Education, Jewish, 70–72, 73, 179–180, 188; in Galicia, 133; Haskalah and, 148–149, 151, 154–156, 158, 160, 162, 165, 172, 179; literacy, 181; of women, 71–72
Edzard, Esdras (Pietist missionary), 82–83, 126
Egmont, Earl of *see* Perceval
Ehe, Johann Friedrich (silversmith), 278
Ehrenberg family, 110
Ehrenberg, Hans ("non-Aryan" pastor, cousin of F. Rosenzweig), 110n, 111, 112n
Eibenschütz [Eybeschuetz], Jonathan (Altona Chief Rabbi, kabbalist), 72
Eichmann, [Karl] Adolf (Nazi war criminal), 297, 300
Einsatzgruppen, 48, 300
ELAS *see* EAM
Elbaum, Jacob, 171n
Elbe, Joachim von, 57
Eliav, Mordechai, 179n
Elijah ben Solomon Zalman (the Vilna Gaon), 138
Elisha ben Avuyah (Tanna, heretic), 254
Elliott, Thompson (clergyman), 239
Emancipation, 90, 102, 172–173, 174, 176, 179, 185–208; and Haskalah, 135, 146; liberals and, 185, 186–189, 193–195, 203–207
Emden, Jacob Israel (Altona rabbi, talmudist), 66n
[L']Encyclopédie, 140n
Endelman, Todd, 69, 85n
Engelmann, Leo (of Kampfgruppe Steiermark), 20n
Enlightenment (Aufklärung), 87, 114, 134, 140, 155, 158, 161–164, 166, 172, 186, 189; in France, 143n
Ensheim [Metz], Moses (mathematician, tutor, Hebrew author), 147
Ensheim Jewish community, 69n
Ephraim family, 150

Ephraim, [Nathan] Veitel Heine (court banker, communal elder), 143, 147, 149
Ephraim, Benjamin Veitel (businessman, son of [N.] Veitel H. E.), 149–150
Epp, Samuel (rabbi in Burgenland), 230
Epstein, Baruch Halevi (rabbi, critic of Mendelssohn), 136n
Erlangen University, 99, 100
Erpel, Simone, 12n
Erzberger, Matthias (Zentrum politician, minister), 121n
Eschwege, Helmut (historian), 3n, 292–293, 311
Ettlinger, Jakob (Altona rabbi, Judaist), 175
Euchel, Gottlob (proposed Copenhagen school, maskil), 142n, 144n
Euchel, Isaac Abraham (teacher, editor, maskil), 133, 137, 139, 140–141, 142, 144, 145, 147, 148, 149, 150, 155, 156, 160, 161, 162–164, 165, 166, 172
Eulenberg, Herbert (playwright), 120
"Euthanasia", 307
Evangelischer Oberkirchenrat, 100
Evangelisches Zentralarchiv, 88n
Evans, Arthur (British MP, officer), 28
Evelyn, F.A. (chaplain in Vienna), 245
"Exodus" (ship), 59

Fauth, Franz Burckhard (anti-emancipationist), 203–204
[E.] Feinberg Collection, Detroit, 286, 287
Feiner, Shmuel, 138n, 149n
Fichte, Johann Gottlieb (philosopher), 86
Fleck, Christian, 20n
Fleckeles, Eleazar (Prague rabbi), 255
Floss Jewish community, 115–116
Foerg, Irmgard, X
Forell (pastor, associate of K.J. Hirsch), 115
Fortuna tobacco factory, 275
Fraenkel, David (Dessau rabbi, teacher), 172
France: emigrants to, 98, 103; French Jewry, 170, 171, 173, 175, 179n
Franck, Joachim Christian (convert), 69n
Frankel, Zacharias (religious leader), 173, 175, 259
Frankfort, Jakob ben Moses & Reische bat Elias Spier (paper-seller and wife, of Arnhem), 284–285
Frankfurt a. d. Oder Jewish community: maskilim in, 143
Frankfurt a. Main Jewish community, 79, 81n, 143, 173, 176, 271; Jewish museum, 265, 285
'Frankfurter Journal', 197
Freiburg University, 189, 192
Freie Deutsch-Jüdische Jugend, 13
Freie Deutsche Bewegung, 295
Freimark, Peter, 184n
Freud, A.W., 22n, 28n, 43–45, 47
Freud, Sigmund (founder of psychoanalysis), 33
Freudenthal, Max (historian), 137n

[Emil] Freund (metal and silverware factory), 286n
Frey, Joseph Samuel C.F. (convert, founded London Society), 69n, 71–72, 83n
Frick, Wilhelm (Nazi minister), 54, 55
Fried, John H.E. (of US Nuremberg prosecution team), 55
Friedberg Jewish community, 283
Friedenthal, Aaron Zechariah (educationalist), 133, 139, 147
Friedländer family (Königsberg), 147
Friedländer, Abraham ben David (maskil), 144n
Friedländer, Bunem (maskil), 144n
Friedländer, David (Berlin manufacturer, Jewish reformer), 114, 133, 135, 136, 137–138, 139, 141, 143–156 passim, 164–166, 172
Friedländer, Joachim Moses (father of David F.), 137n
Friedländer, Joseph Abraham (maskil), 144n
Friedländer, Michal (physician), 145
Friedländer, Moses (maskil), 144n
Friedländer, Rebecca (sister L. Mendelssohn), 92n
Friedlander, Albert H., 7n
Friedrich II (Frederick the Great, King of Prussia), 154
Friedrich Wilhelm III (King of Prussia), 98, 102
Friedrichsfeld, David (maskil), 143, 147
Friends' Emergency Committee for Jews and non-Jews, 234
Fries, Jakob Friedrich (historian, antisemite), 86
Front national pour la Libération, 18
Fuenn, Shmuel Yosef (Russian maskil), 151n
Fürnberg, Friedl (of Kampfgruppe Steiermark), 20n
Fürst, Moses (brother-in-law of M. Mendelssohn), 139n
Fürth Jewish community, 73, 143
Furman Collection, 280

Gaddis, John, 53
Galician Jewry, 133, 144
Gallico, Joseph (correspondent M. Mendelssohn), 156n
Gans family, 274–276
Gans, Abraham (banker, father of Eduard G.), 101, 102
Gans, Angie von, 275
Gans, Eduard (Berlin jurist, philosopher, convert), 87, 92, 101–104, 177, 275; professorship, 101, 102, 103
Gans, Isaac Jacob (Court Jew), 101, 274–276
Gans, Jacob (son of Salomon G.), 275
Gans, Madel (wife of Abraham H. Cohen), 275
Gans, Salomon (Schutzjude in Celle), 275
Ganser, Wilhelm Hubert (writer), 195n
Garbett, Cyril Forster (Archbishop of York), 229–230
Garibaldi Brigade, 15, 16n

General Index

'Gartenlaube', 216
Gay, Peter, 134
Gebhardt (local Nazi leader), 217-218, 220
Geiger, Abraham (religious philosopher), 175, 259
Gelehrtes Kaffeehaus (club), 152
Gemeinschaft für Frieden und Aufbau, 20n
Gerlach, Jens (poet), 298
German Democratic Republic, 4; Deutsches Wirtschaftsinstitut, 295; Historikergesellschaft, 291; historiography in, XI, 291-312; history teaching in, 298, 300-302, 304; and Israel, 310; Rat für Geschichtswissenschaft, 291. *See also* Akademie der Wissenschaften
German Jewry, IX-XII, 266; community structure, 170, 175; post-1945, X, XII, 310; and Reform, 169-184. *See also* Haskalah; *and see* Allied Forces, Ceremonial art, Conversion, Emancipation, Historiography, National-Socialist Regime, Reform Judaism, Persecution, Resistance; *and* Baden, Berlin *and other regions and towns*
German language, 161; Jews and, 146, 147, 173, 174n, 180-181, 188, 260n; "LTI", 294
Germany, after 1945, 45-48; Control Council, 57; de-Nazification, 42, 58, 59, 61; former Nazis in, 305; occupied Germany, 51-62; Office of Military Government for Germany (US) (OMGUS), 57, 60; re-education, 34n, 35, 36, 60, 61, 294, 297; repeal of Nazi legislation, 57; Soviet occupation, 293; US Intelligence in, 51-62
Gerson, Christian (convert), 77
Gesellschaft der Freunde, 143n, 145
Gesellschaft der jungen Hebräer, 145
Gestapo, 11, 13, 14, 18, 20n, 38, 42, 43, 48, 223
Getzler, Israel, 5n
Ghettos, 136, 266; resistance in, 16, 23
Gilbert, Felix, 56-57, 59
Gillon, Meir, 148n
Ginsburg, Ernst (Berlin convert), 115
Ginzel, Günther Bernd, 11n
Giustizia e Libertà, 5n, 15, 16n
Glasneck, Johannes, 310n
Glaubtreu, Christian [Michael David] (convert, reverted to Judaism), 80
Gleiss, Carl Wilhelm (writer), 83n
Globocnik, Odilo (SS- und Polizeiführer Distrikt Lublin), 45
Glogau Jewish Community, 164, 266, 272, 273-274
Glückel von Hameln (memoirist), 66n, 75, 81
Gluckstein, Louis (British Jewish leader), 231
Gobineau, Joseph-Arthur, comte de (orientalist, racist), 110n
Goerdeler, Carl (politician, in resistance), 7, 8n
Görden (Nazi prison), 295
Goethe, Johann Wolfgang von (poet), 110n, 212
Goguel, Rudi (historian), 292, 293, 309

Gold- and silversmiths, Jewish, 266, 274
Goldberg, Jacob, 67n
Goldscheider, Calvin, 173n
Goldsmith, Herbert, 27-28, 31, 33, 35
Goldstein, Moritz (writer), 120n, 121
Gompertz family, 266
Gooch (of World's Evangelical Alliance), 236-237n
Göring, Hermann (Nazi leader), 55
Gossweiler, Kurt, 302n
Gottfried, Johann Adam J.A.C.K. [Nathan] (convert), 73-74
Gottfried, Johann Christoph (convert), 68n, 72, 77
Gottlober, Abraham Bär (Russian maskil), 138, 151n
Graetz, Heinrich (historian), 135, 136, 143n, 175
Graham-Stamper, [Miss] (of SOE), 37
Graml, Hermann, 25n
Gratius, Ortwin (translator), 66n
Grattenauer, Karl Wilhelm Friedrich (antisemitic author), 86n, 87n, 100
Grau, Wilhelm (Nazi writer), 96n
Greek Jewry, 297
Grenville, John, 225n
Grey, Charles Robert (5th Earl), 240, 241, 243
Grigg, James (British minister), 32
Grimes, C.H.D. (chaplain in Vienna), 245
Groehler, Olaf, 392n
Groningen Jewish community, 271
Groß-Glogau *see* Glogau
Grossmann, Rudolf (artist), 214, 215n, 216
Grüneberg, Hans, 25n, 27n, 30n, 31n, 34-35n
Grünhut, David (rabbi), 79
Grynszpan, Herschel (vom Rath's assassin), 222, 237
'[The] Guardian' (Anglican weekly), 239
Gugenheim, Joseph (brother-in-law of M. Mendelssohn), 139n
Guilds, 266
Gulbransson, Olaf (Norwegian cartoonist), 214, 215
Gumpertz, Aaron Salomon Emmerich, (physician, scholar), 172
Gunkel, Hermann (Biblical scholar), 121
[Gebrüder] Gutgesell (silverware firm), 286, 287-288
Gutteridge, Richard, 225n
Gutwein, Franz Anton (silversmith), 279-280
Gypsies, 307

[Den] Haag Jewish community, 282
Haas, Jacob de (correspondent of Herzl), 110n
Habe, Hans (author), 54n
Haber, Fritz (chemist), 116
Ha-Cohen, Shalom (writer), 164
Halle Jewish community, 77, 113, 270
Halle University, 96

General Index

Hamburg Jewish community, 73, 266, 276, 277; maskilim in, 142, 143; Rabbinic Court, 251, 255; Reform Temple, 173, 174, 176, 251, 255
Hamburger, Ernest (political scientist), 6n
'Hame'asef', 133, 137, 140, 141, 142, 143, 144, 147n, 154, 155, 156, 157, 161–162, 164, 166
Hammond, H. (clergyman), 233
Hang, Conrad Jacob (convert, reverted to Judaism), 79
Hannover, David (commentator, maskil), 141
Hanover Jewish community, 141, 143, 271, 281–282
Harden, Maximilian (journalist, editor), 116
Hardenberg, Karl August Fürst von (Prussian statesman), 96, 97–98, 102
Harnack, Adolf von (Protestant theologian), 114
Hashomer Hazair, 5, 11n, 17
Hasidism, 134
Haskalah (Jewish Enlightenment), 71, 123, 133–167, 169, 171–172, 179, 180; "conspiracy", 136. *See also* Maskilim
Hass, Gerhart, 300n
Hebrew language, 70, 71, 72, 75, 110, 133, 139, 140, 142, 146, 147, 151, 162, 167, 171; literature, 140, 146, 164; translation into, 153, 154, 157, 164. *See also* Hevrat Doreshei Leshon 'Ever, Jüdisch-deutsch, Publishing
Hebrew Union College, Cincinnati: Klau Library, 65n
Hecker, Friedrich (Baden liberal, anti-emancipation, revolutionary), 186, 195, 202, 203, 204
Hegel, Georg Wilhelm Friedrich (philosopher), Hegelianism, 101, 102, 112n, 114
Heilwort, Johannes Zacharias (convert), 79
Heine family, 211–224
Heine, Heinrich (poet), 92, 103, 127, 128, 177
Heine, Johanna (daughter of Th.Th. H.), 211, 216, 217, 220, 222–224
Heine, Magdalena (wife of Th.Th. H.), 211, 216, 217, 220–221, 222, 223, 224
Heine, Thomas Theodor (artist, caricaturist), 211–224
Heins, Valentin (lawyer for Heine family), 221, 223
Heise, Wolfgang (philosopher), 304
[Den] Helder Jewish community, 282–283
Heller, Yomtov Lipman (Chief Rabbi of Prague), 66n, 73n, 77n
Hennings (correspondent of M. Mendelssohn), 161n
Henson, Herbert Hensley (Bishop of Durham), 226, 227, 239
Herf, Jeffrey, 9n
Herfurth, Röttger (silversmith), 271
Hermannus quondam Judaeus (medieval convert), 67
Hermlin, Stephan, 298
Hertz, Deborah, 107n, 123, 124, 125, 128, 129, 145

Hertz, Joseph Herman (British Chief Rabbi), 231–232, 233
Hertz, Lorraine Blumenfeld, 85n
Herz Beer family, 92
Herz, Henriette (salon hostess, wife of Marcus H.), 133, 150, 177
Herz, John (interpreter, investigator), 55, 58
Herz, Marcus (physician, philosopher), 133, 139–140, 145, 150, 151, 158, 167, 177
Herzl, Hans (son of Theodor H.), 108
Herzl, Theodor (founder of Zionist movement), 113, 114; and antisemitism, 108–109; and conversion, 108–110, 111, 112, 122
Herzog, Chaim (President of Israel), 15
Hess, Moses (Socialist, Zionist writer), 177
Hess, Rudolf (Nazi leader), 34
Heuss, Theodor (President, Federal Republic of Germany), 59
Hevrat Doreshei Leshon 'Ever (Society for the Promotion of the Hebrew Language), 140, 141, 142, 143, 144, 146, 152, 156, 162
Hevrat Hinuch Ne'arim (Society for Youth Education), 137, 141, 144, 148, 154, 162n
Hevrat Mazdike HaRabim (Society of Righteousness to the Many), 144, 154, 156n
Hevrat Oharei Lashon Ivrit (Society of Lovers of the Hebrew language), 164
Hevrat Shoharei Hatov Vehatushia (Society for the Propagation of Goodness and Virtue), 140n, 141–142, 143n, 144, 154, 162
Heydrich, Reinhard (Nazi leader), 48
Heymann, Felix (of Baum Group), 9n
Heymann, Stefan (journalist, author), 295–297, 304
Heyse, Julie (sister L. Mendelssohn), 92
Hilberg, Raul, 4n
Hildesheimer, Esriel (leader of Orthodoxy), 175, 259, 262
Hildesheimer, Meir, 136n
Himmler, Heinrich (Nazi leader), 47
Hindenburg, Paul von (fieldmarshal, German President), 216
Hinsley, Arthur (Cardinal), 230, 237, 241, 242, 246
Hirsch, Karl Jakob (painter, convert), 111, 115
Hirsch, Paul Wilhelm (writer), 80n
Hirsch, Samson Raphael (rabbi, leader of Orthodoxy), 166, 175, 176, 259
Hirschel, Benedikt (privileged Jew), 272
Hirschel, Philipp Lazarus (Court Jew), 272
Hirscher, Johann Baptist (conservative professor), 192
Hirschlein, Christian Gottlieb (convert), 74n
Historiography, 3–5, 10–11, 13n, 104, 291–312; German-Jewish, XII, 3–5, 119n; in GDR, XI, 291–312; Historikerstreit, 308; local history, 303; M. Mendelssohn and, 161; school-teaching, 298, 300–302, 304; Sonderweg interpretation, 104–105, 123; Soviet his-

torians, 300n; Stuttgart International Historians' Congress, 312
Hitler, Adolf, 25, 26, 29, 44, 54, 55, 214n, 218, 226, 227, 229, 235, 236, 237, 246, 293, 296, 307, 309; Machtergreifung, 212, 213, 224, 225; "Mein Kampf", 236; resistance against, 7, 10
Hitler-Stalin Pact, 9, 13
Hitzig see Itzig
Hoare, [Sir] Samuel (British politician), 228, 230, 231
Höffler, Johann (silversmith), 278n
Höss, Rudolf (Auschwitz commandant), 47
Hoffmann, David Zvi (Professor, head of Rabbinerseminar Berlin), 251–252, 260–263
Holzer, Charlotte (née Abraham, of Baum Group), 9n
Holzer, Richard (of Baum Group), 9n
Homberg, Naphtali Herz (educationalist), 133, 139, 142, 144, 147, 149, 152
Homosexuals, 307
Honecker, Erich (East German leader), 310, 312
Honigmann, Peter, 107n
Honner [Hunner], Franz (of Kampfgruppe Steiermark), 20n
Horn, Otto Franz Max (Austrian anti-Fascist), 19n
Horovitz, Markus (Frankfurt a. Main rabbi), 262–263
Hosmann, Sigismund, 78n
Howes, Justin, 212n
HS (silversmith), 277
Huebner, Carl Friedrich (gold- and silversmith), 279
Humboldt, Karoline von (née von Dacheröden, wife of Wilhelm v. H.), 97
Humboldt, Wilhelm Frhr. von (Prussian statesman), 92, 96, 97
Hume, David (philosopher), 150
Hungarian Jewry, 300
Hurwitz, Jehuda (Vilna physician), 133n
Hutchinson (secretary to Sir S. Hoare), 231
Hyman, Paula E., 175n

I.G. Farben, 275, 306n
Iberian Jewry, 127, 265–266; Marranos, 79, 82; Conversos, 77. See also Sephardim, Portuguese Jewry
Innitzer, Theodor (Austrian Cardinal), 228, 244
Institut für Militärgeschichte der DDR, 292n, 299
Institutum Judaicum, Halle, 83
Inter-Aid Committee for Children from Germany, 234, 235
Intermarriage, 19, 87, 105, 107, 115, 120, 205; "privileged mixed marriage", 294; as solution to "Jewish Question", 109, 120–121, 125. See also Christians
International Brigades, 15, 16n, 17

International Military Tribunal see War Crimes Trials (Nuremberg Trials)
Irgun, 62n
Isaac min Halevi'im (Italian-Jewish writer), 66n
Isaac, Johannes (convert), 76
Isaac, Stephan (son of Johannes I.), 76n
Israelitische Religionsgesellschaft, 176
Isserles, Moses (Talmudic scholar), 253
Italy: emigrants to, 15–16; Italian Jewry, 155, 266
Itzig, Daniel (banker), 91, 93, 95, 143, 154, 156
Itzig, Ephraim (Berlin community leader), 154
Itzig, Isaac Daniel (banker), 144, 156
Itzig, Julius Eduard (publisher, convert), 93, 94
Itzstein, Adam von (liberal, anti-emancipation), 186

Jablonski, Daniel Ernst (Court preacher, orientalist), 80n
Jackson, Robert H. (Chief US Prosecutor, Nuremberg), 54
Jacob ben Israel (of Tarchdorf), 277
Jacobs, Karl Heinz (poet), 298
Jacobson, Isaac Jacob (Talmud Torah administrator), 269
Jacobson, Jacob Meyer (banker), 269
James, William (philosopher of religion), 107, 108n, 109
Jawitz, Zeev (Orthodox historian), 136n
Jensen, Angelika, 17n
Jerocham (wife of Jacob ben Israel), 277
Jewish Agency: Emigration Department, 244
Jewish Christian Union, 243
Joel, Isaac (physician, maskil), 133, 139
Jofen, Jean, 68n
John, Theodore (convert), 67n
Jokes, Jewish, 124, 128
Jolson family, 100
Jones, Griffiths (president, Free Church Council), 230
Joresch, Aaron Meyer (banker), 147
Josel of Rosheim (German communal leader), 66n, 69n, 79
Joseph II (Emperor of Austria), 148, 155, 159, 160, 165, 171, 172, 179; Toleranzpatent, 155, 160, 172
Jost, Isaak Markus (historian, editor), 206n
Journalists, Jewish, 14
'Judaica' (missionary journal), 115n
Judaism: burials, 145, 184n; ceremonial art, 265–288; dietary laws, 32; Einheitsgemeinden, 260; Eruv, 184n; Liberal, 105; liturgical language, 173, 188, 260n; liturgy (translations), 140–141, 144n, 180; organ music, 251–264; Positive-Historical Judaism, 169, 173, 174, 259; ritual, 32, 75, 111, 187; sermons, 171, 173, 260n. See also Orthodoxy (Jewish), Reform, Secularism

Jüdisch-deutsch (German in Hebrew script), 141, 154, 180
'Jüdische Rundschau', IX
Jüdischer Frauenbund, 122n
July Plot, 4, 7, 13n
Jung-Stilling, Heinrich (physician, professor, mystic), 212
Junghanns, Johann Baptist Karl (conservative Catholic), 199

Kabbalah, Jewish mysticism, 171
Kahn, Siegbert (East German economist), 295–297, 304, 305
Kaisersteinbruch POW camp, 42
'Kalendar für Zeit und Ewigkeit' (Catholic almanac), 190
Kaltenbrunner, Ernst (Reichssicherheitsdienst chief), 56
Kampfgruppe Steiermark, 19–20n
Kana, Heinrich (friend of Herzl), 109n
Kant, Immanuel (philosopher), Kantianism, 110, 133, 137, 139, 140, 162–163, 164, 177
Kaplan, Marion, 65n, 119
Kapp, Johann Georg Christian (liberal politician), 205, 207
Katz, Itsik (of Ostrowo), 277
Katz, Jacob, 78n, 82n, 86n, 89n, 178n
Keating, Frank L. (US general, of OMGUS), 61
Keller, Adolf (Swiss ecumenist), 227
Keller, Julius, 15n
Keller, Rudolf (publisher), 216
Kempner, Robert K.W. (political scientist, IMT prosecutor), 53, 54–55
Keslin, Hayim (teacher, Hebraist), 142
Kiel Jewish community, 148
Kirk, Kenneth Escott (Bishop of Oxford), 243
Kirn, Hans-Martin, 67n
Kirsch, Rainer, 298
Kirsch, Sarah, 298
Kirsners, John (of US Intelligence), 58
Kisch, Abraham (physician, teacher), 172
Kisch, Enoch Heinrich (writer), 118n
Klagsbald, V., 283
Klemperer, Victor (philologist), 294–295
Knight, G.A.F. (chaplain in Vienna), 244
Koehler, Max (rationalist philosopher), 118
Königsberg Jewish community, 141, 142, 143, 144, 145, 148, 156
Koestler, Arthur (writer), 26
'Kohelet Musar', 156, 157
Kollwitz, Käthe (artist), 213
Komittee der Widerstandskämpfer der DDR, 312
Kommunistische Partei Deutschlands: and Jews, 8–9; KPD/SED, 295
Kommunistische Partei Österreichs (KPÖ), 19, 20n
'Konkret', 302n
Kopitzsch, Franklin, 138n

Koreff, David [Johann] Ferdinand (physician, convert), 87, 96–99, 102, 103; and mesmerism, 96, 97; professorship, 96, 97, 98, 103
Kornberg, Jacques, 108n, 109
Krakowski, Shmuel, 23n
Kreditbank (Austria), 59
Kreisauer Kreis, 8
Kreutzer, Michael, 9n, 20n
Kroger, Jelka, 269n
Kronstein, Heinrich (jurist, convert), 116n
Krumstroh, Frantz Peter (goldsmith), 276–277
Krumstroh, Hans Hinrich (silversmith), 274, 276, 277
Krupp, Alfried (industrialist), 62n
Kuczynski, Jürgen (economic historian), 291n, 302n
Kuh, Ephraim Moses (Hebrew poet), 96
Kulturbund zur demokratischen Erneuerung, 295
Kunert, Günter, 298
Kunstwart-Debatte, 120n
Kursachsen Jewish community, 80n
Kwiet, Konrad, 3n, 10n, 11n

Lagarde, Paul Anton de (orientalist, antisemite), 110n
Landau, Ezekiel b. Judah [Noda bi-Yehuda] (Chief Rabbi of Prague), 156
Landau, Philippine (née Fulda, convert), 116
Landau, Samuel Segal (Prague rabbi), 255
Landauer, Hans, 17n
Landjudenschaft, 170
Landsberg, Bavaria: Nazi officials, 218–223
Lang, Cosmo (Archbishop of Canterbury), 228–238, 240, 241–244, 246
Langmaid, Janet, XI
Langen, Albert (publisher), 211, 212n
Laqueur, Walter, 53
Lasker, Eduard [Jizchok] (liberal politician), 177
Laski, Nathan (communal leader, Manchester), 235–236
Laski, Neville Jonas (British judge), 231, 235, 242
Lauterbach, Jacob (Orthodox rabbi), 252n
Lavater, Johann Caspar (Swiss theologian, physiognomist), 155, 158
Lawyers, German, 211, 217, 218, 219–220, 221, 222, 223
Laycock, Peter (Pioneer Corps commander), 36
Laycock, Robert (British general), 36
Layton, Julian (British officer), 30n
Le Roi, Johannes F.A. de (theological writer, antisemite), 89n, 107n
Lea, R.A.H. (clergyman), 239
League of Nations Union, 239
Lehmann, Rudolf (teacher, convert), 118
Lehren, Abraham Moses (son of Jacob M. L.), 272

Lehren, Akiba (banker), 272
Lehren, Isaak Abraham Zvi (son of Abraham M. L.), 272
Lehren, Jacob Meier (banker), 272
Lehren, Zvi Hirsch (banker), 272
Lehrensteinfeld Jewish community, 273
Leipzig University, 291n
'Leipziger Pikante Blätter', 212
Leistikow, Walter (painter), 214n
Lemberg Jewish community, 144
Leo Baeck Institute: Archives, 55; Bibliography, X-XI; Conferences, 21n; Year Books, IX-XII, 7n, 51; Year Book indexes, XI; Jerusalem, New York, London, XI, 3, 51
Leon da Modena *see* Modena, Leon
Leonard, F.N. (US Intelligence officer), 60n
Leopold, Großherzog von Baden, 186, 189, 195–196, 199, 200, 202, 207
Leopold, Vern, 58
Lepsius, Juliane, 15n
Leslie, Charles (17th-century writer), 77–78
Lessing, Gotthold Ephraim (poet, dramatist), 158, 163, 297, 301
Levenson, Alan, 123, 124, 125, 126, 129
Levetoff, Paul (wrote to 'Church Times'), 243n
Levi, Avigdor (teacher, of Glogau/Prague), 133n
Levi-[Hannover], Raphael (teacher, philosopher), 172
Levin, Joseph (teacher), 148, 154
Levinstein, Gustav (anti-apostasy writer, industrialist) 112–113, 119n
Levy, Sara (salon hostess, aunt of L. Mendelssohn), 93
Lewin, Zevi Hirschel (rabbi), 156
Lewy-Lingen [Landon], Walter (fought at Arnhem), 41
Leyens, Erich, 12n
Liberal Judaism, 105, 174, 252, 260
Liberals, 7, 11, 90, 98, 174; in Baden, 185–208; and Jews, 185, 186–188, 193, 195, 202–208
Library of Congress, 62
Lichtheim, Clara (mother of Richard L.), 117
Lichtheim, George (father of Richard L.), 117
Lichtheim, Richard (Zionist politician), 117
Liebermann von Wahlendorf, Willy Ritter (brother of convert), 116–117
Liebermann, Eliezer (teacher, preacher), 251, 254, 255, 256, 257, 258, 259, 263
Liebermann, Max (artist), 211, 212, 213–214, 215
Life and Work (ecumenical movement), 227
Lindanus (anti-Jewish writer), 76
Lindau, Baruch (tutor, writer, maskil), 142, 144n, 147n
Lindemann, Frederick Alexander, Lord Cherwell (scientist), 40
Lindenbaum [Priestley] (German-Jewish parachute agent), 42–43
Linn (Nazi Mayor of Landsberg), 221

Lipmann-Rosenthal Bank, 269
Lipschütz, Solomon (writer), 73n
Lithuanian Jewry, 170, 171
Löhr, Alexander (German general), 45, 46
Loewenberg, Peter, 108n, 109
Löwenfeld, Philipp (Social Democratic lawyer), 117n, 118n
Löwenheim [Lowe], Walter "Miles" (founder of Neu Beginnen), 5n
Löwenstamm, Abraham Levy (Emden rabbi), 257–258, 259, 262, 263
Löwenstamm, Jacob Moses (Chief Rabbi of Amsterdam), 271, 282
Lowenthal, Ernst Gottfried (author, editor), XII
Löwenthal, Gerhard, 60
London Society for the Promotion of Christianity among the Jews, 83n, 124
London, Jews in, 75, 83n, 266
Londonderry, Charles S.H.V.-T.-Stewart (7th Marquess of, Nazi sympathiser), 236
Lovett, Ernest Neville (Bishop of Salisbury), 243
Lowenstein, Steven M., 140n, 175n
Lowy, Arthur F., 36n
Lublin ghetto, 298, 301. *See also* Maidanek
Lubliner, Chaim (Amsterdam rabbi), 79
Ludovici (correspondent Don), 245n
Lustiger, Arno, 4n, 15n
Luther, Martin (religious reformer), 70n, 79; Lutherans, 78
Lux, Johann Georg (silversmith), 274
Luza, Radomir, 20n
Luzzatto, Moses Hayyim [Ramhal] (Jewish-Italian mystic), 142
Lyra, Nicholas (possibly a convert), 76
Lytton, Victor A.G.R. (2nd Earl), 39n

Maass, Martin (assimilationist), 121n
McClure, Robert A. (US general), 60
MacLeish, Archibald (of Library of Congress), 62
Maetzig, Kurt (film director), 297
Maggid of Mezritch *see* Dov Baer
Maidanek concentration camp, 301
Maimon, Salomon (philosopher), 66n, 133, 139, 145–150 passim, 152–153, 158, 172
Maimonides, Moses ben Maimon [Rambam] (medieval philosopher), 154, 157
Mainz Jewish community, 143
Makkabiade 1938, 57
Malcolm, Neill (general, League of Nations High Commissioner for German Refugees), 231
Malinovsky, Rodion Jakovlevitch (Soviet marshal), 43
Mallon, J.J. (Warden of Toynbee Hall), 237n
Mamlok, Eva (led resistance group), 13; Mamlok group, 17
Mann, Heinrich (novelist), 213, 301

Mann, Thomas (novelist, essayist), 212
Mann, Vivian, 287, 288n
'Mannheimer Abendzeitung', 203
'Mannheimer Morgenblatt', 203
Maquis, 15, 16, 19
Marcus, Moses (convert), 72, 75–76
Margalioth family, 77
Margalith family, 77n
Margalith, Jacob (Regensburg community leader), 77n
Margaritha, Anthonius (convert), 66n, 77
Margolith, Isaac (Prague yeshiva head), 77n
Margolith, Samuel (moralist), 77n
Mark, Bernhard, 20n
Markov, Walter (historian), 291n
Marks (gave talk at Rucking), 233
Marr, Wilhelm (antisemitic author), 121n
Marriage *see* Christians, Disabilities, Intermarriage
Marx, Alexander (son-in-law of D.Z. Hoffmann), 261
Marx, Assur (dealer in metals and gems), 270
Marx, Karl Heinrich (founder of scientific Socialism), 177; Marxist historiography, 291, 308
Maser, Werner (historian), 54
Maskilim, 114, 133–167, 172; 'Nahal Habesor', 142
Mathieu, Gustave Bording, 60
Matthews, Walter Robert (Dean of St. Paul's), 242
Matteotti Brigade, 15
Maurer, Trude, 169n, 179n, 184n
Mauthausen concentration camp, 312
Max-Planck-Institut, 27n
Mayer, Julius (editor), 196n
Mayer, Paul Yogi, 21n, 27n, 33n, 38n, 39n
Mecklenburg, Frank, 51n, 55
Mederle, F.C. (silversmith), 279n
Medieval Jewry, X, 80n, 81n, 123, 274
Melamed, Jacob [David Hieronymus] (convert), 73, 80n, 83n
Melish, Leib (Prague rabbi), 255
Menasseh ben Israel (Dutch rabbi), 160
Mendel of Buda (convert), 73n
Mendel of Strasbourg (tutor), 152
Mendel, Christoff (convert), 73n
Mendelssohn family, 92–95, 96, 147, 150
Mendelssohn[-Bartholdy], Abraham (banker, son of Moses M.), 92, 93–94, 95, 96, 97, 103, 125, 127, 128
Mendelssohn, Dorothea (daughter Moses M., wife of S. Veit, F. v. Schlegel, convert), 93–94, 96, 177
Mendelssohn, Fanny (sister of F. M.-Bartholdy), 95
Mendelssohn, Joseph (banker, son of Moses M.), 92, 133, 145
Mendelssohn, Leah (née Salomon, wife of Abraham M.[-Bartholdy], convert), 91–93, 94, 95, 96, 97, 103
Mendelssohn, Moses [Moshe ben Mendel Dessau, Rambeman, Moses ben Menahem] (philosopher), 83, 92, 93, 94, 95, 128, 172, 177, 180; and "disciples", 133–167; and education, 155–156, 158; and history, 159, 160–161; "Phaedon", 154, 157
Mendelssohn[-Bartholdy], Rebecca (daughter Abraham M.), 92, 94
Mendelssohn-Bartholdy, Felix (composer, son of Abraham M.), 87, 91, 92, 94–95, 99, 128
Mengele, Josef (physician, war criminal), 55
Metis, Eduard (journalist), 115
Metternich, Klemens Wenzel Fürst von (Austrian statesman), 91, 98
Metz Jewish community, 143
Meusel, Alfred (historian), 291n
Meyding (lawyer for Th.Th. Heine), 220
[H.] Meyen (silverware firm), 286
Meyer, Eduard (opponent of Börne), 110n
Meyer, Friedrich Christian (convert), 76n
Meyer, Michael A., 173n, 257
Meyerbeer, Giacomo (composer), 92, 95
Mez, Karl Christian (Baden emancipationist), 188
Michael (Polish convert), 67n
Michael, Daniel (silversmith), 267
Midgley, Peter, 31n
Milch, Erhard (Luftwaffe general), 55
Military service, 91, 105, 188. *See also* Allied forces
Mischlinge, 19, 37, 57; persecution of, 232, 234, 240, 241. *See also* Johanna Heine
Mischlingsliga, 18–19
Mitau Jewish community, 164
Mittnacht, Hieronymus (silversmith), 279n
Mittwochsgesellschaft, 152, 155, 162
Modena, Leon[e] [da] (Italian-Jewish writer), 66n
Möller, Horst, 161
Mohrmann, Walter (historian), 293
Moltke, von (Kreisleiter), 223
Moltmann, Günter, 181n
Mone, Franz Josef (opposed Catholic dissent), 196n
Moneylending, "Usury", 85, 187, 188
Montesquieu, Charles de (philosopher), 149
Montgomery, Bernard (British field-marshal), 44
Mordechai, Moses (religious commentator), 77n
Morrison, Herbert (British minister), 30
Moser, Moses (banker), 127n
Moses, Siegfried (President, Leo Baeck Institute, Zionist politician), IX, X
Moshe, Gedaliah (maskil, teacher), 141–142, 144n
Mosley, [Sir] Oswald (British Fascist), 39
Mosse, George L., 118, 178n

Mosse, Werner E., 116
Mountbatten, Louis (British admiral, 1st Earl), 36
Mühsam, Paul (jurist), 118, 125, 126
Müller, Armin (poet), 298
Müller, Werner (historian), 293
Munich Pact, 25, 226, 235, 237
Museums, Jewish: Joods Historisch Museum, Amsterdam, 265–288; Frankfurt a. Main, 265, 285; Gemeentemuseum, The Hague, 271; Israel Museum, Jerusalem, 271, 280, 288n; London, 279n, 286; New York, 271, 280, 281n, 283n, 285; Switzerland, 278; B'nai B'rith Klutznick Museum, Washington, 280
Museums, other: Stadtgeschichtliches Museum, Altona, 277, 285; Berlin, 279, 285n; Hessisches Landesmuseum, Cassel, 279, 283n; Musée de Cluny, 283; Victoria and Albert Museum, London, 283n; Kremlin Museum, Moscow, 268

Napoleon Bonaparte (Emperor of the French), Napoleonic Era, 85, 88, 90, 92, 96, 102, 173; Congress of Vienna, 91, 97, 173; Wars of Liberation, 86, 87, 90, 97, 101, 102, 188
Nathan [Howarth], Erich (of X-Troop), 36
Nathanson, Mendel Levin (co-founded Copenhagen Freischule), 142n
National Archives (Washington, DC), 51, 52, 61
National Socialist regime: anti-Communism, 296; British sympathisers, 225, 236; Christians under, 228–229, 238; foreign views, 225–247; Gleichschaltung, 214–216; German language, 294–295; Machtergreifung, 212, 213, 292
National Socialist regime, Jews under, 5; artists, 213–217; in Austria, 16–20, 227–231, 232, 238–239, 240, 241, 244–245: Church of England and, 225–247; historiography of, 291–312; Judenkartei, 88; legal defence, 211, 218–220, 223, 224; underground life, 14. *See also* Persecution, Resistance (Jewish)
Nationalism, German, 86, 99
Nationalsozialistische Deutsche Arbeiterpartei (NSDAP), 307; youth organisations, 291
Nebenius, Karl Friedrich (liberal minister in Baden), 190
Neo, Aaron (businessman), 145–146
Nessler, Walter Horst, 31n
Nestler, Ludwig (editor), 304
Netherlands Jewry, 265–288. *See also* Amsterdam
Netherlands, emigrants to, 266, 274
Neu Beginnen, 5
New York Jewish community, 266. *See also* Museums
'News Chronicle', 36
Nicholson, Godfrey (British MP), 241, 243

Nicolai, Christoph Friedrich (author, bookseller), 152
Niemöller, Martin (pastor), 233
Nietzsche, Friedrich (philosopher), 110n, 111
Nobel, Günter & Genia, 16n
Nordhausen, Richard (writer, journalist), 120–121
November Pogrom, 8, 15, 25, 28, 221, 226, 237–240, 301, 310
Nuremberg Laws, 9, 225, 299, 301

Occupational structure, Jewish, 159, 172
Österreichische Kampffront, 18
Ogorek, Benny, 75n
Ohlendorf, Otto (Einsatzgruppe leader), 48
Oppeln-Bronikowski, Friedrich von (writer), 96n
Oppenheim, Gertrud (cousin of F. Rosenzweig), 110
Oppenheim[er], David (Chief Rabbi of Bohemia), 259, 260, 263
Oppenheimer family, 266
Oppenheimer, Emanuel (Court Jew), 272
Oppenheimer, Nathan (businessman), 145
Org/Neu Beginnen *see* Neu Beginnen
Orientalische Buckdruckerei, 141, 142, 144, 154
Orthodoxy, Jewish, 99n, 105, 115, 174, 176, 179; in Burgenland, 230; in England, 170; and Haskalah, 135, 166; neo-Orthodoxy, 166, 169, 173, 174; and organ music, 251–264; in Vienna, 170
Osterode Jewish community, 277
Ostrowo (Poznań) Jewish community, 277
Otto, Julius Conrad [Naftali Margalita] (convert), 77
Otto, Wilfriede, 310n

Pablo de Santa Maria [Salomo Halevi] (convert), 76, 77
Pace, Eric, 54n
Pacelli, Eugenio (later Pope Pius XII), 242
Pacifism, pacifists, 225; Nazi accusations, 219, 220
Palestine, emigrants to, 22, 113; immigration certificates, 244
Panitz, Michael Edward, 184n
Pannwitz, Helmuth von (German general), 46
Parti Communiste français, 18
Partisans, 4, 15, 16, 18–20, 23, 42–43
Paterna, Erich (historian), 291n, 299n
Paterson, Alec (British official), 30n
Patriotism, Jewish, 99, 100
Paucker, Arnold, XI, 3n, 4n, 5n, 7n, 21n, 26n, 36n, 51n
Paucker, Pauline, 212n
Pelli, Moshe, 137
Penn, A.R. (secretary, Church Mission to the Jews), 227

Perceval, Augustus Arthur, 1st Earl of Egmont, 76n, 81
Perowne, Arthur William Thomson (Bishop of Worcester), 231
Persecution and extermination, 5, 7, 8, 27, 35, 49, 105, 300; Church of England and, 225–247; responsibility for, 296n, 299, 305, 306–307, 309; "euthanasia", 307; forced labour, 12–13, 308; Generalplan Ost, 307; ghettoisation, 300, 301; Gypsies, 307; E. German historiography of, 291–312; homosexuals, 307; legal defence against, 211, 218–220, 223, 224; literary/dramatic depiction, 297–298, 301–302; Madagascar Plan, 300; Slavs, 307. *See also* Aryanisation, Mischlinge, National Socialist regime (Jews under)
Petzold, Joachim (writer), 304
Peyrère [Pereira], Isaac de la (pre-Adamite, convert), 77
Pfefferkorn, Johannes Joseph (antisemite, convert), 67–68, 75n, 77
Pfefferkorn, Meir (rabbi), 77
Pfeiffer, August (theologian), 76
Philippson, Ludwig (editor 'Allgemeine Zeitung des Judentums'), 259
Physicians, Jewish, 96–99, 172
Pick, Josel (teacher, maskil), 142, 144n, 147, 148)
Pieck, Wilhelm (Communist politician, GDR President), 291n
Pietism, 78, 79, 82
Pijade, Mosha (adviser to Tito), 16n
Pikarski, Margot, 20n
Pioneer Corps, 25–34, 37–40, 46. *See also* Special Operations Excutive
Pitt-Rivers, George (racist writer), 245
Pius XI (Pope), 242
Plank [II], Jakob (silversmith), 268
Platz, Christian Friedrich (liberal politician, Baden), 195
Pogroms: Hep! Hep!, 84–85, 86, 95; Kishinev, 109. *See also* November Pogrom
Pohl, Oswald (SS economic leader), 47
Polish Jewry, 150, 153, 170, 171; emigrants from Poland, 147, 266; Rabbinate, 146, 156, 161, 163
Political allegiances, Jewish, 5–6, 7, 8–11; in Austria, 17
Political Warfare Executive, 35
Poole, DeWitt (US official), 57
Popitz, Johannes (Prussian minister, in July Plot), 7, 8n
Porritt, Isaiah (rabbi in Vienna), 230
Porter, Roy, 138n
Portuguese Jewry: in the Netherlands, 265, 267, 268, 269. *See also* Sephardim, Iberian Jewry
Posen Jewish Community, 164
[Silberwarenfirma Lazarus] Posen Witwe, 283–285

'Prager Tageblatt', 216
Prague Jewish community, 164, 251–264; Altneuschul, 252n, 254, 256, 257, 259, 261; Gesellschaft der jungen Hebräer, 144–145; Maisel Synagogue, 252–253, 261, 262; maskilim in, 143, 144–145; Neuer Tempel (Altschul, Spanish Synagogue), 254, 259–260; organ music, 251–264; Pinkas Synagogue, 274; printing houses, 147
Press, German, 198
Press, Jewish, 5, 14, 37, 112, 118, 174n
Prestel, Claudia, 179n
Preußische Akademie der Künste, 213, 214
'Preußische Jahrbücher', 112
Pringle, Annette, X
Prisoners of war, 19, 42, 43, 47, 48, 53, 57, 58–59
Professions, Jews in, 105, 140; career conversion, 104–105, 106: Haskalah and, 140, 146
Proßnitz Jewish community, 65
Prussian Jewry, 143, 173, 176, 179; Edict of Emancipation (1812), 91, 102–103
Publishing, Jewish, 142, 154–155: in Hebrew, 72n, 140, 147, 154, 156n, 270; in Yiddish, 80, 180
Pulitzer, Walter (denazification official), 61
Pulzer, Peter, 6n, 120n
Putik, Alexander, 252n

Rabbinate, 165; in Germany, 156, 174, 175–176; in Poland, 146, 156, 161, 163; rabbinical conferences, 173–174, 175, 176; rabbinical seminaries, 173–174, 251
Rabbinerseminar für das orthodoxe Judentum, 251, 252, 260
Rafaeli, Alex, 62n
Rath, Anton (editor), 215
Ravensbrück concentration camp, 13, 46, 48, 301, 312
Reading, Gerald Rufus Isaacs (2nd Marquess of), 26, 242
Reclam Verlag, Leipzig, 294
'[The] Record' (Anglican paper), 226, 229, 231, 236, 239–240
Rée, Anton (educationalist, politician), 180
Reform Judaism, 92, 99n, 102, 105, 119, 169–184, 188, 251–264; Government opposition, 173, 176; and Haskalah, 135, 136, 146, 167
Reichenau Jewish community, 142
Reichmann, Hans (lawyer, C.V. Syndikus), 7n
Reichssicherheitshauptamt, 300
Reichsvereinigung der Juden in Deutschland, 7
Reichsvertretung der Juden in Deutschland (der deutschen Juden), IX, 7
Reineccius, Christian (writer), 65n, 66–67, 74
Reitlinger, Gerald (art expert, historian), 307n
Remarque, Erich Maria (author), 54
Remba, Isaac (historian), 126n

Rendsburg (Schleswig-Holstein) Jewish community, 276
Rendulic [Rendolitsch], Lothar (Austrian general), 44, 45–46
Resistance, 296, 300, 301, 311–312; Anglican Church (Berlin), 233; Austrian, 43; Belgian, 18; Communist/Socialist, 4, 5, 9, 14n, 18n, 291, 295, 311–310. *See also* Baum Group; Czech, 19; in exile, 298. *See also* Allied Forces; French, 18; Italian, 15–16, 42–43; liberal, 7, 12; by POWs, 19; Right-wing, 6–8; by workers, 4, 10, 296–297, 299. *See also* Anti-Nazi Propaganda, Sabotage
Resistance, Jewish, XII, 3–20, 311; armed resistance, 3, 10, 14–16, 17, 19–20, 23. *See also* Allied forces; Austrian, 4, 15, 16–20; in Belgium 17, 18; ex-soldiers, 12; in France 15, 17, 18, 19; infiltration, 11, 19; in Italy, 16; in Poland, 23; press and propaganda, 5, 9, 11, 14, 18, 19, 24n, 212–213, 214n–215; rabbis, 13–14; in Russia, 23; in Shanghai, 16; Vienna, 18, 19, 20; Warsaw Ghetto uprising, 311; women, 12–13, 15, 18; youth, 9–12, 14, 24; in Yugoslavia, 16, 19
Restitution, XII, 296
Reuchlin, Johannes (humanist), 77n
Revolutions: French, 189; of 1848, 98, 174
'Rhein-Main Zeitung', 59
RIAS Berlin ((Rundfunk im amerikanischen Sektor), 60
Ribbentrop, Joachim von (Nazi Foreign Minister), 55
Richarz, Monika, 107n
Richborough camp, 26–27, 30
Riederer, Johann (writer), 81n
Riesser, Gabriel (liberal politician), 114
Riesser, Lazarus Jakob (maskil), 114
Rindeschwender, Ignaz (liberal, anti-emancipationist), 186, 200–201, 202
Ritchie, J.M., 26n
Rothschild, Eli, XI
Rogers, Daniel E., 62n
Rogers, Guy (clergyman), 233, 238
Romanticism, 86, 87, 102
Rome Jewish community, 123
Rommel, Erwin (German field-marshal), 31
Ronge, Johannes (dissident Catholic), 192, 196, 197
Rose, A.C.W. (Bishop of Dover), 240
Rose, Paul Lawrence, 86n, 97n
Rosenberg, M. (author), 270
Rosenstock-Huessy, Eugen (philosopher), 110, 111n
Rosenthal family, 47–48
Rosenthal, Berthold (writer), 207n
Rosenthal, Georg (banker), 269
Rosenzweig, Adam (uncle of Franz R.), 110
Rosenzweig, Adele (née Alsberg, mother of Franz R.), 110–111

Rosenzweig, Franz (philosopher), 114, 117n, 178; and antisemitism, 110, 111n; and conversion, 108, 110–112, 122
Rosenzweig, Georg (father of Franz R.), 112n
Ross, James R., 16n
'[Die] Rote Fahne', 9n
Rote Kapelle, 20n
Rotenhan, Hermann von (student), 100
Roth, Cecil (historian), 286, 287
Roth, Eugen (editor, author), 214n
Rothschild, [Baron] Wilhelm von (of Frankfurt a. Main), 283
Rothschild, Nathaniel Mayer Victor (3rd Baron), 241, 242
Rotteck, Karl von (liberal, anti-emancipationist), 186
Rühs, Christian Friedrich (antisemitic historian), 86, 102
Ruppin, Arthur (sociologist), 107n, 119
Rural Jewry, 107n, 176, 187, 276; urbanisation, 176
Russia/Soviet Union: emigrants to, 301; persecution of Jews, 48

SA, 217–218, 219, 220, 234, 303
Saaling, Marianne (sister L. Mendelssohn), 92n
Sabbatai Zvi (kabbalist, pseudo-Messiah), 69
Sabbatians, 83
Sabotage, 9, 19, 37, 38, 40, 43
Sachs, Michael (Berlin rabbi, scholar), 259, 260, 263
Sachsenhausen concentration camp, 24, 28, 113n, 312
Salomon, Bella [Bilke] (mother of L. Mendelssohn), 92, 94
Salomon, Ernst von (German nationalist), 58
Salomon, Levin Jacob (father of L. Mendelssohn), 92
Salomon Bartholdy, Jacob *see* Bartholdy, J.S.
Salons, 86, 87, 88, 90, 93, 128, 133, 145, 150, 166, 177
Samosc [Zamosc], Israel (teacher, translator), 172
Samter, Nathan (anti-apostasy writer), 112
Samuel, Herbert Louis (1st Viscount), 242
Sander, Adolf (liberal, anti-emancipationist), 186–187
Sargent, A.E. (C. Lang's secretary, chaplain), 233
Sassin, Horst R., 12n
Satanow, Isaak (teacher, printer, Hebrew author), 133, 139–140, 142, 144, 149, 150n, 154, 155, 156n, 161n, 166
Saunders, Erich, 47n
Scaliger, Joseph Justus (writer), 78
Scandinavia, emigrants to, 217
Schatzker, Chaim, 180
Scheffler, Wolfgang, 12n, 286

Schelling, Friedrich Wilhelm Joseph von (Protestant philosopher), 112n
Scheuer, Oskar (writer), 99n
Scheur, Hirtz (Mainz rabbi), 254–255, 256, 257, 260, 262, 263
Schieb-Samizadek, Barbara, 20n
Schik, Baruch (Jewish functionary in Minsk), 133, 139
Schiller, Friedrich von (poet), 61
Schilling (associate of Th.Th. Heine), 215
Schinkel, Karl Friedrich (architect), 281
Schlegel, Friedrich von (littérateur), 93
Schleicher, Kurt von (general, politician), 216
Schleiermacher, Friedrich Ernst Daniel (Protestant theologian), 90, 110
Schlessmann, Leo (Gauleiter), 62n
Schliemann, E., 274, 276, 277
Schmelz, Usiel O., 107n
Schmiedler, Bernhard (associate of L. Bendix), 118
Schneersohn, Yosef Yitzhak (rabbi), 136n
Schoenberner, Franz (author), 211n, 214n, 215
Schönemann, Shlomo (physician, son of I. Satanow), 142
Scholem, Gershom (philosopher, authority on Jewish mysticism), 117n, 118n
Schrecker, Hans (falsely accused), 310n
Schreiber, Heinrich (Baden professor), 189n
Schudt, Johann Jacob (writer), 77n, 80–81n, 252n
Schulz, Wilhelm (graphic artist), 216
Schumann, Wolfgang (historian), 292n, 304
Schuschnigg, Kurt (Austrian politician), 227
Schutzhaft, 221, 222
Schweder, Alfred (head of Bremen Gestapo), 48
Schweiger, Harry (arrested O. Pohl), 47
Secret Intelligence Service (SIS), 37
Secularism, 166, 169, 176–184; secular learning, 171–172
Seeligman, Christian Gottlieb (convert), 75n
Segal, Alan F., 108n
Self-regard, Jewish, 117, 179
Seligsberger, Sigmund & Sara [née Wolf] (emigrants to Netherlands), 274
"Semi-Gotha", 121
Sephardim, 82, 83; in Amsterdam, 79, 265–266, 267–269
Serapionsbrüder (literary club), 98
Serpilius, Georg (writer), 77n, 80
Seydel, Heinz (poet), 298
Sezession (art movements), 214n
Shabbetai of Yanov (publisher), 142
SHAEF (Supreme Headquarters Allied Expeditionary Forces), 57
Shalome ben Shalomon (convert), 74
Shapiro, Marc, 264n
Sheldon, Max, 57
Shklov Jewish community, 143, 144
Shohet, Azriel, 69n

Sick, Georg Christian Friedrich (silversmith), 281
Silberman, Lou, 252n
Silesian Jewry, 274. *See also* Glogau
Simonov, Konstantin (reported on Maidanek), 301
'Simplicissimus', 211, 212, 214–216, 217, 222
Simpson, [Sir] John Hope (British civil servant), 234
Simpson, William (Methodist clergyman), 241
Sindermann, Horst (GDR politician), 312
Singakademie, Berlin, 92, 95
Singer, Solomon (Prague rabbi), 253, 261
Slánský trial, 310n
Smith, Anthony, 148
Smolenskin, Perez (Hebrew author), 135, 136
Snell, Henry (1st Baron), 229
Sobibor extermination camp, 274, 301
Social status, Jewish, 105–106; embourgeoisement, 178–184
Socialists, 10, 11, 37, 177, 225; in Austria, 17. *See also* Sozialdemokratische Partei Deutschlands
Society for the Protection of Science and Learning, 234
Society of Jews and Christians, 233
Sofer [Schreiber], Moses [Chatam Sofer] (Preßburg rabbi, leader of Orthodox Jewry), 256–257, 258, 260, 261, 262, 263
Soiron, Alexander von (liberal politician), 204, 205
'Soldier', 36
Solomon of Burgos *see* Pablo de Santa Maria
Sonderabteilung "NN" (Jewish anti-Fascists), 18–19
Sorkin, David, 91n, 106, 114, 139n, 157–158, 179n
Sozialdemokratische Partei Deutschlands (SPD), 5, 6n
Sozialistische Einheitspartei Deutschlands (SED), 295, 296, 299, 309
Spaatz, Carl (US Air Force general), 58
Spanish Civil War, 15, 17, 18n
Spanish Jewry *see* Iberian Jewry
Special Operations Executive (SOE), 37–41, 42; parachuted agents, 37, 38–39, 41–44, 48. *See also* Sabotage, Twelve Force, X-Section
Spener, Philipp Jakob (Pietist, historian), 82
Sperling, Benedictus Sebastian [Israel Benediti] (reverted to Judaism), 79
Spiegel, Tilly, 18n
Spielman, Diane, 51n
Spoerl, Johann Conrad (preached on converts), 67n
SS, 15, 44, 46, 47, 234, 303; Aktion Reinhard, 45; imprisonment, 57; trials of, 46; Waffen-SS, 58
Stägemann, Friedrich August von (Prussian official), 97n, 101–102
Stahl, Friedrich Julius [Julius Jolson] (jurist,

conservative politician, convert), 87, 99–101, 103–104
Stammers, Neil, 25n
Stampfel, Franz (athletics trainer), 30n
Stanley, Oliver (British politician), 26n
Stark, Werner, 55–56
Staudenmaier, Franz Anton (opposed Catholic dissent), 196n
Stauffenberg, Claus Philip Schenk Graf von (20th July Plot leader), 6n
Stein, Edith (murdered nun, convert), 115, 116
Steinberg, Lucien, 20n
Steinhardin, Gütgen (convert), 67n, 71
Steinschneider, Moritz (bibliographer, orientalist), 155
Stenglin, Balthasar Friedrich (silversmith), 279n
Stern, Jacob (author), 121n
Stern, Karl (of Floss, convert), 115–116, 124n
Stern, Moritz Abraham (mathematician), 182
Stern, Wilhelm (opposed Catholic dissent), 196n
Sternfeld, Albert, 18n
Stettin Jewish community, 142
Stiefel, Ernst, 55
Stolz, Alban (Catholic, conservative), 190, 196–197, 201
Stopford, Robert (British diplomat), 240
Strabolgi, Joseph Montague Kenworthy (10th Baron), 229
Strasbourg Jewish community, 143
Strauss, Johann (composer), 215
Streicher, Julius (Nazi leader), 5
Streisand, Joachim (historian), 293, 299n
Strobl, Ingrid, 12n
Students, German, 85–86, 90; fraternities, 99–100
Students, Jewish, 99–100, 101, 102, 122, 144, 147, 181, 182
'[Der] Stürmer', 5, 14
Stürz (Dießen police inspector), 221
Suchy, Barbara, X, 121n
'Süddeutsche Zeitung für Kirche und Staat' (Catholic paper), 190, 192, 195, 207
Suicide, 14, 49; in Austria, 227, 229, 234, 239
Sulzbach, Herbert (diplomat, Pioneer), 29, 34
Surnames, 94, 109n, 128; Anglicisation, 33, 36,

Talmud, 70, 72n, 78n, 147, 171
Talmud Torah association, 269
Tarchdorf Jewish community, 277
Tassaert, Jean Pierre Antoine (sculptor), 137
Taylor, Telford (US prosecutor, Nuremberg), 53, 54, 61
Teachers, Jewish, 73; converts, 124, 126; maskilim and, 147–148
Teddern, Clive, 24n, 30n, 31n, 33, 49n
Teller, Wilhelm Abraham (Protestant theologian), 136
Temple, William (Archbishop of York, later of Canterbury), 231, 236, 237, 241, 248

Tesch, Bruno (supplied Zyklon-B), 47
Theodore, David (physician, maskil), 141, 144n
Theresienstadt ghetto (Terezin), 7, 39n, 298
Thöny, Eduard (cartoonist), 214, 215
Thompson, David M., 225n
'[The] Times', 237, 238, 240, 241, 242, 243
Timm, Angelika, 310n
Tito, Josip Broz (Yugoslav statesman), 16n, 19
Tolbukhin (Soviet field-marshal), 43
Toleranzpatent (Austria), 155, 160, 172
Toury, Jacob, 107n, 176n, 178n
Trahner (Mayor of Dießen), 222
Travail-Anti-Allemand, 18
Treblinka concentration camp, 301
Trefurt, Franz Christof[ph] (liberal politician, Baden), 195, 203, 206n
Treitschke, Heinrich von (historian), 91n, 177
Troki, Isaac (anti-Christian writer), 80n
Trützschler von Falkenstein, Heinz (diplomat), 57n
Tsitron, Shmuel Leib (historian), 126n
"[Rabbi] Tuvya (Tobias)" (associate M. Mendelssohn), 157
Twelve Force, 21n, 24n, 28n, 37–41, 47, 49n

Ulbricht, Walter (GDR politician), 299
Ulmann, Naftali Hirz (maskil, philosopher), 158
United Press, 61
United States of America, emigrants to, 27, 51–62, 181, 244; naturalisation, 61
United States of America: Intelligence, Jews in, 51–62; Counter Intelligence Corps (CIC), 55, 59, 62n; Office of Strategic Services (OSS), 37, 52, 54, 57, 60
Universities: Jewish professors, 181–182; Oriental studies, 71n

Varnhagen von Ense, Karl August (diplomat, author), 96, 97n, 101–102
Varnhagen von Ense, Rahel (née Levin, salon hostess), 92n, 96, 97, 101–102, 114, 177
Veil [de] family, 77
Veil, Ludwig Compiègne de [Daniel] (convert), 70, 81n
Venetian Jewry, 266
Verband der Vereine für jüdische Geschichte und Literatur, 183
Verein für Cultur und Wissenschaft der Juden (Culturverein), 102, 103
Verein für jüdische Geschichte und Literatur, 183
Verein zur Abwehr des Antisemitismus (Abwehrverein), 121
Viadrina (Jewish fraternity), 122n
Vicari, Hermann von (Catholic archbishop), 190, 191, 198
Vienna Jewish community, 93, 145, 170, 238–

239; after Anschluß, 227, 228–229, 234, 238–239, 244; maskilim in, 142, 143; printing houses, 147; salons, 93, 145
Vilna Gaon *see* Elijah b. Solomon Zalman
Vilna Jewish community, 143
Vital, Hayim (rabbi), 77n
Vlassov, Andrei Andreievich (led anti-Soviet Russians), 58
Voigt, Klaus, 16n
Volkov, Shulamit, 175n, 178n
Voolen, Edward van, 265
Voss, Philip (secretary), 241
VT (silversmith), 278

Wagenseil, Johann Christoph (writer on religion), 74n
Wagner (US Democrat Senator), 61
Wagner, Adolf (Bavarian Nazi minister), 217, 218n
Wagner, Jakob (Hebraist), 261
Waldegrave, Frances Countess of (political hostess, daughter of J. Braham), 127
Waldmann, Kurt (of Berlin, convert), 114–115
Wallace, [Miss] (secretary of Council on Foreign Relations), 235, 243–244
Wannsee Protocols, 54n, 300, 301
War Crimes and Trials, 46–47; medical crimes, 55; Nuremberg Trials, 53–56, 62n, 294, 304; War Crimes Commission (Washington, DC), 54; War Crimes Executive, 46; War Crimes Group (NW Europe), 47–48
Warnberger [II], Abraham (silversmith), 268
Warner, Frederick Michael [Manfred Werner], 26n, 34, 40, 41, 43, 45–46, 47–48
Warsaw Jewish community, 128–129
Wassermann, Henry, 211n
Wassermann, Jakob (novelist), 120
Weber, Albrecht (of Abwehrverein), 121n
Wedekind, Frank (dramatist), 212n
Weidner, Paul (convert), 76
Weimar Republic, Jews in, 122n
Weinmann, Hans, 51n
Weinsaft, Henry, 59
Weiskopf, F.C. (writer), 301
Weiße Rose (resistance group), 4
Weissmandl, Michael Dov (Czechoslovak rabbi), 230, 235
Weißler, Adolf [Benedictus Levita] (jurist, writer), 112–113, 114, 121n, 122
Weißler, Friedrich (jurist), 113n
Weizel, Franz Gideon (conservative Catholic), 199–200
Weizmann, Chaim (Zionist statesman), 109
Welcker, Karl Theodor (liberal writer), 191n
Weller, Ludwig (anti-emancipationist liberal), 205
Weltsch, Robert (editor 'Jüdische Rundschau', Zionist, founder-editor LBI Year Book), IX, XI

Werner, Johannes (pseud.), 57–58n
Wertheimer family, 266
Wertheimer, Serchen (wife of Herz L. Cohen), 275
"Werwolf", 58
Wessely, Moshe (merchant), 145
Wessely, Naphtali Herz (Hebrew poet, educationalist), 133, 135, 137n, 139, 142n–150 *passim*, 152, 155–156, 157, 164; and education, 148, 155–156, 166, 172
West, Nigel (pseud. of Rupert Allason MP), 37
Westphalian Jewry, 173, 183
Whiston, William (theologian, mathematician), 76n
Whittingham, Walter Godfrey (Bishop of St. Edmundsbury and Ipswich), 239
Wiener Library, X
Wilhelm II (Emperor of Germany), 212
Wilhelm, Robert K. (IMT interrogator), 55
Willstätter, Richard (chemist), 125, 126
Wilson, Henry Albert (Bishop of Chelmsford), 230
Wimmer, Adi, 22n
Winks, Robin W., 59n
Wippermann, Wolfgang, 12n
Wissenschaft des Judentums, 105, 166, 169, 177
Wittels, Fritz (anti-apostasy writer), 112
Wolf, Friedrich (playwright), 301
Wolf, Konrad (film director), 297
Wolf, Robert, 51n
Wolff, Charlotte (memoirist), 117n, 119
Wolfsohn, Aaron Halle (editor, maskil), 137, 141, 144n, 145, 166
Wolkensdorfer (SA official), 219
Women and girls, Jewish, 12–13, 15, 18, 87–88; in Allied forces, 21; assimilation, 141; converts, 66n, 67n, 71, 87–88; dowries, 185n; education, 71–72, 141; and liturgy, 141, 180. *See also* Salons
World Jewish Congress, 232
World's Evangelical Alliance, 236
Württemberg Jewry, 176, 273
Wurm, Theophil (Protestant bishop), 54

X-Section, Special Operations Executive, 37; X/AUS, 37. *See also* Twelve Force
X-Troop, No. 3 (Miscellaneous) Troop, 10; X/AUS, (Inter-Allied) Commando, 35–36
Xeres, John (convert), 70–71, 74

Yagel [Jagel], Abraham (Italian-Jewish writer), 66n
Yehudah Leib of Zelechow (writer), 73n
Yellow badges, 266
Yerushalmi, Yosef Hayim, 81n
Yiddish, 80, 83n, 161, 180–181, 287. *See also* Jüdisch-deutsch

Youth movements, Jewish, 11, 17; Zionist, 11, 14
Youth, Jewish, 9–10, 17, 158; resistance, 9–10, 15; youth movements, 11, 14, 17

Zadek, Alice & Gerhard, 11n
Zedlitz, Karl Abraham Frhr. von (Prussian minister), 156
'Zeitschrift für die Geschichte der Juden in Deutschland', XII
'Zeitschrift für Geschichtswissenschaft', 292n
Zell, Karl (Baden professor), 189n
Zelter, Karl Friedrich (composer, Singakademie director), 92
Zengraf [Zengravio], Johannes Joachimo (writer), 80n
Zentrum für Antisemitismusforschung, Berlin, 309
Zentrumspartei, 6
Zimmermann, Moshe, 312
Zinzendorf, von (Austrian governor of Trieste), 155
Zionism, 105, 109–110, 111, 117; anti-Zionism, 309–310; youth movements, 11, 14
Zionistische Vereinigung für Deutschland, X, 122n, 177, 312
Zittel, Karl (liberal politician, Baden), 193–195, 196, 198, 199, 200
Zobel, Jeremias (silversmith), 271, 285
Zuckerman, Alan S., 173n
Zuckerman, Solly (scientist), 34
Zweig, Arnold (novelist), 293

Published in 1995

On the 40th Anniversary
of the Leo Baeck Institute

LEO BAECK INSTITUTE

YEAR BOOKS
XXI-XXXIX
(1976-1994)

GENERAL INDEX

1995

PUBLISHED FOR THE INSTITUTE
SECKER & WARBURG LONDON

The long-awaited second Index Volume, compiled by Janet Langmaid, comprises Year Book XXI-XXXIX. It represents an invaluable resource for researchers, students and the general reader.

Contents:

Preface by Arnold Paucker
Foreword by Janet Langmaid
Advice to the User
List of Abbreviations
Index of Authors
Index of Subjects
Antisemitism: Detailed Sub-Headings
Register of Illustrations

AVAILABLE AT ALL THREE LEO BAECK INSTITUTES AND THE
PUBLISHERS

FORTHCOMING

Martin Liepach

Das Wahlverhalten der jüdischen Bevölkerung: Zur politischen Orientierung der Juden in der Weimarer Republik

Schriftenreihe wissenschaftlicher Abhandlungen des Leo Baeck Instituts
1996

J.C.B. MOHR (PAUL SIEBECK), TÜBINGEN

NEW FROM MOHR: Hebrew and Aramaic Magic Texts From the Cairo Genizah, a German Translation, and a Detailed Commentary

Magische Texte aus der Kairoer Geniza I
in Zusammenarbeit mit Martin Jacobs, Claudia Rohrbacher-Sticker und Giuseppe Veltri. Herausgegeben von Peter Schäfer und Shaul Shaked

The present volume is the first part of a planned three-volume edition, containing Hebrew and Aramaic magic texts from the Cairo Genizah, a German translation, and an extensive commentary. The texts range from theoretical essays and magical recipes to amulets and incantations. The German translation and the detailed commentary make the texts accessible to a large audience. Significant is also the variety of languages, which change from Hebrew to Aramaic and from both to Arabic. The use of Latin and Greek words is a sign of the age of the writings. The range of subjects covered in the Genizah texts demonstrates that what was often termed 'magic' was in fact misleading. For example one aspect of this are medical prescriptions which point out the parallels between classic Greek and Arabic medicine. The detailed analysis attempts to elucidate the deep and complex interrelations between Greco-Roman magic from Late Antiquity, Arabic tradition and medieval Jewish magic.

1994. IX, 329 pages (Texte und Studien zum Antiken Judentum 42). ISBN 3-16-146272-6 cloth
DM 168.00

J.C.B. MOHR (PAUL SIEBECK) TÜBINGEN

BÖHLAU BÜCHER AKTUELL

Oskar Frischenschlager (Hg.)
Wien, wo sonst!
Die Entstehung der Psychoanalyse und ihrer Schulen
1994. 254 S. Br. DM 58,–. ISBN 3-205-98135-9

Martha Keil / Klaus Lohrmann (Hg.)
Studien zur Geschichte der Juden in Österreich
(Handbuch zur Geschichte der Juden in Österreich, Reihe B, Bd. 2)
1994. 191 S. Br. DM 48,–. ISBN 3-205-98174-X

Rolf Steininger
Der Umgang mit dem Holocaust
Europa – USA – Israel
(Veröffentlichungen des Instituts für Zeitgeschichte
der Universität Innsbruck und des Jüdischen Museums Hohenems, Bd. 1)
2. Aufl., 1994. 498 S., 9 SW-Abb. Br. DM 86,–. ISBN 3-205-98311-4-1

Klaus Hödl
Als Bettler in die Leopoldstadt
Galizische Juden auf dem Weg nach Wien
(Böhlaus Zeitgeschichtliche Bibliothek, Bd. 27, hg. v. Helmut Konrad)
2. Aufl., 1994. 331 S., 13 SW-Abb. Br. DM 68,–. ISBN 3-205-98303-3

Alfredo José Schwarcz
Trotz allem . . .
Die deutschsprachigen Juden in Argentinien
1994. 323 S., 8 S. SW-Abb. Br. DM 68,–. ISBN 3-205-98218-5

Dorit B. Whiteman
Die Entwurzelten
Jüdische Lebensgeschichten nach der Flucht 1933 bis heute
1995. Ca. 432 S., 8 S. SW-Abb. Geb. Ca. DM 98,–. ISBN 3-205-98136-7

Aschkenas
Zeitschrift für Geschichte und Kultur der Juden
Hg. v. J. Friedrich Battenberg und Markus J. Wenninger in Verbindung mit dem Institut
für Geschichte der Juden in Österreich und dem Deutschen Koordinierungs-Rat der
Gesellschaften für Christlich-Jüdische Zusammenarbeit. Erscheinungsweise: ab Jg.4/1994
zweimal jährl. Einzelheft DM 42,50. Abonnement DM 68,–. ISSN 1016-4987

Erhältlich in Ihrer Buchhandlung!

BÖHLAU VERLAG WIEN KÖLN WEIMAR

Lesen Sie weiter auf Deutsch
Literatur zur jüdischen Geschichte und Kultur

Arnaldo Momigliano
Die Juden in der Alten Welt

Momigliano gelingt es, die Wechselbeziehungen aller an der Ausprägung der antiken Welt beteiligten Kulturen sichtbar zu machen. Seine besondere Aufmerksamkeit gilt der Geschichte des Judentums in den Zeiten ihrer stärksten Berührung mit der hellenisch-römischen Umwelt.

Kleine Kulturwissenschaftliche Bibliothek 5. 96 Seiten.

Hannah Arendt
Israel, Palästina und der Antisemitismus

Die wichtigsten Essays der großen Philosophin und politischen Wissenschaftlerin zu zwei – zumal für die Deutschen – entscheidenden Fragen: der Antisemitismus vor wie nach Auschwitz und das Palästinaproblem.

Wagenbachs Taschenbuch 196. 128 Seiten.

Josef Hayim Yerushalmi
Freuds Moses
Endliches und unendliches Judentum

Ist die von Freud begründete Psychoanalyse die jüdische Wissenschaft par excellence? Welche Rolle spielen Judentum und Antisemitismus im Werk und in der Biographie von Sigmund Freud?
»Dieses Buch wird mit Sicherheit für hitzige Diskussionen sorgen, nicht nur unter den Freud-Adepten, sondern auch unter Historikern und Theologen.
Auch jeder interessierte Laie sollte dieses Buch lesen.« Times Literary Supplement

Allgemeines Programm. 192 Seiten.

Klaus Wagenbach
Franz Kafka
Bilder aus seinem Leben

Ein unentbehrliches Kompendium, mit allen Bildern Kafkas und seiner Familie. Diese dritte und stark erweiterte Ausgabe enthält neue Funde, besonders bisher unbekannte Photos der zweiten Braut, Julie Wohryzek, und der großen Unbekannten G.W., die Kafka in Riva kennengelernt hat.
»Der beste Bildband über Kafka.« DIE ZEIT

Leinen. 240 Seiten mit über 500 Abbildungen Duoton.

Franz Kafka
Ein Landarzt

Kafkas berühmteste und umfangreichste Erzählungssammlung, im originalen Wortlaut und Ablauf.
Mit einem Nachwort über die Titelfigur, Kafkas Lieblingsonkel, den Landarzt. Herausgegeben von Klaus Wagenbach.

Gebunden. Bleisatz und Buchdruck durch die Offizin Haag-Drugulin in Leipzig.
80 Seiten mit zweifarbigen Abbildungen.

Josef Hayim Yerushalmi
Ein Feld in Anatot

Ein im heutigen Europa äußerst aktuelles Buch über das Verhältnis der Juden zu ihrer Geschichte, über Erinnern, Hoffen und Vergessen.
»Yerushalmi wäre nicht Salo Barons Schüler, wenn ihm die »weinerliche« Variante jüdischer Geschichtsschreibung nicht zutiefst unsympathisch wäre.« Die Tageszeitung

Kleine Kulturwissenschaftliche Bibliothek 44. 96 Seiten.

Wenn Sie mehr über den Wagenbach Verlag und seine Bücher wissen wollen – schreiben Sie uns eine Postkarte und wir schicken Ihnen gerne unseren kostenlosen Westentaschenalmanach – ZWIEBEL

If you would like to know more about Wagenbach and the wide range of books we publish – please send us a postcard and we will send you our annual almanach – ZWIEBEL free, for a lifetime.

Verlag Klaus Wagenbach
Ahornstraße 4, D-10787 Berlin

ÜBER 30 JAHRE

*Zeitschrift
zum Verständnis
des Judentums*

**Unabhängig
Objektiv
Kritisch**

Beziehbar beim Tribüne-Verlag
60385 Frankfurt/M., Habsburgerallee 72

Gideon Greif

Wir weinten tränenlos...

Augenzeugenberichte der jüdischen Sonderkommandos in Auschwitz

1994. LI, 307 Seiten. Zahlreiche Abbildungen. Broschur. DM/sFr 44,–/öS 343,–
ISBN 3-412-03794-X

50 Jahre nach Auschwitz geben die interviewten jüdischen *Sonderkommando*-Arbeiter in diesem Buch zum erstenmal Zeugnis über ihr Leben in der Todesfabrik des Nationalsozialismus: eine wichtige historische Quelle – nach „Schindlers Liste" ein neuer Beitrag zur Geschichte des Holocaust.

Jürgen Wilke, Birgit Schenk, Akiba A. Cohen, Tami Zemach

Holocaust und NS-Prozesse

Die Presseberichterstattung in Israel und Deutschland zwischen Aneignung und Abwehr

1995. Etwa 300 S. Br. Etwa DM/sFr 48,–/öS 375,– ISBN 3-412-11694-7

Das Buch geht der Frage nach, wie der Holocaust und die Nazi-Ära nach 1945 in der deutschen und israelischen Presse behandelt worden sind. Dazu wird die Berichterstattung über vier große NS-Prozesse untersucht, den Nürnberger Prozeß (1945/46), den Eichmann-Prozeß (1961), den Auschwitz-Prozeß (1963-65) und den Demjanjuk-Prozeß (1987/88).

Thomas Hofmann / Hanno Loewy / Harry Stein (Hg.)

Pogromnacht und Holocaust

Frankfurt, Weimar, Buchenwald
Die schwierige Erinnerung an die Stationen der Vernichtung

1994. XII, 200 S. 6 Abb. Br. DM/sFr 38,–/öS 297,– ISBN 3-412-03293-X

Es braucht kaum betont zu werden, daß die beiden Städte Frankfurt und Weimar in der deutschen Kulturgeschichte viel miteinander verbindet. Doch daß 1938 mehr als 2600 jüdische Frankfurter nach Buchenwald deportiert wurden, ist in beiden Städten kaum bekannt. Was lag also näher, als gemeinsam an dieses Stück Weg „Deutscher Kultur" zu erinnern...

Holger M. Meding

Flucht vor Nürnberg?

Die deutsche und österreichische Einwanderung in Argentinien 1945-1955

1992. 311 S. 11 Abb. Gb. mit SU. DM/sFr 58,– ISBN 3-412-11191-0

Mit diesem Buch wird erstmals der nationalsozialistische Exodus als migrationshistorisches Phänomen, zugleich aber auch als Epilog zur Geschichte des Dritten Reiches, in einer mit bisher unveröffentlichten Archivalien gestützten Studie vorgelegt.

Bitte fordern Sie unseren Sonderprospekt an!

BÖHLAU VERLAG KÖLN WEIMAR WIEN
Theodor-Heuss-Str. 76, D - 51149 Köln

BÖHLAU

THE JOURNAL OF JEWISH STUDIES

Announces A Special Double Issue

Honouring

Geza Vermes

As its Editor for the last twenty-five years

Volume XLVI, 1-2   **AUTUMN 1995**

Annual Subscription: £21.00 ($40.00)
Student Rate: £13.00 ($25.00)
Single Issues: £13.00 ($25.00)
Volume XLVI, 1-2 (Vermes issue)   £21.00 ($40.00)
Back Issues: Please enquire
                             for details.

Cheques to be made payable to JOURNAL OF JEWISH STUDIES
Post Office Giro Account No. 23 672 4002

All correspondence should be addressed to:

The Editor
Journal of Jewish Studies
45 St. Giles'
Oxford OX1 3LP
England
Fax (01865) 311791

Tübinger Atlas des Vorderen Orients (TAVO) Beihefte
Reihe B: Geisteswissenschaften. Herausgegeben von Heinz Gaube und Wolfgang Röllig

B 100 Jerusalem. Baugeschichte der Heiligen Stadt von der Frühbronzezeit
bis zum Beginn der osmanischen Herrschaft
Von KLAUS BIEBERSTEIN und HANSWULF BLOEDHORN
1994. 8°. 3 Bde., 1249 Seiten, 1 Karte, kart. (3-88226-671-6) DM 158,-

Dazu sind erhältlich 4 Karten auf 3 Kartenblättern (Preis pro Kartenblatt: Einzelblätter je DM 28,-):

B IV 7 Jerusalem. Baugeschichte. Jerusalem. Architectural Development
    7.I Von der frühen Bronzezeit bis zur Zerstörung durch Nebukadnezar II (3100-587/586)
    From the Early Bronze Age to the Destruction by Nebukadnezar II (3100-587/586 B.C.)
    7.II Vom Wiederaufbau in persischer Zeit bis zur Zerstörung durch Titus (539 v.-70 n.Chr.)
    From the Re-erection in the Persian Period to the Destruction by Titus (539 B.C.-70 A.D.)

    7.III Vom Wiederaufbau in hadrianischer Zeit bis zum Vorabend der Kreuzzüge (117-1099 n.Chr.)
    From the Re-erection in the Hadrianic Period to the Eve of the Crusades (117-1099 A.D.)

    7.IV Von der Ankunft der Kreuzfahrer bis in frühosmanische Zeit (1099-um 1750 n.Chr.)
    From the Arrival of the Crusaders to the Early Ottoman Period (1099-ca. 1750 A.D.)

    von/by KLAUS BIEBERSTEIN/M. HAMILTON BURGOYNE; 1 : 5 000; 24. Lfg. 1992

Judaica Monographien

Reisen nach Jerusalem - Das Heilige Land in Karten und Ansichten aus fünf Jahrhunderten
Bestandskatalog der Sammlung Loewenhardt. Bearbeitet von ANEMONE BEKEMEIER
[Eine Ausstellung des Jüdischen Museums (Abteilung des Berlin Museums) vom 1. April bis 6. Juni 1993]
1993. 19 x 24 cm. Geb., 172 Seiten mit 72 Abbildungen und 2 Klapptafeln, DM 78,- (3-88226-575-2)

Liebe deinen Nächsten; er ist wie du. Judaica für Josef Guggenheim zum 60. Geburtstag
Herausgegeben von GUSTAV INEICHEN
1990. 152 Seiten und eine Abbildung, Leinen mit Schutzumschlag, (3-88226-488-8) DM 28,-

Veröffentlichungen der Hochschule für Jüdische Studien Heidelberg

Nr. 2 Die Entwicklung der hebräischen Sprache
Von CHAIM RABIN
1988. 8°. 60 Seiten, kart. (3-88226-439-x) DM 9,80

Nr. 4 Jüdische Geschichtsschreibung hundert Jahre
nach Heinrich Graetz
Von MICHAEL GRAETZ
1992. 8°. 18 Seiten, kart. (3-888226-572-8) DM 10,-

Hochschule für Jüdische Studien Heidelberg.
Zeitschriftenverzeichnis
Zusammengestellt und bearbeitet von BETTINA KALDENBERG
1992. 115 Seiten, kart. (3-88226-543-4) DM 14,-

Modernes Hebräisch

Lehrgang für Fortgeschrittene. Von DIETER BLOHM und RACHEL STILLMANN

Teil 1. 1992. 8°. 400 Seiten mit Abbildungen und Karten, gebunden (3-88226-549-3) DM 48,-
Teil 2. 1994. 8°. 342 Seiten mit Abbildungen und Karten, gebunden (3-88226-593-0) DM 58,-
c-90-Sprechkassette zu Teil 1. (3-88226-578-7) DM 34,-
c-90-Sprechkassette zu Teil 2. (In Vorbereitung)

DR. LUDWIG REICHERT VERLAG · TAUERNSTR. 11 · D-65199 WIESBADEN

DAS WERK MARTIN BUBERS IM VERLAG LAMBERT SCHNEIDER

»Diese deutsche Bibel ist eine der höchsten Leistungen der deutschen Sprache in unserer Zeit«.
(Hermann Hesse)

Die Schrift
Verdeutscht von Martin Buber gemeinsam mit Franz Rosenzweig.
DM 198,-/öS 1.545,-/sFr 191,-
ISBN 3-7953-0127-0

Laut müssen die Preisungen gelesen werden.
Diese »Psalmen« sind unendlich viel näher bei den hebräischen heiligen Texten als jede frühere Übersetzung.

DM 32,-/öS 250,-/sFr 32,80
ISBN 3-7953-0184-X

»Vertrauen« oder »Fürwahrhalten«, Martin Buber trennt scharf jüdischen und christlichen Glauben. Dieses Buch ist unverzichtbar für den echten Dialog von Christen und Juden.

DM 42,-/öS 328,-/sFr 42,50
ISBN 3-7953-0123-8

Von Martin Buber kurz vor seinem Tod selbst zusammengestellt, enthält das Buch die Quintessenz seines Schaffens.

DM 36,-/öS 281,-/sFr 36,80
ISBN 3-7953-0915-8

Es gibt »Die Guten« nicht. Aber es gibt das Gute.

Wahre menschliche Existenz und wahrhaftiges Leben: ein immer aktuelles Thema.

DM 26,-/öS 203,-/sFr 26,70
ISBN 3-7953-0924-7

»Alles wirkliche Leben ist Begegnung«.

Gottesbeziehung und Philosophie des Menschen; hier findet sich der Kern des Dialogischen Denkens Martin Bubers.

DM 29,80/öS 225,-/sFr 30,50
ISBN 3-7953-0914-X

VERLAG LAMBERT SCHNEIDER GMBH
Weilimdorfer Straße 76, Postfach 10 01 23, D-70826 Gerlingen, Telefon (0 71 56) 43 08-0, Fax (0 71 56) 43 08-40